The Red Army and the Second World War

In a definitive new account of the Soviet Union at war, Alexander Hill charts the development, successes and failures of the Red Army from the industrialisation of the Soviet Union in the late 1920s through to the end of the Great Patriotic War in May 1945. Setting military strategy and operations within a broader context that includes national mobilisation on a staggering scale, the book presents a comprehensive account of the origins and course of the war from the perspective of this key Allied power. Drawing on the latest archival research and a wealth of eyewitness testimony, Hill portrays the Red Army at war from the perspective of senior leaders and men and women at the front line to reveal how the Red Army triumphed over the forces of Nazi Germany and her allies on the Eastern Front, and why it did so at such great cost.

ALEXANDER HILL is Associate Professor in Military History at the University of Calgary, Canada

Armies of the Second World War

This is a major new series of histories of the armies of the key combatants in the Second World War. The books are written by leading military historians and consider key aspects of military activity for each of the major powers, including planning, intelligence, strategy and operations. As with the parallel *Armies of the Great War* series, military and strategic history is considered within the broader context of foreign policy aims and allied strategic relations, national mobilisation and the war's domestic social, political and economic effects.

Titles in the series include:

The British Army and the Second World War by Jonathan Fennell
The French Army and the Second World War by Douglas Porch
The German Army and the Second World War by Jeff Rutherford

The Red Army and the Second World War

Alexander Hill

University of Calgary

CAMBRIDGE UNIVERSITY PRESS

CAMBRIDGE
UNIVERSITY PRESS

University Printing House, Cambridge CB2 8BS, United Kingdom

Cambridge University Press is part of the University of Cambridge.

It furthers the University's mission by disseminating knowledge in the pursuit of education, learning and research at the highest international levels of excellence.

www.cambridge.org
Information on this title: www.cambridge.org/9781107688155

© Alexander Hill 2017

First published 2017

Printed in the United States of America by Sheridan Books, Inc.

A catalogue record for this publication is available from the British Library

Library of Congress Cataloging-in-Publication Data
Names: Hill, Alexander, 1974– author.
Title: The Red Army and the Second World War / Alexander Hill, University of Calgary.
Description: New York : Cambridge University Press, 2016. | Series: Armies of the Second World War | Includes bibliographical references and index.
Identifiers: LCCN 2016010291| ISBN 9781107020795 (Hardback : alk. paper) | ISBN 9781107688155 (pbk. : alk. paper)
Subjects: LCSH: Soviet Union. Raboche-Krest͡s͡ëiͭanskaëiͭa Krasnaëiͭa Armiͤëiͭa–History–World War, 1939–1945. | World War, 1939–1945–Campaigns.
Classification: LCC D764 .H523 2016 | DDC 940.54/1247–dc23 LC record available at http://lccn.loc.gov/2016010291

ISBN 978-1-107-02079-5 Hardback
ISBN 978-1-107-68815-5 Paperback

To my wife Jody, and children Tamsin and Alistair

Contents

Figures

Maps

Acknowledgements

Many people have provided assistance and support over the years that has in some way contributed to the outcome here, although in these acknowledgements I will largely focus on assistance and support provided specifically during the period in which this book has been written. From the point at which I was asked by Michael Watson of Cambridge University Press to write this book and submit an outline in 2011, my wife Jody has been extremely supportive of the project even after it became apparent that writing such a book was going to be a far more involved and protracted process than she had originally envisioned! With two young kids I was initially wary of taking on such a commission, but Jody's encouragement to take the opportunity undoubtedly contributed to my accepting – little did she know... The last time I produced a book I hadn't met Jody and didn't have children. Life with a young family – on what amounts to being in some ways a small 'farm' – certainly requires a much more focused approach to writing a book than the last time round when I was a single academic! In their ways, my kids Tamsin and Alistair (one still a baby and the other barely conceived when the project began) have been very tolerant of daddy disappearing into his basement office space to write, and particularly so during those periods when a deadline loomed and writing was essentially from dawn till dusk, day after day. I apologise to all of them for my at times grouchy mood as deadlines loomed. Regarding those deadlines, my thanks certainly go to Michael Watson at Cambridge University Press for his tolerance and understanding in allowing a number of extensions! At or through Cambridge University Press, in addition to the commissioning editor Michael Watson, I would like to thank my production editor Amanda George for her assistance in seeing this work through to publication, and Bindu Vinod and Kalai Periassamy at SPi in Chennai who oversaw copyediting and typesetting there.

In terms of the shaping of this work, constructive criticism from the three 'anonymous' reviewers of the initial proposal, and comments by the manuscript reviewer for Cambridge University Press, have certainly all been appreciated. Particularly appreciated is the fact that Drs Roger Reese, Jeff Rutherford and the soon to be Dr, Jan Mann, along with my former undergraduate honours student Aaron Bates, all took time out of their schedules to look over a full draft manuscript. Dr David Stahel was kind enough to find time to review those chapters relating to his published work. Their comments have all helped shape and improve this work. A number of people have provided assistance in obtaining materials for this work. There are far too many archivists and librarians to list all of them, and particularly to include those who helped in obtaining materials used in this project that I collected during the previous decade and even in the late 1990s as a PhD student. Since 2011 the University of Calgary library has been excellent at gaining the necessary interlibrary loans required, and here Rosvita Vaska undoubtedly deserves most of the credit. Dr Sergei Kudriashov – now of the German Historical Institute in Moscow – has continued to send me the latest archival publications from the Russian Presidential Archive that he has edited and are relevant to my work, and I was particularly pleased to be given his latest edited collections of documents while attending a conference he organised in Moscow in the spring of 2015. In this work I also make some use of valuable Soviet archival materials on Lend-Lease to the Soviet Union made available to me by Dr Mikhail Suprun some years ago, and which were important sources in articles and chapters I wrote prior to this book and to which I also refer here. Ralph Gibson of what was RIA-Novosti provided photos from the press agency's archive at a very reasonable rate – many paid for through a start-up grant provided by the University of Calgary when I started there in 2004 and which I had carefully husbanded to finally spend the last funds on photographs for this book. I was also grateful for the six-month research leave provided by the University in 2014 that allowed me to make real headway with writing. At the University of Calgary, I would also like to thank my PhD student, Keith Hann, who was provided with additional funding unbeknown to me on the understanding that he undertake research for a professor – and scoured a number of English-language translations of German memoirs for concepts and terms I had selected that certainly saved me some valuable time. He also provided a brief translation from Polish that I used in Chapter 6. I would also like to thank the Russian historians and enthusiasts who collated archival materials in pdf form from the Russian Central Archive of the Ministry of Defence that were published on the website *Podvig Naroda*, and those who run and contribute to the online library militera.lib.ru, that was extremely valuable in locating materials that I then consulted in hardcopy where possible.

So, thanks to all who have helped this work to see publication. At the end of acknowledgements, it is customary to point out that although a number of people have contributed to this work in a variety of ways, any errors or omissions in the content remain the author's responsibility, and so I have done just that! I hope you find this work interesting and thought provoking, and that any minor errors do not detract in any meaningful way from the whole.

Military Ranks

Approximate comparative Red Army officer-grade ranks over time used in the text with their Wehrmacht equivalents

Red Army (1935–1945)	Political command equivalent	Soviet navy	Wehrmacht
Marshal of the Soviet Union Principal Marshal (of Branch) Marshal (of Branch)			*Generalfeldmarschall*
Komandarm 1st rank/General (of the Army)	Army commissar 1st rank	*Flagman* of the Fleet 1st Rank/Admiral of the Fleet	*Generaloberst*
Komandarm 2nd rank/General-Colonel	Army commissar 2nd rank	*Flagman* of the Fleet 2nd rank/Admiral	*General (of Branch)*
Komkor/General-Lieutenant	Corps commissar	*Flagman* 1st rank/ Vice-Admiral	*Generalleutnant*
Kombrig/*Komdiv*/ General-Major	Brigade commissar/ Divisional commissar	*Flagman* 2nd rank/ *Kontr*-Admiral	*Generalmajor*
Kompolk/*Kombrig*/ Colonel [*polkovnik*]	Brigade commissar/ Regimental commissar		*Oberst*
Kombat/ *Podpolkovnik*	Senior battalion commissar		*Oberstleutnant*
Kombat/Major	Battalion commissar		*Major*
Captain	(Senior) *politruk*		*Hauptman*
Senior lieutenant	*Politruk*		*Oberleutnant*
Lieutenant	(Junior) *politruk*		*Leutnant*
Junior lieutenant			

Sources: Postanovlenie TsIK i SNK SSSR ot 22 sentiabria 1935 g., *O vvedenii personalnikh voennikh zvanii nachal'stvuiushchego sostava RKKA...* (Moscow: Otdel izdatel'stva NKO SSSR, 1935), p.8; M.M. Kir'ian (editor-in-chief), *Sovetskaia voennaia entsiklopediia, 3* (Moscow: Voenizdat, 1977), pp.434–5; Earl F. Ziemke, *Stalingrad to Berlin: The German Defeat in the East* (Washington, D.C: Center of Military History, United States Army, 1987), p.505; http://army.armor.kiev.ua/titul/ [Accessed 10 September 2015].

Introduction

Our appreciation for the strengths and weaknesses of the Red Army during the Great Patriotic War has increased significantly in recent years – and particularly since the end of the Cold War. The opening up of Soviet archives not only to Western historians, but even more so to those of Russia and the former Soviet Union, has fostered considerable enrichment of the historical literature on the subject. The Soviet military archives were for a number of practical and political reasons not opened up to the same extent as many other archives, and access for Western researchers is now arguably worse than it was during the 1990s. Nonetheless, the materials made available during the last years of the Soviet Union and beyond have added considerable colour and nuance to the picture of the Red Army that predominated during the Cold War in the West. That picture, of faceless hordes and overwhelming material might overcoming superior German tactical and operational capabilities, relied heavily on the memoirs of senior German commanders such as Heinz Guderian, Erich von Manstein and others. Although these figures acknowledged improvement in Red Army effectiveness due not only to quantitative but also qualitative factors, they nonetheless understandably focused on comparison between the Red Army and the Wehrmacht at a time at which the latter was at the peak of its capabilities. Such authors also tended to explain German defeat primarily in quantitative terms or in terms of poor leadership on the part of Hitler. In many ways the work of the late John Erickson foreshadowed recent scholarship on the Red Army in the West that has led to questioning of whether the Red Army could really have reached Berlin without significant qualitative improvement. As a teenager in the late 1980s I recall reading Erickson's *The Road to Stalingrad* and *The Road to Berlin* for the first time, and not only recall their richness then despite the relative limitations on his written sources, but looking at them now appreciate what he achieved with the materials available to him.[1] The work of John Erickson, who had access to at least some participants but relied to a considerable extent on a thorough examination of the Soviet memoir and wider published literature, dramatically increased our understanding of the functioning of the Red Army and changes in its organisation and leadership over time. Nonetheless the German memoir-inspired picture of faceless Soviet hordes being almost defeated by the Wehrmacht but for Hitler's meddling – before German forces were overwhelmed by sheer weight of numbers – still coloured popular and even academic views of the war in the east at the end of the Cold War.

During the 1990s the work of David Glantz in particular did much in the English-language literature to shift the historiography of the war on what was Germany's Eastern Front away from Cold War perspectives. Glantz has and continues to highlight a development of the Red Army during the war that suggested that not only did it have increasing material resources after the debacles of the summer and autumn of 1941 saw the destruction many of those vast resources accrued before the war, but was increasingly able to make good use of them. More recently in the West historians such as Evan Mawdsley, Roger Reese, Geoffrey Roberts and David Stone in particular have built on the work that is still underway by David Glantz to add additional diplomatic, social and economic dimensions to our understanding of the development of the Red Army. They have also in many ways done for Stalin – the Soviet leader who held the reins of both the military and economic dimensions to the Soviet war effort – as they have done for the Red Army in highlighting that just as sheer weight of numbers alone does not explain Red Army successes, Stalin contributed more to Soviet victory than ruthless determination. In adding much to our understanding of how Stalin's Red Army became a more effective military machine as the war progressed, and indeed why things went so badly wrong during much of 1941 and 1942, these historians among others in the West have been able to draw on some excellent work undertaken by a new wave of popular and academic Russian military historians. Since the collapse of the Soviet Union many historians writing in Russian have offered a revisionist line critical of the Soviet historiography that glossed over many Red Army failings. Others have offered what might be described as a neo-Soviet view of the Red Army at war in which the focus on the role of the Communist Party as a driving force has been replaced in many ways by Russian patriotism, and in which the focus of work tends to be on successes rather than failures. Regardless of whether such historians are of a revisionist or neo-Soviet bent, they and their Western counterparts agree that the Red Army became a more effective fighting force as the war progressed. This assessment holds whether the benchmark is the increasingly poorly trained and far less combat effective mass of the German armed forces of the end of the war, or the elite but at the end of the war rapidly diminishing core of the German armed forces that has dominated the popular literature on the war in the West. As well as acknowledging at least some improvement in Red Army performance, all would also agree that the Red Army was ultimately led by Stalin, who during the war became a more effective military leader than he had been when it started. The Red Army became a more capable army, but the devil is of course in the detail – just how far did qualitative improvement in the Red Army go and to what extent were those improvements down to human and organisational factors, and to what extent were improved capabilities down to equipment and material factors? To what extent did the bludgeon of 1941 become a sword handled with some skill, or was it that the bludgeon of the early war was by the end of the war still a bludgeon but much better balanced in terms of weight and being wielded with sufficiently improved skill to be far more likely to strike where it mattered? In many ways I have already started to place my cards on the table with this last and indeed slightly rhetorical question. Where the historiography of the Red Army has swung from portrayal of a rather crude and blunt instrument to highlighting the flaws in such a picture by paying attention more to development and strengths, this work certainly highlights that the Red Army was transformed into a more effective fighting force, but makes it clear that transformation could only go so far in the time available. That transformation was, as will be highlighted in this book, well underway by the summer of 1941 from what might be seen as the nadir of Red Army performance in Finland during late 1939. Given the numerical and material strength of the Red Army in the summer of 1941, the Red Army could perhaps even in its June 1941 state have halted the Wehrmacht well before the gates of Moscow had it not been for initial strategic and operational failures that set the Red Army up for mind boggling losses and the debacles of the summer and autumn of 1941. However, had the Red Army been deployed differently and been better prepared to meet the invasion in an immediate sense, halting the initial German advance sooner than was in fact the case would have been one thing – winning the war would still however have been another and a protracted process.

Regardless of whether the Red Army at the end of the war is repre-sented by a swordsman, a bludgeon-wielding warrior or something in between in terms of finesse, in a simple sense the Red Army was by the end of the war effective – where the word effective carries with it the idea of accomplishment of some sort of aim or goal. If the aim was to repel the Nazi-German invader and its allies, and then defeat them, then the Red Army achieved the objective and was effective. In Soviet terms this required only a little help from the Western Allies, although the extent to which the defeat of Nazi Germany required Allied assistance is the subject of some debate. For neo-Soviet Russian-language historians Allied aid was a luxury item that was not required for victory, and even in the West most historians have tended not to go as far as suggesting that it was essential for Soviet victory. Whether the Soviet Union could have defeated Nazi Germany and her allies alone however is a moot point. The reality was that the Red Army did not defeat Nazi Germany alone, and the question becomes one of the relative contributions of the Western Allies and the Soviet Union to the defeat of Nazi Germany. Undoubtedly the Soviet Union played a major role in the defeat of Nazi Germany and those fighting along side her with assistance from her allies. The Red Army could quite reasonably claim to have destroyed the bulk of German field forces, even if the Western Allies can lay claim to the destruction of the bulk of German air and more limited naval power and managed towards the end of the war to undermine to a significant degree the German productive effort required to sustain the field armies. Recently historian Philips O'Brien has questioned the extent to which destroying German divisions on the Eastern Front made that theatre decisive, where he suggests that all the major powers with the exception of the Soviet Union overall invested more heavily in air and sea power than ground forces.[2] However, the Western powers would have struggled to overcome Nazi Germany without the Red Army slogging it out with the Wehrmacht and increasingly the Waffen SS from the summer of 1941, as the Red Army would have struggled much more had the Western powers not deflected a significant or even dominant proportion of German economic effort away from the German Eastern Front. The Red Army certainly fought predominately with Soviet-produced weapons, but the role of Allied and particularly US aid in sustaining their production and keeping the whole Soviet system going – and the Red Army moving forward – should not be ignored.

So in the context of the Allied war effort, the Soviet Union and the Red Army were in a crude sense effective in that they played a leading role in the defeat of the enemy – with a little help from their 'friends'. However, rarely do we consider effectiveness in terms of achieving a goal at any cost. Although the war against Nazi Germany had in many senses to be won – for it was a war that if lost would have resulted in the destruction of the Soviet Union as a geopolitical entity and horrendous suffering for many of its peoples – theoretically even in a *Vernichtungskrieg* or 'War of annihilation' one could imagine a point at which the cost exceeded the benefits. In the Soviet case that would probably have resulted in defeat, but had the Red Army somehow managed to continue to sustain losses on the scale sustained during 1941 and into the spring and summer of 1942 and survive thanks perhaps to greater and earlier sacrifices on the part of her allies, then such a point might hypothetically have been reached. The Soviet Union might, as German general von Mellenthin postulated, have been fought to some sort of stalemate on the Eastern Front. The historical outcome of the Great Patriotic War – Soviet victory – in reality was achieved at a horrendous cost of more than nine million soldiers killed and total population losses of in the region of twenty-seven million.[3] We can of course ultimately blame these losses on the Nazi invasion and the manner in which Nazi Germany conducted the war, although should not forget Stalin's propensity to sanction the killing or allow the death through wilful neglect of millions of Soviet people as indeed occurred in the 1930s. Arguably, some of the more than nine million soldiers killed could have been spared had the Stalinist regime not made some of the very significant mistakes it made prior to and during the war, and indeed had it not shown a far greater disregard towards the lives of its troops than its allies or even its principal opponent. Certainly the losses of 1941 and early 1942 were not sustainable, and the Red Army had to become more effective in its use of resources or lose. Stalin's early war assertions that the Soviet Union possessed limitless resources must have sounded hollow by the time of the infamous Order Number 227 of July 1942 that noted that further retreat for the Red Army was unacceptable if the resource situation was not to become critical.[4] Fortunately, the losses of 1941 – and in particular losses as PoWs who would subsequently die in their millions due to neglect in German prisoner of war camps – would not be repeated even if combat losses and casualties remained relatively high throughout the war.

The Red Army played a leading role – possible the principal role – in the defeat of the Wehrmacht and its allies but at terrible cost thanks to the fact that even allowing for greater German ideological fervour and barbarity on the Eastern Front than the West it was not as effective as its allies in doing what was necessary to win relatively economically. To some extent this was because the Soviet Union could not attack the German capacity to wage war from afar, where it was stuck on the same continent and locked in a sustained and costly ground war. Soviet resources could not be spared for example to develop a strategic bombing capability beyond promising beginnings in part because of this reality, but in part however because within this context it was, and particularly early in the war, inefficient in turning investment and lives expended into results. From strategic miscalculation in the summer of

1941 that contributed to the loss of military resources built up over the previous decade, to an at times one might want to say criminal disregard for the lives of its troops in hammering away at German forces in ill-conceived operations, the Soviet leadership squandered resources that were expended for often less gain that might otherwise have been the case.

From broader societal issues down to the decisions of one man – Stalin – there are many reasons why the Red Army is often perceived as having been a somewhat crude instrument and particularly so earlier in the war. By the end of the war however, it had, as the new historiography of the Red Army suggests, been transformed – even reborn. As overall German effectiveness declined at the tactical and even operational levels the Red Army was often much better matched to its opponent in terms of capability than it had been earlier in the war. This was the case not just for material reasons – the Red Army functioned better as an organisation and was able to 'adapt to the actual conditions of combat'.[5] After the 'wakeup call' of the debacle in Finland in late 1939, the wheels had been set in motion to focus attention on preparing for combat – not showpiece manoeuveres. The disastrous strategic deployment of the summer of 1941 resulted in a situation that could easily have paralysed the Soviet military machine, but nonetheless the Red Army rapidly learnt much from and adapted to actual war against specifically Nazi Germany and her allies. The Red Army learnt much from the Wehrmacht – and adapted what it learnt so that it worked in a Soviet context. However, Soviet losses were all too often horrendous through to the very end of the war, and not just because of stubborn resistance from the enemy. Late in the war Stalin and the Soviet leadership arguably drove the Red Army on for reasons beyond the immediate defeat of the enemy – looking to postwar territorial acquisition and influence for which many Red Army troops were sacrificed. In terms of Marxist-Leninist logic, spreading revolution may have been ultimately the only way to guarantee Soviet security, but even this does not explain, for example, the lives squandered to capture what perhaps epitomizes the throwing away of lives at the end of the war – the capture of the fortress city of Königsberg in April 1945. Here Stalin arguably over asserted political goals – at the expense of thousands of Soviet lives. Ultimately much comes down to the personality of one man – Stalin – whose influence as in the case of his German rival Hitler – be it directly or in terms of the sort of people he chose to lead on his behalf – was considerable and perhaps even greater in the case of Stalin. His strengths and weaknesses are a significant factor in explaining both why the Red Army was ultimately effective, and why effectiveness in getting the job done proved so costly. Why so much was expended – and indeed how so much could be mobilised to be expended to first hold off and then push back the enemy – is an important focus of this book.

This work in many ways not only sits between post-Cold War Western revisionism and the Western Cold War literature in its portrayal of the Red Army and its development, but also endeavours to take from both the old and the new in terms of sources. In contemporary academic history there is, despite the rise of 'history from below', something of a fetishisation of archival sources. Such sources should be central to most serious historical works, and this case is no exception. Although Soviet archival sources preserved in Russian military archives are far from easily accessed by Western researchers, I was fortunate to gain access to many such materials or to be provided them by Russian colleagues in the 1990s and the first years of the new millennium. Many valuable documents for 1941 and 1945 were published online by the Russian Ministry of Defence on the *People's Victory* website, and subsequently collated by Russian historians and military history enthusiasts.[6] These sources are used in this work alongside the many documentary sources that have been published in Russian since the latter phases of Gorbachev's *glasnost'* and *perestroika*. Also available since the late 1980s and early 1990s are a range of until then unpublished Soviet memoirs of the war, and indeed some memoirs first published in the Soviet period in very heavily edited form and now available as written by the author. These memoirs span from the post-Soviet release of Marshal Georgii Zhukov's three-volume memoirs with much material that was not published until the post-Soviet period, to many rich memoirs by participants at the grass roots level written towards the end of their lives in a post-Soviet climate of greater frankness or written earlier but only deemed acceptable for publication during the late 1980s and beyond. These rich sources – as any source – have to be used with care but have their own unique strengths and weaknesses in the case of the memoirs. These memoirs certainly add colour and nuance to a work such as this, and are complemented by interviews conducted after the collapse of the Soviet Union, where particular credit has to go to the work of Artem Drabkin and his colleagues who have done so much to preserve the testimonies of hundreds of Soviet veterans.

Where this work perhaps differs most in terms of sources from other recent work in the West in particular is the extent to which it has sought to make use of the Soviet published sources so effectively mined by John Erickson when alternatives were unavailable – both Soviet era memoirs and academic works that in the light of post-Soviet archival releases and other publications have a new lease of life. These Soviet works – be they journal articles from the premier Soviet military history publication *Voenno-istoricheskii zhurnal*, academic monographs or some of the thousands of memoirs published during the Soviet period – can now be mined much more effectively in the light of new information than they could prior to the collapse of the Soviet Union. The issue with Soviet-era publications was often not typically willful misinformation on the part of authors although there were certainly polemical works, but editorial attempts to censor information that might tarnish the reputation of the Red Army and ultimately the Communist Party. Nonetheless, within what were fluctuating confines of acceptability that were noticeably less constrained during the 'thaw' of the early-mid 1960s and again in the late 1980s, there were still attempts to analyse, explain, understand and set the record straight that led to meaningful discourse and serious academic research. In many ways materials available since the collapse of the Soviet Union are a key to unlocking the value in these sources, of which I have made significant use. This work also makes arguably more use than most of recently published memoirs – typically post-1991 – that add the aforementioned colour and nuance to the picture one can obtain of the Red Army from archival sources and many academic works. I would like to stress here that these contrasts with the existing literature are relative rather than absolute, and that many of my colleagues in the field have put these sources to good use already, although not necessarily using as many of them in a single work and to the extent to which they have been used here.

In this work, as well as using a different blend of sources than used in many others on the Red Army, I have sought to focus attention on certain factors contributing to military effectiveness that overall have perhaps received less attention in the literature on the Red Army to date than they arguably deserve. For example, I have tried to highlight and examine in some detail the role of communications and communications failure and indeed broader issues of command and control in military failure, and developments in these areas contributing to improved Red Army effectiveness. Similar attention has been paid to reconnaissance, logistics, education and training, and more nebulous factors such as organisational culture. I have tried where possible, and in particular for self-contained conflicts prior to the Great Patriotic War and major campaigns and operations during it, to make it such that chapters dealing with them can be read alone without having read the preceding chapters. Here I hope that for those reading the book from cover-to-cover the at times nuanced change over time in Soviet practice in key areas such as reconnaissance, and alternative examples used in making a similar point to one presented earlier, prevent any feeling of repetition. In order to keep something of the flavour of different time periods considered within this work I have kept Soviet ranks for the time period concerned, meaning that there is considerable variation in the terms used over the course of the book. Approximate equivalents over time are provided in the relevant table. I have anglicised words such as general and colonel where it makes sense, although kept the Russian word order in ranks such as general-colonel in part to keep a Russian flavour and further differentiate them from German ranks that I have kept in German. On translation, where there is any scope for significantly different interpretation of a translation than that offered here, I have provided the original Russian in parentheses after the translation concerned.

I certainly spent significant time selecting the photographs for this book, and have attempted to cover the full range of campaigns, battles and themes considered within it in the pictures. Many of the photographs are here published for the first time in the West. To some extent I tried deliberately not to present a sanitised view of war in the photographs – as I have also sought to avoid in the text. It can be all to easy for the historian and subsequently their readers to hide from the death and horror of war behind statistics and top-down description – a criticism I hope cannot reasonably be levelled at this book. The aim here is conversely not to wallow in the misery of war but to analyse and explain how the Red Army evolved over time as a military machine, albeit one run by flesh and blood.

In this work, the varied English- and Russian language sources that have been consulted have been used – along with German archival sources and other materials where appropriate and where space constraints allow – to present a picture of change and continuity within the Red Army from the start of the breakneck industrialisation of the Soviet Union in the late 1920s through to the end of the Great Patriotic War in Europe in May 1945. This change is addressed from Stalin and the upper echelons of the leadership, where possible down through the middle command ranks and at times all the way down to the rank and file. This work does not offer a detailed narrative overview of the war, even if it does examine most of the key operations in chronological order along with analysis of key themes in the development of the Red Army at appropriate points. It is assumed that readers of this work will have read at least one of the many sound overviews of the war, be that the two volumes of John Erickson's seminal history noted earlier, David Glantz and Jonathan House's *When Titan's Clashed*, Evan Mawdsley's *Thunder in the East* or Chris Bellamy's *Absolute War*.[7] This attempt to present the development of the Red Army from top to bottom, providing traditional military-historical analysis of strategy, operations and tactics alongside elements of the 'new' military history and economic history, seeks to provide a wide ranging overview of factors contributing to Red Army success and failure on its long road to Berlin, victory and peace. I hope that it provokes much thought on the nature of Soviet military success and failure, and the human tragedy that was the Great Patriotic War.

1   Of Horses and Men
The Red Army of the Late 1920s

On the eve of the adoption of the First Five-Year Plan for industry and Stalin's 'Great Turn' in Soviet development, the Red Army was a far cry from being the mechanised titan that it had become by the second half of the Great Patriotic War – or indeed even the less nimble colossus it had become by June 1941. The Red Army of 1927 was certainly not small by the international standards of the day – 607,125 strong if one includes air strength and ignores the part-timers, with their mobilisation adding 2,800,000–2,900,000 men to strength. This would have given a planned force of in the region of 3,400,000 men in the event of a war.[1] However, both commanders and men were typically poorly educated peasants, with many personnel fulfilling their service obligations through territorial militia units that offered at best sporadic training. These militia units were in many senses akin to the US National Guard or British Territorial Army except that service was not voluntary. Some of these territorial units were national units, hampered by the fact that the bulk of their personnel did not speak Russian and struggled to communicate with Russian commanders who didn't speak their language. Despite some efforts on the part of the regime, commanders often lacked authority with their men and were at the mercy of political commissars. The Red Army of 1927 was also poorly equipped – for example there were few tanks and aircraft and the former were of First World War vintage, and communications equipment was scarce. In many ways the Red Army was a very different organisation by 1936. During the early-mid 1930s the Red Army would in many senses be transformed by forward thinking elements in its leadership from a somewhat anachronistic product of Civil War experience into a modern military machine. Not only did it have the latest tanks and aircraft to rival those available anywhere else in the world, but it also had coherent ideas on their employment that were innovative and forward looking rather than focusing on fighting the last major war. For many Red Army leaders the last war and the war they wanted to fight again was understandably the Russian Civil War – the war that had made their careers and secured the Soviet state's hold over most of the former Russian Empire. The Russian Civil War was a particularly poor choice for a past war to focus on given that although Western Powers had intervened on the side of the White opposition to the Bolsheviks, their participation was at best half-hearted. The Russian Civil War saw precious little use of the new technologies of the First World War – the tank and aircraft – and with the exception of the armoured train, mobility was provided largely by the horse. There was relatively little positional warfare during the Russian Civil War, and in many ways it was the cavalry that was the dominant arm in the vast expanses of Russia and her neighbours.[2] Fortunately, key thinkers of the early 1930s would focus on the First World War and extrapolate from it. The problem with emergent grand plans for a Red Army that would exploit the new technologies of the First World War to achieve sustained breakthrough of enemy defences was that not only were suitable means for effective command and control lacking in practice, but also the human component of the plan did not match up with the grand theories which the Red Army could at best only pretend to be able to implement.

In 1926 Mikhail Tukhachevskii, then head of the Headquarters of the Red Army, had painted a bleak picture of manoeuvres that took place that summer. Command and control by commanders – knowing what to do and being able to communicate that to the relevant units – were both identified as having been typically poor, where commanders took 'decisions extremely slowly' and were 'very weak in responding to changes in the military situation'. Tukhachevskii went as far as to note, that for commanders 'initiative is an extremely rare phenomenon' – with headquarters units similarly 'passive'. Communications from headquarters to units was entirely dependent on telephone lines, without which 'any sort of communication ceased'. Perhaps unsurprisingly, cadre (regular) rifle divisions were seen as being better prepared than territorial, although this comparison did not necessarily involve comparing units in equivalent states of mobilisation, and comparison between specific units did not always end up favouring the cadre unit. Certainly individual Red Army men were noted to have shown 'high levels of initiative in action' [*visokaia boevaia aktivnost'*], particularly cadre personnel, although the 'initiative' expected of the rank and file was limited. Co-ordination between different arms was poor, with artillery often late in providing fire support for the infantry. Limited communications resources and all but total reliance on the field telephone were certainly a particularly serious hindrance in this instance. As for the infantry, although typically advancing in an orderly manner, instances of infantry tending towards advancing in waves were noted, with supporting machine guns often hiding behind them. The conclusion that inadequacies in military preparation left the Red Army with the task of trying to achieve a 'breakthrough' in 'basic elements of training' for combat was certainly not a ringing endorsement of its capabilities.[3]

Some Red Army leaders saw the part-timers of the territorial divisions as a factor in poor Red Army performance, and Tukhachevskii had indeed suggested that cadre personnel tended to perform better than their part-time counterparts. Certainly territorial divisions lacked the status of their cadre counterparts within the Red Army. According to an interviewee of the Harvard Project on the Soviet Social System (HPSSS) who had held command rank in the Red Army, serving as a cadre commander with a territorial division was considerably less prestigious than serving with a cadre division – and even an indicator of lack of trust in the commander concerned on the part of the regime.[4] Whether the latter applied in all cases is certainly questionable, as the following case of Nikolai Iakovlev, future Marshal of Artillery, suggests, although his stint with a territorial division seems to have been brief. Iakovlev described some of the problems associated with territorial divisions in his 1981 memoirs, *On Artillery and A Little About Myself*:

From May until December 1929 I had to serve as chief of the headquarters of the 13th Artillery Regiment, 13th Rifle Division of the territorial forces, based in the north of the Don *oblast'*. ...

In this regiment, as by the way in the division as a whole, there was a completely different system for the organisation of training than, for instance, in my native 28th Rifle Division. The latter was a cadre formation. In this instance, we commanders of all ranks, in general conducted basic training during so-called musters for new recruits that began in May and continued until September – that is until the time of the general muster. During the general September muster, the territorials who had already completed basic training appeared from towns and railway halts and were now accounted for as members of artillery batteries with different specialties. So it transpired, that for only one month a year the regiment became a fully fledged military unit. At this time, live firing and field exercises were conducted. But in October...In October the conscript element again left for home, and the batteries remained at reduced strength until the spring.

Iakovlev went on to describe the situation during the winter months:

In general middle ranking and junior commanders and a small part of the rank and file were left with the task of looking after equipment, other military assets and the horses. It is true, that on occasion command exercises were conducted with commanders, but that was only from time to time.

Additionally, during the winter some of the commanders of the battery would periodically head out to the farmsteads and railway halts where the soldiers assigned to their units lived and worked. There, at educational centres and primarily in the evenings, commanders conducted military classes with them.

However, all of this also had a primitive and sporadic character. As a result, batteries, *divizions* and of course the whole artillery regiment, had only so-so preparation. This was highlighted in all dimensions by district manoeuvres conducted in the autumn of 1929, in which the 13th, and also 9th Rifle Divisions of the territorials took part. Their units and regiments, in contrast with the cadre units, lacked confidence, acted slowly and showed little manoeuvreability.[5]

As Iakovlev goes on to suggest, the territorial militia system seemed to offer a number of advantages over the more conventional system of conscription that had been adopted in its final form by the Tsarist army in 1874 and was the norm in many other European states. First of all, the territorial militia system offered a large force for low cost, where conscripts were not, for example, billeted with units year round and could be provided for economically during the summer months – for example living in tents rather than barracks. This was particularly important after the dramatic cuts in the Red Army after the Civil War that left it unable to sustain a force over five million strong. By November 1922 strength had been reduced to a nominal 800,000, but an additional 200,000 personnel had still to be cut to provide a sustainable permanent force level.[6] The severity of the cuts to the armed forces is highlighted not only by the slashing of the size of the Red Army, but by the fact that Soviet naval power all but disappeared from the White and Barents Seas.[7]

In the economic climate of the period a traditional conscript-based army simply did not allow the Soviet Union a wartime Red Army of anything like the size that the territorial militia system would provide for the same cost. As the cut in the force level to 600,000 was decided upon, the Revolutionary Military Soviet – the military-civilian body directing Soviet military policy – ordered that the militia system and territorial units be organised with some haste. By January 1924, twenty-two rifle divisions had been formed on a territorial basis.[8] Those fulfilling their military obligations in the regular or cadre forces from 1925 served continuously for 2–4 years depending on the arm – those serving in territorial units supposedly served for 8–12 months in total over a five-year period.[9]

At the same time as being apparently cost effective – or at least cheaper – the territorial militia system seemed to offer other economic and political benefits. First, the territorial militia system did not remove men from the economy for a protracted period – a factor stressed by the head of the Main Board of the Red Army, Levichev to the Revolutionary Military Soviet of the USSR in a report on territorial militia formations in August 1925. Certainly, as Levichev noted, a month a year for training in the territorial militia did not compare in terms of disruption to a two-year period of conscription for peasants, where during that period they might lose their 'agricultural base' in the countryside.[10] Second, the territorial militia system seemed to offer a vehicle for political education in the countryside. In December 1924 Frunze and a colleague, Bubnov, highlighted how 'beyond the purely military significance' of the territorial units they had 'huge significance in the task of Sovietizing our countryside, its political enlightenment and the raising of the cultural and political level of young peasants'.[11] There was however the risk that prevailing norms in peasant regions and proximity to home for such part-time soldiers might mean that the territorial divisions became more peasant than a regular division might have been, with ramifications for discipline. This was certainly an issue aired early on by Trotsky, who was concerned that the non-peasants might be overwhelmed by the peasant mass.[12] It seems that few territorial divisions drew on industrial centres – only 45 per cent according to one source – depriving the territorial divisions of supposedly ideologically more reliable proletarian elements.[13] Campaigns to increase the proportion of workers in the Red Army apparently had some effect – by 1932, 42.9 per cent of conscripts called up were 'workers', but the Red Army, as Soviet society, remained predominately peasant.[14] Similar problems of local cultural sullying of desirable Soviet ways applied in what were seen as the less advanced Soviet republics that combined peasant backwardness with undesirable ethnic cultural practices and values.

By 1928, the Red Army had a mere twenty-two regular rifle divisions compared to forty-one territorial ones. According to Red Army statistics, of approximately 1,300,000 men liable for service at that time, only about 300,000 would serve with regular or cadre units, with another 240,000 serving as non-cadre elements in the territorial forces. So conscription was not actually experienced by a majority of Soviet men of conscription age at this time. If suitable young men did not serve with cadre forces then there was not always the potential for them to serve with the territorials – only about 39 per cent of the Soviet population lived in areas from which the territorial units drew personnel – about 8 per cent of the total area of the Soviet Union or 25 per cent of the 'useful', one assumes populated, territory.[15] Nonetheless, despite the opposition of senior Red Army commanders to the territorial system, during the early 1930s it actually expanded its remit to include specialist units for service both within and outside the territorial divisions.[16] Only as the international situation deteriorated rapidly during the mid-1930s with both Japan and then Nazi Germany emerging as genuine threats did specific weaknesses in not only the equipment but also organisation of the Red Army become issues not only of deep concern to the Red Army but also Stalin and the political

Troops of 46th Territorial Division parade on the eighth anniversary of the October Revolution in November 1925. For financial rather than military reasons the territorial divisions were the mainstay of the Red Army during the late 1920s and early 1930s. (RIA Novosti #22014)

leadership. Where cadre forces were insufficient to guard against attack by a substantial enemy force, territorial units were difficult to mobilise and deploy to border areas in the event of increased international tension. The disruption to the economy of mobilising troops for an unspecified period without provision for their absences was just one issue hampering their mobilisation in a situation that stopped short of war. This factor, on top of the limits to what could be achieved through limited and sporadic training for units that would lack the same cohesion as regular formations if required at short notice in the event of a crisis, meant that regular divisions now had increased appeal not only to the Red Army, but also the civilian leadership. Nonetheless, the military system established in 1925 that obliged many Soviet men of call-up age to serve in either the regular or territorial forces would survive until 1939.

Under the above system some men – often workers – were not required to serve in either the cadre or territorial forces. So that those not serving in cadre or territorial units might be more mobilisable in the event of war, they were supposed to receive some sort of basic military training through OSOAVIAKHIM – a compound of OSO and AVIAKHIM or the Society for Co-operation in Defence and Society for Aviation-Chemical Construction respectively. Formed in 1927 through the merging of the above two predecessors, initially those receiving training through OSOAVIAKHIM were volunteers. This volunteerism was central to the image of OSOAVIAKHIM as a 'social organisation' that was tasked not only with providing the population with military and broader civil defence skills, but also 'patriotic education'. 'Military Knowledge Circles' were supposed to provide 'pre-conscription members with a preparatory stage before for service in the army; for the part-time elements of the territorial units the means to improve their military knowledge between musters; and for command elements and reservists a school to help them retain and reinforce knowledge obtained in the Red Army; and for the remaining mass of workers, not touched by a single type of military preparation the sole venue for them to receive it.'[17]

As OSOAVIAKHIM gained more and more responsibilities for the military preparation of the population it was increasingly militarised. By 1935, as the organisation focused more on its military preparation remit, 'military discipline' was supposed to apply to those undertaking training. In practice, and despite the uniforms, military discipline and standards frequently did not consistently apply. Some of the programmes offered by OSOAVIAKHIM were popular with young people, including some offered in collaboration with the Komsomol or youth wing of the Communist Party. OSOAVIAKHIM provided the means for the chosen few to learn to fly or receive parachute training. However, even with the local will and competence, much of the training provided to 'volunteers' who satisfied their military obligations through the organisation was always going to be second rate given in particular the relatively modest financial inputs during a period when the organisation was expected to train specialists in a range of areas that included the training of tank crews.[18] As the Russian historian of OSOAVIAKHIM, Olga Nikonova, notes in the conclusion to her monograph on the activities of the organisation in the Urals:

Only in a few specific directions did the paramilitary organization facilitate the creation of cadres for the formation of air and airborne units, sniper teams, and in the groundwork for the large scale incorporation of women into auxiliary and frontline units of the Red Army – through the training of parachutists, the activities of flying clubs and the piecemeal preparation of snipers.

Large scale military-political preparation and training in many senses remained at the level of slogans and propaganda, despite the constant highlighting of their importances. Nonetheless, and particularly closer to the Great Patriotic War, at least some meaningful pre-conscription training was clearly offered and no doubt helped when hundreds of thousands of recruits had to be trained very quickly during the early phase of the Great Patriotic War. An example here is radio operator Arkadii Glazunov, who prior to the Great Patriotic War had 'in school' studied the use of 'radio apparatus'.[19] Poor and limited training was nonetheless a problem across the Soviet military system, made worse by the low educational levels of both commanders and men. In 1927, 10.3 per cent of conscripts entering service were 'illiterate', with 30–35 per cent having 'poor literacy' [*malogramotnie*]. Dealing with the problem of literacy was an obvious starting point for improving military effectiveness. Where previously an attempt to tackle this problem within the army had been made through 'reading circles'– during time set aside for 'mass cultural work' – from 1931, time for developing literacy was included in the academic programme. At the same time the level of literacy of the bulk of conscripts was apparently improving, with official figures suggesting that the number of illiterate new recruits had fallen to 6.8 per cent in 1930 and 4.5 per cent in 1932. Improving and prolonged educational provision in schools certainly meant that the Red Army had access to an increasing number of recruits with better general educational preparation, and particularly for specialist arms.[20] Nonetheless, while younger generations were less likely to be illiterate, their elders who would be mobilised in time of war remained illiterate in more significant numbers. According to the 1937 census, just under 10 per cent of 20–24 year old males were illiterate, rising to just over 18 per cent for the 35–39 year old range.[21]

In the case of both commanders and men, it is tempting to speculate that time spent on political education severely limited time available for both training for combat and broader educational goals such as improving literacy. The 200 hours per year that were supposed to be spent by the rank and file on self study in preparation for political classes from January 1932 are a case in point.[22] One respondent to the post–Second World War Harvard University Refugee Interview Project, who lectured in chemical warfare (chemical troops were responsible for smokelaying and flamethrowers as well as toxic gases) suggested that during the 1930s perhaps 'one hour in five' was spent on political education, success in which was often more important for advancement than in actual military matters.[23]

For most of the year – when it occured – education and training took place within a unit. The Soviet military system – and to a large extent its territorial element – meant that for many units field training, and certainly 'manoeuvres', took place only during the summer and autumn. During the summer, tactical training involving more than one unit might take place during camp, before larger scale manoeuvres in the autumn that would see more manoeuvre and engagement between larger formations.[24] Only in the latter case would troops really get a taste of combined arms warfare against a 'real' opponent. As Nikolai Iakovlev points out in his memoirs cited earlier, recalling a period in mid-1920s during which he served as commander of the 3rd *Divizion* [equivalent to a battalion] of the 28th Artillery Regiment, large scale manoeuvres at the military district level 'were conducted relatively infrequently', and 'tactical field exercises', typically lasting two or three days, were largely confined to the summer, noting that 'if these exercises took place in the winter, then they did so as a rule only once [per year]'.[25] Not only were they limited to the autumn, but also manoeuvres seem to have only taken place in good weather. Even in 1936, the first day of manoeuvres of the Belorussian Military District were for example cancelled due to rain as will be discussed further later. The contrived nature of manoeuvres did not stop there. During the period with which this chapter is concerned, according to guidelines for their conduct, manoeuvres were typically to be limited in duration to the daylight hours – with manoeuvres lasting more than seven or eight hours from dawn being atypical. Convenient breaks were allowed between phases of manoeuvres to allow for the repositioning of forces, for whom combat often only involved initial contact and not the breaching of positions in depth. All of this was watched over by umpires, whose role seemed to be as much to make sure that the manoeuvres went according to plan as adjudication.[26]

While low levels of education and limited and unrealistic training undoubtedly hampered the effectiveness of the Red Army as a whole, Tukhachevskii's comments about the 1926 manoeuvres suggested that the problem was far more serious where commanders were concerned. In a decree of the Central Committee of the Party 'On the Command and Political Personnel of the RKKA' of 5 June 1931 it was explicitly stated that 'the level of military-technical training of commanders is clearly inadequate' – the rectification of which was deemed to be 'the fundamental, currently decisive task in raising the combat readiness of the army further'. This would allow them to master the new equipment they were to receive, and the use of such equipment in 'complex forms of modern combat'.[27] Educational levels among potential commanders remained low in the late 1920s – in 1928 among first year students of military schools only 18.8 per cent had previously received seven years of general education, a percentage that had risen to only 24.3 per cent by 1932. This meant that considerable time had to be spent on raising the general level of education of students, before they could focus their attentions on specialist military knowledge. However, by 1936, 73.5 per cent of new recruits had actually received eight years of general education, with the remaining 26.5 per cent receiving seven years. By this time the total number of students in military schools had also increased – from 44,000 in 1932 to 63,440 at the end of 1936. New higher educational institutions created during the 1930s seemed to have the potential to significantly increase the education level of commanders, with 1932 for example seeing the creation of a number of specialised military academies such as the Military Academy for Motorisation and Mechanisation.[28]

This all looked good on paper, but the realities were less impressive. Even if the general educational level of students was increasing, a key problem was having suitable teachers and lecturers for the schools and academies. Such personnel could not be simply conjured up out of thin air, and Red Army schools and academies were competing with the civilian sphere for qualified specialists. The situation was made worse by the fact that by the end of the 1930s, in the era of forced collectivisation and rapid industrialisation, the regime was increasingly concerned with political reliability. Just as being a worker was seen to indicate reliability for new recruits, social origin was a key indicator for teaching staff and other commanders. Many 'military specialists' who had served the Red Army during the Civil War lacked the right social credentials and were 'purged'. According to Voroshilov, speaking at the February–March 1937 plenum of the Central Committee of the Party, between 1934 and 1936 alone 22 thousand personnel had been 'purged' from the Red Army – some for good reason such as alcoholism, but many experienced commanders because of mistrust based on their social origins.[29] It was perhaps positive in many instances for the Red Army that some of those with inappropriate social credentials not 'purged' from the Red Army were deposited in military academies rather than given more sensitive field commands. One respondent to the HPSSS who had taught in military schools suggested that the percentage of non-Party commanders was far higher in military schools – where promotion prospects were poor – than in 'the line'.[30] The contribution of the Soviet military theorist G.S. Isserson to the development of the Red Army was perhaps greater as a lecturer at the Frunze and later General Staff Academy than it would have been as a field commander whose promotion was probably hampered by suspicion about his political reliability – and his outspokenness on military matters that seems not to have been tempered when communicating with superiors. Many commanders that would rise to prominence during the Great Patriotic War were taught by Isserson, including Vasilevskii, Bagramian, Zakharov, Sandalov and Rotmistrov, the latter's academic thesis at the Frunze Academy being written under Isserson's supervision. It is possible that Isserson simply wasn't a good field commander, but as a lecturer it seems he served a valuable role.[31]

Soviet military theorist Aleksandr Svechin – who was killed during the Great Purges – can also be seen to have fulfilled a valuable role as a lecturer in the General Staff Academy, to which he was sent after an earlier arrest and incarceration.[32]

As the Red Army started to expand in the late 1920s and early 1930s, not only was the quality of military educational provision arguably decreasing, but also the time spent on that education – and not only because political education was eating into time available for other learning. As Red Army expansion progressed, according to Roger R. Reese, where previously the curriculum for future commanders had required 3–4 years to complete, during the mid-1930s the military schools were churning out graduates often after only two years, which would probably have been a sufficient period to turn a well educated new intake into commanders. However, the intakes during this period were so poorly educated that it is questionable how much serious military education they received and digested as they were supposed at the same time to be raising their general educational levels and wasting considerable time on political education. Even if taking the education that these future commanders and specialists received as satisfactory, the numbers being trained were always behind demand as the Red Army expanded. By 1936, the overall education level of the Red Army commanders remained low. As Reese again notes, citing figures presented by the then head of the military education administration for the Red Army, as of October 1936, 10 per cent of battalion and regimental commanders had only a primary education – percentages rising to 30 per cent of company-level commanders and 70 per cent of junior lieutenants, highlighting how those passing through the military schools and academies were having only a limited impact in raising the overall educational level of an expanding Red Army.[33]

Combat training for commanders of course suffered from the same limitations as that for the rank and file – for example manoeuvres took place only during the summer and autumn, in good weather, typically in daylight and for only part of the day and so forth. Additionally, although such manoeuvres were supposed to allow commanders to show initiative, in reality they were so tightly choreographed by umpires that this claim was almost farcical. Senior commanders typically directed this pantomime for the benefit of their troops, gaining little meaningful command experience with real formations operating outside parameters that they themselves had defined!

Other than lacking suitable education and 'realistic' training involving the exercising of initiative, commanders with the right social and Party credentials were burdened with responsibility for political education as the Party sought to bring in unitary command in the Red Army from 1925. Unitary command – where a commander had authority over both the political and military affairs of a unit – was to replace dual command that had been instituted during the Civil War. During the Civil War, commanders had been supervised when leading Red Army units by political commissars with whom they shared command – a measure instituted given the lack of trust in the political reliability of former Tsarist officers in particular.[34] A significant 73.3 per cent of corps commanders had the 'privilege' of unitary command in 1925, although only 33.4 per cent of regimental commanders. By 1927, 48 per cent of regimental commanders enjoyed formal unitary command and the demands on their time that came with it, requiring that steps be taken to alleviate the burden that these matters placed on them. Clarification of what unitary command should mean in practice gave commanders deemed reliable responsibility for 'general party-political leadership', and his 'assistant for political affairs' responsibility for the 'practical realization' of policy.[35] Nonetheless, the Party's commitment to the idea that commanders should place political education at the heart of military life meant distraction from other tasks that went beyond the sort of concerns for morale that officers in other armies had to deal with. One respondent to the HPSSS who served as a commander suggested that the combined workload of having to deal with military and political training and education was enough to drive some commanders to suicide – with the political component of their work conducted under the watchful eye of the political organs being the cause of particular anxiety.[36] The revolutionary hostility towards bourgeois distinctions between ranks included undermining the concept of the non-commissioned officer as well as officer, and commanders lacked assistance from a capable NCO class in the day-to-day running of the unit. Only in November 1940 would the rank of sergeant be reintroduced – along with junior sergeant and senior sergeant – titles designed to foster greater 'responsibility' on the part of junior command elements, as well as raising their 'authority'.[37]

One might also argue that Soviet commanders also lacked the sort of privileges and professional status that might act as motivation to really get to grips with issues not only of running a unit on a day-to-day basis but also mastering the military craft. Respondents to the HPSSS suggest that while senior commanders lived at least reasonably well by Soviet standards during the late 1920s–early 1930s, their junior counterparts had all of the work and few compensatory privileges to motivate them. As Reese notes, it was not until 1934 that a lieutenant in the infantry would make more than a factory worker. In 1935, a battalion commander received less than a factory foreman, and a factory supervisor more than a corps commander! Red Army commanders were not necessarily compensated in kind, for instance housing was often in short supply and 'what housing existed was often in a pitiful state'. Reese goes on to suggest that the accommodation provided for the command ranks through to the equivalent of colonel 'equaled those of ordinary civilians – overcrowded and dilapidated'.[38] Conditions were undoubtedly worse in many ways out in the provinces, to which most commanders could be expected to be posted at some point. As a divisional commander in the provincial town of Slutsk in Belorussia, to which he was transferred in the spring of 1933, future Marshal of the Soviet Union Georgii Zhukov and his family were provided with a single '8-meter' room – presumably 8 m/sq – as temporary accommodation, Zhukov noting the 'problems with accommodation' faced then and after the war. He later notes how many families had given up 'nice apartments below Leningrad' with the transfer to Slutsk.[39] On his transfer to Moscow in early 1936, G.S. Isserson – at this stage a brigade commander – was however provided with a four-room apartment in the Chistie Prudi area of Moscow, and was even able to employ a live-in maid. As Harrison suggests, perhaps the mid-1930s were 'the high-water mark of the prewar Red Army's power and influence in Soviet society', when material rewards accompanied the improved social status of commanders.[40] The Great Purges would bring the prestige of the Red Army command corps crashing down, once again presumably making becoming a commander in the Red Army less appealing for many than other employment options in the civilian sector. Certainly, during the late 1920s and early 1930s, where industrial workers and managers seemed to be far more highly rewarded for their labours than army commanders, and being a commander did not bring the social prestige that being an officer had during the Tsarist era, there was a shortage of suitably qualified volunteers for command schools – where choosing to receive such an education as part of military service added years to the service obligation. After appeals to various Party and Soviet organisations for volunteers to make up for a deficit in candidates for command positions in 1929 did not yield the required numbers, in 1931, the Party launched a special mobilisation of members for service as commanders that contributed to the enrollment of 17,000 members for education in the military schools in 1931 and 1932, followed by another 10,000 between 1933 and 1935. At the same time in order to reduce shortfalls in available commanders, the Party propelled men from the ranks with Party memberships into command roles, encouraging others from the ranks to voluntarily apply for military schools, and created an accelerated promotion process for 'NCOs' in training to become lieutenants by examination or short courses. As Reese notes, training and cohesion

were sacrificed through these unorthodox commissioning methods –
undermining the military ethos and contributing to the lack of 'professionalism' of the Soviet officer corps that Reese argues dogged the Red
Army right up to the collapse of the Soviet Union.[41]

In addition to Red Army commanders lacking the motivation of prestige – and for junior commanders material reward – for most of the
period of Red Army expansion from the late 1920s onwards, their ability
to effectively command was undoubtedly hampered by the lack of a stark
formal distinction between commanders and men that was a product of
the revolutionary ideals of 1917. While arguably if commanders are too
detached from the men they lead then they are less likely to be able to
command and lead effectively – as Brian R. Sullivan suggests was the
case in the Italian army – having little more status than the men is
typically not good for enforcing discipline.[42] During the 1920s and early
1930s those who would formally become officers during the late 1930s
and wartime period were known as 'command elements', and hence
those who will later be described as officers are identified as commanders
in this chapter. Commanders were often undermined in attempting to
command by the political correctness of the day that elevated the status
of the rank and file and gave it considerable scope for insubordination.[43]
This was particularly the case when commanders came from pre-
revolutionary middle or even upper class social backgrounds. An
unnamed respondent to the HPSSS, from such a middle class background, gave the following example of a situation in which his authority
was undermined. In 1935, while travelling on a bus that was full to
capacity with Red Army personnel, a 'junior sergeant' tried to board
the bus. The 'officer' concerned had been told to limit those on the bus
to twenty-six. Having been told it was full, and with the 'sergeant' having
forcibly tried to board, the 'officer' concerned had him removed before
the bus continued on its way. For this the 'officer' was called to justify his
actions, deemed inappropriate, in front of the commissar of the military
school at which he served – a note being made on his service record that
he had 'behaved in an unpleasant manner to a Red Army man'. A similar
example is provided by another respondent, who, of lower middle class
origins himself had married the daughter of a former Tsarist officer.
A comment by his wife in 1933 in the club facilities shared by commanders and rank and file personnel that there was 'an odor from the Red
Army men who were close by' resulted in similar trouble with a
commissar.[44]

In theory, Red Army commanders exercised unitary command over
their units by 1927, but as noted earlier when discussing workload, full
unitary command was certainly not 'enjoyed' by all commanders at this

point. By the beginning of 1930, 27 per cent of regimental commanders still did not have *de jure* full unitary command of their units, although by the middle of 1931 the transition to unitary command in the ground forces was reportedly all but complete, even if it was less advanced for naval and air forces.[45] The fact that dual command had meant that political commissars could countermand the orders of commanders on political grounds gave them considerable scope for interference in tactical and operational decision making, and certainly in the day-to-day running of units. Ultimately the commissar had held the reins – and the rank and file knew it – with obvious ramifications for the authority of the commander. By 1925, with at least some commanders with the right social backgrounds having been trained, the regime was confident enough to move towards unitary command in the Red Army, supposedly giving all commanders full control over 'operational-combat, administrative and housekeeping functions'. Nonetheless, responsibility for the 'moral-political state' of many units still gave the commissar something of a blank cheque for interference, particularly given the culture that had developed during the Civil War.[46] Testimony above from the HPSSS certainly suggests that de jure authority did not necessarily apply in practice for some who were nominally in sole command during a period in which the regime was encouraging vigilance over 'class enemies'. In such a situation, a shift in culture and practice away from suspicion of commanders from the wrong social backgrounds to complement changes in regulations was unlikely, even when, in an attempt to create a distinct officer class with greater prestige without actually using the word 'officer', in 1935 the rank structure of the Red Army was revised. That year ranks that had been used in the Tsarist army – from *leitenant* to *polkovnik*, that is direct equivalents to from lieutenant to colonel in the West – were resurrected, even if the regime wouldn't have the stomach to replace more senior titles such as *komkor* or corps commander with their pre-revolutionary equivalents until 1940.[47]

In terms of commanding effectively, language barriers were an added complication for Russian commanders with non-Russian units, the formation of which had been promoted in the 1920s. During this period, although the Soviet leadership had been willing to forcibly incorporate the various nationalities of the former Russian Empire into the Soviet Union, the regime neither had the confidence nor resources to attempt to Sovietise many of these peoples. Having lost Finland and the Baltic Republics from the 'imperial' fold after the Civil War, the Ukraine and Belorussia remained in the west to be incorporated into the federal system that became the Soviet Union in 1924. Taking the Ukraine as a whole, it is easy to exaggerate the extent of Ukrainian nationalism at the time where in a largely peasant republic the tendency beyond urban intellectual circles was arguably more towards the prominence of very local rather than national identity – if anything Soviet policies in the 1920s fostered significant growth in Ukrainian nationalism. Belorussia was similarly rural, but arguably less culturally distinct from Russia. Both were relatively straightforward to incorporate into the Soviet system compared to the Caucasian and Central Asian republics, where both cultural and linguistic differences were serious barriers to integration. Given a degree of tolerance of non-threatening national identity, and the lack of resources both for integration and the military, initially the easiest approach to mobilising many smaller nationalities for military service was not to do so at all and ignore them. For the others the policy of 'nativiza-tion' [*korenizatsiia*] of 1923 pointed to troops being mobilised, trained and deployed along ethnic lines – being trained and led in their local languages and serving alongside their ethnic peers.[48]

A report by Frunze of 29 December 1924 on the incorporation of the nationalities into the Red Army noted how the process of incorporation had to date moved slowly and did not include many of them at all. The report noted the requirement of the plan to have created a number of national formations by 1929, including for example a cavalry division in the Turkmen SSR and a rifle division with cavalry squadron in the Iakutsk SSR. By May 1926, the Red Army could note success in forming the required units in the culturally more similar and indeed economically more advanced western republics, but poor progress in Central Asia. In the case of the Turkmen SSR a single cavalry regiment had been formed out of the four required for a cavalry division, with even a single regiment not yet formed out of the four required for the Kazakh Cavalry Division specified in the plan. Even then, the report went on to note that 'far from all' existing national units provided 'reliable [*prochnie*] cadres for further development' of national formations.[49] Given that the development of national formations would be at the expense of other Red Army units, it was proposed that the Red Army no longer form national units in the Iakutsk and Kazakh republics, and:

Along with the rejection of forming Iakutsk and Kazakh (and also Kalmyk) national units it is necessary to cease to call up these nationalities for military service while suitable military-political preparation has not been conducted amongst this population and while the necessity for bearing such compulsory military service has not been firmly and solidly instilled in them. Until that time pre-conscription preparatory work is to be conducted with the organized youth of these nationalities, and those wishing to undertake military service on a voluntary basis are to be accepted into regular units.[50]

Issues with the performance of existing national units were to be rectified in part through such measures as sending reliable commanders from other Red Army units of that nationality to the national units and actually providing national units with the necessary infrastructure and other means to perform during a time of relative scarcity – particularly providing horses for cavalry units. Language barriers remained, perhaps unsurprisingly, an important issue – and one that would not go away. In a situation where there were insufficient native commanders within a unit, the report noted how Russian commanders had to 'run for the help of interpreters' when giving commands.[51] The bulk of personnel in national units were Ukrainians and Belorussians, and in fact only 18,912 personnel were from other nationalities in May 1927, representing a considerable but still inadequate investment of resources for a very limited outcome in terms of troops.

Despite the expense of the national units and questions about their military value in a broader sense, such units were however a relatively economical means of strengthening the Soviet military presence in the sparsely populated regions of Central Asia and the Far East – a point noted in the 1927 report – alongside the fact that such nationalities offered experience and skills in physical and climatic environments such as mountainous regions that were hardly typical in the Soviet population as a whole.[52] This was certainly reason enough not only to keep such units on the books but continue to foster their developments. A respondent to the HPSSS noted how by 1930 the 'Tatarization' of the Tatarstan Rifle Division was complete, with all of the officers and personnel being Tatars.[53] The extent to which such units had been part of a pro-national development policy is highlighted by the fact that for some, and even for Belorussians, passing through a Belorussian military education had in the mid-1920s meant learning their supposedly native tongue for the first time![54]

A respondent to the HPSSS, an Azeri, and early graduate of the Transcaucasian Military School from which he graduated in 1926, served in the recently formed Azeri Mountain Rifle Division from 1929 as a commander and was elected secretary of the Party Bureau in Baku. However, in 1932 he claims to have been sidelined for expressing support for national units at a divisional Party conference resulting in accusations of 'nationalism' and his being subsequently sent to the 4th Mountain Regiment in Karabakh.[55] The Great Purges saw the final dissolution of the national divisions as Stalin's personal distrust of many nationalities alongside other elements of the Soviet population was violently expressed. Whether such concerns were unfounded is debatable – a respondent to the HPSSS, an Armenian, describes how the Armenian

Mountain Rifle Division was replaced in April 1931 by NKVD troops in fighting with insurgents opposed to collectivisation – having been deemed unreliable.[56] Not only were some national units deemed to be of suspect reliability during the late 1920s and early 1930s, but also some peasant-dominated units of otherwise reliable nationality during a period in which the regime forcibly collectivised Soviet agriculture. The issue of social origin and promotion has already been raised earlier, but here the issue was not one of bourgeois origin, but origins and sympathies with the wrong part of the peasantry – the rich peasants or *kulaks* – a term which became a catch all for any peasant opposing collectivisation.[57] Particularly vehement and widespread opposition to collectivisation from some national groups almost made them kulaks *en masse* in the eyes of the regime.

One exception to the trend during the 1930s towards the dissolution of national formations was the removal of the bar to military service of Cossacks, who had in many ways symbolised the forces of reaction during the revolutionary year 1917. In a Politburo decree of 20 April 1936, a number of existing cadre and territorial cavalry divisions were renamed as Cossack divisions and a new 13th Don Cossack Territorial Division was formed. Personnel from the Caucasian mountain nationalities were to be removed from what became 10th Terek-Stavropol' Division and formed into a separate regiment that would become part of a cavalry brigade of the mountain peoples.[58] With larger cadre elements than other territorial divisions, and their own uniforms, at a time of mounting international tension it seems that the regime was willing to compromise on ideology in order to harness the legendary military prowess of the Cossack peoples.

Many senior Red Army commanders had a soft spot for the cavalry arm, which as suggested earlier had played a significant role in Soviet victory during the Civil War, and there can be no doubt that the experience of the Civil War of 1917–1921 was the formative military experience for many Soviet military leaders of the 1920s and 1930s. The war of manoeuvre that was the focus of Soviet military theory in the late 1920s may superficially seem progressive, but was in fact in many ways quite the opposite. During the Russian Civil War relatively poorly equipped forces had operated in an environment in which there was usually a flank to go round, and in which cavalry were ascendant. In many ways the Red Army had been able to realise the hopes of many cavalrymen during the First World War in the West, for whom the breakthrough allowing cavalry to manoeuvre in the enemy rear came only belatedly. Even with Allied breakthrough in late 1918, it had been the tank that had proven to have

Cavalry at a May Day parade in Khar'kov in 1928. During the 1920s and into the 1930s the cavalry remained the principal manoeuvre arm of the Red Army much as it had been during the Civil War. (RIA Novosti #24980)

the degree of survivability to operate in an environment where a single heavy machine gun could hold up a regiment of cavalry.

For military leaders such as Voroshilov and Budennii, with their more limited intellectual abilities to grasp how the Civil War they fought was not typical of warfare of the era, Soviet military theory of the 1920s developed during a period in which the Red Army lacked modern weapons such as tanks and aircraft. These factors allowed their beloved cavalry to maintain an undeservedly high position in the hierarchy of arms in the Red Army. Voroshilov did at least seem to realise by the mid-1930s that even though substantial cavalry formations might survive the introduction of the tank and armoured cars in large numbers, there could be no going back to the period when the cavalry was the dominant offensive arm. When in August 1937, Budennii all but pleaded with Voroshilov on the subject of the importance of cavalry formations in the Red Army after the arrest of Tukhachevskii and other mechanisers, Voroshilov was swift to issue a resolution that 'it is necessary to and we will cut cavalry strength'.[59] Nonetheless, during the 1920s, cavalry had many advantages for a peacetime Red Army, and particularly where industrialisation was in its infancy – horses were more readily available than motor vehicles, and fodder more than petrol. In a still predominantly peasant society, and particularly among some of the Caucasian and Central Asian nationalities, at least crude skills were readily available. For internal security operations that were in many ways similar to many smaller actions of the Civil War, the horse made sense. Rejection of pre-Soviet elite culture had unfortunately led to some loss of more refined horsemanship skills along with the social baggage of the former officer corps, and horse husbandry and day-to-day care of horses seem to have suffered too. During the late 1920s and early 1930s the cavalry arm, that had in 1924 been described as 'an independent arm of the Soviet Armed Forces', remained central to the offensive in developing doctrine. Attacking largely while still mounted, 'strategic cavalry' formations were the primary means to operate at any depth during offensive operations given the absence of tanks. During the 1930s, cavalry units were incorporated into the combined arms schema for offensive operations alongside tanks, playing a central role in what became known as 'Deep Battle'.[60]

2 Tanks, Aircraft and 'Deep Battle'
The Red Army Transformed 1928–1936

The history of the development of Soviet theories on the use of tanks, and in particular in a tactical schema that became known as 'Deep Battle', is covered elsewhere in some detail – here we are concerned with the application of theoretical work to practice and in particular its influence over Soviet field regulations and organisation.[1] The 1983 Soviet Military Encyclopedic Dictionary succinctly defines the concept of 'Deep Battle' as 'the simultaneous suppression of the tactical defence of the enemy in all its depth, and breakthrough by infantry and tanks supported by artillery and aviation'.[2] Crucial in achieving this breakthrough was the simultaneous use of all of these arms – combined arms – where mobility would be essential for their continued co-operation and co-ordination as the breakthrough progressed. Particular credit is given in the Soviet literature to Mikhail Tukhachevskii and Vladimir Triandafillov for the early development of this conception, that obviously draws and expands on the earlier work of the British theorists J.F.C. Fuller and B.H. Liddell-Hart. Soviet-German military co-operation during the late 1920s and early 1930s prior to the ascendancy of Hitler in Germany gave opportunity for the interchange of ideas between German and Soviet commanders, with 'Deep Battle' and the practice of what would come to be known as Blitzkrieg having obvious similarities. Both these, and the theories of Fuller and Liddell-Hart, stemmed from the problems faced by armies in breaking through enemy defensive positions in depth during the First World War. The key issue was the attacker having sufficient momentum to break through enemy positions in depth before the enemy could bring up significant reserves. In order to break through layers of defence it was necessary to provide the infantry with the fire support both to suppress immediate defences and enemy artillery and then mobile artillery resources to deal with any defensive lines that might exist or crystallise behind them. Where towards the end of the First World War the tank and infiltration tactics both played a role in breakthrough of enemy forward defences, conventional horse-drawn artillery lacked the cross-country mobility and survivability to keep pace with the infantry and tank attack. Infantry and tanks – and particularly one of these without the other – could be halted by a new line consisting of enemy infantry and artillery, where at depth the ability of the defender to reinforce a sector was not hampered by the churned up ground across which the attacker had to advance. Through the use of tactical air support and airborne forces to disrupt the enemy rear as infantry and tanks supported by artillery broke through the enemy frontline, 'Deep Battle' was the Soviet equivalent to the German practice of what came to be known later as 'Blitzkrieg' as a tactical and lower level operational concept, with 'Deep Operations' being the logical wider operational extension of the tactical model that allowed for deep penetration by armoured forces supported by airpower. Certainly reading the minutes of meetings of the Military Council of the People's Commissar for Defence during the early-mid 1930s, it becomes apparent that Tukhachevskii should be given much credit in the practical development of 'Deep Battle' and its operational extension given his broad appreciation of the value of new technology in modern warfare, and in particular the tank and aircraft. His persistence in the promotion of the new arms in the face of a lack of understanding of the potential of new technology and defence of the cavalry arm by those such as Budennii and to a lesser extent Kliment Voroshilov certainly played an important part in the development of the military-industrial capacity that was so important in Soviet victory in the Great Patriotic War.

The Red Army Field Regulations of 1936 – practical instructions for commanders that incorporate the by then developed theory of 'Deep Battle' – are an impressive document. Had the Red Army been able to carry them out during the summer of 1941 it is questionable whether the Wehrmacht would have achieved as much as it did even with flawed Soviet operational and strategic deployment. From the importance of reconnaissance through to the necessity for effective co-ordination of arms, the instructions in the regulations seem a coherent expression of the theoretical developments that had been taking place since the late 1920s. The Red Army was certainly getting closer to Tukhachevskii and his colleagues, aspirations by 1945, but a still predominately peasant society in which top-down control was particularly pronounced was perhaps not the ideal society to implement them. The regulations are in some senses surprisingly realistic about at least some of the limitations of the Red Army in 1936. As will be discussed later, despite the achievements of Soviet industry in many spheres, in terms of communications the Red Army was poorly equipped. In this context, when discussing the 'fundamentals of command and control' [osnovi upravleniia boem] the fact that instructions state that commanders 'should allocate sufficient

Mikhail Tukhachevskii, as its commander, parades on the 10th anniversary of the Leningrad Military District in late 1930. Tukhachevskii would play a pivotal role in the tank rising to prominence over cavalry in the ambitious combined-arms schema developed for the Red Army during the early 1930s and expressed in the 1936 Field Regulations. (RIA Novosti #21806)

daylight before the start of operations in order to raise the quality of command and control of troops and for the decisive reduction of the time required for the giving of orders at corps, divisional and regimental headquarters' is telling. One area where the regulations were weak was in realism about the extent to which – even in 1936 – subordinates were capable of and allowed to exercise genuine initiative in an army that like others seemed in practice to see 'initiative' [*initsiativ*] and 'bravery' as synonyms. The 1936 regulations suggest that 'the greatest success in military operations is achieved when commanders of all ranks are educated in the spirit of bold initiative' – a statement that might seem more appropriate for a German manual on infantry tactics than Soviet field regulations.[3] Indeed, the 1933 German *Truppenführung* manual less dramatically states, along similar lines, that an army and its subordinate units requires 'leaders capable of judgment, with clear vision and foresight, and the ability to make independent and decisive decisions and carry them out unwaveringly and positively'.[4] However, where the notion *Auftragstaktik* or 'mission-type orders' that in theory gave German officers and even NCOs some latitude in how to carry out orders to achieve a given goal within a given timeframe had genuine meaning in practice the Wehrmacht, its Soviet equivalent did not at all but the very highest levels of command – and indeed would not for the bulk of the Red Army even by 1945.[5]

Despite in many ways being a rather optimistic document, the Red Army had nonetheless produced a sound set of field regulations by 1936 towards which it could strive, and also had much of the equipment at least to be able to make headway in implementing them on the ground. In 1936, the Red Army was equipped with modern tanks and aircraft that had simply not existed in the late 1920s. In 1927, the Red Army had a single tank regiment made up of two types of battalion – heavy and light – of thirty tanks each, with strengths of 692 and 438 men respectively. Most of the ninety tanks available had been captured by the Bolsheviks during the Civil War – 45 'Rikardo' or British Mk V, 12 'Teilor' or 'Whippet', and 33 'Reno' or Renault FT-17. In the latter case 15 'Russian Renaults' had been produced by the Bolsheviks over a two-year period during the Civil War, based on a captured example. The first of these tanks entered service in December 1920, and the last 8 had the novelty of combining an 8 mm machine gun with a 37 mm cannon in the turret, although the former was not co-axial but on the plate to the right of the cannon. The 'Russian Renault' did not however see combat.[6] With the last 'Russian Renault' Soviet tank production ceased until the late 1920s.

Unlike tank production, Soviet aircraft production did not collapse after the Civil War, where aircraft that could be used for military purposes had a role to play in the civilian sphere. During the 1927–8 financial year the Soviet aircraft industry produced 644 aircraft and 614 aero engines, rising to 924 aircraft and 861 engines for the 1928–9 financial year.[7] In early 1929 the Red air forces had 909 aircraft in service (126 of which were seaplanes), making the Soviet Union a major power in terms of aircraft production and military air power in these crude terms – by Soviet reckoning at this time having the third largest air force in the world. Of these aircraft, the vast majority were however outdated types, with relatively few fighters and bombers. In fact, of the 909 aircraft, only 112 or 12.4 per cent were fighters and 211 or 23 per cent bombers. The remainder were classed as reconnaissance aircraft. The principal Soviet fighters, Fokker D-XIs, were described in a 1929 report on the state of the Red Army as 'outdated and worn out'.[8] Most Soviet aircraft engines produced up to this point had been based on foreign designs dating back to the First World War, and in fact quality issues in production had contributed to the fact that in 1928, 70 per cent of motors in Red Army aircraft had been manufactured abroad.[9]

The economic 'Great Turn' of the late 1920s and 1930s was funded to a large extent by the peasantry whose forced collectivisation made it possible for the state to systematically extract grain for sale abroad at relatively low cost. With the proceeds, Soviet industry could acquire the technology to advance at a more rapid tempo. The first of many Five-Year Plans that started practically in 1929 but officially in 1928 was more concerned with the broad development of raw materials extraction, processing and the development of core heavy industry. Nonetheless this period would see the Red Army gain new, Soviet-manufactured tanks and aircraft before the plan was deemed fulfilled. However, new equipment during this period was often of questionable quality. In the development of new industries and the capability for the mass production of more advanced aircraft there were inevitably teething troubles – exacerbated by the ridiculous demands placed on developing industries by the Soviet leadership and regular changes in plans. In late 1929 Voroshilov described the aircraft industry as being 'in serious crisis', and in the spring of 1930 Tukhachevskii even raised the idea of buying aircraft abroad. This was perhaps not such a dramatic suggestion as it might superficially have sounded, given that motors, avionics (for example altimeters) and other aircraft parts were being bought from abroad – and particularly the United States – in large numbers anyway.[10] During the 1st Five-Year Plan many foreign specialists had been brought in to assist with the development of Soviet industry, but no doubt as many of their domestic counterparts, were frustrated by disruption and resultant quality issues brought about by the nature of the Soviet planning process. However, improved design and development and quality controls, with some stabilisation in the planning process, would mean that during the Second Five-Year Plan the Red Army was receiving some of the best tanks and aircraft available anywhere in the world – manufactured in Soviet factories, even if often with foreign machine tools and reliant on foreign manufactured or licensed parts.

The first Soviet mass produced tank of this new era was in essence a development of the Renault FT-17. Series production of the MS-1 or T-18 was undertaken from November 1928 until late 1931, by which time up to 900 vehicles had been delivered to the Red Army. The first thirty tanks had been handed over to the Red Army in the spring of 1929, and are reported to have seen action shortly afterwards against the Chinese with the Special Far Eastern Army. A number of these vehicles in modified form apparently saw action with fortified districts during the

Some of the first Soviet-manufactured tanks – derived from the FT-17 of the First World War – are paraded in Kiev on May Day in 1932. (RIA Novosti #28931)

early phases of the Great Patriotic War.[11] Experience gained in manu-facturing, for example of armoured plate, could be applied to the pro-duction of new models with somewhat greater combat value, produced in large numbers, and that in developed forms would make up the bulk of the Soviet tank force at the outset of the Great Patriotic War.

In April 1930 the Soviet Union bought two examples of the American inventor Walter Christie's innovative tank the M1940 that not only offered considerable speed on tracks, but also the apparently useful but ultimately rarely used option of running without tracks. At the same time 20 Carden-Lloyd Mk-IV tankettes, 15 Vickers 6-tonne and 15 Vickers 12 tonne models were purchased in the United Kingdom. These tank designs were used as the bases for the T-27 tankette, T-26 and BT-2 tanks respectively. In addition, British designs were used in the develop-ment of the T-37A amphibious tank, the T-28 medium, and T-35 heavy tanks.[12] Initial plans for the expansion of the Soviet tank force of June 1928 aimed at the Red Army having 1,075 tanks at the end of the 1st

Five-Year Plan, an ambitious enough target given that the Soviet tank industry was starting essentially from scratch. By July 1929, the aim was to have 1,500 tanks in service by the end of the 1st Five-Year Plan – not including at least the same number again for immediate wartime deployments and in reserve. At this point as plans escalated, only a limited number of T-18 tanks had actually been produced and handed over to the Red Army.[13] Production of the T-26 and T-27 tankette started in 1931, with the BT-2 in 1932 and T-35 in 1933. Needless to say, Soviet industry could not meet the increasing demands made upon it, and production fell short of plans. Nonetheless, the 1,050 T-26s and 2,086 lighter T-27s, along with 396 BT-2s – a total of 3,532 tanks – produced by the end of 1932 was a considerable achievement. As the 2nd Five-Year Plan progressed, Soviet industry was churning out tanks that rivaled or exceeded the tanks of foreign powers in their respective classes in terms of core indicators such as speed, armoured protection and firepower – and were being produced in huge numbers. In 1936, even if production was behind absurd targets, Soviet industry produced an impressive 3,935 tanks – 1,313 T-26, 411 T-37, 1,046 T-38 – 'light' tanks – along with 1,049 BT-7 'medium' tanks and 15 T-35 'heavy' tanks. That 101 T-18s are listed in this source as having been produced in 1936 suggests however that upgrades and modifications have been included in these Gosplan figures.[14] Much of this tank park – and even the newer models – would however soon become obviously inadequate as more dedicated infantry anti-tank weapons appeared, where the vulnerability to artillery of tanks with armour only capable of withstanding small arms fire had been shown during the First World War and was reinforced in Spain. At this point the focus on producing tanks without due attention being paid to the more prosaic concern of providing sufficient spare parts was not such an issue as it would become by the end of the decade and into the next, by which point the Red Army would struggle to keep many of these vehicles in operation. Soviet tank losses in 1941 would be greatly exacerbated by a lack of tank repair capabilities and spare parts.

The divide between plans and capabilities was perhaps worse in the aircraft industry, and particularly where aircraft motors were concerned. In July 1929 a key Central Committee resolution on defence had inflated the target for aircraft strength from 2,000 operational aircraft at the end of the 1st Five-Year Plan (from the existing strength of 1,032) in a June draft of the resolution, to a target for a staggering 20,000 aircraft in service at the end of the plan in the final July version of the document. All this was with the expectation that Soviet aircraft, as well as tanks and artillery, would be technically superior to those of an opponent.[15] The production of 5,109 aircraft between 1930 and 1932 was a considerable achievement, even if such production highlighted the absurdity of a 20,000 target by the end of the plan.[16] The overall production of large numbers of aircraft may have looked good when presented as figures for increased production, but could not hide the fact that the Soviet aircraft industry still lagged behind foreign competitors in terms of quality. Foreign aircraft engines, and increasingly more powerful high perform-ance air cooled models were purchased from abroad, but it took time to modify them for Soviet production and then produce them in large quantities whilst not sacrificing quality in a system that initially placed far too much emphasis on the former. The quality controls in the aircraft industry of the early 1930s had to be improved given the sophistication of the product. Particular success was had with the construction of more simple straightforward aircraft such as the ubiquitous U-2 trainer and utility aircraft that would even be impressed into service as a light bomber during the Great Patriotic War.

Perhaps the best Soviet fighter of the early 1930s was the Polikarpov I-5 biplane, design of which took place in 1930 with some haste – Polikarpov no doubt motivated by a death sentence that hung over him like a sword of Damocles. Despite performance being hit by the substi-tution of a Soviet M-22 engine for the French-produced Bristol Jupiter engines used in prototypes, the aircraft was undoubtedly a success com-pared to other fighters of the time, apparently having a better rate of climb and manoeuvrability than the contemporary Heinkel HD-37, Curtiss P-6E and Bristol Bulldog by virtue of its light weight, even if the I-5 lacked the speed of competitors. The I-5 was the principal Soviet fighter of the early 1930s, of which 803 were produced by late 1935. Its success undoubtedly saved the designer Polikarpov's life at a time when the regime was looking for scapegoats, and particular amongst those of bourgeois origin, for industrial failures. However, the I-5 did not go into series production until late 1932, with deliveries from February 1933. In fact, delays in the production of the I-5 led to the licensed production of the Heinkel HD 37c with a BMW (M-17) engine already manufactured in the Soviet Union – in Soviet service the I-7. Consequently, by the time the I-5 was in service in significant numbers, it was already heading towards obsolescence.[17]

Despite the crises in the Soviet aircraft industry of the early 1930s, by the end of 1936 considerable strides had been made in quality control, and Soviet industry was producing some of the best aircraft in the world in large quantities. Overall aircraft production for 1936 stood at 4,270 aircraft, with 11,326 aircraft engines produced.[18] The design process for the Polikarpov I-16 monoplane fighter began in the summer of 1933, meaning that a successor to the I-5 was in the pipeline as it started to look obsolete. With the outdated Soviet M-22 engine initially installed in the new I-16 monoplane fighter replaced by a more powerful Wright Cyclone 1830-F-3 engine that improved performance, particularly at altitude, overall the I-16 performed better than the opposition even if initial production aircraft appearing in 1934 were still powered by the M-22 engine. Performance of the aircraft was sufficiently good for the installation of an 8 mm armoured pilot's seat which did not have a negative impact on performance. The I-16, with production aircraft soon equipped with the improved engine, saw combat in Spain from the autumn of 1936 onwards, comparing favourably with the German Heinkel He-51 and Italian Fiat CR-32 biplanes it faced as discussed in the next chapter. However, by this point foreign manufacturers were developing the next generation of fighters and bombers – improved versions of the Bf 109 started to surpass the I-16 in performance, leaving the Soviet Union with a large aircraft park that in a similar manner to its tanks would soon be outdated.

In 1929, the Party had specified that the Red Army should have technology more advanced than potential enemies for three types of weapons systems by the end of the 1st Five-Year Plan – aircraft and tanks covered above – along with artillery. Here initial targets were perhaps more measured, even if they would still be raised well beyond the point that Soviet industry could hope to meet them during the hectic years of the 1st and 2nd Five-Year Plans. Of 999 artillery pieces ordered for 1929–30 the production of 952 was a considerable success.[19] However, in July 1929, after a measured start, dramatic increases were planned for artillery production, and particularly in a crude numerical sense for light and anti-aircraft artillery. For light artillery slated for deployment at battalion level an increase from 270 pieces to 2,682 pieces by the spring of 1933 was planned. By 1 November 1936 the Red Army had been supplied with 1,620 Obr 1927 76.2 mm regimental guns that could use the same ammunition as the divisional guns of the same caliber. Rate of fire was low given the use of a breech block of outdated design – the weapon was based on a 1913 Tsarist weapon – but this useful weapon continued to be used and produced with minor modifications and new ammunition throughout the 1930s and the Great Patriotic War. In 1929, the Red Army also had few anti-aircraft guns – in fact the Red Army didn't have any modern light anti-aircraft guns and only 528 outdated medium caliber weapons, with targets to have 712 and 1218 weapons in these categories respectively by the spring of 1933. Light automatic anti-aircraft guns would appear in most armies as the 1930s progressed, and meaningful progress in this sphere was initially limited to the production of a Soviet-produced version of a 75 mm weapon initially purchased from a subsidiary of the German firm Rheinmetall. Produced as the 76 mm Anti-Aircraft gun Obr. 1931 (3-K), 1,171 guns had been produced by 1 November 1936.[20]

The only category in which the Red Army was well stocked at the end of the 1920s, even if with weapons that had served during the Civil War, was in regular light and medium artillery. Much of the artillery produced during the early 1930s was based on these older Tsarist weapons – the 76.2 mm Obr. 1930 Divisional Gun was for example a 1902 Tsarist design that had been produced by the Bolsheviks during the Civil War, with modifications. Whilst the ranges of guns were increased, the modifications made in this instance did not go as far as the addition of suspension to the carriage, meaning that it could only be towed at 6–7 km/h! Nonetheless, more than 4,000 of these guns were produced up to 1937. These antiquated looking divisional guns would be replaced in production with the 76.2 mm Divisional Gun Obr. 1936 (F-22) by this point, and during 1937 417 examples of the F-22 were produced. The new carriage allowed towing at up to 30 km/h, meaning that it was a realistic proposition that such weapons might keep up with advancing mechanised forces. Many Obr. 1930 divisional guns, and indeed unmodified Obr. 1902 models, would however face the Germans in 1941.[21] The Bolsheviks had both inherited and then produced 122 mm howitzers in 1909 and 1910 variants that differed in their breech blocks, and these weapons were, as many others, also modernised during the 1930s. Where the old carriage with wooden wheels had only allowed towing at a speed of 6 km/h, the new carriage allowed a towing speed of 18 km/h. The later 122 mm Howitzer Obr. 1938 (M-30) was a superior weapon – a 1930s design on a modern carriage – that could be towed on good roads at up to 50 km/h and would ultimately serve throughout the Great Patriotic War. However, as with many weapons systems of the 1930s, the transition from design and trials to production was a slow one, where despite acceptance in 1938 production was only underway in earnest in 1940.[22]

In terms of heavy artillery, although Soviet industry was particularly slow in producing weapons in this category in quantity, there were a number of successful designs put into production during the early and mid-1930s. The 122 mm Obr. 1931 (A-19), on a new carriage from 1937, would continue in production throughout the 1930s and the war, but by 1 November 1936 only 74 guns had actually been produced. Similarly the ML-20 or 152 mm Howitzer-Gun Obr. 1937, a significantly modified and improved version of a 1910 weapon was in production by 1937, during which year 148 pieces were produced. Ambitious plans of 1929 for artillery production also sought an increase in super-heavy artillery pieces from 31 to 120 pieces. By 1 January 1937 Soviet industry had produced 88 B-4 BM and 31 B-4 MM tracked 203 mm Howitzers Obr. 1931.[23] One might wonder whether, given the state of Soviet industry and Red Army equipment in the late 1920s, the effort expended on super-heavy guns was an unnecessary diversion from basic types. Such weapons certainly however fitted in with the Soviet predisposition towards headline-grabbing monsters in many spheres (such as the Kalinin K-7 bomber). While the democracies were less prone to squandering resources in such a manner – or at least not moving them into production – Nazi Germany would exhibit this same tendency for artillery, aircraft and tanks (the Dornier X flying boat perhaps being the German equivalent of the K-7). These weapons would prove to have some utility in Finland in early 1940, and indeed during the second half of the Great Patriotic War, but are nonetheless indicative of a Soviet penchant for throwing far too many resources into the production of weapons rather than the means to sustain their activities and make their employment more effective.

Material presented earlier on the development and production of tanks, aircraft and artillery – prioritised in Soviet planning – shows how during the 1930s the Soviet Union was able to gradually move from the modification of pre-Soviet or foreign designs or systems based around foreign core components to Soviet designs that were produced to meet Soviet requirements. That this happened first in the design and production of artillery before in the sphere of more complicated weapons systems such as aircraft and tanks is understandable, but by the end of the decade the Soviet Union would be able to both design and manufacture its own equipment in all of these spheres.

For developing concepts of 'Deep Battle' some of this artillery, along with at least some of the infantry, would have to be mechanised. During the1930s Soviet industry did produce limited numbers of self-propelled artillery systems. For example, a number of variants of the SU-5 self-propelled gun were produced, mounting the 76.2 mm Divisional Gun Obr. 1902/1930 – the SU-5-1; the 122 mm Howitzer Obr. 1910/1930 – the SU-5-2; and 152.4 mm Divisional Mortar Obr. 1931– the SU-5-3 – on the T-26 chassis. Only very limited numbers were produced – six SU-5-1, six SU-5-2 and three SU-5-3, a number of which are reported to have seen action with 2nd Independent Mechanized Brigade at Lake Khasan in the summer of 1938. According to A.G. Soliankin et al, despite being accepted for service by the Red Army, numbers produced were limited because the available chassis did not have the power to carry larger weapons along with meaningful armour – the 152.4 mm Divisional Mortar Obr. 1931 was certainly too heavy for the T-26 chassis.[24]

Certainly in the aftermath of the Lake Khasan incident of July–August 1938, it was suggested by Semen Krivoshein, also a veteran of the Spanish Civil War, that the self-propelled artillery available in the Far East had 'shown its poor utility [*neprigodnost'*] (few shells, crews poisoned by fumes, transmission failures) – they need to be removed from production'.[25] Less mobile than the SU-5s were SU-12 self-propelled artillery systems, mounting the 76.2 mm Obr. 1927 gun on a truck – either a US Moreland or GAZ AAA. Produced in only limited numbers – 99 in total – they initially served with mechanised units and saw action at Khalkhin Gol. During first encounters between Soviet and Japanese forces on 28 May four such self-propelled guns apparently played a significant part in disrupting the Japanese advance.[26] Otherwise, during the mid-late 1930s the Red Army would continue to rely almost exclusively on towed artillery, where the carriage of the Obr. 1902/1930 divisional gun further highlights the extent to which during this period theory had developed well ahead of the means to realise it – and Soviet industry was in no position to produce the many vehicles to provide the Red Army with the sort of mobility that theorists envisioned. Certainly the broader mechanisation for the Red Army did not receive anything like the priority that weapons systems did. In his memoirs, Iakovlev describes early mechanisation of the artillery arm. In April 1931 he was appointed commander of the 9th Corps Artillery Regiment – equipped with recently produced 107 mm Obr 1910/1930 field guns and 152 mm howitzers Obr 1909/1930 – on arrival at the unit finding out that it was slated for conversion to mechanised transport. The following month the unit was ordered to give up its horses and to be provided with 100 AMO F-15 lorries, fifty 'Kommunar' tractors produced in Khar'kov, thirty tractors from the Stalingrad Tractor Factory, along with light vehicles, motorcycles and even bicycles.[27] The AMO F-15 was an improved version of a wartime FIAT lorry, and could carry between one and 1.5 tons depending on the road surface. Through a number of variants the Soviet Union had produced a modest 6,971 AMO F-15s from 1925 up to 1931. Newer models, such as the ubiquitous GAZ-AA – a copy of the Ford-AA and that was in series production in the Soviet Union from 1932 – were however in the pipeline.[28] Between 1931 and 1932 production of 'heavy' motor vehicles jumped from around 3,900 to 23,700, and up to 131,500 by 1936. Many of these vehicles were slated for use by the Red Army in the event of war, but in peacetime in particular the Red Army was competing with the civilian sector of the economy for what remained a relatively scarce resource. Soviet production of tractors for agriculture was also low compared to demand in 1931 despite the rhetoric of mechanisation associated with collectivisation, although production was starting to increase dramatically – from in the region of 3,300 in 1929 Soviet industry produced 9,100 in 1930 and 37,900 in 1931. Such vehicles were therefore also available in the system for military use in the event of war, but of course at the expense of agriculture. In 1936, Soviet industry produced in the region of 112,900 tractors, but as for lorries, although such figures may sound impressive when compared to the production of military vehicles, they have to be put in the context of agricultural demand from across the Soviet Union. Vehicles designed specifically for towing artillery were a luxury item that was certainly not a priority during the early and mid-1930s.[29] In the absence of self-propelled artillery or suitable towing vehicles in sufficient numbers, the mechanised corps intended for operations in the enemy rear and for which composition is discussed in Chapter 4, were provided with limited numbers of tanks armed with larger caliber guns to provide fire support – four for each tank and motor rifle battalion. In 1937, a mechanised corps was provided with only four towed 122 mm and four towed 76 mm artillery pieces, with 32 BT-series tanks with 76 mm guns to provide fire support instead.[30]

Superficially, the early 1930s were good for Red Army leaders who wanted to move the Red Army into a mechanized age. The historian David Stone presents the increasingly ambitious plans for defence spending and weapons procurement during the 1st Five-Year Plan – and the resulting production – as a victory for the Red Army leadership.[31] Finally the Red Army was being listened to and would in theory receive the equipment it deserved. As has been illustrated above, the Red Army was indeed receiving new equipment, even if military leaders were increasingly frustrated with the progress of industry in meeting wild targets and with issues of quality – but at least they were not being ignored. However, as R.W. Davies observes, although defence spending and production did increase proportionally in 1931 and 1932 at a time when the threat from Japan had emerged as a genuine concern, and the significance of defence in the Soviet economy would jump again in 1936 in response to the realisation that Nazi Germany was becoming a genuine threat far more quickly than might have been envisioned in 1933, it was 'not until the last couple of years before the German invasion that the economy began to be transferred to a war footing'.[32] The Soviet economic 'Great Turn' was certainly being justified in part by the threat of war – vague proclamations on the seriousness of which had been coming from the mouths of Stalin and other Soviet leaders regularly since the 'war scare' of 1927.[33] However, as historians such as the late Oleg Ken have suggested, it was not until the mid-1930s that the threat of war shifted from being an abstraction to something more concrete for Soviet leaders – prompting not only the increases in defence expenditure and production of the mid-1930s, but according to Khlevniuk being a key motivation for the bloodletting of the Great Purges, to be considered in the next chapter.[34] In the early 1930s the Soviet Union was nothing like as militarised as it would be by 1940. It is tempting to speculate that in some senses the predictable desires of military leaders for more and bigger had been hijacked by Stalin and the Soviet political leadership, who in the early 1930s listened to commanders as far as military requirements could provide momentum for broader industrialisation. Even with civilian factories being established with a view to their being able to switch production to military requirements in the event of war, as Davies suggests, during the early-mid 1930s '*capacities* for production stipulated in the mobilisation claims and requirements, and in the mobplans, were vastly in excess of actual peacetime *current production*' – making the achievement of the mobilisation plans rather unlikely.[35] Other than the persistence of the territorial militia system until the late 1930s, a good example of the regime sacrificing military requirements in order to economise or accelerate projects is the construction of the Baltic-White Sea Canal. Planning for the construction of the canal took place during 1930, and seemed to suggest that the military utility of the canal was an important consideration in construction, with discussion of the sort of naval vessel that might transit the canal including sizeable vessels such as cruisers. When the canal was finally 'completed' in 1933, the largest vessels that could transit the canal were considerably smaller than cruisers – in fact only small destroyers and submarines. In order to pass through sections of the canal destroyers had to be stripped of anything of weight that could be removed to decrease draught, including armament, and submarines had to pass through the canal on purpose built barges.[36]

Despite the limitations of the Baltic-White Sea Canal, its construction made the reintroduction of Soviet naval power in the White Sea and Arctic waters viable where since the early 1920s only the NKVD's predecessor the OGPU had been defending Soviet northern naval borders. In the absence of significant local shipbuilding capacity light vessels and submarines could at least be transferred to the region from the industrial centre of Leningrad and the Baltic Fleet. On 1 June a Northern Flotilla was formed, which became the Northern Fleet in May 1937. By the mid-1930s the Soviet Union had grand plans for its naval forces, plans that if they had come to fruition would have transformed it from a minor to a major naval power. The Northern Fleet alone was to receive sixty-six units over a ten-year period according to the 'Programme for large-scale naval construction' of 1936, with these units to include two small battleships, two new light cruisers, two destroyer leaders, sixteen destroyers and forty-four submarines of various types.[37]

The Pacific Fleet was to receive a staggering 232 new units that were supposed to include six small battleships, with four larger battleships of '35,000 tons' along with four of the smaller 26,000 ton types to go to each of the Baltic and Black Sea Fleets as part of their 137 and 98 additional units over the ten-year period. The Japanese threat in the East seems to have precipitated these far more radical plans for naval transformation.[38] During the mid-1930s the Soviet political and naval leadership clearly moved towards the idea that that the Soviet naval forces, as the ground forces, would not only expand and modernise in the face of now more concrete threats, but to move from being clearly defensive in focus to having much greater offensive potential. The Soviet naval forces were, as the Red Army, clearly by the late 1930s being intended as a tool for the projection of Soviet power beyond its borders. Commensurate with its new ambitions the navy became an independent arm of the Soviet armed forces with its own People's Commissariat.[39] The Soviet naval forces, as the ground and air forces, were being reborn not only in terms of numbers but also their intended use, although on top of problems with delivering planned vessels Soviet naval equipment, along with training to use it had a long way to go to catch up to the Western powers. On the eve of war the Soviet Navy had only a single warship, the cruiser *Molotov*, equipped with any sort of RADAR, and the first crude 'hydroacoustic' submarine detection devices had only appeared on Soviet vessels in 1940, with Soviet destroyers not being fitted with any form of active submarine detection device prior to the war.[40] Naval construction plans of 1936 – that became even more ambitious the following year – were certainly absurd given the state of Soviet shipbuilding – and even more modest plans of 1933 with their focus on light forces had in fact only been partially realised by 1937. Soon, however, the needs of the ground and air forces in the light of the German invasion would off plans for an 'Ocean Going Fleet' that were already dying as war loomed on the horizon.[41] Considerable resources had nonetheless been expended that might certainly have been better used elsewhere.

As will become apparent in later chapters, the political leadership took detailed Red Army requirements far more seriously at the end of the decade than at the beginning, even if as war approached the needs of the navy would have to play second fiddle to the needs of the ground and air forces. Nonetheless, David Stone has argued that even by 1933, 'despite continuing difficulties in the production of artillery shells, the Red Army had matched foreign armies in the state of its communications, optical gear, and other technically advanced equipment and could no longer be described as backward'.[42] While Soviet engineers may have been able to design equipment of relatively high quality, producing that equipment was a different matter – and nowhere was this better illustrated than in the production of communications equipment. By mid-1931 overall average provision for mobilised units of the Red Army in terms of communications equipment was in the region of only 3.7 per cent.[43] According to the Soviet historian Iovlev, during the 1st Five-Year Plan radio communications were only available to regimental and some battalion headquarters. Iovlev could stress that this situation was a considerable improvement over the Tsarist army of the First World War where 'at best radio stations existed a corps headquarters'.[44] The Red Army was however well behind other leading armies, for whom battalion-and even company-level radio communications had been employed, albeit often reluctantly due to concerns with secrecy and reliability, towards the end of the First World War.[45]

Similarly, although by 1936 the Red Army had modern tanks and aircraft in abundance, broader mechanisation of the Red Army was insufficiently advanced for 'Deep Battle' to be executed as conceived, and certainly to allow aspects of 'Deep Battle' to be meaningfully translated to the operational level as 'Deep Operations'. As Uborevich, commander of the Belorussian Military District, railed to colleagues at the October 1936 session of the Military Council of the People's Commissar for Defence, Soviet tank battalions lacked for example suitable reconnaissance vehicles to prevent them from falling foul of enemy anti-tank screens (the T-37 tank being seen as inadequate for the task), and lacked the self-propelled artillery to allow them to be neutralised once located.[46] Even once Soviet forces had broken through enemy defensive positions, the ability of Soviet forces to operate in the enemy rear was not only hampered by the above absence of suitable reconnaissance resources and mobile artillery, but also the ability to resupply as quickly as mechanised warfare would require. Motor vehicles with good cross-country mobility were simply not available in large enough numbers to the Red Army. Undoubtedly the ambitions of Soviet military theorists fell far short of the productive capacity of Soviet industry – and particularly where the tempo of Red Army expansion was increasing.

Perhaps the most significant problem in the translation of the sophisticated military theories developed in the Soviet Union during the late 1920s and early 1930s into reality was the availability of suitably educated and trained human capital with both the ability and freedom of action to realise them. Issues with command and control – relating to both technology and human capital – are apparent when examining the conduct and result of Soviet manoeuvres in 1936. In his 'on the results of preparation for combat for 1936 and on tasks for 1937' of 3 November 1936, Voroshilov, as People's Commissar for Defence, started by painting the achievements of the Red Army in glowing terms. During manoeuvres across the Soviet Union he wrote that 'commanders and headquarters acted with confidence both in directing combat, and in making use of a significant amount of varied equipment' – apparently in stark contrast with Tukhachevskii's scathing comments a decade before. Specifically on the large scale manoeuvres conducted by the Belorussian Military District (BVO) during the summer, Voroshilov went on to write:

Large scale district maneuvers by the Belorussian Military District were conducted in a complex operational-tactical environment with the deployment of large tank, air, artillery and parachute forces. The principal leaders of the maneuvers and commanders and headquarters of units of the BVO, not only managed *well* [Voroshilov's italics] with the organization of what were as a whole complex maneuvers, but in terms of operational and tactical engagements showed continued development of the art of command in modern warfare, in the co-ordination of all arms in a rapidly changing context.[47]

The newspaper *Pravda* similarly had much that was positive, if vague, to say about the manoeuvres of the Belorussian Military District that autumn. Certainly after reading the numerous *Pravda* articles on the subject, one could easily gain the impression that the manoeuvres gave commanders a meaningful opportunity to show initiative in fluid situations.[48]

In September 1936 the later Lieutenant-General Sir Giffard Martel of the British Army had the rare opportunity to watch the manoeuvres praised by Voroshilov and described by *Pravda*. Although Martel had some complimentary things to say about the manoeuvres – recorded in his later book *The Russian Outlook* – his impressions at the time were not all positive and certainly do not correspond with Voroshilov's glowing appraisal – and certainly not *Pravda*'s misleading 'reporting'. On 8th September 1936 Martel witnessed a number of engagements between the opposing 'Red' and 'Blue' teams, including 'a spectacular battle' between the mechanised forces of the opposing sides in the manoeuvres, and was apparently 'impressed with their power when employed in such suitable country'. However he also noted that 'there was little skill shown in the handling of these forces, which appeared just to bump into each other'. Martel had also not been impressed by the use of cavalry in open country alongside and against tanks earlier in the day. On the second day of the maneuvers he was impressed by defensive positions he was shown, but not the fact that communications seemed to rely on 'the mass of telephone wire which extended all over the position which would not have lasted long when heavy shelling began'. Nonetheless, the parachute drop of an infantry brigade in the afternoon was 'a most spectacular affair'. The following day, 10th September saw further evidence of the often contrived nature of the manoeuvres, where tanks crossing a water obstacle immediately in front of enemy positions were guided on to 'corduroy paths of small tree trunks' on the marshy approaches to a small river 'by men with small flags' who 'hid behind bushes and surreptitiously guided the tanks on to these prepared approaches'. During the actual attack 'as far as we could see, no effort was made to umpire the situations as they arose or to assess the effect of the fire of the defence'. Overall Martel concluded that the umpires 'were terribly busy seeing that the troops knew what to do according to plan and any real umpiring was purely incidental'. In further assessing the manoeuvres as a whole, Martel was not convinced of the extent to which junior 'officers' had 'absorbed much tactical training', even if noting the 'excellent schools' seen later in his visit to remedy this situation. Although impressed by the quality of the artillery, 'the tactical handling of tanks...was not high'. Little use of radio and poor reconnaissance before tanks advanced were also noted. Other than the 'essentials', Martel also did not see the sort of additional equipment such as 'small cars or machine-gun carriers or trucks' that would enhance the 'technique' of the Red Army.[49] In conclusion, he wrote:

The main impression which we formed as a result of seeing these maneuvers was that, apart from the formidable array of tanks and aeroplanes, the army, as far as could be seen, had not changed greatly, and still exhibited its former virtues and faults – great hardihood, great endurance but considerable tactical clumsiness. The Russian army was still a bludgeon, quite incapable of rapier work; it had armoured spikes put on the head of the bludgeon and would strike a deadly blow when it landed; but an active and well-equipped enemy should often be able to avoid or counter the blow and would at least inflict heavy damage on the opponent.[50]

Underneath the rhetoric, it is possible that even Voroshilov wasn't convinced that choreographed maneuvers were a solid indicator of actual military capability. Having sugared the pill of negative comment in what was by now a typically Soviet way, Voroshilov in fact continued his November 1936 report beyond the summer maneuvers by highlighting a range of significant issues with wider Red Army capabilities. The large scale maneuvers of the summer were perhaps unusual in bringing together different arms – where he noted the wider 'inadequate participation of artillery and tanks in tactical exercises with elements of rifle regiments and cavalry regiments. There remain many inadequacies in the practicalities of co-operation between infantry, artillery, tanks and cavalry'. Poor reconnaissance was a problem for most units and formations, and with tank and mechanised units 'questions of command and control' had not been 'fully developed', both 'within tank battalions, companies and platoons, as within mechanized formations'. This was perhaps unsurprising given the limited supply of radios, which similarly made it unsurprising that for aircraft 'the direction of units and formations both on the ground and in the air from command posts' had not been 'worked through'. The subtext of comments on airpower was that Soviet aviation was limited to functioning at lower altitudes in good weather not too far away from home bases – and that included bombers and long-range reconnaissance aircraft.[51]

In his November 1936 critique of the military preparation of the Red Army, Voroshilov also noted that the staff work of headquarters of 'a string of formations' did not 'meet the demands of modern war', with orders slow in being given as a result of 'the failure to master' [nesover-shenstvo] staff work, with the transmission of unclear orders and 'insufficiently flexible' communications with units.[52] The Red Army may have had a number of significant military theorists in its senior ranks at this point, but the implementation of their ideas was not only a problem at middle and lower ranking command levels. The issues with staff work about which Voroshilov complained earlier were not just issues with lower-level staffs, but also with staff work at senior and upper levels. In the early 1930s the Red Army lacked an equivalent of the German General Staff, and indeed the Kriegsakademie for the preparation of staff officers.[53] The Headquarters of the RKKA did become the General Staff in 1935, giving the Red Army a body with far broader competence than its predecessor and in particular wide ranging responsibilities for operational and strategic planning.[54] The first chief of the General Staff would be Marshal A.I. Egorov – soon to be purged.[55] In order to improve the quality of staff work and command from the top down staff officers and senior commanders from brigade level and above were by the late 1930s supposed to have attended the Academy of the General Staff created in 1936 – as well as having had a suitable blend of command and staff experience. Previously the Frunze Military Academy had been at the apex of the Red Army educational system, the primary function of which was to train commanders for the tactical and lower operational levels of command – primarily from regimental to divisional level. Operational level courses were provided from 1931 by a special operational faculty, the primary purpose of which became the preparation of officers for assignment to corps, fronts and the Headquarters of the RKKA. The new Academy of the General Staff would have a clear mandate to provide commanders with operational and strategic-level preparation beyond that provided by the courses of the Frunze Academy's operational courses, that had also catered for only small numbers – at first only thirty students. Students would spend a year and a half at the new institution dedicated to operational and strategic preparation that would at any one time provide education for approximately 250 commanders.[56] Students for the Academy of the General Staff would be selected by a Personnel Department of the General Staff that was created the same year, and that would also supervise the distribution of suitably qualified staff officers.[57] The approximately 250 places at the Academy – with 138 commanders selected for the first intake – might have been sufficient for the Red Army in 1936 but a combination of the Great Purges and the need for personnel for an increasingly rapidly expanding Red Army would both decrease the effectiveness of the education provided and mean that the Red Army would once again have too few trained and hopefully competent staff officers.[58] By 1941 the annual intake for the academy of the General Staff was still only about 150.[59]

Despite many outstanding flaws, during the period from the late 1920s to the mid-1930s the Red Army had nonetheless made considerable strides in the development of doctrine and the acquisition of the equipment needed to implement it. The creation of the Academy of the General Staff highlighted the realization that at least at the time it was appreciated that more than doctrine and equipment were required for the Red Army to be an effective force, although this concern for training and education clearly did not extend as far down the chain of command as it might. Not only were places at the Academy of the General Staff few, but the 1700-strong intake in 1941 for the Frunze Military Academy that provided education to typically younger commanders progressing beyond small unit command was clearly inadequate for an army of millions.[60] As Brian R. Sullivan eloquently put it in an essay on the pre-war Italian army, 'well-trained troops, led by competent commanders, can perform extraordinary feats with poor arms and equipment, but the finest weapons are virtually useless in the hands of a badly instructed army'.[61] Certainly, unlike the Italian Army, that continued to lack 'the finest weapons' when it needed them both in the lead up to and during the Second World War, in the case of the Red Army in 1936 the standard of equipment had improved significantly since the late 1920s – and this equipment was in theory to be employed in a coherent manner in accordance with doctrine and field regulations that were undoubtedly advanced. A lack of communications equipment was a limiting factor that alone might not have had devastating impact on Red Army performance in the event of war had the Red Army not been lacking in other areas, and particularly in defence where the scope for the field telephone to be effectively employed was greater. However the inadequate education and training being provided to all but an elite – the quality and quantity of which was being squeezed as the Red Army expanded – could only inhibit mastery of new equipment and ideas, and of course their implementation. That at the beginning of August 1936 only 40.6 per cent of commanders in infantry schools had at least the equivalent of a high school or secondary education is certainly indicative of levels of education within the Red Army that were still far from ideal for the mastery of modern warfare.[62] Even if a commander was able, the Red Army paid only lip service to the idea that commanders, and particularly junior ones, would show or indeed be given the scope to show meaningful initiative. As John Erickson notes, when discussing the viability of the 1936 Field Regulations:

Tukhachevsky demanded 'nerve' and initiative. Yet the very operation of the command method seemed to blanket this at subordinate levels. The emphasis lay upon exact implementation of the plan, which had to be almost rigidly specific in order to compensate for the deficiencies in tactical ability and training at the lower levels. The offensive form adopted called for considerable flexibility (especially in ... the co-operation of the various arms), and yet the danger was dogmatism and even conservatism.[63]

The Red Army of 1936 was clearly not capable of realizing the vision of Tukhachevskii and others of 'Deep Battle'. Whether it could have done so with time had the institutions and personnel of the mid-1930s had the opportunity to develop, hone and pass on skills and knowledge in particular in the light of experience of the small wars of the late 1930s is debatable given that the still predominately peasant Soviet Union would probably not have been able to keep up with this military elite. The development of the Red Army would also have had to have been less rapid to allow Soviet industry to actually provide the Red Army with all the means – and not just focusing on basic weapons systems – to do 'Deep Battle' properly. The removal of experienced cadres during the Great Purges, to be considered in the next chapter, would however leave the Red Army with an elite that although possessing the social credentials for success in Soviet society arguably lacked not only the same intellectual capacity as its predecessor, but also certainly the experience. The resulting situation would further exacerbate issues with inadequate training and education, and particularly where perceived political reliability became an increasingly important criterion for the promotion of survivors, in many instances at the expense of ability. The deaths of so many Red Army commanders also limited the likelihood that those with ability that remained would show even limited initiative given the risks involved – in a system that even prior to the Great Purges had for reasons including the overall poor educational level of many members been wary of allowing much meaningful initiative. Prior to the Great Purges showing initiative and making mistakes could cost someone their career – during and after them it could even cost them their life.

3   The 'Enemy' within

*The Red Army during and in the Aftermath
of the Great Purges, 1937–1940*

During the early summer of 1936 few could have predicted that Stalin
would unleash the NKVD on the Red Army the following year with such
fury, resulting in what one might in many ways appropriately term the
decimation of the Red Army 'officer' corps. For the upper echelons of the
Red Army leadership 'decimation' – the killing of one in ten – does not in
fact, as will become apparent later, do justice to the slaughter. One might
argue that the political situation in the Soviet Union was more stable
during the summer of 1936 than it had been in late 1934 when
the prominent Leningrad Bolshevik Kirov was murdered in suspicious
circumstances. Although there had been disquiet in some Party circles
over the tempo and human costs of collectivisation and rapid industrialisation during the early 1930s, the upper echelons of the Party had been
cleared of meaningful opposition to Stalin by the middle of the decade.
In the wake of the murder of Kirov, 'opposition' figures such as Zinoviev,
Kamenev, Rykov and Bukharin had been accused of conspiring against
the regime with foreigners, were arrested and incarcerated, and had
apparently been neutralised as threats. The situation in the countryside
had stabilised after the upheavals of mass collectivisation and associated
famine, and in the industrial sector one might argue that the Second
Five-Year Plan was somewhat less chaotic than the First. For workers
bread was no longer rationed by early 1935 as consumer consumption
increased after the bleak first years of the 1930s, even if deliberately high
prices set by the state negated any gains for some lower paid workers.
The much trumpeted 1936 Soviet constitution may similarly have been
window dressing in many senses with its promises and rights for workers
and peasants, but nonetheless was no doubt seen at the time by those of
more optimistic disposition as a step in the right direction. Whether the
timing for the start of what would become the Great Purges was cynical
or not, only weeks after the publication of the draft constitution the
purges began.

Purges were nothing new in the Soviet Union – from the period of
Lenin's leadership through to Stalin the Party had periodically been

purged of politically unsatisfactory elements or simply dead wood. In fact, as People's Commissar for Defence Voroshilov stated to a plenum of the Central Committee of the Communist Party during the spring of 1937, during a *proverka* or check on Party members in the Red Army during 1933–4, 3,328 were purged or removed from the Party – 555 for 'Trotskyism or counterrevolutionary agitation', of whom 400 were immediately sacked from the army.[1] What was new in 1936–8, beyond the scale of purging, was the fact that being purged did not only mean losing one's Party membership and job, but frequently led to incarceration in the GULAG system where many died, or for many even execution. During August 1936 the whipping boys of the regime – Zinoviev, Kamenev, and of course Trotsky in absentia – the big names of a '16' – were tried again as they had been in early 1935 for their supposed plotting with foreigners against the regime, but this time were swiftly executed. Although there were not Red Army commanders amongst the '16', there were isolated arrests of Red Army personnel during this period. On 28 May 1936 for example one of the instructors of the Frunze Military Academy – Kombrig E.G. Matson-Igneus – was arrested for having stated in public, in opposition to the official line, that 'German fascism and Hitler had the ability to reflect the national feelings of the German people and hence came to power easily'. A Swede by nationality and former member of the Swedish Social Democratic Party, he had nonetheless fought for the Bolsheviks during the Civil War and had become a Party member in 1918, and had even been awarded the Order of the Red Banner for his efforts. In July Komdiv D.A. Schmidt and Maior V.I. Kuz'michev were arrested, followed by Komkor V.M. Primakov and the until recently military attaché in London Komkor V.K. Putna in August, along with Kombrig M.O. Ziuk and Voeninzhener 2nd rank G.A. Litokh. The trickle of similar arrests continued for the remainder of the year. Their interrogations would bring forth 'evidence' of conspiratorial activities in the Red Army, so that during the summer of 1937 the People's Commissariat for Internal Affairs or NKVD had the justification, if flimsy, to begin mass arrests of Red Army personnel – starting at the top. What the NKVD needed was Stalin's sanction, which according to Peter Whitewood came by mid-1937 as Stalin could no longer ignore the apparent scope for subversion of the Red Army by those hostile to him and the Soviet Union – as identified by the security services.[2] Unsurprisingly, there is evidence of considerable tension and fear in the Red Army as the Great Purges gathered momentum even if they had yet, in late 1936 and early 1937, to hit the Red Army hard. As the Russian historian of the Great Purges and the Red Army Suvenirov notes, the purported testimony of Kombrig K.I. Sokolov-Strakhov on his arrest in January 1937 is suggestive of 'an uneasy [*trevozhnoi*] atmosphere' that had existed in the Red Army since late 1936. Sokolov-Strakhov, deputy head of the Military-Historical Department of the General Staff and editor of the Military-Historical Bulletin had apparently felt prior to his arrest that 'every step I take is observed… To work is difficult, even frightening…the responsibility huge'. Writing history was a sensitive business during a period in which Stalin and his associates sought to rewrite it to bolster their positions. Sokolov-Strakhov's family ties certainly made him a likely candidate for suspicion – he was married to the niece of the former head of the tsarist police, P.G. Kurlov. He was arrested on 22 August 1937. The arrest of a number of well-known commanders over the summer and autumn of 1936, although not publicised in the press, was no doubt known to 'a wide circle of senior commanders', who, as Suvenirov suggests, probably 'could not help but contemplate their own fates'.[3]

The purpose of this chapter is not to provide a blow by blow account of the Great Purges, either in general or specifically relating to the Red Army, nor to speculate more than briefly on the causes of this bloodletting, but to assess the impact of the Great Purges on the Red Army and examine the performance of the Red Army in the immediate aftermath after what was undoubtedly a calamity for an organisation that was in many ways starting to mature. Recent work by historians such as Oleg Khlevniuk has argued that the Great Purges were not only about the fear of opposition on the part of Stalin, but fear of opposition during a period when the threat of war was more than a propaganda tool to drive the 'Great Turn'.[4] During the summer of 1936 the threat of war was far more real than it had been during the 1927 'war scare', or indeed than it had been during the early 1930s. During the late 1920s and early 1930s the regime may, as shown in the previous chapter, have sought to strengthen the Red Army, but was not willing to prioritise military power in economy and society in the way it would from the mid-1930s onwards. Japanese ambitions in the Far East from 1931 certainly added some substance to the idea that Soviet territory was under threat. However, it was the speed with which Hitler's Nazi Germany turned militaristic rhetoric into reality after Hitler's rise to power in early 1933, and the Western powers unwillingness to deal with a resurgent Germany, that led to an escalation in Soviet rearmament and the further expansion of the Red Army. The announcements by Germany of the existence of the Luftwaffe and reintroduction of conscription in the spring of 1935, both in flagrant breach of the Versailles Treaty, were followed by the brazen remilitarisation of the Rhineland the following year. These events, and the Italian invasion of Abyssinia in 1935, were not met with meaningful opposition from the League of Nations. In 1936 the international system turned a blind eye to Italian and German intervention in the Spanish Civil War, where the Kriegsmarine was at the same time ostensibly participating in the enforcement on the arms embargo to the warring sides. Given Hitler's known desire for German eastward expansion, the Soviet Union had reason to be concerned about the pace of German rearmament and the unwillingness of the Western powers to act.

After the arrests of a number of senior Red Army officers during the second half of 1936, the Plenum of the Central Committee of the Communist Party from 23 February–5 March 1937 is widely seen, and for good reason, as a key indicator of the regime's intention to move against the Red Army. Voroshilov, People's Commissar for Defence and a close associate of Stalin – sufficiently close at least that his wartime incompetence did not lead to his death but merely to him being given innocuous prestige positions – was undoubtedly an important actor in bringing down the Great Purges on the Red Army. Voroshilov certainly played an active role in bringing down the Great Purges on rivals in the leadership such as Tukhachevskii, between whom, as Zhukov noted, there was considerable enmity.[5] During the Central Committee plenum, after having described the strength of the Red Army, Voroshilov noted that:

It stands to reason, that the enemy cannot but attempt to penetrate [the Red Army] for the purpose of wrecking and diversionary work. But I repeat, that at this time there is only a numerically small group of people hidden amongst Red Army personnel that is carrying out its underhand counterrevolutionary work.[6]

He went on to discuss, by name, letters he had received from many of those arrested during 1936, claiming their innocence of any crimes, before describing the crimes to which some of those arrested had admitted during interrogation. Particularly prominent was the 'testimony' of Putna, who it was claimed, had described the aims of a 'military Trotskyist organisation' within the Red Army that sought to remove 'in the first instance Stalin and Voroshilov' from their positions as heads of the Party and Red Army respectively. Ominously, Voroshilov noted later how Putna:

Named specific individuals, slated for recruitment, who were perhaps even already enrolled. The traitors counted on the fact, that in the army 'contingents' could always be found, aside for former Trotskyist-Zinovievite bastards on whom they could count and who could be drawn in to their vile organisation.[7]

Tukhachevskii was no doubt one of those Voroshilov was hinting at.

When Stalin put the question of Tukhachevskii's expulsion from the Communist Party to the Politburo on 24 May 1937 after his arrest and the start of the move to mass purging of the Red Army, Tukhachevskii was accused of 'participation in an anti-Soviet, Trotskyist-rightist conspiratorial bloc and in espionage work against the USSR on behalf of fascist Germany' – accusations for which there is no evidence of substance but probably representing real fears on the part of leader and regime – fear of a wartime 'Fifth Column' assisting or exploiting the fact that Nazi Germany and other powers were attacking the Soviet Union.[8] As Molotov stated during interviews with Felix Chuev when justifying the Great Purges during the later years of Molotov's life and decades after Stalin's death:

In that period it was necessary to act mercilessly. I believe our actions were fully justified.

Today such actions would be completely unjustified. By the time the war broke out, when the purges had been completed, . . ., such a danger was gone. But if the Tukhachevskys and Yakirs, with the Rykovs and Zinovievs, had started an opposition during the war, then there would have been cruel internal strife and colossal losses. . . .

I consider Tukhachevsky [to have been] a most dangerous conspirator in the military who was caught only at the last minute. Had he not been apprehended, the consequences could have been catastrophic. He was most popular in the army.[9]

Voroshilov was certainly not alone in seeking to destroy Tukhachevskii – be it because he actually believed the accusations or because of often strained relations going back to the Civil War. As material cited in Suvenirov suggests, Budennii sought in a letter of 29 August 1937 to Voroshilov to associate the activities of 'enemies of the people' with the undermining of his beloved cavalry arm – perhaps trying to suggest that it was not military thinking but 'wrecking' that led Tukhachevskii and others to push mechanisation at the expense of traditional cavalry. He certainly did not hide his enmity, writing that during his period working for the Cavalry Inspection of the RKKA:

I had to fight, of course with your support and that of Comrade Stalin, for the existence of the cavalry... because enemies of the people, and namely Tukhachevskii, Levichev, Mezhenikov and all sorts of other bastards that had worked in the central apparatus, helped by Iakir and Uborevich, strove in a variety of ways right up until the last moment to destroy the cavalry arm in the armed forces of our country.[10]

The copy of the Politburo resolution to expel Tukhachevskii from the Party reproduced in J. Arch Getty and Oleg V. Naumov's collection of documents on the Great Purges is Budennii's copy, on which Budennii wrote emphatically in favour of Tukhachevskii's expulsion – 'unconditionally yes. It's necessary to finish off this scum'.[11]

By 1938 when these T-26 tanks were being paraded on May Day in Palace Square in Leningrad, the Red Army had arguably the strongest tank arm in the world. By this point many of those who had fought for the new mechanised Red Army earlier in the 1930s had already been killed during the purge of the Red Army of 1937 onwards. (RIA Novosti #40691)

Whether Voroshilov and Budennii wanted or expected the Great Purges to take such a heavy toll on the Red Army officer corps as they had by the end of 1938 is another matter – certainly Voroshilov's speech to the Central Committee plenum in the spring of 1937 did not suggest that he saw the Red Army as being riddled with 'spies and wreckers' to use the appropriate Soviet terms. This one might have expected – as People's Commissar for Defence he had held some responsibility for the political and moral state of the Red Army since June 1934. In the case of Sokolov-Strakhov mentioned earlier, it seems that Voroshilov initially did not give his sanction for the arrest of Sokolov-Strakhov, delaying his arrest from late 1936 into 1937 by which time the People's Commissar for Internal Affairs, Ezhov, had become involved. Even once the purges were in full swing, Voroshilov was capable of intervening on behalf of close associates, as in the case of Komdiv M.F. Lukin, previously military commandant for Moscow until his demotion to deputy head of the headquarters for the Siberian Military District in 1937 for 'relaxation [*prituplenie*] of class vigilance and personal ties with enemies of the people'. Lukin was summoned to Moscow for a meeting with one of Stalin's henchmen – Lev Mekhlis – who would, as Voroshilov, make a name for himself in the history of the Great Patriotic War for a degree of incompetence that might have led to the deaths or at least imprisonments of others. Summoned by Lev Mekhlis and the Commission for Party Control – responsible for Party discipline – Lukin may very well have feared the worst, and many commanders were arrested after having been called to the capital, typically without explanation. Fortunately for Lukin, he bumped into Voroshilov in the corridors of the Central Committee offices and explained what was going on to the Commissar for Defence. Voroshilov apparently phoned one of those in charge of the committee, stating that he had known Lukin since the Civil War and that he was 'an honest communist' and that what was going on around him was 'insanity' [*nedorazumenie*]. Requesting that the representative of the committee 'take care to sort the situation out [*vnimatel'no razobrat'sia*]', Voroshilov suggested that if Lukin was indeed innocent to make that plain to his home military district. After having made the call, Voroshilov reportedly told Lukin that he had in fact been asked three times to sanction the latter's arrest'.[12] Lukin would go on to command an army with some distinction during the Great Patriotic War – including during intense fighting on the Smolensk axis and in the Viaz'ma region during the summer and autumn of 1941. Such examples serve to suggest both the extent and limits of Voroshilov's authority, and perhaps suggest that the purges had gone far beyond what Voroshilov had proposed in the spring of 1937. Nonetheless, despite the former's interventions on behalf of associates, Voroshilov and Budennii seem to have made little attempt to slow down the purging of the Red Army as a broader process as it gathered momentum – nor indeed did Stalin until late 1938. Some of those arrested during the purges but spared execution would later rise to prominence during the Great Patriotic War, and one might reasonably suggest were arrested as part of a wider process initiated, broadly directed and allowed to escalate by an obviously paranoid Stalin, but one not subject to his detailed day-day control. Amongst those arrested and later released, perhaps most prominent is Konstantin Rokossovskii. Other than the usual personal and professional connections, and the denunciations of those under arrest, as Rokossovskii himself apparently thought, his nationality counted against him – his mother was Russian but father Polish. On 13 June 1937 Komdiv Rokossovskii was removed as commander of 5th Cavalry Corps of the Leningrad Military District, and placed at the disposal of the Ministry of Defence. By the end of the month he had been removed from the Party, and was arrested in August. He would not be released until March 1940. According to Rokossovskii's recent biographer Boris Sokolov, reporting the testimony of the former's family, Rokossovskii rarely spoke about his arrest and the horrors of incarceration and interrogation. According to his grandson Rokossovskii's subsequent carrying of a pistol at all times was so that 'if they come for me again, I won't give myself up alive'.[13] Despite his experience, Rokossovskii served with distinction during the Great Patriotic War, as no doubt would have many others who were executed and posthumously rehabilitated after Stalin's death.

The reasons for the spread of the purges beyond a narrow leadership group – for whom one can identify personal connections and animosities with Stalin and his close cronies such as Voroshilov and Budennii – are undoubtedly many. Looking for skeletons in the closet often results in more being found than initially anticipated – and if NKVD personnel did not want to be accused of lacking 'vigilance' in rooting out the enemy then they had to be seen to be doing something about the problem. Arrests and interrogations led to more names, suspicion and accusations, and more arrests, with the central authorities providing fuel for the fire by directing local NKVD attentions towards specific but at the same time loosely defined targets such as national groups or kulaks. The regime went as far as to establish quotas for the arrest of members of these groups, who would then be tried not in an open court but by a three-man *troika* – the only record being minutes of their meetings.[14] That the purges started with Stalin and a small clique in the leadership is certain, even if some of the momentum was generated locally. The bloodletting was eventually slowed down by Stalin in late 1938, marked in many ways by the arrest and execution of the head of the NKVD for the bulk of the Great Purges, Nikolai Ezhov, and many of his close associates. Nonetheless, the arrests, imprisonments and executions continued at reduced tempo right up to and during the first months of the Great Patriotic War, and notably so in the Red Army.

Since the collapse of the Soviet Union and a period from the late 1980s through the 1990s of unprecedented archival access and releases of the Soviet Union's documentary 'dirty linen', we have a much clearer quantitative and qualitative picture of the Great Purges than had previously been the case. Previously apologists for Stalin and the Soviet Union had tended to play down the human cost of the Great Purges, and opponents to exaggerate them. Even if the reality – as far as can be identified in the documentary record – did not match the scale of repression suggested by right-wing 'Cold War warrior' historians such as Robert Conquest, the figures for those executed or imprisoned for political crimes are nonetheless staggering. According to contemporary Soviet summary statistics, during 1937 779,056 people were arrested for 'counter-revolutionary' crimes, and a further 234,301 for 'anti-Soviet agitation', out of a total for

NKVD arrests for the year of 936,750. Of these, 790,665 were convicted, leading to 353,074 being shot and 429,311 incarcerated in the prison system – often in GULAG labour camps. During 1938 there was a reduction in the bloodletting, which nonetheless continued at a considerable rate. Of a total of 638,509 NKVD arrests, most, or 593,326 were for 'counter-revolutionary' crimes, with 57,366 for 'anti-Soviet agitation' – suggesting that many had realised the wisdom of silence given that even toeing the Party line was a risky business where the latter might change. Of those arrested 554,254 were convicted – 328,618 shot and 205,509 imprisoned.[15]

Figures for the purging of the Red Army are similarly staggering. Of five Marshals of the Soviet Union in post in 1936, during the period 1937–41 two were shot – Tukhachevskii and Egorov – and one – Bliukher – died in captivity. Bliukher's name alone meant that he was vulnerable. The survivors amongst the marshals were of course Voroshilov and Budennii. For the next ranks down – be it in the navy or army – the statistics are even more shocking in that not only were incumbents of many of these positions in 1936 killed but also their replacements. For fifteen army level commanders in 1936, by 1941 nineteen had been shot – for the naval equivalents for four positions in 1936 there had been five executions by 1941.[16] The commander of the recently formed Soviet Northern Fleet, Flagman 1st Rank Konstantin Ivanovich Dushenov, will serve as but one further example of a key military figure purged.

Prior to his arrest and execution Dushenov's rise through the ranks of the Soviet navy had been impressive – after having been head of the headquarters for the Black Sea Fleet he was sent to command the Northern Flotilla in 1935 and remained in command when it was upgraded to fleet status in 1937. Questioning about his wife – a German by nationality – and his trips abroad to Italy and Germany at the May 1937 Murmansk regional conference of the Party did not lead to his immediate arrest. Regarding his wife, he was apparently at ease because, as he stated, she was 'one of ours', and his trips abroad were after all on state business. On 12 December 1937 he was elected to the Supreme Soviet – and in April 1938 received the Order of the Red Banner. Promotion and awards were however no indicator of safety. One can only speculate that his apparent defence of subordinates under suspicion did not help Dushenov's position – and he himself was arrested in May 1938 after having been summoned to Leningrad. Issues with the development of the Northern Fleet were understandably taken as evidence of 'wrecking' – with foreign trips and family ties allowing communication with foreign powers. His sentencing took some time – not until 3 February 1940 was Dushenov sentenced – with his execution swiftly following the next day.[17]

Appendix 1 provides similar statistical details of numbers purged to those provided previously for victims down to brigade commander or kombrig rank. The proportions of any given rank killed declined as ranks were lower, but nonetheless for 474 brigade-level command positions in 1936 there had been 201 executions, fifteen deaths in captivity and a single suicide.[18] For lower ranking commanders similar factors seem to have contributed to arrest – or at least been pretexts for arrest – as senior colleagues. Certainly testimony from interviews conducted as part of the Harvard Project on the Soviet Social System gives further indication of the sort of 'crimes' that were associated with arrest, from inappropriate class background or past political activity, foreign ties and other politically unacceptable personal connections, to lack of 'vigilance' in dealing with potential threats to the regime. 'Crimes' were sometimes simply mistakes – often along with one or more of the above – that could be interpreted as 'wrecking'.[19]

In addition to those reported killed or imprisoned, the purges saw significant numbers of Red Army personnel forced out of the Red Army because they had connections with the 'conspirators' and foreign ties. Statistics for March 1940 on those removed from the Red Army from 1935–9 (excluding the VVS) provided by Army Commissar 2nd Rank E.A. Shchadenko, head of the board for command cadres of the RKKA, highlight how the cost to the Red Army of the purges as measured in terms of personnel losses should not only be measured in terms of those arrested and sentenced. For 1937, allowing for those removed from the Red Army and subsequently arrested within the year or those reinstated in 1938–9 – 676 personnel were removed from command and political-command positions and the Party for 'ties with the conspirators'. In 1938 a more significant 2,219 were removed from the Red Army and neither arrested within the year nor reinstated in 1938–9 because of their nationality, having been born abroad or foreign ties.[20]

The primary concern of this chapter is assessing the impact that this bloodletting and turnover in personnel had on the Red Army. There is certainly widespread acknowledgement in both memoirs and the secondary literature that the Great Purges had a negative impact on Red Army capabilities and performance. For example, according to the brief mention of the Great Purges in Rokossovskii's memoirs, *A Soldier's Duty*, 'at the end of the 1930s serious blunders were tolerated. Our military cadres also suffered, which could not but be reflected in the organisation and readiness [*podgotovka*] of our forces'.[21] In a conversation with Konstantin Simonov in the mid-1960s, Zhukov stated that if comparison was to be made between Red Army cadres in 1936 and 1939, then:

...the level of military preparation of our forces had fallen sharply. ...starting at regimental level our army had been decapitated .... A terrible decline in discipline could be observed.... Many commanders felt lost [*chuvstvovali sebia rasteriannimi*], unable to bring about order.[22]

Zhukov certainly suggested that the Great Purges saw the loss of considerable talent in the upper echelons of the Red Army leadership, spending some time discussing Tukhachevskii and Uborevich with Soviet journalist and writer Konstantin Simonov. More broadly Zhukov noted how, without focusing on specific people killed during the purges who may or may not have excelled during the war, those lost represented a sizeable cohort of personnel who, in the end, all would have been available to fight. He concluded:

Let's imagine war in 1941 with a different atmosphere...without fear, without mistrust, without spies. If all of that wasn't there, then it stands to reason that the country would certainly not have found itself so unprepared for war as it turned out to be. ... Only ... monstrous terror and its eructation, having been drawn out over a number of years, can explain the absurd prewar state.[23]

These comments make reference to a range of areas in which the purges hit the Red Army to varying degrees. From the loss of able commanders, to a decline in discipline and a climate of fear it is certainly difficult to argue that the Great Purges could not have had a negative impact on the Red Army as an organisation.

Perhaps the most obvious impact to start with is the significance of the loss of those killed from the point of view of losing their skills and knowledge, and particularly where replacements were often not as capable or experienced. Regarding the upper echelons of the Red Army leadership, on being asked by Konstatin Simonov for his opinion of Tukhachevskii and Uborevich, in addition to 'rating them both highly', Zhukov noted that Tukhachevskii was the more 'erudite' on questions of strategy and had a 'deep, calm, analytical mind', and Uborevich the more capable on questions of 'operational art and tactics'.[24] In 1936 Tukhachevskii was 1st Deputy Commissar, or minister, for Defence, with Voroshilov as minister. However, Zhukov suggests that much of the work of running the ministry fell on Tukhachevskii's shoulders – where although Voroshilov was 'popular and had pretensions to consider himself a rounded soldier and with a deep knowledge of military questions' he was, in the role of Minister, 'incompetent'.[25] Both Tukhachevskii and Uborevich, and arguably particularly Tukhachevskii, had already made their marks on the Red Army, with for example the 1936 Field Regulations owing much to Tukhachevskii's efforts. However, as the Great Patriotic War would show, there was still plenty of talent left in the Red

Army despite the scale of the purging. The problem was that more so than ever before, promotion seemed to owe as much if not more to political credentials than military ability. With the Tukhachevskiis, Uboreviches and others gone, the Voroshilovs and Budenniis were left as masters of the military house – and all too often promoted unthreatening mediocrities to join them. As Erickson notes, at the very upper level of Red Army leadership, not only was Voroshilov observed to lack military knowledge by foreign observers, but his deputy commissars for defence did not 'inspire any great confidence by virtue of their military ability – Budenny, Mekhlis, Shchadenko and the upstart figure of Kulik. Shaposhnikov alone was possessed of a high degree of professional competence....' Although noting the limits of Shaposhnikov's authority even as Chief of the General Staff, Erickson does go on to note how under Shaposhnikov 'a new group of talented officers was brought to the fore', although it would take wartime circumstances and a raft of failures on the part of those above them for the likes of Vasilevskii to supplant less able predecessors.[26] Of the first of the courses at the Academy of the General Staff that had begun in 1936, many capable individuals survived the purges – not only Colonel or polkovnik A.M. Vasilevskii but also A.I. Antonov and N.F. Vatutin for example – to progress to the most senior command positions during the war, even if many had their educations at the Academy cut short because of the pressing need for incumbents for newly vacant posts.[27] Such talent was, however, noticeably underrepresented or at best muted in the purge-era and immediate post-purge deliberations of the Military Council or Main Military Council that did so much to set the direction for Red Army development in the late 1930s. As P.N. Bobilev, general editor of a collection of documents on the activities of the Military Council in 1938, notes in his introduction to the volume, only ten of the original eighty members of the council of 1934 were still in evidence at the beginning of October 1938, and of those Bliukher would soon also be arrested. This left the likes of Voroshilov and Kulik to clearly dominate proceedings where initially at least new members were clearly as concerned to not be subject to the repression that had led to their promotion as making meaningful contribution to debate.[28]

One dimension to purge era promotions to the very upper echelons of the Red Army military apparatus was the rising influence of the 'politicals' within the Soviet military machine, who as guardians of the ideological sanctity of the organisation had significant influence over promotions and demotions in part through having the ear of a suspicious Stalin. In his memoirs wartime head of the Soviet navy Nikolai Kuznetsov notes how many were apparently surprised – including no doubt

Kuznetsov himself – at the appointment of former NKVD leader M.P. Frinovskii to the post of People's Commissar for the Navy in 1938 where he had apparently only a 'vague conception' of the navy.[29] In such cases, the most prominent and extreme of which is undoubtedly that of Lev Mekhlis, those concerned all too often lacked the requisite knowledge and often skills but were happy to blur the lines between political and military matters in favour of extending their authority. In fact, as one contemporary commentator suggested, in December 1937 Mekhlis was appointed as head of the Political Board of the Red Army – and at the same time became a Deputy Minister of Defence – in part because he did not have ties with the military elite. He had also become a member of the Main Military Council, further increasing scope for his influence.[30] The Political Board of the Red Army which Mekhlis headed oversaw the work of political commanders in the Red Army – commissars. Whilst during the late 1920s and early 1930s such positions theoretically at least had become increasingly about propaganda work with the move towards unitary command, as described in the last chapter, political commanders could in practice still draw a wide range of military and 'domestic' (here the Russian words *bitovie* or *khoziastvennie* are more effective a description than 'domestic') matters within their remits and had considerable influence over units and formations even without formal dual command. In the climate of suspicion of the Great Purges formal dual command would however once more be introduced at regimental level and above on 10 May 1937 – where at the same time military soviets were brought back to provide for political oversight at military district and army level.[31] As supporting materials noted, the military commissar, as equal to the commander, now shared responsibility for not only 'the political-moral state of a unit', but also for ensuring military discipline and for 'combat, operational and mobilisational preparedness', 'the condition of weapons' and day-day management of units. Both were to prevent 'enemies of the people, spies, saboteurs, wreckers' from 'penetrating or emerging within' their units.[32] As for the military soviets, consisting of the military commander of the military district and two members – political minders – they were to run the districts, fleets and armies in a similar manner to the commander-commissar combinations lower down the chain of command, with any order to be signed by the military commander, head of the headquarters and one of the members of the military Soviet, even if orders were still given in the name of the military commander.[33]

Lev Mekhlis undoubtedly played a significant role in the scale of purging of Red Army command and indeed political cadres during the Great Purges. A caricature might have Mekhlis portrayed as a terrier in pursuit of politically suspect vermin. He also had considerable influence over the replacement of those purged. Hence for example, in May 1938 it was not only Army Commissar 2nd Rank E.A. Shchadenko, also a deputy minister for defence and head of the board for command cadres of the RKKA, who would have to draw up a list of candidates for vacancies to command positions within the sensitive Belorussian Military District, but also Mekhlis.[34] Shchadenko had inevitably played a significant role in the purging of the Red Army command, but had apparently become concerned about the scale of arrests and firings of commanders, and had in early 1938 made some attempt to bring an element of moderation to the process by ordering the removal of compromising material on commanders from their files if it had not been substantiated – an order undermined by Mekhlis.[35]

Even if talented individuals were promoted, it would inevitably take time for them to gain competence in new positions. However, during and immediately after the Great Purges promotion that might otherwise have taken years in peacetime took place in a matter of months – fine only in wartime where intensive hands-on experience was typically available, but not in peacetime. One can only speculate on the impact of having many commanders pass through a series of ranks having had only brief tenures in many of them. One can reasonably assume that many were promoted without having gained a rounded appreciation of the practical requirements and challenges of lower positions. For example, if like for one respondent to the HPSSS three promotions were obtained in only four years – in this instance from senior lieutenant in 1936 to captain in 1938 and major in 1939 – then it is probable in many instances that such commanders did not actually have the opportunity to lead a unit or formation they were commanding during manoeuvres for example before gaining further promotion. Even if manoeuvres were choreographed, getting them right was an important organisational exercise.[36] The rapidity with which many were promoted both during and after the Great Purges is well illustrated by the case of I.M. Chistiakov, who over fifteen years had by 1936 progressed from being a platoon to regimental commander within 37th Rifle Regiment. Between 1936 and the end of 1940 he was to rise from commanding a regiment to a corps before his transfer to the Academy of the General Staff on the eve of war. The needs of an expanding army go some way to explaining such meteoric rises, but their rapidity owed much to the losses of cadres during the Great Purges.[37]

It is undoubtedly difficult to become a competent field commander without practical experience, even if that experience is of command in peacetime. Education and training could provide some compensation for lack of field experience, and indeed provide a theoretical framework to make sense of it, but as noted in the previous chapter, despite expansion of provision during the early 1930s Red Army educational institutions struggled to keep pace with the educational requirements of a growing army even before the purges. During and after the purges the system struggled even more as will be noted below. When L.S. Skvirskii arrived at the headquarters of 14th Army in the far north in late 1939 he noted the apparent absence of a single commander with a higher military education, also noting that 'it transpired that the military preparation of all levels of command was low'.[38] On-the-job training also seems to have suffered. In the post-Soviet edition of his memoirs Zhukov notes how, after the arrest of commander of the Belorussian Military District, I.P. Uborevich and his successor I.P. Belov, 'the academic preparation of the upper echelons of command in the district plummeted [*rezko snizilas'*] and we were almost never summoned to the district for any sort of academic activities'.[39]

Even without commanders struggling with new responsibilities for which they were often not prepared – and quite possibly losing respect of subordinates in the process – the Red Army 'officer corps' through the purges had suffered a major blow to its collective prestige and authority. As one respondent to the Harvard Project on the Soviet Social System highlighted, from 1937 'everywhere fear was sown that the officers were spies for England, France, for Germany, for other bourgeois countries'[40] While material from the Harvard Project on the Soviet Social System suggests that among respondents there was some doubt lower down the chain of command about the complicity of lower ranking commanders in the various conspiracies and other crimes orchestrated by opponents of the regime, nonetheless there seems to have been some acceptance that Tukhachevskii and other senior leaders were guilty. One respondent to the HPSSS went as far as to link Soviet military failures when the Great Patriotic War broke out to 'Soviet mobilization plans which Tukhachevsky had turned over to the Germans in 1936'.[41] Another stated that he believed 'that Tukhacevsky [sic] was involved in some kind of conspiracy but probably no more than two hundred officers at the top were involved in it'.[42] It is of course difficult to assess the psychological impact of believing that as a minimum the senior leadership of an organisation had been traitors for confidence in and support for an institution – certainly Stalin seems to have been aware that this was an issue. During a meeting of political commanders in August 1937 Stalin responded to a claim from the floor that as a result of the purges the authority of the Party and Army had not been undermined that it had in fact been 'somewhat' or 'slightly' undermined [*nemnogo podorvan*]. There is certainly significant anecdotal evidence in the HPSSS that the purges, and particularly the experience of arrest even if not resulting in death, had a negative impact on attitudes towards the Soviet regime – be it on the attitude of the arrested or those close to them. One respondent to the HPSSS noted how her uncle's arrest in May 1937 and subsequent treatment left a previously outwardly assiduously loyal Soviet citizen without his previous Soviet patriotism. The fact that he taught Polish and German at a military communications school prior to his arrest meant he was vulnerable, although it seems that an electrical incident at the school when he was in charge that led to a power outage was the immediate trigger for arrest – accusations that he was a wrecker and a spy followed. After being held for twelve months the commander concerned was released – with a broken rib and a number of teeth knocked out. According to the respondent, 'he was 37 years old when he was arrested, he was a big man, in good health. When he came out he was an old man'. This was somebody with whom 'we could never tell an anti-Soviet anecdote..., not that he would report on you, but simply that he would tell you that you were not conscious [*soznetel'nii*] enough', and who had been 'sold on the Soviet regime, saying that it had put him on his feet'.[43]

During the same August 1937 meeting mentioned previously in which Stalin had noted the negative impact of the purges on the authority of the Party and Army, Army Commissar 1st Rank P.A. Smirnov had noted how discipline had suffered as a result of the purges at a time when they had only recently started to hit the Red Army hard. Smirnov noted the high frequency of crashes, suicides, burns and mutilations, and how the number of recorded infractions was high – in fact describing the figure of 400,000 infractions from 1 January – 1 May 1937 as 'astronomical'.[44] Air accident rates became a particular concern for the Main Military Council of the Red Army in April 1938 where it was noted that the number of accidents in 1937 compared to 1936 was 80 per cent higher, with the number of 'catastrophic' incidents rising by 70 per cent. During the first three and a half months of 1938 there had been thirty-seven catastrophic accidents compared to only seven for the same period the previous year. Other than attributing this situation to 'wrecking and diversion' and a lack of 'vigilance', it was noted how a broader relaxation of military discipline had led to failures to follow orders and breaches of regulations concerning 'military discipline and relations between commanders and subordinates'. Instances of 'false "democratism"' certainly infer reduced authority of commanders. As for the causes of this situation, this telling decree noted how those promoted to command positions, 'young commanders and political cadres, possessing strong personal character-istics, in the main still do not possess the practical experience for the command of units and formations'.[45] As Zhukov noted in conversation with Konstantin Simonov, after the purges the Red Army not only remained in a period of 'incomplete rearmament, but also in a no less difficult period during which it was recovering moral values and discipline'.[46]

As the increased number of suicides noted by Commissar 1st Rank Smirnov earlier suggest – and as one might expect – morale amongst Red Army command cadres was hit by the purging of commanders and other stresses associated with the tumultuous situation. Smirnov's comments refer to the first half of 1937 – before an increasing number of arrests would ratchet up the pressure. Certainly a significant if small number of commanders chose to take their own lives rather than, risk arrest. Hence for example Army Commissar 2nd Rank A.S. Grishin, head of the Political Board of the Red Banner Baltic Fleet chose to take his own life in July 1937, subsequently being declared an 'enemy of the people' – following in the footsteps of Army Commissar 1st Rank Ia. B. Gamarnik, 1st Deputy Minister for Defence and head of the Political Board of the Red Army until his apparent suicide on 31 May 1937. A few managed to kill themselves during or after their arrests, as in the case of Brigade Commissar A.I. Blinov, head of the Leiningrad Military-Political School named after Friedrich Engels, who apparently killed himself as he was being arrested in February 1938, or Divisional Commissar G.F. Nevraev, Deputy head of the Political Board of the Trans-Baikal Military District, Brigade Military Lawyer Kurakin, deputy Military Procurator for the Belorussian Military District, and Divisional Military Lawyer L.I. Maller, Chair of the Military Tribunal of the border and internal security forces of the Far Eastern Region, all of whom killed themselves without having been arrested.[47] The fact that most of those who can be identified as having killed themselves prior to arrest were political or legal personnel perhaps suggest that they had more idea of the fate awaiting them on arrest and the nature of the purges than many others. Statistics for suicides and attempted suicides for the Special Red Banner Far Eastern Army provided by V.S. Mil'bakh in his study of political repression in that formation during 1937–8 show an increasing number of such acts that are difficult to explain without reference to the purges. Where in May 1937 five instances of suicide or attempted suicide were recorded for the formation, in two reports for 12 June were reported. By early 1938 such events were even more frequent – in January 1938, twenty-six such events were recorded, with fourteen for February.[48]

It is hardly surprising that given the fear that permeated the Red Army and particularly command ranks, that many turned to alcohol for release from the tension – which no doubt led to other disciplinary infractions and contributed to high accident rates. On 23 November 1938 Komkor Shtern, by this time head of 1st Far Eastern Army, reported that forces of the Far Eastern Front and 1st Far Eastern Army had and continued to suffer from 'a very large number of negative phenomena in relation to the political-moral state' of the troops, including drunkenness, something that was 'well developed and typically accompanied by debauchery and sometimes murder'. The problem of drunkenness had predated and possibly contributed to poor performance during the Lake Khasan incident, with 40th Rifle Division singled out for particular criticism. This unit had apparently 'always suffered from many defects and outrageous conduct', with roll calls conducted after alerts before the Lake Khasan incident revealing platoons with only eight members present, with the whereabouts of the remainder unclear.[49] Certainly the problem of drunkenness had become sufficiently serious across the Red Army by late 1938 for the People's Commissar for Defence to issue a special order on 'The Fight Against Drunkenness in the Red Army' on 28 December 1938. The order starts by noting how drunkenness had recently reached 'genuinely threatening proportions' in the Red Army, and that it had 'taken root' in particular amongst command elements.[50] In 1937, 1,030 command personnel were removed, and not subsequently reinstated in 1938–9, for 'political-moral reasons' that included drunkenness, 'moral corruption' and 'misappropriation of the people's property', rising to 2,350 for 1938.[51]

It perhaps also seems intuitive that fear amongst command cadres looking not to draw negative attention on themselves in a climate where many failures would be interpreted as 'wrecking' would limit the extent to which they would have been willing to show initiative. As one respondent to the HPSSS stated, in the climate of the purges 'soldiers and officers now feared doing anything for fear of being arrested'.[52] Certainly being newly promoted and inexperienced in such a climate would in many instances not have been likely to foster initiative, and certainly once it had become apparent that those moving up through the ranks as a result of the purges could also themselves fall victim to them. Many things could foster low morale – fear and inability to deal with new responsibilities being two significant factors – and low morale could also have an impact on 'initiative'. As Army Commissar 1st Rank P.A. Smirnov noted during the same August 1937 meeting mentioned earlier in which Stalin had identified the negative impact of the purges on the authority of the Party and Army, even at that point 'a certain confusion has taken hold amongst a portion of commanders, who have lost willpower and let go of the reins'.[53]

With so many experienced cadres killed or imprisoned, one of the most significant impacts of the purges on the Red Army was the loss of cadres with the knowledge and experience to train an expanding army. In 1935–6 the cadre or peacetime strength of the Red Army had been in the region of 930,000.[54] On 29 November 1937 the mobilisation plan for 1938–9 set the peacetime strength of the Red Army at 1,495,310 men – a dramatic increase and in particular given the purging that had been taking place over the previous months. These figures for strength were not cast in stone – events in the Far East described later would see Red Army standing strength increased to 1,565,020 in February 1939. In November 1937 a target for mobilised strength for 1938–9 was set at 6,244,500 – with a longer range aim for 1940 of a mobilised strength of a staggering 7,068,900.[55] By 1939 it was planned, in the event of mobilisation, to be able to field 159 standard rifle, 1 motorised rifle and 13 mountain rifle divisions, along with for example 24 cavalry and 5 mountain cavalry divisions; 17 fast tank (BT) brigades, 19 brigades equipped with the T-26 tank, three with the T-28 medium and one with the T-35 heavy tank; and 57 corps artillery and 36 corps anti-aircraft artillery regiments along with other artillery units.[56] Not only would these units need providing with the necessary equipment, but their personnel would need training to use it and this massive force would need to be led by suitably knowledgeable and skilled commanders. Training and education would unfortunately be hit at all levels by the loss of experienced cadres during the purges.

Those rapidly promoted during the purges and concurrent expansion of the Red Army, who would have to lead the training of new personnel, would certainly be hampered in gaining even the theoretical knowledge for new assignments by the fact that the purges had hit the Red Army educational system particularly hard. Education would be provided by recently promoted cadres offering truncated programmes geared to fill the huge number of command vacancies. As discussed in the previous chapter, by the mid-1930s future commanders were often receiving only two years of education where they had previously received 3–4 years. This shortening of such education was in part justified by rising general education levels amongst a younger new intake, but it is difficult to imagine that all that was cut or truncated could be compensated for by increased non-military education. One respondent to the HPSSS who entered training to be an artillery commander in 1938 described his education during this period, which included a considerable amount of the political education that had become prominent in the curriculum even prior to the purges. According to the respondent, during the first half of the first year mornings were spent doing physical training, and the afternoons mathematics, Russian and German – the former geared to artillery computation and the latter to 'military terms, German commands and tactics'. During the second half of the first year he began to receive instruction on artillery. After two hours of free time in the early evening and then supper, there was 'an hour and a half which was devoted to study, theory, languages, but most of all to the political questions' – success in dealing with having considerable significance for 'the future status of the trainee'. After summer manoeuvres, the second year was spent on 'practice to insure that all we had learned could be done automatically and we learned how to command'. After having graduated in February 1940 the respondent was sent to an artillery regiment, where, in addition to assisting the colonel in charge of the regiment ended up being sent to the 'regimental school to give lectures in tactics and other military matters'.[57]

The speed with which many passed through their educations was not just about need for commanders for units and formations, but also the less than adequate numbers of suitably qualified lecturers that meant that after the Great Purges fewer had to teach greater numbers for less time. Military educational institutions suffered heavily as a result of the purges. In March 1938 the Frunze Military Academy had only 106 teaching staff out if 167 positions – a more striking deficit when the then planned number of teaching staff was according to Suvenirov more than 300. This was before intensive investigation into 61 of the teaching staff, where 15 staff were already slated for removal from the academy and a further 18 being considered for removal. By May 1939, according to Suvenirov, of 544 teaching staff positions at the Frunze Military Academy only 358 had incumbents – with their being only 2 incumbent professors out of 40 positions, 19 associate professor equivalents [*dotsent*] out of 105 positions, and 9 incumbent assistant professorial level [*ad"iunkt*] staff out of 75 positions. The staffing situation at the Academy of the General Staff was sufficiently serious during the purge period for 'the best young cadres from amongst students in the second year' to be promoted to teaching positions! Prominent deaths from amongst teaching staff included divisional commander Aleksandr Svechin – arrested on 20 December 1937 and tried and executed on 29 August 1938.[58] In his memoirs future Marshal Vasilevskii notes how in August 1937 he was appointed by the then acting head of the Academy of the General Staff as head of the Department for Rear Area Services in place of the previous incumbent, 'a significant expert in the matter, I.I. Trutko' – also purged. For Vasilevskii this appointment was 'completely inexplicable', given the fact that he lacked expertise in this particular field, highlighting perhaps not only the shortage of appropriate and available candidates but also the relative disdain with which the Red Army treated rear area services.[59] As mentioned in the previous chapter, theoretician and divisional commander G.S. Isserson was also arrested as part of the continuation of the Great Purges, but survived.

In the light of the deficit in commanders at junior levels caused both by the expansion of the Red Army and the rapid promotion of junior commanders into more senior positions as a result of the purges, attempts were made to fill vacant positions with promotees from 'NCO' ranks. Even in July 1937 when the extent to which the purges would thin out the senior command ranks cannot have been fully apparent, but at which time the demands for personnel of Red Army expansion were being felt, 'long-service [*sverkhsrochnii*] junior commanders' – specifically the equivalents of NCOs in other armies- that possessed appropriate 'military, political and general educational preparation' were being encouraged to take short courses lasting from 15 September 1937 to 15 January 1938 that could lead to their being made junior lieutenants, that is attaining command rank.[60] Such expediencies were not dissimilar to those practiced in wartime, including by the democracies, and indeed by Nazi Germany as the Wehrmacht expanded rapidly during the late 1930s.[61] However, in the former case combat experience was an important consideration, and Nazi Germany had the significant advantage in 1937–8 that it was not in the process of slaughtering a significant proportion of its existing commanders and nor was promotability as dependent on political factors. Certainly in the Red Army social and to a lesser extent ethnic origin mattered more than ever for promotion. In a sense the promotion of socially acceptable candidates for command during and after the Great Purges may ultimately have increased their authority where they could display competence, in that their promotions removed class inferiority as a factor undermining the authority of a commander. That competence and authority would first however have to be gained in less than conducive circumstances.

In the late 1930s, not only was the Red Army expanding, but also moving away from the territorial system to an all cadre army manned according to new laws governing military service. The Red Army had also to incorporate the many non-Russian nationalities in the wider military system rather than their continuing to serve in national units. It is this latter reform that will be considered first given its association with the purges and the regime's attempt to neutralise potential internal threats to its security that would be more likely to act against the regime in the event of attack by foreign powers. On 7 March 1938 a joint decree of the Central Committee of the Party and Council of People's Commissars ordered that:

1) National units, formations and military schools and academies of the RKKA be reformed as all-Union bodies with extra-territorial compositions, changing accordingly the dispositions of units and formations.

2) Citizens of national republics and regions are to be conscripted on the same general basis that applies to all nationalities of the USSR.[62]

Some of the justifications for this change provided in the document are less than convincing. Yes – in some instances the national units probably did not foster promotion for commanders from the nationalities trapped within them, and did limit the experiences and preparation of troops to specific locales, something that had been lauded as a strength of the units in the past as noted in the previous chapter. That being said, able commanders were promoted out of the national formations prior to their final abolition, as in the case of one respondent to the HPSSS, a Tatar, who after having served in the Tatar national division and associated military-educational system, studied at the Frunze Military Academy and the Sumy artillery academy in the Ukraine prior to a series of promotions that left him apparently as a *podpolkovnik* – equivalent to a US lieutenant-colonel – in a unit stationed on the Soviet border with East Prussia on the eve of war with Germany.[63] The vague assertion that 'differences in the cultural and material conditions of specific national republics and autonomous regions cannot provide for the educating and necessary military preparation of national formations' not only refers to practical issues in running separate infrastructures for the national formations, but also points to the continued concern of the regime for the integration – and loyalty – of these nationalities to the Soviet regime.[64] The purges of 1937–8 certainly hit some nationalities hard – not only were many members of national minorities killed but many were also expelled from the Red Army. Certainly being identified as German or Polish put someone in the line of fire. More than 4,000 (4,138) commanders were expelled from the Party in 1937 on the basis of their nationality, and although nearly half (1,919) had been reinstated by March 1940, more than half (2,219) had not.[65]

Removing conscripts from the nationalities from their local milieus may have offered the more capable and ambitious opportunities and in the right circumstances encouraged the development of a Soviet identity, but language barriers and cultural understandings and prejudices were understandably impediments to military effectiveness, discipline and broader integration. That national units were reintroduced early in the Great Patriotic War, as will be discussed later, is testimony to the seriousness of the problem of integration that continued to plague the Soviet armed forces right up until the collapse of the Soviet Union where there were advantages to raising and training such units in home areas before sending them to the front. That the role for national units was reduced after the desperate months of 1941–2 is testimony to continued issues with the employment of many nationalities *en masse*. Certainly the abolition of the national units before or during 1938 added further burden to an already administratively complex situation. If national units had survived in 1938, they would have had to have been converted to cadre formations then or in the near future, where national formations had also been territorial formations that had all but ceased to exist in the Red Army by 1939.

Key problems with territorial formations were discussed in the first chapter of this book. However, by the XVIII Party Congress, Voroshilov could announce that 'now our whole army is built exclusively on what is the only appropriate principle – the cadre principle', noting how the territorial system that provided 'weak cadres' had become inadequate in an environment where the imperialist powers were increasing the size of their armies and bringing them to combat readiness even in peace-time.[66] Territorial units had certainly been unpopular with many Red Army leaders during the period of their existence, and their impact on Red Army combat readiness lasted beyond their formal demise. After the war Zhukov suggested that the survival of territorial units until 1939 'played a role alongside other factors in our unpreparedness for war with the Germans', where the territorial divisions were 'poorly trained, without either a conception of modern war, or experience of co-operation with artillery or tanks'.[67] The experience of Aleksei Gavrilovich Maslov provides illustration for Zhukov's assertion, where the former served in a territorial unit during the late 1930s. Drafted in October 1936, Maslov saw his first period of continuous service during the summer of 1937, during which, after a two-week period of training at camp his unit was used to construct defences along the then state border. From the middle of the autumn of 1937 until June 1941 Maslov was available to be called up – a reservist who had supposedly been trained – but in reality 'had no idea about modern battle'. Maslov goes on to note that, 'I had held a rifle in my hands and had studied its assembly, but I had never fired a single shot'.[68] Another reason noted by Voroshilov for switching to a cadre force – reliant on conscripts serving for a continuous period of two or more years, depending on specialism, before becoming reserves – was the inability of the part-time territorials to master the new technology being employed by the Red Army during the 1930s. In speeches of the late 1930s the Red Army was master of the new technology that Stalin's new industrialised Soviet Union had provided, but the extent to which the Red Army had actually made the leap from an army of peasant part-timers to a force able to face potential opponents of the modern industrial age had yet to be put to the test. In many ways Red Army performance in the incidents and interventions of the late 1930s was far from encouraging. Certainly the divide between theories of 'Deep Battle' and PU-36 and practice were vast – and the Great Purges and military expansion made this divide even worse for an authoritarian regime and still predominately peasant society that would have struggled to create such an army even without some of the impediments of the late 1930s. The new military leadership that now dominated the Red Army was capable of identifying this divide between theory and reality, and in fact some of the measures taken to improve the situation would actually bring theory and reality closer together than might have otherwise have been the case. Unfortunately the intellectual capacities of many of this new elite were insufficient, and ambitions too great, for the net result to be a more effective Red Army by the end of the decade. Yet more significant changes to organisation and practice – alongside new equipment – would be required to remedy changes that would take place in the aftermath of the Great Purges. These changes had been instigated by politicals such as Voroshilov and Kulik in the face of little dissent – instigated by those whose competence would be shown to be inadequate for the task of making Tukhachevskii's Red Army that looked so good in theory into some sort of practical reality in the absence of those who had provided the blueprints.

In many ways Stalin's direct influence on the development of the Red Army to this point had been – relative to what was to come – limited. Stalin had been the driving force behind the economic development in part motivated by the need for the Soviet Union to defend itself and possibly even to export revolution by force of arms in order to ultimately do so more effectively. Stalin had certainly wanted the Red Army, as Soviet society, to enter a modern era – for the Red Army one of tanks and aircraft produced by the new heavy industry of the 'Great Turn'. His interest in the detail – and willingness to provide the Red Army with what it wanted – prior to the late 1930s was probably limited by the fact that the threat of war was rather abstract. With the threat of war now taking on a much more concrete form, Stalin's interest in its reliability and effectiveness in addition to loyalty would increase significantly even if Stalin's understanding of military affairs remained, for now, rather limited. As his understanding of and confidence in the Red Army grew so would his ability to choose not only politically reliable but also more capable commanders for senior leadership positions, but this process would take years and continue into the Great Patriotic War before Stalin was frequently making sound decisions on senior personnel. In the meantime the politicals that Stalin had done so much to advance held significant sway. Nonetheless, after the Great Purges and in the face of the deteriorating international situation the Red Army was starting to become

Stalin's army not only in the sense that in terms of political culture it reflected a Soviet Union that was now very much Stalinist, but also as Stalin became more involved in the minutiae of its development. With the politicals in charge, this was not always a bad thing, and Stalin the military outsider was even before the war able to successfully arbitrate in decision making against the politicals to the benefit of the Red Army as in the case of the production of mortars discussed in Chapter 8. On matters of equipment Stalin's increased involvement was arguably more often than not positive – but equipment does not alone make for an effective army.

As a result of the Great Purges, the pool of senior talent on which the Red Army could draw was now notably smaller and valuable experience that could undoubtedly have helped mould an expanding army into a more capable fighting force had been lost. There were capable future replacements, but in many cases they would be preceded by promotees who owed their advancement more to political acceptability and acumen than military ability of any sort. More or less capable alike would be propelled through the leadership ranks at considerable speed given the sheer number of vacancies to fill thanks to the loss of personnel and new positions emerging as a result of expansion of the Red Army. Provided with at best truncated educations from educators who themselves had all too often been catapulted into teaching positions, they would have little opportunity to gain experience when appointments were so short before they moved on up to the next rung of the ladder. With the prestige of command ranks tarnished, their authority suffered as discipline in the Red Army sank. The Great Purges were undoubtedly a calamity – and one that would cost the Red Army dearly during the early stages of the war before command cadres could increasingly frequently be filled with capable commanders with proven wartime experience.

4   More than Manoeuvres

Red Army Experience in Spain and at Lake Khasan

During the early 1930s, as concepts of 'Deep Battle' and later 'Deep Operations' were being developed and the Red Army was receiving the new equipment to carry them out, the Soviet Union had little conventional military experience since the Russian Civil War to draw on. Military operations by the Independent Far Eastern Army in late 1929 for control over the Chinese-Eastern Railway did involve significant Soviet strength, for example the Transbaikal Group of Forces committed three rifle divisions (21st, 35th and 36th) and a cavalry brigade (5th) – with MS-1 tanks and air support.[1] Elsewhere, in the Primor'e region, Cherepanov's 1st Pacific Division was also committed along with 9th Cavalry Brigade and air support.[2] Despite significant numbers Chinese forces were clearly overall poorly equipped, trained and organised and the panic amongst Chinese forces under Soviet pressure described by Cherepanov and Chuikov is probably not apocryphal. The fighting certainly provided some early experience for some Soviet commanders who would rise to prominence during the Great Patriotic War, particularly prominent later being Vasilii Chuikov who would command 62nd Army at Stalingrad and Konstantin Rokossovskii who would be in command of 2nd Belorussian Front at the end of the Great Patriotic War. During the fighting in late 1929 Chuikov served with the headquarters of the Independent Far Eastern Army, and Rokossovskii commanded 5th Cavalry Brigade. In an article on the subject Chuikov highlights how the single company of MS-1 tanks supporting 36th Rifle Division on the attack on 17 November was able to break through Chinese positions without loss and advance deep into the Chinese rear, despite the fact that the tanks had outrun their supporting infantry. The tanks were something of a spectacle for many Soviet troops, for as Chuikov describes rather than advancing some Soviet infantrymen simply stared in wonder at the 'steel tortoises spewing fire' as they moved forward, never having seen a tank before where tractors were only just appearing in the Soviet countryside.[3] Two of the tanks had evidently fallen beyond the remainder of the company as it advanced, and apparently ended up supporting

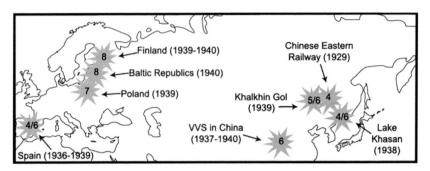

Map 1: Soviet military commitments prior to the Great Patriotic War considered in this book – where, when, and in which chapters they are discussed.

I.I. Fediuninskii's 6th Rifle Company, 106th Rifle Regiment, 36th Rifle Division on his insistence.[4] In the absence of meaningful resources for command and control there was perhaps scope for commanders even of Fediuninskii's rank to seize at least some initiative in carrying out orders at a time when Red Army actions were in many ways more akin to the chaos of the Civil War era than they would be by the end of the 1930s. After the Great Purges there was certainly far greater scope for superiors to at least attempt – often counterproductively – to micromanage the conduct of a battle where there was now something of an obsession with control and better although still hopelessly inadequate means to do so.

Somewhat later, during the second half of the 1930s, participation in the Spanish Civil War from the summer of 1936, as well as that of Soviet pilots and aircraft in the war in China from 1937, would give more modern Soviet aircraft and tanks their first battlefield testing. Soviet participation in the Spanish Civil War did not involve the commitment of large numbers of troops, where those that were committed were required to blend in with the Spanish Republican forces as much as possible in order for the Soviet Union to maintain the appearance of neutrality. Although the Soviet Union sought to placate the British and French with whom it sought alliance against an emergent Germany with its charade of non-intervention, it could not however sit by and watch a left-wing government crushed by fascists of various persuasions. Consequently considerable quantities of Soviet equipment were provided to the Spanish Republicans as detailed later, even if not as much as the Republican government might have liked and even if they ended up having to pay handsomely for this 'support'. During the summers of 1938 and 1939 the Red Army would be able to use much of this equipment during the Lake Khasan and Khalkhin Gol incidents, where Japanese occupation of Manchuria and the often poorly defined borders in the region brought Japan and the Soviet Union to blows that although falling short of wider war saw border clashes that were arguably far more than typical border incidents in scale. Clashes at Lake Khasan on the Soviet Far-Eastern border and Khalkhin Gol on the border with the Soviet client state of Mongolia gave Red Army units and formations the opportunity to utilise some of the equipment sent to Spain to achieve limited objectives of their own in what, in the case of Khalkhin Gol involved a whole army supported ultimately by sizeable air assets. Although most Soviet observers were at pains to highlight that the small scale of even the Khalkhin Gol incident limited the utility of these experiences in discussion on doctrine and organisation being developed with a view to large-scale war in Europe, nonetheless they highlighted many strengths and weaknesses of the developing Red Army. These experiences also prompted and justified a flurry of reform, re-equipment and reorganisation that even if sound would be difficult to implement for an expanding army that had just rid itself of so much experience and at least some ability – and cowed many of the survivors.

The Spanish Civil War gave the Red Army the opportunity to try out new equipment for the first time, even if the contribution of Red Army personnel to the Spanish Republican cause was certainly not on a large enough scale for it to be used to assess broader Soviet capabilities. According to Colonel G.F. Krivosheev and his colleagues who worked on *Soviet Casualties and Combat Losses in the Twentieth Century*, the Soviet Union sent about 3,000 personnel to Spain to aid the Republicans as advisers, tank crews, pilots, sailors and other specialists. These personnel were often used to train and advise Republican personnel, although Soviet pilots for example flew combat missions as part of all-Soviet units with Spanish ground personnel and many tanks were manned at least in part by Soviet personnel. Between 1936 and 1939, 158 Soviet military personnel in Spain were killed or missing in action, assumed dead. More significant was the equipment provided to the Republic – according to the first volume of the Soviet Khrushchev-era official history of the Great Patriotic War cited by Krivosheev between October 1936 and January 1939 the Soviet Union supplied 648 aircraft, 347 tanks and 60 other armoured vehicles, 1,186 artillery pieces, 20,486 machine guns and 497,813 rifles.[5] Some of these tanks and equipment did not necessarily arrive, with Steven J. Zaloga suggesting that 331 tanks actually arrived.[6] Nonetheless, although the Soviet Union supplied the Republic with relatively little equipment compared to demand – for which the Republic often had to pay – the tanks supplied were certainly superior in most respects to those available to the fascist forces.

The Soviet experience of tank use in Spain is worth looking at in some detail. Unlike in Germany, where little was made of experience in tank use in Spain in part because the inadequacies of the Panzer Is deployed were obvious even before they had seen combat, in the Soviet Union the employment of tanks in Spain was the subject of considerable discussion. This seems to a large extent to have been as a result of the fact that some of the conclusions of Soviet personnel involved in tank deployments in Spain suited the post-purge leadership's opposition to armour used *en masse* – where alternative experience was lacking. Particularly important here is the fact that Kombrig D.G. Pavlov, who advised the Republican government on tanks and commanded 1st Republican Tank Brigade until late May 1937, in July 1937 became deputy, and in December head of the Main Auto-Armour Board of the Red Army. Admiral N.G. Kuznetsov, appointed as military attaché in Spain in August 1936, certainly notes in his memoirs in a critical outburst unusual for Soviet books of the genre but in keeping with the spirit of *perestroika* when the version was published, that the man who would subsequently head Soviet armoured forces seemed, on the basis of his infrequent contact with him in Spain, 'to be insufficiently organised and hadn't got it together enough [*ne khvatalo organizovannosti i lichnoi podtianutnosti*] for military affairs.... I was surprised...when I found out about his promotion to a high ranking post....'[7] A survivor and indeed beneficiary of the purges in terms of promotion, Pavlov was willing – for whatever reasons – to emphasise those aspects of the Spanish experience that suited Voroshilov, Budennii and other likeminded leaders. Such leaders included future Marshal of Artillery G.I. Kulik, who at the rank of Komkor similarly served in Spain as an 'adviser' to Republican forces. He would, like Pavlov, contribute to the shift in Soviet armoured doctrine away from the idea that tanks used *en masse* could be used effectively in deep penetrations of the enemy's tactical and operational rear. Using the tank effectively *en masse* in such a manner as part of a combined-arms schema may have been beyond Soviet capabilities, but abandoning such a goal completely however would leave the Red Army in an even worse position to deal with a capable opponent.

The first significant use of Soviet tanks in combat occurred on 29 October 1936 in and around the village of Sesena south of Madrid – the same month that the first Soviet tanks had arrived in Spain. In this instance, according to Soviet sources, a company of fifteen tanks entered the village of Sesena, without infantry, believing that it was not in enemy hands. After establishing that it in fact was – through conversation with enemy officers who thought that the tanks were Italian – the T-26s were able according to Soviet accounts to wreak a certain amount of havoc against unprepared infantry and cavalry in the area. Returning to the village later that day the tanks this time however met organised resistance. With Fascist troops enjoying protection from stone buildings, against which the 45mm guns and machine guns of the T-26s were relatively ineffective, and without infantry support, three Republican tanks were lost to 'organised anti-tank defences' – where amongst other weapons the defenders used Molotov Cocktails. Certainly poor reconnaissance, poor infantry-tank co-operation and in general a failure to combine arms effectively were all dimensions to this battle that would plague the Republican side to a greater or lesser degree throughout the war and were rightly identified as issues in a subsequent Soviet analysis of the battle. The episode might also have been taken as indication of the weakness of unprepared infantry and cavalry to tanks – particularly outside the village – but the loss of three tanks or 20 per cent of the force seems to have led the Soviet authors of the 1937 Ministry of Defence publication concerned to focus on the vulnerability of the tanks.[8]

Despite the nominal growth of the Soviet tank force in Spain to brigade strength during the winter of 1936–7, the tanks were typically employed in small packets. As Polkovnik B.M. Simonov noted in a report published under another name after his arrest and execution, Republican tanks were during this period 'used exclusively in an infantry support role'. Noting how the outcome of actions depended on the activities of tanks, he also noted the clear superiority of Soviet tanks over those available to the fascists.[9] The use of 'two dozen' or so tanks in the storming of Mount Garabitas during early 1937 as mentioned by Manfred Shtern, a.k.a. General Kleber, representative of the Comintern in Spain, was a typical case of tank deployment in an infantry support role. Shtern reported in this instance the tanks seem to have been squandered, be it because they had gone into action with insufficient fuel as Shtern suggested, or they had been employed in unsuitable terrain as Kombrig Pavlov commanding Soviet tanks in Spain, claimed. Having become bogged down or run out of fuel before enemy positions, he suggested that at least some were then picked off by enemy anti-tank guns.[10] Alternative sources on the Mount Garabitas engagement note how in this case Republican tanks – including some of the survivors of twelve antiquated Renault FT-17 tanks – struggled to make headway in far from ideal terrain against prepared positions, with far from smooth co-operation with other arms and against an enemy now better equipped with anti-tank weapons. In fact, over three days 23 out of 36 tanks involved were knocked out.[11] In the case of Mount Garabitas, Pavlov's

apparent point about the suitability of the terrain for tanks is not without
foundation – the hilly and wooded terrain was not ideal tank country, but
was certainly better than much of the terrain fought over in Spain. But
terrain was only one factor in the often poor showing and high loss rates
for tanks – and well supported tanks would regularly operate effectively in
less suitable terrain during the Second World War.

Certainly the use of relatively lightly armoured tanks for infantry support
as the enemy became better equipped with anti-tank weapons was bound
to lead to vehicle losses. As the war progressed Nationalist forces certainly
seem to have made good use of the German-supplied PaK 36, of which
thirty companies of six guns were apparently available to von Thoma of the
German Condor Legion by 1938.[12] Zaloga notes how in a section of a
report on operations in Spain on the Central Front from October 1936 to
February 1937 – later published by the People's Commissariat for Defence
(NKO) – Komkor G.I. Kulik noted sarcastically 'how 'the anti-tank gun
could sweep the battlefield of tanks the same way that machine-guns swept
it of infantry.'[13] Kulik's section of the full published report, not formally
attributed to him, in fact provides a little more detail on the appropriate
circumstances for the success of tanks, noting that in the aftermath of
fighting in rugged terrain along the River Jarama and heavy tank losses:

In the face of well organised anti-tank defence tanks can suffer significant losses
from anti-tank fire if such weapons are not supressed by artillery and infantry fire.
Anti-tank weapons are a similarly dangerous enemy for tanks as the machine-gun
is for infantry. Yet tanks can operate with considerable effect against infantry and
cavalry that have not organised reliable anti-tank defences.[14]

In public Soviet observers often seemed to be looking to condemn tanks
to an infantry support role in line with the prevailing political wind back
at home. Observers were often unwilling to emphasise in oral presenta-
tions what they often inferred in the body of reports, that as Soviet
doctrine of the Tukhachevskii era suggested, in the right circumstances
tanks could act as the principle arm in the exploitation of a breakthrough
or fluid situation akin to the aftermath of breakthrough. Kulik's remarks
to the Military Council of the People's Commissar for Defence in
November 1938 are certainly different in tone to his above written
remarks, where he later noted rather dogmatically in front of his peers
what many of them wanted to hear, that:

We need to bear in mind, that the wars in Spain and China do not give a full
picture of modern combat. . . .
    The role of the infantry has recently been somewhat downplayed. We have to
resurrect [vozrodit] the infantry and put it in its rightful place.
    . . .

We have to demand that different arms provide for and give timely assistance to the infantry.

... It is necessary for tanks to act in close co-operation with the infantry, not breaking away from them.[15]

After his return to the Soviet Union, in late 1937 Pavlov would go as far as to emphatically condemn the whole concept of tanks as an exploitation force, referring to the Battle of the Jarama in February 1937. Here Republican tanks were apparently initially concentrated near the town of Arganda before being parcelled out, with for example the 15th International Brigade being provided with nine T-26s – a company – according to the memoirs of the British volunteer Jason Guerney.[16] Pavlov stated:

Experience has shown, that tanks thrown in independently (and a DD[17] group is a group for independent action) are destroyed. If you want to convince yourselves of this, then I ask you to ask Comrade Kulik sitting right here – he remembers such independent action below Arganda. Here also sits Comrade Petrov[18], who almost didn't escape from that episode.[19]

Pavlov actually then went on to rail against the concept of infantry riding on tanks – a practice that would become typical for Soviet troops during the Great Patriotic War given the lack of alternative transport despite the obvious failings of such a practice – on the basis of a botched operation the previous month, stating that:

Such [tank] riders consisting of 250 of the best antifascist sons were shot in recent fighting on the Aragon Front. They were put on machines, the machines were thrown in to the attack, the tanks with this infantry moved up to the front line and all the infantry, sitting on the tanks, were shot. Then something else. I won't give a figure, ... for the number of DD tanks than were left to the enemy and destroyed.[20]

Certainly the failure of the bulk of the 50 BT-5 tanks supplied to Spain when employed in October 1937 – tanks intended to act as exploitation forces in mid-1930s Soviet doctrine - gave the naysayers such as Pavlov further ammunition to downplay the scope for the tank to play a leading role in offensive operations. The operation in question, to which Pavlov refers above, is described in some detail in a 1969 article written by future General-Lieutenant of Engineers A.A. Vetrov, who in October 1937 commanded the so called International Tank Regiment of the Republican Army – a force of BT-5s. The regiment was ordered to attack the town of Fuentes del Ebro along with the 15th International Brigade as part of attempts to divert Nationalist forces from operations elsewhere. The town region had been attacked by Republican forces in August, and was well fortified and with positions manned by experienced Moroccan

Soviet 'volunteer' tankmen near the graves of fallen comrades in Spain in July 1937. That tanks such as the BT-series and T-26 were very vulnerable to artillery and contemporary anti-tank weapons was very much apparent to Soviet observers in Spain. (RIA Novosti #53963)

troops. On 13 October, with only poor reconnaissance of Nationalist positions and with the 15th International Brigade understrength and poorly equipped, three tank companies with a total of forty-eight tanks rushed against prepared positions with infantry of the 24th Spanish Battalion who had never ridden into battle on tanks doing so for the first time against prepared positions. The tank riders suffered heavy losses, and the tanks soon lost contact with the infantry as they struggled to manoeuvre. Ultimately any gains – including positions overlooking the town – had to be surrendered given the lack of infantry reserves for consolidation. In what had been a reckless attack, the regiment had lost nineteen tanks and thirty-seven tankers.[21]

So the fighting in Spain seems to have been used to justify the idea in the Red Army that tanks were so vulnerable to anti-tank fire that they needed to be used exclusively in close co-operation with infantry and artillery, on the infantry's terms. On the negative side, this experience certainly contributed to the decline of the idea of large armoured forces conducting deep penetrations into the enemy's tactical and certainly operational rear – even in favourable circumstances – that had figured in the ideas of many now dead theorists who had contributed to the spirit of the 1936 Field Regulations. This was despite the fact that in Spain it had been shown, and reported on numerous occasions, how successful tanks could be when operating against enemy forces in disarray, even if such operations were difficult to follow up on. This was particularly the case for the Red Army that had not invested in the provision of tracked and armoured vehicles for the infantry and artillery that it was acknowledged would have to accompany tanks in any sort of deep penetration. In his memoirs Petro G. Grigorenko writes about the increasingly side-lined military theorist Isserson's stubborn defence of the doctrinal thrust that was being undermined during and in the immediate aftermath of the Great Purges by the 'Spaniards' – those who served in the Spanish Civil War – and their interpretation of 'the Spanish experience'.[22] Certainly post-Soviet archival releases and in particular the publication of the records of bodies such as the Military Soviet advising the People's Commissar for Defence highlight how significant the experience of the Spanish Civil War was for the development of Soviet doctrine in the late 1930s.

With the idea of deep penetration of the enemy rear by formations in which the tank was the principal actor increasingly discredited, the tank corps – until 1938 mechanised corps – that were to have undertaken such operations were ripe for disbanding, a step eventually taken in November 1939. Mechanised (soon known as motorised) rifle divisions, with their two motorised rifle regiments, would have a tank regiment with 240 tanks in four battalions. The tanks that had been part of the tank corps – with a staggering 560 tanks each – were to be formed into independent tank brigades – 42 in total – where the 21 equipped with T-26s and the 17 with BT-series tanks would still have 258 tanks each.[23] Clearly the reforms were not about moving away from the concentration of tanks – and indeed Pavlov's experiences in Spain seem to have convinced him of the need for tanks to be used *en masse*. In late November 1938, after having railed again against the use of fast or DD tanks for deep penetration of the enemy rear with reference to the debacle at Fuentes del Ebro, but with a little more nuance than the previous year, Pavlov pointed this need for concentration out to his colleagues:

In the attack against a static enemy tank companies should not be broken up [*dolzhna bit' nedelimoi edinitsei*].
   A tank brigade, thrown against a static enemy or in a meeting engagement should without fail co-operate with infantry and aviation and be accompanied by

an artillery barrage. The throwing of DD tanks 150 km into the enemy rear through an unbroken enemy anti-tank defence should cease. The experience of the Aragon Front confirms this....

...Our tanks can only carry out their role when released *en masse*.[24]

Tanks were deployed by the Red Army during the border incident at Lake Khasan or Changkufeng in late July and early August 1938, although they played only a minor role in an action fought on unsuitable terrain. Although this event was of relatively little significance in terms of impact on Soviet doctrine and organisation, it did highlight a number of issues hampering Red Army performance – and arguably some of the detrimental ramifications of the recent purging of Red Army personnel in the Far East.

The Soviet commitment of forces to the fighting incident at Lake Khasan was not insignificant – although only an 'incident' in that it did not lead to war, it was more than a skirmish. At Lake Khasan Soviet forces ultimately committed 39th Rifle Corps, consisting of 32nd and 40th Rifle Divisions, along with elements of 2nd Mechanised Brigade. Whilst the tank battalions from the latter saw action, its infantry was used, along with 39th Rifle Division and 121st Cavalry Regiment for protecting the left flank of forces committed to the fighting.[25] Theoretically Soviet forces enjoyed the support of the available artillery assets of 39th Rifle Corps – according to Soviet sources these increased from an initial 217 up to 237 pieces of various calibres including 58 of the 45 mm anti-tank guns and eventually 179 pieces of 76 mm and above. By the first days of August, 39th Rifle Corps had 245 T-26, 79 BT-series and 21 T-37 tanks on strength, and Soviet forces were also provided with air support from a number of fighter and bomber regiments, with a total of about 250 aircraft in the region.[26] Impressive as the artillery figures might sound, 39th Rifle Corps did not have the artillery assets it was supposed to have at list strength, with at the outset 40th Rifle Division for example having ninety-four artillery pieces compared to the 132 it was supposed to have. The 32nd Rifle Division only had the transport capability to bring in only 25 per cent of a full reload or *boekomplekt* of ammunition. An additional problem was personnel shortages discussed later, the end result of all of this being that not all artillery brought in actually participated in the fighting.[27]

Soviet forces were faced by a Japanese force that, as the fighting escalated, committed only three of four infantry regiments of the 19th Division – supported by a maximum of thirty-seven artillery pieces of undisclosed calibres at the tail end of the fighting.[28] As such, Japanese forces committed about 7,000–7,300 men out of at most 10,000 men for 19th Division, with Soviet ground forces committing in the region of

15,000 men to combat, out of a probable 22,950 men in the vicinity.[29]
The fact that the Japanese ground forces did not receive air support
where the Japanese Imperial General Headquarters sought to prevent
an escalation of the fighting, meant that Soviet forces were fighting an
enemy with one hand tied behind his back.[30] However, despite Soviet
material superiority, after the initial Soviet force consisting of border
troops that were soon reinforced by two battalions of 40th Rifle Division
had been ejected from and failed to recapture hilltop positions in late
July, one might argue that the hilly and marshy terrain in the immediate
vicinity favoured the soon to be well entrenched defender. Additionally,
the deployment of Red Army forces to the area was hampered by poor
transport infrastructure in the region, where the Red Army relied on a
single gravel road for supplies and did not have a railhead nearby as the
Japanese did.[31] Nonetheless, despite these factors, the Red Army was
ostensibly victorious although in the aftermath of the incident Soviet
forces were not deemed to have functioned at all effectively in what were
in many ways favourable circumstances.

Initial Soviet attacks were hurried and poorly planned and organised.
Future Marshal M.V. Zakharov notes in his unusually critical Soviet-era
memoirs, that initial Soviet attacks on Japanese positions on 2 August by
three regiments of 40th Rifle Division lacked significant artillery or any
air support – with only a few artillery batteries available and with fog
apparently preventing air operations.[32] Tret'iak et al's history of the Red
Banner Far Eastern Military District suggest that two *divizions* of artillery
were available to support the attack, and border guards actually reported
some Soviet air support that morning, with thirteen aircraft hitting the
heights and twelve the Japanese rear. In fact Japanese troops had been hit
by Soviet air attacks the previous day – as noted in both Soviet and
Japanese sources.[33] Nonetheless, Soviet efforts to expel Japanese forces
were poorly organised at this point. A description of operations in the
Lake Khasan region produced by the headquarters of the Red Banner
Border and Internal Security Forces of the Far Eastern Military District
produced shortly after the incident describes the situation as the attack
was about to commence, as one where 'part of the artillery that had
arrived during the night was not ready; the enemy's disposition, and
particularly forwards positions, had not been studied; communications
had not been set up fully; and the left flank of the force was not in a
position to start the attack at the appointed hour'.[34] Certainly the decision to attack an enemy in prepared positions might under the circumstances have been questioned, but in a manner to be repeated so many
times during the Great Patriotic War delay was apparently unacceptable.
Hampered by orders not to cross the border, the commander of the 40th

Rifle Division launched a frontal assault from the north on the Japanese positions to the west of Lake Khasan – supported by tanks of 32nd Independent Tank Battalion – that soon stalled. According to Zakharov the tanks, whose crews had not been familiarised with the terrain, 'got bogged down in the marshes and ditches' – as reported at the time by the head of artillery for 39th Corps Kombrig P.N. Iaskin, who noted how they got 'stuck in marshes, and were shot up by the Japanese whilst stationary'.[35] A number of commanders apparently abandoned their men and the battlefield – including the commander of 40th Rifle Division's tank battalion along with one of its platoon commanders.[36]

The attack on Japanese positions was renewed with greater strength and success a few days later. This time Japanese forces could be attacked from more than one direction and greater artillery and air support was now available. On 6 August in preparation for the Soviet ground assault and after a delay for fog to clear Japanese forces were attacked in a number of waves by bombers, including now somewhat antiquated TB-3s.[37] According to Mil'bakh however, these air attacks were delayed not by the weather, but by poor preparation and readiness on the part of units involved, where they did not even have the necessary maps.[38] The ground assault was also preceded by artillery preparation – interrupted by air attacks, before elements of 40th Rifle Division supported by the division's own tank battalion and a second from 2nd Mechanised Brigade attacked Japanese positions from the south-west whilst the bulk of 32nd Rifle Division attacked from the north also supported by two tank battalions.[39] Once again, it seems that many tanks were lost – on 6–7 August only 'individual tanks made it to their objectives, but very few made it back. They got stuck in the marshes and were shot up by Japanese 37–40 mm guns'. According to Kombrig Iaskin, presumably by the end of the day on 7 August, of the thirty-two T-26 (and twenty T-37) tanks listed for 32nd Rifle Division on 3 August, only seven were operational, 'the remainder burnt out, standing in the marshes. Four to five tanks were bombarded by their own artillery by order of the divisional commander'. By 8 August 40th Rifle Division was apparently no longer fighting in organised regiments and battalions, with small units fighting it out for the heights with the enemy.[40] After heavy fighting Soviet forces had gained some ground, and Japanese troops fought to try to recapture lost positions during counterattacks over subsequent days. On 11 August, when a ceasefire was agreed upon, Japanese troops had been pushed back, although at significant cost. Soviet forces are reported to have lost 717 killed and 75 missing, along with 2,752 wounded. Japanese losses were in the region of 526 killed and 913 wounded.[41] According to one Soviet source the Red Army apparently lost twenty-four tanks presumably completely destroyed, with a further fifty-six damaged.[42] Thirty-two artillery pieces – more than 10 per cent of the total force – were either destroyed or broken.[43] It is important to stress, that Japanese withdrawal from the area – and territory deemed Soviet by Soviet leaders – was not because they were convincingly defeated on the battlefield, but because the Japanese leadership wanted to prevent an escalation in the fighting.[44]

Initial assessment of Soviet performance during the Lake Khasan fighting was certainly damning, Protocol Number 18 of the Main Military Soviet of 31 August 1938 stating that:

Events of these few days have uncovered considerable defects in the state of the Far Eastern Red Banner Front. The military preparation of troops, headquarters and the commanders of the front was of an unacceptably low standard. Military units were not coherent [razdergani] and not ready for action; supply for combat units had not been organised. It was discovered that the Far Eastern theatre was poorly prepared for war (roads, bridges, communications).[45]

The above protocol heaped particular blame on the commander of the Far Eastern Red Banner Front, Marshal V.K. Bliukher, and removed him from command of the front leaving him 'at the disposal of the Main Military Soviet of the RKKA' – a situation that was often, as in this case, a precursor to arrest.[46] Bliukher was subsequently arrested on 22 October 1938, before being killed whilst in custody on 9 November 1938.[47] Making Bliukher the scapegoat for failures at Lake Khasan was certainly convenient, where Moscow had certainly made the tasks of local commanders more complicated than need have been the case. Bliukher had been told to oversee operations at Lake Khasan while simultaneously bringing all of the forces of the Far Eastern Front and Trans-Baikal Military District to full readiness with poor administrative resources. Lower down the chain of command at the time of the first attack on Japanese positions at the beginning of August the commander of the 40th Rifle Division apparently told the head of the General Staff that he had received objectives from front, army and corps level command![48] Not only confusion over the chain of command but the hunt for enemies within it by Red Army political organs made the task of commanders more difficult. The arrival of Lev Mekhlis at the headquarters of 40th Rifle Division on 1 August can certainly not have made the tasks of the divisional commander easier, and Mekhlis's attentions were not limited to 40th Rifle Division.[49]

Too many commanders involved in the fighting at Lake Khasan had only taken up new appointments recently thanks to the purging of Soviet forces in the region. A significant number of arrests had hit units and formations involved in the fighting at Lake Khasan during the summer of 1937, but the arrests did not stop there. During July 1938, 599 commanders were arrested from amongst those of the Far Eastern Front, with the number of arrests that month being 4.5 times higher than the average for the previous twelve months. One of the victims that month was Polkovnik V.G. Burkov, commander of 2nd Mechanised Brigade, who was arrested on 28th July 1938! He was actually released on 23 May 1939 and returned to duty, reaching the rank of General-Major of Tank Forces on 3 May 1942 suggesting a certain competence.[50] As noted by the Russian historian V.V. Diatlov, the artillery of the Special Red Banner Far Eastern Army had been hit hard by the purging of 1937–8, with victims including the head of the artillery department for the army, Kombrig V.L. Leonovich and the army's head of artillery supply Polkovnik I.S. Dubovnik – both arrested in September 1937.[51] Many replacements did not have suitable experience or qualification for the positions they were undertaking – and sometimes immediate replacements could not be found. The 40th Rifle Division lacked 40 per cent of its list-strength medical personnel immediately prior to the Lake Khasan incident, with the heads of medical services for all its regiments having been arrested. In the absence of alternatives, Senior Dispensing Assistant Voenfel'dsher Salikhov was head of the division's medical department, and Senior voenfel'dsher B.P. Begoulev, a dentist, was head of medical services for 120th Rifle Regiment.[52]

From supply through to battlefield command and control and co-ordination between arms, the Red Army performed poorly at Lake Khasan. On the former the Protocol Number 18 of the Main Military Soviet of 31 August 1938 was extremely scathing, suggesting that 'forces were completely unprepared as they moved out towards the border after the alarm was raised'. Failure to organise the distribution of material held back for use in the event of crisis meant that 'in many instances whole artillery batteries appeared at the front without munitions', with further examples of failures to equip troops for combat including the extreme case of one of the units of 32nd Rifle Division 'arriving at the front without any rifles or gas masks at all'. That commanders and headquarters units had insufficient maps of the combat zone certainly hampered the conduct of operations.[53]

Poor supply and a lack of maps could not bode well for the quality of artillery support, the poverty of which was highlighted by Kombrig P. N. Iaskin, head of artillery for 39th Rifle Corps. Panic under Japanese artillery fire resulted in the execution of three artillerymen – presumably including the commander – from 2nd *Divizion* of 40th Light Artillery Regiment early in the incident. The attack that begun on 2 August was

Soviet commanders on the shore of Lake Khasan in the summer of 1938. Soviet victory could not hide the many glaring deficiencies of the purge-wracked Red Army. (RIA Novosti #59244)

apparently undertaken without artillery preparation, and there was no co-operation during the attack between the artillery and the infantry. Tanks of 2nd Mechanised Brigade were also reported as not having received support from their own artillery assets during the renewed offensive.[54] The Main Military Soviet protocol of 31 August went on to consider the performance of other arms in combat, and was similarly critical, noting how 'all branches, but especially the infantry, revealed an inability to function on the battlefield, to manoeuvre, to integrate fire and manoeuvre, and to make use of the terrain.' Tanks units were 'used in a clumsy manner, as a result of which they suffered heavy material losses'.[55] Regarding airpower, aircrews were reported as being insufficiently familiar with new equipment, namely DB-3, SB and R-10 aircraft, and tracer and incendiary ammunition was lacking, but many problems were attributed to the lack of experience of new commanders.[56]

Although much of the Main Military Council protocol of 31 August on events near Lake Khasan that became the NKO order of 4 September was concerned with passing responsibility for failures to Bliukher, behind the scenes there were wider recriminations, and attempts to remedy some deficiencies. Komkor G.M. Shtern, by now commander of 1st Independent Red Banner Army, for example explained to the Military Council how training at all levels was remedying some of the inadequacies shown at Lake Khasan. It was also acknowledged that communications in the region could be improved. Nonetheless, reading the transcripts of meetings of the Military Council, it is difficult to avoid the conclusion that although focus on some 'political-moral' factors was constructive in that discipline would be required to deal with many issues, the subversive activities of traitors still provided too convenient an excuse to explain away many issues.[57] This, once again, would occur all too frequently during the dark months of the summer of 1941. Focus on finding scapegoats over seeking solutions would characterise the Red Army of the Great Patriotic War when the chips were down during the crises of the summer of 1941 and when early in the war Stalin would continue to place considerable reliance on the zeal of the military incompetent politicals who still had the ear of the dictator.

5   Khalkhin Gol

Border tensions with the Japanese, whose often poorly defined shared border with the Soviet Union or the latter's Mongolian satellite now extended for thousands of kilometres, did not end with the incident at Lake Khasan. Far more successful for the Red Army than operations at Lake Khasan were Soviet operations on the River Khalkha in July and August 1939, in that in the latter case the outcome was a clear Soviet victory – and the encirclement of a significant Japanese force. Soviet tanks were employed in brigade strength and provided the Red Army with a mobility that their opponent lacked. The Red Army performed relatively well, but in favourable circumstances. At Khalkhin Gol not only was the terrain far more favourable to the Red Army than it had been at Lake Khasan, but the Soviet commander on the spot, Zhukov, had time to both prepare and amass resources for the offensive that would prove decisive – time that would all too frequently not be made available during the Great Patriotic War. Zhukov also did not have to worry about orchestrating and providing for deep operations on a battle-field of limited size where the enemy ultimately held a very static defensive posture. Japanese equipment, doctrine and local leadership were all inadequate in the circumstances, during an episode that had resulted from the pushing for activity by local Japanese commanders against the better judgement of at least some involved. As Coox notes, the Chief of the Japanese Army General Staff operations section had apparently suggested before the battle to commanders of the Kwantung Army – elements of whose 23rd Division were being committed to offensive operations – that it was 'senseless for a second-line division that was not 'operational' to become involved in large-scale combat in a meaningless locale', but that is what it did.[1] The ordnance chief of the Japanese 23rd Division actually shot himself in June as the bulk of the division was committed, apparently because of the 'awful equipment' that the division possessed. The local Japanese command did not have the wholehearted support of the chain of command as events reached a climax – although it had overconfidently turned down resources as the incident had been developing – where Zhukov certainly did have the support of his superiors.[2] The resulting encirclement of Japanese forces was a major victory for the Red Army but one that even Zhukov was not to overstate in his memoirs.

In a similar manner to the Lake Khasan incident, a Japanese border incursion – this time into Mongolian territory – in May 1939 saw an escalation in forces committed by both sides. By July, by which point Komkor G.K. Zhukov had taken over command of Soviet forces, Japanese forces had committed a significant force to offensive operations in the region consisting not only of the 23rd Division – a second line unit – but also elements of 7th Division and two tank regiments. According to Soviet sources, at this stage a Japanese frontline strength of nearly 22,000 infantry and approaching 5,000 cavalry in the area was countered by a Soviet force with just over 11,000 infantry and 1,000 cavalry. Despite having approximately only half the artillery assets compared to the Japanese, according to Soviet sources the Red Army had as many machine guns as the Japanese and could deploy 186 tanks and 266 armoured cars against the supposedly 130 tanks available to the Japanese – an exaggeration of Japanese armoured strength by about one third as will become apparent later.[3] By the time that Zhukov launched his offensive in mid-August Red Army material superiority was apparent not only in terms of armour. Not only did Japanese force no longer have any tank units at this point, the reasons for which will become apparent later – and with as many as 498 tanks available to Soviet forces along with 385 armoured cars – but the Red Army enjoyed considerably greater artillery support. By the 20 August Soviet offensive, the Red Army had committed significant artillery assets to the region. Although losses in action and due to their intensive use had not been insignificant up to this point – in part perhaps as a result of a Japanese 'artillery offensive' in late July – the Red Army probably fielded in the region of 540 guns and mortars by 20 August.[4] The 'more than 300' artillery pieces identified in one of the more realistic Soviet assessments of local Japanese strength not only meant fewer guns and often lighter guns than available to the Soviets, but ammunition supplies available to the Japanese gunners were extremely limited as well – and particularly after intensive artillery bombardment of Soviet positions from 23–25 July.[5] Despite the inadequacies of many of the older Soviet pieces – with only the four A-19 guns having particularly long range capabilities of over 20 km – Soviet fire support was certainly impressive and at least included many modernised pieces.[6] Japanese artillery was often of Russo-Japanese War vintage and sometimes not even modernised. Hence Japanese artillery was forced to fire at ranges of only up to 6,800 metres for unmodernised 75 mm guns and only 5,000 metres for similarly antiquated 12 cm howitzers.[7]

Fighting in early July saw the end of the Japanese advance, but this was only achieved at considerable cost and in fighting that did not suggest that the Red Army had moved on much beyond the Lake Khasan experience in terms of the co-ordination of arms. Part of the problem may have been the loss of many of the communications resources that had initially been available, where in a telegram to Voroshilov the commander on the spot – Zhukov – in the face of the loss of radio and field telephone communications making it 'very difficult to command' over the distances involved asked for a signals battalion to be sent by Moscow. By the late afternoon of 8 July in actions from 2 July 57th Special Corps had apparently lost twenty-five telephonists in addition to twenty-five radio operators.[8] During the morning of 3 July after Japanese engineers had constructed a pontoon bridge over the River Khalkha, the Japanese had committed two infantry regiments – 71st and 72nd, with artillery support – across the river and seized the heights of Bain Tsagan. They were later reinforced by 26th Regiment, bringing the Japanese commitment up to seven and a half battalions with supporting units, or in the region of 8,000 men.[9] The Soviet counterattack on the morning of 3rd July was in theory to have seen the commitment of 11th Tank Brigade, supported by 24th Motor Rifle Regiment and 7th Armoured Motor Brigade with its armoured cars – which together may have been able to overwhelm the Japanese in open country without sustaining horrendous losses. In his memoirs, Zhukov stressed the importance of counterattacking without delay so that Japanese troops could not fortify their positions. However, 'the bulk' of 11th Tank Brigade was initially committed alone at about 10:45 a.m. after a 60–70 km drive to engage the enemy. The 24th Motor Rifle Regiment – 'critically needed for co-operation with the tank brigade, which without infantry suffered unnecessary losses', ended up not entering the fray until 12:00 due to being misdirected, and 7th Armoured Motor Brigade was committed later still at around 15:00.[10]

Fighting for Bain Tsagan continued throughout 4 July, before Japanese forces retreated across the river that night and supposedly destroyed their pontoon bridge behind them. The Japanese had taken heavy losses – nearly 10 per cent of those troops committed were killed or wounded, but Soviet losses were also heavy. According to the Soviet author E. Gorbunov 11th Tank Brigade 'lost half of its personnel. Of 182 tanks 82 had been lost. No less serious losses were suffered by other Soviet and Mongolian armoured units. During July, in the main at Bain Tsagan, losses consisted of 175 tanks and 143 armoured cars'.[11]

During the fighting on 3 July, tank-infantry co-operation had been poor and as the previous figures suggest, the tanks initially committed alone suffered accordingly despite the poor anti-tank capabilities of Japanese units involved. As Zhukov later noted in conversation with Konstantin Simonov regarding the attack of 11th Tank Brigade, 'I knew that without infantry support it would take heavy losses, but took the decision aware of the situation [*soznatel'no shli na eto*].'[12]The testimony of Vasilii Filatov, commanding a tank company of 11th Tank Brigade, highlights the vulnerability of Soviet tanks during the battle. Having received the order to attack at 10:45, Filatov was in action sometime around 11:20 – without infantry support and of course with artillery support ceasing after the initial barrage once the tanks were engaged at close quarters with Japanese infantry. He described the confusion as tanks charged around trying to avoid attacks from Japanese infantry and what Soviet and Japanese sources agree as having been the most effective weapon against them available in any quantity – Molotov cocktails. After the battle he noted that his company had lost five tanks, possibly the five tanks he had earlier seen on fire surrounded by Japanese troops.[13] Japanese sources describe how Soviet tankers often charged forward at great speed – sometimes at an estimated 45–50 km/h – and 'since the vehicles were overheated in the sun and were mainly light types and gasoline-fuelled, they tended to burn easily when hit at any point'. An early Soviet attack on 71st Infantry Regiment consisting of '50 tanks and armoured cars' had apparently been halted by noon, 'leaving behind more than 20 machines stopped by rapid-fire weapons and by a platoon of the newly arrived field guns from 3rd Battalion of the 13th Field Artillery Regiment, which knocked out 14 vehicles in 20 minutes, at ranges as great as 700 meters and as close as 30 metres'.[14] Certainly early in the day on 3 July, with Japanese troops relatively fresh and well supplied, a number of successful engagements with Soviet armour were recorded. On a more positive note for the Red Army, the impact of Soviet heavy artillery – outranging Japanese pieces available – is worthy of note even if Zhukov had at the time complained to Moscow of having insufficient artillery resources.[15]

Soviet tanker Vasilii Rudnev arrived in the region in mid-July after the fighting for Bain Tsagan, and commanded a tank of 11th Tank Brigade during later fighting that had been recovered from the battlefield at Bain Tsagan. The previous crew of his tank had all been killed, but the tank was patched up leaving visible signs of battle damage. Perhaps unsurprisingly, it was initially 'terrifying' to be 'climbing into someone else's crypt', although the new crew apparently got used to it. Rudnev notes how the 37 mm anti-tank gun used by the Japanese – and committed in limited numbers at Bain Tsagan – could penetrate the weak front armour of the BT-5 at even medium ranges, although the solid shot would not necessarily cause significant damage if it didn't start a fire. He also noted the ineffectiveness of the Japanese light tanks committed elsewhere during the fighting at Khalkhin Gol, and indeed of Japanese airpower against tanks, where likelihood of a direct hit with bombs from a medium or light bomber on relatively dispersed armour was low. He goes on to note however how Soviet tanks with their petrol engines 'took genuinely heavy losses from bottles filled with an inflammable mixture, although heavy losses were suffered 'only initially', with infantry support and tanks advancing in a 'chessboard' formation limiting the effectiveness of Japanese infantry attacks with Molotov cocktails and anti-tank mines and grenades.[16] According to Maksim Kolomiets, using Soviet after action analyses, overall at Khalkhin Gol 5–10 per cent of Soviet tank and armoured car losses were to Molotov cocktails – many early on in the fighting- compared to 75–80 per cent to anti-tank guns. With 15–20 per cent of armoured vehicles losses to field artillery, only 2–3 per cent were due to hand grenades or mines – where Japanese anti-tank mines had apparently often simply been pushed down and failed to detonate in the sand. Japanese aircraft were responsible for the loss of 2–3 per cent of tanks as well.[17] Hits from anti-tank guns and Molotov cocktails often led to fires and ultimately total destruction of vehicles. From 3 July–5 August 11th Tank Brigade alone lost sixty-nine tanks 'burnt out [*sozhzheno*]' – compared to the same number otherwise knocked out. A significant number of the latter could be repaired – most of the former could not. During fighting from 20–30 August 11th Tank Brigade lost only twenty-two tanks burnt out – with 102 otherwise knocked out. Of twenty-two burnt out and fifty-six otherwise knocked out tanks – and one that did not make it into combat – 6th Tank Brigade was able to repair forty-nine during the period from 21 August–1 September.[18]

The Japanese advance in the region of Bain Tsagan in early July was repulsed, albeit at significant cost. In many ways this was achieved in a manner that would characterise many Soviet successes of the Great Patriotic War, where overwhelming force compensated for ineffective combined arms. As reported by 36th Motor Rifle Division, poor co-operation between arms during the July fighting was not limited to poor artillery support from divisional artillery 'that lacked forward command posts', but could be identified within infantry battalions where 'machine-gun companies operated in the majority of instances cut off from the battalion, not receiving orders and without communications with the battalion commander'. In the former instance the artillery lacked organic communications resources. Adding to the confusion was the fact that reconnaissance was sporadic and not being conducted 'actively', with even passive observation of the enemy 'poorly organised'.[19] Soviet integration of arms would be more effective the following month and highlight what could be achieved by the Red Army in a well-planned operation against a relatively static enemy – but frequently would not be achieved during the Great Patriotic War in circumstances where enemy capabilities and initiative were higher. Fortunately for Soviet forces in the Far East, as Coox notes, the Japanese High Command was 'not interested in a war against the USSR as a means of settling the Nomonhan dispute. Dislodging the Russians from the right bank of the Halha would suffice'.[20] Consequently the Japanese did not launch attacks elsewhere. Additionally, Zhukov could certainly draw on far more significant wider resources than local Japanese commanders. Japanese inactivity elsewhere in the region allowed Soviet forces to concentrate on conducting an offensive to take place in many senses favourable operational circumstances against an enemy with few operational options – and in particular few mobile reserves. The Japanese did commit armoured forces during the early stages of the fighting in the region. The 3rd Tank Regiment (Medium) fielded twenty-six Type 89 (Otsu) medium tanks in two companies, and four Type 97 (Chi-ha) mediums along with seven Type 94 (TK) with four Type 97 (Ke-te) tankettes. The 4th Tank Regiment (Light) had thirty-five Type 95 (Ha-go) light tanks organised into three 'line' and one reserve companies, with a company of eight Type 89 (Kō) medium tanks and three Type 94 (TK) tankettes. These two regiments essentially represented the entire armoured strength of the Japanese Kwantung Army.[21] Japanese tanks arguably performed admirably during fighting in the central section of the Khalkhin Gol battlefield on 2–3 July – despite being committed hurriedly – with tank–tank combat taking place on a scale only rivalled up to that point during fleeting episodes during the Spanish Civil War. Despite the superiority of Soviet tanks over the predominately light and undergunned Japanese models – and the fact that the Japanese tankers lacked the level of motorised infantry support enjoyed by the Soviet side – Japanese tanks inflicted casualties on their Soviet armoured opponents and provided a counterbalance to the significant Soviet armoured units being fielded. However, in a matter of days Japanese armoured strength was dwindling – on 9 July the 3rd Regiment's fielding of 'the half-dozen tanks of the supply and maintenance company represented what was left of the whole regiment operationally'.[22] That day the commander of the Japanese armour received orders to deactivate the tank detachment the next morning, although Japanese tanks were not actually pulled back until around 20 July – and released from local command on 26 July.[23] Coox provides 'best data' for Japanese tank losses during the July fighting – thirteen 'wrecked irreparably by gunfire', with 11–14 repaired on return to home bases, along with seventeen more restored to working order before being pulled out. As such, the Japanese tank force had seen 60 per cent of its vehicles immobilised during the fighting, but could have provided a meaningful mobile reserve in the August fighting. Certainly, as Coox suggests, the presence of Japanese tanks might have 'restrained' Soviet forces, even if, as Zhukov later apparently suggested to Stalin in conversation in May 1940, they were on the whole little better than the MS-1 tanks that the Red Army had removed from frontline service.[24]

During the Soviet offensive operation that began on 20 August, and that resulted in the encirclement of the bulk of Japanese forces in the region, Soviet forces unleashed a well-prepared attack against a passive opponent caught in many senses by surprise. Both Japanese and Soviet accounts point to careful Soviet *maskirovka* – concealment of preparations for the offensive and deception as to Soviet intentions – that although it did not convince all frontline Japanese commanders nonetheless seems to have convinced their superiors that the Soviet posture was defensive. Certainly limited Soviet radio traffic before the offensive was

Soviet infantry and tanks advance in the Khalkhin Gol region in July 1939. Red Army superiority in armour and artillery was increasingly apparent during operations fought in a relatively confined but nonetheless open area that allowed the Red Army to take advantage of its relative strengths. (RIA Novosti #41696)

ominous.[25] When the Soviet attack finally came, Soviet forces enjoyed both superior mobility and firepower. Japanese forces were initially hit by air strikes – easily directed against fixed positions. Japanese anti-aircraft batteries had revealed themselves by opening fire on aircraft sent ahead for the purpose of exposing the anti-aircraft guns – and were suppressed by Soviet artillery. The subsequent Soviet artillery barrage lasted for more than two hours before more airstrikes hit Japanese positions. Japanese fighter aircraft were kept at bay, and there is little evidence of meaningful Japanese counterbattery fire.[26] Perhaps adding an element of the surreal to the drama – and the horror – was the fact that these events were apparently accompanied by the 'Internationale', 'March of the Pilots' and March of the Artillerymen' blaring from Soviet loudspeakers.[27]

With the beginning of the ground advance, Zhukov initially committed all but one of his tank and armoured car brigades to offensive operations on the flanks, with infantry in the centre supported by their organic tank battalions and a tank brigade. Delays were experienced on the first day in getting armoured formations across the Khalkha, and the strength of Japanese positions on the left flank on the Fui Heights had clearly been underestimated. Soviet troops spent at least four days hammering away at Japanese positions on the Fui Heights – much to Zhukov's apparent consternation – before organised resistance ceased, but during the night of 21 August Zhukov had already committed mobile reserves on this sector to continue the advance – leaving only 212th Airborne Brigade in reserve. Soon the newly committed 9th Armoured Motor Brigade with a battalion of 6th Tank Brigade was able to work its way behind Japanese positions and wreak havoc in the Japanese rear. On the Soviet right flank by the end of the day on 21 August any line of retreat for Japanese forces deployed forward south of the Holsten River had been severed by elements of 6th Tank and 8th Armoured Motor Brigades.[28]

Japanese troops fought tenaciously – even fanatically – but were often defending isolated positions that were at best poorly supplied. The Japanese simply did not have the mobile reserves to do much to either meet Soviet penetrations or to seize the initiative and counterattack with any speed. One by one, key Japanese positions – often not mutually supporting or in depth – were reduced as the Red Army where necessary bludgeoned and elsewhere traversed its way towards an envelopment of the bulk of Japanese forces, – an envelopment which had taken place by 24 August when Japanese sources confirm the linking up of the left and right pincers of the Soviet encirclement.[29]

Superior Soviet equipment available in quantity played a significant role in Japanese defeat. Soviet units employed not only conventional gun tanks but also flamethrower tanks that both Soviet and Japanese accounts suggest caused not only significant casualties, but perhaps as importantly contributed to the psychological overwhelming of many Japanese troops. Central to Soviet success both in the destruction of enemy forces and the psychological wearing down of the enemy was artillery, with a majority of Japanese casualties – just over 50 per cent of those killed and wounded – being reported as having being caused by artillery fire. In many instances isolated Japanese positions were reduced by artillery fire – both indirect and from weapons being fired over open sights.[30] Artillery of up to 152 mm calibre was deployed in a direct fire role in the destruction of such Japanese positions –with the Fui Heights on the left flank of the 20 August offensive being subjected according to one eyewitness to artillery preparation lasting about two and a half hours before the final storming of the positions by Soviet troops.[31] Weak Japanese logistics – even before Soviet units had penetrated the Japanese rear – meant that Japanese guns could provide only limited return fire. When the Japanese did finally counterattack in force against Soviet forces on edges of the rapidly developing envelopment, the Soviet offensive was already on its fifth day, and poorly supported Japanese infantry struggled to make headway against entrenched Soviet troops enjoying more significant artillery support than available to the Japanese. During the period from 24–26 August, with Japanese counterattacks having failed, the encirclement of the bulk of Japanese forces remained intact.[32] With Red Army troops on the outside of the encirclement dug in to protect the Soviet-claimed border, Soviet forces could move towards destroying remaining Japanese resistance on Mongolian territory.

Japanese 'fighting spirit' was not sufficient to halt a Red Army that although far from a well-oiled machine, had nonetheless been training and equipping for warfare in a different league – and had a coherent plan to be set in motion against a passive opponent. Red Army troops – often of peasant origin and hardly suffering from the effects of Western decadence – and with the experience of the Great Purges and harsh penalties for failure to motivate them – would not simply crumble in the face of Japanese will power. Japanese forces may have been engaging in warfare in many ways on a large scale in China (and not clinging to an atoll without a land flank to turn as they would be in so many instances later on), but faced a second rate opponent in the Chinese forces they had been fighting since 1931 – allowing them to get away with practices and the employment of equipment far from as suitable for use against a major European power as the Chinese. An equivalent to the Japanese situation might be seen to be the employment of inadequate light tanks by the British for imperial policing, and that even First World War experience suggested were unsuited for most combat roles. Neither the Japanese or Chinese had participated in or developed doctrinally from the victories and defeats and attempts to break the stalemate on the Eastern and Western Fronts during the First World War, with the prevailing wind in the Japanese army being more akin to the commitment to 'hard steel' shared by both the Japanese and Russian sides at Mukhden in 1905 than the mechanised combined arms schema that incorporated the tank as an important element and a focus on mobility that was developing at least in some European armies. The extent to which the Japanese Army learnt from the experiences of Khalkhin Gol seems to have been limited – defeat led to the suicide or side-lining of many often competent Japanese officers involved in the incident, and 'lessons' from the battle often seemed to be perceived to insult the 'manhood' of Japanese troops for whom, for example, 'caution was equated with a lack of courage'.[33] According to Drea, in the light of the Nomonhan fighting Japanese army investigative committees concluded that 'fighting spirit still retained its absolute priority in battle, although more firepower might be necessary in future engagements'.[34]

Japanese 'fighting spirit' did not lead to victory during the summer of 1939, but it did contribute to the exacting of a significant toll on Soviet forces. According to G.F. Krivosheev and his colleagues, 6,831 Soviet troops were killed in action or died during casualty evacuation during the fighting in the region, with a further 1,143 missing in action. During the whole 'incident' Soviet tank troops alone lost 659 killed on the battlefield, with 36 missing and 864 wounded. Overall, in addition to those killed, and those who died during evacuation or were missing, 15,251 were wounded, concussed or suffered burns and were admitted to medical facilities – and a further 701 were removed from duty due to sickness. At least 720 of these later died. Kolomiets provides a figure of 9,703 killed, missing or died from wounds and 15,952 wounded.[35] These losses were from a force with an average monthly strength for the four-month period from June – September of just under 70,000 men – with Soviet strength for 1st Army Group being reported in Soviet works as being around 57,000 at the time of the Soviet offensive of 20 August. On the basis of archival sources Maksim Kolomiets accounts for at least 51,950 frontline troops for 1st Army Group at this point – with the strength of the three rifle divisions committed alone – 57th and 82nd Rifle and 36th Motor Rifle – in the region of 28,690 troops.[36] Losses during the initial phases of the 20 August offensive were understandably particularly high, with Shtern reporting 3,637 wounded on 24 August according to figures provided by medical services for 20–23 August. Shtern also reported 30–32 tanks and armoured cars burnt out, with a further 70–75 knocked out although with many already repaired by the time he reported.[37]

Although irrecoverable Soviet tank and armoured vehicles losses declined between July and August – in part it seems thanks to tactics limiting the scope for infantry attacks on tanks – overall Soviet armoured vehicles losses were significant as figures for casualties amongst their crews provided earlier suggest. Armoured vehicles that were burnt out or totally destroyed, or had to be sent from units for 'capital repair' included 59 BT-7 and 157 BT-5, along with 8 T-26, 12 flame tanks and 17 T-37 tankettes. Certainly the armour of BT-series tanks was shown – as it had been in Spain – to be inadequate, and their vulnerability to fire highlighted once again. Nonetheless, the close-support version of the BT-7 tank – the BT-7A – had proven its worth in the suppression of anti-tank fire, and the T-26 tanks had proven to have good battlefield survivability compared to the BT-series vehicles. It was identified in after action reports that more tanks might have been evacuated from the battlefield before being lost completely – with the single vehicle per company detailed to tow damaged vehicles from the battlefield being clearly inadequate.[38]

Armoured car losses were high – in part because early in the incident they were used in intensive combat roles for which they were not suited rather than being used for reconnaissance and flank security. In such circumstances in particular the limited infantry support allocated to such units was a serious problem. Eight BA-3, 44 BA-6, 41 BA-10, 21 FAI and 19 BA-20 armoured cars were lost – a total of 133.[39] Certainly the importance of the armoured car in the Red Army would decline significantly in Soviet thinking by the time of the Great Patriotic War, with productive resources seen to be better invested in more heavily armoured and more mobile tracked vehicles.

At Khalkhin Gol Japanese forces suffered considerable casualties, with a very high proportion killed. 'At least' 8,000 were killed and 8,800 wounded, with a further 1,200 incapacitated due to sickness out of a total commitment of what Soviet sources claim as 75,000 men including Munchurian troops – although in his post-Soviet work the Russian historian Gorbunov accepts that local Japanese strength at the time of the late August offensive – for the recently formed 6th Army – was in fact similar to Soviet local strength at 55,000 men. This figure is certainly more realistic when attempting to assess opposing forces on the battlefield in late August. Coox notes that the Kwantung Army came up with an incomplete figure for troops committed as 75,738, but including units that certainly did not participate in the late August fighting such as the tank corps. Medical services for 6th Army came up with an incomplete figure of 58,925 – with total participation according to Coox 'that exceeded 60,000'. Certainly combined strength for 23rd and 7th Divisions – including the bulk of the Japanese combat troops that bore the brunt of the late August fighting – comes to 25,753. Japanese infantry units suffered particularly severe casualties, 71st Infantry Regiment for example losing 93.5 per cent of its strength during the fighting, and 26th Infantry Regiment 91.4 per cent. That 23rd Division suffered a loss of 76 per cent of troops committed during the period is in many ways a more frightening statistic, given that the divisional strength included all arms and some support personnel.[40]

It is interesting to note the significant role that snipers – or perhaps more accurately marksmen – seem to have played on both sides, and particularly in singling out officers or commanders who in both armies were sufficiently distinctly dressed to make them obvious targets.[41] In his memoirs I.I. Fediuninskii, at the time a colonel or *polkovnik*, recalls an apparently jocular conversation with some rank and file Red Army men on the matter after he had made his way to forward positions with them and they had come under fire on their approach. In his memoirs he wrote, paraphrasing the purported conversation of 1939:

Fediuninskii: Lads – it is not beneficial to go with you – the Samurai shoot at us! Better to move individually.

Red Army soldier: Comrade Polkovnik…, one has to consider for whom it is beneficial, and for whom not. Perhaps it is not to our benefit. When we were moving on our own, we were not shelled, but as soon as you joined us it then started. You there are so decked out [*raznariaz-hennii*] that you are visible from a kilometre away!

Fediuninskii goes on to note how this was something about which something was done only during the Great Patriotic War.[42]

Kombrig M.P. Iakovlev, commanding 11th Tank Brigade, was, according to at least one account, killed by a Japanese sniper.[43] As snipers, both Japanese and Soviet troops could display a degree of initiative not typically encouraged elsewhere – and seem to have also had some success as an organic part of infantry units the previous year at Lake Khasan.[44] Fediuninskii describes how his regiment employed snipers on the flanks and in front of the core positions of the regiment as a way of providing both warning against and disrupting Japanese attacks before they gained any momentum.[45]

Although at Khalkhin Gol circumstances and the opponent were in many ways favourable, there were many positive aspects to Soviet performance in the region, even if some of them would be difficult to replicate in a wider war in the west. The 20 August offensive was planned, and resources amassed to give significant superiority over the enemy in particular in artillery and armoured vehicles – despite poor communications between the region and the Soviet Union and in particular European territory. The nearest rail head was as much as 700 km away, and the 2,636 automobiles of various types used according to Zhukov by the 1st Army Group to bring in supplies were alone insufficient although additional automotive transport from the Trans-Baikal Military District and indeed other parts of the Soviet Union were apparently employed. In his memoirs Zhukov stated that in addition to the above 2,636 vehicles, 1,250 trucks – along with 375 tankers – had been received 'from the Soviet Union' by 14 August.[46] In fact, 1st Army Group had been unusually well provided for in terms of vehicles from its inception as 57th Special Corps in September 1937. According to Maksim Kolomiets, referencing archival sources, in June 1939 57th Special Corps had a total of 4,342 lorries on strength as part of transport units, 720 of which were tankers. Total vehicle strength for the formation as of 1 February 1939 was 5,208 trucks, 193 light vehicles, 679 'specialised' vehicles, 631 tankers, 245 mobile repair shops, 91 tractors and 265 motorcycles in addition to 284 tanks and 370 armoured cars.[47] To put this in context, the entire Red Army vehicle park on 22 June 1941 was in the region of 272,000 vehicles.[48] Artilleryman Nikolai Kravets recalls making the long journey across the steppe from Borzia at night, with his unit and their new 152 mm ML–20 gun howitzers being pulled by tractors from the Cheliabinsk Tractor Factory that were waiting for them along with trucks.[49] Whilst Khalkhin Gol might be seen as suggesting considerable Soviet mobility and supply capability, as figures presented previously certainly suggest, that was with 1st Army Group not only being well-equipped to start with but also being able to draw on wider resources that in the event of a broader war would not be available to your average formation.

Also positive at Khalkhin Gol were attempts to deceive the enemy of Soviet offensive intentions, where significant effort went in to the operational *maskirovka* noted above. As Coox's monograph on the battle suggests, primarily from a Japanese perspective, many Soviet troops certainly fought hard. At the same time Japanese sources seem to highlight the skill of Soviet troops in tactical concealment, including of defensive positions, even if this skill did not however, according to then Colonel I.I. Fediuninskii, typically extend to commanders![50] By the time of the 20 August offensive co-operation between arms seems to have been better than during the hurried Lake Khasan attacks or indeed during the Bain Tsagan fighting in early July, but here improvement from a very low level should be stressed. Shtern's report to Voroshilov of 24 August on the progress of operations suggested that in attacks against enemy positions there were still instances of tank attacks without the requisite infantry support, even if he suggested that 'on the whole our people have adapted to this positional warfare'.[51] Certainly a Soviet after-action report cited by Kolomiets suggested that combined arms or co-operation primarily between infantry, artillery and armour remained a particular weakness. Attacks were deemed to have often been poorly organised, with units often going into the attack straight from the approach march. Infantry battalion commanders were also deemed to be poorly equipped to co-ordinate the sort of co-operation required – with attempts to do so being made by commanders at regimental level and above.[52]

Many Soviet units were poorly trained on the outset of hostilities, where training typically bore little resemblance to the realities of war. In his memoirs future Marshal of Artillery N.N. Voronov described a case at Khalkhin Gol prior to the 20 August offensive of an infantry company failing to take advantage of artillery preparation against Japanese positions only a couple of hundred metres in front of them and remaining heads in the sand until well after the barrage had lifted and the Japanese defence had recovered. According to Voronov, their support weapons made no attempt to suppress Japanese machine gun fire. This is perhaps a good example of where more meaningful training might have paid dividends. Voronov goes on to describe another, more positive incident with a different unit where a Japanese machine gun was silenced by a 45 mm anti-tank gun that had moved up on the initiative of its commander. It apparently took days to identify the junior commander concerned, where 'the point was that the commander of the weapon had acted on his own initiative, and was now concerned that he might be punished for it [*samovol'stvo*]'. Of course, had things not worked out, he probably would have been.[53] Fortunately for the Red Army Japanese troops were under pressure to follow orders to the letter – regardless of changing circumstances – even more than their opponents.

Also on a more critical note, indirect artillery support that could be provided to relatively rapidly advancing units fighting an entrenched enemy was limited to relatively few long range pieces that in this instance fortunately did not have to move forward with the tanks and infantry where the battlefield was limited to the contested border region. Had this artillery had to move forward, then its effectiveness might have been more limited, for as Coox notes, 'though Soviet artillery was very good at pre-planned firing, it was not very effective against targets of opportunity'.[54] Lighter pieces could to a limited extent avoid fire-control issues through being employed in a direct fire role as part of the process of softening up Japanese defensive positions, even if their mobility still left much to be desired.[55]

The Red Army as a whole might have lacked modern heavy artillery and the means to tow it effectively, but for this particular engagement more might have been found – despite the situation in Europe – where Moscow was willing to throw resources at 1st Army Group, as the additional trucks mentioned earlier suggest. Certainly the Russian historian Gorbunov is critical of Zhukov in this regard, suggesting that even if the operation could not have been delayed further given circumstances in Europe and pressure from Moscow, nonetheless Zhukov might have 'asked for Moscow to send..., even if as a temporary measure, a few corps artillery regiments'. That he didn't seem to have requested more of such resources is attributed to the fact that 'apparently, having received immense power over tens of thousands of people, even then Zhukov showed signs of disdain for soldiers and commanders under him.' Gorbunov goes as far as suggesting that for Zhukov troops were 'cannon fodder [*pushechnoe miaso*], which could be expended as suited [*kak emu ugodno*]'.[56] This sentiment may be difficult to find in the Soviet literature, but echoes that expressed by Petro G. Grigorenko in memoirs published in the United States in 1982. Grigorenko was on the staff of the front group co-ordinating Soviet forces in the Far East and Mongolia during the early stages of the Khalkhin Gol incident, and indeed made a brief visit to the Khalkhin Gol region before the August offensive. Komandarm 2nd rank Shtern was head of the front group, and as Grigorenko suggested, may very well have played a role in the planning of the Khalkhin Gol offensive – in addition to certainly playing a role in the supply of Soviet forces in the region as even Zhukov suggested to Stalin after the event as reported in his memoirs.[57] Shtern did not get the opportunity to write his own memoirs, being executed in late October 1941 after having been arrested on 7 June – accused of the usual participation in a Trotskyist conspiracy and of spying for the Germans.[58] In his chapter covering the period including the Khalkhin Gol fighting, Grigorenko suggested that 'Zhukov didn't care about any losses we suffered'.[59] Certainly Zhukov and many other successful Red Army commanders of the Great Patriotic War era were successful because they were willing to provide what Stalin wanted – results when demanded – and often regardless of the immediate human cost. Khalkhin Gol was a good example of such a victory. Certainly there are times in war when taking heavy casualties to achieve a result quickly might ultimately save lives – and in the case of Khalkhin Gol had Zhukov listened to the advice Shtern apparently offered to him early on in the offensive to regroup and delay further offensive action for two-three days in the light in part of the heavy casualties being taken by Soviet forces, then the result might have been far less decisive and more lives lost. Certainly pushing forward resolutely on the confined battlefield at Khalkhin Gol was unlikely to lead to the sort of encirclements of attacking forces that would prove all too typical for the Red Army for much of the Great Patriotic War where providing support for such thrusts at the operational level was often beyond the limits of Soviet command and control. The relatively poor mobility of Soviet artillery and supply services would early in the Great Patriotic War further increase the chances of the resolute attacker pressing on into enemy operational depths being encircled – neither was a particular issue at Khalkhin Gol given the confined nature of the battlefield, limited mobility of the enemy and relatively short duration of the battle. Zhukov's self-reported reply to Shtern, that 'war is war, and in war there can't not be casualties' nonetheless does seem to suggest an attitude to the lives of those under him that would often contribute to the horrendous losses suffered by Soviet forces in operations throughout the Great Patriotic War.[60]

The relatively confined geographical limits and positional warfare of the Khalkhin Gol battlefield had in many ways meant that with a capable albeit ruthless commander in Zhukov a number of limitations of the Red Army had not been brought to the fore, limiting the scope for lessons to be learned from the experience. Although supply to the Khalkhin Gol region was an issue, this was less of a problem on the actual battlefield and certainly compared to the Japanese. As regards communication, on the battlefield for much of the time the Red Army could rely on the telephone and pre-planned actions modified as required with orders at times transmitted by hand against an enemy with even less effective command and control. In a situation where an observer with binoculars or other similar instrument could glean much about enemy dispositions without having to move far from a command post, the fact that the Red Army paid inadequate attention to reconnaissance and in particular reconnaissance after operations had begun was also less critical than it would be in different circumstances.

The Khalkhin Gol experience did not figure as prominently in pre-Great Patriotic War deliberations on the use of war experience as might be supposed, although 'inadequacies in the organisation of medical provision' not only at Khalkhin Gol, but at Lake Khasan and in Finland did lead to changes in the nature of medical services in the Red Army. Although calls for more surgeons for example would be difficult to act upon given the limited availability of suitable personnel for a rapidly expanding army, elsewhere there was more that could be done. A lack of appropriate preparation for civilian doctors called up into army service, the deployment of doctors too far forward where casualties were unacceptably high, and a lack of specialised medical provision within a less than coherent system were all issues at least partially addressed in the lead up to the Great Patriotic War. Hence, for example, where doctors had served at battalion level at Lake Khasan, they were moved to regimental level at Khalkhin Gol leaving fel'dsher at battalion level. By the summer of 1941 the divisional medical point, staffed by up to fourteen doctor-surgeons was seen as the basic level for the provision of field medical services.[61]

Despite having little apparent impact on Soviet military theory or practice beyond perhaps for military medicine, the Khalkhin Gol experience was certainly important in providing an example to the Japanese as to what might happen if Japan was to continue to focus its ambitions outside China on the Soviet Union rather than the Western powers to the south. The Khalkhin Gol victory also of course helped Zhukov's career – a man who along with Stalin would do so much to set the tone for Red Army operations during the Great Patriotic War.

6   Keeping up with the Schmidts and the Suzukis

Soviet Military Equipment and the Small Wars of the 1930s

Just as experience in Spain provided valuable testing of equipment for the Red Army and German armed forces alike, then so did the Soviet Union's other small wars of the late 1930s and 1940. It is in this regard that Red Army seems to have gained most from its experience of war to the end of the summer of 1939. Experience in Spain was certainly used to justify a certain undermining of the doctrinal developments fostered by those such as Tukhachevskii during the early 1930s – and particularly their ideas on the role of armour and other arms in their 'Deep Battle' schema – but at that point such application of Soviet experience to doctrinal discussions all but ceased. It is sometimes argued that changes to the organisation of armoured forces of November 1939 discussed in Chapters 4 and 9 that saw the mechanised (briefly 'tank') corps disbanded flew in the face of experience at Khalkhin Gol that summer. Although at Khalkhin Gol Zhukov had apparently shown the potential for the tank to take the lead in encirclement of enemy forces, the November reforms were however not out of sync with Zhukov's experience. At Khalkhin Gol operations had taken place in a relatively confined geographical area in which the tank brigades used did not undertake deep penetrations of the Japanese operational rear. The large tank brigades of November 1939 intended primarily for infantry support would in fact have been in a good position to carry out the sort of local encirclement – in co-operation with other arms – achieved by Zhukov at Khalkhin Gol.

Experience in Spain in particular – reinforced in fighting with the Japanese – undoubtedly led Soviet leaders to increase focus on the vulnerability of tanks – where in both Spain and the Far East only moderately armoured tanks had been pitted in frontal assaults against defensive positions with little support. Thus experience seems to have encouraged the development of heavy breakthrough tanks designed to support infantry. Alexander Alexandrovich Vetrov, who had been deputy commander of the Republican International Tank Regiment during the Fuentes del Ebro fiasco, claims in his memoirs to have highlighted many of the deficiencies of Soviet tanks employed in Spain to Stalin and a meeting of the Sovnarkom Committee for Defence on 4 May 1938. Vetrov was certainly concerned by the armour of the BT-5, which was 'not in a position to resist German anti-tank artillery that had appeared in the hands of Franco's forces', apparently requesting that new tanks not only have increased armour, but also improved firepower, radio communications and electrical equipment as well as improvements in mechanical reliability.[1] The government Committee for Defence would subsequently, on 7 August 1938 approve the plan 'On the System of Tank Armament of the RKKA' that had been in development since early in the year, dealing with concerns over the multitude of tank types in the Red Army, the need to improve existing models and the need for a new tanks – a heavily armed and armoured breakthrough tank and a tank for work with other arms to replace the T-26 and BT series.[2] Ultimately these projects would result in the KV series and T-34, which will make their first appearances in the next chapter. In the process multi-turreted tanks, petrol-engined tanks and tanks able to run on both wheels and tracks were abandoned.

During the mid-1930s, and despite issues with the production of high performance engines, the Soviet Union could not only field some of the best tanks available, but also possessed some of the best fighter aircraft. During the early fighting in the air over Spain the Soviet I-15 and I-16 bi- and mono-plane fighter aircraft compared favourably to their German and Italian equivalents available to the Nationalists. The Italian CR-32 biplane was more manoeuvrable than either Soviet aircraft and was well-armed by the standards of the day, although the fact that it lacked the speed of the I-16 was significant – during a period in which it was becoming apparent in many air forces that the manoeuvrability of biplanes was typically no compensation for the speed advantages enjoyed by new monoplane fighters. The German Heinkel 51 biplane initially fielded as a fighter by the German Condor Legion was, even in the autumn of 1936, inadequate for air combat and soon relegated to other roles. During a brief period in late 1936 and early 1937 the Republic and its Soviet allies could enjoy air superiority over the battlefield thanks to the quality of and numerical superiority in equipment and pilots, where much of the Spanish Air Force had gone over to the Republic rather than the Nationalists. In such favourable circumstances Republican forces could use antiquated R-5 and successor R-Z biplanes in daylight bombing in support of ground forces, in a war in which both the Republicans and Nationalists made considerable use of airpower in direct support of ground forces. During the Spanish Civil War the value of close air support of ground forces became apparent to many participants – not only in terms of the material damage and dislocation that could be inflicted on the enemy, but also in terms of the psychological impact of air support on friend and foe alike. The defeat of the Italian [Guadalajara] offensive in March 1937 was certainly aided by Republican airpower, with Republican fighters operating in a ground attack role playing a notable role in the disruption of the Italian advance on 12 March.[3] On 18 March the Republican counterattack was supported by both fighters and 'ground attack aircraft' – including recently arrived R-Z aircraft with Spanish crews – hitting Brihuega and positions around it.[4] Certainly Italian historians have pointed to the importance of Republican air supremacy during the battle in the defeat of the Italina offensive – where that supremacy seems in part to have been made possible by inopportune basing of Italian aircraft.[5] Republican R-5 and R-Z aircraft – of which 31 and 93 respectively were supplied to the Republic – are reported as having carried out 166 out of 226 missions – involving 1,271 of 3,686 sorties – against enemy ground forces to 1 January 1939, with the 92 SB bombers supplied carrying out 405 missions against enemy ground forces involving 3,306 sorties during the same period. The R-5s and R-Zs were slow and vulnerable to both ground fire and enemy fighters – although the 31 R-5 SSS aircraft with Soviet crews apparently undertook a number of successful daylight attack missions after their arrival in November 1936, they started to take heavy losses and were relegated to night missions, with the Republicans declining further deliveries. Increasingly close support of ground forces by day was conducted by fighters – with I-15 and I-16 aircraft reported as having conducted 23,066 sorties – 405 missions – against enemy ground forces.[6] Certainly German 88-mm and automatic 20 mm anti-aircraft guns deployed by the Condor Legion seem to have made their presences increasingly felt during the war. Hugh Thomas suggests that the Condor Legion's 88-millimetre anti-aircraft batteries 'limited the extent' that Soviet superiority in the air at Jarama in February 1937 could play in support of the Republican offensive.[7] Republican forces reported having lost thirty-six aircraft to fire from the ground between October 1936 and 15 December 1938, five of which were R-5 and nine of which were R-Z aircraft.[8] As noted by one Soviet observer reporting on the war up to the spring of 1937, 'the work of aviation . . .has been severely complicated by the appearance of high speed fighters and the increased effectiveness of anti-aircraft resources'.[9]

The appearance of series-production German Bf 109 aircraft in early 1937, along with German and Italian training of Nationalist aircrews, contributed to the fact that as 1937 progressed it was Nationalist forces that were increasingly able to enjoy superiority in the air. German fighter pilots in the faster Bf 109s could, with the benefit of surprise, get in a first attack on I-15s and even I-16s before leaving regardless of the outcome of the brief engagement. For Soviet pilots the solution was to try to use better manoeuvrability in the horizontal plane to get behind German aircraft, with the machine-gun armed aircraft engaging in an aerial version of circling the wagons. The war certainly highlighted the need to improve the firepower of fighter aircraft, beyond the only two machine guns of early I-16 aircraft – soon doubled to four – for example. The appearance of I-16 armed with 20 mm cannon gave them a better chance of causing damage if 'jumped' by German fighters, but with the arrival of the Bf 109E 'with three bladed variable pitch propeller and 20 mm cannon, superior to the I-16 of all types by all measures, the situation changed drastically'. The superiority of the Bf 109E was such that 'in an engagement with such aircraft I-16 pilots could pin their hopes only on luck or their skill'. Even if attacking from above and gaining the speed benefits of a dive, the vertical manoeuvrability of the Bf 109E typically meant that 'if the pilot of an I-16 wasn't successful during his first attack, then to repeat it was a tall order'. The chances of Soviet fighters being surprised was increased by the lack of radio communications between aircraft, where co-ordination in the air was consequently poor.[10]

An I-16 fighter, in this case in naval service. What had been state of the art in the mid-1930s was looking increasingly outdated by the end of the decade. Despite its increasing obsolescence, the VVS would have to place considerable reliance on this fighter during the early stages of the Great Patriotic War. (TsVMM #65163)

Combat experience for Soviet aircrews and aircraft would also be provided in the war against the Japanese in China from late 1937. The first Soviet aircraft – a squadron of I-16 fighters and another of SB bombers – were flown into China in October 1937, and by the end of November the first combat between Soviet 'volunteers' and the Japanese is recorded as having taken place in Soviet accounts. By late April 1938 there were more than 100 Soviet-crewed I-15 and I-16 aircraft operating in the Hankou area. Soviet aircraft increasingly engaged with new Japanese I-96 (Mitsubishi A5M) monoplane fighters that were far more effective than the biplane I-95s (Kawasaki Ki-10) also in action and with which Soviet pilots had been familiarised back at home. New Japanese I-97 fighters (Nakajima Ki-27) made the situation worse – Soviet bombers supporting Chinese forces and operating without fighter escort could apparently outrun the I-95 and even I-96 – but not the I-97. Bombing soon took place from 7–9,000 metres as a result of the threat from Japanese fighters, rather than the 2–4,000 metres that had initially been undertaken. Soviet losses to Japanese fighters were significant – in one incident alone on 12 August 1938 five SB bombers were lost. As in Spain, co-operation between Soviet aircraft once airborne was poor given that there weren't radio communications within a section.[11] Soviet assistance to the Chinese Nationalists had petered out by early 1940 as a result in part of Soviet rapprochement with Japan and Chinese failure to support the Soviet Union as it faced expulsion from League of Nations over the invasion of Finland, although aid continued to be provided in 1941.[12] During the brief period of active Soviet involvement in China from 1937–9, Krivosheev et al suggest that 195 Soviet personnel were killed or reported missing. Alternative sources suggest that a total of 211 out of the more than 3,500 that served were lost.[13]

In contrast with the incident at Lake Khasan, where air combat between Japanese and Soviet forces did not take place, and indeed where Japanese air forces play no part in the fighting, at Khalkhin Gol local Japanese commanders pushed restrictive rules of engagement. In the air Japanese forces had fared better than their colleagues on the ground – at least initially – as even Zhukov apparently acknowledged to Stalin.[14] As a result of fighting in China, Soviet forces were aware of Japanese capabilities, even if Soviet air forces in the region were initially poorly equipped. Escalation of the aerial war mirrored that on the ground, with something of a small arms race seeing initial Japanese success with Type 96s and Type 97s – with the latter in –a and –b variants soon becoming the standard Japanese fighter in the region – over Soviet I-15bis aircraft, requiring the Soviet dispatch of more I-16 fighters to the region and I-153 biplanes with superior performance. Soviet I-16 Type

5s were soon augumented by improved Type 10s and 17s – the latter with 20 mm cannon to be used primarily for ground attack.[15]

At around the time of the first fighting in the air on 22 May the VVS in the region consisted of 100th Mixed Air Brigade consisting of 70th Fighter Air Regiment and 150th Mixed Bomber Air Regiment, with thirty-eight I-15 and I-16 fighters, twenty-nine SB bombers and seventeen LSh-5 ground attack aircraft. In a region that was in many ways a backwater, pilots had apparently flown particularly infrequently even by Soviet standards prior to the conflict and were poorly trained – with discipline 'as low as it gets', and where many aircraft were not serviceable. In fact, by 20 May only twenty-one fighter aircraft – thirteen I-16 (twin machine gun equipped Type 5) and nine I-15bis – out of thirty-eight could be put in the air. Mongolian forces could, theoretically, also deploy thirty-six aircraft – all R-5 or R-5Sh (a ground attack variant). However, the VVS would receive rapid reinforcement. In fact, on 21 May the transfer of 23rd Fighter Air Brigade with twenty-eight I-16 Type 10 and thirty-five I-15bis from the Trans-Baikal Military District began.[16] On 14 May, when Japanese air operations began, 2nd Japanese Air Division had according to Coox provided a light bomber squadron (nine aircraft) and two fighter squadrons (nineteen aircraft) to support the Khalkhin Gol enterprise – with two further fighter (twenty Ki-27) squadrons transferred on 23 May – at this point giving the Japanese nine light bombers, forty-eight fighters and nine scout aircraft at Hailar.[17] Both Japanese and Soviet accounts agree on Japanese superiority at this point, with well-trained Japanese pilots in superior aircraft taking a heavy toll on the VVS. Anton Iakimenko, an I-16 pilot of the second squadron of 22nd Fighter Air Regiment brought in from the Trans-Baikal Military District, recalls virtual destruction of the 4th Squadron of his regiment in a single sortie during the latter part of May – elsewhere noted as having taken place on 28 May. On that day the VVS lost 11 I-15bis aircraft and eight pilots in combat – with Soviet sources not recording a single Japanese loss.[18] Some sources suggest that a temporary ban on Soviet air operations in the region was instituted that day. Certainly the next day, on 29 May, forty-eight experienced Soviet pilots and engineers were dispatched to the region from Moscow, many with experience from the Spanish Civil War and over China.[19] Many Soviet pilots were not however experienced, and lacked particularly thorough training. A.V. Vorozheikin, a future Soviet ace of the Great Patriotic War, recalled how at Khalkhin Gol against capable opponents he realised how little – how very little – they had flown during peace time – 'and in difficult meteorological conditions we hadn't flown at all'. In these recollections, he noted how at the time he had 'with bitterness noted how he did not have mastery of the difficult art of aerial gunnery and how my skills as a pilot needed to be honed'. Not alone in lacking key skills, it was apparent to him that in training 'often we spent time on things that were not necessary for war'.[20] As was typically the case in wartime, such pilots had to learn quickly or be killed.

By the second half of June the VVS had 151 fighters and 116 bombers available – ninety-five I-16 and fifty-six I-15bis on 21 June – where the Japanese had only seventy-eight Ki-27 fighters in the region, and where only nineteen were deployed forward approximately 40 km from the frontline, with the bulk 150–600 km away![21] Two major air battles are recorded as having taken place on 22 June involving tens of fighters on each side, with Japanese sources acknowledging losses of seven aircraft (with possibly more later written off), and Soviet fourteen – out of a total of seventeen aircraft lost in battle that day. Of course, pilots on both sides exaggerated enemy losses.[22] Soviet authors tended to exaggerate Japanese strength in the air at this time where increasing Soviet strength had actually given the VVS a subtantive numerical advantage in the region. With the VVS conducting attacks on the Japanese side of the border, and in an attempt to reduce Soviet strength, on 27 June a Japanese air strike hit Soviet air bases in a shift away from a policy of only operating over what was deemed to be Japanese airspace. Three Soviet aircraft of 22nd Fighter Air Regiment were apparently lost for the loss of five Japanese aircraft, with losses for 70th Fighter Air Regiment being acknowledged as sixteen aircraft for no Japanese losses. Total Soviet combat losses for the day were twenty-two aircraft and ten pilots. In the attacks on airfields some Japanese sources record the loss of four aircraft, with one badly damaged aircraft limping home. This attack was a success – catching Soviet air forces off guard – despite the fact that Japanese orders for attacks on Soviet airfields in the region had been captured only a few days earlier.[23] Despite the success of this attack however, the VVS continued to maintain and increase its numerical superiority.

In his late-Soviet work on Khalkhin Gol, Gorbunov claims that by the time of the Bain Tsagan fighting in early July 'Soviet aviation had been able to win air superiority, and that superiority was maintained until the end of the conflict'.[24] Certainly by 1 July Soviet strength far exceed that of the Japanese, with Soviet air strength including ninety-three combat ready I-16s and forty-five I-15bis of 70th and 22nd Fighter Air Regiments – where at the end of June overall Japanese strength was, according to conflicting Japanese sources, probably somewhere around 100 aircraft. Certainly it seems that by mid-July Japanese fighter strength was still around eighty aircraft as it had been in late June.[25] As Soviet pilots gained experience – some of which could be passed on to colleagues and lead to the improvement of wider practice – increasing disparity in numerical terms could not be compensated for as often as it had been by the greater prowess of Japanese pilots that had been evident earlier. Without question the VVS had achieved air superiority by the beginning of August, with the VVS fielding 532 Soviet aircraft – including 57 I-15bis, 70 I-153 and 194 I-16. By the start of the Soviet offensive of 20 August the VVS in the region had 580 aircraft on its books, with the figure 515 appearing in a number of Soviet sources perhaps referring to combat ready aircraft. Japanese frontline strength 'totaled 145 planes at most'.[26] Japanese aircraft were unable to play a meaningful role in support of Japanese ground forces over the battlefield during most of the Soviet offensive. On the morning of 20 August around 150 SB bombers were able to attack Japanese positions from a height of 2500–3000 meters with heavy fighter escort (144 fighters), as 46 I-16 fighters engaged in flak suppression. After artillery preparation another 52 SBs attacked, covered by 162 fighters, with Japanese fighters unable to do more than damage three bombers.[27] Japanese forces did launch attacks on troops concentrations and Soviet airbases on 21–22 August however, the latter planned before the Soviet offensive struck. Japanese success against ground targets was apparently limited – and losses high – with the Japanese losing eight aircraft on 21 August and six on 22 August. On 21 August a Soviet tank concentration 'near the river' was apparently bombed by Japanese aircraft that had not located their target during the attack on the airfields – and Soviet troops concetrations near Fui Heights were apparently attacked late that afternoon – but these cases of Japanese aircraft hitting Soviet ground forces were the exception.[28] On 21 August Soviet forces lost a total of sixteen aircraft, including to ground fire, but losses would remain at three or less per day from 22–27 August, and only one per day from 28–31 August before fresh Japanese resources were thrown into the region in early September.[29] Twenty-nine Japanese aircraft were recorded as lost from 23–31 August – losses that the Japanese could ill afford.[30]

In addition to the medium SBs, the increasingly aged heavy TB-3 bombers had appeared, as they had at Lake Khasan, over the skies of Khalkhin Gol, but had been used in a night bombing role with single aircraft bombing at intervals – more for the purpose of disrupting the sleep of Japanese troops than causing material damage. Japanese sources suggest that night attacks did indeed serve this purpose, and the tactic would be used again during the Great Patriotic War by light bombers.[31] As for the effectiveness of bombing in causing material losses rather than having psychological effect, although troops caught in the open were vulnerable on the open steppe, it is unsurprising that accounts of the battle do not describe significant damage – relative to other arms – as

having been caused by medium and light bombers. Soviet strafing attacks
are certainly mentioned far more frequently in Japanese testimony cited
by Coox – and indeed strafing by Japanese light bombers seems to have
been relatively effective compared to their bombing. The testimony of a
Japanese soldier in a diary subsequently seized by the Red Army certainly
suggests in entries for 20 and 25 August 1939 prior to his death that
Soviet air attacks were certainly frequent, although caused little damage
compared to the Soviet artillery.[32] Although the Red Army had a conception of close air support, at the beginning of the incident neither side
had the means to accurately deliver more than machine-gun fire against
enemy targets where AA fire and enemy fighter attack were considerations. The arrival of 20 mm cannon-armed I-16s gave the VVS a little
more firepower, where by this time the lightly armoured Japanese tanks
against which they might have been effective had left the battlefield. In
fact I-16s armed with rockets were used for the first time during the
battle, but against Japanese aircraft rather than ground targets.

At Khalkhin Gol the Red Army had both a quantitative and often
qualitative edge over the Japanese when it came to equipment. Even
munitions were – particularly when the isolation of the battlefield is
considered – plentiful. Certainly when the Soviet Union had mobilised
troops at the time of the Munich crisis, as Hugh Ragsdale details in his
monograph on the subject,[33] Soviet ground troops at least were typically
still equipped with what were first-rate weapons systems for the time by
European standards – that were often as yet not worn out. In September
1938 A. A. Vetrov was deputy commander of 8th Independent 'Tank'
Brigade, and recalls in his memoirs how his unit equipped with T-26
tanks and T-37 tankettes was ordered to move westwards at short notice
as part of Soviet mobilisation for possible intervention, moving from the
settlement Starie Dorogi deep inside Belorussia to a forest on the Polish
border. His unit remained there 'for a number of days' before returning
to their previous quarters.[34] Whilst the survivability of the T-37 was
questionable – its production had already ceased – the T-26 was better
armoured and armed than the bulk of German tanks available in
September 1938. German experience in Spain had however highlighted
the poor performance for the calibre of the 45 mm gun that armed most
Soviet tanks, thanks to the poor quality of Soviet ammunition. Quality
issues with Soviet munitions in many ways reflected wider issues with
quality control and the focus on gross output. Quality issues were to
some extent however masked by the fact that whether installed in a tank
or as an anti-tank gun the Soviet 45 mm gun was nonetheless effective
against the German tanks being fielded at the time. The PzKpfw I – the
only German tank in Spain and still most numerous type in September

1938 – was vulnerable to the Soviet 45 mm guns at ranges beyond the effective range of the 37 mm PaK anti-tank guns used to accompanying and protect them in Spain. However, in late 1937 and into 1938 the German tank force was receiving more and more PzKpfw III and IV tanks armed with 37 mm and 75 mm guns able to penetrate the armour of a T-26 or BT-series tank at meaningful ranges – with the 2cm gun of the PzKpfw II effective at shorter ranges. Whereas as of 1 October 1937 the Wehrmacht had received only 12 PzKpfw III tanks to go with the 1,468 PzKpfw I and 238 PzKpfw IIs available, as of 1 October 1938 the German Wehrmacht was equipped with 1,468 PzKpfw I, 823 Pzkpfw II, 59 PzKpfw III and 76 PzKpfw IV.[35] In February 1938 the Red Army could, in theory, field 6,748 T-26 tanks; along with 618 BT-2, 1,841 BT-5 and 2,346 BT-7; and 262 T-28 and 41 T-35.[36]

Soviet experience in Spain and against the Japanese in the Far East provided important pointers for the future development of tanks and aircraft. Even if in the latter case Soviet tanks were far superior to their Japanese counterparts, the vulnerability of lightly armoured gasoline-fueled tanks to a variety of threats had been reiterated. Development work on new tanks that would culminate in the KV series and T-34 – vehicles that would ultimately cause so many problems for the Wehrmacht during the summer of 1941 even though these new models were available in relatively small numbers – was still very much in progress at the time of the Munich crisis and indeed at the time of the Khalkhin Gol incident and on the outbreak of the Second World War in Europe. Regarding aircraft, in Spain the Bf-109E had clearly proved superior to the I-16, even if later models of the latter could still hold their own against the Japanese I-97 in both China and Manchuria in 1939. However, by 1940 – by which point the next generation of Soviet fighter aircraft had yet to supersede their mid-1930s predecessors – even the Chinese viewed the I-16 (and SB bomber) as outdated.[37] Nonetheless, the Soviet Union would have thousands of these aircraft on strength in June 1941. David Stone, author of *Hammer and Rifle: The Militarization of the Soviet Union, 1926–1933*, has suggested, that 'in a sense the Soviet Union rearmed for World War II six or seven years too early. . . . For both economic development and military effectiveness, the correct policy would have de-emphasised current production, turning instead toward building capacity and improving design and technology'.[38] Certainly the Soviet Union had rearmed at a time and with an energy that was not in sync and commensurate with either official or actual threats. If the Soviet Union had intended to strike first such an approach might have had a military rationale – as events unfolded the Soviet Union did not and any rationality in the Soviet approach remained political. In the mid-1930s, at a stage in development at which the Red Army had reached a point of considerable relative strength over Germany, Stalin and his associates launched the Great Purges. In the aftermath of the purges the Red Army was not only in a worse position to make effective use its vast equipment park than it had been a couple of years before, but that park had lost much of its potency – at least on a tank-tank or fighter-fighter basis when the principal Soviet models were being compared to new German ones, and in a situation where the next generation of Soviet designs were some way from mass production. Older models in the BT-series and earlier versions of the T-26 tank of this period would, as Stone suggests, in many senses be 'obsolete tanks choking the Soviet army in the earlier days of the war' during the summer of 1941. However German tanks – be they Panzer I or IIs – were of the same vintage as Soviet vehicles in terms of design and even more poorly armed and armoured than their Soviet opponents. In addition to reliability and supply, for the Red Army the problem was in their use – for in the summer of 1941 Germany could still pull off operational and tactical successes with poorly armed and armoured tanks.

Where German equipment was particularly superior – enhancing the effectiveness of otherwise inferior tanks – was in terms of communications and optical systems. Soviet production of and the quality of such elements of tanks and aircraft as communications equipment and optics was also far behind future enemies and allies alike. The short-wave 5-AK divisional and 6-PK regimental radio sets introduced in the early 1930s and in widespread service in 1939 and indeed on the outbreak of war are good examples. The 5-AK set weighed in total 130.2 kg and had a range – presumably a maximum in favourable conditions – of only 15 km for speech or 30 km for morse when used in mobile vehicle – mounted form with a 2.7 m wide antenna. Ranges of up to 50 km could apparently be achieved for morse with an umbrella aerial of 5.6 m height in a static set up, or 25 km for speech. The 24.2 kg (including battery) 6-PK set had a range of up to 8 km for speech or 16 km for morse with its 30 m long aerial set up – without which, using a 1.5 m antenna ranges were down to 4 and 8 km respectively – or 3 km for speech without the antenna.[39] Not that maximum range in favourable conditions was the only issue with sets such as the 6-PK – as radio operator Leonid Gurvits – who served in the war against Finland of 1939–40 and into the Great Patriotic War – noted in his memoirs:

The primitive portable short-wave radio set 6-PK was intended to provide radio communications between battalion commanders and the regimental command. Unfortunately, this equipment was not up to the task. ... The issue was that short waves...cannot provide reliable communications over short distances. For such purposes it was necessary to use very high frequency, but we did not manufacture such sets. Right up until the end of the war the development of infantry radio sets was along the lines of perfecting specifically short wave sets.[40]

At least more advanced Soviet short wave sets had been designed by 1939, with new sets including the RAT (obr. 1935), RAF (obr. 1937), and the RSB (obr. 1936) for service at divisional level, the latter with an optimum range of 60 km for morse or 30 km for speech with a 4 m antenna.[41] Also in service was the 21.5 kg RB (obr.1938) set used by rifle regiments, which had a stated range of 8 or 12 km for speech or morse respectively with 170 cm antenna, or 10 and 15–17 km for speech and morse respectively in average conditions with an aerial for static use. The Soviet source in this instance notes that the RB radio's range could be reduced significantly depending on whether it was day or night, the time of the year and the amount of interference.[42] As one of the few Soviet monographs on the subject of military communications covering the pre-war period notes, of the newer sets 'by the end of 1939, only the RB radio station had been produced in large batches, with the remaining examples serving in the army in very limited numbers'.[43] General-Major N.I. Gapich, head of the Communications Board for the Red Army, noted in a report to the by then People's Commissar for Defence Marshal S.K. Timoshenko of October 1940, that the powerful RAF radio set for the command of formations – with a range of up to 600 km for morse or 300 speech – was only actually being produced in 1940 despite having existed since 1936. In fact, 1940 saw a production target of only ninety-five examples to satisfy a requirement for 1,500, with only fifteen examples actually produced during the first nine months of the year.[44] Consequently, older, outdated sets continued in service in large numbers.

Not only were available Soviet radio sets often outdated, and available in inadequate numbers, but they were according to pre-war Soviet sources often poorly used. During a November 1938 meeting of the Military Soviet for the NKO during discussion of the state of technical troops, one Kombrig I.A. Naidenov noted how 'in stable conditions all forms of communication work well, but in dynamic circumstances of combat they fail. This can be explained by the fact that commanders of units and communications are themselves insufficiently prepared in a tactical-technical sense'. He went on to note, how 'the training of radio operators and the use of radio equipment is still not acceptable. Radio specialists have to prepare themselves for work in conditions that hinder the functioning of radio stations'.[45] Such critical comments were however few – not only because of the risks of being critical but also because in the Red Army, as in many others, communications were not high on the agenda. In reading pages of material from the Military Soviet and other similar materials of the pre-war period, the relative absence of discussion about communications is striking.

At Lake Khasan Soviet communications had been poor – with radio communications apparently going no further down the chain of command than divisional level – with the exception of 2nd Mechanised Brigade where although individual tanks lacked radios there were at least radios for command vehicles. At Khalkhin Gol Soviet forces had much more time to prepare before the August offensive, and significant communications resources could be brought in. At Khalkhin Gol – within a relatively small and defined area – considerable reliance could be placed on telephone communications for all but the mechanised forces conducting the encirclement, where radio communications seem to have played a more significant role down to battalion level – with intra-unit radio communications down to company or platoon level at the very best. Legitimate fears about radio security certainly further limited Soviet use of radio communications beyond their availability – and considerable use seems to have been made of motorcyclists and tanks to deliver orders at Khalkhin Gol.[46] Certainly during the Great Patriotic War Soviet reticence to use even available radio communications systems would contribute to effective *maskirovka*, but this certainly hampered tactical effectiveness in more fluid situations. Certainly, radio was used at Khalkhin Gol, and Japanese sources suggest that Soviet use of radio during the 20 August offensive gave away little of value – with radio communications being used 'mainly at regimental or battalion level' where enemy interception would not provide information on which the enemy would have time to act.[47] Despite the benefits of the presence of commanders on the spot for motivation Soviet commanders at Khalkhin Gol certainly spent far too much time charging about giving orders to be acted on immediately that might otherwise have been given by radio where available. The wounding of Polkovnik I.I. Fediuninskii at Khalkhin Gol as he tried to make it back to an armoured car in order to return to his regimental observation post after having moved forward to encourage a battalion to press home an attack on an enemy's strong point certainly highlights how commanders delivering orders in person were vulnerable.[48]

Insufficient provision of radio communications equipment for armoured vehicles certainly hampered the responsiveness of armoured units to changes in tactical circumstances. As Kolomiets notes, command within companies or platoons was at the time of Khalkhin Gol typically on the basis of 'do as I do'. The absence of lower level radio communications – be it between tanks or between armoured units and infantry – could often have tragic consequences. One example during the Khalkhin Gol fighting concerned a group of seven BT-7 tanks of one of the companies of 6th Tank Brigade, which on 23rd August was wiped out by Soviet anti-tank guns of one of the batallions of 602nd Rifle Regiment – its vehicles taken for those of the Japanese. The junior commander of the anti-tank gun battery was able to seek confirmation of the order by telephone from the battalion commander – but not communicate with the tanks. Of the seven tanks all were burnt out and twenty-one tankers were killed.[49]

At Khalkhin Gol reticence to use and limited scope for the use of radio communications – particularly at a tactical level – often did not have as serious ramifications as it might have in different circumstances, where in this instance the enemy was often static or slow moving within a very defined area in open terrain. Certainly during the summer of 1941 effective German use of communications technology and superior optics would often make it easier for German armoured forces to gain local numerical superiority in those instances where tank versus tank combat could not be avoided – or to bring anti-tank weapons to bear.

For the Red Army, analysis of events in Spain and even the Far East certainly prompted changes in equipment that would serve the Red Army well in the longer term, even if the opponents faced did not highlight inadequacies in Red Army use of the equipment in the way an overall more capable opponent might have done. Even glaring inadequacies in maintenance and supply were hardly starkly outlined where forces committed were relatively small, resources relatively abundant or where in the case of Spain issues could be blamed on the Spanish. Analysis of events from September 1939 into 1940 would however make it plain that in many spheres the Red Army had some catching up to do in the way it organised resources if it would be able to challenge the Wehrmacht that would perform so effectively in Poland. Stalin and Soviet leaders would push forward re-equipment stemming to a large extent from experience prior to September 1939 – and re-organisation stemming very much from that after this point – and even tinker with some of the cultural issues in the Red Army that might enhance battlefield performance. However, even if Nazi Germany would give the Red Army the time it needed for grandiose re-equipment and reorganisation, it would take longer to improve more nebulous human dimensions to military performance. As Lenin had emphasised back in 1921 after the Russian Civil War had been won by the Bolsheviks, the cultural change required for the new society to function effectively could not take place in only a short period of time, and the same applied now to the Red Army.[50] The fear integral in the system after the Great Purges ironically had rapidly led to negative changes in the way the Red Army functioned and those that led it – one can easily spoil a dog but positive training takes time. Not only did the Soviet Union under Stalin not have the time for such changes to transform the system were it willing to make them, but at this point did not have the will to do more than tinker with a highly centralised system that paid only lip service to lower level initiative as a crucial element of its functioning.

In many ways the Soviet invasion of Poland in September 1939 would be a better test of Red Army effectiveness and functioning than Khalkhin Gol in that Soviet forces would be expected to operate over a much wider area in less open terrain and against a much less predictable even if far less aggressive enemy. Issues with supply, maintenance, reconnaissance and command and control – and the ability to practice combined-arms warfare in what was a much less set-piece context – would all come to the fore, highlighting just how the Red Army was some way from being able to execute the 1936 field regulations in less conducive circumstances.

7   Voroshilov's 'Lightning' War
The Soviet Invasion of Poland

On 17 September 1939 Soviet troops crossed the border into eastern Poland or what in Soviet terms was Western Ukraine and Western Belorussia.[1] The Soviet Union had just signed the Nazi–Soviet or Molotov–Ribbentrop Pact with National Socialist Germany but weeks before, a pact which with its secret protocols was not only a non-aggression pact, but also saw the two powers divide Eastern Europe into spheres of influence. The Soviet Union could make a case for claiming at least some territory in Eastern Poland that had been lost after the Soviet–Polish War with the 1921 Treaty of Riga. Seizing the remaining Polish territory agreed upon with Nazi Germany as the Soviet allotment would require somewhat different justification. Whilst for the Polish leadership the Red Army was a second invader participating in the dismemberment of the fledgling Polish state, the Soviet version presented to the Red Army was that it was 'liberating' the population – undertaking a 'march of liberation' [*osvoboditel'nii pokhod*] that would result in both the reuniting of ethnic Belorussians and Ukrainians with their fellow nationals, and of course liberating workers and peasants from capitalist servitude. Order Number 005 of the Military Soviet of the Belorussian Front of 16 September 1939 was read out to units on the eve of invasion and stated that the troops would be liberating 'brother Belorussians and Ukrainians' – 'the working people of Western Belorussia and Western Ukraine' – who had been enslaved by 'Polish landowners and capitalists'.[2] The fact that Polish forces found 'triumphal arches' in some villages awaiting the Red Army suggests that this claim was perhaps not entirely without justification, with there being numerous reports of the Red Army being welcomed by non-Polish nationalities.[3] That in the aftermath of the Great Patriotic War Poland was incorporated into the Soviet sphere not only all but silenced Cold War–era historians in Poland on the matter, but also provided good reason for Soviet historians to play down military aspects of the 'liberation'. For Soviet and Soviet-dominated Polish historians it was important to stress the lack of fighting between Polish forces and the Red Army in September 1939, where later co-operation between Poles and the Soviet regime was certainly a politically more desirable focus for historical work. Consequently Soviet-sponsored Polish units that fought in increasing numbers as the Great Patriotic War progressed were a more popular topic for research.[4] Although a relatively significant amount has been written on Polish engagements with Soviet forces in Polish since 1989,[5] little has been written on the subject in English even in recent years – and particularly with referenced sources.[6] Where the Soviet invasion of Poland in September 1939 is mentioned in general English-language histories of the Second World War, it tends to be very brief. The 1991 translated second volume of the semi-official German history of the Second World War that remains a significant source on the German invasion of Poland simply refers readers to Janusz Piekalkiewicz's useful but nonetheless less than scholarly *Der Zweiter Weltkrieg* and *Polenfeldzug* for information on the fighting between Soviet and Polish forces.[7] Post–Cold War works that would greatly enhance our understanding of Polish activity have not unfortunately been translated from Polish into English. In Russian fortunately Mikhail Mel'tiukhov's post-Soviet study of Soviet–Polish wars provides a well-researched and critical analysis of Soviet operations produced in an academic climate where such critical analysis is not the norm.[8]

Gerhard L. Weinberg rather clinically wrote in his history of the Second World War *A World At Arms*, that Soviet casualties of 2,600 in Poland 'barely justified Stalin's proud assertion of December 1939 that the friendship of Germany and the Soviet Union had been 'cemented with blood'. Soviet losses were indeed small compared to those of Germany, where according to Weinberg Germany suffered 45,000 casualties during the invasion of Poland.[9] Nonetheless, even a relatively low number of Soviet casualties taken in order to seize a significant portion of Poland have to be assessed in the light of the scale of resistance faced. The Soviet history of the Belorussian Military District goes as far as to suggest that 'as units of the Red Army entered Western Belorussia many Polish troops laid down their arms and surrendered without a fight'.[10] Polish resistance was certainly far more limited than it might otherwise have been given that the Wehrmacht had destroyed a significant proportion of the Polish armed forces before the Soviet invasion, with much of the remainder committed to fighting it in central Poland as Soviet troops rolled across the border on 17 September. In addition, the commander-in-chief of the Polish Army, Marshal Edward Śmigły-Rydz, had on 17 September ordered the Polish Army not to 'fight the Soviets except in case of their [attack] or attempts to disarm our units', with Polish units to head for 'Romania and Hungary by the shortest routes' and to 'negotiate' with Soviet forces over passage. This order seems to have reached at least some Polish Army units.[11] Certainly some Soviet units participating in the 'liberation' saw little or no combat according to the reminiscences of veterans. Vasilii Danilov Kirdiakin, a junior commander of 229th Corps Heavy Artillery Regiment, noted in a post-Soviet interview that his battery had deployed their guns on a number of occasions, but had only fired them in one instance during the campaign in Poland and hadn't come under enemy fire.[12] In his Soviet-era memoirs future Marshal of Artillery Iakovlev certainly suggests that on the L'vov axis during the first days of the 'liberation' the Red Army met little resistance – singling out harassing fire from 'isolated groups of Polish gendarmes' on 18 September at Tarnopol' as an example of what little resistance there had been.[13] Ivan Valdimirovich Maslov, a tanker of 139th Independent Tank Battalion of 25th Tank Brigade, commented that 'no battles of note' took place in Poland, but did nonetheless see and participate in 'the repulsing of an attack by Polish cavalry' on his battalion – apparently a brief encounter.[14] Army Commander 1st Rank Grigorii Kulik's report of 21 September 1939 to Stalin, Molotov and Voroshilov, suggested that the Polish Army had been 'so demoralised that it offered almost no resistance, with the exception of minor isolated instances of resistance by border forces, the *Osadniki* [Polish military settlers], and retreating units under the leadership of the high command'.[15] Some of this resistance apparently took an irregular form, with one example reported in the Soviet literature being future Marshal of Artillery Voronov's claim that in the Soviet-occupied town of Novogrudok there was night time anti-Soviet activity by 'police and paramilitaries' [*politseiskikh i zhandarmov*] who had changed out of their uniforms and who attacked Soviet troops with both small arms and grenades.[16] Certainly, when assessing the scale of resistance, Kulik's report was perhaps accurate in broadly describing the first days of the Soviet invasion where many Polish Army units seem to have surrendered without offering resistance, and where by 20 September forces of the Ukrainian Front alone claimed to have captured '60,000 men, including 4 generals'.[17]

However, despite Marshal Edward Śmigły-Rydz's order and the critical military situation to the West, some Polish units did resist the Soviet invasion both on or near the border and as Soviet troops penetrated deeper into Poland. Polish border troops of the *Korpus Obrony Pogranicza* or KOP, which were not under Army command and from 30 August were under the command of General Orlik Rückermann, had not been ordered to evacuate to Rumania and seem frequently to have put up resistance. Nonetheless, the KOP had been weakened by needs to the west, where some officers had apparently been reassigned to duties with the Army there before the German invasion, and the invasion itself predictably saw the transfer of some KOP units westwards. With a strength before the war of in the region of 11,000 men according to Jan T. Gross, the KOP was, as its name suggests, a paramilitary border security force and one neither large enough nor equipped with the artillery and anti-tank weapons to deal with Red Army formations. As the Red Army moved into Poland, Rückermann nonetheless ordered KOP units to resist.[18] Resistance by KOP units in the east was however hampered by confusion that resulted to a large extent from the fact that Rückermann's order to resist the invaders evidently didn't get through to all KOP units just as Śmigły-Rydz's order not to seek confrontation did not get through to all those of the Army. There was evidently confusion on the ground over whether the Red Army was entering Poland as a conquering force or in fact in order to assist the Poles in the war against Germany.[19] In one instance where such confusion was apparently manifested, Soviet troops entering Tarnopol' were reported as having 'shouted to a passing Polish Army detachment that they were on their way to fight 'the krauts', and as Gross suggests 'they might actually have believed that'. When negotiating a ceasefire and the eventual surrender of L'vov, Colonel Kazimierz Ryziński was apparently told by one Colonel Ivanov that once Soviet forces had entered the city 'they would fight the Germans together with us, but that they wanted first to enter the city'.[20]

Despite this confusion over whether the Red Army was friend or foe, the failure to get orders through to units and Marshal Edward Śmigły-Rydz's orders to the Army not to engage the Red Army, there were nonetheless engagements of note during the first days of the Soviet invasion which seem not only to have involved the KOP but also Army units. Certainly former commander of the Soviet 52nd Rifle Division, Ivan Nikitin Russiianov, even in Soviet-era memoirs noted that 'isolated groups of Pilsudksii's defeated forces...did offer resistance', recalling incidents near 'Nesvizh, Pinsk, Kobrin, Brest-Litovsk and Shat'sk'.[21] Other more recent reminiscences of veterans contain some references to encounters with Polish forces, be they KOP or Army. Aleksei Andreevich Shilin, a junior commander in the armoured forces, suggested in a post-Soviet interview that his unit took casualties in the Belovezhsk area, and had to engage in combat for the city of L'vov.[22] Certainly at L'vov on 19 September there was at least brief fighting between Soviet and Polish forces – with Soviet tanks entering the city coming under fire – an incident described in further detail later in the chapter.[23] Later that day there was an incident during which Soviet forward units and advancing German forces exchanged fire and took casualties – fighting portrayed as German 'provocation' in many

Soviet works even during the era of *glasnost'* and *perestroika*, but which was most probably the product of misunderstanding.[24]

One of the most significant of the clashes between Polish forces and the Red Army – and certainly more significant than the one at L'vov – was during the defence of Grodno between 20 and 22 September 1939. On the basis of Polish sources Halik Kochanski provides a brief description of the fighting for the town, defended by 'army' units and 'a number of boy scouts', who as Soviet tanks advanced 'darted between the tanks throwing Molotov cocktails'. She goes on to note how ten Soviet tanks were destroyed in this fighting on 20 September.[25] Soviet accounts also note the participation of 'youth' in attacks on Soviet tanks of 27th Tank Brigade operating without infantry support in the town that day, where the defence employed 'only a few guns and bottles of inflammable liquid'.[26] These attacks led to the destruction of part of a Soviet force that had initially consisted of fifty tanks, with the remainder being forced to retreat back across the River Niemen that runs through the town. With the defence broken on 21 September, during the night of 22 September many of the remaining defenders left the town, having killed 57 Soviet personnel and wounded another 159, and having knocked out 19 tanks and 4 armoured cars, according to Soviet sources. Soviet sources report that after the battle 644 Polish corpses were buried, with 1,543 military personnel having been taken prisoner – leaving 514 rifles, 50 revolvers, 146 machine guns, one anti-aircraft gun and a single mortar to the Red Army.[27] Certainly Polish forces had been poorly equipped, but the Soviet decision to initially throw unsupported tanks into an urban environment had been a reckless one.

According to G.F. Krivosheev and his colleagues, the Soviet, Ukrainian and Belorussian Fronts lost a total of 996 men during the 'liberation' of Western Belorussia and Ukraine – 852 killed or who died during casualty evacuation, and 144 missing. In addition, 2,002 were wounded – a total of more than 3,000 men killed or wounded.[28] Post-Soviet Russian historian of the Soviet–Polish wars Mikhail Mel'tiukhov suggests that 81 of these were killed and 184 wounded during another relatively significant engagement that took place near Shats'k, or in Polish Szack, involving the Soviet 52nd Rifle Division and its 411th Tank Battalion. During the morning of 28 September 411th Tank Battalion was advancing along the east-west road south-east of Shats'k having apparently alerted by a civilian source of a Polish cavalry squadron in the woods to the east that was supposedly looking to surrender. The KOP cavalry squadron 'Bystrzyce' was indeed in the area, along with other Polish units, but apparently was not intent on surrendering. Mel'tiukhov notes how that morning the Soviet tank battalion came under anti-tank fire and lost seven men before retreating. According to General Orlik Rücker-mann, early that morning these Soviet tanks were allowed to advance to 500–600 metres before being engaged by Polish forces from the edge of forest, resulting in the loss of a number of tanks. Then, later that morning according to Rückermann forward Soviet elements including tanks were ejected from the town of Szack and pushed back to the north, leaving behind in the panic not only tanks and other equipment but also staff materials.[29] With the Soviet divisional headquarters advancing in column to the north, command and control of Soviet forces was initially particu-larly poor, Mel'tiukhov noting how in 'forested and marshy terrain' units of the division 'often lacked communication with each other and were practically out of command'. Both Soviet and Polish sources agree on the panic that spread amongst Soviet conscripts of 58th Rifle Regiment caught in fighting in marshy terrain to the north of the town with Polish troops that struck from the east – according to Mel'tiukhov a panic sparked by news of the wounding of the divisional commander.[30] The Soviet-era memoirs of the divisional commander, Russiianov, unsurpris-ingly contain little information on the incident, although he did note that:

Near Shat'sk we were shot at from the forest. I was wounded in the left arm by shrapnel. I fell from my horse and lost consciousness. However I quickly came around. The orderly bandaged up my arm as best he could, and I continued to direct units of the division until morning.[31]

The fighting for Shat'sk and its environs lasted into the following day, but by 9:00 on the morning of 29 September, the divisional commander Russiianov had apparently brought order to the chaos, and with the arrival of further troops and with artillery and air support Soviet forces were quickly able to gain the upper hand and retake the town that had been occupied by Polish troops. As Mel'tiukhov suggests, complacency certainly seems to have played a part in the failures of 28 September, where 'having got used to the relatively calm progress they had made through territory of Western Belorussia' Soviet troops proved to be 'unprepared for fierce enemy resistance'.[32] What had turned into a relatively costly and sustained encounter with Polish forces ended with the surrender of 1,100 Polish servicemen – some of whom may have been rear-area personnel given Soviet recovery of only 500 rifles and 34 machine guns. According to Soviet sources Polish troops surren-dered with 524 of their comrades dead on the battlefield – a figure consistent with data provided by the popular Polish historian Czesław Grzelak. Elements of the Polish force had escaped across the River Bug. In additional to the Soviet personnel losses noted earlier and that included the commander of 411th Tank Battalion killed and the divisional commander wounded, 52nd Rifle Division had lost – 'knocked out' [*podbito*] – five T-26 and two T-38 tanks, two tractors and three anti-tank guns.[33]

In his memoirs Russiianov notes how 52nd Rifle Division had been engaged in the construction of fortified regions along the Soviet border prior to the move into Poland. He and other commanders and political workers may have given military training 'the maximum possible attention', but it is unclear what that maximum was and it is likely that the military preparation of many conscripts such as those of 52nd Rifle Division was poor.[34] One can certainly speculate that 21st Rifle Division of the Belorussian Front was also in poor shape for combat. When moving up to the border on 19 September it had, according to Front command, '400 men in its ranks who were not fully kitted out, of whom many were in bast shoes, barefoot, in civilian trousers and caps'. During a 'disorganised' approach march some sub units of the division had seemed more like a 'crowd without direction'.[35] The fragmented manner in which 52nd Rifle Division had advanced on Polish territory was perhaps also not atypical. According to an NKVD report of 24 September Red Army units were often not in a position to provide support to each other should resistance be encountered, with units moving forward in columns 'with intervals of 10–15 km between them', without the columns having communications with each other, and with headquarters units not in a position to command given poor communications and their often being separated from subordinate units.[36]

Inadequate reconnaissance was arguably a major contributor to many of the losses taken by the Red Army in Poland. Poor reconnaissance – be it aerial or otherwise – had been an early problem at Khalkhin Gol that summer and would continue to plague the Red Army into the Great Patriotic War.[37] Good reconnaissance required in the first instance the sort of freedom of action by relatively junior commanders that was an anathema to the post-Purge Red Army – and the ability to communicate findings. Certainly General-Lieutenant Golikov, by December 1940 head of the Reconnaissance Board of the Red Army, during the December 1940 conference of senior leadership elements of the Red Army bemoaned the lack of aerial reconnaissance resources available to him as a frontline army commander in Poland.[38] Perhaps the absence of radio equipment contributed to the use of reconnaissance battalions more as forward detachments. It is certainly debateable whether tanks like the BT-7s of such units, or indeed any other Soviet tank of the period, were ideal reconnaissance vehicles given the poor visibility from within with hatches closed.

A reconnaissance battalion commanded by A.V. Egorov, part of 24th Tank Brigade, was one such reconnaissance unit that 'functioned as a forward detachment' for 6th Army, apparently being the first Soviet unit to enter the key city of L'vov. As noted earlier, the Soviet move into L'vov saw combat between Red Army and both Polish and German troops. According to Egorov his unit 'during the night of 19 September entered L'vov' – without adding any mention of coming under Polish fire although describing the subsequent exchange of fire with the Wehrmacht.[39] Detail is however added by the testimony of Petr Veniaminovich Bobrov, a senior lieutenant and assistant to the chief of the headquarters of 218th Independent Reconnaissance Battalion, 24th Light Tank Brigade – Egorov's unit. His battalion had apparently arrived on the outskirts of L'vov by the small hours of 19 September, on the way one company having encountered and destroyed two Polish barricades on each of which had been emplaced a 75 mm gun.[40] According to a report of the Ukrainian Front of 20 September, those elements of 218th Independent Reconnaissance Battalion that pressed on through to the centre of the city – ten tanks and three armoured cars - 'were met with fire from a single [artillery] battery and machine guns, and with return fire one artillery piece was knocked out and the crew scattered; the battalion moved out of the centre of the city to its eastern outskirts in expectation of the arrival of the principal strength of the brigade'.[41]

Both Bobrov and the report of the Ukrainian Front describe how as 218th Independent Reconnaissance Battalion was making its way out of the city it encountered German units seeking to encircle the city from the east. According to Bobrov 218th Independent Reconnaissance Battalion lost two BA-10 armoured cars burnt out and three knocked out in the encounter, along with a BT-7 tank, with nineteen members of the battalion killed or wounded. The report by the Front confirms two armoured cars burnt out and a third knocked out, with three killed and five wounded. The encounter had been with troops of a German mountain division, and armoured car losses were primarily as a result of hits from German 37 mm anti-tank guns, two of which were according to Bobrov captured intact and shipped off by air with their ammunition for testing – perhaps the two guns deemed destroyed by the Front. As suggested by the testimony of Aleksei Andreevich Shilin and Bobrov, fighting in the city did not stop with the surrender of the bulk of the Polish garrison on 21 September, where afterwards 'in some parts of the city there was resistance from Polish officers who opened fire with machine guns on our tanks and armoured cars, but did not have a significant impact on the liberation'.[42] This incident – or series of incidents – in and around L'vov has been described in some detail in order to illustrate the confused nature of the Soviet advance as forward units charged headlong in what Voroshilov described – not knowing that it would later sound ironic – as a 'lightning' strike, during which Soviet forces frequently took casualties as a result of their speed as opposed to haste.[43] This speed seems to have been motivated as much by political concerns as military, where it was politically undesirable that the Soviet Union be gifted vast tracts of territory under the terms of the Nazi–Soviet Pact that had recently been conquered by German forces. The Soviet desire to take L'vov was a case in point.

The idea that resistance such as that described by Bobrov in L'vov was on the part of 'Polish officers' seems at least on occasion – even if not necessarily in L'vov – to have been an attempt by Soviet commanders to follow the party line, that in line with the Red Army's mission of class and national liberation resistance was coming neither from the working classes nor Ukrainians and Belorussians, but bourgeois Polish officers. That instances labelled as such were not always so is highlighted by the fact that KOP forces under Rückermann's command apparently seized orders after a successful skirmish with the Red Army that described such KOP detachments being encountered as 'bands of Polish officers'.[44] It is also possible that at least some irregular activity attributed to 'Polish officers' or the 'police and paramilitaries who had changed out of their uniforms and who attacked Soviet troops with both small arms and grenades' described earlier by Voronov was in fact undertaken by civilians in the strictest sense, where according to Gross 'volunteers frequently joined detachments of the Polish army', and where 'civilians sometimes fought on both sides'. Some Polish civilians were organised into Citizens' Guard (*Straż Obywatelska*) militia units. In L'vov the militia had apparently relied heavily on 'members of the Association of Reserve Officers who were too old to be conscripted into the army', where elsewhere the Citizens' Guard was formed from 'patriotically inclined Polish citizens – the so called settlers (*osadnicy*) in the countryside' and others such as 'petty officials' to maintain order in towns and villages, and from which more committed armed volunteers no doubt gravitated towards the KOP or Army units.[45] Jan Węgrzyn, head of the Welfare Department of Baranowicze or Baranovichi recalled organising a Citizens' Guard 'exclusively from Poles I knew personally; I armed 186 people with rifles left at the police station; they put on blue armbands'. Later, under the influence of 'armed workers from the Socialist party' the armbands were to be changed to red ones – by the time they had actually changed authority having apparently passed to local communists. In this instance the Citizens' Guard was by agreement between Węgrzyn and the communist leader to defend 'against robberies and excesses until the Soviet authorities arrived'.[46]

In reports of fighting during the 'liberation' with which the Russian historian Mel'tiukhov worked in providing what is probably the most comprehensive account of the campaign from a Russian perspective, we certainly have reason for Soviet historians to have written little about the Soviet 'liberation' of eastern Poland from a military performance perspective. As has already been pointed towards in examples provided here, during a hurriedly organised operation Red Army performance was often poor, both in combat and in transit. Poor Soviet reconnaissance and the use of tanks without infantry support have already been illustrated – and as Russian historian Mil'bakh suggests the limited use of Soviet artillery during the fighting was however not necessarily because there were no opportunities but because 'the poor march capabilities of the artillery, inadequate equipment, supply and organisation of fire control for co-operation with rifle, tank and mechanised forces hampered the ability of the artillery to have meaningful impact in suppression of the enemy and in the results of military action' What use was made of artillery tended to be in a direct or semi-indirect fire role.[47] Command and control was undoubtedly a significant issue – as was an overconfidence that stemmed in part from Soviet propaganda and the overall limited scale of Polish resistance.

Soviet troops including BA-10 armoured cars in what in Soviet terms was Western Belorussia in September 1939. The rushed Soviet invasion of eastern Poland highlighted many Red Army weaknesses when operating over a wide area in fluid circumstances. (RIA Novosti #101829)

Even before Soviet troops crossed the Polish border preparations for the campaign in Poland had not gone well, with the spectacle of 21st Rifle Division moving forward being just one example of how the organisation and execution of the transfer of Soviet troops to the border and the move into Poland had certainly not been as polished as they might have been. Admittedly, before the signing of the Nazi-Soviet Pact and German invasion of western Poland, the Red Army was certainly not poised to move westwards. From a peacetime state, according to the Ukrainian historian Andriy Rukkas, on 3 September 1939 Commissar for Defence Marshal Voroshilov had ordered Military Soviets of seven military districts to undertake a series of preliminary measures to increase the combat readiness of troops that included moving military units to combat-ready status, recalling commanders and political workers from vacation, and barring the release of soldiers in their final year of service into the reserves. This was followed on 6 September by orders for a 'partial secret mobilization' justified by 'large-scale training exercises' to begin the following day – meaning that mobilisation would be conducted without fanfare. By 8 September orders had been given for the deployment of forces of the Belorussian and Kiev Special Military Districts towards the Polish border.[48] S.M.Shtemenko, future head of the Operational Board of the wartime General Staff, had initially been led to believe that he was being transferred from the Academy of the General Staff to the Kiev Military District at the beginning of September so that he could participate in manoeuvres, although district commanders had understandably been made aware of the plan to move into Poland by the time the military districts involved became fronts on 11 September. On 14 September the Ukrainian Front received orders to be ready by 16 September to cross the international border the following day.[49]

As detailed by Rukkas, in early September 1939 there was considerable chaos on the roads and railways of western Belorussia and the Ukraine as men and equipment moved westwards from home bases for the impending move into Poland. Rukkas goes as far as suggesting that in practice 'no traffic control ever existed', giving poorly trained drivers who frequently 'utterly neglected basic traffic regulations' plenty of scope to contribute to the confusion.[50] There was predictably chaos with the mobilisation of reservists and their transfer to units already on the move – for whom much of their automotive transport also had to be mobilised from the civilian economy at short notice.[51] Hence, for 14 September although many formations of the Belorussian Front had more than 90 per cent of their personnel strengths, the availability of automotive transport was often only around 50 per cent of mobilised strength. Both 22nd and

25th Tank Brigades for example had only 55 per cent of their automotive transport at this point.[52] Although 36th Tank Brigade received more than the number of motor vehicles planned, in theory giving it the capability to move a slightly greater tonnage, it did so for example by accepting 307 1.5-ton GAZ AA trucks instead of a planned 6, and did not receive 187 3-ton ZIS-6 trucks as planned, actually receiving only 15. With overall fuel consumption having increased, the absence of the planned number of specialised vehicles that included tankers – 26 instead of 66 – restricted the ability of the unit to refuel using its own transport resources.[53] Available horses were not always up to the task of pulling artillery that might be required to support other arms, where for example horses of 54th Artillery Regiment were apparently of such 'poor quality' that they prevented the regiment from being in a position to accompany the infantry they were supposed to be supporting as the latter moved into Poland. By 7 October the regiment recorded that the situation regarding horses was 'threatening'.[54]

Given the limited time available for preparation and the fact that conscripts had to be mobilised it is perhaps unsurprising that the bulk of the Soviet forces earmarked for the invasion were not ready to move across the border on 17 September. The inadequate pace of mobilisation prompted the Soviet military leadership to limit the first wave of the invasion to a number of assault groups that were defined on 13 September. Many of those formations that did cross the border on 17 September were nonetheless far from ready for combat, lacking personnel, equipment, and even whole sub-units. Hence on 16 September 13th Rifle Corps' 99th Rifle Division that was part of one of the assault groups leading the advance into Poland 'had neither its regular 71st Artillery Regiment nor the three artillery batteries assigned to support its three rifle regiments. It also did not have its required tank and engineer battalions or the supply train assigned to its 197th Rifle Regiment'.[55]

The advance of many units that did make it across the border on time was not only hampered by lack of fuel and transports, but as Army Commander 1st Rank Kulik noted in his report of 21 September, Soviet forces were also slowed down further once they moved across the border by the condition of many dirt roads in Poland during the opening days of the invasion – the 'General Mud' that a Time Life article of 28 August had described as a 'natural ally' of the Poles.[56] Although Polish forces did not apparently engage in widespread sabotage of lines of communication that might have slowed down the Soviet advance, resupply by rail was hampered by the fact that since the separation of Poland from the former Russian empire it had converted to the narrower European gauge for railway lines.[57] Even in his 'censored' Soviet-era memoirs future Marshal of Artillery Nikolai Iakovlev hints at the disorder as the Red Army advanced when he states that the move of Soviet forces into what was at the time eastern Poland had taken place 'according to plan [*plano-merno*]', 'if of course one doesn't take into account isolated misunder-standings [*otdel'nikh nedorazumenii*]'.[58] In order to maintain the tempo of the advance near Baranovichi at the beginning of the campaign, according to the commander of 29th Tank Brigade S.M. Krivoshein tanks of the first battalion had to fuel from other battalions of the brigade because even at this early stage of the campaign 'lorries with fuel lagged behind together with the rear area services of the brigade'.[59] Shtemenko describes an instance where a tank unit waited two hours at Tarnopol' for a column of tankers that had been stuck in a traffic jam – hardly unusual in any war but apparently the sort of event that happened far too fre-quently as Soviet troops advanced into Poland as it had done on Soviet territory.[60] In his memoirs Future Marshal of Artillery Voronov describes how on the approach to the town of Novogrudok during the advance he encountered a large traffic jam, forcing him to abandon his transport and make his way into the town on foot.[61]

During the hurried mobilisation it seems that combat units had tended to be better provided for with resources than often poorly trained rear area units – exacerbating logistical issues and the chaos both in the Soviet rear and at the front. Rukkas gives the example of signals units for the Northern Army Group of Soviet forces moving in to Poland, where on 18 September – the day after the start of operations – 360th Independent Signals Battalion was at only 60 per cent strength, 362nd Independent Radio Battalion at 82 per cent strength and 364th Separate Line (Wire) Battalion at 65 per cent strength. The situation was apparently even worse where 'cable-pole, operational-telegraph, and telegraph construc-tion companies' was concerned. Such shortfalls have to be put in the context of an army short on communications equipment and specialist personnel to start with, making it perhaps not unsurprising that the end result was sometimes 'the complete silence of military radio stations' even where they were ostensibly available.[62]

Fortunately for the Red Army as it advanced westwards in far from ideal or even reasonable order, in addition to there being only sporadic resistance on the ground, there was little Polish activity in the air. Although there may have been in the region of 150–170 serviceable Polish combat aircraft in eastern districts of Poland on the eve of the Soviet invasion, fuel shortages were apparently an acute problem. Add-itionally, similar orders to those issued by Marshal Edward Śmigły-Rydz to the Polish Army had apparently been issued to the Polish Air Force on 17 September as well, meaning that the escape of aircraft to Rumania further limited resistance in the air beyond the fact that the Polish Air Force had taken heavy losses fighting the Luftwaffe and fuel was in short supply.[63] By 20 September the Ukrainian Front alone claimed to have captured fifty aircraft of undisclosed types, with a further eleven shot down [*sbito*].[64] The Red Army air forces or VVS committed significant air assets in support of the 'liberation' – The VVS of the Belorussian Front alone had 1,018 operable aircraft as of 12 September 1939, along with 148 out of service. Of a total of 1,166 aircraft, 423 were I-16, 325 SB, 185 I-15 and 94 R-Zet – with the remainder being 62 Di-6, 36 TB-3, 28 R-5 SSS and 13 R-10. Initially the VVS seems to have been focused on neutralising Polish airpower, but with reconnaissance sorties and attack missions against Polish ground forces also being flown. On the first day of the invasion the VVS of the Ukrainian Front committed 194 sorties to 'the bombing of objectives in the enemy rear' with a further 81 for 'the bombing of enemy troops concentrations' – the majority of attacks being undertaken by SBs. Eighty-eight reconnaissance sorties were reported as having been flown – approaching 15 per cent of a total of 618 sorties.[65] It seems that many of the Soviet aircraft losses were due to accidents – considered a serious problem in the VVS at the time and one highlighted in a report of the headquarters of the VVS for the Belorussian Front at the end of September 1939.[66] In post-war testimony Nikolai Ivanovich Petrov, an I-16 pilot with 21st Fighter Air Regiment recalled how at the time of the invasion the Soviet ace and two-time Hero of the Soviet Union Major S.I. Gritsevets was killed in an accident as a result of a collision with another aircraft landing from the opposite direction.[67] Certainly by the end of September VVS commanders of the Belorussian Front had identified a number of issues with VVS deployment against the Poles that included problems with command and control, the deployment of rear area services and the ability of air units to keep up with the ground advance.[68] Although problems with navigation were not exclusive to the VVS – as the loss on 10 January 1940 of elements of German plans for the invasion of France and the Low Countries attests[69] – nonetheless prior to the invasion widespread issues with navigation and in particular in poor weather had been flagged in the VVS. An instance described by Shtemenko where his U-2 pilot got lost on the way to Kiev from in fog on 23 September with Shtemenko carrying important documents – a report on the performance of the Ukrainian Front during the 'liberation' – provides an anecdotal supporting example.[70]

That the Soviet invasion of eastern Poland was launched at such short notice obviously made an operation involving approaching half a million men challenging. However, even if we make some allowance for the fact that Soviet units had little time to prepare for this specific operation, that does not solely explain how such overwhelming force suffered the losses it did where its opponent actually committed only a fraction of the limited forces available to combat. The unpredictable nature of Polish resistance certainly made what was ostensibly a traditional military campaign more complicated, where as Soviet accounts suggests many Polish units were encountered that did simply surrender. However, the fact that sporadic and at times irregular resistance caused such difficulties owed much to the fact that Red Army leaders seem to have been overconfident both in the capabilities of the Red Army and perhaps had swallowed their own propaganda about the likelihood of the Red Army being treated as liberator. That in border areas some Red Army units did indeed report being treated as liberators can only have exacerbated any blasé attitudes. The fact that the Red Army had in recent years over focussed on the development of frontline combat capabilities at the expense of supporting functions such as reconnaissance and communications and the even less glamorous provision of rear area services played a role in making the Soviet invasion of eastern Poland less than a ringing endorsement of its capabilities, and poor communications of course played a significant part in the poor co-operation between arms that characterised the Red Army in any sort of fluid situation. As Russian historian V.S. Mil'bach notes with regard to the poor showing of the artillery arm during the invasion, the fact that Polish resistance was so light and hence failures did not result in significant casualties by Soviet standards seems to have prevented critical reflection on performance. Consequently, as Mil'bach goes on to note, poor performance would be repeated again at the beginning of the Soviet war with Finland but weeks later, albeit this time with more serious consequences.[71]

8   The Finnish Debacle

Unfortunately for many men of the Red Army, the inadequacies in practice, organisation and preparation that had been displayed in Poland would be shown again later the same year against Finland. Whilst there might be some debate as to whether the primary motivation for the occupation of eastern Poland was to provide cushioning on the Soviet western border from attack or a jumping off point for further operations westwards, in the case of Finnish territory demanded by the Soviet government in the autumn of 1939 there is little evidence to suggest that the territory being sought was being acquired with anything other than defensive intent. Certainly the threat from Finnish territory in early 1918 had contributed to the moving of the capital of the fledgling Soviet republic from Petrograd to Moscow, and the Royal Navy had been able to attack the Kronstadt naval base in the Gulf of Finland in 1919. In the autumn of 1939 after what amounted to an ultimatum for the transfer of much of Karelia and bases on Finnish coastline on the Gulf of Finland in exchange for territory further north was not accepted by the Finnish government, the Soviet Union moved to acquire the territory it sought by force.[1]

In both Poland and Finland the Soviet leadership launched an invasion of foreign territory at relatively short notice using inadequately prepared forces. However, whilst in the case of Poland resistance was limited, the same was not the case against Finland. Certainly key figures in the Soviet military and political leadership – and particularly Stalin and the initial commander of the operation, Meretskov – underestimated the Finnish capacity for resistance and conversely overestimated the capabilities of the Red Army. Chief of staff Shaposhnikov's more cautious approach that did not underestimate the Finnish capacity for resistance in the same way was not adopted for the initial invasion. Four armies of the Leningrad Military District – 14th Army near Murmansk, 9th Army near Kandalashka, 8th Army near Petrozavodsk and 7th Army immediately north of Leningrad – were from 30 November 1939 to seek to occupy Finnish territory from the Petsamo region in the far north all the way down to the Karelian Isthmus in the south through a number of thrusts in operations that were certainly not intended to drag on through most of the winter. Initially there wasn't deemed to be the need to pull better units from elsewhere in the USSR, although there was a certain logic to using units from the Leningrad region even with the large number of reservists involved where in theory at least they were more likely to be familiar with the type of terrain and conditions to be faced fighting the Finns. Whilst in the barren tundra of the far north 14th Army was able to quickly occupy the Petsamo region, in the far south on the Karelian Isthmus Soviet forces struggled with dense forest, few roads and stubborn Finnish resistance even before reaching significant fortifications. After having taken considerable losses for little gain in typically road-bound operations across a broad front, in early 1940 Soviet forces concentrated their attention on the Karelian Isthmus under the command of the perhaps less than inspirational but nonetheless competent Timoshenko.

Initially the Red Army had deployed insufficient troops for an advance on a broad front in close terrain against an enemy often both dug-in and well concealed. As Carl van Dyke notes, at the start of the invasion on 30 November 1939 all of those troops intended for the invasion were not ready to participate, where the Soviet 'strategic reserve had not yet been fully concentrated: only four out of nine first-echelon divisions were ready for combat on 30 November due to mobilisation delays and the unexpectedly early date set for the invasion'.[2] As the war progressed, the scale of the Soviet military commitment increased significantly. As chief of the General Staff Shaposhnikov noted during the April 1940 Soviet command conference organised to assess conduct of the war, 'having started the war with 21 divisions, we increased strength at the front up to 45 divisions, and ended the war with 58 divisions concentrated at the front...to which have to be added a further four rifle divisions that were transferred but not committed' – an overwhelming force.[3] That such a numerically superior force – one that by most indices out-gunned its opponent – took so long to break through Finnish defences on the key Karelian axis did considerable damage to the international reputation of the Red Army. However, poor tactical and operational performance in Finland would also provide a sufficient jolt to the post-purge military leadership and Stalin for what by Stalinist standards was soul-searching in the aftermath of the war. Stalin's crony, Voroshilov, who despite his lack of military education and significant intellectual ability had risen to become Commissar for Defence, would visibly fall from grace – albeit in the first instance not far – giving others the opportunity to try to amend some of the weaknesses of the Red Army before the 'inevitable' war with Germany finally came.

The fact that the invasion of Finland was launched with the onset of winter certainly contributed to what by the end of the year had become something of a debacle. Basic equipment and logistical support available to many units were not up to the task of breaking through significant defensive positions in winter conditions – nor for action against an enemy that was not only at times heavily fortified but at other times also highly mobile. A reconnaissance soldier of 17th Independent Ski Battalion recalled the equipment provided to his unit and in particular reconnais-sance elements, noting how they had apparently thought at the time, '"what sort of scouts are we" – we thought as we went along on our skis – "we are asses or camels loaded up and unable to turn around... Our kit hampered us – we were neither manoeuvrable nor particularly mobile and operating in biting frost and deep snow!"'.[4] Future General E.E. Mal'tsev, then a political commander, noted in his memoirs that soldiers of 78th Rifle Regiment from his 74th Rifle Division being prepared for participation in the war in Finland in late November and early December 1939 were certainly burdened by considerable clothing, rations and equipment during forced marches in the snow. With their many items of clothing, and with 'food for two weeks and a reserve of cartridges along with their personal weapon', they were 'far from agile [nepovorotlivim] and incapable of close combat'.[5] The quality of at least some of the equipment being used by the Finns came as an unpleasant surprise to some Red Army troops – from the apparently widely available sub-machine guns or SMGs to lightweight plastic covered telephone cables that were easier to lay than the heavy Soviet steel ones with thick insulation – at times Finnish troops seemed much better equipped to operate in the terrain and conditions being faced even if it was the Red Army that had the far more artillery and tanks.[6] Certainly in some senses the Red Army faced a better equipped opponent in Finland than it had against the Japanese, where for example the relative availability of auto-matic weapons to 36th Motor Rifle Division in July 1939 at Khalkhin Gol had been identified as a Soviet strength.[7] At the April 1940 Soviet command conference held to analyse performance in the war Meretskov, Commander of the Leningrad Military District at the start of the invasion and subsequently 7th Army, complained how in Finland – in forest and snow – his infantry were 'poorly armed', with rifle-armed Soviet infantry with their clumsy supporting machine guns being no match for the sub-machine guns of the Finns.[8] The raiding tactics employed by many Finnish troops proved problematic for the Red Army as it advanced along the few roads, where Finnish troops would descend on Soviet forces on skis from the forest, spray them with fire from sub-machine guns and disappear back into the trees. Such was the case in one incident described by M.I. Lukinov, then a junior artillery commander with an infantry division, when he and other commanders were on an ill-conceived reconnaissance outing and surprised by Finnish ski troops with SMGs.[9] Tanker Ivan Vladimirovich Maslov describes an incident where some Red Army men who were utilising a makeshift *bania* in the forest were surprised by three Finns on skis equipped with SMGs who killed a number of those inside.[10]

The winter of 1939–40 was a relatively severe one across Europe, with temperatures recorded as dropping as low as –50 degrees Celsius on the Karelian Isthmus during January, although low temperatures should hardly have been a shock to the Red Army.[11] Snow certainly hampered supply from railheads, and particularly where most Soviet manufactured trucks were not all-wheel drive and where there were roads few. As Carl van Dyke writes in his seminal study of the Soviet invasion of Finland regarding supply and reinforcement in January 1940 and particular on supply for 8th and 9th Armies operating north of Lake Ladoga:

Once the troops reached their rail termini they had to be transported to the front line by large convoys of trucks which saturated the few existing snow-bound roads and formed enormous traffic jams. Stavka's reaction to this specific problem had been to order the 8th and 9th Armies... to economise on the number of truck trips to the rear, but this policy had effectively reduced those armies' ability to continue their operations.'[12]

The fact that vehicles engines had to be kept running so that they did not freeze up was another ramification of the cold – increasing fuel consumption and stretching inadequate rear area services even further. Even Soviet tanks then in service struggled in deep snow.[13]

With Soviet equipment often less than ideal, the fact that Soviet troops involved in the invasion were not necessarily used to conditions in the region was apparently an additional problem. Meretskov noted in his memoirs how one division, 'transferred to the front from the Ukrainian steppe without prior training for operations in terrain with forest, marshes, hills and deep snow...found itself in a completely unfamiliar situation and took heavy losses, and the divisional commander was killed'.[14] Here it is unclear to which division Meretskov was referring. One possibility is 75th Rifle Division.[15] He may have been referring to 44th Rifle Division, which by the time it was committed was as Meretskov notes no longer under his command since he had become commander of 7th Army rather than the operation as a whole, and 44th Rifle was part of 9th Army that at this point had just been handed over to Chuikov. The 44th Rifle Division had been formed at Zhitomir in the Ukraine in September and after service in Poland transferred to the

Leningrad Military District.[16] If indeed referring to this division, then Meretskov did not note in his memoirs that the divisional commander, Vinogradov was in fact executed by his own side – along with his commissar and chief of staff in front of his remaining staff members – after his division had taken heavy losses having been dispatched to aid another division in trouble, 163rd Rifle Division. For this debacle the divisional commander Vinogradov was in many ways a scapegoat not only for wider failings of the Red Army but also more immediate mistakes on the part of those higher in the chain of command. That Vinogradov's division was mauled by Finnish forces in late December and early January had certainly not been helped by the fact that unciphered orders had been sent to him by radio by 9th Army headquarters and apparently utilised by the Finns, and the fact that with his division in trouble he was not given permission to withdraw as suggested by the commander of 9th Army, Komkor V. Chuikov, for more than a day after requesting assistance from 9th Army headquarters.[17] That Vinogradov had chosen to split his force into two elements – one combined-arms and mechanised and the other infantry moving on foot – was also a product of a shortage of transport and pressure to move forward quickly. That the infantry moving on foot included reconnaissance and sapper battalions was however a major blunder on his part. The result was, as noted in a subsequent report by procurators and 9th Army on the circumstances surrounding the virtual routing of the division, that as the division arrived to assist 163rd Rifle Division 'the independent reconnaissance battalion that was supposed to provide deep reconnaissance of the enemy, and the independent sapper battalion that was in local conditions essential for the clearing of forest along the road, the construction of blockhouses, bridges and other structures, arrived at the tail end of the division rather than being in the vanguard'.[18] Vinogradov had, like many of his colleagues, been rapidly promoted during the purge era and was quite probably out of his depth commanding a division in such circumstances. From June 1937, as a major, Vinogradov commanded a rifle regiment before in February 1938 receiving accelerated promotion to the rank of polkovnik. In January 1939, after having been 'at the disposal of the Board for Command and Leadership Elements of the RKKA' since March 1938 he gained command of 44th Rifle Division and was promoted to kombrig.[19] Vinogradov's subsequent execution owed much to the appearance of Lev Mekhlis on the scene – as head of the Main Political Administration he had descended on 9th Army on the orders of the Stavka. As those implicated in the embarrassing disaster during Mekhlis's investigation increased in number it became apparent that Vinogradov's superiors at 47th Rifle Corps and 9th Army headquarters had also played their part in the unfolding disaster, with arrests following.[20]

At least some commanders were willing at the time to point at wider issues in explaining the poor performance of 44th Rifle Division and 9th Army. Chuikov had in early January pointed to the 'road strategy' employed by the Red Army as part of the problem, and his chief of staff noted that Red Army troops were limited in their mobility – 'frightened by the forest and cannot ski'.[21] In the case of 163rd Rifle Division the terrain of the region in which it had been formed south of Moscow was no excuse, with plenty of winter snow and forest, but of course little field training took place outside the summer months.[22] In fact, the bulk of the divisions committed in Finland were from north-western European military districts of the Soviet Union. Even for those that could ski, there was a shortage of skis in 9th Army anyway – on 20 January 1940 it was short 10,896 pairs![23] The fact that 44th Rifle Division was thrown into such a frontline role without more and particularly theatre specific training when it was made up largely of recently mobilised reservists can only have contributed to the heavy losses taken by the division. Of 3,229 men of the 25th Rifle Regiment of the division, only 900 were cadre personnel with the remainder mobilised just before the invasion of Poland in which the division had participated.[24] By the 7 January 1940 44th Rifle Division had in fact lost more than the mobilised strength of 25th Rifle Regiment, having lost 1,001 killed, 1,430 wounded, 82 frost-bitten and 2,243 missing in action.[25]

Part of the problem for the Red Army was locating the enemy – in this instance including in particular key defensive positions. Poor reconnaissance or *razvedka* – the Russian word incorporating all aspects of reconnaissance from the tactical to strategic – was particularly obvious in Finland. Effective *razvedka* does not of course just require the collecting of information, but its processing to provide useful intelligence for use in the planning and execution of military operations. As David Glantz notes in one of his earlier works, by 1940 the Red Army theoretically had a good appreciation for the value of intelligence and the various means by which it could collect it. In practice however, 'theory was often difficult to transform into practice' and Red Army intelligence, and particularly field intelligence, was nothing like as valuable an asset as the regulations suggested.[26]

In the Red Army at the time of the invasion of Finland strategic and some operational intelligence was carried out by the 5th Board of the People's Commissariat for Defence, ultimately becoming the Main Reconnaissance Board of the NKO, or GRU. For the 5th Board the primary source of intelligence was 'agents', be they military attaches or more covert human sources of intelligence on foreign territory. As I.I. Proskurov, head of the 5th Board at the time of the invasion of

Finland noted during the April 1940 command conference, the board had provided intelligence prior to the war on both the Finnish armed forces and fortifications on Finnish territory.[27] In his memoirs Meretskov claimed that he had asked Moscow for intelligence on Finnish fortifications on the Karelian Isthmus on more than one occasion prior to the invasion, to be provided with information that suggested that the Mannerheim Line defences were less significant than they transpired to be. According to Meretskov the Red Army 'unfortunately literally had to bump into it [*uperet'sia*] [the Mannerheim Line] in order to appreciate what it actually was'.[28] Here it is unclear whether Meretskov was being a little disingenuous and covering up his own mistakes, or whether the intelligence provided was indeed wildly inaccurate. Certainly, as Erickson suggests, out of either 'overconfidence or incompetence' Meretskov's December 1939 offensive appears to have been poorly prepared.[29] Meretskov's offensive had been thrown together in a very limited timeframe in order to placate Stalin, who had apparently questioned the need for the far more significant resources that had been deemed necessary in a first plan for operations put to him by Chief of Staff Shaposhnikov in July 1939. Meretskov quite possibly ignored information that might have challenged the wisdom of the rapid advance that was supposed to have taken place.[30] For the planning of operations by the Leningrad Military District by his own admission Meretskov had some details of Finnish fortified zones collected by agents before the war 'on his desk' – an 'album' on the subject. This information was, according to Meretskov, the means by which his forces 'orientated themselves'. The information had been gathered over a significant period prior to the war – and apparently delivered to the General Staff on 1 October 1939 as the Finns continued construction.[31] During the April 1940 command conference on the war, Proskurov understandably stood by its accuracy – at least in terms of placing fortifications identified up to that point in the right place in the majority of cases.[32] That this intelligence seems to have been used on Meretskov's own inference initially without being corroborated and added to through tactical military reconnaissance was a serious failing on his part, but one that was indicative of negligent attitudes towards operational and tactical intelligence within many frontline Red Army formations. According to Meretskov's own testimony at the command conference, providing an example of the need for corroboration of strategic and higher level operational intelligence, troops of 123rd Rifle Division made a number of assaults against enemy positions on 'Height 65,5' considering – on what basis is not explicit but context suggests perhaps on the basis of pre-war intelligence – that the height was protected by a single wood and earth bunker. It transpired – only after 'extended reconnaissance by fire by small independent groups with constant observation' – that there were indeed concrete positions.[33]

That the 5th Board 'album' on Finnish defences referred to by Meretskov was on an Army commander's desk no doubt limited its value. As deliberations at the April 1940 command conference go some way to highlighting, a likely combination of incompetence, typical Stalinist obsessive secrecy and inadequate staff work probably prevented at least some information such as that contained within the 'album' on Meretskov's desk, even if incomplete, from finding its way to those who could have made good use of it.[34] Certainly Proskurov and Meretskov were more than happy to follow Stalin's lead in challenging the need for the sort of obsessive secrecy that meant that even publications freely available abroad were then secret in Soviet hands and not readily available within the Red Army – ironically a situation that Stalin had done much to foster and would continue to do so.[35] Although obsessive secrecy may have hampered the dissemination of information collected under the auspices of the 5th Board, the Board does seem to have been effective at gathering strategic – and at times operational – intelligence. Events leading up to the German invasion of the Soviet Union in June 1941 would highlight that the issue was often not with the gathering of strategic and a significant amount of operational intelligence, nor indeed with its analysis lower down the chain of command, but with its interpretation at the highest levels of the command structure and in particular by Stalin.

The competence of the 5th Board in the gathering of strategic and operational intelligence did not exist in the gathering of operational and tactical intelligence by frontline formations, where the starting point for the provision of meaningful intelligence – collection – was hopelessly inadequate to start with. The 1936 Field Regulations may have stressed the importance of battlefield reconnaissance, but the idea that 'the collection of information on the enemy and on the situation in general is the broad responsibility of all military units, headquarters, boards and individual military personnel in all instances of their military activities' is the sort of statement that would guarantee that on top of other responsibilities reconnaissance would gain little attention from most commanders, units and formations with more pressing and often more prosaic concerns.[36] According to Proskurov, field reconnaissance was in fact 'not being carried out by anybody'. Meretskov also highlighted this glaring deficiency, noting at the conference that simply 'we do not have genuine [nastoiashchaia] battlefield reconnaissance'.[37] In theory, and not unreasonably, by the summer of 1940 heads of intelligence existed down the chain of command from those of a Reconnaissance Board of the General

Staff and of staffs of fronts, and were subordinated to operational planning and organisation. At their disposals – technically at the disposal of formation and unit commanders – they supposedly had dedicated reconnaissance units, from the independent reconnaissance battalions of the infantry divisions for example to aerial reconnaissance assets at corps level.[38] The fact aerial reconnaissance was described in PU-36 as 'the principal resource available to commanders for operational reconnaissance and one of the main resources for tactical reconnaissance' was fine in theory, but in practice aircraft were few and pilots often poorly trained, with reconnaissance being limited to daylight in part because of the obvious need to see the enemy, but also because of the limits of pilot training.[39] It is worth recalling here how, as noted in the previous chapter on Poland, General-Lieutenant Golikov, by December 1940 head of the Reconnaissance Board of the Red Army that had replaced the 5th Board that summer, during the December 1940 conference of senior leadership elements of the Red Army bemoaned the lack of aerial reconnaissance resources available to him as a frontline army commander in Poland.[40] In Finland about 5 per cent of the total number of air sorties were made for reconnaissance purposes, a total of 4,358 sorties. Given that 22 days in December were deemed to have been 'non-flying' days – with a further 16 such days in January – the limits of this reconnaissance resource are clear.[41] There was clearly scope for meaningful input from other intelligence gathering assets, and indeed the 1939 Field Regulations (PU-39) that were developed but not officially implemented took a more balanced approach to intelligence collection that better considered the strengths and weaknesses of different means for intelligence gathering.[42] Radio interception will be considered later, but here we will focus on other means for finding out about the enemy that required visual contact between observer and observed.

Most obvious amongst these other assets were the reconnaissance units such as the independent reconnaissance battalions of the infantry divisions, which were according to PU-36 tasked with 'deep reconnaissance' up to a depth of 25–30 km from the primary force where the unit was not in contact with the enemy, and 'close reconnaissance' in circumstances where the main force was engaged with a substantial enemy grouping. In the latter case artillery and even rifle units could be provided as support – and capturing enemy prisoners was a primary concern.[43] Certainly, if operating up to 30 km from the main force, the scope for intelligence to get back to commanders in a timely manner was limited by the availability of radio communications where transmission by courier could take some time.

The fact that in the deployment of 44th Rifle Division its commander Vinogradov had allowed its reconnaissance battalion to trail behind

other elements betrays the attitude apparent in Poland that reconnaissance battalions were far from being specialised units for reconnaissance
tasks and in fact just another combat battalion – and certainly did
not always engage in deep reconnaissance as PU-36 directed. During
the April 1940 command conference on the war in Finland, the fact that
reconnaissance battalions were specialist units in name more than practice was pointed out by Proskurov, who suggested that reconnaissance
battalions were in combat 'just the same sort of battalion as any other'
and deployed as such.[44] As former *razvedchik* or scout Aleksei Sobolev
noted in his memoirs, some pre-war commanders considered that there
was no need for specialist scouts where 'a well-trained Red Armyman
could carry out reconnaissance perfectly well'. Specialist skills such as
capturing enemy troops for interrogation were deemed unnecessary in at
least one pre-war lecture attended by Sobolev because the enemy would
include workers and peasants who would voluntarily go over to the
Soviets.[45] The creation of small, dedicated units for specialised tasks
such as reconnaissance at lower organisational levels was also certainly
not practice for a Red Army that struggled with command and control
and one might also speculate struggled with the concept – particularly
immediately after the purges – of encouraging the sort of initiative and
autonomy amongst junior commanders – especially on enemy territory –
that was important for any arm but essential for reconnaissance. On an
ad hoc basis such tactical reconnaissance assets were created in Finland
in the field however, out of necessity. During assaults against enemy
positions on 'Height 65,5' mentioned earlier, where according to
Meretskov it emerged contrary to existing intelligence that there were
concrete fortifications, the sort of tactical reconnaissance assets required
for the task of determining the exact nature of Finnish defences did not
exist and hence enemy defences had not being reconnoitred prior to
being attacked. After initial setbacks, 'reconnaissance by battle' – a costly
process – was employed, by it seems non-specialist forces, to ascertain
that Finnish positions were indeed more robust than pre-war intelligence
had suggested.[46] Apparently during the war it had been argued in the
military press that, as van Dyke notes, the 'basic element of reconnaissance organisation should be the infantry section operating in small
groups of either a section or platoon in size' – not that the military press
saw particularly informed or open discussion of battlefield problems.[47]
As future General Mal'tsev noted in his memoirs, during this period the
military press discussed military actions 'with a certain superficiality
[*legkost'iu*]' – focusing on for example heroism and sacrifice without
dealing with the sort of 'difficulties met during combat, the heavy losses
taken by our troops during the storming of enemy fortifications, ... , and

with the unnecessary surveillance of junior commanders by their seniors [*izlishnei opeke starshimi nachal'nikami mladshikh*]'. Material in the military press contrasted with the testimony of eyewitnesses – and did not tackle such predictable phenomena as the 'exaggeration of enemy strength and in particular his omnipresent [*vezdesushchikh*] "Cuckoos"'. Such an approach understandably had ramifications for morale – leading to 'confusion' amongst in particular younger soldiers – as well as not facilitating learning.[48]

The inadequacies of Red Army intelligence did not end with inadequate provision for frontline collection of intelligence. According to Proskurov reconnaissance as a wider task lacked an 'owner' – with the Russian term *khoziain* used here by Proskurov inferring responsibility. Nobody was tasked with putting all of the pieces of the intelligence puzzle together, or ensuring suitable dissemination of the range of intelligence information that would allow the best decision making. Proskurov's suggestion that there should be a single body of the General Staff responsible both in peacetime and wartime for the collection, processing and distribution of all forms of intelligence would certainly potentially have solved many issues that continued to plague Soviet military intelligence.[49] A single 'owner' or *khoziain* of intelligence might have solved the problem that in the Red Army there was not a meaningful vertical structure for the processing and dissemination of that information as there was in many foreign armies. It is indicative of the poor vertical integration between those tasked with *razvedka* that the distribution list for the 9 October reconnaissance report of the headquarters of the Leningrad Military District on Finland did not note the report distributed to the heads of reconnaissance departments of rifle corps, but to their commanders – in addition to the head of the General Staff and the head of the 5th Board. Hence it seems that whether this information found its way to the intelligence 'officer' or not was dependent on the overall commander of the formation, who was at best overworked and typically not focused on intelligence, in a system that liked to keep meaningful responsibility in as few hands as possible. In April 1940 Proskurov railed at the fact that personnel under the chief of staff of the North-Western Front,[50] Army Commander 2nd Rank Smorodinov, did not see fit to distribute pertinent information on the sectors of armies to their neighbours.[51] In the Wehrmacht the intelligence officer or Ic and his staff from division upwards were subordinated to operations to a similar extent as in the Soviet case, and in both the case of the Wehrmacht and the Red Army intelligence staff were not necessarily well trained specifically in intelligence matters. One might argue that the preparation of general staff officers in the Wehrmacht, who at least early in the Great Patriotic War filled all Ic staff posts, was higher than for Soviet counterparts, although Wehrmacht Ics were during the first half of the war in the East also burdened with a 'psychological guidance' role carried out in the Red Army by political staff.[52] Certainly as the Great Patriotic War approached, as Proskurov complained, Soviet intelligence personnel were too few, lacked experience and indeed training.[53] As well as keeping authority highly concentrated the Soviet military system did not yet value specialist personnel as much as it might – and as much as seems to have been the case in for example the British or US armies. In all cases one should not exaggerate the value placed on intelligence personnel – officers and commanders of combat arms were the ones most likely to gain promotion to key leadership positions higher up the chain of command, although former intelligence officers could sometimes do well in the staff hierarchy.

Hampered by poor reconnaissance, with Red Army mechanised units crammed on the few snow covered roads, it didn't take much to halt the Soviet advance during the first days of the campaign. Particularly significant in delaying the advance during the first days were Finnish mines, for which the Red Army in the region at least seems to have been hopelessly unprepared. As noted by future General-Colonel of Engineers A.F. Khrenov in his memoirs, mines of a variety of types – be they sown along the sides of roads or 'booby traps' in dwellings – took a significant toll. He recounts a particular incident in early December, where on the main road to Viborg the advance of a rifle division had been halted after two lead trucks had been blown up by anti-tank mines, and their drivers killed. Khrenov and the head of the sapper battalion accompanying him were it seems both surprised and disappointed that those gathered round had not noticed three more anti-tank mines that were barely concealed having perhaps been placed in a hurry. There followed instruction on the removal and disarming of such mines to nearby commanders.[54] Ivan Vladimirovich Maslov, then commanding a tank of the recently formed 25th Tank Regiment, in post-Soviet testimony describes how in an attack on Finnish fortifications at the end of 1939 or beginning of 1940 the second company of three in action on the Petrozavodsk axis was lost to a minefield – all seventeen tanks destroyed by mines or Finnish artillery.[55] The Red Army did apparently possess mine detection devices contrary to some accounts, but few were available, although their rapid production in Leningrad during December apparently improved the situation.[56]

Finnish snipers – used in large numbers – caused considerable consternation and loss of life amongst Soviet troops. The so called 'Kukush-kas' or 'Cuckoos' were often hidden high up in trees or otherwise well concealed and took a considerable toll and particularly of commanders who were often clearly identifiable – particularly in the sheepskin coats that only they had received.[57] Apparently commanders were ordered to remove insignia of rank from outerwear in response to this threat from snipers. Armed not only with rifles but also sub-machine guns, tactical use of snipers seems to have varied from lone 'snipers', sometimes with sub-machine guns, harassing Soviet troops before making away on skis to groups of snipers operating together to create killing squares with fire from multiple directions that would relocate at night. Finnish snipers – as Soviet snipers during the Great Patriotic War – would sometimes be women, as in one instance described by junior artillery commander Lukinov. This 'young red-haired girl, white as death' apparently offered no resistance when located, which along with her gender may have helped her cause, for Lukinov's description hints that many Finnish snipers were shot on capture.[58] Soviet desperation in dealing with the problem of snipers is perhaps highlighted by the fact that artillery was used to rake areas of forest in an attempt to clear them of snipers.[59]

By mid-December 1939 Soviet forces on the Karelian Isthmus had reached the main line of Finnish defences – the so-called Mannerheim Line – and according to Meretskov attempted to break through 'off the march[s khodu]' – and failed.[60] This 'main defensive zone' consisted of 'a discontinuous series of concrete fortifications...machine-gun nests, anti-tank traps, and anti-personnel barriers of various types interconnected by a system of trenches located in defiles between lakes and swamps or on high ground overlooking major roads and railways'. Even the 'obstacle zone' that preceded the 'main defensive zone', with its 'scattered mine fields and machine gun nests', had highlighted in early December how poorly prepared Soviet troops were.[61] Soviet forces continued to throw poorly trained units in to costly frontal assaults on prepared positions – be they against the concrete bunkers of the 'main defensive zone' or wood and earth nests, without the sort of support – or appropriate support – from specialist troops and other arms that would be the norm during the later stages of the Great Patriotic War. Initially poor support from sappers has already been noted in dealing with mines – where at the beginning of the campaign the integration of small groups of specialist troops in to combined-arms groups for specific tactical missions seems not to have taken place with any regularity. As commander of 8th Army during the war Komandarm 2nd rank Shtern noted at the April 1940 command conference, there was a need to allow for the organisation of co-operation between arms at lower levels of the chain of command, suggesting that co-ordination – 'above all with artillery, and in a number of instances with tanks, should conclude not at the level of battalion and *divizion*, but at the level of the rifle company and battery'.[62]

Certainly attempting to integrate arms at the planning stage lower down the chain of command would have helped mitigate deficiencies in communications and in particular with the artillery.

In Finland, and particularly as the war progressed and provision increased, artillery was certainly often seen as the key to success. On the last day of the command conference of April 1940 on the war, Stalin suggested that 'in modern war artillery is God' – with the idea of that 'artillery is God of war' being subsequently frequently repeated in Soviet military circles both during and beyond the Great Patriotic War.[63] During the early stages of the war in Finland Soviet artillery had certainly not achieved such elevated status in practice. In his memoirs Meretskov describes how artillery preparation for the initial assault on the defensive positions of the 'main defensive zone' had failed to damage or even reveal many fortifications, with artillery fire landing at best on field defences between bunkers. When attacking the main defensive line for a second time in December after five days of artillery preparation the defences 'were not suppressed'.[64] This was hardly surprising in part given the initially limited provision of heavy – and absence of superheavy artillery. However, problems were about more than just having suitable heavy and super heavy artillery – with poor reconnaissance as outlined above, many enemy positions were not identified and specifically targeted – and even where targets were identified fire control was often poor as will be discussed further later.

Finnish Marshal Mannerheim's comments about Soviet artillery in his memoirs were certainly less than adulatory, with the suggestion that the relative position of the artillery arm had sunk in the Bolshevik-led successor to the Tsarist army. Mannerheim noted that:

In the Tsarist army, the artillery had, from a technical as well as from a tactical point of view, been regarded as an elite arm. Now its level had naturally sunk because of the lack of education of the officer corps. But the material had kept well up to modern development. This was illustrated by the astonishingly great mass of modern artillery of great rapidity of fire and range as well as by the apparently inexhaustible stocks of ammunition.

Inspite of tactical deficiencies, it was the enormous mass of artillery which formed the base of the Russian's activity on the isthmus, but their artillery, such as it was, was not capable of meeting the demands of a war of movement.[65]

As noted in Chapter 2 artillery was one area in which by the period of the Great Purges the Red Army was receiving new and effective ordnance – and Mannerheim was correct to highlight that deficiencies in Soviet artillery effectiveness were not about having modern guns. Certainly by 1940 the Red Army was indeed increasingly well equipped with modern artillery – even if there were certainly not enough such pieces to go round and their use left much to be desired. The 76.2 mm gun Obr. 1936 (F-22) for example gave the Red Army its first modern field piece with a carriage suitable for a period in which tracked and wheeled vehicles could move such pieces forward far more rapidly over rougher terrain than the horse teams of the previous decade. By the end of 1938 1,429 F-22 guns had been produced, with a further 1,503 being manufactured in 1939. Its successor, the 76.2 mm divisional gun Obr. 1939 (USB) followed, both improving on the F-22 and being more straightforward to produce – the latter quality general tendency in the development of Soviet weapons systems in the late 1930s and into the 1940s and one that would put Soviet industry in a much better position to replace the horrendous losses of the summer and autumn of 1941 than it would otherwise have been.[66]

However, although Soviet units were increasingly receiving modern artillery pieces, training and practice in their use had not kept up with technological development. For example, during the early phases of the campaign in Finland, Soviet long-range artillery fire had, according to van Dyke, been conducted exclusively by map co-ordinate, where 'no provisions had been made for the organisation of artillery observation points to correct artillery fire and verify the destruction of targets'. Whilst efforts were made to provide this as part of broader attempts to improve co-operation and co-ordination at battalion and company level, here of course the shortage of communications equipment – and particularly radios for troops on the offensive – was a limiting factor.[67] According to Lukinov even telephone cable was in short supply, at least for his battery.[68] Direct fire on enemy positions was one solution to the problem of fire control and co-ordination that received considerable attention during the Finnish campaign, although direct fire obviously placed artillerymen in a far more vulnerable position than would otherwise have been the case.[69] Lukinov describes an instance where at one point their 'guns had to be rolled out from under cover to fire over open sights right under the fire of Finnish soldiers armed with submachine-guns and our men were getting killed to no purpose'.[70]

In addition to Soviet units being increasingly equipped with modern field artillery, Soviet investment in super-heavy artillery seems to have proven to be of some value in dealing with Finnish defences once such weapons were actually deployed. It is apparent from the transcripts of the April 1940 command conference on the war that 203 mm guns were at least in some instances brought forward through the forest, screened with other assets, and fired over open sights at ranges as low as 200 metres on Finnish bunkers or DOTs. Although they did not necessarily destroy them as in the instance described to Stalin by Colonel Mladentsev, commander of 387th Rifle Regiment of 136th Rifle Division, such fire in this case compelled the Finnish garrison to flee. The sheer scale of artillery support provided to Mladentsev's regiment later in the campaign was impressive. His single rifle regiment had the support of thirteen *divizions* of artillery – more than a hundred artillery pieces![71] As Meretskov notes in his memoirs, by February 1940 7th Army advancing up the Karelian Isthmus could field on average fifty artillery pieces for a kilometer of front.[72] At one point 8th Army could field an impressive 719 artillery pieces of varying calibres, with each rifle company apparently being allocated a divisional artillery battery with the remainder held for use higher up the chain of command. This compared to the poor state of 8th Army artillery at the beginning of the campaign, where three divisions out of six – 155th, 139th and 168th Rifle – had only a single artillery regiment. The 56th Rifle Corps didn't apparently have any corps-level artillery, and 1st Rifle Corps a single artillery regiment of 107 mm guns. Additional artillery resources made available to 8th Army consisted of a single independent artillery *divizion* of 122 mm guns and 108th Super Heavy (BM) Howitzer Regiment – the latter equipped with 203 mm howitzers.[73] More guns, improved fire-correction even if firing over open sights, and better supply of ammunition would all make it increasingly likely that Soviet artillery could actually suppress Finnish defences for other arms as the campaign progressed.

Soviet field artillery had been supplemented at Khalkhin Gol with mortars – fifty-two in total – and their use would be even more significant during the war in Finland even if their availability to the Red Army as a whole was still fairly limited.[74] In mid-January 1940 three mortar companies had apparently been formed by 8th Army within a period of 15–20 days, being sent straightaway to the front and according to Kombrig Klich, head of artillery for 8th Army, subsequently having 'in combat showed themselves in a favourable light'.[75] Klich's enthusiasm for the mortar per se as expressed at the April 1940 symposium to review war experience was fairly novel – during most of the 1930s there was, as Novikov et al note, a tendency by many Red Army leaders to see mortars as cheap and easily manufactured 'surrogate' artillery pieces, although with 'it following that, if the armed forces had a sufficient number of artillery pieces, then mortars would not be required'.[76] At the April 1940 command conference on the war in Finland opposition to Klich's proposal to provide every infantry company with three mortars of undisclosed calibre, with mortars also at battalion, regimental and divisional level was evident from the rather conservative and less than able Kulik – head of the Main Artillery Directorate of the Red Army.[77] Given the

Soviet 203 mm super heavy artillery fires on Finnish positions during the Soviet-Finnish War of 1939-40. The artillery – Stalin's 'God of War'– played a crucial part in ultimately breaking the stalemate despite poor direction of indirect fire in particular. (RIA Novosti #45604)

preference for conventional artillery on the part of the old guard, production of mortars had therefore been limited prior to 1939, with only seventy-three 82 mm Battalion Mortars Obr. 1936 having been produced by 1 November 1936, with a further 1,587 and 1,188 following in 1937 and 1938 respectively.[78] Limited production of a new weapon for the Red Army – often on Stalin's initiative – did not of course mean acceptance within it – as was also the case with sub-machine guns during the late 1930s as will be discussed later. In the case of mortars, a meeting between the designer B.I. Shavirin and Stalin on 27 November 1938 is often identified in Russian-language literature as having significance in the decision to increase production of mortars and to have led to the acceptance in to service of the improved 82 mm Battalion Mortar Obr. 1937 and its series production in a decree of 26 February 1939 – it is not that the Red Army leadership had pressed for this outcome.[79] Certainly in the conditions met in Finland the mortar no doubt had much appeal for troops on the ground, being relatively easy to move through difficult terrain, and offering infantry units close support under the authority of commanders lower down the chain of command that was typically the case for artillery. The 50 mm Company Mortar Obr. 1938 – followed by the Obr. 1940 and Obr. 1941 – was put in to series production in 1939 and would offer Soviet rifle companies their own, albeit limited fire-support with three being allocated per rifle company as Klich had suggested – even if Klich may have had the 82 mm mortar in mind. Inadequate production of 1,720 50 mm mortars during 1939 saw a major drive to increase production the following year, which saw 23,105 produced. Of course demand was considerable – for each infantry division eighty-one – at a time when the Red Army was expanding. During this period production of the 82 mm mortar was also stepped up, along with production progressing of the even larger calibre 120 mm mortar to be allocated higher up the chain of command. However, production of the bombs for the mortars now being turned out in increasing numbers did not necessarily keep up with production of the tubes, where the Red Army would have in the region of 13,000 of the 82 mm and 3,000 of the 120 mm mortars by June 1941.[80] Producing weapons, without suitable quantities of ammunition, would soon be a major problem.

Inadequate artillery support was not the only problem in co-ordinating arms for the Red Army in advancing in the face of fortifications in Finland during December 1939. In his memoirs Meretskov goes on to characterise infantry and tank attacks on fortified positions during the early stages of the invasion that followed the ineffective artillery preparation. Meretskov notes how unsuppressed 'concrete bunkers were silent until our tanks pressed forward, when they opened fire and knocked them out from the side and rear. Machine guns separated off the infantry from the tanks and the attack stalled'. As Meretskov rightly notes, the Soviet tanks of the period 'lacking powerful guns could not suppress bunkers on their own and in a best case scenario could block the embrasures with their hulls'. With few specialist 'storm groups' to take out pillboxes and bunkers, aircraft 'bombing only the depths of enemy defences and providing little assistance to ground forces', artillery ammunition that could not penetrate bunkers and 'poor provision of field radios not allowing commanders to maintain operational communications', at the front line Soviet forces fared badly.[81] An alternative was to try to go round Finnish defences. Attempts by one commander – Kombrig N. Belaev of 139th Rifle Division – to outflank Finnish positions after an abortive frontal assault did, by his own admission, unfortunately indicate 'weaknesses in troops control and tactical training' that would make frontal assaults more likely. The Finnish High

Command was nonetheless apparently impressed by the fact that Belaev had even attempted an outflanking maneouver during a campaign in which the frontal assault was the norm.[82]

Meretskov's analysis of early attacks on Finnish positions of the Mannerheim Line – written with the value of hindsight – does not show how under pressure for results he probably made the situation worse by pushing commanders forward in unfavourable circumstances. As is apparent in Carl van Dyke's analysis of events based on Soviet archival sources, in early December Meretskov put considerable pressure on commanders to advance more rapidly despite the many issues that were emerging regarding such matters as intelligence and support from sappers in the face of the threat from mines to name just two. To 8th Army at the time he stated that 'we can no longer bicker with Finland, going four to five kilometers a day' – the aim being for 8th Army to cut Finland in to two and prevent the unloading of Swedish aid at Uleaborg. This problem of pushing units forward in what might be seen as sufficiently unfavourable circumstances to warrant a more measured approach was endemic in a Red Army ultimately geared towards satisfying the demands for results – and sometimes whims – of Stalin and his inner circle, where the pressure was passed down the chain of command to commanders on the spot where all knew the possible cost of failure. All down the chain of command little dictators sought to threaten commanders below them in the same manner they were being threatened from above. A good example of this that occurred early in the war with Finland concerns Belaev's relatively effective 139th Rifle Division, where in early December Belaev had requested that he be able to throw the weight of an attack behind encircling troops, but was ordered by his corps commander to throw troops in to a more rapidly organisable frontal assault. The day before the corps commander had received a directive from the NKO that had reprimanded him not only for having his corps headquarters too far back in the rear – on Soviet territory – but also, as Dyke notes for not 'conducting the offensive quickly enough'.[83] It is difficult to imagine that this directive did not influence his decision.

Reading the transcripts of the April 1940 command conference on the war, one can only have sympathy for many commanders who were under pressure to achieve results and pushed subordinates to press on regardless. Such commanders were subsequently at best chastised – often worse – for undertaking unsuccessful operations without sufficient resources or preparation. At what level of command the axe would fall in response to failure was often unclear. In a discussion during the April 1940 conference on the war – perhaps better described as a cross-examination – Chuikov of 9th Army was challenged by Stalin on both his failure to expend significantly more artillery ammunition, and then his ability to budget ammunition in what was at the time a typical exchange with a Stalin who toyed with his commanders as part of the process of gaining an understanding of a situation and finding scape-goats.[84] Vinogradov's execution was a stark reminder of the price of serious failure, although typically failure to advance quickly enough and requests for more resources seem to have led to demotion and damage to ones career rather than death. In the game of Russian roulette that was command in Stalin's Red Army, one could leave the game by showing insufficient resolve or stay and play and throw one's chips in – succeed and win the favour of the *vozhd* but with the risk of losing more than promotion if things went wrong.

Often there were limits to the extent to which senior commanders and political figures could influence what was going on at the front line and particularly once orders for an assault had been given, to a large extent because of the lack of communications resources. At times this may have been a good thing, as the meddling by different elements of the chain of command had shown at Lake Khasan – but generally it both exacerbated and was a partial cause of the lack of tactical and operational flexibility that characterised the Red Army during this period. This absence of communications resources hampered effective Soviet command and control at all, but particularly lower levels of the chain of command. As Meretskov, commanding 7th Army complained in his memoirs, 'poor provision of field radio sets did not allow commanders to maintain operational communications' during the war, where it was only after the war had begun that army commander Meretskov first received his own 'personal' radio set.[85] Even when radios were available they were typically not particularly effective models. The 6-PK sets in widespread use and already noted as somewhat outdated by the end of the 1930s were as artillery commander Lukinov notes from experience at this time, 'cumbersome with little power, transmitting only short distances, and were often jammed by various types of interference'.[86]

In theory at least, the dovetailing of the actions of different arms was supposed to be co-ordinated primarily at the regimental level, but par-ticularly in the sort of terrain encountered in Finland this co-ordination was almost impossible to maintain once troops were committed where telephone cables had not been laid or had been broken and radios were scarce.[87] Even where communications resources were ostensibly avail-able, poor maintenance and training of reservists in particular meant that communications were often broken with formations. As Brigade Com-missar Murav'ev of the Communications Board of the Red Army noted during the April 1940 command conference on the war, contact was lost with a number of substantial units in Finland through, one can only assume, in many instances broken radios or the inability to use them effectively. At one point 19th Rifle Corps lost communications with its divisions and its army headquarters after a number of moves of its command post – where radio communications should have provided some communication before landlines were laid. Contact was also temporarily lost with both 20th Tank Brigade and 10th Tank Corps, where in both instances it proved necessary to 'seek them out on the roads and send a special commander with a radio' to restore communications. The 18th Rifle Division had apparently 'discarded [*brosila*]' its radio set on Soviet territory and crossed the border without radio communications. Even at divisional level there wasn't redundancy in radio communications.[88]

Poor quality sets and fear of interception of radio communications further limited the value of radio communications in combat situations, where there were according to Murav'ev instances of 'radio fear' [*radioboiazn'*] – fear of using radio communications.[89] Lukinov suggests that – in theory at least – 'all transmissions had to be encrypted, which hindered the flexibility of their usage'.[90] If indeed the case, then such requirements born out of at times legitimate fears of interception of messages, showed an obsessive secrecy that failed to take in to account the fact that certain types of tactical communication could be transmitted without encryption and the enemy not have time to make use of them even if intercepted. Under utilisation of radio communications can however be contrasted with their misuse in a panic situation as in the case of 8th Army and 44th Rifle Division discussed earlier.

Whilst there were obvious issues with communications for the vertical chain of command, Murav'ev suggested that 'particularly weak was the business ... of organising communications for co-operation with artillery, aviation and neighbouring units'.[91] The weaknesses of Soviet artillery fire control have already been noted, but weaknesses in the direction of air assets have not. The Red Army possessed doctrine that allowed for relatively close support of frontline ground forces with airpower, but as with so many aspects of Red Army activity there was a considerable gulf between theory and practice. Particularly in Finland where the location of front lines and enemy positions was more difficult than it had been in either Spain or the Far East, limited use seems to have been made of close air support early in the campaign to a large extent due to issues regarding ground-air communication. In his memoirs Meretskov complained that apparently in general 'aviation bombed only the depths of the enemy defences and provided little support to frontline forces'.[92] Even Komkor Ptukhin, commander of the air forces of the North-Western Front, admitted that at the beginning of the campaign the

VVS was unable to bomb enemy frontline positions because crews were frightened of hitting their own troops and were also not capable of such precise bombing.[93] At times inaccurate bombing was a blessing – in his monograph *Soviet Air Force Theory, 1918–1945,* James Sterrett notes an episode on 26 December 1939 where three DB-3 bombers mistakenly attacked Red Army positions on a hill, but none of the thirty bombs dropped hit their target.[94] Certainly without meaningful air-ground communications the chances of timely information making its way from frontline ground units through the chain of command and resulting in an air strike that would hit enemy rather than friendly forces was extremely low. It was in fact deemed necessary according to van Dyke – at least at some undisclosed point in the campaign – in the face of communications problems that 'aviation required a minimum distance of one kilometre between their targets and the front line in order to avoid bombing their own infantry'.[95] Ptukhin claimed at the April 1940 conference that later in the campaign the VSS was at least at times bombing 300–400 metres from the Soviet frontline, although it is difficult to imagine that this was the norm given the terrain and communications issues.[96] These communications problems were not just about the lack of radio communications – better staff work and co-operation between the VVS and ground forces at many levels would have allowed for better co-operation, including for example pre-arranged target identification for pilots through such means as signal flares and tracer fire.[97]

At the time of the war in Finland the Red Army lacked a light or tactical bomber suitable for modern warfare where rapid-fire anti-aircraft weapons above machine-gun calibre in particular made slow moving and at best poorly armoured aircraft such as the R-Zet – a development of the R-5 – extremely vulnerable. Their vulnerability was no doubt made worse by the tendency noted by Sterrett for Soviet aircraft to use the same route of approach to a target during subsequent attacks.[98] Soviet medium bombers – and namely the SB – were however fast and modern, even if not particularly suited to close air support. In the region of 40 per cent of sorties by the VVS during the war were 'in support of ground forces' – a total of 33,704 sorties.[99]

Although not in a position to offer ground forces much in the way of close air support, the VVS did commit significant resources to the bombing of targets further in to the Finnish rear, and including population centres. Of VVS sorties during the war, 10,879 or 13 per cent were categorised as having been 'activity against enemy communications and reserves' and 2.7 per cent or 2,193 'the bombing of military-industrial objectives'.[100] Such strikes seem to have had more success than missions in immediate support of frontline troops, but even here accuracy was also a serious problem. In a report to Voroshilov, one Komkor R.S. Shelukhin damningly reported:

Hundreds of bombers are sent, thousands of bombs are dropped, and tens of aircraft are lost, in order to destroy some object (for example a radio station, a bridge, etc), the accomplishment of this mission drags on for weeks and in the end loses its intended purpose... a single flight of aircraft should be sufficient for the destruction of one of these objects, if it were well trained with dive bombers...[101]

Early in the war, as the Finnish ace Ilmari Juutilainen notes, Soviet bombers risked flying on missions without fighter escorts relying on speed for protection – the Finnish Fokker XXI fighter being slower than the Soviet SB. Fortunately for the VVS, the Finns had few aircraft – and their Fokker XXI and few Bristol Bulldog fighters were inferior to the I-16. Subsequently however significant fighter escort was provided to bombers, with Soviet fighter cover typically exceeding the strength of any Finnish attackers.[102] A total of 31 per cent or 26,098 VVS sorties were recorded as having been flown for the purpose of 'the struggle for air supremacy'.[103]

Despite having a number of accomplished pilots who had distinguished themselves in the skies over Spain, China and Khalkhin Gol, the bulk of Soviet aircrews nonetheless unfortunately remained poorly trained and accidents were all too common. In fact, where Soviet forces in the region lost in the region of 269 aircrafts in combat [boevie poteri] – of which 46 were recorded as lost in aerial combat, 106 to anti-aircraft and 117 failed to return from a mission – at least a further 200 were lost in accidents. Seven times the number of R-Zet were recorded as lost in accidents compared to in combat – twenty-eight to four.[104]

Overall, it is reasonable to conclude – and hardly unpredictable – that the contribution of the VVS to the Finnish campaign was more disappointing than it had been over the open Mongolian steppe where pilots enjoyed the luxury of typically operating in fine weather – and when operating against enemy ground forces concentrated in a fairly well-defined area. It is perhaps worth concluding this section with Sterrett's conclusions on Soviet air support over Finland in 1939–40:

The Soviet Air Force did not succeed notably in meeting any of its objectives. Tactical support improved but was often absent. ... The results were in no way commensurate with the effort expended....they appeared to know the effect they wanted to achieve, but were unable to carry out their intentions in practice: an inability to translate theory and doctrine in to execution.[105]

Although Soviet performance in Finland was arguably embarrassing in late 1939, it did improve during the first months of 1940. As both

Mannerheim and Meretskov agree, during the later stages of the war the Red Army showed far greater tactical competence – enough alongside increased resources to break through Finnish defences and force the Finnish government to sue for peace. In his memoirs, Mannerheim noted in particular that 'co-operation of armour with infantry improved considerably in the latter phase of the war', and that Soviet '28 and 45-ton tanks, armed with two guns and four or five machine guns, contributed decisively to the penetration of our lines'.[106] Here Mannerheim seems to be referring to T-28 and T-35 multi-turreted medium and heavy tanks respectively. These vehicles may have assisted the Red Army in the penetration of Finnish lines, but far more potent in part by virtue of its heavier armour was the KV-series heavy tank that first saw limited action in Finland. The development of the KV-series heavy tank had stemmed from experience in Spain and in particular the need for a breakthrough tank with the armour to resist anti-tanks guns then in service with possible opponents such as the 3.7 cm PaK 36. Whilst discussing Soviet tank development in the late 1930s to June 1941 in more detail later, it is worth noting that here according to Meretskov, one such tank undergoing combat testing and crewed by workers and engineers made it through Finnish fortified positions despite being hit by Finnish artillery, which could not knock it out. Meretskov was exaggerating a little in suggesting that the KV-series tanks was 'practically an invincible tank for the period', but it did offer the Red Army a weapon that would require a disproportionate investment of enemy effort in order to destroy it.[107]

Inadequate and insufficient training for combat had been a problem for the Red Army throughout the 1930s, but there were signs during the war in Finland of change. Future General-Major Ashot Vagarshakovich Kazar'ian served as a machine gunner with 286th Rifle Regiment of 90th Rifle Division during the 1939–40 campaign against Finland. He recalls in his memoirs how in late January 1940, companies of his unit were in turn pulled from the frontline and trained for attacking Finnish fortifications: to deal with barbed wire obstacles, isolate bunkers and accurately throw grenades. Of course, one might have expected troops to be trained in some of these skills anyway, but basic military skills were often lacking amongst reservists. Nonetheless, receiving such training in late January was better late than never, despite the fact that the division had been in the line since the beginning of the campaign.[108] Having received this basic training, troops were divided up in to storm groups and practiced assaulting bunkers, with Kazar'ian's Maxim heavy machine gun being allocated to one such group to provide suppressive fire. Tanks pulling armoured sleds were an additional component of the assault, with the armoured sleds allowing infantry to be transported in to the enemy rear behind bunkers in relative safety. When in mid-February the unit was to assault the enemy line, it was supported by whitewashed 152 mm artillery that had been dragged up to the front line under cover of noise generated by a neighbouring unit and responding Finns. This artillery was apparently 'so well camouflaged amongst the snow covered bushes not far from our fox holes, that not only the enemy, but also we didn't notice the appearance nearby of these rather bulky objects'.[109] Instructions for such storm groups specified that the first echelon of the assault was to find a way through the enemy positions and having got behind fortifications utilising the tanks and armoured sleds were to dig in and wait for the storm groups of the second echelon to destroy any enemy bunkers that had not been destroyed by artillery fire. In addition to the infantry and machine guns – a platoon of each – the storm groups were to include snipers, mortars, 45 and 75 mm guns and a section of sappers with explosives, along with at least three gun tanks and one 'chemical' or flamethrower tank. Having forced their way through any obstacles covering the fortifications the storm groups were to either block up embrasures with sand bags or the hulls of the tanks before the sappers blew them up. In practice Soviet tanks in service at the beginning of the campaign were vulnerable to even the lightest artillery and even anti-tank rifles, even if this was not the case with the KV-1s deployed later and about which Meretskov had so enthused.[110] Storm groups certainly overcame some of the problems of combining arms at a higher level where particularly in close terrain such co-ordination in a fluid environment would have benefitted from reliable – or indeed any radio communications that were simply not available towards the bottom of the chain of command. At the level of the multi-platoon storm group co-operation could at least often be furthered in person and with hand signals.

Ideal for use by the infantry of storm groups were the SMGs that were so effectively used by the Finns. According to Soviet works SMGs had been under development in the Soviet Union since the late 1920s, and indeed, in June 1935 the *pistolet-pulemet Degtiareva* – Degtiarev machine-pistol – or simply PPD – was accepted for service with the Red Army as the 7.62 mm Degtiarev machine pistol model 1934. The weapon was provided with a 25-round magazine. Limited service saw a number of minor improvements being made, resulting in the model 1934/1938, with a total of about 4,000 weapons produced between 1934 and 1939. By 1939 the PPD had apparently won the support of the Main Artillery Directorate, which early that year apparently sought wider use of the weapon – one assumes including as an ideal short-range defensive weapon for gun crews. Nonetheless, not all in the Red Army leadership saw the value of such a weapon and it was in fact removed from production in February 1939 and those with the troops taken out of service and put in to storage.[111] As V.V. Bakhirev and I.I, Kirillov's biographical work on the designer, V.A. Degtiarev notes:

It was only with the start of the war with the White Finns in 1939 that the full tactical possibilities and combat potential of the new weapon were demonstrated, showing how in conditions with widespread forest and complex terrain the machine pistol is a sufficiently powerful and irreplaceable means of putting down fire in close combat.[112]

War in Finland saw production resume with a sense of urgency and further development of the PPD such that in early 1940 it was provided with a seventy-one-round drum magazine – motivated by such magazines proving to be both functional and offering more sustained fire without reloading – an advantage enjoyed by Finnish forces with their 'Suomi' SMG. During 1940 in the region of a further 81,100 PPD were produced. Although by Western standards the PPD was simple to produce and effective, the PPD Obr. 1940 was nonetheless to be superseded by the visually similar PPSh, or Shpagin machine pistol in 1941. The PPSh Obr. 1941 not only had improved technical characteristics but was also easier to produce, and would become in many ways the iconic infantry weapon of the wartime Red Army and suited the needs of an army where time for marksmanship training and practice was often at a premium and in which a simple, robust weapon stood more chance of functioning when it was required to do so.[113]

By the second half of February the principal fortifications called Mannerheim Line had been breached, and on 12 March 1940 the Finnish government came to peace terms with the Soviet Union – giving up Karelia as well as part of the Ribachii and Srednii peninsulas in the far north – and providing the Soviet Union with a 30-year lease on the Khanko peninsula and nearby islands.[114] Voroshilov – who had emerged as the dominant figure in shaping the Red Army that emerged from the Great Purges of 1937–8 – tried to end his report of 28 March 1940 to the Central Committee of the Party on lessons of the war on a positive note:

Comrades! The war with Finland uncovered a series of substantial inadequacies in the preparation of the Red Army and unstatisfactory work of the military administration, but at the same time proved the unconquerable strength of our country and the inimitable direction on the part of the Party, government and Comrade Stalin, which is undoubtedly insurance for future victories.[115]

In some ways perhaps Voroshilov was right – despite all the failures. Roger Reese has certainly argued that during the Winter War the Red Army can be described as having been 'effective' for a number of reasons.

Differentiating between military 'effectiveness' defined as 'the willing-ness and ability of small units and soldiers to fight' and 'capability' defined as 'tactical performance', Reese provides more detail on the former component.[116] In Finland, according to Reese:

> The army...forces in theater...and individual soldiers never lost the desire to overcome the foe; unit cohesion, although seriously challenged, remained for the most part intact, while morale waned and wavered but never collapsed; the soldier's investment (interest) in the success of the mission never failed; and discipline, if sometimes tenuous, did not give way.[117]

Even during the debacles of the early stages of the war it is important to highlight, as pointed out by Reese, that although the Red Army showed many deficiencies that have been highlighted above in what for Reese would be largely be matters of 'capability', many troops fought ten-aciously – even in encirclement. That they did so with not only the enemy to worry about but also the sword of Damocles of their own political and military-political leaders to worry about was certainly the case, although it is difficult to assess the relative importance of the stick compared to other variables such as patriotism and other more nebulous factors. That the debacle of Vinogradov's 44th Rifle Division prompted the NKO and NKVD in late January 1940 to organise 'preventative' or 'control-blocking' detachments [*kontrol'no-zagraditel'nie otriadi*] in order to limit desertion and the activities of 'harmful elements' in the rear of active armies was a predictable response for a regime and current leadership that tended to see failure as a product of some sort of lack of commit-ment.[118] The 44th Rifle Division had been destroyed in part because of poor discipline according to Stavka and the Main Military Soviet – but that fact that this poorly prepared division was noted wiped out suggested otherwise.

In early 1940 the fact that the enemy – horrendously outnumbered and outgunned by most indices – was defeated was helped by the fact that the Red Army could in many senses flood the region with firepower and in particular artillery resources. However, although important, increasing the size of the sledgehammer was only one element of Red Army success. The matters of 'effectiveness' highlighted by Reese were essential. How-ever, if the now larger sledgehammer was to actually hit the nut squarely, then it had to be wielded with a little more precision than had previously been the case. Firepower had to be combined with what by Red Army standards were serious attempts to prepare commanders for and allow the exercising of command, control and initiative much lower down the chain of command than had been the case at the beginning of the conflict. Some units had actually to receive some fairly basic military training as a starting point in theater – training that should already have taken place before deployment. Despite the fact that those such as Mekhlis resorted to matters of psychological 'effectiveness' to explain failure during the conflict, there was consideration and even discussion of many other factors from doctrine through to equipment not only during the conflict but particularly important in the aftermath. This discussion and the changes of approach they fostered showed that even the post-Great Purge Red Army could learn and increase 'capability'.

The horrific human cost of the war against Finland is testimony to both the stubbornness of Finnish resistance and the inadequacies of Soviet forces that engaged them – where even towards the end of the campaign as one might expect Soviet casualties were high since the Red Army could hardly be expected to transform its capability within a matter of weeks. Krivosheev and his colleagues report that, during a war that lasted from 30 November 1939 to 13 March 1940, according to contemporary field reports Soviet forces lost at least 65,384 killed or who died during casualty evacuation, with at least an additional 19,610 missing in action. On the basis of these figures, total losses – including sick and wounded, exceeded 333,084. After the signing of the peace treaty 5,468 POWs were returned to the Soviet Union – with a further 99 opting to remain in Finland, making it likely that most of the remaining 14,043 deemed missing in action had been killed. Later figures collated during the period 1947–51 included VVS losses and those who died in hospital after March 1940 for example, in addition to recalculation of figures for those missing in action based on statements by relatives. A figure of 71,214 for those killed or who died of wounds during evacuation was reached at this time, along with 16,292 who died in hospital of wounds or disease, and 39,369 missing in action – a staggering total of 126,875 truly irrecoverable losses.[119] Finnish losses were noted by Mannerheim as 24,923 killed, missing and died from wounds and 43,557 wounded.[120]

From a governmental point of view – where human lives were apparently rarely of any consequence until they were in short supply – the biggest casualty of the war had been the prestige of the Red Army. That victory at Khalkhin Gol and embarrassing Red Army performance at the beginning of the war with Finland had taken place within a matter of weeks should not be seen as that surprising given how their circumstances were so different. That Zhukov was a more capable leader than Meretskov no doubt played a part the relative success of the former, but otherwise as has already been noted the situation at Khalkhin Gol was undoubtedly far more favourable to a successful outcome. In many ways ultimate success against the Finns would be because after the initial invasion the Red Army focused its attentions on winning at the tactical level and grinding forward in terrain that would have made anything else challenging for any army – not least the Red Army of early 1940. Further territorial acquisition stemming from the Nazi-Soviet Pact fortunately took place without bloodshed. Having already pressured the Baltic Republics to accept the basing of Soviet troops on their territories during September and October 1939, by the beginning of 1940 there were already nearly 60,000 Soviet troops, more than 1,000 tanks and just over 150 aircraft on the territories of the Baltic Republics.[121] The occupations of Estonia, Latvia and Lithuania in June 1940 seem not to have been the culmination of some sort of plan reaching back in to 1939, but a response to German successes in the west by early June when forces in the Baltic Republics were removed from subordination to neighbouring military districts and transferred to the direct command of the Commissar for Defence.[122] Forces to move in to the Baltic Republics were in fact concentrated fairly rapidly during the first half of June 1940, so that in excess of 500,000 personnel and nearly 4,000 tanks along with more than 2,500 aircraft were by the middle of June allocated to occupy the Baltic Republics along with NKVD rifle and border troops.[123] With little armour and few aircraft the peacetime armies of the Batlic Republics combined could field fewer than 75,000 personnel, and wartime mobilisation of all three to the limits of their capacities could not have allowed them to field the manpower being deployed against them on their borders.[124] Within days the Baltic Republics were fully occupied after only token resistance – perhaps the most significant being what might be deemed at worst minor skirmishes in the Estonian capital Tallinn. Soviet losses during the occupation of the Baltic Republics consisted, according to incomplete data, of 58 killed – of whom 15 drowned and 15 committed suicide with the remainder killed in 'accidents', and 158 wounded.[125] The occupations of the Baltic Republics were soon followed by their incorporations in to the Soviet Union as the Red Army set about constructing the facilities and defences on recently occupied territory for thousands of Red Army troops and their equipment in preparation for the 'inevitable' war with National Socialist Germany that at some point was bound to take place – but when?

9   Reform and the Road to War

The Red Army may have ultimately prevailed against the Finns, but its tactical and operational performance had neither impressed Stalin nor foreign observers. A British War Office publication of March 1940 noted many failings of the Red Army that had manifested themselves in Finland, where for example it suggested – and not inaccurately – that commanders had tended to show little initiative in unfamiliar situations, slavishly following training manuals even when inappropriate. The document also noted an almost 'child-like faith' in tanks, used 'in very large numbers in support of every major attack quite irrespective of whether the terrain is suitable for the action of such weapons'.[1] When examining the Soviet war against Finland, the German intelligence organisation *Fremde Heere Ost* identified similar issues, such as how a 'lack of initiative,and clumsy formulaic operations' had led to setbacks early in the war. In addition to supply problems, poor co-operation between arms was identified as a major issue and one that could not simply be compensated for by fielding significant numbers of tanks and heavy use of artillery. Nonetheless, the report concluded that the restoration of unitary command, measures to improve discipline and top-to-bottom improvements in education and training showed that the Red Army leadership was committed to dealing with these issues.[2] Certainly relatively well informed German observers were aware that in the light of the Finnish debacle the Red Army was trying to get its act together and improve combat effectiveness. *Fremde Heere Ost*'s subsequent handbook on the Soviet armed forces of 1 January 1941, although suggesting that transformation would take time, was far from writing off the Red Army as an opponent in the shorter term. Noting the shift in focus in training away from the large scale manoeuvres and exercises of previous years to a focus on training individual soldiers and officers that included attempts to foster an appreciation for the value of combined arms, it was clearly being suggested that despite the wide range of specific issues to be tackled from the low levels of initiative to inadequate artillery fire-control, the Red Army was likely to improve in capability. In the meantime the Red Army still drew strength from numbers – be that in equipment or its 'tough, resilient and brave soldiers' that were likely to offer stubborn local resistance on the defence.[3] Certainly for General of Cavalry Köstring, German military attaché in Moscow, even if he had noted in the late 1930s how the purges has impacted Soviet operational capabilities through the loss of experienced commanders, this was certainly not reason to write off the bulk of the Red Army that remained. Although 'the generally tough, undemanding, willing and brave soldier' was no longer the 'good *moujik*' or hardy peasant of the First World War, the Red Army man of 1940 had benefitted from 'cultural improvement' and a 'rise in intelligence'.[4] So at least some foreign observers were accurate in their assessments of the tactical and operational competence of the Red Army of 1940, and noted how attempts were being made to deal with at least some of these issues highlighted in Finland – of the seriousness of which more thoughtful members of the Soviet military elite were only too well aware. Where intelligence sources tended to be inaccurate was in underestimating Soviet resolve to make meaningful changes to the way the Red Army prepared for war with some haste – also not being aware of the new equipment that would give on average better-trained – or at least more appropriately trained – troops much better prospects in battle in the long term. Soviet secrecy may have hampered the functioning of the Red Army as shown in the previous chapter, but it also kept much information from potential enemies. Certainly on the eve of Operation 'Barbarossa', a *Fremde Heere Ost* report on the Soviet armoured forces could only note that 'our knowledge of the Russian armoured forces is sketchy [*lückenhaft*]' – certainly there would be some unpleasant surprises ahead for German forces in terms of Soviet equipment even if not immediately in its employment.[5] However, despite new equipment and more combat-orientated training, in the post-purge Soviet Union meaningful attempts to deal with the only limited initiative shown by commanders at all levels were lacking – and the cumbersome machine would be slow to respond to or often suppress what few flashes of inspiration were actually shown.

Serious attempts to rectify some of the issues that had emerged in Red Army performance in both Poland and Finland were heralded by a change in senior leadership. It is easy to make too much out of Voroshilov's removal from the post of People's Commissar for Defence in May 1940. One might assume that it was clear even to Stalin that Voroshilov was not the man to head the Red Army after the Finnish debacle and what by post-purge standards was the soul searching of the spring. Someone who was not as close to Stalin as Voroshilov would almost certainly have suffered some sort of humiliation for Red Army failure in

December 1939. Voroshilov however escaped overt criticism as he would continue to do so during the early phases of the Great Patriotic War, before Stalin finally ran out of patience with his obvious inability. Announcement of Marshal Timoshenko's promotion to People's Commissar for Defence on 7 May 1940 was not accompanied even by a veiled dressing down for Voroshilov, who van Dyke suggests was rather 'kicked upstairs... where his incompetence could do less harm' and became a deputy chairman of the Council of People's Commissars and chairman of its Defence Committee.[6] On 8 May *Pravda* simply printed the appropriate decrees of the Supreme Soviet without comment.[7] These decrees also saw Marshal Shaposhnikov, until now Chief of the General Staff, removed from his key post to become head of the Main Military Engineering Directorate with responsibility amongst other things for the construction of fortified regions on the Soviet Union's western borders.[8] Shaposhnikov was undoubtedly far more capable a figure than Voroshilov, one who, it should be recalled, had proposed a more robust initial invasion of Finland to that undertaken by Meretskov and in many ways been a voice of reason as Meretskov's forces became bogged down. The fact that the same day as being removed as Chief of Staff Shaposhnikov became a Marshal of the Soviet Union does not suggest disgrace, and in fact in July 1941 Stalin would once again make Shaposhnikov Chief of Staff. Indeed, the fact that Meretskov was appointed Chief of Staff in Shaposhnikov's place suggests, counter to van Dyke's above assertion, that performance in Finland was not the core motivation for personnel changes where it is difficult to envisage Meretskov's initial failures in Finland were seen in a positive light. Politically reliable commanders had nonetheless got the job done in the end, and there is perhaps some truth to Rzheshevskii's suggestion that, as Stalin made clear to Shaposhnikov, the latter was being removed in order to make it plain to the 'public' that lessons of the conflict had indeed been learned.[9] Meretskov's promotion may seem to run counter to this argument, but neither the Soviet public nor foreign observers were privy to debate on the eve of the invasion of Finland that highlighted if anything the new Chief of Staff's poor judgement compared to his predecessor. Voroshilov and Shaposhnikov had technically been in charge – their removal suggested change. Despite Stalin's assertion at the April 1940 command conference on the war in Finland that the experience of and traditions of the Civil War that were so important to Voroshilov, Budennii and the Red Army's senior leadership at the time of the Finnish conflict were of value, he made it plain that such credentials were 'completely inadequate' qualification for command in modern war.[10] Voroshilov and his Civil War cohort would nonetheless be given the chance to adjust to the requirements of modern warfare and not simply replaced because almost puppy-like loyalty and political reliability were still important requirements to serve Stalin in the immediate aftermath of the Great Purges. Stalin had made it clear in the same April speech that modern warfare required the mass use of aviation, tanks, mortars and sub-machine guns in addition to more traditional artillery, and then made one of the most conservative figures in the senior leadership of the Red Army, Kulik, Marshal of the Soviet Union the following month.[11] Kulik was hardly sufficiently capable to serve in upper leadership roles – not only was his competence in question but he was also a bully. In a damning paragraph in his 1963 memoirs, future Marshal of Artillery Nikolai Nikolaevich Voronov – after Finland Kulik's first deputy at the Main Artillery Directorate of the Red Army – recalled Kulik's love of the threatening phrase 'prison or a medal' that often accompanied orders. According to Voronov, Kulik – 'a disorganised man, who thought a lot of himself and considered his actions beyond fault [*nepogreshimii*]' – like many other post-purge leaders liked to rule by fear, and made the lives of subordinates even more difficult and fearful by issuing only vague orders.[12] Voronov was far from alone in noting Kulik's inability to organise – wartime head of the navy Nikolai Kuznetsov was first made aware of Kulik's competence or lack thereof in Spain, and later described him in his memoirs as someone 'who took a certain chaos [*sumatokh*] with him wherever he was sent'.[13] Voroshilov and Kulik were the two men who had worked particularly hard to destroy many of the positive aspects of the legacies of their purged comrades. Unfortunately Stalin's continued trust in such figures – based on their loyalty – would in many instances cost the Soviet Union dearly during the first months of the Great Patriotic War when they would be trusted with field commands on key axes. Fortunately at the very top of the Red Army command Timoshenko combined political acceptability with a certain degree of ability and oversaw reorganisation and reform that would at least push the development of the Red Army towards more effective use of its vast material and human resources.

One of the most significant changes to Red Army practice implemented under Timoshenko and in the light of experience in Finland was to attempt to actually train the Red Army for combat. Under Voroshilov the rhetoric of training for battle remained just that. The *akt* transferring the authority of People's Commissar for Defence from Voroshilov to Timoshenko contained some sharp criticism of Red Army training under Voroshilov where inadequately trained middle- and junior ranking commanders were deemed to have overseen tactical training for their units that bore little relevance to the sort of conditions that troops would face in actual combat.[14] But weeks after the transfer of authority to

Timoshenko detailed instructions for training that summer were issued under his name. Having started with mention of that favourite Stalinist explanation of the time for failure – namely discipline – the order went on to address the serious issues of co-operation between arms in battle, noting a lack of tactical competence in dealing with such elementary battlefield situations as clearing trenches, and the general inability of middle and lower ranking commanders to command. Command failure was deemed to be not only a product of inadequate competence, a particular problem for reservists, but also the inability of junior commanders to maintain their authorities and discipline in units. Senior and higher-level commanders were not let off the hook, where they shared some of the blame for poor co-ordination between arms – in part a product of poor staff work and limited use of the resources that headquarters could provide. Poor reconnaissance, inadequate discipline and organisational chaos in rear areas were all added to a catalogue of failings that was similar to what Voroshilov had railed about. Appropriate and regular combat-orientated training was to be at least a partial cure.[15]

(Left to centre) Marshal of the Soviet Union Timoshenko and Generals of the Army Zhukov and Meretskov observe manoeuvres of 99th Rifle Division in the L'vov region of the Kiev Special Military District in July 1940. That summer training was supposed to take place in conditions far closer to those that might be experienced in actual combat than had previously been the case. (RIA Novosti #53871)

Many memoirs and interviews of Red Army personnel of the period certainly suggest that training during 1940 and beyond had a much more obvious combat focus than had previously been the case. Former anti-aircraft gunner Ignatii Grigor'evich Mel'nikov noted in a post-Soviet interview how 'up to the Soviet-Finnish War of 1939–40 training was not conducted in particularly tough conditions' – something that changed afterwards.[16] Nikolai Nikolaevich Osintsev, also a junior anti-aircraft commander at the name, recalls how in the pre-war period his battery actually practiced relocation and redeployment and the rapid engagement of targets.[17] A significant range of problems had been iden-tified in Timoshenko's order on training – hardly for the first time – with the promise of verification of progress by September to motivate the implementation of a new training regime – with the possibility that the careers of commanders not up to the task would suffer.[18] For those with the ability, Timoshenko was undoubtedly aware that improvement in the authority of commanders would help them get the best out of subordin-ates and in particular the rank-and-file after the damage done to the reputation and authority of command cadres during the purges. Under Timoshenko's leadership all the way down the chain of command to the equivalent of NCOs there was to be an attempt through enhanced status, formal powers and training to improve the ability of commanders to effectively lead those under them.

The reintroduction of the rank of general was, as the replacement of the broader term 'commander' with 'officer' would be during the Great Patriotic War, a significant step back from revolutionary rhetoric. In order to enhance the authority and prestige of senior commanders revo-lutionary ideals would have to be sacrificed.[19] At the other end of the spectrum, the junior command ranks of junior sergeant, sergeant, senior sergeant and starshina were created as part of further revision of ranks in late 1940 in order to 'raise the level of responsibility of . . .and further increase the authority of junior command elements'. Rank-and-file Red Army men could distinguish themselves from their compatriots by earning the rank of *efreitor* – awarded to a Red Army man in his second year of service who would be able to provide basic instruction to new recruits.[20]

During the purges dual command between political and military com-manders – a transition away from which the regime had invested consid-erable time and effort – had been reintroduced. By August 1940, with the worst of the purging now in the past, and the command ranks 'consider-ably strengthened', unitary command could be reintroduced. Senior and middle-ranking commanders would, once again, have the authority to make command decisions on their own rather than sharing that authority with political commanders – commissars and politruks – who again became deputy commanders with a focus on political matters.[21] In February 1941 counter-intelligence within military units by the feared Special Sections was transferred to the NKO from the NKVD. Although the personnel involved remained largely the same, it seems more than likely that this shift was at least in part about the Red Army being seen to supervise itself. Certainly the Central Committee decree on the transfer suggested that it was 'associated with the strengthening of the Red Army and Navy' – and made sense in terms of coherence. Even if it made organisational sense earlier, the transfer was now viable thanks to 'the increase in the number of well-prepared command and political cadres committed to the tasks of the party of Lenin and Stalin'.[22]

Further strengthening commanders – and undermining both revolutionary ideals and rhetoric – was the revision of the Red Army 'temporary' disciplinary code that had been introduced in the relatively heady days of 1925. The tone of Section 6 of the new disciplinary code highlights how dramatic a change in the authority of commanders was being sought from the sort of dynamics that were prevalent between commanders and men during the 1920s and early 1930s described in Chapter 1. Section 6 of the new code for instance noted that 'in cases of disobedience, open opposition or ill-intentioned breaches of discipline and order the commander has the right to take all necessary coercive measures, all the way to the use of force and of firearms'.[23] Anti-aircraft gunner and junior commander Nikolai Nikolaevich Osintsev in a post-Soviet interview certainly suggested that discipline during Timoshenko's pre-war tenure as Commissar for Defence was 'harsh', recalling measures taken to deal with the problem of drunkenness.[24]

During 1940 therefore – formally at least – the authority of Red Army commanders increased – and they were engaged in what was hopefully a more meaningful training regime with their units and formations. Needless to say, the Red Army was not, and could not be transformed overnight. Inspection of the Western Military District during the late summer of 1940 did not suggest that the training of 'the individual warrior able to function at a high level' or 'the well organised, flexible and highly manoeuvrable small unit' was something that those responsible for training 'all levels of command' were taking seriously. Timoshenko went on to state how 'the old over simplifications, indulgences and low expectations continue to figure in the training of soldiers and small units'. Of the many failings identified at the tactical level, the concealment of defensive positions or their *maskirovka* – often identified during the Great Patriotic War as a Soviet strength by German personnel – was but one identified as still being poor despite apparent relative Soviet success in this regard at Khalkhin Gol. Command, control and co-ordination were poor at all levels of command – and poor reconnaissance left 'units functioning in the dark'.[25] Inspections of a number of military districts and the Far Eastern Front in the autumn also highlighted the same old issues – poor reconnaissance, co-ordination between arms, poor communications, and a general lack of initiative even if the situation was not described in such terms, an example in this instance being the failure of infantry commanders to 'quickly assess a situation and clearly set objectives on the spot'. Poor staff work was noted across the board – particularly for rifle regiments and battalions.[26] In January 1941 Timoshenko went to some lengths to make plain the 'poor operational preparation of upper-level commanders, field headquarters, Army and Front command and control organs, and especially aviation headquarters'.[27] Timoshenko's medicine for these ills was to be training and education focused on the practical – including as one might expect staff map-based exercises and those conducted in the field with real troops – alongside individual study and lectures.[28] In his memoirs future General-Colonel Leonid Mikhailovich Sandalov recalled the 'field and headquarters command exercises' that were conducted by 4th Army in Belorussia in late 1940 – including an operational-strategic staff map exercise or wargame led by deputy head of the General Staff General-Leitenant N.F.Vatutin, that ran alongside combined arms tactical field exercises involving artillery, sappers, infantry and tanks and live ammunition.[29] Unfortunately much of this was to take place in an environment where many to be doing the educating had little or no experience of what they were teaching given their rapid promotions. As noted earlier, numerous commanders had been in post for very little time – often having spent little time in lower command positions below their current one.[30] For the VVS the Russian historian A.G. Tsimbalov suggests that on the eve of the Great Patriotic War more than 46 per cent of commanders of the VVS for military districts, VVS formations and units had been in post for less than six months. The struggle to get the VVS in fighting shape will be discussed further later, with the VVS perhaps struggling more than other arms to do so. Many VVS commanders would be removed from their posts on the eve of war – with their replacements not necessarily in a better position to handle the issues facing them. As Tsimbalov documents, in late May 1941 the VVS command for the Moscow Military District was gutted as a result of a catalogue of failings that were not necessarily down to individual command failures.[31]

Timoshenko's demands for reform and transformation in 1940 and 1941 were considerable and not all commanders were up to the tasks in

hand. Particularly as the Red Army was expanding and reequipping, in
the aftermath of the purges, and where Timoshenko could hardly tackle
the key issue of political culture that encouraged commanders to slavishly
follow and wait for direction from above, the scope for change as dramatic as transformation was limited. The failure of commanders to show
initiative – in those instances where they had the knowledge and ability –
and the tendency for their superiors not only to discourage such initiative
but to micromanage their activities evident in Finland were as much
about broader political-cultural impediments as inadequate training
and formal authority. Red Army commanders were typically not only
unable but often simply unwilling to show the sort of leadership and
initiative in fluid circumstances in order to achieve results. If they did
meet objectives they consequently often did so only at terrible cost in
men and material as they pressed on with plans for circumstances that
had now changed rather than face charges of insubordination from
superiors who were fearful for their own skins. Timoshenko's May
1940 orders for training certainly noted how in the context of orders
from above that were often 'rushed and poorly conceived, lacking study
and analysis of circumstances' there was a tendency for 'unnecessary
interference on the part of senior commanders in the work of junior
ones'.[32] Timoshenko's pointing out of the problem was not however
going to lead to fundamental change. Head of the Navy Nikolai Kuznetsov certainly implies in his memoirs that Timoshenko's appointment –
along with Meretskov as Chief of the General Staff – did not bring the
sort of organisational transformation that was required, but whether
someone other than Timoshenko could have achieved more in peacetime
and with the limited time that ended up being available before the
German invasion is debateable.[33] Not only was the time available limited,
but Stalin and his entourage set the tone – and that tone had not changed
as much from that of the period of the Great Purges as might ideally have
been the case to promote what was required. Although repression of Red
Army commanders on fanciful charges of conspiracy had diminished
during 1939 and 1940, the repression continued right up into June
1941 and beyond. In the atmosphere of 'fear' and 'a lack of trust' of
early 1941 described by Georgii Zhukov to Soviet author and journalist
Konstantin Simonov, many more experienced commanders suffered the
wrath of Stalin and the NKVD.[34] In many instance their crime seems to
have been an air of independence lacking in some of their compatriots –
the sort of qualities required to push transformation further. Richagov,
Smushkevich and Shtern were – amongst others – all belatedly arrested
just prior to 'Barbarossa', and executed as the Wehrmacht advanced on
Moscow.[35] As testimony of those such as wartime head of the Navy

Nikolai Kuznetsov suggests – where Kuznetsov for example is typically credited with a certain competence and was well acquainted with many such figures given the geographical diversity of his appointments from Spain to the Soviet Far East – the issue with those such as Smushkevich and Shtern was certainly not one of relative competence.[36]

Even if in the post-purge climate described earlier a cultural shift towards a more flexible command culture in the Red Army was not on the cards, there was much in addition to strengthening the authority of commanders and improving training that could be done to improve Red Army effectiveness. Where, in the immediate aftermath of the Great Purges, Voroshilov and his associates had made certain organisational matters and the doctrine that informed them into highly political issues, soon after Finland it was acceptable to return to the doctrinal and organisational direction established by Tukhachevskii and others who had been purged. One of the most significant organisational decisions that had been pushed through in the anti-Tukhachevskii climate after the purges by Voroshilov – supported by Kulik and Shaposhnikov – had been the abolition of the mechanised corps that it had been envisaged would allow the Red Army to exploit a breakthrough of enemy defences beyond the tactical to operational depth.[37] Voroshilov's November 1939 report to political leaders that incorporated details on their abolition had pointed out, not entirely without foundation, that the 'mechanised' corps had been 'unwieldy formations to manage'.[38] It is certainly debateable whether the Red Army, even prior to the purges, was up to making effective use of formations with 560 tanks in each, with inadequate means of command and control and insufficient attention being paid to logistics.[39] However, the tank brigades created with anything from 238 tanks for those equipped with the BT series to a staggering 538 for those equipped with the T-26 were hardly the solution. Such brigades did not of course mean a lack of concentration of armour, where the T-26-equipped brigades dwarfed their German divisional counterparts in terms of number of vehicles, but were intended to be deployed in support of rifle forces. Consequently the new tank brigades did not have the organic infantry and artillery components for independent action, and were not intended to operate alone in the enemy rear. In the longer term that mobile combined-arms striking power was to be provided by ten mechanised rifle divisions that would 'be fully equipped with mechanised means for towing artillery and integral automobile transport for the conveyance of infantry'. Four tank battalions would provide a total of 240 tanks for each such division.[40] The folly of this reform with its heavy emphasis on a mass of tanks for the tactical support of rifle divisions became apparent after German successes in Poland, where the German

Panzer divisions were clearly not shackled to the infantry. In the Panzer divisions in which German tanks were concentrated motorised infantry clearly supported the tanks in the pursuit of operational goals that were not limited to the sort of depths to which Soviet infantry supported by the tank brigades would effectively have been limited. Although as the Second World War progressed the importance of infantry being supported at the tactical level by armour organic to their units was to be appreciated by all major powers, and indeed late in the war Red Army armoured formations would be giving up armoured units for the direct support of infantry units during the breakthrough phase of an offensive, the issue here was the fact that the reforms essentially abandoned the aspiration for armour-led operations at operational depth.

Having barely scrapped the old mechanised corps, in the summer of 1940 the Red Army reintroduced them. Within weeks a new model for the mechanised corps had been introduced that would provide each corps with two tank divisions (instead of two brigades in the previous incarnation) and a motorised infantry division (instead of a single rifle-machine gun brigade) – nearly doubling the number of tanks, including those with the motorised infantry division, to over 1,000. Each tank division would be provided, as of 6 July 1940, with a total of 386 tanks in two regiments, each with a battalion of heavy, two battalions of medium and a single battalion of flamethrower-equipped tanks in addition to 108 armoured cars. In addition each tank division would be provided with a motorised rifle regiment of three battalions well provided for with mortars, machine guns and sub-machine guns and self-loading rifles and with its own six-gun regimental artillery battery. The tank division would also include an artillery regiment, anti-aircraft *divizion*, reconnaissance battalion, bridging battalion and service units. Alongside the more than a thousand tanks and the infantry, the new corps would include a motorcycle regiment, a road transport battalion [*dorozhnii*] and a signals battalion – along with two light bomber and a single fighter regiment. In all the Red Army was to have eight mechanised corps and two independent tank divisions.[41]

In December 1940 a conference of senior and higher Red Army commanders took place to discuss progress in the development of the Red Army, and provide input into future direction. Understandably the role of the mechanised corps was discussed at the conference, and a particularly sound assessment of their strengths and weaknesses was provided by General-Major M.I. Potapov, commander of 4th Mechanised Corps of the Kiev Special Military District. The issue of close support from the air will be discussed later – here we will focus on issues on the ground. To Potapov, the divide between theory and practice for the mechanised corps was clear, where existing wheeled transport was insufficient to allow motorised infantry to keep up with the tanks – and indeed for their resupply. Existing artillery tractors – here the STZ-5 – were similarly inadequate for keeping up with armoured units. His suggestion that infantry train to ride on tanks as pioneered – somewhat disastrously – in Spain would of course become practice in wartime, and in many ways ultimately a combination of all-wheel drive US-supplied Lend-Lease trucks and Soviet-built assault guns would provide some of the off-road – or poor-road – mobility for fire support that was desired. Potapov's suggestion that the motorcycle regiment of the corps was only of value on its own when chasing down an enemy in disarray would be something German forces would come to appreciate as the war progressed. Soviet perceptions of the value of independent motorcycle units were based on their known use by German forces in Poland and France, without knowledge of the losses such units took. His suggestion that such motorcycle units be combined with tanks and armoured cars in order to provide a deep reconnaissance asset and mobile reserve predicts late-war Soviet practice in forming forward detachments – provided by that point with US-supplied scout cars and half-tracks where possible instead of relying on motorcycles.[42] The mechanised corps of 1940 was however a long way from both the theory of the mid-1930s and the practice of 1945 – and yet many Soviet military leaders seemed blissfully unaware of or willing to accept their inadequacies as long as they contained huge numbers of tanks. In many ways the mechanised corps were once again the gigantism of the Stalinist era applied to the Red Army with little attention paid to utility.

Not only did the new colossal mechanised corps not have the range of vehicles required to function as intended, but as Zakharov notes in his memoirs, these new mechanised corps would be even more difficult to command than their predecessors without the necessary communications equipment and suitably experienced commanders.[43] The lack of communications equipment on the eve of 'Barbarossa', and particularly radios, was an ongoing issue for the Red Army. The *akt* transferring authority at the NKO to Timoshenko back in May 1940 portrayed the situation regarding communications in both Poland and Finland as one where 'reliable and uninterrupted' communications were not maintained as a result of both poor equipment and organisation.[44] In February 1941 Timoshenko ordered better use of available radio communications by the Red Army, having declared radio the 'core means of communication for all arms', where unfortunately 'certain commanders of units, formations and heads of headquarters to this point have not grasped the situation and taken the necessary measures to master the art of command and control of troops by radio'.[45] Availability of equipment – regardless of quality – was however poor. As of 1 January 1941 provision of the regimental 5-AK set had not reached 50 per cent for the Red Army as a whole based on requirements upon mobilisation – and it was expected that only 57 per cent provision would be achieved by the beginning of 1942.[46] In May 1941 provision of radios for the crucial Kiev Special Military District for example was often still less than 50 per cent for many key types – 41 per cent for the 11-AK, 41 per cent for the RAF and 48 per cent for the 5-AK set for example.[47]

Equally serious to the absence of sufficient communications equipment – an absence that was stark even before the rapid expansion of the Red Army undertaken during 1940 and into 1941– was the fact that logistical provision for all arms, and not just the mechanised formations, was inadequate. The inadequacy of logistical provision had been demonstrated in both Poland and Finland. Despite the extent to which logistical inadequacies inhibited frontline operations, logistical provision does not seem to have received the attention it deserved even if it seems in 1940 to have become a more prominent issue than it had been the previous year. In his December 1940 comments on the effectiveness of mechanised corps, General-Major Potapov at least noted the issue of logistics – a theme notably absent in many previous discussions concerning concentrated armoured forces.[48] Certainly the *akt* accompanying Timoshenko's appointment to People's Commissar for Defence had pointed out many inadequacies in rear area provision – including for example the fact that the Red Army lacked the means to transport and deliver the necessary fuel from supply bases to units, but the Red Army was overall still fixated on weapons and such prosaic needs such as fuel tankers would certainly lag behind weapons systems in the battle for factory capacity.[49]

On a more positive note, at least the Red Army was receiving new equipment in 1940 – weapons systems that would be produced in large numbers during the war and which would allow the Red Army to halt the Wehrmacht before Moscow and counterattack before playing an even more prominent role in the offensive operations of late 1942. New artillery – rather than reconditioned Tsarist-era pieces – was equipping an increasing number of units. The 1939 76.2 mm divisional gun or USB – 1,170 of which the Red Army had received before the war – was an excellent artillery piece with for the time good anti-tank potential even with high explosive rounds. Retrospectively premature curtailment of its production before the war did not take into account the losses that the Red Army would suffer during the summer of 1941. By the middle of the war the USB would be replaced by the lighter ZIS-3, but by the standards of 1941 the USB was about as good as it got for a multi-role artillery piece.[50] Stalin's personal involvement in forwarding the production of mortars now meant that in June 1941 the Red Army had not only 34,622 of light 50 mm mortars for direct fire support of infantry units, but 13,569 of the heavier 82 mm mortars.[51] Although the situation for anti-tank artillery was less favourable than that for field artillery as will be discussed later, new tanks were both entering production and in development – vehicles that it was planned would replace the multitude of types in Red Army service that had been shown through experience in Spain, Poland and Finland to be inadequately armed and armoured. In fact, 1940 and early 1941 saw the development and introduction into service of many of the weapons systems that are often used to symbolise the Soviet war effort – T-34 and KV-1 tanks, the Katiusha rocket system and Il-2 Sturmovik ground attack aircraft.

The inadequacies of the slow biplanes and fighter aircraft being used for ground attack in the late 1930s had been obvious from the early phases of the Spanish Civil War where not only enemy fighters but also ground fire from small arms upwards took their toll on the I-15s, -16s, R-5s and derivatives used in such a role. At the end of January 1938 the aircraft designer S.V. Il'iushin had apparently written to Stalin with the suggestion that he design an armoured ground attack aircraft with a speed of 400 kmh at sea level and range of up to 800 km, and the first prototype of the BSh-2 made its first flight on 2 October 1939. Performance of this two-seater was not however as hoped for – speed 362 km/h at sea level and operational range 618 km during state trials in April 1940. Unacceptable to the Red Army, modifying the design meant that state trials of the new aircraft, now designated Il-2, did not take place until 28 February 1941. The new aircraft was a single-seater, offering better protection and visibility for the pilot, better armament having two 20 mm cannon and two machine guns rather than just four machine guns, and better performance and slightly improved operational range despite increased weight – maximum speed was now 419 kmh at sea level and operational range 638 km. Preparations for series production were already underway in February 1941, with the first production aircraft flown on 10 March 1941.[52] Few were in service in June 1941 – a total of only 249 had been manufactured by the outbreak of hostilities – and only eighteen had reached frontline units where given the fact that five were in the Pribaltic, eight in the Western and five in the Kiev Military District they were probably being used for familiarisation and training.[53] The single-seater version of the aircraft would prove vulnerable to fighter attack where fighter escort was often lacking. Although Il-2 losses would be extremely high by Western standards throughout the war, the mid-war two-seater version produced in staggering quantities would provide the

Red Army in due course with the sort of flying artillery envisaged in notions of 'Deep Battle' in the mid-1930s.

Also produced in staggering quantities during the war in the case of the lighter of the two, even if few were available in June 1941, were the two tanks that caused the Wehrmacht such consternation during the summer of 1941 despite their availability in such limited numbers. The heavy KV-1 has already been mentioned in Chapter 8 having been tested in combat in Finland, although it is the medium T-34 that became so iconic for the Soviet military machine during the Great Patriotic War.

Whether advocates of a more independent breakthrough role for tanks, or more inclined towards seeing the tank as a vehicle for infantry support, there was widespread agreement amongst senior Soviet military leaders in the late 1930s of the need for at least some tanks with better armour than those that had been employed in Spain. As early as April 1938 the Main Military Soviet had determined that the Red Army needed a breakthrough tank with armour able to resist anti-tank fire from up to 47 mm anti-tank guns at all ranges, ideally with a diesel engine, a main armament of a 76 mm gun with an initial projectile velocity of 560 metres per second, two 47 mm guns with co-axial machine guns, a speed of 25–35 km/h, range 200–250 km and no more than 55 tons.[54] The requirement for two 45 mm guns as secondary armament was fortunately subsequently dropped – apparently after Stalin had personally intervened during a meeting of the Main Military Soviet on 9 December 1938 and suggested that removing at least one, and possibly two turrets from one of the two competing designs – the SMK (Sergei Mironovich Kirov) – would allow improvement in armour.[55] From this discussion apparently emerged a new set of expectations that would lead to the KV-1 (Kliment Voroshilov-1) – with the session of the Main Military Soviet leaving the requirement that in addition to a two-turreted version, a prototype of a single-turret breakthrough tank of 30–32 tons and also with armour proof against 47 mm anti-tank guns be made available by 1 November 1939.[56] A single-turreted prototype – weighing in at more than 40 tons – was available for trials at the end of September, initially armed with a 45 mm gun co-axially mounted with the 76 mm main armament – the former dropped for a machine gun before the prototype first saw action in Finland. On 17 December 1939 the KV-1 had seen action in Karelia – along with the SMK and competing T-100 multi-turreted prototypes – all manned in part by factory personnel.[57] The KV-1 was not only better armoured, with a maximum of 75 mm of armour compared to 60 mm for the SMK, but presented a smaller target and could reach the same maximum speed of 35 km/h. Two days after first seeing action the KV-1 was formally accepted for service by the Red Army – with an order for the production of 40 vehicles issued for 1940 at the same time, a figure increased to 230 in May 1940.[58] Series production only began however in the summer of 1940 after the design had been both improved and simplified, but during the year as a whole 243 tanks were eventually produced.[59] By 1 February 1941 the total number of KV-series tanks produced had reportedly reached 273.[60]

Development of what would become the T-34 was taking place concurrently with what became the KV-1. The T-34 stemmed from an April 1938 requirement for a fast tank capable of 50–60 km/h with armour 'in vulnerable locations' of 30 mm, with a diesel engine and range of 250–300 km, 45 mm main armament with two machine guns and a weight of 13–14 tons for a straightforward tracked version, 15–16 tons for one capable of running on wheels.[61] By the 9–10 December 1938 session of the Main Military Soviet the A-20 had emerged in two formal variants, a 16.5 ton version (A-20) capable of running on wheels and with a 45mm gun – a clear development of the BT-series – or a solely tracked version of similar weight with a 76 mm gun (A-20G or A-32), both with diesel engines and with armour proof against 12.7 mm rounds at all distances.[62] Apparently the survival of the solely tracked version owed much to Stalin's intervention, where the conservatism of the new Red Army elite was reflected in the fact that many saw little need to pursue the A-32 and move too far beyond the tried and tested BT-series and give up the expectation of movement by wheel and track, despite the fact that the former added complexity for a little used feature. The simplification and weight saving afforded by producing a track-only tank allowed however for the A-32 to have a maximum of 30 mm armour compared to only 20 mm for the A-20.[63] Prototypes of both were ready by May 1939, and state trials and resulting discussion of the merits of the two versions by a state commission had by the end of the summer led to the recommendation for an up-armoured version of the A-32. With experience in Finland in particular highlighting the weak armour of much of the Red Army tank park the heavier A-32 project won through, and on the same day as the KV-1 – 19 December 1939 – it was accepted for service with an initial order for 220 tanks to be produced during 1940. This was in fact before prototypes of the T-34 were even available. Two prototypes of the T-34 were ready for the beginning of March 1940, and series production then began at Factory Number 183 in Khar'kov in June, and at the Stalingrad Tractor Factory during the autumn.[64] By this point the T-34 weighed in at a relatively hefty 26.5 tons, but now with sloped armour up to 45 mm. It also had a maximum speed of 55 km/h despite its heavy armament and armour, thanks to its 500 hp diesel engine, and its wide tracks limited ground pressure.[65] The first series production T-34s were received by the Red Army in September 1940, although the T-34 was not, and certainly not at this point, without a host of deficiencies that would be expected of a weapons system developed and introduced into service in such a short space of time. Moving from prototype to mass production proved far from straightforward, and an increase in orders for the Khar'kov factory from the initial 220 tanks to 600 during 1940 would prove optimistic – during 1940 a total of 117 T-34s was produced by Factory Number 183.[66] By February 1941 the total produced had reportedly reached only the same figure as for the KV-series – 273.[67] Certainly as Ulanov and Shein discuss in some detail, many flaws in early T-34s that fought in the summer of 1941 – from poor radio equipment where provided to localised vulnerabilities in their armoured protection and flaws in their optical systems – would take well into the Great Patriotic War to mitigate.[68] Although the T-34s available in the summer of 1941 were less capable than their 1942 successor, nonetheless even when used poorly they proved an unpleasant surprise for the Wehrmacht.

Finally, of those weapons often seen to symbolise the Soviet war effort, the Katiusha rocket system – the initial variant using the M-13 rocket – was also developed prior to the Great Patriotic War. Development of a rocket or RS (*reaktivnii snariad*) system for ground forces stemmed from the development of aerial rockets such as the RS-82 – that had been first used at Khalkhin Gol in air-air combat – and air-ground RS-132. From the latter in 1939 emerged the M-13 rocket for ground-ground use, launched from what would become the BM-13 launcher – the launch system mounted on a ZIS-6 lorry. During 1940 six launchers were constructed by the Rocket Scientific Research Institute for trials, and only in February 1941 did the Main Artillery Directorate order a trial production run of 40 BM-13 launchers for 1941, with full series production ordered on 21 June 1941, after the weapons system had been demonstrated to notables including Marshal Timoshenko and by then Chief of the General Staff General G.K. Zhukov but days earlier.[69] Development of the BM-13 and M-13 was arguably slower than for the KV-1 and T-34 because military figures, and indeed Stalin, were not sufficiently convinced of the value of the weapon to prioritise its development as would be the case early in the war. Marshal Kulik, as head of the Main Artillery Directorate, seems not to have made particular efforts to promote the system prior to the war after Stalin had given the nod for further investigation in late 1939.[70] In his memoirs, Zhukov was happy to point a finger in the direction of Main Artillery Directorate and Kulik for not appreciating the value of the weapons system earlier.[71] However, the development of the 'Katiusha' seems also to have suffered from the

suspicions and political violence of the late 1930s and early 1940s – its
'proving' in June 1941 perhaps for example saving some of those involved
in its development from the NKVD.[72]

All of these weapons systems became effective elements of the Soviet
arsenal with time, when refined, and when used *en masse* – even if often
flawed early versions were not available in significant enough quantities
during the summer and autumn of 1941 to make a significant difference.
Nonetheless, in 1940 and early 1941 the prospects for the Soviet tank
park and rocket artillery were good – not so however in the short term for
the development of Soviet airpower, despite progress with the Il-2. Not
only in the realm of communications did the Red Army lag behind
foreign powers and namely Germany, but also in the development of
fighter aircraft as already apparent in Chapter 6. Having produced perhaps the best monoplane fighter in service in large numbers in the mid-
1930s in the I-16, by 1940 the I-16 was looking out of date. However, the
next generation of Soviet fighter aircraft was slow in development during
the late 1930s and then rushed as the new decade began. These aircraft
suffered from the relative inadequacy of Soviet aero engine development,
and the most numerous new type, the MiG-3, was arguably designed and
entered production without a clear conception of why it was actually
needed in the large numbers planned given that the VVS was very much
orientated towards the support of ground forces and the MiG-3 was a
high-altitude interceptor. The suggestion by V.A. Belokon' that the
progress of the MiG-3 (developed from the I-200) project owed much
to the possibility of war with Great Britain during late 1939 and first half
of 1940 in particular is certainly intriguing – and plausible.[73] The MiG-3
suffered from poor performance at the low altitudes it would typically be
required to operate at, poor firepower and proved extremely difficult for
less experienced pilots to fly – resulting in many accidents. Nonetheless,
Soviet desperation for new aircraft types meant that it moved through
operational trials to mass production rapidly leaving many unresolved
issues, the resolution of which often led to worse rather than better
performance. Operational aircraft in the early summer of 1941 had to be
worked on by brigades of workers from the factories in order to iron out
problems.[74] By 22 June 1,289 MiG-3 had been produced – making it the
most numerous of the new fighter types. Also available – at least having
been produced – by 22 June 1941 were 322 LaGG-3 and 335 Yak-1
fighters.[75] As of 27 May 1941 however only 158 LaGG-3 for example
had been formally handed over to the VVS, from which only two units had
received aircraft – 37 with 24th Fighter Air Regiment and two with 19th
Fighter Air Regiment. Most of those supposedly handed over remained at
the factory 'in the process of being properly finished [*v protsesse dodelki*]'.

Those with field units were riddled with problems.[76] The LaGG-3 (developed from the I-301) ended up in service after similarly rushed development – with problems being experienced with production aircraft having actually been identified prior to the decision to mass produce. Enthusiasm for production of the aircraft has been seen as relating more to the fact that it was manufactured using a significant amount of wood rather than 'strategically valuable materials'.[77] Perhaps the best of the bunch was the Yak-1 (initially I-26), which despite the inevitable range of issues one might expect with a project that saw mass production initiated before many flaws in the operational trial aircraft had been ironed out, was apparently easy to fly and to convert to from the I-16. Nonetheless, even the Yak-1 was inferior to the Bf 109F in Luftwaffe service to a large extent because of the weakness of its engine rather than the basic design.[78]

Despite issues with the development of fighter aircraft to match the Bf 109F, in terms of tanks, artillery and small arms the Red Army was receiving weapons that were overall at least as good as if not better than those that would be fielded by the Wehrmacht during the summer and autumn of 1941. To a large extent this was due to the acceptance of the need for increased armour and firepower – needs to a large extent identified thanks to the small wars of the late 1930s and 1940. However, despite the fact that the Soviet Union was ramping up production – increasing working hours, curtailing labour freedoms and moving towards what might reasonably be seen as a war footing – Soviet industry was far from able to keep up with the absurd demands being placed on it by the Soviet leadership.[79]

In terms of the provision of weapons in order to meet the requirements of current tables of organisation and equipment, the Soviet Union was struggling throughout 1940 and moving into 1941 with what was a colossal task. For example, there was a vast gulf between production of both the KV-1 and T-34 during 1940 and demand, where the new mechanised corps from July 1940 were supposed to be provided each with a total 546 KV-1 and T-34 tanks – each tank division having sixty-three KV-1 and 210 T-34. The nine mechanised corps, two independent tank divisions, twenty-eight independent tank brigades and tank units of infantry divisions planned during the second half of 1940 were to require a total of 6,354 heavy and medium KV- and T-34 tanks.[80] On 1 February 1941 many formations had yet to receive a single KV-series or T-34 tank. Those that had been received by the Red Army by 1 February – 240 KV-series and 183 T-34 – were concentrated in the military districts of the western Soviet Union, with the Kiev Special Military District holding the lion's share or 104 KV-series and 115 T-34. Alongside these new vehicles hundreds of outdated and often worn out tanks continued to serve, with for example 546 BT-2 and 1,742 BT-5 on strength for the Red Army as a whole.[81] As Bagramian noted in his memoirs, these tanks that exclusively equipped some of the later mechanised corps were 'no longer in production, spare parts for them were almost unavailable and every serious breakdown meant, as a rule, that the vehicle went out of service for good. Troops were supposed to train with these vehicles until receipt of KV and T-34 tanks'.[82] The breakdown of such vehicles in the event of having to move was far from unusual. In the case of such tanks of 4th Mechanised Corps, ordered by the commander of the Kiev Special Military District, General Kirponos to deploy to their concentration areas one night in late May 1941 as part of 'training', there were, according to future Marshal I.Kh. Bagramian, a significant number of breakdowns. The commander of the tank division concerned protested when challenged, stating that those T-26 and BT-series tanks that broke down were training tanks, although this understandably met with little sympathy from Kirponos. To the unfortunate commander of the tanks, Bagramian recalls Kirponos exclaiming, 'Why Colonel, is your unit in such disarray? With tanks breaking down on the march, what will happen in battle!?'.[83] The colonel concerned did not of course decide upon the scope to which he was provided with field repair resources or indeed spare parts – the Mobile Repair Bases of the Great Patriotic War were yet to come, and as head of the Main Auto-Armour Board of the Red Army General Fedorenko noted in January 1941 the fact that 'the entire repair system is based on the sending of vehicles to industrial factories in the depths of the country for repair' was a poor solution to the problem of repair in operational and wartime circumstances. Units didn't even receive sufficient spares for day-day maintenance.[84] Hence, although according to figures for 1 June 1941 about 10 per cent of Soviet tanks were deemed to require overhaul at central repair facilities or factories, and might be deemed along with a similar percentage of tanks requiring repair at military district level to have been not fit for employment, some of the approximately 16,080 tanks requiring day-to-day servicing and light repairs were also most probably not likely to have been ready to meet the Wehrmacht, where 8,383 of these vehicles were in the western military districts. Nonetheless, this still left the Red Army with 2,157 fully functioning and essentially recently manufactured tanks and a significant proportion of the 8,383 tanks requiring servicing and light repairs with field units in the western districts ready, on paper at least, to meet the enemy as of 1 June 1941.[85] However, as units moved up to the border as tensions rose, the number of serviceable tanks would inevitably decline further, and Soviet problems were of course not limited to vehicle serviceability.

For the tanks that were available, and indeed serviceable, munitions were in short supply, and particularly armour piercing rounds for the guns of the T-34 and KV-1. Certainly the 76 mm guns of the latest tanks and field guns could not rely on high explosive rounds in combat with enemy tanks that had been up armoured in the light of experience in 1940. Soviet production of 76 mm armour piercing rounds had been extremely limited prior to 1940, in which year of 150,000 ordered only 28,000 were delivered. Even in 1941, by 2 June of 400,000 76 mm armour piercing rounds ordered only 1,18,000 had apparently been delivered.[86] The 33rd Tank Division of the Western Special Military District reported on 18 June 1941 that for 76 mm regimental and tank guns it had only 3 per cent of the stipulated requirement for munitions, even if by this point it had 100 per cent for 7.62 mm, mortar and 45 mm rounds.[87] As of 29 April 1941 for every 76 mm gun on a KV-series tank of the Kiev Special Military District there were only twenty-five armour piercing rounds available, and for T-34s only thirteen. The 76 mm guns of the district's rifle divisions had only six rounds a piece.[88] The need for more 76 mm armour-piercing rounds was apparently particularly acute where the 45 mm anti-tank and tank guns, of the latter of which the Red Army had more than 15,000 of the 1937 and earlier 1932 version at the beginning of the war,[89] were increasingly being shown to be less effective than no doubt hoped against the heavier German tanks such as the Panzer III and IV. An October 1940 report to Deputy People's Commissar for Defence Marshal Kulik stressed that the '45 mm tank and anti-tank gun Obr. 37 with an armour-piercing round weighing 1.435 kg with an initial velocity of of 760 m/s penetrates armour of contemporary quality angled at 30 degrees from the vertical as follows: 30 mm of armour… at a distance of 1,000 m and 40 mm of armour…only at a distance of 150 m'.[90] One can assume here that the ammunition being used was of good quality, for problems with munitions – and particularly anti-tank rounds – did not stop with quantity. The quality of many rounds available in relatively large numbers such as for the 45 mm guns left much to be desired. As noted in Chapter 6, German troops had discovered in Spain that Soviet 45 mm tank guns did not have the predicted penetrative capabilities in part because of relatively poor quality anti-tank rounds that greatly reduced the distance at which the armours of German tanks could be penetrated. Indeed, a German assessment of 30 March 1939 that claimed that Soviet armour-piercing shells could only penetrate 40 mm of armour plate at a range of 100 metres was close to the October 1940 Soviet assessment.[91] The problem with poor quality rounds – thanks no doubt to the need to rely on stocks of poor quality ammunition – had not gone away by 1941.[92] On the assumption that Germany was producing heavy tanks along the lines of the T-34 and KV-1 Marshal Kulik sought to cancel production of 45–76 mm guns in early 1941 with a view to the Soviet Union switching production to more powerful 107 mm guns – in the first instance developing a tank variant. In this instance Stalin – the final arbiter in decisions that he didn't particularly at this stage always grasp – apparently sided with Kulik against the protestations of People's Commissar for Armaments B.L. Vannikov, apparently influenced by the fact that the calibre of the new gun proposed by Kulik – 107 mm – was the same as a field piece of the Civil War era. Vannikov had apparently believed that use of the already available 85 mm anti-aircraft gun would have made better sense – and indeed when heavier German tanks did appear in late 1942 it was this gun that was provided for the KV-85, SU-85 and T-34/85 variant. Shortly after the outbreak of the war the decision to cancel production of 45 mm guns – along with 76 mm guns – was reversed in the light of the heavy losses of anti-tank guns in the border regions where more than half of Soviet stocks – 7,520 out of 15,468 – had been concentrated.[93] Certainly it made sense at a time of dire need to produce the 45 mm anti-tank gun for which production could be resumed quickly and which was effective against most German tanks as well as having an infantry support role with high explosive rounds – than developing a new weapon and having to produce ammunition for it. Indeed, the improved 1942 version of this gun would serve for the remainder of the war thanks to its greater velocity with standard anti-tank rounds for it and in 1942 a sub-calibre [podkalibernii] round.[94] The October 1940 report on the penetrative capabilities of Soviet anti-tank guns cited earlier also suggested that in the face of 40 mm armour the available 76 mm guns – Obr. 02/1930, L-11, F-32 and F-34, as the 45 mm guns, were 'unable to successfully combat medium and heavy tanks with armour of more than 50 mm' – no doubt providing stimulus not only for the abortive shift to 107 mm calibre but also for the production of the 57 mm ZIS-2 anti-tank gun.[95] The 57 mm ZIS-2 was not in service when the war began but 371 would be produced by the end of 1941, and was designed to be able to penetrate the armour of heavy tanks like the KV-1. With ammunition being produced for this gun from scratch there would not be the same quality issues that affected stocks of 45 mm ammunition produced in the 1930s. In June 1941, however the 45 mm Anti-Tank Gun Obr. 1937 was the principal dedicated anti-tank weapon of the Red Army and more than capable of dealing with the tanks that the Wehrmacht was actually fielding, supported by the anti-tank rifles being introduced that were still potent against the lighter German tanks. Additionally 37 mm and 85 mm anti-aircraft guns were also slated for anti-tank roles in which the latter was a potent if less than mobile weapon where the Red Army was short of suitable tractors, and if used in an anti-tank role they would then not be available for air defence. In the spring of 1941 it was decreed that ten anti-tank artillery brigades for the High Command Reserve be formed that would rely heavily on these anti-aircraft guns with 48 85 mm anti-aircraft guns in each, but their formation had not been completed prior to the outbreak of war in part because of a shortage of tractors.[96] In June 1941 the Red Army certainly did not want for anti-tank weapons even if in some instances suitable munitions were in short supply.

Worse however in many ways than for many munitions was the situation with fuels and lubricants that could prevent functioning tanks – even if with inadequate munitions – from actually engaging the enemy. The 33rd Tank Division of the Western Special Military District reported for example that for 18 June it had only 15 per cent supply for 1st grade petrol and 4 per cent for automobile fuel, and for diesel fuel it had 0 per cent.[97] The situation for 33rd Tank Division was not as bad as it got – 31st Tank Division of the Pribaltic Military District had it even worse with only 2 per cent of required automobile fuel and no diesel.[98] In both instances the availability of supply vehicles for fuels and lubricants was under 10 per cent, although both had relatively plentiful supplies of steel drums even if little to fill them – 31st Tank Division having 204 per cent of requirement![99] Aviation fuel production was inadequate for growing needs – and according to the Russian historian M.A. Bobrov, only 61 of 155 aerodromes of the Western Special Military District were equipped with fuel storage tanks (open type) on 22 June 1941 that were required for effective storage of that fuel that was available. Storage in drums apparently led to significant fuel wastage.[100]

The supply crisis had certainly been exacerbated by the Red Army's move forward into territory that had been occupied from September 1939 through to the summer of 1940. Although describing the training taking place from the tactical through to operational-strategic levels of command, future General-Colonel L.M. Sandalov noted in his memoirs how in the autumn of 1940 an unusually dry and warm period in Belorussia allowed 'all units of the army to engage in construction work' – much of which was required because of the forward deployment of much of the Red Army into recently occupied territory.[101] For the VVS the move required the construction of new airbases – of 626 of which in the western military districts 135 were undergoing 'reconstruction' and 141 under construction on 22 June 1941. The supply situation, the move of Soviet forces westwards and shortages of aviation fuel undoubtedly limited the scope for aircrew training – as did technical issues with the new types. By 22 June 1941 the VVS of the western border military districts could theoretically field 1,448 aircraft that were new types (Yak-1, MiG-3, LaGG-3, Pe-2 and Il-2), but only 208 crews had actually been retrained to fly these types – of whom four crews were trained for combat missions in either difficult weather or at night.[102]

Also moving forward were the fortifications that were supposed to provide the necessary cover along with screening forces – rifle formations covering mechanized forces – to allow the Red Army time to gather strength in the event of enemy attack and deliver a counterstrike. Future Marshal of Artillery N.D. Iakovlev had this to say about these fortified districts in his memoirs:

As a result of my service in the Belorussian and Kiev military districts I knew such fortified districts as the Polotskii, ... very well. Up to 1940 each of these had a number of machine-gun battalions, artillery units and corresponding headquarters. Troops of the fortified districts were in general well-trained and had detailed fire-plans prepared...[103]

After the Red Army moved westwards in September 1939 the construction of new fortified districts was started on the new border, and the old fortified districts to the rear were stripped of personnel. In late 1939 the 9th, 10th and 11th Independent Machine-Gun Battalions manned the Polotsk Fortified District – with these three battalions subsequently collapsed into two, one of which – the 9th – was subsequently transferred along with the communications battalion to the new Grodno Fortified District in August 1940. In October the Polotsk and Sebezh Fortified Districts were merged, and manned by a total of two independent artillery-machine gun and one independent machine gun battalion.[104] Iakovlev was certainly convinced that having at least one line of completed and appropriately manned defences would have been of value, acknowledging the limitations of such fortified lines. In his memoirs, he suggested that:

It was a big mistake that a situation existed where on the old border units that had been based there for many years were removed with almost all their weapons (a certain proportion of weapons were left behind) and the fortified districts mothballed.[105]

Whilst the Soviet Union was utilising some of its finite resources in order to move fortifications westwards, by the spring of 1941 more effort was undoubtedly being made to mobilise Red Army reservists and bring rifle and mechanised units up to strength as the Red Army expanded. Sometime around 12 February 1941 a new Soviet plan for the mobilisation of forces – MP-41 – was accepted by Stalin and replaced the mobilisation plan of 1937 that envisaged a wartime strength for the Red Army of

6,826,642.[106] MP-41 had been in development since the late summer of 1940 alongside, as one would expect, deployment planning.[107] MP-41 now envisaged a wartime strength for the Red Army of a staggering 8,682,827 troops in 300 divisions and other units. This was now to include sixty tank and thirty motorised divisions which would now require 1,065,230 personnel as opposed to 181,461 in the previous plan.[108] With MP-41 in place a new plan for the deployment of the Red Army followed in March, that envisaged up to an impressive 200 German divisions being deployed against the Soviet Union.[109]

In order to increase strength in the west after partial mobilisation in September 1939 the Soviet Union could not, it was assumed, resort to a general mobilisation of reservists given that this might be provocatory – and Stalin was clearly concerned with not giving Hitler and Germany cause to start a war before the Soviet Union was ready. The September 1939 law on universal military service enshrined many changes in mobilisation and conscription that had already been made in the Soviet constitution, recent changes that greatly increased the number of conscripts theoretically available for full-time service at any one time through such changes as extending conscription periods and the length of summer training camps.[110] The mobilisation of reservists for summer training – as ordered for example for the Kiev Special – and Western Special Military Districts on 31 March 1941 – would allow at least some additional strength to be assembled without a general mobilisation, with orders for this mobilisation formally envisaging reservists for both front-line and rear-area services being held in the army into the autumn.[111] Units and formations could also be moved westwards from the interior and the Far East, with for example from 26 April 1941 the Trans-Baikal Military District and Far Eastern Front sending one mechanised corps, two rifle corps and two airborne brigades to the west. On maps in Moscow coherent units and formations could no doubt be seen to be moving westwards to join those already there, but the units being moved were typically manned at peacetime rather than wartime levels.[112]

Manning new units, and filling out partially manned unit, was not an easy task – particularly when the latter were on the move and not taking new personnel in their home areas, and where there was a chronic shortage of experienced commanders – or indeed suitably trained commanders – who would supposedly not only lead but train those below them. In May 1940 when Timoshenko took over from Voroshilov at NKO, he noted a shortfall in commanders – particularly in the infantry – reaching 21 per cent of list strength as of 1 May 1940.[113] The shortage of junior commanders was, as had been the case since the late 1930s, to be solved in part by educating far more in an increasing number of institutions for less time – significantly increasing output but diluting quality. In 1938 the Red Army had received 57,000 new commanders of junior leitenant rank and above from military academies, schools, from the ranks of what in other armies were termed 'NCOs' and from recalled reserve commanders. In 1939 nearly double the figure for 1938 was received – 101,147. Over the two-year period from 1938–9 two and a half times the number of commanders had been received than for the previous decade.[114] Nonetheless, still commanders and particularly experienced commanders were in short supply. Many junior commanders from the reserves were rapidly upgraded to middle-grade ranks – 106,065 for the period from 1938–40 – making it hardly surprising that it was deemed that 30–40 per cent of middle-ranking commanders in the military districts were deemed to have inadequate military preparation. About 70 per cent of regimental-level commanders of ground forces had held their current rank for less than a year.[115] In the light of the shortage of commanders and particularly experienced commanders – it was apparently ordered on the eve of war that central and military district staffs were to be cut by 20 per cent – an order that Bagramian notes with some relief was not carried out.[116] These staff positions may have been spared, but many commanders were still on the move to new postings – with obvious ramifications for continuity. In January 1941 11,632 'officers' were moved to new postings in order to bring existing units up to strength – in June 17,144. In January 1941 only 235 were moved for the formation of new units, but by April this had risen to 10,356 and stood at 7,252 in June.[117]

As well as lacking personnel – and with many fresh and not only inexperienced but less than adequately trained faces amongst the those they had – many formations being moved westwards did so despite their lacking the equipment they were supposed to receive. Where the mechanised corps formed in the western military districts lacked equipment to meet list table of organisation requirements, they had as noted above at least received the lion's share of the new tanks and equipment. For the mechanised corps formed further eastwards, the situation was typically even worse. In his Soviet-era memoirs General D.D. Leliushenko describes how at training camp in the early summer of 1941 21st Mechanised Corps – formed initially in the Moscow Military District starting in March 1941 before relocating to summer camp near Idritsa and Opochka from late April – had only ninety-eight BT-7 and T-26 tanks – and had yet to receive any of the new T-34s or KV-series tanks. Lacking small arms, artillery, and short on transport, 21st Mechanised Corps nonetheless made plans in mid-June to concentrate forces further westwards.[118] In fact, by June 1941 on paper only 16,555 of the 31,574 tanks required for the mechanised corps were available, with it being predicted that a total of 19,825 would be available by the beginning of 1942. The head of the Main Auto-Armour Board of the Red Army noted that the full strength – with older types still inevitably prominent – would only be available by current reckoning in early 1943. The situation regarding tractors for artillery was similarly dire – of the 94,584 required in the event of war only 42,931 were available as of 1 June 1941 – a figure not even covering the peacetime requirement for 49,552 tractors.[119] Stalin was in early May 1941 apparently willing to pretend that all these armoured and mechanised units that were forming were in fact ready for war – in a speech to graduates of Red Army academies of 5 May 1941 Stalin suggested that at that point the Red Army did indeed have the 300 divisions of MP-41 – noting that a third of these were mechanized – two thirds of the mechanised divisions being tank divisions.[120] Exaggeration of Soviet strength may have provided some comfort for Soviet leaders even if there was still so much to be done, and certainly where in the March plans for Soviet deployment it was envisaged that Germany might deploy 12,000 tanks against the Soviet Union – 7,500 to the south and up to 2,000 in the north.[121]

By the early summer of 1941– on the eve of the start of Operation 'Barbarossa' – many units and formations of the Red Army that existed as meaningful combat-capable entities on paper only were sitting inadequately equipped, supplied, trained and often undermanned in poorly prepared positions or camps along the Soviet western border – including the mechanised corps. At this point available Soviet strength was not concentrated in what might seem to have been the obvious region to defend against what Soviet plans of September 1940 had identified as the most likely avenue for a principal German attack. These plans stated that

The board for the graduation of Red Army commanders on 5 May 1941, including now Chief of Staff Zhukov, People's Commissar for Defence Timoshenko and Marshals Voroshilov, Budennii and Kulik, along with Stalin at the podium. Infamous 'political', Lev Mekhlis, has a prominent place for the proceedings. (RIA Novosti #3098)

'Germany is most likely to deploy her principal strength to the north of the river San in order to develop a principal blow towards Riga and Kovno and on to Dvinsk-Polotsk, or to Kovno-Vilnius and on to Minsk'.[122] The Minsk axis was the obvious route to Moscow. The March 1941 deployment plan for the Red Army seems to have identified it as being likely that principal German strength would be deployed to the south. The plan saw the principal thrust of a German attack most likely as coming from primary strength concentrated 'from the south-west of Sedlets to Bulgaria' in a 'strike towards Berdichev and Kiev to capture the Ukraine', accompanied by 'a supporting blow in the north from East Prussia towards Dvinsk and Riga or with concentric blows from Suvalki and Brest towards Volkovisk and Baranovichi'. The plan did not however rule out 'that Germany might concentrate her main strength in East Prussia and on the Warsaw axis'.[123] There Soviet reconnaissance had indeed identified significant German concentrations – suggesting at the end of May 1941 that there were 23–4 German divisions in East Prussia, of which two were Panzer and three motorised divisions, and thirty divisions 'on the Warsaw axis' facing the Western Special Military District, of which four were Panzer and one motorised. This was in addition to the 35–6 divisions in the Liublin-Krakow region facing the Kiev Special Military District – including six Panzer and five motorised divisions – where the Pripiat Marshes would be a major hindrance to those forces moving northeastwards instead of southeastwards towards Kiev. Further south were two more Panzer and five motorized divisions in addition to infantry, mountain and cavalry divisions.[124] The Soviet high command had not left the region north of the Pripiat Marshes denuded of forces, where in terms of mechanised forces for example the Pribaltic Special Military District had 3rd and 12th Mechanised Corps, Western Special Military District 6th, 11th, 13th, 14th and Kiev Special 4th, 8th, 15th and 16th in the first echelon. However, where the Pribaltic Special didn't have a single mechanised – and indeed only a single corps of any type in the second echelon – and the Western Special 17th and 20th Mechanised Corps and two other corps in its second echelon, the Kiev Special Military District had 5th, 9th, 19th, 22nd and 24th Mechanised Corps along with nine other corps in its second echelon – likely exploitation forces.[125] As Evan Mawdsley has argued, the fact that the Red Army was concentrated in depth on the southern sector of the western border regions – south of the Pripiat Marshes – in the summer of 1941 stemmed most probably not from discussions during the autumn of 1940 about how the Red Army could best defend on Soviet territory, but about how it could best attack westwards.[126] The March 1941 deployment plan implied that the September 1940 proposal to amass strength to the south rather than the north was with a view to potentially being able to strike northwards towards Berlin or East Prussia, or alternatively Prague and Vienna, after German forces had been destroyed in the Liublin-Radom-Sandomir region. The alternative was that 'the deployment of the principal forces of the Red Army in the west with principal strength grouped against East Prussia and on the Warsaw axis brings the serious risk that the struggle on this front could lead to protracted fighting' – where certainly terrain and fortifications, and quite possibly awareness of the precedent of the First World War played a part in such an assessment.[127]

Given Soviet dispositions in the early summer of 1941, it is understandable how some historians in the 1980s – and in particular the Russian émigré Vladimir Rezun writing under the pseudonym Viktor Suvorov – saw the Red Army deployed ready for offensive operations to the west in the near future – and indeed in July 1941 – even before details of Soviet war plans were widely available and added further weight to arguments that Soviet posture was far from wholly defensive.[128] However, at the same time archival and other testimony made available from the late 1980s onwards allowed historians such as David Glantz to show more clearly – that the Red Army simply wasn't ready for offensive operations in the summer of 1941 – and certainly wasn't 'planning pre-emptive war against Germany in July 1941' – a notion that Glantz suggested was 'totally unfounded'.[129] If Soviet intentions were wholly defensive, then the Red Army certainly did not lack the resources to mount a meaningful defense of the western regions of the Soviet Union in 1941, but forward deployment ready for offensive operations at some undisclosed point in the future was not the best way to use resources available for defence – and nor was the continued creation and mobilisation of new units and formations rather than fully equipping and manning existing units to list strength first. Here continued overestimation of German strength on her eastern border can only have fueled the desire to spread resources far too thinly in the creation of the bases of future formations. Dominant ideas in the Soviet camp on how war would begin – that assumed that German forces could be held in border regions whilst the remainder of the Red Army mobilised – conveniently fitted in with the forward deployment of Soviet mechanised forces that would ultimately sweep into German territory. Voices such as G.S. Isserson's, that suggested on the basis of the German invasion of Poland that this need not be the case and that German forces might attack without due warning and with considerable initial strength and force, were conveniently ignored.[130]

Although Suvorov's suggestion that the Red Army was preparing for war against Germany in July 1941 is certainly untenable given the evidence available, in June 1941 the Red Army was undoubtedly mobilising for war against Germany, just not a war in 1941. We can only speculate that in May 1941, when plans for a preventative strike against German forces massing on the border were considered, that Stalin deemed – in many ways correctly – that the Red Army was simply not ready for such an operation. Given the lack of Red Army preparedness such an operation was unlikely to be a knockout blow, and certainly not against, what the plan itself describes as an army 'in a fully mobilized state, with fully deployed rear-area services'.[131] By this point Soviet intelligence estimated German strength at 112 divisions in situ on the Soviet border – including 13 Panzer and 12 motorised – with Germany being 'able to put as many as 137 infantry, 19 armoured, 15 motorized, 4 cavalry and 5 airborne divisions against us, in all up to 180 divisions'. With the fragmented manner in which Soviet units and formations were being brought up to strength, the Red Army had a long way to go to take on that sort of mobilised force on enemy territory.[132] The completion of MP-41 can be seen to be a requirement for the Soviet military and political leadership to initiate hostilities against Germany, and most key targets of MP-41 were not going to be met until well into 1942 and even 1943. Stalin's response to this situation was to pretend that Germany would not attack first – despite increasingly strong evidence to the contrary – and continue with the mobilisation and deployment of under strength and poorly supplied units that would be topped up before being thrown against the enemy. These units were concentrated where it would be convenient for them to go on to the offensive when the Red Army was ready – despite significant and growing evidence that an attack was likely well before that and not necessarily directed conveniently against principal Soviet strength. Stalin's probable wishful thinking that Hitler would not risk an invasion when still at war with Britain and when he was receiving the sort of natural resources he might gain from occupation of Soviet territory anyway involved a surprising degree of ignorance of the ideological drive of Nazi foreign policy for a man who claimed to be a Marxist-Leninist.

The Red Army that sat concentrated along the new Soviet border with its likely foe, had been placed in an extremely vulnerable position by Stalin and the senior Soviet military leadership. Reorganising, requipping, understrength units with inadequate supply sought to train and prepare for war in circumstances where Soviet mobilisation was only partial. That Germany and her allies attacked when they did – with Britain still in the war – seems retrospectively to have been folly, but as subsequent events would highlight the Red Army was far from fighting fit but only likely to get in better shape. For Germany, the problem with

Troops of 70th Rifle Division, ostensibly on manoeuvres, in May 1941.
In reality the Red Army was mobilising for the inevitable war, just not by
Hitler's timetable. (RIA Novosti #634807)

'Barbarossa' was not timing – it is difficult to imagine it achieving more
than it would. Certainly German underestimation of the sheer size of the
Red Army and Soviet mobilisation potential was a significant factor in its
ultimate failure. In many senses it shouldn't have mattered for the Soviet
defence whether Soviet forces were concentrated more to the south or
north of the Pripiat Marshes, where in the end it ended up being the
former – the concentration of forces north on Pripiat Marshes was still on
paper at least impressive but too far forward and without a second
echelon in situ.[133] The problem was forward deployment of undermanned and underequipped units that might not have time to be brought
up to full strength in time to meet an enemy attack. Nonetheless, even
without units and formations having the strengths they were supposed to
have – and even allowing for serviceability issues for example with the
tanks – the Red Army could field phenomenal strength. Considering
tanks alone, on 1 June 1941 the Red Army had a tank park with a
staggering 23,106 tanks and a few self-propelled guns. Of these, to
reiterate figures presented in part earlier, 12,782 were in the western
military districts ready – supposedly – to engage the enemy. Of the tanks
in the west 10,540 were deemed to be in sufficiently good state of repair
to remain with frontline units, even if 8,383 apparently needed some sort

of light repairs or servicing that was supposed to take place with these field units. Only 2,157 tanks were considered fully operational without any caveats, but even allowing for some of the light repairs being sufficiently serious to keep at least some of these tanks out of action and others breaking down as Soviet units moved up, the Red Army in the west was still formidable.[134] The Wehrmacht would launch more than 3,500 tanks and self-propelled guns at the Red Army – they would be met by at the very least a similar number of tanks. Most of the Soviet tanks were theoretically capable of dealing with their German opponents – some would be a shock to them even if their crews far too frequently had little time to familiarise themselves with their new equipment.[135] Locally however it would be Soviet tanks that would often be outnumbered in those instances where tank actually fought tank, thanks to command and control and the host of other issues that hampered the Red Army making the most of what it had on paper. However, once they were lost there were still thousands of tanks in the Soviet interior to be fed – often piecemeal – into the fray.[136]

Despite its many flaws, the Red Army was much larger than at least some German leaders were convinced, and despite having the likes of Voroshilov and Kulik at the very top the Red Army had actually learnt much from the small wars and conflicts of the late 1930s and in particular assessment of Germany's success in Poland and the West. This experience – as reflected not only in organisation but also equipment – was only just being meaningfully incorporated into an army that had experienced so much change and turmoil that in such a large organisation could not simply be reversed or undone overnight. Not only did the Red Army need time to fully mobilise the manpower for, but also to provide the equipment required by its mass of new units and formations to bring them to the sort of material strengths they were supposed to have. It also needed time bring itself to order in terms of functioning as a coherent organism – time Hitler was unwilling to give it. The Red Army – a product of the top-down society that Stalin was building – was never going to be able to emulate the elite German formations that spearheaded 'Barbarossa', but it didn't have to. When Germany and her allies did attack the sheer size of the Red Army was certainly a factor in whittling down inadequate German strength, but so also was the resolve of many of its troops who fought hard despite the predicament in which their leaders had put them. Sometimes this initial resolve would be fostered by the barrel of a gun, sometimes by patriotism, sometimes by the sort of factors that could motivate soldiers in any army like loyalty and commitment to comrades in arms. The important thing – and particularly for Stalin – was that they fought, and they fought on regardless.

Despite losses that might have seemed calamitous, the Red Army would stubbornly whittle down German strength as it added wartime experience to that accrued prior to the war, and mobilised fresh resources to make up for losses suffered during the summer of 1941 that need not have been suffered on that scale. With different deployment, and aided by more balanced approach to raising units that did not leave them as skeletons of their intended selves, it is quite possible that even without the new equipment hoped in MP-41 that was just starting to reach the Red Army in the summer of 1941 the Wehrmacht could have been stopped earlier. In many ways it would be critically stalled well to the west in a bloody war of attrition – at Brest – at Smolensk – and only ultimately stopped in 1941 at Rostov, Moscow and Tikhvin.

10 'Barbarossa'
From Minsk to Smolensk

On Saturday 21 June 1941 the Red Army was certainly not ready for war – and certainly not ready for the sort of offensive westwards that Suvorov had proposed was imminent. Much of the field strength of the Red Army sat, often only recently mobilised and poorly trained, in inadequately supplied and understrength units along the Soviet western border. Much of the remainder was on the move westwards. As mechanised corps waited for their new tanks – with insufficient fuel and munitions for those they had that were also often in a poor state of repair – many units in summer camps in the west didn't even have some of the basic equipment and munitions to hand that had been provided to their units, as much of it was still stored at their winter billets. As one veteran who served close to the western border in Belorussia at the beginning of the war noted in a letter to the Soviet historian Samsonov during the early days of Mikhail Gorbachev's *glasnost'* – in June 1941 'Enemy attack found us unforgivably unaware. Commanders were on leave. Weapons were in deep conservation in stores. Equipment had not been assembled.'[1] Aleksandr Efimovich Shvarev, a junior commander with 236th Fighter Air Regiment that had only that Friday arrived at its current base, was initially convinced that as anti-aircraft guns opened up during the night of 21–22 June a training exercise had started – a burning hangar soon suggesting otherwise.[2] As former Red Army man Velerii Vakhromeev describes in his memoirs, when he and his recently mobilised colleagues back in the Soviet rear heard Molotov declare the state of war to the Soviet peoples on 22 June, 'silent and suppressed, we stood and listened. His words were bitter and unexpected. From childhood we had been convinced, that we were ready to repel any aggressor with a powerful and decisive blow'.[3] Although some higher up the chain of command were aware of the apparently rapidly increasingly likelihood of a German invasion, secrecy and fear of 'provoking' Germany prevented that information from penetrating down the chain of command where, as in the case of radio operator Arkadii Glazunov, troops moving westwards were told they were on maneuvers.[4] Even when there were

202

belated attempts to ready the Red Army to meet the German attack – such as in the case of the establishment of a field headquarters for what would become the North-Western Front on the outbreak of war that will be discussed further later – secrecy at times prevented those who should have been 'in the know' from becoming so as soon as they might otherwise have done. Head of communications for what would become the North-Western Front, Petr Kurochkin, describes an incident shortly before the war where in attempting to establish field communications with the future Western Front he was forced to phone his counterpart there by civilian telephone at night, but could not apparently make it plain – one assumes to the operator – why the latter needed to take a call from the middle of nowhere in the middle of the night.[5] Obsessive Soviet secrecy might have kept the Germans in the dark, but it was certainly a double-edged sword.

Undoubtedly, and understandably, some resentment against the regime was held by at least some for the predicament they and their country were soon in at the end of June 1941. The psychological impact for those under fire of the much vaunted Red Army being caught apparently unaware by an erstwhile ally – and not only unable to take the war to foreign territory but lurching from crisis to crisis in retreat – is difficult to assess. It is likely, as one respondent to the HPSSS suggested, that complacency and overconfidence before the war were 'paid for with interest' in the coming weeks for those who harbored any serious doubt or resentment towards the regime.[6] I.I. Fediuninskii – at the time a rifle corps commander – certainly suggested in his memoirs that many younger Red Army personnel in particular expected that if war came the Red Army would 'easily' be victorious 'against any enemy', and that such attitudes contributed to the 'underestimation of the Hitlerite military machine that in the first battles inflicted so much damage on us'.[7] It is easy to exaggerate the scale of any doubt and resentment held by the population towards the regime at this time – the Western historiography of the Stalinist era during the Cold War relied to a considerable extent on Soviet émigrés for assessment of popular mood – and even after the collapse of the Soviet Union has made considerable use of the materials of the security services whose task in was to find discontent. As Catherine Merridale notes in *Ivan's War*, although for younger Soviet troops there might have been 'resentment of the collectives and of harsh working conditions in factories and on construction sites', they were nonetheless 'born into the Soviet system and knew no other' – and did not have 'opportunity to develop a different political outlook . . . on a public scale'. Older people might not have been 'reconciled to the new world', but that did not mean that they would resist it.[8] Those that had shown such a tendency had, in the Red Army at least, been likely victims of the purges. Certainly at times draconian measures would be required to keep units fighting – even if in other instances the shock of the perfidious attack intensified resistance as was apparently the case for Valerii Vakhromeev and many others.[9]

Attempts by the Soviet leadership to minimise the threat of war during the last days of the spring of 1941 are perhaps best typified by the infamous TASS communiqué of 14 June that sought to play down rumours of 'the proximity of war between the Soviet Union and Germany'.[10] Many Soviet memoirs and interviews conducted both before and after the collapse of the Soviet Union suggest however that many Red Army commanders at least, and particularly in border regions, were increasingly aware of the possibility of war during the summer of 1941 even without their being in a tightly controlled loop of very senior commanders taking more explicit steps to ready the Red Army to meet the enemy. Both archival sources and memoirs suggest that proximity to the border and seniority in the chain of command were factors in increased awareness of the threat, and we therefore have no reason to believe that what was recalled in memoirs was all hindsight. There were certainly documented appeals from the frontline for permission to take more robust defensive measures. Such requests came from the commander of 125th Rifle Division of 11th Rifle Corps, 8th Army, Pribaltic Special Military District on 18 June to be able to take such measures as allowing troops to keep sixty rounds of ammunition with them in order to reduce the time required to move to combat readiness to 10–15 minutes – and for units to be more likely to be able to man forward positions before they were breached by enemy mechanised forces. In this instance these requests were preceded by the latest alarming intelligence of German buildup as tension heightened on the border.[11] In material from his memoirs that was only published during the *glasnost'* era Rokossovskii – then commanding 9th Mechanised Corps – suggested that during the summer of 1941 as he talked with other senior commanders 'our opinions came together to conclude that we were on the eve of war. The air reeked of war, and only the blind and deaf did not notice it or want to notice it...'.[12] L.S. Skvirskii, a staff officer with 14th Army in the far north, was apparently convinced of German preparations for an attack in the region when questioned on the matter by People's Commissar for Foreign Affairs, Molotov in early 1941.[13] Certainly, on the eve of the German Operation 'Barbarossa' many units were on the move westwards to deployment areas as the Wehrmacht struck – having only recently been ordered to do so – in what was clearly some sort of response to the intensified threat from higher up the chain of command. Immediately prior to the war Ivan Bagramian headed the Operations Department of the Kiev Military District, and in his memoirs noted how on 15 June he received orders from Moscow to start moving the five rifle corps of the second echelon of the district to deployment areas closer to the border according to plans for such deployment that had been worked out the previous month. Moving only at night, they were to require anywhere from eight to twelve nights to be in their new positions that were still far enough back from the border to be less likely to be noted by German reconnaissance.[14] Rokossovskii noted how a few days prior to the war he became aware of the relocation of the headquarters of the Kiev Special Military District from Kiev further west to Tarnopol' – the reason for which he and colleagues around him were not informed. In a damning indictment of the situation being created by the high command, also in material from his memoirs that was also only published during the *glasnost'* era, Rokossovskii suggested that 'if there was some sort of plan, then it obviously did not correspond to the situation that was developing as war approached, and from which followed the heavy defeats of our forces during the initial period of the war.'[15]

Thanks to a large extent to what seems to have been cognitive dissonance on the part of Stalin the strategic and operational deployment of the forward echelon of the Red Army was far from appropriate to meet the onslaught about to begin, a second echelon was barely in position and the fortified regions along the new border only in the process of being augmented, although clearly there was at least some realisation and response to the possibility of attack even if denial still had the upper hand.[16] Despite being *vozhd'* – the supreme leader – Stalin did not and could not devise and implement Soviet strategy alone. Those in senior leadership positions in the Red Army such as Timoshenko and Zhukov were most probably not just going along with the plan through fear – their ambitions and hubris also no doubt played a part in the creation of the situation the Red Army found itself in mid-June 1941 – just as they did for senior German leaders who supported 'Barbarossa' despite the many arguments that could be made about its folly.

As 'Barbarossa' was days rather than weeks away from being launched an increasing weight of intelligence had suggested that a German invasion was imminent and that Germany was not working to the same timetable as Stalin. This intelligence picture was increasingly devoid of clutter and noise as one-by-one indicators pointed to invasion. From overflights of Soviet territory of the Western Special Military District by numerous German aircraft within a short period of time on 20 June to the removal of barbed wire entanglements on the German side of the border by the evening that same day, such indicators meant little on their own but much when combined.[17] As one might expect, the choir of intelligence sources reached something of a crescendo late on 21 June and into the small hours of Sunday 22 June as invasion was but hours away where to strategic intelligence from the likes of Sorge in Tokyo – that were unable to pinpoint a date for invasion – were added reports from border units on activity on the German side of the border and even deserter testimony.[18] A German NCO and pioneer, Alfred Liskow, during the night of 21–22 June had crossed the state border to Soviet territory having been told by his company commander of the impending attack the next morning.[19] Nonetheless, even with tactical intelligence alarm bells sounding at ground level some fairly elementary preparations to meet enemy attack would not be taken even by units but kilometers from the border because the Soviet leadership – under pressure from Stalin – was determined to make their preparations for the 'inevitable' war with minimal provocation so, one assumes, that war might ultimately start according to a Soviet timetable, not the German one.

Some Soviet commanders apparently took measures to increase combat readiness before the first bombs were dropped – against the tone and even the letter of orders that had at that point been received from on high – including two apparently unrelated Kuznetsovs. Admiral N. Kuznetsov in command of the navy had, with the apparent encouragement of a 'particularly unsettled' Vice-Admiral V.F. Tributz of the Baltic Fleet, decided to move the Baltic and Northern Fleets to Operational Readiness Number 2 on 19 June.[20] Tributz had apparently been concerned about suspicious German naval activity in the Baltic for some time, having made this plain to his superior Nikolai Kuznetsov by phone on a number of occasions.[21] As Tributz suggests in his memoirs, indicators that something was afoot were many, including the fact that after 14 June no German transport vessels entered Soviet ports, with those that were already there leaving. At the same time the departures of Soviet vessels in German ports were apparently being stalled by German authorities.[22] Operational Readiness Number 2 as ordered on 19 June meant readiness to go to sea within 4–6 hours for ships, with command posts fully manned – not combat readiness. Tributz had apparently increased naval patrols at the mouth of the Gulf of Finland and Irbensk Strait. Full combat readiness was not ordered by Kuznetsov until just before midnight on 21 June – and even then he did not give clear instructions on what to do in the event of incursions and stressed the need to avoid provocation.[23] On 18 June 1941 General-Colonel F.I. Kuznetsov, commander of the Pribaltic Special Military District issued orders that included preparations for the destruction of bridges by 8th and 11th Armies on the border by 21 June and the stripping of petrol tankers from non-VVS or mechanised units in order to provide them to 3rd and 12th Mechanised Corps by the same date.[24] Whilst taking such measures, commanders such as Kuznetsov were of course under pressure not to rock the boat – in orders of 19 June he ordered the completion of work on forward positions for example, but that they only be occupied by troops (in the case of 125th Rifle Division above based further away from such positions than the positions were from the border) in the event of enemy breaching of the border – at the same time reiterating the need to avoid provocation of the enemy.[25] In the case of F.I. Kuznetsov, as Glantz suggests, these limited measures seem to have made little difference – and the navy was of little relevance to what was going on in the border regions.[26] Only at 00:30 Moscow time on 22 June did Timoshenko and Zhukov send out orders to commanders of the western military districts that noted 'the possibility of surprise attack by the Germans' – an attack that might start with 'provocative activities', to which Soviet forces were not to respond. They were nonetheless to move to 'full battle readiness in order to meet the possible surprise blow by the Germans or their allies'. This meant manning firepoints of the fortified districts on the state border during the night of 22 June, as well as dispersing and camouflaging aircraft, bringing ground units to combat readiness and dispersing and camouflaging them too and readying anti-aircraft defences.[27] What became the Western Front – as distinct from the Western Special Military District that contrary to many secondary sources continued to exist for mobilisation purposes and was only disbanded in early September[28] – is recorded as having received this coded telegram at 01:00 local time – with armies and units of the fortified districts being sent these orders between 02:00 and 02:30. Whilst 3rd and 4th Armies had apparently time to take at least some sort of action as a result of these orders, '10th Army only decoded the warning after military operations had begun'.[29] According to L.M. Sandalov, then colonel and chief of staff for 4th Army, his deputy had the telegram in his hands as German aircraft hit the military town on the edge of Brest at which his headquarters was situated. Only after the air attack – and the first casualties of which Sandalov was aware – was he read the telegram.[30]

'Barbarossa' began with Luftwaffe strikes against airfields and other targets. Although on 19 June orders had been issued by Timoshenko for the camouflaging of airfields, supply dumps and other potential VVS targets during the first half of July, these and other measures to ready the VVS for war had clearly not been completed by the time the German bombers struck.[31] The first attacks reportedly hit Soviet territory as early as 3:30 a.m. – the Western Front recorded starting to receive 'an endless stream of reports, in the main from the air defence network, on bombings' at around 4:00 a.m. local time.[32] That day Soviet sources record the Luftwaffe as having hit sixty-six Soviet airfields – eleven of the Pribaltic Special Military District, twenty-six of the Western Special, twenty-three of the Kiev Special and six of the Odessa Military District. Soviet histories of the VVS during the war identify a number of factors in the high losses for the VVS of the western military districts that day that would leave more than 1,100 Soviet aircraft destroyed – in the region of 800 on the ground. The result was the loss of nearly 50 per cent of strength for the Western Special Military District (728 aircraft) that suffered most, and only 3 per cent (twenty-three aircraft) for the Odessa Military District in the region. Included in those factors explaining high losses that day was the fact that Soviet airfields in the west were often crowded with aircraft – sometimes with 100–120 aircraft on a single airfield. This was in part because many airfields in the region were still under construction and in part because some units were converting to new types and in a number of cases still had the older types to hand. It was also a result of the fact that the basic Soviet unit for airpower at this point was the air division, whose regiments were often kept on the same airfield rather than dispersed in part given poor communications available to co-ordinate the activities of aircraft across airfields. The proximity of many airfields to the border meant that the Luftwaffe was able to easily achieve surprise in many instances, with some airfields being close enough to the border to be shelled by German artillery.[33] The destruction of large numbers of aircraft on the ground brought with it one positive for the VVS – many pilots survived to be sent to the rear for the formation of new aviation regiments.[34] The Luftwaffe rapidly achieved air superiority on the principal axes, but as many German memoirs confirm, the VVS was not silenced even during the first days of the war, although Soviet airpower did not have the sort of impact that the Luftwaffe was having over events on the ground. From the first days of 'Barbarossa' Hans Roth of 299th Infantry Division, 6th Army, Army Group South noted regular Soviet air attacks on German forces, particularly from low-flying fighter aircraft, as indeed did Erich Hager of 39th Panzer Regiment, 17th Panzer Division of 2nd Panzergruppe, Army Group Centre albeit noting little Soviet air activity in late June.[35]

Hit hardest from the air was the VVS of the Western Front, the sector of the front on which we shall focus our attention. At the same time as German bombers were reported to be hitting airfields and other targets the Western Front recorded artillery opening up on Soviet positions. At 05:00 the war diary for the Western Front reported that German forces were advancing across the whole front.[36] Whether units had received the order regarding combat readiness or not, the Soviet response was not necessarily to fight back – some units were apparently ordered to hold their fire, as in the case of 313th Artillery Regiment of 115th Rifle Division on the Finnish border. According to N.V. Ogarev, his unit was initially ordered 'not to open return fire', despite being under air attack.[37] The German Chief of Staff for 4th Army Günther Blumentritt recalled German interception of a Soviet radio message declaring to superiors 'We are being fired on, what shall we do?' – the response from the headquarters being 'You must be insane. And why is your signal not in code?'.[38] Only at 07:15 Moscow time was there clarification of the situation from the Soviet capital, where having noted German air attacks on airfields and positions along the border, artillery bombardment of Soviet territory and the crossing of the border by German forces 'in a number of places', Soviet forces were ordered to fight back – the VVS was to strike enemy airfields to the west to a depth of 100–150 km, although ground forces were not given permission to cross the state border.[39]

Even before the second of the three key directives that would see Soviet forces in the west ordered by Moscow to move from cautious preparation to reckless counterattacks within the space of a day, the Soviet communications network in the west was starting to fail. On the key Minsk axis at 04:30 the Western Front recorded losing telephone communication with 3rd, 4th and 10th Armies. Radio communications with subordinate units were sporadic. For the 23 June, the Western Front recorded that 'communications between the headquarters of the front and headquarters of armies functioned, as on the first day of the war, with extreme irregularity (and only by radio) and with large and prolonged breaks'.[40] In his memoirs, then head of the operational section for the headquarters of the South-Western Front and future Marshal Ivan Bagramian described the collapse of communications for what had been the Kiev Special Military District during the first days of the war. Bagramian recalled how commander of the South-Western Front General-Colonel M.P. Kirponos, had exclaimed that 'if communications are to work so poorly, then how on earth are we going to be able to command our forces!'.[41]

Telephone and telegraph communications were not only vulnerable to being severed or intercepted en route, but also simple failure – and particularly so where considerable reliance was placed on the civilian network for communications over longer distances. For example, the field headquarters for the North-Western Front that was set up at Panevėžys in Lithuania just before the Axis invasion was able to establish telephone communications with the headquarters of the military district in Riga, the headquarters of the subordinate 8th and 11th Armies and the General Staff in Moscow, but it struggled even before the invasion to maintain communications with the Western Special Military District to the south – communications that soon it seems 'for technical reasons ceased to function at all' before the first bombs dropped. Given the 'technical specificities' of the telephone systems of the three Baltic Republics that lay between it and the Leningrad Military District, the new field headquarters at Panevėžys was unable at all – even temporarily – to establish telephone communication with its neighbour to the north-east.[42] It was of course, not only in the north that new territory had recently been incorporated into the Soviet Union, and where there had hardly been time to make sure that infrastructure was compatible with Soviet equivalents.

At the beginning of the war, problems with Red Army communications by the key alternative to telephone or telegraph – radio were not just down to shortages of radios or their technical limitations, but hampered by a combination of poor training and understanding of the appropriate use of radio, Soviet secrecy and the fact that Stalin and the Soviet military leadership did not sanction an escalation of defensive preparations that might be deemed provocative until it was too late. Although the field headquarters for the North-Western Front was established in great secrecy during the last few days before 'Barbarossa', there was not, for example, sufficient time for the full distribution down the chain of command of secret documents that included codewords, frequencies and other key information that would allow the network to function effectively in wartime. The head of communications for the soon to formally be North-Western Front Petr Kurochkin notes in his memoirs that the distribution of this information from military district down to individual frontline radio sets would take at least a week and the situation was apparently sufficiently tense by somewhere around 20 June for the system to be deemed to have to be in operation sooner. The decision was taken that the radio network within the confines of what would become the North-Western Front would continue to function as in peacetime. Given inevitable greater enemy appreciation of the peacetime network, here a security measure in the given circumstances was actually undermining security.[43] The tendency in the Red Army to make too much rather than too little use of code in radio communications has already been noted as having been an issue during for example the war in Finland. Although transmission of information was at times unnecessarily delayed, at least in such instances radio was being used and there was a chance that information might get through. At the beginning of the war – as Petr Kurochkin notes in his memoirs – although radio communications suffered less from enemy attack than telephone, 'often it was not used as a result of inadequately prepared staff personnel' and where 'some commanders sought to avoid using radio at all through fear of the enemy pinpointing a transmitting radio set and hence their headquarters'.[44] This was indeed a legitimate concern, and radio communications needed to be used sparingly and headquarters moved with sufficient frequency to avoid being hit by air attack or artillery – or even located by ground forces. There were no easy solutions to command-and-control – moving headquarters frequently led to disruption in communications. Not using radio communications was however hardly a viable solution to this problem where given the difficulties in maintaining communications by telephone would all too often mean units effectively lacking any direction from above – a particular problem for an army in which the exercising of lower level initiative was hardly encouraged. Using dispatch riders and other runners did offer an alternative over shorter distances – and even over longer ones where the orders or information were not too time-sensitive. However, frequently time was of the essence, and dispatch riders were not guaranteed to get through.[45]

Soviet ground forces had received permission to counterattack in the second of the three directives of 22 June, but they had often started the day in poor shape to execute their orders and were certainly not in a position to finally take the war to enemy territory as planned after a number of hours of war. Nonetheless, Soviet ground forces were ordered later on 22 June in the third key directive from Moscow to do just that – to take the war beyond Soviet borders.[46] Not only were the ground forces hardly in a position to strike beyond the Soviet border, but the VVS was also not in a state to take the war to enemy territory in any meaningful way and initially to participate in the fighting on Soviet territory. Before midday on 22 June the VVS for 4th Army of Western Front deployed near Brest had taken 30–40 per cent losses and reported that the enemy already had 'air superiority'. By the end of the day the Western Front as a whole had recorded the loss of 738 aircraft – 528 destroyed on the ground. These losses were described – and this was not exaggeration – as 'catastrophic'. The commander of the VVS for the Western Front, General-Major Kopets, committed suicide that evening.[47] On the ground, where communications were established, mechanised units moved to counterattack as per instructions from Moscow. For what was now the Western Front 14th Mechanised Corps of 4th Army – 22nd and 30th Tank Divisions – was for example on 22 June ordered to concentrate and attack enemy forces in the direction of Brest and, together with 28th Rifle Corps and 10th Mixed Air Division to 'restore the situation' and deal with enemy penetrations – a counterattack to take place at dawn on 23 June. In reality, 22nd Tank Division consisted of only 29th Tank Brigade near Brest, and 30th Tank Division of only 32nd Tank Brigade at Pruzhani – nonetheless fielding a total of 462 T-26 tanks between the two.[48]

According to Sandalov, 22nd Tank Division was deployed only 3–4 km from the border at the outset of hostilities, and when German artillery opened up at 04:00 on 22 June its commander immediately raised the alarm without waiting for orders and deployed duty tank units to the River Bug – where the division 'lost a significant portion of its equipment'. The previous day 30th Tank Division had been out training and had to return to base at Pruzhani before the first tank regiment moved out at around 07:00 that day – followed soon by the second and 'elements of the motor rifle regiment that had automotive transport'. Unfortunately 'a significant proportion of the personnel of the division, not provided with automotive transport, and also the artillery regiment that had yet to receive munitions, were left where they were to defend Pruzhani' – back on which the formation would soon fall. Starting out with 'around 120 T-26 tanks', on-the-march units of the division had lost some vehicles as a result of German air attack before engaging the enemy. After having been blooded on the first day of 'Barbarossa', on the evening of 22 June, with its air division having already lost 'a large portion of its aircraft', and with 22nd Tank Division 'down to around 100 tanks', 14th Mechanised Corps readied itself for their counterattack to begin at 06:00 on 23 June, having already seen heavy fighting.[49]

The counterattack by 14th Mechanised Corps was typical of engagements across the front where Soviet mechanised units were thrown into combat with little idea of opposition – taking little or no advantage of the prepared positions that had been constructed – and according to Sandalov in the case of 14th Mechanised Corps against the better judgement of many commanders. Fleeting communications with the Front command and to a lesser extent army commands provided little comfort – combat formations such as 14th Mechanised Corps received frantic requests for information as higher commanders expressed their exasperation at the failure of subordinate units to counterattack and stem the German advance as they were all under orders to do from above. By the end of the day on 23 June the Western Front recorded that enemy forces 'continued to develop success on the left flank of the Western Front, meeting insignificant opposition from the disorganised and almost uncommandable units of 4th Army'. As German armoured spearheads to the north and south pushed eastwards 'command and control of forces was made extremely difficult as a result of the complete absence of telephone communications and insufficient (as a result of losses) radio communications and the relocation of resources'. Whilst front headquarters was certainly exercising only limited command, on the ground the situation was perhaps slightly better where 4th Army commanders had been forced to join combat units by the collapse of communications. Unit strengths, supply and cohesion were deteriorating rapidly in the face of enemy attack both on the ground and - perhaps as significantly if Soviet memoirs are to be believed - from relentless air attack. Many valuable supplies still at dumps were either destroyed by the enemy or the Red Army in retreat.[50]

By the end of 24 June the Western Front reported that the Luftwaffe had achieved local 'air supremacy' [*polnoe gospodstvo aviatsii protivnika*]. That night, according to the headquarters for 4th Army, under combined attack from enemy armour and air forces '28th Rifle Corps and 14th Mechanized Corps, having failed to bring themselves to order did not withstand this attack...and started a retreat which turned into a rout...'. By the late evening of 25 June the Headquarters of the Western Front was describing 14th Mechanised Corps as 'no longer combat effective'.[51] To the north what was described as the principal striking force of the Western Front – 6th Mechanised Corps of 10th Army initially 'equipped with a full complement of KV and T-34 tanks' – had on day one failed to engage the enemy spearheads and had to be redeployed in the face of a rapidly deteriorating situation – wasting fuel and being subjected to air attack. Redeployed, 6th Mechanised Corps was nominally part of a 'shock group' commanded by the deputy commander of the Front, I.V. Boldin, and ordered to attack towards Grodno to the north. Essentially forces of 3rd and 10th Armies along with much of the Western Front were already fighting to prevent the encirclement of Soviet forces in the Brest region. By late afternoon on 25 June a battered 6th Mechanised Corps – where 4th Tank Division reported being without munitions although was as would be shown later relatively intact even if corps losses had reached 50 per cent – was ordered by Front command to disengage from the enemy and move rapidly eastwards the following day as encirclement loomed – and indeed 3rd, 4th, 10th and 13th Armies were all ordered to retreat during the night of 25–6 June.[52]

In the crisis that was unfolding for the Western Front, there was little hope of the remaining mechanised corps of the first eschelon of the Front or indeed of neighbouring fronts from transforming the situation. The two remaining mechanised corps of the first eschelon of the Western Front had only recently been formed. The 11th Mechanised Corps to the east had started on 22 June with only 241 tanks – largely T-26 and BT – with the corps as a whole having received only 15 per cent of its lorries and with understrength artillery regiments. In effect, as Drig suggests, 11th Mechanised Corps was a division. The 13th Mechanised Corps was similarly of barely divisional strength, at least in terms of tanks, and was also equipped largely with 'light' tanks – T-26s.[53] In the front's operational summary for the evening of 24 June only 'remants' of 13th Mechanised Corps were identified near Baranovichi. To the north forces of North-Western Front were in no position to assist in preventing encirclement for much of the Western Front. By the end of the day on 25 June the Western Front could note that 5th Tank Division of 3rd Mechanised Corps near Vilnius was down to only three tanks, twelve armoured cars and forty lorries. On 20 June it had 50 T-34s, 30 T-28s, 170 BT-7 and 18 T-26s on strength – and now three tanks remained in operation.[54]

The retreat of much of the first echelon of the Western Front – although not all units of course received orders to retreat such as 21st Rifle Corps of 13th Army – continued into 26 and 27 June as the front command desperately tried to organise defences further eastwards. The second echelon – including 17th and 20th Mechanised Corps – failed to halt German forces at key river crossings more than briefly and with the rapidly resurrected fortified districts of the old border also seemingly having little impact in slowing down the German advance. Attempts to bring the Slutsk Fortified District to readiness for defence by units including 'remnants' of 14th Mechanised Corps were 'short lived' and consequently did not 'bring the desired results' – Slutsk was abandoned by the night of 26 June as German forces penetrated further eastwards on the southern flank.[55] Concentration of armoured forces near Baranovichi – now itself threatened with inclusion in a large encirclement – included much of 4th Tank Division of 6th Mechanised Corps that had taken relatively light losses and reported 20–26 per cent losses 'in the main on account of light tanks', where its KV tanks 'did not always take losses even from direct hits'.[56] Nonetheless, the new tanks seem to have made far less of a contribution than their numbers might have predicted. Soviet counterattacks certainly seemed to have little impact at Front headquarters. Soviet commanders claimed that they were outnumbered – and tactically they often were – but in a given region often outnumbered their opponents but simply could not concentrate where required as German forces looked for gaps and worked their way eastwards. The Western Front command was by 28 June having to worry about German forces seizing a bridgehead over the Berezina River to the southeast of Minsk – well to the east of the fighting involving most of the Front's strength.[57] That day Bobruisk fell and the front command started to think about the defence not only of the Berezina River line, but also the Dnepr. Attacks on the exposed German flanks were of course ordered to try to stop the German drive eastwards – of the mechanised corps 13th and 17th Mechanised Corps were ordered to attack in the south and 20th Mechanised Corps in the north near Minsk. By 29 June however, it was reported by the head of the Auto-Armour Board of the Western Front that 'the overall material losses' for 6th, 11th, 14th, 17th and 20th Mechanised Corps had reached 70–80 per cent, and that 6th, 17th and 20th Mechanised Corps 'in general function as rifle [units]'. Remnants of 14th Mechanised Corps were being sent to the rear to Smolensk, although 7th Mechanised Corps was arriving in the region from the east.[58] In early July it would be thrown into the counterattack after a German crossing of the Berezina River along with 5th Mechanised Corps – and like its counterparts further to the west would achieve little for considerable losses.[59] The scope for the surviving mechanised units to punch through the German flanks was extremely limited both due to low strength and supply and maintenance issues, but also the well documented issues of poor reconnaissance, command and control and co-operation between arms. Nonetheless, the remnants of the mechanised corps along with their rifle counterparts could bring considerable disorder to the German rear. By this point German spearheads had not only crossed the Berezina but also encircled Minsk – albeit far from 'hermetically sealing' the pocket that had been formed. Many Soviet troops broke out of the encirclement whilst many fought on in the forests in the pocket as German commanders argued over whether to push eastwards or more effectively seal and reduce the huge pocket containing much of the Western Front.[60]

Despite the less than impermeable nature of German encirclements in the west, by the end of June – in a matter of days – hundreds of thousands of men, thousands of vehicles, artillery pieces and other assets had been squandered – destroyed or captured for far less military benefit than had they been organised and deployed more appropriately and some fairly elementary precautions taken in a timely manner. During what was subsequently described as the Belorussian Strategic Defensive Operation deemed to have taken place between 22 June and 9 July, forces of the Western Front numbering in the region of 625,000 men at the outset of hostilities suffered in the region of 417,729 casualties, of which 341,000 were 'irrecoverable' – killed, missing and captured – and where a significant proportion of the 76,716 sick and wounded would also not be fit for frontline service again.[61] Troops of the Western Front left behind or destroyed huge quantities of supplies – stockpiled in forward areas but often not available to units fighting for their existence. In early July for example the Western Front reported having destroyed, left behind or been destroyed by the enemy more than seventeen million rounds of rifle ammunition.[62] These supplies could not easily be pulled back thanks not

A KV-series tank on a Leningrad street, in this instance during the autumn of 1941. Such heavily armoured and armed tanks, despite their limited numbers, proved a considerable shock for advancing German forces even when deployed piecemeal. These tanks could have had more significant impact had they been deployed in greater concentration and with better support. (RIA Novosti #601304)

only to unreality on the part of those higher up the chain of command who often only realised the need for such measures by the time it was too late, but also thanks to the fact that the Red Army's motor transport resources in particular were spread hopelessly thinly – hampering the distribution of supplies to troops and in particular where German air attacks were frequent. Super heavy artillery such as the B-4 introduced in Chapter 2, on which the Soviet Union had expended considerable resources, was deployed forward as if it might soon be required for offensive operations, and was not necessarily provided with suitable transport resources to move it and evacuate it to the rear. Hence more than one heavy howitzer artillery regiment equipped with 203 mm B-4 howitzers but not the means to move them to the rear in a timely manner was based at Dubno at the beginning of the war. After the capture of Dubno German forces reported having acquired a total of forty-two '21 cm' howitzers along with 215 tanks and other equipment there.[63] The lack of field repair and evacuation resources for Soviet armoured units – an issue to which we will return later – meant that many Soviet tanks would be captured intact by German troops. Although there is not space to detail it, the Dubno region had just seen intense fighting between forces of the South-Western Front and German forces of both 1st Panzergruppe and the German 6th Army at the end of June. German Army Chief of Staff Franz Halder noted in his war diary for 26 June how 'Army Group South is advancing slowly, unfortunately with considerable losses', noting how 'the enemy on this front has energetic leadership' and that the Red Army was 'continuously throwing new forces' against the German 'tank wedge' not only from the front but also on the flanks. The commitment of 'strong tank forces' had led to 'local enemy successes'. By 29 June Army Group South was still reporting 'heavy fighting' in the area, where a deep Soviet armoured penetration had 'caused a lot of confusion in the area between Brody and Dubno'. The next day Halder recorded continued 'local crises' until finally on 1 July he could record that the 'Dubno episode seems to be over'.[64] By this point Soviet forces in the region had been ordered to fall back after significant but 'piece-meal' attacks by the Soviet mechanised corps had resulted in the loss of strength not only to enemy action but to breakdowns and fuel short-ages.[65] Although losses had been inflicted on German armoured forces and were in this case significant, Soviet mechanised forces in the region soon all but ceased to exist. Future Marshal M.E. Katukov's under-strength 20th Tank Division, as part of Rokossovskii's 9th Mechanised Corps of the Soviet 5th Army, had in attempting to strike the German flank almost been encircled, but managed to retreat in time – despite exhortations from above not to do so.[66] Despite the calamity unfolding on the borders, even in the bleak weeks of June and early July 1941 there would be numerous indicators for the Soviet and German leaders and foreign observers that despite what on paper might have seemed to be cataclysmic losses and rapid German progress eastwards, the Wehrmacht was not able to achieve enough with its tactical and operational advan-tages to overcome Soviet strategic preparation and the problems associ-ated with conquering such vast expanses in the face of often stubborn, even if poorly organised, resistance.

Even before 'Barbarossa' had begun, the Soviet Union was in the process of mobilising its vast human and material resources for war – invasion accelerated the process. Soviet plans for war and mobilisation may have been on paper ridiculously ambitious, but chasing such targets still meant that even with the losses of the summer of 1941, the situation was such that it was, to quote the German Army Chief of Staff Franz Halder in an oft quoted passage in his war diary of 11 August 1941:

... increasingly plain that we have underestimated the Russian Colossus, who consistently prepared for war with that utterly ruthless determination so characteristic of totalitarian states. ... At the outset of war we reckoned with about 200 enemy divisions. Now we have already counted 360. Those divisions indeed are not armed and equipped according to our standards, and their tactical leadership is often poor. But there they are, and if we smash a dozen of them, the Russians simply put up another dozen.[67]

As important as force regeneration was the fact that although some Soviet units surrendered *en masse* in often hopeless circumstances, Soviet morale typically held through a combination of factors that included both carrot and stick. Hitler's suggestion of the previous summer, apparently overheard by Albert Speer, that 'a campaign against Russia would be like a child's game in a sand box by comparison' to defeating France was certainly not the case, and soon the Wehrmacht was taking significant losses that were sustainable only if it was assumed that the bulk of Soviet strength had been destroyed in the border regions.[68] Armoured vehicles and mobility was a central element to German success, and armoured vehicle losses during July were heavy, with the 732 tanks, assault guns and armoured command vehicles lost during July, along with the 118 lost at the end of June giving frontline formation a theoretical strength of 2,889 vehicles that does not factor in serviceability.[69] Soviet losses to the end of July had of course been far worse. Losses suffered by the mechanised corps of the South-Western Front alone were shocking. The six mechanised corps for the front, 4th, 8th, 9th, 15th, 19th and 22nd had started the war with 272 KV, 494 T-34, 1,378 BT-series tanks, 1,326 T-26, 49 T-35, 126 T-28 and 65 T-37 and similar light tanks. By 1 August these formations had on strength only 7 KV, 57 T-34, 121 BT-series tanks, 74 T-26, 22 T-28 and 8 T-37 and similar light tanks.[70]

As already identified, an important element in the poor performance of Soviet forces during the first days of the war – and making a significant contribution to the disaster experienced by the Western Front – was undoubtedly inadequate communications, and particularly radio communications. The problems with communications described earlier in this chapter were exacerbated once Soviet units and headquarters were no longer static. Men were willing to fight – they had equipment to do so even if supplies were low – but were not in the right place at the right time to maximise their impact even where weak Soviet reconnaissance had identified where that might be. Where possible the Red Army preferred to rely on telephone communications where land lines were more secure, but in a fluid situation it would be difficult to maintain them even without enemy disruption. It is not difficult to imagine how much cable alone would be required for the establishment and re-establishment of telephone communications as command posts moved in response to the military situation and where there were competing demands for resources – and not just at the front. For example, as the North-Western Front headquarters along with subordinate units and formations were pushed back again and again during the first days and weeks of the war the materials to keep re-establishing cable-based networks were used up – sometimes having to be destroyed where they had been stored in the absence of sufficient transport to move them. Part of the problem was that higher level headquarters were often situated too far forward – theoretically easing communications issues as long as the Red Army was holding ground – and probably preventing accusations of cowardice towards senior commanders. However, forward deployed command posts were vulnerable to the enemy and likely to have to relocate frequently if the enemy was advancing.[71]

Shortages of communications equipment were not just a problem at the front as a result of what might be described as supply chain issues. The Soviet regime had paid insufficient attention to communications in general prior to the war the Red Army soon simply found itself with insufficient cable and field telephone sets to meet wartime needs. On 20 July for example GKO ordered that the People's Commissariat for Communications pull twenty thousand telephone sets from the civilian sector so that they could be used to replace field sets that were in service at military hospitals, with the PVO and in other rear-area roles – releasing these field sets for frontline use.[72] Field telephone sets might be replaced with civilian ones, but the shortage of cable remained and must have hit lower priority users such as the PVO particularly hard. According to a note of no later than 22 July 1941 the air defences forces for Leningrad lacked not only 1,000 telephone sets but also 3,000 km of cable – along with lacking large numbers of radio sets.[73] It is quite likely that the shortage of telephone equipment and cable experienced by anti-aircraft forces contributed to the fact that 158th Fighter Air Regiment in the Leningrad Region reported losing almost as many aircraft from 22 June to 8 August to Soviet anti-aircraft fire as German – three to Soviet and four to German.[74] The fact that as of 10 July, as noted later, the 1st Leningrad Militia Division only had telephone cable for a single set of fixed positions highlights the acute shortages of cable not only for the PVO.

Not only did the Red Army have far fewer radio sets at the beginning of the war than it should have done – as in the case of the Kiev Special Military District noted in the previous chapter – but their quality and capabilities remained poor. For communications at higher levels, the Red Army had the 11-AK radio set, although KOVO for example only had 41 per cent of the requirement for 306 in early May 1941.[75] The 11-AK truck-mounted set was apparently rather delicate and far from suitable for use with tank formations that nonetheless employed it, where even in late 1938 a more modern set was being demanded.[76] Nonetheless, at least the tank formations had in principle communications resources intended for a high degree of mobility, with radio communications far more widely available and penetrating lower down the chain of command. Nonetheless, of 832 T-34 tanks available to the Red Army as of 1 June 1941, 197 were described as radio tanks for communication with those higher up the chain of command. Even approximately a third of older model tanks were equipped with some sort of radio equipment.[77] Unfortunately the effectiveness of these as other radio sets often left much to be desired. For example the 71-TK-3 radio set used for two-way communication from tanks although theoretically having a range on the move with voice of 'up to 15 km' in practice had a range on the move of 'about 6 km', and was according to one tanker 'a complex, unreliable radio set. Very often it failed, and it was very difficult to get it working again'.[78] Later, Lend-Lease sets with the capability for higher frequency operation for effective short-range communication would highlight just how inadequate Soviet radio equipment all too often was.

On top of insufficient sets to start with, many sets not only broke but were of course lost to the enemy or destroyed – where for example by 1 September, after it had been transferred to the command of the Northern Front, 48th Army had few surviving radio sets. As a whole 48th Army was down to barely divisional strength, and had only seventeen radio sets in total remaining. The 1st Mountain Rifle Brigade apparently lacked any sets, despite a strength of more than a thousand men.[79] Radio operator Arkadii Glazunov on the Western Front describes in his memoirs how he and his compatriot were forced to destroy the truck-mounted 5-AK radio set of their regiment and the vehicle because it ran out of petrol during the retreat during the first days of the war.[80] On 16 August the war diary for the North-Western Front noted for 48th Army how the 1st People's or Leningrad Militia Division 'wasn't being commanded by anyone' and for 18 August noted 'the Military Soviet of 48th Army in essence is not in command of the Army. It does not have communications with divisions....'.[81]

The collapse of the Western Front and the fall of Minsk at the end of June were significant blows to Stalin who had even been temporarily been left in the dark about developments on that key axis thanks to a breakdown in communications. More than happy to blame others for the situation – including Zhukov as head of the General Staff for the loss of communications with the Western Front – Stalin undoubtedly lost focus for a couple of days and fell into some sort of depression. According to his what might be deemed close colleague Anastas Mikoian, Stalin went as far as suggesting that all might be lost, stating that 'Lenin left us with a

Map 2: The German advances of 1941 and 1942.

great inheritance, and we, his successors, have squandered it all. . .'. This was perhaps said for effect, but nonetheless apparently had impact. Stalin is subsequently recorded as having briefly retreated to his dacha for a couple of days before being coaxed back by to the helm by his colleagues.[82] Stalin was now head of the new State Defence Committee that would from 30 June run the Soviet war effort as a whole. Stalin was also Commissar for Defence from 19 July and would be self-promoted from member of the Headquarters of the High Command created on

23 June, to Supreme High Commander of the armed forces at the head
of the Supreme High Command created on 8 August, after the brief
existence of a Headquarters of the Supreme Command in between.
Typically, all of these headquarters are referred to as the *Stavka*.[83] By
this point it was not only the thrust by the German Army Group Centre
on the Moscow axis that was making significant headway – Army Group
North was making dramatic progress towards Leningrad and even Army
Group South was making headway in its drive loosely towards Kiev and
beyond despite heavy opposition.

In true Stalinist fashion, someone lower down the chain of command
would have to pay for the calamity on the borders with their life, even if
Stalin himself had to a large extent been responsible for the flawed
deployment of the Red Army that meant that the Western Front was in
essence partially encircled before war had even started! The search for
scapegoats started quickly, and senior commanders of the Western Front
were obvious targets. On 28 July 1941 Stalin, in this instance wearing the
hat of People's Commissar for Defence, announced the execution not
only of General D.G. Pavlov, who had commanded the Western Front
during the late June debacles, but also former chief of staff for the
Western Front General-Major V.E. Klimovskii, former head of communications General-Major Grigor'ev and former commander of 4th Army
General-Major A.A. Korobkov. The list of accusations against them was
long, with Pavlov being accused not only of cowardice but also for of
such crimes as 'allowing command and control to collapse', 'handing
weapons and supplies to the enemy' and 'on his own initiative for having
given up positions with units of the front and allowing the enemy to break
through'. The announcement concluded with a warning that all those
who betrayed their oaths of loyalty, forgot their duty to the Motherland
and brought shame on the upper warrior ranks of the Red Army –
'cowards and panicmongers' who gave up positions and weapons to the
enemy 'on their own initiative and without a fight' – would be 'mercilessly punished according to the full weight of wartime laws', regardless
of who they were.[84] Lower down the chain of command there were more
executions for cowardice. On 6 July 1941 a number of middle-ranking
commanders of the Western Front were handed over to military tribu-
nals, such as the head of Medical Depot Number 848, Military Veterin-
arian 2nd Rank Beliavskii, who 'not having taken appropriate measures
for the evacuation of resources and not having destroyed them, ran away
leaving reserves of medical supplies to the enemy'.[85] On 7 July 1941
Army Commissar 1st Rank Mekhlis, as a member of the Military Soviet
for the Western Front and who had signed off on the order for the above,
made it clear that 'depending on circumstances, I authorize executions in

front of the troops' and indeed sanctioned the publication of 'more typical' cases in army and divisional newspapers, although forbidding that more than one case be publicised in any given edition.[86]

As had been the case during the 1930s, alongside the search for scapegoats ran the belief that failure was not just due to incompetence or betrayal, but also due to lack of resolve on the part of commanders and Red Army men, despite much evidence to the contrary. Where there had been a clear appreciation in the spring of 1940 that dual command and political interference in military decision making had hampered effective command, in what was deemed to be an absence of the latter there was again the need for closer political supervision of commanders and men. On 16 July 1941 dual command was reintroduced in the Red Army after little over a year without it – with commissars down to battalion level, and politruks below, once again sharing responsibility for military decision-making with commanders, and providing the moral leadership to make sure that units would be willing to 'fight to the last drop of blood' to 'defend every last inch of Soviet ground' regardless of whether it made obvious military sense.[87] On 16 July Smolensk fell. According to Zhukov, as one might expect, the fall of Smolensk was a significant blow to Stalin who was apparently 'beside himself' over the situation.[88] The next day counter-intelligence within the Red Army by the Special Sections was transferred back from the NKO to the NKVD – the Special Sections being provided with NKVD troops in order to carry out their 'struggle with espionage and treachery in units of the Red Army and the liquidation of desertion directly in the prefrontal zone'. In dealing with the latter the Special Sections not only had the power to arrest deserters, but 'where necessary to shoot them on the spot' – a punishment that could also be meted out to those suspected of causing self-inflicted wounds.[89] In August the encirclements and mass surrenders by Soviet troops often in militarily hopeless circumstances prompted the Headquarters of the Supreme High Command to issue the infamous Order Number 270 that essentially made surrender treason and that promised particularly severe punishment for commanders and 'political workers', who could expect to be shot for desertion and cowardice.[90]

Whether dual command and increasingly harsh discipline in the Red Army during the summer of 1941 were entirely detrimental to its functioning is difficult to assess. Commanders at all levels were undoubtedly less likely to exercise tactical and operational initiative and for example order timely withdrawals when under the watchful gaze of a commissar under pressure to make sure that positions were indeed held – even when convinced that it was the right thing to do. The military competence of many commissars was certainly limited – from Lev Mekhlis at the top down to those at lower levels even if at times it wasn't a question of ability but lack of training. All too frequently authorisation for withdrawal from above came too late to save units and formations from encirclement, where here the ultimate example is the encirclement of more than 600,000 men in the Kiev region in September to be considered in the next chapter. Accusations of 'cowardice' could stick all too easily and much resort was undoubtedly made to the pistol or firing squad in order to maintain 'discipline'. In his important work that focuses on issues of Red Army motivation during the Great Patriotic War, Roger Reese cites the example of one Josef Finkelshtein, a junior commander in a Leningrad militia division, who recalled witnessing the execution of three tank crewmen accused of desertion at the beginning of October 1941. 'They undressed and stood submissively in the snow in their trousers. . . . The one wearing the tankers helmet covered his eyes with his hands. They went up to him and moved his hands down. "At the traitors to the Motherland – fire!". . . . They all fell, two were still moving. The NKVD man went up to them and shot them in the head with his revolver'.[91] Il'ia Grigor'evich Sokolov, a rifleman, recalls on two occasions later in the war having witnessed the shooting of Red Army personnel intended to reinforce discipline through their being made an example of, in one case it was because of a self-inflicted wound, 'the second time they shot a soldier who had hacked a finger off his left hand with an entrenching tool [*sapernaia lopatka*]. . . .Commanders told us, "Better that a German bullet kills you, than your own kill you for cowardice!". This phrase made it through into our consciousness, and in some way helped us fight'.[92] That, as Sokolov suggests, 'too much blood of soldiers was wasted without purpose' by the special sections is perhaps highlighted by the fact that at times the scale of killing prompted intervention from higher up the chain of command, such as an order from Stalin as People's Commissar for Defence of 4 October 1941 that sought to limit the use of repression as an 'educational tool' rather than an 'extreme measure' to be used sparingly – something of a case of do as I say, not as I have done.[93]

Repressive factors were probably more effective where more positive factors such as nationalism also had a role to play. The Soviet Motherland or Rodina needed defending, and not only the few acceptable Soviet wartime leaders such as Lenin and Chapaev, but also their many historical forebears from who had defended what was now Soviet territory were soon mobilised to rally the troops. As *Pravda* noted early in the war, 'first among the equal peoples of the USSR' were the Russians, whose imperial heroes were soon at the vanguard of the propaganda struggle that would soon have hatred of an increasingly obviously brutal invader as a potent theme.[94] Certainly hatred of the enemy that had inflicted so much death and destruction on the Soviet Union would be an important motivational tool to encourage Red Army personnel to fight past the point of liberating Soviet territory – fostering the sort of crimes on German territory that have figured prominently in some recent histories before belatedly draconian measures were taken to halt them.[95] The Soviet writer Ilia Ehrenburg soon made it plain that the war was being fought not only against 'Hitlerites' or 'Nazis', but against 'the Germans' as a whole. His promotion of almost indiscriminate violence against Germans probably seemed to have been in keeping with much of the violence meted out on German-occupied territory of the Soviet Union, and can only have reinforced any understandable hatred and bitterness that already existed.[96] Vengeance for German and Axis crimes could be something of a unifying mantra – neither Soviet nor Russian nationalism would appeal to some 'subject' peoples no matter how things were dressed up, and it is easy to imagine how in the context of an erstwhile ally gaining the upper hand against the much trumpeted Red Army after having caught it apparently napping that those with less than positive feelings towards the regime would have plenty of ammunition – figuratively at least – to undermine resolve.

Unsurprisingly the Western Front early in the war sought to deal with an apparent problem with the reliability of Red Army personnel from the recently occupied districts of the western Ukraine and Belorussia – along with other potentially less than reliable troops who for example had relatives who had suffered at the hands of the NKVD. The solution was to be dispatch to the Soviet rear for some, but for the 'more active anti-Soviet elements decisive repressive measures'.[97] Particularly problematic in terms of reliability – and understandably so when their histories are appreciated – were the territorial rifle corps of the Baltic Soviet Republics. After the incorporation of the Baltic Republics into the Soviet Union during the summer of 1940 their armies were not disbanded and arms taken elsewhere as suggested by Soviet officials on the spot, but reformed as 22nd Territorial Rifle Corps for Estonia, 24th for Latvia, and 29th for Lithuania, subordinate to the Pribaltic Military District. Given concerns about reliability, dual command had been maintained for these formations and in addition to local communist commissars they were provided with commissars from the Red Army.[98] As one might expect, these formations were subjected to considerable purging, with for example hundreds of commanders being removed from their positions in 22nd Territorial Rifle Corps in June 1941, leaving the formation according to historian of these formations S.B. Buldigin 'not fit for combat' on 22 June 1941.[99] It was probably not a surprise for many Red Army personnel involved with the units concerned that their reliabilities were poor, even after 22nd and 24th Territorial Rifle Corps had been provided with non-native troops from the east. Elements of 29th Territorial Rifle Corps were the first to see action, the formation starting the war, albeit not in a fully mobilised state, close to the Soviet border. Soon remnants of 184th Rifle Division initially deployed forward were falling back on Vilnius, at which point according to Soviet sources at around 16:00 on 23 June 'having sensed the close proximity of German units the reactionary element of the division rebelled, took up arms against commanders of Russian nationality', who 'in the main were killed'. Meanwhile in Vilnius itself elements of the corps were engaged in combat with those loyal to the Soviet regime, knocking out a number of artillery pieces and destroying supplies and munitions.[100] In a report on the state of 180th Rifle Division of 22nd Estonian Corps (now no longer Territorial), it was noted on 14 July how 'a significant portion of commanders and Estonian Red Army men have gone over to the Germans', on 15–16 July a representative of the Military Soviet of the North-Western Front noted how 'in the division there have been instances where elements of the Estonian command and rank-and-file have gone over to the Germans, making it very difficult to accurately confirm divisional losses'.[101] When a unit was not made up of significant numbers of pre-1939–40 non-Soviet nationalities or other Soviet national groups that lacked the same stake in the Soviet empire as their Russian, eastern Ukrainian and eastern Belorussian colleagues, then when the military situation was not hopeless Red Army units typically fought hard. The issue of nationalities and Red Army military effectiveness is something to which we will return later when significant numbers of troops drawn from the Caucasus and Central Asia would see action.

In the main, both the stubbornness of Soviet resistance and the new Soviet tanks were clearly a shock to many German officers and men. Although operationally Soviet forces were overwhelmed during the battles in the border regions, and Soviet armour in particular performed poorly on the counterattack at the tactical level as well, Soviet forces nonetheless frequently fought hard. In his diary, Hans Roth of 299th Infantry Division, 6th Army, Army Group South describes resistance in the village of Lokacze on 24 June 1941 where he reported how 'house after house must be cleansed with hand grenades. Fanatics fire at us until the roofs collapse over their heads and they are buried under the rubble. Others escape their houses at the last minute as human torches'. As German forces pushed forwards pockets of stubborn resistance continued from rallying points in the forests. Roth noted on 25 June how 'time and time again there are small battles to the rear of the front line', writing on 26 June how 'we are no longer safe anywhere', and how 'over the past few days the Reds have shot many messengers on their motorcycles, dragging them off their bikes....'.[102] Perhaps the strongest symbol of Soviet resistance during the first days of 'Barbarossa' became the defence of the Brest fortress. The reduction of meaningful resistance at the citadel took, according to a report by the chief of staff of the German 4th Army, from 22 to 29 June, during which time the Red Army and NKVD personnel resisted 'stubbornly and fiercely'. Despite the disparity in firepower and local resources- German forces ultimately employed 'artillery, assault guns, the "Karl" piece [a super-heavy mortar], captured armoured cars, ..., 8.8 cm anti-aircraft guns, flamethrowers, petrol, oil and so forth'- the reduction cost 32 German officers and 421 rank and file killed and 31 officers and 637 men wounded.[103]

In the face of often fierce resistance the much vaunted German armoured units suffered not inconsiderable attrition – a situation alleviated by the fact that typically the battlefield would be German and many knocked-out vehicles could be salvaged. In his diary, Erich Hager of 39th Panzer Regiment, 17th Panzer Division describes not only the fierce nature of Russian resistance during the fighting in June 1941 on the Minsk axis described earlier, but also the destruction of his PzKpfw IV tank, quite possibly to anti-tank gun fire and from close range, on 28 June 1941 as they entered a village. Other tank losses he mentions during the fighting in the border regions during the first weeks of 'Barbarossa' include the loss of three tanks to artillery on 2 July.[104] 4th Panzer Division had also been deployed against the Soviet Western Front, and had taken heavy losses, such that by 21 July it had suffered eleven Panzer II, twenty-seven Panzer III, three Panzer IV and one command vehicle as total losses, with a further eighty-nine vehicles out of operation – forty-nine being repaired and forty awaiting spare parts before repairs could take place. Consequently only forty-four vehicles – including only six Panzer IV with its short-barrelled but nonetheless 75 mm gun that was far more useful than the Panzer IIs and even IIIs when facing potent Soviet anti-tank guns and gave slightly more hope in favourable tactical circumstances when the latest Soviet tanks were encountered.[105]

Fortunately for the Wehrmacht during the first weeks of the war the new T-34 and KV-series tanks were typically not encountered in any numbers – their crews often poorly trained on new vehicles sometimes only delivered days and weeks before, lacking sufficient fuel and munitions along with appropriate support from other arms. Disorganised counterattacks by Soviet armoured forces blundered headlong into enemy units and anti-tank defences. As suggested by A.A. Kamentsev, a veteran of the first days of the war, 'during the early battles we took terrible losses in tanks and personnel because of a lack of knowledge of and ability to conduct manoeuvre. We only knew one thing – "Forward!"'.[106] There can be little doubt that through a combination of technical deficiencies, particularly in communications, weak leadership, and weak logistics, the Red Army was for the first weeks of the war unable to gain any sort of meaningful initiative more than fleetingly despite possessing far greater mechanised strength than the Wehrmacht. In fact, it is debateable whether the Red Army had a practical conception of 'initiative' that suited the type of fluid warfare in which it was now engaged. The sort of 'elastic command and control' that Zhukov had noted was crucial in German military successes of 1939 and 1940 would not only have been technically difficult for the Red Army, but went against an organisational culture that paid lip service to initiative. It is certainly unclear what Zhukov meant by 'sensible initiative' in December 1940 and whether there was much scope for that to be displayed where 'no retreat' and 'forward!' were mantras.[107] These terms continued to be a stock response all too frequently for the remainder of the war, where as the Soviet Union gained the upper hand the former was of course required less frequently. As artilleryman N.N. Nikulin who served from 1943 onwards bitterly wrote in his post-war memoirs – 'Attack! – phoned the boss in the Kremlin, attack! – telephoned the general from his warm office, attack! – ordered the colonel from his solid dugout.'[108]

Not only had much of the Soviet tank park been thrown into the fray with the advancing Wehrmacht with reckless abandon during the first days and weeks of the war, but also many men who could certainly have been better used. This reckless squandering of lives was perhaps most obvious with the militia divisions. Moves to form volunteer militia divisions began even before the end of June 1941 – with the primary constituencies for such divisions being factory workers in urban areas. The drive for the formation of such divisions was certainly not from the Red Army, but if Soviet sources are to be believed from factory workers and the local Party machinery. In Leningrad, on 30 June 1941 a headquarters was formed for the Leningrad Army of the People's Militia that would nominally include ten militia rifle divisions, five worker's brigades and sixteen artillery-machine-gun battalions – in the region of 224,000 men.[109] As of 10 July 1941 1st Division of the Leningrad Army of People's Militia had 'in the main been provided with personnel, received weapons released to it and principal items of material-technical provision'. With a high proportion of Party members and candidate members (1,693), along with members of the Komsomol (1,800) – enough for 12–15 per cent Party members and 10–12 per cent Komsomol members in units – the division had only twenty cadre command personnel. Of the remaining commanders the majority at least had 'combat experience from the last war', despite their 'theoretical preparation being low' and where 'the basic core of commanders has an insufficiently clear conception of the character and nature of contemporary combat, and especially the use of technical combat resources'. Of the rank and file 'a significant number were completely lacking military education or had not gone through pre-conscription training' – later in the document noted as being up to 50 per cent. With little artillery, sufficient light machine guns for only two per rifle platoon and without heavy machine guns for the rifle companies, it was noted that 'the division completely lacks anti-tank artillery and anti-aircraft resources'. The report on the division went on to note that with extremely limited communications resources – with telephone communications at best down to battalion level for a single set of fixed positions, and without radio communications between rifle battalions and higher headquarters – the 'limited quantity of auto-transport resources and the absence of horses means that the mobility of units is extremely limited'. Brief, and extremely optimistic concluding remarks for the report were as follows – '1st Division is in the main prepared for dealing with the requirements of defensive battle. It requires 1–2 days for practical integration when concentrated'.[110]

Supposedly making up for lack of training equipment, and supplies with patriotic zeal, divisions such as 1st Division of the Leningrad Army of People's Militia were thrown into the defensive battles of the summer of 1941 and predictably performed poorly and took heavy losses. In a report of 29 July 1941 to the head of the Political Department for the Leningrad Army of People's Militia, one Battalion Commissar Moiseichenko described the actions of the second rifle regiment of the division a few days earlier where the first battalion of the regiment had seen heavy combat over 12 hours on 26 July that saw it ultimately retreat without authorisation – losing in the region of fifty men killed and wounded. Apparently as a result of poor communications – where it lacked not only telephone communications with its own companies but also communications with the regimental command and the artillery – the battalion was not only subjected to fire from the artillery that was supposed to be supporting them, and one of its own companies ended up firing on another as it moved positions – but was also unable to co-ordinate its actions with the neighbouring cadre unit. The battalion was also not effectively supported by its own mortars that lacked sufficient munitions – even though there were munitions available at regimental level. The battalion was thrown unsuccessfully into the attack on two occasions, starting from about 1,000 metres from enemy positions, before the battalion commander, senior lieutenant Moraev, ordered a withdrawal without the sanction of the regiment. This withdrawal was, according to Moiseichenko, conducted 'in an utterly disorganised manner' that saw intermingled sections and companies pull back without 'following rules for conducting a withdrawal'. Somehow one of the company politruks received orders from the regiment not to pull back, and was able to hold the line with sixty men he withheld – preventing the enemy occupying the battalion's positions. Subsequently both regimental and divisional commanders were slow to bring the situation to order, coming under heavy criticism for their lack of leadership, although Moiseichenko did note that he had seen similarly disorderly withdrawal from cadre units nearby and namely 835th and 841st Rifle Regiments of 16th Rifle Corps.[111] Still, despite the poor performance of the militia divisions committed early on as the autumn arrived there were on paper more than sixty militia divisions in the Soviet Union.[112] Many of these militia divisions were ground down before their remnants were sensibly converted to conventional rifle divisions, before such militia divisions appeared again the following year as German forces once again threatened to capture key urban areas that were inadequately defended by conventional forces.

Nonetheless, as Soviet divisions were being chewed up and replaced with new albeit weaker ones, they were whittling down German strength bit by bit. As Generaloberst Franz Halder, Chief of Staff for the German Army recorded in his war diary on 4 August 1941, in the war against the Soviet Union to the end of July the Wehrmacht had lost 205,175 NCOs and enlisted men, along with 8,126 officers killed, wounded or missing – a total of 213,301. As of 19 July for the period to 16 July total non-medical losses had been less than half that at 102,588. Three days further into August and casualties to 3 August were 231,801 and 9,188 for NCOs and other ranks and officers respectively as German losses mounted steadily, and particularly amongst officers, where Halder recorded that more than 10 per cent of those lost had been commissioned. The Wehrmacht had now suffered total losses to 3 August of 242,000 men from a strength of approximately 3.35 million – more than 7 per cent of strength.[113]

Perhaps the greatest German failures in launching 'Barbarossa' were both underestimation of Soviet resolve, and not only underestimation of initial Soviet strength but also of the Soviet Union's ability to mobilise new units. The German spearheads may have danced round the Soviet infantry and even many mechanised formations during the first weeks of the war, but avoiding them still left them fighting in the rear – sometimes for days – with German infantry soon torn between dealing with Soviet troops to the rear and moving forward to deal with the units ahead.

Soviet militia from the Kirov Factory in Leningrad march past a statue of their factory's namesake in the summer of 1941. Such poorly prepared units suffered heavy casualties in action for relatively little obvious gain. (RIA Novosti #371)

As German forces pushed eastwards the Red Army was not trading space for time, but as Soviet units were bypassed or retreated this unintentionally made German operational problems worse thanks to ever extended lines of communication vulnerable to Soviet attack. By late July it was apparent not only to many German leaders, but also Western observers, that despite the territory and resources lost, the Soviet Union and the Red Army were not about to collapse – something on which German plans rested. German operational successes would continue through the summer and into the autumn, but every success limited German potential to concentrate resources for the next as losses mounted and supply lines were increasingly strained. With hindsight it was a battle of attrition that the Red Army was actually winning, albeit at horrendous cost.

11   'Barbarossa'

From Smolensk to Moscow

During the summer battles of 1941 the Red Army was, in terms of the narrow concept of military effectiveness used by Roger Reese discussed in Chapter 8, an effective fighting force – Soviet troops fought stubbornly despite a catalogue of deficiencies in reconnaissance, command and control and logistics to name just a few. It would not be long before that resolve would be increased for many as it became apparent that the invaders – and the Red Army – were fighting what both sides in different ways described as 'a war of annihilation' – for Stalin in his speech to the Soviet people by radio of 3 July 1941 a 'fight to the death' [*smertel'naia skhvatka*] with German fascism.[1] With German forces soon at Smolensk on the central axis of advance – two-thirds of the way to Moscow from Brest-Litovsk – and approaching Leningrad in the north, Soviet resistance if anything intensified. Certainly in his diary entry for 26 July, or the 36th day of the German war with the Soviet Union, German Chief of Staff for the Army General Franz Halder noted under the heading 'Over-all picture' that 'Enemy defense is becoming more aggressive; more tanks, more planes' – with of course far more to come – and far more than expected by initial optimists such as Halder.[2] German artillery officer Siegfried Knappe noted from a somewhat different and grass roots perspective to Franz Halder, how 'from Smolensk on, the Russian resistance grew stronger'.[3] Undoubtedly Soviet resistance intensified as the summer progressed in the sense of being more consistently fierce as the relative paralysis of Soviet forces in the border regions during late June and early July no longer applied. Despite the destruction of much of the Soviet mechanised strength on the borders – vast material resources amassed over years of intensive rearmament – the Red Army and the Soviet Union had much more still to throw at the advancing Wehrmacht and her allies even if tanks in particular would be a relatively scarce commodity over the coming months. During the late summer counter-attacks of varying sizes such as that being conducted in the Smolensk region by amongst others 19th Army from mid-August into September[4] or led by 34th Army in the Staraia Russa region during mid-late August

233

would cause concern for over extended German forces, but their local significances did not contribute to immediate change in the wider operational and strategic situation. Such counterattacks certainly whittled down German strength and had a cumulative effect, but Soviet losses were all too frequently so heavy that whole units and formation ceased to be combat effective. Near Staraia Russa, after initial success on 15–16 August in the face of apparently overwhelming German air support from 16 August onwards by 20 August 'after having lost more than 50 per cent [of its strength] killed and wounded' 34th Army was apparently 'so demoralized that it retreated in disarray'. By 28 August, in what was essentially a damning indictment by a member of the army's military soviet of 34th Army's commander, General-Major Kachanov, the army had lost most of its artillery and heavy machine guns – with only 20,000 of 86,000 personnel remaining with the army.[5]

The Wehrmacht undoubtedly suffered particularly significant losses as a result of stubborn Soviet resistance in the protracted fighting around Smolensk that continued from July–September, as German forces sought to seal a large pocket of Soviet troops there and then hold positions to the east for when the advance on Moscow might be resumed. During the second half of July the bulk of German mechanised strength in the centre was sent both northwards and southwards in accordance with Hitler's controversial directive of 19 July 1941. Army Group Centre was theoretically 'after the destruction of the many pockets of enemy troops which have been surrounded, and the establishment of lines of communication' to continue 'to advance on Moscow with infantry formations', but was soon very obviously on the defensive despite the fact that Army Group Centre was not totally denuded of its armour.[6] It was in this region that Soviet forces launched perhaps the most widely trumpeted Soviet counterattack of the summer in late August and early September at El'nia, that saw according to celebratory announcement to the troops of 7 September 'a crushing blow' struck against the Wehrmacht with 'the broken enemy, having suffered huge losses, bleeding to death...retreating in disarray'.[7] The reality was that German forces withdrew in relative order back across the Desna and fell back on previously prepared positions, although under considerable pressure and after having in the German commander of Army Group Centre Fedor von Bock's own words been 'bled white' defending their bridgehead that had now been lost.[8] With the armoured forces that had destroyed the Western Front in June to a significant extent dispersed from north-south along the Eastern Front, the Red Army perhaps had an opportunity on this sector, despite its weaknesses in command and control, to concentrate resources for a major victory. Much like the Wehrmacht, too many major and indeed offensive operations were however being run at once –essentially along the whole front – for overwhelming force to be concentrated against Army Group Centre. Even in the centre it was questionable whether there were sufficient resources for major operations from the north-east, east and south-east of Smolensk.

Soviet forces had already been hammering away at German forces in the Smolensk region for weeks by late August.[9] Certainly preparations for offensive operations by Zhukov's Reserve Front in mid-August, as he suggested in his memoirs, had been rushed under pressure from Stavka – with Zhukov feeling the sort of pressure that he would frequently apply in similar circumstances.[10] I.N. Russiianov, then commanding 100th Rifle Division noted in his memoirs, how 'fierce, exhuasting fighting had been taking place day and night for about a month' by the time that Zhukov visited the division towards the end of August, dissatisfied with the failure of the division to take the village of Ushakovo on the northern extremity of the German El'nia salient – by this point particularly unlikely with Russiianov apparently reporting to Zhukov that rifle companies were now down to 10–15 men and commanded by junior [*mladshie*] commanders.[11] After brief respite Soviet forces would go over to the offensive again. On 25 August 1941 the Headquarters of the Supreme High Command directed the Reserve Front, as part of wider operations to recapture the whole Smolensk region, to 'from the morning of 30.08 to go over to the offensive and liquidate the enemy's El'nia group of forces, striking blows with 24th Army towards Pochinok and 43rd Army towards Roslavl' (between Briansk and Smolensk) with the aim of destroying the enemy and occupying these points', by 8 September holding a line to the west of these objectives.[12] Soviet strength for the renewed offensive – against well dug-in enemy forces – was hardly overwhelming at any given point – with Russiianov noting how it was really only in artillery that 24th Army had superiority over opposing German forces. When the offensive began on 30 August Russiianov's division was soon bogged down in fighting that saw little progress for high casualties for the first couple of days, although by 4 September had finally made significant progress in breaching enemy defences and advancing plans for encirclement of German forces in the El'nia salient.[13] Further west 102nd Tank Division and 107th Rifle Division initially made little progress, prompting the commander of 24th Army K.I. Rakutin to resort to threats against the 'disorganised' commands of these divisions, which received 'strong reprimands with warnings [*strogie viguvora s preduprizhdeniiam*]'.[14] Things were also not going well on the Roslavl' sector – on 1 September Zhukov reported that 211th Rifle Division had retreated 3–6 km in panic during the night of 30 August–1 September, creating a difficult situation for its neighbour, 149th Rifle Division.[15] The problem was to a large extent the fact that the Reserve Front was trying to do too much with too little, with Zhukov not unreasonably insisting to Stalin on 4 September that he not focus more resources for operations on the Roslavl' sector with the Briansk Front heavily engaged with Guderian's 2nd Panzer-gruppe heading southeastwards, and exploit emerging successes against the El'nia salient first.[16] Zhukov's conversation with Stalin late in the evening of 29 August had highlighted the extent to which there was too much juggling with resources between competing offensive priorities – in this case with aircraft – where Zhukov was to give up all but twenty aircraft for operations to the south before himself receiving reinforce-ments over the next two days – with offensive operations to be launched on the ground during that period.[17] Nonetheless, despite the dissipation of available Soviet strength the Soviet El'nia offensive hit German forces also denuded of strength hard, such that by 2 September von Bock commanding Army Group Centre had decided to pull out of the sali-ent.[18] After the recapture of El'nia Soviet propaganda claimed that 'as a result of the fighting eight German divisions were smashed [razgrom-leno]', including 10th Panzer, although the El'nia offensive was perhaps more significant for the morale boost that it provided.[19] Certainly the trophy materials seized by the Reserve Front from German forces did not suggest a 'broken' enemy who was 'retreating in disarray' as Zhukov had suggested, even if German forces had taken heavy losses.[20] Even allowing for the frequent shooting of PoWs and the fact that the unit concerned was a tank division, five NCOs and twelve rank-and-file as PoWs was a low tally for 102nd Independent Tank Division for the period from 8 August to 12 September where considerable effort was often expended to highlight the scale of the haul seized in such documents. The padding of this list of 'trophies' even by the standards of such lists is highlighted by the listing of three pairs of boots [sapogi] amongst the weapons, muni-tions and other equipment.[21] Nor was the El'nia operation a glowing endorsement of Red Army capabilities in modern combined arms war-fare. In his memoirs Zhukov wrote of the Red Army at El'nia – under his command of course – 'using all forms of weaponry, blending fire and manoeuvre, our rifle units, artillerymen, pilots and tankers struck power-ful blows against the enemy in close co-ordination with each other'.[22] This was perhaps how Zhukov would have liked it to have been, but the reality was somewhat different. In a communication with the commander of the Reserve Front, namely Zhukov, on 13 September 1941 Shaposh-nikov, once again Chief of the General Staff, talked of 'unnecessary losses in both men and material' for 24th and 43rd Armies due to poor mar-shalling of forces available, and described artillery and air support for the attack by infantry and tanks as 'disgracefully organised'.[23] Losses for the Reserve Front had indeed been significant during the operation. The 43rd Army's losses on the Roslavl' axis had been relatively light by Soviet standards with total losses including medical recorded as 960 for the period from 8 to 10 September 1941 alone.[24] During the heavy fighting from 30 August to 4 September against the El'nia salient 100th Rifle Division of 24th Army alone recorded the loss of 2,986 men.[25] Armoured units also suffered heavy losses – 102nd Tank Division had lost a total of 5,034 men from 17 July to 12 September 1941 – and its tank regiments had few operable vehicles by 11 September. With list strengths of ten heavy, twenty-one medium and sixty-nine light (BT-series and T-26) tanks per regiment, on 11 September 204th Tank Regiment had preserved barely half of its list strength, and 205th Tank Regiment retained just over a third.[26] Command and control had certainly been an issue during the offensive – 24th Army had an operational section of only nine men, of whom 'a number were inexperienced staff officers' for the command and control of forces including twelve rifle divisions. The chief of staff for the army, General-Major Kondrat'ev essentially pleaded with the chief of staff of the front for ideally 'eight operationally literate commanders' to join them, that could not be drawn from divisional staffs as they were also short on personnel.[27] Here, the fact that the Academy of the General Staff had been created only in 1936 with a relatively small intake per year would alone have been a limiting factor, but the number of experienced and even recently trained staff officers had also been whittled down by the Great Purges. Even before the rapid expansion of the Red Army in 1940–1, as suggested by the aforementioned testimony of former staff officer L.S. Skvirskii with regard to the case of 14th Army during the war with Finland, the Red Army lacked the sort of staff cadres that would soon be required in even greater numbers.[28]

In the aftermath of the El'nia fighting, Russiianov's 100th Rifle Division was one of the first divisions of the Red Army to receive the Guards designation. In an order of 18 September 1941 Stalin made 100th, 127th, 153rd and 161st Rifle Divisions 1st–4th Guards Rifle Divisions respectively for their 'military achievements, their organisation, discipline and exemplary order' – with increased pay for their personnel and the promise of distinct uniforms.[29] The distinct uniforms did not in the end materialise, although a guards badge was introduced.[30] Guards units and formations would subsequently receive better equipment and a greater number of supporting elements, even if their theoretically increased strengths would not always translate to manpower on the ground given their intensive use and heavy losses. How these losses were replaced could influence the continued performance of a Guards unit. Feeding 'just any reinforcements' into Guards units could and did lead to a dilution of quality and *esprit de corps* as one Major Zayonchkovsky notes for 38th and 41st Guards Rifle Divisions near Stalingrad in late September 1942, and particularly when there wasn't time to integrate them into the unit before they were thrown into combat. Such expedients may have contributed to 62nd Army commander Chuikov's suggestion in January 1943 that Guards divisions weren't 'really all that different' from other divisions, highlighting desertions from 13th Guards Rifle Division.[31] Quality was at least in some instances threatened later in the war as the Red Army advanced westwards by the local recruitment of personnel from liberated territory 'without preliminary checks' being made. Consequently, according to the General Staff, 'criminal elements and traitors to the Motherland' were finding their way into such units.[32] In April 1943 the Stavka issued an order that explicitly sought to preserve Guards corps and armies for offensive operations or counterattacks, otherwise pulling them back from the front line in order to train.[33] At least in such circumstances new recruits could be more effectively incorporated into such units, and their wounded personnel would be more likely to rejoin their unit. In December 1941 the NKO had specified that wounded Guards personnel with all but the most serious injuries were to be kept in medical facilities as close to the front line as possible in order to facilitate their return to their Guards units to preserve the 'special nature of their cadres' and to 'preserve their military traditions'. The need to return wounded Guards troops to their own units or at least another Guards unit was stressed in the same February 1944 General Staff document that raised concerns about locally recruited 'criminal elements and traitors to the Motherland' from occupied territory finding their way into Guards units.[34]

Although the Guards designation was first applied to the infantry divisions just mentioned, it would also be applied to other arms. In many ways the institution of the Guards designation was part of the first wartime phase of cultural shift away from the symbolism and ideals of the Revolution that had started in the late 1930s – revolutionary ideals and symbolism that had amongst other things for example hampered the authority of commanders and prevented the development of a Soviet General Staff and the training of staff officers through the Academy of the General Staff or equivalent. The Red Army was now returning to tsarist and bourgeois symbolism and practice in a significant way. Where this first phase saw both the institution of the Guards designation and the resurrection of tsarist military heroes in Soviet propaganda for example, the second in late 1942 and early

1943 would see the wholesale return of the title 'officer' and the associated divide between officers and men that had been an important marker of revolutionary change in the armed forces. In the case of the Guards designation, if Russiianov's memoirs are any indicator of his feelings in September 1941, the designation was certainly a source of pride, as he recalls it being for men of the division. Such devices probably often provided a boost to motivation – particularly when they came with material benefits as well as prestige.[35] The Guards designation certainly seems to have been far more significant – both materially and in terms of prestige – than the increasingly less significant Red Banner designation that had been awarded to units and formations of the Red Army since 8 May 1919. Initially awarded relatively sparingly – eighteen regiments were awarded the Red Banner designation for their performance during the Civil War – the designation was handed out more readily by the late 1930s and early 1940s where for example nine regiments were awarded the designation after Khalkhin-Gol and forty-six after the war with Finland. During the early phases of the Great Patriotic War relatively few units received the designation – only seven regiments during the summer and autumn campaigns of 1941 – when one might assume that the designation therefore had more meaning. However, during the Great Patriotic War as a whole a staggering 1,496 regiments would receive the designation for service on the Soviet-German front – the bulk during the final phases of the war.[36]

The institution of the Guards designation was perhaps not an act of desperation – the El'nia victory was for example a genuine, even if subsequently exaggerated, victory. Despite heavy losses 100th Rifle Division had achieved some success and as a meaningful unit survived to fight another day. Despite heavy losses and issues with command and control, when comparing the Red Army in September 1941 to June and July, it is apparent that by September the Red Army was no longer on the back foot in the same way that it had been but weeks before, even if there was still something of a scramble to mobilise new units and throw them into the battle with inadequate training. The Red Army command had certainly learnt much from the initial period of the war, but would require time and the more stable winter period of 1941–2 and into the spring of 1942 for many of these 'lessons' to be applied. In a directive of 15 July the Headquarters of the Supreme High Command made it plain to the commanders of fronts, armies and military districts that the mechanised corps were 'far too massive amalgamations' that were 'not very mobile, nimble and suitable for manoeuvere' and also 'vulnerable targets for enemy aviation'. The directive went on to note how 'large and cumbersome armies' made it complicated for commanders of relative 'youth and limited experience' to exert command and control in battle.' – 24th Army earlier with its inadequate staff being a case in point here.[37] Not only would these young and inexperienced commanders propelled up the chain of command both by the purges and the rapid expansion of the Red Army require time to gain the necessary experience, but it would also take a little time to weed out the many commanders who would probably not have occupied senior positions or had as much authority had it not been for the Great Purges. Despite the many inadequacies of the Red Army, German commanders certainly noted the ability of the Soviet artillery and air force to inflict increasing casualties on German forces both at El'nia and elsewhere.[38] If the Red Army could get the various arms to co-operate a little more effectively then it should be able to make something out of what were individually far from refined but nonetheless not entirely incapable pieces of the jigsaw.

The Red Army still did not however function well as a conglomeration of components at any level – including the tactical – although at this point in the war the grim determination of many Soviet troops who fought tenaciously and literally to the death was militarily at least a positive factor that stood out in sharp contrast to the many inadequacies of the Red Army as an organisation. Unfortunately poor reconnaissance, inadequate and rushed planning and poor co-ordination between arms made the costs of the sort of unimaginative frontal assaults all too frequently launched by Soviet units excruciating. Hans Roth for example recalls a number of instances from the perspective of a frontline combatant, one on 3 July 1941 during which he described how 'the masses charge with a loud "hurrah!"…with our concentrated fire we mow them down row after row.'[39] Later that year on 4 December, artillery officer Siegfried Knappe recalled a series of frontal attacks by Soviet troops that started as what might be described as a reconnaissance in force in platoon strength before being repeated in company and later battalion strength.[40] Not only German sources record the frontal assaults all too frequently carried out by Soviet forces, but even Rumanian forces at Odessa discussed later noted how Soviet infantry 'acted without particular initiative and creativity' on the offensive in all too often launching frontal assaults.[41] Some German troops apparently thought that the capacity for Soviet troops to push forward as they often did, apparently regardless, was because they were 'either drugged or drunk'[42] – and on occasion that might have been the case as vodka, watered down spirit or sometimes cognac or wine were provided to Soviet frontline troops for most of the war. As an interlude from operations, the impact of vodka rations on Soviet combat performance is worth considering.

Soviet troops fight on the approaches to Odessa in the late summer of 1941. With the pre-war 1936 model helmet still in evidence as a vestige of the army of the 1930s, these troops reliant on the rifle lacked the sort of small arms firepower that their later war successors would be able to employ, and were all too often thrown into poorly supported frontal assaults. (RIA Novosti #59232)

A regular portion – perhaps dose would be a better term – of vodka or equivalent was first provided to Soviet troops during the war with Finland. Future popular Soviet actor and comedian Iurii Nikulin, then a young Red Army soldier, recalls in his memoirs receiving his 100 grams of vodka in Finland, but preferred to exchange it for the portion of *salo* – a fat – that was also provided. Nikulin first drank his 100 grams on his eighteenth birthday in late December 1939.[43] On 22 August 1941 in a brief decree the State Defence Committee authorised the provision of 100 grams of 40 per cent proof vodka per day from 1 September for Red Army personnel of all ranks 'in the front line of the field army', elaborated on in an NKO order of 25 August to include aircrews and supporting personnel on field airfields as frontline personnel.[44] What exactly constituted being in the front line was unclear, and the end result seems to have been to provide the entire field army with vodka – where the initial intent seems to have been to provide some relief from the stress of being under fire or in combat – be that to raise courage before or foster relaxation after combat.[45] On 11 May 1942 the State Defence Committee would limit daily vodka provision from 15 May 1942 'only to military personnel in units at the frontline who have been successful in action', for whom the norm for vodka provision would rise to 200 grams per day! The remainder of the field army would have to make do with 100 grams on a number of days a year worthy of celebration, including of course the anniversary of the October Revolution and International Worker's Day.[46] One can only assume that not only was this unpopular, but that 200 grams a day was, depending on when it was consumed, enough to hinder military effectiveness for what were supposed to be the better units, and the rules were changed again at the beginning of June to allow for the provision of 100 grams a day for those units at the front line engaged in 'offensive operations'.[47] Still, the formula was not right – those under enemy attack did not get the appropriate relief from stress that might have helped them at least get a good night's sleep, and having tried to cut dramatically back from the initial August 1941 decree the GKO decided in November 1942 to provide rations for a larger number of personnel of the field army whilst not providing it for everyone all of the time. In detailed rules open to abuse, now the 100 grams was to be provided to those 'engaged directly in combat and dug-in in forward positions', along with those engaged in reconnaissance, artillery and mortar units providing fire support to those mentioned earlier and air-crews after completion of combat missions. Others – including regimen-tal and divisional reserves and the wounded in field hospitals could – in the latter case with the agreement of doctors – receive 50 grams per day. The field army as a whole was to be limited to 5,691,000 litres of vodka for the period from 25 November to 31 December 1942, excluding in the Caucasus where 1,200,000 litres of wine could be consumed instead.[48] With further minor tweaks, such as the provision of 50 grams for person-nel servicing aircraft for combat missions regardless of their location, the GKO had finally settled on a formula for vodka provision.[49] Abuses of the system were of course far from unusual – the NKO railed about commanders in the rear abusing their authority to gain access to vodka rations in an order of 12 June 1942, and attempts were made to tighten controls over vodka supplies.[50] In practice sometimes troops did not receive their due daily ration, at others commanders sought to provide more for units that were engaged in combat at the expense of those in the immediate rear who qualified for 50 grams, giving frontline troops 150 grams that would more likely have the desired effect for someone who was used to regularly drinking vodka. Sometimes there wasn't the opportunity to drink the ration – or as will be illustrated shortly to do so safely.[51] As General Antipenko, a deputy front commander with respon-sibility for rear services notes, there wasn't a consensus on when the best time to provide the ration was – was it better to provide it 'before raising people for the attack so that they were more courageous and impulsive', or was it better to provide it after battle, before dinner, 'when at which point vodka was provided above norms, and the soldier would sleep soundly'. In the evening vodka could often be provided above norms because if a unit received its quota on strength at the start of the day, the portions for the dead and wounded would be available for the survivors at the end of the day. According to Antipenko 'the majority of commanders of formations and units came to the conclusion that vodka before an attack was not always stimulating, but more frequently suppressive and even encouraged sleepiness'.[52] This might explain – along with the fact that receiving the 100 gram norm would not be sufficient to make most drunk and particularly having eaten prior to an attack – why German accounts of combat with drunken Soviet troops are not as easy to find as might be thought. One example in the literature involves German troops of 258th Infantry Division before Moscow in early December 1941 as described by controversial German military historian Paul Carrell.[53] As Soviet general Antipenko suggests, sometimes troops were provided with their ration before an attack, and often above the norm, and one can reasonably assume that this was more likely earlier in the war before negative experiences influenced practice. Certainly 8th Guards Rifle Corps was to distribute vodka rations prior to attacking as part of the failed Operation 'Mars' against the German Army Group Centre in November 1942, although it is unclear whether rations were to actually be consumed prior to or after the initial day's fighting.[54] Troops could of course find themselves in combat again after having consumed their ration after earlier fighting, since German forces were not required and Soviet commanders sometimes not willing or able to give Red Army soldiers respite for vodka, supper and sleep and often in that order in order to gain the maximum soporific effect. As tanker Ivan Maslov recounts, in one instance in early 1942 after the Kerch' landings in the Crimea his unit consumed the wine that they had been provided in lieu of vodka after a night action, only to be roused by their ambitious commander for an attack for which they were unfit – 'we were all drunk'. Unwilling to delay the attack by an hour, Maslov's unit 'lost 50 per cent of its tanks in the attack'. Maslov himself was in no state to perform as required.[55] Certainly the vodka ration above norms would not fit in with high tempo operations in which there might be little respite, and hence it is understandable why commander of the 1st Belorussian Front Marshal Zhukov sought in April 1945 to prohibit the consumption of vodka until otherwise ordered for 1st and 2nd Guards Tanks Armies and 9th Tank Corps on 17 April as they pressed forward during the Berlin Operation.[56] Overall, it is actually possible that vodka rations improved Red Army effectiveness. Certainly if they were consumed at an appropriate time then they might have offered some respite from the hell that many experienced at the front line. Certainly fighter pilot Sergei Gorelov appreciated the ability to use vodka to relax after the stresses of combat, but as a fighter pilot he was fortunately not consuming his ration at the front line.[57]

Although in 1941 Soviet problems at the tactical level were significant regardless of whether and when the vodka ration had been consumed, problems at the operational and operational-strategic levels were perhaps greater where, after all, at the tactical level time and time again Soviet units were able to overwhelm German forces and inflict local reverses on the Wehrmacht – albeit at horrendous cost. Thanks to numbers and a certain zeal, and at times even superior equipment, the Red Army was often able to temporarily gain the upper hand at the tactical level. However, despite poor German logistics – an increasing problem as the Wehrmacht pushed deeper into the Soviet Union – at the operational level with mechanised forces in the vanguard the Wehrmacht was typically able to manoeuvre around Soviet forces blocking their path eastwards and then either encircle them or force them to fall back – often in disarray. For the Red Army poor communications and command and control took their toll in a war of manoeuvre, as did the fact that Soviet armour lacked the sort of mobile infantry and artillery support that the German spearheads enjoyed. However, perhaps the biggest obstacle to being able to deal with the German methodology was Stalin and the senior leadership who insisted and continued to insist on counterattacking at almost every available opportunity across a wide front whilst at the same time insisting that Soviet units hold territory even when it made little or no military sense, at best only belatedly authorising withdrawal. Nowhere was this better illustrated than in the encirclement of over 600,000 Soviet troops in the Kiev region in mid-September 1941. That the German conduct of the encirclement was at the expense of operations elsewhere and in particular on the Moscow axis, and highlighted the Wehrmacht's inability to focus on something that would be the knockout blow, could only provide retrospective consolation to some of those Soviet commanders struggling in the Kiev region who would survive the ordeal to fight on.

The crisis in the Kiev region developed rapidly as 2nd Panzergruppe headed there from the Moscow axis. In late August and early September the Briansk Front had engaged primarily with forces of Guderian's 2nd Panzergruppe to the south of Zhukov's successful recapture of the El'nia salient. In many ways faith placed in these counterattacks in Moscow – and in particular by Shaposhnikov and Stalin – was crucial in action not being taken in the Kiev region by South-Western Front to avoid planned German encirclement. With 2nd Panzergruppe soon pressing on forces of the Kiev region from the north, 1st Panzer Army's advance from the south subsequently made it plain that there was risk of encirclement for much of the Soviet South-Western Front in the Kiev region. The Briansk Front's counterattacks against Guderian's forces ran out of steam during the second week of September, giving 2nd Panzergruppe far greater room for manoeuvre against the South-Western Front.[58] By 11 September, the day after Zhukov's forces in the El'nia region had been ordered on to the defensive, it was apparent to both Marshal Budennii commanding the South-Western Direction, and his subordinate General Kirponos commanding the South-Western Front, that a withdrawal to the east was required for the westernmost armies of Soviet-Western Front where Soviet forces were simply unable to consistently hold river lines and parry the German spearheads that kept finding their way round Soviet defences.[59]

Bagramian suggests in his memoirs that even if Soviet reconnaissance had provided Soviet forces with the information to allow them to concentrate local resources against the spearheads threatening South-Western Front – which it clearly did not – German forces would with hindsight still have broken through. For Bagramian the explanation was overwhelming German strength, although the reality was strength where it mattered.[60] Command and control was all too often the key, where facing a local crisis German forces were more likely to be reinforced on the ground in a timely manner or the Luftwaffe was able to intervene. Soviet and German sources alike highlight this reality where even the much vaunted T-34s and KV-1s could be overwhelmed by local German strength, as apparently was the case with the KV tank of lieutenants V.I. Sokol'ev and F.P. Kosenko of 142nd Tank Brigade on 10 September who were apparently overwhelmed by four German tanks and supporting infantry where no mention is made of their having meaningful assistance.[61] In the interrogation report of Stalin's eldest son, Iakov, captured by German forces earlier in the summer, Iakov was undoubtedly being candid when apparently noting to his captors how 'the German tanks and their tactical use' were 'praiseworthy', also highlighting the impact on morale of attack by Ju 87 or Stuka dive bombers on Soviet troops that would play their part in the destruction of Soviet forces near Kiev and frequently saved German forward units from crisis.[62] Certainly in early September 1941 the command and control apparatus of the South-Western Front was struggling to manage the situation. Air attack had hit 38th Army's headquarters on 7 September killing some personnel including those who could code and encode messages, and who could not be replaced. The headquarters was soon in communication with only the right flank of its forces.[63] The counterattack in which lieutenants Sokol'ev and Kosenko had been overwhelmed represented what had been a fairly typical Soviet response to crisis during the war to date – if in doubt counterattack – even without sufficient information of the enemy and without having marshalled forces sufficiently to give an attack a meaningful chance of success.

The counterattack by 38th Army launched on 10 September against 1st Panzer Army advancing from the south did initially at least made headway in pushing German units back towards the Dnepr but soon ran out of steam, despite the commitment of far from insignificant tank strength during this operation, including 3rd and 142nd Tank Brigades and 47th Tank Division. However, resources being thrown into the counterattack were in typical fashion for this period being done so often without appropriate preparation and sufficient strength. In the case of the only just formed 142nd Tank Brigade for example, equipped with both KV and T-34 tanks, 'many of its crews did not have experience in operating heavy and medium tanks, and at least a portion of its commanders arrived to their sub-units only at the point at which it was being loaded for transit'. Infantry units committed to the attack were often understrength, such as 300th Rifle Division that had already seen heavy losses, or the recently arrived 304th Rifle Division that was however only able to commit two out of three regiments to the attack because the third was still in transit. The 1974 history of 38th Army claims that the attack took place where it was the enemy who had the numerical advantage, and where as Bagramian notes 'our air and artillery support were clearly inadequate'. In fact, at least some units transferred from other sectors of the front for the attack were unable to get their artillery relocated in time.[64] According to German sources as cited by David Stahel, 68 of up to 100 attacking Soviet tanks were reported as destroyed as German forces were pushed back.[65] As Bagramian notes in his memoirs, on 12 September offensive operations by 38th Army were called off. Soon the bulk of the mobile assets of 38th Army were transferred northwards to face 2nd Panzergruppe and the remaining strength of 38th Army faced its own issues with encirclement as they were forced to retreat.[66] On 11 September Kirponos and other members of the South-Western Front's command were in communication with Stalin, and were told how they were to deal with the unfolding crisis by counterattacking to the north in co-ordination with Eremenko's Briansk Front against Guderian's spearheads threatening their rear, and create a new defensive line along the River Psel – already breached – before even conducting a minor withdrawal from Kiev back across the Dnepr. Although at this point in the south 38th Army's attack had not yet run completely out of steam, the Briansk Front was clearly increasingly unable to press home continued counterattacks and the South-Western Frontly lacked the sort of mobile resources in the north that might have made the Stavka's plans plausible. In his memoirs Bagramian – who escaped the Kiev encirclement – noted how according to an eyewitness after having received the end of Moscow's communication that 'finally, you are to cease looking for lines of retreat, and start looking for avenues for resistance' 'Kirponos had lost all colour from his face and twice spelt out this phrase' from the telegraph ribbon.[67] South-Western Front, without timely authorisation to withdraw a meaningful distance to the east, would suffer the same fate as much of the Western Front at the end of June – with permission to withdraw only finally being received after Budennii had been removed from command of the South-Western Direction to be replaced by Timoshenko. On 14 September 1st and 2nd Panzergruppe had nominally completed the encirclement with the establishing of contact between elements of 3rd and 16th Panzer Divisions, the next day the encirclement becoming much more meaningful with the linkup of 9th and 3rd Panzer Divisions just south of Lokhvitsa. On 16 September, with the front 'having gone over to fighting in a state of encirclement with all lines of communications cut' – belatedly the Stavka accepted that withdrawal was the only option.[68]

To reinforce the resolve of Soviet forces in the region to hold their ground and one assumes foster a positive outcome to the crisis, late on 12 September the Headquarters of the Supreme High Command issued orders for the creation of blocking detachments in all rifle divisions – a measure that had been first sanctioned in a Stavka directive of 5 September in response to a request from the Briansk Front.[69] The blocking detachments to be created across all fronts – distinct from NKVD 'blocking detachments' mentioned in Chapter 10 and further discussed in Chapter 15 – were to be made up of 'reliable warriors, of no more than battalion strength' in total, under the direct control of the divisional commander and consisting not only of troops and lorries for transportation but also 'a few tanks or armoured cars'. These troops were to prevent 'panicmongers and simply hostile elements' from fomenting retreat and the collapse of units – arguably a waste of resources at a time when such mobile elements could have achieved more fighting the enemy.[70] The blocking detachments were to be ready within five days, although on 14 September the Kiev encirclement had already nominally taken place. By the end of the so called Kiev Strategic Defense Operation that had lasted from 7 July through to 26 September, Soviet forces in the region had lost more than 600,000 men as 'irrecoverable losses', with South-Western Front losing more than 500,000 men.[71]

Although the Red Army was fighting with the luxury of falling back on railheads, supply was a serious issue for Red Army units. When considering Soviet operations Stalin in particular seems to have engaged in the sort of map-based fantasies engaged in all too often by Hitler as well that failed not only to take account of the actual strength of Soviet units, but also the ability of the system to provide for them. Particularly serious was the provision of munitions, both in getting what munitions there were to the troops that needed them but also producing munitions to meet demand in the face of having to evacuate existing plant from the path of advancing German forces. Losses of transport resources were both heavy and difficult to replace. A rifle division was supposed to have more than 3,000 horses for more than 14,000 personnel according to list strength at the beginning of the war, but few did. A few examples from a report by the South-Western Front for 15 July 1941 highlight shortages of horses experienced by units of the front, where for example although 45th Rifle Division had 9,114 personnel, it only had 2,196 horses, and 139th Rifle Division was down to 1,026 personnel and only 167 horses.[72] From 22 June to 20 July the North-Western Front alone lost –killed, wounded or missing– in the region of 38,830 horses.[73] Inadequate transport resources were not however left with mountains of munitions to move. In Chapter 9 it was noted how prior to the war the Red Army lacked sufficient armour-piercing rounds for 76 mm anti-tank guns – but at least in June 1941 units might have had their full initial supply of at least some munitions. However, as N.A. Antipenko notes – who was in the autumn of 1941 deputy commander of 49th Army with responsibility for rear services – 'mobilisation stocks of munitions and weapons were soon used up'.[74] Significant stocks were lost to the enemy or destroyed to prevent them falling into enemy hands, and soon limited stocks of munitions from the Trans-Baikal, Central Asia and Far Eastern Military Districts had been 'gobbled up' by the fronts in the west. If before the war production of munitions had not kept pace with the production of weapons, at the beginning of the war this imbalance got worse leading to 'a shell shortage' reminiscent of that experienced by the Russian Army during the First World War. Certainly the 26 million artillery shells produced during the second half of 1941 represented barely 50 per cent of planned production which itself was far less than desirable. If as N.D. Iakovlev notes increased production of shells during the first full year of the war was almost four times production for 1940 then it should he suggests have been more like twenty times greater 'as a minimum' where the production of artillery pieces had increased proportionally even more. Consequently, in the face of shortages of munitions by the autumn 'strict limits had to be set for the release and using up of munitions' – as many expedients such as modifying outdated stocks of ammunition for use in contemporary weapons systems were tried. Militia divisions were being provided with artillery pieces of foreign production stored since the period of the First World War and Civil War with the hope that they would not actually have to use them and that the enemy would be halted by regular units – but use them in anger they all too often did.[75] Relocation of plant was also having significant ramifications not only for munitions production but also for the production of weapons systems. Fortunately for the Wehrmacht production of T-34 and KV-1 tanks that went some way towards compensating for Soviet tactical failings would also decline significantly the third quarter of 1941 as plant was evacuated in the face of the advancing Germans. Factory Number 183 originally in Khar'kov – the principal producer of the T-34 in early 1941- was evacuated to Nizhnii Tagil in the Urals according to a GKO decree of 12 September 1941, having produced 1,560 T-34 tanks before it moved (of which 1,025 had been handed over to the Red Army by 2 August) only to produce meaningful numbers again in 1942. The Kirov Factory – the primary producer of the KV tank in early 1941 was also evacuated.[76] Production of spare parts for tanks had been inadequate before the war – a problem that did not improve during the early months of the war. Of 11,500 units of spares for BT-series tanks that Factory 183 was supposed to have provided to the Red Army by 1 July 1941 only 7,000 had actually been provided. The commissar for the Main Auto-Armour Board of the Red Army reported in mid-August 1941 that failure to produce planned quantities of spare parts continued into the war, with Factory 183 that was producing T-34 tanks having only produced 30 per cent of planned 'deficit spares' for BT-series tanks in July in circumstances where it was claimed that more than 300 BT-series and T-26 tanks of the Western Direction could not be repaired because of a lack such spares and engines.[77]

In the aftermath of the Kiev encirclement the German flanks in the centre were now a little more secure. The Red Army was now more than half a million men weaker and often struggling to provide those it had with the means to fight, and the economic assets of the Ukraine had been secured for the protracted war Germany was seeking to avoid and relatively ill-equipped to fight. Now, the Wehrmacht could finally move on Moscow. German Chief of Staff for the Army Halder and others had hoped that an attack on Moscow would take place earlier, but the real problem was that the Wehrmacht didn't have the resources to both take Moscow and deal with the fact that on the flanks there were still sizeable Soviet forces. By the time that the Wehrmacht was ready to press forward again in the centre the Red Army had thrown new troops and defences in its path, which the German mechanised forces would either penetrate or avoid and end up encircling in the same old way. After the start of the principal component of Operation 'Typhoon' on 2 October 1941, it was but a matter of days before the bulk of Soviet forces defending the direct route to Moscow had been encircled at Viaz'ma and Briansk. The bulk of the defending Soviet forces had – including armoured – been deployed too far forward making the possibility of encirclement far more likely. Indicative of poor Soviet reconnaissance and communications – as well perhaps of fear of being the bearer of terrible news or being seen to be responsible for it – was the fact that the Stavka was not aware of deep German penetrations of Soviet lines until German forward elements were more than 100 km behind where the front line was supposed to be on 5 October as encirclement loomed for so many units and forma-tions.[78] The Stavka was unaware – or unwilling to accept – the reality of the situation until later that day, then ordering a withdrawal that was poorly organised and came too late.[79] By 12 October German com-mander of Army Group Centre von Bock was apparently euphoric on hearing of events near Viaz'ma, where despite their encirclement large numbers of Red Army troops fought on stubbornly. The ferocity of Soviet attempts to break out of the pocket is described in some detail from a German perspective by David Stahel in his *Operation Typhoon*, where breakout attempts often took the form of frontal assaults by massed infantry – with predictable carnage.[80] Soviet losses in the Viaz'ma and Briansk pockets were horrendous – by 15 October alone with the Briansk pockets yet to be eliminated Army Group Centre claimed to have taken 558,825 Soviet troops prisoner – but losses for German forces of Army Group Centre that had engineered them were also far from trivial with Army Group Centre losing a total of 'no less than 48,000 men' during the first half of October. The vital German armoured spearheads predictably suffered heavy losses, where as Stahel notes 'Guderian's 2nd Panzer Army had lost more than 2,000 men in only the first ten days of October and another 2,300 by 20 October'.[81]

Although the Wehrmacht had ripped the heart out of Soviet forces immediately before Moscow and provoked something of a crisis for the Soviet high command in early October, the scene was not set for a dash for the capital that had already seen panic at the prospect in mid-October. The road to Moscow might have appeared open, but Soviet resistance no matter how costly had more than blunted the German spearheads and German logistical issues made worse by the mud and snow that would replace the summer dust were just one factor slowing down the advance. Attrition – along with the continued ability of the Red Army to throw at least something in the way – meant that once again

German units would have to both lick their successive wounds and at the
same time fight their way forward against the apparently inexhaustible
manpower of the Red Army. Despite the Soviet collapse to the south
near Kiev and the subsequent encirclements at Viaz'ma and Briansk
significant Soviet forces still existed on the flanks of the push on Moscow
and in particular to the north. As Jack Radey and Charles Sharp suggest,
the German High Command was understandably not solely focused on
taking Moscow but also for example dealing with Soviet forces in the
gap once again developing between Army Groups North and Centre.
Even without considering any participation of Army Group North in an
encirclement of Soviet forces between the two, Army Group Centre
certainly did not have the resources in mid-October to strike towards
Torzhok to the north, move on Moscow in the centre and Kursk to the
south, and with Moscow ultimately the focus German forces inevitably
found themselves subjected to continued Soviet counterattacks on the
flanks with those taking place near Kalinin including the incident
described later involving 21st Tank Brigade.[82]

The Red Army had still not been broken – far from it – and significant
Soviet forces continued to fight hard during October on all axes – to
which many German memoirs are testimony. One such memoir is that of
Hans Schäufler of 35th Panzer Regiment. Schäufler describes how he
and his tank crew were holed up in a basement for six days during the
fighting for Mzensk in October and were subjected to heavy and well-
directed artillery fire. Soviet heavy tanks roamed the street, in response to
which Schäufler and his crew had placed 'teller mines at the entrance
to the basement, armed and ready, since they were the only means with
which we could combat those heavy monsters'.[83] As Hermann Hoβ, an
Oberleutnant and signals officer with 5th Panzer Brigade recounted, in
addition to relying on the support of Stukas to deal with superior Soviet
tanks, German ground forces relied on 88 mm anti-aircraft guns and
artillery in the direct fire role despite the time required to reposition
them. The superiority of the Soviet tanks meant that German armoured
forces even advanced at night – usually an undesirable option given that
the night gave more opportunities for infantry to knock out their tanks,
but better than facing the superior firepower and armour of the new
Soviet tanks.[84] German losses in the war against the Soviet Union were
now significant – Generaloberst Franz Halder reporting in his war diary
on 30 September 1941 noted that total losses for the 'Eastern Army'
fighting the Soviet Union – excluding medical casualties – had reached
15 per cent of a strength of 3.4 million up to 26 September – 17,866
officers and 517,086 NCOs and other ranks killed, wounded and missing.[85] By the end of September the German armoured force level had

Soviet tanks pass through a village in the Moscow region in mid-
October 1941. By this point most of the pre-war tank stocks available
in the west had been squandered and production of new types that had
replaced the older models was still relatively limited. Although proportionally there were now more KV-series and T-34 tanks, the Red Army
had to throw the old and worn out from further east into action alongside the new. (RIA Novosti #2551)

dropped from around 3,648 tanks, assault guns and armoured command
vehicles on 22 June 1941 to in the region of 2,044 by the end of
September, although an injection of OKH reserves would bring strength
back up to around 2,480 for 'Typhoon'.[86] With the bulk of the German
armour now concentrated on the Moscow axis, on 1 October 1941 there
were only 47 Soviet 'heavy' (largely KV) and 94 'medium' (largely T-34)
tanks, along with 641 'light' (largely BT-series and T-26) tanks actually
with combat units for the Soviet Western, Reserve and Briansk Fronts on
the key Moscow axis – a total of 782.[87]

Although still relatively few in number overall, nonetheless Soviet
T-34 and KV-1 tanks were making their presence felt on the battlefield
thanks to their armour, potent 76 mm guns and also use in more
meaningful numbers at any one time than had been the case some
months ago. There were also signs of somewhat more responsible and
effective Soviet use of tanks than had been the case in the summer. The
fact that in a directive of 15 October Zhukov ordered armoured forces of
the Western Front to ambush German forces before counterattacking

was relatively novel.[88] On 22 October after the fierce fighting near Mzensk the divisional commander for the German 4th Panzer Division noted how German forces had started to encounter Soviet heavy tanks used *en masse*. Whereas in the past the few such tanks might have been 'driven off by concentrated artillery fire or bypassed', or even on occasion single tanks might have been 'destroyed by direct hits from artillery', now Soviet tanks were not to be so easily driven off by artillery fire. In tank-to-tank combat they exhibited their 'absolute superiority' over the German Panzer IIIs and IVs, opening up with their main armaments at ranges well beyond those at which the German guns had a hope of penetration.[89] In mid-November the German 112th Infantry Division was in the words of Heinz Guderian commanding 2nd Panzergruppe in a state of 'panic' when faced by tanks – by inference T-34s – along with 'Siberian troops', although such a response was not the norm.[90] In his memoirs Guderian also noted that Soviet tanks were – at least sometimes – being used not only in greater concentration but also more effectively by the autumn than they had been in the summer, and how by the beginning of 'Typhoon' 'The Russians attacked us frontally with infantry, while they sent their tanks in, in mass formation, against our flanks. They were learning.'[91] It is with good reason that German memoirs, such as those of Major-General F.W. von Mellenthin, often single out Soviet armoured forces as being more capable than other arms with the possible exception of the artillery – and particularly as the war progressed.[92] Tank crews were certainly supposed to consist of better quality recruits in terms of political reliability – and were supposed to be able to speak Russian well to avoid language being an issue in effectiveness. In instructions for the selection of tank crews from the Main Political Board of the Red Army of 12 August 1941 personnel from territories in the west only recently incorporated into the Soviet Union were for example, along with those who had made their way alone or in small groups from behind German lines but whose conduct in encirclement raised suspicion, excluded from consideration as tank crew.[93] Nonetheless, even if their crews were to some extent cherry-picked, Soviet tanks were still easily separated from the infantry and their use all too frequently still left much to be desired and meant that the Red Army gained less from its wonder weapons than it otherwise might.

During the autumn of 1941 Soviet tanks were still, all too frequently, used not only in isolation from infantry support but all other arms. Nowhere was this better illustrated than in the case of 'raids' launched by Soviet tank and sometimes cavalry units into the German rear. In *The Defence of Moscow 1941* Radey and Sharp describes a 'raid' by 21st Tank Brigade of 30th Army, Kalinin Front in the German rear that began on

17 October near Kalinin – captured by German forces on 17 October.
The 21st Tank Brigade was actually mentioned in Zhukov's directive
to the Western Front of 15 October that suggested ambush as an appropriate tactic for Soviet armour, having been given the task of reconnoi-
tring the Turginovo region, ascertaining enemy armoured strength in the
area, and destroying it.[94] As 21st Tank Brigade moved north it was
transferred to 30th Army of the Kalinin Front – the Kalinin Front having
been created on 17 October and pulling units and formations from both
its neighbours with the aim of 'cleansing the Kalinin region of enemy
forces and liquidating enemy attempts to go round Moscow from the
north in co-operation with the Western and North-Western Fronts'.[95]
On 15–16 October 21st Tank Brigade had apparently enjoyed significant
success in defence against German armour from ambush positions, with
the unit claiming the destruction of eighteen German tanks during that
two-day period.[96] 21st Tank Brigade had fought defensively instead
of immediately launching itself into attack towards Kalinin as ordered
by 30th Army but countermanded by a deputy head of the General
Staff, General-Major Golubev, on behalf of the commander of the
Western Front.[97] According to the war diary for the newly created
Kalinin Front 21st Tank Brigade was on 17 October 'engaged in battle
to destroy enemy motorized infantry and tanks in the region of Efremovo
and Pushkino', to the south of Kalinin, where 30th Army as whole was
'preparing for an advance on Kalinin from the north and south-east'.[98]
Most of 21st Tank Brigade – excluding its BT-series tanks – was however
that day to charge towards Kalinin with only a few tank riders as support,
an operation that despite causing disruption to German supply lines and
destruction of German vehicles and even aircraft en route, was however
perhaps not only reckless but indicative of the poor command and
control being exercised over Soviet forces. The attack certainly benefitted
from surprise – as both Soviet and German accounts concur the episode
saw one T-34 actually make it through occupied Kalinin before returning
to Soviet lines –with German forces having few resources to deal with the
wild ride of the T-34s if they kept moving.[99] As Radey and Sharp note,
the attack was nonetheless 'poorly co-ordinated' and 'suffered heavy
casualties', and indeed 'failed to meet its objective' – that is to 'seize
the south-western portion of Kalinin'. However, more broadly the brigade was supposed to disrupt German offensive operations towards
Moscow, and may have contributed something to this in 'buying time'
through distracting German forces.[100] That the unit had been bombarded with orders from a range of sources prior to brigade orders being
written, that included Zhukov as commander of the Western Front, was
perhaps symptomatic of the sort of command chaos that had reigned at

Lake Khasan and elsewhere where overlapping authorities and poor communications fostered command chaos. By the evening of 16 October Zhukov was technically in command of all forces engaged in the 'liquidation of the enemy in the Kalinin area' – by which point 21st Tank Brigade had already been committed to a course of action based on the erroneous assumption based not on reconnaissance but wishful thinking, that Kalinin was occupied by only forward German detachments.[101] That the response of the unit was to draw up dramatic orders to charge off alone towards Kalinin was perhaps as a result of the 'oh well,...' [*da ladno*] response that was often the alternative to paralysis or caution. The fact that the attack saw 'significant losses' inflicted on the German 36th Motorised Division, severed a key supply line, dealt 'a serious psychological blow' to German forces under attack in their rear and demonstrated that the Red Army was neither giving up or out of reserves was of some value. Now however, 30th Army had however lost most of its tanks.[102]

Zhukov's order of 15 October to forces of the Western Front mentioned earlier was in response to the collapse of the central sector of the Front and the Soviet attempt to fall back on new positions on a line including Naro–Fominsk and the River Nara. The Mozhaisk Defence Line, which had been under construction since July and soon expanded – and on which much hope had rested – had been unable to hold back German forces.[103] When German forces reached Soviet positions in the Naro-Fominsk region towards the end of October, as the Soviet 1942 General Staff history of the Battle of Moscow notes, the Wehrmacht was more than 200 km east of its positions at the start of 'Typhoon' and now constituted 'a real threat to the capital of the Soviet Union – Moscow'. To the south German forces of 2nd Panzergruppe pushed towards Tula, and its defence was soon made the responsibility of the Western Front.[104] The German advance had clearly stalled in the face of Soviet resistance, reduced strength and supply issues exacerbated by the *rasputitsa*.[105]

It would be mid-November by the time that Wehrmacht forces were in sufficient order on the central Moscow axis for a final lunge towards the Soviet capital, by which point once again the Soviet regime had been able to throw new units against what by now were relatively small – and increasingly manageable German spearheads. Fresh – even if weak – Soviet rifle divisions and indeed brigades were being formed across the Soviet Union, and with little training been thrown from railheads into the fighting with almost reckless abandon. As Stalin had apparently conveyed to General Ivan Tiulenev, in a meeting of mid-October 1941, 'the situation at the front now depends on how quickly and how well we can prepare reserves'.[106] In terms of the organisation of these new units, by this point in the war gone were the Soviet mechanised corps that had proven not only so difficult to command but also to supply, and even new tank divisions were supposed not to be formed from late August onwards – tank brigades and battalions were the norm – despite apparently abortive orders to cease forming independent tank battalions of 13 September that may simply have referred to those intended for rifle divisions as in the 23 August decree. According to these instructions of 13 September – primarily for the formation of tank brigades – the number of tanks in a brigade had already fallen, and the fifteen armoured cars supposedly included, the absence of which was 'not to hold up the formation of brigades', were indeed often missing.[107] By December 1941 the tank brigades were two-battalions strong compared to three back in August, and with forty-six tanks instead of more than ninety, but still had their motorised infantry battalion. Gone for example was the reconnaissance company and anti-tank guns, the latter essentially replaced with the new PTRD anti-tank rifles.[108]

In late 1941 infantry divisions were now also smaller, leaner entities than they had been at the beginning of the war – with less artillery and with only limited anti-tank assets beyond anti-tank rifles. Gone was the separate heavy artillery regiment (howitzers) of the pre-war incarnation, although a list-strength mortar battalion was some compensation by December – and the anti-aircraft battalion had also gone to be replaced by a battery. List strength in terms of personnel had – at least on paper – increased from 10,859 at the end of July to 11,626 by 6 December, but was considerably lower than the pre-war 14,483. Perhaps most negative was the drop in anti-tank capability and mobility. Compared to the 54 37 or 45 mm anti-tank guns that a pre-war division was supposed to have, there were now at best only eighteen – losses replaced in essence once again with the new PTRD anti-tank rifle of which there were supposed to be eighty-nine for a division. The 12 57 mm anti-tank guns as list strength in early December and that appear in the GKO decree of 25 October on 'The Wartime Rifle Division' soon disappeared from the table of organisation of a rifle division as their production was curtailed in essence because they were deemed to be too powerful to be as effective as the alternatives. During 1941 there had been only 371 57 mm ZIS-2 anti-tank guns in existence for example – barely enough for thirty divisions! Overall mobility of a rifle division – assuming that it had the fuel for motor vehicles – had dropped significantly from pre-war list strength, with the April 1941 incarnation nominally fielding 558 cars and trucks compared to 248 by December – with 3,039 horses on strength having dropped to 2,410. No longer – at least for now – would a rifle division have any sort of organic armoured vehicle component, be that armoured cars or light tanks, despite the fact that back in July the attachment of such had been seen as necessary to stiffen the infantry and indeed where instructions for the formation of independent rifle brigades had as late as 22 October included provision for a tank company of three T-34 and 12 T-60s.[109]

These list strengths had of course as has already been shown been something of a fantasy prior to the war, and continued to be in December 1941. Not only had there been too few ZIS-2 57 mm anti-tank guns produced during 1941 for even a handful of divisions, but that the rifle battalion in which Mikhail Suknev commanded a machine-gun company had only two PTRD in the spring of 1942 further highlights how tables of organisation were in particular for early war Soviet divisions very much best case scenarios or aspirations.[110] Changes to organisation also took time, and particularly for frontline units. On 17 September 1941 the Stavka ordered the stripping of the second artillery regiment from rifle divisions of the old table of organisation 'at the first available opportunity in accordance with the military situation', but it would be some time before this had taken place across the board.[111] Although less potent in terms of firepower and mobility the new infantry divisions were undoubtedly easier to command given they consisted of fewer distinct sub-units – particularly important in the absence of due experience on the part of often reservist commanders, and in the absence of sufficient means of communication. Ironically given the panic about anti-tank capability in the Red Army, Soviet rifle divisions were arguably still more capable of dealing with enemy tanks than their German rivals if both were equipped at list strength, where the Soviet divisional artillery was in theory more than capable of dealing with tanks – if armour-piercing rounds were available – and the new PTRD anti-tank rifles were effective against most German tanks of the period at close ranges. For the Red Army the apparent problem with anti-tank capability and certainly the fact that what a unit supposedly had according to list strength was often not available was in part to be dealt with through the widespread use of Molotov cocktails – often by 'tank destruction detachments' formed from within rifle regiments.[112] In many ways by December 1941 the Red Army had reached the sort of level of organisational complexity that suited the means for command and control at its disposal and the education and experience of most Red Army commanders at this point – a far more suitable starting point for development of operational effectiveness than the monstrous formations that had existed at the beginning of the war.

Whilst the Red Army of late November was both organisationally and in terms of equipment not a force likely to destroy a major German formation that had freedom to manoeuvre and could escape or effectively counter encirclement, it was nonetheless capable of launching offensive operations of limited depth and with clear objectives that could push German forces back – with operations for the recapture of Rostov-on-Don in the far south offering such an opportunity before the Soviet counteroffensive near Moscow. At Rostov-on-Don, as north-east of Leningrad at Tikhvin and at Moscow the German spearheads were by the late autumn and early winter now significantly weaker than they had been but weeks before, and the Wehrmacht was compelled – much to Hitler's displeasure – to pull back from Rostov behind the Mius River. The Red Army in this instance engaged the Wehrmacht in significant urban fighting where German forces neither had the same room to manoeuvre as had often enjoyed and nor indeed the strength to use mobility elsewhere to relieve forces locally.

Although fighting in urban areas would – and had already – proven a great leveller in the fighting between the Red Army and the Wehrmacht – it was something in late 1941 that the Soviet high command identified as not taking place frequently enough. As Shaposhnikov's directive on the subject of 24 November 1941 pointed out, towns that had been prepared for defence 'demand considerable expenditure of military strength and resources by the enemy'.[113] The reticence of Red Army commanders to defend towns was perhaps at least in part because of fear of encirclement for troops holed up in built-up areas – a factor Zhukov at least identified in a subsequent directive on the matter to forces of the Western Front.[114] Nonetheless, at Odessa for example against primarily Rumanian forces, and at Sevastopol', Soviet defence of urban areas would tie down significant Axis forces for protracted periods in capturing urban areas ringed by increasingly extensive defences. Rumanian losses in capturing Odessa were heavy before many of the defenders were evacuated by sea in early October, and having broken into the Crimean Peninsula after 'ten days of the most bitter fighting' to break through narrow access points that might have held longer had they been better fortified, by 16 November Axis forces had occupied 'the whole of the Crimea except for the fortified area of Sevastopol.'[115] The first assault on the fortress city itself failed in late November and early December 1941. By the period of the battle of Moscow both sides tended to operate from and defend towns – in part because of the protection buildings offered from the bitter cold.

It is perhaps not coincidental that the protracted defences of both Odessa and Sevastopol' occurred in circumstances where despite Germany typically enjoying air superiority the Soviet navy enjoyed superiority in the Black Sea over the limited Axis naval forces in the region. On 21 June 1941 the Black Sea Fleet could dispose of a total of twenty-three 'sea-going' and fifteen smaller surface ships that included two recently constructed cruisers, three similarly recent destroyer leaders and eight Project 7 or 7-U destroyers also of Soviet construction – not counting light vessels – in addition to six large, nineteen medium and nineteen small submarines.[116] Initially their opposition either on or below the surface consisted of the much smaller Rumanian navy, although the transfer of German and Italian light craft and a few small submarines to the region would complicate the situation in 1942.[117] More sizeable Soviet naval resources were available in the Baltic, where the Baltic Fleet had two out of three of the navy's old battleships, two out of seven cruisers, 28 out of 54 destroyers and 71 out of 212 submarines – not counting 656 out of 2,429 aircraft under navy control.[118] During the Great Patriotic War the Soviet navy was forced to rely largely on these vessels constructed prior to the war as during the war naval production all but ceased as resources and facilities were thrown into the production of equipment for the war on land. The Soviet navy did however receive significant naval resources from her allies – and in the Arctic at least support from Allied vessels operating from Soviet territory – that in contrast to tanks for example were far superior to Soviet equivalents thanks to a large extent to equipment such as RADAR and ASDIC and in the case of those operated by the Allies crewed initially in particular by far better trained personnel. The Soviet Navy also lagged behind other powers in terms of mine warfare where once again foreign equipment and expertise would prove valuable in improving Soviet capabilities.[119] Nonetheless, the issue once again was not just equipment but organisation, training and command and control that as head of the navy Admiral Kuznetsov noted when discussing poor and insufficient use of mines and minefields in April 1942 were all sadly lacking. It didn't help apparently that some specialist personnel in mine warfare had been committed to fighting on land.[120] In terms of competence the purges had if anything hit the Soviet navy harder than the Red Army, where the requisite skills were perhaps even more difficult to replace.[121]

Despite the many failings of Soviet vessels and crews, in the Black Sea conditions were otherwise relatively favourable for use of the naval power that was available, and certainly more so than in the Baltic. In Baltic waters not only did the Baltic Fleet have to deal with the German navy where its mine warfare capabilities would prove particularly damaging, but was also early on in the war in particular less likely to be able to avoid attentions of the Luftwaffe. By the end of the summer the Baltic Fleet had been bloodied in retreating from forward naval bases, and was soon bottled up in besieged Leningrad. As Andrei Platonov notes in his *Tragedies of the Gulf of Finland*, the losses sustained by the Soviet navy in the retreat from Tallinn to Kronstadt in late August 1941 'were some of the most tragic... in the history of the Russian and Soviet navies'. The loss of five destroyers, three 'guardships', two submarines, a gunboat, and a few minesweepers and fast attack craft was bad enough, but the loss of forty-three other vessels and nearly 11,000 passengers in addition to the crews of the above was a tragic manner in which to highlight the inability of the Baltic Fleet to sustain surface operations in the Baltic Sea.[122] The Baltic Fleet was now having to function in an era where operations in confined waters – and particularly involving the convoying of slower vessels – would typically prove costly without in particular the requisite air superiority. With its surface forces bottled up in Leningrad, and submarines struggling to break through German minefields, although its vessels could provide some fire support to ground troops they did not need all their crews to do so, and many sailors of the Baltic Fleet would find themselves fighting as infantry by early 1942 as the ground forces faced shortages discussed in Chapter 14.

In the Black Sea however – despite the overrunning of Soviet naval bases during 1941 and particularly 1942 – Soviet naval forces had far greater scope than in the Baltic for support of ground operations in providing fire support, landing supplies and indeed the landing and disembarkation of men and material. The Kerch' landings of December 1941 were a significant undertaking, where although operations on land became a fiasco the naval component was, despite the lack of specialised landing craft for example, relatively successful.[123] Landings in the area again in late 1943 were similarly a success for the navy and this time on land, where fortunately the landings involved only brief passage across the Kerch' Straights.[124] German airpower was the principal threat in the region, with the Black Sea Fleet taking significant losses to German aircraft not only in port but also at sea, as in the case of Flotilla Leader *Khar'kov* and destroyers *Besposhchadnii* and *Sposobnii* in October 1943 that is described further below.

In the Arctic the Northern Fleet would have, in theory at least, an important role in participating in the defence of Allied convoys with aid arriving to Murmansk and Arkhangel'sk, although British naval officers often lamented the very limited scope of such assistance and the distance from Soviet bases from which assistance was provided.[125] By late 1944 there was considerable scope for the use of Soviet naval power not only in the Black Sea and Arctic waters, but also in the Baltic. However, despite increased opportunities, Soviet naval surface forces were undoubtedly underemployed compared to those of other powers. Despite the strength of the Soviet Baltic Fleet, the German navy still maintained the upper hand in the southern portion of the Baltic in late

1944 and even early 1945 where it was able for example to provide fire support for ground forces in Kurland and indeed supply German forces in that pocket. Soviet submarines were certainly more heavily engaged than larger surface vessels – and caused more damage – where the sinking of the *Wilhelm Gustloff* by the Soviet submarine *S-13* in early 1945 is perhaps the most infamous sinking by a Soviet submarine of the period, for the sinking of which along with another transport *S-13* was understandably in the circumstances awarded the Order of the Red Banner.[126] In the Black Sea, after the evacuations of Odessa and then Sevastopol' had required the risking and loss of significant naval assets, the Stavka was certainly subsequently reticent to take unnecessary risks with remaining strength and in particular after the loss of the Flotilla Leader *Khar'kov* and destroyers *Besposhchadnii* and *Sposobnii* for little gain during the morning of 6 October 1943 as they were making their way back to the port of Tuapse in the Caucasus after having shelled Axis positions in the Crimea the previous night. Despite having some air cover, all three were sunk for the loss of 780 lives.[127]

In the Arctic region the Soviet navy – reinforced with vessels from her allies either under Lend-Lease or in lieu of a share of the Italian fleet – was perhaps most active towards the end of the war and did launch the successful Petsamo-Kirkenes Landings in October 1944, but as Mikhail Suprun notes, despite an impressive Northern Fleet that now included the aged British battleship Royal Sovereign renamed Arkhangel'sk, and the US cruiser Milwaukee renamed Murmansk, German destroyers were not only able to cover German withdrawal by sea but also bombard Soviet ground forces. Although it is possible that Admiral Golovko commanding the Northern Fleet was under orders not to risk his major units unnecessarily – and perhaps particularly those borrowed from the Allies – Suprun's suggestion that reticence to make use of such assets was perhaps due to what he terms 'Beria syndrome' is convincing and may very well be applied to the use of Soviet surface vessels in the Baltic at the end of the war as well. For a commander of ground forces to take heavy losses might raise questions where the likelihood of a unit or formation being completely destroyed in a single battle was lower by the end of the war, but for a naval commander to lose a ship – and particularly a larger unit – was not only more likely than the destruction of a large ground unit but also bound to lead to more intensive questioning and greater damage to his career. As Suprun notes, 'not everyone would have dared, for the sake of glory, to risk their life and career, especially at the end of the war'.[128]

Overall, compared to pre-war investment and the cost of that investment of resources not being available elsewhere, the performance of the

Type 7 destroyers of the Northern Fleet, here pictured in 1944. Many personnel of the other fleets in particular and especially the crews of larger vessels had by this point been killed or wounded in combat on land. (TsVMM #23634-6)

Soviet Navy and its contribution to the defeat of the Axis was disappointing. Arguably the least effective arm of the Soviet armed forces, nonetheless thanks in part to Allied aid it was significantly more capable by the end of the war than it was at the beginning – when commanders were willing to make good use of at least its smaller ships and other vessels.

Returning to Rostov-on-Don and dry land – here in late November 1941 Soviet troops were of course not just engaged in defensive operations, but had taken the offensive at the operational level in part in an urban environment where intense fighting provided a brief taster of what was to come at Stalingrad the following year. In fighting for the city itself for once however Soviet forces had – not by intent where German strength was assumed to be far greater – managed to gain considerable local superiority over the defenders.[129] Although strengthened with additional artillery resources and a meaningful concentration of armour – some still however en route as the offensive began – the communications resources available to 56th Army for the Rostov offensive were inadequate for the command and control of the fighting, and particularly once Soviet forces were making meaningful progress beyond Rostov itself. As of 25 November 56th Army only had a fraction of the communications resources that it should have had, where although some units were well provided for this

Red Army soldiers fight on the streets during the liberation of Rostov-on-Don in late November 1941, in what was an important victory for the Red Army that preceded German reverses near Moscow and Tikhvin further north. The Red Army had all too often failed to take advantage of urban areas in slowing down the German advance during 1941. (RIA Novosti #59606)

seems to have been through stripping others. So acute were shortages of communications equipment that the collection of captured communications equipment gained 'serious significance', although fear of interception of radio communications is recorded, as was all too often the case, as having been a factor in the less than effective use of the radio resources that were available.[130] Nonetheless, outside Rostov as well the Soviet infantry made headway in achieving their defined objectives. German forces were pushed back beyond Rostov – although mobile forces that included 64th and 70th Cavalry Divisions and 54th Tank Brigade failed in achieving their planned objective of preventing the withdrawal of German forces across the River Sambek that would have significantly increased German losses, in part because of the intervention of the Luftwaffe.[131]

Despite not having destroyed the German strength that it might – a product in part of poor reconnaissance and command and control – the

Rostov offensive was of considerable significance. The liberation of Rostov-on-Don on 29 November 1941 was the first liberation of a significant population centre by the Red Army, and although soon eclipsed by events near Moscow, nonetheless provided a major boost to morale. Meanwhile, before Moscow the German advance was being halted as the weekend of 5–7 December approached – a weekend that would retrospectively seem so significant for the course of the war.

12   The End of 'Typhoon'

The Soviet Moscow counteroffensive that would drive German forces from the gates of Moscow is typically recorded in the literature as having started during the weekend of 5–7 December 1941. Although the weekend of 5–7 December would certainly see the start of a series of initially successful major counterattacks by the Red Army across an increasingly wide front, as had been the pattern for the duration of the war so far many of the Soviet troops soon to be committed to the headline offensive had been engaged in local counterattacks for some time preceding it and it is very difficult to separate these off from the main event. The choice of the weekend of 5–7 December for the start of wider and more co-ordinated counteroffensive operations can be justified by a significant increase in the force and scale of counterattacks – not a sudden swing over to the offense for the Red Army. In the aftermath, both generals and historians are for often different reasons apt to bring order to events of the time, and the Moscow counteroffensive is a good example of this. The successful Soviet counterstrokes were undoubtedly born out of a process whereby Soviet reserves being fed into the region made it apparent by late November in the light of waning German momentum and strength that the pendulum was swinging in Soviet favour, and that the situation could be exploited and the immediate threat to Moscow removed. Just as the success of the initial operational-scale counterattacks near Moscow suggested the possibility of wider successes, the success of smaller operations prior to those of 5–7 December highlighted that circumstances were now ripe for more than just local counterattacks. The fact that there wasn't a grand plan that had been in the pipeline for weeks, and for which resources were being amassed, no doubt contributed to the surprise factor for senior German commanders when the weight of Soviet attacks increased significantly during that first weekend in December in operations planned only days before.[1] The emergence of plans for wider and more co-ordinated counteroffensive operations in late November that would take place during the first weekend in December will be considered in some detail in the next chapter. In this chapter we will look at the local operational successes and a shifting resources situation that made them increasingly feasible, as well as looking at Soviet efforts to conduct the war not only at the frontline but also in the German rear.

During counterattacks on the Moscow axis that preceded the main event that began on 5–7 December, Soviet infantry supported by available tank battalions and brigades had sought to eliminate increasingly weak German spearheads that moved forward from village to village seeking a way round Soviet units to continue the advance on Moscow. By this point the German advance was clearly running out of steam and the Red Army was increasingly enjoying local numerical superiority. One such incident – the rebuff of one of the last attempts by German forces to break through towards Moscow – occurred during operations in the Naro-Fominsk region to the west of Moscow. Part of the German 478th Infantry Regiment, 258th Infantry Division with support including anti-aircraft guns and elements of 191st Sturmgeschütz-Abteilung had in an attempt to breach Soviet lines by 2 December pushed forward from the Nara River. Having pushed aside 76th Rifle Regiment of the NKVD part of the German regiment held positions on both sides of the Desna River in the vicinity of the villages of Petrovskoe, Burtsevo and Iushkovo, with further elements covering their flank from heights to the west.[2] According to 33rd Army later that day, from 14:30 an 'armoured group' under the command of the head of the armoured forces for the army Colonel Safir – 'with 11 tanks of 5th Tank Brigade, 30 tanks of independent tank battalions and a composite detachment from 183rd Reserve Rifle Regiment' – engaged the enemy forces of 'two companies with 10–12 tanks and around 200 enemy sub-machine gunners' in the Petrovskoe area, what was in fact a second attack.[3] Soviet operations here on 2 and indeed 3 December 1941 to deal with the German incursion showed some of the glaring weaknesses in organisation and command and control that had plagued the Red Army since the beginning of the war. Infantry support for the component of the Soviet operation by 33rd Army to eliminate the forward bridgehead over the Desna for example was limited to relatively small numbers of tank-riding troops – on 2 December only sixty-five infantrymen accompanied 136th Independent Tank Battalion as it went over to the defence that night, and even the next day Soviet operations did not for example include the two ski battalions (23rd and 24th) and 18th Rifle Brigade allocated as support, where apparently according to Soviet after-action reports even on 3 December 'the concentration of the infantry was delayed' and 'at the allotted time the infantry did not attack'.[4] Fortunately for the Red Army German troops in the area had few anti-tank resources. Heavy fighting apparently took place at Iushkovo later on 2 December where a detachment of 16th Border Regiment of 5th Army with six tanks – most probably of 20th Tank Brigade that were apparently T-34s – engaged German infantry and elements of 191st Sturmgeschütz-Abteilung – perhaps three vehicles with the support from an 88 mm anti-aircraft gun as well. It seems that 33rd Army was not aware of this attack from the north – and certainly the commander of 33rd Army's tanks on the spot, Safir was unaware. By the end of the evening and night time engagement, all six T-34s were apparently destroyed, along with two of the German vehicles and the Soviet attack repulsed albeit apparently with heavy German losses amongst the infantry.[5] The next day, after Safir had been in communication with 5th Army whose 20th Tank Brigade was it transpired not to participate in any attack with his forces presumably after the losses it had taken the previous night, with limited support from Katiusha rockets his 136th and now also 140th Independent Tank Battalion attacked Petrovskoe from the south-east without significant infantry support for which Safir felt he could no longer wait as daylight hours remaining were few and he apparently hoped to prevent German forces from being able to withdraw to the west. Despite the lack of infantry support, Safir's force was nonetheless able to make inroads into German positions on the flank and on both 2 and 3 December had played an important role in providing the necessary pressure to compel a full German withdrawal behind the Nara under considerable Soviet pressure as was ordered early on the afternoon of 3 December.[6]

These Soviet attacks in the vicinity of Iushkovo were subsequently recorded as having been part of wider operations with ambitions to destroy – 'liquidate' and indeed 'envelop' – significant German forces in the area, although Zhukov's orders to 33rd Army for the operation merely called for 'an attack towards Iushkovo' that would then push on towards Goloven'ki (north of Naro-Fominsk) and 'restore the situation' to that before 258th Infantry Division had pushed forward.[7] Soviet operations might have led to greater German losses than was the case given a Soviet armoured strength in the area of in the region of 100 tanks, but being seen to be decisive seems to have been the order of the day for Soviet commanders that had led all too frequently to premature counter-attacks in the preceding months.[8] That 258th Infantry Division was able for example to pull back behind the Nara River in what was described in a German after action report as a retreat that 'could easily have turned into a catastrophe' reflected poorly on Soviet operational planning, execution and command culture.[9] The outcome for the Red Army might have been improved had Soviet forces not launched attacks piecemeal on the sector of the front over a number of days prior to the German withdrawal on 3 December, and perhaps had the tanks amassed waited

for suitable infantry support as apparently commander of 33rd Army
Efremov had advised the commander of the tank force and attached
infantry, Safir.[10] Certainly had the forces of 5th Army that attacked
during the night of 2–3 December been co-ordinated with those of
33rd Army the German defeat might have been much more resounding.
That Efremov exercised little control over and provided little higher-level
co-ordination for the operations concerned was due to a large extent to
the poor state of communication, where 'in the absence of radio- and
telephone communications' communication between Safir and Efremov
was in writing only, delivered by hand and in fact by a Moscow militia-
man – a professor – on motorcycle. So poor were communications that
Safir could only report on the repeated bombing of his tanks by the VVS
after the operation had concluded![11] Soviet intelligence of German
strength was apparently good in this instance according to German
assessments based on captured orders, thanks apparently largely to
PoWs, but of course the use to which this intelligence could be put was
hampered by the communications bottleneck.[12] Some of the information
available in this instance had been gleaned through radio interception. In
Soviet Intelligence in War David Glantz notes that by mid-1942 'Soviet
communications units at every level routinely monitored German radio
transmissions' in addition to their interception by specialist units radio
battalions formed from the end of 1942 that were also tasked with the
location of enemy transmitters and jamming.[13] Some attention had been
paid to radio reconnaissance earlier on, and it is indeed discussed in the
1936 Field Regulations.[14] According the Hans Schäufler of 4th Panzer
Division during a German advance in late October 1941 engineers from
the division had found a 'Russian radio intercept station'.[15] There is
perhaps a question mark over the extent to which specialist personnel
were available to run such stations, and particularly early in the war. It is
interesting to note how for example in a commendation of October
1942 for senior lietenant Vasilii Kozlov – a 'translator from German of
394th Independent Radio *Divizion* "OSNAZ"' on the Don Front – it was
noted that he was 'the sole specialist on our front who was good at
intelligence gathering on very high frequencies'. In the original of the
commendation this point has been underlined in pencil.[16] Such intelligence where available was undoubtedly valuable where reconnaissance
by Red Army units was not only limited but resultant information difficult to relay to those who might use it thanks to poor communications
and an intelligence structure that, as will be discussed later when it was
reformed, was poor at processing and dissemination.

In the case of the elimination of the Naro-Fominsk breakthrough
detailed earlier, with better command and control and a little restraint,

the Red Army might quite possibly have been able to marshal the sizeable force available to overwhelm a German infantry division with only limited mobility without having provoked withdrawal beforehand – the sort of outcome far more common later in the war. Many factors in addition to improved communications would play a part in making encirclement a far more likely result of Red Army operations, such as improved Red Army mobility and the inverse for a Wehrmacht increasingly subject to mindless orders to hold ground. Changing attitudes towards what was deemed acceptable delay before attacking in order to achieve a more satisfactory outcome would also have a major role to play. Nonetheless, during the retreat of 3 December 1941 258th Infantry Division suffered heavy losses. During operations from 1–4 December 1941 258th Infantry Division had lost ten officers killed and nine wounded, along with 160 NCOs and other ranks killed, 568 wounded and 148 missing – a total of 895 casualties. In addition, the division had lost equipment and transport resources that included 6 light and 2 heavy infantry guns, 3 light field howitzers, 7 assault guns, 4 3.7 cm anti-tank guns and 12 radio sets, along with 203 horses and a number of light vehicles.[17]

Although it tends not to be publicised, at least not by the victors, most armies at some point – and particularly what are now termed special forces – end up shooting prisoners. However, during the Second World War in the West arguably nowhere was the practice more prevalent than on the Eastern Front where the shooting of prisoners – already disarmed and not just at the point of surrendering when anger and adrenalin could get the better of any combatant – was probably endemic. In the above fighting near Naro-Fominsk Soviet documents captured by the German 258th Infantry Division suggest that 'in view of the difficult situation' 100 PoWs were shot by 1st Moscow Rifle Division on the order of the commissar, where another 15 PoWs had been shot by other units nearby.[18] On the other side, even in 1945 the German Field Marshal Schörner, commander of Army Group Centre, was apparently 'praising soldiers who took no prisoners'.[19] Snipers were often singled out in any theatre, but the infamous German commissar decree singled out all Soviet political commissars for special treatment, and if not shot after capture, the chances of survival for Soviet and Axis PoWs in their opponent's camp systems were overall poor.[20] In this 'fight to the death' [smertel'naia skhvatka] with German fascism – or for Hitler and his associates 'war of annihilation' [Vernichtungskrieg] with both Soviet Communism and the Jews apparently behind it – the 'rules of war' than at least partially governed or moderated the war in the West were often ignored. Not only was this the case in the treatment of PoWs, but there were also far more non-combatants killed in face-to-face encounters than in the West thanks to the intensity of the Soviet struggle in the German rear than ran concurrently with National Socialist attempts to cleanse occupied territory of the politically and racially undesirable and make way for German settlers.[21] Whilst this violence – or its effects – was often undoubtedly significant in motivating resistance in the Soviet Union, here we are primarily concerned with the effectiveness of the Soviet military in its contribution to bringing down Nazi Germany and its allies. Part of the Soviet military effort that fueled, was fueled by and early in the war often inhibited by German-led violence was the Soviet partisan movement. Here the Soviet partisan movement will be discussed not so much with focus on its social and political dimensions – on which readers may look at works recommended in the notes but will necessarily be considered in passing – but with a view to assessing its contribution to the defeat of German and allied armed forces in the East.

From the first days of the Great Patriotic War Stalin and the Soviet leadership sought to foster 'popular' resistance to the Axis invasion not only at the front line but in Axis rear areas. Whilst the Soviet authorities could draw on a Russian tradition of partisan warfare on which they had drawn during the Civil War and intervention, with the shift in Soviet doctrine in the late 1930s towards the primacy of the offensive, preparations for partisan warfare on Soviet territory in the event of foreign invasion were curtailed. As Panteleimon Ponomarenko, wartime head of the partisan movement recalled:

Despite a rich tradition and experience of partisan warfare and underground activity in previous wars, we did not have a single academic work putting this experience in context. The preparations being carried out during peacetime for partisan warfare were cut short in the mid-1930s, and caches of weapons, supplies and technical equipment created for this end were liquidated. The reason for this was without a doubt the unrealistic thrust of our military doctrine, stating that if the imperialists unleash war against the Soviet Union, then it will only take place on enemy territory. Even if it wasn't accepted unconditionally by the military leadership in planning, this doctrine was nonetheless promoted in the press and in the speeches of prominent political and military figures, and supplanted the idea that war could be transferred to our territory.[22]

Many of those involved in such preparations seem to have perished during the Great Purges of 1936–8 – many others during the debacles of the summer and autumn of 1941.[23] This did not mean the Red Army and even the NKVD would not have sent or dropped personnel into the enemy rear in the event of Soviet offensive operations from the outset for reconnaissance or sabotage, and such forces were undoubtedly as will become apparent a part of Soviet anti-Axis activity on occupied territory of the Soviet Union. For the enemy the result of their activities might easily have been confused with those of partisans drawn from the local Party apparatus and population, and indeed as the war progressed the distinction between 'regular' and 'irregular' forces was greatly diminished.

As the scale of the Axis invasion of 22 June 1941 became apparent, the Soviet leadership soon sought to resurrect previous plans to hamper an enemy advance through partisan activity issuing a directive on 29 June 1941 to local Party organisations that not only sought to 'bring an end to placidity and a carefree attitude and mobilize all of our organizations and all the force of our people for the total defeat of the enemy' but specifically to bring about the creation of 'partisan detachments and diversion groups' that would on occupied territory create 'intolerable conditions' for the enemy.[24] More detailed instructions were provided on 18 July in a decree concerned specifically with partisan warfare, that in addition to calling for the establishment of an underground on German occupied territory called for local Party organisations to 'in all haste organise armed bands and diversion groups from amongst participants in the Civil War and from those comrades that have already proved themselves in the destruction battalions,[25] in militia units and also from amongst the NKVD, NKGB and others'.[26]

At the same time some partisan detachments or diversion groups, sometimes called partisan-diversion groups, were formed primarily on the initiative of the NKVD. In fact, a directive of 29 July for the NKVD/NKGB of the Kalinin region for example had, in the light of the failure of many partisan detachments formed under Party auspices, suggested by implication that partisan detachments be formed solely from personnel from the destruction battalions, a responsibility of the NKVD, and from members of the NKVD and NKGB. Such detachments would however require the assistance of military formations for supply and equipment.[27] Meanwhile, whilst the Party and NKVD were taking measures for the establishment of a front in the enemy rear with varying degrees of co-operation between them depending on location, the Red Army through the military soviets was also taking steps to establish a presence on enemy occupied territory. The military soviets, re-established in 1937 at the beginning of the Purges, were a key vehicle for political control over the Red Army, with, at front level for instance, both the civilian Party apparatus and political organs of the Red Army being represented. They were indeed useful organs for the co-ordination of different arms, for instance at front level formally bringing together front commanders, commanders of artillery and of the air armies, and hence had value in operational planning.[28] Given both the political sensitivity of a partisan movement which gave its members unprecedented scope for independent action and hence required close political supervision, and political and military interests in its activities, the military soviets were, if they had the time after dealing with other concerns, the most suitable existing organs for directing partisan activity. Without sufficient time for dealing with detailed issues concerning the partisan movement, the military Soviets kept track of and facilitated partisan activity before their respective fronts and armies through subordinate organs. Initially of particular importance were the political boards of fronts and armies, under Lev Mekhlis's Main Political Directorate, and also reconnaissance organs.

With the Party, NKVD and political administration of the Red Army all sponsoring partisan detachments of varying quality, it became increasingly apparent that command and control needed to be more unified. Apparently moves had been taken within days of the German invasion to provide some sort of central direction to the organisation and activities of partisan detachments. According to Ponomarenko, who at the end of May 1942 would become a key figure in the further development of the partisan movement, before the end of June 1941 the Central Committee of the Party had taken the decision to establish a special commission for the direction of underground activity on German occupied territory. Ponomarenko was, it seems, to have been a member of this commission, along with Mekhlis, although Ponomarenko only apparently became aware of this after the war since no further action was taken.[29] On 12 August 1941 General I.V. Boldin was apparently approached by Stalin with the suggestion that Boldin assume the position of head of a board for the direction of the partisan movement being set up in Moscow.[30] Other than being seen as politically reliable, Boldin had on 10 August 1941 just escaped with 1,650 men from forty-five days on German occupied territory following encirclement, which was no doubt an important factor in his being approached.[31] Boldin apparently turned down the position on the grounds that he ought to remain with the field army.[32] Recently published documents from the Russian Presidential Archive certainly shed some light on the machinations taking place during the summer and autumn for the establishment of some sort of overall leadership of the partisan movement. As battalion komissar I. Anan'ev of the Political Board of the Western Front pointed out in a letter to Stalin of 27 October – a letter that sought to establish a headquarters under Party auspices not dissimilar to the Central Headquarters of the Partisan Movement ultimately established – there were too many organisations doing there own thing without co-ordination with other, what in our contemporary terms might be described as 'stakeholders'. Anan'ev apparently first made such his suggestion in early July, and was consequently sent with his idea to the Military Soviet of the Western Front and Party Secretary for Belorussia – Ponomarenko – who clearly knew more than he would subsequently let on.[33] Ponomarenko was clearly an interested party in expanding his influence over the partisan movement in 1941 – and Beria was keen to keep his finger in the pie. With Mekhlis also involved – and even Malenkov possibly in the mix, there was undoubtedly the sort of intrigue often associated with Hitler's court.[34] Also suggesting a leading role for their organisation was E.A. Shchadenko, head of the Main Board for the Formation and Equipping of the Forces of the Red Army, who in a series of proposals started to make the case even before the autumn that the Red Army to take the leading role in the organisation of the partisan movement.[35] According to Ponomarenko, ultimately appointed head of the Central Headquarters of the Partisan Movement or TShPD the following year, he had first been approached by Stalin regarding the creation of a headquarters for the partisan movement in November 1941, having pushed for a 'department for work in the enemy rear' of the Central Committee of the Party at the beginning of October that would see the Party take responsibility for training of for example saboteurs [*diversanti*] in schools across the western part of the Soviet Union.[36] However, despite arrangements for the central training of radio operators and other preparatory work having apparently been made, 'without warning a decree ordering the curtailment of the organisation of the headquarters was received'. According to Ponomarenko, the reason for this decree was 'a memorandum by Beria regarding the inexpediency of the creation of such a headquarters, since, in his opinion, he himself could provide leadership for the movement, without a specialist headquarters'.[37] Although the intrigues may have continued, with high expectations for the December 1941 Soviet counteroffensive, the need to further develop organs of the partisan movement could perhaps have been seen to have passed, although in December Shchadenko went as far as proposing the formation by mid-January of so called 'partisan armies' for operations in the enemy rear. One of two proposed armies would be formed in the North Caucasus and Stalingrad region and be primarily cavalry based, and the second, in the Moscow region, infantry. At 33,008 and 26,465 strong respectively, these partisan armies would, even if causing significant disruption, no doubt have been destroyed if they had managed to get behind German lines given their lack of heavy weapons and relatively poor training.[38] However, at this point Stalin did not have to decide who to reward with responsibility for a partisan movement that would hopefully not be required for too much longer anyway.

As will be shown in the next chapter the Soviet winter offensive of 1941–2 was far from the knockout blow hoped for by the Soviet leadership, and the need to improve the organisation and functioning of 'partisans' operating in the German rear remained. In many ways December 1941 saw the nadir of the Soviet partisan movement. Typically small detachments with poor communications with the Soviet rear during this period often struggled with supply in winter conditions and German attempts to suppress them where they had done sufficient to bring attention to themselves. As is apparent for the Leningrad and Smolensk regions for example, although a significant number of partisan detachments were formed for operations on enemy territory, many didn't actually make it into the German rear, and many of those that did were destroyed or achieved little. In a report of 22 November 1941 the Smolensk regional committee of the Communist Party could note that for 45 districts of the region 48 partisan detachments had been formed with somewhere in the region of 1,650–1,700 partisans in total. To start with detachments had not been formed for a number of regions where the terrain was unsuited to partisan warfare because it was largely steppe, and in four districts including two categorised as steppe the partisan detachments had 'fallen apart' after German forces occupied the districts concerned. Two more were identified as having made their way to Soviet lines after a month in the enemy rear, and one noted as destroyed by German forces, leaving forty-two detachments for forty districts, with 1,450–1,500 men supposedly still operating in the enemy rear. However, of twenty-four detachments formed in August and September in the eastern districts of the region, the regional Party committee only had information that thirteen remained on enemy territory, where only five were described as having 'gone over to active operations against the enemy', and where the eleven detachments with which communications had not been maintained being considered in operation 'only because nobody from these detachments made their way to our rear, . . . and there is neither direct nor indirect information of their exit' from enemy territory.[39] In the El'nia and Dorogobuzh districts there were partisan detachments 30–35 men strong recorded as active in late November, but German reports suggest that the partisan threat in the region remained largely limited to 'attacks on collaborators', 'acts of sabotage' and 'quite a few attacks on German soldiers either individually or in small groups', where it is unclear which 'partisans' were actually carrying out such attacks.[40]

These 'partisans' were operating relatively close to the frontlines where NKVD or Red Army detachments sent into the enemy rear for reconnaissance or sabotage purposes were more likely to be operating than deep in German occupied territory. At the same time, during the summer and autumn of 1941 there were frequently Red Army units that had escaped encirclement attempting to break through to Soviet lines and engaging German forces in the process, such as those accompanying General Boldin earlier. Although the partisan detachments formed as such during the summer and autumn of 1941 seem to have achieved little during that period, the Soviet winter counteroffensive – and the activities of Belov's regular cavalry and the airborne forces in the enemy rear discussed in the next chapter – seem to have emboldened many 'partisans' in a region where alongside the partisans there were now many regular troops who played a part in organising partisan activity in the area.[41] Here interesting parallels can be drawn with the partisan war of 1812, where regular troops such as Colonel Davidov's hussars along with Cossacks seem to have played an important and arguably leading role in making the 'partisan' menace increasingly meaningful for the enemy.[42] During early 1942 German security forces may all too frequently have taken out their frustrations on the local civilian population, but the fact that between March and June 1942 the German 221st Security Division in the region lost 278 men is testimony to a now genuine 'partisan' threat in the region.[43]

Partisans of the Pskov region on the move, September 1941. Such partisan units were far more militarily effective when they included professional military cadres, as was increasingly the case as the war progressed. (TsMVS 21323-n)

In the face of poor organisation, equipment and supply, and without the prospect of the return of the Red Army and Soviet power to an area, the willingness of civilians to join the partisans and the activity levels of partisan detachments in existence in late 1941 and early 1942 seems to have been limited, as was certainly the case in the forests and marshes of the Leningrad region. German success in suppressing the widely-dispersed Party and state functionary-dominated partisan movement in the Leningrad region during the autumn and winter of 1941 contrasts starkly with Leningrad partisan claims of having killed 11,493 Germans and destroyed seventy tanks and seventy-one aircraft in the little over six months of the war in 1941, where the number of 'active' partisans on 10 December 1941 was only 2,430. Leningrad partisans lost no fewer than 616 killed and missing during 1941 (officially reported), but this does not include the many units that simply gave up in the face of the hardships of winter and under German pressure and sought to cross back to Soviet lines.[44] Across the Soviet Union German security and frontline forces were overall successful in suppressing the partisan threat during 1941 thanks to the fact that the movement was not only poorly organised, equipped and supplied but also at best poorly supported by a primarily rural population that even in Russian heartlands was not willing to throw its lot in with the partisans and face the consequences. At times hostile to the Soviet regime – and particularly older peasants and those who had been labelled 'kulaks' – many peasants seem to have opted to wait and see whether Germany and her allies would win or Soviet power would return before throwing in their lot with either side. Often however German forces and local partisans attempted to force the local population to take sides through intimidation, where for much of 1941 at least German forces are more likely to have appeared the stronger and more likely to be on the winning side.

After the organisational chaos and relatively inactivity of the so called 'partisan movement' during 1941 and the winter of 1941–2, during 1942 and into 1943 considerable progress was made in providing the Soviet partisan movement with a coherent and effective organisational structure to replace a situation where in many areas the Party, NKVD and Red Army were all involved in fostering partisan activity in the German rear. These organisations were engaged in the development of partisan units in the German rear at best without effective liaison with other organisations concerned, at worst in competition with each other. On 30 May 1942, a GKO order for the creation of a Central Headquarters of the Partisan Movement [*Tsentral'nii shtab partizanskogo dvizheniia* or TsShPD] was given, a body which would take overall responsibility for the partisan movement across the Soviet Union. The principle task of the

partisan movement at this point was identified as 'the disorganisation of
the enemy rear', attacking German lines of communication but also
providing intelligence for the Red Army. The eventual creation of the
Central Headquarters of the Partisan Movement in May 1942 would be
followed in September 1942 by what can be deemed the basic Union-
wide instructions for the conduct of partisan warfare for the remainder of
the war, and which will be referred to further later.[45] The effective
professionalisation of the partisan movement that had occurred locally
in the El'nia-Dorogobuzh region in early 1942 thanks to the presence of
1st Guards Cavalry Corps and Soviet airborne forces in the region was
gradually to be emulated for the movement as a whole that would
increasingly lose its 'irregular' character as mufti was replaced by uniforms to go with military organisation and equipment. Better organised,
equipped and supplied, it also became apparent later in 1942 or during
1943 depending on the region concerned that the Red Army would not
be defeated, and in fact would no doubt return and bring with it Soviet
power that had never entirely disappeared and particularly so where the
partisan movement was stronger such as in the forest of Belorussia.
Under heavy pressure to become or support the partisans lest they face
the consequences of awkward questions, when the Red Army was on the
advance from late 1942 onwards the ranks of the partisans would as in
the case of the Leningrad region in early 1944 be swelled with new
recruits to a movement that was by this point much more like a regular
army in the enemy rear than the obviously amateurish movement of
1941. In the Leningrad region in early 1944, with the prospect of major
Soviet offensive operations and the liberation of the territory concerned
and with Soviet partisans now giving many collaborators the opportunity
to redeem themselves by joining the partisans at a time when the alternative was often forced evacuation by the German authorities, the number
of partisans swelled within a matter of weeks. From 4,836 partisans in
72 detachments at the beginning of October 1943 by mid-January
1944 there were 25,062 partisans in 182 detachments although there
were not necessarily arms for all these new recruits. By this time Leningrad partisans were able to inflict meaningful damage on German forces,
including for example delaying elements of 12th Panzer Division on their
way to the front.[46]

Calculating the damage caused by the Soviet partisan movement to the
German war effort in the East is far from straightforward. Much of the
contribution of the partisan movement to the defeat of Nazi Germany
and her allies in the East cannot be measured in the way that many Soviet
accounts did with inflated claims for German forces destroyed directly
by partisans. Although the partisans were often engaged with German

security forces – be they Wehrmacht close to the front lines or SS-run further in the rear – a significant proportion of those casualties actually inflicted by partisans on the German war machine were not inflicted on security forces. In late 1941 approximately 4,000 partisans of the Leningrad and Kalinin regions fighting against forces of Army Group North faced no more than a total of 30,000 security troops, whose numbers declined dramatically during the winter.[47] For the whole of 1942 Leningrad partisans alone claimed to have killed 28,450 Germans and destroyed 70 tanks and 19 aircraft, where partisan strength reached a high of 5,700 on 15 August 1942, from a low of 2,391 on January 1942 (Leningrad region partisan losses for 1942 were no lower than 1,267 killed and 286 missing according to Soviet figures).[48] Yet in 575 anti-partisan operations between 29 December1941 and 28 September 1942 281st Security Division, one of three allocated to Army Group North, lost only 161 killed, with 128 wounded and 12 missing.[49] Even factoring in any propensity on the part of German forces to kill civilians and count them as partisans, it is apparent that lightly armed partisans unsurprisingly tended to fare badly when in combat situations even with poor quality security troops in any concentration, as during anti-partisan operations. As late as in the spring of 1943, during Operation 'Spring Clean' in the Army Group Rear Area of Army Group North it is reasonable to assume that more than a hundred partisans were killed by troops of 281st Security Division on the basis of weapons recovered and where partisan units admitted 'heavy...fighting' for the loss of eleven Germans killed and forty-five wounded.[50] Undoubtedly many of those killed in partisan attacks other than on trains or on troops in transit by road were not actually German troops that could otherwise have been fighting at the front. Local garrisons of security troops were made up of troops that were certainly not the best the Wehrmacht had to offer. The most combat-effective elements of the security divisions were soon fighting on the front line, as for example the 368th Infantry (Jaeger) Regiment of 281st Security Division, fighting 'almost without interruption' at the front as part of 30th Jaeger Division from July 1941. Replacements received by the end of November 1941 were deemed unsuitable for aggressive anti-partisan operations.[51] Increasingly guard duties were carried out by local collaborators, who would not otherwise have been deployed to the front. A significant proportion of German losses were undoubtedly brought about during attacks on trains, and losses to frontline units in transit are difficult to distinguish from losses in combat at the front, and an area where further detailed research might be revealing. There are however other key measures of partisan military effectiveness – the extent to which partisan tied down German resources in rear-area security that might have been used for some other purpose even if not in frontline combat, the extent to which their activities disrupted frontline operations, be this through hampering the ability to move reinforcements to where they were needed in a timely manner and indeed the withdrawal of German forces, or German ability to resupply frontline troops.

As has already been suggested when looking at German losses due to partisan activity, many of those troops committed to anti-partisan work would not otherwise have been deployed at the front at the time they were engaged in anti-partisan work in the absence of the partisan threat (even if as the German manpower situation deteriorated increasingly less combat effective troops were in frontline combat). Additionally the numbers committed for a sustained period remained relatively small compared to the size of the Wehrmacht and the size of the territory concerned throughout the occupation. At the beginning of Operation 'Barbarossa' the Wehrmacht allocated nine security divisions to rear area security, that is 207th, 281st and 285th for Army Group North, 213th, 286th and 403rd for Army Group Centre, and 221st, 444th and 454th for Army Group South, with a total of fifteen security divisions being created for service on former Soviet territory.[52] Based on an initial total of in the region of 11,449 men for 281st Security Division on 1 June 1941, this gives a total of approximately 100,000 troops initially committed. In the case of the three security divisions allocated to Army Group North their attentions were focused on Russian territory of the Leningrad and Kalinin regions by the end of the year. Even before fighting had begun 281st Security Division was down to 7,827 men, at the end of 1941, on 21 December 1941, 7,053 men according to its war diary.[53] As noted earlier, in the region of 4,000 Soviet partisans operating against Army Group North faced no more than 30,000 security troops at the end of 1941, with the security divisions being assisted by forces of the Reichsführer SS, in this case elements of Einsatzgruppe A and 2nd SS Infantry Brigade for instance.[54] Before the widespread use of collaborators the situation for the Army Group Centre Rear Area on 5 October 1941 where 'after static rail line guards were posted there were too few troops remaining to mount any offensive action against the partisans or exercise effective control' was certainly not an exaggeration.[55] It is also worth noting that not only were limited numbers of increasingly second-rate troops allocated to rear-area security, but they were also poorly equipped, particularly with transport resources.[56]

Whilst partisan strength dropped dramatically during the winter of 1941–2, the fall in available security forces was even more dramatic. US historian of the Soviet partisan movement Edgar Howell suggests that of thirty-four battalions initially allocated to rear-area security for

Army Group North, all but four were in frontline service during the by the spring of 1942 – on 22 April 1942 only elements of 207th and 281st Security Divisions were actually engaged in rear-area security duties.[57] By 1 October 1943, according to Ponomarenko, there were fourteen German divisions allocated to rear-area security, of which six were security divisions (201st, 203rd, 207th, 281st, 285th, 286th), four he describes as Luftwaffe field divisions (153rd, 388th, 390th, 391st) that were in fact field training divisions, and four reserve divisions (141st, 143rd, 147th, 151st). In addition German allies provided security troops – another fourteen divisions, nine of which were Hungarian, three Rumanian and two Slovakian, along with 3rd Rumanian Mountain Corps.[58] This list ignores non-divisional units of up to regimental strength, where, for instance, partisans identified 356th Infantry Regiment, apparently of 228th Infantry Division, as operating in the Ostrov region deep in the rear of Army Group North in the summer of 1943, where the division had apparently been disbanded.[59] Whilst some of these divisional types had or would shortly see front-line service, most were operating in rear-area security roles due to their apparent inadequacies in frontline roles. Despite increasing partisan strength Army Group North could not field more regular troops against the partisans in late 1943 than late 1941 – with somewhere between 25–30,000 troops in regularly organised units down to below company strength being available for security functions in late 1943.[60] Anti-partisan operations did on numerous occasions however temporarily draw off troops from frontline service, as in the case of the frontline capable 2nd SS Infantry Brigade mentioned earlier. Partisans for instance identified ('confirmed') 27th Infantry Regiment of 12th Infantry Division in the rural Kudever' district in the Army Group Rear Area of Army Group North in December 1943.[61] Even in the autumn of 1941 at least 691st Infantry Regiment of 339th Infantry Division seems to have been deployed in a rear-area security role in the Rear Areas of Army Group Centre, before the crisis period of the Soviet winter counteroffensive of 1941–2.[62]

Many local security functions were carried out by former-Soviet collaborators, who undoubtedly suffered heavily in partisan raids and who certainly made up a significant proportion of 'enemy' losses reported by partisans, only sometimes distinguished from German losses. The 281st Security Division alone could claim 778 EKA (*Einwohner-Kampf-Abteilung*) personnel and 480 OD (*Ordnungsdienst*) personnel carrying out security and police functions within its jurisdiction in March 1943.[63] On the territory of Army Group North more reliable security and police units from the Baltic Republics were frequently deployed in significant numbers. Kalinin partisans for instance identified the 273rd,

515th and 615th Latvian Police Battalions as operating on the territory
of Army Group North in the summer of 1943.[64] Partisan activity also
undoubtedly tied down non-combat units such as those identified by
partisans in intelligence reports e.g., construction and railway units,
which could have been deployed on other tasks had it not been for acts
of sabotage.

A significant proportion of the casualties inflicted by partisan on
German and allied forces did not actually damage German frontline
operations in any meaningful way, or indeed draw substantial force away
from frontline duty for sustained periods of time, as was the Soviet
intention. Arguably far more significant than killing or tying down
second- or even lower grade units was partisan disruption of German
lines of communication through rear areas. Summary data for the
Leningrad Headquarters of the Partisan Movement of April 1944, suggests that Leningrad partisans alone 'destroyed' 1,050 steam locomotives
and a staggering 18,643 railway trucks.[65] Ukrainian partisan claimed to
have brought about a total of 4,958 train derailments up to 1 September
1944, including 61 armoured trains.[66] Once again, these figures are
exaggerated, although damage done to German communications was at
times significant. Much of the damage to German railway communications, broader troop movements and resupply efforts took place either
during focused operations such as during the 'war of the rails' of the
summer and autumn of 1943, or later in the war when the numerical
balance between partisan and security-force strength was most favourable to the partisans. Of the 1,050 locomotives claimed as 'destroyed' by
Leningrad partisans for their war as a whole, only 66 were supposedly
'destroyed' during 1941, rising to 266 for 1942, and 440 for 1943, with a
278 for 1944 where much of the Leningrad region had been liberated by
the spring.[67]

In late 1941, when partisan units remained small in size and were often
less than resolute in their activities, German security forces focused on
railway security at the expense of other dimensions to rear-area security
given the supply crisis. As Howell notes, on 20 December 1941 281st
Security Division ordered, in order to secure the Pskov–Ostrov–Rezenke
and Pskov–Dno railway lines, that 'all bridges and culverts less than
40 feet long were to have double sentries, longer structures to be guarded
by a squad of one non-commissioned officer and six men'. In addition
'all stretches of rail in closed terrain were to have one sentry every 100
yards; in open terrain every 200 yards; sentries were to remain in sight of
one another. . . . This security schedule was not to be deviated from, even
if the last man in the division was used.'[68] Only during 1942 would
increasingly large, well-trained and equipped partisan units start to do

significant damage to the German transportation network in rear areas. In the Army Group North Rear Areas partisan attacks on railway lines and bridges increased during the summer of 1942, with a particular increase in the number of partisan attacks being noticed between May and June. From 1 May to 31 July in the rear of 16th Army partisans destroyed '30 bridges, broke rails in 84 places, and damaged or destroyed 20 locomotives and 113 railroad cars'. Attacks on railway lines were not however necessarily on the key transport arteries, and less well defended road bridges were, at least in the Opochka region, apparently more likely to be hit that rail bridges.[69]

Order Number 00189 of the People's Commissar for Defence entitled 'On the tasks of the Partisan Movement' of September 1942 increased the emphasis of partisans on attacks on railway lines, with for instance a series of derailments taking place on key railway lines in the rear areas of Army Group North in September–October 1942, with sixteen derailments on the key Pskov–Dno–Staraia Russa line in September and six in October. Nonetheless this intensity of attacks could not be maintained, no doubt to a large extent because partisan strength typically dropped dramatically during the winter of 1942–3 as it had done during 1941–2, in the case of the Leningrad region with 5,700 partisans officially accounted for on 15 October 1942, dropping to 2,472 on 1 December 1942. Even Ponomarenko, head of the Central Headquarters of the Partisan Movement, was forced to admit to Stalin, that before the start of the 'War of the Rails', 'despite the considerable importance of the partisan struggle against [enemy] lines of communication disorganization of enemy movement on the railways has still not reached such an extent as to have operational impact on the German frontline'.[70] This would change as an increasingly strong partisan movement was thrown into intensive operations aimed at destroying railway track faster than the Germans could replace it in the summer of 1943.

Ordered on 14 July 1943, what would subsequently be described as the 'War of the Rails' began on 21 July for Orlov partisans and on 3 August for Leningrad, Kalinin, Smolensk and Belorussian partisans. According to figures received up to 13 August Leningrad partisans destroyed 3,271, Kalinin 7,224, Smolensk 8,279, Orlov 7,935 and Belorussian a staggering 75,227 lengths of railway track.[71] Whilst the above figures are certainly exaggerated, they do give some indication of the areas in which partisan attacks were most heavy. Certainly the rear areas behind Army Group Centre were worst hit as German troops withdrew in the face of the Soviet counterattack after the German attack on the Kursk salient had been blunted. According to German sources during the night of 2–3 August partisans behind Army Group Centre, that is in the Army

Group Centre Rear Area and Reichskomissariat Weissruthenien, set 10,900 demolition charges and mines, 8,422 of which detonated, the remainder disarmed (of which 6,519 detonations were for the Army Group Centre Rear Area). For August the total was 15,977 detonations (12,717 for the Army Group Centre Rear Area) with an additional 4,528 removed by the Germans. According to Howell, the effect of these demolitions 'while never disastrous, was considerable', although a total of 2,951 supply and troop trains were successfully moved during the month in the area concerned.[72]

Across the front, as German fortunes waned partisan strength increased – the relationship between the two being strong and where German and allied forces were only able to provide viable security for an increasingly limited number of railway lines. The onset of winter, in burdening a growing partisan movement with increasingly complex supply issues had some impact on the frequency and intensity of partisan attacks. However, the fact that the tide had clearly turned against Germany and the impact of Soviet incitement to join or assist the partisans or face punishment later gave the partisans new recruits and helped, on the surface at least, ease or hide tension between hungry partisans and the civilian population on which they depended for most of their food, increasing partisan effectiveness.[73]

The September 1942 order 'On the tasks of the Partisan Movement' also increased emphasis on partisans serving the needs of the Red Army in other ways, and in particular in providing intelligence. After a period during which the Red Army, NKVD and Party were all sponsoring partisan units in the German rear during 1941 and into 1942, during the second half of 1942 the organizational structure of the partisan movement under the Central Headquarters of the Partisan Movement sought to foster links between the partisan movement and Red Army through the Military Soviets and Operational Groups at Front and Army level respectively – a process of integration very much along the lines of a model established in the Leningrad region during late 1941.[74] The potential value of partisan intelligence reaching the Red Army through the above organisation is obvious but difficult to measure – partisans frequently identified regular and frontline capable units resting, being redeployed or engaged in anti-partisan operations in the German rear. For instance, the loss of 27th Infantry Regiment to 12th Infantry Division, identified by partisans as being in the Kudever' region in December 1943, would have been a major blow to the strength of the division.[75] The effectiveness of this intelligence provision increased as more partisan units were equipped with radios, for instance the timeliness of intelligence allowing better use of Soviet airpower, although German intelligence

Soviet partisans of the Leningrad region operating a radio set in May 1943. Earlier in the war the availability of such equipment to partisans had been very limited. (TsMVS 50183)

also gained a better appreciation of partisan activities at the same time.[76] Certainly poor or often non-existent radio communications during the early part of the war limited not only the value of the partisans as a means of gathering intelligence but also their ability to co-ordinate their activities with each other and for example arrange for supply drops by air. As I.N. Artem'ev notes, having been responsible for partisan communications as part of the TsShPD apparatus – before more widespread availability of radio equipment communication with Soviet lines was often through messengers sent through the frontlines who could all too easily be captured by the enemy.[77]

Better communications also facilitated attempts to co-ordinate partisan sabotage activities with Red Army operations, a co-operation noticeably more effective at the time of the 'War of the Rails' of the summer of

1943 and the Soviet winter offensive of 1944 below Leningrad compared to attempts at co-ordination during the Moscow counteroffensive of 1941–2.[78] The Soviet historian Andrianov suggests that the first attempt to co-ordinate partisan attacks with Red Army operations was planned during November for December 1941 for operations against German forces in and near Demiansk, although he suggests that the frequency and scale of such co-operation was limited until 1943 to activity barely of operational significance. During the 'War of the Rails' of the summer of 1943, large-scale partisan activity behind more than one front and to a considerable distance behind German lines was of operational and even operational-strategic significance, being geared to the hampering of German movement in the face of the Soviet counteroffensive in the aftermath of the German Operation 'Citadel' and very much reliant on the sort of radio networks then available to many partisan brigades.[79]

Whilst the broader impact of the partisan movement on the German economy is not the principal concern of this work, it is nonetheless worth noting that given the extent to which the Wehrmacht was forced to 'live off the land' in the East, partisan disruption of the German collection of agricultural products and other resources (e.g. lumber) from the occupied territories of the East is of some significance. As early as 19 June 1942 WiIn Nord, the German military agency responsible for the exploitation of the territory occupied by Army Group North, considered agricultural activity in all areas of the Army Group North Rear Area to have been at least partially disrupted, with agricultural activity having been considered impossible in a number of districts of the Kalinin region in the south of the area occupied by Army Group North in the border region with Belorussia. Limited German authority over the hinterland also limited the extent to which German forces could mobilise the local population for labour service for the Wehrmacht. It is in this broader regard that the partisan movement had the most sustained influence on the German military effort, contributing for example, along with broader German administrative weakness on occupied territory, to the fact that German grain collection from the occupied territories was never as great as had been predicted.[80]

German security resources were focused, from the first year of the war, on keeping key railway arteries open, very rapidly to the exclusion of other tasks. In doing so German forces enjoyed short-medium term success with limited resources in achieving their key aim of keeping key supply arteries to the front open. In focusing in on this key task, German forces however, despite sporadic large-scale anti-partisan operations, gave over potential base areas for partisans in the hinterland where Soviet power could be rebuilt and from which increasingly large, well-equipped and organised partisan units could attack and often overwhelm the defences of the precious transport arteries. In Belorussia, the existence of districts administered more or less continuously by the partisans was by the middle of the Great Patriotic War certainly not a fiction, from which region by 1 January 1944 according to statistics of the Central Headquarters of the Partisan Movement 121,282 partisans were operating out of a total of 145,038 participants in the Belorussian partisan movement since 15 June 1942 – 55.5 per cent of total participants recorded. Highlighting the professionalisation of the partisan movement by this point is the fact that at the beginning of 1944 3,841 Belorussian partisans were Red Army officers, with another 9,403 being Red Army personnel of other ranks, to whom can be added 833 personnel either from the police or NKVD and NKGB. In fact overall at this point there were 56,435 Red Army personnel recorded as serving in the partisan movement.[81]

That the Soviet historiography of the partisan movement inflated the achievements of the partisans whilst at the same time downplaying the human cost of their activities is beyond doubt. However, in 'clinical' terms the Soviet partisan movement was, by Soviet standards, a cost effective means of causing military and economic damage to the German war effort on the Eastern Front. Damage to the Axis war machine and assistance provided to the Red Army were apparently achieved at a remarkably low cost by Soviet standards, that is by the standards of the slaughter at the front. In the case of the Leningrad region, according to Petrov 13,000 'Soviet patriots gave their lives in the struggle against the Hitlerite occupiers,'[82] of whom according to alternative figures 4,326 were partisans identified as such by the Central Headquarters of the partisan movement and lost up to 15 February 1944,[83] out of a total of 39,905 total official participants in the Leningrad partisan movement from the start of the war.[84] As of 15 February 1944 the partisan movement as a whole, excluding the Ukraine, had apparently lost 30,047 killed and missing, out of a total of 208,206 official participants.[85] Many Soviet citizens were killed, in addition to official partisan losses, who considered themselves partisans and were considered as such by German forces. To these deaths have of course to be added the tens of thousands of civilians killed by German forces of occupation during anti-partisan operations and indeed in reprisals for partisan activity who did not see themselves as partisans, but also those 'collaborators' with the Germans killed by the Soviet partisans particularly early in the war whose collaboration may have been less than enthusiastic but difficult to avoid.[86] We might assume that for every officially recognised partisan three or even five unofficial 'partisans' or civilians were killed, giving a total of in the region of 120,000–180,000 'partisans' killed for Soviet territory excluding the Ukraine over the entire period of occupation. If making such an assumption, then a rather cold cost-benefit analysis of partisan activity relative to other Soviet military activity suggests that 'partisans' achieved much – difficult to quantify as their impact often was – for relatively limited cost compared to some of their frontline compatriots. For example, Soviet forces facing Army Group North alone (taken as the North-Western, Leningrad and Volkhov Fronts) suffered 476,450 irrecoverable losses (including 213,557 killed) during 1942 for little territorial gain even if they did draw significant German resources from other operations.[87]

Other professional 'soldiers' operating in the German rear included both Red Army and NKVD troops that were sent into the German rear either for reconnaissance, sabotage or both – units that we would now describe as special forces. Where Red Army units in the enemy rear were, once the Red Army was on the offensive more likely to be for reconnaissance purposes, there were 'elite' or 'special forces' operating in the German rear with the intention of engaging in sabotage originating both from the Red Army and NKVD. Such units had already been employed during the second half of the war with Finland, when for example at the end of January 1940 a number of detachments for the creation of, to use the Soviet term, 'diversions' in the enemy rear were formed on the initiative of the head of the then 5th Board of the NKO Komkor I.I. Proskurov. A special ski detachment was formed from students from the Institute for Physical Education named after P.F. Lesgaft and other volunteers in Leningrad, which subsequently engaged in raids in the Finnish rear.[88] Students from the Lesgaft institute would subsequently form a partisan detachment during the Great Patriotic War – 1st Vounteer Partisan Detachment formed at the end of June 1941.[89] The NKVD would also be involved in sabotage and raids in the enemy rear from the early part of the Great Patriotic War through OMSBON or the Independent Special Service Motor Rifle Brigade born out of immediate predecessors of the summer of 1941 when it was formed in October 1941. Ultimately OMSBON detachments would end up conducting reconnaissance, diversion and other similar activities in the enemy rear for the Stavka across the entire front, although from October to December 1941 OMSBON operated in support of the Moscow Defence Zone.[90] Certainly a tidy divide between Soviet partisans, what might be termed 'special forces' or in Soviet terms 'Spetsnaz' troops and front line combatants – particularly from a German perspective – is difficult to make and particularly with the propensity for regular Soviet troops, including cavalry units and formations, and during the winter ski battalions, to be launched on what amounted to 'raids' into the Axis rear as Belov's 1st Guards Cavalry Corps in the next chapter. These regular frontline formations were nonetheless supposedly participating in broader operations of the field army, and were not in the Soviet rear merely to cause disruption as 'partisan' units such as Kovpak's partisan cavalry division, whose deep raid into Galicia in early 1943 may have achieved little that was concrete and resulted in the destruction of much of his force but certainly added new meaning to the notion of raiding behind Axis lines.[91] The Soviet winter offensive of 1941–2 would see not only Soviet cavalry and ski troops, but also airborne forces alongside specialist Red Army and NKVD units, all operating in the German rear for protracted periods of time along with those partisans who were able continue their activities.

One of the few arms that was not engaged in protracted operations in the German rear was the armour given its reliance on fuels that could not even hypothetically be easily sourced locally like food and fodder might, and that could not be airdropped in meaningful quantities. By late November and early December 1941, in many ways the Red Army was scraping the bottom of the barrel in terms of the tanks it was mobilising to throw at the Wehrmacht where although there was new production of the latest models such as the T-34 and KV-series much productive capacity had been evacuated to the east and was yet to resume production. As would be the case in 1945 in Germany, aged vehicles and development vehicles were thrown into the fray such as the A-20 prototype mobilized from the testing area at Kubinka in to an independent tank battalion incorporated in to 22nd Tank Brigade.[92] Nonetheless, proportionally newer models were playing a more significant role than they had been during the summer, and that included foreign vehicles that were new to the Red Army at least.

The autumn of 1941 had seen the nadir for Soviet tank strength and indeed by many measures strength more broadly, where on 1 October 1941 for example the Western, Reserve and Briansk Fronts on the Moscow axis could muster a total of 782 tanks that were with combat units, of which only 141 were medium and heavy types, that is by this point predominately T-34s and KV-series tanks respectively.[93] By 1 December 1941 the Kalinin, Western and left wing of the South-Western Front defending the capital could still nonetheless field more than 667 tanks with combat units, where of more than 600 tanks concentrated with the Western Front 205 were T-34 or KV-series.[94] That relative Soviet material strength had improved by the end of the year such that on 1 January 1942 the Soviet tank park stood at somewhere around 7,700 vehicles owed much to the ability of the Red Army to throw everything it still had from pre-war stocks in with continued albeit disrupted production of new equipment for what were often newly formed units.[95] It also owed something to the support it now enjoyed from its allies, Great Britain and the United States, and at this stage particularly the former. The British government during the summer of 1941 moved toward a position where it opted to support the Soviet Union with equipment and supplies at the expense of its own operations elsewhere. For Churchill, Beaverbrook and other British leaders Soviet survival was crucial for the British who at a minimum needed time to ensure the defence of the British Isles in case they would once again be left essentially alone with the empire facing Nazi Germany and her allies as had been the case from June 1940–June 1941. In the fighting near Naro-Fominsk described above, 136th Independent Tank Battalion was equipped with British-supplied tanks, just one of a number of units so equipped that participated in the later phases of Soviet defensive operations near Moscow and the subsequent counteroffensive.

The first action during the defensive battles near Moscow involving Soviet units equipped with British tanks seems to have been an engagement between the German 252nd Infantry Division and 146th Tank Brigade, where three British-supplied tanks were recorded as knocked out in German sources near Petrovskoe near the River Istra north-west of Moscow on 25 November 1941. On 20 November 1941 General Nikolai Biriukov of the Main Auto-Armour Board of the Red Army recorded in his service diary that 146th Tank Brigade had been equipped with British-supplied Valentine or 'Mk-III' tanks, and was soon according to the commander of 78th Rifle – soon 9th Guards Rifle – Division Afanasii Beloborodov attached to his command and provided assistance during withdrawal and subsequent defensive action.[96] The presence of British tanks on the Eastern Front was confirmed by the German OKH on 27 November, where it was recorded that 'Reports during the last few days of the appearance of British tanks...have been confirmed. Five British tanks (type Mark-III) have been knocked out by forces of 3rd Panzergruppe'.[97] By 9 December 1941 the British Military Mission in Moscow noted that about ninety British tanks had seen action with Soviet forces – in all likelihood 146th Tank Brigade equipped initially with forty-two Valentines, 131st Independent Tank Battalion with twenty-one, with 136th and 138th Independent Tank Battalions that had also seen action as of 20 November having been provided with three Matilda and nine Valentine for the former and fifteen Matilda and six Valentines for the latter. By the end of 1941 the Soviet Union had in fact received 187 Matilda and 259 Valentine tanks from the UK – with more than 350 having reached the Red Army by that point.[98] Whilst certainly slow for a Red Army that had abandoned the infantry support tank concept before the war, the Matilda and Valentine were nonetheless certainly better armoured and with a main armament of equivalent or superior anti-tank capability to much of the Soviet tank strength even if their two-pounder guns lacked high-explosive rounds. In terms of suitability for service in Russian conditions, their abilities to deal with snow and ice were relatively poor for example the capabilities of the British tanks to deal with deep snow was worse than for the KV, T-34 and indeed BT-7 (50 cm), but comparable to the T-60 (35 cm), where the Matilda was deemed in a report by the Auto-Armour Board of the Western Front of early 1942 to be capable of dealing with 35 cm, and Valentine 40 cm

Map 3: The Moscow region in early December 1941, with the locations of Soviet tank units equipped with British-supplied vehicles indicated.

Matilda and Valentine infantry tanks being loaded in Britain for shipment to the Soviet Union, exact date unknown. A meaningful number
of such vehicles arrived in late 1941 at a time when the Soviet Union
was experiencing an acute shortage of medium and heavy tanks.
(Tank Museum #8097-A1)

of snow.[99] From a crew perspective, the high nickel content of British
armour was likely to mean less fragmentation when hit, giving a better
chance of survival in such circumstances.[100] Particularly where used in
defensive roles and for infantry support where they could play to their
strengths, British tanks were undoubtedly a useful addition to the Soviet
tank park at a crucial juncture.

Also of some value – and in particular given Soviet struggles to get an
effective new-generation fighter aircraft in to service in meaningful
numbers – were British-supplied aircraft. By the end of 1941 the Soviet
Union had received 484 Hurricanes, 216 British-supplied albeit
US-manufactured Tomahawks and 11 similarly sourced Airacobras.
As early as 12 October 1941 Tomahawks were in service with 126th
Fighter Air Regiment of the Soviet PVO or Air Defence Forces, the first
Soviet unit to be equipped with foreign-supplied aircraft. By the end of
the year British-supplied aircraft had seen action in the far north near
Murmansk, in defence of the 'Road of Life' supplying the besieged city
of Leningrad, and in the skies over Moscow. At the very end of 1941
British-supplied aircraft – Hurricanes and Tomahawks – made up

approaching 10 per cent of the fighter strength of the Soviet PVO, with the 99 Hurricanes and 39 Tomahawks serving alongside not only 136 of the more capable Yak-1s but also 264 rather antiquated I-153 biplanes and 351 of the problem-plagued MiG-3. Despite the heavy losses suffered by the VVS in the war to the end of 1941 – with losses of in the region of 5,100 fighters out of an initial strength on 22 June 1941 of 11,500 – both domestic and foreign replacements left the VVS with around 7,900 fighter aircraft at the end of 1941 – of which nearly 10 per cent had been provided by the allies.[101]

Certainly of note in reinforcing the Soviet position before Moscow and then providing troops for the winter counteroffensive were units drawn from the Urals, Siberia and the Far East. For example, between July and November twelve divisions are recorded as having been transferred from the Far Eastern Military District to the west by the 1985 third-edition of the history of that district. In July 1941 107th Motor Rifle Division had arrived in the west, and was soon fighting near El'nia and subsequently in defence of the Mozhaisk Line before Moscow. The 32nd Red Banner Rifle Division arrived in the west in October and as part of 5th Army also fought in the defensive battles around Mozhaisk, and 78th Rifle Division also from the Far East fought in the Istra region with 16th Army in late October.[102] From Siberia in time for the winter counteroffensive came not only rifle forces but also recently raised ski battalions.[103] If the German Tiger tank would become the bogeyman for Allied forces in 1943 and 1944, then for the Wehrmacht in late 1941 the bogeymen were perhaps not only the T-34 and KV-1, but also Siberian rifle divisions. As noted in the previous chapter the 'panic' experienced by the German 112th Infantry Division on 17 November 1941 was according to Guderian supposedly as a result of attack by a combination of T-34 tanks and 'new Siberian troops', although it is unclear just what proportion of Soviet forces engaged in the immediate area were actually Siberian and indeed T-34s where they remained relatively few in number.[104] The Soviet 112th Tank Division operating in the area was for example 'armed in the main with the T-26 light tank', even if 131st Independent Tank Battalion attached to it was equipped with what were in many sense more intimidating KV-1s.[105] Certainly, in these regions deep in the Soviet rear the call up of reservists had, as elsewhere, begun prior to the war and Siberian troops, both experienced and otherwise, would find their way westwards as, just as the 185 T-34s produced in October and 253 and 327 vehicles in November and December respectively would find their way very quickly to combat units.[106]

The mobilisation of specific armies during the spring and 805,264 troops for 'large-scale training exercises' in May had brought the Red

Army to a nominal strength of 5,707,116 men by the start of the war, although many of those called up for the training exercises had not as David Glantz notes been immediately allocated to field forces. The general mobilisation that was initiated at the beginning of the war meant that by 1 July 1941 there were 9,638,000 men in the Soviet armed forces, including 3,533,000 in field forces and 532,000 in the navy, with a further 5,562,000 in the military districts in the rear.[107] By the end of September the Red Army had already lost more than two million men as irrecoverable losses, to which would be added more than another million during the last three months of 1941.[108] Also lost were those of call up age on enemy occupied territory, many of whom would later be conscripted as the Red Army liberated them. As of September 1942 E.A. Shchadenko – in charge of new unit creation for the Red Army – suggested that more than five and a half million personnel of call up age were on enemy occupied territory, with much of the territory concerned having been occupied since the first weeks of the war.[109] Nonetheless, there were still 3,627,000 men with the fronts and other formations as of 10 September out of a total strength of just over eight million.[110] During the summer and autumn of 1941 the GKO would issue numerous decrees on mobilisation that would increase manpower available and lead to the creation of new fighting units, be that through the creation of the militia divisions discussed in the previously, through to very specific decrees for unit formation such as one of 14 July 1941 for the creation of a single mountain rifle division in the North Caucasus Military District 'for the screening of the border along the Black Sea coast'.[111] The ages of those being called up predictably both decreased at the lower end and increased at the upper such that during 1941 – and particularly from areas at the frontline that were threatened by enemy activity – men of up to 45 years old were already being called up along with young men born in 1922 and 1923. Hence for example a GKO decree of 20 August 1941 authorized the NKO to mobilise men of this age range from Zaporozhskaia region of the Odessa Military District, with men of up to forty being directed towards 'march' battalions as immediate and supposedly trained replacements for frontline units, and those born in 1922 and 1923 and those from 40–45 years old being sent to reserve units.[112] Older conscripts would often be used to replace younger personnel in the rear before women would then replace many of these men the following year as they were shunted off to field units. In his memoirs General Ivan Tiulenev describes being sent by Stalin to the Urals in October 1941 in order to supervise the formation of fourteen rifle and six cavalry divisions that were to be 'fully combat capable' within two months by GKO mandate. In total he recalls how he was expected to supervise the formation of not only these fourteen rifle and six cavalry divisions, but also ten rifle brigades and twenty-one ski regiments. Roughly a third of these units were to be organised and equipped for 1 November, the remainder for 20 November. They were then supposed to be trained for 'contemporary combat' taking in to account war experience to date, and with particular attention being given to combat with enemy tanks. These divisions were, still during November, subsequently transferred to the rear areas of the Moscow region where they were to train and prepare defences, assisted by 2nd Sapper Army that was one of six such armies supposedly fielding a total of 300,000 personnel formed from 13 October 1941 for construction work.[113] At the end of December Tiulenev reported to Stalin that the rear defence line had been prepared, and the reserve units had 'matured and raised their combat preparation and could now successfully carry out combat assignments'. In January 1942 these units would be sent to participate in the now snowballing Soviet counteroffensive near Moscow, Kalinin and Tikhvin.[114]

The resources described earlier – both human and material, domestic and foreign in origin – would put the Red Army in an advantageous material position for the larger-scale counteroffensive operations about to be launched near Moscow during the weekend of 5–7 December – a weekend in many ways that retrospectively would prove to be pivotal for the course of the war. However, it is not unreasonable to argue that in terms of the likelihood of German victory, the worst had actually passed before that weekend. It is difficult to imagine how the Wehrmacht could have achieved more during the summer and autumn of 1941 in order to defeat the Soviet Union. Although debate still rages over whether taking Moscow in the late summer as promoted by those such as Halder would have brought about Soviet collapse, many factors including the precedent for losing Moscow and winning the war as had been the case in 1812 would have made it less than a foregone conclusion had German forces actually done so. The German plan for taking the war as far as the Ural Mountains and then stopping – launching periodic forays further east to keep whatever remained to the east down – was in the light of evidence from the summer of 1941 sheer fantasy. The German leadership showed a complete and utter disregard for the resolve of the Soviet regime and the ability of it to get the peoples of the Soviet Union to fight for it – even if the stick was required to get them to do so – and where it was rapidly becoming apparent that what the Nazi regime might offer would probably be far worse. The Nazi leadership also chose to underestimate the sheer mobilisation potential of the Soviet regime – based once again on ideological prejudice rather than rational analysis. To use a sporting analogy of a duel between Germany and the Soviet Union as popularised by David Glantz in *When Titans Clashed*, in many ways Germany was the lithe and fit Aryan of the German propaganda movies who in his arrogance had been far less committed to broader fitness training as opposed to swordplay than his somewhat stockier but equally complacent Slavic opponent who had for far too long heard that he was unbeatable. Unless overwhelmed quickly with a flurry of the blade by his German opponent, the Soviet swordsman could all too easily wake up from his stupor and even if less nimble nonetheless parry his opponent for long enough to exhaust him and then seize the initiative. By December 1941 the Soviet Union was ready to seize the initiative and did so – even if this first opportunity to gain the upper hand was to be squandered in the snows of the winter of 1941–2.

13   Lost Opportunity

For the Red Army the psychological significance of the successful defence of Moscow was undoubtedly considerable. As one respondent to the Harvard Project on the Soviet Social System who served in the Red Army during the period concerned suggested, with Moscow held 'The soldiers in the Red Army realized that the Germans could be stopped'.[1] Our respondent – a commander in the Red Army prior to the war – went on to note how success in defending Moscow undoubtedly 'revived morale', that as another former Red Army participant in the HPSSS and General Meretskov both noted had predictably declined as the Red Army was pushed back towards Moscow and deeper into the Soviet Union. Meretskov was in a good position to judge the change in mood – he had been arrested in July apparently as a result of association with the doomed commander of the Western Front, Pavlov, only to be released in September.[2] Stalin had done much to give the Soviet Union and the Red Army the material resilience to still be in the war at this point, as he had done much to squander many of the resources that had been amassed prior to the war. More recently Stalin had played a part in rallying the troops – his decision to stay in Moscow rather than evacuate, and hold the annual parade in celebration of the October Revolution despite the approach of German forces, was certainly a propaganda victory – with Soviet units literally heading to the front line after having paraded through Red Square. The 40 KV-series, 49 T-34 and 69 T-60 tanks to participate in the parade as of 4 November represented a significant proportion of Soviet armoured strength before Moscow.[3] Now, operations near Moscow such as those in the Naro-Fominsk region described in the previous chapter, that had started as defensive, ran almost without pause into a local counteroffensive that had been planned in earnest only days before. The counteroffensive was launched on the 5–6 December 1941, and soon escalated into offensive operations across a broad front. Combined with offensive operations taking place near Leningrad to relieve that beleaguered city, and operations in the far south near Rostov, the Red Army was soon on the offensive across almost all of the German

Eastern Front. Stalin would certainly play a central role in the spreading of the Red Army's resources too thinly, underestimating the enemy, and continuing with offensive operations long after they might have been called off. With the value of hindsight – and of course putting all responsibility on Stalin – in his unexpurgated memoirs Zhukov not unreasonably suggested that:

> ...events showed the folly of the decision by the Supreme Commander to go over in January to the offensive on all fronts. ....
>
> Had the ten armies of the reserve of the Headquarters of the Supreme High Command not been scattered across all the fronts, and had been committed to the tasks of the fronts of the Western Direction, then the central grouping of Hitlerlite forces would have been defeated, which would without doubt have influenced the further progress of the war.[4]

Although A.M. Vasilevskii notes that the idea for a significant counteroffensive near Moscow first emerged at the Headquarters of the Supreme High Command early November 'after the first enemy attempt to break through to the capital had been broken', renewed offensive operations by the Wehrmacht in mid-November 'required the reserves that we had to hand'.[5] Some of the cavalry discussed later was indeed thrown into counterattacks at this point. According to Zhukov's memoirs the formulation of concrete plans for a major counteroffensive – and not just attacks geared to spoiling German offensive operations and in particular dealing with breakthroughs towards Moscow – began at the end of November 1941. Zhukov – commanding the Western Front - requested forces from reserves for a counteroffensive in a telephone conversation with Stalin on 29 November. With the General Staff in apparent agreement by his rather self-serving account that fails to give the Stavka due credit for its role, Zhukov was allocated 1st Shock Army and 10th Army as requested – along with all formations of 20th Army.[6] The so called shock army – where 1st Shock Army was indeed the first to be named as such – was as David Glantz notes formed to spearhead the Red Army's winter counteroffensive, and was indeed followed by four more by late 1942. In late 1941 and through 1942 the designation was more than just a title – shock armies were better provided for with tanks and artillery in particular, although the extent to which this was the case declined during the mid-war period.[7] By the standards of late 1941 1st Shock Army was indeed relatively well provided with resources for its breakthrough role – as of 29 November it consisted of seven rifle brigades with two more on the way, along with twelve ski battalions, an army artillery regiment, a tank battalion, a company of KV tanks along with two *divizions* of Katiusha rocket mortars.[8]

That day – 29 November 1941 – the Western Front's plan for the counteroffensive was approved in principle, with more detail provided the next day. The plan called for 1st Shock, 20th and 16th Armies to go over to the counteroffensive on 3–4 December and 30th Army on 5–6 December, with dates for the start of their offensive operations based on the predicted times for formations to detrain, unload and concentrate their forces. Thrusts towards Klin and Solnechnogorsk to the north-west of Moscow, and Uzlovaia and Bogoroditsk to the south with the aim of destroying enemy forces on the flanks were to be accompanied by 'offensive operations with limited goals' by the remainder of the front in order to pin down German forces. Neighbouring fronts would also have to support the Western Front with limited offensive operations.[9] Although Zhukov was not provided with the extra 200 tanks he apparently asked for in order to 'develop the counteroffensive quickly' – 'we don't have the tanks at the moment, we can't give them to you' being Stalin's response – Zhukov was given additional air support.[10] Strengthened with reserves of the Supreme High Command, and with the support of less well reinforced neighbours, the counteroffensive, rather than the counterattacks that had taken place to date, began only slightly later than planned on the 5 and 6 December 1941.

Although Zhukov was not immediately provided with the extra 200 tanks he requested from Stalin for the start of his counteroffensive – and indeed didn't receive that number as reinforcements during December – nonetheless Zhukov had little to complain about compared to other fronts or his opponent. Despite the fact that much Soviet production was still dislocated due to the evacuation of plant to the east the Red Army was still favourably provided for with armour compared to the Wehrmacht at the beginning of the counteroffensive and indeed after its first weeks. As noted in the previous chapter, the Soviet tank park stood at in the region of 7,700 vehicles at the beginning of January 1942, although this figure does include significant numbers of older tanks in the Far East. Included in the 7,700 were approximately 600 'heavy', 800 'medium' and 6,300 'light' tanks, and Zhukov's Western Front had on 1 December at least 607 tanks with frontline units out of a total of 618 – of which at least 205 were as previously noted KV and T-34. During December it would receive three more independent tank battalions – 123rd, 133rd and 140th. The 133rd Independent Tank Battalion was for example equipped with ten KV, one T-34 and twenty T-60s, and was dispatched to 1st Shock Army on 28 November 1941.[11] Serviceability for these at this point is unclear – although it is worth noting that many Soviet vehicles were new production or recently received from Britain, whereas a great proportion of German vehicles had seen significant service by this point. Nonetheless even with a high proportion of recently produced or delivered tanks, by 19 February 1942 the Western Front reported that for nine tank brigades that had started with a combined strength of 709 tanks only 153 remained operational on 15 February 1942, with a further 264 needing repair either with units or repair bases – a total of 417, and with 322 reported as requiring recovery from the battlefield, of which some would presumably be repairable.[12]

When considering the fresh resources available to each side during this period, it is worth noting that the additional strength of 133rd Independent Tank Battalion for the Soviet Western Front in early December with its new tanks exceeded total German replacements for the dry month of December, when only 15 Panzer II and one assault gun were apparently provided to Wehrmacht divisions in the East. Total German replacement tanks and self-propelled guns added to divisional strength on the Eastern Front during 1941 and just into 1942 would be only 693 by the end of January 1942 – where 2nd and 5th Panzer Divisions had arrived in October with a further strength of in the region of 450 tanks. Total German armoured strength for the Eastern Front as a whole, excluding the few tanks fielded by Germany's allies and the above French vehicles, was still 1,803 tanks and self-propelled guns at the beginning of January 1942, down from 2,177 at the beginning of the previous month, although many were reported as being out of service.[13] Opposite the Soviet Western Front at the start of the Soviet counteroffensive German forces certainly had few operable tanks, where for example at the end of November 1st Panzer Regiment, 1st Panzer Division reported only thirty-seven operational tanks, predominately Panzer III. The 7th Panzer Regiment, 10th Panzer Division also reported a similar number of operational tanks – forty on 1 December – actually increasing to forty-two by 11 December. On 22 December 1941 the 16 Panzer divisions of Army Groups North and Centre reported a total of 254 Panzer II, 286 Panzer 38(t), 434 Panzer III and 211 Panzer IV on strength – 1185 tanks, of which 66, 84, 180 and 75 – respectively were operational – a total of 405, the remainder repairable.[14] A crude comparison between these figures and those for nine brigades of the Soviet Western Front on 15 February 1942 gives in both cases just over a third of strength as operational.

Significant as German issues with the recovery and repair of tanks were – and particularly with the supply of replacement engines – Soviet battlefield recovery and repair capabilities were as yet even more inadequate. Only in October 1941 did the Western Front for example start to receive Mobile Repair Bases, the creation of which had belatedly been ordered by the GKO despite the obvious pre-war need for such resources. As former General-Major of Engineers A. Tarasenko noted in a 1982 article on the subject, the Western Front had lost considerable repair assets in the Viaz'ma pocket, leaving it apparently with only three Independent Repair-Restoration Battalions (77th, 102nd and 132nd ORVB) as repair resources beyond repair by combat units themselves, before it received recently formed Mobile Repair Bases – more of which would be ordered in early 1942 as noted in the next chapter.[15] Many Soviet tanks were now either new Soviet production or new production provided by Soviet allies – easing at least some maintenance issues. The importance now being placed on tank repair is highlighted in a NKO order of 25 February 1942, where in order to accelerate the repair of tanks, personnel of repair units were offered bonuses for the 'rapid and high quality ... repair of tanks within timeframes established by command'.[16] Nonetheless, despite issues with repair capabilities, Soviet forces could still, despite their horrendous losses during 1941 and large numbers of tanks out of service at any given time, field at least twice, possibly three times the number of tanks as the Wehrmacht and her allies on the Eastern Front, even if they tended not to be concentrated in the same manner as the available German tanks and were particularly during this period handed out in battalion and brigade-sized parcels in support of infantry units and formations.

As regards manpower, Soviet superiority was at least in crude numerical terms also substantial – and unlike the situation for armour acknowledged even in Soviet era sources. With the Soviet Union recovering from the horrendous losses that included the mass encirclement on the borders, at Kiev and in the aftermath of the start of German Operation 'Typhoon' the balance in terms of manpower in the respective field armies was shifting even more in Soviet favour. Where average monthly list strength for the Soviet field forces is given by Krivosheev and his colleagues as 2,818,500 for the final quarter of 1941, during the first quarter of 1942 that had increased to 4,186,000 and would increase again to 5,060,300 during the second quarter of 1942 – where the Red Army during the first months of the war had an average field strength of approximately 3,335,400.[17] At the end of 1941 and into 1942 the German army in the East was now overall 3,200,000 men strong according to Halder – an average strength that had increased from 2,500,000 at the start of the campaign.[18] Germany's allies, and particularly Rumania added meaningful strength to this force, but hardly enough to alter the fact that the Soviet Union maintained a crude numerical superiority. Soviet manpower, as tanks, was now being managed in smaller units – not only had the rifle divisions a lower list strength than at the beginning of the war, but new rifle forces were also being raised in brigade-sized units.[19]

Many Soviet units thrown into the fighting near Moscow were not only hurriedly trained, and often far from suitably clothed, but also not necessarily well-equipped. Even Soviet tanks – superior as many of them were in many respects to their German counterparts could only deal with snow that was so deep. Hence although the KV series tank could apparently deal with snow of around 60–70 cm deep – and the T-34 around 70 cm – the ST-2 tractor that might tow artillery to support them could cope with only 15–20 cm. Resupply by truck would often be by the GAZ-AA, which could cope with only 10–15 cm of snow without chains, perhaps 20 cm with them.[20] The war with Finland during the winter of 1939–40 had at least prompted the Red Army to pay more attention to fighting in winter conditions. The State Defence Committee had, for example, issued a decree on the supply of the Red Army with warm clothing for the winter of 1941–2 in mid-July 1941. The July GKO decree had for example called for the concentration of more than six million pairs of baggy trousers [sharovar] by 1 September.[21] Soon however it was apparent that there would nonetheless be shortages of winter clothing. Although a request from the Western Front for 340,000 sets of winter clothing was met in full, a further request for 558,000 sets on 29 October was only partially fulfilled – 410,000 sets were supposed to be provided but the Western Front ended up receiving barely more items than it had requested sets. A shortage of field kitchens was also inhibiting the ability of the front to provide hot food to the troops.[22] Of the aforementioned trousers, many in storage had by this point been lost or damaged, with the transfer of stocks of clothing threatened by the enemy in early October adding to the chaos in the Soviet rear.[23] On 15 January 1942 production of baggy trousers by industry was more than two million short of orders issued by NKO, and the manufacture of warm clothing by civilians at home provided with the necessary materials, and donations from the populace still did not mean that all Soviet units went it to battle suitably dressed for the weather – even Guards units and formations.[24] In the case of 1st Guards Rifle Corps in early 1942, on 26 January 1942 chief of the General Staff B.M. Shaposhnikov had noted after visiting the formation that '1st Guards Rifle Corps is in a material-technical sense not suitably provided for in order to carry out combat missions' – including according to Soviet historian V. Zhelanov poor provision of warm clothing and the ubiquitous felt boots. Shaposhnikov requested that its commitment to battle be delayed, but on 29 January it was nonetheless thrown into battle without all of its component units.[25]

As regards the provision of weapons, future Marshal Golikov notes in his memoirs how during this period 10th Army to the south of Moscow was well below list strength in terms of provision of artillery, anti-aircraft guns, machine guns and small arms – with Soviet tanks concentrated elsewhere. Cavalry would at least provide some mobility, although in the case of 10th Army, 57th and 75th Cavalry Divisions arrived at the front without weapons and mounts. Nonetheless, 10th Army would be thrown into the counteroffensive on 6 December over a wide front.[26] Such forces would be widely dispersed and soon squandered in repeated attacks that failed to achieve the sort of results either hoped for and indeed that might have been possible had Stalin and the Stavka taken a different approach to the counteroffensive of the winter of 1941–2. Future General-Colonel Khlebnikov was certainly damning in his memoirs on the manner in which the Red Army would all too frequently conduct offensive operations during the period of the Moscow counteroffensive, noting how:

> Theoretically, in principle, everyone agreed that what would provide for the success of the offensive was decisive superiority over the enemy on the decisive sector of the front. However, in practice… this axiom of military theory was certainly not adhered to in all instances. It hence often happened, that a well thought out deep thrust turned into a series of frontal attacks which only 'expelled' the enemy, rather than resulting in his encirclement and destruction.[27]

General Golikov notes in his memoirs in what is a damning indictment of the readiness of 10th Army at least for the offensive, how meeting far more fierce German resistance than seems to have been expected 10th Army functioned poorly from top to bottom. Part of the problem here was the fact that 10th Army had only a 'superficial knowledge of the enemy' – with Golikov suggesting that 'of all the army and front level operations that I conducted during the Great Patriotic War we were most poorly informed of the enemy in this instance'.[28] Not only were head-quarters staff at all levels, including army level 'poorly selected and of low competence', but:

> The poor tactical capabilities of forces led to many mistakes in combat: to frontal assaults, sluggish action, inadequate provision of fire-support when advancing, to inadequacies in co-operation and also to unnecessary losses. The Army operated without a fully prepared rear, without regular deliveries of munitions, fuel and provisions. Divisional and army-level horse-drawn transports fell behind.[29]

The lack of information about the enemy about which Golikov complained in his memoirs certainly continued to be a significant problem for the Red Army beyond the Moscow counteroffensive. However, by the end of 1941 there were at least signs that reconnaissance was being taken more seriously than it had been both prior to and during the first months of the war. Given the absence of radios that might be provided to partisans and agents in the enemy rear utilisation of the civilian population and the few partisan detachments on enemy territory for information would prove difficult, and would be far more meaningful sources of information later in the war when the partisan movement was stronger and radios more plentiful. Front commands were, as noted in a directive of 14 November 1941, to receive air regiments equipped with U-2 and R-5 biplanes for reconnaissance and liaison work with partisans and the civilian population on occupied territory, where these aircraft with their short take-off and landings might feasibly land in the enemy rear.[30] Given the vast expanses of the Eastern Front the scope for aerial reconnaissance was still significant for the VVS despite the fact that the Luftwaffe had the upper hand in the air. In addition to aerial reconnaissance assets, the Red Army had of course on paper significant reconnaissance forces as part of its field units, even if the idea that they might actually engage in reconnaissance was relatively new. Near Tikhvin to the east of Leningrad, where German troops sought to link up with the Finns to their north and widen the encirclement the reconnaissance company of 44th Rifle Division commanded by N.A. Moiseenko seems to have engaged in meaningful reconnaissance in late November 1941, where they at least 'seized "tongues"' and 'gathered information on the enemy defences'.[31] Reconnaissance could also take the form of a 'reconnaissance in force' or 'reconnaissance by battle' – at a potentially much higher cost that does not seem to have dissuaded Soviet commanders from regularly employing it to little effect during this period of the war. One such 'reconnaissance' of enemy positions by a rifle platoon of 225th Rifle Division in January 1942, according to assistant chief of staff for 1100th Regiment of 327th Rifle Division P.Ia. Egorov, saw 'in the dead of night soldiers in white camouflage smocks approach enemy fortifications unnoticed', before they then 'burst into the enemy trenches' and pushed their way deeper into the enemy defences by force. Unfortunately fire from three hidden bunkers apparently took the platoon by surprise, and having already used up their grenades three of their number are noted as having sacrificed themselves to allow for the escape of others.[32] Such exploits may have been heroic, but their value often seems questionable. German NCO Helmut Pabst, with the artillery of Army Group Centre recalled Soviet reconnaissance of their battalion's positions at the beginning of January 1942 by three 'reconnaissance groups', the last of which was 20-strong, and one of which made it to the wire in front of their positions. The next morning he saw numerous small mounds in no-man's land – the bodies of many of these 'scouts'.[33] In late June 1942 the Southern Front was chided by the General Staff for instances where one battalion had lost 180 men, and another 311 without having captured a single prisoner – the problem apparently being the location of enemy firepoints in advance and their suppression.[34] Moiseenko's company mentioned earlier that spent at least some time on covert reconnaissance activities also seems to have been used as a raiding force against an enemy garrison, an airfield and a monastery used as a strongpoint during the fighting near and in Tikhvin, where the collection of information seems at times to have been tertiary to the destruction of enemy assets.[35] Such a use of better troops might have been economical in lives for the destruction caused, but no doubt meant that reconnaissance assets were not available for reconnaissance – including during an offensive – because they were too busy fighting. That Meretskov identifies the need for reconnaissance during offensive operations as a lesson of the fighting around Tikhvin suggests that such reconnaissance was certainly not the norm at the time.[36]

At the start of the Soviet winter offensive of 1941–2 offensive operations near Moscow were, despite their rather straightforward head-on approach and underestimation of the German ability to resist, nonetheless initially successful in pushing overextended German forces back and destroying significant German strength, even if encirclement of significant German strength was unusual, as in the case of German XXXIV Corps near Elets.[37] On 8 December 1941 in Führer Directive Number 39 Hitler had already ordered that the Wehrmacht abandon major

Soviet SMG-armed troops head out on a reconnaissance mission in the Leningrad region in early 1942. Soviet battlefield reconnaissance was all too often inadequate, but at least the Red Army was typically better provided for with winter clothing at this point than its opponent, even with considerable shortages in the Red Army. (RIA Novosti #572)

offensive operations for the winter and indeed make some adjustments to the front line in the interests of 'easy quartering and defence and simplification of supply problems'. His order of 16 December prohibiting a general withdrawal to pre-prepared positions to the west in the face of Soviet breakthroughs and a now exacerbated poor supply situation was certainly in tone a step back from the directive of 8 December that did not however provide details of what positions would be held, instead offering vague guidelines such as the need to 'hold areas which are of operational or economic importance to the enemy'.[38] Retreat would no doubt have led to significant German losses of material in particular given the impact of deep snow on German mobility, although Hitler was nonetheless forced to his dismay by developing Soviet offensive operations to order a withdrawal akin to that proposed by von Brauchitsch in December in the middle of January. Had the Red Army continued to throw fresh resources primarily at the Western Front, then there would have been a considerably increased likelihood of the Red Army being able to isolate and destroy significant German forces regardless of where they stood and fought. No doubt aware of the precedent of 1812, when the retreat of the *Grande Armée* from Moscow had resulted in its virtual destruction, Stalin had sought to turn a regional counteroffensive into something much wider – in fact encompassing all fronts – with the ambitiousness of objectives increasing during a period in which Stalin was apparently rebounding from the doom and gloom of previous months. According to Zhukov, only he resisted the widening of offensive operations to a general offensive as Stalin proposed in an evening meeting on 5 January 1942 – with Chief of the General Staff Shaposhnikov bending readily to Stalin's will. Zhukov's raising of doubts perhaps would have carried more weight had it not been that he was proposing reinforcing forces under his command.[39] The Red Army was soon overstretching itself even more with ambitious offensive operations all the way from Lake Ladoga near Leningrad down to Kerch' on the Crimean Peninsula – operations that often had operational objectives that were not only beyond available frontline strengths, but beyond the capabilities of the rear-area services to sustain them. Even before the January counteroffensive across the whole front the resupply of frontline forces was far from adequate. Near Tikhvin Meretskov noted how 4th Army had superiority in artillery over German forces but didn't have the munitions to match the numbers of guns and mortars available. If indeed accurate, then the average of seven rounds per day per 120 mm mortar or 122 mm howitzer, or fourteen for the 82 mm mortars, was hardly generous for forces on the offensive or defensive.[40] More limited objectives during the counteroffensive of the winter of 1941–2 might certainly have allowed

Soviet forces to achieve more with the advantages they had – from cavalry formations and ski troops to heavy KV and medium T-34 tanks – that afforded considerable tactical mobility to frontline forces that were frequently able to break through German lines.

Soviet cavalry – accepting Soviet willingness to regularly take heavier losses than most armies – certainly proved to have some value on the Eastern Front where the vast expanses often prevented the maintenance of an impermeable front line and breakthroughs could open up considerable space for maneuver. Despite a reduction in the number of cavalry divisions and formations prior to the war, and as in many armies their conversions to mechanized formations, the Red Army had started the war with a total of 13 cavalry divisions – six of which were part of three cavalry corps. At this point a cavalry division had a list strength 9,420 men – thirty-four light tanks, eighteen armoured cars, thirty-two field and sixteen anti-tank guns, twenty-two anti-aircraft guns and sixty-four mortars. The reality for the cavalry divisions, as many others, that their strength was well below list strength – on average more like 6,000 men according to Zhukov. The corps structure added a little more firepower at corps level, with a corps having in theory a total of 128 light tanks, 44 armoured cars, 64 field- and 32 anti-tank guns, 40 anti-aircraft guns and 128 mortars. For both cavalry and the mobility of these other assets a cavalry corps was supposed to be provided with in the region of 16,000 horses.[41] Deployed largely in the border regions, these forces were hurled into the counterattack along with the mechanized corps.[42]

In the fluid war of manoeuvre of the early phases of the German invasion, cavalry units clearly had inadequate firepower to engage in modern mechanised warfare where the enemy was able to bring the firepower of a non-cavalry division to bear. If caught mounted cavalry were vulnerable from both the air and on the ground – and in principle horses constituted a mode of transport, and were no longer part of a weapons system. That the Civil War traditions that glorified the latter were not dead would unfortunately be illustrated on more than one occasion described later. Cavalry also suffered from the same command, control and supply issues of any large Soviet formation – perhaps worse. Cavalry participating in the Soviet counteroffensive near Rostov in late November 1941 were for example typically poorly provided with communications resources – with four out of five cavalry divisions only being provided with four 5-AK sets for use up to divisional level and four RB/6-PK sets for use within regiments as of 25 November 1941.[43] This did not mean however that cavalry was not seen to have a meaningful place in the Red Army order of battle – frontlines during the war in the east were rarely as impermeable as in the west, and once a cavalry unit had broken in the enemy rear it could operate with some success against enemy lines of communications for as long as it was neither cornered nor forced to seek to make its way back to Soviet lines as a result of supply issues. The latter would of course be less likely in the summer, when horses at least might be at least poorly fed from locally available resources. In this role, cavalry divisions would have to be large enough to deal with meaningful resistance, but small enough to be relatively nimble and reduce vulnerability to air attack for instance. In a directive on war experience for the first weeks of the war Chief of the General Staff Zhukov suggested regarding cavalry that:

Our forces have to some extent underestimated the significance of cavalry. In current circumstances at the front, where the enemy rear is extended for hundreds of kilometers in forested regions and completely unprotected against major raids from our lines, raids by Red cavalry... could play a decisive role in the task of disorganising command and control and the supply of German forces....[44]

For such a task, the Red Army would require 'a few tens [*desiatki*] of light cavalry divisions of raiding type of 3,000 men each, with light supply trains...'. It would therefore be required that the existing cavalry corps and cavalry divisions be restructured – along with new cavalry divisions of the new type also being formed for raiding purposes.[45] Thanks to the development of 50 mm and 82 mortars, these cavalry division would have relatively greater firepower than their pre-war counterparts – by 9 August each cavalry division was supposed to be provided with a total of forty-eight 50 mm mortars that would be horse-mobile – one per platoon – with each cavalry regiment having a battery of 6 82 mm mortars moved in carts with a total of eighteen for the division.[46] Additional firepower for the division included thirty-six heavy and fifty light machine guns – twelve 45 mm anti-tanks guns and twelve 76 mm guns – with the largely rifle-armed cavalry also being provided with 200 SMGs.[47]

In the raiding role, the cavalry divisions can certainly be seen at times to have been successful in causing meaningful disruption in the German rear, even if the destruction caused by such raids tends to be exaggerated in the Soviet literature. In his war diary Franz Halder notes on 3 August in the situation report for Army Group Centre how 'The enemy cavalry that was romping around in our rear seems to be at the end of its rope...; it is bottled up in so small an area that it can do no harm from now on'.[48] He was quite probably referring to the activities of 43rd, 47th and particularly 32nd Cavalry Divisions that had been engaged in the German rear since mid-July and had indeed caused significant disruption, although when cornered losses for such cavalry units were high. Even before encirclement a few days earlier 32nd Cavalry Division had apparently clashed with forward units of the German XLIII Army Corps in 'bitter fighting' that lasted a full day – also unlikely to have gone well for the cavalry division.[49]

Soviet cavalry divisions – now explicitly intended for raiding – were also however used in the role for which they had been to a considerable extent intended prior to the war, that is as mobile infantry. Soviet cavalry had undoubtedly played a meaningful role in compelling German forces to pull back from Tikhvin to the east of Leningrad in mid-December where they were able to sever German lines of communication. Final Soviet offensive operations by 4th Army that led directly to the ejection of German forces from Tikhvin started in earnest on 5 December. However, as near Moscow, counterattacks and offensive operations had been hammering away at the German penetration on the Tikhvin axis for some time – operations to cut German lines of communications to Tikhvin for example had in fact started on 13 November when an understrength 27th Cavalry Division that had been in action since September and 60th Tank Division had been launched westwards from starting positions to the south-east of the town.[50] On 19 November future Marshal P.K. Koshevoi's green and recently arrived 65th Rifle Division was launched against Tikhvin itself from the east where forces of the Northern Operational Group of the three such groups of 4th Army that included 46th Tank Brigade had already been attacking towards the town from the north since 11 November.[51] Poor co-ordination between the activities of the operational groups of 4th Army and indeed units within them is perhaps unsurprising given the poor state of Red Army communications and difficult terrain. As Meretskov notes, the three operational groups of 4th Army 'functioned independently of each other', and in 'the complicated conditions of a forested and marshy area' headquarters with little experience of operations in such terrain 'lost command' – how frequently is not made clear.[52]

Armoured support was obviously important to give the cavalry that were to cut German lines of communication to the south a little more resilience and firepower – particularly against tanks where horse-drawn field and anti-tank guns would be difficult to move in deep snow and not yet fully frozen marshland that was problematic for the cavalry as well. Soviet armour was on most sectors of the front in short supply although the fact that 4th Army had been provided with 60th Tank Division put it in a relatively privileged position for forces away from Moscow. The 60th Tank Division had arrived at Tikhvin on 29 October – transferred from 30th Mechanised Corps that until its disbanding had been in the Far East. According to Russian historian Evgenii Drig on 1 November the division had 179 tanks on strength – 13 BT-7, 139 T-26, 25 KhT flamethrowers tanks and 2 T-37 – with thirty-one armoured cars. These tanks were soon largely parcelled out in support of rifle and cavalry units, including 27th Cavalry Division.[53] After a brief artillery bombardment on 13 November 27th Cavalry Division and supporting units went over to the offensive south of Tikhvin. After having severed the key approach artery to Tikhvin from Kotelevo by the evening of 14 November after an abortive attack on German defensive positions further east at Goro-dishche, on 27 November cavalry, tanks and motor rifle troops of 60th Tank Division once again pushed further west after a brief artillery bombardment. After more bitter fighting – and having hammered away at German forces defending the road on 27 and 28 November without success – by 4 December the key Budogosh'-Tikhvin artery further west was also finally severed – by the start of the day on 5 December according to Meretskov. The capture of the main road to Budogosh' left the more minor Tikhvin-Lipnaia Gorka road as the sole meaningful access road to Tikhvin. By the time this road had been reached by Soviet cavalry with infantry of 1st Guards Rifle Brigade on 9 December the chances of preventing the withdrawal of the bulk of the German forces still defending Tikhvin had slipped away and indeed that day the town was recaptured.[54] During attempts to sever communications with Tikhvin Soviet cavalry took heavy losses not only where cavalry were thrown in against dug-in enemy troops but also where German forces typically with less cross-country mobility but fighting from the roads and with more firepower were faced by dismounted cavalry on the defence.

The sacrifices of cavalry and tanks pushing through or moving round the as yet not fully frozen marshland and negotiating deep snow to the south only made sense when combined with pressure on Tikhvin from more robust formations. Near Tikhvin itself, rifle forces had, as noted earlier, been hammering away at German defences since mid-November. There is little doubt that despite Hitler's displeasure, German withdrawal from Tikhvin itself was imminent by the time 4th Army had launched what are often seen in the Soviet literature as renewed offensive oper-ations against the Tikhvin and German positions to the west of the town along the Tikhvinka River on 5 December.[55] That day Generaloberst Halder noted how Army Group North was preparing to withdraw from the Tikhvin salient, although it had been ordered not to pull back beyond artillery range from the town itself. Tikhvin – and control over the railway line to Volkhov – was seen – as relayed by head of the OKW Field Marshal Keitel – as an important element to preventing the reinforce-ment of Soviet forces that might hamper the 'finishing off of Leningrad' [endgültige Abschließung von Leningrad]– and of course giving up the salient would prevent the linking up with the Finns to the north so important to Hitler. Army Group North could only highlight the fact that 12th Panzer Division and 18th Motorised Infantry Division were weak, and even 61st Infantry Division that had only recently been moved from occupation duties had 'suffered heavily' [*schwer gelitten*] in the fighting for Tikhvin itself.[56] In a report of 8 December XXXIX Army Corps reported that 61st Infantry, 12th Panzer and 18th Motorised Infantry Divisions had between 4–6 December alone lost 488 men as a result of enemy action, although they had lost approaching twice as many due to frost-bite. The three infantry regiments of 61st Infantry Division (151st, 162nd and 176th) had a combined combat strength of fewer than 2,000 men.[57] By 8 December Halder recorded – as Soviet forces noted – that the evacuation of Tikhvin was underway. In his war diary entry for 9 December Halder was forced to come to terms with the fact that German attempts to widen the Tikhvin corridor had failed and that a wider withdrawal would indeed be necessary.[58] Despite heavy German losses, Soviet forces had lost an opportunity to destroy whole divisions in part because Soviet forces in the region were pursuing too many and broader aims that were beyond their means – a key theme in the failure of Soviet operations during the winter of 1941–2 at all levels.

It is worth noting here that although Soviet forces had failed to destroy German forces defending Tikhvin, during the fighting in and around the town there was at least some evidence of more astute use of Soviet resources than had been typical in the summer – even if the almost stereo-typical repeated assaults against dug-in German troops ready and waiting for the Soviet infantry were still very much in evidence at Tikhvin as they were near Moscow. That M.A. Fishchev, commanding mortars of 1061st Rifle Regiment in fighting near Tikhvin noted supporting infantry making repeated attacks against German positions at Lazarevichi 'a number of times per day' is certainly a case in point.[59] At least however ambush, infiltration and camouflage can be noted as having being employed – reflecting at least an anecdotal increase, even if hardly an overwhelming one, in such practices that economised on human lives and resources where local leadership was competent and given some freedom and time – often not by design. Here one can note instances of effective tactical reconnaissance, cases of tanks used in ambush, and a concealed ice bridge made in part out of man-made ice reinforced with straw as positive devel-opments taken by a Red Army that had at least caught its breath – and when allowed a little composure – could start to think. However, troops had previously been and all too often continued to be thrown with reckless abandon into the counterattack.[60]

As near Tikhvin, Soviet cavalry would also have a significant role to play during both defensive and offensive operations near Moscow in a frontline role, although their misuse would at times lead to losses that were heavy even by Soviet standards. For example, during the defensive phase of the fighting near Moscow – which nonetheless of course saw numerous Soviet counterattacks – 17th Cavalry Division of 16th Army's engagement on 16 November 1941 with the advance of 'up to 80 enemy tanks' did not go well – 'after heavy fighting towards the end of the day only around 800 troops remained'.[61] In a different Soviet work it was noted having first been hit by a German air attack the cavalry division engaged 'around 80 tanks with motorized infantry. There began an unequal battle between cavalry and tanks'. Exaggerated claims of German armoured and infantry losses to the division's horse artillery *divizion* that had rapidly deployed are followed by the note that 'almost all of the artillerymen died at their guns'.[62]

Even worse was the fate of 44th Cavalry Division that same day, which according to German accounts launched two cavalry regiments in succession over open ground against dug-in German troops of 106th Infantry Division near Musino on the approaches to Klin. That day, after 60–70 cavalry had emerged from and disappeared back into forest about 3 km away from German troops after a number of salvoes from German artillery, four Soviet tanks of undisclosed type approached German positions without infantry support and were knocked out by German anti-tank guns.[63] Then the Soviet cavalry appeared in greater numbers:

Suddenly 3,000 metres away from us on the edge of the forest cavalry were emerging. To start with there were few , then 50, 100, 300 and in the end, from left to right from the depths of the forest to the west even greater masses of cavalry bring themselves forward. We still cannot believe that the enemy intends to attack us over this wide field, suited so it seems only to parades. . . .

. . .The mass of cavalry that had appeared from the forest in disorder quickly and unobtrusively took up combat formation. Now they are already in three ranks, echeloned side-by-side. . . .

It is an unbelievably beautiful sight as on a clear sunny winter landscape, saddle to saddle, . . ., with gleaming sabres above their heads the cavalry regiment goes over to the attack.[64]

What followed was undoubtedly horrific. Artillery rounds landing amongst the cavalry were soon recorded as being joined by high-explosive anti-tank rounds as man and beast were slaughtered in their droves. Then, almost unbelievably to the German observer, 'from the forest a second regiment went over to the attack' and the 'nightmarish performance is repeated' – 'the destruction of the second regiment takes place even more quickly than the first. Only about 30 cavalrymen led by an officer on a beautiful horse leap forward almost to the village itself, and here they perish in the fire from our machine guns'.[65] Soviet sources understandably provide little detail on the engagement, one noting only that 44th Cavalry Division sustained 'serious losses' before pulling back.[66]

Cavalry undoubtedly proved most useful as part of combined-arms formations, be they ad-hoc or as later in the war provided for with meaningful support at the formation level. Many authors note the use of Cavalry-Mechanised Groups or KMGs during Soviet defensive operations near Moscow and during the subsequent counteroffensive, where cavalry provided infantry support for or were provided with armoured and artillery elements for their support – the latter often from High Command Reserves. These early KMGs were slightly more coherent combined-arms entities than for example the cavalry provided with some armoured support below Tikhvin – and the KMGs tended from the outset to be given clear operational objectives ahead of rifle forces such as encirclement and the cutting of transport arteries. These early KMGs, as opposed to the cavalry supported by tanks below Tikhvin, superficially at least had the core components of a Panzergrenadier or Panzer division – a significant concentration of armour, infantry support and higher-level artillery support and not just that artillery organic to smaller units. Given the resources available to the Red Army they were a sound idea, even if they were particularly early on typically given far too ambitious objectives as was all too often the case for other formations as well. An example here might be the mobile group established in mid-December 1941 as part of operations by 49th and 50th Armies for the 'destruction of the Aleksin enemy group of forces and the liberation of Kaluga'. Here 112th Tank Division was to operate with 154th Rifle and 31st Cavalry Divisions, along with 447th Artillery Regiment RGK, a flamethrower company and a *divizion* of Guards rocket mortars.[67] Despite the successful liberation of Kaluga in this instance, the capacity of such conglomerations to achieve the same sort of results as a Panzergrenadier or Panzer division was however often limited by the fact that their constituent parts were far more likely to be separated from each other, and the early would be KMGs lacked the equivalent of the higher level logistical and other support, no matter how inadequate, provided to a German armoured or motorised formation. As an example of the former, as commander of 112th Tank Division Getman also noted in his memoirs citing a member of the military soviet for 49th Army, during the first day of a counterattack by forces of 49th Army that was to see cavalry general Belov's combined arms force including 2nd Cavalry Corps and 112th Tank Division strike German forces near Serpukhov on 16 November, the preceding day as operations by 49th Army had begun 'artillery got bogged down in the forest and did not manage to get into firing position on time, cavalry did not reach their start points, and having suffered losses the infantry returned to their start positions'.[68] In this instance there were good reasons to strike through a highly forested region that was deemed to be relatively lightly defended – and forest provided some protection to vulnerable cavalry where much of a cavalry force could nonetheless pick its way through. In winter, the depth of snow in forest tended to be significantly less than on open ground, actually therefore facilitating movement for infantry and cavalry. However for the horses, carts and lorries that would haul the cavalry's heavy weapons –and the tanks and artillery units – heavily forested areas without meaningful roads were far from ideal. The horrific case of 44th Cavalry Division described earlier might have been ameliorated had the cavalry been accompanied by even a portion of the limited artillery and fire-support assets technically available to them.

Although Soviet cavalry divisions would continue to serve in the Red Army for the remainder of the war, their proliferation during the second half of 1941 was a product of both continued attachment to tradition and the fact that the Red Army lacked the mobility that it would later achieve thanks to automotive transport – much of it provided under Lend-Lease. As one of the few Soviet works on cavalry notes, in the region of 500,000 cavalry were added to Soviet strength during the summer and autumn of 1941. During the Moscow counteroffensive fifteen cavalry divisions would participate. As the authors of *Sovetskaia kavaleriia* note, 'being poorly provided for with military equipment and weapons, the cavalry divisions suffered heavy losses. Consequently many of them were as a result disbanded, and those remaining at the start of 1942 incorporated into cavalry corps'.[69] Losses to cavalry divisions participating in the Soviet counteroffensive near Rostov in late November and early December 1941 highlight their vulnerability where air attacks are noted as having brought particular losses for cavalry units lacking anti-aircraft assets. From 20 November to 5 December 70th Cavalry Division lost 2,100 men and 1,246 horses killed wounded and missing; by 4 December 62nd Cavalry Division had only 680 active troops – 181st Cavalry Regiment had only 176, 183rd Cavalry Regiment 210 and 185th Cavalry Regiment 203. The 62nd Cavalry Division was on 15 December replaced in the line by rifle units.[70]

Cavalry corps – with full rather than light cavalry divisions – may have made such cavalry forces more robust in theory, but particularly in winter conditions the problem of keeping supporting arms and the logistical train in contact with the cavalry and particularly during deeper penetrations remained. Heavier snow by late December 1941 hampered the use of cavalry formations during the Moscow counteroffensive – and indeed the offensive as a whole. At this point the ski troops discussed in the previous chapter could come into their own, although would suffer from the same limitations as the cavalry formations faced, namely the inability to sustain operations from a logistical perspective and with only limited firepower. Hence, although the five ski battalions provided to Belov's cavalry group – centred on 1st Guards Cavalry Corps – increased the mobility of forces under his command at a point at which the flexibility of cavalry was suffering due to the deep snow, the addition of these battalions could not overcome the basic problem for such formations of sustaining operations after a breakthrough.

During the second half of January 1942, Belov's force consisted of five cavalry and two rifle divisions – along with the five aforementioned ski battalions – a force of in the region of 28,000 men according to Belov, although a force apparently with only eight tanks. Three of the cavalry divisions, as noted by Lieutenant-Colonel A.K. Kononenko – chief of intelligence for 1st Guards Cavalry Corps – were only light cavalry divisions (41st, 57th and 75th Cavalry Divisions), 'about half the size of our guards cavalry divisions', and without meaningful organic artillery. According to Kononenko, such divisions were 'practically non-combat-capable' and had to be paired with the guards divisions.[71] Belov suggests in his memoirs that opposing his force as it attempted to break across the Warsaw Highway into the German rear in late January was a force of similar strength of the German 4th Army, although with more armour than his own. This alone did not bode well for Belov's force, where the German divisions were infantry, motorised or Panzer divisions with greater proportional firepower even without the armour. Hammering away at German forces defending settlements achieved little. The capture of the village of Trushkovo on 18 January by 131st Cavalry Regiment and a company from 115th Ski Battalion for example was soon followed by a successful German counterattack apparently supported by tanks that left the ski company with ten men.[72] The solution, was predictably, to avoid dug-in enemy forces around the settlements and to breach enemy lines through forest, a breakthrough which occurred on 26 January and was reinforced on subsequent days as behind 115th Ski battalion, initially operating in a reconnaissance role, followed a second ski battalion and a rifle regiment. They were soon followed by the second echelon – 2nd Guards Cavalry Division and 75th Cavalry Division. Despite poor artillery support the cavalry also broke through, but 'without mortars, divisional artillery, and without even mentioning the supply carts' that certainly did not make it. The deep snow also prevented a radio truck making it through.[73] Despite penetration by additional elements of Belov's force including much of 1st Guards Cavalry Division and at least some artillery and supplies, the force in the enemy rear not only lacked much of its infantry component and some of its cavalry, but also had to leave behind much of its artillery and supply train – even if the corps headquarters made it through dragging its radio equipment on sledges.[74] As Kononenko noted, the result was that 'we conducted combat in the enemy rear area with 3–5 bombs per mortar tube, and insufficient grenades and bullets'. Hungry men and horses with inadequate supplies and munitions – harried by enemy airpower and lacking anti-aircraft – were nonetheless ordered deeper into the enemy rear and to take Viaz'ma by their superiors – Zhukov and his deputy General G.F. Zakharov. Belov's force stood at about 7,000 men, and was still about 90 km from its objective which would not be reached.[75] The Soviet General Staff study of the Moscow battle certainly noted how cavalry formations such as Belov's were vulnerable to air attack – and Belov's forces were indeed plagued by the Luftwaffe – and that if they were to 'conduct large scale actions on the enemy flanks and in the rear' then they would require 'reinforcement with a rifle division and one or two tank brigades'.[76]

Issues with the firepower and air defence capabilities of cavalry units and formations were addressed by the Stavka even before the end of the

Cavalry of General Belov's cavalry corps on the move in mid-December 1941. Despite their valuable manoeuvrability, such forces all too often struggled against both German infantry and armoured forces alike. (RIA Novosti #2548)

winter of 1941–2. On 16 March 1942 the Stavka issued a directive geared to increasing the combat effectiveness of cavalry formations and units that would see the disbanding of a number of cavalry divisions and corps in order to provide men and material for surviving cavalry formations, and the further incorporation of cavalry divisions into existing corps. Additionally, every cavalry division was to be provided with a battery of six 37mm automatic anti-aircraft guns.[77] With further reform, Soviet cavalry would still have a role to play in mid-twentieth century warfare on the Eastern Front throughout the war – and indeed German divisions would regularly use cavalry for reconnaissance functions for example, to which they were ideally suited. Nonetheless, the role of cavalry formations in breakthrough and exploitation operations by the Red Army would decline as alternative forces became available. Attaching a rifle division to a cavalry corps as suggested earlier in the Soviet General Staff study of the Moscow battle was certainly not a solution to the need for cavalry formations to have robust support, and it would be when working with the large armoured formations of the latter period of the war or with their own substantial armoured components that Soviet cavalry formations such as 1st Guards Cavalry Corps would perhaps be most effective as mobile infantry that could keep pace with the tanks in the face of continued shortages of motor vehicles – and particularly armoured vehicles. They were however also used as an exploitation force in their own right – as in the case of 1st Guards Cavalry Corps in late April 1945 when it seems to have relied on the armoured regiments that were attached to its cavalry divisions for armoured support even though before commencing offensive operations in mid-April two of the three regiments were down to only five tanks, the third with eight. On 15 April 1945 1st Guards Cavalry Corps would consist not only of 1st, 2nd and 7th Guards Cavalry Divisions, but also supporting units that relied on a combination of horses and vehicles to move their mortars, artillery and anti-tank weapons that gave it significant firepower but in many ways less than a rifle division.[78] With only limited fire support – and by their very nature as cavalry with man and horse being but flesh and blood – the cavalry were still extremely vulnerable, and would take the sort of losses that many other armies would not have tolerated, even if Stalin and the Soviet leadership were willing to in the same manner as they were with other arms. Between 15 April and 1 May 1945 as the corps pushed over the Elbe River it suffered a total of 2,332 casualties out of a starting strength of 18,412. The corps would also suffer 1,150 casualties amongst its horses from a starting strength of 12,699, losing 435 mounts killed from the cavalry divisions during the same period during which 823 personnel of the cavalry divisions had been killed or were missing.[79]

Not only man, but also beast, would suffer as they were driven forward with all too often scant regard for the cost ultimately from those safely to the rear. Certainly the Soviet Union would struggle to mobilise the requisite numbers of horses for its forces not only as cavalry mounts, but also to continue to pull artillery and move supplies forward even with the large numbers of American trucks that would be available later in the war. The 1st Guards Cavalry Corps had more than 10,000 horses in April 1945 – and a rifle division according to list strength established at the end of 1944 still required more than 1,100, down from 2,410 in December 1941 or 1,850 in April 1942.[80] At the same time Soviet agriculture was more reliant than ever on horses that were not available in the requisite numbers because of demand elsewhere.

Despite the vulnerability of cavalry, they did often offer greater mobility during the winter of 1941 than the rifle forces that otherwise predominated. Similarly appealing in providing opportunities beyond the ground forces literally bogged down in the snow were Soviet airborne forces, in which the Soviet Union had invested considerable resources both prior to and during the early phases of the war. At the beginning of the war the Red Army had three airborne corps in the western districts, and in September 1941 went as far as to aim to mobilise 50,000 volunteers from the Komsomol into the airborne forces despite manpower needs elsewhere.[81] Often used as elite infantry without having been airdropped – as they had been at Khalkhin Gol and would frequently be used during the Great Patriotic War – they were nonetheless employed in some strength in their intended air-dropped role during the winter of 1941–2 near Moscow. As David Glantz and Jonathan House note, the commitment of Soviet airborne forces to the winter counteroffensive began in early January when they were used to assist in the advance of 33rd and 43rd Armies, and indeed was supposed to assist Belov's 1st Guards Cavalry Corps in breaking through enemy defences by attacking southwards. According to Belov, little assistance was provided by the paratroops in crossing the highway as intended, and only subsequently did Belov's cavalry link up with the parachutists of 8th Airborne Brigade. Of a strength of 2,100, only 1,300 apparently rallied to the brigade commander, and given that Belov's cavalry had crossed Warsaw Highway without accompanying rifle divisions, heavy equipment and its supply train, the combined force of Belov's cavalry and the paratroopers still lacked the means to deal with significant opposition.[82] Two more brigades of 4th Airborne Corps would subsequently be dropped in the area in mid-February after an initial plan for their commitment had been aborted, but with only about 70 per cent of strength at best, after the paratroops had been dropped after initial successes 4th Airborne Corps would fight to little effect in the German rear for the next few months although German forces were unable to evict them from their marshy base area. Airborne forces were also committed elsewhere that winter to little effect, including in operations near Demiansk to be considered below where they were dropped into the pocket centred on the town that was occupied by encircled German forces.[83] They would again be used in significant strength during the Dnepr River crossing in 1943, but the Soviet Union lacked the transport aircraft for them to be used in anything like the strength they would be employed by their allies to the west during Operation 'Market-Garden'. The British and Americans went to far greater lengths to provide their airborne forces with heavy equipment that still proved clearly inadequate at Arnhem for the British when combined with resupply issues and German armour – Soviet airborne troops fought with much less. Only during the Cold War would the Soviet Union provide its airborne forces with the sort of heavy equipment that was obviously lacking during the Great Patriotic War.

Soviet forces would hammer away with inadequate local strength across most of the Eastern Front for the duration of the winter of 1941–2. It is not my intention here to list every offensive operation, but to show with examples just how overstretched the Red Army was and how poor central direction of Soviet forces was. Undoubtedly Stalin, Zhukov and others failed to come to terms with the capabilities and strength of the Red Army relative to the Wehrmacht now strategically and operationally defending in winter conditions favouring the defence. From below Leningrad and the Demiansk pocket in the north to Rzhev and southwards Red Army troops were hurled into attacks against well-entrenched German troops again and again, and took terrible losses in pursuit of wildly ambitious goals. The Stavka – and in particular Stalin – railed at the incompetence of commanders often provided with inadequate resources and pushed for renewed efforts. Regarding the central sector of the front for example, in a Stavka directive of 20 March 1942, after the Red Army had been hammering away at Army Group Centre for months, Stalin and Vasilevskii complained that 'the liquidation of the Rzhev-Gzhatsk-Viaz'ma group of enemy forces has dragged on unacceptably long'. The directive went on to complain how Belov's 1st Guards Cavalry Corps and 4th Airborne Corps were still cut off in the enemy rear and 39th Army and 11th Cavalry Corps were threatened with 'isolation' – demanding that the enemy forces in the region be 'destroyed' [*razgromit'*] and the former Soviet defensive line to the west including El'nia be reached and fortified by 20 April.[84] Needless to say, this did not happen, and heavy losses were taken by worn down troops attempting to achieve hopelessly overambitious goals. Losses were certainly horrendous – during the 'Rzhev-Viaz'ma Strategic offensive

Operation' that ultimately lasted from 8 January to 20 April 1942 of a total of 1,059,200 troops committed 272,320 were irrecoverable losses – with a further 504,569 sick and wounded and at least temporarily out of action.[85] On 30 March Zhukov railed about 'the criminally negligent attitude of commanders of all levels to the preservation of Red Army men of the infantry', where 'poorly prepared attacks' led to the losses of hundreds and thousands of Red Army troops.[86] Zhukov was however part of the problem – under pressure from Stalin for results he and other senior Red Army commanders pushed Soviet forces forward often with insufficient resources and time for preparation as if all that was needed was just a little more commitment to achieve decisive results. The 20 March directive from the Stavka mentioned earlier that was concerned with the delay in destroying German forces in the Rzhev-Viaz'ma region was aimed at Zhukov, commander of the Western Direction, and he in turn applied unreasonable pressure on his subordinates. As Lieutenant Colonel A.K. Kononenko, chief of intelligence of 1st Guards Cavalry Corps in early 1942 noted in post-war memoirs that went unpublished during the Soviet period:

Army General G.K. Zhukov continuously demanded that General P.A. Belov explain why he had not encircled the enemy and why he had not taken Viaz'ma. Georgii Konstantinovich did not wish to hear any of his arguments or any reports about the offensive against us by the large enemy force and did not want to learn about the real conditions. Was it really not clear to him that to attempt to 'encircle and destroy' the enemy Viaz'ma group,..., was fantasy?[87]

After the war Colonel V.T. Lobashevskii, the chief of the political section for 1st Guards Cavalry Corps, had apparently written that 'The 'red thread' of G.K.Zhukov's ruthlessness ran through all the front orders. He was not stopped by any sort of loss which he had not counted on. He limited General P.A. Belov's initiative in every possible way'. In one instance where Belov had moved his corps command post without authorisation from Zhukov and was subsequently chided, Belov had apparently described Zhukov as 'such a cruel and heartless man'.[88] In their recent biography of Zhukov, Lopez and Otkhmezuri are certainly damning of a Zhukov who 'led with the help of fear, like Stalin' – subordinates were simply expected to submit to his impervious will and continue with his plan or face the consequences. An appeal to higher authority, namely Stalin, might have seemed risky, but Stalin was often apt to rule in favour of Zhukov's subordinates in order to keep the latter in his place.[89]

During the winter of 1941–2, if offensive operations were to have taken place across the whole front, then the encirclement and destruction of a number of individual German divisions and corps would have been a

realistic target – the destruction of whole Army Groups was not. Nonetheless, as Soviet forces near Moscow sought the destruction of Army
Group Centre, to the north Soviet forces below Leningrad sought the
destruction of Army Group North.

On the northern sector of the Eastern Front forces that included 1st
Guards Rifle Corps, mentioned above as being poorly equipped when
thrown into offensive operations in late January 1942, were able to
encircle a German force of approximately 100,000 in a pocket centred
on the town of Demiansk in early February 1942. As the Soviet historian
Zhelanov notes, the tasks set for fronts such as the North-Western Front
in December and that were translated into orders for the front in early
January were 'unrealistic' given the resources available, where the North-
Western Front was according to broad Stavka plans in mid-December to
participate in both the destructions of Army Groups North and Centre –
as well as to at least 'pin down' German forces opposite the central
sector of the front near Demiansk whilst hopefully participating in the
undermining and even destruction of German forces in the area with
operations on its flanks.[90] When German forces of 16th Army outside
the pocket are considered, it is apparent that the approximately 180,000
men, 559 artillery pieces of more than 76 mm or greater calibre, only
75 anti-aircraft guns, 186 operable tanks and 89 operable aircraft of the
Soviet North-Western Front at the start of winter offensive operations on
7 January hardly provided overwhelming strength. Clearly many Soviet
units were understrength, where the front could on paper field eighteen
rifle divisions and ten rifle brigades, twenty-two ski-, six tank- and
seventeen engineer-sapper battalions in addition to artillery and airpower – to be joined by 1st and 2nd Guards Rifle Corps in the process
of formation – and as noted earlier for 1st Guards Rifle Corps hurriedly
thrown into offensive operations. Without any reserves, the front undertook offensive operations in often difficult forested and marshy terrain
with poor access to supplies by rail – at the same time 34th Army in the
centre was given the task by the front of encircling German forces near
Demiansk alone – with five rifle divisions, an anti-tank artillery regiment
and three sapper battalions against the five German infantry divisions
and SS troops in the Demiansk area.[91] Penetrations on the left and right
flanks of the front soon offered the possibility of encirclement of German
forces in the Demiansk salient, a notion supported by the Stavka but
where the North-Western Front would not be able to focus on this task as
the Stavka continued to sustain the idea that the broader operational-
strategic aims of the winter counteroffensive could be achieved. The
North-Western Front would have to destroy German forces near
Demiansk simultaneously with participation in the destruction of the

remaining strength of Army Group North to the north and with much of the North-Western Front's strength on its left wing transferred to the Kalinin Front for its principal operations against Army Group Centre – but where it was to assist in the destruction of the German forces in the Demiansk region.[92] With additional strength in the form of 1st and 2nd Guards Rifle Corps in late January the North-Western Front was able to finally complete its portion of what was supposed to be an inner encirclement, and would be further reinforced with 1st Shock Army in February. Operations to destroy German forces near Demiansk had nonetheless made slow process where there was a lack of unitary command and where the Kalinin Front was focused on its primary mission further south.[93] For II German Army Corps in and around Demiansk 'the last truck from the rear area reached II Army Corps at 7:00p.m', with the encirclement complete later that evening. Encirclement and the destruction of a well entrenched force were two different things where the German High Command was willing to throw significant resources into holding these positions and resupply them by air, where German forces in the area had been receiving at least some supplies by air for a week before the encirclement was finally compete.[94] On 25 February the Headquarters of the Supreme High Commander or Stavka noted slow progress in the reduction of the pocket given the lack of unitary command for forces involved – and gave the head of the North-Western Front temporary command over significant forces of the Kalinin Front in order to achieve this end. With permission granted to use one of the arriving 'Siberian divisions' to strengthen the encirclement, the destruction of the pocket was to take no more than 4–5 days.[95] On 9 March the pocket was still in existence, a Stavka directive that day suggesting that was the case because 'forces of the [North-Western] Front are incapable of fighting for population centres', with their commanders relying solely on infantry without utilising the artillery and air assets at their disposal. New resources were to be provided for the liquidation of the pocket, including 2nd and 204th Airborne Brigades and a significant quantity of artillery including rocket mortars.[96] Belatedly, on 15 March the Stavka ordered the creation of 'Number 2 Shock Aviation Group of the Headquarters of the Supreme High Commander' in order to facilitate the destruction of enemy forces near Staraia Russa and of the Demiansk Pocket. The force was to be concentrated by the end of the following day, and to consist of 568th and 299th Assault Air Regiments, three fighter regiments and 20 DB-3 bombers. The commander of the formation was also able to call on assets of the North-Western Front as required.[97] A similar Shock Air Group would be formed to assist 1st Guards Cavalry Corps and other formations near Moscow.[98] Soviet airpower in the region was not only used to attack German forces – when in March Soviet ski troops near Staraia Russa were themselves encircled aircraft of the Soviet long-range aviation were required to resupply them and assist them in linking back up with Soviet forces, dropping 750 tonnes of supplies in late March.[99] That the German II Army Corps – a force of approximately 100,000 men – was able to hold out at Demiansk from initial encirclement on 8 February to relief on 22 April 1942 was undoubtedly a significant achievement both for the ground forces and aerial resupply that nonetheless left German forces in the pocket poorly supplied.[100] The success of the Demiansk airlift undoubtedly contributed to the decision to resupply the German 6th Army and other forces encircled at Stalingrad in November 1942, to which we will return in the next chapter. In late 1942 the Luftwaffe resupply effort at Stalingrad would not only be on a far greater scale, but be significantly hampered by the Soviet VVS – far moreso than at Demiansk where as Hayward suggests VVS strength was, relatively at least, 'negligible'.[101] As the Soviet historian V. Zhelanov notes in his article on the Demiansk encirclement, 'the North-Western Front did not have the necessary fighter strength for the establishment of an air block-ade of the encircled forces. On the primary route for flights by enemy transport aircraft there was almost no anti-aircraft artillery, and the fight with aircraft was conducted solely with infantry weapons to only very limited effect'.[102] Not only on the ground but in the air did the Stavka spread resources too thinly for significant results anywhere, with add-itional air resources for the Demiansk encirclement being committed far too late.

Even where offensive operations were launched with adequate initial supplies these supplies were soon depleted as frontline units, and not just those such as Belov's cavalry operating behind enemy lines, rapidly lost combat effectiveness. Soviet problems with supplies getting through started with the railways. As I.M. Golushko noted in his study on *The Headquarters of the Rear of the Red Army during the War Years, 1941–1945* citing a report by Divisional Commissar V.A. Baiukov of the Main Board for the Rear, in January 1942 of 5,422 railway truckloads of munitions planned for delivery to all fronts, only 4,281 were actually loaded – 79 per cent. Of these fronts and independent armies received only 1,866 truck-loads in January – only 35 per cent of the planned deliveries. The situation was similarly bad for foodstuffs, where of 15,201 planned truckloads only 4,216 or 27.7 per cent were actually unloaded. The transfer of men and equipment was similarly well behind plans.[103] Then of course these resources had to be transported from the rear areas of fronts and independent armies to frontline units by lorry or often using horse-drawn transport, where lorries with good cross-country mobility were in short supply and motorised and horse-drawn transport struggled to reach units that had often made inroads into enemy positions where communications were particularly poor. The Red Army 'autopark' may have increased in size from 272,600 vehicles at the beginning of the war to 318,500 on 1 January thanks largely to the draining of vehicles from the civilian economy rather than new production, but the Red Army was considerably larger by this point and provision of motor vehicles had been grossly inadequate even in June 1941.[104] Attempts to improve the supply of frontline forces included the formation of independent horse-drawn transport battalions – Stalin apparently noting the irony of resorting to the formation of such units 'in a century of machinery [*tekhnika*]'. On 24 December 1941 the first seventy-six such battalions were sent to the front.[105] Aircraft were an ideal means to transport supplies to less accessible areas, but the Soviet Union had as noted when discussing airborne forces invested relatively little in transport aircraft in the pre-war period where licensed production of the DC-3 as the Lisunov-2 had for example amounted to only fifty-one units during 1940 after production had started late the previous year, and where increasing production in 1941 was disrupted by evacuation of the factory producing them to the east.[106] In winter conditions powered sledges with aircraft engines and propellers providing thrust had potential in areas with sufficient snow, although payloads were small. By 1 January 1942, twelve air sledge battalions were reported as having been sent to the front along with an additional three by 14 January at which point another fifteen were apparently ready for deployment. Each battalion consisted of 40–50 air sledges and 90–100 personnel.[107] Such measures were, however, not enough to provide the supplies required by Soviet forces to maintain the sort of advances being demanded of them from Moscow.

In the snows of the winter of 1941–2 the Red Army could undoubtedly have achieved far more than it did had resources been used differently. Regardless of issues with command, control and supply, had available forces been better concentrated and provided with clear and typically more limited goals, then even if German forces were not to be completely routed before Moscow then far more damage could have been inflicted on them for lower cost than was in fact the case. Balancing goals and means would remain a problem for the Red Army for the remainder of the war and an often impatient Stalin would press ambitious lieutenants for rapid and dramatic results well beyond the capacity of available forces.

14   More Men, Women and Machines

Horrendous losses amongst Soviet forces during the winter of 1941–2 perhaps for the first time brought about something of a manpower problem for the Red Army – the resolution of which required amongst other measures a greater role for women. By the spring of 1942 men were also being drawn from a wider pool than they had been at the beginning of the war. In this chapter we will firstly look at the increasing role for women in the Red Army before turning our attention to the widening mobilisation of men. Regarding firstly the role of women in the Red Army, our primary concern is to consider the extent to which the influx of women contributed to the military effectiveness of the Red Army, be that through their own direct participation or their replacement of men in auxiliary roles who could then typically be fed into the meat grinder at the front.

Regardless of the enthusiasm of women to volunteer for service in the Red Army, it took until the spring of 1942 for women to be conscripted *en masse* into the Red Army itself. According to G.F. Krivosheev, out of a total of 490,235 women called up for service with the Red Army during the war, only 5,594 were called up in 1941, but these figures are clearly misleading in not including many of those who will have ended up working as civilians [*vol'nonaemnii sostav*] with the Red Army and were often slated for service with it even if not part of it prior to the war.[1] In September 1941 there were 57,905 medical personnel of both sexes in medical units and formations of the fronts, and 64,962 military and 45,469 civilian personnel in facilities of both the People's Commissariat for Defence and People's Commissariat for Health of the military districts.[2] Marwick and Cordona suggest that including both those conscripted into the Red Army and all civilians employed by it on the assumption that most were women would give a figure of 'just in excess' of one million women serving in or with the Red Army during the war, with 318,980 of the 490,235 conscripted into the army serving with the fronts. Marwick and Cordona's assumption that essentially all civilians serving in the Red Army were women is clearly inaccurate where for example many men drafted in from industry to repair tanks and other vehicles are included in this civilian count. However by the time female partisans and other women serving in military or paramilitary roles are added it is quite likely that the number of women serving with the Soviet armed forces broadly defined during the war totalled somewhere in the region of the 'more than 900,000' estimated by Krylova.[3] Certainly prior to the outbreak of the war many women were already serving with or in the Red Army in medical roles, and indeed the number and proportion of women allocated to Red Army medical services had increased significantly between 1939 and 1941. Hence, of 68,593 *fel'dsher* subject to call up to the Red Army in mobilisation plans by 1941, 59,744 were women – compared to 10,552 *fel'dsher* in 1939, of whom only 2,408 were women. There was not however the desire in the NKO to see women perform frontline medical roles. During the invasion of Finland the NKO had issued a directive on 11 January 1940 that all female doctors and *fel'dsher* be removed from the immediate prefrontal zone to units and establishments further to the rear. Of 100,301 doctors subject to call up as of 6 May 1941 only 36.8 per cent were however men. This desire to keep women away from the front line nonetheless continued into the war. With the formation of new Soviet units extra to planning for MP-41 during the first weeks of the war – and where the Red Army medical services already lacked in the region of 35 per cent of doctors and *fel'dsher* prior to the war – the medical services for a rifle division were soon cut from 45 doctors, 54 *fel'dsher* and 4 dentists to 27 doctors, 36 *fel'dsher* and a single dentist.[4] Even if early in the war it was deemed desirable to keep women away from the front line, in many situations they could be found closer than perhaps intended. The nursing sister encountered by anti-aircraft gunner Iurii Vladimirov during the Khar'kov debacle of May 1942 is a case in point – medical services following behind frontline units could be caught in encirclement or might fail to retreat quickly enough during periods of rapid enemy advance.[5]

Although some of the 5,594 women conscripted during 1941 will nonetheless have served in medical units and establishments, many also served as communications personnel and drivers for example. In a decree of 19 August 1941 10,000 young female volunteer 'radio enthusiasts' were sought for Red Army service from the Komsomol – with 14,430 women being sought as drivers in a decree of late August.[6] A significant number of these women would actually see service in 1942, when the total number of women actually called up had leapt to 235,025.[7] Certainly, as highlighted by a 2007 article by Korovin et al on women of the Kursk region in volunteer formations such as the militia divisions, many more women took up arms during the war and served in frontline roles in

1941 than Krivosheev's figure suggests.[8] Many women fought as partisans or had a role in the partisan movement, where officially about
10 per cent of participants were women as of 1 January 1944.[9]

There was a flurry of mobilisation of young women for service with the
armed forces towards the end of the winter of 1941–2 and into the spring
of 1942. On 25 March 1942 the GKO ordered the mobilisation of
100,000 young women aged 19–25 for service with the Air Defence
Forces or PVO as replacements for men in a range of roles from radio
and telephone operators to observers and the crews of searchlights and
guns.[10] According to an NKO order following on from the GKO decree
the previous day, 30,000 women were to be called up, primarily for
service as communications personnel in the Red Army. These women
were to serve at front and army levels, freeing up men who were 'to be
used in the first instance for the manning and replacement of losses
amongst signallers of rifle divisions and rifle brigades' and other frontline
units.[11] On 18 April GKO issued a further decree that required the
replacement of 40,000 men with the same number of women of 19–25
years of age for service in rear area units and establishments in roles from
driver, bookkeeper and cook to communications personnel.[12] Orders for
the employment of women and older men in headquarters and other
units of the Red Army in the rear in place of younger men were not
necessarily acted on with enthusiasm.[13] According to Krivosheev, during
the war as a whole, 177,065 women would for example see service with
the PVO – with a further 70,458 also participating in the air defence
effort as part of the local air defence network, what might be termed civil
defence network, supervised by the NKVD.[14] A total of 41,224 women
would be conscripted into frontline military medical units and establishments during the war as a whole, where the need was undoubtedly acute.
Before large numbers were used in frontline medical roles there had been
further cuts to the medical services of frontline formations, where an
army could expect according to list strengths in place by 25 February
1942 to have 42 per cent fewer doctors, 20 per cent fewer *fel'dsher* and
27 per cent fewer medical sisters than at the beginning of the war. These
cuts took place despite the emptying of medical schools to satisfy the
needs of the Red Army.[15] A total of 14,460 women would see service
with automobile units and 41,886 with communications units, with
20,889 women serving in these and similar rear-area roles in the navy
or VMF, and 40,229 with the air forces or VVS.[16] In this last case women
would serve in what were clearly combat roles in a number of units, most
famously in light bomber units that often harassed German forces at
night. The 588th Night Aviation Regiment, with U-2 aircraft, was
ordered to be formed in October 1941, somewhat earlier than the mass

mobilisation of women into the Red Army of the spring of 1942.[17] Combat roles were also undertaken by women in the ground forces, where female snipers served in increasing numbers. The Central Women's School for the Preparation of Snipers created in May 1943 on the base of existing courses for women would send 1,061 female snipers to the front line, as well as producing 407 female instructors in sniping.[18] On 3 November 1942 the GKO went as far – for a still predominately peasant country that during the social 'Great Retreat' of the 1930s had taken a *de facto* step back from the egalitarian ideals of the revolution – as creating a 6,983-strong women's volunteer rifle brigade, 1,000 of the personnel for which would be women drawn from the field army who already had frontline experience. However, the Stavka was not willing to see it subjected to the slaughter at the front line being endured by predominately male units, and the brigade was ultimately incorporated into the internal security forces of the NKVD.[19]

The Red Army undoubtedly gained significantly from the mobilisation of substantial numbers of women from 1942 onwards, both in terms of the contributions they made to its effectiveness and in allowing the

A Soviet medical sister tends to a Red Army soldier in what is probably a posed picture – taken apparently in the summer of 1941. By the spring of 1942 an increasing number of young women were performing such dangerous, although technically non-combat roles, at the frontline. (RIA Novosti #65721)

redeployment of many men. Many male Soviet commanders and troops certainly developed the highest regard for the capabilities of their female comrades. In January 1943 General Chuikov commanding 62nd Army at Stalingrad for example had high praise for the women under his command. Although he apparently sent female staff to the east bank of the Volga River during intense fighting for the city, this decision was he suggested not based on negative assessment of their 'moral qualities' but rather the 'physical' requirements of such circumstances where one assumes he had in mind the fact that his army and other headquarters were far more vulnerable in Stalingrad than they might have been in other circumstances outside the city. Chuikov certainly suggested that those women employed in frontline 'non-combat' roles often outdid men 'in terms of courage' and 'in their fortitude, heroism, honesty and loyalty'.[20]

Undoubtedly the Red Army was overall a more effective organisation due to the participation of large numbers of women. However, there were some drawbacks to the increasing mobilisation of women into in particular frontline roles where unit cohesion undoubtedly suffered in some instances thanks to competition between men over them – whether their attentions were wanted or not. There were of course genuine and positive male-female relationships that resulted in lasting relationships and marriages that resulted from meeting at the front, where of course both could survive the slaughter and interventions of others in their romance. Nina Arsent'evna Smarkalova, having been sent to the front it seems for having been less than accommodating to a male commander there met her husband. Their regimental commander was against marriages at the front, and so their 'marriage' was at that time unofficial – the regimental commander also assuming that their relationship would be fleeting and suggesting that Nina's husband would want to be rid of her if she was wounded. That he was committed – apparently exclaiming to the regimental commander when seeking permission to visit her when he had heard that she was wounded and had just had a leg amputated that he wasn't about to give up on her and was 'interested in a person, not a leg' – is from a human perspective obviously touching, and was not necessarily the norm. Nina was evacuated and her husband fought on at the front, and did not, tragically as in so many cases, survive the war. Nina and her husband had served in the same regiment, but not the same sub-unit where their 'marriage' might have caused tensions given that one might reasonably expect loyalty first to go to one's spouse as opposed to the unit.[21]

As Oleg Budnitskii notes in an article on 'Men and Women in the Red Army', there were certainly women who refused to be involved in the sexual milieu at the front in any sense – often paying some sort of price for their lack of accommodation with male 'superiors'. In his memoirs artilleryman Isaak Kobilianskii describes the sexual affairs of his unit and its female members. Medical sister Olia Martinova consistently refused sexual advances that might have been exploited to improve her safety, and was soon killed in action.[22] Translator Irina Dunaevskaia notes the achievements of saninstruktor Tania Kaznova at the front in a 1943 entry to her diary, who nonetheless went without the awards that might have followed given her refusal to accept the advances of her immediate superior.[23] Certainly, without protection, rape was, as might be expected, not unusual. Nina Fedotovna served in the women's volunteer rifle brigade of Vera Krilova, and managed to fight off a pilot when she returned alone to check for items left where her all-female company had been bathing in a river.[24] At the other end of the spectrum to those who refused consensual sexual relations there were at least some women who sought to use sex as a tool to obtain privilege or social advancement. As noted by translator Irina Dunaevskaia, there was competition between women for higher ranking male companions even if for her other factors were more important, and some women were proud of their status within units as 'Mobile Field Wives', or PPZh – usually of commanders.[25] As tanker Boris Kuz'mich Koshechkin rather flippantly put it in a recent interview, his brigade commander – with access to telephone and radio operators at brigade headquarters – would often send pregnant 'casualties' to the rear.[26] For some at least being PPZh to a senior figure within a unit offered protection from other predatory men – including from rape.

All of this sexual activity – be it consensual or otherwise or indeed even if it didn't involve sex – undoubtedly caused some tensions within units both between men and women, men and men, and women and women – that was often not positive for unit morale or cohesion. Artilleryman Isaak Kobilianskii describes one of undoubtedly many 'love triangles' – typically involving two men and a woman – that could only have a negative impact on a unit.[27] If it did not cause tension it may have also caused some distraction for both men and women that might not always have been positive either. Here the attraction of one of the central male characters to the recently arrived fel'dsher in V. Bogomolov's short story Ivan, on which Tarkovskii's 1962 Soviet movie Ivan's Childhood is based, comes to mind and is indeed portrayed in the movie. The male character and officer concerned is advised by a colleague on his relationship with the 'stately, 20-ish year old beautiful blonde with bright blue eyes…' 'not to see her during the day', so as not to lose authority.[28] These factors – along with practicality where even sanitary provision was and remains more difficult in co-ed units – may have contributed to the formation of female only units such as the volunteer rifle brigade and light bomber units.

Not only would the Red Army be able to increase frontline strength as a result of the employment of large numbers of women in the Soviet armed forces, but also by combing the navy and NKVD for personnel and even whole units that might have been better employed in the field army – as well as employing older male personnel in headquarters roles for example and other similar expedients. At the start of the war the NKVD had significant numbers of men under arms, from the border troops that are recorded by both German and Soviet observers alike as often having fought stubbornly during the first hours of Barbarossa, to infantry units of the internal security forces that often ended up fighting as frontline infantry. In total 379,782 NKVD troops were serving in various NKVD forces on 1 June 1941, with their numbers swelling rapidly during the first months of the war despite transfers to the Red Army.[29] The NKVD troops should not be seen as equivalent to the troops of the Waffen SS in the German armed forces, for not only were even their lightly equipped rifle divisions not supposed to be first echelon frontline troops but in no way were they seen as elite even at the beginning of the war. The NKVD did not for example field meaningful numbers of tanks. Nonetheless, in their role in providing security behind the front line they often ended up being close to it, either because they were carrying out security functions on recently liberated territory or ended up being engaged in combat at the front line as a result of rapid German advances or deep penetrations. Certainly as David Stahel notes, during the fighting near Kiev German forces apparently met 'fanatical resistance' for the town of Lubni that was defended in part by NKVD forces. Here it seems the units concerned were 94th Border Detachment and 6th NKVD Regiment, which together with a rifle regiment defended a line on the Sula River near Lubni.[30] During the fighting for Stalingrad the performance of 10th NKVD Rifle Division seems to have been more questionable, and during the Naro-Fominsk breakthrough by German forces in early December 1941 detailed in Chapter 12, 76th Rifle Regiment of the NKVD doesn't seem to have offered significant resistance.[31] Certainly it didn't make sense to have two organisations competing for resources as with the Waffen SS and the Wehrmacht, and Stalin was willing to chip away at Beria's nonetheless growing empire even when the chips were down apparently primarily in the interests of efficiency. Although many NKVD units such as a first incarnation of 10th NKVD Rifle Division formed from NKVD personnel in other units would be converted into Red Army units, in this case in the autumn of 1941, they were nonetheless replaced with new NKVD rifle units that were often of lower combat potential as 10th Rifle Division's subsequent incarnation.[32] As the Red Army advanced this was less of an issue than it was in 1942 when the new 10th Rifle Division of the NKVD fought at Stalingrad, where on the advance such units were far less likely to face frontline German units even if they had to deal with their remnants. NKVD forces of the OMSBON also discussed in Chapter 12 were in a different category however and might reasonably be described as 'elite'.

Much of the Soviet navy was by mid-1942 bottled up either in or near Leningrad or in Black Sea ports, and cutting the strength of the navy certainly made sense. Hence in a GKO decree of 26 July 1942 through cutting the strength of the navy to 450,000 men it was intended to transfer 100,000 men in the ranks and at the equivalent of NCO level who had already received training to the field army for frontline service. The NKVD was also to provide personnel not only from reserved positions within the ministry, but also selected inmates sentenced for domestic and property crime from within correctional labour camps and colonies, and labour exiles. In this particular instance that was supposed to lead to the transfer of 35,000, 30,000 and 15,000 men respectively to the Red Army – aged up to 35 or 40 depending on the category. Finally, all suitable males born in 1924 'regardless of place of work or position' would be called up and transferred not only to military academies and reserves units, but 100,000 to the navy and 75,000 to the NKVD to free up further existing personnel from these organisations for frontline service with the Red Army.[33] How much additional training these personnel received for their move from the Navy and NKVD to field army is unclear – General Chuikov commanding 62nd Army at Stalingrad would note at the beginning of January 1943 how his army didn't receive marine brigades, but did receive 'sailors from the Far East who had come in as reinforcements. They were good men but poorly trained. Their morale was good. You'd give one of them a submachine gun and he'd say: 'First time I've seene one of these.'[34]

Underutilised had also been the manpower of many of the nationalities of the Caucasus and Central Asia, where as previously noted not only political reliability but also language were barriers to their effective integration into the Red Army. As commander of the Trans-Caucasian Front, Ivan Tiulenev noted in his memoirs regarding the formation of national units in early 1942, although the Transcaucasus region had population reserves it was difficult to rapidly incorporate them into conventional Soviet military units given that 'many comrades from the conscriptable contingent did not speak Russian, and this factor complicated the conduct of accelerated military training'.[35] One respondent to the Harvard Project on the Soviet Social System, an Armenian, had prior to the war been deemed 'politically unreliable' and not suitable for service in the Red Army was in September 1941 sent to a unit of 53rd

Army manned by men of various nationalities aged 35–45 who had not previously been drafted for 'political or other reasons'. With little training these men were sent to the front line in December 1941 and thrown into action the following month. Apparently, in part due to the poor discipline explicable because 'the majority of the soldiers did not understand Russian and the commands were given in Russian' these men were from February 1942 incorporated into national units such as those then being formed under Ivan Tiulenev's command.[36] Although prior to November 1941 a number of national divisions and regiments had been reconstituted in Transcaucasia and Central Asia along the lines of their pre-1938 predecessors, in November 1941 the GKO ordered the formation of a number of national units to be drawn where possible from the local populations and topped up as required with Russians. A total of twenty cavalry and fifteen independent rifle brigades were to be formed, including for example five cavalry divisions and nine independent rifle brigades from The Uzbek SSR and two cavalry divisions from the Chechen-Ingush and Kabardino-Balkarian ASSRs.[37] A number of these units reached the field army in the spring of 1942, including 110th – Kalmyk, 112th – Bashkir and 115th Kabardino-Balkarian Cavalry Divisions, although a total of fifteen national cavalry divisions and ten national rifle brigades would be disbanded during 1942 and elements transferred to other national units or used as replacements for them. As German forces approached and entered the Caucasus during the summer and autumn of 1942 the need to raise national units in the region increased. However, particularly as the war progressed many national units were actually multi-national, even if the core personnel were of the nationality by which the unit was identified. Many national groups could not provide sufficient specialist personnel and commanders both because of their sizes and because the likelihood of personnel being excluded on political grounds was still considerable. Some non-national units were moved to republics in the Caucasus and Central Asia, taking on a national identity even if elements of the previous division were part of the reformed unit. Hence in 276th Georgian Rifle Division formed during the autumn of 1942 more than 38 nationalities were actually represented, and in 416th Azerbaijani Rifle Division formed during the spring of 1942 only 52.6 per cent of middle-ranking commanders were Azerbaijani, dropping to 30 per cent for senior commanders.[38] That national units continued to be formed throughout the war suggests a certain utility – concentrating a given nationality in a single unit would ameliorate the language problems that had plagued the incorporation of many nationalities into all-union formations prior to the war. Certainly the amount of translation required for a unit to run effectively would be reduced in such circumstances.

Rules regarding language use for units forming under the auspices of the Trans-Caucasian Front in early 1942 for example saw the national language of the unit as the acceptable medium for communication in military matters only to and between the rank and file and NCO-level commanders and for political and cultural matters – with commanders required to interact with non-Russian speakers requiring translators.[39] According to Russian historian V.V. Gradosel'skii, a total of twenty-six national rifle or mountain rifle divisions were formed during the Great Patriotic War, along with twenty-two cavalry divisions and eighteen rifle brigades or regiments. The rifle divisions included two Estonian, two Latvian and one Lithuanian rifle divisions that included the first of the wartime wave of national formations to be formed during from the late summer of 1941, being formed despite issues of reliability for such national formations during the initial phase of the German invasion. New units formed with a core of personnel from the Baltic Republics were formed in a completely different context than their territorial predecessors, in the sense that they were not formed on home territory and their national components were often drawn from personnel who by choice were outside the Baltic Republics.[40] All of these divisions from the Baltic Republics saw combat – many units from the North Caucasus and Central Asia did not. It is certainly unlikely to be coincidental that units culturally closer or more sympathetic – often based on religion – to the Russian cultural core of the Soviet Union were more likely to see combat than those further away. Hence, according to Gradosel'skii, where all four Armenian rifle divisions saw action, and eight out of eleven Georgian units also saw actionas formed, only three out of fifteen Uzbek units saw action and the Chechen-Ingush cavalry division did not.[41]

Also formed at this time during which the Soviet leadership was broadening the search for military manpower was a Czecholslovak Brigade and a Polish Army. The latter, as decreed by the State Defence Committee on 25 December 1941 was by this point to be 96,000 strong, consisting of six infantry divisions and other elements, a dramatic increase in planned strength from the two divisions and other elements totalling a strength of 30,000 planned on 3 November that year.[42] In accordance with the Sikorski-Maiskii pact of 30 July 1941 and the Polish-Soviet military agreement of 14 August 1941, the Polish armed forces forming on Soviet territory would 'owe allegiance to the Polish government' but would be 'operationally subordinate to the Red Army'. For air support they would be reliant on the VVS. Service in the army would be open to 'all Polish citizens who had been resident in Poland on 1 September 1939' – with a preference for those who had been serving in the Polish armed forces in 1939. Former Soviet PoWs would be available for service as a result of a Soviet amnesty on PoWs and other Polish prisoners of 12 August 1941, although many had already perished whilst in the care of the NKVD.[43] Unsurprisingly, Soviet enthusiasm for such a Polish army was limited and interference and manipulation in its formation predictably rife – with many Poles understandably hostile towards their Soviet hosts. On 2 February 1942 the commander of the Polish Army, Władysław Anders, had apparently been pressed by 'the Soviet military authorities' to send a Polish division, 5th Division, to the front, but not only did it lack the necessary equipment beyond small arms, but was supposed according to orders from the Polish government in exile in London to be sent to the front as part of the Polish Army as a whole. Relations between the Polish Army and Soviet authorities deteriorated, and with British assistance by the end of August the Polish Army, along with a significant number of civilians, had been evacuated across the Caspian Sea and on to Iraq and beyond.[44] It would be 1943 before a new Polish army would be formed in the Soviet Union that would fight alongside the Red Army and was very much under Soviet control, first committed in divisional strength in the autumn of 1943.[45] Soviet-sponsored Polish, Czechoslovak and other national formations such as Rumanians and Yugolavians fighting alongside and effectively as part of the Red Army would, understandably given increasing Soviet manpower issues, all see heavy action later in the war.[46] Their roles were not however only military – they could also serve a political purpose by making it apparent that it was not just a foreign power 'liberating' their homelands. As the war progressed national identity was increasingly fostered within such units where for example many units and formations were often provided with nationally specific uniforms – as in the case of the Poles for example.[47] Regardless of their motivations to fight – and these certainly included a range of considerations from getting out of PoW camps, sympathies with the Soviet project and fighting to liberate their homelands – such forces made a meaningful contribution to the Allied war effort on the Soviet-German front. In the case of the Rumanian forces after Rumania switched from the Axis to the Allied side in 1944, Rumanian personnel would probably have been better off fighting with Soviet equipment as part of the Red Army than with typically inferior or insufficient Rumanian equipment as part of the army of a far from trusted new Soviet ally[48]

A much more positive experience for both Soviet and non-Soviet parties than the early history of the formation of Polish forces on Soviet territory, albeit on a very much smaller scale, was the formation of the Free French 'Normandie' – ultimately 'Normandie-Niemen' – fighter squadron on 4 December 1942. The squadron was formed as part of the

Soviet VVS with Soviet equipment and rations, and initially equipped with Yak-1s.[49] Whilst of minimal military impact – despite the skill of a number of the pilots – one might argue that the well-publicised 'Normandie-Niemen' fighter squadron was a morale booster for Soviet forces in highlighting the fact that the Soviet people were not fighting Nazi Germany alone and indeed in publicising a well-functioning inter-allied relationship.

One further measure taken to economise on manpower was to utilise machine-gun artillery battalions for the covering of quiet sectors of the front as part of fortified districts – small headquarters units would command units with significant firepower and capable of making considerable noise, but with relatively few men for the coverage possible. On 18 April 1942 the GKO ordered the creation of 100 independent machine gun-artillery battalions for such purposes, each with a strength of 667 men. Headquarters units for the fortified districts would be only 93-strong.[50]

As many of the earlier new units were being equipped and trained in early 1942, despite the further heavy losses of men and materiel during the counteroffensives of the winter of 1941–2, the Red Army's material situation was improving significantly compared to the previous autumn, although there were still considerable shortages in many areas of equipment and supply. Although falling well short of unrealistic plans, during the first quarter of 1942 Soviet industry had produced 1,990 T-34s, 730 KV-1s and 902 T-60 light tanks – at total of 3,622 tanks. By the end of the second Soviet industry had produced a further 2,716 T-34, 933 KV-1, 861 T-70 and 2,245 T-60 light tanks – a total of 6,755 tanks.[51] On 1 April it was recorded that for 36 tank brigades forming during March – in addition to four sent to the front towards the end of the month – there were 160 KV-series, 200 T-34, 560 T-60, 100 British-supplied Matildas and 40 Valentines being formed into brigades of various compositions from that included many permutations that excluded the mixing of KV-series and T-34 with the British types or KV-series and T-34s together.[52] Aircraft production was also increasing, where total aircraft production had been 3,633 units during the first quarter of 1942, rising to 5,964 during the second as Soviet industry recovered from the dislocation of evacuation and factories shifted production to those types deemed necessary for the war effort.[53] The cost for these production increases was however felt in other areas of the economy, where for example production of lorries fell from a total production of 118,704 for 1941 as a whole to only 32,409 for 1942.[54] This may not have seemed such a critical issues when the Red Army was in retreat or being pushed back on railheads, but shortages of motor transport were of course far more serious on the offensive where railheads were soon deep in the rear. Here, ultimately during 1943 and 1944 US-produced trucks and other armoured fighting vehicles would fill a gap in the Soviet inventory, but in the interim in early 1942 relatively limited numbers of British and US-supplied vehicles were undoubtedly important for the Red Army along with limited new Soviet production. Supply was one area where such vehicles were crucial, but also in giving the Soviet artillery some hope of keeping up with tanks, cavalry and even infantry. For the formation of artillery regiments for the High Command Reserve in March 1942 for example the State Defence Committee allocated 1,488 GAZ-AA trucks from new production along with 760 Studebaker and International trucks from imports, as well as 250 STZ-5 artillery tractors from the Stalingrad Tractor Factory.[55] The importance of British and US-supplied equipment even in the spring of 1942 – items requested by the Soviet Union – is perhaps best illustrated by the attention the State Committee gave to the distribution of Allied equipment, and not only motor vehicles. When the Allied convoy PQ12 arrived in early March the equipment and materials being delivered were carefully dolled out by the State Defence Committee. From the 136 Hurricane fighter aircraft to be provided to the VVS of the Karelian Front, the Moscow Air Defence Forces and 22nd Reserve Air Regiment, to the 43 Valentine, 75 Matilda and 44 M-3 tanks for the formation of new tank brigades, the State Defence Committee carefully specified who was getting which of these weapons systems. Also of significance was the provision of communications equipment, such as the 300 British Number 18 Mk. III wireless sets intended for communication at battalion level, of which 200 were to go to the navy and 100 to the Main Communications Board of the Red Army.[56] Much of this equipment would find its way to the front within a very short period of time. For example, the anti-aircraft battery of which Iurii Vladimirov was a part – the training of which will be discussed later – received three British Bedford lorries to pull its anti-aircraft guns and move personnel in early April 1942, with the tank corps of which he was ultimately a part – 21st Tank Corps – being equipped in part with British-supplied tanks.[57]

As important as getting new production into service was putting broken down and damaged examples of existing equipment back into the fray. Not only did this require more repair facilities, and particularly in the field, but also the production and distribution of spare parts. Finally, in early 1942 the State Defence Committee was paying serious attention to these matters – and just as well given that as regards aircraft alone as of 25 March 1942 the Red Army air force had according to the GKO 4,938 aircraft out of service requiring repair, along with a staggering 9,752 motors. Part of the solution was the production of spares, but also improvements in the quality of repairs and the mobilisation of skilled civilian workers into Red Army repair at the front.[58] Similar concern was also being shown to the issue of tank and vehicle repair, not only with the provision of mobile repair bases but also the production of spare parts for models both in production but also for those of which there were stocks but were no longer in production.[59] Once again, this was as for aircraft a pressing issue – on 20 April 1942 it was reported by the Main Auto-Armour Board of the Red Army that there were 1,989 tanks – including 410 KV-series and 667 T-34s – that were immobile in the face of shortages of spare parts. Production of spares during the first quarter of 1942 had in most categories fallen far short of planned production.[60]

Not only was Soviet production of core weapons systems increasing, but the Soviet Union was refining existing, introducing new and increasing production of other equipment that in many instances was both effective and suited to mass production. The 1941 variant of the T-34, although with a more potent gun than its 1940 predecessor, was nonetheless improved both in terms of armoured protection, internal arrangement and crew visibility during early 1942 and became the principal variant in the field later that year, subsequently improved the following year with the addition of a commander's cupola.[61] Many weapons included in list strengths for units in 1941 but in which there were often shortages, such as the PPD-40 and subsequent PPSh-41 SMG with a 71-round disc magazine, or PTRD anti-tank rifle were increasingly widely available such that the use of such weapons in concentration was now becoming a reality. In many ways the SMG – which in October 1941 was supposed to have equipped a company in each rifle regiment – was an ideal weapon for a Red Army that could spend little time on training, and was one that relatively speaking required little maintenance. The PPSh-41 was also relatively easy to produce – something of considerable importance to Soviet industry during the early years of the war in particular where there were attempts to cut down both the man-hours to produce weapons and the materials expended in doing so.[62] The ZIS-3 divisional field gun put into mass production during 1942 was considerably easier to produce than its predecessor the USB, and was also lighter and easier to manage in the field.[63] In 1942 Il-2 ground attack aircraft produced were significantly improved over their predecessors with the addition of a second crewman and gunner to the rear, where in circumstances where Soviet fighter protection was scant at best the single-seater Il-2 had proven extremely vulnerable to German fighter aircraft from behind.[64]

The Red Army might have been able to find the men and women to man and indeed service this equipment, albeit with a little more difficulty than in 1941, but finding suitable personnel to lead these new recruits was another matter. The Red Army had started the war with insufficient junior commanders – despite expedients described earlier to increase their numbers. War with Germany and her allies would make the problem worse, requiring once again a range of measures to fill vacancies with personnel who were not necessarily fully trained for the positions they were to fill. Much as in the later phases of and aftermath of the period of the Great Purges, from the summer of 1941 educations and training were being truncated in order to get command personnel into the field. As early as 16 July 1941 cadets in the final year of military schools were to be graduated more than two months early in order to replace losses and provide personnel for new units.[65] Soon 'more experienced in a military sense' political 'workers' were being appointed to command positions by divisional commanders and commissars in part for similar reasons. More sound at least – than committing those with less than intended or indeed little or no military training – were the measures soon to be taken at divisional level for the training of the equivalent of NCOs in the divisional rear, and for the training of junior lieutenants for platoon command at army level from amongst those of NCO-level ranks who had proven themselves at the front.[66]

Training in general had been cut to an absolute minimum in order to get troops into the field. Training received by new recruits during the winter of 1941–2 was undoubtedly all too often rushed, where for example anti-aircraft gunner Iurii Vladimirov, a volunteer in the final phase of his post-secondary studies, received no more than six months training – formally five – as an anti-aircraft gunner with 90th Reserve Anti-Aircraft Artillery Regiment from November 1941 through to early March 1942, not having received significant military training prior to this period.[67] Vladimirov certainly received training better than many did – even in September 1942 the man in charge of new unit formation for the Red Army, Shchadenko, suggested that reserves should get a minimum of only three months training as part of attempts to 'raise the training of reserves for the winter and summer', soon after which they might be thrown into combat.[68] Before being sent to a field unit, and in fact in early February 1942, Vladimirov describes the farcical testing his and other batteries underwent in front of senior commanders. Anti-aircraft gunners had to fire on a tank cutout moving horizontally with one of the two anti-aircraft gunlayers of the 37 mm guns who controlled height having little or nothing to do as part of the exercise. The farce only got worse when a clearly capable gunlayer was borrowed by other batteries

for the purpose of passing the test – this individual not being sent to the
front with the rest of the unit but being kept back with the training unit to
serve a similar function in future.[69] Iurii Vladimirov would, after the
incorporation of his battery into 199th Independent Tank Brigade,
soon find himself in action during the disastrous Khar'kov offensive of
May 1942. Whilst the brigade was being formed from early March to
mid-April 1942 the anti-aircraft gunners did not formally have access
to anti-aircraft guns for training, although their commander was able to
come to agreement with PVO forces near where they were billeted for
them to train with actual guns. Vladimirov's battery only received their
unit's anti-aircraft guns and other equipment shortly before being sent to
the front, and then only two out of a list strength of four 37 mm anti-
aircraft guns fresh from the factory. It seems that it was only whilst at the
front awaiting the start of the offensive that Vladimirov was able to
familiarise himself with the silhouettes of German and Soviet aircraft
that his battery might encounter.[70]

During the spring of 1942 the Red Army started to take a wide range of
further measures in order to try to rapidly promote and provide at least
some supporting education and training for commanders who had
proven themselves at the front, whilst at the same time ensuring that
younger personnel in military schools that included future commanders
would receive sufficient training where previous months had seen so
many of them thrown into combat with woefully inadequate preparation.
In March 1942 as a measure to 'speed up the appointment of those
who have proved themselves in battle to appropriate positions' the field
promotion of combat proven commanders in the infantry was outlined,
where regimental commanders were for example able to promote to
platoon command level, and corps and divisional commanders to company level without reference to higher authority. The previous summer
the military soviet at army level had been required to appoint to command ranks up to senior lieutenant level.[71] From the spring of 1942, in
addition to the Academy of the General Staff – now The Higher Military
Academy – focusing on training senior commanders in all-arms warfare,
at middle command levels the Red Army was able in theory to pull
commanders typically trained in a particular branch of the Red Army
and provide 1,500 of them at a time with a four-month education geared
to making them better all-arms commander at the regimental level. Below
this in the hierarchy, the Red Banner Higher Rifle–Tactical Courses for
the Finishing of Command Elements – understandably shortened to
'Vistrel' – would in addition take 2,000 men at a time for a two-month
period for the retraining of company and battalion commanders – a
reduction in duration from three months in December 1941. All these

course were supposedly to be conducted by 'courageous, capable com-manders who have proved themselves at the front'.[72] Certainly by May 1944 there were few battalion and company commanders without any meaningful training and education for their positions, even if they would often move on to the next tier in the military hierarchy without training for the change in role. From a sample of fourteen armies – 971 battalion commanders – 46.9 per cent – had at least passed through a military school, with 18.8 per cent having taken the 'Vistrel' course. Overall, only 2.2 per cent of the sample had not received any military education.[73] Still, many who had entered the system much earlier before the war were promoted to high positions without what might be seen as the requisite or even an acceptable level of military education – in May 1944 142 generals or 4.8 per cent of the total had not received any military eduction, with a signifi-cant 443 generals or just over 28 per cent not having received any military eduction beyond that received in a military school as a cadet.[74]

At least those entering the system now were typically being better trained and educated than had been the case earlier in the war. By September 1942 cadets in artillery schools who had been sent there straight after call up could expect to receive training lasting for between seven and ten months depending on speciality. For anti-aircraft artillery, that meant training of between 8 to 10 months depending on the gun type. In the engineering schools sappers could expect to receive six months training, personnel for bridging units eight and electro-mechanical personnel ten.[75] Although these periods were considerably shorter than those before the war, they were nonetheless better than being thrown into combat literally from the classroom regardless of the point reached in their education as had been the case all too often when German forces were advancing rapidly during the summer and autumn of 1941. In mid-October 1941 orders for the manning of the Mozhaisk defensive line before Moscow contain far too many mentions of units from military academies and schools.[76] Although during the summer of 1942 the German advance would be similarly rapid, and once again such units would be thrown into the fray, this would not occur on anything like the same scale in terms of the front as a whole, in part because of the fact that there were fewer such establishments in the path of German forces now only advancing with such speed on one sector of the front, but also because the Red Army's need to throw such units into the fray was in a broader sense not quite as pressing.[77] Nonetheless, on the Stalingrad axis – often as their schools were threatened with being overrun – cadets would not be pulled to the rear but thrown into the fray, as in the case of the Rostov Artillery School mentioned later. That they were often poorly equipped – and prepared – to fight forward German units is apparent from testimony presented by Michael K. Jones. In the testimony of one Mereshko who commanded a company of cadets that summer, he notes how half of his company didn't have rifles and that there was only a single machine-gun for the whole company. Having at best been pushed through accelerated training, by September where 'the normal strength of each cadet regiment was 2,500', 'by the beginning of September most were reduced to barely a hundred'.[78]

In the context of growing Soviet material strength in the spring, and despite the losses sustained during the winter of 1941–2, Stalin was undoubtedly keen to get in the first blows of the spring and summer of 1942 in order to hold on to the initiative and maintain pressure on German forces – it would be the following year before he could be convinced to wait for German forces to exhaust themselves before going over to the counterattack at Kursk. Stalin was also keen to continue the approach he had promoted during the winter of 1942 that attacks across much of the front were better than clearly amassing forces on one or two sectors, in a situation where the Soviet Union did not have the resources for 'offensive operations on a strategic scale'.[79] The underestimation of German strength by Stalin that underpinned this approach was perhaps the result of wanting to believe that the costly operations of the winter had brought the German armed forces on Soviet territory close to collapse – and hammering away further should bring that result about. Stalin had, as Evan Mawdsley notes, gone as far as to proclaim the likelihood of imminent German collapse under this sustained if diffuse pressure in his late February Red Army Day speech.[80] Whether Stalin still believed in the possibility of a strategic outcome – German collapse – through a series of smaller operations that cumulatively would break the camel's back by the end of the following month is unclear.[81] Certainly Zhukov claims to have opposed such an approach – as in a sense did Shaposhnikov who according to Zhukov was in favour of 'active strategic defence' before resources could be amassed for operations across a wide front.[82] Local commanders tended to like the idea of having force concentrated on their sector of the front and not spread too thinly and much more widely if they were going to attack, and just as Zhukov saw the need to amass resources near Moscow, others such as Bagramian of the South-Western Direction saw the need to concentrate resources on their sector of the front. Ultimately, the Soviet memoir literature squarely places the blame for Soviet strategy during the period of limited offensive operations across a wide front on Stalin – easier to do after Stalin's death.[83] Zhukov was however unwilling to push the point far enough to get himself into trouble – and nor was the now probably too sick to undertake his duties as Chief of the General Staff Shaposhnikov willing to try to rein Stalin in for the short term – and he would soon be replaced by his deputy, Vasilevskii.

Although distinct plans were being developed for the spring and summer campaigning season, there was hardly a clear break in Soviet offensive operations between the winter counteroffensive of 1941–2 and operations of the spring and early summer. The Khar'kov operation to be discussed shortly was part of a next wave of blows, but, for example, below Leningrad and in the Crimea operations continued from winter through into the spring and both ended in failure at heavy cost. Below Leningrad what became General A.A. Vlasov's 2nd Shock Army that had commenced offensive operations in the snow in January would struggle to make progress in a region where forest and marsh made partisan activity viable – and conventional operations all the more difficult and particularly so once the spring thaw had begun. Here bloody fighting to break through German lines would be followed by encirclement and more bloody fighting to belatedly break out at the end of an operation with grandiose ambitions to relieve Leningrad and destroy significant German forces in the region, but with inadequate means.[84] Politruk V.A. Pavlov of 305th Rifle Division describes the heavy fighting in which his division was engaged from the outset when attacking well dug-in German forces across the Volkhov River on 13 January 1942 on what would be the left flank of 2nd Shock Army. When Pavlov returned to his unit in early March after having been wounded a few days after offensive operations had begun his unit was soon forced over to the defensive and in mid-March was cut off from Soviet territory along with 2nd Shock Army. A corridor was punched through the German encirclement early the next month, but could not be held open indefinitely and the lifeline and escape route was closed again in June. Interestingly, Pavlov places the principal blame for the debacle on betrayal by General A.A. Vlasov – an easy target given his subsequent leading of the German-sponsored anti-Soviet Russian Liberation Army – a very Stalinist approach.[85] By June Captain V.M. Domnichenko's 165th Rifle Division had been thrown into the fray in order to break the encirclement, and was committed to the attack in unfavourable tactical circumstances to little avail in what evidently was slaughter. Soviet troops with insufficient firepower to suppress German defences suffered heavy losses not only to enemy troops on the ground but in the daylight to 'ranks of 10 or more' enemy Ju-87s screened by fighters, that 'struck uninterrupted blows' against the attacking Soviet infantry.[86] For an operation that was supposed to lead to the relief of the siege of Leningrad and the destruction of its besiegers, the forces involved had clearly been inadequately supported from the outset.

Although German forces could be decisively reinforced, with commitments elsewhere the same was not true for Soviet forces.

Also, in the Crimea, despite the initial success of the Kerch' landings at the end of 1941, little was achieved despite a significant Soviet buildup and a belated offensive starting on 28 February 1942 that was renewed in mid-March and mid-April. Subsequently, just prior to Soviet operations near Khar'kov, on 8 May a German offensive in the Crimea – Operation 'Bustard Hunt'– rapidly led to the destruction or entrapment of most of the forces of the Soviet forces committed in the eastern part of the peninsula and evacuation of some of the remainder across the Kerch' Straits. German forces in the region could now focus their attentions on Sevastopol', which on 4 July would finally fall after having held out against German General Manstein's final offensive against the city for nearly a month. Shortly before the final surrender of Soviet forces in Sevastopol' Manstein was promoted to field marshal.[87] The fall of Sevastopol', despite its heroic defence, ended what overall had been a sorry chapter for the Red Army in the Crimea that is further discussed in Chapter 16 with the fall of the 'politicals' from military prominence. In the case of the Crimean debacle the 'political' whose influence had proven so negative had been Mekhlis, who had played a significant part in fostering significant Soviet losses. As Mawdlsey notes, not only had in the region of 150,000 Soviet personnel been lost defending Sevastopol' during what had been a nine-month siege, but in addition nearly 240,000 troops had been lost from the first landings in December through to the collapse of Soviet forces in the eastern portion of the peninsula in May.[88] Here, once again as below Leningrad, the Luftwaffe had played a significant role in Soviet defeat – as it again would near Khar'kov.

If the fighting below Leningrad, in the Crimea, and indeed before Moscow were not enough, there was the question as to where further Soviet blows should fall. In early 1942 Soviet intelligence had provided far from conclusive evidence of German intentions to pursue primarily renewed offensive operations against Moscow, with only secondary operations in the south. In accepting this conclusion Soviet leaders were probably not swayed by a subsequent German deception effort code-named Operation 'Kremlin' – effective as a deception effort in that it fed into existing beliefs – but which probably had little impact over Soviet planning in the spring as opposed to assessments of German intentions during June and July.[89] Acceptance of the line that Moscow was the likely principal German target prior to Operation 'Kremlin' was not limited to Stalin, as General Bagramian, at the time head of operations for the South-Western Direction, clearly suggests in his memoirs, even if German dispositions might have suggested a far from trivial thrust in the south as well aimed at the Caucasus.[90] Zhukov had certainly been in favour during the spring of reinforcing Soviet strength before Moscow, where Soviet forces would continue to hammer away at German forces in the Rzhev region with brief interludes throughout the year and even after it had become apparent that German attentions were focused on the south. According to Zhukov Stalin had suggested in the spring that for German forces to strike primarily towards the Caucasus in the south would be folly without having taken Moscow because of the extended flank that would result. In the light of obvious German strength in the south as well, it was assumed that an attack on Moscow might be made from the south-west and Soviet resources were distributed accordingly, with the Briansk Front that would be in a position to attack the German flank in July being well provided for. In many ways hindsight suggests that Zhukov and Stalin had been correct to assume that Moscow was the likely principal target given the strategic folly of an extended flank in the south.[91]

In the south Timoshenko, the South-Western Direction commander, had in March initially proposed an operation for the spring to liberate the entire Donbass region including Khar'kov. Contrary to Stalin's apparent belief in German collapse during the winter – the attack in the south was to be justified by the longer term benefits of having reincorporated this key industrial and resource rich region back into the Soviet war effort.[92] However, in the light of the threat to Moscow such a plan was not going to be allowed by the Stavka to soak up the sort of resources demanded. The resultant compromise for operations in the south was an attack solely in the Khar'kov area rather than liberation of the whole Donbass region. Pre-emptive strikes on both the Moscow axis and in the south would – supposedly – spoil German offensive plans on both sectors, and attacking in the vicinity of Khar'kov would also contribute to the spoiling of German plans on the Moscow axis, diverting German resources to the south.[93]

Khar'kov and enemy forces in the vicinity were retrospectively hardly important enough to risk the mechanised resources ultimately committed – and there was no need to throw such resources into a risky deep penetration if the primary intention was to deflect German resources from further north. Here there was probably a disconnect between the expectations of the Stavka and hopes of the South-Western Direction that although forced to scale down its plans still had ambitions for an operation of significance. Here perhaps parallels might be drawn with the Anglo-Canadian Dieppe raid where both operations suffered from being neither sufficiently modest to achieve stated objectives with limited losses or well enough supported to justify the risks to the forces ultimately committed.[94] Not only did the Khar'kov operation not have the ground forces hoped for by commanders in the region, but inadequate air support and co-operation with ground forces meant that the Luftwaffe could play a major role in the destruction of what constituted the bulk of Soviet mechanised strength in the south. By the end of April significant VVS resources had been concentrated in the region, and 21st Tank Corps of which anti-aircraft gunner Vladimirov's unit was a part had been allocated 20 fighters, 15 night and 20 daytime bombers for direct support with the front having 117 fighters, 60 ground attack aircraft, 20 'day' and 121 'night' bombers, with in addition 15 DB-3 medium bombers.[95] The airpower committed seems to have made little impact on the ground as Vladimirov testifies.[96] Command and control of air assets, and co-operation between the VVS and ground forces was undoubtedly poor as the Soviet General Staff study of the operation would subsequently conclude, and it was the Luftwaffe that had the resources where they could have impact. Relative Luftwaffe flexibility is highlighted by the fact that much of the Luftwaffe airpower that would wreak havoc near Khar'kov had only just been transferred from Kerch' where it had done similarly. Soviet ground forces also failed to co-operate and co-ordinate effectively, hampered by the continued problem of all too often having little idea what the enemy was doing.[97] As for anti-aircraft gunner Vladimirov, he would finally surrender to German troops on 24 May 1942.[98]

The Soviet pre-emptive strike near Khar'kov, rather than stalling the German summer offensive actually made its initial phases in particular far easier than they should have been. From 10–31 May 1942 forces of the South-Western Front had lost a total of 266,927 troops, along with 652 tanks, nearly 5,000 artillery pieces and mortars and more than 57,000 horses. Of the troops lost more than 200,000 were lost in the encirclement.[99] Soviet losses in the Khar'kov debacle – and particularly when combined with those in the Crimea that same month when Soviet forces had lost in the region of 162,000 men in just two weeks[100] – represented a staggering loss of men and material in the region comparable to one of the major encirclements of the previous summer and autumn. Nonetheless, in many ways Soviet operational failings – pieces of a jigsaw puzzle of strategic miscalculation and mismanagement – hid the realities of a resource balance shifting in Soviet favour and the gradual improvement of Red Army combat effectiveness. German and allied forces should perhaps not have been able to reach Stalingrad and penetrate the Caucasus, much as they should not have been able to reach the outskirts of Moscow in 1941. That they did and would, was not helped by issues at a tactical and operational level in Red Army performance that were not fully compensated for by the fact that the Red Army fielded ever larger quantities of equipment often superior to that being fielded by Germany, from the T-34 and KV-1 tanks to the 'Katiusha' rocket mortar – and the troops using this equipment typically fought stubbornly even if not always with relative finesse. However, strategic misconceptions – stemming from Stalin but ultimately supported by Zhukov and others – in large measure undermined the advantages that the Red Army had. Many Red Army personnel would pay for these misconceptions with their lives, but ironically it was Germany that would, and not by Soviet design, hopelessly overextend its resources and put itself in a position where it would lose the strategic initiative on the Eastern Front. Stalin's squandering of resources in relatively small and both poorly conceived and executed operations in early 1942 would cost the Red Army dearly, but Stalin had a better appreciation for the bigger picture. In June 1941 Stalin had in many senses been justified in believing that for Germany to attack the Soviet Union without first knocking Britain out of the war would be grand strategic folly, just as he was correct to believe that a principal German thrust towards the Caucasus without dealing with Soviet forces in the Moscow region would similarly be folly in 1942, just strategic rather than grand strategic.

15   "Not a step back!"

Germany initially started the summer campaigning season of 1942 with plans not only to strike towards the Caucasus and the resources in that region and en route to it, but also to capture Leningrad. The latter goal, in the light of events, had to be dropped. What was initially Operation 'Blau' – the advance on the Caucasus – would be the German focus even if Stalin and the Soviet leadership would not become aware that German attentions had shifted from Moscow for some time after 'Blau' had begun.[1]

Although in many ways facilitated by the destruction of Soviet forces encircled during the Khar'kov debacle, German Operation 'Blau' – soon developing into 'Braunschweig' – was initially not as successful as had been hoped for by German leaders, despite its apparent success as measured by progress towards the Caucasus. Although in the Crimea, near Khar'kov, and indeed below Leningrad sizeable Soviet forces had been destroyed in the spring, during the summer of 1942 it was soon clear that the April 1942 aim according to Hitler, to 'be absolutely sure to annihilate the enemy' in large numbers through encirclement as German forces headed eastwards would not take place.[2] The summer of 1942 was not to be a repeat of the summer of 1941 – after capturing much of Voronezh on the northern flank of the advance on 6 July in the face at first of only limited resistance and only a little over a week after the start of operations on 28 June, in the forthcoming weeks German forces essentially pirouetted around in pursuit of the sort of encirclement that had taken place during 1941, but to no avail.[3] Despite the operational dance of July the Wehrmacht was nonetheless advancing eastwards, and as it did so it was increasingly difficult for the Wehrmacht and its allies to protect an increasingly long and exposed northern flank. The bulk of Soviet resources were concentrated on the central sector of the front with a view to being able to protect Moscow from the south thanks to Soviet assumptions that during the summer may very well have been reinforced by the German deception effort, Operation 'Kremlin'. This Soviet deployment undoubtedly facilitated the initial successes of Operation

'Blau', but also contributed to its failure as enough of these resources could soon be transferred southward despite Soviet operations against Army Group Centre – joined by yet more newly formed units and formations and with the Soviet position further reinforced with troops from the Far East. Had Soviet forces been deployed differently – and certainly had they been deployed in concentration too far forward – the Khar'kov debacle might have taken place on a larger scale or more sizeable Soviet forces could have been caught preparing for offensive operations in a situation with parallels to June 1941. However, with Soviet strength concentrated on the Moscow axes, and with the Khar'kov disaster leaving the Red Army in the south without much of its mechanised strength, much of the Red Army in the south was soon engaged in what was often unauthorised retreat across the steppe.

Even without significant redeployment that was soon to come, the Red Army did possess significant strength, including armoured, on the northern flank of the principal German advance. Soviet counterattacks near Voronezh could be launched almost immediately after the German offensive had begun. By 1 July these counterattacks had achieved little – much to Stalin and head of the General Staff Vasilevskii's ire – with communications issues clearly playing some role in the failure to achieve meaningful results.[4] At times constraining the German advance and certainly whittling down German strength little by little, these counterattacks did not distract German forces from the drive eastwards and move into the Caucasus. Managed more effectively the resources of the Briansk Front for example should perhaps have had greater impact on German operations in late June and early July than was in fact the case. As General M.E. Katukov, in the spring of 1942 commanding 1st Tank Corps, notes in his memoirs, by May 1942 the Briansk Front could field in the region of 700 tanks – not including Stavka reserves in the area that added in the region of an additional 600 tanks.[5] On 30 June Stalin had already railed at the front command about their lack of success in the light of their superiority in armour.[6] During this period, after having disbanded the large tank formations during the late summer of 1941, Soviet armour was now gradually being concentrated in larger formations once again with high hopes that greater concentration would lead to more significant results. Tank corps began to be created in March, soon being incorporated into tank armies as will be further discussed later. Despite considerable armoured strength, Katukov's 1st Tank Corps that participated in the attacks on the German flank in late June was soon criticised by the Stavka for getting bogged down in the local encirclement of two German infantry regiments rather than pushing on into the enemy rear. Shortly afterwards, Vasilevskii complained that at least some of the tank corps 'had ceased to be armoured and gone over to the combat methods of the infantry'.[7] Certainly, as Katukov notes in his memoirs, 'the tank corps entered the battle piecemeal [*razroznenno*], each of them being given narrow, limited objectives', rather than being concentrated into 'an armoured fist reinforced with air and ground support resources' that might have 'struck a genuinely decisive blow against the Hitlerites in the flank'.[8] At the beginning of July Vasilevskii had held out hope that Katukov's tank corps might nonetheless 'strike a decisive blow to the south into the enemy rear'.[9] For Katukov's corps alone this was over-optimistic, and co-ordination between corps was poor – something for which Katukov could hardly be held solely responsible. German air-power undoubtedly also played a significant part in blunting these poorly co-ordinated Soviet attacks on the flanks, and their efficacy was certainly in early July hampered by the fact that the Soviet command had yet to fully appreciate – despite some defensive deployments to the Stalingrad region – that German efforts were primarily focused on goals to the east, not on finding a way northwards towards Moscow.

Forces that struck from the north in late June and early July included not only recently formed tank corps but also the first of the tank armies to be committed. After the independent tank corps had achieved little in late June they were joined in battle during early July by 5th Tank Army, and attempts were made to unify the command of armoured forces in the region – on 3 July it being proposed for example that the headquarters of 5th Tank Army might co-ordinate the activities of armoured forces operating on the same axis.[10] As the re-emergence of tank corps and armies above suggests, the Soviet command was well aware of the need for the concentration of both armour and infantry in larger and appropriately supported units and formations than had been the norm during the winter of 1941–2. In late 1941 tank battalions and tank and rifle brigades had proven convenient expedients. Formed quickly, the battalions and brigades of late 1941 were relatively easy for their commanders to manage and could usefully plug gaps in the line and conduct local counterattacks in November and early December as the Wehrmacht's advance ran out of steam before Moscow. When the Red Army had gone over to the offensive ad hoc conglomerations of these units proved not only difficult to command and control, but also to supply. With the Red Army having accrued some wartime experience in the command and control of armoured forces, and with the obvious need for their employment in greater concentration and with better support if they were going to achieve deep penetrations into the enemy rear and enact the sort of encirclement operations envisaged, in late March 1942 the formation of tanks corps began, soon followed in late May by the first tank army.[11]

In early April 1942 the list strength of a tank corps included two tank brigades and a motorised rifle brigade, but lacked even a reconnaissance battalion – soon an addition to list strength along with a guards rocket mortar battalion where an additional tank brigade was also added. Tank strength varied from in the region of 150 to closer to 200 during much of 1942, up from an initial establishment at the end of March 1942 of 100 tanks that had increased to 183 on 29 May 1942.[12] The 5th Tank Army was formed in accordance with a Stavka directive of 25 May 1942, and consisted of 2nd and 11th Tank Corps, an independent tank brigade, 340th Rifle Division, a regiment of USB light artillery, a mixed rocket mortar regiment with two *divizions* with M-8 and a single *divizion* with M-13 rocket mortars, and an anti-aircraft *divizion*. As of 29 May total tank strength was to be 431 tanks.[13] 5th Tank Army, and forming at the same time 3rd Tank Army, were to be provided with supporting elements such as supply, repair and medical services according to a directive of 26 May, that would include two army repair and reconstruction battalions, six mobile repair bases and four tractor evacuation companies.[14] 5th Tank Army was transferred from the Elets region where it was forming to the region north-west of Efremov and subordination to the Briansk Front according to an order of 15 June 1942.[15] By 4 July, with 7th Tank Corps attached – 5th Tank Army could field an impressive armoured force of more than 500 tanks – around 600 according to commander of 7th Tank Corps, Rotmistrov, who noted that this strength did not include 18th Tank Corps also in the region.[16]

Concentrating armoured forces in name was easy enough, and may indeed have looked good on paper, but from the provision of appropriate equipment and appropriately organised logistical support to the development of command and staff competencies, the formation of effective tank armies would take some time. The mobility of the corps' rifle division was certainly limited for example – even if its primary role was to facilitate the initial breakthrough of the armoured units in reality their support was required to considerable depth, and personnel for the new tank corps did not necessarily have an armoured background where for example 3rd Tank Army was in late May 1942 to be formed on the basis of 58th Army. In the case of 1st Tank Army formed in January 1943 the headquarters was to be formed on the base of the headquarters of the 29th Army rather than an armoured formation – much to the surprise of its commander Katukov.[17] Soon, in a State Defence Committee decree of January 1943 the formation of a staggering ten tank armies was ordered – each to contain 640 tanks, of which 430 were to be T-34 and 210 T-70s.[18]

The combined strength of the available tank corps and 5th Tank Army did, at least briefly, cause some consternation for German forces as they struck from the north during the first half of July. As Citino notes regarding fighting at the end of June to 4 July, German 2nd Army 'had to ward off a series of heavy Soviet counterattacks from the north that had not been foreseen in the German plan, but the situation was stable' and 2nd Army was able to 'occupy the intended defensive positions from Livny to Voronezh'.[19]

During the night of 4 July 5th Tank Army received orders directly from Moscow, that it was to:

With a blow in the general direction of Zemliansk, Khokhol (35 kilometres south-west of Voronezh) cut the lines of communication of the enemy Panzer group breaking through towards Voronezh across the Don; operations in the rear of this group are to smash his bridgehead across the Don.[20]

According to Rokossovskii, the fact that Moscow did not provide directives to the Front but rather to 5th Tank Army directly, hampered effective co-ordination between 5th Tank Army and other forces of the Briansk Front.[21] The complex Soviet command structure was undoubtedly a factor in poor command and control where often the problem was not the straightforward vertical hierarchy despite the limitations of staff work at corps and lower levels, but the fact that there were so many with fingers in the pie. The solution was not however to ignore key components of the chain of command. The 5th Tank Army was thrown into the counter-attack, although not as a whole and certainly without the desired results. Soon back in Moscow 5th Tank Army's lack of progress was cause for concern, Vasilevskii noting early on 9 July on behalf of the Stavka how '5th Tank Army, facing an enemy force of no more than one tank division, for a third day are marking time in one place. As a result of a lack of decisiveness units of the army have become tangled up in protracted frontal assaults, losing the advantage of surprise and are not carrying out the task demanded of them' – that is they should have broken into the rear of enemy forces operating against Voronezh.[22] Rotmistrov's 7th Tank Corps – attached to 5th Tank Army – was according to Rokossovskii more successful than the remainder of the army – initially however fighting alone.[23] Rotmistrov himself claims that reasons for the relative success of 7th Tank Corps included reconnaissance on a wide front that allowed for relatively effective deployment – with three tank brigades in the first echelon supported by units of a motor rifle brigade, with a battalion of T-34s in reserve. He also notes that the slow progress of 5th Tank Army as a whole can in part be explained by the movement of the bulk of the corps over the 100 km or so to the front line by rail, with loading, unloading and regrouping preventing timely arrival and the effective concentration of force. Where according to Rotmistrov 7th Tank Corps was able to enter the fray on 6 July not having been moved by rail, and 11th Tank Corps was committed the following day, it was 10 July before the same was true of 2nd Tank Corps.[24] Katukov similarly notes the failure to commit 5th Tank Army in concentration, suggesting that with insufficient time for preparation of the operation 'the Army was committed to combat by unit, and in general off the march, without reconnaissance of the area or the enemy.[25] M.I. Kazakov, at the time chief of staff for the Briansk and then Voronezh Front, suggests that the end result was that 5th Tank Army advanced as if passing through an existing breakthrough in the enemy line in a column formation where only battalions in the vanguard could actually engage the enemy.[26] In his memoirs Konstantin Rokossovskii adds to the post-mortem in suggesting that the commander of 5th Tank Army, General Liziukov was not the right man to command this new formation and indeed the tank corps subordinated to him – 'a good tank brigade commander who could have been a reasonable corps commander. But he was not up to commanding tank army' was Rokossovskii's assessment, noting how Liziukov was killed having thrown himself in his KV-1 tank forward in an attempt to spur his tankers on to more decisive action – in an action towards the end of the month described in detail by Katukov.[27] Further armoured strength would soon be thrown into the fighting in the region outside the command of the Briansk Front, where as 5th Tank Army was finally committed in its entirety the Stavka on 9 July ordered the newly formed Voronezh Front to take the city back from the Germans and support 5th Tank Army to the west of the city.[28] As David Glantz notes, in reserve the Voronezh Front also had the recently arrived 25th Tank Corps. The resultant shock group and reserves had a strength of approximately 270 tanks. This attack, as that of 5th Tank Army, soon also stalled.[29] Rushed, poorly organised operations and confused command and control had once again meant that the Red Army could not make good use of material superiority.

Although unsuccessful in meeting their objectives, Soviet operations in the area by what can only be described as unprecedented armoured strength not seen since the destruction of the mechanised corps back in June and July 1941 certainly registered back in Germany. In his war diary Halder reported for example on 5 July how German forces had 'repelled enemy attacks partly supported by tanks but lacking co-ordination'. On 7 July Halder recorded in his war diary how to the north of the German penetration eastwards 'the enemy has resumed his attacks against this defensive front, mainly in its easternmost sector', the following day noting how German forces on this sector were 'repelling the enemy who is again probing with tanks'. By 9 July Halder was reporting 'serious enemy attacks', and on 11 July Halder noted that the front in this area was 'still under sharp attack by large enemy tank forces. The attack was checked after local penetrations', with further pressure continuing for a number of days. Over these next few days Halder noted 'bitter fighting', 'the enemy attacking with large masses of armour', 'intense tank battles', ultimately 'repelled with some effort'.[30] During what would be subsequently described as the Voronezh-Voroshilovgrad Strategic Defensive Operation, from 28 June–24 July 1942 forces of the Briansk Front alone (13th and 40th Armies and 5th Tank Army) would lose 36,883 personnel as irrecoverable losses, along with 29,329 sick and wounded for a total of 66,212 total losses – out of 169,400 committed – for little of value.[31] Along with the Southern Front (26 June–24 July) and Voronezh Fronts (9–24 July), Soviet irrecoverable losses on this sector of the front for this would reach 370,495, along with 197,800 sick and wounded for a total of 568,295 out of 1,301,900 committed.[32]

As Soviet forces of the Briansk and soon Voronezh Fronts massed against German forces from the north, in the south German forces pressed on eastwards on the heels of Soviet forces that at times fought stubbornly and at times voted with their feet. During the summer of 1942 the Red Army in the south did not, as is still sometimes suggested, deliberately draw the Wehrmacht and its allies into the depths of the Soviet south before launching a cunning counteroffensive – the Red Army had been caught wrong-footed and was pushed further and further eastwards much to the chagrin of and despite the exhortations to stand and fight from Stalin and Soviet leaders. At the end of July Rostov fell and German forces once again were in a position to move southwards into the Caucasus. Hitler's orders of 23 July 1942 for the continuation of the German summer offensive – Operation 'Braunschweig' – as well as directing Army Group A to continue operations into the Caucasus, also noted a concentration of Soviet forces in the Stalingrad region and ordered their destruction and the occupation of the city.[33] Stalin's infamous Order Number 227 of the People's Commissar for Defence of 28 July 1942, or 'Not a Step Back', not only destroys any suggestion that the Red Army was trading space for time or military advantage, but also saw a new wave of repressive measures being applied to attempt to boulster what was perceived as insufficient resolve on the part of frontline troops. As the order itself states, having outlined German progress during the summer campaign of 1942 to date:

Certain unintelligent people at the front comfort themselves with talk that we can retreat to the east even further, because we have a huge territory, vast quantities of land, a large population, and we will always have surplus bread. With this they hope to justify their shameful conduct at the front. But such conversations are deceitful and false through and through, of benefit only to our enemies.

Every commander, Red Army soldier and political worker should understand, that our resources are not without limits. ...The territory of the Soviet Union, which has been seized and is in the process of being seized by the enemy is bread and other foodstuffs for the army and rear; metal and fuels for industry; mills and factories...; railway lines.... To retreat further means to ruin oneself together with our Motherland....

From this it follows, that it is time to put an end to the retreat.

Not a step back! Such should now be our principal call.

We must stubbornly defend every position, every metre of Soviet territory to the last drop of blood, cling to every last scrap of Soviet soil and hold our ground until all other possibilities have been exhausted [*do poslednei vozmoszhnosti*].

... We have to restore strict order and discipline in our army if we hope to save the situation and hold on to the Motherland.[34]

Order Number 227 had been read out to all Red Army units, and as many memoirs suggest, certainly made an impression. Future general Evdokim Egorovich Mal'tsev, in July 1942 head of the Political Department for 12th Army, suggested in his Soviet-era memoirs that Order Number 227, that 'in a very short period was hammered into the consciousness of every Red Army man and officer in the army' played a 'significant role in the war'.[35] In many ways Order Number 227 was an unusually open admission of the situation at that point in time from a regime whose propaganda was typically particularly sparing with the perceived truth by the standards of other major protagonists. As a former artilleryman wrote on having heard the order, Order Number 227 'for the first time laid bare the frightening results of the first year of the war'.[36] This bluntness alone may certainly have increased its impact, even without the associated intensification and further systematisation of repressive measures.

As the order goes on to detail, strict order and discipline, and in particular the prevention of unauthorised withdrawal, were to be maintained as required through two key measures. The first was through the threat that 'middle-ranking and senior commanders' who tolerated or led unauthorised withdrawals – those who would soon be called officers and provided with embellishments for their uniforms to highlight this – might be sent to officer-only penal battalions that would be 'placed on the most difficult sectors of the front, so that they might pay back the Motherland in blood for their crimes against her' in their 1–3 months of service in such a unit – in a similar manner to the personnel of penal companies for the rank-and-file. In both instances penal units were under the jurisdiction of the Military Soviets of fronts, with 1–3 penal battalions and 5–10 penal companies per front for allocation out to regiments and above as

"Not a step back!" – Soviet troops defending the Caucasus in late
September 1942. (RIA Novosti #186266)

required. They would be commanded by specially selected personnel –
one of whom would be Mikhail Suknev whose memoirs are cited later
and who became the commander of a penal battalion.[37] The odds of
surviving service in such a penal battalion or penal company for long
enough to win redemption and return to a regular unit were certainly
poor if the unit was committed to action. For example between 4 and
10 February 1944 128th Independent Penal Company would lose
54 killed and 193 wounded – nearly its entire strength.[38]

Despite the existence of penal companies and battalions, summary
execution continued to be applied regularly for a range of crimes. Falling
into the hands of a Special Section of the NKVD without a weapon
regardless of how it might have been lost often ended badly as did
apparent self-mutilation. As Mikhail Shelkov notes in his memoirs for
late 1942 when he was a senior lieutenant commanding a company at the
age of 19, 'more often than not' cases of self-inflicted wounds resulted in
execution by firing squad. If lucky, the guilty party might have been sent
to a penal unit. In the specific instance he notes the punishment was
indeed execution.[39] Although 139 men were sent to penal companies
and battalions by the NKVD 'Special Organs' of the Don Front

according to incomplete figures for the period from 1 October 1942 to 1 February 1943, 169 'cowards and panicmongers' were noted as being executed in front of their comrades.[40] If the guilty party was already in a penal unit, then they could certainly expect little mercy, with regulations governing their functioning allowing for punishment as far as 'shooting on the spot' for 'not following orders, self-mutilation, flight from the battlefield and attempting to go over to the enemy'.[41] Later in his memoirs Suknev notes an instance where self-inflicted wounds within his penal battalion led to summary execution – when one of two soldiers was not killed by the firing squad he was finished off by a 'chekist' with his pistol.[42]

Secondly, in addition to the creation of the penal battalions, Order Number 227 ordered that 'blocking detachments' of essentially company strength were to be formed by armies and subordinated to the Special Sections of the NKVD responsible for counter-intelligence within the Red Army. These blocking detachments were to be positioned behind 'irreso-lute' units and were sanctioned, if required, to fire on their own troops in order to prevent unauthorised withdrawal. This second measure outlined in Order Number 227 did not signal the creation of something new where such detachments had already been used with some effect during 1941 as noted in Chapter 11. So called 'blocking detachments' had been formed both by the NKVD – largely performing functions carried out by military police in other armies but with greater zeal – as well by the Red Army in order to provide spine to units at the frontline. In the case of the former by 10 October 1941 the deputy head of the Special Section apparatus of the NKVD could claim in a report to People's Commissar for State Security, Beria, that 657,364 servicemen 'separated from their units and running away from the front' had been intercepted by special sections and blocking detachments of the NKVD, of whom 10,201 were recorded as having been shot of 25,878 arrested for various crimes including being 'traitors', 'cowards and panicmongers' and 'deserters'.[43] Here NKVD troops attached to the Special Sections as described in Chapter 10 will have done the 'blocking' – and continued to perform this role throughout the war albeit under the auspices of the NKO later in the war.[44] Units raised by the Red Army were created according to a Stavka Directive of 12 September 1941 that called for each rifle division to form Red Army blocking detachments, although these seem to have been reintegrated back into their units of origin by the time Order Number 227 was issued.[45] Order Number 227 did not just mark the re-emergence of these Red Army blocking detachments – Order Number 227 heralded their use on a more permanent basis even if the number of troops involved remained relatively small, and the new detachments differed from their predecessors where in September 1941 they had been subordinate to the commander of a Red Army division and not the Special Sections of the NKVD as in July 1942. According to an NKVD note of mid-October 1942, by 15 October 193 such blocking detachments had been formed across the whole of the Red Army, with 16 for the Stalingrad Front and 25 for the Don Front.

Available documentary evidence suggests that these blocking detachments were busy in the south during the summer and autumn of 1942 rounding up hundreds of would-be deserters. The NKVD note of mid-October claimed that 140,755 personnel had been detained by the detachments during the period from 1 August to 15 October across the whole front, with the bulk, or 131,094 being returned to their units or sent to higher echelon units. Of the remainder 1,189 were shot, 2,776 sent to penal companies and 185 to the officer-only punishment battalions. With the Red Army in the south often in retreat for much of the period concerned it is understandable that 36,109 of those detained were stopped by detachments of the Don Front, and 15,649 by detachments of the Stalingrad Front.[46] Many of those stopped had clearly simply been separated from units, and it seems that for blocking detachments to have to take such drastic action as firing on Soviet units abandoning positions was rare. The note from which the above figures came does cite one clear example where on 14 September 1942 troops of 396th and 472nd Rifle Regiments of 399th Rifle Division, 62nd Army defending Stalingrad apparently fell back 'in panic' under enemy pressure, abandoning their defensive positions. In response:

The head of the blocking detachment (junior lieutenant of state security El'man) ordered his detachment to open fire over the head of those retreating. As a result the personnel of these regiments were halted and within 2 hours the regiments had occupied their previous defensive positions.[47]

The details of an earlier cited incident are more vague, but one can only assume that lives were lost where on 29 August 1942 lieutenant of state security Filatov took 'decisive measures' to stop troops of 29th Rifle Division of 64th Army of the same front from a 'chaotic' retreat. The NKVD document concerned went on to highlight with considerable disapproval how in a number of cases blocking detachments had been used as combat units by frontline commanders.[48] Supposedly consisting of some of the best and most reliable troops, the temptation for commanders to use the detachments in frontline combat roles a crisis is understandable. An NKVD report of 30 October 1942 claims that Konstantin Rokossovksii, then commanding the Don Front, sought to use blocking detachments on the offensive as a means not only of preventing

358 The Red Army and the Second World War

withdrawal, but pushing troops forward, with blocking detachments 'following behind infantry units and by force of arms forcing soldiers to get up and advance [*podnimat'sia v ataku*]', although even if that was the case in this instance there does not seem to be evidence of the systematic use of blocking detachments in this way.[49] As the war progressed and the Red Army was advancing the permanent blocking detachments perhaps became a means to avoid frontline combat for their personnel and had by August 1944 'lost any meaning' in the words of the head of the Political Directorate of the 3rd Baltic Front.[50] On 29 October 1944 an NKO order would finally abolish the independent blocking detachments and see their personnel provided as replacements for rifle divisions.[51]

During the crises of 1941 and 1942, the Red Army blocking detachments – and indeed their NKVD-only counterparts – certainly served a purpose in providing yet another safeguard against the lack of resolve and commitment to the regime so often feared and suspected by Stalin. At the same time the blocking detachments and the repressive apparatus associated with Order Number 227 provided a vehicle through which the unfortunate or even the tactically and operationally literate might pay for what at times might have been sound decisions or the decisions of others with their lives and without due process. Undoubtedly the threat of being sent to a penal unit made some sort of contribution to overall discipline – as did the fear instilled in soldiers on seeing comrades executed before their eyes. Unfortunately, the mechanisms for sending personnel to punishment battalions or companies – be they for the rank-and-file or officers – suffered from similar weaknesses to the mechanisms that determined the fates of those who fell into the hands of the special sections. Certainly many received punishment that was disproportionate, arbitrary and indiscriminate. Although the significance of blocking detachments may have declined as the Red Army advanced rather than retreated, an increasingly wide range of 'offences' could still result in being sent to penal units. Alex Statiev notes in an article on penal units in the Red Army, that by 1 October 1944 16,163 officers had been sent to penal 'assault battalions'.[52] In an order of 16 October 1942 those serving in the rear and sentenced not only for desertion (AWOL) but also guilty of theft of military resources, being drunks and 'malignant breaches of military discipline' but whose sentences had been put on hold till the end of the war were to be sent to penal units – rather than escaping punishment or sullying regular frontline units.[53] Officers and rank-and-file Red Army personnel were sent by Stalin, Zhukov and others to punishment units in fits of rage, in order to cover up the mistakes of superiors and for other less than morally justified reasons and even in flagrant breech of the rules nominally in place. Hence, as Alex Statiev also notes, in November 1944 Stalin 'turned the entire 214th Cavalry Regiment into a penal unit for losing a banner in combat';

on 29 April 1944 Marshal Zhukov sentenced a colonel commanding 324th Guards Regiment to a penal battalion for two months without court martial; and lower down the chain of command 'a commander of a tank that fell into a ravine because of the driver's mistake' and 'a soldier who praised a good German machine gun' were all sent to penal units for their supposed crimes.[54] In penal units the guilty had more chance of using their talents to useful effect than in the case of summary execution, but in many instances would have been more useful continuing to serve in regular units with greater life expectancies after lighter punishment. Making an example out of almost any 'crime' was however the Stalinist way, and particularly so during a period of crisis.

The crisis in the south of the summer of 1942 that prompted Order Number 227 was, despite the fact that it hid the realities of the shifting resource balance in stark favour once again of the Soviet Union, very real even if the regime in what was now typical fashion resorted all too readily to repression as a way of solving problems. The resources for which Hitler was lunging in the south were also important to the Soviet Union, and particularly the oil near Groznii, Maikop and beyond. The loss of so much prime agricultural land in 1941 was already taking its toll before the German summer campaign of 1942, where thanks also to the loss of labour, draught strength and transport capacity as well as land lost during the summer of 1942 the Soviet food supply was even further from being adequate by late 1942 than it had been at the end of the previous year. Even privileged frontline forces did not necessarily eat what might have been acceptably well or according to norms, where the issue was a combination of availability and distribution.[55] Increased attention given to the issue in late 1941 – including the allocation of responsibility for the issue to one of the members of the military soviet of an army and front, may have helped, but Soviet memoirs certainly suggest that particularly during the early period of the war food was short for units both at the frontline and likely to be sent to the frontline soon.[56] An NKVD Special Section report of 27 October 1942 noted that 'it is apparent from materials received that the existing system for the supply of foodstuffs to the field army in a number of cases has . . . had a negative impact on the progress of military operations' did not represent a response to an isolated instance.[57] The performance of frontline troops was probably not helped by the fact that in order to concentrate efforts on troops at the frontline, those in units that were forming for example and soon to be sent to the frontline were relatively speaking starved, and arrived at the front hungry and often in poor health. In his memoirs anti-aircraft gunner Vladimirov describes the pleasure of having been able to eat fresh potatoes sourced from a nearby village when his unit was forming in March 1942, when they were nonetheless still only receiving food by the norm for military personnel deep in the Soviet rear. Hence:

the impact of vitamin deficiency, the absence of strong sunlight for an extended period, very poor food (category three provision) essentially without fresh vegetables and fruit and with a stark inadequacy in milk, meat and fatty foodstuffs – with at the same time also insufficient quantity for everyone – was a weakening of the health of many soldiers.

Arrival at the front did not lead to the expected improvement in sustenance, where an increase in quantity was not matched by an increase in quality.[58] Allied aid would by 1943 have a significant impact on the availability of food for the Red Army, where much of the food being delivered was also in convenient forms for frontline use from dried egg to tinned meat. The tinned meat – 266,000 tons of which sent from the US was even prepared as Russian-style *Tushonka* – was soon nicknamed 'Second Front' in what seems like sarcasm but retrospectively seems to have also incorporated an element of appreciation from many Soviet veterans.[59] Part of the problem for Soviet supply was not just the issue of resources, but also of attitude. As in any army, being given responsibilities for supply did not, as Stalin's close associate and senior politician Anastas Mikoian notes, bring the same prestige as a combat command, and 'not all military commanders appointed to the post of head of rear area services for a front showed interest in this work, and many tried by whatever means to get out of it'. Mikoian also notes – and was in a position to observe given he had a number of supply-related posts – how at least early in the war not all military leaders saw to establish good working relationships with their rear area service personnel.[60]

Returning to the application of the stick in order to motivate, the application of a new wave of such repressive measures during the summer of 1942 may suggest parallels with the situation during the summer of 1941, but much had and was changing. Red Army troops may well have been more often than not hungry, but during the summer of 1942 the wider Soviet material situation was in many ways improving dramatically compared to the situation during 1941. Also, during the period with which this chapter has been concerned, the Soviet military leadership at the very top improved significantly in overall quality, where at the same time during the previous year Stalin still had faith in the pre-war cronies and 'politicals' whose influence remained significant into 1942 despite their seeming lack of operational ability. During 1942 the voices of many of those in position more for their political than military acumen who had held the reins along with Stalin prior to the war were finally sidelined from operational matters, and Stalin began to heed the advice of the new elite.

16   Change at the Top

Despite the fact that the Red Army was falling back to the east on the southern sector of the German Eastern Front during the late summer of 1942, on paper at least the Red Army was as a whole far stronger than it had been at the end of the previous year. Part of this improved situation was material, but it was also due to the fact that the Red Army leadership was changing and gaining the confidence of a dictator prone to distrust.

A comparison between those who met Stalin at the Kremlin during the summer months of June–August 1942 and those who met Stalin during the same months the year before highlights some significant shifts in the relative importance of a number of figures and indeed an overall shift in consultation towards military rather than political figures. By the summer of 1942 a far smaller core of political figures – a core including Molotov and Beria – was being regularly consulted compared to the previous summer. As head of the NKVD Beria obviously continued to be consulted by Stalin on security matters, but his ability to interfere in military matters seems to have been reduced from the time at the very beginning of the war when he was one of only five members of the State Defence Committee. Nonetheless, Beria was certainly able to interfere in operational matters during the apparent crisis in the Caucasus during the late summer and autumn of 1942, where commander of the Trans-Caucasian Front General I.V. Tiulenev wrote in his memoirs of Beria's disorganizing impact on the activities of the front headquarters, from the formation of a separate operational group for the organisation of the defence of the principal mountain range to the issuing of instructions over the front command and without informing it. Presumably out of exasperation Tiulenev claims to have offered Beria command – which he declined.[1] However, by late 1942 the scope for such interference seems to have declined, and one can perhaps suggest that Stalin was seeking to constrain Beria's formal power with the transfer of the Special Sections from the NKVD apparatus to the NKO, even if the move did not mean a change in leadership of the organisation. As the war progressed NKVD personnel lower down the chain of command would have to have more than a little prior military and their NKVD experience to be parachuted into commands in the Red Army. Deputy People's Commissar for Internal Affairs G.G. Sokolov is perhaps a good early-war example of transfer between the NKVD and Red Army. Sokolov had, after serving in the Red Army during the Civil War, continuously served in the NKVD and its predecessor's border guards throughout the 1920s and into the 1930s, and as a result of this he did receive some military education. Sokolov led the NKVD border troops from the summer of 1939 till June 1941, where Soviet border troops were, as their resistance on the border in June 1941 highlights, far more military than their equivalents for many Western states. This experience and education are likely to have been important reasons for G.G. Sokolov landing a series of senior operational commands in the Red Army on the outbreak of war that culminated in command of 2nd Shock Army in December 1941. Whether this experience justified such commands is certainly debateable – he had not participated in any of the small wars of the 1930s and had not really been part of the Red Army intellectual mileu.[2] Sokolov was removed from command of 2nd Shock Army on 10 January 1942 by command of the Stavka after Stalin had given his superior, Meretskov, the opportunity to highlight the former's failings.[3] In his memoirs, Meretskov notes how on the eve of undertaking offensive operations described in the previous chapter, subordinate commanders to Sokolov expressed their ire at the superficial leadership from their army commander, and that:

General Sokolov was completely unaware of the [military] situation, who was doing what and where units of his army were, and was a long way from having an understanding of contemporary battle and operations, clinging to old methods and means for the command of troops. Where those methods didn't work, he would lose motivation.[4]

Sokolov might not have been destined for great things as a frontline commander, but some 'politicals' did have the capabilities to succeed as field commanders. Red Army political officers were not NKVD personnel, but those who we might classify as 'politicals' in the sense that their political reliability was more important that military ability in their appointment. At least some commissars, whose military command role would be removed with the abolition of dual command in October and who had shown potential as military commanders would, with some training, be moved into command positions in the field army.[5]

Significant among the 'politicals' who had been so heavily involved in leading the Red Army in 1941 – and who was still consulted with some frequency by Stalin during the summer of 1942 although less so than the previous year – was the energetic Mekhlis. Fellow 'political' Shchadenko was, with some gaps, also a frequent visitor to Stalin's Kremlin office into 1943. Turning our attentions firstly to Shchadenko, although overall making frequent visits to Stalin's Kremlin office in 1941–3 in his capacity as head of the Board for the Formation and Equipping of the Red Army from the beginning of the war, Deputy Commissar for Defence Shchadenko did not make a single visit in 1944 and 1945, having been removed from his wartime post and subsequently as a deputy Commissar for Defence. Shchadenko's removal from the latter coincided with the abolition of most deputy-ministerial posts – a decision certainly simplifying an at times confusing chain of command.[6] Subsequent roles as a member of the military soviet of a number of fronts suggested that Stalin had not lost trust in Shchadenko, although these did not continue to the end of the war. Certainly then General-Major Gorbatov, in various cavalry inspection positions in the south during the summer of 1942, would have had opportunity to judge Shchadenko's work, which he apparently found lacking where in the revised 1989 version of his memoirs he was critical of the fact that someone such as Shchadenko be responsible for formation and equipping of Red Army units without a sound grasp of military affairs. Gorbatov was also critical of the head of the Main Board of Cadres of the RKKA from October 1940 to April 1943, Alexander Rumiantsev, who in selecting personnel for leadership positions he accused of paying little attention to the man and too much attention to the curriculum vitae. In 1943 Rumiantsev was replaced by Filipp Golikov who had recently commanded the Briansk and Voronezh Fronts, but whose frontline role seems to have been cut short after he was held responsible for the loss of Khar'kov in the spring of 1943. Rumiantsev would actually go on to be a successful field commander and end the war commanding a rifle corps – a case apparently of a man in the wrong sort of job at the beginning of the war rather than lacking ability. Gorbatov – like Meretskov and Rokossovskii for example – would also ultimately be successful in senior leadership positions in the Red Army despite having been repressed prior to the war, ending the war commanding an army.[7]

Mekhlis is in many ways perhaps the best example of the rise of the 'politicals' prior to and during the war given his significant influence over military decision making both directly and indirectly despite his lack of meaningful military experience and training for his subsequent roles. Not only did he wield indirect influence over operations through his role in the removal and often execution of a number of Red Army commanders, but also by early 1942 was essentially taking operational decisions himself. Mekhlis's hunts for scapegoats often took place after defeats in which commanders may or may not have shared responsibility, but where those executed at Mekhlis's insistence would not of course have the opportunity of redeeming themselves and going on to greater things, as in the fortunate case of Tolbukhin described later. At the beginning of the war Mekhlis was made a deputy People's Commissar for Defence and, backdated to 21 June, head of the Main Directorate for Political Propaganda for the Red Army (GUPP). He had already shown his capacity for interference in operational matters at Lake Khasan in 1938 in the role of head of the Main Political Board of the Red Army, the predecessor of GUPP. After a brief holiday from heading the Red Army's political branch before the outbreak of war, with the start of the Great Patriotic War the GUPP was soon the Main Political Board again, with Mekhlis again at its helm. Mekhlis was once more responsible for the political component of dual command from political representatives on the Military Soviets down to commissars and politruks. Mekhlis was in essence chief commissar – and proceeded to meddle in operational matters and conduct witch hunts when he made his frequent visits to frontline commands. Mekhlis had already played a central role in bringing about the arrest and execution of General D.G. Pavlov for the debacle on the Western Front in June and early July 1941, and proceeded to make his presence felt on other fronts during the remainder of 1941.[8] Many of his activities were formally carried out in his capacity as plenipotentiary for the Headquarters of the Supreme High Command – a Stavka representative at the fronts where, as historian Iurii Rubtsov notes, he acted more as Stalin's personal representative than that of the Stavka.[9] In September 1941 for example he descended on the North-Western Front and set about finding scapegoats for the defeat of 34th Army – resulting in the execution of the commander of the Army General-Major K.M. Kachanov and his head of artillery, General-Major of Artillery V.S. Goncharov – both of whom would later be rehabilitated. His *de facto* military career – and we might call it that given the increasing influence he had over operational matters – culminated in early 1942 with his role in the Crimea. After the success of the initial Kerch' landings of late December 1941 hopes for the liberation of the Crimea were soon dashed as German forces counterattacked in mid-January and Soviet forces pulled back. Mekhlis was sent in as Stavka representative in order to 'strengthen command' of what from 28 January was the Crimean Front. Soon Mekhlis was in practice in command, and with significant reserves pushed the front into rushed offensive operations in late February. Without taking any responsibility for the failure of this operation – in which the Red Army had dramatic numerical and material superiority – Mekhlis was soon looking for scapegoats. Although Stalin resisted his calls to remove the commander of the Front, General Kozlov, Mekhlis did manage to get the chief of staff General-Major Tolbukhin removed and his own replacement appointed. Tolbukhin would later become a Marshal of the Soviet Union and led the 3rd Ukrainian Front after Mekhlis's star had waned. With the memberships of the military soviets for the front and three subordinate armies replaced essentially at Mekhlis's insistence, it would be increasingly difficult for Mekhlis to blame others for subsequent failures that would have his fingerprints all over them.[10]

When German operations to push Soviet forces out of the Crimea gained momentum in May, Mekhlis could not escape Stalin's ire. On 11 May Stalin and Vasilevskii addressed criticism for the conduct of the front largely not only at Kozlov but also Mekhlis – both of whom along with the military soviet appointed by Mekhlis had 'lost it [*poteriali golovu*]'.[11] On 15 May, when ordering the stubborn defence of Kerch' along the lines of the defence of nearby Sevastopol' and the regaining of command and control over forces to the west of Kerch', Vasilevskii pointed out to Kozlov that 'You are the commander of the front, and not Mekhlis. Mekhlis should be helping you. If he isn't assisting you, then let us know.'[12] It is difficult to believe that Stalin was not aware of the content of this communication. Having previously given Mekhlis the authority to essentially take command when he saw fit, it is not unreasonable to postulate that by mid-May Stalin was apparently, as Rubtsov suggests, doubting Mekhlis's competence. Reassertion of Kozlov's authority could not save the Crimea – and nor could dispatching Budennii to the area.[13] Finally, Stalin lost confidence in Mekhlis's ability as an operational supervisor, and demoted him – deriding his military competence in a lengthy report on reasons for the failure of the Kerch' operation. In this document, Stalin and Vasilevskii made numerous criticisms of Kozlov and Mekhlis, both of whom had shown 'a complete lack of understanding of modern warfare' – commanding in a 'bureaucratic and paper pushing manner' where the focus was on issuing orders and not facilitating their being carried out. At the end, punishments were meted out – Mekhlis was to lose both his position as a deputy commissar for defence and his headship of the Main Political Board – being demoted down to corps commissar, with Kozlov and others also being demoted and to be assigned to 'less complex tasks'. Mekhlis's demotion – as that of other loyal cronies who had risen so far thanks to Stalin – was certainly not as severe as it might have been where others might even have lost their lives.[14] He would subsequently continue to serve as a political member of the military soviets of a number of fronts, by which point thankfully he could not interfere with the authority that dual command would have previously given him.[15]

Although Mekhlis was still able to get an audience with Stalin during the summer of 1942, notably absent from Stalin's Kremlin office were Marshals Kulik, Timoshenko, and Shaposhnikov.[16] Of these the first was

'Death of a soldier' reads the caption for this photograph taken during the fighting near Kerch' in the Crimea in the spring of 1942. Soviet infantry were still all too frequently being thrown into the attack with inadequate support. Debacles in the Kerch' region in 1941 and 1942 would lead to the falls of both Kulik and Mekhlis respectively. (RIA Novosti #491040)

perhaps the least able of the three as suggested by material elsewhere in this work. His performance during the first months of the war pointed to his lack of organisational ability – he had been sent as Stavka plenipotentiary to the Western Front to little effect, and although one Russian author has suggested that his being given command of 54th Army for the Siniavino Operation to relieve Leningrad in September 1941 – as a Marshal of the Soviet Union – was indicative of the significance of the operation, it was also perhaps indicative that Kulik was not deemed suitable for command of larger scale offensive operations despite Stalin's relative warmth towards him.[17] Very few commanders saw Stalin end their telegraph communications with 'Well, I shake you hand [*zmu ruku*], all the best' as with Kulik on 16 September before it became apparent that 54th Army would not be able to relieve Leningrad. On 20 September he got simply 'all the best' – before on 24 September being removed from the command for 'being unable to handle the carrying out the task set before him'.[18] Although the failure of this operation was down to many factors, including pressure from above to go over to the offensive before 54th Army was ready, Kulik once again showed fairly uninspired leadership and ability to deal with the complexities of the situations with which he was faced. Aware of such issues as the risk of encirclement in both the case of 54th Army and subsequently on the Kerch' Peninsula, Kulik was nonetheless as a result of the fact that he was unable to think and act quickly enough and outthink his opponent less likely than many others to be able to pull some sort of operational or even tactical rabbit out of the hat that might mitigate the impact of poor decision making above him and placate an impatient Stalin.[19] He was nonetheless sent as Stavka representative to assist in the Crimea at Kerch' on 8 November 1941. Here, in a less than favourable situation, his relative closeness to Stalin could not save him from Stalin's ire when contrary to direction from the Stavka he ordered the evacuation of Kerch' which subsequently fell into enemy hands on 15 November. The punishment – demotion from marshal and removal from his position as a deputy People's Commissar for Defence, expulsion from the Party and and loss of orders and medals- was by Stalin's standards of 1941–2 far from severe, but served to highlight that personal loyalty only went so far.[20] Nonetheless, Kulik was given more opportunities to redeem himself at lower rank, firstly with operational commands. After his performance had not been deemed satisfactory – and a later less than successful role in the formation and equipping of new units – in June 1945 he still held the rank of General-Major. He was subsequently executed in 1950 after having been arrested in 1947.[21]

Unlike Kulik, Timoshenko had shown organisational ability prior to the war, and indeed was able to strengthen his status as a commander during the first months of the war thanks to a combination of sufficient ability, decisiveness and avoiding having failure attributed directly to him. After having led the Western Direction Timoshenko was moved first northwards and then to the south, there being associated with the successful Rostov counteroffensive of November 1941 on which he had apparently insisted. Timoshenko's downfall was perhaps his personal drive to see the failed Khar'kov operation of May 1942 through – an offensive that was very much his and on which Stalin had clearly high hopes, despite the fact that Timoshenko's initial plan was very much watered down by the Stavka. Demotion rather than execution followed – Stalin had after all made him marshal and tended to give second chances to those he had promoted particularly enthusiastically. Senior Soviet politician Malenkov's damning indictment of Timoshenko whilst the two of them were on the Stalingrad Front in September 1942, where the former claimed to Stalin that Timoshenko 'looks like a good-for-nothing, indifferent to the fate of the Soviet government and the fate of our motherland', would quite probably have finally put an end to the careers of the less favoured, but not for Timoshenko.[22] Subsequent command of the North-Western Front for the Demiansk Operation did not lead to his rehabilitation given the fact that the operation fell far short of its aims, and in future Timoshenko was not given further front-level commands even if as Stavka representative he continued to participate in the planning and execution of operations.[23] In conversation with the Soviet journalist Konstantin Simonov, Zhukov suggested that in terms of ability Timoshenko was more capable a commander than some of those whose stars subsequently rose above his, namely Eremenko who will be discussed further later. Zhukov also suggests that had Timoshenko fawned over Stalin then he might have gained further front level commands, but apparently to his credit he did not.[24] Historian Roger Reese suggests that Timoshenko – along with Budennii – suffered 'eclipse' by the younger generation of Red commanders.[25] This was certainly the case, in the sense that both lacked the fire and aggression of many of the younger commanders appointed to operational commands during the war. In the case of the older Shaposhnikov, who was appointed as chief of the General Staff on 10 August 1941 in place of Zhukov, the issue was not ability but his failing health – in May 1942 he asked for and was granted a transfer from the demanding post of head of the General Staff.[26] That Stalin addressed Shaposhnikov using the formal first name and patronymic combination rather than the surname alone as in the case of most others was, as Rzheshevskii suggests, indicative of Stalin's respect for Shaposhnikov. Despite having been willing to make a case for a more robust invasion of Finland in late 1939, he undoubtedly vacillated over the evacuation of Kiev in September 1941 in the face of Stalin's obvious desire to hold, and certainly later in the Great Patriotic War and perhaps as a result of his failing health, Shaposhnikov seems to have been unwilling to press views contrary to those held by Stalin. It is difficult to assess whether Shaposhnikov's support for operations across a broad front in January 1942 and essential continuation of the strategy with due preparation in the spring of 1942 were down to poor judgment or the fear of Stalin's ire from a man in poor health. Rzheshevskii suggests that Shaposhnikov was a man of the "officers' code of an earlier generation', where respect for hierarchy *per se* was perhaps greater than during the Great Patriotic War and indeed in Stalin's Soviet Union.[27]

Closest to Stalin of the pre-war marshals – both close associates of Stalin during the Civil War – were undoubtedly Budennii and Voroshilov. Voroshilov's importance – if frequency of visits is an indicator – had declined considerably by the summer of 1942 even if he was still an intermittent visitor to Stalin's Kremlin office. Like Timoshenko, and Budennii, Voroshilov had been entrusted with major commands during

1941, including for example on 10 July 1941 command of the North-Western Direction that was supposed to co-ordinate the activities of the Northern and North-Western Fronts.[28] His subsequent command of the Leningrad Front highlighted the fact that although far from being as incapable as his fellow pre-war Marshal Kulik, he did not nonetheless show the sort of characteristics demanded of operational commanders such as the ability to rapidly grasp the essence of a complex situation and take decisive action. One might argue that Voroshilov lacked the nerve for a frontline command in Stalin's wartime Red Army – on more than one occasion Voroshilov sought to avoid continuing in command of or taking on new commands, as in September 1941 where he sought to be relieved from command of the Leningrad Front.[29] Success in the pre-war politics of the Red Army did not mean that Voroshilov was a particularly good wartime leader – and his intellect did not suit him to staff work.[30] By 1 April 1942 Stalin had clearly had enough disappointment with a man in whom he had relatively speaking considerable faith, based largely it seems on Voroshilov's loyalty, and indeed had a relationship that was by Stalin's standards a friendship. By order of the Central Committee on 1 April 1942 – rather than direct order from Stalin – it was decreed that 'It should be recognized that Comrade Voroshilov has not justified himself in carrying out the frontline tasks entrusted to him', and that as a result it was necessary to 'Dispatch Voroshilov to rear area military work'.[31] On 6 September 1942 Voroshilov was appointed to what sounded like an important position – that of 'Supreme Commander of the Partisan Movement'. However, in reality Voroshilov did little meaningful in this position at the head of what was actually officially a Party rather than military organisation – reflecting that as an organisation its political role was perhaps more significant than its military one. His nominal deputy P.K. Ponomarenko, who nonetheless ran the Central Headquarters of the Partisan Movement, was not from a military background.[32] Voroshilov was actually sent by the Stavka to assist the command of the Independent Coastal Army in October 1943, although criticism of the army for getting bogged down in street fighting in Kerch' of 27 January 1944 – addressed to both the army commander and Voroshilov – was not followed by the sort of successes that might have led to the redemption of Voroshilov as a frontline commander.[33]

Budennii was, similarly to Voroshilov, not particularly academic, and unsuited to staff work. Despite his anachronistic commitment to cavalry during the late 1930s Budennii's early war performance was not glaringly inadequate and it does seem that Budennii was able to incorporate his beloved cavalry into a meaningful combined arms schema. Like Voroshilov, Budennii lacked the personal characteristics for operational command in a war in which Stalin set the tone. That tone set by Stalin and senior commanders such as Zhukov meant that during 1941 and into 1942 offensive spirit and an unwillingness to give ground were key characteristics required for operational commands in the Red Army, along with organisational ability and the capability to rapidly make sense of a situation and take appropriately aggressive action. In the Kiev region in September 1941 Budennii had shown himself too willing to sanction retreat – in this instance the sound but un-Stalinist option. Similarly the following year in the south, as his biographer the popular Russian historian Boris Sokolov notes, Budennii was too willing to give ground, and was unable to perform the sort of command acrobatics that might have produced victories, albeit at high cost in men and materiel.[34] One certainly gets the impression that Budennii remained in essence even in 1942 – despite the incorporation of modern weaponry in to his cavalry-orientated schema – the cavalry commander of the Civil War. Having been removed from the position of First Deputy Commissar for Defence in late August 1942 to be replaced by Zhukov, Budennii's subsequent appointment as chief of cavalry in January 1943 was certainly in many ways fitting for a man whose life as a whole revolved around horses, and probably suited him, despite his disappointment at not receiving a field command.[35]

Hence, by the late summer of 1942 the five Marshals of the Soviet Union of 1940 had lost all or most of the influence they had enjoyed during the previous summer. Similarly as Glantz notes, many generals of the so-called 'class of 1940' that had been promoted to the rank of general by June 1940 had failed to live up to expectations where many of their promotions had been extremely rapid during the purge era. Of these generals, twenty-four commanded fronts during the first six months of the war during a period in which there were typically far too frequent changes of command for sensible continuity. Some were killed – by the Germans or their own side- namely M.P. Kirponos and D.G. Pavlov respectively, but most continued to serve. As Glantz notes, only 11 of 24 were still in command of fronts by the end of 1941. In the cases of those demoted – for example D.T. Kozlov demoted alongside Mekhlis- their demotions in many ways had a positive effect on the military effectiveness of the Red Army. This was not only in terms of improving overall competence but in allowing a new command characteristic – one where resolve was combined with considerable disregard for cost as long as goals were achieved – to dominate as reason to promote to senior command positions. Fewer than half of those commanding fronts during the first six months of the war went on to be considered reliable for such high level command responsibilities throughout the war, be it as commanders of fronts or Stavka representatives at the front, where those commanding fronts or with equivalent or greater responsibility were soon joined by a number of early-war commanders of armies such as A.I. Eremenko who were soon commanding fronts.[36] Whilst perceived loyalty was obviously still a requirement for promotion in the late summer of 1942 this factor was not as personal as it had been during the peculiar circumstances of the Great Purge era. The new military elite was too young to have had either a prior positive or negative history of personal interaction with Stalin – to highlight its youth, it is worth noting that in May 1945 of 3,970 generals 48 were 30–35 years old, 409 36–40, 1,476 41–45 and 2,037 older than 46. Of the marshals, although all of the Marshals of the Soviet Union were older than 46, six other marshals out of 14 were 41–45 years old. Some at the lower end of the general's rank had risen quickly – 61 general-majors and three general-lieutenants had achieved that rank within a five-year period of service. General Ivan Cherniakhovskii's case is of particular note – he ended up commanding a front in April 1944 at only 37 years old.[37]

Loyalty and competence were certainly not however entirely distinct categories for wartime commanders – following orders and getting the job done, despite for example a high cost in terms of the men under one's command- showed both loyalty to Stalin and the sort of effectiveness that ultimately mattered. Here Zhukov perhaps excelled most. As Reese notes, the new senior commanders who rose to prominence during the Great Patriotic War had several other advantages over senior counterparts of the pre-war period. Firstly, the new elite had experience of commanding and training smaller units often lacking for their senior predecessors who had managed to avoid far too many command experiences during the tumultuous Civil War era – arguably giving a greater sense of perspective on Red Army capabilities even if this didn't always show. Secondly, the new elite had not had experience of operational command in the Civil War and taken such Civil War experiences as indicative of how to conduct modern warfare – where their predecessors had not had similar World War I experiences that might have provided better indication of the changing nature of warfare. As Reese goes on to suggest, those such as Voroshilov – and indeed Tukhachevskii and other purged leaders – spent too much time in the mid-late 1930s thinking about and engaged in large scale manoeuvres without due consideration of the limits of and development of the human capabilities of the Red Army at lower levels.[38] This is something different from the brutal pushing of those capabilities in which Zhukov and others so frequently engaged during the war. Timoshenko's reforms of 1940 started to change the situation and introduce greater realism, even if a case of too little too late for Red Army performance during the first year of the war.

372 The Red Army and the Second World War

Of those in prominent positions in the Red Army in late 1942, Zhukov might best be described as having been at the vanguard of the new before the Great Patriotic War had begun – a member of the 'class of 1940' along with Eremenko and Meretskov. Zhukov's capability combined with ruthless willingness to get the job done undoubtedly appealed to Stalin. Comments on Zhukov's strengths and weaknesses as a military commander, as of Stalin, are spread throughout this work and relatively speaking a considerable amount has been written in English about his generalship. In his recent biography of Zhukov, Geoffrey Roberts is undoubtedly sympathetic. Roberts's assertion that Zhukov was 'the best all-round general of the Second World War' is perhaps not justified on the basis of the evidence he presents, and just what being the greatest all-round general entails is a little unclear – Roberts's statement that 'Zhukov's reliance more on energy and vigor than on imagination to achieve his goals was consonant with the prevailing ethos of the whole Soviet system' certainly does not suggest brilliance. Zhukov's 'exceptional will to win' might have served the Soviet Union well during certain times of crisis in 1941–2, but at other times contributed to the squandering of lives. Here, as Roberts infers, Zhukov's 'strategic vision', and particularly so earlier in the war, often meant sacrificing tens of thousands of lives after it should have become apparent that grandiose operational goals were unlikely to be achieved in a particular instance. Pressure from Stalin was obviously a factor here, but Zhukov did exercise some initiative on the matter where Stalin was often the arbiter between rather than the source of operational ideas in the decision-making process. Had someone less able than Zhukov – of whom there were many candidates in the Red Army leadership during the early days of the war – put forward plans and gained Stalin's ear instead, then the results might of course have been far worse. Everyone has their failings, but as Roberts points out with justification, Zhukov was an energetic and capable organiser, learned from many of his mistakes, and ultimately got the job done – and at a price that was acceptable to Stalin.[39] In their recent biography of Zhukov Lopez and Otkhmezuri are at times less favourable when looking at specific instances towards a man whose managerial style was often less subtle than that of even Stalin. Threats, tantrums and ruthlessness made Zhukov a man to be avoided as much as possible, as apparently Rokossovskii attempted to do. At least however Zhukov's threats and tantrums were far more likely to be geared towards subordinates carrying out a coherent plan with a reasonable chance of success than would and indeed was the case with far less capable leaders such as Kulik. Given the requirements of place and time, Lopez and Otkhmezuri certainly align with Roberts in arguing that overall Zhukov was undoubtedly an effective commander, even if not employing the sort of what today would be described as 'emotional intelligence' often credited for example to Rokossovskii.[40] Making more than an isolated appearance in Stalin's appointment diary by 1942 despite having been repressed prior to the war – Rokossovskii had gone from commanding a mechanised corps and then 16th Army in 1941 to the command of fronts by 1942. Rokossovskii and Vatutin – risings stars of the mid-war period – may have proven to be more effective leaders than even Zhukov had the latter not been killed in 1944 and the former had the opportunity to show ability to lead beyond the front level. Of those who we might also call the new of wartime, Vasilevskii was perhaps the first star to rise to upper senior level during the war itself. From being deputy head of the General Staff in August 1941 he was promoted formally to head on 27 June 1942 although had been carrying out the function prior to this point, and was an almost daily visitor to Stalin.[41] Vasilevskii too rivalled Zhukov in ability without quite the same rough edges even if he did not have the same range of experience as Zhukov to show it. Eremenko – who as Zhukov noted after the war was perhaps less capable than Timoshenko – had sufficient ability to work alongside his aggressive – almost bullish – 'can do' attitude that so appealed to Stalin and particularly so early in the war. Eremenko's early war failures after big promises were not sufficiently glaring to bring about his downfall. The failures of the Briansk Front in September 1941 considered in Chapter 11 were in part as a result of such attitude. As Vasilevskii notes in his memoirs regarding the scope for the Briansk Front to defeat Guderian's mobile forces as the Kiev debacle was unfolding, 'Stalin, unfortunately, took the stubborn assurances of commander of the Briansk Front A.I. Eremenko that decisive victory could be achieved over Guderian's forces all too seriously. It didn't happen. B.M. Shaposhnikov and I from the very beginning considered that the Briansk Front lacked sufficient forces for that.' Eremenko, in modern terms 'talked the talk' – and could pull off the 'walk' sufficiently well to get away with not achieving the results promised. According to Vasilevskii, the previous month Stalin had said of Eremenko as he left Stalin's office after having made an earlier commitment to defeat Guderian – 'that is the sort of person we need in these complex circumstances'.[42] Simplification of the situation and a commitment to offensive action as the solution to all ills appealed to Stalin in 1941, although thankfully for the Red Army the supreme commander – and final arbiter in all decision making – would become a little more sophisticated in his thinking as the war progressed.

As chair of the State Defence Committee, and head of the Stavka, Stalin formally and in practice held the reigns in both military and non-military decision-making. For Zhukov at least, operations in the Stalingrad region were something of a transition period in Stalin's grasp of operations and strategy. Stalin's early-war lack of appreciation for the complexities of modern warfare has been well illustrated in the last few chapters. In his memoirs, Zhukov suggested that 'up until defeat of German forces at Stalingrad in practice Stalin was weak on questions of military strategy and even worse on questions of operational art. He was weak on the organisation of contemporary front-level operations, and even worse on those at army level.' Consequently, 'Stalin frequently demanded clearly unrealistic periods of time for the preparation and conduct of operations' – operations that were often unrealistic in their goals. Stalin had been the driving force behind the idea that Kiev should have been defended to the last – based no doubt largely on its political significance, leaving sanction of retreat until it was too late. Stalin had also been the driving force behind the broad front offensive of the winter of 1942 and its continuation long after the Red Army was no longer in a position to meet the demands placed upon it. Despite his lack of know-ledge and experience – with what experience he did have largely being more than twenty years before – at the start of the war Stalin was undoubtedly apt as Zhukov suggests to try to prove his mastery over operational-strategic matters based on his Civil War experiences rather than accept guidance, 'from which nothing positive followed'.[43] On a slightly more positive note, a post-war article attributed to Voroshilov was correct in suggesting that Stalin had paid 'especially serious attention to reserves' during the war – an important factor in Soviet survival during 1941 and 1942, but of course his impetuosity had contributed to their squandering.[44] Zhukov was correct to point out in his unexpurgated memoirs that Stalin had tended during the early period of the war to throw recently mobilised and not yet fully equipped units into combat resulting in 'unnecessary losses'. According to Zhukov, when challenged on the matter in one instance Stalin snapped, 'It's nothing to whine about, such is war. . .'.[45]

Stalin was, fortunately, able to learn – and with that improved under-standing seems to have come not only a respect for the Red Army as a whole but also for the advice of the General Staff. Zhukov certainly notes – in a passage published in his Soviet-era memoirs unlike those earlier – that 'Later Stalin did grasp the basic principles of the organisa-tion of front-level operations and those of groups of fronts, and directed them with appropriate knowledge and understanding. Stalin's capabil-ities as Supreme Commander were in particular revealed starting with the battle for Stalingrad'.[46] Stalin gave Vasilevskii reasonable time to organise the ambitious Stalingrad counteroffensive, even if as will be highlighted later the success of Operation 'Uranus' led to the sort of overconfidence in the Red Army's capabilities that had manifested itself in the winter of 1941–2 after the initial success of the Moscow counter-offensive. By late 1942 Stalin was nonetheless more likely to take advice – now from overall more capable advisers. One small example of this to go with the case of the Stalingrad counteroffensive might be the decision of 9 September 1942 to disband 4th and 16th Tank Corps, sending their tank brigades as separate units to the Stalingrad Front. Part of the reason for their disbanding seems to have been the opinion that their command-ers 'were not compatible with their appointments'. Stalin did, in this instance, ask Zhukov whether he had any misgivings about this course of action – which he apparently did.[47] The next day Stalin issued instruc-tions for them to be reconstituted with new commanders.[48]

Lower down the chain of command improvements in quality and capability to function effectively within the system were more diluted – for as Lenin might have noted, cultural change for a whole organisation would take longer than political or even cultural change at the top. A protracted war certainly weeded out some of the most glaringly incapable commanders of the early war period, who in many instances had also risen more rapidly than they otherwise might have done in the aftermath of the Great Purges – or those who had been able to move into command positions in the Red Army from the NKVD structure without actually possessing the necessary skills for their new post such as in the case of Sokolov discussed at the beginning of this chapter. However, despite the efforts made at the end of the last chapter to train and promote capable junior and middle-ranking commanders of what would soon officially be officer grade, the Soviet system was unable both practically and culturally to produce a desirable number of commanders who could not only show the right amount of ability and initiative when required but also operate and succeed within what was still a very stifling organisational culture. A problem in any army, showing too much initiative early on, was a particular problem in the Red Army that tended to promote those showing an aggressive pursuit of the plan from above without too much thought and too many questions. At times, commanders were removed for not having shown due resolve, only to later be reinstated in equivalent positions from which their careers could then progress, as in the case of A.I. Lopatin who was removed as commander of 62nd Army of the Stalingrad Front in early September 1942 at General Eremenko's sug-gestion for inadequate resolve in the defence, but then the following month given command of 34th Army of the North-Western Front.[49] Certainly, capable commanders were in short supply, and nowhere more so than on the staffs of formations lower down the chain of command as noted elsewhere. Here one might offer one more example of issues with staff work at army and divisional level within the Trans-Caucasian Front in late 1942, where calls for the appropriate training of staff officers within the front were bound to be complicated by the fact that those with competence were in such high demand.[50] Pressure to keep competent troops and commanders at the front seems to have kept the quality of leadership in training and reserve units low, where nonetheless even at the front line the military 'literacy' of many commanders remained low.[51] Infantry officer Mikhail Suknev's description of 1349th Rifle Regiment's commander Ivan Filippovich Lapshin – and suggestion that he represented something of a type – is far from being an exception. According to Suknev, Lapshin was not only without ability and stubborn, but indifferent towards subordinates and merciless with them. Going further, he notes how Lapshin 'apparently hadn't read a book in his life, but in front of the bosses he was anxious to please and looked imposing...'. With only a three-month course for military education at most, he had nonetheless participated in the Civil War that probably gave him some credibility. Suknev concludes his comments on Lapshin, by noting how 'I met the likes of Lapshin in the future, almost on demand'.[52] All armies tend to suffer from the problem that junior commanders require very different competencies than those higher up the chain of command, where personal bravery and resolve in following someone else's orders lower down the chain of command is often justification for promotion to positions where bravery is increasingly less important than intellectual qualities. The 'can do' – and 'has done' – were of course particularly important in the Red Army not only at the top but also lower down the chain of command, where 'has done at what cost' was not necessarily the next question to be asked.

Despite the intensification of repressive measures initiated during the summer of 1942 against perceived failure and lack of loyalty on the part of at least some, one might argue on the basis of further policy developments regarding the status of what had been middle ranking commanders and above that Stalin had increasing confidence in the Red Army leadership as a whole. On 9 October, as fighting for the city of Stalingrad itself raged, dual command in the Red Army was abolished for the third time under Stalin's leadership. In the decree ending dual command it was explained that the war to date had 'tempered our command cadres, pushing forward a deep layer of new and talented commanders experienced in battle and to the very end true to their military responsibilities and the honour of command'. Having shown 'loyalty to the Motherland, and acquired significant experience of modern war, growing and becoming stronger in both military and political respects', it had apparently become 'inevitable that the institute of commissars in the Red Army be disbanded and that unitary command be established'. Commissars would now become 'deputy commanders on political matters', with those most 'militarily prepared' being able to transfer to full command positions.[53] In many instances this was no doubt a relief for commanders, such as for one of the section heads of the operational department for 66th Army one Captain Akhunov, who was recorded by the Special Section of the NKVD for the Don Front as having stated that the decision was sound, and that commissars 'only demoralise and undermine discipline in the Red Army', being 'capable only of a lot of talk and of loafing about and stressing command cadres out without getting down to meaningful business...'. As in the previous instances where dual command had been abolished, it is important not to exaggerate the scope of the change. Political officers would retain considerable influence over all aspect of decision making, just as political representatives on the highest rung of the hierarchy of which commissars had been a part would continue to play a full role in decision making at the military Soviet level for armies and fronts. As Senior Battalion Commissar Dorandin of 24th Army was reported as having noted after hearing of the end to dual command, 'I have already lived through this change twice. Where the commander and commissar worked well together this change won't bring anything new. The deputy commander for political matters will all the same remain as representative of the Party in the army, and will have to be reckoned with...'.[54] As discussed prior to the war, the commissar-commander relationship was not however always a smooth one as suggested by Captain Akhunov above. Certainly Military personnel could now at least in theory assert their authority over in particular military decision making as long as their decisions could be demonstrated to be politically sound as well – allowing at least some commanders to bring an end to the meddling in tactical and operational matters by political overseers that had been exemplified by Mekhlis. Gone perhaps was a check on the decision making of poor commanders, but anecdotal evidence suggest that there were even more militarily incompetent commissars than the commanders they supervised. For example, although Mikhail Suknev liked many of the commissars with whom he served as an infantry officer prior to commanding a punishment battalion, it is apparent that regardless of rank and whether they had been through the military-political education system their military experience and knowledge on arrival was poor to non-existent if, as was often the case, they hadn't become a commissar after service in the Red Army.[55]

Certainly there was a practical benefit in terms of efficiency to the end of dual command. As the deputy commander of the operational department for 66th Army, one podpolkovnik Timoshenko was noted as having stated:

That order should have been issued some time ago. Consider this – yesterday I approached the commander for a signature on a document, he signed it and that seemed to be it, however it was still necessary to go to the end of the earth [*chertu na kulichki*] to find member of the Military Soviet, Brigade Commissar Katkov, in order to complete the signing with him, and he wasn't required for it. Now it will be somewhat more straightforward. . . .[56]

At the same time, in addition to unitary command strengthening the prestige and authority of commanders and providing certain practical benefits such as many orders no longer having to be countersigned by a commissar, the process by which gradually senior and middle-ranking commanders had become 'officers' rather than commanders was completed. By the summer of 1943 there was a firm distinction between the rank and file, sergeants, officers and generals.[57] Visible evidence of the change in status was provided by shoulder boards. The reintroduction of shoulder boards was certainly controversial – according to I.M. Golushko enthusiasm for their reintroduction came more from politician M.I. Kalinin and rear area services General A.V. Khrulev in charge of supply than Stalin, where Khrulev had been toying with the idea of shoulder boards as part of the development of distinctive uniforms for Guards troops that never materialised.[58] The shoulder boards were not universally popular even amongst those who were to wear them. Young officer Mikhail Shelkov was forced after being mildly disciplined for breaching rules on uniform to wear his golden shoulder boards when in the rear in Moscow, parading about in which he 'felt uncomfortable'.[59] Mikhail Suknev, infantry officer, had the following to say in his memoirs about the reintroduction of shoulder boards:

. . .in the army they introduced shoulder boards. They were almost the same as the Tsarist ones! As the son of a Red partisan, was I really to put on White Guard shoulder boards instead of the shevrons on the sleeve and a captain's 'sleepers' (the dream of my youth)!? . . . Without the shevrons a field commander could not be distinguished from a quartermaster. With shoulder boards all were the same. That, I considered, was not for the benefit of discipline in the army. Unacceptable! [*ne poidet!*]

Suknev was apparently subsequently, as Shelkov, forced to wear his new shoulder boards, in Suknev's case by the Smersh representative for his regiment after some argument.[60]

Nonetheless, even if some were uncomfortable with their new attire, others were apparently supportive of the change. An NKVD report for the Don Front on reactions to the introduction of new forms of

distinction between ranks noted that there were positive reactions to the
fact that the new distinctions were essentially tsarist. One Senior Lieutenant Bogomolov apparently suggested that the new 'military look
[*voenstvennii vid*]' provided by the shoulder boards would be good for
discipline, suggesting that 'it reminds us of our forebears – victorious
Russian commanders Suvorov and Kutuzov. Every soldier will fight even
better for the honour of his uniform...'. The deputy commander for
armoured forces of the Don Front apparently thought that the shoulder
boards would 'raise the authority of the command cadres in the Red
Army...'. Of course, as one critical commenter noted, 'shoulder boards
alone would not raise authority...', but the shoulder boards were introduced shortly after the end of dual command and at a time during which
at least some commanders not up to the job of leading had been weeded
out.[61] Higher up the chain of command embellishments to uniforms to
highlight rank would perhaps get out of control after the war. Regarding
the wartime provision of gold braid for officer's uniforms, as then journalist in the Soviet Union Alexander Werth notes in *Russia at War*, at the
time the 'Russian request for vast quantities of it at first struck the British
(as an embassy official told me at the time) as 'absurdly frivolous'. They
did not grasp the full significance of these exports until later'.[62]

In many sense the abolition of dual command was part of a much wider
simplification of Red Army command and control during late 1942 and
into 1943 that saw a simultaneous reduction in the number of different
individuals and organisations interfering in and complicating decision-
making at the same time as the authority of those making the decision
was being bolstered by these reforms and other measures described above.
Where the political apparatus of the Main Political Board no longer had a
de jure role to play in military decision-making, political officers were
however not the only people hovering over and around frontline commanders as they made military decisions. Although typically less invasive,
'Officers of the General Staff' who were the eyes and ears of the General
Staff at front, army and even corps level, would be present at a headquarters
and particularly during the first half of the war casting a scrutinizing eye
over the activities of commanders. As noted by Deputy head of the General
Staff Shtemenko, the 'Corps of Officers of the General Staff', whose title
came from their tsarist predecessors and in fact saw perhaps the first
sustained use of the term officer in the Red Army, came into existence in
1941 in a situation where fronts and armies had little idea where their
troops were and what they were doing, and where 'the General Staff
received the most sketchy and contradictory details of the situation at the
front'. The solution was to send out Officers of the General Staff – initially
for short durations – to find out what was going on and report back. Soon

such officers became permanent fixtures at headquarters, at times even operating down to divisional level.[63] As former officer of the General Staff Nikolai Saltikov notes in his memoirs, in preparation for his assignment as an officer of the General Staff it was made plain that his role was to be to 'personally supervise, without respite, forces at the front and their maintenance in the actual conditions in which they were operating, and see that Stavka orders and directives from the General Staff and its commanders were being executed', in addition to reporting back to the General Staff on the state of affairs at the front as seen with their own eyes.[64] As Shtemenko goes on to note, by the middle of 1943 the activities of the Corps of Officers of the General Staff had been somewhat cut back in circumstances where commanders and their staff had supposedly sufficient experience to manage without the same close supervision. The officers of the General Staff did not disappear, but were incorporated into the operational apparatus where they were presumably to be seen more as a part of the command apparatus serving the commander even if they continued to be responsible to their own hierarchy. They nonetheless continued to report back to the General Staff, and in 1944 Officer of the General Staff N.V. Reznikov's observations on the conduct of operations by 33rd Army of the Western Front commanded by General-Lieutenant V.N. Gordov seem to have played a role in his subsequent removal from command.[65] Stavka representatives at front level continued to overrule commanders on the spot throughout the war – ostensibly in the interests of co-ordination between fronts – but at least their presence was according to perceived need rather than permanent. Arguably such temporary assignments were better than the direction headquarters that supervised the activities of multiple fronts during 1941 and 1942 that added another then effectively permanent level to the command hierarchy to stall decision making and muddle command and control.

Extended German supply lines and a combination of attrition and Soviet resistance had, by the time dual command had been abolished in the Red Army, slowed down the German advance considerably as fighting for what remained the secondary objective on the flanks of the Caucasus advance – Stalingrad – consumed increasing German resources. Increasing Soviet resources were shifted towards the Stalingrad region as the summer progressed – Soviet attempts to recapture Voronezh for example being suspended on 7 September as four rifle divisions from the Voronezh Front were ordered to be transferred to the Stalingrad region.[66] Soon German forces would get a better feel for the strength of the resurgent Red Army than they had during the earlier phases of their advance eastwards that summer, a strength that would be apparent not only amidst the ruins of Stalingrad but on the open steppe that surrounded the city.

17   Stalingrad and 'Uranus'

During the summer of 1942 the Red Army was supposed to have held the Wehrmacht to the west of Stalingrad and prevented Axis forces breaking into the Caucasus across the southern portion of the Don River. Not only did it fail to do so, but considerable Soviet strength was lost in fighting in the Don bend and at the gateway to the Caucasus. Soviet troops were supposed to be defending ground every bit as stubbornly as they had at Smolensk and Moscow the previous year, and indeed they often were. However, in the chaos in the south of the summer of 1942 there was undoubtedly something of a tendency towards retreat even if an unauthorised one, and where in part because of this the German pincers that snapped at times frantically were unable to enact the sort of encirclements that had caused so much damage during the previous summer and autumn.

On the road to Stalingrad and the Caucasus, there was certainly stubborn Soviet resistance. In an unusually frank account for a Soviet memoir – published before the Khrushchev-era political 'thaw' had passed – then commander of 55th Tank Brigade, 28th Tank Corps of 1st Tank Army P.P. Lebedenko describes how under intense pressure to undertake offensive action near Kalach as part of action to relieve pressure from 4th Tank Army he threw his forces forward once again in early August 1942 against German forces. Lebedenko's forces were thrown into the attack despite low strength and limited support and supply, with only eleven tanks for his 55th Brigade, and ten for 39th Tank Brigade, with reinforcements recently arriving in the area consisting of a company of BT-7s and another of T-60s – not the T-34s hoped for. In addition to the participation of the corps' 32nd Motor Rifle Brigade, on the left 131st Rifle Division, and on the right 399th Rifle Division of 1st Tank Army were also to attack. After an initial advance of about half a kilometer in the face of only light resistance the advance was halted by intense enemy fire. After enemy fire subsided the advance resumed, only to be halted again, and again. With infantry pinned and tanks seeking whatever cover they could find, the appearance of German aircraft on the scene only made the situation worse. Nonetheless, the order was to attack, whether Lebedenko thought it appropriate or not[1]:

'Why aren't you advancing?' I angrily asked battalion commanders by telephone.

'We can't make it through the fire, comrade colonel. We literally can't raise our heads.'

I myself could clearly see what was taking place on the frontline, but it was being demanded that I advance, only advance, and I shouted into the handset:

'Forward! Get your people up and moving forward! You will answer with your head if you do not carry out orders!'

'Yes sir, foward!' came the responses from the strained and hoarse voices of the battalion commanders.[2]

The resulting spectacle as viewed by Lebedenko through his binoculars was of course not a pleasant one, as the infantry pushed forward in small bounds and as 'the spouting explosions left gaping holes in their ranks [opustoshaiushchimi smerchami prokhoditsia po ee riadam razrivi]'.[3]

Soviet forces frequently nonetheless escaped encirclement during the summer of 1942 largely because the German infantry simply couldn't keep up with the armoured spearheads – and German losses were also significant. German losses were such that in order to move into Stalingrad, as David Glantz notes, 'Army Group B had no choice but to insert Hungarian, Italian and finally Romanian forces to defend the Don River flank'. Although in the main these held the flanks with German support during August and September, even during this period the Red Army was able to seize, and hold, a number of bridgeheads on the southern bank of the Don.[4] However, despite these local successes, during the late summer, any talk of a major Soviet counteroffensive in the Stalingrad region was, as Zhukov himself acknowledges in his memoirs, 'with the aim of holding the enemy before Stalingrad' – not the destruction of either of the German Army Groups A or B, or both. Zhukov goes on to note that at that point the resources were simply not available for such ambitious goals.[5] This was in part because Zhukov was still focused on operations further north for the final destruction of German forces in the Rzhev region against which Soviet forces had been regularly hurling troops since the end of 1941. Operation 'Mars' – the failed Soviet operation in late 1942 to finally destroy German forces in the Rzhev region – will be discussed further later. Also a factor in the military situation in the Stalingrad region was the fact that even after the region had been deemed sufficiently significant to receive them, the transfer of resources to the area would take time.

By 3 September the prospect of German forces taking the city in the near future was very real as Stalin noted in a tense telegram to Zhukov, who had arrived in the region at Stalin's behest on 29 August.[6] Only with the failure to hold German forces further west and their penetration as far as Stalingrad did the Soviet high command focus, and not out of choice, on the defence of the city itself. By mid-October, after intense fighting, much of the city was in German hands as the Soviet high command belatedly seems to have appreciated the value of a stubborn defence of Stalingrad and its environs. Although the Soviet military leadership had stressed even in 1941 how fortified towns 'demanded considerable expenditure of military strength and resources by the enemy' – and demanded that 'fighting for population centres should be stubborn, fighting for every street, for every building, in order to destroy the maximum enemy human and other resources', it was at Stalingrad that this approach was belatedly applied with a vengeance.[7] On 14 October 1942 the Stavka ordered that for those parts of Stalingrad still in Soviet hands that 'every house, every street and every district become a fortress' – as well as that having cleared German troops from areas of the city that they then also be fortified.[8] On that day, as German forces pushed forwards, Soviet and German losses were heavy. That evening, as commander of 62nd Army Chuikov noted in one version of his memoirs – a figure recorded by 62nd Army in the operational report for 14 October – '3,500 of our wounded were ferried across to the left bank of the Volga. This was a record figure for the whole period of fighting in the city'.[9] Not only had the command post for 62nd Army been hit early in the day – by air attack – but army communications hubs had also been captured by the enemy. As Chuikov notes in a journal article on the subject of 62nd Army communications during the battle, the command post for the army was hit again at 13:10, with more than thirty killed. Subsequently, 'at around 14:00 we lost telephone communications with all of our forces engaging the enemy. Only radio stations functioned, and then with interruptions'.[10] Such issues with communications undoubtedly contributed to the decentralisation of command that will be discussed later. During this period the Luftwaffe was undoubtedly dominant over Stalingrad, and despite the difficulty of target identification in such an environment was able to cause considerable damage to forces of 62nd Army beyond hampering command and control, as in the case of air strikes hitting dug-in tanks of 84th Tank Brigade in the vicinity of the 'Barrikadi' Factory.[11]

It is during this period in mid-October that after stubborn resistance Soviet troops were pushed from the Stalingrad Tractor Factory during some of the most horrific fighting of the struggle for the city – to be followed by protracted fighting over the Barrikadi and Red October factories on the defence of which 62nd Army had chosen to concentrate. During this fighting, as even was made plain in Soviet-era memoirs, Soviet losses were such that whole divisions could be all but wiped out. Hence, on 17 October the combat journal for 37th Guards Rifle Division recorded that 'as a result of 15 days of fierce combat...only the artillery regiment remains. By the evening of 17 October 1942, the division has up to a company and a half of active 'bayonets'.[12] The 112th Rifle Division also suffered horrendous losses. As N.I. Krilov, chief of staff for 62nd Army at the time notes in his memoirs of the Stalingrad battle, this division that 'initially consisted of Siberians', in bloody fighting in September 'shrank to regimental size and then down to a composite battalion', to be reconstituted with the remains of neighbouring units and march or replacement troops from across the Volga. On 20 October 112th Rifle Division was finally moved back across the Volga River into reserve, although the reality was that 'only headquarters and very few frontline commanders' remained.[13] Nonetheless, the Red Army was able to continue to feed troops into the battle for the city – during the night of 15–16 October 138th Rifle Division under the command of General Liudnikov started to be deployed across the Volga. Only 2,646 men strong, the division nonetheless brought with it significant artillery assets. When the remainder of 138th Rifle Division was deployed across the river on the morning of 17 October German forces had already captured most of the positions it was ordered to defend – for which its commander Liudnikov was duly chided. The 138th Rifle Division was soon fighting for the Barrikadi Factory, the route to which it was supposed to have defended, joined by remnants of another Soviet division, 308th Rifle. After intense artillery preparation during the evening of 10 November, on 11 November 138th Rifle Division faced the last major push by German forces to take control of the factory district, and was soon partially encircled and cut off from the main body of 62nd Army. By the end of the day on 13 November 138th Rifle Division was down to approximately 500 men. On 20 November 1942 the isolated division would have faced another major attack that may very well have finally destroyed it, had it not been for events elsewhere.[14]

Despite horrific losses to those units engaged in the city, the advantages to fighting in urban areas for the Red Army were many – and would similarly become advantages for German forces later in the war. Firstly, German losses were for once similarly horrific to those of the Red Army. David Glantz describes losses for 6th Army – 145 killed, 469 wounded and 18 missing – as 'relatively low cost' for German gains made on 14 October – on which day 24th Panzer Division lost 8 out of 33 tanks, some however recoverable.[15] As will be discussed further later, although useful, the armoured forces that had done so much in German operational successes during the war to date were far more vulnerable to infantry in built up areas, and it was far more difficult to deploy air support assets that had previously done so much to support them to their advantage when enemy forces were deliberately operating in very close proximity to their own and it was often extremely difficult to identify a frontline.

The loss of the Stalingrad Tractor Factory in mid-October was a blow to the defenders, but it was during this period after the blunting of the mid-October German offensive that Krilov suggests that 'it was possible [udavalos'], even if only on isolated sectors of the front for the time being, to seize combat initiative from the enemy'.[16] During this period at the end of October 62nd Army received the last divisional-scale reinforcements it was to receive for the duration of the battle remaining, 45th Rifle Division, along with a division returning from the right bank of the river that had received fresh troops, and a company of tanks. Two battalions of 45th Rifle Division crossed the Volga – 1,588 men – on 27 October, out of a total strength of approximately 6,400 on 26 October, with the remainder following over the next few days. A regiment from 45th Rifle Division was thrown into the attack on 31 October along with the remains of 39th Guards Rifle Division and the recently arrived company of tanks. As Krilov notes, the 'scale of the attack was in the grand scheme of things modest, but appeared at the time to be of such significance that in our operational documents it was noted that the army had gone over to the counteroffensive with part of its strength'.[17] Nonetheless, overall German forces were still the ones that were on the offensive within the city even in late October and early November as Soviet forces clung to, and counter-attacked to maintain, their foothold on the western bank of the Volga.

Symbolic of Soviet resistance in the city of Stalingrad both in the West and the former Soviet Union is perhaps the sniper – and in particular the exploits of Vasilii Zaitsev. During the 1930s the importance of marksmanship had been stressed in the Red Army as one might expect, although in the Soviet case the promotion of marksmanship also applied to pre-conscription training and sport. An article in *Pravda* for 25 April 1936 on 'sniping' by one Major I. Khorikov for example stressed the importance of encouraging pre-conscription and in particularly sporting marksmanship, in which young people could earn the distinction of 'sniper' for the accuracy of their shooting and provide suitable cadres for the Red Army. Of course, for the 'sniper' in the Red Army to be given the time to maintain his skill once conscripted as stressed by Khorikov – presumably outside unit-level activities – was unlikely.[18] It is unsurprising that in a *Pravda* article of 6 June 1939 – after the most intense period of the Great Purges – Red Army soldier

M. Moskvin was not rewarded with a distinct role as 'sniper' for his 30/30 scoring but with command of a section, with Moskvin apparently encouraging sniping skills within the context of an average rifle section.[19] Having good marksmen – even 'snipers' in a unit was one thing, but it was apparent that much could be achieved by the sniper acting alone or with other snipers. Although marksmen or 'snipers' had shown their worth at Khalkhin Gol, they had clearly done so as members of rifle units. During the Russo-Finnish War of 1939–40 the Red Army had suffered both in terms of sustaining losses and morale thanks to the widespread use of snipers by Finnish forces, typically operating independently of units. The impact of Finnish snipers on morale is certainly illustrated by the extent to which their activities were subsequently recalled by veterans, for whom Finnish snipers had become something of a bogeyman. Despite their relatively limited numbers, Finnish snipers undoubtedly contributed to a 'fear of forest' for Soviet troops who tended to exaggerate the propensity for snipers to be hidden not only a ground level at which they might make good their escape but also in the trees.[20] So great was this fear that the need to guard against snipers hidden in trees would find itself specifically mentioned in the 1942 regulations for rifle forces.[21] Despite the Finnish example, Soviet practice and that of most armies was subsequently still nonetheless for 'snipers' to operate with units – 'snipers' were the best shots a unit had, and performed sniping functions as part of that unit even if they might be deployed on the fringes of that unit. On the defence and in positional warfare snipers were particularly effective – as shown at Khalkhin Gol and as the 1936 *Pravda* article above noted as part of the trench warfare on the Western Front during the First World War that had been so important for the development of the modern conception of sniping.

During the battle of Stalingrad both sides employed snipers, but the Red Army turned good shots into 'snipers' in large numbers and gave them both far greater significance, status, and finally a more independent role than they had been previously allowed. In part independence was a product of environment – decentralisation of command was obviously desirable in an environment in which command and control was particularly difficult. The development of storm groups will be discussed later, but in many ways the lone sniper was the most extreme expression of this decentralisation. The sniper movement of 1942 in Stalingrad seems to have had antecedents during 1941 in fighting in urban or suburban environments, where 'sniper-destroyers' were at least in the eyes of Party officials troops of almost any arm who showed particular effectiveness in killing German troops and who as part of the exercise were supposed to pass their competency on to their peers in a frontline setting. For Leningrad Party leader Andrei Zhdanov, the 'sniper-destroyer' movement

Snipers await their prey on the Western Front in August 1942. The role of snipers and the glorification of their exploits would become far greater during the fighting for Stalingrad just weeks later. (RIA Novosti #601058)

seems to have been the military equivalent of the Stakhanovite Movement in industry in the 1930s, where the primary purpose of both Stakhanovite workers and the wartime 'destroyers' was as exemplary figures to inspire others – in the latter case complete with ridiculously inflated figures for kills as opposed to production. There was apparently some desire to create special sections and platoons of 'snipers' – with some such units of up to company size apparently operating at the frontline near Leningrad in early 1942.[22] Although, as N. Mal'tsev notes in a 1970 article on the 'Sniper Movement during the Battle for Stalingrad', there were few infantryman 'snipers' operating specifically as such is the late summer of 1942, their numbers increased dramatically during the autumn as the development of a so called 'sniper movement' received support from higher up the chain of command. By 29 October the Stalingrad Front, commanded by Eremenko, had issued an order on the 'Development of the Sniper Movement and the Use of Snipers in the Struggle with the Enemy' that called for every rifle platoon to prepare a sniper command of at least two-three snipers and indeed to promote their exploits. By the time of the anniversary of the October Revolution – on 7 November by the new calendar – 'a significant number of snipers' had been prepared by the Stalingrad Front and 'organised into commands, groups, platoons and even whole companies'. A sniper company of 38th Rifle Division of 64th Army had seventy-nine men in it, and a sniper company of 422nd Rifle Division of 57th Army eighty-six men. There were however insufficient sniper rifles, spares, binoculars and scopes for all – and many had to make do with regular rifles. Of note is the high proportion of Komsomol and Party members amongst snipers – where for 62nd and 64th Armies more than 80 per cent of snipers were apparently Komsomol or Party members. Here one can speculate that the independence demanded of them was seen to require a high degree of perceived loyalty.[23]

Vasilii Chuikov, commanding 62nd Army, had the following to say about the 'sniper movement' during the battle for Stalingrad in his memoirs:

We paid particular attention to the development of the sniper movement amongst our forces. . . .

Political department, Party and Komsomol organisations headed the sniper movement: at Party and Komsomol meetings questions regarding and the means to improve the work of sharpshooters were discussed. Every sniper took on the responsibility to train up a number of marksmen, chose a partner and made a self-sufficient sniper out of them. . . .

Snipers went on the 'hunt' early morning to pre-selected and prepared locations, carefully concealed themselves and patiently waited for the emergence of targets.[24]

In the 1939 (December 1938) development of the regulations for infantry platoons snipers were to operate in pairs – 'with a sniper operating within a sniper pairing, with each in turn carrying out the role of sniper and spotter' – a requirement dropped by the November 1942 regulations that spent greater time on the role of the sniper and suggested a more independent role. In both regulations the targets of a sniper were similar – enemy snipers, officers, artillery observers, gun crew, tank crews (a 1942 addition) and low flying aircraft, that is 'all important targets that appear for a brief period of time before quickly disappearing'. The 1939 regulations had little more to add to the above targets other than the issue of pairing – the 1942 regulations noting for example the importance of camouflage and the need for patience in waiting for a suitable target – 'sometimes for a number of hours' before striking and then moving position.[25] Snipers would play an important role in the Red Army throughout the remainder of the war – as indeed would their German counterparts. The activities of snipers would be a daily menace for troops who got used to stooping as they made their way around positions so that they would not become victim to a sniper's bullet. Lieutenant Gottlob Herbert Bidermann, serving with 132nd Infantry Division below Leningrad, describes in his memoirs how snipers from both sides typically 'engaged each other in deadly duels' – the absence of Soviet snipers in this particular instance in mid-1943 being taken as indicative that a Soviet attack was about to start.[26] The significance of snipers is highlighted by their numbers. After the end of the Stalingrad fighting on 3 February 1943 many rifle divisions of 62nd and 64th Armies would have upwards of forty-eight snipers – and as many as ninety-eight.[27] On 12 July 1943 the General Staff ordered the provision of 1,200 snipers for 52nd Army – 174 per division.[28] Sniper Mikhail Fomich Chechetov served with 1st Belorussian Front towards the end of the war, and in an interview first published in May 2014 describes his training and subsequent activities as a sniper and the sort of sniper-sniper engagement noted by Bidermann above taking place now in Germany in early 1945. 'Kills' were to be carefully recorded in one of two pocket books provided, in this case in the one with the title 'Hunting [*Na okhotu*]' – the second book for recording observations on enemy positions. Chechetov recorded twelve such 'kills' as a sniper.[29]

'Storm groups' were another component of Soviet urban warfare practice that seem to have been systematically used for the first time during the fighting for Stalingrad, and that also decentralised command and control along with providing greater scope for meaningful combined arms warfare further down the chain of command than had previously been the norm. Certainly in the section on fighting in urban areas in the

1936 field regulations meaningful decentralisation of command and control down to company level and below – as would be the case with the employment of 'storm groups' – was not highlighted. Although in PU-36 there was indeed talk of 'small detachments' operating along streets, the principal strength of forces engaged of undisclosed but probably at least of battalion size 'advanced through allotments, parks and across yards'. Support was to be provided by heavy artillery, where there was supposed to be a Infantry Communications Section [OSP] for the artillery with the infantry – and the infantry were to be provided support not only from heavy infantry weapons and individual pieces of artillery, but also sappers with explosives and a 'plentiful [*obil'no*] supply of hand grenades'. On the defence strongpoints were to be created – and in particular at road junctions 'mutually flanking strong points' were to be constructed – and counterattacks launched 'from neighbouring sectors' to regain lost positions. PU-36 highlighted that the destruction meted out by heavy artillery and aviation was the 'basis of success' on the attack in built up areas – not fire support combined with the effective small-unit combined arms approach that not only the Red Army would find out was required to flush the enemy out of the rubble.[30] The tone of instructions for attacking in built up areas issued in this particular instance by 47th Army on 28 December 1942 is somewhat different to the general guidelines in PU-36, with not only emphasis on reconnaissance by combined-arms groups of reinforced company through to battalion strength with the potential to take advantage of enemy weakness and gain ground, but also the acknowledgement that 'fighting for a population centre typically breaks down into a number of isolated local battles for the possession of strongpoints and cornerstones of the defence. The result of combat is decided by the persistence, initiative and skillful and audacious actions of even small subunits'. With fire support over open sights (and not indirect fire by grid once friendly forces were in the area) for the attack on strongpoints within a population centre an infantry regimental commander was to 'organise storm groups from the infantry (up to platoon strength), sappers with explosives, individual artillery pieces, flamethrowers and tanks'. Movement was not only to be across 'parks, gardens [*ogorodi*] and yards' but also through breaches in walls, with tanks accompanied by small infantry sub units to advance along the streets. Infantry equipped with SMGs were to be 'particularly actively utilised', infiltrating behind enemy fortified positions.[31] On the defence a strongpoint was to be typically defended by a reinforced platoon capable of resisting for a prolonged period in isolation from the remainder of a battalion that would counterattack with available reserves.[32] The phrasing here is similar to that in the infantry field manual of 1942.[33]

Vasilii Chuikov, commander of 62nd Army fighting in Stalingrad, in his memoirs lays some claim to the development of storm groups, noting how in response to the specific circumstances encountered in an urban environment:

A military subdivision – the storm group – was created, adapted for the conduct of fighting in an urban environment. Each time they were formed depending on the object under attack and available strength and resources. ... A storm group usually consisted of a platoon or company of infantry (from 20 to 40 riflemen), backed up by 2–3 artillery pieces for direct fire support and 1–2 sections of sappers and chemical troops. All of the troops were provided with sub-machine guns and with large numbers of hand grenades.[34]

Particularly striking perhaps was the decentralisation of artillery. Although Chuikov ignores the use of heavy artillery in a direct fire role in the war with Finland, he was nonetheless correct to stress that the breaking up of artillery batteries for use in a direct fire support role was not typical practice for Soviet units. He notes the particular example of 39th Guards Rifle Division, which:

In the fighting for the 'Red October' Factory used artillery pieces of even 203-mm calibre in a direct fire role from 200–300 metres. If our artillerymen had said earlier, that such powerful artillery would be used in such a manner, they would not have been believed.[35]

Although in the city itself Soviet forces had few tanks, when appropriately protected tanks were also identified by Chuikov as a valuable component to the small unit tactics that were being developed.[36] Here although tanks were, as many analyses of German failures highlight, particularly vulnerable and certainly in the German case of less operational value in the city than outside it, they nonetheless added an important anti-infantry capability to combined arms units. Certainly Chuikov highlights the problems that German armour provided for the defenders.[37] Understandably, commanders of armoured units and formations were less positive above the deployment of their vehicles in the city – the commander of the German 24th Panzer Division was critical of 'the practice of detaching his tanks for use as assault guns to support infantry assaults, claiming 'this unintelligible practice' led to 'completely useless casualties'. On 14 October 1942 24th Panzer Division was able to field 33 tanks – only six Panzer IV with the most useful armament in the form of the long or short barrelled 75 mm gun. By 19 October 24th Panzer Division could field only three Panzer IV.[38] The fact that German forces were advancing and relatively efficient battlefield recovery would nonetheless mean that operational strength would increase again. In both the German and Soviet cases the fighting for Stalingrad, and other urban areas, prompted the development – or in the German case up-armouring and up-gunning – of assault guns, in the early development of which the Soviet Union had participated and then dropped. During 1941, 57 mm anti-tank guns mounted on artillery tractors served with tank brigades during the battle for Moscow but did not continue in production, and it would be late 1942 before the Red Army embraced new models initially for direct support of the infantry. In November 1942 the Board for Mechanised Towing and Self-Propelled Artillery was formed under the auspices of the Main Artillery Directorate and would oversee the introduction of the first self-propelled artillery regiments from the end of the year, initially equipped with light SU-76 self-propelled guns on the same chassis as the T-70 light tank, but also SU-122 guns with a low velocity 122 mm piece on the T-34 chassis. At the same time during early 1943 the development of a self-propelled 152-mm gun-howitzer on the KV-series chassis was underway and that would be seen in small numbers during the summer of 1943. All of these were initially intended for infantry support, to be followed later that year by self-propelled guns – initially the SU-85 essentially mounting the Soviet 85 mm anti-aircraft gun – intended to engage enemy tanks.[39] Given the proximity of much of the fighting in the autumn to the Volga River, armoured fire support could also be provided to Soviet units by *bronekateri* or armoured launches, some of which were sufficiently substantial to mount 76 mm guns, and which could 'quickly appear where infantry required support from the river'.[40]

The fighting for the city of Stalingrad was as is apparent from material presented earlier and elsewhere, intense, and saw increasing German resources sucked into the fighting from outside the city. Fighting was however of course not only taking place inside the city, but also across vast expanses of steppe outside it, as Leonid Fialkovskii describes in his memoir apparently based on a diary of the period written with considerable risk in contravention of rules on the matter. On the periphery of the Stalingrad battle to the south, on the edge of that region for which a front line is typically provided on maps of the battle, 254th Tank Brigade fought Rumanian and German forces on the edge of the Kalmyk steppe. Fialkovskii, then a *feld'sher*, describes the penetration of his rather understrength brigade into the enemy rear in late September 1942, where initially they were opposed by Rumanian forces against which some success was achieved in the ebbe and flow of fighting in the region.[41] Prior to the mid-November counteroffensive, there were many attempts to relieve pressure on the defenders of the city by launching attacks outside it – many of which were hurriedly organised and seemed to squander resources for little noticeable gain. Major Petr Zayonchkovsky was part of 66th Army thrown into fighting to the north of the city in

September 1942. In fighting beginning on 5 September 'our assault, which lasted eight days and cost us heavy casualties, did not result in any real successes. ... We lost nearly all our tanks and a great number of men'. Attacking 'without any intel on the terrain' his unit attacked the day after it arrived at the front where some of the troops involved had just marched from Saratov.[42] Rokossovskii's Don Front was ordered on 15 October 1942 at 05:23 to prepare for an attack towards the city in the direction of Orlovka with a view to linking up with the defenders and indeed destroying German forces in the Orlovka area. Given the urgency of the situation within the city, the plan was to be ready for 23:15 that night.[43] A plan was submitted to Zhukov that day at around 19:45 for an attack on 20 October primarily by 66th Army using four fresh rifle divisions along with a number of other divisions and units that had already been worn down in recent fighting – nine rifle divisions of 66th Army being noted as being of only battalion strength. In terms of armour, 66th Army was provided with three tank brigades (64th, 91st and 121st) that were to be fully equipped by the start of the operation, although 58th Tank Brigade of 66th Army would be of little value being down to eight tanks with no prospect of replacements before the operation was to begin. Frontal air power at the time consisted of sixty-five fighters, eighty ground attack aircraft and sixty light night bombers [nochniki] – deemed 'an insufficient number' by Rokossovskii and his staff.[44] By the night of 16 October – a response provided by 03:00 – the plan had been sanctioned with minor alterations, although 'given the deteriorating situation in Stalingrad' the attack was to be launched on the morning of 19 rather than 20 October.[45] In his memoirs, Rokossovskii suggests that given the strength of the Don Front at the time, even with a total of seven new rifle divisions, without 'any sort of additional reinforcement (artillery, tanks, aircraft)' it was 'difficult to count on success' against a well fortified enemy. Not all of the fresh division had arrived by the start of the operation, and Rokossovskii was apparently only too pleased to be able to place the late arrivals in reserve for more productive use later. As for the operation that started on 19 October, 'as was expected, the attack was unsuccessful', although it did pin German forces in the area.[46] Certainly, as David Glantz notes, these counterattacks did contribute 'markedly to the effort to pin down the invaders and bleed them white', further noting that when the commander of the German 6th Army Paulus 'traded' divisions and regiments from Stalingrad for those on the flanks, the new units had 'only marginally more combat power than those they had replaced'.[47]

At the time during which much German armoured strength was bogged down in the city of Stalingrad weak German armoured and motorised forces continued to be operationally successful in more suitable terrain not only to the south of the city where 254th Tank Brigade was operating, but further to the south east towards Astrakhan. In fighting reminiscent of North Africa the German 16th Motorized Infantry Division fought the Soviet 28th Army in the vast expanses of the Kalmyk steppe.[48] Less suited to the sort of mobile warfare at which the Wehrmacht excelled were the Caucasus mountains, which should have offered better defensive possibilities for the Red Army. However, as Tiulenev and Stavka documents testify, the Red Army failed to take advantage of terrain and units ostensibly trained and equipped for it. To start with, it didn't help that Soviet forces were poorly provided for with maps of the region – in his memoirs Tiulenev noting how Soviet forces were unfamiliar with the main Caucasus mountain range, 'which we had to study from inadequate descriptions [*skudnim opisaniam*] and outdated, very much imprecise maps'.[49] The mapping of internal districts of the Soviet Union even in 1:100,000 scale had been ordered only in July 1941, supposedly for completion by the end of the year for territory as far east as the Volga. The quality of the result was undoubtedly poor, and 1:50,000 scale maps that would have been far more useful were provided simply by enlarging available 1:100,000 scale maps.[50] Fortunately, given the absence of up-to-date maps in many instances and Soviet secrecy, German and Axis forces were also poorly provided for in this regard – picking up a Michelin guide was not an option in the Caucasus as it might have been in France!

Soviet forces undoubtedly performed poorly during the early stages of the battle for the Caucasus – not helped by lack of knowledge of much of the terrain over which they were fighting. As Tiulenev himself admits, during the initial fighting in the region, 'We allowed a lot of tactical mistakes because the mountain troops that, as is well known, we had prepared in peacetime had been in the main transferred to other fronts and units and formations tasked with the defence of mountain passes were not trained for mountain warfare'. Poor reconnaissance was once again a problem for Soviet forces, and meant that 'frequently we launched frontal assaults, and not on the flanks, that is particularly ruinous in mountain warfare'. Failure to occupy the heights led to the undermining of defence of mountain passes – that were initially poorly defended. All of these together led to 'tragic results'.[51] As Tiulenev acknowledges, it was the Stavka that insisted on better defence of the key mountain passes, for example issuing a directive on 20 August 1942 that called for a strengthening of the defence of the main principal range [*khrebet*] of the Caucasus Mountains that was apparently seen by some commanders as a natural barrier to the enemy that didn't need much defending.[52] Despite initial German successes in the mountains and indeed along the coastline of the Black Sea, German strength in the region was insufficient to break through to Baku, and indeed the German advance had stalled by early November – as it might have earlier had the Soviet defence been better thought out. Nonetheless, German progress was even by August slowing – with stubborn Soviet defence along the in many places wide and fast flowing Terek River for example slowing German armoured forces down in late August as they threatened to break through to the oilfields in the Groznii and Bakinsk districts.[53] During fighting in the Mozdok area at this time German forces encountered a number of Soviet armoured trains, and this is an ideal point therefore to briefly comment on one element of the Soviet armoured forces as yet unmentioned.[54] Armoured trains had proven of considerable value to the Bolsheviks during the Russian Civil War, and continued to serve with the Red Army through the Great Patriotic War, although in a direct ground combat role were perhaps better suited to the early phases of the war where the armours of the heavier trains were still meaningful when matched with contemporary tank guns for example. In the Soviet-era version of his memoirs Ivan Tiulenev describes the engagement of 20th Independent Heavy Armoured Train with German armour on 23 August 1942 as it covered the retreat of troops from the Rostov Artillery School across to the southern bank of the Terek River not far from Mozdok. In what was clearly an unequal engagement, and where most armoured trains were better suited to providing indirect fire support rather than directly engaging enemy armour, Soviet accounts claim four-six German tanks knocked out but with the train taking heavy damage.[55] As for German forces, Soviet armoured trains would nonetheless throughout the war provide a useful means to rapidly move limited artillery and anti-aircraft assets in support of ground forces and particularly in defence of or in order to seize railway infrastructure.[56]

Returning to events further north, although according to both Vasilevskii and Zhukov planning for a major counteroffensive near Stalingrad had started in mid-September, it is quite possible that as, David Glantz suggests, any offensive plans at this stage being considered had more modest goals than Operation 'Uranus' would eventually have. Certainly by mid-September the fact that German forces and particularly mechanised forces were concentrated on Stalingrad itself was plain, and as Glantz suggests 'all of the Stavka's offensive planning focused strictly on the need to delay Army Group B's advance and prevent 6th Army from capturing Stalingrad'.[57] It is difficult to believe that at this point any serious consideration for what would become Operation 'Uranus' was taking place. Zhukov was until 26 September present in the Stalingrad region and involved in the planning of counterattacks that in keeping with what had happened before Moscow did slow down German forces but were far too numerous and hurriedly organised, and hit far too significant concentrations of German forces close to the city to make much headway. Although the scope for launching a successful major operation from the north against well entrenched troops in order to trap substantial German forces and link up with the Stalingrad defenders was apparently deemed limited by Zhukov – and noted by Rokossovskii – this did not prevent Rokossovskii's forces of the recently formed Don Front being thrown into the attack close to Stalingrad near Orlovka in mid-October, but according to Zhukov the failure of this attack also prompted planning for operations on the flanks that would develop into Operation 'Uranus'.[58] A proposal in early October for offensive operations by commander of the Stalingrad Front, Eremenko, had suggested striking weaker enemy forces on the flanks and operations on similar axes to those of Operation 'Uranus', although the forces proposed for commitment were considerably weaker and more cavalry-focused than those that would ultimately be committed on 19 November. In fact, reading Eremenko's proposal it is apparent that what he was proposing was more akin to the sort of deep raids that had also been launched near Moscow the previous year than an attempt to encircle and destroy 6th Army and much of 4th Panzer Army, and was proposed for later that same month.[59] It is however quite probable that Eremenko's proposal, along with Rokossovskii's concerns about attacking closer to Stalingrad contributed to the development of Operation 'Uranus'. Detailed plans for Operation 'Uranus' that did indeed aim for a major encirclement and the destruction of sizeable Axis forces after Soviet forces had broken through weaker Axis defences further out from Stalingrad than had been the focus to date were finally presented to Stalin by Zhukov and Chief of the General Staff Vasilevskii on 13 October. This meeting – and Stalin's apparent satisfaction with what had been planned – is described in Zhukov's memoirs.[60] These plans did not however, mean that the Stavka would give up on plans for the Don Front to attack that same month closer to Stalingrad, an attack further discussed later.

Operation 'Uranus' was ultimately to be launched on 19 November rather than 9 November as initially planned, in the light of the difficulty of amassing and deploying significant forces in a region that was not particularly well served by good roads and railways, after what was eventually up to an unprecedented two months of preparation if we accept Zhukov's claims – and certainly more than a month.[61] For Operation 'Uranus' the Soviet high command had amassed considerable resources, including concentrated armour, on the weak flanks of the predominately German forces fighting for the city of Stalingrad itself. According to the Russian historian Zhilin and his colleagues, along with ten combined-arms or infantry-focused armies the Red Army could dispose of a tank army and three air armies – a total of sixty-seven rifle divisions, four tank corps, two mechanised corps, three cavalry corps, fifteen rifle brigades, fourteen tank brigades and three motor rifle brigades along with other units. On the principle axes of attack the Red Army would enjoy an overall at least 2:1 advantage, sometimes 3:1 depending on measure and location. The plan – not appearing in published documents as a single document – was essentially that Soviet forces from the north-west and south-east of the city would encircle German forces in and around Stalingrad by linking up in the Kalach area to the south of the city and constituting an inner encirclement, with a wider outer encirclement preceding the final destruction of the 6th Army and much of 4th Panzer Army in the pocket.[62] On these flanks, Germany's poorly equipped allies with some German support defended often open steppe with some success against Soviet infantry attacks, but certainly lacked the resources to contain mechanised forces thrown in with any resolve. As Richard L. DiNardo notes in his study of the Axis alliance, Germany went into the summer campaign of 1942 with 'a group of allied armies that were sadly deficient in material. Moreover, the Germans were well aware of this'. German promises of the sort of equipment that might have made allied troops more capable of taking on the Red Army, and particularly its armour, 'far exceeded its deliveries'. With only limited mobility, and lacking reserves, the Rumanian 3rd Army for example fielded predominately 37 and 47 mm anti-tank guns that could take on at least part of the Soviet tank park with some success the previous year, but not the T-34 and KV-1s that were now the predominate types. A Rumanian division could, at best, field six potent German 75 mm anti-tank guns, 'a situation that aroused even Hitler's concern'. With the availability of only a few radios hampering command and control, 'constant Soviet probing attacks' made the stockpiling of ammunition for a major battle impossible.[63]

Soviet resources for Operation 'Uranus' included the new mechanised corps, one of which was to be incorporated into each of the ten tank armies ordered to be formed from January 1943.[64] These mechanised corps were first formed as a result of an NKO decree of 8 September 1942, and were undoubtedly a response to the poor showing of the tank corps and tank armies during the spring and summer of 1942 where although they fielded large numbers of tanks the provision of infantry support for these tanks was poor and they had soon got bogged down without having penetrated into the enemy rear. Varying in organisation, the basic principle behind the mechanised corps and their constituent mechanised brigades was to shift the emphasis towards mechanised infantry with strong armoured support compared to the tank corps and brigades for which the reverse was the case. By 1 January 1943 six mechanized corps had been formed.[65] 1st Mechanised Corps was formed from 1st Guards Rifle Division, with the corps to have a personnel strength of 17,437 men – with a full range of supporting units. Three mechanised brigades of just under 4,000 men in each and each incorporating a tank regiment would have the support of two further tank regiments, a guards artillery regiment, anti-tank *divizion*, anti-aircraft regiment, a *divizion* of M-13 RS or 'Katiushas' and machine-gun, sapper, communications, field repair, supply cart and medical battalions – not forgetting a training battalion, field bakery and mobile repair shop. Troops for the unit, as the formation of the corps from 1st Guards Rifle Division suggests, were supposed to be 'suitable' for service in a Guards formation whether they be taken from field units or the training system.[66] As the tank brigades, the mechanised brigades were used outside the mechanised or tank corps structure. The Stalingrad Front was for example sent three mechanised brigades (17th, 61st and 62nd) on 1 November 1942.[67] The 17th Mechanised Brigade was identified by German intelligence as located in reserve south-west of Stalingrad on 18 November.[68] According to a decree of the People's Commissar for Defence of 16 October 1942 on the battlefield use of tank and mechanised units and formations, the mechanised corps was 'a resource for the commander of a front or army' for use 'on the principal axis as an echelon for development of successes...and pursuit of the enemy' – a formation that was 'able to achieve offensive goals independently against an enemy who has failed to fortify himself'. The mechanised corps were therefore to be used for the development of a breakthrough 'after the penetration of the principal enemy defensive belt by general formations and where infantry have reached the area in which enemy artillery positions are located'. The document makes it plain – suggesting that this was often not the case – that mechanised corps were not to be broken up and parcelled out.The tank corps were also for deployment in the exploitation of a breakthrough, but with the 'task of delivering a massive blow with the aim of breaking up and encircling the principal grouping of enemy forces and its destruction in co-operation with aviation and other ground forces of the front'.[69]

By now Red Army units were starting to receive infantry weapons such as the PTRD anti-tank rifle and PPSh sub-machine gun in far more meaningful numbers than had been the case at the beginning of the year despite fictional list strengths that suggested that they should already have had them then. Such weapons – just like the tanks – were gradually being employed *en masse* alongside other weapons such as flamethrowers. Where tank armies and air armies represented concentration of armour and aircraft, the SMG companies and battalions and flamethrower battalions saw concentrated of considerable firepower for the infantry assault as the Red Army approached the peak of its mid-war obsession with the concentration of individual weapons systems and types. As early as the spring of 1942 infantry commander Petr Bograd recalls his battalion being equipped primarily with the PPSh SMG, with a light machine gun in each section and a heavy machine gun and mortar company with 82 mm mortars – along with an anti-tank platoon with three 45 mm guns for the battalion.[70] Such concentration at this stage might have meant shortages elsewhere – Mikhail Suknev's division had as already noted in early 1942 apparently lacked SMGs – and indeed only had two PTRD for the infantry battalion.[71] Nonetheless, the trend was alongside concentration of such weapons in specific units and formations such as the 'shock' forces that would lead the assault, for their wider general availability as well. By 23 May 1943 it was probably realistic for the Stavka to order that every rifle company in a rifle division or brigade have one of its platoons armed solely with SMGs, with SMGs being provided to command elements from section and above.[72] A further example here of the concentration of a particular weapon would be the formation from independent flame-thrower companies of independent flame thrower battalions in both motorised and non-motorised variants. The latter, horse-drawn version, consisted of three flamethrower companies with 216 flamethrowers in each, supported by 363 rifles and SMGs.[73] As the case of the flamethrower battalions highlights however, this concentration differed from pre-war gigantism in that more attention was paid to providing supporting arms in circumstances where the tendency was very much as the war progressed to move towards mass deployment of a given weapon or system with support, before the supporting multi-arm component became the focus with support from significant concentration of a specific weapon or system as in the case of the mechanised corps.

The success of Operation 'Uranus' has been extremely well documented in other works, and the aim of this work is not simply to repeat material readily available elsewhere. David Glantz's recent Stalingrad 'trilogy' provides considerable detail on the course of 'Uranus'.[74] The success of 'Uranus' was not just due to the concentration of Soviet resources for the offensive, but also the fact that German forces had made few preparations to deal with such a possibility. Prior to the operation, although there were strong indicators from frontline Axis units of the impending Soviet offensive, by the time it had struck little had been done to meet it.[75] Soviet *maskirovka* undoubtedly played its part here, as did radio discipline and other discipline such as not engaging in the practice common early in the war for infantry units to fire on enemy aircraft with their small arms – for which infantryman Sergei Drobiazko was chided by his company commander in 1942 after he had tried to shoot down a German aircraft with an anti-tank rifle![76] By late 1942 Soviet forces were also generally, and certainly prior to 'Uranus', paying more attention to reconnaissance, although the nature of Soviet reconnaissance practices often still differed greatly from those of their opponents and indeed the Western allies. Whilst observation did play a role in Soviet reconnaissance, overall Soviet reconnaissance was still much more aggressive than that conducted by other powers. Hence, although frontline Soviet forces were provided with aircraft for the purpose of tactical and operational reconnaissance, as Zhukov notes in his memoirs far too little attention was paid to aerial reconnaissance. Although the VVS did carry out reconnaissance missions deeper into the German rear, according to Zhukov Stalin was unwilling to invest in the sort of dedicated reconnaissance aircraft - and particularly photoreconnaissance assets – deployed by other powers. Aerial reconnaissance was more likely to be used to confirm information from other sources rather than as a starting point. Human intelligence from agents and the partisan movement on German occupied territory was by late 1942 starting to be of some importance partly because reconnaissance had been identified as a core task of the partisan movement, and partly because partisans were more likely to be able to communicate intelligence by radio back to Soviet lines by this point than during 1941 and early 1942. Despite the paucity of radios for communication available to Soviet forces early in the war, radio interception was of some significance in Soviet intelligence efforts. Similarly, observation by frontline units was also important, be it for the identification of enemy positions prior to an offensive or the location of German artillery batteries for their suppression prior to an offensive or broader counterbattery work. At times of course documents of intelligence value would fall into Soviet hands through enemy error, where for example navigation issues on the part of a German pilot led to the shooting down of a German aircraft carrying two officers with plans in the south in June 1942. These captured documents gave the Soviet command at least indication to expect German offensive operations in the south in the short term regardless of German activity elsewhere, even if the result of the capture of this material might actually have reinforced belief that German forces were actually likely to focus their attention on Moscow.[77] Documents were of course seized during operations, and both partisans and frontline reconnaissance forces both engaged in raids with the intention of seizing documents, prisoners and other sources of information. Soviet and German accounts suggest particular persistence and success in seizing prisoners or 'tongues', with commander of the German IX Corps near Belgorod during the summer of 1943 Colonel General Erhard Raus describing how persistence in the 'kidnapping' of German sentries of 320th Infantry Division at night no doubt aided the Red Army in building up a picture of the strength of their defences along the Donets River.[78] Such raids were hardly exclusively Soviet, but Soviet practice and that of Germany and the Western Allies started to differ significantly when it came to such active reconnaissance – sending troops behind enemy lines for the purpose of seizing prisoners and documents, and identifying reserves for example. Active reconnaissance that would see Soviet forces deliberately engage in combat in order to gain intelligence seems to have been the predominant form of tactical reconnaissance for the Red Army even during the middle period of the war. The second issue of the Soviet General Staff 'Collection of Tactical Examples based on Experience during the Great Patriotic War' concerned with tactical reconnaissance issued in May–June 1943 notes in its introduction how Soviet reconnaissance forces were all too often unwilling to utilise 'cunning and concealment' in their reconnaissance activities, and all too frequently showing a lack of discipline and restraint in the use of firearms for example. Nonetheless, the publication then went on to spend the first section on the employment of ambush, often behind enemy lines, as a means not only to destroy enemy resources but also seize documents and prisoners.[79] These reconnaissance activities were often belated, and as has already been noted earlier in the war, all but ceased once offensive operations were underway, by which point specialist reconnaissance assets were very much secondary to frontline units that would provide information on the enemy by engaging them – often with unnecessary losses. In his memoirs Ivan Tiulenev, commander of Trans-Caucasian Front, prints a document provided to senior commanders of the front of May 1942 in which he notes German practice at the time as:

Throwing reconnaissance parties into our rear to a depth of 15–20 km, consisting of a number of armoured cars with infantry. These parties are provided for with radio transmitters. Halting somewhere in deep forest, they put up their antennas on important roads and relay information on troops movements.[80]

German reconnaissance units, and particularly those of the armoured and mechanized units, were equipped with armoured half-tracked vehicles and armoured cars for the purpose of reconnaissance, where their light armament and armour were not supposed to be the means to fight for reconnaissance but to enable units to disengage and defend themselves when discovered and engaged. Such units performed reconnaissance functions during offensive operations, and still did not have obvious Soviet equivalents where the Red Army lacked suitable vehicles for the purpose and indeed the appropriate culture. During the early period of the war the Soviet regime had all but given up on the production of armoured cars, and had lacked armoured personnel carriers from the outset. As significant however was a culture that soldiers fight – the glory being in killing enemy soldiers and destroying material assets – rather than creeping around avoiding the enemy. Only during the final phases of the war would there be evidence of a change of culture and the resources to conduct tactical reconnaissance during offensive operations and particularly after breakthrough in the manner that the Wehrmacht, and for that matter the British, conducted it.

Operation 'Uranus' was finally launched on 19 November, with the Stalingrad Front joining in on 20 November. Despite local setbacks, by 23 November Soviet forces of the Stalingrad and Don Fronts had linked up at Kalach and the race was then on to thicken the encirclement and prevent either those forces within the Stalingrad pocket escaping or those outside breaking through to the defenders.[81] Hitler's insistence on – and the German commander of 6th Army's acquiescence in – the decision to hold Stalingrad, await relief and receive supplies by air certainly played into Soviet hands, where despite a far from perfect supply situation many of the more mobile assets in the pocket might have broken out had then done so promptly. Leaving less mobile forces behind would have been bad for morale, and the fact that 6th Army had sent most of its horses outside the city would have severely hampered a wider withdrawal.[82] Still, the defence of the Stalingrad pocket did tie down sizeable Soviet forces, and it is certainly possible to argue that the stubborn defence of the pocket saved Army Group A in the Caucasus.

In the light of the stunning success of 'Uranus', the Stavka had planned not only to reduce the Stalingrad pocket to free up those forces involved in containing it, but also to launch an even more ambitious operation, 'Saturn' to destroy German and Italian forces to the north-west of Stalingrad along the Don and Chir Rivers and ultimately cut off the German Army Group A in the Caucasus through an thrust in the direction of Rostov.[83] Given that at the same time significant operations were taking place against the German Army Group Centre as well – to be discussed later – it is possible to argue that at the end of 1942 Stalin and the Soviet high command were engaging in the sort of wishful thinking that had led to the snowballing of offensive operations and over commitment of late 1941 and early 1942. Certainly many factors were now more in Soviet favour in the circumstances of late 1942 than the same time the year before – German forces were now at the end of even more stretched supply lines, and the Soviet material resource situation had improved considerably as Soviet industry recovered from relocation of much of its plant. Overall, the Soviet Union was now receiving more significant assistance from its allies than it had the previous year despite the temporary cessation of convoys in the north after the PQ17 debacle. In fact, halting the shipment of aid to the Soviet Union via Iran was of sufficient significance for Germany for it to be asserted as a justification for preparations to be made for the transfer of German light naval forces to the Caspian Sea, where they would harass 'oil tankers and communications with the Anglo-Saxons in Iran'.[84] There was not a meaningful 'Second Front' in the West, but German airpower in particular was being drawn away from the Eastern Front to face British and American forces, where for example in Tunisia 250 Ju 52 transport aircraft were committed that might have made some difference at Stalingrad if their commitment could have been sustained logistically.[85]

The success of 'Uranus' and eventually the destruction of the resulting Stalingrad pocket through Operation 'Kol'tso' was certainly assisted by the resurgence of the VVS, although important in the increased importance of the VVS was the relative decline of the German Luftwaffe that was now being stretched more thinly on the Eastern Front in part because of Allied activity elsewhere. At the beginning of the war the VVS was suffering from a wide range of problems that limited its ability to provide the sort of support expected of it in pre-war doctrine – and which the Luftwaffe seemed to provide the Wehrmacht. As has been mentioned earlier, at the tactical level problems for the VVS were many and varied – from poor pilot training and increasingly outdated aircraft being at best replaced by next generation aircraft plagued by design issues and teething troubles, to cumbersome units and poor communications not allowing the desired degree of flexibility in deployment. At the operational level the concentration of airpower in order to actually make a difference where it mattered had been clearly identified as an issue by the Soviet military leadership, as had the sort of command-and-control problems that plagued all of the Soviet armed forces at almost every level. In March 1942 air forces commander Pavel Zhigarev, had for example in a note to Stalin called for the concentration of airpower in large formations under the VVS command and the Stavka rather than armies and fronts, to then be committed *en masse*.[86] By late 1942 and early 1943 many of these issues were however being addressed. Where even during the summer of 1941 the VVS had never completely disappeared from the skies – and as German memoirs suggest provided regular harassment for German forces – by early 1943 the VVS was able to interdict German resupply of the Stalingrad garrison by air and make its presence felt in more than the isolated incidents in which that had been the case during the summer of 1941.

Although VVS pilot losses during the summer of 1941 had been far lower than aircraft losses, many of these pilots were poorly trained despite exhortations for the improvement of training prior to the war. The testimony of Sergei Dmitrievich Gorelov, in June 1941 a pilot with 165th Fighter Air Regiment, highlights the extent to which the VVS lagged behind the Luftwaffe. Although the training schools turned out large numbers of pilots their flying skills were often rudimentary. Having theoretically progressed from the U-2 to I-5 and I-15 in flight school, Gorelov notes that upon graduation at the beginning of the summer of 1940 after a year and a half rather than two years training he in fact 'other than being able to take off and land couldn't do very much at all'. Moving from the I-153 to I-16 with 165th Fighter Air Regiment prior to the war, after the war had broken out Gorelov converted to the LaGG-3 with about twelve hours flight time on the new aircraft. Soon he was escorting Il-2 ground attack aircraft, despite the fact that in 1941 'we neither possessed the theory or practice for escorting ground attack aircraft'. At this time Gorelov suggests that he was unable either to shoot effectively or manoeuvre – with defending the ground attack aircraft being more about frightening the enemy off and getting between them and the ground attack aircraft than effectively engaging them. Any sort of co-operation in the air was hampered by poor communications, with improvement only coming in 1943. In 1941 as Gorelov notes, it was all too easy to lose contact with the camouflaged ground attack aircraft they were supposed to be protecting. 'Only after Stalingrad' Gorelov notes, was he really capable of either evading the enemy or destroying him, by which time he had received additional training as well as survived to benefit from his own experiences.[87] As Von Hardesty and Ilia Grinberg note, by early 1943 new arrivals to 4th Air Army fighting over the Kuban would benefit from 'a realistic training program – one forged in the context of battle experience. During March and April, experienced pilots instructed the new arrivals in air combat techniques', 'based on careful analysis of Luftwaffe tactics'. In fact, Von Hardesty and Ilya Grinberg go as far to suggest that the VVS 'emulated the hated but tactically and technologically superior enemy'.[88]

By the spring of 1943 not only the tactical divide between the Luftwaffe and VVS was diminishing, but also the technological gap between the two. By early 1943 new Soviet aircraft types were more than a match for their Luftwaffe equivalents and revised organisational structures and improved command, control and communications were starting to better fostered concentration of force where it mattered and tactical effectiveness. The two-seater version of the Il-2 was now somewhat better able to defend itself in the air, and new fighter types such as the La-5 gave – and particularly after initial teething troubles were ironed out – both high speed and manoeuvrability. This was the aircraft with which Gorelov's fighter regiment – now 13th Fighter Air Regiment – was provided during the summer of 1942 before it was committed near Stalingrad as part of 2nd Mixed Air Corps. During 1942 Aircraft Factory Number 21 would produce more than 1,100 of this aircraft – and more than 4,600 the following year. At the end of the war the La-7 development of the La-5 would undoubtedly rival any piston-engined aircraft the Luftwaffe could field.[89] These new types were this point concentrated in air corps and air armies that replaced the army and front-level aviation that was supposed to have fostered better co-ordination with ground forces, but had in fact for example led to the sort of dissipation of resources that as Gorelov suggests from ground level often left the VVS tactically outnumbered. Whether the parcelling out of aircraft to fronts and armies actually hindered tactical concentration as much as Soviet historians suggest is debateable, although it certainly played a part along with extremely poor communications in preventing the VVS from delivering the sort of massive air strikes that the Luftwaffe had regularly inflicted on the Red Army that could have meaningful impact on the outcome of operations on the ground. The two fighter air armies formed during the summer of 1942 were intended to allow the VVS to gain a significant advantage in the air on key axes, but were now made up of smaller and it was assumed tactically more flexible tactical components where fighter air regiments were now half the size of those of the beginning of the war.[90] After their introduction in May–June 1942 air armies were, as the Soviet historian E. Simakov notes, 'the basic operational formation of the VVS and were subordinated to commanders of fronts'. They were made up of air divisions– now consisting of a single aircraft type (bomber, ground attack aircraft or fighter) to ease servicing and repair – with each division initially consisting of two, then three and subsequently even four air regiments. Each regiment was by the autumn of 1942 supposed to be thirty-two aircraft strong (increasing to forty for ground attack aircraft during 1943), with a flight now four aircraft strong for fighters and ground attack aircraft, each flight consisting of two aircraft pairs. Even without the air reserves amassed by the Stavka, at the end of 1942 an air army 'averaged a strength of up to 400 aircraft, by mid-1943 up to 500'.[91] From the autumn of 1942 the air armies could be reinforced with air corps from Stavka reserves – similar in concept to the Shock air groups introduced in the spring of 1942 that brought together a number of air regiments and had been deployed during the Demiansk operation. During 1942 11 air corps were formed, consisting of 2–3 divisions with a list strength of between 120 and 180 aircraft, and could at this stage be single type or of mixed type – later in the war only the former. The VVS also sought to marshal air forces for meaningful activity beyond simply tactical and operational depth with the organisation in March 1942 of Long Range Aviation forces that superseded the Long-Range Bombing Aviation of the beginning of the war that had only rarely struck at enemy strategic targets. However, the VVS lacked suitable heavy aircraft – by the start of the war only 93 TB-7 heavy bombers had been built, with the TB-3 now being hopelessly outdated. Given that her allies were unwilling to provide the Soviet Union with heavy bombers that they themselves were able to use perhaps to greater effect than might have been the case by the VVS, Long Range Aviation tended to carry out the sort of interdiction and similar functions in support of ground forces to which the medium bombers provided to a significant extent by her allies were well suited.[92]

In the Stalingrad region, the VVS was by the end of 1942 making a more sustained challenge to the Luftwaffe than the last time it had really been able to do so in late 1941 near Moscow. During Soviet counter-offensive operations near Stalingrad to the three air armies involved – 8th, 16th and 17th – the Stavka added four reserve air corps of the Reserve of the Supreme High Command.[93] Although the potential significance of an air blockade of German forces in the Stalingrad pocket was perhaps not fully appreciated in late November 1942 when only a single fighter and a ground-attack regiment were allocated to aerial interception and the destruction of transports on the ground by 16th Air Army by order of commander of the VVS General A.A. Novikov, in early December far more significant resources started to be committed in a systematic manner to the task.[94] Although as Hayward notes, the primary inhibitor to the German airlift in support of 6th Army was the weather – and soon the loss of airfields – VVS fighters 'succeeded in destroying a relatively small but steady number' of German transport aircraft.[95] The primary inhibitor to Soviet interception was arguably not the Luftwaffe later in the Stalingrad campaign, where as a Luftwaffe officer noted in a post-war US-sponsored study, during the battle for Stalingrad 'the Russian fighter arm achieved absolute air superiority for the first time, especially after the German fighters could no longer provide air cover above the pocket because of the excessive distances from their air bases'. German transport aircraft were forced initially to try to slip into the pocket in small groups with little hope of survival if actually intercepted, before any flying in daylight even by lone aircraft was too dangerous. Even if some aircraft still got through, Soviet fighter 'interference', as Schwabedissen notes, was by January 1943 causing 'intolerable' cumulative losses.[96] Certainly, the VVS still had a long way to go in terms of command and control to be able to respond to the still inadequate reconnaissance efforts – where for example during 1942 units and formations of frontline aviation as a whole received a total of only 124 ground radio sets – compared to 698 the following year.[97] The VVS was a long way from the sort of taxi-rank approach to ground support that was more feasible by the end of the war, and where as Soviet historian Mikriukov notes during the Stalingrad counteroffensive ground support was limited to relatively small numbers of aircraft being committed to attacks on enemy defensive positions close to the frontline.[98]

As 1942 came to a close, although the Red Army had 6th Army and elements of 4th Panzer Army still in the bag, had undermined the position of Army Group A in the Caucasus and was systematically destroying the armies of Hitler's Eastern Front allies, preventing the escape of Army Group A was beyond Soviet capabilities. Certainly given the many commitments for Soviet forces both within and beyond the region at the end of 1942 there was a renewed urgency to finally deal with the Stalingrad pocket and throw forces involved elsewhere. On 27 December 1942 a plan was submitted by the Stavka representative in the region for the final destruction of the Stalingrad pocket by the Don and Stalingrad Fronts, with an ambitious timetable that was supposed to see the complete elimination of the pocket only seven days after the provisional start date of 6 January 1943.[99]

The reduction of the pocket would, despite the supply situation within it, be a bloody affair. The 254th Tank Brigade in which *fel'dsher* Leonid Fialkovskii participated in the outer encirclement of German forces in Stalingrad as part of 51st Army and then the reduction of the Stalingrad pocket. Having functioned for weeks with only few T-40, T-60 and T-70 light tanks it received reinforcement in the form of 32 T-34 before participating in what Fialkovskii frequently reminds readers was intense fighting for the pocket during January 1943 during which the brigade advanced into Stalingrad itself. Where German forces had taken heavy losses on the offensive in the autumn, now despite the supposedly poor supply situation for German forces on the defence the Red Army took heavy losses in both men and materiel. For 26 January Fialkovskii describes heavy fighting for a railway bridge over the River Tsaritsa in fighting against the southern of now two German pockets, with the brigade having lost five tanks on the approaches to the bridge at this point. The bridge was not finally taken until 28 January as 57th Army advanced a little as 200 metres in a day on some sectors.[100] Not long after

Soviet troops amongst the ruins of Stalingrad after the German surrender on 2 February 1943. Soviet losses had been high, but the victory was significant for morale as well as militarily. (RIA Novosti #602161)

the fighting which Fialkovskii either witnessed or saw the bloody aftermath of, German forces in the Stalingrad pocket surrendered. On 2 February 1943 the Stavka representative in the region head of artillery Voronov and commander of the Don Front Rokossovskii – who had been given responsibility for the final reduction of the pocket over an embittered Eremenko whose Stalingrad Front had been disbanded – reported to the Stavka on the losses that the Axis had suffered on the surrender of the pocket. Those Axis forces 'completely destroyed and in part captured' included in addition to German and Rumanian infantry divisions and 1st Rumanian Cavalry Division, 14th, 16th and 25th Panzer Divisions. They went on to note the 'more than 91,000 prisoners taken, of whom more than 2,500 were officers and 24 generals...'.[101] Soviet losses had been far from low – victory had been won at a high price. According to G.F. Krivosheev and his colleagues the so called 'Stalingrad Strategic Defensive Operation' lasting from 17 July–18 November 1942 had cost the Red Army 323,856 irrecoverable losses out of total losses of 643,842, with the 'Stalingrad Strategic Offensive Operation' from 19 November 1942 to 2 February 1943 a further 154,885 irrecoverable losses out of total losses of 485,777. So in total the Red Army had lost – irrecoverably – approaching half a million personnel out of total losses exceeding a million.[102] For once however, these horrendous losses had led to a significant achievement – not only had the enemy advance been halted and a sizeable enemy force been destroyed in the Stalingrad region – but in the broader fighting German and allied forces had taken, and would continue to take into the spring, losses that for some of Germany's allies would be too much to bear.

18 The Wrath of the Gods

That the successful Soviet counteroffensives of the late autumn and winter of 1942 in the south – Operations 'Uranus' and what became 'Little Saturn' and associated operations – could take place at the same time as Operation 'Mars' taking place further north against the Rzhev–Viaz'ma salient, was stark evidence of the shifting resource balance in favour of the Soviet Union and of Hitler's repeated under-appreciation of Soviet strength and resilience. In fact the Red Army had been hurling troops against Army Group Centre and in particular the Rzhev–Viaz'ma salient for much of the year. In her *The Rzhev Slaughterhouse*, Svetlana Gerasimova provides an overview of the Soviet offensive operations against Army Group Centre in the region that led to staggering Soviet casualties far out of proportion to results even by Soviet standards.[1] The Rzhev–Viaz'ma Strategic Offensive Operation of 8 January–20 April 1942 was followed by the 1st Rzhev–Sichevka (Gzhatsk) Offensive from 30 July–31 September 1942 – even before the 2nd Rzhev–Sichevka Offensive Operation – Operation 'Mars' of 25 November–20 January 1943. As Gerasimova highlights, although only one of these operations subsequently received the label strategic, all three were indeed strategic in aim – to destroy the Rzhev salient and the associated threat to Moscow, and destroy as much of the German Army Group Centre as possible. The Rzhev salient would finally be re-occupied by Soviet forces in March 1943 as German forces pulled out of the salient pursued by the Red Army. The legendary Marshal Zhukov was heavily involved in the planning and execution of operations for much of the fighting as either a front commander, commander of multiple fronts or Stavka representative in the region – and as Gerasimova notes from June 1942 onwards Vasilevskii was chief of the General Staff and Konev a front commander in the region from January 1942 until the re-occupation of the salient.[2] Unsurprisingly the attention given by these prominent figures in their memoirs – and indeed the Soviet historiography – to these battles was limited, although Zhukov's memoirs do make it clear that Operation 'Mars' was a significant enough operation in the autumn of 1942 for

410

Zhukov to take responsibility for its planning. In his memoirs Zhukov presented 'Mars' as having been an operation to pin German forces that might otherwise interfere in the south – to prevent the 'transfer of units of their forces from different regions, and in part the Viaz'ma region, …once a serious situation had developed in the Stalingrad region and in the North Caucasus'.[3] Stavka documents on the operation suggest however more ambitious aims consistent with the aims of previous operations in the region. On 8 December 1942 for example, with Operation 'Mars' already bogged down, a Stavka directive in the names of Stalin and Zhukov to the commanders of the Western and Kalinin Fronts was calling for the 'destruction of the Rzhev–Sichevka–Olenino–Belii group of enemy forces by 1 January 1943'.[4] This ambitious goal was not to be achieved during an operation that highlighted many of the weaknesses that had plagued the Red Army since the beginning of the war. In his memoirs commander of the 6th Tank Corps that participated in the operation noted how:

It is not possible to fail to note the inadequacies of the corps in combat. Such was the case because it was one of the first experiences in the use of major armoured formations, and hence there were issues.

The attack was undertaken to seize fortified positions occupied by the enemy's armoured forces, in a forested and marshy area in complex meteorological conditions. Both of these factors were in the enemy's favour. On our side the necessary co-ordination with the infantry and desirable artillery and air support were lacking. The infantry lagged behind the tanks. The suppression of enemy strongpoints was poorly organised and in particular the suppression of his anti-tank resources by the artillery and aviation. The end result was, that the tank brigades suffered heavy losses.

The corps,…, lacked its own artillery with the exception of an anti-tank regiment. Our reconnaissance and communications resources were poor and this had a negative impact on command and control of our forces. Finally, the desire of the front and army commands to use the corps a number of times on the same axis and with little maneuver was not always justified by the circumstances. All of these factors made carrying out our objectives difficult.[5]

Soviet claims of superior German strength in the region were nonsense – Getman's 6th Tank Corps alone that would spearhead the eastern penetration was equipped with eighty-five T-34s prior to the battle, many recently received, with these T-34s making half of his strength.[6] The 5th and 9th Panzer Divisions operating on that sector of the front – the latter taking the lead from the former later in the battle – were on 18 November 1942 equipped with 78 and 102 operational tanks each, although it is important to note that 38 of the vehicles of the former were still Panzer II or short-barrelled 50-mm gun-armed Panzer IIIs, with

General Mud had arguably switched sides by the autumn of 1942 when the Red Army's largely horse-drawn artillery all too frequently lagged behind the even limited advances made by the infantry and armour. (RIA Novosti #90027)

56 of the vehicles of the latter similarly less than suitable for tank-tank combat against T-34s and KV-series tanks.[7] During the first day of its operations on 26 November 6th Tank Corps would lose 'half of its 170 tanks and just under half of its men' having been perhaps prematurely thrown into attempts to break through to the north-south Rzhev-Sichevka Road. On a particularly confused snow covered battlefield German troops held out in the Soviet rear preventing effective resupply and hampering target identification and fire support. Despite the fact that the artillery assets of 20th Army had been unable to move up to support the advance, Zhukov seems to have been in fine form in ordering that 6th Tank Corps press on regardless despite the lack of artillery or indeed infantry support. That the commander of 6th Tank Corps in Getman's absence, Colonel P.M. Arman insisted that the corps be resupplied before resuming the advance was understandable – as was Zhukov's desire that it press forward and take inevitable heavy losses thanks to its supply situation and lack of support. In the end 6th Tank Corps would resupply and await support – as German forces reinforced the defenders. When the attack finally resumed, David Glantz suggests that Zhukov had decided to 'renew the attack in all sectors with increased ferocity in the belief that, somewhere, German defences would crack' and that an armoured thrust by 6th Tank Corps could in the centre penetrate

Troops of 167th Rifle Regiment of 1st Guards Rifle Division of the
Western Front advance in terrain typical of much of central and northern European Russia in the autumn of 1942. The Red Army would
frequently become bogged down in fighting for such terrain during
1942 and early 1943. (RIA Novosti #297)

through to the key Rzhev–Sichevka road.[8] German defences did crack,
although they certainly did not shatter, and two out of three tank brigades
of 6th Tank Corps did make it across the road along with elements of 2nd
Guards Cavalry Corps, but sustained heavy losses in the process. Given
the battered states of 6th Tank Corps and 2nd Guards Cavalry Corps
others might have taken the decision to pull them back across the road
and admit defeat, but characteristically – sometimes successfully, often
not – Zhukov insisted that the operation continue and that the mobile
forces that had broken through continue to attempt to press forward with
the eastern wing of what was supposed to be an encirclement of German
forces in the tip of the Rzhev salient. Also not unusually, Zhukov apparently saw the continued possibility not only of success against at least part
of the salient that would render holding the salient as a whole untenable,
but also the possibility that Operation 'Jupiter' – a wider operation to
destroy much more of Army Group Centre – might succeed without
the success of the eastern penetration of the Rzhev salient. However, the
reality was that Soviet spearheads had been encircled not only on the

eastern but also western sides of the salient, with weak elements of 6th Tank Corps and 2nd Guards Cavalry Corps fighting in encirclement. Colonel Arman, commander of 6th Tank Corps, had not shown the sort of blind aggression that Zhukov demanded, and had been removed from his command – as had the commander of 20th Army.[9] With 5th Tank Corps still in reserve, and with 20th Army reinforced from neighbouring armies, in early December those elements of 6th Tank Corps not fighting in the pocket to the west were reinforced, where by 11 December according to Getman the corps now had 100 tanks – seven KV, sixty-four T-34, twelve T-70 and seventeen T-60. Although re-equipped, 22nd and 100th Tank Brigades had according to David Glantz tanks 'with barely trained tank crews to man them. Most of the new tank drivers had received fewer than five hours of driver training'. 20th Army now had a mobile group with 'a formidable total of 231 tanks'. Weakened by earlier fighting, or inexperienced, these forces were not apparently suited to 'complicated maneuvers', but could and would at Zhukov, Konev and commander of 20th Army Khozin's insistence 'attack straight ahead and *en masse*' into an enemy expecting them.[10] Overestimation of Soviet capabilities and strength, underestimation of German strength and capabilities, and the usual reliance on resolve to win through would nonetheless mean than on 20 December 1942 Operation 'Mars' would be called off and its intended significance conveniently ignored. Soviet losses had been far from trivial – David Glantz calculates losses during 'Mars' of about 100,000 killed and about 235,000 wounded that are not wildly different from German estimates of Soviet losses, giving 'Operation Mars the somewhat dubious honor of being one of the most costly Soviet offensive failures during the war'. Even before it had resumed the advance in December 6th Motor Rifle Brigade of 6th Tank Corps was down to only 170 active personnel. Tank losses had certainly been heavy – 6th Tank Corps had lost many of its tanks during the initial attack, and then lost many of those that constituted its reinforced strength on 11 December. The 5th Tank Corps started on 11 December with 131 tanks, and was down to twenty-six operable tanks by 13 December.[11] As had been the case during the offensive of the winter of 1941–2, Soviet forces still functioned in the German rear even after the offensive operations of which they had been a part had failed. In this case elements of 20th Cavalry Division of 2nd Guards Cavalry Corps would fight in the German rear for more than a month and at least some would make it back to Soviet lines in early January 1943.[12] To the south there was at least good news – the great victory at Stalingrad was well under way even if 6th Army, elements of 4th Panzer Army and Rumanian forces still held out in the pocket.

Map 4: Soviet territory liberated by the Red Army in late 1942 and 1943.

Having encircled German forces at Stalingrad, the Soviet high command had the choice of whether to focus on the destruction of the pocket, or seek to prosecute wider operations in the region with more ambitious goals, namely cutting off Army Group A in the Caucasus from Axis forces north of Rostov. On 27 November Stalin was certainly of the opinion that the focus should be the destruction of the Stalingrad pocket, stating in conversation with Vasilevskii it 'didn't make sense to not complete one task before throwing oneself into another' and that it was necessary to 'liquidate' enemy forces at Stalingrad in order to free up the three armies engaged there.[13] Nonetheless, planning for 'Saturn' continued, and Stalin approved the operation – to begin on 10 December.[14] Whether Stalin was correct to see the destruction of the Stalingrad pocket as a competing priority with the more ambitious 'Saturn' is debateable – containment of the pocket and pursuit of wider aims can certainly be seen as having been a viable option once it had become apparent that Germany intended to try to hold Stalingrad. As the supply situation deteriorated, so would the mobility of German forces in the pocket, but Stalin may have been aware of the possibility of overextension and the benefits of 'a bird in the hand...'. It could certainly not be guaranteed that the encirclement would hold, and it has to be remembered that up until this point Soviet forces had not seen through an encirclement on anything like this scale – where for example at Demiansk Soviet forces had not been able to eliminate those forces contained within the pocket. In the end, Operation 'Kol'tso' or 'Ring' that was to see the destruction of the pocket had briefly to be put on hold as German forces sought to break through to the increasingly beleaguered 6th Army and accompanying units. On 14 December 1942 the Stavka ordered that General Malinovskii's forces, and in the first instance mechanised, were by forced march to be transferred from the north to the south to face Hoth's relief attempt whilst Rokossovskii and Eremenko's forces 'continued with the systematic destruction of enemy forces' in the Stalingrad region.[15] On 13 December the plan for 'Saturn' – 'thought up in what were favourable military circumstances' – was amended so that the aim of what was now 'Little Saturn' was the destruction of more modest but still sizeable Axis forces, including the Italian 8th Army, whilst covering Soviet operations against counterattack from the west. The revised operation was to begin on 16 December, with the option of course that if 'Little Saturn' progressed particularly well that 'Saturn' might be resurrected.[16] The destruction of Army Group A was not however on the cards given in part gross underestimation of German capabilities and the fact that even Hitler was not willing to see Army Group A sit in the Caucasus region and be cut off and ultimately destroyed. On its first day, 16 December, 'Little Saturn' did not make the progress it was supposed to – Soviet airpower was constrained by fog and penetration of Axis defences by forces of the South-Western Front stalled.[17] The problem was not German armour – German and Axis armoured strength in the region was certainly limited at the beginning of December and at the beginning of 'Little Saturn' – Group

Hollidt, with 22nd Panzer Division and 1st Rumanian Armoured Division – could certainly field few operational tanks. On 10 December 22nd Panzer Division could apparently field one Panzer II, two 38(t), five long-barrelled Panzer III and two short-barrelled, and two long and one short barrelled Panzer IV – with the 1st Rumanian Armoured Division fielding a paltry lone Panzer III and five R II.[18] Nonetheless, even if Axis forces lacked the sort of mobile armoured reserves at the start of 'Little Saturn' that would have helped check penetrations, Soviet forces would first have to get through frontline defences. Future General-Colonel Zheltov, as a member of the military soviet of the front, describes how after having made his way to the front on 16 December to investigate why the tank corps had not passed through enemy defences, he saw through the firing slit of the bunker he was in 'Twenty or so [*desiatka dva*] of our tanks had been knocked out. One of them was burning, the rest stood still, disabled in the minefields'. As he goes on to note, early on 17 December 18th and 25th Tank Corps were able to penetrate into the rear of 8th Italian Army, and elsewhere there were also penetrations into the enemy rear. Deep penetrations, such as that conducted by 24th Tank Corps, were impressive – as Zheltov notes 'within five days of fighting the corps had advanced 240 kilometres and on 24 December occupied the railway station at Tatsinskaia, destroying a supply dump and a significant number of aircraft on an airfield. However, what was subsequently described as a raid resulted in a period of encirclement for 24th Tank Corps where Soviet follow on forces, including 346th Rifle Division that apparently lacked armoured support, could not break through.[19] On 28 December 1942 Stalin and Zhukov consulted with Vatutin on the situation on the South Western Front and with particular attention being paid to the encircled 24th Tank Corps which was fighting with thirty-nine T-34 and fifteen T-70s in all round defence of its position at Tatsinskaia, under apparently heavy German air attack. At this point the Supreme High Command had not lost hope that 'Little Saturn' could be turned into 'Big' 'Saturn' – and although the commander of 24th Tank Corps had asked for permission to break out this was only to be allowed as a last resort – ideally 5th Tank Army and Russiianov's 1st Guards Mechanised Corps would break through to 24th Tank Corps. In order to foster the transition from 'Little Saturn' to 'Big' 'Saturn' it was noted that the South Western Front had already been provided with 2nd and 23rd Tank Corps, and was promised another two tank corps in a week along with 3–4 rifle divisions and additional air support. Limited resupply was promised by air for 24th Tank Corps.[20] The situation with 5th Tank Army to the east will be discussed further later, but 24th Tank Corps would not however be relieved and after having held Tatsinskaia for a number of days only elements of 24th Tank Corps eventually broke back through to Soviet lines.[21]

Certainly Axis defence of the Chir River was stubborn – and the Supreme High Command premature again in assuming scope for victory at German army-group rather than army scale. Further east 5th Tank Army, with 5th Mechanised Corps at the fore, struggled to break through and then expand penetration of the Axis line along the river. Having been transferred to the region in great secrecy in late November from the Briansk Front according to an order of 25 November, the bulk of 5th Mechanised Corps was launched against Axis defences along the Chir as day broke on 10 December.[22] Facing 5th Mechanised Corps on 10 December, as the former chief of staff for the corps noted in a 1982 article on the December 1942 operations of the corps, the enemy lacked tanks 'either on the front line or at tactical depth' – and was according to the author outnumbered by more than three to one in terms of infantry. Problematic however was the fact that 5th Mechanised Corps lacked overwhelming artillery support – chief of staff for 5th Mechanised Corps M. Shaposhnikov suggesting that in terms of artillery resources both sides were 'more or less' equivalent. Also a serious issue was the lack of bridging equipment that would allow 5th Mechanised Corps to rapidly deploy its armoured strength on the southern bank of the river in support of the infantry where the thickness of the ice on the river was insufficient to support heavy equipment. This was a particularly serious issue where considerable reliance was to be placed on the armoured assets of the corps used in concentration – 193 tanks – for the storming of German positions. So tanks and infantry were to be thrown across the Chir – piecemeal in the case of the tanks – with inadequate artillery support for the suppression of enemy defences and in particular key strongpoints – hardly a plan to inspire confidence. For M. Shaposhnikov a further issue was apparently the fact that 5th Mechanised Corps was equipped with British Lend-Lease tanks – Matildas and Valentines, that did indeed have 'limited speed and poor cross-country mobility' by the standards of the T-34 and KV-1 – and their 40 mm guns were certainly a poor weapon for fire support even if it would transpire during the battle that they were still sufficient to deal with Panzer III tanks at ranges of 400–500 metres. Certainly with poor artillery support – and their slow speeds – these vehicles could not charge about the battlefield with relative impunity in the same manner in which T-34s and KV-1 were still apt to do in many instances, although Shaposhnikov's claim that they had weak armours was certainly inaccurate for the Matilda. Despite poor artillery support – and issues in feeding armour into the battle across the river – 5th Mechanised Corps was able to break through enemy defences even if

German reserves prevented exploitation by a formation hardly equipped for such a task. By 21 December 5th Mechanised Corps's advance had ceased in the face of enemy counterattacks.[23] Although a large bridgehead over the Chir was in Soviet hands, 5th Mechanised Corps had gained little for what were undoubtedly significant losses. On 28 December 5th Tank Army's commander during the earlier fighting was replaced by order of the Stavka.[24] Certainly the aforementioned October 1942 instructions on the use of mechanised forces had specified the use of mechanised corps for the initial exploitation of a breakthrough created by rifle forces, where here the mechanised corps had been thrown into create it and had little or no strength for exploitation in an operation – and tanks not designed for that purpose. The almost textbook operational successes of 'Uranus' were certainly far from being the norm in late 1942 even where Soviet forces enjoyed meaningful superiority according to a number of key indices. Facing the sizeable Soviet forces amassed for Saturn and Little Saturn were German forces of Army Detachment Hollidt – with four battered infantry divisions reinforced with remnants of two Luftwaffe field divisions – along with 6th and 11th Panzer Divisions and the recently arrived 7th Panzer. The 22nd Panzer Division had by now been disbanded. As Soviet forces struck often blindly – their reconnaissance poor at best – they were either halted or parried for long enough into 1943 for the bulk of Army Group A to make its escape from the Caucasus.[25]

Although 'Little Saturn' did not become 'Saturn', 'Little Saturn' and associated operations did disrupt German intentions to try to break through to Stalingrad from the west, draw in German reserves from elsewhere and destroy considerable Axis strength – all but ending the participation of Italian forces on the Eastern Front for example. If 'Uranus' hadn't alone been enough – certainly not a guarantee with Hitler at the helm of the German armed forces – 'Little Saturn' also made the German position in the Caucasus untenable. Certainly the casualties inflicted on Italian, Rumanian and Hungarian forces during this period of the war were horrific. As Richard L. DiNardo notes in his study of the Axis alliance, by the end of January 1943 'the Romanian, Hungarian and Italian forces on the eastern front were in tatters'. The Italian 8th Army had suffered from 75,000–80,000 killed and missing; Rumanian forces committed to the campaign had perhaps lost 140,000 killed, wounded or captured; Hungarian forces had between April 1942 and March 1943 lost a total of 176,971 as casualties, where 'the winter battles alone cost the Hungarians close to 100,000 casualties'. All had lost the bulk of their vehicles and equipment Rumanian forces involved here were pulled back to Transnistria, Italian forces withdrawn altogether from the Eastern Front in the spring, and the 'Hungarian presence on the Eastern Front would continue in a limited sense until the summer of 1943'.[26]

In many ways Operation 'Uranus' highlighted a number of improvements in Red Army military effectiveness. The Red Army was undoubtedly materially gaining the upper hand – with exceptions in communications, fire control and armoured transport Soviet military equipment was proving to be not only as effective as German equivalents, but there was of course more of it. At Stalingrad Stalin and the Soviet leadership had allowed forces for a major offensive to be amassed before being thrown in – contrary to the piecemeal deployments that had characterised the first year of the war. Stalin was listening to a number of competent senior commanders and staff officers who were capable of devising coherent plans and organising and amassing the necessary forces for their execution. From the Stavka and the General Staff down, these operations were launched with better intelligence than had been the case the previous year. During the opening phases of operations – and indeed on the defence – Soviet artillery often provided heavy and concentrated fire support, Soviet tanks were now used in concentration and less likely to be squandered in mindless frontal assaults and concentrated Soviet airpower was available to suppress the Luftwaffe and provide support beyond the range of the artillery. Certainly during the opening phases of operations there were attempts to co-ordinate arms that involved greater decentralisation of command in order to facilitate effective combined arms, including, in addition to artillery and air support, to provide infantry support for the tanks. On the flanks at Stalingrad all of these were combined and pitted against an enemy – and particularly the Axis satellite nations – that lacked the artillery and anti-tank assets, and for the first time the air support, to be able to stall Soviet operations early on and prevent breakthroughs in defences that often lacked meaningful depth. Breaking through into the operational depth near Stalingrad allowed Soviet armoured forces to effect an encirclement that did not involve penetrative operations too deep and prolonged in the enemy rear to overtax the logistical chain and those rear services that struggled to keep the Red Army going.

Much may have changed to increase Red Army military effectiveness, but much had not. Stalin was still prone to over ambition in the aftermath of success, and the same criticism might for example be applied to Zhukov and others. The sustaining of offensive operations remained a significant issue for the Red Army in late 1942 and early 1943, and particularly so when they were successful and the Red Army was advancing significant distances. Staff work lower down the chain of command was not of the same quality as that at the top that would frequently become even more plain in more fluid situations, and intelligence that would act as an effective force multiplier and allow the Red Army to concentrate force most effectively started to dry up rapidly once offensive operations were underway. If German and Axis defences could withhold the initial onslaught and upset initial Soviet plans, then the chances of a Soviet operation failing increased dramatically. With both the Stavka and frontline commanders increasingly in the dark, smaller German armoured forces in particular were able to deal with penetrations by Soviet armoured units and formations that were soon increasingly unsupported by other arms. Soviet artillery was still not as mobile as it would become, although American vehicles in particular were changing that, and mobile communications were still less readily available than the sort of fixed communications that could be employed at the start of an operation. Soviet infantry were all too easily separated from the armour – the infantry that had proven so vulnerable riding tanks in Spain was still vulnerable – and the Red Army lacked the armoured transport vehicles to provide infantry protected from at least small arms fire to accompany forces breaking out into the enemy rear. Soviet airpower was supposed to provide airborne artillery support deep into the enemy rear, but communications and liaison were issues that continued to hamper the effective utilisation of the considerable air support assets now concentrated in support of Soviet operations. At this stage of operations, in all but the most favourable circumstances, the Red Army proved far less effective in turning tactical success into operational success than it would be by the end of the war. At Stalingrad the Red Army achieved a stunning operational victory in favourable conditions, but things would not necessarily go as smoothly further west as they were also not doing further north.

Running concurrent large-scale operations was not just about having the manpower and equipment – with which the Red Army was increasingly well equipped – but also the capacity to sustain them. Although the material situation for the Red Army had improved dramatically by this point over that in late 1941 – at least regarding arms and munitions, even if not food – the ability of the Red Army to resupply units with these resources on the offensive had not improved to the same extent. At the very front rifle divisions had clearly had inadequate transport resources for their needs from the beginning of the war. Although theoretically provided with the capacity to simultaneously lift 1,340 tons of supplies, as the Soviet historian N. Maliugin notes, even near the border rifle divisions were provided with only 30–40 per cent of their transport resources. By the end of 1942 the list strength capacity of divisional

transport was three and a half times lower than pre-war list strength as
rear area services were formally stripped of personnel and transport
resources that they often only theoretically had anyway. More effective
use of transport resources could certainly help alleviate the situation, and
in late 1942 divisional and regimental transport resources were no longer
dedicated to particular roles but pooled to be allocated to particular tasks
as required.[27] As noted by I. Golushko, by mid-1943 a clear chain of
responsibility for the delivery of supplies existed. With a member of the
Military Soviet of a front responsible for supply, responsibility for the
delivery of supplies to the front line led from the head of rear area services
at army level who was responsible for the delivery of supplies down to
divisional level, where his divisional equivalent took over and so forth.[28]
The fact that deputy People's Commissar for Defence and head of rear
area services for the Red Army A.V. Khrulev had participated in the
planning for Operation 'Uranus' is another indicator of the realisation –
at last – that supply was a crucial element of operational success.[29]
Nonetheless, resources remained far from adequate for rapid offensive
operations over large distances. The success of Operation 'Uranus' had
been fostered in part by amassing supplies in close proximity to frontline
forces – where those supplies amassed had not necessarily reached levels
deemed desirable according to norms established at the time. Hence,
forces of the South-Western, Don and Stalingrad Fronts were provided
on the eve of the offensive with somewhere between 1.8 and 3.2 *boekomplekti* or full reloads of rifle ammunition, 1.2–2.7 *boekomplekti* of 120 mm
mortar rounds, 1.8–4.0 *boekomplekti* of 76 mm shells and 0.9–3.3 *boekomplekti* of 122 mm shells. Although the Red Army's supply organisation had proven sufficient for 'Uranus', as I. Golushko notes in a 1974
article, 'during the offensive operations of the Soviet Army of the spring
of 1943 instances of supply bases and dumps lagging behind frontline
forces were noted', with frontline rear area services 'not having coped
with transshipment over large distances'.[30]

As has already been noted, inadequate Soviet support services
included poor field repair facilities for tanks at the beginning of the
war. At the beginning of the war Soviet tank repair evacuation and repair
facilities had been hopelessly inadequate – such that field repair services
'with the start of operations were unable to cope even with the day-to-day
maintenance of tanks'.[31] The lack of spare parts was a major limiting
factor in keeping the vast Soviet tank pool operational – even one of the
standard Soviet histories of the wartime tank forces noted that on 1 June
Soviet industry could only provided about 11 percent of the required
spare parts. As of 15 June nearly a third – 29 per cent – of older tank
types, that is primarily BT and T-26 series tanks, required complete

overhauls.[32] Urgent measures to provide field evacuation and repair facilities did mean that during the second half of 1941 48 mobile field repair bases (prb) were formed for significant servicing of vehicles in the field – with more serious repairs requiring that vehicles be sent to their fixed counterparts based, typically, at a variety of factories in the rear. The personnel for these mobile repair bases were to consist, according to an NKO decree of 20 February 1942 at least, of 30 per cent specialist workers from industry, with the remainder of the personnel provided by the NKO.[33] By 1 January 1943 there were according to the Soviet historians S. Lipatov and V. Kolomiets 108 field repair bases in operation along with twenty-three independent repair and reconstruction battalions and nineteen army repair and reconstruction battalions – served by fifty-six field evacuation companies. Nonetheless, as these authors acknowledge, although more tanks were by this stage being repaired the facilities available in the field were not capable of major overhauls of tanks, and a 'severe shortages of tank spares, and particularly engines' meant that not only could field repair facilities not repair many vehicles, but nor could they be repaired in a timely manner in the rear. Even if an engine was available, getting the tank to the engine or vice-versa was problematic given the already strained transport network. In 1943 the problem of tank repair became 'particularly severe' as a result of the formation of tank armies that were now involved in major offensive operations. Ultimately, in the aftermath of the final destruction of 6th Army at Stalingrad the inadequacies of Soviet rear areas services including tank repair would contribute to the overextension that would allow German forces to successfully counterattack near Khar'kov, where on paper Soviet forces could dispose of far greater assets than were operable and indeed than could be effectively supplied. Regarding the operability or lack thereof of tanks, Lipatov and Kolomiets provide the example of 2nd Tank Army of the Central Front, which between 12 and 19 February 1943 moved from the Efremov region to Fatezh – 200 km – in winter conditions and on poor roads, as a result of which it left 226 out of 408 tanks along the route 'for technical reasons' – i.e. they had broken down. At the start of the German counterattack by Army Group South that began on 19 February 1943, four tank corps of the South-Western Front could field only twenty operational tanks – with those lacking motive power being dug in as immobile firepoints.[34] Gary Dickson provides the example of 3rd Tank Army, which started to deploy over a 400 km distance at the end of 1942 in order to undertake offensive operations, and which left 122 out of its 426 tanks on its route 'in various stages of disrepair'. After it had started offensive operations on 14 January 1943 operational strength dropped rapidly from 306 vehicles on 1 January 1943 to eighty-five on 31 January. After a subsequent period of relatively stable operational strength that nonetheless did not see the formation's operational strength frequently exceed 100 vehicles the German counteroffensive of 2 March led to what might be described as catastrophic losses. With forty-seven operational tanks on 2 March out of a total of 455, by mid-March 3rd Tank Army did not have a single operational tank through a combination of irrecoverable losses and vehicles out of action. Many of the irrecoverable losses will have been as a result of the formation being unable to recover damaged vehicles overrun by the enemy.[35] The crisis situation with tank repair during this period led to the creation of Mobile Tank-Aggregate Repair Factories – PTARZ – that would be introduced later that year as the Red Army finally dealt with the problem and started to move from having woefully inadequate resources for maintenance and repair to a situation whereby Soviet capabilities exceeded those of their opponent.[36]

That German forces were able to successfully counterattack in early 1943 and retake the much fought over city of Khar'kov is retrospectively unsurprising. Stalin and the Soviet military leadership had already shown that they were prone to swinging towards overconfidence after having survived a crisis. Stalin and Zhukov were certainly prone to ignoring pleas from frontline forces that it was time to slow down or halt and regroup, although such pleas would however be made increasingly infrequently as 'can do' – and might actually do with extremely heavy losses – men were promoted to key commands. With the destruction wrought by 'Little Saturn', subsequent operations 'Gallop' and 'Star' launched by the South-Western and Voronezh Fronts on 29 January and 2 February respectively sought to capitalise on success.[37] In the optimistic post-Stalingrad push westwards and in the light of the initial success of Operation 'Gallop' by South-Western Front plans were soon put forward by its commander, Vatutin, for the defeat of Axis forces in the Donbass region by cutting off their line of retreat across the Dnepr River by striking with a mobile group in the direction of Melitopol', in an operation that if successful would also ultimately see the South-Western Front gain a jumping off point into the Crimea south of Perekop.[38] In his memoirs Chief of the General Staff Vasilevskii was critical of that fact that 'the commanders of the South-Western and Voronezh Fronts incorrectly assessed the strategic situation that had arisen [slozhivshuiusia] on that wing of the Soviet-German front by mid-February'. German troop redeployments were taken by the front commanders 'as the start of the withdrawal by the enemy of his Donbass group of forces to the other side of the Dnepr', rather than what they soon were – preparations for counterattack. Having stalled plans for racing German forces for the

Dnepr only days before – Operation 'Gallop' – on 17 February after
Soviet forces had finally captured Khar'kov Stalin had personally sanctioned toned down operations with what were nonetheless similar aims
and assumptions about the enemy to Vatutin's proposal that would see
Soviet forces continue to advance and overextend – without additional
strength.[39] Soon however enemy activity was disrupting snowballing
plans and 3rd Tank Army was being transferred from the Voronezh to
the South-Western Front for an attack on the flank of a counterattack by
the German 4th Panzer Army supported by elements of 1st Panzer
Army – in the supposed blunting of which the overextended 3rd Tank
Army would soon be without a single operational tank.[40] Khar'kov had
been captured by Soviet forces in mid-February, but would be retaken by
the SS Panzer Corps on 14 March as German forces struck again at
exposed Soviet forces in an operation that further embellished the reputation of the commander of now unified German forces in the south,
Manstein, who had nonetheless tried to avoid focus on the city itself.[41]
Facing a new threat from German armoured forces from the south, at
this point the Voronezh Front to the north put forward plans to formally
go over on to the defensive – accepted the following day – as Soviet forces
had to fight to defend gains including in the Kursk region to the north of
Khar'kov, rather than destroying German forces in the Donbass or even
seeking the collapse of the entire German position in the south.[42] Stalin,
Vasilevskii and the front commanders could all be deemed to have played
a part in this bout of over-optimism which they either fuelled or acqui-
esced in. Certainly, as was all too often the case, senior commanders
pouring over their maps had failed to consider the actual potential of the
Red Army to execute plans at the operational and operational-strategic
levels that included fancifully rapid redeployment of forces that had just
participated in the destruction of the Stalingrad pocket and an expansion
of ambitions to include Army Group Centre.[43]

Despite German operational success in the Khar'kov region in what
had certainly been a bold counterstroke, when combined with the fact
that the Red Army was gradually increasing in effectiveness from the
operational level down to a lesser extent to the tactical level during late
1942 and into 1943, Soviet material superiority had, by the spring of
1943, all but crushed the German ability to ever again seize the strategic
initiative on the Eastern Front. Manstein's suggestion in his memoirs – of
course benefitting from hindsight – that after the recapture of Khar'kov
Army Group South should have eliminated Soviet forces in the Kursk
region in co-operation with Army Group Centre and shorten the line
would obviously have been desirable, but with Soviet forces in the region
receiving reinforcement operational dexterity by elite formations

exploiting enemy overextension could only carry German forces so far.[44] By this point the tide had certainly in many senses turned, at least with the value of hindsight. As both Soviet and German ground forces recouped in the south and centre – and with a corridor finally linking Leningrad in the north with the bulk of Soviet held territory – it was the turn of the VVS, in the Kuban, to highlight how qualitatively improved Soviet armed forces could use a dramatically improved material position to gain the upper hand. Over the Kuban 4th and 5th Air Armies attached to the North-Caucasian Front were in the spring of 1943 substantially and rapidly reinforced by the Stavka. For example, 5th Air Army a had on 17 April 190 aircraft, of which 90 were fighters, on that day being reinforced with 2nd Mixed Air Corps with a fighter and ground-attack division and a total of 136 aircraft, receiving an additional fighter division three days later with 98 Yak-1 fighters.[45] 4th Air Army added a further 250 aircraft, and the VVS for the Black Sea Fleet a further 70, where with additional strength from Stavka reserves by 20 April the VVS for the North-Caucasian Front with that of the Black Sea Fleet could field in the region of 900 aircraft with up to 200 more yet to arrive and which would do so in late April and early May. Soviet fighter strength in the region that spring consisted to a large extent of new or recent models, from the Yak-1 and -7b to the La-5, and also about 11 per cent Lend-Lease aircraft including Aerocobras and even Spitfires. The new Tu-2 bomber also made an appearance.[46] Of strength in late April in the region of 1,100 aircraft - with 826 for 4th Air Army, 106 for the VVS of the Black Sea Fleet and seventy-eight for aircraft of Long-Range Aviation – a significant number were however out of action, with 24 per cent of aircraft for 4th Air Army and approximately half of the aircraft of the Black Sea Fleet under repair. Soviet aircraft were crammed into a relatively limited number of airfields, with two to three regiments to a single airfield and as many as eight regiments at Krasnodar.[47] Nonetheless, the VVS was able to rapidly concentrate strength.

Attempts had earlier been made to co-ordinate the activities of the air armies attached to the North-Caucasian Front with the formation of a headquarters of the VVS of the North-Caucasian Front, but on 24 April this headquarters was disbanded and the air assets of 5th Air Army transferred to 4th Air Army, with the headquarters of the former transferred elsewhere. This fitted in with the wider trend described earlier of cutting down on formal links in the chain of command above front level, and undoubtedly simplified command and control.[48] During offensive operations in May, although air-ground communications had been improved over those typically available earlier in the war, ground sets were few and fighter direction was hampered by the absence of radar.

Representatives of 4th Air Army were present at the headquarters of 37th and 56th Armies – and rifle corps on the principal axes – although it seems that ground sets were used primarily for fighter direction.[49] Nonetheless, as the air war in the Kuban progressed, Soviet forces were undoubtedly able to better concentrate airpower to gain local superiority and cause meaningful damage to German ground targets. During this period from late 1942 and on into 1943, one can also identify attempts to concentrate – and not subsequently unnecessarily dilute – the quality of elite air units that might be given key tasks. Just as there were Guards units amongst the ground forces – with attempts to keep their personnel to some extent 'elite' with for example attempts to return previously wounded Guards troops to Guards units – there were Guards air units.[50] This designation often had real meaning, where for example in the case of 8th Air Army involved in the Stalingrad blockade the previous year, seven aces with more than ten victories from 9th Guards Fighter Air Regiment, along with three from 296th Fighter Air Regiment and two from 11th Fighter Air Regiment were subsequently concentrated in 9th Guards Fighter Air Regiment that was re-quipped with Yak-1 aircraft instead of LaGG-3s.[51] Soviet ace Aleksandr Pokrishkin's 16th Guards Fighter Air Regiment of 4th Air Army in the fighting for Kuban was initially supposed to take poorly trained replacements from local reserve air regiments during the spring of 1943, but subsequently took replacements from regiments slated to reequip from older fighters such as the I-15 and I-16 instead.[52] These pilots and units that had already shown their capabilities in air combat were given more scope to exercise initiative and rival the Luftwaffe tactically having learnt from it. As Von Hardesty and Ilya Grinberg note, the new tactics being employed by the VVS during this period that included the adoption of flexible pairings of fighters along German lines 'marked the growing maturity and combat effectiveness of the VVS in 1943', and 'once embraced…shaped the VVS's combat role for the rest of the war'. Compared to prescribed tactics of the previous year that dictated speeds, altitudes and manoeuvres, by 1943 'experienced VVS pilots were now given previously unthinkable liberties – the ability to select group composition, optimal formations, methods of engagement, and the most advantageous speed and altitude for a given assignment'.[53]

    In the Kuban, in the spring of 1943 the VVS was committed in what in the Soviet literature is described as the first Soviet 'air offensive' – with the VVS tasked with winning air superiority and then providing appropriate support to ground forces.[54] Although Soviet accounts tend to exaggerate achievements over the Kuban, as Von Hardesty and Ilya Grinberg note 'VVS air units had employed innovative tactics on a large scale and achieved some measured success' even if 'air superiority remained an elusive goal' and losses had been high.[55] Certainly in late 1942 and early 1943, as German sources note, 'Russian fighter operations became more systematic and straightforward' – that is focused – 'with forces concentrated at the points of main effort' as the VVS and particularly the elite units became more aggressive in engaging the Luftwaffe. With increased strength, improved organisation and tactical flexibility the VVS was soon actually hitting German bombers that had often previously got through relatively unmolested and where 'the division of units into attack and cover elements' was more effective than it had previously been. The VVS was also able to more effectively protect their own attack aircraft, in stark contrast to the situation in 1941.[56] Although typically still not penetrating deep into the German rear, Soviet ground attack operations were not only more likely to get through, but were being conducted by larger groups of aircraft that were increasingly likely to inflict meaningful damage on German ground forces when they struck.[57] Not only on the ground, but also in the air, was the Soviet military fist by late 1942 and early more likely to land a weighty punch where it mattered than had been the case only months before, even if the blow was typically not a knockout one.

From late 1942 through the spring of 1943 the course of the war in the East and overall was, with the value of hindsight, turning decisively in Soviet and Allied favour. Unless one believes that events are predetermined, then during 1943 the Soviet leadership might have made strategic errors on such a scale as to allow Germany to once again gain the upper hand on the latter's Eastern Front. However, by the spring of 1943 the chances of Stalin and the Soviet military leadership making errors of such magnitude as to undermine the benefits of qualitative improvement and quantitative superiority were clearly reduced compared to the summer of 1941 when strategic miscalculation had cost the Red Army so dearly – as it had done so again to a lesser extent during the winter of 1941–2. The German defeat at Kursk in the summer of 1943 would make Soviet ascendancy clear not only to historians of any persuasion, but also to an increasing number of those on both sides embroiled in events at the time.

19 The Defence of the Kursk Salient and the Battle for Prokhorovka

Stalingrad was undoubtedly a significant victory for the Red Army – and a major blow for Nazi Germany. The Soviet leadership did not however at the time see it as a clear turning point in the war. The resounding success of Operation 'Uranus' at Stalingrad is also perhaps misleading as an indicator of overall Soviet tactical and operational capabilities in late 1942 in that the German command had done so much to facilitate its success in overextending Axis forces – including there being insufficient reserves to seriously attempt to deal, in a timely manner, with a Soviet offensive on the flanks. Similar Soviet operational-strategic success would arguably not be achieved again until mid-1944. By the time Operation 'Uranus' was launched 6th Army in Stalingrad was suffering from reduced mobility thanks to the loss of most of its horses that would have hampered a breakout even if one had been sanctioned. With those elements of 4th Panzer Army also trapped in the Stalingrad pocket along with 6th Army denied the opportunity to break out whilst resources gave even a chance of some units escaping, the cards were stacked very much in Soviet favour for an up until then elusive large-scale encirclement that would hold. At the point at which it was conceived, Soviet success in Operation 'Uranus' was not of course guaranteed despite the increasingly favourable resource situation – such an operation had to be well-planned on the basis of reasonable intelligence, Soviet forces had to be effectively concentrated and supplied, and particularly for the initial breakthrough rifle and mechanised forces well supported by other arms. Soviet armour could then complete the initial encirclement relatively unmolested by their German armoured counterparts. That all of these factors applied to 'Uranus' was undoubtedly an achievement for the Red Army that had failed in 1941 and early 1942 to tick most of these boxes in any operation. However, Operation 'Mars' further north was an abject failure, and painful and only limited progress – at least in terms of expectations – was made in general in the centre and north during late 1942 and early 1943 despite the significance of the narrow corridor punched through to Leningrad in January 1943.

The Red Army had not been reinvented in order to achieve success at Stalingrad, but it was – as one would hope it would be – developing at all levels in the light of wartime experience. When dealing with the period from Stalingrad onwards it is important however to stress both the ways in which the Red Army had changed since the summer of 1941 but also the shifting resource balance in Soviet favour as explanation for the operational and indeed strategic victories that it was now scoring. That Soviet military leaders set slightly more realistic goals by the summer of 1943 is important here – although in 1943 success at and in the aftermath of Kursk would once again snowball into offensive operations across most of the Eastern Front that were perhaps a little broad in their scope. The ability to concentrate, supply and support the breakthrough of tactical defences by large mechanized formations and the setting of more realistic operational goals – even being willing to scale plans back in the light of events as in the case of 'Saturn' – certainly contributed to the fact that by the summer and autumn of 1943 the Red Army was winning battle after battle and pushing the Axis back. However, compared to other major powers it was still doing so at a painfully high material and human cost – a relative cost that cannot simply be explained away by the ferocity of the 'war of annihilation' on Germany's Eastern Front.

During 1943, as had been the case in 1941 and 1942, Soviet troops typically fought hard, with weapons that were frequently overall at least as good as those of their opponents – now increasingly with more of them to complement a widening relative manpower advantage. The German field army in the East – with the exclusion of Luftwaffe and Waffen-SS forces – had barely changed in overall strength on 1 July 1943 when it stood 3,115,000 strong compared to 22 June 1941 when it had a strength of 3,206,000. Luftwaffe and Waffen-SS troops added far greater numbers by the summer of 1943 than they had in late June 1941, but the increase in German manpower committed had certainly not been as great as that for the Red Army. As of 9 July 1943 the Soviet field army – here deemed troops of the operating fronts – stood at a strength of about 6,724,000 personnel compared to in the region of 2,700,000 on the outbreak of war. In terms of armour, Soviet armour concentrated on the Kursk axis alone rivalled total German armoured strength in the East where 2,269 tanks and 997 assault guns gave a combined strength of 3,266 as of 30 June 1943. Of these, most might not be considered outdated types, with the long-barelled Panzer IIIs and particularly IVs being a match for the 76 mm-gun armed T-34s that made up the bulk of the Soviet tank park.[1] However, although there were many improvements in Red Army leadership from the very top down, and many organisational improvements, these were changes that could not suddenly transform the Red Army overnight into an organisation that functioned as intended at all levels. At the bottom of the system for example Soviet infantry units – and particularly run-of-the-mill as opposed to Guards units – still displayed many of the inadequacies that they had gone to war showing. Many of the issues were not particular to the Red Army – rifle platoons were under-strength as many tried to avoid being fed into the meatgrinder by taking on other roles within their units, where personnel were in infantry units often because they were not wanted by other arms. Complaints such as that 'many commanders of companies, platoons and even sections do not know their people' can be explained in part by the high turnovers in personnel and the short life expectancies – or at least periods without being wounded – of infantrymen in action. Exhortations to push personnel hiding in the rear into core rifle units and maintain company strengths, improve discipline, food, training and the quality of personnel and particularly command elements could only achieve so much given the demands of other arms and the often poor educational and peasant backgrounds of so many personnel who had been unable to escape to other roles.[2] At least the firepower of Soviet rifle units was improving, even if the situation on the ground didn't always keep up with orders from above. As already noted, for example, as of 23 May 1943 all Soviet rifle companies were supposed to re-equip one of their platoons entirely with sub-machine guns, significantly increasing their firepower – and providing units with a simple and effective weapon suited to use by poorly trained troops often fighting at close quarters.[3]

Many developments in Red Army effectiveness deemed desirable by the Soviet military leadership would require changes in organisational culture that often were in opposition to an established broader political culture. Nowhere were exhortations from above more obviously not being realised on the ground than in the display of the sort of initiative that was much talked about but in reality difficult to show in a system still far more obsessively top down than that of its opponent. Few Red Army commanders were willing or able to regularly exercise any real initiative even in more prestigious and privileged units, although the storm groups at Stalingrad had for example been a pointer to the fact that allowing Soviet troops a taste of the sort of decentralisation and autonomy in the execution of orders enjoyed by their opponents might actually be productive in the right circumstances. Certainly at the very lowest levels of the Red Army organisation in battle there were numerous small acts involving initiative, but they typically involved initiative in attempting to carry out orders in which there was often little scope for lower level input despite the fact that troops on the ground might have a better appreciation for the actual tactical circumstances faced. By the end of the war there would be signs in the Red Army of the sort of 'mission tactics' typically seen as most effectively being employed by the Wehrmacht and Waffen SS, but they were still little in evidence in late 1942 and early 1943 with the possible exception of reconnaissance forces engaged in raids for 'tongues' in which Soviet scouts excelled. Nonetheless, during the period after Stalingrad until the end of the war there was subtle cultural change within the Red Army – and to some extent in wider society – where during the war the Soviet population was more likely to be left to get on with it than prior to the war. The regime's fleeting wartime acceptance of greater albeit still very limited autonomy for its citizens – born more out of necessity than ideology – would play a role in gradually fostering increased military effectiveness. At the same time this effectiveness was being enhanced through both continued organisational and technological improvements, and material advantage, that meant that a gradually more effective Red Army was increasingly able to overwhelm the Third Reich and its allies through a combination of sufficient quality to make meaningful use of quantity. During 1944 the Red Army would be able to run major overlapping operations, that unlike 'Uranus' and 'Mars' would both be successful thanks to a favourable resource situation, organisational changes instigated from above, and valuable accrued experience below, with these components being blended together to maximise potential.

By the spring of 1943 the likelihood of Germany and her allies being able to seize the strategic initiative in the East had declined considerably from the previous year. Nonetheless German tactical and operational capabilities had not yet been degraded to the extent they would be by the same time the following year, and could have allowed Germany to achieve far more on the Eastern Front during 1943 than was to be the case. This achievement might have been less than dramatic – timely retreat to the Dnepr and the Panther and Wotan lines might have allowed Nazi Germany to drag out the war in the East for far longer than was the case – but then had that been opted for then one would have to remove Hitler from the equation leading most probably to Barbarossa not having being launched in the first place! The reality was that Hitler and the German leadership were unwilling to go over to the defensive until they had little choice, and the major German offensive actually launched in 1943 – Operation 'Citadel' – lacked the sort of rationale ideally required to justify the expenditure of resources in circumstances that ended up in far too many ways favouring the defender. Destruction of the Kursk bulge and Soviet forces concentrated within it as a precursor to finally seizing Moscow – the plan – would have been unlikely in most scenarios that involved Stalin and the Soviet military leadership keeping their heads. The fact that the Red Army was to be on the defensive – and had not launched an operation such as that launched near Khar'kov the previous year before Operation 'Blau' – did represent significant progress in Soviet military leadership at the upper levels. However, as fighting in the Kursk region would show, limited improvements at the top were not to be matched by sustained relative capability at the operational and tactical levels, and particularly when troops at the bottom were pushed forward with the sort of distain for their lives all too often shown by Stalin and Soviet military leaders. Kursk would be another glowing endorsement of the tactical and at times operational capabilities of German arms against an opponent that although catching up in many aspects of competence at these levels would reap the rewards of material superiority, improved organisation and favourable operational and operational-strategic circumstances.

As discussed in the previous chapter, the German counterattack in the Khar'kov region – combined with repair, maintenance and supply issues – had brought Soviet post-Stalingrad offensive operations in the south to a halt in March 1943. Stubborn resistance and an apparently early spring thaw had brought Soviet offensive operations elsewhere to a halt that same month or early the next, but certainly earlier than had been the case the previous year. During the previous year Soviet forces had in some instances continued to hammer away at German forces throughout the spring and even during the thaw – squandering resources such as Vlasov's 2nd Shock Army below Leningrad in the process. We will move north again in the next chapter, but for now it is worth noting, as Zhukov notes in his memoirs for example, how in mid-March 1943 operations by the North-Western Front to force the River Lovat' were called off that spring thanks to conditions that previously did not seem to have been seen as an impediment.[4]

In the south, after the successes of the winter of 1942–3 and resulting overextension, by the spring of 1943 the Red Army was in need of time for recuperation. Although initial gains in territory had been reduced by the German counterattacks, the Red Army had nonetheless made dramatic gains in the region having advanced since the beginning of the year as much as 500 km. However, not only were armoured formations now typically mere shadows of their initial selves, but Soviet forces had outrun their supply lines such that on 5 March 1943 General-Major Kuznetsov of the Military Soviet of the Voronezh Front would describe the front's fuel situation as 'catastrophic'.[5] In terms of manpower the Voronezh Front for example had also sustained substantial losses, and in particular during the German counteroffensive in March. From 13 January to 3 March 1943 according to Krivosheev the Voronezh Front suffered

33,331 irrecoverable losses out of total losses of approaching 100,000 men from a strength of in the region of 350,000 – and the left wing of the front alone (3rd Tank Army and 40th and 69th Armies) would lose 29,807 men as irrecoverable losses out of total losses for these units and formations of nearly 60,000 men during what became known as the Khar'kov Defensive Operation from 4–25 March 1943.[6] As of 30 March amongst the infantry alone the front was short 4,591 commanders of all ranks, including 74 battalion, 673 company and 2,844 platoon commanders, along with 179 staff officers. Some of these could be drawn from within the front or were en route, but 566 company and 790 platoon commanders were being requested from the centre. These were not the only living creatures in short supply and that were being lost in large numbers – the front was requesting 16,200 horses for the cavalry, artillery and supply.[7] Replacement troops for existing units from outside the front, front reserve units, from hospitals and amongst liberated PoWs would certainly not cover personnel losses even where the front resorted to what would be standard practice as territory was liberated – mobilising personnel from what had been occupied territory into reserve units or sometimes straight into combat units. In January-February 20,902 personnel would be drawn from liberated territory, along with 10,885 from personnel collection and distribution points and those liberated from captivity – which along with 14,480 from front reserve units and 1,812 from hospitals would provide just under 50,000 personnel from front resources. During this period the front would receive fewer than 10,000 replacements in the form of 'march' replacements, that is trained replacement troops from the rear. In March the nearly 24,000 personnel drawn from the front's resources, and just over 14,000 as 'march' replacements would not cover losses for the left wing of the front.[8] It is worth noting that the front received penal troops as reinforcements [*popolnenie*] for frontline units in January and February.[9] Certainly by mid-March 1943 the Red Army was running out of the sort of reserves that could be fed into operations that it was clearly now acknowledged at Stavka and General Staff level were required for operational success and would be built up for the offensives in the aftermath of the defence of the Kursk salient.

Regarding tanks, as of 30 March the Voronezh Front's tank formations and units had only 116 tanks out of a total list strength of 837 tanks. Of material resources, not only available tanks were well below list strength, but various items of equipment were in short supply with frontline units and where stocks in front and army supply bases and committed by the centre would only cover part of the shortfall. The availability of communications resources – although far better than in equivalent circumstances in 1941 – remained something of an issue where the Voronezh

Front was at this time experiencing particular shortages of the sort of sets most likely to be lost in action. Although having 160 of the 175 RSB sets of list strength that were typically used for the command armoured forces or by higher level infantry formations, the front lacked for example 1,177 of 2,381 RB and 12-RP sets typically used by infantry or artillery regiments respectively, with the bulk of requirements being requested from the centre.[10]

Vague Soviet plans as of late March and the beginning of April for the summer were seemingly to amass resources for a principal offensive in a south-westerly direction from the Voronezh region where the Reserve Front was to be formed by the end of the month according to a Stavka directive of 6 April.[11] In early April however, Soviet intelligence had alerted the Soviet military leadership to German preparations for an offensive in the Kursk region that it was expected would commence before the arrival of summer. Whether recalling the Khar'kov debacle of the previous year or not, Zhukov seems to have taken the lead in fostering the decision of early April for the Red Army to stand on the defensive and receive the German attack before itself going over to the offensive, although this likely involved some discussion with the General Staff as Vasilevskii suggests. On 8 April Zhukov certainly proposed such an approach to Stalin having offered an appreciation of likely enemy plans for the near future, and concluding that 'for our forces to go over to the offensive in the forthcoming days with the aim of pre-empting the enemy is not in my opinion expedient [*netselesoobraznim*]', and that it would be better for the enemy to wear itself down [*izmotaem*] against Soviet defences – and particularly its armoured strength – before 'with the introduction of fresh reserves to go over to a general offensive and decisively sieze [*dob'em*] the core enemy grouping'.[12] Having received Zhukov's report Stalin sought the opinions of front commanders on likely enemy intentions and their thoughts on future action both by telephone and through the General Staff before committing to Zhukov's proposal – a proposal supported by Vasilevskii and the General Staff. Certainly front commanders in the Kursk region were aware of the concentration of German armour and other resources being amassed opposite them, and the likelihood of their being used in some sort of major offensive in the coming weeks.[13] On the evening of 12 April at a meeting attended by Stalin, Zhukov, Vasilevskii and deputy chief of the General Staff A.I. Antonov, the decision was actually taken to prepare to meet the German attack first, although as Vasilevskii notes with the possibility that Soviet forces might 'go over to the offensive in the case that the fascist command did not launch an offensive in the Kursk region in the near future and delay it for a protracted period'.[14] As plans were being made for defence of the Kursk salient, offensive plans were being formulated for Operation 'Kutuzov' by the left wing of the Western and Briansk Front in co-ordination with the Central Front on the Kursk Salient with a view to seizing Orel – to be launched 'at the most advantageous moment'. In mid-May Vasilevskii reported the probable readiness of forces for the operation by the end of the month, by which point there had already been two 'scares' that German forces were about to launch offensive operations against the Kursk salient.[15]

Stalin and a number of other senior commanders were undoubtedly concerned about Germany seizing the initiative on the Eastern Front during the spring of 1943. Preparing to meet a German offensive was undoubtedly contrary to the offensive tone that had been set for the Red Army in the late 1930s – Stalin's statement to graduating commanders on 5 May 1941 that a 'modern army is an offensive army' springing to mind.[16] Obsession with taking the offensive where possible – and particularly on the part of Stalin – had cost the Red Army dearly since June 1941. It is understandable how there were many concerns over the idea of meeting an enemy offensive before going over to the offensive, despite the fact that Red Army successes to date had generally occurred in that context even if not by choice. Despite the fortification of the Kursk salient, the Reserve Front, which became the Steppe Military District on 13 April was to amass forces for eventual offensive operations be they after an enemy attack or not. A Stavka directive of 23 April 1943 highlighted that although the defence of the left bank of the Don was to be prepared for by mid-June with contingency plans for enemy offensive operations in the meantime, 'troops, headquarters and commanders of formations are in the main to make preparations for offensive action and operations with a view to breaking through enemy defensive belts, and similarly for the creation of powerful counterstrikes by our forces...'.[17] In May Stavka nerves about the possibility of a German offensive beginning earlier than was deemed desirable were certainly apparent as they were in the above Stavka directive on the tasks of the Steppe Military District. On 5 May Vasilevskii and Antonov had sent a directive to the Central Front on German forces massing near Orel and requiring that enemy movements not take place 'without punishment' and that air forces and indeed ground forces engage them from the air and with both artillery and infantry weapons and increase reconnaissance activities.[18] On 8 May in two separate directives the Stavka warned the Briansk, Central, Voronezh and South-Western Fronts – and the Steppe Military District – of the possibility of enemy attack between 10–12 May from either the north, south or both north and south of the Kursk salient, and requiring that Soviet forces – and particularly the VVS – be ready to meet them. On 13 May the Stavka ordered the cessation of attacks on enemy airfields and lines of communication, but this would not be the last 'scare' of May, with a subsequent warning of a possible enemy offensive going out on 20 May for the period 19–26 May.[19] It was by this point that Zhukov suggests Stalin's 'vacillation' over whether the Red Army was capable of holding the Wehrmacht before going over to the offensive had ceased and firm plans for offensive operations both immediately north and south of the Kursk salient and more broadly that were to follow defence of the bulge were accepted.[20] Nonetheless, the option that Soviet forces might go over to the offensive prior to a German attack if the latter had not occurred as expected – as indeed it didn't seem to be doing – did not go away. Initially planned for May, Operation 'Citadel' would in fact be delayed until July. By mid-June Soviet reconnaissance – to be discussed in more detail in a moment – suggested German readiness for offensive operations that had yet to come, and as Vasilevskii notes in his memoirs the commander of the Voronezh Front, N.F. Vatutin pressed for the Red Army to launch its offensive whilst it was still summer and indeed seems to have provoked sufficient doubt in Stalin's mind for him to suggest that such a suggestion 'deserves the most serious consideration'.[21] Despite fears of German intentions and missing an opportunity, the Soviet command nonetheless held its nerve – this time with Vasilevskii apparently taking a lead in pressing that the Red Army retain its defensive posture to meet an enemy attack that was bound to come soon.[22]

Undoubtedly an increasingly clear picture of German intentions from Soviet intelligence – even if there were issues with timing relating not to the quality of the intelligence but Hitler's changes of plan – was a crucial factor in Soviet offensive operations being held off. Soviet intelligence had a wide range of sources that as the spring progressed pointed to German offensive operations against the Kursk salient. By April 1943 the bulk of this information was being fed into a unified and centralised Red Army intelligence hierarchy that had, as discussed in Chapter 8, previously been lacking. As a result of a series of changes taking place from late 1942 into 1943, by the time NKO order Number 0071 was issued on 19 April 1943 the Red Army was already moving towards merging intelligence from agents both at home and abroad and other methods within a more unified system.[23] The NKO order of 19 April 1943 led to the creation of a Reconnaissance Board of the Red Army under the command of General-leitenant F.F. Kuznetsov that would handle some of the intelligence previously handled by the GRU in addition to that from military units. A 1st Department would handle intelligence from frontline units, a 2nd intelligence from agents – although would only run agents abroad. A 3rd Department would handle intelligence from agents being handled by fronts, and a 4th Department would handle radio-intelligence. Under the auspices of the General Staff however groups of officers were to be formed for the 'wider application [*obobshcehniia*] and analysis of incoming intelligence on the enemy from all organs of intelligence and counter-intelligence (NKO, NKVD, the People's Commissariat for the Navy (NKVMF), the Main Board "Smersh" and partisan headquarters)'. At front level departments would run intelligence from frontline forces (1st), agents (2nd), air reconnaissance (5th) and radio (6th), with a 3rd Department handling sabotage and diversion activities in the enemy rear. Staffing for intelligence was specified all the way down to regimental level, where a deputy chief of staff responsible for reconnaissance would have a translator and both an infantry and cavalry reconnaissance platoon for reconnaissance.[24] As has been noted in numerous instances throughout this work already, existing frontline reconnaissance assets were not necessarily being used effectively, and NKO Order Number 0072 that same day covered their activities, where it was noted that 'commanders of units and formations do not give frontline reconnaissance sufficient attention' and still reconnaissance units 'were frequently not being used for their intended purposes', 'were not being provided with material resources', their personnel were not being 'prepared as they should' and where there wasn't 'stimulus' – material or in the form of awards – 'for the best frontline commanders and soldiers to want to move to reconnaissance units and organs'. The damning introductory section of the order from which the above comes finished by noting how overall the activities of reconnaissance were of 'low quality [*na nizkom urovne*]', provided 'insufficient information on the enemy' – including inadequate interrogation of prisoners on the capture of which much effort was expended – and didn't process information that included captured documents appropriately. The solutions proposed included using reconnaissance assets only for reconnaissance – and being 'inventive and cunning' in all spheres of intelligence where this included the use of scouts as well as 'ambushes and raids'. That these 'ambushes and raids' were not only about 'capturing prisoners and operational documents' but also assassinating officers and destroying headquarters still highlights a somewhat different Soviet emphasis in intelligence gathering at the front line that could all too frequently devolve into combat, but at least overall stress was being placed on gaining information. Certainly reconnaissance forces were now to be better compensated for their efforts – better paid and fed – and their prestige increased in part through their promotion in the press and literature. From the top to bottom of the hierarchy intelligence staff and frontline personnel were to be better selected and trained for intelligence work, and the system provided with more reconnaissance assets subordinated directly to intelligence personnel. Reconnaissance aviation regiments equipped with Yak-7 and Pe-2 aircraft at front level were to subordinated to heads of reconnaissance, and all fronts provided with motorized reconnaissance companies with 6–10 armoured cars (increasingly light BA-64s), 30–40 motorcycle and sidecar combinations and 15–20 'jeeps' 'for use on the principal axes of offensive operations'.[25] Partisan units had already been told to focus more on intelligence gathering in the September 1942 'On the Tasks of the Partisan Movement' as discussed in Chapter 12 and a further NKO order of 19 April ordered the better integration of Red Army intelligence personnel with the separate, Party-run partisan movement by placing Red Army intelligence officers within the partisan movement's hierarchy.[26] These changes to Red Army reconnaissance gathering were significant, and would provide an organisation that would function without significant change until the end of the war. That these changes would take time – and a little cultural change – for the Red Army to reap the full rewards is perhaps well illustrated by a General Staff document of 25 December 1943 that chided reconnaissance personnel for a series of failings that included taking intelligence at face value, failure to corroborate sources, and a tendency to pass raw intelligence information higher up the chain rather than analysing it – all predictable for an organisation within a wider system that hardly encouraged inquisitiveness and questioning and in which sticking ones neck out might prove costly.[27] Nonetheless, during the spring and summer of 1943 this new structure would provide significant material that would contribute to the decision to prepare for and wait for 'Citadel' before striking back.

By mid-June – and certainly by 22 June 1943 – Vasilevskii suggests that the Voronezh and Central Fronts consisted of 'a strong grouping of forces' that had finally been massed in appropriate strength in expectation of German operations in the region. Both Zhukov and Vasilevskii who spent time supervising preparations in the Kursk region were aware of the need for forces in the Kursk salient to be echeloned in sufficient depth to absorb the expected German attack. They were also aware that in addition to artillery and airpower being brought together for use *en masse* anti-tank resources had also to be sufficiently concentrated to have meaningful impact. Massed indeed they were, both within the defensive positions in the salient, and behind it. In his memoirs, for the end of June Vasilevskii writes of more than 1,336,000 troops in the Voronezh and Central Fronts, along with more than 19,000 guns and mortars, 3,444 tanks and self-propelled guns and 2,172 aircraft not including long-range bombers and U-2 light night bombers. We can assume that the bulk of this equipment was operational – as that for

German forces below – in particular given the often meaningful period of time since units concerned had been in combat or transit under their own power. Behind the Central and Voronezh Fronts the Steppe Military District could field another 573,000 personnel, 7,401 guns and mortars and 1,551 tanks and self-propelled guns.[28] Alternative figures note that of these troops of the Voronezh and Central Fronts nearly a million were with combat units. According to Soviet-era published statistics about 160,000 Soviet troops of the Voronezh and Central Fronts – including 15 rifle divisions, along with 3,160 guns and mortars of 76 mm calibre and above and 440 tanks and self-propelled guns – were deployed forward in the 'tactical zone' of the defences along just over 100 km of front. Along with 179 heavy tanks – primarily KV-series – the Central and Voronezh Fronts alone fielded 2,033 medium tanks – primarily T-34 – and 961 light tanks, many of which were T-70s, giving a total of in the region of 3,500 tanks and self-propelled guns. The Steppe Military District – soon to be a front – could add another 1,034 medium – primarily T-34 – tanks with combat units.[29]

New to the Red Army for the defence of the Kursk salient were the next generation of self-propelled guns that followed abortive developments of the 1930s. On 4 January 1943 the GKO had ordered the development of a prototype heavy self-propelled ML-20 gun based on the KV chassis within twenty-five days, and trials were ordered on 10 January to last only seven days from the arrival of the prototype at the testing grounds! With trials actually completed by 7 February, a GKO decree of 14 February 1943 ordered the formation of sixteen heavy self-propelled artillery regiments of the High Command Reserve – the first to be ready supposedly by 28 February, and each with 320 men and twelve ML-20-armed self-propelled guns.[30] A regiment for the training of crews would be formed at the Kirov factory producing the guns in Cheliabinsk, and the units would be provided with amongst other support services 'specialized mobile repair workshops'.[31] The Central Front fielded twenty-five of the new SU-152 assault guns intended primarily for infantry support but with potent anti-tank capability as well, along with fifty-six medium and fifty-two light self-propelled guns – the SU-122 and SU-76 also primarily being intended for infantry support but with at least limited anti-tank capabilities in the case of the former – more so for the latter. More SU-152s would be used in the Soviet counteroffensives after Operation 'Citadel' had been blunted – assault gun crewmember Elektron Priklonskii and his unit did not receive their SU-152s until the German offensive was underway on 11 July 1943, but would participate in Soviet offensive operations from the beginning of August.[32] As regards anti-tank guns, relatively few of the more potent ZIS-2 anti-tank guns were available for the Kursk defence given that production had only recently been resumed with the 1943 variant of a gun first introduced and then removed from production in 1941 – but along with nearly 4,000 (3,869) 45–57 mm guns including available ZIS-2s much of the Soviet field artillery available including the new ZIS-3s had good anti-tank capabilities against all but the latest German heavy tanks and assault guns from the front. Certainly many of the 756 76–85 mm anti-aircraft guns available, and particularly the larger 85 mm guns, were potent anti-tank weapons. The Red Army had deployed 3,107 field guns of 76 mm calibre or above on the Central Front and 2,279 on the Voronezh Front, in addition to a total of more than 10,000 mortars of various calibres and where additional firepower – primarily against personnel and lighter vehicles – was provided by 518 BM-8 and BM-13 'Katiusha' rocket launchers.[33] In addition to guns and mortars, considerable stocks of ammunition had also been stockpiled, with frontline artillery units from 76 mm regimental to 203 mm howitzers being stocked with between 1.6 and 2.5 *boekomplekti* of ammunition. In the case of ammunition for 152 mm guns and howitzers for example, for the former there were approximately 2.5 *boekomplekti* with units, 1.2 at army-level dumps and 0.4 at front level dumps – for the howitzers 1.6, 0.7 and 0.2 respectively. An indicator of the significance of these figures for stockpiled munitions is provided below with the statistic that the 30-minute intensive barrage intended to be unleashed on German forces preparing for attack was supposed to use about half a *boekomplekt* of ammunition.[34]

Much of the anti-tank and artillery strength massed for the defence of the Kursk salient was formed into large units – for the Red Army of mid-1943 mass deployment was seen as a crucial element to success even if many such units and formations would on the advance in particular prove somewhat unwieldy. Early 1943 saw a flurry of GKO decrees for the formation of artillery brigades and corps. For example, on 12 April 1943 the GKO decreed the formation of four breakthrough artillery corps and eight independent heavy gun artillery brigades. Each artillery corps was to consist of two breakthrough artillery divisions and a Guards rocket mortar *divizion*, with a total of 244 guns and 108 mortars in each of the two breakthrough divisions made up of one light artillery brigade of three regiments each with twenty-four 76 mm guns; one howitzer brigade with three regiments of twenty-eight 122 mm howitzers; two heavy howitzer brigades with thirty-two 152 mm howitzers in each; one super heavy artillery brigade with twenty-four 203 mm howitzers; and one mortar brigade with three regiments of thirty-six 120 mm mortars.[35] An add-itional breakthrough corps was ordered on 23 April, along with changes to the structure of the breakthrough divisions replacing a 32-gun 152 mm howitzer brigade with a 36-piece brigade.[36] That same day the GKO issued a decree for the creation of ten independent 'anti-tank destruction brigades' for the High Command Reserve that would see a similar concentration of anti-tank assets. Each brigade was to consist of two 20-gun regiments equipped with 76 mm guns, and one 20-gun regiment with 45 mm guns to be formed from late April through to late May and to be provided with many appropriately-sized Lend-Lease vehicles, be they jeeps or trucks, able to provide considerable mobility.[37] As veteran Viktor Nikolaevich Mat'ianov notes in a post-Soviet interview, Lend-Lease vehicles were by the summer of 1943 starting to have significant impact on the mobility of at least certain types of Red Army unit and formation, even if overall the Red Army still had what was deemed to be inadequate motor-vehicle provision. After having been trained to drive 'Shevrole' – Chevrolet – lorries and 'Dodzh ¾' for pulling anti-tank guns near Kiubishev with an automobile training regiment Viktor Nikolaevich Mat'ianov eventually ended up with 238th Independent Anti-Tank Destruction *Divizion* with 18–20 guns being pulled by Dodge ¾ ton trucks. Unsurprisingly, Mat'ianov's unit was subject to frequent enemy air attack as it and others like it were thrown to where they were needed, requiring that the guns and trucks never congregate in more than twos or threes.[38] By now Mat'ianov's unit was far from unique in having received vehicles from the Soviet Union's Western allies. The Soviet Union had been sent more than 4,500 Dodge ¾ ton trucks by the end of June 1943 out of a total of more than 23,000 shipped during the war as a whole. By the end of June 1943 the Soviet Union had also been sent more than 35,000 Studebaker 6x4 or 6x6 2½ ton trucks that on arrival – and the vast majority did arrive – were also undoubtedly making a meaningful contribution to getting the Red Army moving forward more quickly.[39]

At the beginning of Operation 'Citadel' German forces could field 1,632 tanks and assault guns, along with 230 self-propelled anti-tanks guns as part of Panzer or Panzergrenadier divisions of the Wehrmacht and SS, including 57 Tiger or Panzer VI tanks out of a total of 146 participating in the offensive. Additionally the Panzer and Panzergrenadier divisions could field seventy-eight Wespe and fifty-four Hummel self-propelled artillery pieces. More than 600 of these tanks were Panzer III, with 58 lighter models still serving. Not only most of the new Tiger tanks, but also the new Panthers and assault guns were fielded outside the Panzer and Panzergrenadier divisions, with the bulk of the 466 StuG III and all of the 89 Ferdinands fielded as such. Ultimately, according to Niklas Zetterling and Anders Frankson German forces were able to deploy in the region of 2,451 tanks and assault guns for 'Citadel', along with approximately 777,000 men, 7,417 guns and mortars and 1,830 aircraft.[40] Clearly, in crude statistical terms, German forces did not have numerical superiority in the region even if local superiority in men and armour would be achieved during the early phases of the attack. Such circumstances had not stopped the German armed forces from achieving dramatic operational successes in 1941 and 1942, but these had been achieved in circumstances where there was room for maneuver and against a less capable Red Army.

Not only had troops and equipment been massed by the Red Army in preparation for the expected German attack, but there had perhaps been more time for training than before the many rushed or almost continuous offensives that characterised 1941 and 1942. In July 1943 recently graduated junior officer Elektron Priklonskii and his colleagues did at least get to familiarise themselves with their new equipment on the firing range before being thrown into battle – something that had certainly not been guaranteed in the desperate weeks of the autumn of 1941 before Moscow for example. After completing his training at the training school by May 1943, by June Priklonskii had been in uniform for a whole year. His training might have been more limited than might have been desirable due to material concerns such as not 'wasting' ammunition during only two live firing exercises in late 1942 and early 1943, but at least he had spent the full allotted time in training. Two weeks spent in the Cheliabinsk Tank Factory in the Urals near where they were training seems certainly to have been of value in gaining an appreciation of the workings of the sort of vehicles in which he would serve. During June his unit – '1548th Heavy Self-Propelled Artillery Regiment of the High Command Reserve' – was provided with the necessary NCOs and rank and file personnel before receipt of their new equipment in early July and subsequent dispatch to the front.[41] Former border guard Aleksandr Sergeevich Shlemotov had entered the 2nd Gor'kov Motorcycle School by early July 1942, which then became 2nd Gor'kov Tank School, where despite similar cold and poor food he apparently 'studied alot and with enthusiasm [*okhotno*]' prior to graduation at the end of May 1943 as a lieutenant and T-34 platoon commander. He was soon a platoon commander of 1st Company, 2nd Battalion, 243rd Molotov [Perm'] Tank Regiment as part of which he participated in further training at Kubinka near Moscow before being sent to the front in late July where he would participate in offensive operations on the Orel axis.[42] One of the recently formed armoured formations to be committed in the aftermath of Operation 'Citadel' would be 4th Tank Army, formed for a second time in late June and into which Shlemotov's brigade as part of 30th Urals Volunteer Tank Corps would be incorporated.[43] In command

would be General-Leitenant V.M. Badanov, who had led the deep penetration or raid to Tatsinskaia at the end of 1942. Unfortunately, although
some of its tank crews may have received adequate training, formed only
in late June and early July, by the time it was committed 4th Tank Army
had been a formation for far too little time to function effectively. Future
Marshal A. Kh. Babadzhanian, at the time a brigade commander, notes
in an article on tank and mechanised forces at Kursk that the headquarters elements of such a recently formed army were 'staffed by young
officers were not functioning as a team and prepared for the firm direction of forces. Even in higher level headquarters there was far from
sufficient clarity regarding how tank armies of the new type should be
used operationally'.[44] With an increase in the number of corps in the Red
Army in early 1943 capable and experience staff officers remained in
short supply. Russian historian of the Kursk battle Valerii Zamulin cites
the chief of staff of 40th Army of the Voronezh Front who reported that
staff officers at corps level were apparently often provided from a reserve
pool and that 'the overwhelming majority' had no experience of the Great
Patriotic War to this point, going on to note how at Kursk:

> They did have academic training, but the practical responsibilities of a
> headquarters staff were not studied. Their theoretical knowledge adjusted to
> the realities of combat very slowly; in the first days of the battle they controlled
> their forces so poorly that army headquarters was forced to completely take over
> their duties.[45]

Fortunately, fixed Soviet defences were well-prepared, with significant
efforts in terms of deception and *maskirovka* limiting German appreciation of the true strength of Soviet forces in the region. German forces
certainly had considerable time to study Soviet defences from the ground
and air – with future Major-General or *Generalmajor* F.W. von Mellenthin,
then with XLVIII Panzer Corps, going as far as suggesting that 'air photos
were available for every yard of the Kursk salient'. In the light of Soviet
camouflage von Mellenthin goes on to note how Soviet 'strength was
considerably underestimated'.[46] Camouflage and deception – in combination *maskirovka* – were something that was being improved by the Red
Army after considerable dissatisfaction with concealment in particular
having been voiced prior to the war. The General Staff continued to
complain about inadequate measures on the Kursk salient and elsewhere
during the summer of 1943 – on 20 June 1943 Antonov of the General
Staff complaining about a number of instances of Soviet positions being
identified by German aerial reconnaissance after German aircraft had
been shot down.[47] Chief of the General Staff Vasilevskii both praised
and criticised efforts in both camouflage and deception at the end of the

month, noting that on the Voronezh Front out of the last twenty-five German air attacks on airfields only three had hit operational airfields and the remainder decoys, and called for more to give *maskirovka* 'due attention'.[48] In order to disguise troops movements within the Steppe Military District training units had been ordered at the end of May to march southwards during the daylight and return at night.[49] Some appreciation for the resources now thrown into *maskirovka* can be gained from efforts of 38th Army on the Kursk salient, where whole units including a rifle division and three different types of engineering battalion – contributed to deception efforts that included seven radio stations functioning as if they were for units that weren't actually there and for whom there were 450 dummy tanks and with 18 lorries, eight tanks and a rail detachment consisting of 20 wagons being used to create the impression troops movements.[50]

Future Marshal K.S. Moskalenko, then commanding the 40th Army of the Voronezh Front, provides a useful description of the defences on the south-western sector of the Kursk salient defended by forces under his command. As Moskalenko notes, particular attention was paid in preparing defences to anti-tank and anti-aircraft defence – to the latter more than 50 per cent of machine guns apparently being allocated in addition to dedicated anti-aircraft forces – with the preparation of battalion-strength strongpoints and company positions being a particular focus in defensive preparation. According to Moskalenko, on the principal defensive belt five trench lines were linked by communications trenches, with each division on average having prepared 70–80 km of trenches with 6–7 bunkers for every kilometer of frontage, with such positions and shelters for troops against air attack and artillery bombardment being camouflaged from both the ground and air. On those axes on which principal enemy attacks were expected anti-tank ditches were dug, on river banks escarpments were created, and in wooded areas trees were felled and mines added to these barriers. These earthworks and defences were complemented by barbed wire and minefields, where 40th Army alone is recorded as having placed nearly 60,000 anti-tank and more than 70,000 anti-personnel mines in total across not only as part of the above first defensive belt, but also as part of a second, which 'on the more important axes did not differ from the first in terms of defences, only the concentration of mines was reduced'. In addition to the anti-tank and anti-personnel mines, more than 6,000 shells were also used as mines, with delayed action mines being used to block roads and bridges and cover any retreat by Soviet forces. Barbed wire was apparently set up before positions as much as 3–4 rows deep. Covering in particular key probable axes of advance and potential choke points created not only by the terrain but also the defences were anti-tank strongpoints, where in addition to average divisional concentrations of eleven anti-tank guns and up to ten PTRD per kilometer, from at best regimental level and above commanders had the support of reserve anti-tank units for deployment to meet enemy attacks and breakthroughs, but also units of sappers tasked with sowing additional mines in front of actual enemy advances. In direct subordination to the front command there were five sapper battalions provided with lorries and 2–5,000 mines and up to 500 kg of explosives.[51] German forces did not attack the positions established by 40th Army, but did attack neighbouring positions that had similarly been prepared in accordance with instructions from above. In a 1978 article in the Soviet *Military History Journal*, Z. Shutov provides a detailed description of the defences occupied by the 3rd Rifle Battalion of 228th Guards Rifle Regiment, 78th Guards Rifle Division as part of the defences on the southern face or Belgorod-Kursk axis of the Kursk salient. For defence of its positions the battalion was allocated, in addition to core strength, a sub-machine gun company, an anti-tank rifle company, an anti-tank battery and a sapper platoon, with fire support to be provided by an artillery *divizion*.[52]

In the light of discussion of the use of penal forces in Chapter 15 it is worth noting, according to former medic A. Bublikov, the presence of an officer's penal battalion in positions in front of regular battalion defenses near the village of Lukhanino also on the Belgorod-Kursk axis in the south.[53] Anti-tank resources beyond those that were list strength of infantry units were typically in part forward deployed in anti-tank strongpoints, in part held in reserve. Hence of ten independent anti-tank artillery regiments allocated to 6th Guards Army of the Voronezh Front – against which enemy strength was expected to be concentrated along with against 7th Guards Army – two were held in reserve and ten provided to rifle divisions in the first echelon of the defences, where with the exception of elements of one regiment they were used together in regimental strength (in the region of twenty guns) in anti-tank zones within rifle company or battalion defensive positions.[54] As for tanks, as part of the defences they were, as the Soviet General Staff study of the Kursk battle notes, used in regimental and brigade strength under army control and used 'to reinforce the second, and partially the main defensive belt'. At times tanks were deployed on key axes in platoon and company strength to reinforce infantry units. In some instances – the study citing the case of 6th Guards Army – tanks were used as mobile anti-tank guns as part of anti-tank strong points with 10–15 tanks.[55] Supporting these forces were not only their organic artillery assets, but also assets from Supreme High Command Reserve that by 5 July would for example give 6th Guards Army of the Voronezh Front a concentration of artillery (guns and mortars) of in the region of twenty-six pieces per kilometer, thirty-one per kilometer for 7th Guards Army, and thirty-two per kilometer for 40th Army. In a piece on artillery during the battle of Kursk former commander of artillery for the Steppe Front, General-Colonel N.S. Fomin, suggests that this concentration was in the case of 6th Guards Army for example more than twice the concentration available at best during defensive fighting on the Moscow axis in October 1941. Such a concentration of artillery assets was, as he notes, unusual for a defensive operation, where overall, even if not necessarily at the points at which German forces actually attacked, Soviet superiority in terms of artillery was in the region of 2:1.[56] Such a concentration of assets was of course, as discussed later, with a view to not only dealing with German offensive operations – but also facilitating the Soviet counterattack in conditions where although Soviet artillery enjoyed improved mobility compared to late 1941 for example, it was nonetheless provided with at best only 60 per cent of the transport resources deemed necessary in list strengths.[57] As Fomin notes, in the event of enemy attack it was planned to unleash a 30-minute barrage on enemy forces – the focus of one of the armies of the Central Front in the north being on enemy artillery assets, of 6th Guards Army in the south on enemy infantry and tanks. In either case the intention was as noted above to expend half a *boekomplekt* or reload of ammunition on this counterpreparation alone.[58]

During the early hours of 2 July 1943 the Stavka once again warned the Soviet fronts on the Kursk salient and indeed more broadly to the north and south of the possibility that German forces would go over to the offensive between 3–6 July, requesting increased reconnaissance activity and readiness to meet the enemy attack.[59] A German prisoner captured during German probing attacks on the afternoon of 4 July on the Voronezh Front provided, along with deserters from German forces opposing the Central Front, strong evidence that the German attack would start in earnest the following day and Soviet artillery counter preparation was planned for that night.[60] As noted by Colonel General Erhard Raus, commander of the German XI Corps on the southern side of the salient along the Donets, during the small hours of 5 July Soviet forces did lay down 'a destructive fire on suspected crossing sites around Belgorod, resulting in considerable German casualties'. Almost immediately after this bombardment nonetheless forces of Armeeabteilung Kempf on the right flank of German forces in the south started crossing the Donets.[61] Further west von Mellenthin notes how the Panzergrenadier division 'Großdeutschland', assembling in dense formation, ..., was heavily shelled by Russian artillery' and that 'many tanks fell victim to the Red Air Force' despite German air superiority.[62]

Troops of an anti-tank company in frontline positions on the Central Front on the Kursk salient on 5 July 1943. Their anti-tank rifles remained effective against more lightly armoured German vehicles such as armoured personnel carriers even at this stage of the war. (RIA Novosti #611205)

The purpose of this chapter is not to give a blow-by-blow account of the battle for the Kursk salient, but to highlight where the Red Army proved more or less effective. It is firstly worth noting that Soviet fixed defences 'with an intricate system of minefields and anti-tank defences' did indeed prove effective in, as von Mellenthin suggests, taking the 'sting' out of the German attack even if particularly in the south they did not prove successful at restraining German forces to the extent intended in part because of the incorrect intelligence assessment that the principal German blow would be from the north.[63] Uncharacteristic-ally, there seems to have been an element of accepted give or elasticity in the Soviet defences where von Mellenthin writing of Soviet forces 'yielding ground adroitly' was not without foundation. The rifle regiment served by medic A. Bublikov mentioned above eventually retreated 5–6 km from positions including Lukhanino after having been partially encir-cled.[64] 3rd Rifle Battalion, 228th Guards Rifle Regiment, 78th Guards Rifle Division, whose defensive positions are described earlier, also did not fight until overwhelmed on the left wing of the southern flank of the salient, but was eventually 'pulled out of the battle' from positions of the first defensive belt by the regimental commander towards the end of the day on 5 July.[65] The give in the defences should not be exaggerated however – Soviet troops more often than not fought to defend positions until overwhelmed. Soviet infantry positions were provided for with anti-tank defences but typically fought without obvious armoured support – and with anti-tank regiments fighting as an almost separate entity within infantry defensive positions. The new German 'heavy' tanks that spear-headed German attacks – and particularly the Tiger – gave German attacks considerable momentum despite the considerable anti-tank defences built up by Soviet forces. One problem with the Kursk defences was the failure to allocate control of resources in a given location to a single commander on the ground. Anti-tank guns from outside the regiment and armour used as part of anti-tank strongpoints were, for example, not typically at least under the authority of an infantry com-mander – be it at the battalion or regimental level – within whose defensive positions the anti-tank assets were positioned. Consequently co-ordination was often poor. This was not a problem that would be resolved by the end of the war. Infantry commanders were able to control all the assets within a given area typically only in the very specific circumstances of storm groups and detachments formed in an urban environment. Even a divisional commander could not expect to control all resources deployed within either defensive positions or on a sector on which his division was to attack, even if corps, army or other assets including air assets had theoretically been deployed to support his troops. As a Soviet post-war manual with historical examples from the Great Patriotic War notes, from Kursk onwards co-operation in defence was organised higher up the chain of command 'in the interests of' rifle battalions as units that by now were acknowledged as being the basic building blocks of the defence, although this was not the same as giving them control over assets allocated to support them. This section on the regiment on the defence can usefully be compared to that dealing with the regiment on the attack in an urban area where different elements such as even the tanks were incorporated 'in the combat grouping' [*v boevom poriadke*].[66] As the commander of 121st Rifle Division noted in a May 1944 letter to Zhukov concerned with issues in Red Army performance, the end result of a situation where an infantry commander did not have authority over assets deployed in support of his troops was not just poor co-ordination but more 'friendly fire' incidents. Ladigin's letter to Zhu-kov is in many ways a damning indictment of some of the worst failings of the Red Army that persisted throughout the war and that stemmed from the culture of mistrust that permeated the system. For Ladigin, there was a need to trust officers down the chain of command, not constantly be checking up on them – in Russian pithily stated as '*nado doveriat'*, *ne proveriat*".[67] Such was typically not however the case, and was certainly not the case for many infantry commanders at Kursk whose battalions and regiments would face the German onslaught.

Despite the toll that Soviet defences took on the German attackers during the first days of 'Citadel' the principal German blow from the south was faced by Soviet forces with inadequate front reserves to adequately reinforce the defences there. In the north, where reserves were greater, armoured reserves were committed to the defence relatively early on where there was, in the case of 2nd Tank Army and 19th Tank Corps on 6 July for example, attempt to restore the front line after German penetration with far from overwhelming success in a battle of attrition in which German forces were still able to inflict more sizeable casualties on their opponent despite the advantages enjoyed by the Soviet side.[68] In the south, as Zamulin notes, despite the nonetheless significant defence lines Manstein's Army Group South took 'only 18 hours to overcome the first line and even less for the second'. Despite Vatutin and the staff of the Voronezh Front having a fairly good appreciation of broad German intentions on that sector of the front, counterattacks during the early part of the defensive period of the battle from 6–8 July – planned according to Zamulin at army level with broad direction from above – showed 'poor preparation, unjustified haste and an exaggerated idea of the troops' capabilities (especially the tanks')'.With the enemy seemingly having the initiative, Zamulin suggest that Vatutin and the front command rushed into attempting to rectify the situation – a product of Vatutin's personality according to Zamulin but also the sort of behaviour typical of the 'can do' generals that Stalin had promoted and had frequently threatened in the past for not taking decisive action soon enough.[69] On 9 July the Steppe Military District was activated as a front as a response to the tense situation in the south where German forces had penetrated two defensive lines and were engaging a third, including Soviet forces in the Prokhorovka area.[70] On 8 July 5th Guards Army had been transferred from reserves to the Voronezh Front and required to move 140 km westwards in order to man defences on the River Psel along a 45–50 km front from Oboian' to Prokhorovka. By first light on 11 July 5th Guards Army's forward units were only just starting to take up positions.[71] Also transferred from reserves for deployment in the south was 5th Guards Tank Army which was transferred to the Voronezh Front on 6 July. At this point 5th Guards Tank Army consisted of 18 and 29th Tank and 5th Guards Mechanised Corps, 53rd Guards Tank, 1st Guards Motorcycle, 678th howitzer, 689th Anti-Tank Destruction Artillery and 76th Guards (Rocket) Mortar Regiments and supporting elements.[72] 5th Guards Tank Army received orders to move more than 300 km westwards during the second half of 6 July. By the morning of 10 July 5th Guards Tank Army had taken up positions north-west of Prokhorovka, by which time German forces had already penetrated up to 35 km into the Soviet defences.[73] It is probably not a surprise to readers that in the face of a situation where only the broad thrust of German plans were apparent, and where German forces had seized a meaningful degree of tactical and operational initiative despite Soviet defences, that Soviet command and control was slow to respond to changing circumstances and that a significant degree of confusion reigned. The Soviet chain of command – hampered by the poor staff work noted above as well as communications – was slow to pass information and orders up and down. Only limited reconnaissance as German operations progressed also contributed to the fact that the Soviet response to German thrusts was often far from timely, well directed and even well informed. For example, with 5th Guards Tank Army in position to the north-west of Prokhorovka, during the early evening of 11 July at about 5:00 p.m. Stavka representative Marshal Vasilevskii was according to its commander, Pavel Rotmistrov, at the army's command post when he pointed out 'a few dozen tanks' moving down the road near the 'Komsomolets' Sovkhoz. According to Rotmistrov a stern Vasilevskii looked at him and asked 'what is going on? Why have you released your tanks earlier than planned?' Having looked through his binoculars, Rotmistrov reported that the tanks were in fact German! Two tank brigades of 29th Tank Corps were apparently therefore committed to halt the German advance. The next morning –12 July – after a fifteen minute barrage and air attacks, units of 5th Guards Tank Army were thrown into the attack in concentration in what even the Soviet General Staff study of the Kursk fighting describes as a 'frontal attack against crack German panzer divisions'.[74]

What subsequently became known as the battle of Prokhorovka was undoubtedly one of the largest and most significant tank battles in history, although both the size and significance of the engagement were undoubtedly exaggerated in the Soviet historiography.[75] As is apparent from the exchange between Rotmistrov and Vasilevskii, the Prokhorovka battle in many ways did not start on 12 July when 5th Guards Tank Army was to be thrown in the counterattack, but had been in progress for a number of days. The 2nd Tank Corps had reached the Prokhorovka area by the night of 8 July and that day, along with 2nd Guards Tatsinskaia Tank Corps and other units, met advancing German forces. In addition to 29th Tank Corps – two tank brigades of which were committed by Rotmistrov above – 2nd Tank Corps on their left flank that was now to be subordinated to 5th Guards Tank Army was also in

action on 11 July and indeed its 99th Tank Brigade was encircled by
enemy forces that day– an encirclement from which it broke out after
remaining encircled during the night of 11–12 July. On the morning of
12 July after Soviet air strikes and artillery preparation the first echelon
of 5th Guards Tank Army – 18th, 29th and 2nd Guards Tank Corps –
moved off to engage advancing German forces of II SS Panzer Corps
consisting of 1st, 2nd and 3rd SS Panzergrenadier Divisions.[76] Of these
German divisions 3rd SS Panzergrenadier Division 'Totenkopf' was
committed on the left flank primarily against forces of 5th Guards Army,
and 1st SS Panzergrenadier Division 'Leibstandarte' faced the bulk of
5th Guards Tank Army and subordinate units in the centre moving
towards the village of Prokhorovka. 'Das Reich' – 2nd SS Panzergrenadier Division – operated on the right flank.[77] According to Zetterling
and Frankson, on 12 July, depending on the geographical confines set
for the battle, 'from 294 German (II SS Panzer Corps) and 616 Soviet
AFV (those engaging II SS Panzer Corps) up to a maximum of
429 German and 870 Soviet AFV' participated in the battle of Prokhorovka – which Zetterling and Frankson see as having continued up until
16 July.[78] During the battle neither side achieved what it set out to
achieve – II SS Panzer Corps did not take Prokhorovka and advance,
but nor did 5th Guards Tank Army and other Soviet units and formations push back and destroy II SS Panzer Corps.

Rotmistrov's explanation as to why 5th Guards Tank Army did not
achieve its objective of 12 July to advance to the south-west contains
some truths, although the claim that German forces had a numerical
advantage 'on the principal axis' in fielding 'up to 700 tanks including
more than 100 heavy tanks' compared to 'slightly more than 500 tanks'
on the Soviet side, 'of which 200 were light' is certainly misleading.[79]
After repeating the fiction of more than 100 heavy tanks ('Tigers') and
self-propelled 'Ferdinand' guns in the Prokhorovka region the Soviet
General Staff study analysis of the battle on 12 July notes a German
counterattack by thirteen 'Tiger' tanks during the morning, but the
remaining German heavy tank strength is not in evidence.[80] There were
not in fact, any Ferdinands on the whole of the southern sector of the
Kursk salient.[81] That, as Rotmistrov suggests, German operations on
11 July disrupted Soviet preparations for offensive operations on 12 July
is undoubtedly the case, as is Rotmistrov's claim that the desired forces
could not be concentrated on the principal axis because of the need to
defend the flanks. Rotmistrov's final explanation for not achieving
objectives of 12 July is a lack of air and artillery support – with of course
no mention of the capabilities of what in fact was a smaller German force
as a factor.[82] In fighting in which Soviet armoured forces had a numerical

advantage, and during which both sides attacked and defended during the wider battle beyond 12 July, Soviet forces undoubtedly came off worse. Wild Soviet claims for German losses on 12 July for example – with 'up to 400 tanks lost' by German forces that day alone in the Prokhorovka region according to Ivanovskii who was chief of intelligence for 2nd Tank Corps at the time – were far from accurate.[83] 5th Guards Tank Army had been thrown into the counterattack with a very poor appreciation of enemy strength which seems subsequently to have been exaggerated to justify the heavy losses sustained by Soviet forces. Rotmistrov's 1970 claim that during that day both sides lost 'around 300 tanks' is relatively close to the mark for Soviet losses, where Zamulin calculates that 5th Guards Tank Corps lost 194 tanks burnt out and 146 otherwise knocked out for 12 July, a total of 340 tanks or just over 50 per cent of the force committed.[84] Military soviet political member Nikita Khrushchev would report on 14 July that during 12 July 18th and 29th Tank Corps 'lost' 113 T-34, 48 T-70 and 15 Churchills or 176 tanks in total along with 3 self-propelled guns, with 261 killed and 720 wounded personnel.[85] German losses were certainly significantly lower. On the evening of 12 July 2nd SS Panzergrenadier Division 'Das Reich' could actually field more tanks and assault guns than the previous evening – 103 compared to 95 – and although figures for 1st SS Panzergrenadier Division 'Leibstandarte' do not seem to be available for the evening of 12 July, the following evening its operational strength had dropped only slightly from seventy-seven on 11 July to seventy in a situation where there was certainly an insufficient number of tanks under repair on 11 July whose return to operational status could hide subsequent battlefield losses as high as those claimed by Rotmistrov.[86] Interestingly, in Stavka representative Vasilevskii's report to Stalin of 14 July on events in the Prokhorovka region in which he noted the loss during two days of fighting – both total write offs and repairable – of up to 60 per cent of the tanks of 29th Tank Corps and 30 per cent of 18th Tank Corps, assessment of German strength on the basis of prisoner interrogation is in part fairly accurate. As of 14 July 'Das Reich' was noted to have up to 100 operational tanks – 107 according to German figures for the previous evening. It was however suggested that 19th Panzer Division of III Panzer Corps was able to field around seventy tanks, where German figures for that morning however note an operational strength of twenty-eight tanks.[87]

On 13 July 5th Guards Tank Army committed additional strength to the Prokhorovka fighting, the following day Vasilevskii reporting to Stalin that on 13 July he himself had witnessed an engagement between 18th and 29th Tank Corps and 'more than 200 enemy tanks on the counterattack'. As a result of this engagement Vasilevskii noted that within an hour 'the battlefield was strewn with our own burning tanks and those of the Germans'.[88] At 19:00 that day 18th Tank Corps had only 15 T-34 and 18 T-70s operable, having had 159 operable tanks at 16:00 the previous day.[89] By 16 July 5th Guards Tank Army had taken very high losses both in men and material, but had nonetheless blunted the German attack on the Prokhorovka axis. Personnel losses for 5th Guards Tank Army as a formation were very high – perhaps in the region of 14,000 total casualties to 23 July.[90] For the period to 16 July the Voronezh Front as a whole reported irrecoverable losses of 1,204 tanks, with a further 655 knocked out [podbito] – along with 29 self-propelled guns as irrecoverable losses. Soviet equipment losses were not only heavy in tanks, but also artillery, where during the period of enemy advance up to 16 July the front lost a staggering 1,605 artillery pieces of all calibres in addition to 1,734 mortars. The front reported 18,097 personnel killed, 47,272 wounded and 24,851 missing – with 29 known to have been captured by the enemy.[91] Fortunately during the 'Kursk Strategic Defensive Operation from 5–23 July' overall losses of personnel, whilst still utterly horrendous, were perhaps modest by Soviet standards given the scale of the fighting where of more than 1.25 million personnel committed approximately 70,330 ended up as irrecoverable losses with 107,517 wounded.[92] In some senses material losses were restraining lives lost. For the other side, the Soviet General Staff analysis of the battle suggested German losses in tanks and assault guns of around '300 tanks and 20 assault guns' over five days of fighting against 5th Guards Tank Army alone, although German losses were undoubtedly dramatically lower than Soviet estimates.[93] Soviet claims for overall German losses are probably closer to Soviet losses for 5th Guards Army of 334 tanks and assault guns as total write offs to 16 July, where during the Prokhorovka battle Zetterling and Frankson calculate German losses at most at 54 tanks and assault guns destroyed.[94] Although German historian Friesner suggests that only thirty-three tanks and self-propelled guns can be identified as total losses in German archival sources for the whole of 'Citadel', his section in the semi-official German history of the Second World War ultimately gives total German losses for Operation 'Citadel', from 5–16 July, as 252 tanks and 54,182 personnel – far lower than Soviet losses but nonetheless a significant blow.[95]

Although 'Citadel' had not seen the sort of German losses that might have been hoped for by the Soviet high command, in many ways it was still a momentous operational failure for the German armed forces and considerable Soviet success. Despite a considerable massing of resources by Germany – including the latest tank and assault gun types even if they were not available in the sort of exaggerated numbers portrayed in Soviet accounts and suffering inevitable teething troubles – the Red Army had held and inflicted significant losses on the enemy. Soviet losses had been high, but materially at least they had been sustainable and the Red Army had the reserves to exploit its defensive success. For the last time in the East the German armed forces would be able to even claim to hold anything that might be termed the initiative on an operational-strategic scale – and even then to claim that was the case at Kursk might be considered an exaggeration.

20   To the Dnepr and Beyond

12 July 1943 was a significant date for the Soviet war effort not only in that it saw 5th Guards Tank Army thrown into the counterattack on the southern sector of the Kursk salient, but more because it saw the start of broader Soviet counteroffensive operations on the northern side of the Kursk salient where German forces had been held after penetrating only 15 km into Soviet defences. On 12 July Operation 'Kutuzov' was finally launched – the first of the major Soviet counteroffensives to be launched on the back of the defence of the Kursk salient – and that would see the Briansk and part of the Western Fronts begin operations to destroy German forces in the Orel region. On 15 July the Briansk and Western Fronts would be joined by forces of the Central Front on the Kursk salient, with Orel falling to Soviet forces in early August. While Zhukov as Stavka representative could be genuinely pleased with the initial progress in breaking through German defences on 12 July, Soviet forces were initially able to play to what were arguably becoming strengths – the mass employment of artillery as part of prepared operations to break through reasonably well reconnoitred enemy forward defences.[1] When the southern side of the Kursk salient went over to the counteroffensive on 5 August as part of Operation 'Rumiantsev' or the Belgorod-Khar'kov Offensive there was similar initial success in breaking through German defences, where despite criticism of 5th and 6th Guards Armies by front command for poor reconnaissance in force of enemy defences Zhukov praised the Voronezh and Steppe Fronts for 'the appropriate use of breakthrough artillery divisions'. Zhukov also praised their use of concentrated artillery during the initial phase of the pursuit of enemy forces before running into prepared enemy defences once again, by which point the breakthrough forces were no longer concentrated.[2] Soon Soviet forces would be on the offensive across the whole of the south as Soviet forces were tasked not only with the destruction of German forces in the Khar'kov region but also the liberation of the Donbass.[3] Despite initial successes both north and south of the Kursk salient in breaking through enemy defences and introducing tank armies that could then exploit the

breakthrough and penetrate into operational depths, soon Soviet operations were losing their initial momentum. Vatutin, commanding the
Voronezh Front was on 5 August critical of the frontal assaults being
conducted by 5th Guards Army and 5th Guards and 6th Tank Corps as
they advanced, and on 7 August the General Staff was critical of 5th
Guards Army and 1st Tank Army of the Voronezh Front for not concentrating forces but instead dissipating strength in a number of different
directions.[4] The Stavka certainly played a part in the loss of concentration of Soviet forces and loss of operational momentum as it sought to
amend operational plans to exploit initial successes without taking into
consideration the limitations of the large and to some extent unwieldy
formations involved. Part of the problem in maintaining momentum
nonetheless certainly remained poor frontline reconnaissance once an
operation was already underway – adding to command and control woes
that meant that Soviet forces were less likely to be concentrated where it
mattered during an operation than at the beginning – and particularly
when objectives kept changing. In just one of numerous examples of
criticism from above of issues relating to reconnaissance and command
and control, the senior officer of the General Staff on the Western Front
noted when discussing operations by 11th Guards Army for the period
from 12 July to the end of the month how insufficient attention was paid
in this instance by infantry and artillery forces to reconnaissance, with
poor communications both between units of the same arm and units of
other arms supposed to be co-ordinating their activities with them. Poor
communications and co-ordination was an issue for armoured forces not
only in terms of the lack of control being exercised by tank corps commanders, but all the way down to company and platoon level where 'in
the main tank crews carry out tasks on their own as a result of weak
control over tank forces on the battlefield'. Artillery, 'and particularly
corps and High Command Reserve artillery' lagged behind the infantry,
with the motorised infantry or cavalry available to tank corps being
insufficient to provide them with suitable support. When discussing
1st Tank Corps it was similarly suggested that the tank corps needed
support from mechanised forces and artillery if they were to be successful in their operations at operational depth. For 1st Tank Corps there
were at least a few examples of the sort of resources required – eleven
'American armoured transports (MK-3)' – presumably M3A1 scout
cars – and a regiment of what were probably SU-122 represented the
sort of support that later in the war would facilitate operations still often
dominated by tanks but with more appropriate support. Having started
operations with 204 tanks plus reserves – although most with more than
200 motor hours on them – by 24 July the corps was down to 40, one

assumes operable, tanks.[5] Forward units – such as 112th, 49th and 1st Guards Brigades of 1st Tank Army – were vulnerable to being cut off by German forces as they advanced with little effective reconnaissance, as indeed was the case for these units in the face of counterattacks by the 'Totenkopf' and 'Wiking' Panzergrenadier Divisions in mid-August near Bogodukhov after 1st Tank Army had changed the direction of its advance as a result of orders from above. By 22 August losses for 1st Tank Army had been so high that after having pulled six tank brigades from combat the remaining forces of the formation provided support for rifle divisions of 4th Guards Army as 1st Tank Army's participation in the Belgorod-Khar'kov Operation effectively ended.[6] On the Orel axis during this period 3rd Guards Tank Army of the Central Front was noted to have lost 100 tanks out of 110 within the space of a matter of hours in an attempt to take heights defended by enemy forces – an incident that was far from being an exception despite taking place in general circumstances where the enemy was retreating and lacked pre-prepared defensive positions. The problem – according to Antonov of the General Staff – was not unreasonably seen to be a lack of co-operation with other arms where the commander in this instance had 'thrown tanks to their fates [*na proizvol sudbi*] without any sort of support'.[7] As Soviet forces ploughed forward – pushed forward by senior commanders all the way to top and with inadequate reconnaissance – there was not only considerable scope for Soviet forces to blunder into enemy defences without appropriate support, but also for ambushes. One such ambush is described by infantryman Mansur Abdulin of 66th Guards Rifle Division, 32nd Guards Rifle Corps, 5th Guards Army as his unit advanced in the aftermath of Kursk. Despite regimental reconnaissance having declared the next two kilometres clear of German forces, Abdulin's battalion and regiment advancing in column were caught in an ambush by German tanks. As infantry, at least Abdulin and his unit could dig in – Soviet tanks could not.[8]

Soviet armoured losses were consistently far heavier than those of German forces during the Great Patriotic War and certainly during the summer of 1943 to a large extent because decision-making was poorly informed by intelligence and then Soviet forces poorly co-ordinated – what in modern terms would be described as inadequate C3I. From 5th Guards Tank Army being thrown into the counterattack with only a poor appreciation of German strength, to at the tactical level target allocation and engagement being hampered by poor communications, massed Soviet armoured forces and indeed concentrations of any arm were still a rather blunt instrument. In mid-1943 Soviet armoured forces could frequently, and particularly early on in an offensive, apply assets *en masse* and achieve local superiority – often overwhelming defences. As the German commander of 17th Panzer Division noted in April 1943, weight of numbers could win the day – if heavily losses were an acceptable cost – and indeed Soviet tank formations would achieve much taking such losses.[9] Certainly, as noted in a report from 103rd Panzer Artillery Regiment concerned with both offensive and defensive action south of Orel from 5 July–18 August 1943, German infantry divisions did not have the available anti-tank resources to stop massed Soviet attacks alone, the author comparing an infantry division to a corset requiring the boning of tanks and other more - anti-tank capable branches for support.[10] However, despite successes in penetrating German lines, during this period of the war the Red Army was finally able to deploy armour *en masse* and at times in concentration as part of large formations during a period however where massed armour even when supported by, but in the Soviet case in particular not necessarily well integrated with, other arms was increasingly vulnerable. As the German commander of 17th Panzer Division noted in late April 1943:

The Panzer tactics that led to the great successes in the years 1939, 1940 and 1941 must be viewed as outdated. Even if today it is still possible to breach an anti-tank defensive front through concentrated Panzer forces employed in several waves behind each other, we must consider past experience that this always leads to significant losses that cannot be endured by our production situation.[11]

What could perhaps not be endured by German forces was however being endured by Soviet forces, which during 1943 as a whole would lose in the region of 23,500 tanks and self-propelled guns – about half of available stocks.[12] Such losses were suffered before the widespread use of infantry anti-tank weapons such as the *Panzerfaust* that would provide German infantry units with far greater anti-tank capabilities against tanks operating with inadequate infantry support than they had previously had.

By the end of 1943 a Soviet tank corps could, at least if at list strength, field more than 200 tanks and approaching fifty self-propelled guns, with a mechanized corps fielding only slightly fewer tanks and self-propelled guns.[13] Still all too often Soviet tank attacks by these formations even when forces had been suitably concentrated did not hit a weak spot in enemy defences, with Soviet forces often attacking frontally due to the weakness of reconnaissance and command and control, and all too often poorly supported by other arms. Valuable fire support in such break-throughs was fortunately on the horizon in the form of the heavy self-propelled guns that saw limited service at Kursk and in greater numbers in the subsequent counteroffensives. This fire support would certainly increase the chances of anti-tank assets being destroyed – and indeed in the battle between armour and anti-tank weapons new heavy tanks would further increase the number of tanks likely to survive a breakthrough of enemy defences.

Soviet tanks employed *en masse* were vulnerable not only to concentrated anti-tank defences, and particularly in depth, but as had become apparent by mid-1943 in engagements that included meeting engagements, by this point Soviet tanks were more vulnerable to the fire of German armoured vehicles than they had been the previous year. By mid-1943 the T-34 tanks and to a lesser extent KV-series tanks that were the principal medium and heavy Soviet tanks no longer had the superiority in armour and firepower that had taken poorly handed armoured forces as far as was often the case the previous year. The Tiger and Panther tanks fielded at Kursk, despite the teething problems of the latter in particular, were superior in both regards to Soviet tanks and particularly where tactical control prevented Soviet armour from being able to engage them on the flanks. However, there were relatively few of these tanks at Kursk – and certainly far fewer than Soviet accounts suggest where production of the Tiger had only just passed 50 per month, and the Panther 100 per month, compared to well over 200 per month for production of the long-barreled gun-armed version of the Panzer IV. Nonetheless, even the up-gunned Panzer IV – the principal variant armed with the long-barreled L/48 75 mm gun – was more than capable of knocking out T-34s at reasonable combat ranges, with the StuG III assault gun by now, and indeed from the 1942 F variant, armed with such a capable weapon along with many of the German self-propelled anti-tank guns on tank chassis such as the H and M variants of the Marder III. Although it would take time, the late 1943 model Panzer division, with a mix of long-barrelled Panzer IV and ultimately Panthers as they became available, would prove not only more than capable of combating Soviet units still equipped with the 76 mm gun armed variant of the T-34 but also as something of a shock to Allied forces in the West where it would take time to make meaningful numbers of 17 pounder-armed Sherman tanks available.[14] The up-gunning of existing German tanks, new tanks with better armament, and larger calibre and higher velocity German anti-tank guns such as the PaK 40 both self-propelled and otherwise, meant that at Kursk and in the subsequent offensive towards Orel Soviet forces noted a far higher proportion of tanks completely destroyed as opposed to simply damaged. Where during operations near Stalingrad only 25–30 per cent of tanks knocked out by German and allied forces were total write-offs, during the 'Orlov-Kursk Operation' during July and August 1943 that percentage was more like 60–65 per cent. Of 7,942 Soviet tanks identified as having participated in the operation, 2,971 or nearly 40 per cent were identified as having been knocked out, with a staggering total of more than 1,700 total write offs.[15]

The first IS-2 heavy tanks would roll off the production lines at the end of 1943 – perhaps later than need have been the case where development of the IS-2 tank had only begun in February 1943. According to V.A. Malishev, then People's Commissar for the Tank Industry, in June 1942 Stalin had delayed the development of new tanks for a number of months in the interests of focusing attention on the improvement of existing models, noting the need to improve visibility from the 76 mm gun-armed T-34 and reduce the weight of the KV-1 in order to improve manoeuvrability. The 85-mm gun armed T-34 would only enter production in at the end of 1943, by which point Stalin was well aware of the inadequacies of the 76 mm gun version and insistent that production switch to the up-gunned one that would also be up-armoured at the front. By this point Stalin had enthusiastically embraced the production of self-propelled guns, having suggested on 24 December 1943 that without Soviet tanks having better firepower Germany might be able to seize the initiative after it had amassed heavy tanks for offensive operations. The upgunning of existing tanks, and production of the IS-2, had become 'a matter of life and death'.[16]

Given the increasing vulnerability of tanks on the battlefield in general, the commander of the German 17th Panzer Division went on to note in his analysis of the role of the tank by mid-1943 how in the German case, in part out of necessity 'the Panzers no longer build the core of the Panzer division around which other weapons are grouped more or less as supporting weapons. The Panzer is a new weapon that is to be employed together with the older weapons and is equal to them'. The importance of tanks was not primarily due to their 'being indestructible or less destructible because of their armor' but due to their 'mobility and firepower'.[17]

Increasingly in the German armed forces tanks would be but one part of a *Kampfgruppe* – a battle group in which the other components were not simply there to serve the needs of the tanks. Only late in the war, as will be discussed later, would the Red Army employ in any meaningful numbers what might be seen as equivalent to these German groupings of forces that were often ad hoc in their organisation. In mid-1943 the forward detachments that led Soviet advances were all too frequently dominated by tanks in a similar manner to the larger tank corps and armies. From the summer of 1943 such forward detachments were typically based around a tank brigade, where the attachment of other components with similar manoeuvrability was particularly initially constrained by the availability of suitable vehicles.[18] The new reconnaissance

units were more likely to function as a coherent combined-arms unit –
and would later in the war operate with tanks – but were nonetheless
rather small. It is also worth noting the trend in the German armed forces
during this period towards providing infantry formations with more
meaningful armoured anti-tank assets. In a document that was very
much promoting the assault gun in the German armed forces, the commander of Sturmgeschütz Replacement and Training Abteilung 200 was
not unreasonable in highlighting the importance of the role of assault gun
battalions [Abteilung] in the support of infantry during the period from
30 August to 22 September 1943.[19] As well as maintaining relatively
concentrated armoured assets for the counterattack or assault, German
forces would take the lead in providing armour for infantry units and
formations as Soviet concentration of tanks in the tank armies was
reaching its peak. New assault guns – including the light SU-76 – would
serve the same purpose for the Red Army as their numbers increased
during late 1943 and early 1944 as the Soviet leadership also realised
that in the circumstances of late 1943 and 1944, the use of tanks and
armour was not a question of deciding between concentration and parcelling out armoured assets as in the pre- and early-war debates, but one
of providing both.

In addition to massed Soviet armour still being poorly co-ordinated
with other arms in fluid situations, the exploitation of the tank's 'mobility
and firepower' remained less than might have been the case for the Red
Army in mid-1943 at the tactical level in particular because most Soviet
tanks were still not equipped with radio communications between
vehicles within tactical units, and communications higher up the chain
of command were also less well provided for than they would be by the
final months of the war. Although during this period assault gunner
Priklonskii's SU-152s all had radios, as indeed did all of the vehicles
supplied by Britain and the United States, the same was not true of
T-34s.[20] As Boris Kuz'mich Koshechkin suggests in an interview published in 2014, as platoon commander of Soviet tanks having to 'climb
out of the hatch and wave little flags' had been 'nonsense'. At Kursk
Koshechkin commanded a platoon of Valentine tanks – with radios –
allowing tanks in his words to 'engage in combat the right way [voevat' po
nastoiashchemu]: 'Fedia, where have you gone [vilez] – let's move forward!... Petrovich, catch up to him.... . Everybody follow me'.[21]
According to Koshechkin, the Valentine was 'like a restaurant' in terms
of comfort compared to the T-34 even if less well armed and armoured.
His subsequent comment to the notion that the Valentine was comfortable – 'like a restaurant...But we had of course to fight...', not dine, is to
some extent reasonable, but add ons like radios were not meaningless

luxuries. Nor perhaps were other refinements enjoyed by Allies and Germans – Koshechkin apparently typically wore German tank overalls rather than Soviet ones because they were more comfortable and did not need to be all but removed in order to go to the toilet like their Soviet equivalent. One can only speculate on the cumulative benefits of such overalls for reducing the time spent, and associated risk, of being outside the tank in a hostile environment.[22]

Returning to the subject of C3I and the radio communications, in many ways issues with C3I in the Red Army were worse beyond than at the tactical level – where at least at the tactical level 'waving flags around' was an option that perhaps gave better chances of positive result than alternatives for timely longer range communication such as runners or pigeons. For a 1943 tank brigade two RSB radio sets were clearly inadequate for longer range communication – and did not reflect significant improvement over the situation in 1941. A whole tank army in 1943 was likely to have only 26–27 radio sets and receivers, 3–4 RAF primarily for communication outside the formation, 16 RSB primarily for communication within the army, 6 radio receivers and a single 'Sever' set. By 1945 a tank brigade would be more likely to have a total of 6 radio sets and receivers – four RSB and one RAF and a receiver – and a tank army a total of 44–45 sets and receivers.[23] Certainly by the end of the war Allied deliveries of radio equipment had greatly enhanced the communications of the Soviet armed forces, where by the end of the war the Soviet Union had received 43,148 radio sets of less than 1 KW power, and where during the second half of the war when the bulk of these were received losses of such equipment were relatively low.[24] Not only were effective long-range sets provided under Lend-Lease, but also sets for employment at the tactical level such as the Anglo-Canadian No. 19 set for armoured vehicles that provided higher frequency communications than equivalent Soviet sets, contributing to making them far more effective at short ranges.[25]

Unfortunately still relatively poor Soviet communications and command and control undoubtedly increased the incidence of 'friendly fire' – a horrendous euphemism if ever there was one. The problem of 'friendly fire' remains, even in this electronic age a problem for all armies, but was certainly a particular problem for the Red Army. On 8 and 9 July for example 183rd Rifle Division of the Voronezh Front was on two separate occasions attacked by Soviet forces. During the evening of 8 July a tank brigade of 2nd Tank Corps assaulted heights occupied by units of 183rd Rifle Division, with both 'sides' taking losses before the next morning when 183rd Rifle Division was hit again by an attack with 60 Il-2 and again took casualties.[26] Post-Soviet memoirs published after the collapse of the Soviet Union make reference to many similar situations, and anecdotally more frequently than German memoirs.[27]

Despite the increasing relative effectiveness of German armour and anti-tank capabilities the Red Army was able to liberate considerable swathes of Soviet territory from Axis forces during the second half of 1943. In favourable operational circumstances for Soviet forces – and particular in the more open terrain in the south – Axis forces struggled to contain a Red Army bounding forward a leap at a time. An article by German historian Walter Bußman describes the difficulty with which XXXXVI Panzer Corps resisted Soviet attacks involving concentrated armoured forces in the aftermath of Kursk on the Orel axis, and how the order to retreat at the beginning of August 'came not an hour too soon'.[28] During the retreat that followed Kursk, eventually to the Dnepr and the incomplete Panther Line, German forces had by both their own and Soviet accounts typically retreated in relatively good order, with XXXXVI Panzer Corps finally crossing the Dnepr with Soviet forces on its heels during the night of 25 September. Despite the relative order of the retreat by German and Axis forces, losses had been heavy – such that the war diary for XXXXVI Panzer Corps described the formation as being 'at the end of its strength' after it had crossed the Dnepr. Between 15 August and 30 September the Panzer corps had lost 32 officers and 714 men killed, 100 and 2,685 respectively wounded, with 12 officers and 368 men missing. Despite including a formidable waterway, German defences of the southern part of the Panther Line had not been built up in good time thanks to Hitler and others being unwilling to accept the reality of the situation on the Eastern Front until it was too late to make the line meaningful – that is in August 1943.[29] As commander of the XXXXVI Panzer Corps at the time, Generalleutnant Friedrich Hoßbach subsequently noted, 'the upper levels of the German leadership had not made any sort of provisions in advance for a decisive defensive battle on the Dnepr'.[30]

Although the German Panther Line that included much of the Dnepr River was largely a fiction by the time it was reached by Soviet forces, the Dnepr was nonetheless a major obstacle even when the opposing bank was less than thoroughly fortified. As Soviet forces reached the river on the heels of German forces there were understandably numerous attempts to force the river – often off the march – and in circumstances where supplies were low and bridging materials or boats initially well to the rear of advance elements. As commander of 40th Army at the time, future Marshal K.S. Moskalenko notes, forward and reconnaissance elements of 40th Army had already begun to cross the Dnepr River during the night of 22 September using 'whatever was at hand', where list strength crossing equipment either arrived later or not at all, with on this sector of the river available crossing resources under front control apparently going to 3rd Guards Tank Army.[31] The Stavka certainly encouraged commanders to push troops across the Dnepr as soon as possible, going as far as to note in a directive of 9 September 1943 that senior commanders and indeed other officers lower down the chain of command could expect to be rewarded with the title Hero of the Soviet Union if their forces were in the vanguard of successful crossings of the Dnepr below Smolensk and other water obstacles of a similar size.[32] Subsequently the net was cast more obviously widely – on 12 October the General Staff required that in accordance with the above directive the Voronezh Front and 60th and 13th Armies provide the Stavka with lists of candidates for the award that included at least 40–50 persons of sergeant and other ranks per division that had been in the first echelon forcing the Dnepr.[33] According to Moskalenko, the focus of political work prior to attempting to force the Dnepr was primarily on the prospect of being awarded the title Hero of the Soviet Union![34] During the night of 23 September forces of Moskalenko's 40th Army started large-scale crossings of the river, starting with storm groups and detachments from platoon up to battalion size – in his memoirs Moskalenko describing the dispatch of a storm group of company strength from 161st Rifle Division across the river – on three small boats and two rafts. In this particular instance, after one of the boats was destroyed by artillery fire the remainder apparently reached the far bank. After having heard the fire of automatic weapons and explosions of grenades, all apparently went quiet. After a brief period of concern for the fate of those who had made it to the opposite bank signal rockets were soon seen indicating a successful crossing and that it was time for the next wave to cross. However, it would take until the following night for reinforcements to reach the company on the other bank, where in the meantime it was supported only by artillery and the VVS in fighting off German attempts to destroy the fledgling bridgehead. The following night however 'a number of battalions' were able to cross and expand the bridgehead to a depth of 1.5 km. Tank support on the right bank required the construction of ferrys, with Moskalenko crossing to the far bank with a T-34 of 3rd Guards Tank Army on 26 September.[35] Later tanks would cross on pontoon bridges, like the tank of tanker Georgii Nikolaevich Krivov, who joined 362nd Tank Battalion of 25th Tank Brigade, 29th Tank Corps, 5th Guards Tank Army as a replacement in October 1943. His units crossed the Dnepr on a pontoon bridge into a bridgehead 3–4 kilometres deep in order to provide support for the rifle battalion that had captured the bridgehead. Krivov's unit was subsequently thrown into the attack without having assessed the terrain before them or any sort of reconnaissance. As Krivov describes, soon on his left one of their tanks was burning, with two more on the right. Returning to Soviet lines he found out that much of his unit had been destroyed.[36] Poor reconnaissance, combined with the problem of landing paratroops in the right place at night, meant that paratroops were not necessarily as effective as hoped in supporting the Dnepr River crossing, as in the case of the dropping of 3rd and part of 5th Airborne Brigades in support of the crossing operation of 40th Army and 3rd Guards Tank Army. During the night of 24 September these units were dropped 'where the front headquarters did not have a clear appreciation of the enemy, and where the drop zones were incorrectly determined'.[37] Head of the Soviet airborne forces General-Major Kapitokhin's report on the operation to Stalin highlighted just how badly the operation had gone. The commander of one of the brigades, 3rd Brigade, was along with more than 200 others dropped 20–30 km from their intended dropzones, and co-ordination between the airborne forces and other components of the operation was poor. Poor co-ordination between the airborne forces and others was far from surprising given 'the absence of radio communications with the landing'.[38]

Dropping the paratroops during the day would have been extremely risky where the Luftwaffe was far from beaten and particularly where Soviet forces had advanced rapidly away from existing VVS facilities. On the right bank of the Dnepr Krivov's unit, 362nd Tank Battalion, was soon subjected to German air attack – a core component of the German defence.[39] Certainly during the earlier phases of crossing operations, with VVS airfields not yet moved forwards, the Luftwaffe was during the day a significant impediment to crossing the river and holding positions on the right bank. In his recollections of the Dnepr crossing, former artilleryman Ivan Novokhatskii describes an attack by German Ju 87 aircraft on forces crossing the river that followed enemy artillery bombardment of the crossing point. Soviet anti-aircraft cover was limited, and Soviet fighters were too busy engaging their German counterparts higher up to deal with the German bombers attacking the crossing point. After the destruction of their raft and 300–350 metres from the river bank Novokhatskii and others made it to a sandy 'island' 30–40 m long and 4–5 metres wide only to be further subjected to air attack. He eventually made it to the far bank – 'Eventually the aircraft flew off. A small launch with a pontoon ferry came up to the island. They gathered up the wounded and took off the living – and took them to the opposite bank.'[40] Despite the bloodshed in crossing the river – and many unsuccessful attempts – during September and October Soviet forces gained a number of footholds on the right bank of the river. In this instance the tendency of the Soviet leadership to attack first, ask questions afterwards probably paid off. For forcing the Dnepr 47 generals, 1,123 other officers and 1,268 'NCOs' and soldiers became Heroes of the Soviet Union – gaining not only the prestige that this award brought but the prospect of longer term material perks.[41]

For Soviet troops the supply situation on the far bank was of course worse than on the Soviet side, with foodstuffs competing with ammunition and fuel for transport space. Fortunately for the Red Army at this point it was summer, and Soviet forces could to some extent 'live off the land'. According to infantryman A. Ovsienko, regarding food supplies, 'the period from August 1943 till March 1944 was particularly stressful when our division was fighting in the Ukraine. On the retreat the enemy destroyed railway lines, bridges and torched depots. Our rear area services were required to ... prepare and process agricultural products.' During this period, he goes on to suggest that from army stores the division received 'in the main only fats, tinned foods, sugar, salt, tobacco [*makhorka*] and a variety of spices [*razlichnie spetsii*].[42] There was indeed something of a food crisis in the Soviet Union by 1943, in part compensated for through Allied deliveries of food aid. By this point an increasing number of dried and tinned foodstuffs from North America that were relatively easily transportable could be utilised by the Red Army. Their delivery to frontline troops, by late 1943, was also more likely to be in Lend-Lease vehicles than it had been the previous year.[43] The supply

Heavy artillery being ferried across the Dnepr River in late September 1943. The Dnepr River failed to provide the sort of obstacle to the Soviet advance belatedly expected of it by German leaders, although Soviet losses during the initial crossings were high. (RIA Novosti #60265)

situation undoubtedly contributed to some extent to the failure of Soviet operations to break out of the Bukrin bridgehead in mid-October, the Stavka however claiming that resources were not the issue but rather the choice of terrain for the offensive use of tanks. After this failure 3rd Guards Tank Army was to be redeployed further north, where it would participate in more successful operations and the liberation of Kiev.[44] German attentions were undoubtedly at this time in late October and early November focused on preventing the expansion of the Soviet bridgehead to the south that included Dnepropetrovsk. The marshy territory south of Chernobyl' and north of Kiev was far from ideal for armoured operations, but here 3rd Guards Tank Army would again be thrown across the Dnepr.

The Kiev operation involved forces not only to the north of the city, but also once again an attack from the Bukrin bridgehead that was, all going well, supposed to provide at least part of the encircling ring that would trap much of 4th Panzer Army in the Kiev region, although this attack would not be of the strength that Soviet deception efforts suggested that it would be, and the Stavka had certainly ordered on 24 October that the principal focus of this attack be deflecting German strength.[45] The Soviet intention was to deceive German forces into thinking that 3rd Guards Tank Army was still in the Bukrin bridgehead through such devices as mock up tanks and false radio traffic. To the north the principal enveloping blow was to be in a south-westerly direction. Significant forces would also attack to the north-west, where once again deception efforts were employed to portray Soviet strength on this sector as being greater than it was to hide the direction of the principal thrust. The 3rd Guards Tank Army had little over a week to move the 200 km north and cross the river twice where there were few functioning crossing points in part thanks to the scarcity of bridges, and the fact that German air and artillery attack either knocked out or damaged some of those that had been thrown across the river. Also, in order to conceal the redeployment from the enemy, movement was to take place only at night.[46]

Commander of 91st Independent Tank Brigade future Marshal Ivan Iakubovskii notes in his memoirs how efforts were made to amass supplies for the Kiev operation and even pushed its start back, but when operations to the north of Kiev began on 3 November 1943 some calibres of artillery were still not provided with the ammunition it was intended they would use on the first day of the operation. Although the tanks had 1–1.5 refuels, the reserve artillery of the Stavka was provided with only 0.5–0.7 refuels.[47] Nonetheless, with German attentions focused further south – including on renewed Soviet attacks from the Bukrin bridgehead that had begun on 1 November – at least the northern component of the

Kiev operation would see German defences broken through, albeit after intense fighting – and the insertion of mechanised forces for the exploitation phase despite the less than desirable supply situation. Here perhaps however, as was not unusual, successes were not as rapid as hoped for back in Moscow. Moskalenko, now commanding 38th Army that would in fact liberate Kiev on 6 November with forces which included 1st Independent Czech Rifle Brigade, by Soviet published standards was vociferous in venting his frustration at the General Staff and in particular its deputy head General Antonov for the removal of chief of staff of what was now the 1st Ukrainian Front General S.P. Ivanov later that month for inadequate organisation of command and control.[48] Ivanov's removal took place despite commander of the front, Vatutin, leaping to his defence. Certainly there were, as Moskalenko notes, issues with communications as there often were with the front command having to send front-level staff officers and members of the Military Soviet with radios to sustain communications and command and control over subordinate formations much as the Stavka did with its representatives at front level.[49] In this case the Stavka representative of the spot was Zhukov, who when present could provide advice and be a conduit for information to the Stavka as well as being in a position to be criticised for local failures – possibly more than an unintended benefit of such positions for a supreme commander wanting to keep ambitious generals and marshals in their place. The bullying from above and scapegoating of subordinates that had been so typical early in the war – often with tenuous cause – had certainly not ceased by late 1943, although in this case the fact that Antonov was apparently acting alone – or could be seen to have been – made protest from below at least that bit less risky.

The capture of the Fastov railway junction by the morning of 7 November as Soviet mechanized forces advanced around Kiev to the south-west was undoubtedly a success for the 1st Ukrainian Front, against which was thrown the inexperienced German 25th Panzer Division, at first without its Panzer regiment. With German troops initially thrown back in disarray, renewed German attacks with the Panzer regiment took 25th Panzer Division to the outskirts of the town but no further. After the fighting for Fastov, as Major-General Mellenthin notes in his memoirs, 25th Panzer Division was unfit for participation in offensive operations for some time. The losses sustained by the 'untrained' – or at least poorly trained division – that had been committed apparently against the advice of Inspector General of Panzer Troops Guderian – were according to Mellenthin indicative of committing such units against what were by inference increasingly experienced Soviet units.[50] Commander of Army Group South, Field Marshal Manstein makes a similar point without giving the development of the Red Army due credit. In the case of 25th Panzer Division at Fastov Manstein suggests that 'once again we saw what price a newly drafted division had to pay for its initiation into war conditions in the East'.[51] The fact was that the Red Army was as a whole gaining experience quickly – and able to preserve enough of that experience as units were reincarnated for their new incarnations often at least not to be starting quite as relatively green as many of the fresh German divisions that were being formed without a sufficient veteran component. During the defence of Fastov Iakubovskii's 191st Independent Tank Brigade had however also unsurprisingly took heavy losses, with the self-propelled artillery regiment of the brigade – 1893rd Self-Propelled Artillery Regiment – left with only four guns and few more than 100 personnel active after three days of fighting for the town.[52] German forces were unable to break through towards Kiev or elsewhere, but Soviet forces were forced over to the defensive, subsequently losing ground in particular to the west as German reinforcements were thrown in, but the Red Army did not lose Kiev. Elsewhere along the Dnepr the Soviet advance was also halted by the German armoured fire brigades, with Soviet attacks towards Krivii Rog and then beyond Novgorodka further north also defeated as the end of the year approached, with their forward elements suffering heavy losses as Soviet mechanized forces reached the point of overextension. By 8 December 1943 for example, 18th and 29th Tank Corps of 5th Guards Tank Army operating on the Krivoi Rog axis were down to only 37 and 22 tanks and self-propelled guns respectively compared to authorised strengths of in excess of 250 each.[53] Further to the south Soviet forces of Steppe, South-Western and Southern Fronts (subsequently 2nd, 3rd and 4th Ukrainian Fronts) had successfully advanced along and seized a bridgehead over the lower Dnepr and cut off German and Rumanian forces in the Crimea. German commander of Army Group South, Manstein, had sought to use XL Panzer Corps to attack this Soviet penetration in the flank, but the speed of the Soviet advance and withdrawal of the reconstituted German 6th Army behind the Lower Dnepr perhaps fortuitously for German forces prevented it. The armoured forces provided to Army Group South by a Hitler bent on preventing the loss of the Crimea could certainly be used to better effect elsewhere, where German forces simply did not have the Panzer divisions to blunt every Soviet leap forward and where the formation of a defensive line on the steppe in the far south would have been challenging and resource intensive.[54] Significant as this success in the far south was for the Red Army, it had nonetheless been achieved with horrendous losses – more than 750,000 lost out of a force of in the region of 1,500,000 between 26 September and 20 December 1943 – with nearly 175,000 of the losses 'irrecoverable'.[55] During this period Soviet forces also once again launched an amphibious assault on the Kerch' peninsula, this time however not being ejected. Although the aim of liberating the entire Kerch' Peninsula was not achieved that year, Soviet forces did however hold a jumping off point for future operations. Whether this warranted approximately 29,000 total casualties inflicted on Soviet forces in the region through November and into December is debateable, but at least the gap between enemy and Soviet casualties was far smaller than was typically the case earlier in the war, where total German and Rumanian losses were perhaps in the region of 14,000 for a similar period and where both figures cover the period of the most intensive fighting.[56]

By the end of 1943 it was certainly clear that where Soviet commanders had time to plan operations, amass supplies, and had a suitable superiority in strength by most indicators, then particularly where Soviet armour was being pushed through and into relatively open terrain the likelihood of successful penetration into German operational depth was good. These leaps were however limited by the capacity to supply units beyond railheads – made more difficult by the fact that German forces employed a scorched earth policy on the retreat leaving not only bridges destroyed but also railway lines systematically wrecked. Regardless of terrain, the Soviet advance did also ultimately reach points at which force and momentum were insufficient to parry counterattacks by German 'fire brigade' armoured elements or overcome the next defended major river line, where at times German mobile forces could do significant damage to exposed and already weakening Soviet forward elements far ahead of the bulk of the infantry and artillery behind them.

Further north, where terrain was typically more favourable to the defence given the density of woodland and frequently also marshland, in late 1943 and early 1944 the Red Army fared less well than in the south, and things could and still all too frequently did go badly when operations were rushed and under-supported. An aggressive Stavka – and aggressive commanders on the ground such as Vatutin – still did not have the sort of relative superiority to launch major offensives at multiple-points on the Eastern Front with them all having good prospects for success. Soviet academic works tended, understandably, to focus on the dramatic victories in the south rather than the more limited gains for higher cost on the Smolensk axis for example, or particularly further north near Leningrad. Between 7 August and 2 October 1943 forces of the Kalinin and Western Fronts did indeed advance, in the end, up to 225 km, but during the early phases of operations struggled to overcome German defences. During what one of the few Soviet studies on the Smolensk Offensive Operation identifies as the first phase, from 7–20 August Soviet forces advanced up to 40 km, and during the second from 21 August – 6 September up to a similar distance. During both periods German defences were indeed breached as planned on some sectors of the front, but ambitious operational goals were difficult to achieve given both the terrain, resources available, stubborn enemy resistance and reinforcement.[57] On some sectors of the front during this period Soviet forces hammered away at German defences for weeks as they had done all too often during the winter of 1941–2. General A.P. Beloborodov, moved to 2nd Guards Rifle Corps from 5th Guards Rifle Corps of 39th Army of the Kalinin Front just prior to the start of offensive operations, describes the attack by his corps towards Dukhovshchina, north-east of Smolensk, in early August 1943. Attacking along a 6 km front, the corps was to break through enemy defences and cross the River Tsarevich, penetrating to a depth of 15 km. Attached to the corps were 28th Guards Tank Brigade, 203rd Heavy Tank Regiment, an anti-tank destruction brigade, an assault engineer brigade and a number of mortar regiments along with army-level artillery assets – 21st Breakthrough Artillery Division and a number of Guards rocket mortar units.[58] By 13 August 39th Army as a whole had a total of 2,439 guns and mortars of all types from 82 mm mortars and above, including 806 guns of calibres ranging from 203 down to 76 mm divisional artillery – and 265 rocket mortar launchers. Regarding tanks, 102 operational tanks were ready to participate and support the Army's 8 rifle divisions, a rifle brigade and a fortified district, the rifle divisions with strengths approaching 7,000. The 2nd Guards Rifle Corps alone fielded in the region of 556 guns and mortars – with 290 heavier guns from army strength on its sector of the front.[59] The Western Front could field a staggering 13,374 guns and mortars of all calibres as of 7 August 1943 – along with 961 tanks – alongside 58 rifle divisions with an average strength of 7,200. According to Soviet historian Istomin, Soviet forces of 39th Army of the Kalinin Front on the right flank, and forces of the Western Front, had the benefit of an overall superiority in men and equipment somewhere in the order of 2–3.5:1 in terms of manpower and 1.5–3:1 in terms of equipment at the start of operations.[60] Specialist units, such as 1st Komsomol Engineer-Sapper Assault Brigade were provided for the Smolensk operation – with two engineer-sapper assault brigades and ten such battalions provided to the Western Front.[61] 1st Komsomol Engineer-Sapper Assault Brigade arrived in the region on 16 July, having been recently reformed on the basis of 38th Komsomol Engineer Regiment. The brigade was committed to the assault on a German strongpoint on heights on 10th Guard Army's sector at the beginning of the offensive, where it was hoped that its equipment and élan as described by head of engineers for the Western Front Ivan Pavlovich Galitskii, would facilitate the breaching of German defences:

The brigade's personnel consisted of Komsomol members and Red Army troops of Komsomol age. It was intended for the assault of heavily fortified enemy positions alongside the infantry, supported by artillery and tanks. The principal task of assault units was to destroy bunkers and pillboxes with high explosives and flamethrowers. The personnel of the assault brigade were armed with sub-machine guns, sapper's bayonets, steel bullet-proof breastplates and steel helmets. . . . They had good engineering training and were battle hardened.[62]

The brigade had apparently failed with other units to take German positions on 'Height 233,3' on the Roslavl' axis on 7 August – with a second follow-on attack also having failed in the face of German defences clearly not sufficiently suppressed by artillery. In this instance, the brigade had been employed as sappers, clearing minefields, and not as assault troops – a role in which they were employed when the heights were subsequently actually taken. The brigade was again committed in late August after the focus of Soviet operations had been shifted from the Roslavl' direction towards El'nia and Smolensk and after Soviet forces had been reinforced. This time the brigade captured German positions on 'Height 244,3' near Matveevshchina, allowing elements of 10th Guards and 21st Armies to advance on that sector.[63]

The attack on Dukhovshchina further north by forces of 39th Army was initially similarly unsuccessful. Beloborodov's degree of candour about the August attack on Dukhovshchina and its failure was perhaps in part because the basic plan of attack was not his but his predecessor's, but nonetheless the continuation of offensive operations despite initial failures was under Beloborodov's command. Strong artillery support was supposed to suppress enemy defences, including the ability of the enemy to lay fire upon 91st Guards Rifle Division as it advanced along a tributary of the Tsarevich – the Velenia – under the guns of enemy forces on heights on the opposite bank. A 'strong but brief' artillery bombardment lasting 35 minutes on 13 August did indeed facilitate the occupation of first and second line enemy trenches, but did 'not achieve the desired effect' – with 91st Guards Rifle Division 'pinned' by flanking fire. By 17 August what amounted to a frontal assault on Dukhovshchina had stalled with 9 km out of 15 remaining to be covered. Beloborodov apparently sought to shift the focus of the attack towards outflanking the well-defended town, only apparently to be ordered by the Army commander General-Lieutenant Zigin to throw the second echelon, 9th Guards Rifle Division, into the frontal assault on the town across the Tsarevich as forces that had penetrated furthest in a southerly direction sought to envelop it. In the face of German defences these attacks failed, but 39th Army continued to launch attacks, 'with breaks between them of one-three days', in intense fighting by the corps that continued until late August without the capture of Dukhovshchina. A further attempt was launched to capture the town in early September by neighbouring corps after 2nd Guards Rifle Corps had gone over to the defence on 28 August.[64] It was not just the Kalinin Front that was experiencing difficulties in overcoming resistance during the operation – on 21 August the Stavka representative on the Western Front and its commander informed the Supreme High Command how despite deeper penetrations than further north on 39th Army's sector, German reserves were contributing to intensified resistance with new defensive lines under construction in the German rear, and how the front would need to regroup before renewing the offensive at the end of the month after fourteen days of intense operations.[65] Not only German forces were however being reinforced – in August the Kalinin Front was provided with two medium, one light self-propelled artillery regiment and three tank regiments along with seventy tanks as replacements in September. The Western Front in August received 2nd Guards Tank Corps along with a number of other units, and in September additional units and 349 replacement tanks.[66]

In his analysis of the failure of operations of 39th Army in August, Beloborodov notes the hurried preparations made for it that had characterised so many Soviet operations before it. Artillery batteries continued to move into position right up to the final hours before the offensive was launched, with time for artillery observation and reconnaissance consequently being limited in many instances. Rushed preparations may have limited the scope for *maskirovka* – certainly Beloborodov suggests on the basis of PoW testimony that German forces were expecting a Soviet attack on 39th Army's sector where it finally came and had moved reserves accordingly.[67] For this – apparently as a result of inadequate *maskirovka* – the commander of the Kalinin Front was duly chided by the General Staff.[68] Beloborodov's view is certainly echoed by then head of artillery for the Kalinin Front, Nikolai Mikhailovich Khlebnikov, who in his memoirs notes the failure both to concentrate artillery assets and suitably reconnoitre enemy defences in depth. A lack of communications resources also apparently hampered artillery support, where 'the possibilities for the artillery were severely hampered by insufficient means of communication. The cable communications that we had barely covered ten percent of needs, and radio communications resources were few. We ended up having to use the communications resources of the rifle forces, that led to considerable difficulties in the operational use of artillery'.[69]

Soviet historian Istomin notes, that the Western Front to the south spent insufficient time on preparing the operation whilst it was participating in the Orel operations, only switching to focus on the Smolensk operation after 30 July – with only seven days remaining – after forces participating in the Orel operation were transferred to the Briansk Front. Apparently, in the interests of maintaining secrecy in preparing the operation, many orders that would otherwise have been on paper were given orally. This may have aided the maintenance of secrecy, but hampered effective preparation.[70]

On the Kalinin Front, renewed offensive operations by 39th Army would take place in September – now with a new commander General-Lieutenant N.E. Berzarin, a younger wartime promotee to the command of formations who was apparently still not forty years old – 'a typical representative of the new pleiad of Great Patriotic War commanders' not only in his relative youth but also in that he was an 'erudite, very willful and decisive person'.[71] General-Lieutenant A.I. Zigin had been moved to command 20th Army, and would soon replace General-Lieutenant G.I. Kulik – formerly marshal – as commander of 4th Guards Army and so was therefore however hardly moved in disgrace. By the end of the month Zigin had been killed by a road mine.[72] In new plans the attack was to be across, not along the River Velenia, with a mobile group being pushed on to enemy lines of communications after the attack of rifle corps on the right flank, with 2nd Guard Rifle Corps – with 9th and 17th Guards Divisions replaced with 97th and 184th Rifle Divisions – following them with a view to attacking Dukhovshchina from the north-west. The revised plan may have been positive in dealing with some of the more critical flaws in the first, but increased artillery support was also no doubt of significance. East of the river Velenia, in woods, there was for the mid-September renewal of the attack apparently an impressive concentration of artillery that had been reinforced since early August and that included six batteries of 203 mm howitzers of 103rd Super Heavy Artillery Brigade, sixteen batteries of 152 mm guns or howitzers, and more than 200 rocket mortar launchers, with Stavka representative and Marshal of Artillery Voronov involved in ensuring that the artillery preparations were more effective.[73] This time round, as head of artillery for the Kalinin Front Nikolai Mikhailovich Khlebnikov infers in his memoirs, far greater attention was paid to artillery reconnaissance, with Khlebnikov claiming some credit for extra time being provided for preparations. In his memoirs, he notes:

Having been given the necessary time for preparatory work, we launched wide reconnaissance of targets in the enemy defences. On the sector of the principal blow this was conducted by 830th and 827th Independent Artillery

Reconnaissance *Divizions* attached to the front and 629th Independent Artillery Reconnaissance *Divizion* ... .Additionally the front's artillery spotting air reconnaissance regiment and balloon observation *divizion* were both active.[74]

On 14 September at 9:00 a.m. Soviet artillery once again rained down on German positions, but this time for a total of about 90 minutes with greater effect in suppressing German guns. By the end of the day 2nd Guards Rifle Corps had advanced as much as 10 km into the breach. By the night of 18 September Dukhovshchina had been cleared of German forces in an encirclement that although had failed to trap the defenders had finally seen the objectives of early August achieved, for which 91st Guards and 184th Rifle Divisions became 91st and 184th 'Dukhovshchina' Rifle Divisions.[75]

After the successes of mid-September – that in the centre included the liberation of Briansk on 17 September and in the south had seen the liberation of the Donbass region – the Stavka set its sights on a series of major objectives that included ambitious goals in the central region of the Eastern Front. In the face of obvious German withdrawals it was understandable that the Stavka drove the Red Army forward, but as usual paid little attention to the state of Soviet forces involved. In a series of directives on 20 September the Stavka directed the Briansk Front towards Minsk, the left wing of the Kalinin Front to Vitebsk and the Western Front towards Smolensk and then Orsha and Mogilev.[76] On 1 October the Central Front was tasked with the capture of Minsk itself with the Western Front advancing towards Orsha on its right with the ultimate aim of reaching Vilnius – the Briansk Front being abolished on 10 October.[77] Smolensk had already fallen by this point – for once ahead of the Stavka's demand that it be captured by 26–27 September – but Vitebsk, Orsha, Mogilev, Minsk and certainly Vilnius were beyond immediate Soviet reach, with the turning of summer into fall and bringing the rain and mud certainly hindering progress alongside the Germans. The liberations of all of these would have to wait for the following summer where in the meantime the focus of Soviet attentions would be on exploiting more favourable terrain in the south. Soviet losses on the central sector of the Eastern Front in the aftermath of Kursk had, as usual, been significant. During what would subsequently be described as the Smolensk Strategic Offensive Operation, Operation 'Suvorov', lasting from 7 August till 2 October, forces of the Kalinin and Western Fronts lost a total of more than 450,000 personnel out of a total of about 1,250,000, of whom more than 107,000 of the losses were 'irrecoverable' and the remainder 'sick and wounded'.[78]

Further north, the bloodbath associated with breaking the siege of Leningrad and attempts to destroy significant German forces in the region continued into 1944. Evan after a corridor had been punched through to Leningrad along Lake Ladoga in January 1943 – Operation 'Spark' – the resulting land corridor was narrow and subject to at times intense air and artillery bombardment. 'Spark' had at least achieved its core goal – to punch through to Leningrad – and at a cost of what in Soviet terms was relatively low, even if 33,940 irrecoverable losses and 81,142 wounded were nonetheless horrific.[79] In broad Soviet plans since the siege of Leningrad had begun in September 1941 it is often difficult to separate plans to relieve the siege from plans to destroy a significant portion of German Army Group North, although successful attacks in the region of Siniavino and Mga to the south-east of Leningrad were – regardless of broader plans – supposed to either punch a land corridor through to the city or in 1943 both widen the existing corridor and enhance its security by gaining control of the higher ground in the Siniavino region. Both Soviet and German losses during the continued heavy fighting in the broader region were heavy – the Soviet 2nd Shock Army was effectively destroyed as a coherent formation twice in 1942 for example – both in the late spring further south towards Novgorod between Liuban' and Chudovo, and then again in the summer of 1942 in fighting in the Siniavino region to the south of Leningrad. In this latter case Soviet forces ran up against German preparations for their own offensive in the region, for which 11th Army had been moved from Sevastopol' after its capture in July 1942. Here German Tiger tanks made their appearance, albeit with little impact in what was hardly ideal terrain.[80] In both instances penetrations of German lines turned into encirclements, from which at least some of the Soviet forces trapped were able to break out. Fighting near Novgorod and for the heights in the Siniavino region and key railway junction of Mga continued in 1943 as once again Soviet forces were hurled against well-prepared German defences. In his memoirs, German soldier William, or Wilhelm, Lubbeck describes a series of Soviet attacks across the ice of Lake Ilmen' that rarely got close to German positions thanks to Soviet troops being so clearly visible and the impact of German artillery.[81] During these attacks near Novgorod Mikhail Suknev's battalion went from a strength of 450 down to fifteen in attacks during which he bitterly notes poor reconnaissance, unimaginative and often frontal assaults and poor artillery support.[82]

Another German soldier who fought in north-west Russia, Gottlob Bidermann, describes in his memoirs fighting in mid-August 1943 involving his 132nd Infantry Division near Gaitolovo – a much fought over gateway to the Siniavino Heights. Once again the slaughter was horrendous for both sides, but particularly the Red Army. Bidermann describes a series of Soviet attacks starting on 11 August, on which two Soviet attacks, the first in regimental strength, were launched against his unit's positions. The following day, on 12 August 'at exactly 09:00, the enemy launched an attack along the entire front in full strength. It consisted of numerous waves of brown-clad infantrymen heavily supported by artillery fire, tanks and overwhelming airpower'. Subsequent attacks over the next few days ultimately saw Bidermann's unit withdraw to new positions that were apparently more defensible and to avoid local encirclement, at the end of which, on 16 August, 132nd Infantry Division started to be pulled from the front line.[83] Certainly, as Kirill Meretskov, during this period commanding the Volkhov Front, notes in his memoirs, Soviet operations in the Mga-Siniavino region had caused significant casualties for the German 18th Army, and denuded it of reserves, but Soviet forces in the region did not have the reserves of either men or materiel to move beyond the limited gains made during a month of operations that had begun on 22 July and were brought to a close on 22 August.[84] Meretskov's claim that Stalin had told him before the operation that the primary purpose of the operation was grind down German forces – pinning forces in the north – like Zhukov's similar claims about Operation 'Mars' seem like partial retrospective justification. In the 22 August Stavka directive bringing an end to the last bout of attacks it was noted how the Volkhov and Leningrad Fronts had 'attracted significant enemy operational reserves', inflicted heavy losses, and attained some of their objectives.[85] Plans by the Volkhov and Leningrad Fronts from the spring onwards suggest nonetheless that the aim from the perspective of front commanders at least was not to pin the enemy but to finally link up forces of the Leningrad and Volkhov Fronts in the Siniavino-Mga region, destroy enemy forces to the north, and achieve what they had been trying to achieve over so many months.[86] Meretskov's disillusionment in his memoirs with not having had a clear intelligence picture of the damage done to German forces through the bloodletting in late July and August 1943 may be genuine, but knowing otherwise might not have led the Stavka to release significantly greater resources for the region.[87] Part of the problem for Soviet forces in the north was that relatively speaking, the region was of secondary importance. The fall of Leningrad could not be tolerated, but throwing resources into the region did not make sense beyond a certain point where the decisive battles were being fought further south. With Stalin and the Stavka's tendency to try to do too much with available resources – and some pressure to relieve Leningrad – operation after operation was nonetheless launched in the north with a mix of hopes of relieving Leningrad or strengthening its land communications with the rest of the Soviet Union and destroying significant

German forces in the region but with insufficient resources to actually get the job done. Back in Moscow, pinning down German forces and any losses sustained by the Wehrmacht were at least partial compensation for losses sustained near Leningrad, even if losses were far more severe than they need have been for that purpose. Krivosheev et al record irrecoverable losses of more than 77,000 for the Volkhov Front during 1943, with irrecoverable losses for the Leningrad Front of more than 88,000 that same year. When one considers the more than 83,000 irrecoverable losses for the Leningrad Front during 1942, and the staggering irrecoverable losses of 208,509 for the Volkhov Front that year, the scale of Soviet losses in the region for fairly limited gains becomes apparent – more than 450,000 soldiers irrecoverably lost – with total losses being in excess of 1.5 million.[88] German losses had also been significant – the German 18th Army had lost 118,950 troops killed, wounded and missing in 1942, and a further 166,500 in 1943 – but such German losses hardly justified Soviet casualties, and Soviet gains on the ground had also been far from impressive.[89]

During the January 1944 offensive that would see the final liberation of much ground that had eluded Soviet forces for months and even years, Soviet irrecoverable losses would from 14 January–1 March 1944 be in excess of 75,000. These losses were primarily sustained by the Leningrad and Volkhov Fronts, a figure including however nearly 7,000 for part of 2nd Baltic Front.[90] Nonetheless, at least this time the siege of Leningrad was finally completely lifted, even if after January 1943 the food crisis in the city had passed thanks in part to resources being brought in but also the horrendous death toll during the winter of 1941–2 meaning there were fewer mouths to feed. In many ways the success of the January 1944 offensive was due to the success of Soviet operations further south that made the German position below Leningrad increasingly untenable. Certainly the Leningrad-Novgorod Strategic Offensive Operation as it came to be known was not conducted with the same drive and élan that by early 1944 was characterising operations further south despite the heavy losses involved. In many ways this is understandable – Soviet forces and commanders in the north to this point had little experience of a war of movement except on the retreat, and had apparently learnt little from the accrued war experience of others to date where this heavily documented experience did not permeate down the chain of command to all those who actually needed to know.[91] The lack of the sort of hard won personal experience of operations that involved significantly more than tactical depth that had been gained in the south was compounded in the north by the terrain that hampered mobile operations – forest and marshland dominating the region. Consequently much of 18th Army of

Army Group North was able to escape encirclement and destruction as it retreated into the Baltic Republics. On 1 June 1944 the Army Group could still field in the region of 700,000 troops excluding *Hilfswillige* – former Soviet troops operating in auxiliary roles often as an alternative to the misery of German PoW camps rather than due to any particular desire to serve the Third Reich.[92]

By the second half of 1943, German forces along the whole of the Eastern Front were starting to feel the weight of a resurgent VVS as had been the case in the Kuban in the spring of 1943 and was discussed in Chapter 18. On the Eastern Front the Luftwaffe would not however all but collapse as it did in the West, and it continued to at times offer meaningful local opposition and support to German forces even in late 1944 and even into 1945. Nonetheless, increasingly on the principal axes of a Soviet advance German ground forces were subjected to a ferocity of air attack that had not been experienced in previous years, although at no point had the VVS completely disappeared from the skies. The 'overwhelming airpower' noted by Gottlob Bidermann as being thrown at German ground forces near Gaitolovo on 12 August 1943 was by this period of the war far from unusual, and German rear areas had been subjected to bombing by Soviet 'long-range aviation' in the region for fifteen days of air attacks that had begun on 29 July. Although Soviet commander of the Volkhoz Front saw the force committed as small – with an average of only 100 sorties per day – the commander of Soviet long-range aviation 'provided almost unlimited fuel and was generous in the provision of bombs'.[93] This was on what for the Stavka was supposedly a relatively unimportant sector of the front. At Kursk and beyond on the key axes air support for Soviet ground forces was far more lavish than below Leningrad. Where the Soviet DB-3 was increasingly outdated and direct replacements few, the provision by the United States of in particular Boston medium bombers by this stage of the war greatly enhanced the capabilities of Soviet 'long-range' aviation where the Soviet focus during the early period of the war had been very much on close tactical air support. Soviet aircraft capable of striking deeper into the German rear than the Il-2 such as the Pe-2 were often employed in a tactical role, to which they were well-suited given for example their capabilities as dive bombers. US-supplied medium bombers gave the VVS a far more meaningful capability to strike at targets such as railway junctions and other such targets deeper in the enemy rear with a higher payload than the Pe-2 for example – and were also easier to fly. By 1 May 1945 the VVS had more than 900 Bostons in service, with nearly 600 of these in service with the field army. The Soviet navy also operated large numbers of the aircraft.[94]

Il-2 ground attack aircraft, here serving with the Northern Fleet in 1944. Such Soviet tactical airpower was by mid-1943 having an impact both over land and sea – at least in the former case where it was deployed in concentration. (TsVMM #31482)

The memoirs of both Soviet and German frontline troops tend to suggest frequent attack by enemy air power during the middle period of the Great Patriotic War. On the Belgorod-Khar'kov axis in the aftermath of 'Citadel' Elektron Priklonskii's SU-152 unit was subjected to frequent German air attack, be it by Heinkel 111s engaged by rocket fire from a 'Katiusha' launcher or the Ju 87s that were ubiquitous as the Soviet Il-2s.[95] At the same time Soviet aviation was also active nearby, on more than one occasion during the same period Priklonskii recalling attacks by Pe-2s – in early August in possibly regimental strength against German forces, a few days later Soviet bombers abortively attacking Priklonskii's unit before signal flares alerted them to their error.[96] By this stage of the war both sides could, with the requisite commitment, gain the upper hand in air engagements where both possessed experienced pilots and recently trained novices and where neither side now had obviously superior aircraft – as long as aircraft could be directed where they were needed. Fighter-fighter contact in the vast expanses of Soviet territory was most likely over or near a defended target as for example over the Dnepr bridgeheads, where high above fighters engaged as ground forces were attacked below. Elsewhere the vast expanses of the Soviet Union meant that concentration of one side in a given area inevitably left others at best poorly served. During this period of the war, as Major-General F.W. von Mellenthin notes, although the VVS was 'growing into a formidable power' the Luftwaffe could still 'gain air superiority over limited sectors and for limited periods' where although 'Russian planes in increasing numbers swarmed over the battlefield' their 'efficiency in no way corresponded with their numbers'. Nonetheless, as he goes on to note, 'in spite of German air superiority' during the first days of 'Citadel' 'many tanks fell victim to the Red Air Force'.[97]

Certainly, nowhere was concentration of air assets more apparent than over the Kursk salient, where as the commander of 16th Air Army at the time of the Kursk fighting S.I. Rudenko notes 2nd and 16th Air Armies of the Voronezh and Central Fronts that had been strengthened with air corps from Stavka reserves could field 881 and 1,034 aircraft, which along with forces of 17th Air Army of the South-Western Front also committed gave Soviet forces in the region 2,650 aircraft for operations over the salient at the beginning of July. According to Rudenko, this gave a Soviet numerical superiority of in the region of 1.4:1. In reserve the Stavka had 5th Air Army of the Steppe Front to hand.[98] Nonetheless, despite Soviet forces being able to as Mellenthin notes caused significant damage to German ground forces overall, as Vitalii Gorbach notes for Rudenko's 16th Air Army at the beginning of the German offensive the impact of Soviet airpower on stemming German ground operations and limiting the scope of the Luftwaffe to support German ground forces was not what had been hoped for.[99] Soviet losses were heavy – 16th Air Army lost a total of 391 aircraft between 5 and 11 July – 535 for July as a whole that included the loss of 269 fighters (primarily LaGG-5 and Yak 1, -7 and some -9s), 161 Il-2 ground attack aircraft, 48 Pe-2 and 38 Boston bombers, 13 U-2 and six reconnaissance aircraft. At the start of the 'Kutuzov' counteroffensive proper on 12 July a reinforced 16th Air Army could still field 706 aircraft, where the VVS could commit as many as 3,323 aircraft in total to the operation including long-range aviation and 1st and 15th Air Armies.[100] Gorbach nonetheless concludes, that despite Soviet strength if considering the two defensive and two offensive operations associated with the northern and southern faces of the Kursk salient, that only Operation 'Rumiantsev' on the southern face of the salient began with Soviet air superiority even if this could not be sustained.[101] In the south 17th Air Army participated in operations after 12 July with the 'defence' of the salient continuing until 23 July. At the start of the German offensive of the 881 aircraft of 2nd Air Army – 389 fighters, 276 ground-attack, 172 bombers with a further thirty-four night bombers, and 110 reconnaissance aircraft – were alone seen to have enjoyed approximate overall numerical parity with the enemy. Despite more than 15,000 sorties by 2nd and 17th Armies by 17 July, during the defensive phase of operations the senior General Staff officer on the Voronezh Front recorded afterwards that 'passive' and largely defensive use of Soviet fighters meant that the VVS did not gain air superiority. Although ground attack aircraft were deemed to have been effective in particular when employing 1.5 kg armour piercing bombs against enemy armour – and undertook 2,644 sorties during the whole defensive period concerned – bombers were noted to have been used less frequently than they might have been due to still inadequate fighter cover.[102] The apparent effectiveness of ground attack aviation, and particularly in less fluid circumstances, may be partly explained by improved air-ground co-operation, where at Kursk for the first time command points for ground attack air formations were situated forward with corps or even divisional commanders being able to summon air support either from airbases or already in the air. Fighter direction by radio from army-level command posts as had been the case over the Kuban was arguably less effective – albeit offering more opportunities than the very much cable based command and control of the beginning of the war that did not allow effective control of aircraft once airborne. A radio-based system was an innovation, but still offered relatively limited scope for meaningful direction of fighter resources where weather could be a major impediment to location and vectoring and where Soviet use of radar was still limited.[103] Certainly the general role of the German Luftwaffe liaison officers down to divisional level can only have provided a more coherent response to changing circumstances than distinct ground attack and fighter control of the VVS. Certainly German ground attack formations seem to have been used more intensively than their Soviet counterparts.[104] The limits of Soviet fighter control certainly contributed to Soviet losses – losses of 437 aircraft for 2nd Air Army by 23 July were significant, with eighty-three lost on 5 July alone in the face of the initial German air attacks. During July as a whole 2nd Air Army was recorded as losing in combat missions – be that to enemy aircraft, AA fire or unspecified reasons for failure to return – more than 400 aircraft, and in August just under a further 300. It is also worth noting how limited resources given over to aerial reconnaissance remained. Between 12 July and 18 August 1st, 15th and 16th Air Armies (from 15 July for 16th Air Army) launched only 3,441 sorties out of a total of 60,995 for reconnaissance purposes.[105] Nonetheless, as with the artillery, although heavy losses were taken by the VVS the mass employment of Soviet airpower proved effective in particular where pre-planned attacks could be launched against fixed German positions or known concentrations. During the attack on the southern sector of the front Commander of IX Corps, Colonel General

Erhard Raus noted even at the start of the southern portion of 'Citadel' that Soviet bombers 'attacked the IX Corps area incessantly', with Soviet aircraft beginning to 'participate in the battle with ever-increasing intensity' as the first day progressed. The German IX Corps attacked initially at least without air support - with Luftwaffe assets committed to supporting 4th Panzer Army – although IX Corps was provided with significant Flak assets for the engagement of both air and ground targets.[106] The fact that Raus does not mention Soviet airpower again during the German offensive and does not single out Soviet airpower as a specific factor in the failure of the German attack is no doubt due in part to the greater fluidity of the situation hampering the effective use of Soviet airpower. In slightly different circumstances, with Soviet offensive operations on the Belgorod axis of late July and early August, Raus mentions the the 'continuous air raids' supporting Soviet attacks south of Belgorod in early August that did not nonetheless apparently distract heavy flak from engaging primarily tanks. With the subsequent retreat towards Khar'kov 'low-flying hostile planes in great numbers dropped fragmentation bombs and machine-gunned troops on the march', Raus noting how in a situation reminiscent of that faced by many Red Army units at the same time during 1941 'suffering heavy casualties, our soldiers edged towards panic'.[107] This did not stop the Luftwaffe at the same time in the same region inflicting significant losses on Soviet forces, such as the twenty-four T-34 and five T-70s of 5th Guards Tank Army knocked out in enemy air attacks between 3 and 10 August.[108] Only the following summer, as noted by Mellenthin, would the VVS enjoy 'unquestioned command of the air' over the central sector of the Eastern Front in part because of the drain of Luftwaffe resources westwards.[109]

Soviet operations in 1943 and into 1944 were characterised by the deployment of tanks, aircraft and artillery support on a hitherto unprecedented scale and concentration, with the former proving particularly effective in the more suitable tank terrain of the south. Not unreasonably did documents from the reconnaissance battalion of the German 167th Infantry Division captured by the Soviet side characterise Soviet offensive operations of mid-1943 in three initial points – as involving large tank formations, strong artillery support from heavy artillery and mortars and massed infantry attacks in co-ordination with the tanks and ground attack aircraft.[110] The ability to concentrate these resources, and co-ordinate their deployment in particular during the early phases of operations, marked a substantial development over the use of such resources in 1941, although where breakthrough wasn't achieved the Red Army still all too frequently hammered away at the same point. When doing so, Soviet troops could display considerable cunning in seeking to achieve a given goal – as in a lengthy description by Raus of intense and sustained fighting in close terrain along the Donets in the aftermath of the Kursk offensive that saw Soviet troops apparently break into German positions in German uniforms, infiltrate German positions across marshy terrain and bring in tanks across a rapidly constructed submarine bridge supported by T-34s driven into the river.[111] On occasion this could be described as 'initiative', but all too often involved its employment to overcome a poor or at least inflexible plan.

That documentation from an infantry division such as 167th Infantry might present such a view of the Red Army involving the mass use of different arms with a reasonable degree of co-ordination is understandable given that such units typically faced the initial and by now relatively well co-ordinated Soviet onslaught. However, after the initial breakthrough of German defences manned by such units Soviet command and control often started to break down, with the armour operating increasingly 'with only weak infantry and artillery forces' and without effective air support, as noted before Khar'kov in the summer of 1943 by Colonel General Erhard Raus, commander of German IX Corps.[112] In early 1943, and to a lesser extent late that year, German forces were frequently able to deploy the sort of armoured reserves over much of the Eastern Front required to prevent major encirclements planned by the Soviet command, with anti-tank defences having taken a significant toll on the attacker's massed tanks even before such counterattacks. In the north terrain and German defences limited the scope for the mass employment of tanks, but the staggering concentrations of artillery were present initially at least to support the Red Army as in slogged its way forward. The timely German redeployment of armoured reserves all too often proved crucial in holding the line and even on occasion pushing Soviet forces back. The 103rd Panzer Artillerie Regiment – which above noted the importance of armour for stiffening German defences – was certainly not alone in asserting the need for infantry units to be stiffened with armoured assets of some sort – armoured assets that years earlier Soviet leaders had deemed should be incorporated into every rifle division. XXXXVI Panzer Corps, whose retreat to the Dnepr is noted above, recorded for 25 July on the Orel axis how 'at the current time successful defence against enemy breakthrough is essentially on account of the assault guns, Tigers and Panthers'.[113] However, although these resources had proven sufficient in the spring of 1943 to push the exhausted Soviet spearheads back near Khar'kov, such successes would as 1943 progressed, and into 1944, be increasingly localised. Certainly, if German forces could not, so to speak, throw a large enough – and typically armoured – spanner in the works of a major Soviet offensive in the south and centre in particular, then increasingly such offensives had sufficient weight and momentum for them to be able to punch through German defences and penetrate deep into the German operational depth regardless of local German counterattacks – assisted by the greater mobility afforded to the Red Army by Lend-Lease trucks and lorries by the thousand and despite high losses. Increasingly during 1944 the German armoured 'fire brigades' that sought to destroy Soviet spear-heads – blunting them and diminishing their penetrative power – were insufficient to deal with their weights where Soviet offensives would run out of momentum as much because of supply and maintenance issues as continued levels of attrition that were staggering compared to those being suffered by their opponent. The final buffer for Soviet offensive oper-ations was increasingly a major river line, which would be the jumping off point for the next bound forward. The '*feste Plätze*' decreed by Hitler in March 1944 and discussed in the next chapter, would certainly hinder Soviet progress on key axes to a large extent from a supply perspective, as did a ruthless 'scorched earth' policy, but not as much it they might have done in previous years and not enough to prevent the Red Army making huge bounds westwards that would as 1944 progressed bring the Red Army to the Reich itself. On the way, for the first time, the Red Army would achieve what had been so frequently aimed for from the first year of the war – the destruction of a German Army Group – the focus of the next chapter.

21   The Ten 'Stalinist' Blows of 1944

On 6 November 1944 Stalin gave a speech to Party and Soviet government officials cataloging Red Army victories over Germany and her allies since the beginning of the year. These ten 'blows' to the enemy – that later would be described as 'Stalinist blows' after Stalin's cult of personality had been further invigorated by wartime successes – were indeed all significant and marked not only destruction of the German armed forces and liberation of territory, but also the collapse of the Axis and the German alliance system.[1] By mid-1944 there could be no doubt which side had the upper hand on the Eastern Front. If at the beginning of the year there were still the German armoured units of sufficient quality to cause meaningful damage to the spearheads of Soviet thrusts and play a major role in preventing collapse, by the end othe year they were all too frequently no longer there in circumstances where Germany's last available assets that might have been used as such were being thrown into hopeless last-ditch offensive operations. By the end of the year from a German perspective stopping the Soviet hordes on the battlefield could clearly be no more than a fantasy that also required the Allied alliance to fracture – the sort of fantasy that could only be sustained by the most ardent of the true believers.

The first of these Soviet blows of 1944 was considered in the previous chapter – the liberation of the Leningrad region and conclusive lifting of the siege of Leningrad in January 1944. German Army Group North's position was becoming increasingly precarious in late 1943 where south of Novgorod Soviet forces had managed to seize the key railway junction of Nevel' on the boundary with Army Group Centre that had been a Soviet objective for months. The risk of encirclement undoubtedly contributed to the German decision to withdraw in the face of the Soviet January 1944 offensive below Leningrad, denying Soviet forces in the region the sort of encirclement of the German 18th Army that had been hoped for since 1941. Although militarily the Leningrad operation was far from the best illustration of Soviet capabilities at the time, it did nonetheless not only lead to the liberation of significant Soviet territory

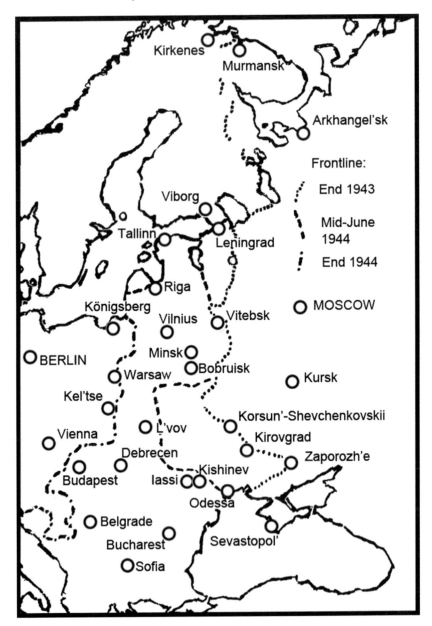

Map 5: The Soviet advance during 1944.

but also contributed to the loss of a German ally in Finland – albeit not a member of the Axis. After the January Soviet offensive below Leningrad Finland was increasingly isolated in the north, and in June Soviet forces pushed the Finns out of Karelia in the fourth of the blows. In September 1944 Finland was able to extricate itself from the war. Even further north, at the end of October German troops were pushed back from Murmansk and into northern Norway in the final blow of the year during the Petsamo–Kirkenes Operation, which included as noted when discussing the navy in Chapter 11 an amphibious component. To these three blows might be added the eighth – the liberation of much of the Baltic region that freed the Baltic Fleet from its imprisonment in the Gulf of Finland. Significant as these four blows were, the more important successes for the conclusion of the war were in the centre and south, where the latter facilitated the former and then vice-versa.

In the south the 1st Ukrainian Front had already advanced to the Bug River in the 'Dnepr-Carpathian Strategic Offensive' Operation of late 1943 and early 1944 before the start of the 'ten blows' of 1944. The 'Dnepr-Carpathian Strategic Offensive' Operation is often broken down into a series of smaller operations that included the Korsun'–Shevchenkovskii Operation about which more later, and which cumulatively saw the Red Army advance up to 450 km to the west.[2] During February and March 1944 Soviet forces advanced from the Bug River to the Dnestr, liberating the right bank of the Dnepr and for the first time entering what in 1940 had not been Soviet territory – back to the east liberating the Crimea in the third blow of April and May. Soviet forces again bounded forward on this southern sector of the front during the seventh blow of the year in August, and pushed into Rumania. This thrust in the south prompted not only a coup in Rumania and its defection to the Allied camp, but also opened the way for Soviet forces to push into Bulgaria and bring about the defection of a somewhat passive member of the German coalition. Soon Soviet troops would also push into Yugoslav territory, and into Hungary with the hope of a repeat of the Rumanian experience. With all of her allies that had been squarely in Soviet sights up to this point having deserted the Third Reich, this time Germany acted to prevent defection – a German coup in Hungary saw the installation of a puppet regime that would keep Hungary in the war until the bitter end. Soviet offensive operations between the Tisa and Danube Rivers – the last of the ten blows of 1944 – were still in progress when Stalin gave his November speech, and although saw Soviet forces make progress in Yugoslavia and the Carpathians was soon bogged down at the end of the year in the bloodbath that was the fighting for Hungary. In fact the following spring Nazi Germany would hurl its last meaningful armoured reserves into the fighting in Hungary. Consequently, although Soviet forces had overall made most progress in the far south during late 1943 and much of 1944, they ended up striking at the heart of the Reich not through Vienna but on the more obvious Minsk-Warsaw-Berlin axis that was relatively denuded of forces.

With German armoured reserves in mid-1944 tied down in the south attempting to deal with Soviet breakthroughs there – and with the much vaunted 'Second Front' now with a foothold in France – the Red Army was in a favourable strategic and operational-strategic position to undertake what is arguably the most successful of the ten blows of 1944 against Army Group Centre. Operation 'Bagration' or the Belorussian Operation will be discussed in some detail later, but here it is important to note that in this instance during the fifth of the blows of 1944 Soviet forces were actually able to achieve the encirclement of and destruction of a significant part of a major German formation that had been the aim of many of the operations of 1943. Vitebsk, Mogilev and Minsk would all finally fall to the Red Army that was in the aftermath of the collapse of Army Group Centre as a meaningful entity able to push on into Poland and Lithuania and indeed for the first time reach German territory in East Prussia. Slightly to the south, the success of the sixth blow was, in the context of the fifth from which it was supposed to deflect enemy reserves, even more likely where in what in Soviet terms was Western Ukraine the Red Army captured L'vov and the Red Army pushed forward to the Vistula River on this sector of the front as well as further north.

During what was undoubtedly a momentous year, the Red Army seemed to have a broadly successful formula for success that was arguably more tweaked than changed as the year progressed and the war dragged on into 1945. What was perhaps as important as any reform from on high during this period was the cultural change within the Red Army as an organisation that would allow the Red Army to make the most of the reforms of late 1942 and 1943. Gradually the exercising of what by the Soviet standards of 1941 was meaningful initiative – that meant that the Soviet bludgeon was wielded with a little more finesse – became less a hollow exhortation and more of a reality on the ground. Soviet forces were still pushed forward and into operations by Stalin and the senior leadership that on a macro level were either launched prematurely or made little sense in terms of defeating Germany, but in their execution there was now more likelihood that the tactically or operationally 'literate' [*gramotnie*] might be able to mitigate some of the broader flaws. At the same time the combat capabilities of the German armed forces as a whole were undoubtedly declining in a manner not dissimilar to the situation for the Red Army in the summer of 1941 where inexperienced and insufficiently trained were thrown into combat without the sort of veteran components necessary to increase their survivability long enough to gain experience themselves. As Mellenthin noted regarding the performance of the fresh 25th Panzer Division near Kiev at the end of 1943, by this point whilst veteran units could outmaneuver Soviet forces, 'yet untrained units' had 'little chance against them' – thanks not only to numerical strength but also the improved quality of the better quality Soviet units that led major offensives.[3] Nonetheless, even if the quality of German resistance was decreasing, the intensity of German resistance increased as the Red Army approached and then penetrated not only the Reich but also the German heartlands. Fighting against a stubborn defence in often close country or built up areas would take a terrible toll on the Red Army, where at times the battle need not have been fought.

During 1944 and into 1945 the effectiveness of the Red Army would undoubtedly be enhanced by both the introduction of the next generation of Soviet military equipment and the increasingly significant quantities of material aid arriving primarily through Iran from the United States and to a lesser extent from the Commonwealth. Where during 1943 the T-34 tank armed with a 76 mm gun remained in many ways an effective weapons system, German anti-tank capabilities had as noted in the previous chapter increased significantly over the previous year. The effectiveness of the T-34's 76 mm gun against the Tiger and Panther tanks was clearly inadequate – where the Tiger's 88 mm main gun and Panther's high velocity 75 mm gun were both even more potent that those of the Panzer IV and Pak 40 anti-tank gun. The SU-152 assault gun on the KV chassis that had made its debut at Kursk provided increased armoured firepower – as indeed did the SU-85 tank destroyer mounting an 85 mm high-velocity gun on the T-34 chassis. By the end of 1943 this gun had been mounted, in a new turret, on the T-34. However, the T-34 chassis was reaching the limits of its up gunning and up armouring. The IS-2 tank provided heavy armour and considerable firepower, even if the rate of fire of the 122 mm gun was low in part because of the separation of the charge from the round. The IS-2 chassis would become the basis for a series of tank destroyers and assault guns that even given the appearance of the Tiger II or King Tiger would remain potent. The ISU-122 and -152 followed the format of the SU-152 but could be provided with far better armour than their predecessor. The SU-100 introduced slightly later mounted a high velocity 100 mm gun on the T-34 chassis, providing a potent tank hunter even if overloading the T-34 chassis despite the absence of a turret. A high

Soviet forces on the streets of Viborg on the Karelian Isthmus in June 1944. Pictured are an IS-2 tank and a BA-10 armoured car apparently converted into an armoured personnel carrier in order to try to redress the lack of Soviet armoured infantry transport vehicles. The IS-2 went some way to compensate for the temporary superiority of German armour of the second half of 1943, although functioned best as a breakthrough tank in support of infantry. (RIA Novosti #389)

velocity 100 mm gun was also fielded as an anti-tank gun by late 1944 as the BS-3. In the tank gun versus armour race, the Soviet Union had once again caught up with Germany in terms of the primary indicators of equipment capability.

By 1944 Soviet armour was being handled in a far superior manner to that in which it had been handled at the beginning of the war even if communications still hampered command and control. The February 1944 combat [boevoi] regulations for Armoured and Mechanised Forces did highlight the need for co-operation between the armour and other arms, but nonetheless still wrote that 'armoured and mechanised forces are intended both for joint action with infantry or cavalry and for independent action', where the latter was 'in the exploitation of success on the offensive'.[4] 'Mechanised forces' of course included infantry accompanying the tanks, be they riding on them or motorised infantry – and the assault guns now available in significant numbers that could offer the tanks significant fire support. Infantrymen riding on tanks were of course very vulnerable when under fire, and despite the increased mobility afforded to the infantry by Lend-Lease vehicles, most of these were not armoured and the armoured transport vehicles very limited in number. The 3,068 M3A1 armoured scout cars received by the Soviet Union from the United States during the war gave some mobility to reconnaissance forces for example, and were undoubtedly used intensively where more than half or 1,662 were recorded as lost during the war in Europe. Such vehicles were however relatively few in number and the Western Allies kept most of the armoured half-tracks that essentially superceded them in production for themselves. A Soviet postwar report on Lend-Lease deliveries described these and other armoured transports such as US half-tracks and British carriers as had 'good operating characteristics', noting how they were successfully adopted by the Red Army that would otherwise not have had access to such types.[5] In practice however, few Soviet personnel could be transported in armoured personnel carriers, and it remained all too likely that Soviet armour would become separated from the infantry if advancing too quickly. In the new regulations gone completely was any differentiation between tanks for infantry support or breakthrough and tanks for exploitation, although the functions of the heavy tanks included attacks on 'a heavily fortified enemy' and the medium tanks were considered suitable for carrying out reconnaissance roles carried out by armoured cars or light tanks in other armies.[6]

When tanks were deployed *en masse* in suitable terrain and even where they were separated from the bulk of their infantry support they could continue to overwhelm defending forces after tactical defences had been breached, although sometimes at high cost. As the Red Army moved further westwards the terrain was however less likely to be suited to the sort of operations that the regulations envisaged – the success of which further east and particularly in the south had informed their creation. In the face of the plethora of infantry anti-tank weapons fielded by the German armed forces in late 1944 and early 1945 the instances in which the Red Army could in practice successfully employ such tactics without taking what even by Soviet standards were unacceptable losses diminished. During the relatively brief Rogachev Operation in early 1944 1st Belorussian Front subsequently noted that 30 per cent of the tanks had been knocked out, of which a staggering 84 per cent were total losses in the main due to explosions. The explanation for such losses here was given as the use by the enemy of a large number of hollow charge projectiles 'and in particular the "*Faust*" hollow charge anti-tank grenade'. Many of the losses – 40 per cent – were unsurprisingly caused by 75 mm hits.[7] During the six-day breakthrough phase of operations of

'Bagration' in June 1944 losses of in the region of 60 per cent of attacking tanks were recorded in some units, dropping dramatically during the extended exploitation phase and rising again as Soviet forces reached the Narev and Vistula Rivers. The bulk of losses were primarily to 75 and 88 mm guns. During the breakthrough and exploitation phases few tanks had been lost to the numerous '*Faust*' and '*Ofenrohr*' or *Panzerschreck* infantry anti-tank weapons available to German infantry – 'barely' 3 per cent of losses – rising to 9 per cent for T-34s by the time the Narev and Vistula Rivers had been reached. With less significant use of hollow charge weapons there were significantly fewer total losses. Here it was suggested that the lack of 'resilience' [*stoikost'*] of German infantry earlier on explained the difference in losses to the hand-held weapons compared for example to the later phases of the operation, despite the availability of 'the few hundred thousand' large and small '*Faust*' and '*Ofenrohr*' weapons discovered at the beginning of the summer offensive. Although this may have been the case, it was no doubt due in part because of the impact of the greater artillery and infantry support available to the tanks earlier on – less relevant during the exploitation phase but once again required although less readily available as the key Narev and Vistula rivers and associated defences were reached.[8]

In the air the VVS had arguably overtaken the Luftwaffe in terms of the quality of its aircraft according to basic indicators by late 1944. Although the Luftwaffe had been the first to use jet aircraft in a meaningful operational sense, their numbers were few and even when belatedly shifted to fighter functions were employed in the west. In the East the Bf 109 soldiered on, with later variants serving there looking increasingly outdated like the Panzer IV gun tank in its final J version. The Fw 190 had – like the new tanks of the mid-war period – briefly given the Luftwaffe an edge during the mid-war period, but was also by the end of the war no longer the superlative weapon that it had been despite modifications. Even more outdated was the Ju 87, that although enjoying something of a renaissance as a tank-busting aircraft from Kursk onwards was hopelessly vulnerable if caught by Soviet fighter aircraft without adequate cover. The armoured Hs 129 was in many ways a German version of the Il-2, which despite its armour was also relatively slow – and vulnerable to fighter attack. The Il-2 was also vulnerable – but could be produced and fielded in far higher numbers – with horrendous losses also being sustained not only due to German fighters but also the larger calibre automatic anti-aircraft fire to which they were increasingly subjected as the war progressed. During 1943 Dmitrii Degtev and Dmitrii Zubov suggest that 3,515 Il-2 aircraft were lost, where despite production of nearly 9,000 Il-2 aircraft during 1943 according to Mukhin, between

1 July 1943 and 1 January 1944 the total number of available frontline Il-2 aircraft apparently dropped from 2,815 to 2,413 aircraft. By 1 June 1944 numbers available had climbed to 3,797 – and indeed had climbed further to 4,171 by 1 January 1945. Nonetheless, in the 'year preceeding the final year of the war', one assumes here referring to 1944, 3,344 aircraft are noted as having been lost.[9]

At the time of the Korsun'–Shevchenkovskii Operation in early 1944, Soviet armoured forces were yet to enjoy the full weight of the new equipment that was available in relative abundance by the middle of the year, and so in many ways relied more than ever, in terms of tanks at least, on the abundance of the satisfactory. Relative abundance there was however, despite the fact that the Soviet 1st and 2nd Ukrainian Fronts involved had since the last days of 1943 been engaged in intensive operations in the Berdichev region on the Vinnitsa axis and towards Kirovgrad respectively. German counterattacks had, along with the depth of the advance, both played a part in the halting of the late December operations of 1st and 2nd Ukrainian Fronts. Despite Soviet operations west of the Dnepr at the end of 1943 and into 1944, in late January 1944 German forces still clung to a bridgehead extending to the Dnepr at Kanev, with the town and the river being at the tip of a salient that was obviously a tempting target for Soviet forces. Unsurprisingly, the German commander of 1st Panzer Army that occupied the salient was not given authorisation for even limited withdrawal away from the river as the ominous but predictable signs of a Soviet buildup appeared and were followed by preliminary attacks. These preliminary attacks in mid-January were contained, albeit with some effort, and even left some of the attacking forces themselves encircled.[10] On the eve of the Soviet operation proper in the Korsun' salient German forces could field in the region of 142 tanks and assault guns, 493 artillery 'tubes' and 178 anti-tank guns including self-propelled – an undoubtedly inadequate force to defend a long front against the Soviet forces of 1st and 2nd Ukrainian Fronts being redeployed for the operation against the salient.[11]

On the Soviet side, a directive for the operation had been issued by the Stavka to the fronts and Stavka representative in the region, Zhukov, on 12 January, calling for the 'encirclement and destruction of the enemy grouping of forces in the Zvenigorodka-Mironovka salient' through a linkup of forces of 1st and 2nd Ukrainian Fronts 'somewhere near Shpola'.[12] Redeployment of forces was not necessarily straightforward, where for example as Konev notes for 1st Ukrainian Front German counterattacks were being held off on the Vinnitsa axis.[13] Nonetheless, by the start of the operation Soviet forces could commit significant forces to the destruction of the salient, including 6th Tank Army for the 1st Ukrainian and 5th Guards Tank Army for 2nd Ukrainian Front. This gave Soviet forces 451 tanks and 62 self-propelled guns for the operation, more than a quarter of a million men with the support of nearly 5,000 guns and mortars of 45 mm and 82 mm calibre or more respectively in addition to nearly 588 of the heavy M-30 rocket mortar launchers and 166 BM-8 and BM-13 launch systems.[14] As Rotmistrov notes, when forces of the 2nd Ukrainian Front, including 5th Guards Tank Army, attacked during the afternoon of 25 January, the first echelon of the army was to assist in the achievement of a breakthrough rather than being inserted into a breakthrough. With a breakthrough of defences achieved 20th and 29th Tank Corps of 5th Guards Tank Army were actually all but cut off from the main Soviet forces by German counterattacks at the neck of the penetration before the second echelon of 5th Guards Tank Army, 18th Tank Corps and rifle forces pushed through to them in confused fighting. On 28 January 155th Tank Brigade of 5th Guards Tank Army and 233rd Tank Brigade of 6th Tank Army that had begun the attack on 26 January linked up at Zvenigorodka and were along with 53rd Army to form the outer layer of the encirclement.[15] Although Soviet sources claimed the encirclement of a force of around 80,000 German troops and 230 tanks and self-propelled or assault guns, the German forces encircled were probably just below 60,000 strong, and certainly contained fewer than 200 tanks and self-propelled or assault guns given that German strength within the salient was under 150 at the start of the Soviet attack.[16] Nonetheless, the German force in the Korsun' pocket was significant both quantitatively and psychologically, and it is important to note that despite Soviet successes since Stalingrad, this was in fact the first major encirclement by Soviet forces since 'Uranus'. Although postwar Soviet historians would suggest that encirclement or envelopment was 'the Red Army's main form of manoeuvre' and 'claim a complete mastery of the technique', the reality was that envelopments were frequently not the primary focus of Soviet operations and often failed to come to fruition despite Hitler's apparent best attempts to facilitate them in all to often insisting beyond reason on holding ground.[17]

During this period the German Army Group South was well provided for with Panzer divisions, and a German counterattack further west that had been planned prior to the Korsun' encirclement, Operation 'Watutin' – launched on 24 January with the aim of encircling and destroying Soviet forces attacking west of the Korsun' salient in a southerly direction east of Vinnitsa. This attack saw the deflection of the Soviet 5th Mechanised Corps from 1st Ukrainian Front and the Korsun' encirclement, and saw the Soviet 40th Army badly mauled and elements of 1st Tank Army encircled, but nonetheless the subordination of 5th Mechanized Corps to 40th Army to the west was only brief, and 5th Mechanised Corps was moved back westwards to participate the containment of German forces in the Korsun' pocket.[18] Soon significant armoured forces available to Army Group South were committed to the relief of the Korsun' pocket in early February, including those forces that had destroyed much of 1st Tank Army but days before. Here primarily Hermann Breith's III Panzer Corps was tasked with breaking through to the pocket, and could field what by German standards for 1944 was an impressive force of 126 tanks and assault guns, sixty-four of which were Tigers or Panthers, where as Niklas Zetterling and Anders Frankson note in their study of the battle 'more than half of all Tigers and Panthers on the Eastern Front were either with Breith's corps, or on the way to it'.[19] That such a force should make some progress in a relief attempt is perhaps unsurprising, but part of the problem for the encircling Soviet forces was the fact that the encirclement was less than tight with the seal on the southern side of the pocket far from impermeable. Here the Stavka was undoubtedly correct to see co-ordination between 1st and 2nd Ukrainian Fronts as an issue, and particularly given that command and control within the fronts was still sluggish. Zhukov's presence in the region as Stavka representative was supposed to smooth co-operation between the fronts but the role was obviously hampered by the fact that the fronts were being commanded from different locations. After elements of the German forces caught in the pocket had broken out, Zhukov was forcibly chided by Stalin and Antonov in a directive of 12 February for the fact that this had not been foreseen and countered, that same day command of all forces engaged in the containment and reduction of the pocket was passed to Konev and 2nd Ukrainian Front.[20] The Korsun' encirclement certainly highlighted the continued clumsiness of the Soviet chain of command where the Stavka communicated with fronts both directly, through the General Staff and Stavka representatives, and where the latter two were not always singing from exactly the same hymn sheet and indeed one identical to that of the Stavka. It must have been appar-ent to informed Soviet readers in comparison between the upper level command organs for the Red Army and Wehrmacht that despite praise for the 'flexibility, reliability and operability' of the Soviet system and despite the inadequacies of the OKH/OKW divide for Germany, on the Eastern Front German direction was far more straightforward and in many senses more likely to lead to the sort of decisive action sought by Stalin that could make up for the limits of Soviet vertical communication by any channel. In the Soviet system the message would certainly get through in some form – but with greater likelihood of mixed messages confusing the conduct of operations at front level and hampering an already less than lightning response to changing circumstances.[21] Stalin's chiding of Stavka representatives for not keeping the Stavka sufficiently informed of events was an attempt to keep the reins firmly in the hands of the Stavka and Stalin – as in the case of chiding of Vasilevskii for not informing the Stavka of events in the Donbas in August 1943.[22] Certainly, as Evan Mawdsley notes, despite being Chief of Staff Vasilevskii had spent an inordinate amount of time as a Stavka representative at the front.[23] Vasilevskii role as a Stavka representative might be taken as an indicator of trust, but one might argue that the fact that the dispatch of those such as Zhukov and Vasilevskii as Stavka representatives was also perhaps about maintaining Stalin's position at the apex of the chain of command by denying them a consistent overall picture. Certainly their roles as Stavka representatives were complicated by the fact that their provision of timely advice to front commanders might conflict with Stalin and the Stavka. If Stalin's aim was indeed to maintain ascendancy over those such as Zhukov and Vasilevskii, then the result was often dysfunctional in a manner not dissimilar to that which resulted from the confused chain of command in areas of the German war effort.

Despite the breakout of elements of the encircled German force from the Korsun' pocket, significant German forces were ultimately destroyed, with Konev able to report the final destruction of the pocket on 17 February 1944. Konev's and 2nd Ukrainian Front's claim of nine infantry divisions, one Panzer division and a Panzergrenadier brigade totally destroyed in the pocket were excessive – contrary to Konev's 17 February report, some German troops were able to break out of the encirclement. German sources suggest that 40,423 men survived the encirclement without becoming PoWs.[24] German losses had nonetheless been heavy and particularly so if including the relief forces, and German forces had been torn away from the Dnepr. Zetterling and Frankson suggest that German forces both within and outside the pocket engaged in the fighting lost about 300 tanks and assault guns – along with losses of personnel in the region of 30,000 in the pocket.[25] The cost for the Red Army had, as always, been heavy, but fortunately more in terms of material than men – where Soviet losses were particularly heavy in tanks if the losses sustained by 1st Tank Army to the west are also considered. According to Zetterling and Frankson, Soviet tank losses were in the region of three for every German loss in the Korsun' fighting – somewhere in the region of 850 in total. Total Soviet personnel losses were in excess of 80,000 – with 24,286 irrecoverable losses and 55,902 medical losses, that is wounded and sick.[26] Nonetheless, in the war of attrition that Stalin was in practice waging, the exchange was relatively speaking favourable to the Red Army and undoubtedly furthered the prospect of victory. As the Red Army now bounded forward, the Red Army was not only however destroying the German field army, but moving towards the borders of the Reich and its allies. Soon the territory being taken would have greater economic and military significance for Germany than it had to date – soon it would mean the loss of Rumanian oilfields and other assets of importance for the continuation of the war. Soon territory lost would mean loss of German population, agricultural land and factories. The Soviet strategy was undoubtedly in practice quite different than the series of intentional encirclements by German forces that threatened to leave remaining Soviet territory insufficiently well defended from the German Blitzkrieg in the summer and autumn of 1941. Despite at times aspirations towards the grand envelopment, in practice more often than not the Soviet strategy was one of 'breakthrough and advance until the enemy was exhausted or until, as in fact happened, he simply ran out of space'.[27] Gradually being sapped of strength, the German armed forces and their allies would soon have their backs against the wall.

Although during the Korsun'–Shevchenkovskii Operation Soviet forces had failed to completely seal the pocket in which German troops had been trapped, Operation 'Bagration' further north during the summer of 1944 did however achieve the sort of encirclement that Soviet commanders had aspired to achieve not only at Korsun' but on so many previous occasions. Success on the same scale would not be repeated. As the semi-official German military history of the war notes, during the first phase of the Soviet Belorussian operation from 22 June to 10 July to the destruction of the Minsk pocket the German armed forces took losses on a scale where 'never - neither before or after –would the Wehrmacht have to swallow such horrendous losses as during these 19 days', with the Wehrmacht losing close to 250,000 men during this brief period.[28] Soviet losses were of course far from light – and the Red Army would lose far more men killed and wounded during the operation than the Wehrmacht even if the balance of irrecoverable losses was in Soviet favour, where during the entire Belorussian Strategic Offensive Operation from 23 June to 29 August Soviet losses were 178,507 irrecoverable out of a total of 765,815 that includes wounded and sick.[29] Nonetheless, in terms of destroying German strength for Stalin and the Soviet leadership the 'Bagration' operation was an overwhelming and relatively economical success that also saw the Red Army liberate Belorussia in one fell swoop. The Red Army was in many ways at the peak of its effectiveness in terms of balancing cost and clear benefit – the Belorussian operation was not a distraction or an attempt to win postwar influence as many operations later in the year and into

Soviet troops advance to the west of Minsk in mid July 1944 during the successful Operation 'Bagration'. Note both the camouflage and use of smoke that were both increasingly prevalent by this stage of the war and reduced the likelihood of being successfully targeted. (RIA Novosti #67351)

1945 – it both led to the destruction of significant German strength and the liberation of territory – and was conducted relatively economically.

Operation 'Bagration' was arguably the most significant achievement for Soviet arms not only of 1944 but of the second half of the war, that took place in favourable operational-strategic circumstances that the Red Army and the Soviet Union had done so much to create. Initially supposed to be launched slightly earlier, being launched towards the end rather than in mid-June still meant that the Normandy landings and 'Bagration' were mutually beneficial and supporting in denying Nazi Germany the freedom to switch the armoured forces that were so essential for the German defence from one front to the other. The German armoured fire brigades that were on the Eastern Front could not be in both the south and centre, and it was undoubtedly wishful thinking where it was believed that the Army Group Centre 'balcony' would not be attacked by the Red Army whilst the focus of Soviet operations was in the south. On 31 May 1944 the Stavka had issued a series of directives that set out constituent parts for what would be the initial moves of the first phase of the liberation of Belorussia – and which would hopefully see the Red Army finally capture Mogilev and Vitebsk that had eluded it since the previous year. Operations were to begin after 10 June.[30] Zhukov was to co-ordinate the activities of 1st and 2nd Belorussian Fronts, and Vasilevskii 1st Baltic and 3rd Belorussian Fronts. According to Vasilevskii at this stage the Stavka was to act more as facilitator than overseer – with the GKO and General Staff making sure than the operation was materially provided for. By 10 June, with additional forces for the offensive operations not yet in place they were delayed, by now the Stavka aware of the initial success of the landings in Normandy. Ultimately, the operation would begin with reconnaissance in force on 22 June, and in earnest on 23 June.[31] There are hints for example from Zhukov that for Stalin the initial successes of the Allied landings in Normandy and the successful completion of the first phase of the Belorussian operation increased pressure for a rapid Soviet advance 'to start the liberation of Poland and without halting reach the Vistula'.[32]

German forces of Army Group Centre were far from insubstantial in terms of manpower, albeit far from adequate for the defence of the lengthy front line of the 'balcony'. Extremely problematic were however the relative immobility of the German defenders, the inadequate armour available to deal with breakthroughs and Hitler's insistence on not giving ground. In the region a significant number of towns had been designated as *feste Plätze*, and fortified as such, including Minsk, Mogilev and Vitebsk. Their garrisons of battalion to reinforced regimental strength were in the event of enemy advances to be reinforced to a strength of 1–3 divisions, meaning that as the German semi-official history of Germany in the Second World War notes, 12–13 German divisions were being offered up as a guaranteed haul for the Red Army.[33] According to this work, supporting the 336,573 men of 3rd Panzer, 4th and 9th Armies defending the 'White Russian balcony' at the beginning of June were 118 tanks and 377 assault guns, 2,589 pieces of artillery of various calibres but including 1,305 field pieces. The right-wing of 2nd Army to the north included another 149,920 men, 647 artillery pieces and seventy-five assault guns. On the 'balcony', 3rd Panzer Army was something of a fiction given that it lacked Panzer divisions, had in the region of 60,000 horses and could field only seventy-six assault guns. In fact for the northern half of the German Eastern Front at the beginning of June there was only a single meaningful Panzer unit, that is 12th Panzer Division of Army Group North. Army Group Centre could dispose of few frontline combat formations from reserve at the start of the operation other than the relatively potent 20th Panzer Division along with the 'Feldherrnhalle' Panzergrenadier Division and 14th Infantry Division. Security divisions in the rear such as 201st Security Division of 3rd

Panzer Army or 286th Security Division of 4th Army were by now far less capable than they had been at the start of the war in the East, where training units could also of course be thrown into the fray in the same sort of way that they had been by the Red Army in 1941 and 1942 even where they were not deemed ready. By 22 June, with armour moved in from the south, Army Group Centre as a whole could field just short of half a million men in combat units and formations – 486,493 – along with 3,236 artillery pieces, 118 combat tanks, 452 assault guns and supported by about 602 combat-ready aircraft.[34] That the Soviet General Staff Study of the operation claims German strength opposing Soviet forces at 'one million men, 7,000 guns, 1,300 airplanes, several hundred tanks, etc' is certainly to include forces of questionable utility such as the more than 100,000 former Soviet auxiliaries available who at this time were being encouraged to go over to the partisans before it was too late.[35] Certainly, if German security divisions and 'native' auxiliaries are to be included in German strength then it would seem only reasonable to include Soviet partisans operating in the region. According to the operational department of the representation of the Belorussian Headquarters of the Partisan Movement with the 1st Baltic Front as of 1 May 1944 there were approximately 21,175 partisans operating in the Vitebsk region before forces of the front, out of a total of 40,935 in all regions bounded by the front. That there were barely small arms for half of them certainly limited their effectiveness, as indeed did the fact that for fifty-two partisan 'brigades', one 'regiment' and seven independent detachments there were only thirty-two radio sets.[36] However, the disruption caused by Soviet partisans to German lines of communication and particularly the railways was significant by the summer of 1944, even if far from threatening to undermine German forces at the front. As Alexander Brakel notes for the Baranovichi region, through which key transport arteries ran, 'the vital main lines remained in working order until the end of the occupation', where although in the summer of 1944 significant railway track was destroyed, lines were typically repaired quickly.[37] After partisan base areas had been overrun, German historian of the Soviet partisan movement Erich Hesse suggests that during the last months of the war on Soviet soil at least some of those partisans not mobilized into the Red Army 'hunted the thousands of fugitive German soldiers who, in the smallest of groups, sought an escape route to the west', giving them something of a post-liberation security role.[38] Partisans were also used to deal with nationalist insurgents in the Soviet western border regions that also posed a security risk to lines of communication.[39]

Whilst the German semi-official history of the war tends if anything to downplay German strength, it is perhaps unsurprising that Soviet sources at times do the same for Red Army strength where the motive for doing so is perhaps that the scale of the victory looks all the greater if the Soviet numerical superiority is not seen as too overwhelming. The Soviet General Staff study for 'Bagration' does not include for example tanks and self-propelled guns for the development of a penetration of Soviet defences in the correlation of forces at the start of the operation on the principal axes for 3rd Belorussian Front, although does in other instances where consequently the correlation of forces could then reach as much as 16:1 as on the principal breakthrough sectors such as south of Parichi for 1st Belorussian Front.[40] Regardless of possible attempts to play down respective strengths be they by historians or those at the time for whatever reasons – or indeed if such vagaries in the statistics available were not intended to deceive – what is apparent from the statistics presented by either is the extent to which Soviet forces enjoyed far more significant numerical superiorities in men and particularly material than they had during offensive operations earlier in the war. German forces undoubtedly had few immediately available reserves to match the considerable Soviet exploitation forces available. Overall, Krivosheev et al suggest that Soviet forces committed approximately 2,331,700 personnel to the Belorrusian Strategic Offensive Operation from 23 June to 29 August 1944 without the nearly 80,000 personnel of 1st Polish Army. The numerically strongest front, 1st Belorussian Front committed less than a third of the total forces it committed to the operation during the initial breakthrough phase where 39 divisions or 315,346 men are noted to have been committed along the 240 km sector front out of a total of 1,071,100 personnel committed during the operation as a whole.[41] On the principal axes of attack both north of Rogachev and south of Parichi the initial correlation of forces in terms of personnel was by Soviet calculations more than 4:1 for the former and nearly 6:1 for the latter, rising to a staggering 16:1 for tanks as noted earlier and with an even greater superiority of 22:1 in field artillery south of Parichi. Here on a 28 kilometer sector 24 rifle divisions, 806 tanks and self-propelled guns, 2,469 field guns from divisional up to high command reserve strength and 1,910 mortars were concentrated. The fact that these forces had been provided with rations for men and horses for 10–15 days at the start of operations along with four and a half *boekomplekti* or combat loads of ammunition and three full refuels also contrast starkly with earlier operations, even if these resources would soon be used up.[42] At the beginning of the Stalingrad operation for example, as noted earlier, the South-Western, Don and Stalingrad Fronts were provided on the eve of the offensive with somewhere between 1.8 and 3.2 *boekomplekti* of rifle ammunition, 1.2–2.7 *boekomplekti* of 120 mm mortar rounds,

1.8–4.0 *boekomplekti* of 76 mm shells and 0.9–3.3 *boekomplekti* of 122 mm shells.[43]

Soviet *maskirovka* undoubtedly played a part in increasing local superiority – and particularly where in June even after Army Group Centre had become increasingly aware of the likelihood of Soviet offensive operations against it there seems to have been an unwillingness to accept the potential scale of any attacks from the east and north. The Soviet General Staff study of the operation notes, citing PoW testimony, that although the German command for Army Group Centre ultimately correctly predicted that the principal Soviet thrust in upcoming offensive operations would be on the Orsha axis the strength of Soviet forces of 3rd Belorussian Front to the south-east of Vitebsk was not predicted and nor was there a clear picture of when an offensive might occur.[44] It certainly seems that the concentration of Soviet forces to the north-west of Vitebsk was not fully appreciated at least by Army Group Centre prior to the start of Soviet operations, even if there were warnings of the likelihood of such an attack from other sources and from the beginning of June there was a broader awareness of the likelihood of Soviet offensive operations against the Army Group. Hence, as the German semi-official history notes, on 19 June Army Group Centre intelligence saw it as unlikely that there would be a concentric attack on the fortress of Vitebsk, it being noted only three days later that the onset of a major Soviet attack north-west of Vitebsk was 'an unmitigated embarrassment [*eine vollständige Überraschung*]'.[45] On the Orsha axis however, as commander of 11th Guards Army that was to assault German positions on this sector notes on the basis of the testimony of the commander of the German 78th Infantry Division defending this sector, the Soviet attack had been expected. In fact an additional infantry regiment and reconnaissance battalion had apparently been sent to reinforce the division prior to the offensive, and German bombardment during the night before the attack seemed to indicate some German awareness of what was afoot.[46] Here however, it is important to stress that even a wider appreciation of Soviet intentions within the Army Group would probably not have changed the outcome without a similar appreciation of the situation higher up the chain of command leading to a significant influx of resources in advance, where for example Army Group Centre had not only such limited reserves but also had to commit to the defence of so many fortresses or *feste Plätze*. Once the scale of the offensive was apparent, then reserves from outside the Army Group were thrown into the region, such as 35th Panzer Regiment as part of 4th Panzer Division that was transferred from Army Group North Ukraine, which would soon be hit by a Soviet offensive on the L'vov axis. Now equipped with Panther as well as Panzer IV tanks,

4th Panzer Division was a potent force that might have achieved more if committed earlier.[47] As Hans Schäufler noted in his memoirs, on 28 June the first units of the division were transferred to the central sector of the front – a journey taking four days as a result of partisans blowing up railway lines. Attacked by Soviet fighter-bombers as the unit detrained, from 2–16 July they were involved in 'hard defensive fighting' in attempting to delay the Soviet advance. A battle group or *Kampfgruppe* consisting of 35th Panzer Regiment, an armoured reconnaissance *Abteilung* or battalion, an armoured infantry and an artillery battalion and a company of engineers became a 'mobile fire brigade' that achieved some success in slowing down the Soviet advance.[48] Certainly, in his 1952 history of the Belorussian Operation, M.M. Minasian noted the significance of the resistance met by 1st Belorussian Front near Baranovichi, where with a 'fresh Panzer division' and organised resistance from a number of retreating infantry divisions 'the enemy put up fierce resistance for a four-day period' in early July before Baranovichi – a *fester Platz* – fell on 8 July.[49]

During the first phase of the Belorussian Operation – before significant German reserves had been brought into the region – Soviet exploitation forces were generally able to make good progress in the face of the limited German armoured and more mobile units available – and indeed the breakthrough of German defences in less defended sectors had been a far less painful experience than was often the case. As the Soviet General Staff study of the Belorussian Operation notes, on the Bogushevsk axis south of Vitebsk the success of the reconnaissance in force of the second half of 22 June that was supposed only to capture the first line of enemy positions and clarify the depth of enemy defences was such that the forward battalions of 72nd and 65th Rifle Corps on the principal axis of attack 'overcame not only the first trench with all the obstacles which had been constructed in front of it, but also captured the second and third trenches'. Such was the relative initial success near Vitebsk at the beginning of the offensive that 5th Guards Tank Army would be redeployed from the Orsha axis to exploit the initial penetrations to the north-west that had penetrated German defences from between 30 and 50 km during the first three days as German forces pulled back to the Berezina River. Within only five days five German divisions – three infantry and two Luftwaffe field divisions – were claimed destroyed in the Vitebsk area after being encircled by the Soviet pincers.[50] Lend-Lease vehicles available in large numbers, along with the inevitable widespread use of infantry riding on the tanks, helped the artillery and infantry keep pace with the tanks to some extent, although bridging rivers in particular slowed down both the advance and perhaps more so resupply. On 27 May for example, 3rd Guards Mechanised Corps that was part of the forward mobile forces of

3rd Belorussian Front had not only 196 tanks and 255 guns and mortars of various sizes – along with eighteen 37 mm anti-aircraft guns – but also ninety-nine armoured cars and Allied-supplied armoured transports and 1,223 motor vehicles to move this equipment and its 16,090 personnel forward.[51] Nonetheless, at the beginning of July after 3rd Guards Mechanised Corps had crossed the Berezina, and with resources held within the corps already used up, advancing units were forced temporarily on to the defensive by the lack of for example fuel. After the crossing of the Berezina commander of the corps General-Colonel V.T. Obukhov suggests however that the corps was at least able to benefit from a new resource and possibly one leading to economy of fuel, where partisans were able to not only provide intelligence and local knowledge but also act as tank-borne infantry for forward elements.[52]

Where German forces were relatively concentrated on the Orsha axis and had established more imposing defences, initial progress was slower and more painful. The 3rd Guards Mechanized Corps that was bounding forwards towards Minsk in early July after its insertion into the breach further north, had earlier been ordered to attack southwards to assist the first echelon on the Orsha-Borisov-Minsk axis that had struggled at first to break through German defences.[53] On that axis on the morning of 23 June Galitskii's 11th Guards Army went over to the attack after the inevitable reconnaissance in force by four battalions the previous day. Despite a more than 90 minute artillery bombardment and air attack first by 300 bombers and then 250 ground-attack aircraft only the first line of German trenches that had suffered most from the bombardment could be taken quickly – within an hour. Soon the attack had stalled in the fighting for the subsequent defensive lines where in a candid piece Galitskii notes the slow response of Soviet artillery under very centralised control to local circumstances, where by the time it became available considerable damage had already been done to those units requiring support. Soviet tanks took heavy losses from mines, anti-tank guns and fire from dug-in German assault guns. The 35th Tank and 345th Self-Propelled Artillery Regiments lost a 'large part' of their strengths to these defences and *Panzerfaust* fire. This frontal assault along the Moscow-Minsk highway soon ceased to be the principal effort in the face of the intensity of resistance and penetration of German defences on the right flank where Soviet forces would find greater success in less well defended marshy and forested terrain. It would take three rather than the planned two days to breach German tactical defences on this sector – but they were breached. In Galitskii's analysis of the relative failure of the attack the issues in his mind were far from unusual – in the face of strong German defences provided with the bulk of local reserves there were failures in both the Soviet 'planning and execution' of the attack. From insufficient strength for the supporting attack until far too late to insufficient depth for the artillery bombardment that was no doubt in part due to the limits of reconnaissance and that meant that the second German line was not suppressed, the attack by 11th Guards Army's attack showed many of the failings that had plagued the Red Army to date. To these factors Galitskii adds poor co-operations between tanks and assault guns and what he describes as 'insufficient manoeuvre by rifle divisions and supporting equipment, and also poor timing in the augmentation of attacks within divisions and particularly regiments'.[54] Soviet material superiority, coupled with what in comparison to the sort of inflexibility that characterized many similar incidents earlier in the war was reasonably timely acknowledgement of the failure of the attack on the principal axis, had facilitated success, even at high cost.

The Belorussian Operation did not come to an end until the end of August. Although there had been brief pauses in an operation that can certainly be broken down into phases and smaller operations, it is none-theless meaningful to describe it as a single strategic operation. After the breakthrough phase the encirclements in the east did not bog significant Soviet forces down in the same way as they had at Stalingrad, where I.V. Timokhovich notes the Vitebsk pocket took only two days to reduce, Bobruisk three, and even the Minsk pocket only six and where the depth of the encirclement was rapidly expanded by the outer and mobile elements of the encirclements preventing the sort of breakout of German forces that had occurred during the Korsun'–Shevchenkovskii Oper-ation.[55] The success of the Belorussian Operation depended not only on successful breakthrough, nor indeed only on the successful encircle-ment of such significant German forces on the eastern sector of the balcony, but also on the ability of the Red Army to sustain the pursuit all the way to the Vistula River. All too often during the first years of the war even when the Red Army had broken through German defenses the exploitation forces would be halted by the German 'fire brigades', allowing a new defensive line to then be created. With the German 'fire brigades' now weaker the Soviet armoured spearheads were more likely to be able to push them aside or thanks also to improvements in com-mand-and-control possibly even avoid them. Soviet armoured forces certainly suffered heavy losses as they pursued the enemy, and particu-larly in the case of 11th Tanks Corps of 47th Army of the 1st Belorussian Front that lost seventy-five tanks as it was thrown forward on the Kovel' axis in mid-July without appropriate support or reconnaissance. How-ever, as long as blunders such as this were not the norm Soviet material superiority could mean continued progress.[56] Whereas in the past Soviet communications had often failed during rapid movement either on the advance or during a retreat, now greater resources and redundancy in the system facilitated more continuous communication, even if such communication might have to avoid the normal and clumsy chain of command. Here for example the all-important mobile forces – the tank and cavalry forces – maintained communication with front command theoretically at least not only through the standard chain of command but also directly with front command via communications groups consisting of reserve officers from the operational directorate of the front along with a radio, reconnaissance and tank officer and cipher clerk. As the operation progressed the Stavka had registered its disapproval at the poor functioning of the chain of communications through a chain of command where the failure to organise communications before headquarters moved forward and the ignoring of radio communications had contributed to poor communications with cavalry and tank formations in particular.[57] It is perhaps no surprise that in this context as the Soviet General Staff study of the operation suggests the communications groups 'were the primary channels through which communications were maintained between the front headquarters and the mobile formations'.[58] Communications at lower levels were also being enhanced through the greater availability of the means of radio communications – by the Belorussian operation for example E.I. Fillipov's battery of 305th Howitzer Artillery Regiment enjoyed radio communications between observer and battery, although it seems that the battery often carried out direct fire missions in part because of encounters with enemy tanks for example as a result of inadequate reconnaissance. At least Filipov's battery and regiment had not been all but wiped out because of such negligence, as apparently had 719th Light Artillery Regiment of their artillery division that had been ambushed by German armour as it advanced through close terrain at night. In a candid memoir, Filipov describes a subsequent such incident where his battery encountered a German tank, subsequently coming under mortar fire from Soviet infantry nearby who were apparently unaware of their presence.[59] It is apparent from Filippov's memoirs how the scope for Soviet artillery keeping up with the advance of the armour had improved since earlier in the war. His battery's Studebaker trucks were by now far from being the exception, where much of the Soviet artillery and anti-tank capability at least for advance units was towed by Lend-Lease vehicles. Indeed, the significance of Lend-Lease vehicles by this point is illustrated not only by the frequent mention of Studebaker and other trucks in post-Soviet memoirs in particular, but in this instance by the gathering of his unit and other forward elements in a forest clearing prior to their engagement in 'Bagration', with his unit's

Studebaker trucks apparently standing near Sherman and Valentine tanks.[60] Infantry were also frequently moved to the front line in Lend-Lease vehicles, although often moving forward in a hostile environment on tanks and self-propelled guns, as with Aleksandr Fedorovich Pankin's ISU-152 assault gun of 344th Guards Heavy Assault Gun Regiment during the Belorussian operation. The five SMG-equipped infantrymen who accompanied his gun were all young men born in the main in 1926 or 1927 who had been conscripted from recently liberated territory.[61] Further south, Apollon Grigor'evich Zarubin's anti-tank gun battery that participated in the L'vov–Sandomierz Operation had its guns towed by both Lend-Lease and 'trophy' vehicles captured from German forces. Whilst his unit was equipped with ZIS-3 guns the brigade of which it was a part also had ZIS-2 guns that had been reintroduced after their production had ceased prematurely in 1941. By this point of the war each anti-tank battery in his brigade was equipped with a radio set.[62]

Not only was the communications network better able to keep up with the pace of advance than earlier in the war thanks in part to avoiding much of it – and artillery and anti-tank units enjoying greater tactical flexibility thanks to the greater availability of radio sets – but the Soviet supply system was also more likely to be able to keep them moving forward. During the Belorussian operation not only was the Soviet capacity to resupply facilitated by the increasing size and manoeuvrability of the Soviet truck park – capacity to be discussed at greater length below when looking at operations on the L'vov axis – but meaningful use was made of the relatively small Soviet air transport fleet for the resupply of Soviet armoured spearheads with fuel, munitions and spares. According to Timokhovich, citing an archival source from the Central Archive of the Ministry of Defence, the VVS was able to supply tank armies and corps with 1,182 tons of fuel, 1,240 tons of munitions and about 1,000 tons of 'technical equipment and spares for tanks'.[63] Such quantities were of course small, and it took time to integrate transport aviation into a front-level supply network that to date had not incorporated such a component. During the operation as a whole as N.A. Antipenko, a deputy front commander with responsibility for supply, notes in his memoirs, the supply of fuel was so bad, 'that it was necessary to provide it to armies in small doses – in 30–40 ton units where the demand was for 300–400 tons'. Additional bottlenecks in the system for the speed of the advance for forward elements were not only the bridging capacity of military formations, but also the speed with which the railways could be repaired and put into use to limit the distances over which automotive transport had to travel to supply frontline troops. As Antipenko notes, it was always a difficult decision to make whether to send forward fuel tankers up to 300 km from frontline troops – returning a shorter distance as the repaired railway lines caught up but burning 100s of tons of fuel in the process, or waiting for a couple of days for the railway lines to bring the offloading points forward to save fuel.[64] Timokhovich's praise for the use of resources 'to-hand' during bridging operations may very well be legitimate testimony to the ability of Soviet forces to improvise in such circumstances, but there was a limit to the extent to which heavy and equipment and supply could be sustained through improvisation.[65] Available bridging units, for example during the crossing of the Niemen River in mid-July by forces of 3rd Belorussian Front, struggled to maintain bridgeheads in the face of Luftwaffe air attack that knocked many bridges out.[66] When combined with a solidification of German resistance, stretched supply lines, the failure of infantry and much of the artillery to keep up with the pace of advance and human and material losses along with wear and tear on equipment over the course of a bound forward explain the halt on the Vistula – where the Red Army was also now active in the far south as well. Over the Vistula the Red Army held two large bridgeheads, into which significant Soviet forces had been moved and which would require considerable supply moved in across the inadequate number of available bridges at the end of the Belorussian operation. As Antipenko notes, at this point the operation may have been over in many respects, but it was not over for the rear area services that now had to improve on the tenuous lines of communication and supply that in some instances extended for up to 500 km from railheads.[67] Certainly Red Army forces involved were in need of a halt in high tempo operations, and the Vistula line was an obvious point. That the Soviet halt was before Warsaw where the August uprising would be put down by German forces with less assistance from the Red Army than the Poles might have liked was unfortunate, although the halt made military sense. Certainly the Red Army could had done more to assist the insurgents, and Stalin was typically hardly sensitive about expending the lives of Red Army troops in operations pushed beyond the point at which they should have been halted. However, to do so hardly made sense for a dictator whose forces would ultimately quite probably had to suppress the insurgents themselves had the German forces not done it for them. From the perspective of Soviet troops the respite was undoubtedly welcome, even if for Polish forces with the Red Army it was no doubt painful to hear the SS brutally suppressing the uprising.[68]

The crisis for German forces in the centre during the summer of 1944 required, as noted earlier, the drawing of forces from the south. Soviet resources were however sufficient for the striking of another major blow in this region as operations in the centre continued, even if sustaining operations over extended supply lines at full tempo was still not possible in too many places at once. In fact, as Soviet sources are often apt to point out, during the operation 1st Ukrainian Front was considerably stronger than 2nd and 3rd Belorussian Fronts combined during 'Bagration', with 1st Ukrainian Front fielding more than 2,000 tanks and self-propelled guns and more than 3,000 aircraft.[69] With the Belorussian operation seeing an advance as much as 600 km during its 68 days, the L'vov–Sandomierz Operation by 1st Ukrainian Front that began to the south on 13 July also saw advances of up to 350 km within 48 days.[70] It would also see the encirclement of sizeable enemy force in the Brody Pocket that included 14th Waffen SS Division 'Galician' that drew from the population of western Ukraine. The encirclement of XIII Corps alone, including 14th Waffen SS Division 'Galician', would cost the German armed forces in the region of 40,000 men, where Soviet irrecoverable losses for the operation as a whole were just over 65,000 personnel. Once again, the Red Army was reducing German strength far more economically than it had been earlier in the war, thanks to a combination of its increased effectiveness and other factors such as Hitler now being the one to throw away troops with attempts to hold territory at any cost.[71] On the L'vov axis too a key bottleneck in keeping supplies moving was the restoration of railway lines destroyed by the retreating enemy, although as the Soviet General Staff study of the operation noted, Soviet reconnaissance photos showed that the enemy had done much to increase overall rail capacity since 1941. With planning to restore destroyed railway at just over 9–10 km per day, the rate of railway reconstruction would struggle to keep up with the advance that ultimately averaged at 3–10 km per day and where actual rates of restoration varied between 5.4 km and 12.8 km per day – rates that the Soviet General Staff study of the operation notes were overall 'lower than planned'. The 56,331 lorries available to the front – 74 per cent of authorised strength – would certainly struggle to keep up with shipping supplies from railheads to frontline troops, and particularly in the case of 13th Army that advanced 10–12 km on the first day of the offensive and 5–8 on the second – far less than intended but nonetheless rapid by the standards of most Soviet operations. By the end of July 13th Army had supply lines extending back 180 km over dirt roads.[72] By the end of August 1944 the Military Soviets of the Karelian, Leningrad, 3rd, 2nd, 1st Belorussian and 1st and 4th Ukrainian Fronts were being ordered to economise in their use of munitions in order to build up reserves during a period in which 2nd and 3rd Ukrainians Fronts in the very south were pushing into Rumania.[73] Here once again as during 'Bagration', Soviet forces were trying to reach objectives that they had already pushed for before, in this case in the spring of 1944 during the Iassi–Kishinev Operation, but where already overextended Soviet forces had been pushed too far and suffered accordingly.[74] The subsequent and brief August Iassi–Kishinev Strategic Offensive Operation saw the Red Army this time throw overwhelming resources into Rumania – including as of 20 August 1,428 tanks and 446 self-propelled guns – where German strength in the region had been significantly weakened in July as a result of the crises further north.[75] Soon Rumania would change sides, and Rumanian troops would push into Hungary alongside those of the Red Army.

During 1944 the Red Army had, as Stalin's speech of 6 November legitimately highlighted, achieved a great deal and shown what a combination of qualitative improvement and quantitative might could achieve. Former Soviet territory had been all but 'liberated', and Hungary alone stood alongside the Third Reich that now faced war on home soil. Even if by the end of the year the Red Army was clearly becoming bogged down in operations on the flanks that were arguably of questionable military necessity, it was nonetheless poised to bring the would be 1000-year Reich to an end after little more than a decade.

22   The End in Sight

By the second half of 1944 the Red Army – and particularly the infantry – was suffering from acute manpower shortages. Those reserves that might have seemed almost bottomless in 1941 had proven otherwise thanks to a large extent to the operational and operational-strategic failures of Stalin and the high command earlier in the war, and in particular during 1941–2. Even later in the war the Red Army continued to take high casualties by the standards of both its opponent and allies, even if it was being far more efficient – and indeed effective – in destroying the enemy's armed forces at the same time as closing in on his economic assets and political heartlands. As the Red Army advanced the need for replacement troops drained the manpower pool on Soviet-controlled territory, and forced Soviet units to look for replacement troops on territory that they had only just liberated. Soviet forces were soon combing recently liberated Soviet territory for new conscripts who were all too often thrown in almost immediately into the fray with little training in a practice that by the second half of the war had become routine. This practice in some ways echoed the squandering of lives in militia divisions early in the war, although fortunately in this later case the uninitiated were often able to learn from their comrades, the more experienced frontline troops or *frontoviki*. Certainly future scout Vladimir Adamovich Storozhuk claims to have learnt little of value during a brief period with a reserve rifle regiment to which he was sent after being liberated by the Red Army as he was attempting to find a partisan detachment to join in the Ukraine during 1943. After only ten days the reserve riflemen were sent to field units, in his case 545th Rifle Regiment. In Storozhuk's case it would be March 1944 before he would see combat, giving him time to learn within a field unit, although the availability of such a period before seeing action was far from guaranteed.[1]

On Soviet territory Red Army units often overran partisans fighting in the German rear, offering a source of personnel who hopefully at least had some sort of combat experience. Partisans were something of an anathema to the Stalinist system that was uncomfortable with the idea of relatively poorly supervised armed bands running around in the forest, and on the liberation of territory partisans were typically quickly mobilised into Red Army units. In Lithuania Mikhail Suknev's understrength infantry battalion of 854th Rifle Regiment received replacement troops from liberated Belorussia, including former partisans, but this still left the rifle component of the battalion at barely company strength.[2] Later his battalion was provided with replacements from Western Ukraine – 'in the main peasants, religious people, and as a rule of low literacy' who often fought with little enthusiasm and 'sometimes even deserted'. He then recounts the tragic case of a father and son from such a background who arrived to the unit together – the father having fought in the First World War and the son not more than 18 years old. A lapse in judgement and the son was killed by a German sniper within sight of his father.[3] Mobilisation of such individuals was supposed to be conducted through the Military Soviets – but it is clear that despite the early protestations of the Stavka, at divisional level and below commanders continued to incorporate such personnel directly into their units. It is apparent in the case of 1st Ukrainian Front noted below at the very end of the war, that at this point there was no need to attempt to conceal the practice. Stavka concerns on the matter, expressed in October 1943 for example, were not however that such personnel might not receive appropriate training, but that they might not end up being allocated where there was greatest need.[4]

Both the urgency of the manpower situation, and at the same time the load on the rail network, seemed to be factors fostering a certain toleration of local mobilisation. These factors are highlighted by a GKO decree of March 1944 ordering the creation of four reserve rifle brigades for the training of conscripts from recently liberated territory of western Belorussia and Ukraine in the region as opposed to their being transported eastwards for training and then back again to fight.[5] Certainly although considerable feats had been achieved in terms of rail transport keeping up with the advance westwards, as General N.A. Antipenko noted, if the delay between bounds forward was not long enough as would be the case between the Vistula–Oder and Berlin Operations, and the railway lines remained at times up to 400–500 km to the Soviet rear, then the limitations of vehicle transport from railhead to front line were increasingly significant for supply.[6] Transporting personnel to the east and back for training and equipping was apparently not something that the Stavka was going to make too much of an issue where there was a desperate and immediate shortage of manpower at the front and where transport resources were at a premium. Certainly the manpower shortages at the front line also had an impact on the availability of personnel for rear area services. Attempts continued to be made late in the war to reduce the number of personnel involved in running the rear areas. Hence for example, as a result of successive reorganisations of the rear area services for rifle divisions up to December 1944 rear area personnel for a rifle division had been reduced to 1,852 persons from 3,359 at the beginning of the war. More efficient organisation can only have partially compensated for the reduced manpower available in the rear, although the greater capacities and capabilities of US-supplied trucks compared to their Soviet counterparts also made for greater efficiency.[7]

Not only were recently liberated and rear areas being combed for personnel, but they were being combed for personnel who earlier in the war might not have been considered suitable for service by virtue not only of factors such as age but also potential political reliability. In late October 1944 the GKO decreed the mobilisation of manpower from the western Ukraine, western Belorussia and Moldavia of up to 45 years of age who were not engaged in war work, with it being apparent that many of those of even 45 years of age would end up at the front line after training in reserve units if the war lasted long enough.[8] Of course, once the Red Army was operating on clearly foreign territory, these sources of immediate replacements to a considerable extent dried up, although what constituted foreign and therefore potentially hostile territory was clearly at times dictated by theory rather than reality. Hence during 1944 Lithuanians were drafted into 50th Lithuanian Reserve Rifle Division from those who had been combed from the forests of Lithuania by the NKVD. That 830 such individuals ended up deserting from the division in late 1944 might have in part been due to the poor state of material conditions in the unit as claimed in one Soviet report, but may also have been at least influenced by nationalist sentiment. Despite the issues with at least some troops from the Baltic Republics early in the war noted in Chapter 10 it seems that Stalin was unwilling to accept that personnel from what was nominally a liberated Soviet republic might be less than reliable.[9] As Soviet forces reached other territories only incorporated into the Soviet Union in 1939 and 1940, then those fit for service were pulled into the Red Army, such as for example into 25th Guards Rifle Division of 7th Guards Army – 2nd Ukrainian Front, that in January 1945 had 60 per cent Bessarabian or Moldavian troops. This mobilisation, and that of personnel from western Ukraine noted earlier, can certainly be contrasted with the restrictions on the employment of conscripts from such regions in 1941 noted earlier. There was also obviously different use of the peoples of Central Asia and the Caucasus in the Red Army later in the war, where after the enthusiasm for their mobilisation into national formations in 1941–2 had passed they were increasingly incorporated into multi-national units from the second half of 1942 onwards. Hence, to give just a few examples, where the second incarnation of 112th Rifle Division was apparently primarily manned by Siberian Russians and penal troops in April 1942, by February 1943 after blooding at Stalingrad it had only 30 per cent Russian personnel, with of the remainder 10 per cent Ukrainian and 60 per cent Turkmen. Some mixed units at one point including large numbers of troops from Central Asia saw such losses that they ceased to have significant numbers of such troops, such as 15th Guards Rifle Division that had 50 per cent Russian and 50 per cent Tajik and other Central Asian personnel in April 1943, but by November 1944 was 90 per cent Ukrainian and in January 1945 two-thirds Russian and a third Ukrainian.[10]

On enemy territory there were at least sometimes locally available replacement troops where Soviet forces liberated Soviet citizens from German imprisonment or labour service. In this category were not only PoWs but also *Ostarbeiter* – the latter foreign workers who had been conscripted from German-occupied territory for labour in the Reich. By early 1945 the manpower situation was so bad that former PoWs and *Ostarbeiter* were being mobilised directly into Red Army units on German territory. Hence in an lecture on the activities of 4th Guards Tank Army from 12 January to 22 February 1945 its commander noted that his formation was able to get Soviet citizens liberated on German territory into 'a fit state for service [*stavit' ikh v stroi*] and incorporate them into our forces as replacements' – after they had been screened by counter-intelligence.[11]

In the light of continuing personnel shortages at the front further mobilisation of women from Soviet territory also took place late in the war, although women were still not to be used as replacements in the infantry where need was most acute and the slaughter most intense. Female snipers continued to serve in relatively small numbers, and larger numbers of women served in dangerous medical and communications roles. The number of men the mobilisation of more women into accept-able roles could free up was limited by the fact that women were already serving in large numbers in many of the roles deemed suitable for them. 'Casualties' amongst women at the front – be they as a result of enemy action or pregnancy – would soak up some of these replacements. Further mobilisation of female volunteers in the spring of 1944 as decreed by the GKO was supposed to bring 25,000 women aged 21–35 into frontline non-combat roles, and specifically radio and telephone operators, cooks, orderlies and laundresses[*prachek*], but would certainly not have released this number of men for frontline service as similar mobilisation had early in the war.[12] Despite inputs of fresh personnel be it into frontline service or into rear area roles, many frontline units continued to be chronically under strength. After heavy fighting in East Prussia Shelkov's infantry battalion was again down to barely fifty men – and a depressed Shelkov and colleague drank what vodka they could find.[13]

Personnel shortages that were most acute in the infantry could have serious ramifications – and particularly when combined with poor decision-making by commanders. The self-propelled gun regiment for which Boris Zhurenko was acting commander was forced to take up defensive positions on heights most probably somewhere near Budapest without the guns having their attached SMG gunners, because the company had been 'bled white' [obeskrovlena]. In this instance the decision to put the regiment in such a position and subsequent actions led to the loss of five self-propelled guns.[14] As will be made plain later, in particular where German forces were increasingly well equipped with infantry anti-tank weapons such as the *Panzerfaust*, the shortage of infantry in mechanised and armoured units or their inability to keep up with the tanks without engaging in the risky and often costly riding on them would cost Soviet armoured forces dearly. The shortage of infantry was not only being felt in the south – as Soviet General S.M. Shtemenko – head of the Operational Section of the General Staff – notes in his memoirs, after reaching the Oder River in early 1945 regiments of 8th Army of 1st Belorussian Front for example could often only muster 'two battalions apiece, with only 22–45 men per company'.[15] The tempo of operations during 1945 did not give time to effectively rebuild units. Understandably, a certain consolidation of units was often required – for example on 19 April 1945 756th Rifle Regiment of 150th Rifle Division spent the day reorganizing in order to raise the strength of rifle companies from a paltry 40–50 men and three MG teams for the intensive fighting that inevitably stood before it in the battle for Berlin. The regiment's first battalion was disbanded, allowing strength for remaining companies to rise to 80–85 men with six MG teams for each. This reorganisation also allowed the better use of experienced command personnel.[16]

By the latter period of the war the availability of tanks was undoubtedly relatively far better compared to manpower than had been the case earlier in the war, and major armoured formations were increasingly used alongside infantry formations rather than the latter breaching enemy defences for the former to then be inserted into the breach. During both the Vistula–Oder and Berlin strategic operations tank formations were thrown in alongside infantry formations before the latter had broken through enemy defences, even if after breakthrough tank formations were able to press ahead of the infantry. A brigade from 31st Tank Corps had been used alongside infantry formations during the initial breakthrough phase of the attack by 5th Guards Army during the opening phase of the Vistula–Oder Operation during the morning of 12 January 1945, with the remainder of the corps supposed to be engaged during the final phases of the breakthrough. These mobile forces were however thrown into the breakthrough of the third layer of German defences early that after-noon.[17] As commander of 5th Guards Army A. Zhadov notes, this operation had benefitted from considerable time for preparation of the Sandomierz bridgehead for the launching of the Vistula–Oder offensive – in fact from late August 1944 through to mid-January 1945.[18] Many units had been brought up to full strength for the final push and many units at least started the offensive with a full complement of personnel even if they would soon be back to operating at significantly reduced strength. Artillery brigade commander Viktor Makar'evich Zhagala notes how on his return to his brigade of 1st Ukrainian Front after a period in Moscow at the end of 1944 it had been brought up to full list strength both in terms of men and equipment, but would soon take heavy losses in the fighting for Kel'tse.[19]

The release of tanks from armoured formations during the break-through phase where they were typically intended for exploitation was increasingly frequent. As Marshal I.S. Konev commanding the 1st Ukrainian Front notes in his memoirs for 1945, during the Upper Sile-sian Operation in mid-March 1945 he had released armoured forces simultaneously with the infantry in an operation to encircle five German divisions near Oppeln. Here, as to the north, relatively concentrated German armour was apparently seen to threaten the flanks of any advance on the Berlin axis, and hence had to be dealt with. Konev's motivations for committing armoured formations alongside the infantry during the breakthrough phase, according to his memoirs, were mani-fold. Although speeding up the breakthrough in order to increase the chances of success was one reason, limiting the losses in rifle divisions was another. This desire to limit infantry casualties was in part because of awareness of shortages and the requirements of the Berlin Operation soon to be launched, but also 'the moral responsibility of the commander for the unnecessary loss of life'. He goes on to suggest that 'by 1945 it was unacceptable – as a matter of principle – to throw infantry into the attack without tanks'.[20] The northern pincer for the encirclement was to consist of a rifle corps from 5th Guards Army, 21st Army, 4th Guards Tank Corps and 4th Guards Tank Army. The southern pincer would consist of 59th and 60th Armies with 93rd Rifle, 7th Guards Mechanised and 31st Tank Corps and 152nd Independent Tank Brigade.[21] This and other rushed operations in the spring of 1945 saw heavy tank losses – with losses for tanks being particularly high in proportion to infantry losses during the latter phase of the war not only due to rushed planning but also because of the use of major armoured formations during the break-through phase – armour that would then often charge forward without due infantry support. During 1945 – barely more than four months – the Red Army would lose somewhere in the region of a staggering 8,700 tanks and 5,000 self-propelled guns.[22]

In the case of the Upper Silesian Operation of mid-March 1945 the 'serious losses' suffered by 7th Mechanised and 31st Tank Corps that were supporting 59th and 60th Armies – and indeed also 'unnecessary losses' suffered by 4th Guards Tank Army – were also because in a typically hurried operation for the period reconnaissance had been poor that had resulted in 'an insufficiently powerfully working over of enemy anti-tank defences by the artillery'.[23] Commander of 4th Tank Army, D.D. Leliushenko, notes in his memoirs how the tank army had only seven days to plan for the operation with the need for redeployment on the back of recent intensive fighting.[24] This operation was on the back of the Lower Silesian Offensive slightly further north that had been launched the previous month as the tail end of the Vistula–Oder offensive, and that had seen both 3rd Guards Tank and 4th Tank Armies suffer significant losses. By this point 1st Ukrainian Front's operations – often presented in Soviet works as part of an almost seamless run of offensive operations forming a coherent whole – were undoubtedly losing steam and conducted in a much more reactive and less systematic and thought out manner than they had begun in January.

A significant limiting factor in the third phase of the Vistula–Oder Strategic Operation in Silesia in early February 1945 had been the fact that infantry forces of 13th Army in support of 4th Tank Army could not keep up with the advance of the armoured units, and indeed where although armoured formations had advanced to the Neisse 'the enemy had been able to separate off infantry of 13th Army from 4th Tank Army at the River Bober'. Indeed, it seems that all motor vehicles within 4th Tank Army were required for supply meaning that even within the Tank Army itself 'there wasn't motor transport for the motorised infantry'. As a result of the failure of the supposedly motorised infantry to keep up with the tanks it was subsequently noted how a bridge over the Oder seized by elements of 62nd Tank Brigade on 24 January had been subsequently destroyed by the enemy, along with five tanks, thanks to the 'limited number of infantry' in the infantry detachment riding on the tanks.[25] By the end of the third phase of the operation it is unsurprising that both tank and personnel losses had become significant. During the operation as a whole to 24 February 4th Tank Army had lost 236 tanks and 50 self-propelled guns including 10 SU-57 as total write-offs, with 2,467 killed and 6,223 wounded. That during the operation an equivalent number of repairs to total strength – that is 620 – had to be carried out on the tanks and self-propelled guns of the army would at the beginning of the war have been well beyond the capacity of repair services and strained them even now.[26] By 10 March 1945 as Soviet forces slugged away at the German forces in Silesia in the region of Lauban in what was not part of the Vistula–Oder offensive as it had been planned even if it followed on from it without meaningful pause, 3rd Guards Tank Army as a whole was down to only 120 operable T-34/85 tanks out of a list strength of 375.[27] As commander of 55th Tank Brigade of 7th Guards Tank Corps David Abramovich Dragunskii noted of the fighting between the Bober and Neisse Rivers of the Lower Silesian Operation of February and early March 1945, despite the fact that brigades resources had been 'depleted' it continued to receive orders from above driving it 'Forward! Forward!'.[28] With the intensity with which tanks and other armoured vehicles had been used after the operational lull of late 1944 there were predictably problems with breakdowns. Between 1 February and 10 March 3rd Guards Tank Army recorded sixty-two T-34 breakdowns, the majority of these according to the formation being as a result of manufacturing defects.[29]Although 3rd Guards Tank Army was no longer fit for combat by early March and was pulled out of the line, its compatriot formations continued to be heavily engaged. During the first day of the Soviet attack on the Oppeln salient that began on 16 March Soviet forces were able to advance at most 10 km and as Soviet forces battered their way forward 7th Mechanized and 31st Tank Corps for example lost, according to Konev, a quarter and a third of their armour respectively. Konev suggests that in this case Soviet forces – at least of 1st Ukrainian Front – met for the first time concentrated defence against tanks reliant to a large extent on the *Panzerfaust*, often in built-up areas and in spring conditions hampering the mobility of tanks.[30] Certainly the bulk of Soviet tanks were being lost to or damaged by anti-tank guns and *Panzerfaust* by this time. The 3rd Guards Tank Army recorded that of 1,479 instances of battle damage to tanks and self-propelled guns from 12 January through to 12 March 1945 only 42 were due to mines and 75 due to enemy air attack, with the remainder due to artillery – be it anti-tank or otherwise – and *Panzerfaust*. Tanks were lost outright in similar proportions – 530 out of a total of 556 to artillery and *Panzerfaust*.[31]

Understandably, time for preparation – including for reinforcement, training, artillery reconnaissance and the amassing of munitions and other supplies – was an important factor in achieving success whilst minimising losses. All too often, as apparent in previous chapters, Soviet forces were pushed forward before they had what might be deemed suitable time for recovery since the last major operation, and before they had time to prepare for the specifics of the next. In many ways the Vistula–Oder Operation was an exception, and in the case of the early phases of the Vistula–Oder Offensive Soviet forces arguably reaped the benefits of time for preparation. As commander of 4th Tank Army Leliushenko notes in his lecture on the formation's activities from 12 January–22 February 1945 as part of the Vistula–Oder Operation and breakout from the Sandomierz bridgehead, the formation had in this instance considerable time for recovery and preparation for the offensive from the point at which it went over to the defensive after the L'vov–Sandomierz Operation on 1 September 1944, to the beginning of the Vistula–Oder Offensive on 12 January. On 1 September 1944, as was typical after a major offensive, the army's operational tank strength was low – in fact only 17 per cent of list strength in that it had only 106 operational tanks and self-propelled guns rather than the authorised 605, in addition to having fifty Lend-Lease SU-57 self-propelled anti-tank guns. The situation was better for manpower – with the army having 82 per cent of authorised strength, that is 33,305 personnel out of 40,415, although had only 69 per cent of the list strength for automotive transport or 3,375 out of 4,911 vehicles. In the next few months the army apparently had time to cycle troops through two firing ranges established for training, where preparations for the forthcoming operation focused on knocking out enemy anti-tank weapons, fighting at night, river crossing and other relevant training. That thirty rounds of large-calibre ammunition were allocated for every tank, self-propelled gun or gun crew represented a significant allocation of ammunitions for training. Time was similarly available for map exercises for staff officers that could transition into planning for the actual operation. By the time the operation was launched the army was at full list strength as far as tanks and self-propelled guns were concerned – with a total of 620 tanks and self-propelled guns – 482 T-34, 113 SU-76 and SU-85, and 63 IS-2 along with 61 SU-57 – and where most of the replacement T-34 tanks were armed with 85 mm guns. Units had the appropriate command elements largely through promotions from within the army. At the beginning of the Vistula–Oder Offensive the supplies available to 4th Tank Army were considerable compared to those available at the start of offensive operations earlier in the war. At the beginning of the operation 4th Tank Army had three or more refuels per tank or self-propelled gun and close to three *boekomplekti* for infantry arms – with three *boekomplekti* of ammunition per armoured vehicle.[32] Commander of 3rd Guards Tank

Army Ribalko also noted in a subsequent lecture how before the start of the Vistula–Oder Strategic Operation the four months preparation had been 'quite sufficient in order to fully prepare forces', where in such instances the 'quality of preparation is directly proportional the time available'.[33]

Certainly, after intense planning and preparations in late 1944 forces of the 1st Ukrainian Front were extremely successful in operations during the first weeks of the Vistula–Oder Offensive. During the first phase of the operation from 12–19 January forces of 4th Tank Army of 1st Ukrainian Front advanced up to 220 km and 6th Guards Mechanised Corps participated in closing the Kel'tse-Radom pocket with 9th Tank Corps of 1st Belorussian Front. Losses of 102 tanks and self-propelled guns were heavy but far from excessive by the standards of earlier in the war. That during the second phase of the operation to 3 February the army was able to seize a bridgehead over the Oder – advancing up to 300 km or more – was also a significant achievement. The crossings of the Oder were particularly significant in the light of the fact that not only were supply lines starting to strain in the face of the continued shortage of motor transport and in particular tankers, but also given the inevitable lack of infantry that was becoming an issue for forward units where available infantry beyond the tank riding infantry who tended to suffer appalling losses had often yet to catch up either due to enemy action or because of the lack of suitable transport for them to keep pace with the tanks.[34] Here the shortage of armoured personnel carriers in particular– be they wheeled or half-tracked – put the Red Army at a disadvantage. Nonetheless, a pause of a week from 30 January–7 February on the Oder between the second and third phases of the operation was apparently enough for supply services to catch up the at least 24–48 hours they apparently lagged behind forward elements, so that when the third phase of the offensive began on 8 February 4th Tank Army had three *boekom-plekti* of munitions and three refuels available for the 415 tanks and self propelled guns still in operation.[35] However, such figures hide other factors such as the fact that reconnaissance information was increasingly lacking as operations continued without respite in the wear and tear on man and machine. As in previous instances in which Soviet armoured formations had been pushed forward relentlessly – such as in the spring of 1943 – in early 1945 they would pay very dearly for gains made during the latter phases of a major strategic operation. What was however different in 1945 compared to 1943 was the fact that German forces did not have the capacity to take advantage of the situation in the way they had in 1943 when, as noted at the end of Chapter 18, 3rd Tank Army had been all but destroyed.

During the Soviet late-war offensives in which the tank would often take the lead, inadequate reconnaissance, and in fact the use of armoured units for reconnaissance at the head of forward detachments, would often mean that encountering the enemy would lead to significant tank losses. During the Upper Silesian Operation of March 1945 Konev candidly notes how many German anti-tank positions consisting of 'dug-in tanks and self-propelled and anti-tank guns hidden in population centres ended up being a surprise to us' – 'difficult to locate from the air' and where 'ground reconnaissance forces were unable to provide full details of the enemy's fire system within the limited preparation time available for the operation' meaning that in particular anti-tank defences were not suppressed by Soviet artillery.[36] Certainly when operations had actually begun, just as BT-series tanks had proven to be poor reconnaissance vehicles in 1939, so the T-34 was similarly poor in that role in 1945. Nonetheless, during the exploitation and pursuit phase by 47th Guards Tank Brigade of 2nd Guards Tank Army of 1st Belorussian Front on the Sokhachev axis during the Vistula–Oder Operation for example, tanks – with at best tank riding infantry – were at the head of the advance. Although on the left and more exposed flank 'a group of scouts' operated in front of a forward detachment consisting of a reinforced company of tanks that was followed by a tank battalion reinforced with a battery of self-propelled guns, a company of SMG gunners and section of sappers, on the right flank it seems that reconnaissance elements did not precede the reinforced tank company that was effectively scouting ahead of a battalion with supporting elements.[37] When 47th Guards Tank Brigade entered Sokhachev – in what former chief of staff for 2nd Guards Tank Army A.I. Radzievskii describes as a 'raid' and with what can only have been very limited infantry support – it is apparent that it took heavy losses to German infantry armed with *Panzerfaust* anti-tank weapons. In his recollections of early 1945 Radzievskii suggests, in a manner similar to Konev slightly later as noted above, that at Sokhachev 'we for the first time met with the mass use of the *Panzerfaust* by the fascists, and initially suffered losses given that we did not have experience of fighting against them'.[38] Soviet forces, including of 1st Ukrainian Front, had of course encountered the *Panzerfaust* in meaningful numbers prior to both of these engagements, and claims of their first use '*en masse*' seem to provide a convenient excuse for very heavy losses amongst tanks used without appropriate support. Even the heavy Soviet tank were vulnerable without due support. A Swedish volunteer with the 11th SS Panzergrenadier Division 'Nordland' fighting on the approaches to Berlin in April 1945 describes an incident in which three Soviet tanks – most probably IS-2s from his description – were destroyed in relatively open terrain by

German infantry occupying what seemed to be abandoned positions with *Panzerfaust* as they pursued apparently retreating German troops without close infantry support.[39] Soviet tanks all too frequently – be it because there were insufficient infantry or negligence – charged forward without the necessary infantry support. Whether because of a shortage of infantry or leaving the situation *na avos'* – leaving the situation to fate – in a post-Soviet interview scout Vladimir Adamovich Storozhuk described how in January 1945, somewhere in the region of Kel'tse, his reconnaissance section entered a town that unknown to them had been reached first by Soviet tanks of the tank battalion attached to their infantry division. Those tanks had not been accompanied by infantry, and late in the evening in an urban environment were of course vulnerable. Three shots from anti-tank weapons or artillery that Storozhuk and his men had heard had been directed at these tanks, two of which were as a result burnt out.[40] This incident is reminiscent of similar ill thought out use of tanks in an urban environment in Poland in September 1939 in Chapter 7 when Soviet forces were similarly being instructed to press forward almost regardless.

During this period in particular '*stremitelnost''* – translatable usually as 'speediness' although the alternative 'rushed' might often be more appropriate – was the order of the day and would see Soviet forces pushed forward relentlessly once an operation had begun. Radzievskii describes 47th Guards Tank Brigade's 'raid' towards Sokhachev as such [*stremitel'nii reid*].[41] Available dedicated reconnaissance assets were typically used to reconnoitre a line of advance. Reconnaissance assets were often too limited to undertake what might have been more valuable reconnaissance of a sector instead of axis, as in the case of reconnaissance forces of 7th Guards Tank Army during the Berlin Operation. In this case, prior to reaching the city itself both a shortage of suitable vehicles and communications assets hampered reconnaissance activities that much to the chagrin of the reconnaissance officer concerned had not been conducted on a sector basis.[42] Certainly that such dedicated tactical reconnaissance assets were all too often poorly provided for with radio communications limited their utility, where in the above case 'communications were in the main provided through mid- and short-range radio sets, and when the mid-range sets broke down normal communications could not be sustained'.[43] Where, in the face of identified anti-tank defences and particular in built up areasm Soviet armoured units were encouraged to bypass them and move on, and where reconnaissance was weak, it was all too likely that such units would blunder into ambushes or otherwise unidentified defences and take heavy losses. We will return to the issue

Soviet assault guns in early October 1944 poised to move into Hungary. Such assault guns went some way to compensate for the poor mobility of much of the Soviet artillery – and could function in an anti-tank role. (RIA Novosti #61805)

of reconnaissance a little later, but will note here how not just reconnaissance assets, but also manpower might have been more effectively employed had the Red Army not been pushed forward so relentlessly across the whole of the German Eastern Front. In late 1944 and early 1945 Soviet forces were not only engaged in intensive operations on the key Berlin axis, but also on the flanks – for example both East Prussia and Hungary.

From a strategic point of view the protracted fighting in Hungary from the autumn of 1944 through the winter of 1944–5 may have benefitted the Soviet Union in the stated aim of defeating Germany in drawing away much needed German reserves from the key Berlin axis further north, but the cost was high both on the offensive and in dealing with the fierce German counterattacks in the region. It is questionable whether here the Red Army need have been pushed forward quite so ruthlessly once it had become apparent as the end of the year approached that significant German strength was being transferred to the region and indeed once

Germany had been separated from the natural resources there. However, the motivation here was apparently not just the destruction of the Reich, but to strengthen post-war Soviet claims on Eastern Europe. As such, the Red Army was a potent tool in achieving broader political goals that had not been brought about by other means, although the material and human costs were high. Certainly many of these lives need not have been lost in achievement of what was undoubtedly the principal aim of many of those doing the fighting – defeating the German invader and its allies that had caused so much misery for the Soviet population. The Budapest Strategic Offensive Operation alone cost 80,026 Soviet irrecoverable losses and a further 240,056 sick and wounded – a total of just over 320,000. At the end of the operation, as Krivosheev and his colleagues note, the German puppet Hungary had been defeated and the road to the Reich through Czechoslovakia and Austria was indeed relatively open, but neither was hardly crucial for defeating Nazi Germany by this stage.[44]

By late September 1944 Soviet troops had ostensibly been poised to knock Hungary out of the war if the Hungarian government did not remove itself first. The Soviet 2nd Ukrainian Front had struck from Rumania to the south into Hungary on the back of the successful Iasi-Kishenev Offensive, and the 3rd Ukrainian Front had made good progress with Yugoslav forces[45] in Yugoslavia further west, with Belgrade falling on 20 October. To the north east, although planned operations to seize the eastern portion of the Carpathian Mountains had in late August been shelved in the light of the success of operations to the north and south that seemed to negate the need for such a slog, the uprising in Slovakia seems to have rekindled plans for operations there that also offered the prospect of Soviet forces entering Hungary and the Hungarian plain from the north.[46]

After the pro-German Szálasi coup on 15 October it soon became apparent that Hungary would not go the way of Romania and its army and join Soviet forces – Horthy's attempt to go over to the Allies failed even to yield up defection *en masse* by formations of the Hungarian army despite for example the best efforts of General Béla Miklós commanding 1st Hungarian Army, although apparently 'a considerable number of soldiers' did desert even if not *en masse*.[47] Nonetheless, on the assumption of shaky Hungarian morale and the continued focus of German forces to the north success in the region could still potentially offer a less well defended route into Germany through Austria or draw German forces southwards, where there was undoubtedly fear of a race for Vienna with the threat of a British-inspired landing in the Balkans in the autumn.[48] Hopes of reaching Vienna by the end of the year would soon however evaporate in the face of slow progress not only in southern Hungary as 2nd Ukrainian Front advanced in a north-westerly direction, but also given the initial lack of support for the front from the flanks. The redeployment of forces of the 3rd Ukrainian Front to the east of the Danube after their success on the Belgrade axis took some time, where they would then be operating against German forces between the Danube and Tisa Rivers. To the north-east Soviet progress through the Carpathian Mountains was slow in terrain not only very much suited to the defence, but also where all too often advancing Soviet forces 'lacked experience in the conduct of mountain warfare' – as had been the case in the Caucasus. The fact that this operation followed closely on the heels of the L'vov–Sandomierz Operation had meant that the forces committed – principally 38th Army – had little time to recover from the former operation and prepare for the next, with rifle division strengths apparently not exceeding 4.5–5,000 men.[49] Even if not offering the Soviet Union its equivalent of the 'soft underbelly' of the Reich about which Churchill had spoken with regards to Italy, the fighting in Hungary none-theless was soon seen as offering the prospect of diverting German resources from elsewhere as well as the securing of postwar influence in a region in which Churchill and the British also had what retrospectively seem naive aspirations. General S.M. Shtemenko of the Soviet General Staff certainly suggests that for the Stavka a key role of forces on the flanks both in Hungary and East Prussia was in late 1944 to draw off German forces from the key central axis – the most direct route to Berlin – and if this was indeed a key reason for such operations, then those in Hungary would certainly be successful.[50]

Although drawing German resources from the key Berlin axis may have been a motivating factor for operations in the south, knocking Hungary out of the war was a meaningful goal in its own right – depriving Germany of its last ally, further limiting German access to raw materials including the Hungarian oilfields, and also winning the Soviet Union post-war influence in the region. Hopes of a rapid occupation of the region – and even of southern Hungary – were not however to come to fruition. The Soviet advance from the south on Budapest had already been given a bloody nose below Debrecen during the first half of October, when as commander of Army Group South Hans Frießner notes Soviet tank and mechanised forces that were advancing on the town had been cut off from Soviet lines on 10 October. These units would subsequently break out of what threatened to become encirclement in fighting that saw German forces also take heavy losses, but this would not be the first such encircle-ment as Soviet forces sought to punch through to Budapest.[51] After the coup in Budapest, plans for a dash to Budapest of 2nd Ukrainian Front in order to take advantage of relative Hungarian disarray were shelved and the prospects for a quick fix solution to the Hungarian problem had come and gone. On 18 October Malinovskii's 2nd Ukrainian Front was ordered to resume its advance – and advance that had been all but continuous anyway according to Frießner – and destroy the Debrecen group of enemy forces to the east of the city. The destruction of the Debrecen grouping of enemy forces was to be undertaken with a view to 46th Army advancing from the south along the Danube to its west and then taking Budapest.[52] Budapest, as the capital of Hungary, was not only a significant political objective with possible bearing on the willingness of Hungarian forces to continue fighting, but also as one might expect a communications hub. At this stage 2nd Ukrainian Front had at least gained additional mechanized strength – 4th Guards Mechanised Corps that had just participated in the capture of Belgrade with 3rd Ukrainian Front, and 2nd Guard Mechanized Corps that had been intended for 3rd Ukrainian Front. Although a counterattack by the German LVII Panzer Corps of 19 October on Rumanian forces that saw an entire Rumanian division effectively destroyed[53] required the commitment of 7th Guards and 6th Guards Tank Armies, it did not prevent the Soviet capture of the key communications hub of Debrecen that finally fell on 20 October to forces that included the Soviet-sponsored Tudor Vladimirescu Division fighting with the Red Army. The Soviet Pliev Cavalry-Mechanised Group (4th, 5th and 6th Guards Cavalry Corps, 7th Mechanised and 23rd Tank Corps) then advanced northwards on the Budapest axis in an attempt to encircle 8th German and 1st Hungarian Armies and cut off German forces to the east, but its spearhead forces were actually themselves encircled by counterattacking German armoured and other German and Hungarian forces during the small hours of 23 October. According to Frießner, south of Nyíregyháza 23rd Panzer Division destroyed the Soviet 30th Cavalry Division and 3rd Tank Brigade and the town was recaptured by German forces. His claims that three Soviet corps had all but lost their heavy equipment and only elements escaped may be exaggerated, but once again German forces had been able to severely damage Soviet spearheads that had pushed forward prematurely.[54] The cavalry component of the cavalry-mechanized groups might have been able to keep up with the tanks, and could in the right conditions perform a valuable exploitation role, but even with their organic tank components a cavalry corps was hardly a match for even a late-war German Panzer division without timely assistance. Nonetheless, despite this setback, Soviet forces advancing to the east along the Danube had at least made progress where German armour couldn't be everywhere and on 28 October Stalin ordered that the following day 2nd Ukrainian Front must finally strike a 'decisive blow against enemy forces defending Budapest'.[55]

Commander of the 2nd Ukrainian Front Malinovskii's apparent protestations that he needed an additional five days for preparations for a push on Budapest fell on deaf ears – and there was a logic to striking sooner rather than later before the transfer of greater German strength to the south of the city and the occupation of defensive positions protecting it. This logic would certainly justify pushing forward with relative disregard for human life not only in Hungary but also elsewhere – on occasion probably saving lives, often at the tail end of a period of sustained operations not. In this case Stalin and the Stavka had better military grounds to insist on haste than they would perhaps later have near Berlin when the Reich was on its last legs and pressure for quick results was arguably more politically motivated. At the same time however, fighting near Nyíregyháza and earlier in the month near Debrecen had certainly hit the Front's armoured strength, and as Kamen Nevenkin notes, forces on the left flank had only just crossed the Tisza River after having advanced up to it, and in such circumstances consolidation was desirable.[56] Such consolidation was certainly made more desirable where the attack would take place without wider immediate support from neighbouring fronts be it from the east or west. Under pressure from the Stavka for results, the 2nd Ukrainian Front formulated a plan at short notice that was once again wildly over optimistic in its objectives and that as was the case more often than not underestimated the capabilities not only of German but particularly Hungarian forces in the region – and the attack soon stalled.[57] On 29 October Soviet forces attacked, but after initial success the attack stalled before Budapest.[58] On 29 October 2nd Ukrainian Front could field in the region of 545 operational tanks and self-propelled guns, the bulk of which were concentrated in the recently arrived 2nd Guards Mechanised Corps with 181 T-34, 21 IS-2 and 21 each for SU-76 and SU-85s.This was hardly overwhelming strength, where on 1 November Army Group Fretter-Pico facing them could field as of 1 November a force of over 100 operational tanks and assault guns – not considering the other anti-tanks assets available.[59] By the second half of November, as commander I.A. Pliev of the cavalry-mechanised group bearing his name notes in his memoirs:

Our losses started to have an impact on the speed of the advance. The fighting was unusually bloody in character. In 4th Guards Corps a number of units lost large numbers of officers. ... Many platoons were commanded by sergeants, and in 9th Guards Cavalry Division two of the squadrons were led by old, experienced sergeants. The picture was similar for 6th Guards Cavalry Corps. In 23rd Tank Corps by 23 November there were unfortunately only an insignificant number of tanks left operational.[60]

Dead enemy troops lie beside a SU-76 assault gun knocked out in the Polish town of Elbing in early 1945. Soviet armour suffered greatly at the hands of German light anti-tank weapons such as the *Panzerfaust* when such vehicles were deployed with inadequate infantry support in an urban environment. The SU-76 was in many ways particularly poorly suited to urban fighting with its light armour an open-topped crew compartment into which hand grenades could be thrown. (RIA Novosti #2544)

Stalin and Antonov, always apt to point out what seemed obvious with the value of hindsight, in the light of the failure to seize Budapest with this single thrust suggested that 2nd Ukrainian Front attack across a broader front using the right wing of the front to strike from north and north-east in co-ordination with a renewed attack from the south.[61]

Given the significance that was being given to the region by Hitler who was fixated on the possibility of being able to secure valuable oil as well as maintaining access to other natural resources – and was sensitive to losing 'allies' – German strength in the region increased significantly. The German Army Group South as a whole increased dramatically in strength from September 1944 through to mid-March 1945, where if taking armoured strength as an indicator of commitment to the region a strength of 66 operational German and 231 Hungarian tanks as of 4 September 1944 can be compared to 475 German and 53 Hungarian by the end of the year on 30 December. By 15 March 1945, with the German counteroffensive Operation 'Spring Awakening' in the Lake Balaton region reaching its conclusion there were an impressive 742 German and 48 Hungarian operational tanks on strength for Army Group South, even if fuel shortages would limit their utilities.[62] These figures might usefully be compared to total German armoured strength – tanks and assault guns – at these points. On 1 September 1944 total frontline armoured strength for the Wehrmacht was 10,639, rising to 12,336 on 1 January 1945 and 12,524 on 1 February 1945, even if many of these vehicles would struggle to move very far in the light of fuel shortages. Not only the numbers in Hungary, but the fact they were relatively well provided for with fuel highlighted the increasing significance of the region.[63] Despite some reinforcement to a considerable extent in response to German activity, Soviet forces in the region would not be fighting with the sort of numerical superiority that they had enjoyed in August. Hence, in mid-August at the start of the Iassi–Kishinev Operation 2nd Ukrainian Front could field 959 tanks and 329 self-propelled guns, with 4th Ukrainian Front adding a further 474 tanks and 117 self-propelled guns for a total of 1,428 and 446 respectively. By 1 August 1944 German Army Group South Ukraine could field only 155 tanks, 294 assault guns and 30 assault howitzers.[64] Soviet superiority in terms of both manpower and tanks was somewhere in the region of 4:1 for 2nd Ukrainian Front at the beginning of December 1944, with in the region of 140 German tanks and assault guns opposing in the region of 565 Soviet tanks and self-propelled guns.[65] At this point the ratio of armoured strength for example was certainly more in Soviet favour on the key Berlin axis, where for example Army Group A as of 10 January 1945 could field in the region of 1,104 tanks, assault guns and tank hunters – not including other anti-tank assets – compared to a total of the 4,230 tanks and 2,234 tanks and self-propelled guns fielded by 1st Belorussian and 1st Ukrainian Fronts for the Vistula–Oder Operation starting only days later.[66]

At the beginning of November 1944 2nd Ukrainian Front was no longer operating alone against German and Hungarian forces in the region between the Danube and Tisa, with 3rd Ukrainian Front now also in a position to advance northwards. Budapest was encircled by Christmas, although the capture of the city would be more than two months away. As of 24 December approximately 41,000 German along with a similar number of Hungarian troops were trapped in the city, which was stubbornly defended until a bloody breakout attempt effectively ended the siege in mid-February.[67] The encirclement had been followed by a series of German counterattacks in order to attempt to lift the siege, meaning that even before the more infamous Operation 'Spring Awakening' in March the region had seen significant armoured engagements in early 1945.[68] In fighting in the region from 29 October to 13 February forces of the 2nd and 3rd Ukrainian Fronts had lost in the region of 80,000 irrecoverable losses along with more than 240,000 sick and wounded.[69] They had deflected significant German resources from the key Berlin axis and destroyed many of them – including almost the entire force defending Budapest, prised Germany from important natural resources and knocked Germany's last ally of any note out of the war. As hoped for by Soviet leaders, the collapse of the Hungarian war effort had effectively soon followed the fall of Budapest. The Hungarian army had undoubtedly put up stiffer resistance than had been expected, and the capture of Budapest and the removal of the bulk of the Hungarian army from the equation in the south certainly freed up significant Soviet forces for a push on Vienna – by now more of political rather than military significance. Nonetheless, that push would not take place until late March as a result of the last major German offensive of the war that followed the transfer of assets from the West after the failure of the Ardennes offensive of December 1944.

By this point a significant proportion of German armour committed in Hungary was heavy – including Tiger IIs. Although the IS-2 was now in service in significant numbers – 2,210 would be produced in 1944 compared to only 35 at the tail end of the previous year – on a tank-tank basis it was inferior to the heavy German tanks in part because of the low rate of fire of its main gun.[70] Not that the primary purpose of the IS-2 was tank-tank combat – it was ideally used as a breakthrough tank. Fortunately for the Red Army – and particularly on the defensive – the preponderance of large-calibre anti-tank guns had by late 1944 and early 1945 increased significantly, be they self-propelled as in the case of the

ISU-122 or SU-100, or towed as in the case of the 100 mm BS-3. The anti-tank capabilities of the 2nd and 3rd Ukrainian Front were significantly strengthened during the winter of 1944–1945 for example with the allocation of a number of self-propelled artillery units. On 12 February 1945 3rd Ukrainian Front was for example allocated 208th Self-Propelled Artillery Brigade equipped with SU-100s, and the 2nd Ukrainian Front with 207th and 209th Self-Propelled Artillery Brigades also equipped as such, and subsequently transferred to the former.[71] By this point German determination to fight for the region and to throw in significant resources was obvious, and there seems little indication that the German Lake Balaton offensive of early March 1945 came as a surprise to Soviet commanders. Soviet forces were preparing to strike towards Vienna before the offensive hit, and with the Kursk example undoubtedly fresh in many minds and most probably at the Stavka receiving the German blow before launching the offensive made sense. That men and materiel were deliberately withheld from the blunting of the German offensive like artillery officer N.N. Velikolepov's 19th Breakthrough Artillery Division may have preserved units for subsequent offensive action, although probably increased the depth of the German penetrations and cost of the defence for those Soviet forces involved.[72] However, this was Stalin's army – saving lives *per se* was certainly a secondary concern. Certainly 3rd Ukrainian Front was not permitted to throw 9th Guards Army from reserve into the defence of the sector between Lake Balaton and Lake Velence as its commander Fedor Tolbukhin had requested. German spearheads did break through to Dunapentele – now Dunaújváros – on the Danube, but with armoured spearheads supported according to the head of rear area services for 3rd Ukrainian Front A.I. Shebunin only by tank riding infantry with the bulk of available infantry separated off from them, their capturing and holding a bridgehead over the Danube was unlikely. Despite the withholding of assets for forthcoming offensive operations 3rd Ukrainian Front had considerable anti-tank assets to throw in against the German armour – more than 250 self-propelled guns according to Shebunin in the fighting near Dunapentele. So rapid had been the German advance that Soviet forces had not had time to evacuate rear-area services, including hospitals, from the path of the German advance that ultimately was so narrow and focused on the seizure of a bridgehead over the Danube that after the penetration had been eliminated most rear area services had not been touched.[73] Supply deep into Hungary – and in particular where there was ice and enemy damage to bridges – focused very much on fuel and munitions with Red Army units on the right bank of the Danube being fed 'from local resources'.[74] Soviet forces could also apparently benefit from petrol and other petrochemical products from regional production. This left the supply chain going back to the Soviet Union to focus on munitions, which for the offensive towards Vienna that began on 16 March were not excessive thanks to a combination of continued need for reconstruction of the rail network in the southern regions of the Soviet Union and the relatively low capacities of the rail networks of Rumania and Hungary even when functioning. According to Shebunin the principal strike forces of 3rd Ukrainian Front for the attack towards Vienna – 4th, 6th, and 9th Guards Armies – had only one and a half *boekomplekti* of munitions at one assumes the start of the offensive, with forces on the flanks 'for some time' being provided with only a single *boekomplekt* for forward units.[75]

Although the Lake Balaton offensive by German forces did not come as a surprise, the Soviet intelligence picture in late 1944 and early 1945 was in many ways less clear than it had been but months before. On Soviet territory Soviet intelligence had been able to make good use at times of an often favourably disposed populace – and an increasingly well organised partisan and underground movement – in order to gain intelligence on German troops movements and concentrations that could be relayed in a timely manner to Soviet forces thanks to the growing number of radios available. On Polish territory German policies had hardly disposed the population by and large towards Germany, and in Slovakia and later on Czech territory such human intelligence sources also had some potential. However, in the Baltic Republics and Hungary – and certainly on Germany territory – the scope for obtaining such intelligence increasingly dried up and the Red Army was forced to rely on its own frontline reconnaissance assets far more than had previously been the case. Soviet intelligence on German forces at operational depth was now less rich than it had been. The Soviet neglect of reconnaissance aviation, as noted by Zhukov, that otherwise might have at least partially compensated for the removal of human intelligence sources, has already been noted. Tactical aerial reconnaissance was largely conducted by fighter aircraft and apparently typically relied on pilot observation rather than footage or photographs. Operational reconnaissance conducted by larger aircraft such as the Pe-2 seems to have involved few specialized aircraft – two Pe-3R with built-in cameras and extra fuel capacity delivered to 39th Independent Aerial Reconnaissance Regiment seem to have been the exception rather than the norm for equipment, with Pe-2s with cameras installed in the bomb bays being the norm. Operational reconnaissance was often conducted from around 3,000 metres with equipment that made high quality results difficult to achieve. Best results could apparently be achieved by starting to take pictures with the aerial cameras at

---

the point at which the aircraft was coming out of a shallow dive at 4–500 km/h in order to avoid distortion![76]

When faced with fortified enemy positions, as on the Oder line, considerable reliance had however to be placed on the conduct of 'reconnaissance by battle' that had cost the Red Army so many lives earlier in the war. On 11 April – for the offensive planned for 16 April – Zhukov issued orders to 1st Belorussian Front for the conduct of 'fighting reconnaissance' at 06:00 on 13 April with a view to the testing the strength of defences and to encourage the enemy to reveal artillery assets. Armies were to allocate two infantry battalions, to be supported by 5 tanks and 4–6 self-propelled guns along with two artillery regiments along with mortars and rocket mortars that were to deliver a ten minute barrage before the 'reconnaissance' forces attacked identified weaker points in the enemy line under the watchful gaze of commanders seeking to gain valuable information from the attacks. Around 30–40 sorties by ground attack aircraft were to be provided by 16th Air Army to each attack where at the same time reconnaissance aircraft were to be conducting continuous reconnaissance of the battlefield and enemy positions.[77] How much was actually gained from this is apparent is unclear, although with the attacks only probing forward defences that were often abandoned by German forces in the face of the offensive proper what in theory might have been useful in practice probably proved less so.

Gaining an accurate appreciation of German strength in urban areas was perhaps more difficult than elsewhere, and the Red Army was all too frequently forced into fighting for such areas. Here the Red Army's characteristic means of gaining primarily tactical but at times also operational intelligence – the seizing of prisoners in raids – was an important source. Anecdotally the seizing of 'tongues' was of even greater absolute and relative value now than it had been where German troops drawn from an ever widening pool were more willing to talk with Germany now clearly approaching defeat. In his memoirs former reconnaissance officer M.A. Voloshkin of 39th Army describes the capture and interrogation of a far from unwilling 'worker' who had in early 1945 recently been mobilised into 1141st Infantry Regiment defending Königsberg as part of a general mobilisation of men aged 16–60 in the city. The prisoner's description of the state of the city was apparently of some value, although not as significant as the testimony gained after seizure of a colonel from an artillery regiment who was able to provide valuable information on the fortification of the city.[78]

Despite the large numbers of German armoured vehicles still available in the spring of 1945, 'Spring Awakening' had exhausted the German capacity to launch a major counteroffensive as much due to dwindling

Soviet troops on the streets of Vienna at the end of the war. Such US-supplied armoured transports were heavily used by Soviet reconnaissance forces that now served more effectively than they had early in the war in the scouting role, even if they were still far more likely to get bogged down in combat than many of their foreign counterparts. (RIA Novosti #64991)

fuel reserves as anything else – a situation that had been brought about jointly by the Allies in East and West thanks to the Soviet capture of the Rumanian and Hungarian oilfields and Allied bombing of synthetic manufacturing capacity and fuel stocks. Prudence dictated a certain caution about the possibility of German counterstrikes on the main axes of the Allied advances from east and west, but the fact that the initiative not only at the strategic but also operational levels was now firmly in Allied hands could not be hidden. It would soon be time for the Red Army – that had fought so hard, and for so long to liberate Soviet territory – to deliver the coup de grace to the Nazi regime and seize Berlin. With Stalin at the helm however, much effort – and many lives – would be expended manoeuvring the Soviet Union into the best possible position for post-war domination of Eastern Europe. How much of this fighting was actually necessary for the Soviet Union to secure the postwar influence it did in the region is debateable, but Stalin was apparently unwilling to take any chances.

23 The Fall of Berlin and the End of the Reich

The Vistula-Oder and the initial phase of the Berlin Operation had played to strengths that the Soviet Union had been able to wield for many months, and that included the mass employment of armour and increasingly effective direction of massed artillery used during the initial breakthrough phase of an offensive. Soviet forces were now literally at the gates of Berlin, even if on the ground and particularly on the flanks of the Berlin axis the end must have seemed that little bit less tangible to the troops than it looked on a map back in Moscow.

German General Weidling, who after having commanded LVI Panzer Corps of 9th Army during the Soviet advance on Berlin became its garrison commander, had only recently experienced the full weight of the push by the Red Army from the Oder when he was interrogated by Soviet forces at some point in May 1945. In his interrogation he noted that this, as other Soviet operations, had been characterized by 'the concentration and insertion of major forces – in the first instance tank and artillery used *en masse* – on those sectors of the front where successes had been identified, and rapid and energetic action for the development of these breakthroughs in the German front'.[1] The success of such operations partly depended on planning and preparation, but with as Zhukov notes the 'military-political situation' dictating the tempo for preparations for and the execution of the Berlin Operation, the Berlin Operation would begin without the support of 2nd Belorussian Front on the northern flank rather than it being delayed perhaps 'five-six' days to give 2nd Belorussian Front time to finish dealing with German forces in the Danzig and Gdansk regions and redeploy.[2] The advance by 1st Belorussian Front that began on 16 April initially stalled and in fact even after the breakthrough continued to exhibit the speed rather than haste that had characterised too many preceding Soviet operations. A.V. Gorbatov commanding 3rd Army had apparently at the time noted his concern over Zhukov's plan for forces of 1st Belorussian Front to breakthrough German defences on the Oder before Berlin over the Seelow Heights in an offensive launched at night, where searchlights

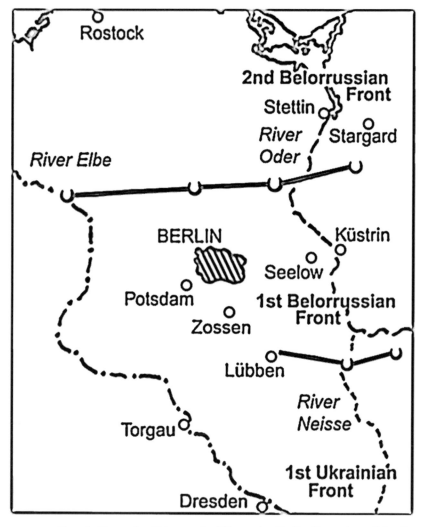

Map 6: From the Oder to the Elbe – the Berlin Operation of April–May 1945.

were supposed to dazzle the defence. With the scope for the four rifle and two tank armies attacking along a narrow 24 km front to become intermingled at night Gorbatov had apparently suggested that it might simply be better to wait for daylight. Zhukov was however apparently satisfied that the concentration of '270 artillery and mortars barrels per kilometre and more than 30 tanks for direct support per kilometre should provide for success'. Berlin was supposed to fall by on D+5, or five days after the start of the operation, and Soviet forces were supposed to reach the Elbe River by 26 April.[3] Certainly the Soviet artillery bombardment preceding the initial Soviet assault had been phenomenal in its ferocity, but where German forces had pulled back from forward positions at least some of the weight of the initial bombardment did not hit German forces. The bombardment was apparently cut short – saving valuable munitions that could not easily be replaced given the fact that the Berlin Operation had been launched with some haste due to the perceived need to race the British and Americans for the city, meaning that the rail network was as yet unable to deliver supplies as far westwards as would have been desirable given the need to breakthrough a now fortified German line. The fuel situation may have been acceptable, but 2–2.5 *boekomplekti* or reloads of munitions for the front as a whole at the start of the operation was far lower than the 3.5–4 that experience had apparently suggested would be desirable in such circumstances.[4] The ammunition spared from the initial bombardment was soon raining down on manned German positions – where by the following day staff officer Siegfried Knappe of the German LVI Panzer Corps notes that 'incessant artillery and aircraft bombardment was now beginning to devastate our positions'.[5]

The 1st Belorussian Front was bogged down in heavy fighting for the Seelow Heights for three days from the morning of 16 April. The Seelow Heights were essentially at first simply assaulted frontally – only belatedly was serious attempt made to outflank them. In a political report for 69th Army of 18 April on successes and failures of the first day of the Berlin offensive using the testimony of wounded Soviet personnel interviewed in hospital, the ferocity of the bombardment was noted even if it was concluded that as a result of German forces pulling back into the depths of the defences and the failure of the artillery bombardment to effectively strike those depths that 'the core of the enemy's fire system was not disrupted as a result of our artillery'. The confusion that Gorbatov claims he feared as a result of attacking at night came to pass on some sectors of the front at least. The searchlights that were supposed to blind the enemy and light the way for Soviet forces were reported by wounded personnel in the aforementioned report by 69th Army to have had varying effects. Some tank and self-propelled gun crews apparently benefitted from them in being less blind in the dark than they otherwise would have been. Alternative testimonies suggested that with smoke and dust from the artillery bombardment and early morning mist the searchlights actually hindered visibility and even provided direction for enemy fire to principal axes of the Soviet advance. In the dark it was apparently all too easy for troops to stray from narrow paths through minefields – and the fact that the tank accompanying one sergeant Safronov of 916th Rifle Regiment of 247th Rifle Division and his men crushed four of them in the dark was probably not an isolated incident. Loss of order in the advance apparently led to heavy losses amongst troops in the second echelon in the Lebus region.[6] For Zhukov forces of 69th Army, along with 1st and 2nd Tank Armies, despite 'colossal strength and resources', had 'conducted themselves inefficiently and indecisively, marking time in the face of a weak enemy'.[7] Whether this lack of decisiveness was motivated in part by the concern of subordinates to save lives is debateable, although General Katukov commanding 1st Tank Army, and criticised by Zhukov in the above, claims in his memoirs prior to the attack to have been concerned with 'how to avoid unnecessary losses and spilling of blood' in the attack, a matter which he claims 'occupied all of my thoughts'.[8] Katukov's 1st Tank Army was thrown into the assault before the defences had been breached – contrary to what was considered desirable – perhaps speeding up their breaching but adding to the heavy losses in tanks that the Red Army experienced during the operation and during 1945 as a whole. The insertion of the tanks may have saved infantrymen's lives, but a better solution might have been a more systematic or imaginative plan without the pressure from above for rapid results that was not primarily underpinned by military justifications. With 2nd Belorussian Front only joining the Berlin offensive on D+4, the frontal assault by 1st Belorussian Front that had stalled and lacked support on its northern flank was unfortunately also characteristic for the Red Army during the war as a whole. At the time Zhukov was not going to take responsibility for any failings in the plan, and his initial response was to resort to the usual calls for greater efforts as the means to overcome them. Further to the south 1st Ukrainian Front under the equally competitive Konev fared better against initially weaker defences thanks in part to terrain, and broke through them on the second day, although had much further to go to reach Berlin and soon faced stiffening resistance around Zossen.[9]

At the planning stage for the Berlin Operation, 1st Ukrainian Front was not necessarily to be committed to the battle for Berlin, even if the option that it might in the light of slower than planned progress of 1st Belorussian Front remained open. Konev had apparently been aware of the scope for 1st Ukrainian Front to make relatively good progress compared to 1st Belorussian Front on its sector where crossing the Neisse further away from Berlin meant weaker defences but with good prospects for maneuver and progress once they had been breached. The 1st Ukrainian Front's principal role at the planning stage was encircle the city on its western side and press on to the Elbe, but when given the chance by Stalin, Konev was understandably keen to redirect 3rd and 4th

Guards Tank Armies towards Berlin, as was done during the night of 17–18 April.[10] For Stalin, the option that 1st Ukrainian Front might also move on the city itself, despite problems relating to two fronts fighting in the city simultaneously noted below, nonetheless made a certain sense. Firstly it would undoubtedly foster the capture of the city as early as possible by whatever means – be it 1st Ukrainian Front receiving the honour or by fostering a race for the city between Zhukov and Konev's forces that would speed up the former. Certainly the purpose of the competition between the marshals that was fostered by Stalin in mid-April 1945 and no doubt baited 'can do' and ambitious leaders such as Zhukov and Eremenko was not military effectiveness as many of Zhukov's frontline subordinates might have defined it – getting the job done whilst minimising losses. Stalin encouraged a competition between commanders in part not just in order to get the job done, but to get it done by Stalin's timetable, where political factors were now increasingly as prominent as military and justified heavy losses that would have been intolerable for the democracies fighting to the west. Stalin's order of 17:50 on 17 April 1945 for the capture of Berlin as soon as possible was explicitly motivated by fear that as the Third Reich was in its death throes it might be able to provoke discord between the Allies by fiercely resisting the Red Army to the east whilst tolerating the rapid advance of Allied forces from the west. In order to deal with this risk, the Red Army would have to capture Berlin and finish off the Reich as quickly as possible.[11]

As well as spurring his generals to push forward with greater resolve, the battle of the egos fostered by Stalin ultimately prevented any one of them from growing too prominent and challenging the position of the *vozhd'*. Here perhaps the only real threat to a paranoid dictator might be seen to have been Zhukov, who was denied the opportunity for his front to take the city alone but undoubtedly drove 1st Belorussian Front as best he could to get there first. Zhukov's orders of 17 April as forces of 1st Belorussian Front struggled to break through the Seelow Heights echoed Stalin's call to deal with German resistance 'without mercy' [*bez posh-chadi*] in order to seize Berlin as soon as possible – 'mercilessly' in Zhukov's case [*besposhchadno*].[12] Arguably this order contained a sense of urgency that was as much for reasons of personal glory as avoiding Stalin's ire. Similarly, just as Zhukov of 1st Belorussian Front and Konev of 1st Ukrainian Front were competing for glory at front level, the same sort of scenario was undoubtedly being played out at lower levels where being first on an objective made some sort of decoration highly likely and brought fame and prestige to commander and unit. Co-ordination for the purpose of saving lives between units and formations that might take time to organise had to be consciously promoted from above if the need for such co-operation was not to be brushed aside in a heady mix of ambition and things being left *na avos'* – giving chance and 'fate' a greater role in the outcome than need have been the case. If Soviet forces at a given level could break through without such co-operation then they were all too often pushed to do so at the first available opportunity and took heavy losses in the process. Although disrupting the German rear, the 'raids' that were all too often launched by Soviet forward detachments often also seemed to have glory and prestige behind them as much as military utility. It is in the context of this driving forward of forces that Zhukov's reasons for not attempting to take Berlin in February 1945 considered below will be discussed.

All too frequently even late in the war Stalin and the Stavka sent Soviet forces into the attack where operations lacked clear military justification. The assaults on major urban areas such as Budapest, Königsberg and Berlin – fortunately not experienced by the Allies in the West – were characteristic of the war in late 1944 and 1945 and certainly undesirable for a Red Army that was starting to seriously struggle with shortages in manpower that had been so profligately squandered earlier in the war. Nobody will have had the temerity – or indeed stupidity – to point out to Stalin how hollow the words in his speech of 3 July 1941 now must have seemed. Then Stalin had spoken of the Soviet Union's 'numberless' forces, where manpower was now a resource more scarce than the tanks that at that point were the commodity in short supply.[13] The ability to employ massed armour in open terrain was perhaps the option that best suited Soviet material superiority and the manpower situation in 1945. Rifle forces would have to be used alongside armour – and suffer heavy casualties – for breaking through German frontline defences in depth as they had done along the Vistula and Oder Rivers, but their sacrifice would at least enable mechanised forces to push on through and out of the breach. Although in urban areas personnel losses were inevitably particularly high and Berlin would be fought for block by block, psychologically Red Army troops could justify that cost where they were fighting for the political nexus of the Reich. The capture of Budapest made some and indeed similar sense – and for senior commanders opened up operational possibilities in the region that would at least distract Germany from events further north, and might even offer an alternative route to the heart of the Reich. Operations in and around Königsberg were not however as clearly justifiable from a military perspective. Simply looking at a map is it apparent that in the light of an advance by 2nd Belorussian Front protecting the flank of 1st Belorussian and 1st Ukrainian Fronts on the key central axis, 3rd Belorussian Front could arguably simply have contained German forces in East Prussia and the Baltic Region rather than seek to destroy them in early 1945. Vasilevskii's attempt to justify the destruction of the Königsberg enemy group of forces of 16 March 1945 is far from convincing. Having noted that more than a third of the enemy force on the Zemland Peninsula consisting of eight infantry and a single Panzer division was defending Königsberg, he suggested that the capture of Königsberg would hopefully lead to 'further enemy resistance on the Zemland Peninsula losing any justification, or at least meaning' – a resistance that had lost all but symbolic meaning by the spring of 1945.[14] A threat on the flanks of the advance in the centre could not unreasonably be postulated from Pomerania, for which 2nd Belorussian Front and indeed much of 1st Belorussian Front fought in February-March 1945, and the German attack from Stargard in mid-February indeed added at least some substance to the idea of a German attack on the flank on the Berlin axis that seemed plausible on a map. The Stargard attack ultimately made little progress involving far weaker forces than intended – the norm for German forces by this stage – but is often credited with delaying the Soviet advance on Berlin.[15] Zhukov certainly highlights the threat in his memoirs – retrospectively promoting a caution to justify dealing with any possible threat to the flanks that he rarely showed. Chuikov's assertion in his 1965 version of his memoir of the end of the war, *The End of the Third Reich*, that Berlin might have been taken in February 1945 warrants some consideration, for as even Zhukov admits German defences before this point were 'rather weak', and in late January the Stavka did indeed make plans to take Berlin the following month. Certainly as Ziemke notes, on the back of the embarrassing failure of the Stargard attack the German command fully expected the resumption of the Soviet advance on Berlin. According to Zhukov, who was apparently having a bout of caution, what prevented these plans from being carried out was the German threat to the flanks from East Pomerania in the context of weakened Soviet forces after the Vistula-Oder Operation and extended supply lines – where it was known that Germany was transferring forces from the West.[16] Zhukov's argument is certainly plausible – and came subsequently to dominate the Soviet literature. Chuikov was forced to back down in the argument with Zhukov, such that his criticism of the failure to try to take Berlin in February does not appear in the 1973 version of his memoirs and part of Zhukov's justification for the course of action taken is reproduced – verbatim – in this later edition of Chuikov's work. By the time of this later edition of Chuikov's memoirs the relatively open historical discourse of the Khrushchev era had certainly passed.[17] The supply situation does not seem to have prevented Soviet operations on the flanks in February and

March 1945 – and it certainly seems unlikely that Zhukov had strong intelligence of German capacity and plans to launch a major counter-stroke from the Stargard region by 10 February when Soviet forces were supposed to have been ready to strike at Berlin. Indeed as Earl Ziemke notes, by 10 February of trains loaded to move troops to the area for the German offensive 'less than half had arrived'.[18] Debate surrounding whether the Red Army might have struck at Berlin in February or even early March 1945 is in some ways similar to the debate as to whether the Wehrmacht might have struck for Moscow in August 1941 – except in the former case the Nazi regime and the German armed forces had fewer options if Berlin should fall than their Soviet opponents would have had in the late summer of 1941 had Moscow been taken.

Although operations on the flanks and a delay in the advance on Berlin can at least be justified in military terms, there was certainly no threat from the Königsberg region that could not even for the pessimist be contained. Preventing the transfer of German forces from the region to the key central axis could have been better undertaken solely by the VVS and Baltic Fleet that by now was at least more active and was interdicting German communications with forces in East Prussia and the Baltic after their land communications with the German heartland had been severed. Here one can reasonably speculate that once again Stalin had an eye on the post-war political landscape, in which Soviet destruction of forces defending the seat of German militarism in East Prussia would carry political weight. Certainly with Berlin not having fallen in February, or with its fall not yet imminent, this ultimately strengthened Stalin's position at the negotiating table with the Allies. It also allowed the Red Army to further strengthen Soviet post-war claims to influence and indeed territory, for example not only in East Prussia but also through operations by 2nd, 3rd and 4th Ukrainian Fronts in Austria and Czechoslovakia.[19]

By the time that Königsberg was assaulted in early April, Soviet forces at least had considerable experience of assaulting heavily fortified urban areas on all axes. The German *feste Plätze* such as Küstrin, Poznan and Breslau may not have been able to prevent deep penetration of German lines by Soviet forces, but their locations were intended to prevent the exploitation of key lines of communication and would not only hamper immediate exploitation, but certainly also the sort of supply efforts required to break through the next major fortified river line. German resistance at Poznan until its fall in late February is used by Zhukov as further reason not to strike at Berlin in February 1945.[20] At least some fortress cities such as Poznan would ultimately have to be taken even if they had been encircled and their garrisons could otherwise have been contained without the commitment of exorbitant resources. Soviet

Königsberg in early April 1945 after its capture by Soviet forces. By this stage of the war the city had little military significance. Note the US-supplied truck in the background, hundreds of thousands of which did so much to enhance Red Army mobility and resupply capabilities. (RIA Novosti #1706)

assault or storm groups that had been so infantry-heavy at Stalingrad could now place more reliance on equipment than flesh and blood, although the relative intensity of urban warfare and the ferocity of German resistance meant that in the fighting for many German towns and cities storm groups and detachments took horrendous losses in a short space of time. The armoured vehicles that were few in Stalingrad for much of the battle were now used in large numbers but were more vulnerable than they had been in 1942, and particularly so without suitably close co-operation with the infantry given the threat from ranged German infantry anti-tank weapons such as the *Panzerfaust* and *Panzerschreck*.

By the spring of 1945 experience accrued by most fronts seemed to point to a similar approach to street fighting. Assault or storm groups of platoon to company strength – and their larger up to reinforced battalion-sized assault detachment counterparts – were to be provided with what amounted to a platoon or company respectively of tanks or self-propelled guns for fire-support, with each tank or self-propelled gun requiring the protection of 4–5 soldiers armed with SMGs from German infantry that might otherwise stalk them. Sappers with explosives were typically attached to storm groups, with as in the case of Aleksandr Naumovich Budnitskii's sapper company at Königsberg their personnel being parcelled out in as small units as sections to storm groups.[21] Such groups or detachments would, as in Stalingrad, also be provided with artillery support – with one of three broad types of storm group noted as being employed by 1st Belorussian Front in Berlin being equipped with a range of artillery pieces from two 45 mm anti-tank guns, a single 76 mm regimental gun, a single divisional 76 mm gun and one or two 122 mm howitzers in addition to either a couple of light SU-76 self-propelled guns or a single IS-2 tank. Varied forms of storm groups employed by the front in Berlin included differing proportions of towed artillery, self-propelled guns, tanks and infantry weapons including flamethrowers.[22] It is also worth noting the use of M-31 rockets – fired not from launch vehicles but used individually and fired from launch frames, at times from windows both upwards and down below.[23] In street fighting the larger artillery pieces such as the 203 mm howitzers in which the Red Army had invested prior to the war came into their own when used appropriately. Such weapons were widely used for the destruction of particularly large or well fortified buildings, although the use of super heavy artillery in a direct fire role was not always effective where the large shells sometimes only exploded after having passed through a target building and where their use demanded wide streets.[24] Such 'super heavy' weapons, into which the Soviet Union had invested considerable resources, had not been widely employed earlier in the war through fear of them being captured when the Wehrmacht was on the advance, but they could subsequently be dragged out of storage in the rear. On 29 November 1944 for example 2nd Belorrussian Front was provided with 317th Independent Super Heavy [*osoboi moshchnosti*] Artillery *Divizion* equipped with 280 mm howitzers constructed in the late 1930s, being provided along with 74th Anti-Aircraft Artillery Division.[25] During the advance on Berlin Zhukov insisted that such artillery keep up with the advance.[26] Anti-aircraft guns were noted to be of value in urban fighting where enemy forces were able to fire from upper floor windows down on infantry and armour alike. Mortar fire could not only be used in order to isolate an enemy position but was also valuable in subjecting courtyards and other open spaces to fire that might not only be crossed but also be occupied by artillery and anti-tank assets. When advancing, infantry would inevitably have to take the lead and serve as scouts, with the tanks or self-propelled guns following a suitable distance behind and spaced so as to provide mutual support – from opposite sides of the street to the next where wider streets allowed. Having located enemy forces the available firepower – including flamethrowing tanks where available – might be sufficient to destroy enemy positions or force surrender, but all too often infantry assault would be required leading to the horrors of hand-to-hand combat. Ideally equipped with appropriate weaponry from grenades through to flamethrowers, darkness and sometimes smoke would, where possible, provide cover for approach and assault and in particular in the case of the latter from enemy forces on the flanks. Instructions for the conduct of street fighting do not portray the particular horrors of fighting in an urban environment, although it is perhaps apparent that with the cover provided to the enemy and fighting in three dimensions that heavy losses were inevitable. Former infantryman Matvei L'vovich Gershman describes how on 20 April 1945 his unit was formed into storm groups for fighting in Berlin. With a strength of approximately fifty men his group was provided with flamethrowers, artillery support from the regimental battery and the support of a platoon of tanks. There followed ten days of street fighting during which they suffered such horrendous losses that although every day the group would be reinforced 'all the same by the evening fewer than half of us remained'. The horror of hand-to-hand combat was clearly something that Gershman did not want to talk about.[27] In order to provide the storm groups with the necessary armoured support whole tank corps were subordinated to rifle formations for the battle for the city, where for 1st Belorussian Front example on 23 April 1945 11th Tank Corps was subordinate to 5th Guards Army, and 9th Tanks Corps to 3rd Shock Army on Zhukov's orders.[28]

A smokescreen was one of those luxuries that the Red Army had rarely enjoyed during the first years of the war. Like communications equipment, armoured transport vehicles and dried or canned foods, smoke candles were delivered to the Soviet Union in large numbers by the United States and were used with some effect during river crossings for example and during the opening phases of offensive operations to breach German defensive positions. At Kielce or Kel'tse in Poland in January 1945 during the Vistula-Oder Operation former sapper Natan Markovich Levin recalls the use of smoke candles to provide thick smoke over a small square in the town so that sappers could blow up the wall of a fortified building defended by German troops.[29] Smoke certainly played an important role in the initial advance of 1st Ukrainian Front on 16 April, where Soviet artillery was firing on targets being hit by map co-ordinate.[30] Slightly later, former tank technician Anton Dmitrievich Bukin describes how during the fighting for Berlin after sappers had removed mines from a bridge on Potsdamerstraße smoke candles were set on a tank that was then driven across the bridge billowing smoke that provided some cover for infantry behind it.[31] The provision of a couple of 'chemists' or chemical warfare troops for the provision of smoke cover as one of their functions was presented by the 1st Belorussian Front as typical during the fighting for Berlin. Towards the end of the battle, when some of the fighting was taking place underground, small storm groups of up to only fifteen men that included chemical troops were apparently being used as forward elements by units such as 286th Guards Rifle Regiment of 94th Guards Rifle Division. From 27 April through to 2 May the regiment was employing storm groups consisting of 3–5 SMG gunners, 1–2 snipers, a light machine gun, 2–3 sappers and 1–2 chemical warfare troops.[32] Certainly after the fighting for Berlin 1st Ukrainian Front would record that 'the use of smoke in street fighting fully justified itself and it is particularly important to use smoke at street intersections' in order to cover the movement of troops.[33]

Measures to provide genuinely combined arms units at the lowest tactical level and tolerance of decentralised tactical initiative undoubtedly saved lives and led to meaningful local results. The capture of the damaged Brommybrücke over the River Spree situated off the Mühlenstraße in Berlin during the night of 23–24 April 1945 – a bridge that although soon damaged was still crossable for infantry – was certainly seen retrospectively by 1st Belorussian Front as highlighting the value of lower level initiative by small multi-arms groups. The head of the department for the use of war experience of the Operational Board of the headquarters for the front noted that in the capture of the remains of the bridge:

The initiative of small groups of SMG gunners and snipers (3–5 men), which thanks to their limited size could make it across the bridge to the opposite bank unnoticed and destroy the crews of enemy fire points with small arms fire at the same time as the river was forced by rifle units, had significant importance.[34]

In this instance during the late afternoon on 23 April units of 60th Guards Rifle Division were advancing along the northern bank of the River Spree in Berlin west of the Rummelsburg district, with 185th Rifle Regiment advancing to the bridge on the left wing. The intact bridge was under fire from the opposite bank of the river, which it would later transpire was being defended by police and *Volksturm* militia with a strength for the defending force of 'up to' eighty 'police' and seventy *Volksturm* according to Soviet sources. An initial attempt to seize the bridge by the 4th Company of 2nd Rifle Battalion supported by fire from 82 mm mortars was unsuccessful with the company taking losses and the bridge being damaged in the process – perhaps as the result of the detonation of a demolition charge by the mortar fire. Later in the evening with the support of 45 mm anti-tank guns a group of riflemen was able to make it to the bridge – a group of SMG gunners having earlier done the same although their fate is unclear. The riflemen and observation from the battalion command point on the roof of one of the buildings on the northern side – combined with information accrued during the fighting to date – allowed it to be established that the southern exit to the bridge had been barricaded with a 4–5 metre passage left in the centre of the barricade, and that there was an enemy tank in the courtyard of barracks on the German side of the river. In order to prevent the total destruction of the bridge by the enemy, the commander of 2nd Battalion and the regimental commander opted to try to seize the bridge the next morning in a surprise attack that would mean gaining a foothold on the other side with a view to the forcing of the river by the remainder of the regiment. From 4th Company of 2nd Battalion two groups were formed for the assault. The first consisting of eight SMG gunners and four snipers was to cross the bridge under the cover of mortar and anti-tank gun fire and establish itself in a building on the other side from which enemy heavy machine gun positions in a neighbouring building could be supressed, allowing a second group consisting of a full company of infantry, heavy machine guns and anti-tank rifles to make it across and seize that building. At 04:30 regimental artillery and 120 mm mortars, along with two artillery *divizions* attached to the regiment bombarded 'Object 158' – the building with heavy machine guns positions covering the bridge – as the first group of infantry moved forward along with 45 mm guns for direct fire support. Five SMG gunners and two snipers apparently made it across the bridge – cutting demolition cables in the process and managed

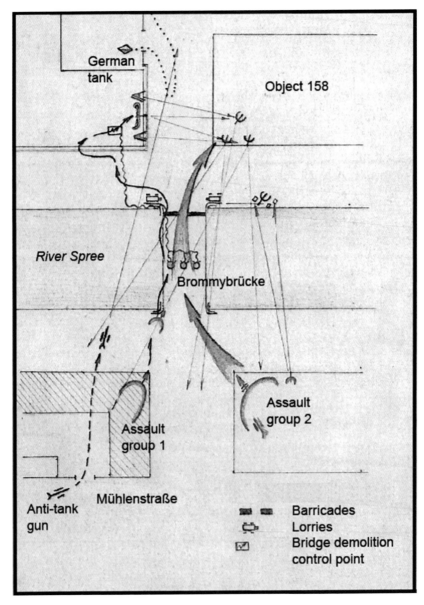

Map 7: Street fighting in Berlin – the capture of the damaged Brommybrücke in April 1945
(adapted from TsAMO f.233.o.2356.d.775.l.50).

to capture the barracks building. With the snipers on the roof of the barracks, at 06:30 4th Company made an abortive attempt to cross the bridge where although the snipers were able to reduce the fire from 'Object 158', a further German machine-gun position further along the river and out of sight on the snipers had to first be neutralised. Only then was 4th Company able to make it across the bridge and seize 'Object 158' after the German tank previously identified in the area had apparently been beaten off by the 45 mm anti-tank guns.[35]

Troops of 32nd Rifle Corps of 5th Shock Army – of which 60th Guards Rifle Division was a part – managed to gain a foothold on the southern bank of the Spree, but were unable to push deeper into the rear of enemy forces that faced 9th Rifle Corps to the east. The 9th Rifle Corps had crossed the Spree to the south-east and was pushing west-wards – able to make relatively rapid progress through the more open terrain of Treptower Park. The nature of the Soviet assault on Berlin – where a principal thrust was not apparent – certainly meant that the bogging down of forces on one sector did not necessarily stall the advance as pressure was being applied not only elsewhere by forces of 1st Belorussian Front, but also soon by forces of 1st Ukrainian Front. If the memoirs of commander of 9th Rifle Corps, 301st Rifle Division and the war diary for 1st Belorussian Front are any indicator, the crossing of the Spree by 9th Rifle Corps had initially exhibited the sort of reckless approach that at times paid off but had all too often led to disaster for Soviet forces. An initial crossing had been made into Treptower Park more or less off the march. In this instance speed at the expense of preparation had fortunately paid off where German forces defending the river bank had apparently fled back into the park. 'Reconnaissance' for this initial crossing had been conducted in typical Soviet fashion, where as a reconnaissance company was crossing the river follow on forces were already moving up. Given that the reconnaissance company – in small boats brought up from the rear by whatever means possible – had not been wiped out, the rest of the division could clearly follow. The subsequent crossing in force was a more measured and planned affair, and was executed with the help of small skimmers – boats – of the 1st River Boat Brigade of the Dnepr Naval Flotilla that had been brought in by lorry from the Oder. That it had apparently taken 15 minutes to raise the 'sailors' by radio highlights once more the relatively fragile communications on which co-ordination often depended. The powered vessels of the 1st River Boat Brigade were, once they had arrived, clearly valuable in allowing the construction of pontoon bridges that allowed heavy equipment to follow behind the infantry, 301st Rifle Division enjoying the support for example of 220th Tank Brigade, 92nd Heavy Tank

Soviet tanks and infantry on a German street at the end of April
1945 prior to the final stages of the battle for Berlin. The up-gunned
T-34 of late 1943 was a valuable addition to the Soviet tank park, being
an effective vehicle for both infantry support and in tank-tank combat.
(RIA Novosti #41236)

Regiment and 337th Independent Self-Propelled Artillery *Divizion*.
German counterattacks, apparently including tanks, could therefore be
beaten off.[36] Inexorably – even if not necessarily systematically – the Red
Army pushed on to the centre of Berlin.

One benefit of capturing new ground was first pickings of goods to loot
and send home – undoubtedly a valuable distraction and morale boost
after the horrors of war and particularly the intensity of urban warfare.
There were other releases, although evidence seems to suggest that as
the fighting continued frontline troops were less likely to engage in rape
than their second line counterparts who certainly often had more time
and opportunity to do so. Mark Edele has certainly argued that the
lower prevalence of rape amongst 'elite units' might be explained by their
having 'a higher level of cohesion and purpose' than existing in 'second-
grade' units. However, at the same time he suggests that high losses
'undermined discipline and group cohesion' and were more likely to
foster rape – particularly by groups rather than individuals. Significant
incidence of rape was certainly not limited to German or even wider

Soviet light craft of the Dnepr Flotilla transport small groups of troops
on the River Spree in Berlin during the fighting for the German capital.
Lower level initiative would play a far more significant role in fighting
for Berlin and other such cities than in fighting in more open terrain.
(RIA Novosti #159)

'enemy' territory – and indeed the rape of female Red Army personnel
has already been discussed – although it does seem that rape was more
prevalent against 'enemy' women be that because it was a form of revenge
or that there was less intolerance towards their rapes by the authorities.[37]
Most armies do not encourage rape and wider uncontrolled violence – it
undermines wider discipline needed on the battlefield – and the Red
Army was in the main no exception. However only belatedly does there
seem to have been a serious clamp down on rape on German territory and
an attempt and enforce the sort of wider discipline that would serve the
Red Army well in relations with the civilian population. Certainly at the
end of the war it was rapidly becoming apparent that the tarring all
Germans with the same negative brush in the vein of the Soviet writer
Ehrenburg was now increasingly counterproductive as the Red Army
became a force of occupation as well as having to destroy the last vestiges
of resistance.[38]

Despite the benefits of decentralisation in securing tactical objectives and improved use of combined arms it is perhaps unsurprising
that Soviet losses in men and materiel remained high – in particular in

urban areas. High losses were thanks not only to the intensity of enemy resistance and the nature of the environment, but also due to approach. The sort of systematic approach to the advance that might have been employed more regularly continued to give way to the sort of pressure for quick results from above that continued to drive forward the Red Army, and all too often drive up losses. Greater initiative at lower levels made it more likely that such an approach would ultimately be successful where opportunities to exploit a situation arose, but continued and undoubtedly costly issues with co-ordination of arms during the street fighting in Berlin pointed to by 1st Ukrainian Front were for example, as had been the case in the past, no doubt in part because sufficient time was not allowed for the establishing of such co-ordination.[39] There was often not time for command and control mechanisms vital for the co-ordination of different arms to keep up with the pace of the advance. As formations pushed forward – and certainly in urban areas – communications suffered a greater number of interruptions. In assessing the actions of 4th Tank Army during the Vistula-Oder Operation in a lecture later that year, its commander Leliushenko noted how the tank and mechanised brigades often used as forward detachments were often 40–50 km ahead of corps and army headquarters, distances that even in open terrain were beyond the capabilities of the RSB radiosets that were supposed to maintain communications. More powerful RAF sets were only available 'in limited numbers'.[40] In an urban environment the maintenance of communications became even more difficult and not only for mechanised units and formations. F.M. Zinchenko's 756th Rifle Regiment of 150th Rifle Division had fought on the outskirts of Berlin without communications with divisional headquarters from the second half of the day on 22 April through to the middle of the next day. At this point the regiment was ordered to change the direction of its attack towards the centre of Berlin.[41] The wider availability of communications resources compared to earlier in the war nonetheless allowed commanders, like commander of 65th Army of 2nd Belorussian Front at the time of the Berlin Operation P.I. Batov, to much more frequently get a better feel 'for the pulse of the fighting in all its subtleties and react to its course in a timely manner' where an army commander was now much more likely to be able to communicate directly as required with the commanders of regiments and battalions than had been the case earlier in the war.[42] Communications were of course not seamless as noted earlier, but at least by this stage of the war there was a strong likelihood that communications could be maintained with inevitable interruptions, as opposed to units enjoying only fleeting communications at best as had been the case all too often in 1941.

At times the extent to which the front command was directing the fighting within the city is unclear – units and formations inevitably had considerable autonomy. As Chuikov, who had it should be recalled commanded 62nd Army at Stalingrad that had become 8th Guards Army by the battle for Berlin notes:

Fighting in an urban area, and especially in such a major one like Berlin, is significantly more complex than fighting out in the field. Here the influence of the headquarters and commanders of major formations on the course of the fighting is significantly less. Therefore an awful lot depends on the initiative of junior unit commanders and each and every one of the rank and file.[43]

This point is reiterated by V.M. Shatilov, at the time commanding 150th Rifle Division, who noted in his memoirs how the commanders of storm or assault detachments that were being formed for the assault on Berlin in the case of his division on or after 22 April 1945 'had the possibility to command powerful firepower and gain considerable independence and freedom of action' – that was of course far from typical elsewhere.[44]

With the end of the war in sight, the extent to which Soviet troops pushed forward during the fighting for Berlin is perhaps surprising – and particularly where it is born in mind that repression was far less likely to be the response to failure or perceived failure than it had been earlier in the war. In his memoirs commander of 150th Rifle Division V.M. Shatilov– whose division would storm the Reichstag – describes approaching a number of tanks on Molktestraße on the Reichstag side of the Molkte Bridge near the Swiss Embassy building. These tanks had not moved up to jumping off positions for the storming of the Reichstag itself. Having summoned their crews from within their tanks by banking on their armours, Shatilov apparently chided the young tankers, who had yet to move forward since they were concerned that they too would be burned alive in their tanks like their comrades whose three tanks had been destroyed ahead of them.[45] Understandable at the best of times, on the approaches to the Reichstag with the war apparently all but won a reticence to hurl oneself forward might be seen as even more reasonable. Whether Shatilov's conversation with the tankers – whom he apparently shamed for being unwilling to advance and support infantry who did not have the benefit of armour – was as delicate as he presents is perhaps in doubt, although certainly by the later stages of the war the use of fear as the principal tool to drive troops forward was less likely to be the first response.

Reward undoubtedly played a greater role in the driving forward of Soviet forces in late 1944 and early 1945 than had been the case earlier, where later in the war the penalty for all but the most gross failure was more likely to be demotion or even a chiding than execution. It is for example difficult to imagine that commander of 7th Guards Army of 2nd Ukrainian Front General-Colonel Shumilov would have got away with a formal reprimand during the summer of 1941 had he then lost 'an operationally important bridgehead' despite being deemed to have had 'sufficient strength and resources to hold it' as he had over the River Hron near Komárno towards the end of the war. Having lost the bridgehead and 8,194 personnel, 459 guns and mortars including 374 of 76 mm calibre and above, and 54 tanks and self-propelled guns in the process, he got away with an official reprimand for 'carelessness and poor organisation of the defence' [*za bespechnost' i plokhuiu organizatsiiu oboroni*].[46] By 1945 the Red Army had a system of rewards that did not just promise status, but also far more significant wider ramifications than equivalent decorations might have had in Western armies and that included financial perks, soon after the war apparently removed by a less than grateful Stalin.[47] The award of Hero of the Soviet Union for example appears to have been of considerable meaning. General Leliushenko commanding 4th Tank Army (subsequently Guards) of 1st Ukrainian Front during the Vistula-Oder Operation suggested that highlighting to frontline troops that outstanding performance during the forcing of the Oder could lead to this award – a line pushed by the Stavka – 'increased the troops' ...decisiveness'.[48]

Competition for accolades and glory could of course as has already been suggested, be both productive and counterproductive. The fact that both 1st Belorussian and 1st Ukrainian Fronts were involved in the fighting for Berlin undoubtedly contributed to overwhelming the defence, even if the competition added to haste and limited the scope for a more systematic approach that might have saved lives. Whilst blows on the Berlin axis from the south-east and north-east with a view to encircling the city made sense, both fronts fighting for the city itself certainly made less sense where problems with command and control in such an environment made 'friendly fire' incidents for example more likely with both fronts engaged. As staff officer G.G. Semenov notes in his memoirs, by the time forces of 1st Belorussian and 1st Ukrainian Fronts were only 2–2.5 kilometres apart 'there was the real prospect of the advancing forces firing on each other'. Consequently 3rd Shock Army's headquarters had to 'take urgent action to deal with such a possibility – the areas on which the artillery of each army could fire were clarified'.[49] In the case of Berlin once encircled there was arguably little need to rush as opposed to make haste – and indeed, one might question the necessity of fighting for the city at all. As German General Weidling – commander of German forces in Berlin noted in his interrogation by Soviet forces shortly after its surrender, the city had only food and munitions for 30 days.[50]

General Aleksandr Gorbatov claims in the second edition of his memoirs published in 1989, that he had thought when being told by Zhukov of plans for the breakout from Küstrin and both encirclement and assault on Berlin that it was better not to storm Berlin but simply to seal it off and push on to the Elbe River.[51] Had he suggested this to Zhukov he would of course have gained short shrift – Berlin was the political prize that for the regime at least was worth additional casualties, and for Zhukov would bring considerable prestige.

Although one issue with both 1st Belorussian and 1st Ukrainian Front fighting for Berlin was the issue of 'friendly fire', fortunately for the Red Army, command and control, including of artillery, was far better than it had been earlier in the war thanks to the availability of communications resources and organisational structures to make better use of them. Although in part a question of organisational change and the centralisation of co-ordination of artillery assets, the fact that after August 1944 the artillery commander for a front could dispose of a *divizion* for artillery direction with 129 personnel that included a 65-person telephone communications battery and 41-person radio communication battery along with service sections that included transport resources was a dramatic improvement over the situation earlier in the war. Transport resources available to the *divizion* included eight light vehicles including two jeeps, eight GAZ-AA trucks, five specialised vehicles and four motorcycle combinations. Former commander of artillery for the 1st Belorussian Front G.S. Nadisev was probably not exaggerating when he described such dedicated resources as 'such riches, of which earlier we could only have dreamt'. Now the front command and artillery commander could communicate directly not only with army-level artillery commanders – as Nadisev recalls with reference to the Modlin axis in October 1944 – but also with the commanders of subordinate units.[52] More effective artillery support saved lives, although the final weeks of the war would still cost the Red Army dearly.

What on paper might look like overwhelming Soviet superiority in the air also provided considerable fire support to Soviet commanders, even if here the scope for 'friendly fire' incidents was high. Certainly as Siegfried Knappe of LVI Panzer Corps notes for the fighting over the Seelow Heights on day two at the beginning of the Berlin Operation, it was not just 'incessant' artillery bombardment that took its toll on the defenders, but also aerial bombardment.[53] The VVS was now adept at throwing considerable assets at pre-identified targets. The VVS could on paper field what might have looked like overwhelming air assets by 1945 – on 1 January 1945 2nd Air Army supporting 1st Ukrainian Front alone could dispose of 2,582 aircraft including 1,172 fighters and 775 ground attack aircraft giving it by its own estimations an overall advantage of 4.3–1 over the enemy. By the Berlin Operation Soviet forces of the 1st and 2nd Belorussian, and 1st Ukrainian Fronts could field between them a staggering 6,696 aircraft excluding 800 bombers of 18th Air Army operating on the sector of 1st Belorussian Front. This strength included 3,275 fighters and 1,709 ground attack aircraft, although only 245 'scouts' [*razvedchikov*] presumably with a dedicated reconnaissance role.[54] In practice there continued to be many inhibitors to the effective use of Soviet air assets. Not only were there continued limitations in command and control thanks in part to centralisation but also the fact that as it advanced it struggled to find and construct sufficient facilities for their deployment. Hence, as noted in a lecture on the activities of 2nd Air Army in support of 1st Ukrainian Front during the L'vov-Sandomierz, Vistula-Oder and Berlin Operations given apparently by its commander S.A. Krasovskii, 2nd Air Army struggled with 'extended rear areas' and 'a limited network of airfields' that led to 'difficulties in moving airpower in full over to new hubs' not only during the first of these operations to which the quotes refer, but also subsequently as well.[55] By April 1945 and the breaching of the Neisse ground attack aircraft could contribute to the smoke screen covering the assault, and ground attack aircraft could 'as planned' attack enemy artillery and command and control infrastructure, but as circumstances became more fluid effectiveness diminished. Although it was noted that during the initial phases of the Berlin Operation 'the enemy air force showed little activity' during a period when weather and smoke were soon hampering Soviet activity, by the time forces of 1st Ukrainian Front had reached the Spree the Luftwaffe 'was active to a relatively significant degree'.[56] Certainly, a highly centralised command and control system allowed for concentration of ground attack assets in support of ground forces, with VVS representatives operating down to army level and at times corps level, but hardly facilitated for example timely response by fighter aircraft to attacks by relatively small groups of enemy aircraft. Nonetheless, by this stage of the war radar and SCh-3 equipment for the identification of friendly aircraft were at least providing the VVS command with additional tools for the direction of resources – as did a much wider availability of communications equipment for both air-to-air and air-to-ground communication.[57] Also significant was the fact that the best of the Soviet fighters available were now better than any of the piston-engined aircraft the Luftwaffe could field, with the Yak-3 and La-7 now being fielded in meaningful numbers.[58] Losses for 2nd Air Army were relatively light during the Berlin Operation – 165 aircraft – even if results did not perhaps seem as proportional to investment compared for example to armoured forces and particularly so after the breakthrough phase.[59]

Berlin fell to Soviet forces on 2 May 1945. A subsequent source of pride for the Soviet empire and many of its troops alike, its capture had nonetheless cost the Red Army dearly. The Berlin Strategic Offensive Operation from 16 April to the end of the war had cost the Red Army nearly 80,000 irrecoverable losses and a further almost 275,000 sick and wounded – a total of more than 350,000. This was on the back of the Vistula-Oder Strategic Offensive Operation from 12 January–3 February 1945 – more than 40,000 irrecoverable losses and nearly 150,000 sick and wounded, not discounting associated with this axis of advance the East Pomeranian Strategic Offensive Operation from 10 February to 4 April with irrecoverable losses of more than 50,000 and approaching 175,000 sick and wounded. In East Prussia, including fighting for Königsberg, from 13 January to 25 April 1945 at least a further 126,464 irrecoverable losses combined with 458,314 sick and wounded starts to make plain just how bloody the final phases of the defeat of Nazi Germany were for the Red Army, as were Stalin's attempts to mop up territory and accrue influence in the region in the post-war world. Even in the very last days of the war – from 6 May until after Germany's official surrender – more than 11,000 Soviet irrecoverable losses were sustained along with nearly 40,000 sick and wounded.[60] Nonetheless, from the regime's perspective the Red Army had not only dealt the final blow to the Reich in a war that would provide a new legitimacy to Soviet power and indeed Stalin's rule, but was now in *de facto* control of most of Eastern Europe. Where the Soviet Union had failed to export revolution westwards in 1920, it had now all but succeeded in doing so now.

Conclusion

Victory in the Great Patriotic War came at a horrendous cost for the Soviet people. Along with the more than nine million soldiers who were either killed or died in enemy captivity up to an additional eighteen million Soviet citizens lost their lives according to the most widely cited figures today. Regardless of the exact number killed, on top of those killed there were the many millions who suffered physical wounds of varying degrees of severity, with mental scars often hidden behind those of the flesh.[1] The Soviet armed forces, supported by Soviet society, had nonetheless proven their basic military effectiveness in taking the lead in destroying German ground forces, even if at a mind boggling human cost that the Soviet government did its best to hide from the Soviet people until the period of *glasnost'*. To some extent the horrendous cost of Soviet victory was a result of National Socialist ideology that meant that the war on the Eastern Front was fought with a brutality that took the horrors of war to even greater heights than was the norm in the West – or perhaps that should be lows. However, although the impacts of abhorrent German policies and the duration over which the Red Army was engaged with the bulk of German ground forces go some way to explain the difference between the human cost of the war for the Western allies and the Red Army, such arguments hide the extent to which Stalin and the Soviet system under Stalin exacerbated the price of what under any circumstances would have been a costly struggle. Whilst the Stalinist system could claim to have built up the Red Army and effectively mobilised the vast human and material resources of the Soviet Union for victory, it also showed an inhumanity and at times incompetence in the squandering of those resources even late in the war that owed much to both the personalities of Stalin and those he promoted, as well as their commitment to the ideology that they espoused.

The worst of Soviet losses came during the early part of the war – the sort of losses that would have been unsustainable if the war was to continue for years. During the summer and autumn of 1941 the Red Army was certainly not in many senses an effective fighting force – not only was it unable to halt the enemy but was not doing so in an unsustainable way. Unsustainable here refers not only to the unsustainable losses in manpower that had they continued would have bled the Soviet Union white within a matter of months, but also unsustainable material losses that would leave the Red Army with only 782 tanks on the Moscow axis at the beginning of October 1941 – predominately light tanks.[2] Failures at the strategic and operational levels – and poor performance at the upper end of the tactical – masked the fact that at the lower tactical levels small units often fought stubbornly with some effect and exacted a high local price for wider German victories. Had they been able to do so in more favourable operational and strategic circumstances, they might have achieved more earlier on, and bled the Wehrmacht white before the winter – sparing the Soviet Union the loss of quite as much territory as was in fact lost by the beginning of December. By the summer of 1942 and Order Number 227, or 'Not a step back!', the Soviet Union could not, as Stalin stated, afford to lose much more territory for any length of time where that territory was as valuable in terms of agricultural resources and raw materials as the eastern Ukraine and southern Russia – and then there was the Caucasus and oil. Fortunately, Axis forces did not reach the principal oilfields, for capturing and holding them for any length of time would have put the Soviet Union in a difficult position even with whatever her allies might have delivered via the north. By the time the German advance was stalling in the late summer of 1942 the Red Army was already making good some of the inadequacies that plagued the conduct of operations in unfavourable circumstances during the summer of 1941. At the same time operational circumstances now favoured the Red Army where the German armed forces and those of her allies were so hopelessly overextended by the late summer of 1942. As the Red Army matured in the light of wartime experience, and even though it was later on the offensive, losses were noticeably lower in proportion to those suffered by the enemy during 1943–5 than during the 1941–2. At the same time, in 1943–5 the Red Army was winning an increasing proportion of battles and the war – both in destroying the German armed forces and 'liberating' territory with not only political and economic significance, but also valuable population. Soviet losses continued to be high, but could be sustained for the duration given the progress that was being made in bringing the war to a conclusion. How long they could have been sustained in slightly different circumstances is debateable – as German General F.W. von Mellenthin suggests, had Germany not launched Operation 'Citadel' in the summer of 1943 then perhaps if 'combining strategic withdrawals with tactical offensives' and hence playing 'havoc with the Russian masses, while conserving our own manpower and material' the Red Army might have been fought to some sort of stalemate. However, fascinating as this counterfactual is, it not only perhaps underestimates Stalin's and wider Soviet resolve but requires a German leader other than Hitler, that might have resulted in Operation 'Barbarossa' – the invasion of the Soviet Union – not being launched in the first place![3] Economic historian Mark Harrison has certainly suggested that without Allied material assistance Nazi Germany might have been able to fight the Soviet Union to some sort of stalemate.[4] Not all German generals shared von Mellenthin's view of what might otherwise have happened and how the Red Army might have been halted. In an in many ways glowing appraisal of Red Army performance during the war given as a lecture to fellow imprisoned officers shortly after the end of the war in Europe, veteran of the Eastern Front Generalleutnant Heim suggested that 'had the war been conducted differently, it might have lasted another six months or a year but the outcome would have been exactly the same'. Heim certainly suggests that German successes in the war against the Soviet Union were down to a large extent to Germany holding the initiative early on.[5] That this was the case was not just because of Soviet dispositions and a poor state of readiness, but because of organisational and cultural inhibitors to the Red Army taking and maintaining the initiative that were gradually ameliorated.

By the end of the Great Patriotic War the Red Army was certainly in many ways a very different creature than it had been in June 1941 or by the summer of 1936. By late 1945 the Red Army had developed organisational structures that played to what had become Soviet strengths and in particular in the employment of tanks and artillery *en masse*, where in the case of the former *en masse* was not taken to the absurd and indeed unmanageable degree that it had been immediately prior to the war. Indeed, arguably even in 1936 Tukhachevskii and others who were the principal proponents of the mass use of armour as part of a complex combined-arms schema – and who would soon be purged – had overestimated the capacity of the Red Army as an organisation and Soviet society at the time to realise their vision. At least Tukhachevksii and other proponents of 'Deep Battle' and 'Deep Operations' were able to heavily influence the 1936 Field Regulations that outlived them, and orientated the Red Army towards fighting a future war rather than the Civil War that had remained far too prominent for far too long in the minds of the likes of Voroshilov, Budennii and Kulik. The theoretical conception of 'Deep Battle' of the period of the 1936 Field Regulations had certainly proven to be beyond the capabilities of both the Red Army as an organisation and Soviet industry by 1941, but by 1945 given the right circumstances was being implemented in modified form with considerable success – thanks to a large extent due to experience accrued at considerable cost during the war. When given suitable time for preparation, including bringing units to strength, the amassing of supplies, conducting operation-specific training, marshalling reserves, undertaking reconnaissance and organising pre-planned co-operation between the different arms, the Red Army was extremely effective in both the breakthrough of enemy defences and initial exploitation phases. In many ways Zhukov had ideal circumstances at Khalkhin Gol in August 1939 for even the purge-battered Red Army of the time to perform well. At Khalkhin Gol the Red Army faced a more or less static enemy in a confined geographical area that would not stretch Soviet command and control mechanisms – allowing for the employment of superior Soviet armoured strength and artillery in meaningful concentration in order to breakthrough enemy defences and exploit those breakthroughs. What the Red Army tried to do with massed armour in far less favourable circumstances in the summer of 1941 exceeded Soviet capabilities, but by 1942–3 the Red Army was building up the concentration of armoured and artillery resources – and indeed airpower – more in line with command and control capabilities than had been the case in 1941.

Central to the success of the Red Army during the late war period in carrying out a modified version of 'Deep Battle' was the tank – even if the relative importance of the tank compared to other arms had perhaps declined by 1945 compared to the vision of Tukhachevskii and others during the 1930s. By 1945 all but gone was the distinction of 1936 between tanks for infantry support and the fast but more lightly armoured tanks for exploitation. It was clear even in Spain – and made plain at Khalkhin Gol – that lightly armoured tanks were very vulnerable to the anti-tank weapons then available that were typically not even being deployed in depth. In some ways the heavy tanks of the late war period, and primarily the IS-2, had replaced the infantry support tanks in the 1936 schema although they had greater value in tank-versus-tank combat despite their slow rate of fire. By 1945 the 85 mm gun-armed version of the T-34 was the principal medium tank of the Red Army that although typically undertaking the exploitation role had the capability to undertake most other battlefield roles even if not as well as more specialised vehicles might have done. Certainly by 1945 even the heaviest tank was far more vulnerable on the battlefield than it had been in 1941 and was much more dependent on close co-operation with other arms than had been the case before the advent of the array of man-packed and towed anti-tank weapons of the later war years and their use in depth that had been mastered by the Red Army and German forces alike. No longer could a few heavy tanks trundle around the battlefield almost impervious to most enemy anti-tank weapons as KV-1 and T-34 tanks had done on occasion in 1941 before running out of fuel or breaking down and finally being destroyed. The infantryman and tanker needed each other, and late in the war the contrast between the idea that rifle armies with their organic armoured support would breakthrough enemy defences to then allow the insertion of the tank armies with their organic infantry support, as effectively mandated in October 1942, had become less clear cut. Tank armies were seeing some of their tanks attached to infantry formations from the beginning of operations, with the tank armies as a whole being committed before the breakthrough phase had been completed. Although the tank armies were then the principal exploitation force, in practice they were often forced to wait for the infantry formations to catch up and particularly when fighting in the dense terrain of Germany. When the tanks charged ahead, although at times they achieved meaningful success in keeping the enemy on the back foot, they also often took horrendous losses even past the point in the war at which German forces might have been able to encircle and destroy armoured spearheads.

In focusing on the production of tanks, Soviet industry unfortunately did not have the capacity to produce the host of other armoured vehicles required to provide the tanks with the appropriate support during the exploitation phase. Suitable Lend-Lease vehicles – be they armoured scout cars or half-tracks – were as has been noted certainly not available in sufficient numbers to provide the motorised infantry with the sort of capability to keep up with the tanks with the degree of protection provided by such vehicles in the elite formations of the German armed forces and even more widely for the Western Allies. Only after the war would the Red Army add such vehicles to its inventory in the requisite numbers. In the meantime Soviet infantry could be moved forward in unarmoured vehicles that were in demand for other roles, but they of course did not offer protection from even shell splinters and small arms fire. For close co-operation with tanks the Red Army continued the practice toyed with by the Red Army despite negative experience in Spain, and adopted whole-sale during the war in the absence of a suitable alternative, of riding into battle on the tanks themselves. What had been shown to be a dangerous and costly practice in Spain continued to be so throughout the war, although at least by 1945 larger tanks offered better cover for the infantry clinging on to them. Even if Soviet industry was not providing the Red Army with the 'bells and whistles', it was of course, like the Soviet system as a whole, good at throwing vast resources at a particular problem and achieving results even if peripheral issues were not being dealt with and there were limits to the extent that Lend-Lease aid could fill in all of the gaps. Certainly, Soviet tank production is an ideal example here, where Soviet industry churned out a staggering total of almost 100,000 tanks and self-propelled guns during the war – which is just as well given losses of almost as many for the war as a whole. By the end of the war the PPSh and other SMGs were available in abundance after more than five million had been provided to the Red Army, and were ideally suited to Red Army methods and practices. Certainly, the mass production of a particular weapon or weapons system followed by its use *en masse* is well illustrated by Soviet artillery and perhaps most obviously in a relative sense compared to any other army by its concentrated use of the many rocket systems collectively known as 'Katiushas'.[6]

Soviet artillery was by 1945 not only available *en masse* for the breakthrough phase, but also far better directed than it had been – as was indeed the case for the Red Army as a whole. The self-propelled and assault guns developed from the middle of the war onwards allowed for direct fire support for the tanks and infantry alike not only during the breakthrough phase, but also exploitation phase. Although the Red Army's towed artillery was more mobile than it had been thanks largely to US-supplied trucks, indirect fire support during the exploitation phase was hampered by the fact that, as well as not producing armoured troop carriers, Soviet industry was unable to provide the sort of self-propelled artillery available to elite armoured formations in the German armed forces and more broadly to the British and Americans. In theory airpower could compensate for this situation, and indeed the Red Army was supported by large numbers of ground attack aircraft and light-medium bombers of various types of both domestic and foreign manufacture. However, despite improvements in command-and-control of air and artillery assets alike, both in terms of organisation and the provision of communications equipment, the VVS was unable to provide the Red Army with the sort of relatively flexible tactical air support provided to both US and British forces by the end of the war that earlier in the war had been developed primarily by the Germans. As former Luftwaffe commander Generalleutnant a. D. Walter Schwabedissen notes in his postwar study of the Soviet air force in the eyes of German commanders, despite VVS successes and in particular on the principal axes of advance 'field commanders of the German army agree unanimously that air warfare in the West produced far more telling effects on the German troops' than in the East.[7] When Soviet air support was available and struck, the results could be psychologically and materially devastating, but all too frequently the air support was not available in a timely manner and all too often ended up being used against the Red Army.

In 1929 the Red Army had striven to be equipped with tanks, artillery and aircraft that were more advanced than those of their likely opponents. In terms of towed artillery this had perhaps been achieved by the beginning of the war, even if fire direction and mobility remained limiting factors in their effectiveness. Certainly in terms of tanks, although German tanks late in the war were technologically more refined, and provided with better communications and optical equipment, in terms of basic characteristics – mobility, firepower and armour – Soviet tanks were not inferior. Similarly in terms of aircraft, after having fallen behind in the late 1930s, by the end of the war Soviet aircraft, and particularly fighter aircraft, were as good as if not superior to developments of the Fw 190 and Bf 109 that continued to provide the principal fighter strength of the Luftwaffe. The La-7 fighter, available in meaingful numbers in 1945, was undoubtedly superior to the German piston-engined fighters that it faced. On the whole Soviet weapons were certainly by the end of the war – and often even at the beginning – well-conceived, relatively simple, robust and at the same time effective – and often far easier to produce than their German counterparts. Although Soviet weapons systems continued to be plagued by quality issues throughout the war, some of the more glaring quality issues were dealt with as for example in the case of poor quality munitions. By the end of the war, when they did go wrong, they were more likely to be repaired closer to the frontline and in a timely manner than they had been early in the war – and indeed the spare parts for repairs were more likely to be available.

In some ways the late war Red Army was like the weapons it was using – organisationally well-conceived but not overly complex. In terms of organisation many typically unnecessary complications from dual command through to unnecessary additional elements to the chain of command such as the direction headquarters of the early war period had been replaced for example by unitary command supported by political officers and Stavka representatives carrying out multi-front co-ordination as required. However, the late-war Red Army was still man-for-man, tank-for-tank or aircraft-for-aircraft all too often not as effective as either its principal opponent or key allies in terms of the ability to destroy the enemy – be that literally or forcing him to surrender – without first being destroyed. Having the appropriate military assets in the right place at the right time was still a particular problem for the Red Army despite dramatic improvements in communications and mobility. When assets were suitably located – often at the beginning of major operations – Soviet forces increasingly achieved much, but all too often they were not and particularly as operations in progress became more fluid. Even prior to the launching of a major operation Soviet reconnaissance was still not providing the sort of detail that the reconnaissance apparatus of her allies was able to provide and particularly on foreign territory, so knowing where to concentrate resources was the first problem. This problem was exacerbated during the mobile exploitation phase of operations where in many ways the Red Army had not moved on from Poland in 1939 where the distinction between reconnaissance assets and other mobile resources was often far from clear, and dedicated reconnaissance assets were relatively few. Soviet aerial reconnaissance was, even by the end of the war, far less significant an asset than it might have been as even Marshal Zhukov noted.

Where the need to bring resources to bear against the enemy in a particular location had been identified, relatively speaking the Red Army was slow to respond thanks in part to the fact that radio communications in particular still only penetrated down as far as battalion level for infantry formations for example, although the situation was better for the armour. Infantry units – and particularly Guards units – were now well provided at least on paper with organic artillery and anti-tank components, where as of 18 December 1944 a Guards rifle division could in theory count on the support of forty-four 76 mm field guns and twenty 122 mm howitzers, along with thirty-six 45 mm and eighteen 57 mm anti-tank guns. The eighty-nine 82 mm and thirty-eight 120 mm mortars added considerable additional fire support that was more decentralised.[8] However, with the exception of storm groups formed for specific circumstances, Soviet infantry units all too often lacked heavier artillery and armoured assets on which they could call directly in the manner in which a German *Kampfgruppe* commander might have been able. With the exception of storm groups and detachments where the allocation of assets to infantry commanders was at times, as for example in the case of the 1st Belorussian Front during the Berlin operation, decreed from on high, senior commanders of particular assets concentrated in increasingly large units and formations as the war progressed seem to have been predictably unwilling to parcel them out. The situation at Kursk where infantry commanders had no authority over anti-tank assets within their positions was far from the exception through to the end of the war. Just like Soviet ground attack aircraft, when such assets were deployed *en masse* in an appropriate location they could be devastating, although such concentration meant that they were at times not in evidence elsewhere where there might have been a need. Hence, as Schwabedissen notes, although concentrated Soviet airpower functioned to often good effect on the key Soviet axes of advance to the north in early 1945, in February in Hungary Soviet airpower was less in evidence.[9] Indeed, even during the Berlin

Operation – despite on paper overwhelming Soviet strength – German fighter aircraft were in more than token evidence during the exploitation phase. Air and other assets, be they anti-tank, artillery or armour were frequently distributed in large parcels from the centre and down the chain of command with often great local impact – as long as you were the recipient of what amounted to a military lottery win.

In some ways concentrating assets in the manner so frequently practiced by the Red Army made sense in the context of a Red Army still struggling with command and control, with there being little choice but decentralisation in those cases where it was typical. Certainly the storm groups and detachments first used in their infancy in Finland when attacking fortified positions were developed throughout the war and increasingly frequently employed in fighting in built-up areas. By April 1945 commanders at the battalion level fighting in urban areas were often able to make use of a considerable array of assets from heavy artillery to sappers, even if even at this level their co-ordination remained problematic in a fluid situation where telephone communications could not be established. It was nonetheless at the equivalent of battalion level where storm detachments were employed that the Red Army was able to best dovetail varied resources under a single commander even without the sort of communications resources enjoyed by German and Western Allied forces. Except for in the case of mobile reconnaissance forces or forward detachments often barely distinguishable from them, relatively junior commanders rarely had this array of sources at their disposal. Perhaps many junior commanders – including many promoted from the ranks – were not equipped to handle many potentially complex combined-arms situations, but the resulting centralised system for the bulk of Soviet troops for most of the time did deny those that were capable to do so. The Soviet Union had certainly made great strides in educating its population during the 1930s, and the Red Army had made great efforts to provide training for commanders as they progressed up the hierarchy, but nonetheless high quality military educations were arguably only available to a military elite. Even prior to the war the Red Army struggled to provide this education in the face of a rapidly expanding force – and particularly where the sort of person with education and possibly a less than ideal class background who held a position within the Red Army's higher educational system was particularly likely to be purged. During the war the needs of the frontline and the high turnover in personnel exacerbated existing trends, where the sort of training courses for which junior commanders were pulled from the frontline in meaningful numbers by the middle of the war were necessarily short and focused on the immediate practical needs of the next appointment. Better field commanders who already had experience were undoubtedly produced by improved training programmes from 1943 onwards, but field command and staff work were two very different things.[10] In the latter case in particular perhaps the anti-intellectual culture fostered by Stalin and close associates in Soviet society at large up to the late 1930s played a part in limiting the breadth of the education provided by Red Army's educational system. In the case of the Red Army, and despite the creation of the Academy of the General Staff that continued to only be able to educate tens of commanders at any time during the war, anti-intellectualism arguably plagued the Red Army into the Great Patriotic War thanks in part to the fact that the likes of Voroshilov and Kulik maintained prominence, and despite the efforts of Shaposhnikov. Nowhere were these inadequacies in education and training more obvious than at the middle levels of command and in staff work, and particularly at corps level, where those with obvious ability were soon promoted upwards and where inevitably many new promotees were not prepared for the particular demands of being a staff officer.

Stalin's Red Army, like any army to varying degrees, struggled to come to terms with genuine initiative at middle to lower levels of command. Unwillingness to decentralise command was not just about perceived competence and the benefits of concentration, but also a question of political reliability and the clearly obsessively controlling mindset of Stalin and many of his compatriots that continued beyond the point that many of the measures introduced early in the war for surveillance and supervision had been abandoned or modified. Nonetheless, in many ways in a manner reminiscent of the Civil War era, even during the latter part of the mid-war period Soviet command and control was complicated by the many mechanisms for supervision and monitoring used in Stalin's army to make sure that the centre was both informed and nominally in control, even if to a lesser extent than it had been. In mid-1943 organisations from the military soviets to Officers of the General Staff continued to complicate decision making and command even if they served useful functions in offering expertise and support. By 1945 Soviet military commanders nonetheless had unprecedented freedom from such interference, even if Stalin still continued to exercise perhaps more influence over the conduct of operations than should have been the case. Stalin's micromanagement of the war – at least of its operational aspects – certainly continued throughout the war. Stalin may have been increasingly willing to take advice, but the key decisions even at the operational level remained his. Even the likes of Vasilevskii had to remember that Stalin was ultimately in command, where Stavka representatives at the front had to report back to Stalin at least daily and consult with the

Stavka before taking meaningful decisions. Fortunately, Stalin had learned much about the conduct of military operations.

Although by the end of the war Stalin may have had a meaningful grasp of the conduct of operations, operations are of course made up of tactical components about which Stalin seems to have had little grasp. Stalin conducted the war primarily from the Kremlin, the Ministry of Defence and his *dacha* or country house – he made few trips either to units in training or the front line. In fact, only in August 1943 did Stalin once visit the front – and even then the headquarters of the two fronts closest to Moscow.[11] If an operation looked plausible on a map – and had been provided with resources that looked appropriate – then Stalin was all too likely to push commanders forward regardless of pleas concerning unfavourable circumstances at the tactical and even operational levels. Immediately below Stalin were senior commanders such as Zhukov who although capable of thoughtful planning and of course with military experience and understanding from a long career to Marshal of the Soviet Union still resorted to barking out orders to advance when they must at times have known the futility of doing so but either feared Stalin's wrath or the impact on their career of being seen as weak. Even Marshal Konstantin Rokossovskii, often attributed as having a more modest and in many ways humane personality than Zhukov for example, of course had to toe the line when it came to launching operations with little chance of success. Such was the case near Stalingrad in the autumn of 1942, as discussed in Chapter 17. During the second half of February 1944 when under Rokossovskii's command, as General Gorbatov discussed with Soviet historian G.A. Kumanev in 1970, Rokossovskii had refused Gorbatov's request to halt the advance in what had clearly become unfavourable circumstances, a request that apparently became a refusal on Gorbatov's part but was subsequently and fortunately for Gorbatov supported by the Stavka.[12] Pushing forward almost regardless was the norm and perhaps became second nature for many senior Soviet commanders given that was all too often what was expected.

Even late in the war and in circumstances where there was time for preparation and indeed ample resources, there were limits to Soviet tactical and operational effectiveness that were a product of the fact that organisational, technological and doctrinal developments were not being supported by the sort of cultural changes within the Red Army that would have been required to gain further improvement in military effectiveness. Although in certain circumstances commanders as low down the chain of command as at the regimental or even battalion level were being provided with both the means and freedom of action to display meaningful initiative in the achievement of tactical goals, not only political but

The winning team: senior Soviet commanders at the end of the Great Patriotic War, pictured shortly after its conclusion. (Bottom row, left to right) Ivan Konev, Aleksandr Vasilevskii, Georgii Zhukov, Konstantin Rokossovskii, Kirill Meretskov, and (top row, left to right) Fedor Tolbukhin, Rodion Malinovskii, Leonid Govorov, Andrei Eremenko, Ivan Bagramian. (RIA Novosti #90221)

also broader cultural factors meant that all too often talk of initiative lower down the chain of command was rather hollow. Despite the initiative that could be shown by the commander of a storm group or detachment in urban warfare during the latter part of the war or the commander of a reconnaissance company at the head of a forward detachment – the nearest a Soviet commander was likely to be able to get to the much vaunted German *Auftragstaktik* – the late war Red Army was as a whole a far from flexible beast. Although there was undoubtedly meaningful initiative shown and improvisation at lower tactical levels, like its British counterpart for example the Red Army was not very good at higher level tactical and lower level operational improvisation where inflexibilities in the chain of command became apparent. Improvisation or 'adaptability' in the chain of command would be more likely at times to save German forces in a tricky situation whereby a commander might 'pick up a battalion here, the contents of a leave train there, a machine gun *abteilung* from one division and a couple of batteries from another, and fling them in ... to save a local situation'.[13] David French's characterisation of the late war British army in this regard is worth noting in part to highlight that many issues noted here for the Red Army were not peculiarly Soviet even if they had a particularly Soviet context. Like the Red Army the British Army was at the end of the war able 'to make their own system work' – in the British case a more methodical and lives-conscious one that was reliant on well-directed firepower and successful logistics rather than an 'audacity' that typified many successful German commanders that as David French suggests in the British context in particular 'would not necessarily have yielded better results'. What the British did not have was:

...a doctrine that decentralized decision-making to subordinate commanders. The British Army retained its commitment to autocratic, top-down managerial control. This did severely constrain the initiative of subordinates and it did confer a major advantage on the Germans. Despite all the improvements the German C3 system continued to be better suited than the British system to cope with the inherent chaos of the battlefield.[14]

Although by the end of the war Soviet commanders – now officers – had been freed from the shackles of dual command and the regime had done much to increase their prestige and authority, this all too often meant burdening the commander with sole responsibility for carrying out rigid detailed orders from above. On many occasions, no amount of initiative within acceptable confines was going to save frontline units from horrendous losses resulting from a bad plan executed with undue haste. Even in urban fighting and when performing reconnaissance functions – when the scope to display meaningful initiative was often the greatest – Soviet units were supposed to display initiative in the use of the resources at their disposal in order to achieve what were often extremely very tightly defined ends such as reconnoitering on or advancing in an urban environment along a narrowly defined axis. The impacts of displays of initiative were impeded by the limitations of broader operational plans and timetables imposed from above, and ultimately by Stalin. Often ruthless both for themselves and their country, Soviet commanders from Stalin down even during the last weeks of the war issued orders that drove forward offensive operations beyond the point at which they should have been halted, and indeed they were all too often undertaken in the first place without serious military grounds to launch them at all. Initiative at lower levels increasingly frequently helped these sometimes bold plans to at least succeed by 1945, albeit at high cost. It is important to highlight that pressing forward as the default option once operations were underway at times prevented German and Axis forces from recovering to reform a meaningful defence where otherwise they might have done – and was more likely to do so later in the war when the Red Army was better able to respond to changing circumstances and the capability of the German armed forces as a whole to respond had been degraded. However, the point is here that in many instances the decision to press on was not taken because of a sound judgement call – all too often the only politically acceptable order was to press forward and all too frequently led to losses that would have been considered far out of proportion to any benefits in most other armies. This was not the calculated 'risk taking' that David French has argued the British lacked – this was almost institutionalised risk taking. Although it is difficult to factor in the myriad of variables that made British circumstances different and often more favourable to those of the Soviet Union, it is certainly nonetheless worth noting that during the Second World War British losses of 385,000 killed and wounded represented a comparatively economical investment of lives for results even if each one lost was a tragedy. Although British infantry losses were high[15] – and the 'British army's reliance on overwhelming fire-power did have the disadvantage that it led to a slow rate of advance' – it did however have the 'great advantage that it enabled troops to reach their objectives without intolerable losses. . .'.[16] The same was increasingly the case for the Red Army during the initial and well-orchestrated phase of Soviet offensive operations when materially the Red Army often held the greatest ascendancy.

Particularly after the initial phases of an operation, and even late in the war, in response to pressure to continue or maintain an advance Soviet forces would mindlessly hammer away at enemy positions or launch themselves forward with reckless abandon and little idea of what lay ahead. Prior to the First World War Russian military culture – as many others – had stressed the primacy of the offensive and in many ways stressed bravery and manhood over the sorts of intellectual or technical approaches to warfare that might have improved chances of success, even if at the tip of the bayonet at the frontline there was a point at which the crude aggression was certainly required. Late in the Great Patriotic War, generally competent senior commanders could when allowed force a considerable degree of planning and considered preparation on the forces under their command that increased the chances of tactical and operational success, but in the more fluid circumstances of operations as they progressed and in the face of pressure from Stalin downwards for rapid results Soviet commanders at all levels made often hurried decisions relating to pressing home the attack that resulted in needless losses. Particularly lower down the chain of command in the face of orders to advance in unfavourable circumstances commanders would all too often metaphorically throw up their hands and cry '*da ladno. . .!*' – 'oh well. . .!'

and resort to the sort of ill thought out and gung ho approach that ostensibly – on paper at least – the Red Army had done so much to reduce since the days of the Civil War. In a situation in which those at the bottom of the hierarchy in particular faced a core problem forced on them and which they were powerless to change, any attempts to ameliorate the situation were in peasant fashion all too often abandoned to fate or *na avos'* – a colloquial expression meaning 'in hope of good fortune by chance'. As one participant in the fighting for Stalingrad noted in May 1943, 'one negative aspect' of the 'heroism – if you can put it that way' – being show by many Soviet troops was 'its rash, senseless aspect, and a readiness to take what is[sic] at times completely unnecessary risks'. As this observer noted, Soviet troops were all too often killed because they walked in circumstances that demanded that they crawl – 'Vanya, give me a smoke' could all too often lead to Vanya's death as he ran straight over to his comrade.[17] The psychology of such circumstances often undoubtedly contained some element of denial – perhaps a psychological defence against the true horror of what was often taking place and limited scope to do anything about it. Although such tendencies on the part of individuals were far from uniquely Soviet or Russian, deeply rooted Russian cultural attitudes associated with *na avos'* would it seems all too often contribute to making a bad situation worse and more costly in terms of men and materiel.[18]

There was unsurprisingly some resistance to being pushed forward – quite possibly to one's death – by ruthless superiors. At times, and despite the many mechanisms for monitoring, commanders at the frontline could go through the motions and claim to be following orders whilst in fact doing the bare minimum. Certainly the capacity for the centre to monitor in a timely manner did not necessarily, and particularly as the war progressed, extend all the way down the chain of command and where even political officers might feel more affinity with the men for whom they were responsible than mindless orders from above. Of course, such an approach could all too easily make the plight of neighbouring units even worse.[19] In a slightly different context, in a January 1943 interview 62nd Army commander Chuikov complained of the problem of subordinates lying – 'lying and the bad leadership that comes from our commanders not knowing what's what. They don't know something, but they pretend they do. ...They're not man enough to say they don't know'.[20] The climate of fear that still pervaded the Red Army into the war probably encouraged subterfuge in similar situations to both of these despite the risks involved. At the top of the chain of command that all too often ended up encouraging such dysfunctional responses by committing units and formations to absurd tasks, was

Stalin – a supreme commander almost oblivious to the problems faced by troops on the ground.

Stalin's relentless driving forward of the Red Army to the very end of the war was not only about defeating an enemy that had wrought so much damage on the Soviet Union, but seemingly about advancing the revolution to which Stalin had given most of his life. Once the Soviet Union was not fighting for its very survival, and particularly when it was clear that German defeat was a when rather than if, Stalin undoubtedly attempted to achieve the sort of revolution beyond Soviet borders that had neither happened spontaneously after the October Revolution nor which the Red Army had been able to bring by force of arms as during the invasion of Poland in 1920. The Eastern European territory for which so many Soviet soldiers died, the conquest of which made little contribution to the defeat of the Third Reich, may have offered the Soviet Union greater security, but arguably Stalin was not only a pragmatist but also an ideologue. Soviet conquests in Eastern Europe – and the subsequent attempts to mould Eastern European nations into Soviet satellites – were a continuation of the revolution. Stalin certainly justified the expansion of the Red Army and associated industrialisation in defensive terms, and it was only pragmatic that these had begun prior to the emergence of specific threats. Stalin was viewing the world through the prism of a Marxism-Leninism that acknowledged that a showdown between the Soviet Union and the capitalist world was inevitable, and it was important to be prepared for it. Despite having started to prepare early, with associated problems such as having an outdated tank and aircraft park that needed to be replaced as other powers developed the next generations of these weapons systems, the Red Army in June 1941 was an imposing even if in many ways flawed military machine. Not only was the Red Army huge and backed up by a system to provide additional strength from a vast pool of reserves now organised without the territorial system that worked so poorly in a Soviet context, but it was despite its aging tank and aircraft parks nonetheless well-equipped with basic weapons systems. As doubtful Western observers soon realised, the Red Army was able to function far more effectively than many had assumed it could in such a short space of time after the Great Purges. Stalin was in many ways by this point a key architect of this army and the principal architect of the system that supported it and able to claim much credit for the capacity for its regeneration, but at the same time was responsible for the squandering of resources to hand in June 1941 that had taken so much time and effort to accumulate. Stalin and his compatriots were also responsible for the fact that as was all too often the case within the Stalinist system, quality had been sacrificed for size and huge numbers of weapons at the expense of the means to make effective use of them.

Had Red Army deployment been different in June 1941 – had the Red Army assumed a clearly defensive posture with forces arrayed in appropriate depth rather than being forward deployed and then launched headlong into the attacking enemy – the Red Army of 1941 would still have struggled with co-operation between arms both as a result of organisation, communications, training and leadership, and what experience to date had also shown were hardly prosaic concerns such as supply, maintenance and training. Its often inexperienced commanders who had risen so quickly during the purge era and subsequent expansion would still have struggled to display the sort of initiative and all too often capabilities required, even those expected within the stultifying command structure of the Red Army, to translate orders from above into battlefield success and particularly operational success. However, the Red Army fought hard – at times fanatically – and would similarly have done so and no doubt to greater effect had its deployment and lack of immediate preparedness not opened it up to the loss of much of its mechanised strength on the borders within a matter of days and weeks during the summer of 1941. In fact, given the likelihood that doubts or animosities towards the Stalinist system would be less likely to flourish in less catastrophic circumstances than those faced by many Soviet units during the summer of autumn of 1941 then alternative Soviet deployment in June 1941 would quite probably have had both positive military and psychological ramifications.

The often noted stubbornness of Soviet resistance during 1941 and 1942 was not just about the repressive measures used by the Stalinist regime to attempt to keep the Red Army from wavering, although at times these measures were arguably both necessary and had the desired effect. As authors such as Mark Edele and Roger Reese have noted, and indeed I have discussed elsewhere with relation to the Soviet partisan movement, often in practice few soldiers or civilians are particularly enthusiastic or hostile towards their government and country regardless of its nature. Keeping the majority – the middle ground – motivated to fight is particularly important. In the case of the Soviet Union at the time there may have been a particularly large minority disposed to be hostile to the regime – from those labeled kulaks in the Soviet heartlands who suffered as such, to members of national groups forcibly incorporated into a USSR that then inflicted collectivisation on them as well as attempting to destroy existing and potentially hostile elites. At the same time there were those who had benefitted from or perceived their country – particularly in Russia – as having benefitted from Soviet rule and who were more enthusiastically willing to fight, often having volunteered to do so rather than having to be conscripted. Draconian measures may have been important in keeping individuals less than favourably disposed towards the Soviet regime on side and in particular in circumstances such as the summer of 1941 that could only exacerbate existing negative dispositions, but also provided a mental barrier to defeatism for Soviet soldiers who were otherwise neither particularly positively or negatively disposed towards the regime. Russian and Soviet patriotism may have been a significant motivational factor for the committed from the beginning of the war, but when this was supported by a hatred for an invader whose brutality surpassed that of even Stalin this patriotism gained additional and wider traction. In such circumstances the Soviet 'us' could more readily be contrasted with the brutal Nazi 'them'.[21] The Stalinist regime was also apt to use a wide range of financial and material incentives to help motivate Red Army personnel, from bonuses for the speedy repair of tanks mentioned earlier through to tolerance of a certain amount of looting on enemy territory towards the end of the war. In fact, by the end of 1944 the practice of looting on enemy territory had been clearly condoned when all personnel were authorized to send looted goods home by post – with seniority increasing the allowance. The latter might be seen as recompense for what had been inflicted on the Motherland, but also undoubtedly helped keep troops on side after they had already accomplished the crucial task of liberating Soviet territory.[22] Through a variety of means, the Stalinist regime was remarkably successful in encouraging or forcing its troops to choose to be on the side of the Soviet 'us' rather than Nazi 'them' and then spur them on with a blend of carrot and stick – otherwise rooting out those who could neither be convinced or threatened into sufficiently enthusiastically being on the right side. As the summer of 1941 progressed the Soviet 'us' was soon a much broader church than it had been on 22 June – fighting for the Soviet side was no longer just fighting for Lenin and Stalin but for the Motherland, whose heroes of the Soviet and indeed Tsarist past were mobilised to motivate the warriors of the present. Certainly the shift in Soviet propaganda that could only broaden its appeal made it more likely that those fighting could identify with it and that it could reinforce other reasons to be committed to fight that might vary from fighting for ones friends and compatriots within the unit to seeking revenge for a loved one killed by the enemy. In the case of groups with many reasons to feel hostility towards the regime, as in the case of many members of a number of national groups, where the threat from such persons and groups to the regime did not warrant their being killed or imprisoned, it was also possible simply to keep them away from the front line. Although there was pressure to employ many national groups of questionable loyalty *en masse* during 1941–2 and to a lesser extent in mixed units from 1943 onwards, where possible the Red Army relied on more reliable core constituent peoples of the Soviet Union to do the fighting alongside selected members of other nationalities, where this also mitigated issues with language that might hamper military effectiveness. When the deteriorating manpower situation during the mid-war period onwards forced the Soviet regime to look at these manpower categories again, the fact that Soviet victory was looking increasingly likely by this point was in itself an important constraining factor for those who might otherwise have held negative attitudes towards the regime.[23]

In the context of measures taken to keep the Red Army fighting, with much of the Red Army's initial strength squandered in a matter of weeks during the summer of 1941, it was the capacity to mobilise fresh units and provide them with the means to fight that to a large extent saved the Soviet Union from defeat. Poorly trained, often poorly led and poorly equipped compared to list strengths, fresh units were thrown in the way of the Wehrmacht and its allies and gradually whittled away at enemy strength. Having underestimated Soviet fighting spirit and capacity for force regeneration, the German armed forces had also themselves paid insufficient attention to more seemingly prosaic concerns such as supply and maintenance required to sustain any army, and particularly one operating over the vast expanses of the Soviet Union. By late November 1941 the counterattacks that had been launched again and again throughout the summer and autumn and into the winter, and that had chipped away at the Wehrmacht even if not stopping it, had brought the frontline situation to a point where superior Soviet resource mobilisation could foster at first tactical and then operational successes. Although these successes might have been greater had Stalin and the Stavka had more limited ambitions for the winter offensives of 1941–2, and despite the horrendous losses that the Red Army suffered during this period, the Red Army had nonetheless saved the Soviet Union. With evacuated plant and new production – and further mobilisation of human resources – the Red Army had prevented the German war machine from using its operational and tactical prowess to achieve a rapid victory that would probably have been even less likely in the first place had it not been for the folly of Soviet deployment in June 1941.

With the initial crisis over, Soviet leaders could pay more attention not only to the mobilisation of quantity, but also providing the appropriate organisational forms, support services, leadership and training to make better use of resources that although in terms of manpower were still abundant – and in terms of material resources improving rapidly – could in particular in the case of the former not be squandered indefinitely in the way they had been in 1941. From mobilising easily commanded brigade-sized infantry and battalion-sized armoured units in late 1941 that were poorly integrated into larger formations and an effective combined-arms schema, increased material resources and accrued command experience in particular allowed for the creation of formations of manageable size and complexity with far greater operational potential than the conglomerations of smaller units of late 1941 and early 1942 or the bloated mechanised corps of the summer of 1941. Staff work however, and in particular at corps level, seems to have continued to be an inhibitor to effectiveness even late in the war where the capacity to train suitable staff officers was lacking.

The Red Army would, as the war progressed, invest considerable time and effort into attempting to learn from war experience, be that in understanding the enemy or developing its own doctrine and practice. As in many aspects of Red Army activity the translation of higher level understanding into grass roots and even mid-command level understanding and action left much to be desired in a system that was still used to obsessive secrecy and spent too few resources on the training and education of in particular middle ranking commanders. A good starting point was knowing the enemy. By September 1941 it seems that the situation had in some sense improved over that which had existed particularly early on during the war against Finland of 1939–40, where Red Army troops were poorly informed about their opponent. There were certainly attempts even early in the Great Patriotic War to get across the basics on the enemy and how to fight him to troops in the field – be the basics the understanding of enemy practice, or more frequently enemy equipment and effective use of Soviet equipment against it.[24] However, beyond these often equipment-related basics the situation was still far from satisfactory. In September 1941 General-Lieutenant Eremenko commanding the Briansk Front had complained in an order on the subject of the use of war experience that 'regarding the study and recording of combat experience the situation is not satisfactory, where valuable military experience of units at the front remains to a large extent only in the memories of participants in the fighting and is not made accessible to field units, educational facilities and the whole of the Red Army'.[25] The reams of paper subsequently dedicated to recording and learning from war experience may have had impact at the top, but were not necessarily effectively disseminated lower down, and if broader materials were available they were not necessarily reaching an audience either able or with the time to process them. In 1944 the chief of staff of 8th Army below Leningrad noted when discussing operations at the beginning of the year as part of an exercise for commanders that 'we do not know the enemy – we are poor at studying the enemy and war experience', where 'the rich experience that we have accrued over three years of war... is not studied'. He indeed went on to suggest that Party-political work should focus on this problem. To some extent such experience was being incorporated into field regulations, but not only was it questionable how well these were actually known as the same staff officer noted, but there was a long lead time for experience to be incorporated into new regulations.[26] Fortunately experience was being processed at the top, and particularly somewhat south of Leningrad individual experience of conducting offensive operations beyond tactical depth was far greater at all levels. In the south and centre the Red Army had become extremely good at using its vast resources for the breakthrough of enemy defences and to a lesser extent subsequent exploitation with or without the matter being studied in detail at all levels of the chain of command.

The growing Soviet ability to deploy larger formations with a reasonable degree of success – and indeed use them to achieve success in 'Deep Battle' and to an often lesser and more costly extent in 'Deep Operations' – in many ways went hand-in-hand with Stalin's development as a military leader. Despite his lack of appreciation for issues at the tactical level that often had ramifications for wider plans, at the operational and strategic levels Stalin learnt a great deal as the war progressed. Stalin's development as a military leader included taking advice from the General Staff and Stavka to which he had promoted an increasingly competent cohort of commanders. The capacity for planning of capable senior staff officers such as Vasilevskii, Antonov and Shtemenko was increasingly frequently allowed by the *vozhd'* or supreme leader to be employed in the preparation of well thought out and resourced operations that could be executed by aggressive field commanders such as Vatutin and Meretskov. At this level of command, although gone was the incompetence of the likes of Kulik, the 'can do' at times seems to have been more important than the 'can do well', but as long as commanders such as Meretskov, Vatutin and Eremenko achieved operational goals most of the time the costs of such operations could be largely ignored. Stalin undoubtedly retained a degree of disregard for human life that went well beyond that of field commanders who had little choice but to accept the losses that following Stalin's orders and achieving operational objectives entailed. Late in the war not only were hurried operations often launched more for political than military reasons, but were launched using under strength units that had often had to draft fresh blood in with little training provided before they were thrown into battle. On the flanks of the Berlin axis not only were units more likely to be understrength, but also less than adequately supplied for the sort of task expected of them – often assaulting well fortified enemy positions in far from favourable circumstances.

Stalin pushed Soviet troops on until the very last days of the war – hounding his commanders who then hounded their subordinates. Still, in May 1945, perhaps later than need have been the case and at horrendous cost, Stalin and his Red Army had played what can be argued to have been the dominant role in the defeat of Nazi Germany. The Red Army had in the end achieved what Stalin had probably hoped to achieve all along – the Red Army had finally exported revolution westwards and the Soviet Union was *de facto* master of Eastern Europe. Stalin's bludgeon was indeed a far more effective weapon by May 1945 than it had been at any other time – better crafted and still with the sort of weight that when it struck it would be likely to cause significant damage if it hit somewhere worthwhile. It was certainly, when initially on the attack, more likely to strike the enemy where it would do significant damage than had been the case at the beginning of the war, but was still a bludgeon, and subsequent swings in the same attack would be more difficult to land where it mattered. By 1945, powerful as the Soviet warrior was, nearly four years of war had taken their toll, and the Red Army was probably not in a position to roll across Western Europe even if Stalin had wanted it to. Had Stalin pushed it to do so, the effectiveness as defined by Reese – willingness to fight – may actually have collapsed. Millions of Soviet service personnel wanted to go home, hopefully to reap some sort of war dividend as recompense for their efforts, although many would first be sent eastwards to fight the Japanese, and more than 10,000 would not return.[27] By and large the expectations of those that did make it home would not be met as the austerity demanded in the interests of reconstruction soon became a more sustained austerity similar to that demanded during the Great Turn of the 1930s. For a fearful Stalin, the Red Army had to remain strong in order to at least hold on to the territorial gains of recent years. The Cold War with the West that had essentially begun when the Bolsheviks came to power in Russia resumed after a relatively brief hiatus, but now the United States had emerged from its isolation as very soon erstwhile allies with sizeable armies even after post-war demobilisation watched each other with suspicion. Nuclear weapons no doubt played a significant role in preventing a 'hot' war between the superpowers and their allies in Europe. Nonetheless, a sizeable Red Army was available at any given time – and army for which doctrine and organisation were heavily dependent on analysis of the Soviet victory in the Great Patriotic War. That victory in many ways provided a legitimacy to sustain a regime and provide example to an army that in many ways were stuck looking backwards towards what both were inclined with some justification to see as their finest hours. Both the Red Army and the Soviet system had passed the test of total war – a considerable achievement when one considers the state of the Red Army and Soviet economy in the 1920s. Millions had paid the ultimate price for that victory – a sacrifice on an unprecedented scale that stands as a chilling reminder of the potential of modern industrial states to wage intensive, sustained and total war.

Notes

INTRODUCTION

1 John Erickson, *The Road to Stalingrad...* (London: Weidenfeld and Nicholson, 1975) and *The Road to Berlin...* (London: Weidenfeld and Nicholson, 1983). There have been a number of reprints by different publishers. I have used a later paperback edition of the former in this work.

2 See the introduction to Phillips Payson O'Brien, *How the War Was Won: Air-Sea Power and Allied Victory in World War II* (Cambridge: Cambridge University Press, 2015).

3 See Conclusion.

4 See Chapter 15.

5 Allan R. Millett and Williamson Murray (eds), *Military Effectiveness. Volume 3: The Second World War. New Edition* (Cambridge: Cambridge University Press, 2010), p.xv.

6 www.podvignaroda.mil.ru/ [Accessed 15 July 2015]

7 The editions I have to hand being Chris Bellamy, *Absolute War: Soviet Russia in the Second World War* (London: Pan Books, 2009); David Glantz and Jonathan House, *When Titan's Clashed: How the Red Army Stopped Hitler* (Lawrence, KA: University Press of Kansas, 1995); Evan Mawdsley, *Thunder in the East: The Nazi-Soviet War 1941–1945* (Oxford: Hodder Arnold, 2005).

CHAPTER 1

1 Figures from Iz doklada nachal'nika GU RKKA V.N. Levicheva predsidateliu RVS SSSR K.E. Voroshilovu o vnov' razrabotannikh shtatakh voennogo vremeni stroevikh chastei Sukhoputnikh i Voenno-vozdushnikh sil, avgust 1927 g., in V.A. Artsibashev et al (eds.), *Reforma v Krasnoi Armii. Dokumenti i materiali. 1923–1928 gg. V 2 kn. Kn. 2* (Moscow/Saint Petersburg: Letnii sad, 2006), p.115.

2 See Evan Mawdsley, *The Russian Civil War* (London: Allen and Unwin, 1987).

3 Doklad nachal'nika Shtaba RKKA M.N. Tukhachevskogo v RVS SSSR 'Itogi manevrov 1926 goda', ne pozdnee 27 noiabria 1926 g., in V.A. Artsibashev et al (eds.), *Reforma v Krasnoi Armii. Dokumenti i materiali. 1923–1928 gg. V 2 kn. Kn. 1* (Moscow/Saint Petersburg: Letnii sad, 2006), pp.645–9.

4 Harvard Project on the Soviet Social System (hereafter HPSSS). Schedule A, Vol. 13, Case 175 (interviewer A.P., type A4), p.12.

5 N.D. Iakovlev, *Ob artillerii i nemnogo o sebe* (Moscow: Voennoe izdatel'stvo Ministerstva Oboroni SSSR, 1981), pp.25–6.

6 See Protokol No. 37 [Revoliutsionnogo voennogo soveta Respubliki], 6 dekabria 1920 g., and Protokol No. 165 [Revoliutsionnogo voennogo soveta Respubliki], 3 noiabria 1922 g., in M.A. Molodtsigin et al (eds.), *Revvoensovet Respubliki. Protokoli. 1920–1923 gg. Sbornik dokumentov* (Moscow: Editorial URSS, 2000), pp.159 and 305.

7 See Alexander Hill, 'Russian and Soviet Naval Power in the Arctic from the XVI Century to the Beginning of the Great Patriotic War', in *The Journal of Slavic Military Studies* (hereafter *JSMS*), Volume 20, Number 3 (July–September 2007), pp.375–6.

8 See Protokol No. 165 [Revoliutsionnogo voennogo soveta Respubliki], 3 noiabria 1922 g., in M.A. Molodtsigin et al (eds.), *Revvoensovet Respubliki. Protokoli. 1920–1923 gg. Sbornik dokumentov*, pp.305–6 and Tezisi nachal'-nika mobilizatsionnogo otdela Shtaba RKKA N.L. Shpektorova o sostoianii Krasnoi Armii, 20 ianvaria 1924 g., in Artsibashev et al (eds.), *Reforma v Krasnoi Armii...Kn.1*, pp.68–70.

9 D. Artamonov, 'Iz istorii razvitiia sovetskogo zakonodatel'stva o voinskoi obiazannosti', in *Voenno-istoricheskii zhurnal* (hereafter *Vizh*), Number 4 (1968), p.110.

10 Doklad nachal'nika GU RKKA V.N. Levicheva v RVS SSSR o militsionno-territorial'nikh formirovaniiakh RKKA, 15 avgusta 1925 g., in Artsibashev et al (eds.), *Reforma v Krasnoi Armii...Kn.1*, p.394.

11 Doklad M.V. Frunze i A.S. Bubnova v TsK RKP(b) I.V. Stalinu o neobkho-dimosti podderzhki i dal'neishego ukrepleniia territorial'noi sistemi kak osnovi organizatsii vooruzhennikh sil, 19 dekabria 1924 g., in Artsibashev et al (eds.), *Reforma v Krasnoi Armii...Kn.1*, p.305.

12 See for example his concerns on this matter in a speech to military workers in Yekaterinburg, 17 February 1921. www.marxists.org/archive/trotsky/1921/military/ch03.htm [Accessed 29 July 2015]

13 Obzor GU RKKA o sostoianii Krasnoi Armii v 1927–1928 gg., 30–31 oktiabria 1928 g., in Artsibashev et al (eds.), *Reforma v Krasnoi Armii...Kn.2*, pp.274–5.

14 A. Iovlev, 'Deiatel'nost' Kommunisticheskoi partii po ukrepleniiu politiko-moral'nogo sostoianiia Krasnoi Armii (1928–1932 gg.)', in *Vizh*, Number 6 (1973), p.74.

15 Obzor GU RKKA o sostoianii Krasnoi Armii v 1927–1928 gg., 30–31 oktiabria 1928 g., in Artsibashev et al (eds.), *Reforma v Krasnoi Armii...Kn.2*, pp.269, 274.

16 I. Berkhin, 'O territorial'no-militsionnom stroitel'stve v Sovetskoi Armii', in *Vizh*, Number 2 (1960), p.18 and Postanovlenie RVS SSSR ob izmeneniiakh v territorial'nom stroitel'stve RKKA, 15 avgusta 1931 g., in 'K istorii territor-ial'nogo-militsionnogo stroitel'stva v Krasnoi Armii', in *Vizh*, Number 11 (1960), pp.96–7.

17 L. Borisov, 'Oboronno-massovaia rabota OSOAVIAKHIM (1927–1941 gg.)', in *Vizh*, Number 8 (1967), p.42.

18 O.Iu. Nikonova, *Vostanie patriotov: Osoaviakhim in voennaia podgotovka nase-leniia v ural'skoi provintsii (1927–1941 gg.)* (Moscow: Novii khronograf, 2010), chapters 2, 3 and conclusion.

19 O.Iu. Nikonova, *Vostanie patriotov...*, p.434; Arkadii Glazunov, *Voina: v plenu, v partizanakh, v deistvuiushchei armii* (Moscow: "Kanon+", ROOI "Reabilitatsii", 2002), p.5.

20 A. Iovlev, 'Deiatel'nost' Kommunisticheskoi Partii po ukrepleniiu...', pp.74–5.

21 Iu.A. Poliakov et al (eds.), *Vsesoiuznaia perepis' nasileniia 1937 goda: Obshchie itogi. Sbornik dokumentov i materialov* (Moscow: "Rossiiskaia politicheskaia entsiklopediia" (ROSSPEN), 2007), p.114.

22 A. Iovlev, 'Deiatel'nost' Kommunisticheskoi partii po ukrepleniiu...', pp.75–6.

23 HPSSS. Schedule A, Vol. 22, Case 433 (interviewer S.H., type A4), pp.7–8.

24 See M. Gareev, 'Iz istorii razvitiia metodiki provedeniia takticheskikh uchenii i manevrov v Sovetskoi Armii', in *Vizh*, Number 10 (1975), pp.13–17.

25 N.D. Iakovlev, *Ob artillerii i nemnogo o sebe*, p.19.

26 Gareev, 'Iz istorii razvitiia metodiki...', pp.15–17.

27 Postanovlenie TsK VKP(b) 5 iiunia 1931 g. O Komandnom i politicheskom sostave RKKA, in *KPSS o Vooruzhennikh Silakh Sovetskogo Soiuza. Dokumenti 1917–1981* (Moscow: Voennoe Izdatel'stvo Ministerstva Oboroni SSSR, 1981), p.263.

28 A. Iovlev and A. Cheremnikh, 'Razvitie voenno-uchebnikh zavedenii v 1929–1937 gg.', in *Vizh*, Number 7 (1980), pp.73–5.

29 See the introduction to N.S. Tarkhova (gen.ed.) et al, *Voennii sovet pri narodnom kommissare oboroni SSSR. 1–4 iiunia 1937 g.: Dokumenti i materiali* (Moscow: ROSSPEN, 2008), p.3.

30 HPSSS. Schedule A, Vol. 22, Case 433 (interviewer S.H., type A4), p.4.

31 Richard W. Harrison, *Architect of Soviet Victory in World War II: The Life and Theories of G.S. Isserson* (Jefferson, NC: McFarland and Company Inc., 2010), pp.71, 171–3, 235.

32 See O.F. Suvenirov, *Tragediia RKKA 1937–1938* (Moscow: Terra, 1998), pp.47–8 and below. On the contribution of Svechin and others to Soviet military theory in the interwar period, see Richard W. Harrison, *The Russian Way of War: Operational Art, 1904–1940* (Lawrence, KA: University Press of Kansas, 2001).

33 Roger R. Reese, *Red Commanders: A Social History of the Soviet Army Officer Corps, 1918–1991* (Lawrence, KS: University Press of Kansas, 2005), pp.102–4.

34 Ob edinonachalii v Krasnoi Armii. TsK RKP(b), 6 marta 1925 g., in *KPSS o Vooruzhennikh Silakh*, p.228.

35 Iu. Petrov, 'Deiatel'nost' Kommunisticheskoi partii po provedeniiu edinonachaliia v Vooruzhennikh Silakh (1925–1931 godi)', in *Vizh*, Number 5 (1963), pp.19–21, and Tsirkular RVS SSSR o rasshirenii otvetstvennosti komandirov-edinonachal'nikov, 13 maia 1927 g., in , in Artsibashev et al (eds.), *Reforma v Krasnoi Armii...Kn.2*, pp.88–9.

36 HPSSS. Schedule A, Vol. 13, Case 175 (interviewer A.P., type A4), p.7.

37 'O vvedenii serzhantskikh zvanii v Krasnoi Armii', in *Vizh*, Number 10 (1979), p.72.

38 Roger R. Reese, *Red Commanders*, pp.94–5.

39 G.K. Zhukov, *Vospominaniia i razmishleniia. V 3-x tomakh. T.1 – 12-e izdanie. Tom 1* (Moscow: AO Izdatel'stvo "Novosti", 1995), pp.194–5.

40 Richard W. Harrison, *Architect of Soviet Victory in World War II: The Life and Theories of G.S. Isserson*, p.180.

41 Roger R. Reese, *Red Commanders*, pp.96–101. For Reese's notion of what is required for professionalism in this instance, see pp.3–4.

42 Brian R. Sullivan, 'The Italian Armed Forces, 1918–1940', in Allan R. Millett and Williamson Murray (eds.), *Military Effectiveness. Volume 2: The Interwar Period, New Edition* (Cambridge: Cambridge University Press, 2010), p.200.

43 Even if it also prevented 'command elements' from abusing Red Army personnel. Reese, *Red Commanders*, pp.57–63.

44 HPSSS. Schedule A, Vol. 22, Case 433 (interviewer S.H., type A4), pp.5–6; HPSSS. Schedule B, Vol. 9, Case 497 (interviewer J.R.), p.3.

45 Petrov, 'Deiatel'nost' Kommunisticheskoi partii po provedeniiu...', pp.21–2.

46 Ob edinonachalii v Krasnoi Armii..., in *KPSS o Vooruzhennikh Silakh*, p.228.

47 See *O vvedenii personal'nikh voennikh zvanii nachal'stvuiushchego sostava RKKA.... Postanovlenie TsIK i SNK SSSR ot 22 sentiabria 1935 g.* (Moscow: Otdel izdatel'stva NKO SSSR, 1935), pp.8–9.

48 For a brief introduction to Soviet nationalities policy during this period, including 'nativization', and on specific nationalities, see Graham Smith (ed.), *The Nationalities Question in the Soviet Union* (London and New York: Longman, 1990), pp.1–7 and other chapters by nationality.

49 Doklad nachal'nika GU RKKA V.N. Levicheva v RVS SSSR o national'nikh formirovaniiakh, 8 maia 1926 g., in Artsibashev et al (eds.), *Reforma v Krasnoi Armii...Kn.1*, p.559.

50 Ibid., p.560.

51 Ibid., p.563.

52 Doklad zam. Nachal'nika Shtaba RKKA S.A. Pugacheva v RVS SSSR o national'nom stroitel'stve RKKA, 30 aprelia 1927 g., in V.A. Artsibashev et al (eds.), *Reforma v Krasnoi Armii...Kn. 2*, pp.65–6.

53 HPSSS. Schedule B, Vol. 1, Case 77 (interviewer Michael Luther), p.3.

54 HPSSS. Schedule B, Vol. 9, Case 497 (interviewer J.R.), p.1.

55 HPSSS. Schedule B, Vol. 7, Case 135 (interviewer M.L.), p.2.

56 HPSSS. Schedule B, Vol. 9, Case 375 (interviewer M.L.), p.2.

57 On this matter, see Roger R. Reese, *Stalin's Reluctant Soldiers: A Social History of the Red Army, 1925–1941* (Lawrence, Kansas: University Press of Kansas, 1996), pp.84–92.

58 Postanovlenie Politburo TsK VKP(b) o formirovanii kazach'ikh divizii, 20 April 1936, in L.S. Gatagova et al (eds.), *TsK VKP(b) i natsional'nii vopros. Kniga 2. 1933–1945* (Moscow: ROSSPEN, 2009), pp.178–80.

59 O.F. Suvenirov, *Tragediia RKKA 1937–1938*, p.72.

60 See A. Ia. Soshnikov et al, *Sovetskaia kavaleriia: Voenno-istoricheskii ocherk* (Moscow: Voenizdat, 1984), pp.142–51.

CHAPTER 2

1 See for example John Erickson, *The Soviet High Command: A Military-Political History, 1918–1941* (London: Macmillan and Company Ltd, 1962); Mary R. Habeck, *Storm of Steel: The Development of Armor Doctrine in Germany and the*

Soviet Union, 1919–1939 (Ithaca and London: Cornell University Press, 2003); and Richard W. Harrison, *Architect of Soviet Victory in World War II: The Life and Theories of G.S. Isserson* and also his *The Russian Way of War: Operational Art, 1904–1940.*

2 Ministerstvo oboroni SSSR. Institut voennoi istorii, *Voennii entsiklopedicheskii slovar'* (Moscow: Voennoe izdatel'stvo, 1983), p.198.

3 Narodnii Komissariat Oboroni Soiuza SSR, *Vremennii Polevoi Ustav RKKA 1936 (PU 36)* (Moscow: Gosudarstvennoe voennoe izdatel'stvo Narkomata Oboroni SSSR, 1937), p.69.

4 Bruce Condell and David T. Zabecki (trans. and ed.), *On the German Art of War: Truppenführung* (Mechanicsburg, PA: Stackpole Books, 2009), pp.17–18.

5 Ibid., pp.3–4.

6 Iz doklada nachal'nika GU RKKA V.N. Levicheva predsidateliu RVS SSSR K.E. Voroshilovu o vnov' razrabotannikh shtatakh voennogo vremeni stroevikh chastei Sukhoputnikh i Voenno-vozdushnikh sil. August 1927, in V.A. Artsibashev et al (eds.), *Reforma v Krasnoi Armii... Kn. 2*, p.104; A. G. Soliankin et al, *Otechestvennie bronirovannie mashini. XX vek.: Nauchnoe izdanie: V 4 t. Tom 1. Otechestvennie bronirovannie mashini. 1905–1941 gg.* (Moscow: OOO Izdatel'skii tsentr "Eksprint", 2002), pp.11–13 and 67–8; A Rizhakov, 'K voprosu o stroitel'stve bronetankovikh voisk Krasnoi Armii v 30-e godi', in *Vizh*, Number 8 (1968), p.105.

7 M.Iu. Mukhin, *Aviapromishlennost' SSSR v 1921–1941 godakh* (Moscow: Nauka, 2006), p.113.

8 Sostoianie i perspektivi v stroitel'stve vooruzhennikh sil SSSR. Otchetnii doklad v Politbiuro TsK VKP(b) za period mai 1927 g. – iiun' 1929 g., ne pozdnee 27 iiunia 1929 g., in S. Kudriashov (ed.), *Krasnaia Armiia v 1920-e godi* (Moscow: Vestnik Arkhiva Prezidenta Rossiiskoi Federatsii, 2007), pp.210–11.

9 Mukhin, *Aviapromishlennost' SSSR v 1921–1941 godakh*, p.105.

10 Ibid., p.114.

11 Soliankin et al, *Otechestvennie bronirovannie mashini. XX vek....1905–1941 gg.*, pp.61, 68–70; A. Rizhakov, 'K voprosu o stroitel'stve bronetankovikh voisk Krasnoi Armii v 30-e godi', p.106; Erickson, *The Soviet High Command*, p.241.

12 Soliankin et al, *Otechestvennie bronirovannie mashini. XX vek....1905–1941 gg.*, p.13.

13 Postanovlenie Politburo TsK VKP(b) o sostoianii oboroni SSSR (Utverzhdeno Politburo TsK VKP(b) 15.VII.29 g.), in S. Kudriashov (ed.), *Krasnaia Armiia v 1920-e godi*, p.238; Rizhakov, 'K voprosu o stroitel'stve bronetankovikh voisk Krasnoi Armii v 30-e godi', pp.105–6.

14 I.V. Bistrova, *Sovetskii voenno-promishlennii kompleks: problem stanovleniia i razvitiia (1930–1980-e godi)* (Moscow: Ros. Akad. Nauka, In-t ros. istorii, 2006), p.644. The terms 'light', 'medium' and 'heavy' with regard to tanks relate as much to use as weight, where with the 'light' tanks the focus tended to be on speed rather than armour and armament (and hence an initial Soviet designation as 'fast' tanks), and with the 'heavy' tanks focusing on armour

and armament rather than speed. 'Medium' tanks tended to be a compromise – having a balance of speed, armour and armament compared to their 'light' and 'medium' counterparts. An additional classification, that of 'Infantry' or 'Direct Infantry Support' tank applies to typically slow and relatively well-armoured tanks intended to provide direct and close support for infantry, where in terms of their armours, armaments and weights they might be deemed equivalent to 'medium' or 'heavy' tanks depending on the period.

15 Proekt postanovleniia Politburo TsK VKP(b), 29 iiunia 1929 g.; and Postanovlenie Politburo TsK VKP(b) o sostoianii oboroni SSSR (Utverzhdeno Politburo TsK VKP(b) 15.VII.29 g.), in Kudriashov (ed.), *Krasnaia Armiia v 1920-e godi*, pp.230 and 238.

16 Mukhin, *Aviapromishlennost' SSSR v 1921–1941 godakh*, p.115.

17 Mukhin, *Aviapromishlennost' SSSR v 1921–1941 godakh*, p.208; Bill Gunston, *Aircraft of the Soviet Union: The encyclopaedia of Soviet Aircraft since 1917* (London: Osprey Publishing Limited, 1983), pp.237–9; Yefim Gordon and Dmitri Khazanov, *Soviet Combat Aircraft of the Second World War. Volume One: Single-Engined Fighters* (Earl Shilton, Leics: Midland Publishing Limited, 1998), p.86.

18 Mukhin, *Aviapromishlennost' SSSR v 1921–1941 godakh*, p.115.

19 Nikolai Simonov, *Voenno-promishlennii kompleks SSSR v 1920–1950-e godi* (Moscow: ROSSPEN, 1996), p.84.

20 Postanovlenie Politburo TsK VKP(b) o sostoianii oboroni SSSR (Utverzhdeno Politburo TsK VKP(b) 15.VII.29 g.), in Kudriashov (ed.), *Krasnaia Armiia v 1920-e godi*, p.238; V.N. Shunkov, *Artilleriia Krasnoi Armii i Vermakhta Vtoroi mirovoi voini* (Moscow: AST/Minsk: Kharvest, 2005), pp.60–2 and 259–60.

21 Postanovlenie Politburo TsK VKP(b) o sostoianii oboroni SSSR..., in Kudriashov (ed.), *Krasnaia Armiia v 1920-e godi*, p.238; V.N. Shunkov, *Artilleriia Krasnoi Armii i Vermakhta Vtoroi mirovoi voini*, pp.72–6.

22 V.N. Shunkov, *Artilleriia Krasnoi Armii i Vermakhta Vtoroi mirovoi voini*, pp.87–90.

23 Postanovlenie Politburo TsK VKP(b) o sostoianii oboroni SSSR..., in Kudriashov (ed.), *Krasnaia Armiia v 1920-e godi*, p.238; V.N. Shunkov, *Artilleriia Krasnoi Armii i Vermakhta Vtoroi mirovoi voini*, pp.124–5.

24 See A. G. Soliankin et al, *Otechestvennie bronirovannie mashini.1905–1941 gg.*, pp.261–8 and Il'ia Moshchanskii and Ivan Khokhlov, *Boi u ozera Khasan (29 iiulia – 11 avgusta 1938 goda)*, (Moscow: OOO "BTV-MN", 2002), p.36.

25 Protokol'naia zapis' vechernogo zasedaniia 23 noiabria 1938 g., in P.N. Bobilev (gen.ed.), *Voennii sovet pri narodnom komissare oboroni SSSR. 1938, 1940 gg.: Dokumenti i materiali* (Moscow: ROSSPEN, 2006), p.125.

26 Maksim Kolomiets, 'Boi u reki Khalkhin-Gol mai-sentiabr' 1939 goda', *Frontovaia illiustratsiia*, Number 2 (2002), pp.18, 23–4; Alvin D. Coox, *Nomonhan: Japan against Russia, 1939* (Stanford, California: Stanford University Press, 1985), pp.246–7.

27 Iakovlev, *Ob artillerii i nemnogo o sebe*, pp.26–7. Having noted his joy at leaving the territorial division with which he had briefly served.

28 Evgenii Kochnev, *Avtomobili Velikoi Otechestvennoi* (Moscow: "EKSMO", 2010), pp.38–9 and 106.

29 Production figures from Mark Harrison, *Soviet Planning in Peace and War, 1938–1945* (Cambridge: Cambridge University Press, 1985), p.253.

30 O.A. Losik (gen.ed.), *Istoriia tankovikh voisk Sovetskoi armii. V trekh tomakh. Tom pervii. Zarozhdenie i razvitie tankovikh voisk Sovetskoi armii do Velikoi Otechestvennoi voini (1917–1941 gg.)* (Moscow: Izdanie Akademii bronetan-kovikh voisk imeni Marshala Sovetskogo soiuza Malinovskogo, 1975), pp.139–140.

31 See David R. Stone, *Hammer and Rifle: The Militarization of the Soviet Union, 1926–1933* (Lawrence, Kansas: University Press of Kansas, 2000).

32 R.W. Davies, 'Planning for Mobilization: The 1930s', in Mark Harrison (ed.), *Guns and Roubles: The Defense Industry in the Stalinist State* (New Haven, CT and London: Yale University Press, 2008), p.120.

33 See Alexander Hill, *The Great Patriotic War of the Soviet Union, 1941–1945: A documentary reader* (London and New York: Routledge, 2009), pp.6–7.

34 For a review and summary in English of Oleg Ken's important work, see Alexander Hill, Review of Oleg Ken's *Mobilizatsionnoe planirovanie i politicheskie resheniia. Konets 1920 – seredina 1930-kh godov*, in *The Journal of Strategic Studies*, Volume 9, Number 5 (2005), pp.894–5. ; Oleg Khlevniuk's argument is presented in English as 'The Objectives of the Great Terror, 1937–1939' in both J. Cooper , M. Perrie and E.A. Rees (eds.), *Soviet History 1917–1953: Essays in Honour of R.W. Davies* (New York: St Martin's Press, 1995), and in D. Hoffman (ed.), *Stalinism: The Essential Readings* (Malden, MA: Wiley Blackwell, 2003), and more recently in his *Stalin: New Biography of a Dictator* (New Haven and London: Yale University Press, 2015), chapter 4.

35 R.W. Davies, 'Planning for Mobilization: The 1930s', pp.120–1.

36 See for example Preparatory Materials of the Council of People's Commissars of the USSR, 'Towards a justification for the construction [*obosnovaniiu sooruzheniia*] of the Baltic-White Sea Canal', no later than May 1930, in Alexander Hill, *The Great Patriotic War*, pp.11–12. Detailed materials relating to the military utility of the proposed canal as of 1930 are contained within RGA VMF f.r-1483.o.3.d.49. Measures taken to get submarines and destroyers through the canal in April-May 1933 are described in Spravka po EONu, 27 May 1933. RGA VMF f.r-1483.o.1. d.200.ll.13–18.

37 Alexander Hill, 'Russian and Soviet Naval Power and the Arctic', pp.379–83.

38 V.Iu. Gribovskii, 'Na puti k "bol'shomu morskomu i okeanskomu flotu" (korablestroitel'nie programmi Voenno-Morskogo Flota SSSR v predvoennie godi)', in *Gangut*, Number 9 (1995), pp.11, 14.

39 Gunnar Åselius, 'The naval theatres in Soviet grand strategy during the interwar period', in *JSMS*, Volume 13, Number 1 (2000), pp.82–5.

40 Alexander Hill, 'British Lend-Lease Aid and the Soviet War Effort, June 1941-June 1942', in *The Journal of Military History*, Volume 71, Number 3 (July 2007), pp.803, 805.

41 See Jürgen Rohwer and Mikhail S. Monakov, *Stalin's Ocean Going Fleet: Soviet Naval Strategy and Shipbuilding Programmes 1935–1953* (London/Portland, OR: Frank Cass, 2001), pp.54, 119–20.

42 Stone, *Hammer and Rifle*, p.210.

43 I.V. Bistrova, *Sovetskii voenno-promishlennii kompleks*, p.118.

44 A. Iovlev, 'Tekhnicheskoe perevooruzhenie Krasnoi Armii v godi pervoi piatiletki', in *Vizh*, Number 12 (1964), p.8

45 See for example Shelford Bidwell and Dominick Graham, *Fire-Power: British Army Weapons and Theories of War 1904–1945* (London: George Allen and Unwin, 1982), pp.141–2.

46 Dokladi i vistupleniia uchastnikov zasedaniia Voennogo soveta pri NKO SSSR ob itogakh boevoi podgotovki RKKA za 1936 g. i zadachakh na 1937 g., 13–19 oktiabria 1936 g. Vechernee zasedanie 14 oktiabria 1936 g., in I.I. Basik et al (eds.), *Voennii sovet pri narodnom kommissare oboroni SSSR. Oktiabr' 1936. : Dokumenti i materiali* (Moscow: Rossiiskaia politicheskaia entsiklopediia (ROSSPEN), 2009), pp.161–2.

47 Prikaz NKO SSSR ob itogakh boevoi podgotovki za 1936 god i o zadachakh na 1937 god, 3 noiabria 1936 g., in ibid., pp.445–6.

48 For example, manoeuvres on 10 September 1936 are reported in *Pravda*, 11 September 1936, p.2 ('Svodka "boevikh" deistvii na manevrakh Belorusskogo voennogo okruga za 10 sentiabria').

49 Lieutenant-General Sir Giffard Martel, *The Russian Outlook* (London: Michael Joseph Ltd, 1947), pp.16–23.

50 Ibid., pp.23–4.

51 Prikaz NKO SSSR ob itogakh boevoi podgotovki za 1936 god i o zadachakh na 1937 god, 3 noiabria 1936 g., in I.I. Basik et al (eds.), *Voennii sovet pri narodnom kommissare oboroni SSSR. Oktiabr' 1936*, pp.447–9.

52 Ibid., p.448.

53 See Manfred Messerschmidt, 'German Military Effectiveness between 1919 and 1939', in Allan R. Millett and Williamson Murray (eds.), *Military Effectiveness. Volume 2: The Interwar Period*, pp.243–4.

54 V. Danilov, 'General'nii shtab RKKA v predvoennie godi (1936–iiun' 1941 g.)', in *Vizh*, Number 3 (1980), p.68.

55 Discharged from the Red Army in February and arrested in April 1938, before being executed – the day after sentencing – on 23 February 1939. See O.F. Suvenirov, *Tragediia RKKA 1937–1938*, p.373.

56 M.M. Kozlov (ed.), *Akademiia General'nogo shtaba. Istoriia ...akademii General'nogo staba Vooruzhennikh Sil SSSR imeni K.E. Voroshilova. Izdanie vtoroe...* (Moscow: Voennoe izdatel'stvo, 1987), pp.26–7, 31–2; M.V.Zakharov, *General'nii shtab v predvoennie godi* (Moscow: Voennoe izdatel'stvo, 1989), p.119.

57 V. Danilov, 'General'nii shtab RKKA v predvoennie godi (1936–iiun' 1941 g.)', p.69.

58 M.M. Kozlov (ed.), *Akademiia General'nogo shtaba*, p.35; M.V.Zakharov, *General'nii shtab v predvoennie godi*, pp.117–20.

59 A.P. Beloborodov (gen.ed.), *Voennie kadri sovetskogo gosudarstva v Velikoi Otechestvennoi voine 1941–1945 gg. (spravochno-statistichekie materiali)* (Moscow: Voennoe izdatel'stvo Ministerstva oboroni SSSR, 1963), p.216.

60 Ibid.

61 Brian R. Sullivan, 'The Italian Armed Forces, 1918–1940', in Allan R. Millett and Williamson Murray (eds.), *Military Effectiveness. Volume 2: The Interwar Period*, p.201.

62 A.P. Beloborodov (gen.ed.), *Voennie kadri sovetskogo gosudarstvo*, p.237.

63 Erickson, *The Soviet High Command*, p.444.

CHAPTER 3

1 'Plenum TsK VKP(b), 23 fevralia – 5 marta 1937 g. Stenograficheskii otchet. Vipusk II', in *Voenno-istoricheskii arkhiv*, Number 1 (1997), p.166.

2 Peter Whitewood, 'Subversion in the Red Army and the Military Purge of 1937–1938', in *Europe-Asia Studies*, Volume 67, Number 1 (January 2015), p.121.

3 O.F. Suvenirov, *Tragediia RKKA 1937–1938*, pp.54, 56, 72–3, 412.

4 See most recently Oleg V. Khlevniuk, *Stalin: New Biography of a Dictator*, chapter 4.

5 Konstantin Simonov, *Glazami cheloveka moego pokoleniia* (Moscow: Izdatel'stvo Agenstva pechati Novosti, 1988), p.383.

6 'Plenum TsK VKP(b), 23 fevralia – 5 marta 1937 g. Stenograficheskii otchet. Vipusk II', pp.153–4.

7 Ibid., pp.161–2.

8 Document 156: Politburo resolution to expel Rudzutak and Tukhachevsky, 24 May 1937, in J. Arch Getty and Oleg V. Naumov (eds.), *The Road to Terror: Stalin and the Self-Destruction of the Bolsheviks, 1932–1939* (New Haven and London: Yale University Press, 1999), pp.448–9.

9 Albert Resis (ed.), *Molotov Remembers: Inside Kremlin Politics. Conversations with Felix Chuev* (Chicago: Ivan R. Dee, 1993), pp.275 and 280.

10 O.F. Suvenirov, *Tragediia RKKA 1937–1938*, p.72.

11 J. Arch Getty and Oleg V. Naumov (eds.), *The Road to Terror*, p.449.

12 O.F. Suvenirov, *Tragediia RKKA 1937–1938*, pp.72–3.

13 Boris Sokolov, *Rokossovskii* (Zhisn' zamechatel'nikh liudei, vipusk 1415) (Moscow: Molodaia gvardiia, 2010), pp.68–74.

14 See in particular J. Arch Getty and Oleg V. Naumov (eds.), *The Road to Terror*, pp.471–81.

15 Ibid., p.588.

16 Alexander Hill, *The Great Patriotic War of the Soviet Union, 1941–1945: A documentary reader*, p.17

17 A.A. Kiselev, 'Sud'ba flagmana 1-go ranga K.I. Dushenov', in *Voprosi istorii*, Number 2 (1999), pp.138–41.

18 Alexander Hill, *The Great Patriotic War of the Soviet Union, 1941–1945: A documentary reader*, p.17 and appendix 1.

19 See for example HPSSS Schedule A, Vol. 22, Case 433 433 (Interviewer S.H., type A4), p.14; Schedule A, Vol. 18, Case 341, pp.13–14 and Schedule A, Vol.5, Case 56 (interviewer A.D., type A2), p.8.

20 Totals for those removed (not considering any subsequent reinstatements) – including those arrested, invalided out or who died while serving, and those

removed for 'political-moral reasons' that included drunkenness – were 6,198 for 1935 (4.9 per cent list strength); 5,677 for 1936 (4.2 per cent list strength), 18,658 for 1937 (13.1 per cent list strength) and 16,362 for 1938 (9.2 per cent list strength). Spravka o kolichestve uvolennogo komandno-nachal'stvuiushchego I politicheskogo sostava za 1935–1939 gg. (bez VVS), 24–25 marta 1940 g., in N.S. Tarkhova (gen.ed.) et al, *Voennii sovet pri narodnom komissare oboroni SSSR. 1–4 iiunia 1937 g.*, pp.548–9.

21 K.K. Rokossovskii, *Soldatskii dolg* (Moscow: Voenizdat, 1972), p.5.

22 Konstantin Simonov, *Glazami cheloveka moego pokoleniia*, pp.348–9.

23 Ibid., pp.402–3.

24 Ibid., p.382.

25 Ibid., p.383.

26 John Erickson, *The Soviet High Command*, pp.508–9.

27 M.M. Kozlov (ed.), *Akademiia General'nogo shtaba*, pp.35, 41.

28 P.N. Bobilev (gen.ed.), *Voennii sovet pri narodnom komissare oboroni SSSR. 1938, 1940 gg.*, pp.3–4.

29 N.G. Kuznetsov, *Nakanune* (Moscow: Voennoe izdatel'stvo Ministerstvo oboroni SSSR, 1966), p.213.

30 Iu. V. Rubtsov, *Iz-za spini vozhdia. Politicheskaia i voennaia deiatel'nost' L.Z. Mekhlis. Izd. 2-e, ispravl.* (Moscow: OOO "Kompaniia Ritm Esteit", 2003), p.66.

31 Prikaz Narodnogo komissara oboroni SSSR s ob"iavleniem postanovleniia TsIK i SNK SSSR 'O sozdanii voennikh sovetov voennikh okrugov i ustanovlenii instituta voennikh komissarov RKKA', 10 maia 1937 g., in V.A. Zolotarev (gen. ed.) et al, *Russkii arkhiv: Velikaia Otechestvennaia:* (hereafter RA) *Prikazi Narodnogo komissara oboroni SSSR [1937–21 iiunia 1941 g.]. T.13 (2–1)* (Moscow: TERRA, 1994), p.11.

32 Prikaz s ob"iavleniem postanovleniia TsIK i SNK SSSR 'ob utverzhdenii polozheniia o voennikh komissarakh Raboche-Krest'ianskoi Krasnoi Armii', 20 avgusta 1937 g. – Polozhenie o voennikh komissarakh…, in ibid., pp.24–5.

33 Prikaz s ob"iavleniem postanovleniia TsIK i SNK SSSR 'ob utverzhdenii polozheniia o voennom sovete okruga (flota, armii) RKKA', 17 maia 1937 g. – Polozhenie o voennom sovete okruga…, in ibid.

34 Protokol No. 6 zasedaniia GVS RKKA 16–21 maia 1938 g., in P.N. Bobilev (gen.ed.) et al, *Glavnii voennii sovet RKKA. 13 marta 1938–20 iiunia 1941 gg.: Dokumenti i materiali* (Moscow: ROSSPEN, 2004), p.53.

35 Iu. V. Rubtsov, *Iz-za spini vozhdia*, pp.72–3.

36 HPSSS Schedule A, Vol. 5, Case 56 (interviewer A.D., type A2), p.4.

37 I.M. Chistiakov, *Sluzhim otchizne* (Moscow: Voennoe izdatel'stvo Ministerstva oboroni SSSR, 1975), pp.23, 35, 40–2.

38 L.S. Skvirskii, 'Vospominaniia. V predvoennie godi', in *Voprosii istorii*, Number 9 (1989), p.65.

39 G.K. Zhukov, *Vospominaniia i razmishleniia. …Tom 1*, p.246.

40 HPSSS. Schedule A, Vol. 18, Case 341 (Interviewer M.L., type A4), p.14.

41 HPSSS. Schedule A, Vol.5, Case 56 (Interviewer A.D., type A2), p.7.

42 HPSSS. Schedule A. Vol.22, Case 433 (Interviewer S.H., type A4), p.14.

43 HPSSS. Schedule A, Vol. 21, Case 431 (Interviewer J.R., type A4), pp.10–12.

44 O.F. Suvenirov, 'Vsearmeiskaia tragediia', in *Vizh*, Number 3 (1989), p.43.
45 Postanovlenie Glavnogo voennogo soveta RKKA 'ob avariinosti v chastiakh VVS RKKA', appendix to Protokol No. 4 zasedaniia GVS RKKA 20 aprelia 1938 g., in P.N. Bobilev (gen.ed.) et al, *Glavnii voennii sovet RKKA. 13 marta 1938–20 iiunia 1941 gg.*, pp.41–2.
46 Konstantin Simonov, *Glazami cheloveka moego pokoleniia*, p.296.
47 O.F. Suvenirov, *Tragediia RKKA 1937–1938*, pp.374–5, 396, 400, 415 and 426.
48 V.S. Mil'bakh, *Osobaia Krasnoznamennaia Dal'nevostochnaia armiia (Krasnoznamennii Dalnevostochnii front). Politicheskie repressii komandno-nachal'stvuiushchego sostava, 1937–1938 gg.* (Saint-Petersburg: Izdatel'stvo Sankt-Peterburgskogo universiteta, 2007), p.198.
49 Protokol utrennogo zasedaniia 23 noiabria 1938 g., in P.N. Bobilev (gen. ed.), *Voennii sovet pri narodnom komissare oboroni SSSR. 1938, 1940 gg.*, pp.115–6.
50 Prikaz o bor'be s p'ianstvom v RKKA, 28 dekabria 1938 g., in *RA T.13(2–1)*, p.84.
51 Spravka o kolichestve uvolennogo komandno-nachal'stvuiushchego i politicheskogo sostava za 1935–1939 gg. (bez VVS), 24–25 marta 1940 g., in N.S. Tarkhova (gen.ed.) et al, *Voennii sovet pri narodnom komissare oboroni SSSR. 1–4 iiunia 1937 g.*, pp.548–9.
52 HPSSS. Schedule A, Vol. 18, Case 341 (Interviewer M.L., type A4), p.14.
53 O.F. Suvenirov, 'Vsearmeiskaia tragediia', p.43.
54 N.E. Eliseeva, 'Plans for the development of the workers' and peasants' Red Army (RKKA) on the eve of war', in *JSMS*, Volume 8, Number 2 (1995), pp.356 and 358.
55 Doklad po planu razvitiia RKKA 1938–1939 gg., 20 fevralia 1939 g., in P.N. Bobilev (gen.ed.) et al, *Glavnii voennii sovet RKKA. 13 marta 1938–20 iiunia 1941 gg.*, pp.425–6 and Zapiska NKO SSSR i Genshtaba Krasnoi Armii v Politburo TsK VKP(b)...s izlozheniem skhemi mobilizatsionnogo razvertivaniia Krasnoi Armii (ne pozzhe 12 fevrailia 1941 g.), in V.P. Naumov (gen.ed.), *1941 god: V 2 kn. Kn. 1* (Moscow: Mezhdunarodnii fond "Demokratiia", 1998), p.612.
56 Zapiska NKO SSSR i Genshtaba Krasnoi Armii v Politburo TsK VKP(b)...s izlozheniem skhemi mobilizatsionnogo razvertivaniia Krasnoi Armii (ne pozzhe 12 fevrailia 1941 g.), in V.P. Naumov (gen.ed.), *1941 god: V 2 kn. Kn. 1*, pp.632–3.
57 It is worth noting that the respondent concerned was, after previous employment in the agricultural sector, pleased with the pay and conditions for both a trainee and serving commander. HPSSS Schedule A, Vol. 22, Case 445 (Interviewer R.S., type A4), pp.7 and 10–12.
58 O.F. Suvenirov, *Tragediia RKKA 1937–1938*, pp.320–1 and 390.
59 A.M. Vasilevskii, *Delo vsei zhizni. Kn.1. 6-e izd.* (Moscow: Politizdat, 1989), p.89. On Trutko, see ibid., p.440.
60 Prikaz o sozdanii kursov dlia podgotovki mladshego komsostava sverkhsrochnoi sluzhbi RKKA, 7 iiulia 1937 [NKO No. 115], in *RA T.13 (2–1)*, pp.19–20.

61 See for example Manfred Messerschmidt, 'German Military Effectiveness between 1919 and 1939', in Allan R. Millett and Williamson Murray (eds.), *Military Effectiveness. Volume 2: The Interwar Period*, p.245.
62 Postanovlenie TsK VKP(b) i SNK SSSR 'O natsional'nikh chastiakh i formirovaniiakh RKKA', 7 marta 1938 g., in in L.S. Gatagova et al (eds.), *TsK VKP(b) i natsional'nii vopros. Kniga 2. 1933–1945*, pp.382–3.
63 HPSSS Schedule B, Vol. 1, Case 77 (Interviewer Michael Luther), p.0.
64 Postanovlenie TsK VKP(b) i SNK SSSR 'O natsional'nikh chastiakh i formirovaniiakh RKKA', 7 marta 1938 g., in in L.S. Gatagova et al (eds.), *TsK VKP(b) i natsional'nii vopros. Kniga 2. 1933–1945*, p.383.
65 Spravka o kolichestve uvolennogo komandno-nachal'stvuiushchego i politicheskogo sostava za 1935–1939 gg. (bez VVS), 24–25 marta 1940 g., in N.S. Tarkhova (gen.ed.) et al, *Voennii sovet pri narodnom komissare oboroni SSSR. 1–4 iiunia 1937 g.*, p.549.
66 '...Rech' t. Voroshilov', in *Pravda*, 15 March 1939, p.3.
67 Konstantin Simonov, *Glazami cheloveka moego pokoleniia*, pp.320–1.
68 Aleksei Gavrilovich Maslov, 'I Returned From Prison! 1', in *JSMS*, Volume 18, Number 2 (June 2005), pp.306–8.

CHAPTER 4

1 V. Chuikov, 'O konflikte na KVZhD', in *Vizh*, Number 7 (1976), p.53.
2 A.I. Cherepanov, *Pole ratnoe moe* (Moscow: Voenizdat, 1984), pp.180–1.
3 V. Chuikov, 'O konflikte na KVZhD', p.54.
4 I.I. Fediuninskii, *Na Vostoke* (Moscow: Voenizdat, 1985), pp.23–4.
5 Colonel-General G.F. Krivosheev (ed.), *Soviet Casualties and Combat Losses in the Twentieth Century* (London: Greenhill Books, 1997), p.46.
6 Steven J. Zaloga, 'Soviet Tank Operations in the Spanish Civil War', in *JSMS*, Volume 12, Number 3 (September 1999), p.142.
7 Probably referring here to Pavlov's later appointment to head the Western Military District that became the Western Front in June 1941. See N.G. Kuznetsov, *Na dalekom meridian. Vospominaniia uchastnika natsional'n-revolutsionnoi voini v Ispanii. 3-e izd., ispr.* (Moscow: "Nauka", 1988), p.150.
8 'Grazhdanskaia voina v Ispanii: Deistviia na Tsentral'nom fronte (oktiabr' 1936-aprel' 1937 goda)', in V. Goncharov (ed.), *Grazhdanskaia voina v Ispanii: Deistviia na Tsentral'nom fronte (oktiabr' 1936-aprel' 1937 goda)* (Saint Petersburg: Izdatel'stvo Sankt-Peterburgskogo universiteta, 2006), pp.42–8; Steven J. Zaloga, 'Soviet Tank Operations in the Spanish Civil War', pp.136–7.
9 P. Samoilov, 'Gvadalakhara. Razgrom ital'ianskogo ekspeditsionnogo korpusa', in V. Goncharov (ed.), *Grazhdanskaia voina v Ispanii*, p.206.
10 'Otchet generala Klebera, 14 dekabria 1937 g.', in ibid., p.457.
11 'Grazhdanskaia voina v Ispanii: Deistviia na Tsentral'nom fronte (oktiabr' 1936-aprel' 1937 goda)', in V. Goncharov (ed.), *Grazhdanskaia voina v Ispanii*, p.156; P. Samoilov, 'Gvadalakhara. Razgrom ital'ianskogo ekspeditsionnogo korpusa', in V. Goncharov (ed.), *Grazhdanskaia voina v Ispanii*, p.206.

12 B.H. Liddell Hart, *The Other Side of the Hill* (London: Pan Books, 1983), p.123.

13 Steven J. Zaloga, 'Soviet Tank Operations in the Spanish Civil War', p.141.

14 'Grazhdanskaia voina v Ispanii: Deistviia na Tsentral'nom fronte (oktiabr' 1936-aprel' 1937 goda)', in V. Goncharov (ed.), *Grazhdanskaia voina v Ispanii*, p.138.

15 Protokol'naia zapis' vechernogo zasedaniia 23 noiabria 1938 g., in P.N. Bobilev (gen.ed.), *Voennii sovet pri narodnom komissare oboroni SSSR. 1938, 1940 gg.*, p.130.

16 Hugh Thomas, *The Spanish Civil War. Third Edition. Revised and Enlarged* (London: Penguin Books, 1986), p.590; Jason Gurney, *Crusade in Spain* (London: Faber and Faber Ltd, 1974), pp.92–3.

17 An abbreviation for *dal'noe deistvie* or deep action – fast tanks expected to exploit a breakthrough, not create one.

18 Kombat M.P. Petrov.

19 Vechernee zasedanie 22 noiabria 1937 g., P.N. Bobilev (gen.ed.), *Voennii sovet pri narodnom komissare oboroni SSSR. Noiabr' 1937 g.: Dokumenti i materiali* (Moscow: "Rossiiskaia politicheskaia entsiklopediia" (ROSSPEN), 2006), p.209.

20 Vechernee zasedanie 22 noiabria 1937 g., P.N. Bobilev (gen.ed.), Voennii sovet pri narodnom komissare oboroni SSSR. Noiabr' 1937 g., p.209.

21 A. Vetrov, 'V boiakh na Ebro', in *Vizh*, Number 4 (1969), pp.72–82.

22 Petro. G. Grigorenko, *Memoirs* (New Yor/London: WW. Norton and Company, 1982), p.93.

23 I.M. Anan'ev, *Tankovie armii v nastuplenii: Po opitu Velikoi Otechestvennoi voini 1941–1945 gg.* (Moscow: Voenizdat, 1988), pp.25–6; Doklad narkoma oboroni SSSR K.E. Voroshilova v Politburo TsK VKP(b) I.V. Stalinu i v SNK SSSR V.M. Molotovu ob osnovakh reorganizatsii Krasnoi Armii, 15 noiabria 1939 g., in N. Bobilev (gen.ed.) et al, *Glavnii voennii sovet RKKA. 13 marta 1938–20 iiunia 1941 gg.*, pp.441–4.

24 Spravka po vistupleniiam na Voennom sovete za 21–26.XI.1938 g. (po p. 1-mu povestki) [ne pozdnee 1 dekiabria 1938 g.], in , P.N. Bobilev (gen. ed.), *Voennii sovet pri narodnom komissare oboroni SSSR. 1938, 1940 gg.*, p.194.

25 I.M. Tret'iak et al (eds.), *Krasnoznamennii Dal'nevostochnii: Istoriia Krasnoznamennogo Dal'nevostochnogo voennogo okruga. 3-e izd., ispr., dop.* (Moscow: Voenizdat, 1985), p.122.

26 M.M. Kir'ian (editor-in-chief), *Sovetskaia voennaia entsiklopediia, 8* (Moscow: Voenizdat, 1980) [hereafter *SVE* 8], p.367 and M.V. Novikov, 'U ozera Khasan', in *Vizh*, Number 8 (1968), p.206; V.V. Diatlov, '"Odnoi artilleriei mozhno bilo vse reshit'"'. Primenenie sovetskoi artillerii v vooruzhennom konflikte u ozera Khasan', in *Vizh*, Number 7 (2012), pp.44, 46–7.

27 V.V. Diatlov, '"Odnoi artilleriei mozhno bilo vse reshit'"', pp.44, 48.

28 Coox, *Nomonhan*, p.135.

29 Ibid. ; *SVE* 8, p.367; and G.F. Krivosheev (ed.), *Soviet Casualties and Combat Losses in the Twentieth Century*, p.48.

30 Coox, *Nomonhan*, pp.134–5.

31 M.V. Zakharov, *General'nii shtab v predvoennie godi*, p.135.

32 Ibid., p.137.

33 I.M. Tret'iak et al (eds.), *Krasnoznamennii Dal'nevostochnii*, p.120; Iz soobsh-cheniia...ob obstanovke v raione oz. Khasan, 1 Avgusta 1938 g. and Done-senie...ob obstanovke v raione boevikh deistvii na visote Zaozernaia, 2 avgusta 1938 g., in P.A. Ivanchishin and A.I. Chugunov (eds.), *Pogranichnie voiska SSSR, 1929–1938. Sbornik dokumentov i materialov* (Moscow: "Nauka", 1972), pp.630 and 632; Coox, *Nomonhan*, p.134.

34 Iz kratkogo opisaniia Khasanskoi operatsii 29 iiulia-11 avgusta 1938 g., sos-tavlennogo shtabom Krasnoznammennikh pogranichnikh i vnutrennikh voisk Dal'nevostochnogo okruga, ne ranee 13 avgusta 1938 g., in P.A. Ivanchishin and A.I. Chugunov (eds.), *Pogranichnie voiska SSSR, 1929–1938*, p.666.

35 M.V. Zakharov, *General'nii shtab v predvoennie godi*, p.137; V.S. Mil'bakh, *Osobaia Krasnoznamennaia Dal'nevostochnaia armiia*, p.187.

36 V.S. Mil'bakh, *Osobaia Krasnoznamennaia Dal'nevostochnaia armiia*, pp.205–6.

37 I.M. Tret'iak et al (eds.), *Krasnoznamennii Dal'nevostochnii*, p.123.

38 V.S. Mil'bakh, *Osobaia Krasnoznamennaia Dal'nevostochnaia armiia*, p.188.

39 Iz kratkogo opisaniia Khasanskoi operatsii, in P.A. Ivanchishin and A.I. Chugunov (eds.), *Pogranichnie voiska SSSR, 1929–1938*, p.667.

40 V.V. Diatlov, "'Odnoi artilleriei mozhno bilo vse reshit'"', p.47.

41 Krivosheev (ed.), *Soviet Casualties and Combat Losses in the Twentieth Century*, p.48 and Coox, *Nomonhan*, p.136.

42 E.A. Gorbunov, *Vostochnii rubezh. OKDVA protiv iaponskoi armii* (Moscow: Veche, 2010), p.265.

43 V.V. Diatlov, "'Odnoi artilleriei mozhno bilo vse reshit'"', p.48.

44 Coox, *Nomonhan*, p.137.

45 Protokol No. 18 zasedaniia GVS RKKA 31 avgusta 1938 g., in P.N. Bobilev (gen.ed.) et al, *Glavnii voennii sovet RKKA. 13 marta 1938–20 iiunia 1941 gg.*, p.135. See also Prikaz o rezul'tatakh rassmotreniia Glavnim voennim sove-tom voprosa o sobitiiakh na ozere Khasan i meropriiatiiakh po oboronnoi podgotovke Dal'nevostochnogo teatra voennikh deistvii, No. 0040, 4 sentiab-ria 1938 g., in *RA T.13(2–1)*, pp.56–61.

46 Protokol No. 18 zasedaniia GVS RKKA 31 avgusta 1938 g., in P.N. Bobilev (gen.ed.) et al, *Glavnii voennii sovet RKKA. 13 marta 1938–20 iiunia 1941 gg.*, p.140.

47 V.S. Mil'bakh, *Osobaia Krasnoznamennaia Dal'nevostochnaia armiia*, p.305.

48 M.V. Zakharov, *General'nii shtab v predvoennie godi*, pp.138–40.

49 E.A. Gorbunov, *Vostochnii rubezh*, p.263 and V.S. Mil'bakh, *Osobaia Kras-noznamennaia Dal'nevostochnaia armiia*, p.195.

50 Mil'bakh, *Osobaia Krasnoznamennaia Dal'nevostochnaia armiia*, pp.67, 186, 269 and 326.

51 V.V. Diatlov, "'Odnoi artilleriei mozhno bilo vse reshit'"', p.44 and O.F. Suvenirov, *Tragediia RKKA 1937–1938*, pp.408 and 431.

52 Mil'bakh, *Osobaia Krasnoznamennaia Dal'nevostochnaia armiia*, p.194.

53 Protokol No. 18 zasedaniia GVS RKKA 31 avgusta 1938 g., in P.N. Bobilev (gen.ed.) et al, *Glavnii voennii sovet RKKA. 13 marta 1938–20 iiunia 1941 gg.*, p.137.

54 Mil'bakh, *Osobaia Krasnoznamennaia Dal'nevostochnaia armiia*, pp.186–7.
55 Protokol No. 18 zasedaniia GVS RKKA 31 avgusta 1938 g., in P.N. Bobilev (gen.ed.) et al, *Glavnii voennii sovet RKKA. 13 marta 1938–20 iiunia 1941 gg.*, p.137.
56 Protokol utrennogo zasedaniia 23 noiabria 1938 g., in P.N. Bobilev (gen. ed.), *Voennii sovet pri narodnom komissare oboroni SSSR. 1938, 1940 gg.*, pp.122–3.
57 See in particular Protokol utrennogo zasedaniia 23 noiabria 1938 g., in P.N. Bobilev (gen.ed.), *Voennii sovet pri narodnom komissare oboroni SSSR. 1938, 1940 gg.*, pp.114–124 and Protokol'naia zapis' doklada komanduiushchego 1-i Krasnoznamennoi armii komkora t. Shterna o sobitiiakh v raione ozera Khasan na zasedanii Voennogo soveta pri narodnom komissare oboroni ..., 26 noiabria 1938 goda..., in P.N. Bobilev (gen.ed.), *Voennii sovet pri narodnom komissare oboroni SSSR. 1938, 1940 gg.*, pp.206–16.

CHAPTER 5

1 Coox, *Nomonhan*, p.196.
2 Coox, *Nomonhan*, pp.263–4.
3 T.S. Busheva and AV. Seregin, *Khalkhin Gol. Issledovaniia, dokumenti, kommentarii. K 70-letiiu nachala Vtoroi mirovoi voini* (Moscow: IKTs "Akademkniga", 2009), p.54.
4 Artillery assets that included 64 76 mm Obr. 1902/30, 4 122 mm A-19, 36 107 mm 1910/1930 and 12 152 mm Obr. 1934 guns, along with 68 122 mm Obr. 1910/1930 and 24 152 mm Obr. 1909/1930 howitzers. Ibid., p.59 and V.S. Mil'bakh, 'Red Army artillery and the armed conflict on the Khalkhin-Gol river', in *JSMS*, Volume 15, Number 4 (2002), pp.61–3.
5 Gorbunov, *Vostochnii rubezh*, p.346; Coox, *Nomonhan*, pp.520–1, 1026.
6 V.S. Mil'bakh, 'Red Army artillery and the armed conflict on the Khalkhin-Gol river', pp.63–4.
7 Coox, *Nomonhan*, p.368.
8 Donesenie Komandovaniia 57-go Osobogo korpusa K.E. Voroshilovu ob otkhode protivnika na vostochnii bereg r. Khalkhin-Gol i prodolzhaiushchikhsia ozhestochennikh boiakh vostochnee g. Bain-Tsagan, 5 iiulia 1939 g., 17:15 (mong.vrem.), Tamtsak, No. 1170, in A.R. Efimenko et al (eds.), *Vooruzhennii konflikt v raione reki Khalkhin-Gol. Mai- sentiabr' 1939 g. Dokumenti i materiali* (Moscow: Novalis, 2014), p.166 and Boevoe donesenie komandovaniia 57-go Osobogo korpusa K.E. Voroshilovu ob otrazhenii nochnoi ataki protivnika i ozhestochennikh boiakh v raione visoti Remizova, 8 iiulia 1939 g., 17:35, g. Tamtsak, No.1236, p.175.
9 Coox, *Nomonhan*, p.342.
10 G.K. Zhukov, *Vospominaniia i razmishleniia. ...Tom 1*, pp.258–9; Gorbunov, *Vostochnii rubezh*, p.184; Konstantin Simonov, *Glazami cheloveka moego pokoleniia*, p.313.
11 Gorbunov, *Vostochnii rubezh*, p.185; Coox, *Nomonhan*, p.342.
12 Konstantin Simonov, *Glazami cheloveka moego pokoleniia*, p.312.

13 A.I. Koshelev (ed.), *Sovetsko-iaponskie voini 1937–1945: sbornik* (Moscow: Iauza; Eksmo, 2009), pp.94–8.

14 Coox, *Nomonhan*, p.300.

15 Coox, *Nomonhan*, pp.299–312 and Boevoe donesenie komandovaniia 57-go Osobogo korpusa K.E. Voroshilovu ob otrazhenii nochnoi ataki protivnika i ozhestochennikh boiakh v raione visoti Remizova, 8 iiulia 1939 g., 17:35, g. Tamtsak, No.1236, in A.R. Efimenko et al (eds.), *Vooruzhennii konflikt v raione reki Khalkhin-Gol*, p.175.

16 Koshelev (ed.), *Sovetsko-iaponskie voini 1937–1945*, pp.123–6.

17 Maksim Kolomiets, 'Boi u reki Khalkhin Gol', p.67; Coox, *Nomonhan*, p.308.

18 It is likely that the nine vehicles repaired by 9th Armoured Motor Brigade during the fighting from 20–30 August – where it was no longer being thrown in to combat situations as if a tank brigade as it had previously – were the nine reported as knocked out, and not the three burnt out. Maksim Kolomiets, 'Boi u reki Khalkhin Gol', pp.52, 63, 66.

19 Analiticheskii obzor komandovaniia 36-i motostrelkvoi divizii ob osobennos-tiakh taktiki protivnika v boiu i nedostatkakh v deistviiakh divizii v iiule 1939 g., 15 avgusta 1939 g., in A.R. Efimenko et al (eds.), *Vooruzhennii konflikt v raione reki Khalkhin-Gol*, pp.297–8.

20 Coox, *Nomonhan*, p.572.

21 *Ibid.*, pp.349–50.

22 *Ibid.*, p.418.

23 *Ibid.*, pp.419, 424.

24 Coox, *Nomonhan*, p.426; G.K. Zhukov, *Vospominaniia i razmishleniia. ...Tom 1*, p.284.

25 Gorbunov, *Vostochnii rubezh*, pp.342–5; Coox, *Nomonhan*, pp.580–7; G.K. Zhukov, *Vospominaniia i razmishleniia. ...Tom 1*, pp.262–5.

26 Gorbunov, *Vostochnii rubezh*, p.350; Coox, *Nomonhan*, p.663.

27 As recalled by artilleryman Nikolai Kravets and tanker Dmitrii Mal'ko, in Koshelev (ed.), *Sovetsko-iaponskie voini 1937–1945*, p.155 and S.V. Gribanov et al (eds.), *Na zemle, v nebesakh i na more [Vip. 8]* (Moscow: Voenizdat, 1986), p.322, respectively.

28 Coox, *Nomonhan*, pp.662 map, and pp.680–81; Gorbunov, *Vostochnii rubezh*, pp.351–4; G.K. Zhukov, *Vospominaniia i razmishleniia. ...Tom 1*, pp.267–8 maps and 269–71.

29 Coox, *Nomonhan*, p.681.

30 Coox, *Nomonhan*, pp.669, 676, 678–9 and 918.

31 N.N. Voronov, 'Stranitsi korotkoi voini', in V.Ia. Shoror (ed.), *Khalkhin-Gol: Kniga druzhbi i pamiati* (Moscow: Voenizdat, 1990), p.30; M.N. Bogdanov, 'V bor'be za pobedu', in V.Ia. Shoror (ed.), *Khalkhin-Gol: Kniga druzhbi i pamiati*, p.59.

32 Coox, *Nomonhan*, pp.699, 740.

33 Coox, *Nomonhan*, pp.977–8 and 1025–6.

34 Edward J. Drea, *Japan's Imperial Army: It's Rise and Fall, 1853–1945* (Lawrence, Kansas: University Press of Kansas, 2009), p.205.

35 Krivosheev (ed.), *Soviet Casualties and Combat Losses in the Twentieth Century*, pp.52–3, 55; Maksim Kolomiets, 'Boi u reki Khalkhin Gol', p.64.

36 Maksim Kolomiets, 'Boi u reki Khalkhin Gol', p.54; E. Gorbunov, *20 avgusta 1939* (Moscow: Molodaia gvardiia, 1986), p.200; Gorbunov, *Vostochnii rubezh*, p.347.

37 Donesenie komandovaniia Frontovoi gruppi K.E. Voroshilovu ob obstanovke na fronte k iskhodu chetvertovogo dnia operatsii po okruzheniiu i unichtozheniiu gruppirovki protivnika..., 24 avgusta 1939 g., 10:00 (mong. vremia), No. 971, in A.R. Efimenko et al (eds.), *Vooruzhennii konflikt v raione reki Khalkhin-Gol*, p.358.

38 Maksim Kolomiets, 'Boi u reki Khalkhin Gol', pp.65–8, 71–2.

39 Maksim Kolomiets, 'Boi u reki Khalkhin Gol', pp.65, 70.

40 *SVE* 8, p.353; Coox, *Nomonhan*, pp.914–16; Gorbunov, *Vostochnii rubezh*, p.346.

41 Testimony of Mikhail Popov, sniper, in Koshelev (ed.), *Sovetsko-iaponskie voini 1937–1945*, pp.107–8; for Soviet sniping of Japanese forces, see for example Coox, *Nomonhan*, pp.208, 487, 768 and numerous other examples throughout that work. See also Maksim Kolomiets, 'Boi u reki Khalkhin Gol', p.47.

42 I.I. Fediuninskii, *Na Vostoke*, p.116.

43 P.M. Rizhov, 'Tanki vedut boi', in V.Ia.Shoror (ed.), *Khalkhin-Gol: Kniga druzhbi i pamiati*, pp.112–13. According to Fediuninskii his body recovered after fighting on 12 July with two fatal wounds of unspecified origin. I.I.Fediuninskii, *Na Vostoke*, pp.103–4.

44 See for example I.N. Moshliak, *Vspomnim mi pekhotu* (Moscow: Voennoe izdatel'stvo Ministerstvo oboroni SSSR, 1978), pp.45–6.

45 I.I. Fediuninskii, *Na Vostoke*, p.133.

46 G.K. Zhukov, *Vospominaniia i razmishleniia. ...Tom 1*, p.262.

47 Maksim Kolomiets, 'Boi u reki Khalkhin Gol', pp.15–16.

48 V.F. Vorsin, 'Motor Vehicle Transport Deliveries Through 'Lend-Lease', in *JSMS*, Volume 10, Number 2 (June 1997), p.169.

49 Koshelev (ed.), *Sovetsko-iaponskie voini 1937–1945*, p.152.

50 Coox, *Nomonhan*, pp.740–1 and I.I.Fediuninskii, *Na Vostoke*, p.116.

51 Donesenie komandovaniia Frontovoi gruppi K.E. Voroshilovu ob obstanovke na fronte k iskhodu chetvertovogo dnia operatsii po okruzheniiu i unichtozheniiu gruppirovki protivnika..., 24 avgusta 1939 g., 10:00 (mong. Vremia), No. 971, in A.R. Efimenko et al (eds.), *Vooruzhennii konflikt v raione reki Khalkhin-Gol*, p.358.

52 Maksim Kolomiets, 'Boi u reki Khalkhin Gol', p.70.

53 N.N. Voronov, 'Stranitsi korotkoi voini', in V.Ia.Shoror (ed.), *Khalkhin-Gol: Kniga druzhbi i pamiati*, pp.26–7.

54 Coox, *Nomonhan*, p.488.

55 Donesenie komandovaniia Frontovoi gruppi K.E. Voroshilovu ob obstanovke na fronte k iskhodu chetvertovogo dnia operatsii po okruzheniiu i unichtozheniiu gruppirovki protivnika..., 24 avgusta 1939 g., 10:00 (mong. vremia), No. 971, in A.R. Efimenko et al (eds.), *Vooruzhennii konflikt v raione reki Khalkhin-Gol*, p.358.

56 Gorbunov, *Vostochnii rubezh*, p.348.

57 Petro. G. Grigorenko, *Memoirs*, pp.105, 107; G.K. Zhukov, *Vospominaniia i razmishleniia. ...Tom 1*, p.286. See also T.V. Bortakovskii, *Rastreliannie Geroi Sovetskogo Soiuza* (Moscow: Veche, 2012), pp.190–1.

58 T.V. Bortakovskii, *Rastreliannie Geroi Sovetskogo Soiuza*, pp.214–15.

59 Petro. G. Grigorenko, *Memoirs*, p.110.

60 T.V. Bortakovskii, *Rastreliannie Geroi Sovetskogo Soiuza*, pp.192–4, citing Zhukov, Konstanin Simonov and others.

61 V.V. Kovanov, *Soldati bessmertiia* (Moscow: Politizdat, 1986), pp.28–30.

CHAPTER 6

1 A.A. Vetrov, *Tak i bilo* (Moscow: Voennoe izdatel'stvo Ministerstvo oboroni SSSR, 1982), pp.8 and 13. See also A.A. Vetrov, 'Neprevzoidennaia "Tridtsat'chetverka"', in *Voprosi istorii*, Number 5 (1982), pp.89–100.

2 See Protokol No. 4 zasedaniia GVS RKKA, 20 aprelia 1938 g. and Doklad nachal'nika ABTU RKKA D.G. Pavlova...narkomu oboroni SSSR K.E. Voroshilovu o neobkhodimosti korennogo peresmotra sistemi tankogo vooruzheniia, 21 fevralia 1938 g., in P.N. Bobilev (gen.ed.) et al, *Glavnii voennii sovet RKKA. 13 marta 1938–20 iiunia 1941 gg.*, pp.37–40, 48 and 336–44.

3 P. Samoilov, 'Gvadalakhara. Razgrom ital'ianskogo ekspeditsionnogo korpusa', in V. Goncharov (ed.), *Grazhdanskaia voina v Ispanii*, pp.309–11; Hugh Thomas, *The Spanish Civil War*, p.600.

4 P. Samoilov, 'Gvadalakhara. Razgrom ital'ianskogo ekspeditsionnogo korpusa', in V. Goncharov (ed.), *Grazhdanskaia voina v Ispanii*, pp.356–7; Hugh Thomas, *The Spanish Civil War*, p.602; S.B. Abrosov, 'Sovetskaia aviatsiia v grazhdanskoi voine v Ispanii', in *Vizh*, Number 8 (2012), p.37.

5 Brian R. Sullivan, 'Fascist Italy's Military Involvement in the Spanish Civil War', in *The Journal of Military History*, 59 (October 1995), p.707; James S. Corum, 'The Luftwaffe and the coalition air war in Spain, 1936–1939', in *Journal of Strategic Studies*, 18:1 (1995), p.77.

6 S.B. Abrosov, 'Sovetskaia aviatsiia v grazhdanskoi voine v Ispanii', pp.37–8.

7 Hugh Thomas, *The Spanish Civil War*, pp.589–90.

8 S.B. Abrosov, 'Sovetskaia aviatsiia v grazhdanskoi voine v Ispanii', p.39.

9 'Grazhdanskaia voina v Ispanii: Deistviia na Tsentral'nom fronte (oktiabr' 1936-aprel' 1937 goda)', in V. Goncharov (ed.), *Grazhdanskaia voina v Ispanii*, p.175.

10 S.I. Shevchenko, 'Boevoe primenenie sovetskoi istrebitel'noi aviatsii vo vtoroi polovine 1930-x godov', in *Vizh*, Number 2 (2010), p.21. On developments of the I-16 see Gordon and Khazanov, *Soviet Combat Aircraft of the Second World War. Volume One: Single-Engined Fighters*, pp.100–102.

11 Iu. V. Chudodeev (ed.), *V nebe Kitaia. 1937–1940. Vospominaniia sovetskikh letchikov-dobrovol'tsev. Izd. 2-e* (Moscow: Glavnaia redaktsiia vostochnoi literaturi izdatel'stva "Nauka", 1988), pp.8–10, 155, 251, 348; Alexander Koshelev (ed.), *Sovetsko-iaponskie voini 1937–1945*, pp.162, 185, 209, 247; V.V. Gagin, *Vozdushnaia voina v Kitae i Mongolii* (Voronezh: 1999), p.8.

12 As discussed in some detail in John W. Garver, *Chinese-Soviet Relations, 1937–1945: The Diplomacy of Chinese Nationalism* (New York: OUP, 1988), chapter IV.

13 Krivosheev (ed.), *Soviet Casualties and Combat Losses*, p.47; Alexander Koshe-lev (ed.), *Sovetsko-iaponskie voini 1937–1945*, p.166; Iu. V. Chudodeev (ed.), *V nebe Kitaia. 1937–1940*, p.13.

14 G.K. Zhukov, *Vospominaniia i razmishleniia. ...Tom 1*, p.284.

15 V.I. Kondrat'ev, *Bitva nad step'iu. Aviatsiia v sovetsko-iaponskom vooruzhen-nom konflikte na reke Khalkhin – Gol* (Moscow: Fond sodeistviia aviatsii "Russkie vitiazi", 2008), p.31; V.V.Gagin, *Vozdushnaia voina v Kitae i Mon-golii*, 47–8; Testimony of fighter pilot Anton Iakimenko, in Alexander Koshe-lev (ed.), *Sovetsko-iaponskie voini 1937–1945*, p.53.

16 V.I. Kondrat'ev, *Bitva nad step'iu*, pp.9–10, 12.

17 Coox, *Nomonhan*, pp.194, 202.

18 Alexander Koshelev (ed.), *Sovetsko-iaponskie voini 1937–1945*, p.47; V.V.Gagin, *Vozdushnaia voina v Kitae i Mongolii*, p.49; V.I. Kondrat'ev, *Bitva nad step'iu*, pp.15, 122.

19 V.I. Kondrat'ev, *Bitva nad step'iu*, p.17.

20 A.V. Vorozheikin, 'Krutie virazhi', in V.Ia.Shoror (ed.), *Khalkhin-Gol: Kniga druzhbi i pamiati*, p.66.

21 V.I. Kondrat'ev, *Bitva nad step'iu*, p.19.

22 Coox, *Nomonhan*, pp.266–7; V.I. Kondrat'ev, *Bitva nad step'iu*, pp.20–5, 122; Iakimenko in Alexander Koshelev (ed.), *Sovetsko-iaponskie voini 1937–1945*, pp.48–50.

23 Coox, Nomonhan, pp.256, 273–7; V.I. Kondrat'ev, *Bitva nad step'iu*, pp.28–30, 122.

24 Gorbunov, *20 avgusta 1939*, pp.186–7.

25 V.I. Kondrat'ev, *Bitva nad step'iu*, pp.31–2, 38; Coox, *Nomonhan*, p.632 n.22.

26 V.I. Kondrat'ev, *Bitva nad step'iu,*, pp.46,49; Gorbunov, *20 avgusta 1939*, p.200; Coox, *Nomonhan*, p.1133 n.17.

27 V.I. Kondrat'ev, *Bitva nad step'iu*, p.50.

28 Coox, *Nomonhan*, pp.685–7

29 V.I. Kondrat'ev, *Bitva nad step'iu*, pp.51–3, 123.

30 Coox, *Nomonhan*, p.755.

31 Testimony of Pavel Tsarev and Konstantin Samarskii, commander and senior engineer of a heavy bomber regiment respectively, in Alexander Koshelev (ed.), *Sovetsko-iaponskie voini 1937–1945*, p.110; Coox, *Nomonhan*, p.583, 660 n.37.

32 Vipiski iz dnevnika voennosluzhashchego Ivata (Evato) Fukuto s kharateris-tikoi boev za 20 i 25 avgusta 1939 g., in A.R. Efimenko et al (eds.), *Voor-uzhennii konflikt v raione reki Khalkhin-Gol*, pp.326–30.

33 See Hugh Ragsdale, *The Soviets, the Munich Crisis, and the Coming of World War II* (Cambridge: Cambridge University Press, 2004), pp.112–26.

34 A.A. Vetrov, *Tak i bilo*, pp.19–22.

35 Thomas L. Jentz (ed.), *Panzertruppen: The Complete Guide to the Creation and Combat Employment of Germany's Tank Force, 1933–1942* (Atglen, PA: Schif-fer Military History, 1996), pp.46, 50 and 57.

36 Not including 3,851 T-37 and T-38 light amphibious tanks. See Doklad nachal'nika ABTU RKKA D.G. Pavlova...narkomu oboroni SSSR K.E.

Voroshilovu o neobkhodimosti korennogo peresmotra sistemi tankogo voor-uzheniia, 21 fevralia 1938 g., in P.N. Bobilev (gen.ed.) et al, *Glavnii voennii sovet RKKA. 13 marta 1938–20 iiunia 1941 gg.*, pp.337–8.

37 John W. Garver, *Chinese-Soviet Relations*, p.105.
38 Stone, *Hammer and Rifle*, p.216.
39 Voennaia elektrotekhnicheskaia akademiia sviazi im. SM. Budennogo. Kafe-dra voennoi radiotekhniki, *Kratkii spravochnik po voennim radiostantsiiam (dlia nachal'nika sviazi polka)* (Leningrad: Izdanie VETAS, 1941), pp.21–2 and 25–6.
40 On the outbreak of war Gurvits was responsible for his regimental 6-AK set for communication with battalion level 6-PK and divisional RSB sets. L.A. Gurvits, *Vospominaniia frontovogo radista. Ot KV-radiostantsii - do morskikh krilatskikh raket* (Saint-Petersburg: "Kul't-inform-press", 2008), pp.64, 67.
41 I.P. Grishin (gen.ed.) et al, *Voennie sviazisti v dni voini i mira* (Moscow: Voennoe izdatel'stvo Ministerstvo oboroni SSSR, 1968), pp.96 and 123.
42 Voennaia elektrotekhnicheskaia akademiia sviazi im. SM. Budennogo. Kafe-dra voennoi radiotekhniki, *Kratkii spravochnik po voennim radiostantsiiam*, pp.17–18.
43 I.P. Grishin (gen.ed.) et al, *Voennie sviazisti v dni voini i mira*, p.96.
44 Dokladnaia zapiska Narodnomu komissaru oboroni SSSR Marshalu Sovets-kogo Soiuza tov. Timoshenko S.K, in V.S. Khokhlov, 'V predchustvii neotv-ratimosti nadvigaiushcheisia ugrozi – Sistema sviazi i upravleniia Krasnoi armii nakanune Velikoi Otechestvennoi voini', in *Vizh*, Number 5 (2008), p.46.
45 Spravka po vistupleniiam na Voennom sovete za 21–26.XI.1938 g. (po p. 1-mu povestki) [ne pozdnee 1 dekabria 1938 g.], in P.N. Bobilev et al (gen.ed.), *Voennii sovet pri narodnom komissare oboroni SSSR. 1938, 1940 gg.*, p.177.
46 A.I. Belov (ed.), *Voennie sviazisti v boiakh za rodinu* (Moscow: Voennoe izdatel'stvo, 1984), pp.78–85; Maksim Kolomiets, 'Boi u reki Khalkhin Gol', p.68.
47 Coox, *Nomonhan*, p.584.
48 I.I. Fediuninskii, *Na Vostoke*, pp.166–7.
49 Maksim Kolomiets, 'Boi u reki Khalkhin Gol', pp.59 and 68.
50 V.I. Lenin, The New Economic Policy and the Task of the Political Educa-tion Departments. Report to the Second All-Russia Congress of Political Education Departments, October 17, 1921, in *Collected Works, 2nd English Edition* (Moscow: Progress Publishers, 1965), pp.60–79. www.marxists.org/archive/lenin/works/1921/oct/17.htm. [Accessed 23 March 2013].

CHAPTER 7

1 Much of this chapter was first published as 'Voroshilov's 'Lightning' War – The Soviet Invasion of Poland, September 1939', in *JSMS*, Volume 29, Number 3 (2014), pp.404–19.
2 Order no. 005 of the Military Council of the Belorussian Front, 16 September 1939, Smolensk, in Anna M. Cienciala et al (eds.), *Katyn: A Crime without Punishment* (Annals of Communism) (New Haven and London: Yale Univer-sity Press, 2007), pp.42–3.

3 Jan T. Gross, *Revolution from Abroad: The Soviet Conquest of Poland's Western Ukraine and Western Belorussia*. Expanded Edition (Princeton and Oxford: Princeton University Press, 2002), pp.20 and 29.

4 For example V.A. Radzivanovich, *Pod pol'skim orlom* (Moscow: Voenizdat, 1959).

5 The many works of Czesław Grzelak serve here as an example, where his *Szack-Wytyczno 1939* (Warsaw: Dom Wydawniczy Bellona, 2001) has been referred to in this chapter.

6 Steven Zaloga and Victor Madej, *The Polish Campaign 1939* (New York: Hippocrene Books inc., 1985) is regularly cited, and perhaps the most significant English-language work to date on Polish resistance to Germany in September 1939, but provides relatively little information on the Soviet invasion and does not unfortunately reference sources.

7 Klaus A. Maier et al, *Germany and the Second World War, Volume 2: Germany's Initial Conquests in Europe* (Oxford: Oxford University Press, 1991), pp.118–9, referring to Janusz Piekalkiewicz, *Der Zweite Weltkrieg* (Düsseldorf: Econ, 1985), and *Polenfeldzug: Hitler und Stalin zerschlagen die polnische Republik* (Bergisch-Gladbach : G. Lübbe, 1982).

8 Mikhail Mel'tiukhov, *Sovetsko-pol'skie voini*. 2-e izd. Ispr. i dop. (Moscow: "Iauza", "Eksmo", 2004).

9 Gerhard L. Weinberg, *A World At Arms: A Global History of World War* (Cambridge: Cambridge University Press, 1994), p.57.

10 A.K. Sul'ianov et al, *Krasnoznamennii Belorusskii voennii okrug*. 2-e izd., ispr., dop. (Moscow: Voenizdat, 1983), p.80.

11 Order of the Commander in Chief of the Polish Army, Marshal Edward Śmigły-Rydz, Regarding the Entry of Soviet forces into Poland, 17 September 1939, Kuty, in Anna M. Cienciala et al (eds.), *Katyn: A Crime without Punishment*, p.48.

12 Testimony of Vasilii Danilov Kirdiakin. http://iremember.ru/artilleristi/kirdya kin-vasiliy-danilovich.html [Accessed 7 May 2013].

13 Iakovlev, *Ob artillerii i nemnogo o sebe*, p.39.

14 Testimony of Ivan Valdimirovich Maslov. http//iremember.ru//tankisti/maslov-ivan-vladimirovich.html [Accessed 7 May 2013].

15 Report of the USSR Deputy People's Commissar of Defense, Army Commander 1st Rank Grigory Kulik, on the Actions of Red Army Units and Formations in Western Ukraine..., 21 September 1939, Stanisławów, in Anna M. Cienciala et al (eds.), *Katyn: A Crime without Punishment*, pp.56–7.

16 N.N. Voronov, *Na sluzhbe voennoi* (Moscow: Voennoe izdatel'stvo Ministerstva oboroni SSSR, 1963), p.133.

17 A.N. Sakharov and V.S. Khristoforov (gen.eds.), *K 70-letiiu nachala Vtoroi mirovoi voini. Issledovaniia, dokumenti, kommentarii* (Moscow: Institut rossiiskoi istorii RAN, 2009), p.202.

18 Jan T. Gross, *Revolution from Abroad*, pp.17–18. See also Halik Kochanski, *The Eagle Unbowed: Poland and the Poles in the Second World War* (London/New York: Allen Lane, 2012), pp.79–80.

19 See for example Jan T. Gross, *Revolution from Abroad*, p.18; Mikhail Mel'tiukhov, *Sovetsko-pol'skie voini*, p.466; and Kochanski, *The Eagle Unbowed*, p.79.

20 Jan T. Gross, *Revolution from Abroad*, p.23.
21 I.N. Russiianov, *V boiakh rozhdennaia…*(Moscow: Voenizdat, 1982), pp.3–5.
22 Testimony of Aleksei Andreevich Shilin. http://iremember.ru/tankisti/shilin-aleksey-andreevich.html [Accessed 7 May 2013].
23 Mel'tiukhov, *Sovetsko-pol'skie voini*, pp.485–6.
24 Ibid., p.487 and A.V. Antosiak, 'Osvobozhdenie Zapadnoi Ukraini i Zapadnoi Belorussii', in *Vizh*, Number 9 (1989), p.56.
25 Kochanski, *The Eagle Unbowed*, p.80.
26 Mel'tiukhov, *Sovetsko-pol'skie voini*, p.473.
27 Ibid., pp.473–6.
28 G.F.Krivosheev et al, *Soviet Casualties and Combat Losses*, p.58.
29 Sprawozdanie gen. bryg. Wilhelma Orlika- Rückermanna, dowódcy KOP, bez daty (praw-dopodobnie koniec lutego – początek marca 1940), in Ryszard Szawłowski (ed.), *Wojna Polsko-Sowiecka 1939… Tom 2* (Warsaw: 1995), pp.108–9. Thanks to my PhD student Keith Hann for providing a translation of part of Rückermann's description of this engagement.
30 See Mel'tiukhov, *Sovetsko-pol'skie voini*, pp.518–20 and Czesław Grzelak, *Szack-Wytyczno 1939*, pp.148–64.
31 Russiianov, *V boiakh rozhdennaia…*, p.5.
32 Mel'tiukhov, *Sovetsko-polskie voini*, p.519.
33 Mel'tiukhov, *Sovetsko-polskie voini*, pp.519–20, and Grzelak, *Szack-Wytyczno 1939*, p.167.
34 Russiianov, *V boiakh rozhdennaia…*, pp.3–4.
35 Sakharov and Khristoforov (gen.eds.), *K 70-letiiu nachala Vtoroi mirovoi voini*, p.188.
36 Ibid., p.201.
37 See for example Doklad Voennogo soveta 1-i Armeiskoi gruppi Narkomu oboroni ob organizatsii razvedki v raione r. Khalkhin-Gol, 16 iiunia 1939 g., in V.A. Gavrilov (ed.), *Voennaia razvedka informiruet. Dokumenti Razvedupravleniia Krasnoi Armii. Ianvar' 1939-iiun' 1941 g.* (Moscow: Mezhdunarodnii fond "Demokratiia", 2008), p.158.
38 F.I. Golikov, general-leitenant, zamestitel' nachal'nika General'nogo shtaba Krasnoi Armii, nachal'nik Razvedivatel'nogo upravleniia, in V.A. Zolotarev (gen.ed.), *Nakanune voini Materiali soveshchaniia visshego rukovodiashchego sostava RKKA 23–31 dekabria 1940 g. RA T. 12 (1)*, p.166.
39 A.V. Egorov, *S veroi v pobedu (zapiski komandira tankovogo polka)* (Moscow: Voenizdat, 1974), p.7.
40 Testimony of Petr Veniaminovich Bobrov http://prukvo.ru/Bobrov.php [Accessed 18 May 2013].
41 Sakharov and Khristoforov (gen.eds.), *K 70-letiiu nachala Vtoroi mirovoi voini*, pp.183–4.
42 Testimony of Petr Veniaminovich Bobrov. http://prukvo.ru/Bobrov.php [Accessed 18 May 2013] and Sakharov and Khristoforov (gen.eds.), *K 70-letiiu nachala Vtoroi mirovoi voini*, p.184.
43 Andriy Rukkas, 'The Red Army's Troop Mobilization in the Kiev Special Military District during September 1939', in *JSMS*, Volume 16, Number 1 (March 2003), p.113.

44 Jan T. Gross, *Revolution from Abroad*, p.19.

45 Ibid., pp.19 and 25–6.

46 Ibid., pp.27–8.

47 V.S. Mil'bakh, 'Artilleriia Krasnoi Armii v pokhode v Zapadnuiu Ukrainu i Zapadnuiu Belorussiiu v 1939 godu', in *Vizh*, Number 9 (2014), pp.48–9.

48 Rukkas, 'The Red Army's Troop Mobilizatio', pp.105–6.

49 S.M. Shtemenko, *General'nii shtab v godi voini. Ot Stalingrad do Berlina* (Moscow: AST/Tranzitkniga, 2005), pp.18–19. Also see Rukkas, 'The Red Army's Troop Mobilization', pp.105–6, 112.

50 Rukkas, 'The Red Army's Troop Mobilization', p.109.

51 Ibid., pp.108–10.

52 Sakharov and Khristoforov (gen.eds.), *K 70-letiiu nachala Vtoroi mirovoi voini*, p.156.

53 Rukkas, 'The Red Army's Troop Mobilization', pp.122–3.

54 V.S. Mil'bakh, 'Artilleriia Krasnoi Armii v pokhode v Zapadnuiu Ukrainu i Zapadnuiu Belorussiiu v 1939 godu', p.46.

55 Rukkas, 'The Red Army's Troop Mobilization', pp.110–11, 118.

56 'Nationalism and 'General Mud' are on the Polish Side', in *Life*, Volume 7, Number 9 (28 August 1939), p.12.

57 I.V. Kovalev, *Transport v Velikoi Otechestvennoi voine (1941–1945 gg.)* (Moscow: Nauka, 1981), pp.23–4.

58 Iakovlev, *Ob artillerii i nemnogo o sebe*, p.38.

59 Sakharov and Khristoforov (gen.eds.), *K 70-letiiu nachala Vtoroi mirovoi voini*, p.163.

60 Shtemenko, *General'nii shtab v godi voini. Ot Stalingrad do Berlina*, p.22.

61 N.N. Voronov, *Na sluzhbe voennoi*, p.133.

62 Rukkas, 'The Red Army's Troop Mobilization', p.121.

63 A.S. Stepanov, 'Pol'skaia kampanii 1939 goda – pervii opit primeneniia VVS Krasnoi Armii vo Vtoroi Mirovoi voine', in *Vestnik Sankt-Peterburgskogo Universiteta*, Ser.2. 2008. Vip.3, pp.50, 52.

64 Sakharov and Khristoforov (gen.eds.), *K 70-letiiu nachala Vtoroi mirovoi voini*, p.202.

65 A.S. Stepanov, *Razvitie sovetskoi aviatsii v predvoennii period (1938 god – pervaia polovina 1941 goda)* (Moscow: Russkii fond sodeistviia obrazovaniiu i nauke, 2009), pp.520–1.

66 A.S. Stepanov, 'Pol'skaia kampanii 1939 goda', p.53.

67 Testimony of Nikolai Ivanovich Petrov. http://iremember.ru/letchiki-istrebi teli/petrov-nikolay-ivanovich.html [Accessed 7 May 2013].

68 A.S. Stepanov, 'Pol'skaia kampanii 1939 goda', p.53.

69 See Karl-Heinz Friesner with John T. Greenwood, *The Blitzkrieg Legend: The 1940 Campaign in the West* (Annapolis, MD: Naval Institute Press, 2005), p.62.

70 Shtemenko, *General'nii shtab v godi voini. Ot Stalingrad do Berlina*, pp.23–4.

71 V.S. Mil'bakh, 'Artilleriia Krasnoi Armii v pokhode v Zapadnuiu Ukrainu i Zapadnuiu Belorussiiu v 1939 godu', p.49.

CHAPTER 8

1 On the diplomatic and strategic background to the war, see Carl van Dyke, *The Soviet Invasion of Finland, 1939–1940* (London/Portland, OR: Frank Cass, 1997), chapter 1.
2 Ibid., p.39.
3 E.N. Kul'kov and O.A. Rzheshevskii (gen.eds.), *Zimnaia voina 1939–1940. Kniga vtoraia. I.V. Stalin i finskaia kampaniia (Stenogramma sovershchaniia pri TsK VKP(b))* (Moscow: Nauka, 1999), p.180.
4 Sakharov and Khristoforov (gen.eds.), *K 70-letiiu nachala Vtoroi mirovoi voini*, p.388.
5 E.E. Mal'tsev, *V godi ispitanii* (Moscow: Voennoe izdatel'stvo Ministerstva oboroni SSSR, 1979), p.43.
6 M.I. Lukinov, 'Notes on the Polish Campaign (1939) and the War with Finland (1939–1940)', in *JSMS*, Volume 14, Number 3 (September 2001), p.134.
7 Analiticheskii obzor komandovaniia 36-i motostrelkvoi divizii ob osobennostiakh taktiki protivnika v boiu i nedostatkakh v deistviiakh divizii v iule 1939 g., 15 avgusta 1939 g., in A.R. Efimenko et al (eds.), *Vooruzhennii konflikt v raione reki Khalkhin-Gol*, p.298.
8 E.N. Kul'kov and O.A.Rzheshevskii (gen.eds.), *Zimnaia voina 1939–1940. Kniga vtoraia*, p.147.
9 M.I. Lukinov, 'Notes on the Polish Campaign (1939) and the War with Finland (1939–1940)', p.136.
10 Testimony of Ivan Vladimirovich Maslov, in A.V. Drabkin (ed.), *Ia dralsia na T-34. Obe knigi odnim tomom!* (Moscow: Iauza/Eksmo, 2010), p.394.
11 Temperatures for the Karelian Isthmus were recorded on a daily basis for the Karelian Isthmus by commander of the Finnish IInd Army Corps. See Evgenii Balashov (ed.), *Prinimai nas Suomi krasavitsa! "Osvoboditel'nii" pokhod v Finlandiiu 1939–1940 gg. (Sbornik dokumentov i fotomaterialov). Chast' I* (St Petersburg: OOO "Galeia Print", 1999), p.181.
12 Carl van Dyke, *The Soviet Invasion of Finland*, pp.192–3.
13 Ibid., p.107.
14 K.A. Meretskov, *Na sluzhbe narodu. Stranitsi vospominanii* (Moscow: Izdatel'stvo politicheskoi literaturi, 1968), p.181.
15 Sakharov and Khristoforov(gen.eds.), *K 70-letiiu nachala Vtoroi mirovoi voini*, p.266.
16 Evgenii Balashov (ed.), *Prinimai nas Suomi krasavitsa!. . .Chast' I*, pp.248–9.
17 Carl van Dyke,*The Soviet Invasion of Finland*, p.86.
18 O.A. Dudorova (ed.), 'Neizvestnie stranitsi "zimnei voini"', in *Vizh*, Number 9 (1991), p.13.
19 Ibid.
20 Carl van Dyke,*The Soviet Invasion of Finland*, pp.88–9.
21 Ibid., p.88.
22 Evgenii Balashov (ed.), *Prinimai nas Suomi krasavitsa!. . .Chast' I*, p.252.
23 O.A. Dudorova (ed.), 'Neizvestnie stranitsi"zimnei voini"', p.13.
24 Ibid.
25 Carl van Dyke,*The Soviet Invasion of Finland*, p.88.

26 David Glantz, *Soviet Military Intelligence in War* (Abingdon, Oxon/New York: Frank Cass, 1990), p.29.
27 E.N. Kul'kov and O.A. Rzheshevskii (gen.eds.), *Zimnaia voina 1939–1940. Kniga vtoraia*, pp.203–4.
28 K.A. Meretskov, *Na sluzhbe narodu*, p.182.
29 Erickson, *The Soviet High Command*, p.544.
30 Carl van Dyke, *The Soviet Invasion of Finland*, p.214, note 11. See also Vasilevskii's testimony on the matter, in Simonov, *Glazami cheloveka moego pokoleniia*, pp.442–3. At this time Vasilevskii was deputy head of the Operational Board of the General Staff and was involved in the formulation of the initial, more resource-intensive plan submitted by Shaposhnikov.
31 E.N. Kul'kov and O.A. Rzheshevskii (gen.eds.), *Zimnaia voina 1939–1940. Kniga vtoraia*, pp.149 and 203.
32 Ibid., p.203.
33 Ibid., p.149.
34 In the literature, see for example K.V. Iakimovich, *Na flange linii Mannergeima. Bitva za Taipale* (Moscow: Veche, 2010), p.21.
35 E.N. Kul'kov and O.A. Rzheshevskii (gen.eds.), *Zimnaia voina 1939–1940. Kniga vtoraia*, pp.205–7.
36 Narodnii Komissariat Oboroni Soiuza SSR, *Vremennii Polevoi Ustav RKKA 1936 (PU 36)*, p.21.
37 E.N. Kul'kov and O.A. Rzheshevskii (gen.eds.), *Zimnaia voina 1939–1940. Kniga vtoraia*, pp.151 and 210.
38 David Glantz, *Soviet Military Intelligence in War*, pp.21–2 and 29.
39 Narodnii Komissariat Oboroni Soiuza SSR, *Vremennii Polevoi Ustav RKKA 1936 (PU 36)*, p.22.
40 F.I. Golikov, general-leitenant, zamestitel' nachal'nika General'nogo shtaba Krasnoi Armii, nachal'nik Razvedivatel'nogo upravleniia, in *RA T.12(1)*, p.166.
41 A.S. Stepanov, *Razvitie sovetskoi aviatsii v predvoennii period*, pp.522–3.
42 See Narodnii Komissariat Oboroni Soiuza SSR, *Proekt Polevoi Ustav RKKA (PU 36)* (Moscow: Gosudarstvennoe voennoe izdatel'stvo Narkomata Oboroni Soiuza SSR, 1939), chapter 6.
43 Narodnii Komissariat Oboroni Soiuza SSR, *Vremennii Polevoi Ustav RKKA 1936 (PU 36)*, pp.25–6.
44 E.N. Kul'kov and O.A. Rzheshevskii (gen.eds.), *Zimnaia voina 1939–1940. Kniga vtoraia*, pp.151 and 210.
45 A. Sobolev, *Razvedka boem. Zapiski voiskovogo razvedchika* (Moscow: Moskovskii rabochii, 1975), p.45.
46 E.N. Kul'kov and O.A Rzheshevskii (gen.eds.), *Zimnaia voina 1939–1940. Kniga vtoraia*, p.149.
47 Carl van Dyke, *The Soviet Invasion of Finland*, pp.109–10.
48 E.E. Mal'tsev, *V godi ispitanii*, pp.44–5.
49 E.N. Kul'kov and O.A. Rzheshevskii (gen.eds.), *Zimnaia voina 1939–1940. Kniga vtoraia*, pp.210–11.
50 Formed on 7 January 1940.
51 Meropriiatiia Finlandii nakanune voini: razvedivatel'naia svodka shtaba Leningradskogo voennogo okruga, 9 oktiabria 1939 g., in V.A. Gavrilov

(ed.), *Voennaia razvedka informiruet*, p.196; E.N. Kul'kov and O.A. Rzheshevskii (gen.eds.), *Zimnaia voina 1939–1940. Kniga vtoraia*, p.211.

52 See Generalmajor Hellmuth Reinhardt, *Size and Composition of Divisional and Higher Staffs in the German Army* (Foreign Military Studies MS No. P-139) (Historical Division, Headquarters, US Army, Europe, 1954), pp.7–8, 18–19.

53 E.N. Kul'kov and O.A. Rzheshevskii (gen.eds.), *Zimnaia voina 1939–1940. Kniga vtoraia*, p.207.

54 A.F. Khrenov, *Mosti k pobede* (Moscow: Voennoe izdatel'stvo Ministerstvo oboroni SSSR, 1982), pp.47, 49.

55 Testimony of Ivan Vladimirovich Maslov, in A.V. Drabkin (ed.), *Ia dralsia na T-34*, p.394.

56 A.F. Khrenov, *Mosti k pobede*, p.48.

57 Testimony of Aleksei Andreevich Shilin. http://iremember.ru/tankisti/shilin-aleksey-andreevich.html [Accessed 7 May 2013]; M.I. Lukinov, 'Notes on the Polish Campaign (1939) and the War with Finland (1939–1940)', p.143.

58 M.I. Lukinov, 'Notes on the Polish Campaign (1939) and the War with Finland (1939–1940)', pp.141–2.

59 Carl van Dyke, *The Soviet Invasion of Finland*, p.112.

60 K.A. Meretskov, *Na sluzhbe narodu*, p.184.

61 Carl van Dyke, *The Soviet Invasion of Finland*, pp.35, 38.

62 E.N. Kul'kov and O.A. Rzheshevskii (gen.eds.), *Zimnaia voina 1939–1940. Kniga vtoraia*, p.166.

63 Earlier in the conference Stalin had suggested that when talking about modern war 'the matter is decided by artillery'. E.N. Kul'kov and O.A Rzheshevskii (gen.eds.), *Zimnaia voina 1939–1940 Kniga vtoraia*, pp.109, 278.

64 K.A. Meretskov, *Na sluzhbe narodu*, p.184.

65 Marshal Mannerheim, *The Memoirs of Marshal Mannerheim* (New York: E.P. Dutton and Company, inc., 1954), p.368.

66 V.N. Shunkov, *Artilleriia Krasnoi Armii i Vermakhta Vtoroi mirovoi voini*, pp.75–8.

67 Carl van Dyke, *The Soviet Invasion of Finland*, pp.112–14.

68 M.I. Lukinov, 'Notes on the Polish Campaign (1939) and the War with Finland (1939–1940)', p.140.

69 See for example, N.N. Voronov, *Na sluzhbe voennoi*, pp.144–50.

70 M.I. Lukinov, 'Notes on the Polish Campaign(1939) and the War with Finland (1939–1940)', p.140.

71 E.N. Kul'kov and O.A.Rzheshevskii (gen.eds.), *Zimnaia voina 1939–1940. Kniga vtoraia*, pp.130–1.

72 K.A. Meretskov, *Na sluzhbe narodu*, p.187.

73 E.N. Kul'kov and O.A. Rzheshevskii (gen.eds.), *Zimnaia voina 1939–1940. Kniga vtoraia*, pp.73, 76–7; M.N. Khlebnikov, *Pod grokhot soten baterei* (Moscow: Voenizdat, 1974), p.86.

74 V.S. Mil'bakh,'Red Army artillery and the armed conflict on the Khalkhin-Gol river', p.

75 E.N. Kul'kov and O.A. Rzheshevskii (gen.eds.), *Zimnaia voina 1939–1940. Kniga vtoraia*, p.75.

76 V.N. Novikov (gen.ed.), *Oruzhie pobedi* (Moscow: "Mashinostroenie", 1987), p.118.

77 E.N. Kul'kov and O.A. Rzheshevskii (gen.eds.), *Zimnaia voina 1939–1940. Kniga vtoraia*, p.75.

78 V.N Shunkov, *Artilleriia Krasnoi Armii i Vermakhta Vtoroi mirovoi voini*, pp.227–8.

79 V.N. Novikov (gen.ed.), *Oruzhie pobedi*, pp.123–4; V.N. Shunkov, *Artilleriia Krasnoi Armii i Vermakhta Vtoroi mirovoi voini*, p.231.

80 V.N. Shunkov, *Artilleriia Krasnoi Armii i Vermakhta Vtoroi mirovoi voini*, p.224; V.N. Novikov (gen.ed.), *Oruzhie pobedi*, p.126.

81 K.A. Meretskov, *Na sluzhbe narodu*, p.185.

82 Carl van Dyke, *The Soviet Invasion of Finland*, p.51.

83 Ibid., pp.68–9.

84 E.N. Kul'kov and O.A. Rzheshevskii (gen.eds.), *Zimnaia voina 1939–1940. Kniga vtoraia*, pp.108–9.

85 K.A. Meretskov, *Na sluzhbe narodu*, pp.185–6.

86 M.I. Lukinov, 'Notes on the Polish Campaign (1939) and the War with Finland (1939–1940)', p.140.

87 Carl van Dyke, *The Soviet Invasion of Finland*, p.113.

88 E.N. Kul'kov and O.A. Rzheshevskii (gen.eds.), *Zimnaia voina 1939–1940. Kniga vtoraia*, p.84.

89 Ibid., p.83.

90 M.I. Lukinov, 'Notes on the Polish Campaign (1939) and the War with Finland (1939–1940)', p.140.

91 E.N. Kul'kov and O.A Rzheshevskii (gen.eds.), *Zimnaia voina 1939–1940. Kniga vtoraia*, p.83.

92 K.A. Meretskov, *Na sluzhbe narodu*, p.185.

93 E.N. Kul'kov and O.A. Rzheshevskii (gen.eds.), *Zimnaia voina 1939–1940. Kniga vtoraia*, p.135

94 James Sterrett, *Soviet Air Force Theory, 1918–1945* (Abingdon, Oxon/New York: Routledge, 2007), p.71.

95 Carl van Dyke, *The Soviet Invasion of Finland*, p.201.

96 E.N. Kul'kov and O.A. Rzheshevskii (gen.eds.), *Zimnaia voina 1939–1940. Kniga vtoraia*, p.135.

97 Ibid., p.85.

98 James Sterrett, *Soviet Air Force Theory, 1918–1945*, p.72.

99 A.S. Stepanov, *Razvitie sovetskoi aviatsii v predvoennii period*, p.523.

100 Ibid.

101 James Sterrett, *Soviet Air Force Theory, 1918–1945*, pp.71–2.

102 Ilmari Iutilainen [Ilmari Juutilainen], *Ia bil "stalinskikh sokolov". Luchshii finskii as Vtoroi Mirovoi* (Moscow: Iauza press, 2013), pp.17, 22.

103 A.S. Stepanov, *Razvitie sovetskoi aviatsii v predvoennii period*, p.523.

104 Ibid., p.524.

105 James Sterrett, *Soviet Air Force Theory, 1918–1945*, pp.73–4.

106 Marshal Mannerheim, *The Memoirs of Marshal Mannerheim*, p.369.

107 K.A. Meretskov, *Na sluzhbe narodu*, p.188.

108 A.V. Kazar'ian, *Prisiaga na vsiu zhizn'* (Moscow: Voennoe izdatel'stvo, 1988), p.15; Evgenii Balashov (ed.), *Prinimai nas Suomi krasavitsa!...Chast' I*, p.250.

109 A.V. Kazar'ian, *Prisiaga na vsiu zhizn'*, pp.15–17.

110 Carl van Dyke, *The Soviet Invasion of Finland*, pp.115–17.

111 V.V. Bakhirev and I.I. Kirillov, *Konstruktor V.A. Degtiarev: Za strokami biografii* (Moscow: Voenizdat, 1979), pp.105–7 and V.N. Novikov (gen. ed.), *Oruzhie pobedi*, p.251.

112 Bakhirev and Kirillov, *Konstruktor V.A. Degtiarev*, p.107.

113 Ibid., pp.107–111 and V.N. Novikov (gen.ed.), *Oruzhie pobedi*, pp.251–2.

114 F.F. Viktorov (gen.ed.), *Istoriia Ordena Lenina Leningradskogo voennogo okruga* (Moscow: Voennoe izdatel'stvo Ministerstva oboroni SSSR, 1974), pp.161, 165.

115 This final paragraph of the report was apparently omitted from Stalin's copy. Iu. G. Murin (ed.), 'Uroki voini s Finlandiei. Neopublikovannii doklad narkoma oboroni SSSR K.E. Voroshilova na plenume TsK VKP(b), 28 marta 1940 g.', in *Novaia i noveishaia istoriia*, Number 4(1993), p.122.

116 Roger R. Reese, 'Lessons of the Winter War: A Study in the Military Effectiveness of the Red Army, 1939–1940', in *Journal of Military History*, Volume 72, Number 3 (July 2008), p.850.

117 Ibid., p.826.

118 Carl van Dyke, *The Soviet Invasion of Finland*, p.88.

119 G.F. Krivosheev (ed.), *Soviet Casualties and Combat Losses*, pp.65–6, 68, 77.

120 Marshal Mannerheim, *The Memoirs of Marshal Mannerheim*, p.370.

121 58,599 personnel, 1,063 tanks and 154 aircraft, as well as 150 armoured cars, 554 peices of artillery or mortars, and over 5,215 motor vehicles. Mikhail Mel'tiukhov, *Pribaltiiskii platsdarm (1939–1940 gg.). Vozvrashchenie Sovetskogo Soiuza na berega Baltiiskogo moria* (Moscow: Izdatel'stvo Algoritm, 2014), p.233.

122 Ibid., p.339.

123 Including those Soviet forces already in the Baltic Republics, no fewer than 541,722 personnel, 7,158 guns and mortars, 3,938 tanks, 720 armoured cars and 26,816 motor vehicles. Ibid., p.353.

124 According to Russian historian Mikhail Mel'tiukhov in statistics compiled from Russian archival and other sources, the three Baltic Republics could field a total peacetime force of approximately 73,000 – in the region of 427,000 in wartime. Ninety-five tanks, 41 armoured cars and 292 aircraft could be fielded along with 1,546 pieces of artillery of various calibres. Ibid., p.358.

125 Ibid., pp.456, 512–13.

CHAPTER 9

1 Avram Lytton, *In the House of Rimmon: British Aid to the Soviet Union, June-September 1941*. Unpublished thesis, University of Calgary, September 2012, pp.18–19.

2 Oberkommando des Heeres. O Qu IV GenStdH Abt. Frd. Heere Ost (IId). Nr. 3535/40 geh. H.Qu., den 2.10.1940. Erfahrung aus dem finnisch-russischen Kriege. TsAMO f.500. o.12451.d.271.ll.1–8. See also Horst Boog et al, *Germany and the Second World War. Volume IV. The Attack on the Soviet Union* (Oxford: Clarendon Press, 1998), p.233.

3 Oberkommando des Heeres. GenStdH O Qu IV - Abt. fremde Heere Ost (II). Nr. 100/41 geh. H.Qu.O.K.H, den 15 Januar 1941. Die Kriegswehrmacht der Union der Sozialistischen Sowjetrepubliken (UdSSR). Stand 1.1.1941. Teil I., pp.61, 65, 72. TsAMO f.500.o.12451.d.279. See also Andreas Hillgruber, 'The German Military Leaders' View of Russia prior to the Attack on the Soviet Union', in Bernd Wegner (ed.), *From Peace to War: Germany, Soviet Russia and the World, 1939–1941* (Oxford: Berghann Books, 1997), pp.179–80.

4 Horst Boog et al, *Germany and the Second World War. Volume IV*, p.233 and Andreas Hillgruber, 'The German Military Leaders' View of Russia...', p.178.

5 Oberkommando des Heeres. Gen St d H. O Qu IV – Abt. Fremde Heere Ost.... Nr 1951/41 geh. H.Qu., den 17.5.1941. Betr.: Die russische Panzerwaffe. United States National Archives (NARA), T-315, Roll 206, frame 00077.

6 Prikaz s ob"iavleniem ukazov...o naznachenii K.E. Voroshilova Zamestitelem predsedatelia SNK SSSR i predsedatelem Komiteta oboroni pri SNK SSSR, S.K. Timoshenko – Narkomom oboroni SSSR, 8 maia 1940 g., in *RA T.13 (2–1)*, pp.132–3 and Carl van Dyke, *The Soviet Invasion of Finland*, p.203.

7 *Pravda*, 8 May 1940, p.1.

8 Carl van Dyke, *The Soviet Invasion of Finland*, p.203.

9 Oleg Rzheshevsii, 'Shaposhnikov', in Harold Shukman (ed.), *Stalin's Generals* (London: Weidenfeld and Nicholson, 1993), p.225.

10 E.N. Kul'kov and O.A. Rzheshevskii (gen.eds.), Zimniaia voina 1939–1940. Kniga vtoraia, p.277.

11 Ibid.,, pp.278–9 and *Pravda*, 8 May 1940, p.1.

12 N.N. Voronov, *Na sluzhbe voennoi*, p.166.

13 N.G. Kuznetsov, *Nakanune*, p.244.

14 Akt priema Narkomata oboroni SSSR S.K. Timoshenko ot K.E. Voroshilova, undated, in *RA T.13 (2–1)*, pp.301–2. A version of this document is also reproduced in Iurii Veremeev, *Povsednevnaia zhizn' vermakhta i RKKA nakanune voini* (Moscow: Eksmo/Algoritm, 2011), pp.34–63.

15 Prikaz o boevoi i politicheskoi podgotovke voisk v letnii period 1940 uchebnogo goda, 16 maia 1940 g., in *RA T.13 (2–1)*, pp.134–48.

16 Testimony of Mel'nikov Ignatii Grigor'evich. http://iremember.ru/zenitchiki/melnikov-ignatiy-grigorevich.html [accessed 19 January 2014].

17 Testimony of Osintsev Nikolai Nikolaevich. http://iremember.ru/zenitchiki/osintsev-nikolay-nikolaevich/stranitsa-3.html [accessed 19 January 2014].

18 Prikaz o boevoi i politicheskoi podgotovke voisk v letnii period 1940 uchebnogo goda, 16 maia 1940 g., in *RA T.13 (2–1)*, p.148.

19 Prikaz s ob"iavleniem ukaza Prezidiuma verkhovnogo soveta SSSR "Ob ustanovlenii voinskikh zvanii visshego komandnogo sostava Krasnoi armii", 8 maia 1940 g., in ibid., pp.133–4.

20 Prikaz on ustanovlenii voinskikh zvanii dlia riadovogo i mladshego nachal'stvuiushchego sostava Krasnoi armii..., 2 noiabria 1940 goda, in ibid., pp.188–9.

21 Prikaz s ob"iavleniem ukaza Prezidium verkhovnogo soveta SSSR "Ob ukre-
    plenii edinonachaliia v Krasnoi armii i Voenno-morskom flote", 14 avgusta
    1940 g., in ibid., p.163.
22 Postanovlenie TsK VKP(b) i SNK SSSR "O peredache Osobogo otdela iz
    NKVD SSSR v vedenie Narkomata oboroni i Narkomata voenno-morskogo
    flota SSSR", 8 fevralia 1941 g., in V.N.Khaustov et al (eds.), *Lubianka. Stalin
    i NKVD-NKGB-GUKR "Smersh". 1939–1946. Dokumenti...* (Moscow:
    Mezhdunarodnii fond "Demokratiia"/izdatel'stvo "Materik", 2006), p.240.
23 Prikaz o vvedenii v deistvie distsiplinarnogo ustava Krasnoi armii, 12 oktiabria
    1940 g., in *RA T.13 (2–1)*, p.181.
24 Testimony of Osintsev Nikolai Nikolaevich. http://iremember.ru/zenitchiki/
    osintsev-nikolay-nikolaevich/stranitsa-4.html [accessed 19 January 2014].
25 Direktiva voennim sovetam okrugov (fronta) o rezul'tatakh inspektirovaniia
    Zapadnogo osobogo voennogo okruga, 27 sentiabria 1940 g., in *RA T.13
    (2–1)*, pp.176–7.
26 Prikaz o rezul'tatkh osennikh inspektorskikh smotrov shtabov i voisk riada
    voennikh okrugov i Dal'nevostochnogo fronta, 6 noiabria, 1940 g., in ibid.,
    pp.193–4.
27 Komanduiushchim voiskami okrugov i DVF. Nachal'niku Glavnogo avto-
    bronetank. upr. KA. 30 ianvaria 1941 goda. p.p. ...S. Timoshenko....K
    Meretskov. TsAMO f.38.o.11351.d.5.l.218.
28 Ibid., ll.225–6.
29 L.M. Sandalov, *Perezhitoe* (Moscow: Voennoe izdatel'stvo Ministerstva obor-
    oni SSSR, 1966), pp.66–7.
30 For data on the Red Army in this regard, see David Glantz, *Stumbling
    Colossus: The Red Army on the Eve of World War* (Lawrence, Kansas: Univer-
    sity Press of Kansas, 1998), p.55 and later.
31 A.G. Tsimbalov, 'Za chto postradal General-leitenant aviatsii P.I. Pumpir v
    mae 1941 goda', in *Vizh*, No, 12 (2006), pp.33–41.
32 Prikaz o boevoi i politicheskoi podgotovke voisk v letnii period 1940 ucheb-
    nogo goda, 16 maia 1940 g., in *RA T.13 (2–1)*, p.135.
33 N.G. Kuznetsov, *Nakanune*, p.245.
34 Konstantin Simonov, *Glazami cheloveka moego pokoleniia*, p.402.
35 See for example T.V. Bortakovskii, *Rasstrelianie geroi Sovetskogo soiuza*,
    pp.124–6, 156–9, 214–15.
36 Nikolai Kuznetsov's 1966 memoirs *Nakanune* – written during a relatively
    liberal period in Soviet historical writing under Nikita Khrushchev's premier-
    ship – are something of a hall of fame for the apparently capable fallen – both
    those lost in 1936–1938 and indeed in to 1941.
37 See for example M.V. Zakharov, *General'nii shtab v predvoennie godi*, p.178.
38 Doklad narkoma oboroni SSSR K.E. Voroshilova v Politburo TsK VKP(b)
    I.V. Stalinu i v SNK SSSR V.M. Molotovu ob osnovakh reorganizatsii
    Krasnoi Armii, 15 noiabria 1939 g., in .N. Bobilev (gen.ed.) et al, *Glavnii
    voennii sovet RKKA. 13 marta 1938–20 iiunia 1941 gg.*, p.444.
39 See Chapter 4, p.85.
40 Doklad narkoma oboroni SSSR K.E. Voroshilova v Politburo TsK VKP(b)
    I.V. Stalinu i v SNK SSSR V.M. Molotovu ob osnovakh reorganizatsii

Krasnoi Armii, 15 noiabria 1939 g., in P.N. Bobilev (gen.ed.) et al, *Glavnii voennii sovet RKKA. 13 marta 1938–20 iiunia 1941 gg.*, pp.441–4.

41 Vopros Narkomata oboroni, 6 iiulia 1940 g., in Iurii Veremeev, *Povsednevnaia zhizn' vermakhta i RKKA nakanune voini*, pp.76–7.

42 M.I. Potapov, general-maior, komandir 4-go mekhanizirovannogo korpusa Kievskogo osobogo voennogo okruga, in *RA T.12(1)*, pp.64–6.

43 M.V. Zakharov, *General'nii shtab v predvoennie godi*, p.188.

44 Akt priema Narkomata oboroni SSSR S.K. Timoshenko ot K.E. Voroshilova, undated, in *RA T.13 (2–1)*, p.304.

45 Prikaz o podgotovke vsekh rodov voisk po radiodelu, 15 fevralia 1941 g., in ibid., p.236.

46 Zapiska NKO SSSR i Genshtaba Krasnoi armii v Politbiuro TsK VKP(b) – I.V. Stalinu i SNK SSSR – V.M. Molotovu s izlozheniem skhemi mobilizatsionnogo razvertivaniia Krasnoi armii, ne pozzhe 1 fevralia 1941 g., in V.P. Naumov (gen.ed.), *1941 god: V 2 kn. Kn.1*, p.622.

47 Spravka o potrebnosi i obespechennosti vooruzheniem sviazi chastei KOVO po sostoianiiu na 10 maia 1941 g., ne pozdnee 10 maia 1941 g., in V.P. Naumov (gen.ed.), *1941 god: V 2 kn. Kn.2*, p.190.

48 M.I. Potapov, general-maior, komandir 4-go mekhanizirovannogo korpusa Kievskogo osobogo voennogo okruga, in *RA T. 12(1)*, p.65.

49 Akt priema Narkomata oboroni SSSR S.K. Timoshenko ot K.E. Voroshilova, undated, in *RA T.13 (2–1)*, p.307.

50 V.N. Shunkov, *Artilleriia Krasnoi Armii i Vermakhta Vtoroi mirovoi voini*, pp.77–8.

51 N.P. Zolotov et al, *Boevoi i chislennii sostav vooruzhennikh sil SSSR v period Velikoi Otechestvennoi voini (1941–1945 gg.). Statisticheskii sbornik No.1 (22 iiunia 1941 g.)* (Moscow: Institut voennoi istorii MO RF, 1994), p.71.

52 A.S. Stepanov, *Razvitie sovetskoi aviatsii v predvoennii period*, pp.434–5 and Yefim Gordon and Dmitri Khazanov, *Soviet Combat Aircraft of the Second World War. Volume Two: Twin-Engined Fighters, Attack Aircraft and Bombers* (Earl Shilton, Leics: Midland Publishing Limited, 1999), pp.44–6 and 164.

53 M.N. Kozhevnikov, *Komandovanie i shtab VVS Sovetskoi Armii v Velikoi Otechestvennoi voine 1941–1945 gg.* (Moscow: Izdatel'stvo "Nauka", 1977), p.16 and N.P. Zolotov et al, *Boevoi i chislennii sostav vooruzhennikh sil SSSR v period Velikoi Otechestvennoi voini (1941–1945 gg.)*, p.249.

54 Protokol No. 4 zasedaniia GVS RKKA, 20 aprelia 1938 g., in in P.N. Bobilev (gen.ed.) et al, *Glavnii voennii sovet RKKA. 13 marta 1938–20 iiunia 1941 gg.*, pp.37–8.

55 N.S. Popov (gen.ed.), *Konstruktor boevikh mashin* (Leningrad: Lenizdat, 1988), p.69.

56 Protokol No. 28 zasedaniia GVS RKKA, 9–10 dekabria 1938 g., in in P.N. Bobilev (gen.ed.) et al, *Glavnii voennii sovet RKKA. 13 marta 1938–20 iiunia 1941 gg.*, p.163.

57 A. G. Soliankin et al, *Otechestvennie bronirovannie mashini. 1905–1941 gg.*, pp.171–2 and N.S. Popov (gen.ed.), *Konstruktor boevikh mashin*, pp.92–4.

58 O.A. Losik (gen.ed.), *Istoriia tankovikh voisk Sovetskoi armii … Tom pervii …(1917–1941 gg.)*, pp.201–3.

59 N.S. Popov (gen.ed.), *Konstruktor boevikh mashin*, p.90 and A. Iu. Ermolov, *Gosudarstvennoe upravlenie voennoi primishlennost'iu v 1940-e godi: Tankovaia promishlennost'* (Saint-Petersburg: Aleteiia, 2013), pp.66, 75.

60 Ob"iasnitel'naia zapiska. K svedeniiam o nalichii boevoi motchasti v Krasnoi Armii po sostoianiiu na 1.2.41 g. 13.2.1941 g. [BTU KA]. TsAMO f.38. o.11355.d.236.l.126.

61 Protokol No. 4 zasedaniia GVS RKKA, 20 aprelia 1938 g., in in P.N. Bobilev (gen.ed.) et al, *Glavnii voenniii sovet RKKA. 13 marta 1938–20 iiunia 1941 gg.*, pp.38–9.

62 Protokol No. 28 zasedaniia GVS RKKA, 9–10 dekabria 1938 g., in ibid., p.162.

63 K.M. Slobodin and V.D. Listrovoi (eds.), *T-34: put' k Pobede: Vospominaniia tankostroitelei i tankistov. 2-e izd., dop.* (Kiev: Politizdat Ukraini, 1989), p.28 and O.A. Losik (gen.ed.), *Istoriia tankovikh voisk Sovetskoi armii ... Tom pervii ...(1917–1941 gg.)* , pp.194–7.

64 K.M. Slobodin and V.D. Listrovoi (eds.), *T-34: put' k Pobede*, pp.29–30, 201–3, 244; O.A. Losik (gen.ed.), *Istoriia tankovikh voisk Sovetskoi armii ... Tom pervii ...(1917–1941 gg.)*, pp.196–7; A. G. Soliankin et al, *Otechestvennie bronirovannie mashini. 1905–1941 gg.*, 129, 144; A. Iu. Ermolov, *Gosudarstvennoe upravlenie voennoi primishlennost'iu v 1940-e godi: Tankovaia promishlennost'*, p.70.

65 O.A. Losik (gen.ed.), *Istoriia tankovikh voisk Sovetskoi armii ... Tom pervii ...(1917–1941 gg.)*, p.197.

66 K.M. Slobodin and V.D. Listrovoi (eds.), *T-34: put' k Pobede*, pp.203–5 and A. Iu. Ermolov, *Gosudarstvennoe upravlenie voennoi primishlennost'iu v 1940-e godi: Tankovaia promishlennost'*, p.66; Alexander Hill, *The Great Patriotic War of the Soviet Union, 1941–1945: A documentary reader*, p.186.

67 Ob"iasnitel'naia zapiska. K svedeniiam o nalichii boevoi motchasti v Krasnoi Armii po sostoianiiu na 1.2.41 g. 13.2.1941 g. [BTU KA]. TsAMO f.38. o.11355.d.236.l.126.

68 A. Ulanov and D. Shein, *Poriadok v tankovikh voiskakh* (Moscow: Veche, 2011), chapter 3.

69 V.N. Novikov (gen.ed.), *Oruzhie pobedi*, pp.158–64.

70 Mikhail Pervov, *Rodilas' v Moskve "Katiusha". Istoricheskii ocherk* (Moscow: Izdatel'skii dom "Stolichnaia entsiklopediia, 2010), pp.84–6.

71 G.K. Zhukov, *Vospominaniia i razmishleniia. ...Tom 1*, p.326.

72 Mikhail Pervov, *Rodilas' v Moskve "Katiusha"*, pp.87–8.

73 A.S. Stepanov, *Razvitie sovetskoi aviatsii v predvoennii period*, pp.324–5.

74 Gordon and Khazanov, *Soviet Combat Aircraft of the Second World War. Volume One: Single-Engined Fighters*, pp.67–9 and Stepanov, *Razvitie sovetskoi aviatsii v predvoennii period*, pp.439–40.

75 M.N. Kozhevnikov, *Komandovanie i shtab VVS Sovetskoi Armii v Velikoi Otechestvennoi voine 1941–1945 gg.*, p.16.

76 Zapiska Nachal'nika GU VVS Krasnoi Armii v TsK VKP(b)- I.V.Stalinu o defektakh samoletov LAGG-3, 27 maia 1941 g., in V.P. Naumov (gen.ed.), *1941 god: V 2 kn. Kn.2*, pp.266–7.

77 Gordon and Khazanov, *Soviet Combat Aircraft of the Second World War. Volume One: Single-Engined Fighters*, pp.24–27 and Stepanov, *Razvitie sovetskoi aviatsii v predvoennii period*, p.440.

78 Gordon and Khazanov, *Soviet Combat Aircraft of the Second World War. Volume One: Single-Engined Fighters*, pp.122–4 and Stepanov, *Razvitie sovetskoi aviatsii v predvoennii period*, pp.440–1.

79 Alexander Hill, *The Great Patriotic War of the Soviet Union, 1941–1945: A documentary reader*, p.28.

80 O.A. Losik (gen.ed.), *Istoriia tankovikh voisk Sovetskoi armii ... Tom pervii ...(1917–1941 gg.)*, pp.212–14.

81 Ob"iasnitel'naia zapiska. K svedeniiam o nalichii boevoi motchasti v Krasnoi Armii po sostoianiiu na 1.2.41 g. 13.2.1941 g. [BTU KA]. Svodnaia vedomost' na 1.II 1941 g. TsAMO f.38.o.11355.d.236.ll.127–8.

82 I.Kh. Bagramian, *Tak nachalas' voina* (Moscow: Voenizdat, 1971), p.75.

83 Ibid., p.66.

84 Tezisi doklada nachal'nika GABTU Glavnomu voennomu sovetu KA po voprosu sistemi organizatsii remonta boevikh i vspomogatel'nikh mashin v voennoe vremia, 28 ianvaria 1941 g., in A.M. Radionov et al (eds.), *Glavnoe avtobronetankovoe upravlenie. Liudi, sobitiia, fakti v dokumentakh – 1940–1942 gg.* (Moscow: GABTU, 2005), pp.16–17.

85 Total Soviet tanks stocks as of 1 June 1941 stood at a staggering 23,106 vehicles, of which 12,782 were in the western military districts. N.P.Zolotov and S.I. Isaev, 'Boegotovi bili... Istoriko-statisticheskoe issledovanie kolichestvenno-kachestvennogo sostoianiia tankovogo parka Krasnoi Armii nakanune Velikoi Otechestvennoi voini', in *Vizh*, Number 11 (1993), pp.76–7.

86 A. Ulanov and D. Shein, *Poriadok v takovikh voiskakh*, p.117.

87 Nachal'niku orgmobotdela shtaba ZapOVO, 18 iiunia 1941 g., in P.N. Knishevskii (gen.ed.), *Skritaia pravda voini: 1941 god. Neizvestnie dokumenti* (Moscow: "Russkaia kniga", 1992), p.34.

88 Iz direktivi nachal'nika shtaba Kievskogo osobogo voennogo okruga Generalleitenanta M.A. Purkaeva, 29 aprelia 1941 g., in P.N. Knishevskii (gen.ed.), *Skritaia pravda voini: 1941 god*, p.23.

89 N.P. Zolotov et al, *Boevoi i chislennii sostav vooruzhennikh sil SSSR v period Velikoi Otechestvennoi voini (1941–1945 gg.). Statisticheskii sbornik No.1 (22 iiunia 1941 g.)*, p.68.

90 Glavnoe artilleriiskoe upravlenie Krasnoi armii. Upravlenie vooruzheniia nazemnoi artillerii. Otdel 1-i. 16 oktiabria 1940 g. No. 383714 ss. Zamestileliu narodnogo komissara oboroni SSSR Marshalu sovetskogo soiuza t. Kulik. TsAMO f.81.o.12104.d.9.l.284.

91 Thomas L. Jentz (ed.), *Panzertruppen. The Complete Guide to the Creation and Combat Employment of Germany's Tank Force. 1933–1942*, pp.46–7.

92 Aleksei Isaev, 'Goriachii sneg "pakfronta"', in Artem Drabkin, 'Ia dralsia s Pantservaffe', in Artem Drabkin and Petr Mikhin (eds.), *Mi dralis' s "Tigrami"*(Moscow: Iauza/Eksmo, 2010), pp.11–12.

93 B.L. Vannikov, 'Zapiski narkoma', in *Znamia*, Number 1 (1988), pp.139–40; N.P. Zolotov et al, *Boevoi i chislennii sostav vooruzhennikh sil SSSR v period Velikoi Otechestvennoi voini (1941–1945 gg.). Statisticheskii sbornik No.1 (22 iiunia 1941 g.)*, p.73.

94 V.N. Novikov (gen.ed.), *Oruzhie pobedi*, pp.413–14.

95 Glavnoe artilleriiskoe upravlenie Krasnoi armii. Upravlenie vooruzheniia
    nazamnoi artillerii. Otdel 1-i. 16 oktiabria 1940 g. No. 383714 ss. Zames-
    tileliu narodnogo komissara oboroni SSSR Marshalu sovetskogo soiuza t.
    Kulik. TsAMO f.81.o.12104.d.9.l.287.
96 Aleksei Isaev, 'Goriachii sneg "pakfronta"', p.11.
97 Nachal'niku orgmobotdela shtaba ZapOVO, 18 iiunia 1941 g., in P.N.
    Knishevskii (gen.ed.), *Skritaia pravda voini: 1941 god*, p.34.
98 Nachal'niku orgmobotdela shtaba PribOVO, 9 iiunia 1941 g., in ibid., p.33.
99 Ibid., pp.33–4.
100 M.A. Bobrov, 'Strategicheskoe razvertivanie VVS Krasnoi armii na zapade
    strani pered Velikoi Otechestvennoi voinoi', in *Vizh*, No.5 (2006), p.6.
101 L.M. Sandalov, *Na Moskovskom napravlenii* (Moscow: Veche, 2010), p.62.
102 M.A. Bobrov, 'Strategicheskoe razvertivanie VVS Krasnoi armii', pp.4–6
    and Stepanov, *Razvitie sovetskoi aviatsii v predvoennii period*, p.348.
103 N.D. Iakovlev, *Ob artillerii i nemnogo o sebe*, p.55.
104 S.I. Poliakov and S.P. Kopil, *"Liniia Stalina". Polotskii ukrepraion
    1919–1941 gg.* (Polotsk: Polotskoe knizhnoe izdatel'svto, 2009), p.26.
105 N.D. Iakovlev, *Ob artillerii i nemnogo o sebe*, p.55.
106 Vedomost' shtatnoi chislennosti Krasnoi Armii, razvertivaemoi po mobplanu
    1941 goda, v sravnenii s mobplanom 1938–1939 gg. (ne poszhe 12 fevralia
    1941 g.), in V.P. Naumov (gen.ed.), *1941 god: V 2 kn. Kn.1*, p.632.
107 M.V. Zakharov, *General'nii shtab v predvoennie godi*, p.226.
108 Vedomost' shtatnoi chislennosti Krasnoi Armii, razvertivaemoi po mob-
    planu 1941 goda, v sravnenii s mobplanom 1938–1939 gg. (ne poszhe
    12 fevralia 1941 g.), in *V.P. Naumov (gen.ed.), 1941 god: V 2 kn. Kn.1*,
    pp.631–2 and Vedomost' kolichestva osnovnikh chastei i soedinenii Krasnoi
    Armii razvertivaemikh po mobilizatsionnomu planu 1941 goda, po sravne-
    niiu s mobilizatsionnim planom 1938–1939 gg. (ne poszhe 12 fevralia 1941
    g.), in ibid., p.633.
109 Plan strategicheskogo razvertivaniia Krasnoi Armii (mart 1941 goda), in
    Iurii Veremeev, *Krasnaia Armiia v nachale Vtoroi mirovoi: Kak gotovilis' k
    voine soldati i marshali* (Moscow: Eksmo/Algoritm-izdat, 2010), p.130. See
    also V.N. Kiselev (ed.), '...variantov planov strategicheskogo
    razvertivaniia...', in *Vizh*, Number 2 (1992), p.19.
110 Ob"iasnitel'naia zapiska k proektu Zakona o vseobshchei voinskoi obiazan-
    nosti [ne pozdnee 4 iiunia 1939 g.], in P.N. Bobilev (gen.ed.) et al, *Glavnii
    voennii sovet RKKA. 13 marta 1938–20 iiunia 1941 gg.*, pp.430–7. See also
    p.256 n.3.
111 General'nii shtab Krasnoi armii. Mobilizatsionnoe upravlenie.... 31 marta
    1941 g. Voennomu sovetu Zapadnogo osobogo voennogo okruga. TsAMO
    f.38.o.11351.d.5.ll.50–54, and ...Voennomu sovetu Kievskogo osobogo
    voennogo okruga. TsAMO f.38.o.11351.d.5.ll.65–68.
112 David Glantz, *Stumbling Colossus*, pp.102–3.
113 Akt priema Narkomata oboroni SSSR S.K. Timoshenko ot K.E. Voroshi-
    lova, undated, in *RA T.13 (2–1)*, p.301.
114 F.B. Komal, 'Voennie kadri nakanune voini', in *Vizh*, Number 2 (1990),
    p.23.

115 Ibid., p.27.

116 I. Kh. Bagramian, *Tak nachalas' voina*, p.79.

117 F.B. Komal, 'Voennie kadri nakanune voini', p.28.

118 D.D. Leliushenko, *Zaria pobedi* (Moscow: Voennoe izdatel'stvo Minis-
     terstva oboroni SSSR, 1966), pp.3–6. See also Evgenii Drig, *Mekhanizir-
     ovannie korpusa RKKA v boiu: Istoriia avtobronetankovikh voisk Krasnoi Armii
     v 1940–1941 godakh* (Moscow: AST/Tranzitkniga, 2005), pp.502–3.

119 Doklad nachal'nika GABTU Glavnomu voennomu sovetu KA o sostoianii
     obespecheniia avtobronetankovoi tekhnikoi i imushchestvom Krasnoi
     Armii, iiun' 1941 g., in A.M. Radionov et al (eds.), *Glavnoe avtobronetanko-
     voe upravlenie. Liudi, sobitiia, fakti v dokumentakh – 1940–1942 gg.*,
     pp.49–51.

120 Jürgen Förster and Evan Mawdsley, 'Hitler and Stalin in Perspective: Secret
     Speeches on the Eve of Barbarossa', in *War in History*, Volume 11, Number
     1 (2004), pp.90–1.

121 Plan strategicheskogo razvertivaniia Krasnoi Armii (mart 1941 goda), in
     Iurii Veremeev, *Krasnaia Armiia v nachale Vtoroi mirovoi*, pp.131–2.

122 Zapiska Narkoma oboroni SSSR i nachal'nika Genshtaba Krasnoi Armii v
     TsK VKP(b) – I.V.Stalinu i V.M.Molotovu ob osnovakh razvertivaniia
     vooruzhennikh sil Sovetskogo soiuza … na 1940 i 1941 godi, 18 sentiabria
     1940 g., in V.P. Naumov (gen.ed.), *1941 god: V 2 kn. Kn.1*, p.238.

123 Plan strategicheskogo razvertivaniia Krasnoi Armii (Mart 1941 goda), in
     Iurii Veremeev, *Krasnaia Armiia v nachale Vtoroi mirovoi*, pp.131–2.

124 Spetssoobshchenie Razvedupravleniia Genshtaba Krasnoi Armii o gruppir-
     ovke nemetskikh voisk na 1 iiunia, 1941, 31 maia 1941 g. in V.P. Naumov
     (gen.ed.), *1941 god: V 2 kn. Kn.2*, p.289.

125 See map, David Glantz, *Stumbling Colossus*, p.12.

126 Evan Mawdsley, 'Crossing the Rubicon: Soviet Plans for Offensive War in
     1940–1941', in *The International History Review*, Volume 25, Number 4
     (December 2003), pp.822–5.

127 Plan strategicheskogo razvertivaniia Krasnoi Armii (mart 1941 goda), in
     Iurii Veremeev, *Krasnaia Armiia v nachale Vtoroi mirovoi*, p.135 and Mawds-
     ley, 'Crossing the Rubicon: Soviet Plans for Offensive War in 1940–1941',
     pp.822–3.

128 Suvorov's thesis was first introduced in V. Suvorov (pseud.) 'Who was
     Plannig to Attack Whom in June 1941, Hitler or Stalin?', in *Journal of the
     Royal United Services Institute for Defence Studies*, Volume 130, Number 2
     (1985), pp.50–5. On the 'Suvorov debate', see Alexander Hill, *The Great
     Patriotic War*, pp.26–37.

129 David Glantz, *Stumbling Colossus*, pp.xii–xiii.

130 See Bruce W. Menning and Jonathan House, 'Soviet strategy', in John
     Ferris and Evan Mawdsley (eds.), *The Cambridge History of the Second World
     War. Volume I. Fighting the War* (Cambridge: Cambridge University Press,
     2015), pp.225–31.

131 …considerations for a plan for the strategic deployment of the armed forces
     of the Soviet Union in the event of war with Germany and her allies. No
     earlier than 15 May 1941, in Alexander Hill, *The Great Patriotic War*, p.30.

132 Ibid., p.29.
133 On this issue, see Bruce W. Menning and Jonathan House, 'Soviet strategy', in John Ferris and Evan Mawdsley (eds.), *The Cambridge History of the Second World War. Volume I. Fighting the War*, pp.222–4. See also Alexander Hill, 'Offense, Defence, or the Worst of Both Worlds? Soviet strategy in May–June 1941', in *The Journal of Military and Strategic Studies*, Volume 13, Number 1 (Fall 2010), pp.61–74. As an indication of Soviet concentration of strength to the south, as of 1 June the Kiev Special Military District that would become the South-Western Front was provided with 5,465 out of 12,782 nominally available tanks, with the Western Special Military District that would become the Western Front having 2,900 tanks. See N.P. Zolotov et al, *Boevoi i chislennii sostav vooruzhennikh sil SSSR v period Velikoi Otechestvennoi voini (1941–1945 gg.). Statisticheskii sbornik No.1 (22 iiunia 1941 g.)*, p.17.
134 See N.P.Zolotov and S.I. Isaev, 'Boegotovi bili... Istoriko-statisticheskoe issledovanie kolichestvenno-kachestvennogo sostoianiia tankovogo parka Krasnoi Armii nakanune Velikoi Otechestvennoi voini', pp.76–7 and N.P. Zolotov et al, *Boevoi i chislennii sostav vooruzhennikh sil SSSR v period Velikoi Otechestvennoi voini (1941–1945 gg.). Statisticheskii sbornik No.1 (22 iiunia 1941 g.)*, p.17.
135 Like the 469 KV-series tanks in the western military districts on 1 June, which along with 51 multi-turreted T-35 tanks made up the 520 'heavy' tanks in the theatre. Serviceability rates for the KV-series and indeed T-34 were far higher than for other types, with for example 420 KV-series tanks being deemed ready for immediate action as of 1 June, with a further 129 requiring only light repairs or servicing. N.P. Zolotov et al, *Boevoi i chislennii sostav vooruzhennikh sil SSSR v period Velikoi Otechestvennoi voini (1941–1945 gg.). Statisticheskii sbornik No.1 (22 iiunia 1941 g.)*, pp.16–17, 132. Many of vehicles had only recently been delivered to units, and where an additional 41 KV-series vehicles would be delivered directly to front line units by Soviet industry from 31 May to 21 June 1941. See N.P.Zolotov and S.I. Isaev, 'Boegotovi bili... Istoriko-statisticheskoe issledovanie kolichestvenno-kachestvennogo sostoia-niia tankovogo parka Krasnoi Armii nakanune Velikoi Otechestvennoi voini', p.76.
136 For example, as of 1 June there were 1,173 tanks with the Moscow Military District alone, where although only 29 were deemed ready for immediate use, 920 required only light repairs or servicing with their units. There were 5,697 tanks in the Far East, and a further 1,240 in the southern military districts – primarily the Trans-Caucasus Military District. N.P.Zolotov and S.I. Isaev, 'Boegotovi bili... Istoriko-statisticheskoe issledovanie kolichestvenno-kachestvennogo sostoianiia tankovogo parka Krasnoi Armii nakanune Velikoi Otechestvennoi voini', p.77. On principal German strength, see Alexander Hill, *The Great Patriotic War*, p.74.

CHAPTER 10

1 P.M. Chaplin, letter of 15 March 1987, in A.M. Samsonov, *Znat' i pomnit': Dialog istorika s chitatelem* (Moscow: Politizdat, 1988), p.41.

2 Shvarev, Aleksandr Efimovich, in Artem Drabkin, *Ia dralsia na istrebitele. Priniavshie pervii udar. 1941–1942* (Moscow: Iauza, Eksmo, 2007), pp.68–9.

3 Valerii Vakhromeev, *Vizhit' i vernut'sia. Odisseia sovetskogo voennoplennogo. 1941–1945* (Moscow: ZAO Izdatel'stvo Tsentrpoligraf, 2011), p.12.

4 Arkadii Glazunov, *Voina: v plenu, v partizanakh, v deistvuiushchei armii*, p.6.

5 P.M. Kurochkin, *Pozivnie fronta* (Moscow: Voenizdat, 1969), p.117.

6 HPSSS, Schedule B, Vol. 6, Case 193 (Interviewer S.H.), p.9.

7 I.I. Fediuninskii, *Podniatie po trevoge* (Moscow: Voennoe izdatel'stvo Ministerstvo oboroni SSSR, 1961), p.9.

8 Catherine Merridale, *Ivan's War: Life and Death in the Red Army, 1939–1945* (New York: Picador, 2006), p.40.

9 Valerii Vakhromeev, *Vizhit' i vernut'sia*, p.12.

10 See TASS communiqué of 13 June 1941, published in the newspaper *Izvestia* the following day, in Alexander Hill, *The Great Patriotic War*, pp.26–7.

11 Donesenie komandira 125-i strelkovoi divizii komanduiushchemu Pribaltiiskim osobim voennim okrugom, 18 iiunia 1941 g., 20 ch 10 min, in V.P. Zhuravlev et al (eds.), 'Pervie dni voini v dokumentakh', in *Vizh*, Number 5 (1989), p.47.

12 K.K. Rokossovskii, 'Soldatskii dolg', in *Vizh*, Number 4 (1989), p.55.

13 L.S. Skvirskii, 'Vospominaniia. V predvoennie godi', pp.66–7.

14 I.Kh. Bagramian, *Tak nachalas' voina*, p.77.

15 K.K. Rokossovskii, 'Soldatskii dolg', p.55.

16 For more detail on deployments immediately prior to the German invasion, see David Glantz, *Stumbling Colossus*, pp.102–6.

17 Donesenie shtaba Zapadnogo osobogo voennogo okruga nachal'niku General'nogo shtaba ot 21 iiunia 1941 g. o narushenii gosudarstvennoi granitsi germanskimi samolotami i sniatii nemtsami provolochnikh zagrazhdenii [otpravlen 21 iiunia 1941 g. v 2 chasa 40 minut], in P.P. Gnedovets (ed.), *Sbornik boevikh dokumentov Velikoi Otechestvennoi voini* (hereafter SBD). *Vipusk 35* (Moscow: Voennoe izdatel'stvo Ministerstva oboroni SSSR, 1958), pp.10–11.

18 For example, a useful list of intelligence information from agents in Berlin from 6 September 1940 to 16 June 1941 is provided in a document dated 20 June, in V.P. Naumov (gen.ed.), *1941 god: V 2 kn. Kn.2*, pp.400–7.

19 Iz Telefonogrammi UNKGB po L'vovskoi oblasti v NKGB USSR, 22 iiunia 1941 g., in V.P. Naumov (gen.ed.), *1941 god: V 2 kn. Kn.2*, p.422.

20 N. Kuznetsov, 'Voenno-Morskoi Flot nakanune Velikoi Otechestvennoi voini', in *Vizh*, Number 9 (1965), p.72.

21 N.G. Kuznetsov, *Nakanune*, p.294.

22 V.F. Tributz, *Baltiitsi srazhaiutsia* (Moscow: Veche, 2015), p.12.

23 See N. Kuznetsov, 'Voenno-Morskoi Flot nakanune Velikoi Otechestvennoi voini', p.72; Gunnar Åselius, *The Rise and Fall of the Soviet Navy in the Baltic, 1921–1941* (London/New York: Frank Cass, 2005), p.3; Donesenie komanduiushchego Krasnoznamennim baltiiskim flotom komanduiushchim Leningradskim i Pribaltiiskim osobim voennim okrugam, nachal'niku pogranvoisk, 20 iiunia 1941 g, in V.P. Zhuravlev et al (eds.), 'Pervie dni voini v dokumentakh', p.48; V.F. Tributz, *Baltiitsi srazhaiutsia*, p.13.

24 Vipiska iz prikaza shtaba Pribaltiiskogo osobogo voennogo okruga, 18 iiunia 1941 g., in V.P. Zhuravlev et al (eds.), 'Pervie dni voini v dokumentakh', p.46.

25 Direktiva shtaba Pribaltiiskogo osobogo voennogo okruga, 19 iiunia 1941 g., in ibid., p.47.

26 David Glantz, *Stumbling Colossus*, p.105.

27 Directive [Number 1]... 21 June 1941, in Alexander Hill, *The Great Patriotic War*, p.40.

28 See Gosudarvtvennii komitet oboroni. Postanovlenie No. GKO-652ss ot "10" sentiabria 1941 g. Moskva, Kreml'. O rasformirovanii Zapadnogo, Kievskogo i Odesskogo voennikh okrugov. www.soldat.ru/doc/gko/scans/0652–1.jpg [Accessed 5 January 2015].

29 Zhurnal voennikh deistvii voisk Zapadnogo fronta za iiun' 1941 goda. TsAMO f.208.o.2511.d.206.l.2.

30 L.M. Sandalov, 1941. *Na moskovskom napravlenii*, p.83.

31 Prikaz Narodnogo komissara oboroni SSSR, 19 iiunia 1941 g., in V.P. Zhuravlev et al (eds.), 'Pervie dni voini v dokumentakh', p.43.

32 Zhurnal voennikh deistvii voisk Zapadnogo fronta za iiun' 1941 goda. TsAMO f.208.o.2511.d.206.l.8, and M.N. Kozhevnikov, *Komandovanie i shtab VVS Sovetskoi Armii v Velikoi Otechestvennoi voine 1941–1945 gg.*, p.36.

33 See M.N. Kozhevnikov, *Komandovanie i shtab VVS Sovetskoi Armii v Velikoi Otechestvennoi voine 1941–1945*, pp. 21–2, 36–7, and I.V. Timokhovich, *Operativnoe iskusstvo Sovetskikh VVS v Velikoi Otechestvennoi voine* (Moscow: Voenizdat, 1976), pp.21–4; M.A. Bobrov, 'Strategicheskoe razvertivanie VVS Krasnoi armii na zapade strani pered Velikoi Otechestvennoi voinoi', pp.5–6.

34 I.V. Timokhovich, *Operativnoe iskusstvo Sovetskikh VVS*, p.23.

35 Hans Roth (Christine Alexander and Mason Kunze (eds.)), *Eastern Inferno: The Journals of a German Panzerjäger on the Eastern Front, 1941–43* (Havertown, PA and Newbury: Casemate Publishers, 2010), pp.27–64 ; Erich Hager (David Garden and Kenneth Andrew, eds.), *The War Diaries of a Panzer Soldier: Erich Hager with the 17th Panzer Division on the Russian Front 1941–1945* (Atglen, PA: Schiffer Military History, 2010), pp.31–44.

36 Zhurnal voennikh deistvii voisk Zapadnogo fronta za iiun' 1941 goda. TsAMO f.208.o.2511.d.206.l.8.

37 Samsonov, *Znat' i pomnit'*, p.74.

38 General Günther Blumentritt, 'Moscow', in William Richardson and Seymour Freidlin (eds.), *The Fatal Decisions: Six Decisive Battles of WWII from the Viewpoint of the Vanquished* (Mechanicsburg, PA: Stackpole Books, 2013), p.47.

39 Directive Number 2... 22 June 1941, in Alexander Hill, *The Great Patriotic War*, pp.41–2.

40 Zhurnal voennikh deistvii voisk Zapadnogo fronta za iiun' 1941 goda. TsAMO f.208.o.2511.d.206.ll.9, 24.

41 I.Kh. Bagramian, *Tak nachalas' voina*, p.90.

42 P.M. Kurochkin, *Pozivnie fronta*, pp.117–18.

43 Ibid., p.118.

44 Ibid., p.119.

45 For an excellent discussion of this issue in the context of the October fighting in the Viaz'ma area in October 1941, see Lev Lopukhovsky (trans. and ed. Stuart Britton), *The Viaz'ma Catastrophe, 1941: The Red Army's Disastrous Stand against Operation Typhoon* (Solihull: Helion and Company, 2013), pp.223–5.

46 Directive Number 3...22 June 1941, in Alexander Hill, *The Great Patriotic War*, p.42.

47 Zhurnal voennikh deistvii voisk Zapadnogo fronta za iiun' 1941 goda. TsAMO f.208.o.2511.d.206.l.20. It is worth highlighting that Kopets was only thirty-two years old when he committed suicide as commander of air forces for the Western Front, highlighting the scope for rapid promotion during the period of the purges and expansion of the Red Army. He had received the title Hero of the Soviet Union in 1937 for his service in Spain. See E.N. Kul'kov and O.A. Rzheshevskii (gen.eds.), *Zimniaia voina 1939–1940. Kniga vtoraia*, p.286, for a brief biography, although here his date of birth is incorrectly noted as 1888 rather than 1908!

48 Zhurnal voennikh deistvii voisk Zapadnogo fronta za iiun' 1941 goda. TsAMO f.208.o.2511.d.206.ll.5,11; Evgenii Drig, *Mekhanizirovannie korpusa RKKA v boiu*, p.375; L.M. Sandalov, *1941. Na moskovskom napravlenii*, p.98.

49 L.M. Sandalov, *1941. Na moskovskom napravlenii*, pp.89, 94, 99–100.

50 Zhurnal voennikh deistvii voisk Zapadnogo fronta za iiun' 1941 goda. TsAMO f.208.o.2511.d.206.ll.30, 41–2; Operativnaia svodka shtaba Zapadnogo fronta No.5 k 22 chasam 24 iiunia 1941 g. o boevikh deistviiakh voisk fronta, in *SBD35*, p.40; L.M. Sandalov, *1941. Na moskovskom napravlenii*, pp.97–8.

51 Zhurnal voennikh deistvii voisk Zapadnogo fronta za iiun' 1941 goda. TsAMO f.208.o.2511.d.206.l.37; Operativnaia svodka shtaba Zapadnogo fronta No.7 k 22 chasam 25 iiunia 1941 g. o boevikh deistviiakh voisk fronta, in *SBD35*, p.46.

52 Zhurnal voennikh deistvii voisk Zapadnogo fronta za iiun' 1941 goda. TsAMO f.208.o.2511.d.206.ll.4,30–31; Boevoe rasporiazhenie komanduiushchego voiskami Zapadnogo fronta ot 25 iiunia 1941 g. komandiru 6-go mekhanizirovannogo korpusa na sosredotochenie korpusa v Slonim, in *SBD35*, p.43; Boevoe doenesenie shtaba Zapadnogo fronta No. 008 k 16 chasam 45 minutam 25 iiunia 1941 g. o polozhenii soedinenii i chastei fronta, in ibid, p.45; Direktiva voennogo soveta Zapadnogo fronta ot 25 iiunia 1941 g. na otvod voisk fronta na rubezh Iliia, Gol'shani, Lida, r. Shara, Biten', Pinsk, in *SBD35*, pp.46–7.

53 Evgenii Drig, *Mekhanizirovannie korpusa RKKA v boiu*, pp.323–4, 363–4.

54 Operativanaia svodka shtaba Zapadnogo fronta No.7 k 22 chasam 25 iiunia 1941 g. o boevikh deistviiakh voisk fronta, in *SBD35*, p.45; Operativnaia svodka shtaba Zapadnogo fronta No.8 k 20 chasam 27 iiunia 1941 g. o boevikh desitviiakh voisk fronta, in *SBD35*, p.50; Evgenii Drig, *Mekhanizirovannie korpusa RKKA v boiu*, p.135.

55 Operativnaia svodka shtaba Zapadnogo fronta No. 9 k 20 chasam 28 iiunia 1941 g. o boevikh deistviiakh voisk fronta, in *SBD35*, p.58; Operativnaia svodka shtaba Zapadnogo fronta No.8 k 20 chasam 27 iiunia 1941 g. o boevikh desitviiakh voisk fronta, in *SBD35*, pp.49–50.

56 Operativnaia svodka shtaba Zapadnogo fronta No.8 k 20 chasam 27 iiunia 1941 g. o boevikh desitviiakh voisk fronta, in ibid., pp.49–50.

57 Boevoe rasporiazhenie shtaba Zapadnogo fronta No.1 ot 28 iiunia 1941 komandiru 4-go vozdushno-desantnogo korpusa na oboronu vostochnogo berega r. Berezina odnoi brigadoi korpusa, in ibid., p.55; Operativnaia svodka shtaba Zapadnogo fronta No. 9 k 20 chasam 28 iiunia 1941 g. o boevikh deistviiakh voisk fronta, in ibid., p.59.

58 Boevoe rasporiazhenie komanduiushchego voiskami Zapadnogo fronta ot 29 iiunia 1941 g. komandiru 17-go mekhanizirovannogo korpusa..., in ibid., p.61; Chastnaia direktiva... Zapadnogo fronta No. 1 ot 29 iiunia 1941 g. na unichtozhenie gruppirovki protivnika zapadnee Minska, in ibid., p.62; Donesenie nachal'nika avtobronetankovogo upravleniia Zapadnogo fronta... o sostoianii avtobronetankovikh voisk fronta na 29 iiunia 1941 g., in ibid., p.65.

59 For a detailed analysis of this counterattack, see Gary A. Dickson, 'The Counterattack of the 7th Mechanized Corps, 5–9 July 1941', in *JSMS*, Volume 26, Number 2 (2013), pp.310–40.

60 See David Stahel, *Operation Barbarossa and Germany's Defeat in the East* (Cambridge: CUP, 2009), pp.178–83.

61 Krivosheev, *Soviet Casualties and Combat Losses*, p.111.

62 Iz doneseniia o poteriakh boepripasov Zapadnogo fronta, [ne pozdnee 10 iiulia 1941 g.], in P.N. Knishevskii (ed.), *Skritaia pravda voini: 1941 god*, p.86.

63 Shunkov, *Artilleriia Krasnoi armii i Vermakhta*, P.133. Franz Halder, *War Journal of Franz Halder. Volume VI* [21 February 1941 – 31 July 1941] (Historical Division, SSUSA, 1950), entry for 27 June, p.178.

64 Franz Halder, *War Journal of Franz Halder. Volume VI*, entries for 26, 29, 30 June and 1 July, pp.173–4, 181, 188.

65 Evan Mawdlsey, *Thunder in the East*, pp.76–7.

66 M.E. Katukov, *Na ostrie glavnogo udara* (Moscow: "Visshaia shkola", 1985), pp.13–17.

67 Franz Halder, *War Journal of Franz Halder. Volume VII*, p.36.

68 Albert Speer, *Inside the Third Reich* (London: Phoenix, 1995), p.250.

69 Alexander Hill, *The Great Patriotic War*, p.74.

70 Dokladnaia zapiska pomoshchnika komanduiushchego voiskami Iugo-zapadnogo fronta v GABTU o boevikh deistviiakh chastei za period s 22 iiunia po 1 avgusta 1941 g., 5 avgusta 1941 g, in A.M. Radionov et al, *Glavnoe avtobronetankovoe upravlenie. Liudi, sobitiia, fakti v dokumentakh – 1940–1942 gg.*, pp.91–2.

71 P.M. Kurochkin, *Pozivnie fronta*, pp.118–28.

72 Gosudarstvennii komitet oboroni. Postanovlenie No. GKO-227/ss ot "20" iiulia 1941 g. O postavke Narkomatu oboroni svedstv sviazi. RGASPI f.644. o.1.d.3.1.209.

73 Zapiska Veonnogo soveta Severnogo fronta I.V. Stalinu ob usilenii PVO g. Leningrada, ne pozdnee 22 iiulia 1941 g., in S.V. Kudriashov (gen.ed.), *Vestnik Arkhiva Prezidenta Rossiiskoi Federatsii. Voina: 1941–1945. Vipusk 2* (Moscow: Izdatel'stvo "Istoricheskaia literatura", 2015), p.50.

74 Overall combat losses were recorded as 26 aircraft in aerial combat (12 I-16 and 14 Yak-1), 4 to enemy AA (2 I-16 and 2 Yak-1), 2 failed to return (1 I-16

and 1 Yak-1), 3 lost to enemy bombers on the ground (2 I-16 and 1 Yak-1), 3 lost to Soviet AA (3 Yak-1), 1 lost to Soviet aircraft in aerial combat (1 Yak-1), and one lost in extreme weather conditions (1 I-16). E.A. Aframeev, *Khronika 158 istrebitel'nogo aviatsionnogo polka. Oborona Leningrad v 1941 godu* (Saint Petersburg: Izdatel'skii dom "Petropolis", 2011), p.74.

75 Spravka o potrebnosi i obespechennosti vooruzheniem sviazi chastei KOVO po sostoianiiu na 10 maia 1941 g., ne pozdnee 10 maia 1941 g., in V.P. Naumov (gen.ed.), *1941 god: V 2 kn. Kn.2*, p.190.

76 Protokol'naia zapis' vechernego zasedaniia 23 noiabria 1938 g. Speaking: Kombrig S.M. Krivoshein, in P.N. Bobilev (gen.ed.), *Voennii sovet pri narodnom komissare oboroni SSSR. 1938, 1940 gg.*, p.125.

77 N.P. Zolotov et al, *Boevoi i chislennii sostav vooruzhennikh sil SSSR v period Velikoi Otechestvennoi voini (1941–1945 gg.). Statisticheskii sbornik No.1 (22 iiunia 1941 g.)*, pp.132–3.

78 Artem Drabkin (ed.), *Ia dralsia na T-34*, p.36 and Glavnoe upravlenie sviazi, *Spravochnik po voiskovim i tankovim radiostantsiiam. Chast' 2 iz 3* (Moscow: Voennoe izdatel'stvo Narodnogo komissariata oboroni, 1943), p.89.

79 Alexander Hill, *The Great Patriotic War*, p.61.

80 Arkadii Glazunov, *Voina: v plenu, v partizanakh, v deistvuiushchei armii*, p.14.

81 Polevoe upravlenie Glavkoma voisk SZN. Zhurnal boevikh deistvii SZF. Nachato"11" 6 1941 g. Okoncheno "28" 8 1941 g. TsAMO f.249.o.1544. d.33.ll.11, 14.

82 Anastas Mikoian, *Tak bilo. Razmishleniia o minuvshem* (Moscow: Tsentrpoligraf, 2014), pp.421–3.

83 Alexander Hill, *The Great Patriotic War*, pp.44–5 and 47–8; M.M. Kir'ian (editor-in-chief), *Sovetskaia voennaia entsiklopediia, 7* (Moscow: Voenizdat, 1979), p.516.

84 Prikaz s ob"iavleniem prigovora Verkhovnogo suda SSSR po delu General armii D.G. Pavlova, General-maiorov V.E. Klimovskikh, A.T. Grigor'eva i A.A. Korobkova, No.250, 28 iiulia 1941 g., in *RA T.13 (2–2)*, pp.37–8.

85 Prikaz voiskam Zapadnogo fronta, No.01, 6 iiulia 1941. Sekretno. ...Soderzhanie: Ob otdache pod sud lits nachal'stvuiushchego sostava Zapfronta za proiavlenie trusosti, in P.N. Knishevskii (gen.ed.), *Skritaia pravda voini: 1941 god*, p.301.

86 Direktiva chlena Voennogo soveta Zapadnogo fronta Armeiskogo komissara 1 ranga L.Z. Mekhlisa o glasnosti i ispolnenii prigovorov s visshei meroi nakazaniia. NP-01. 7 iiunia 1941 g. ... Voennim sovetam 22,20,21,4 i 13 armii, in ibid., pp.302–3.

87 Decree of the Presidium of the Supreme Soviet...on the reorganisation of organs of political propaganda and the introduction of the institute of military commissars..., 16 July 1941, and The position of military commissars in the...Red Army (July 1941), in Alexander Hill, *The Great Patriotic War*, pp.53–4.

88 G.K. Zhukov, *Vospominaniia i razmishleniia...Tom 2*, p.64.

89 Decree of the State Committee of Defence No, 187ss on the re-establishment of organs of the 3rd Board of the NKO SSSR as special sections of the NKVD

SSR, 17 July 1941, and Decree of the State Defence Committee No. 377 ss, 2 August 1941..., in Alexander Hill, *The Great Patriotic War*, pp.54–6.

90 Order of the Headquarters of the Supreme High Command of the Red Army, Number 270, 16 August 1941, in ibid., pp.55–6. The extracts in this English translation were taken from the full version of the document in O.A. Rzheshevskii (gen.ed.), *Velikaia otechestvennaia voina , 1941–1945. Sobitiia. Liudi. Dokumenti: Kratkii istoricheskii spravochnik* (Moscow: Politizdat, 1990), pp.423–4.

91 Roger R. Reese, *Why Stalin's Soldier's Fought: The Red Army's Military Effectiveness in World War II* (Lawrence, KA: University Press of Kansas, 2011), p.161 and Iosif Isaakovich Finkel'shtein, http://iremember.ru/svya zisti/finkelshteyn-iosif/stranitsa-2.html [Accessed 24 February 2014].

92 Il'ia Grigor'evich Sokolov, http://iremember.ru/pekhotintsi/sokolov-ilya-gri gorevich/stranitsa-4.html [Accessed 24 February 2014].

93 Iz prikaza Narkoma oboroni SSSR No.0391 o faktakh podmeni vospitatel'noi raboti v Krasnoi Armii repressiiami, 4 October 1941 g., in V.P. Iampol'skii (gen.ed.) et al, *Organi gosudarstvennoi bezopasnosti SSSR v Velikoi Otechest-vennoi voine. Sbornik dokumentov. Tom vtoroi. Kniga 2. Nachalo. 1 sentiabria – 31 dekabria 1941 goda* (Moscow: Izdatel'stvo "Rus'", 2000), pp.164–5.

94 Karel C. Berkhoff, *Motherland in Danger: Soviet Propaganda in World War II* (Cambridge, Massachusetts/London, England: Harvard University Press, 2012), p.202.

95 See Chapter 23 and the Conclusion.

96 Karel C. Berkhoff, *Motherland in Danger*, pp.182–93.

97 O krasnoarmeitsakh – urozhentsakh Zapadnikh oblastei BSSR, USSR [signed Nachal'nik Politicheskogo Upravleniia Zapadnogo fronta divizionnii komissar D. Lestev], 20 iiulia 1941 g., in P.N. Knishevskii (gen.ed.), *Skri-taia pravda voini: 1941 god*, pp.266–7.

98 S.B. Buldigin, *Istoriia pribaltiiskikh territorial'nikh strelkovoikh korpusov* (Saint Petersburg: Izdatel'stvo "Gangut", 2013), pp.28–32.

99 Ibid., pp.44–50.

100 Ibid., pp.85–7.

101 Iz doklada o sostoianii 180-i strel'kovoi divizii 22-go Estonskogo korpusa, 14 iiulia 1941 g., in P.N. Knishevskii (gen.ed.), *Skritaia pravda voini: 1941 god*, pp.131–2.

102 Hans Roth (Christine Alexander and Mason Kunze (eds.)), *Eastern Inferno: The Journals of a German Panzerjäger on the Eastern Front, 1941–43*, pp.28–9, 31.

103 P. Aliev, *Brestskaia krepost'. Vospominaniia i dokumenti* (Moscow: Veche, 2010), pp.413–14.

104 Erich Hager (David Garden and Kenneth Andrew, eds.), *The War Diaries of a Panzer Soldier: Erich Hager with the 17th Panzer Division on the Russian Front 1941–1945*, pp.34–6.

105 Hans Schäufler (ed.), *Knight's Cross Panzers: The German 35th Panzer Regiment in WWII* (Mechanicsburg, PA: Stackpole Books, 2010), p.93.

106 A.A. Kamentsev, letter of 25 March 1987, in A.M. Samsonov, *Znat' i pomnit'*, p.85.

107 'Kharakter sovremennoi nastupatel'noi operatsii'. Doklad komandiush-chego voiskami Kievskogo osobogo voennogo okruga general armii G.K. Zhukova, in *RA T.12 (1)*, p.145.

108 N.N. Nikulin, *Vospominaniia o voine* (Moscow: AST, 2014), p.42.

109 A.D. Kolesnik, 'Opolchentsi gorodov-geroev', in *Voprosii istorii*, Number 12 (1973), p.102.

110 Voennomu sovetu Severnogo fronta. Doklad o boevoi gotovnosti 1-i divizii Leningradskoi armii narodnogo opolcheniia, 10 iiulia 1941 g. [signed Komanduiushchii Armiei narodnogo opolcheniia g. Leningrada general-maior Subbotin...]. TsAMO f.217.o.1221.d.93.ll.1–9.

111 Nachal'niku Politotdela Leningradskoi Armii Narodnogo Opolcheniia – polkovomu komissaru tov. Verkhoglazu ot batal'onnogo komissara Moisei-chenko. Dokladnaia zapiska. 29/VII 41g. TsGAIPD f.2281.o.1.d.22. http://centralsector.narod.ru/arch/1dno_1.htm. [Accessed 23 December 2014].

112 A.D. Kolesnik, 'Opolchentsi gorodov-geroev', p.103.

113 Franz Halder, *War Journal of Franz Halder. Volume VI*, p.258; and *Volume VII*, pp.16, 27.

CHAPTER 11

1 Vstuplenie I.V. Stalina po radio 3 iiulia 1941 g., in V.P. Naumov (gen.ed.), *1941 god: V 2 kn. Kn.2* , p.450. Some of this speech is available in English translation in Alexander Hill, *The Great Patriotic War*, pp.49–50.

2 Franz Halder, *War Journal of Franz Halder. Volume VI*, p.271.

3 Siegfried Knappe with Ted Brusaw, *Soldat: Reflections of a German Soldier, 1936–1949* (New York: Dell Publishing, 1992), p.224.

4 See Lev Lopukhovsky (trans. and ed. Stuart Britton), *The Viaz'ma Catastrophe, 1941: The Red Army's Disastrous Stand Against Operation Typhoon*, pp.37–48.

5 Zapiska I.P. Voinova I.V. Stalinu o polozhenii del v 34-i armii, 28 avgusta 1941 g., in S.V. Kudriashov (gen.ed.), *Vestnik Arkhiva Prezidenta Rossiiskoi Federatsii. Voina: 1941–1945. Vipusk 2*, p.67.

6 Führer Headquarters, 19 July 1941. Directive No. 33. Continuation of the war in the East, in Hugh Trevor-Roper (ed.), *Hitler's War Directives, 1939–1945* (London: Pan Books Ltd, 1966), p.141.

7 Order of the military Soviet of the Reserve Front to the troops due to the expected victory near El'nia, ..., 7 September 1941, in Alexander Hill, *The Great Patriotic War.*, p.65.

8 David Stahel, *Operation Barbarossa*, p.412.

9 For a broader picture of the Soviet counteroffensives of August and early September across much of the front, with documentary sources, see David Glantz, 'Forgotten Battle of the German-Soviet War (1941–1945), Part II', in *JSMS*, Volume 13, Number 1 (2000), pp.172–237.

10 G.K. Zhukov, *Vospominaniia i razmishleniia... Tom 2*, p.131.

11 I.N. Russiianov, *V boiakh rozhdennaia*, pp.98–9.

12 Direktiva Stavki VGK No.001254 komanduiushchemu voiskami Zapadnogo fronta o razvitii nastupleniia pod Smolenskom, 25 avgusta 1941 g. 02 ch 30 min, in *RA T.16 (5–1)*, p.135.

13 I.N. Russiianov, *V boiakh rozhdennaia*, pp.100–3.

14 M.D. Lubiagov, *V boiakh za El'niu. Pervie shagi k pobede* (Moscow: Veche, 2013), pp.310–13.

15 Zapis peregovorov po priamomu provodu A.N. Poskrebisheva s G.K. Zhukovim, 1 sentiabria 1941 g., in *RA T.16(5–1)*, p.155.

16 Zapis' peregovorov po priamomu provodu Verkhovnogo glavnokomanduiushchego i nachal'nika General'nogo shtaba s komanduiushchim voiskami Rezervnogo fronta, 4 sentiabria 1941 g. Nachalo 03 ch 50 min. Konets 04 ch 30 min, in *T.16(5–1)*, pp.162–3. See this conversation translated in to English in Lev Lopukhovsky (trans. and ed. Stuart Britton), *The Viaz'ma Catastrophe, 1941: The Red Army's Disastrous Stand Against Operation Typhoon*, pp.53–5, as part of a wider and useful discussion of the El'nia fighting.

17 Zapis' peregovorov po priamomu provodu Verkhovnogo glavnokomanduiushchego s komanduiushchim voiskami Rezervnogo fronta, 29 avgusta 1941 g. Okonchanie – 23 ch 04 min, in *RA T.16(5–1)*, pp.147–8.

18 David Stahel, *Operation Barbarossa*, p.412.

19 As for example reported in the newssheet Vesti s Sovetskoi Rodini for 11 September 1941, published by GlavPU, under the subheading 'Razgrom Nemtsev pod gorodom El'nia'. TsAMO f.217.o.1217.d.127.l.58.

20 Order of the military Soviet of the Reserve Front to the troops due to the expected victoty near El'nia, …, 7 September 1941, in Alexander Hill, *The Great Patriotic War*, p.65.

21 Svedeniia o plennikh i trofeiakh zakhvatchennikh u protivnika za ves' period Elenskoi operatsii s 8.8.1941 po 12.9.1941 goda, no earlier than 12 September 1941. TsAMO f.219.o.679.d.26.l.79.

22 G.K. Zhukov, *Vospominaniia i razmishleniia. …Tom 2*, p.141.

23 Direktiva Stavki VGK No.001941 komanduiushchemu voiskami Rezervnogo fronta o nedostatkakh v organizatsii nastupleniia, 13 sentiabria 1941 g. 06 ch 00 min, in *RA T.16(5–1)*, pp.181–2.

24 Donesenie o poteriakh lichnogo sostava soedinenii 43 Armii s "8" sentiabria po "10" sentiabria 1941 goda, no earlier than 10 September 1941. TsAMO f.219.o.679.d.26.l.117ob. Losses amongst horses had also been very high – from 30 August to 10 September a total of 960. Donesenie o poteriakh konskogo sostava soedinenii 43 Armii s "30" avgusta po "10" sentiabria 1941 goda, no earlier than 10 September 1941. TsAMO f.219.o.679.d.26.l.117.

25 Svedeniia o poteriakh lichnogo sostava v chastiakh 100 ordena Lenina str. div. s 30 avgusta po 4 sentiabria 1941 g.[handwritten], no earlier than 4 September 1941. TsAMO f.219.o.679.d.26.l.97.

26 Donesenie o poteriakh lichnogo sostava 102 otd. tankovoi divizii s "17" iiulia po "12" sentiabria 1941 goda, no earlier than 12 September 1941. TsAMO f.219.o.679.d.26.l.78; O chislennom boevom sostave 204 tankogo polka 102 OTD po sostoianiiu na "11" sentiabria 1941 goda. TsAMO f.219.o.679.d.26.l.87, and …205 tankogo polka…. . TsAMO f.219.o.679.d.26.l.88.

27 Nachal'niku shtaba fronta rezervnikh armii general-maioru tov. Anisovu. Undated [dated according to position in delo]. TsAMO f.219.o.679.d.26.l.100.

28 See Chapter 3.
29 Prikaz o pereimenovanii 100, 127, 153 i 161-i strelkovikh divizii v 1,2,3,4-iu gvardeiskie divizii, No.308, 18 sentiabria 1941 g., in *RA T.13 (2–2)*, pp.85–6.
30 I.M. Golushko, *Shtab tila krasnoi armii v godi voini 1941–1945* (Moscow: Izdatel'stvo "Ekonomika i informatika", 1998), p.164.
31 Transcript of interview with Major Pyotr Andreyevich Zayonchkovsky, May 28, 1943, in Jochen Hellbeck (trans. Christopher Tauchen and Dominic Bonfiglio), *Stalingrad: The City that Defeated the Third Reich* (New York: Public Affairs, 2015), p.385, and Transcript of interview with Comrade Lieutenant General Vasily Chuikov, Stalingrad, January 5, 1943, p.282.
32 Komanduiushchim voiskam frontov i otdel'nimi armiiami o poriadke popolneniia gvardeiskikh chastei, 10 fevrailia 1944 g., in *RA T.12 (4)*, pp.65–6.
33 Vsem komduiushchim frontov. Kopiia: Nachal'niku Glavnogo politicheskogo upravleniia Krasnoi Armii. ... 18 aprelia 1943 g. 22 chasa 30 minut. No.30095. in *SBD5*, p.17.
34 Prikaz o poriadke napravleniia iz gospitalei voennosluzhashchikh gvardeiskikh chastei i kursantskikh brigad posle ikh vizdorovleniia, No. 354, 13 dekabria 1941 g., In *RA T.13 (2–2)*, pp.128–9 and Komanduiushchim voiskam frontov i otdel'nimi armiiami o poriadke popolneniia gvardeiskikh chastei, 10 fevrailia 1944 g., in *RA T.12 (4)*, pp.65–6.
35 I.N. Russiianov, *V boiakh rozhdennaia*, pp.106–9.
36 K. Cheremukhin and S. Petrov, 'Krasnoznamennie (K 60-letiiu uchrezhdeniia ordena Krasnogo Znameni)', in *Vizh*, Number 8 (1978), pp.77–80.
37 Directive of the Headquarters of the Supreme Command to commanders of the forces of fronts, armies and military districts, 15 July 1941, in Alexander Hill, *The Great Patriotic War*, p.58.
38 David Stahel, *Operation Barbarossa*, pp.329, 414–15.
39 Hans Roth (Christine Alexander and Mason Kunze (eds.)), *Eastern Inferno: The Journals of a German Panzerjäger on the Eastern Front, 1941–43*, p.45.
40 *Siegfried Knappe with Ted Brusaw, Soldat: Reflections of a German Soldier*, pp.232–3.
41 V.A. Savchenko and A.A. Filippenko, *Oborona Odessi. 73 dnia geroicheskoi oboroni goroda* (Moscow: ZAO Izdatel'stvo Tsentropoligraf, 2011), p.392.
42 David Stahel, *Kiev 1941: Hitler's battle for supremacy in the East* (Cambridge: Cambridge University Press, 2012), p.255.
43 Iu. V. Nikulin, *Sem' dolgikh let* (Moscow: AST, 2014), pp.22–3.
44 Gosudarstvennii Komitet Oboroni. Postanovlenie No. GKO-562ss. ot "22" avgusta 1941 g. Moskva, Kreml'. O vvedenii vodka na snabzhenie v deistvuiushchei Krasnoi Armii. www.soldat.ru/doc/gko/scans/0562-1.jpg [Accessed 28 December 2014] and Prikaz o vidache voennosluzhashchim peredovoi linii deistvuiushchei armii vodka po 100 grammov v den', 25 avgusta 1941 g., in *RA T.13(2–2)*, p.73.
45 N.A. Antipenko, *Na glavnom napravlenii. Zapiski zamestitelia komanduiushchego frontom* (Moscow: Izdatel'stvo "Nauka", 1967), p.149.
46 Gosudarstvennii Komitet Oboroni. Postanovlenie No. GOKO-1727s ot "11" maia 1942 g. Moskva, Kreml'. O poriadke vidachi vodka voiskam

deistvuiushchei armii. www.soldat.ru/doc/gko/scans/0562–1.jpg [Accessed 28 December 2014].

47 Gosudarstvennii Komitet Oboroni. Postanovlenie No. GOKO-1889s ot "6" iiunia 1942 g. Moskva, Kreml'. O poriadke vidachi vodka voiskam deistvuiushchei armii. www.soldat.ru/doc/gko/scans/1889-1.jpg [Accessed 28 December 2014].

48 Gosudarstvennii Komitet Oboroni. Postanovlenie No. GOKO-2507s ot "12" noiabria 1942 g. Moskva, Kreml'. O vidache vodka voiskovim chastiam deist-vuiushchei armii s 25 noiabria 1942 goda. www.soldat.ru/doc/gko/scans/2507-01-1.jpg [Accessed 28 December 2014], and Prilozhenie k postanovleniiu GOKO No. 2507 s ot 12.XI.42g. Limit raskhoda vodki dlia voiskovikh chastei deistvuiushchei armii s 25 noiabria po 31 dekabria 1942 g. www.soldat.ru/doc/gko/scans/2507-02-1.jpg [Accessed 28 December 2014].

49 Prikaz s ob"iavleniem norm i poriadka vidachi vodka tekhnicheskomu sostavu chastei VVS deistvuiushchei armii. No. 31 13 ianvaria 1943 g., in Artem Drabkin (ed.), Ia dralsia na istrebitele, p.494.

50 Prikaz o poriadke khraneniia i vidachi vodka voiskam deistvuiushchei armii, No. 0470, 12 iiunia 1942 g, in RA T.13 (2–2), pp.252–3.

51 See for example comments on the matter by one veteran, in Ivan Novokhats-kii, Vospominaniia komandira batarei. Divizionnaia artilleriia v godi Velikoi Otechestvennoi voini. 1941–1945 (Moscow: ZAO Tsentropoligraf, 2007), p.44.

52 N.A. Antipenko, Na glavnom napravlenii, p.149.

53 Paul Carrell, Hitler Moves East, 1941–1943 (New York: Bantam Books, 1966), p.193.

54 To the commanders of the 8th Guards Rifle Corps' formations, 20 November 1942, in David M. Glantz, Zhukov's Greatest Defeat: The Red Army's Epic Disaster in Operation Mars, 1942 (Lawrence, Kansas: University Press of Kansas, 1999), p.327.

55 Testimony of Ivan Vladimirovich Maslov. http://iremember.ru/tankisti/maslov-ivan-vladimirovich/stranitsa-2.html [Accessed 28 December 2014]. An English-language version is available here: http://english.iremember.ru/tankers/69-maslov-ivan-vladimirovich.html [Accessed 28 December 2014].

56 Rasporiazhenie komanduiushchego voiskami 1-go Belorusskogo fronta komanduiushchim 1-i i 2-i gvardeiskimi tankovimi armiiami, komandiru 9-go tankogo korpusa o zaprete vidachi vodka vsemu lichnomu sostavu. No.10388, 17 aprelia 1945. 22:45. In RA T.15 (4–5), p.86.

57 Gorelov Sergei Dmitrievich, in Artem Drabkin (ed.), Ia dralsia na istrebitele, p.346.

58 By 1 October the Briansk Front could field only 18 'heavy' (largely KV), 33 'medium' (largely T-34) and 32 'light' (including BT-series and T-26) tanks – a total of only 83 tanks. See 'Moskovskaia bitva v tsifrakh (period oboroni)', in Vizh, Number 3 (1967), p.71.

59 I.Kh. Bagramian, Tak nachalas' voina, p.324–7.

60 Ibid., p.321.

61 I.Ia.Virodov et al, V srazheniiakh za pobedu (Moscow: Izdatel'stvo "Nauka", 1974), p.38.

62 Heersgruppe Mitte. Ic/A.O. Dolm. H.Qu., dem 19.7.1941. Vernehmung des Gefangenen russischen Oberleutnant Jakob Josifowitsch Dschugaschvilli, vom 14. Haub-Art. Regiment. NARA T-315 roll 205 frame 000248; Stahel, *Kiev 1941*, pp.227–8.

63 I.Ia. Virodov et al, *V srazheniiakh za pobedu*, p.43.

64 Ibid., pp.38–40, 44; I.Kh. Bagramian, *Tak nachalas' voina*, p.319.

65 David Stahel, *Kiev 1941*, p.217.

66 I.Ia. Virodov et al, *V srazheniiakh za pobedu*, pp.42–6 and I.Kh. Bagramian, *Tak nachalas' voina*, p.331.

67 I.Kh. Bagramian, *Tak nachalas' voina*, pp.328–9.

68 Ibid., pp.333–5 and Stahel, *Kiev 1941*, pp.228–9.

69 Direktiva Stavki VGK No. 001650 komanduiushchemu voiskami Brianskogo fronta, razreshaiushchaia sozdanie zagraditel'nikh otriadov, 5 sentiabria 1941 g., in *RAT.16 (5–1)*, p.164.

70 Direktiva Stavki VGK No. 001919 komanduiushchim voiskami frontov, armiiami, komandiram divizii, glavnokomanduiushchemu voiskami Iugo-zapadnogo napravleniia o sozdanii zagraditel'nikh otriadov v strelkovikh diviziiakh, 12 sentiabria 1941 g. 23 ch 50 min, in ibid., p.180.

71 Krivosheev, *Soviet Casualties and Combat Losses*, p.114.

72 K.A. Kalashnikov et al, *Krasnaia armiia v iiune 1941 goda (statistichesii sbornik)* (Novosibirsk: Sibirskii khornograf, 2003), p.62 and Svedeniia shtaba Iugo-Zapadnogo fronta o boevom i chislennom sostave soedinenii i otdel'nikh chastei fronta po sostoianiiu na 15.7.41 g., in *SBD38*, p.37.

73 I.M. Golushko, *Shtab tila Krasnoi Armii v godi voini 1941–1945*, p.64.

74 N.A. Antipenko, 'Til v Moskovskoi bitve', in A.M. Samsonov (ed.), *Proval gitlerovskogo natupleniia na Moskvu* (Moscow: Izdatel'stvo "Nauka", 1966), p.328.

75 N.D. Iakovlev, *Ob artillerii i nemnogo o sebe*, pp.79, 83–7 and V.N. Novikov (gen.ed.), *Oruzhie pobedi*, pp.402–3.

76 Alexander Hill, *The Great Patriotic War*, p.186; A.Iu. Ermolov, *Gosudarstvennoe upravlenie voennoi promishelnnost'iu v 1940-e godi: tankovaia promishlennost'*, pp.121–2 and 163, 382; Politdonesenie v Glavnoe politupravlenie o sostoianii raboti Bronetankovogo upravleniia po obespecheniiu Krasnoi Armii boevim mashinam i zapchastiami k nim, 11 avgusta 1941 g., in A.M. Radionov et al (eds.), *Glavnoe avtobronetankovoe upravlenie. Liudi, sobitiia, fakti v dokumentakh – 1940–1942 gg.*, p.96.

77 Politdonesenie v Glavnoe politupravlenie o sostoianii raboti Bronetankovogo upravleniia po obespecheniiu Krasnoi Armii boevim mashinam i zapchastiami k nim, 11 avgusta 1941 g., in A.M. Radionov et al (eds.), *Glavnoe avtobronetankovoe upravlenie. Liudi, sobitiia, fakti v dokumentakh – 1940–1942 gg.*, pp.96–7.

78 See Lev Lopukhovsky (trans. and ed. Stuart Britton), *The Viaz'ma Catastrophe, 1941*, pp.181–90.

79 Ibid., pp.193–201.

80 David Stahel, *Operation Typhoon: Hitler's March on Moscow, October 1941* (Cambridge: Cambridge University Press, 2013), p.143.

81 Ibid., pp.151, 153, 160.

82 Jack Radey and Charles Sharp, *The Defense of Moscow 1941: The Northern Flank* (Mechanicsburg, PA: Stackpole Books, 2012), pp.58–63 and David Stahel, *Operation Typhoon*, pp.127–8, 130, 134, 139.

83 Hans Schäufler (ed.), *Knight's Cross Panzers: The German 35th Panzer Regiment in WWII*, pp.141–3.

84 Ibid., pp.147–9.

85 Franz Halder, *War Journal of Franz Halder. Volume VII*, p.131.

86 Alexander Hill, *The Great Patriotic War*, p.74. These figures, regularly cited as representing total German armoured strength, do not include miscellenous units consisting of captured, largely French, equipment, such as Pz. Abt.(F) 101 with Char B1 tanks with flamethrower conversions. Some of these units were however withdrawn before the winter. See Thomas L. Jentz (ed.), *Panzertruppen: …1933–1942*, pp.193, 214–15, and Franz Halder, *War Journal of Franz Halder. Volume VII*, p.148.

87 See 'Moskovskaia bitva v tsifrakh (period oboroni)', p.71.

88 Directive of …the Western Front to commanders of the 16, 5 and 43 Armies…, 15 October 1941, in Alexander Hill, *The Great Patriotic War*, p.72.

89 Thomas L. Jentz (ed.), *Panzertruppen: …1933–1942*, p.205.

90 Heinz Guderian, *Panzer Leader* (London: Arrow Books Limited, 1990), pp.248–9.

91 Ibid., p.235.

92 F.W. von Mellenthin, *Panzer Battles* (London: Futura Publications Ltd, 1973) pp.356–62.

93 Ukazaniia GLAVPU RKKA po otboru tankovikh ekipazhei, 12 avgusta 1941 g., in *RA T.17–6 (1–2)*, p.61.

94 Directive of …the Western Front to commanders of the 16, 5 and 43 Armies…, 15 October 1941, in Alexander Hill, *The Great Patriotic War*, p.72.

95 Direktiva Stavki VGK komanduiushchim voiskami Severo-Zapadnogo i Zapadnogo frontov, zamestiteliu komanduiushchego voiskami Zapadnogo fronta general-polkovniku I.S. Konevu o sosdanii Kalininskogo fronta, No.003053, 17 oktiabria 1941 g. 18:30, in *RA T.15 (4–1)*, p.108.

96 I.E. Krupchenko (gen.ed.), *Sovetskie tankovie voiska 1941–1945 gg. Voenno-istoricheskii ocherk* (Moscow: Voennoe izdatel'stvo Ministerstva oboroni SSSR, 1973), p.44.

97 Donesenie chlena Voennogo Soveta 30-i armii Brigadnogo komissara N.V. Abramova o boiakh za gorod Kalinin, chlenu Voennogo Soveta Zapadnogo fronta tov. Bulganinu, 17 oktiabria 1941, in P.N. Knishevskii, *Skritaia pravda voini: 1941 god*, p.171.

98 Operativnii otdel shtaba Kalininskogo fronta. Zhurnal boevikh deistvii voisk fronta za oktiabr' 1941g. 17 oktiabria. TsAMO f.213.o.2002.d.31.l.1ob.

99 Jack Radey and Charles Sharp, *The Defense of Moscow 1941: The Northern Flank*, pp.85–9 and S. Fligel'man, 'Vsem smertiam nazlo', in M.Ia. Maistrovskii (ed.), *Na pravom flange Moskovskoi bitvi* (Tver': Moskovskii rabochii, 1991), pp.95–6.

100 Jack Radey and Charles Sharp, *The Defense of Moscow 1941: The Northern Flank*, p.89 and S. Fligel'man, 'Vsem smertiam nazlo', pp.94, 98.

101 S. Fligel'man, 'Vsem smertiam nazlo', pp.92–4 and Direktiva Stavka VGK komanduiushchim voiskami Zapadnogo i Severo-Zapadnogo frontov o podchinenii voisk Severo-Zapadnogo fronta v raione g. Kalinin komanduiushchemu voiskami Zapadnogo fronta, No. 003037, 16 oktiabria 1941 g. 19:45, in *RA T.15 (4–1)*, p.107.

102 Jack Radey and Charles Sharp, *The Defense of Moscow 1941: The Northern Flank*, p.89.

103 Decree of the State Defence Committee No. 172 ss concerning the Mozhaisk defence line, 16 July 1941 and …on the composition of forces on the Mozhaisk defensive line, 13 October 1941, in Alexander Hill, *The Great Patriotic War*, pp.63, 70; Gosudarstvennii komitet oboroni. Postanovlenie No. GKO-565ss ot "23" avgusta 1941 g. Moskva, Kreml'. O Mozhaiskoi linii oboroni. www.soldat.ru/doc/gko/scans/0565-01-1.jpg [Accessed 3 January 2015]; and David Stahel, *Operation Typhoon*, p.177.

104 A.V. Vasil'ev, I.S. Korotkov and N.E. Podporozhnii (General'nii shtab Krasnoi armii. Voenno-istoricheskii otdel), *Razgrom nemtsev pod Moskvoi. Operativnii ocherk* (Moscow, 1942), p.13. TsAMO f.450.o.11158.d.89.

105 David Stahel, *Operation Typhoon*, p.305.

106 Ivan Tiulenev, *Cherez tri voini. Vospominaniia komanduiushchego Iuzhnim i Zakavkazkim frontam. 1941–1945* (Moscow: ZAO Tsentpoligraf, 2007), p.275.

107 Prikaz o formirovanii otdel'nikh tankovikh brigad, No.0062, 12 avgusta 1941 g., in *RA T.13 (2–2)*, pp.51–3; Gosudarstvennii komitet oboroni. Postanovlenie No. GKO-570ss ot "23" avgusta 1941 g. Moskva, Kreml'. O tankovikh chastiakh. www.soldat.ru/doc/gko/scans/0570–1.jpg [Accessed 3 January 2015]; Gosudarstvennii komitet oboroni. Postanovlenie No. GKO-671ss ot "13" sentiabria 1941 g. Moskva, Kreml'. O formirovanii tankovikh brigad v sentiabre mesiatse s.g. www.soldat.ru/doc/gko/scans/0671-01-1.jpg and www.soldat.ru/doc/gko/scans/0671-02-1.jpg [Accessed 3 January 2015]; David Glantz, *Colossus Reborn: The Red Army at War, 1941–1943* (Lawrence, KA: University Press of Kansas, 2005), pp.220–4.

108 Glantz, *Colossus Reborn*, p.252.

109 Gosudarstvennii komitet oboroni. Postanovlenie No. GKO-833ss ot "25" oktiabria 1941 g. Moskva, Kreml'. O strelkovoi divizii voennogo vremeni. www.soldat.ru/doc/gko/scans/0833-01-1.jpg [Accessed 3 January 2015]; Gosudarstvennii komitet oboroni. Postanovlenie No. GKO-828ss ot "22" oktiabria 1941 g. Moskva, Kreml'. G..K..O… postanovliaet: 1. Utverdit' organizatsiiu otdel'noi strelkovoi brigade…. www.soldat.ru/doc/gko/scans/0828-01-1.jpg [Accessed 3 January 2015]; Valerii Vakhromeev, *Vizhit' i vernut'sia*, p.18; David Glantz, *Colossus Reborn*, pp.195–6; Directive of the Headquarters of the Supreme Command…, 15 July 1941, in Alexander Hill, *The Great Patriotic War*, p.58; P.V. Mel'nikov (gen.ed.), *Razvitie taktiki sukhoputnikh voisk v Velikoi Otechestvennoi voine* (Moscow: Izdanie akademii [imeni M.V. Frunze], 1981), pp.296–7; V.N. Shunkov, *Artilleriia Krasnoi Armii i Vermakhta*, pp.23, 26.

110 Mikhail Suknev, *Zapiski komandira shtrafbata. Vospominaniia kombata. 1941–1945* (Moscow: ZAO Tsentrpoligraf, 2006), p.37. List strength for a

rifle division as of 18 March 1942 was 279 PTRD. See David Glantz, *Colossus Reborn*, p.196.

111 Direktiva Stavki VGK No.002059 glavnokomanduiushchemu voiskami Iugo-Zapadnogo napravleniia, komanduiushchim voiskam frontov i armiiami... ob izmeneniiakh v shtate strelkovikh divizii, 17 sentiabria 1941 g., in *RA T.16 (5–1)*, p.188. At the same time motor rifle divisions were renamed as rifle divisions.

112 See for example orders for the creation of such detachments by the Western Front of 19 and 21 October 1941 in *RA T.15 (4–1)*, pp.111 and 114.

113 To military soviets of fronts and armies on the defence of population centres, 24 November 1941, in Alexander Hill, *The Great Patriotic War*, p.78.

114 Rasporiazhenie Voennogo soveta Zapadnogo fronta po organizatsii oboroni v naselennikh punktakh, No.01126, 27 noiabria 1941 g., in P.N. Knishevskii, *Skritaia pravda voini: 1941 god*, p.215.

115 Richard L. Dinardo, *Germany and the Axis Powers: From Coalition to Collapse* (Lawrence, KA: University Press of Kansas, 2005), pp.118–20; Field Marshal Erich von Manstein, *Lost Victories* (Minneapolis, MA: Zenith Press, 2004), p.220.

116 Jürgen Rohwer and Mikhail S. Monakov, *Stalin's Ocean Going Fleet*, p.137.

117 Richard L. Dinardo, *Germany and the Axis Powers*, pp.109–10, 142–4.

118 Gunnar Åselius, 'The Naval Theatres in Soviet Grand Strategy during the Interwar Period', p.70.

119 Alexander Hill, 'British Lend-Lease Aid and the Soviet War Effort, June 1941-June 1942', pp.802–5.

120 Prikaz ob ispol'zovanii minnogo oruzhiia VMF v voine s germanskim fashizmom, No.00111, 18 aprelia 1942 g., in *RA T.21 (10)* , pp.121–3.

121 On the purges and the Soviet navy, and for the Baltic Fleet, see Gunnar Åselius, *The Rise and Fall of the Soviet Navy in the Baltic*, pp.238–48, and for the Northern Fleet see Alexander Hill, 'Russian and Soviet Naval Power in the Arctic from the XVI Century to the Beginning of the Great Patriotic War', pp.384–5.

122 Andrei Platonov, *Tragedii Finskogo zaliva* (Moscow: Veche, 2010), pp.109, 191–2.

123 See Chapters 14 and 16.

124 See Chapter 20.

125 See for example, S.W. Roskill, *The War at Sea, 1939–1945. Volume II: The Period of Balance* (Uckfield, East Sussex: The Naval and Military Press, Ltd, 2004), pp.133–4.

126 V.F. Tributz, 'Baltiiskii flot v zavershaiushchikh operatsiiakh voini', in A.M. Samsonov (ed.), *9 maia 1945 goda* (Moscow: Izdatel'stvo "Nauka", 1970), p.611.

127 Alexander Hill, *The Great Patriotic War*, pp.137–8.

128 Mikhail Suprun, 'Operation "West": The Role of the Northern Fleet and its Air Forces in the Liberation of the Russian Arctic in 1944', in *JSMS*, Volume 20, Number 3 (July–September 2007), pp.446–7.

129 V. I. Afanasenko and E.F. Krinko, *56-ia armiia v boiakh za Rostov. Pervaia pobeda Krasnoi armii. Oktiabra'-dekabr' 1941* (Moscow: ZAO Izdatel'stvo Tsentrpoligraf, 2013), pp.190–2, 206–7.

130 *Organizatsiia sviazi v Rostovskoi nastupatel'noi operatsii (s 24 noiabria po 12 dekabria 1941 g.)* (Shtab 56 deistvuiushchei armii – otdel sviazi, 1942), pp.24, 41, 58.

131 Ibid., p.7 and V. I. Afanasenko and E.F. Krinko, *56-ia armiia v boiakh za Rostov*, p.226–7.

CHAPTER 12

1 Here I think that John Erickson's chapter covering this period in *The Road to Stalingrad* is worth looking at despite having been written without many sources available now and being rather long for a single chapter. The chapter is entitled 'The Moscow Counter-stroke: November-December 1941', and covers events from the eve of the anniversary of the Revolution on 6 November through to 5 January and the broadening of the scope of Soviet offensive operations. The chapter is successful in showing how successful local counter-attacks and fresh troops contributed to the relatively rapid development and implementation of more ambitious plans. See John Erickson, *The Road to Stalingrad: Stalin's War with Germany: Volume One* (London: Weidenfeld and Nicholson, 1993), pp.249–96.

2 258. Division Abt. Ia. Div.Gef.Stand, im Februar 1942. Gefechtsbericht der 258. J.D. über die Nara an die Desna bei Burzewo und anschliessenden Rückzug in die Ausgangsstellung in der Zeit vom 1.12.-4.12.1941. NARA T-315 Roll 1817 frames 418–419 and Karte 5. Stand bei XX.A.K. am 2.12.41 abends., frame 458; Paul Carrell, *Hitler Moves East*, p.193; V.M. Safir, 'Oborona Moskvi. Narofominskii proriv 1–5 dekabria 1941 goda (chto bilo i chego ne bilo v deistvitel'nosti)', in *Voenno-istoricheskii arkhiv*, vipusk 1 (1997), p.84; Alexander Hill, *The Great Patriotic War*, pp.79–80.

3 Operativnaia svodka shtaba 33-i armii o boevikh deistviiakh soedinenii i chastei armii po unichtozheniiu prorvavshegosia protivnika . . . v raione Naro-Fominsk, No. 210, 2 dekabria 1941 g. 17:00, in *RA T.15 (4–1)*, p.158 and V.M. Safir, 'Oborona Moskvi. Narofominskii proriv 1–5 dekabria 1941 goda', p.84.

4 V.M. Safir, 'Oborona Moskvi. Narofominskii proriv 1–5 dekabria 1941 goda', p.84 and Alexander Hill, 'British Lend-Lease Tanks and the Battle of Moscow, November-December 1941 – Revisited', in *JSMS*, Volume 22, Number 4 (October–December 2009), pp.578–80.

5 Gefechtsbericht der 258. J.D. über die Nara an die Desna bei Burzewo und anschliessenden Rückzug in die Ausgangsstellung in der Zeit vom 1.12.-4.12.1941, frame 424–5; Paul Carell, *Hitler Moves East*, pp.193–4; V.M. Safir, 'Oborona Moskvi. Narofominskii proriv 1–5 dekabria 1941 goda', p.85.

6 Alexander Hill, *The Great Patriotic War*, p.80 and V.M. Safir, 'Oborona Moskvi. Narofominskii proriv 1–5 dekabria 1941 goda', p.88; Alexander Hill, 'British Lend-Lease Tanks and the Battle of Moscow, November – December 1941 – Revisited', p.580.

7 See General'nii shtab Krasnoi armii. Voenno-istoricheskii otdel, *Razgrom Nemtsev pod Moskvoi. Operativnii ocherk (Moscow: 1942)*, pp.36–7, in TsAMO f.450.o.11158.d.89 and V.M. Safir, 'Oborona Moskvi. Narofominskii proriv 1–5 dekabria 1941 goda', p.81.

8 V.M. Safir, 'Oborona Moskvi. Narofominskii proriv 1–5 dekabria 1941 goda', p.83.

9 Gefechtsbericht der 258. J.D. über die Nara an die Desna bei Burzewo und anschliessenden Rückzug in die Ausgangsstellung in der Zeit vom 1.12.-4.12.1941, frame 433.

10 V.M. Safir, 'Oborona Moskvi. Narofominskii proriv 1–5 dekabria 1941 goda', p.88.

11 Ibid., p.83.

12 Gefechtsbericht der 258. J.D. über die Nara an die Desna bei Burzewo und anschliessenden Rückzug in die Ausgangsstellung in der Zeit vom 1.12.–4.12.1941, frames 431 and 450–1.

13 David Glantz, *Soviet Military Intelligence in War*, pp.127–8.

14 See for example V.V. Kondrashov, *Znat' vse o protivnike. Voennie razvedki SSSR i fashistskoi Germanii v godi Velikoi Otechestvennoi voini (istoricheskaia khronika)* (Moscow: Izdatel'skii dom "Krasnaia zvezda", 2010), pp.117, 133 and *Vremennii polevoi ustav RKKA 1936 (PU36)*, pp.21–2.

15 Hans Schäufler (ed.), *Knight's Cross Panzers: The German 35th Panzer Regiment in WWII*, p.144.

16 I.L. Burnusov (ed.), *Frontovie i voiskovie razvedchiki v Stalingradskoi bitve (v dokumentakh i litsakh)* (Moscow: "Kuchkovo pole", 2013), pp.281, 283.

17 Gefechtsbericht der 258. J.D. über die Nara an die Desna bei Burzewo und anschliessenden Rückzug in die Ausgangsstellung in der Zeit vom 1.12.–4.12.1941, frame 452.

18 Ibid., frame 450.

19 Christian Streit, 'Soviet Prisoners of War in the Hands of the Wehrmacht', in Hannes Heer and Klaus Naumann (eds.), *War of Extermination: The German Military in World War II, 1941–1944* (New York/Oxford: Berghann Books, 2004), p.89.

20 See for example Bernd Boll and Hans Safrian, 'On the Way to Stalingrad: The 6th Army in 1941–42', in *Hannes Heer and Klaus Naumann (eds.), War of Extermination: The German Military in World War II, 1941–1944*, pp.240–5 and ibid., pp.80–9.

21 In addition to the other essays in Hannes Heer and Klaus Naumann (eds.), *War of Extermination: The German Military in World War II, 1941–1944*, for a short overview of many of these issues, see Jonathan Steinberg, 'The Third Reich Reflected: German Civil Administration in the Occupied Soviet Union, 1941–4', in *English Historical Review*, Volume 110, Issue 437 (June 1995), pp.620–51.

22 P.K. Ponomarenko, 'Bor'ba Sovetskogo naroda v tilu vraga', in *Vizh*, Number 4 (1965), p.34 and Alexander Hill, *The Great Patriotic War*, p.193.

23 Alexander Hill, *The War Behind the Eastern Front: The Soviet Partisan Movement in North-West Russia, 1941–1944* (Abingdon, Oxon: Frank Cass, 2005), p.40.

24 Decree of the TsK VKP(b) on the organisation of the struggle in the rear of German forces, 18 July 1941 in Alexander Hill, *The Great Patriotic War*, p.194.

25 Created by the NKVD and charged with such activities as combating enemy agents parachuted into the Soviet rear.

26 Decree of the TsK VKP(b) on the organisation of the struggle in the rear of German forces, 18 July 1941, in Alexander Hill, *The Great Patriotic War*, p.195.
27 Direktiva UNKGB i UNKVD po Kalininskoi oblasti No.807 nachal'nikam MRO NKGB, GO i RO NKVD o merakh po uluchsheniiu organizatsii partizanskikh otriadov i diversionnikh grupp, napravliaemikh v til protivnika, 29 iiulia 1941 g., in V.P. Iampol'skii (gen.ed.) et al, *Organi gosudarstvennoi bezopasnosti.... Tom vtoroi. Kniga 1. Nachalo. 22 iiunia – 31 avgusta 1941 goda*, p.417.
28 M.M. Kir'ian (editor-in chief), *Sovetskaia voennaia entsiklopediia, 2* (Moscow: Voenizdat, 1976), pp.201–2. In English see C. Van Dyke, *The Soviet Invasion of Finland 1939–1940*, p.208.
29 G.A. Kumanev 'Otvet P.K. Ponomarenko na voprosi G.A. Kumaneva. 2 noiabria 1978 g.', in *Otechestvennaia istoriia*, No. 6 (1988), p.141.
30 Ibid.
31 David Glantz, 'Boldin', in H. Shukman (ed.), *Stalin's Generals*, pp.48–9.
32 Kumanev, "Otvet P.K. Ponomarenko", p.141.
33 Pis'mo I.Anan'eva I.V. Stalinu o nedostatkakh v organizatsii partizanskogo dvizheniia, 27 oktiabria 1941 g., in S.V. Kudriashov (gen.ed.), *Vestnik Arkhiva Prezidenta Rossiiskoi Federatsii. Partizanskoe dvizhenie v godi Velikoi Otechestvennoi voini* (Moscow: Izdatel'stvo "Istoricheskaia literatura", 2015), p.93.
34 See Zapiska P.K. Ponomarenko I.V. Stalinu, 'K voprosu o postanovke diversionnoi raboti', 21 sentiabria 1941 g., in ibid., pp.74–7 and later, and for example Zapiska L.P. Beria I.V.Stalinu ob organizatsii partizanskikh otriadov i diversionnikh grupp, No. 2408/b, 8 avgusta 1941 g., in ibid., p.48. Malenkov is mentioned in Anan'ev's letter of 27 October as having provided some initial support for his initial proposal back in July.
35 See Zapiska E.A. Shchadenko I.V. Stalinu o sozdanii partizanskikh otriadov i organizatsii rukovodstva imi s prilozheniem proekta postanovleniia GOKO, No. 719520, 3 sentiabria 1941 g, in ibid., pp.62–6.
36 Zapiska P.K. Ponomarenko I.V. Stalinu s prilozheniem dokumentov ob organizatsii podpol'noi partiinoi raboti i partizanskoi bor'bi v tilu nemetskikh voisk, 4 oktiabria 1941 g., in ibid., pp.77–88.
37 Ponomarenko, 'Bor'ba sovetskogo naroda', p.34.
38 V. I. Boiarskii, *Partizani i armiia: Istoriia uteriannikh vozmozhnostei* (Minsk: Kharvest; Moskva: AST, 2003), p.260; Zapiska E.A. Shchadenko I.V.Stalinu o zadachakh po organizatii formirovanii dlia vedeniia partizanskoi bor'bi, No.00167ss, 7 dekabria 1941 g., including Proekt...postanovenie GKO...o formirovanii partizanskikh armii, in S.V. Kudriashov (gen.ed.), *Vestnik Arkhiva Prezidenta Rossiiskoi Federatsii. Partizanskoe dvizhenie v godi Velikoi Otechestvennoi voini*, pp.99–103.
39 Dokladnaia zapiska sekretaria Smolenskogo obkoma VKP(b) zaveduiushchemu orginstruktorskim otdelom TsK VKP (b) o sostianii partizanskogo dvizheniia v oblasti, 22 noiabria 1941 g., in *RA T.20 (9)*, pp.66–7.
40 Ibid., p.69 and Gerhard L. Weinberg, 'The Yelnya-Dorogobuzh Area of Smolensk Oblast', in John A. Armstrong (ed.), *Soviet Partisans in World*

War II (Madison, Wisconsin: The University of Wisconsin Press, 1964), p.410.

41 Ibid., pp.411–22.

42 See Alexander Hill, *The War behind the Eastern Front*, pp.37–8.

43 See Ben Shepherd, *War in the Wild East: The German Army and Soviet Partisans* (Cambridge, MA/London: Harvard University Press, 2004), pp.192–3.

44 Svedeniia Leningradskogo shtaba partizanskogo dvizheniia o poteriakh protivnika, ponesennikh v resul'tate deistvii partisan Leningradskoi oblasti v godi voini, 4 aprelia 1944 g., in V.M. Koval'chuk (gen.ed.), *V tilu vraga. Bor'ba partisan i podpol'shchikov na okkupirovannoi territorii Leningradskoi oblasti. 1944 g.: Sbornik dokumentov* (Leningrad: Lenizdat, 1985), p.249 and Alexander Hill, *The War behind the Eastern Front*, pp.165, 176.

45 GKO Decree Number 1837ss on the formation of a Central Headquarters of the Partisan Movement…, 30 May 1942, in Alexander Hill, *The Great Patriotic War*, p.198.

46 Alexander Hill, *The War behind the Eastern Front*, pp.160, 165.

47 Ibid., p.86.

48 Svedeniia Leningradskogo shtaba partizanskogo dvizheniia o poteriakh protivnika, ponesennikh v resul'tate deistvii partisan Leningradskoi oblasti v godi voini, 4 aprelia 1944 g., in V.M. Koval'chuk (gen.ed.), *V tilu vraga. Bor'ba partisan i podpol'shchikov na okkupirovannoi territorii Leningradskoi oblasti. 1944 g.*, p.249 and Alexander Hill, *The War Behind the Eastern Front* , pp.165, 176.

49 Alexander Hill, *The War behind the Eastern Front*, p.117.

50 Ibid., pp.140–1.

51 Ibid., p.48.

52 N. Miuller[Müller], *Vermakht i okkupatsiia (1941–1944)* (Moskva: Voenizdat, 1974) p.107.

53 Alexander Hill, *The War Behind the Eastern Front*, p.48.

54 Ibid., p.86.

55 E.M. Howell, *The Soviet Partisan Movement 1941–1944. DA Pam 20–244* (Washington DC: Department of the Army, 1956), p.73.

56 See for instance Alexander Hill, *The War behind the Eastern Front*, pp.47–8 and Ben Shepherd, *War in the Wild East*, pp.76–7, 104–5.

57 E.M. Howell, *The Soviet Partisan Movement 1941–1944*, p.85 and Alexander Hill, *The War Behind the Eastern Front*, p.94.

58 P.K. Ponomarenko, *Vsenarodnaia bor'ba v tilu nemetsko-fashistskikh zakhvatchikov 1941–1944* (Moscow: Nauka, 1986), p.377.

59 Reconnaissance summary material, presumably of the Central Headquarters of the Partisan Movement, in the personal fond of Panteleimon Ponomarenko, Russian State Archive of Socio-Political History (RGASPI) f.625.o.1. d.38.l. 332 and S.W. Mitcham, *Hitler's Legions: German Army Order of Battle, World War II* (London: Leo Cooper/Secker and Warburg, 1985) p.174.

60 Alexander Hill, *The War behind the Eastern Front*, p.160.

61 Reconnaissance summary material, presumably of the Central Headquarters of the Partisan Movement, in the personal fond of Panteleimon Ponomarenko, RGASPI f.625.o.1.d.38.l. 337 and S.W. Mitcham, *Hitler's Legions: German Army Order of Battle, World War II*, p.50.

62 E.M. Howell, *The Soviet Partisan Movement 1941–1944*, p.73 and Ben Shepherd, *War in the Wild East*, p.92.

63 Alexander Hill, *The War behind the Eastern Front*, p.95.

64 Reconnaissance summary material, presumably of the Central Headquarters of the Partisan Movement, in the personal fond of Panteleimon Ponomarenko, RGASPI f.625.o.1.d.38.l.331.

65 Svedeniia Leningradskogo shtaba partizanskogo dvizheniia o poteriakh protivnika, ponesennikh v resul'tate deistvii partisan Leningradskoi oblasti v godi voini, 4 aprelia 1944 g., in V.M. Koval'chuk (gen.ed.), *V tilu vraga. Bor'ba partisan i podpol'shchikov na okkupirovannoi territorii Leningradskoi oblasti. 1944 g.*, p.249.

66 P.K. Ponomarenko, *Vsenarodnaia bor'ba v tilu nemetsko-fashistskikh zakhvatchikov 1941–1944*, p.434.

67 Svedeniia Leningradskogo shtaba partizanskogo dvizheniia o poteriakh protivnika, ponesennikh v resul'tate deistvii partisan Leningradskoi oblasti v godi voini, 4 aprelia 1944 g., in V.M. Koval'chuk (gen.ed.), *V tilu vraga. Bor'ba partisan i podpol'shchikov na okkupirovannoi territorii Leningradskoi oblasti. 1944 g.*, p.249.

68 E.M. Howell, *The Soviet Partisan Movement 1941–1944*, p.76.

69 Ibid., p.94 and Alexander Hill, *The War behind the Eastern Front*, p.132.

70 Alexander Hill, *The War behind the Eastern Front*, pp.132–3 and 139.

71 Prikaz Nachal'nika TsShPD o partizanskoi rel'sovoi voine na kommunikatsiiakh vraga, 14 iiulia 1943 g., and Soobshcheniie Tsentral'nogo shtaba partizanskogo dvizheniia o nekotorikh itogakh operatsii "Rel'sovaia voina", 15 avgusta 1943 g., in *RA T.20 (9)*, pp.300–2 and 304–6.

72 E.M. Howell, *The Soviet Partisan Movement 1941–1944*, pp.163–5.

73 Ibid., pp.173–80 and Alexander Hill, *The War Behind the Eastern Front*, pp.154–60.

74 Alexander Hill, *The War Behind the Eastern Front*, pp.75 and 121–2.

75 Reconnaissance summary material, presumably of the Central Headquarters of the Partisan Movement, in the personal fond of Panteleimon Ponomarenko, RGASPI f.625.o.1.d.38.l. 337.

76 See E.M. Howell, *The Soviet Partisan Movement 1941–1944*, p.168.

77 I.N. Artem'ev, 'Radiosviaz' v sovetskom partizanskom dvizhenii v godi Velikoi Otechestvennoi voini', in *Voprosii istorii*, Number 5 (1969), p.108.

78 See for example G.L. Weinberg, 'The Yelnya-Dorogobuzh area of Smolensk Oblast', in J. Armstrong (ed.), *Soviet Partisans in World War II*, pp.411–22; E.M. Howell, *The Soviet Partisan Movement 1941–1944*, pp.77–80 and 182–8; and Ben Shepherd, *War in the Wild East*, p.122.

79 V. Andrianov, 'Operativnoe ispol'zovanie partizanskikh sil', in *Vizh*, Number 7 (1969), pp.24–7; I.N. Artem'ev, 'Radiosviaz' v sovetskom partizanskom dvizhenii v godi Velikoi Otechestvennoi voini', pp.110, 116.

80 Alexander Hill, *The War Behind the Eastern Front*, pp.100–2.

81 Iz otcheta o rabote Otdela kadrov Tsentral'nogo shtaba partizanskogo dvizheniia za period s 15 iiunia 1942 g. po 15 fevralia 1944 g., 28 fevralia 1944 g., in *RA T.20 (9)*, pp.480–1, 485.

82 Iu. P. Petrov, *Partizanskoe dvizhenie v Leningradskoi oblasti 1941–1944* (Lenigrad: Lenizdat, 1973), p.439.

83 Iz otcheta o rabote Otdela kadrov Tsentral'nogo shtaba partizanskogo dviz-
    heniia za period s 15 iiunia 1942 g. po 15 fevralia 1944 g., 28 fevralia 1944
    g., in *RA T.20 (9)*, p.485 and Alexander Hill, *The War Behind the Eastern
    Front*, p.176.
84 Ibid., p.480.
85 Ibid., pp.481 and 485–6
86 For examples, see Alexander Hill, *The War Behind the Eastern Front*,
    pp.116–17 and 145–6.
87 G.F. Krivosheev, *Soviet Casualties and Combat Losses*, pp.166, 175, 179 and
    W. Haupt, *Army Group North – The Wehrmacht in Russia 1941–1945* (Atglen,
    PA: Schiffer Military History, 1997), p.382. Total losses inflicted on Army
    Group North for 1942 were apparently 259,950, including losses caused by
    partisan activity.
88 V. Stepakov, *Russkie diversanti protiv "kukushek"* (Moscow: Izdatel'stvo
    Iauza/Izdatel'stvo Eksmo, 2004), p.36.
89 Alexander Hill, *The War Behind the Eastern Front*, p.74.
90 David Glantz, *Colossus Reborn*, pp.168–9 and ibid., p.74.
91 See Aleksandr Gogun, *Stalinskie commandos. Ukrainskie partizanskie formir-
    ovaniia. Maloizuchennie stranitsi istorii. 1941–1944* (Moscow: ZAM Tsentr-
    poligraf, 2008), pp.110–12.
92 M.V. Pavlov, I.G. Zheltov and I.V. Pavlov, *Tanki BT* (Moscow: OOO
    Izdatel'skii tsentr "Eksprint", 2001), p.181.
93 'Moskovskaia bitva v tsifrakh (period oboroni)', in *Vizh*, Number 3 (1967),
    p.71.
94 'Moskovskaia bitva v tsifrakh (period kontrnastupleniia)', in *Vizh*, Number
    1 (1967), p.92.
95 Alexander Hill, *The Great Patriotic War*, p.173.
96 Alexander Hill, 'British Lend-Lease Tanks and the Battle of Moscow,
    November-December 1941 – Revisited', p.577 and Alexander Hill, *The
    Great Patriotic War*, p.85.
97 Izvlechenie iz operativnoi svodki No. 165 Glavnogo komandovaniia sukho-
    putnikh voisk Vermakhta. General'nii shtab. 4-I ober-kvartirmeister. Otdel
    po izucheniiu inostrannikh armii Vostoka (II). No. 4316/41 ..., 27.11.1941
    g., in V.A. Zhilin (gen.ed.), *Bitva pod Moskvoi. Khronika, fakti, liudi: V 2-x
    kn. Kn.1* (Moscow: OLMA-PRESS, 2001), p.793. See also David Stahel,
    Operation Typhoon, pp.177–8 and 293.
98 Alexander Hill, *The Great Patriotic War*, pp.83–5 and 173.
99 Soobrazheniia ABTU Zapadnogo fronta v operativnii otdel Genshtaba KA
    po ABTB, sostavlennie na osnove opita boevikh deistvii tankovikh chastei,
    19 ianvaria 1942 g, in A.M. Rodionov et al, *Glavnoe avtobronetankovoe
    upravlenie. Liudi, sobitiia, fakti v dokumentakh – 1940-1042 gg.*, p.168. On
    other technical issues, see Alexander Hill, 'British "Lend-Lease" Tanks and
    the Battle for Moscow, November-December 1941- A Research Note', in
    JSMS, Volume 19, Number 4 (2006), p.291.
100 Artem Drabkin (ed.), *Ia dralsia na T-34*, pp.13–14.
101 Alexander Hill, *The Great Patriotic War*, pp.174–5.
102 I.M. Tret'iak et al (eds.), *Krasnoznamennii Dal'nevostochnii*, pp.153, 155–7.

103 See Nikolay Rostov, 'The Deployment of Reserve Units and Formations of the Territory of Siberia During the Great Patriotic War (1941–1945)', in *JSMS*, Volume 23, Number 4 (December 2010), pp.641–55.

104 See Heinz Guderian, *Panzer Leader*, pp.248–9; David M. Glantz and Jonathan House, *When Titans Clashed: How the Red Army Stopped Hitler*, p.83 and p.337 n24; A. Getman, '112-ia tankovaia diviziia v bitve pod Moskvoi', in *Vizh*, Number 11 (1981), p.49.

105 Getman, '112-ia tankovaia diviziia v bitve pod Moskvoi', p.50.

106 Alexander Hill, 'British Lend-Lease Tanks and the Battle of Moscow, November-December 1941 – Revisited', p.581.

107 David Glantz, *Stumbling Colossus*, p.538.

108 G.F. Krivosheev, *Soviet Casualties and Combat Losses*, p.94.

109 Prilozhenie No.5. Rashet utrachennikh resursov voennoobiazannikh na vremenno zaniatoi protivnikom territorii (Doklad E.A. Shchadenko I.V. Stalinu 'O mobilizatsionnikh resursakh i ikh ispol'zovanii za god voini', No. 778183, 10 sentiabria 1942 g.), S.V. Kudriashov (gen.ed.), *Vestnik Arkhiva Prezidenta Rossiiskoi Federatsii. Voina: 1941–1945. Vipusk 2*, p.236.

110 Doklad E.A. Shchadenko I.V. Stalinu o shtatnoi i spisochnoi chislennosti Krasnoi armii, No. Org./8/540326, ne posdnee 29 sentiabria 1941 g., in ibid., p.79.

111 Gosudarvtvennii komitet oboroni. Postanovlenie No. GKO-146ss ot '14' iiulia 1941 g. Moskva, Kreml'. O formirovanii gornoi strelkovoi divizii i bronepoezdov v SKVO. www.soldat.ru/doc/gko/scans/0146–1.jpg [Accessed 5 January 2015].

112 Gosudarvtvennii komitet oboroni. Postanovlenie No. GKO-533ss ot '20' avgusta 1941 g. Moskva, Kreml'. Razreshit' NKO provesti mobilizatsiiu... www.soldat.ru/doc/gko/scans/0533–1.jpg [Accessed 5 January 2015].

113 Gosudarvtvennii komitet oboroni. Postanovlenie No. GKO-787ss ot '13' oktiabria 1941 g. Moskva, Kreml'. O sformirovanii sapernikh armii obshchei chislennost'iu v 300 000 chelovek. www.soldat.ru/doc/gko/scans/0787-01-1.jpg [Accessed 5 January 2015] and Ivan Tiulenev, *Cherez tri voini*, pp.276–80.

114 Ivan Tiulenev, *Cherez tri voini*, pp.280–1.

CHAPTER 13

1 HPSSS, Schedule B, Vol.6. Case 193 (Interviewer S.H.), p.11.

2 Ibid., and HPSSS, Schedule A, Vol.22, Case 445 (Interviewer R.S., type A4), p.14; K.A. Meretskov, *Na sluzhbe Narodu*, p.236; Geoffrey Jukes, 'Meretskov', in Harold Shukman (ed.), *Stalin's Generals*, p.129.

3 Entry for 4 November 1941, in N. Biriukov, *Tanki frontu! Zapiski sovetskogo generala* (Smolensk: Rusich, 2005), p.48.

4 G.K. Zhukov, *Vospominaniia i razmishleniia. ...Tom 2*, p.276.

5 A.M. Vasilevskii, *Delo vsei zhizni. Kn.1*, p.161.

6 G.K. Zhukov, *Vospominaniia i razmishleniia... Tom 2*, pp.254–5.

7 David Glantz, *Colossus Reborn*, p.144.

8 Direktiva Stavki VGK No. 005241 komanduiushchim vosikami Zapadnogo fronta i 1-i udarnoi armiei o podchinenii armii frontu, 29 noiabria 1941 g. 14 ch 30 min, in *RA T.16 (5–1)*, p.312.

9 Ob"iasnitel'naia zapiska k planu-karte kontrnastupleniia armii Zapadnogo fronta, 30.11.41 g., in *RA T.15 (4–1)*, p.160 and G.K. Zhukov, *Vospominaniia i razmishleniia... Tom 2*, pp.254–5.

10 G.K. Zhukov, *Vospominaniia i razmishleniia... Tom 2*, p.259.

11 N. Biriukov, *Tanki frontu! Zapiski sovetskogo generala*, p.59.

12 Order to forces of the Western Front, 19 February 1942 – on the battlefield use of and preservation of tanks in units of the Western Front, in Alexander Hill, *The Great Patriotic War*, p.87.

13 Horst Boog et al, *Germany and the Second World War. Volume IV. The Attack on the Soviet Union*, pp.1120–2, 1129.

14 Thomas L. Jentz (ed.), *Panzertruppen...1943–1945*, pp.209–11.

15 A. Tarasenko, 'Tankisti-remontniki v boiakh pod Moskvoi', in *Vizh*, Number 1 (1982), p.53.

16 Prikaz o premirovanii lichnogo sostava avtobronetankovikh remontnikh chastei za bistrii i kachestvennii remont tankov, No.0140, 25 fevrailia 1942 g., in *RA T.13 (2–2)*, pp.159–60.

17 G.F. Krivosheev, *Soviet Casualties and Combat Losses*, p.101.

18 *War Journal of Franz Halder. Volume VI*, 5 Jan 1942, p.248 and 5 July 1942 p.341; and *War Journal of Franz Halder. Volume VI*, 3 July 1941, p.198.

19 See for example GKO postanovlenie No. GKO-810ss ot '18' oktiabria 1941 g. Moskva, Kreml'. www.soldat.ru/doc/gko/scans/0810–1.jpg [Accessed 11 January 2015], that ordered the creation of 25 independent rifle brigades by 15 November, that would along with other categories be formed from 35,000 sailors and 40,000 troops who had recovered from wounds.

20 Soobrazheniia ABTU Zapadnogo fronta v operativnii otdel Genshtaba KA po ABTB, sostavlennie na osnove opita boevikh deistvii tankovikh chastei, 19 ianvaria 1942 g, in A.M. Rodionov et al, *Glavnoe avtobronetankovoe upravlenie. Liudi, sobitiia, fakti v dokumentakh – 1940–1042 gg.*, p.168.

21 GKO postanovlenie No. GKO-196/ss ot '18' iiulia 1941 g. Moskva, Kreml'. O meropriiatiiakh po obespecheniiu Krasnoi armii teplim veshchami na zimnii period 1941/42 goda. www.soldat.ru/doc/gko/scans/0196-01-1.jpg [Accessed 15 May 2014].

22 Doklad intendanta Zapadnogo fronta chlenu voennogo soveta fronta ob obespechenosti voisk zimnim obmundirovaniem, No.02321, 9 noiabria 1941 g., in *RA T.25(14)*, p.168–9.

23 Ibid.; [NKO] Prikaz o rezul'tatakh proverki khraneniia, sberezheniia, remonta i sostoianiia ucheta veshchevogo imushestva..., No.0404, 11 oktiabria 1941 g., in *RA T.13 (2–2)*, pp.114–16.

24 I.M. Golushko, *Shtab Tila Krasnoi Armii*, p.88; N.A. Antipenko, 'Til v Moskovskom bitve', in A.M.Samsonov (ed.), *Proval gitlerovskogo nastupleniia na Moskvu*, p.328.

25 V. Zhelanov, 'Iz opita pervoi operatsii na okruzhenie', in *Vizh*, Number 12 (1964), p.28.

26 F.I. Golikov, *V Moskovskoi bitve. Zapiski komandarma* (Moscow: 'Nauka', 1967), pp.46–7, 84.

27 N.M. Khlebnikov, *Pod grokhot soten batarei*, p.141.

28 F.I. Golikov, *V Moskovskoi bitve*, p.47.

29 Ibid., pp.83–4.

30 Direktiva Stavki VGK No.004837 komanduiushchim voiskami frontov, otdel'nimi armiiami. . .i nachal'niku Razvedivatel'nogo upravleniia General'- nogo shtaba ob organizatsii aviatsionnoi razvedki, 14 noiabria 1941 g., in *RA T.16 (5–1)*, p.291.

31 N.A. Moiseenko, 'Tochka na karte', in D.K. Zherebov (ed.), *Tikhvin, god 1941-i* (Leningrad: Lenizdat, 1974), p.360.

32 P.Ia. Egorov, 'Nastuplenie prodolzhaetsia', in ibid., pp.363–4.

33 Gel'mut Pabst [Helmut Pabst], *Dnevnik nemetskogo soldata. Voennie budni na vostochnome fronte. 1941–1943* (Moscow: Tsentpoligraf, 2011), p.47.

34 Nachal'niku shtaba Iuzhnogo fronta o providenii razvedki boem, 2 iiulia 1942 g., in *RA T.23 (12–2)*, p.202.

35 N.A. Moiseenko, 'Tochka na karte', in D.K. Zherebov (ed.), *Tikhvin, god 1941-i*, pp.360–1.

36 K.A. Meretskov, *Na sluzhbe Narodu*, p.249.

37 David Glantz and Jonathan House, *When Titans Clashed*, pp.90, 339 n38.

38 Führer Directive Number 39, 8th December 1941, in H.R. Trevor-Roper (ed.), *Hitler's War Directives*, p.166–7; Franz Halder, *War Journal of Franz Halder. Volume VII*, p.227.

39 G.K. Zhukov, *Vospominaniia i razmishleniia. . . Tom 2*, pp.263–5.

40 K.A. Meretskov, *Na sluzhbe Narodu*, p.241.

41 A.Ia. Soshnikov et al, *Sovetskaia kavaleriia. Voenno-istoricheskii ocherk*, p.161.

42 Ibid., pp.164–70.

43 *Organizatsiia sviazi v Rostovskoi nastupatel'noi operatsii*, p.58; Glavnoe upravlenie sviazi. *Spravochnik po voiskovim i tankovim radiostantsiiam. Chast' 1 iz 3*, pp.10 and 37.

44 Directive of the Headquarters of the Supreme Command. . ., 15 July 1941, in Alexander Hill, *The Great Patriotic War*, p.58.

45 Direktiva Stavki Verkhovnogo Glavnokomandovaniia kom[anduiushchim] [voiskami] frontov, armii, okrugov, No.1, 15 iiulia 1941 g. in V.P. Naumov (gen.ed.), *1941 god: V 2 kn. Kn.2*, pp.471–2.

46 GKO postanovlenie No. GKO-446ss ot "9" avgusta 1941 g. Moskva, Kreml'. O shtatakh strelkovoi i kavaleriiskoi divizii. www.soldat.ru/doc/gko/scans/ 0446–1.jpg [Accessed 27 August 2015]

47 GKO postanovlenie No. GKO-459ss ot "11" avgusta 1941 g. Moskva, Kreml'. O formirovanii strelkovikh i kavaleriiskikh divizii. www.soldat.ru/ doc/gko/scans/0459-02-1.jpg [Accessed 27 August 2015]

48 Franz Halder, *War Journal of Franz Halder. Volume VII*, p.15.

49 A.Ia. Soshnikov et al, *Sovetskaia kavaleriia. Voenno-istoricheskii ocherk*, p.174–5.

50 P.Filippov, 'Kavaleristi v boiakh pod Tikhvinom', in *Vizh*, Number 1 (1976), pp.34–6.

51 P.K.Koshevoi, 'Shturm', in D.K. Zherebov (ed.), *Tikhvin, god 1941-i*, p.279 and K.A. Meretskov, *Na sluzhbe Narodu*, p.237.

52 Ibid., p.236.

53 Evgenii Drig, *Mekhanizirovannie korpusa RKKA v boiu*, pp.653–7.

54 P.Filippov, 'Kavaleristi v boiakh pod Tikhvinom', pp.35–39, Meretskov, *Na sluzhbe Narodu*, pp.245–6.

55 See for example Meretskov, *Na sluzhbe Narodu*, p.245.

56 Anruf Generalfeldmarschall Keitel an Chef des Genst H.Gru., 7.12.1941. (15,40 Uhr). NARA T-311 Roll 51 frame 064614–5.

57 Lagebeurteilung. 8.12.41. [draft] NARA T-311 Roll 51 frame 064625.

58 Franz Halder, *War Journal of Franz Halder. Volume VII*, pp.206, 208, 210.

59 M.A. Fishchev, 'Ogon' vedut minometchiki', in D.K. Zherebov (ed.), *Tikhvin, god 1941-i*, p.346.

60 See for example N.G. Kosogorskii, 'Tank gorit...vipolniaiu zadachu', in ibid., pp.259–62 and V.Ia. Fokin, 'Pereprava', in ibid., pp.334–5.

61 V.D. Sokolovskii (ed.), *Razgrom nemetsko-fashistskikh voisk pod Moskvoi* (Moscow: Voenizdat, 1964), p.82. http://militera.lib.ru/h/razgrom_pod_mosk voy/03.html [Accessed 24/04/2014].

62 A.Ia. Soshnikov (gen.ed.), *Sovetskaia kavaleriia. Voenno-istoricheskii ocherk*, p.186.

63 Opisanie khoda boevikh deistvii 4-i tankovoi gruppi s 14 oktiabria po 5 dekab-ria 1941 g., in *RA T.15 (4–1)*, pp.50–1.

64 Ibid., p.51.

65 Ibid., p.52.

66 A.Ia. Soshnikov (gen.ed.), *Sovetskaia kavaleriia. Voenno-istoricheskii ocherk*, p.187.

67 A.L. Getman, *Tanki idut na Berlin (1941–1945)* (Moscow: Izdatel'stvo "Nauka", 1973), p.27.

68 As well as 415th Rifle Division and 15th Guards Rocket Mortar Regiment. Ibid., p.13.

69 A.Ia. Soshnikov (gen.ed.), *Sovetskaia kavaleriia. Voenno-istoricheskii ocherk*, pp.173, 197.

70 V.I. Afanasenko and E.F. Krinko, '"Vse rvalis' v boi s protivnikom". Deistviia kavalerii RKKA na iuzhnom fronte v oktiabre-dekabre 1941 goda', in *Vizh*, Number 1 (2012), p.32.

71 P.A. Belov, *Za name Moskva* (Moscow: Voennoe izdatel'stvo Ministerstva Oboroni SSSR, 1963), p.178 and memoirs of A.K. Kononenko in F.D. Sverdlov, 'What's new about a well-known raid: A selection from a sup-pressed memoir', in *JSMS*, Volume 8, Number 4 (1995), p.861.

72 P.A. Belov, *Za name Moskva*, pp.178–9.

73 Ibid., pp.180–1.

74 Memoirs of A.K. Kononenko in F.D. Sverdlov, 'What's new about a well-known raid', p.864, and ibid., pp.183–4.

75 Memoirs of A.K. Kononenko in F.D. Sverdlov, 'What's new about a well-known raid', p.864 and P.A. Belov, *Za name Moskva*, pp.188–9.

76 General'nii shtab Krasnoi armii. Voenno-istoricheskii otdel, *Razgrom Nemt-sev pod Moskvoi. Operativnii ocherk (Moscow: 1942)*, TsAMO f.450.o.11158. d.89, p.143.

77 Prikaz Stavki VGK No.0054 o merakh po povisheniiu boesposobnosti kava-leriiskikh soedinenii i chastei, 16 marta 1942 g., in *RA T.16 (5–2)*, p.132.

78 See Zhurnal boevikh deistvii 1 Gvardeiskogo Krasnoznamennogo Zhitomirs-kogo Kavaleriiskogo korpusa im. SNK USSR za period s. 1 po 30.4.45 g. TsAMO f.236.o.2673.d.2736 and on armoured strength on 15 April specif-ically Svedeniia o boevom i chislennom sostave 1 Gv.KZhKK po sostoianie na 15 aprelia 1945 g., l.60.

79 Svedeniia o poteriakh lichnogo sostava s 15 po 30 aprelia 1945 goda. TsAMO f.236.o.2673.d.2736.l.62; and Svedeniia o poteriakh konskogo sostava s 15 po 30 aprelia 1945 goda., l.63; Svedeniia o boevom i chislennom sostave 1 Gv.KZhKK po sostoianie na 15 aprelia 1945 g., l.60.

80 Svedeniia o boevom i chislennom sostave 1 Gv.KZhKK po sostoianie na 15 aprelia 1945 g. TsAMO f.236.o.2673.d.2736.l.60 and P.V. Mel'nikov (ed.), *Razvitie taktiki sukhoputnikh voisk*, p.296.

81 N.P. Zolotov et al, *Boevoi i chislennii sostav vooruzhennikh sil SSSR v period Velikoi Otechestvennoi voini (1941–1945 gg.). Statisticheskii sbornik No.1 (22 iiunia 1941 g.)*, p.13; Gosudarvtvennii komitet oboroni. Postanovlenie No. GKO-654ss ot "10" sentiabria 1941 g. Moskva, Kreml'. Ob otbore 50.000 dobrovol'tsev-komsomol'tsev v vozdushno-desantnie voiska Krasnoi armii. www.soldat.ru/doc/gko/scans/0654-01-1.jpg [Accessed 6 January 2015].

82 David Glantz and Jonathan House, *When Titan's Clashed*, pp.95–6; P.A. Belov, *Za name Moskva*, pp.188 and 193–4; Memoirs of A.K. Kononenko in F.D. Sverdlov, 'What's new about a well-known raid', p.864–5.

83 David Glantz and Jonathan House, *When Titans Clashed*, pp.96–7; Jeff Rutherford, *Combat and Genocide on the Eastern Front: The German Infan-try's War, 1941–1944* (Cambridge: Cambridge University Press, 2014), p.257.

84 Direktiva Stavki VGK No.153589 glavnokomanduiushchemu voiskami Zapadnogo napravleniia ob uskorenii razgroma Rzhevsko-Viazemsko-Gzhats-koi gruppirovka protivnika, 20 marta 1942, in *RA 16 (5–2)*, p.137.

85 Alexander Hill, *The Great Patriotic War*, p.91.

86 Directive Number 3750 of the military soviet of the Western Front, 30 March 1942, in Alexander Hill, *The Great Patriotic War*, p.88.

87 F.D. Sverdlov, 'What's new about a well-known raid', p.865.

88 Ibid., p.868.

89 Zh. Lopez [J. Lopez] and L. Otkhmezuri, *Zhukov. Portret na fone epokhi* (Moscow: ZAO Izdatel'stvo Tsentrpoligraf, 2015), p.369.

90 V. Zhelanov, 'Iz opita pervoi operatsii na okruzhenie', pp.20–22; Directive of the North-Western Front commander to the commanders of the 11th, 34th, and 3rd and 4th Shock Armies…, …2 January 1942, in David Glantz, 'Forgotten battles of the German-Soviet War (1941–45), part 4: The winter campaign (5 December 1941-April 1942): the Demiansk counteroffensive', in *JSMS*, Volume 13, Number 3 (2000), 148–50, and p.146.

91 V. Zhelanov, 'Iz opita pervoi operatsii na okruzhenie', pp.22–4 and Jeff Rutherford, *Combat and Genocide on the Eastern Front*, map, p.256.

92 Direktiva Stavki VGK No.170072 Komanduiushchemu voiskami Severo-Zapadnogo fronta o pererabotke plana operatsii po razgromu Leningradsko-Volkhovskoi i Novgorodskoi gruppirovok protivnika, 28 ianvaria 1942 g., in *RA T.16 (5–2)*, p.75; V. Zhelanov, 'Iz opita pervoi operatsii na okruzhenie', p.26.

93 Direktiva Stavki VGK No.170044 komanduiushchemu 1-i udarnoi armiei o peregruppirovke armii na Severo-Zapadnii front, 25 ianvaria 1942 g., in *RA T.16 (5–2)*, P.61 and Direktiva Stavki VGK No.170035 komanduiushchemu voiskami Kalininskogo fronta ob izmenenii sostava fronta i utochnenii zadach, 19 ianvaria 1942 g., in *RA T.16 (5–2)*, pp.54–5.

94 Jeff Rutherford, *Combat and Genocide on the Eastern Front*, pp.225–6.

95 Direktiva Stavki VGK No.170123 ...ob ob"edinenii upravleniia voiskami, privlekaemimi dlia razgroma Demianskoi gruppirovki protivnika, 25 fevralia 1942 g., in *RA T.16 (5–2)*, p.109.

96 Direktiva Stavki VGK No. 8467/Zh komanduiushchemu voiskami Severo-zapadnogo fronta...o razgrome Demainskoi gruppirovki protivnika, 9 marta 1942 g., in ibid., pp.120–1.

97 Direktiva Stavki VGK No.170146...o sozdanii Udarnoi aviatsionnoi gruppi No.2, 15 marta 1942 g., in ibid., p.126.

98 Direktiva Stavki VGK No.170157 komanduiushchemu VVS Krasnoi armii o sozdanii udarnoi aviatsionnoi gruppi Stavki Verkhovnogo Glavnokomandovaniia, 17 marta 1942 g., in ibid., p.133.

99 A.E. Golovanov, *Dal'niaia bombardirovochnaia... Vospominaniia Glavnogo marshala aviatsii. 1941–1945* (Moscow: ZAO Tsentrpoligraf, 2008), p.161.

100 Jeff Rutherford, *Combat and Genocide on the Eastern Front*, pp.226, 257, 260.

101 Joel S.A. Hayward, *Stopped at Stalingrad: The Luftwaffe and Hitler's Defeat in the east, 1942–1943* (Lawrence, Kansas: University Press of Kansas, 1998), p.235; Generalmajor a.D. Fritz Morzik, *German Air Force Airlift Operations* (Research Studies Institute, Air University, USAF Historical Division, June 1961), pp.142–3.

102 V. Zhelanov, 'Iz opita pervoi operatsii na okruzhenie', p.32.

103 I.M. Golushko, *Shtab tila Krasnoi armii v godi voini 1941–1945*, pp.83–4.

104 Ibid., p.85 and V.F. Vorsin, 'Motor vehicle transport deliveries through 'lend-lease", p.169.

105 I.M. Golushko, *Shtab tila Krasnoi armii v godi voini 1941–1945*, p.62.

106 Production was 237 units in 1941, 423 in 1942, 618 in 1943 and 626 in 1944. M. Iu. Mukhin, *Sovetskaia aviapromishlennost' v godi Velikoi Otechestvennoi voini* (Moscow: Veche, 2011), p.343 and Bill Gunston, *Aircraft of the Soviet Union*, p.165.

107 I.M. Golushko, *Shtab tila Krasnoi armii v godi voini 1941–1945*, p.63.

CHAPTER 14

1 G.F. Krivosheev, 'O poteriiakh sredi zhenshchin-voennosluzhashchikh i vol'-nonaemnogo sostava', in *Vizh*, Number 1 (2005), p.5.

2 P.F. Gladkikh and A.E. Loktev, *Ocherki istorii otechestvennoi voennoi meditsini. Sluzhba zdorov'ia v Velikoi Otechestvennoi voine 1941–1945 gg.* (St Petersburg: "Dmitrii Bulganin", 2005), p.189.

3 Roger D. Marwick and Euridice Charon Cardona, *Soviet Women on the Front-line in the Second World War* (Basingstoke, Hampshire: Palgrave Macmillan, 2012), p.150; Anna Krylova, *Soviet Women in Combat: A History of Violence on the Eastern Front* (New York: Cambridge University Press, 2010), p.169. For example, on male civilian workers drafted in to repair vehicles, see below.

4 P.F. Gladkikh and A.E. Loktev, *Ocherki istorii otechestvennoi voennoi meditsini*, pp.93, 99, 188–9.

5 Iu. V.Vladimirov, *Voina soldata-zenitchika: ot studencheskoi skam'i do Khar'-kovskogo kotla. 1941–1942* (Moscow: ZAO Tsentrpoligraf, 2010), p.250.

6 N.A. Kirsanov, 'Mobilizatsiia zhenshchin v Krasnuiu armiiu v godi fashists-kogo nashestviia', in *Vizh*, Number 5 (2007), p.15.

7 G.F. Krivosheev, 'O poteriiakh sredi zhenshchin-voennosluzhashchikh i vol'-nonaemnogo sostava', p.5.

8 V.V. Korovin, A.N. Manzhosov, N.N. Pozhidaeva, 'Zhenshchini Kurskoi oblasti v antifashistskikh dobrovol'cheskikh voenizirovannikh formirova-niiakh', in *Vizh*, Number 5 (2007), pp.18–22.

9 Iz otcheta o rabote Otdela kadrov Tsentral'nogo shtaba partizanskogo dviz-heniia za period s 15 iiunia 1942 g. po 15 fevralia 1944 g., 28 fevralia 1944 g., in *RA. T.20 (9)*, p.481.

10 State Defence Committee Decree No. GOKO-1488ss of 25 March 1942. ... On the mobilization of young women [*devushek*]- from the Komsomol [*Komsomolok*] to units of the PVO, in Alexander Hill, *The Great Patriotic War*, p.93.

11 Prikaz o mobilizatsii v voiska sviazi zhenshchin dlia zameni krasnoarmeitsev, No. 0284, 14 aprelia 1942 g., in *RA T.13 (2–2)*, pp.212–13.

12 Gosudarstvennii Komitet Oboroni. Postanovlenie No. GOKO-1618ss ot "18" aprelia 1942 g. Moskva. Kreml'. O zamene v tilovikh chastiakh i uchrezhdeniiakh VVS KA voenno-sluzhashchikh muzhchin zhenshchinami. www.soldat.ru/doc/gko/scans/1618-01-1.jpg [accessed 4 May 2014].

13 Prikaz o zamene v shtabakh, uchrezhdeniiakh i tilakh armii, frontov i okrugov godnikh k stroevoi sluzhbeogranichenno godnimi, zhenshchinami i starshimi vozrastami, No. 0678, 6 sentiabria 1942 g., in *RA T.13 (2–2)*, pp.295–6.

14 G.F. Krivosheev, 'O poteriiakh sredi zhenshchin-voennosluzhashchikh i vol'-nonaemnogo sostava', p.5.

15 Ibid., and P.F. Gladkikh and A.E. Loktev, *Ocherki istorii otechestvennoi voennoi meditsini*, p.189.

16 G.F. Krivosheev, 'O poteriiakh sredi zhenshchin-voennosluzhashchikh i vol'-nonaemnogo sostava', p.5.

17 Prikaz o sformirovanii zhenskikh aviatsionnikh polkov VVS Krasnoi Armii, No.0099, 8 oktiabria 1941 g., in *RA |T.13(2–2)*, pp.112–13.

18 N.A. Kirsanov, 'Mobilizatsiia zhenshchin v Krasnuiu armiiu v godi fashists-kogo nashestviia', p.16.

19 Gosudarstvennii Komitet Oboroni. Postanovlenie No. GOKO-2470ss ot "3" noiabria 1942 g. Moskva. Kreml'. O formirovanii zhenskoi dobrovol'cheskoi strel'kovoi brigade. www.soldat.ru/doc/gko/scans/2470-01-1.jpg [Accessed 11 January 2015] and Roger D. Marwick and Euridice Charon Cardona, *Soviet Women on the Frontline in the Second World War*, p.184.

20 Transcript of interview with Comrade Lieutenant General Vasily Chuikov, Stalingrad, January 5, 1943, in Jochen Hellbeck (trans. Christopher Tauchen and Dominic Bonfiglio), *Stalingrad: The City that Defeated the Third Reich*, p.284.
21 Smarkalova Nina Arsent'evna, in Artem Drabkin and Bair Irincheev (eds.), *"A zori zdes' gromkie"*. *Zhenskoe litso voini* (Moscow: Eksmo: Iauza, 2012), pp.19–20 and 26–31, 130.
22 Oleg Budnitskii, 'Muzhchini i zhenshchini v Krasnoi armii (1941–1945)', in *Cahiers du Monde russe*, April-September (2011), pp.410–11 and Isaak Grigor'evich Kobilianskii, *Priamoi navodkoi po vragu* (Moscow: Iauza/Eksmo, 2005), pp.233–4.
23 Irina Dunaevskaia, *Ot Leningrad do Kenigsberga. Dnevnik voennoi perevodchitsi (1942–1945)* (Moscow: ROSSPEN, 2010), p.258.
24 Nina Fedotovna Afanas'eva (Solov'eva), in A.V. Drabkin and Bair Irincheev (eds.), *"A zore zdes' gromkie"*. *Zhenskoe litso voini*, pp.272, 284.
25 Oleg Budnitskii, 'Muzhchini i zhenshchini v Krasnoi armii (1941–1945)', p.412 and Irina Dunaevskaia, *Ot Leningrad do Kenigsberga. Dnevnik voennoi perevodchitsi (1942–1945)*, p.226.
26 Testimony of Koshechkin Boris Kuz'mich. http://iremember.ru/tankisti/koshechkin-boris-kuzmich/stranitsa-2.html. [Accessed 23 August 2014]
27 Isaak Grigor'evich Kobilianskii, *Priamoi navodkoi po vragu*, pp.235–6.
28 V. Bogomolov, *Ivan. Rasskaz* (Moscow: Gosudarstvennoe Izdatel'stvo Detskoi Literaturi Ministerstva Prosveshcheniia RSFSR, 1959), pp.32, 35.
29 See David Glantz, *Stumbling Colossus*, pp.159, 164–6.
30 David Stahel, *Kiev 1941*, p.221 and I.Kh. Bagramian, *Tak nachalas' voina*, p.400.
31 See Frank Ellis, '10th Rifle Division of Internal Troops NKVD: Profile and Combat Performance at Stalingrad', in *JSMS*, Volume 19, Number 3 (2006), pp.601–18.
32 David Glantz, *Stumbling Colossus*, p.165–6.
33 Decree of the State Defence Committee on the manning of the field army, GKO Number 2100ss, 26 July 1942, in Alexander Hill, *The Great Patriotic War*, p.92.
34 Many of these sailors were identified by Chuikov as having been particularly young by the standards of combatants in the city. Transcript of interview with Comrade Lieutenant General Vasily Chuikov, Stalingrad, January 5, 1943, in Jochen Hellbeck (trans. Christopher Tauchen and Dominic Bonfiglio), *Stalingrad: The City that Defeated the Third Reich.*, pp.275, 284.
35 Ivan Tiulenev, *Cherez tri voini*, p.288.
36 HPSSS. Schedule B, Vol.9, Case 375 (interviewer M.L.), pp.3–4.
37 GKO postanovlenie No.GKO-894ss ot "13" noiabria 1941 g. Moskva. Kreml'. O formirovanii natsional'nikh voiskovikh soedinenii. www.soldat.ru/doc/gko/scans/0894-01-1.jpg [Accessed 6 May 2014], and V.V. Gradosel'skii, 'National'nie voinskie formirovaniia v Velikoi Otechestvennoi voine', in *Vizh*, No.1 (2002), p.18.
38 See N.A. Kirsanov, 'Natsional'nie formirovaniia Krasnoi Armii v Velikoi Otechestvennoi voine 1941–1945 godov', in *Otechestvennaia istoriia*, Number

4 (1995), pp.122–3 and V.V. Gradosel'skii, 'National'nie voinskie formirovaniia v Velikoi Otechestvennoi voine', p.19.

39 N.A. Kirsanov, 'Natsional'nie formirovaniia Krasnoi Armii', p.123.

40 See V.V. Gradosel'skii, 'National'nie voinskie formirovaniia v Velikoi Otechestvennoi voine', pp.18, 22–3 and N.A. Kirsanov, 'Natsional'nie formirovaniia Krasnoi Armii', pp.117–20.

41 V.V. Gradosel'skii, 'National'nie voinskie formirovaniia v Velikoi Otechestvennoi voine', p.24.

42 GKO postanovlenie No. GKO-863ss ot "3" noiabria 1941 g. Moskva.
Kreml'. O pol'skoi armii na territorii SSSR. www.soldat.ru/doc/gko/scans/
0863-01-1.jpg [Accessed 6 May 2014]; GKO postanovlenie No. GKO-
1064ss ot 25 dekabria 1941 g. Moskva, Kreml'. O pol'skoi armii na territorii
SSSR. www.soldat.ru/doc/gko/scans/1064-01-1.jpg [Accessed 6 May 2014];
GKO postanovlenie No. GKO-1096ss ot "3" ianvaria 1942 g. Moskva,
Kreml'. O Chekhoslovatskoi brigade na territorii Soiuza SSR. www.soldat.ru/
doc/gko/scans/1096-01-1.jpg [Accessed 6 May 2014].

43 Halik Kochanski, *The Eagle Unbowed*, pp.168–80.

44 Ibid., pp.187–93.

45 Ibid., pp.376–83.

46 As for example the case of the 1st Independent Order of Suvorov II Class and
Order of Bogdan Khmel'nitskii I Class Czechoslovak Rifle Brigade, that saw
heavy fighting with 1st Ukrainian Front through the winter of 1943–4. General Svoboda's troops had been committed in battalion strength in March
1943 on the Voronezh Front, taking heavy losses in defensive fighting. See
Zapiska G.S. Zhukova I.V. Stalinu s prilozheniem doneseniia L. Svobodi o
deistviiakh chekhoslovatskogo batal'ona, No.2/4/6345, 26 marta 1943 g., and
the attached after action report from Svoboda (20 March 1943), along with
Zapiska G.S. Zhukova I.V. Stalinu ob otvode chekhoslovatskoi otdel'noi
brigade s fronta, No.149/s, 1 marta 1944 g., in S.V. Kudriashov (gen.ed.),
Vestnik Arkhiva Prezidenta Rossiiskoi Federatsii.Voina: 1941–1945. Vipusk 2,
pp.287–90 and 400 respectively.

47 See for example consideration of the number of national uniforms required
for Polish forces in Zapiska G.S. Zhukova I.V. Stalinu ob izgotovlenii natsional'noi formi dlia pol'skikh i chekhoslovatskikh chastei, No.111/s, 17 fevralia
1944 g., in ibid., p.397. At this point in February 1944 the Polish Corps had
33,000 men.

48 On the formation of the 1st Rumanian Rifle Division on Soviet lines, drawing
on PoWs, see Zapiska L.P. Berii I.V. Stalinu o formirovanii 1-i Ruminskoi
pekhotnoi divizii, No.140/b, 7 fevralia 1944 g., in ibid., pp.393–4. This
division would subsequently be named after late nineteenth century
Wallachian-Rumanian revolutionary Tudor Vladimirescu and also given the
honourific title 'Debrecen' for its participation in the capture of the Hungarian town. See Mark Axworthy et al, *Third Axis, Fourth Ally: Romanian Armed
Forces in the European War, 1941–1945* (London: Arms and Armour Press,
1995), pp.166, 195, 197, 200–1, 207, 209, 211.

49 See Sergei Dibov, *"Normandiia-Neman". Podlinnaia istoriia legendarnogo avia-
polka* (Moscow: Iauza, Eksmo, 2011), p.76.

50 State Defence Committee Decree No. GOKO-1619ss of 18 April 1942. ...
On the formation of units for fortified districts, in Alexander Hill, *The Great Patriotic War*, p.94.

51 A. Iu. Ermolov, *Gosudarstvennoe upravlenie voennoi promishlennost'iu v 1940-e godi*, pp.191–2.

52 Spravka o nalichii tankov v tankovikh brigadakh, formiruemikh v marte mesiatse 1942 g., 1 aprelia 1942 g., in A.M. Rodionov et al, *Glavnoe avto-bronetankovoe upravlenie. Liudi, sobitiia, fakti v dokumentakh – 1940–1042 gg.*, pp.241–2.

53 M. Mukhin, *Sovetskaia aviapromishlennost' v godi Velikoi Otechestvennoi voini*, p.171.

54 Alexander Hill, *The Great Patriotic War*, p.188.

55 Gosudarstvennii Komitet Oboroni. Postanovlenie No. GOKO-1421ss ot "11" marta 1942 g. Moskva. Kreml'. Ob obespechenii mekhtiagoi i avtotransportom formiruemikh artilleriiskikh polkov reserva glavnogo komandovaniia. RGASPI f.644.o.1.d.24.l.47.

56 Alexander Hill, 'The Allocation of Allied "Lend-Lease" Aid to the Soviet Union arriving with Convoy PQ-12, March 1942 – A State Defence Committee Decree', in *JSMS* Volume 19, Number 4 (2006), pp.732–5. On the Wireless Set No.18 see Louis Meulstee, *Wireless for the Warrior. Radio Communications Equipment in the British Army. Compendium 1. Spark to Larkspur (Wireless Sets 1910–1948)* (Groenlo: Emaus Uitgeverij, 2009), p.205.

57 Iurii Vladimirov, *Voina soldata-zenitchika*, p.182; Spravka o nalichii tankov v tankovikh brigadakh, formiruemikh v marte mesiatse 1942 g., 1 aprelia 1942 g., in A.M. Rodionov et al, *Glavnoe avtobronetankovoe upravlenie. Liudi, sobitiia, fakti v dokumentakh – 1940–1042 gg.*, p.241.

58 Gosudarstvennii Komitet Oboroni. Postanovlenie No. GOKO-1527ss ot "3" aprelia 1942 g. Moskva. Kreml'. O khode i sostoianii remonta samoletov i motorov v voenno-vozdushnikh silakh Krasnoi Armii. RGASPI f.644.o.1. d.26.l.76.

59 Gosudarstvennii Komitet Oboroni. Postanovlenie No. GOKO-1287ss ot "15" fevralia 1942 g. Moskva. Kreml'. O formirovanii dlia Krasnoi Armii 63 podvizhnikh remontnikh baz po polevomu remontu tankov, avtomobilei i traktorov. RGASPI f.644.o.1.d.21.l.87 and Postanovlenie No. GOKO-1416ss ot 9 marta 1942 g. ... Ob usilenii proizvodstva zapasnikh chastei k tankam. RGASPI f.644.o.1.d.24.l.25.

60 Dokladnaia zapiska nachal'nika GABTU zampredu SNK SSSR o vipolnenii plana postavok zapasnikh chastei i agregatov, 1 maia 1942 g., in A.M. Rodionov et al, *Glavnoe avtobronetankovoe upravlenie. Liudi, sobitiia, fakti v dokumentakh – 1940–1042 gg.*, pp.266–7.

61 Soliankin et al, *Otechestvennie bronirovannie mashini. XX vek. ...1941–1945 gg.*, pp.161–6.

62 Prikaz o vvedenii v shtat strelkovikh polkov rot avtomatchikov, No.0406, 12 oktaibria 1941 g., in *RA T.13 (2–2)*, p.117; V.N. Novikov, *Oruzhie pobedi*, p.252; see also comments by a former British army officer on the weapon itself, in John Weeks, *World War II Small Arms* (London: Macdonald and Co (Publishers) Ltd, 1988), pp.111–12.

63 V.N. Shunkov, *Artilleriia Krasnoi Armii i Vermakhta Vtoroi mirovoi voini*, pp.76–82.

64 Yefim Gordon and Dmitrii Khazanov, *Soviet Combat Aircraft of the Second World War. Volume 2: Twin-Engined Fighters, Attack Aircraft and Bombers*, pp.46–9.

65 Prikaz o dosrochnom vipuske kursantov starshego kursa voennikh uchilishch, No. 0230, 16 iiulia 1941 g., in *RA T.13(2–2)*, p.28.

66 Prikaz o dosrochnom vipuske kursantov starshego kursa voennikh uchilishch, No.0230, 16 iiulia 1941 g.; Prikaz o naznachenii politrabotnikov na komandnie dolzhnosti, No.0392, 4 oktiabria 1941 g.; Prikaz o sozdanii pri shtabakh armii i diviziiakh kursov po podgotovke mladshego i srednego komandnogo sostava, No. 0393, 4 oktiabria 1941 g.; in *RA T.13 (2–2)*, pp.28 and 109–10 respectively.

67 Iurii Vladimirov, *Voina soldata-zenitchika*, pp.110–11, 137–8, 140, 168–71.

68 Doklad E.A. Shchadenko I.V. Stalinu 'O mobilizatsionnikh resursakh i ikh ispol'zovanii za god voini', No. 778183, 10 sentiabria 1942 g., in S.V. Kudriashov (gen.ed.), *Vestnik Arkhiva Prezidenta Rossiiskoi Federatsii. Voina: 1941–1945. Vipusk 2*, p.233.

69 Iurii Vladimirov, *Voina soldata-zenitchika*, pp.169–70.

70 Ibid., pp.179, 182, 214.

71 Prikaz o poriadke naznacheniia na dolzhnosti nachal'stvuiushchego sostava pekhoti, No.0225, 30 marta 1942 g.; Ukaz presidium Verkhovnogo Soveta SSSR o prisvoenii voennikh zvanii nachal'stvuiushchemu sostavu i krasnoarmeitsam, otlichivshimsia v boiakh za Rodinu, Moskva, Kreml'. 18 avgusta 1941 g.; in *RA T.13 (2–2)*, pp.189 and 65 respectively.

72 Prikaz o podgotovke obshchevoiskovikh komandirov, No.0263, 9 aprelia 1942 g.; and Prikaz o podgotovke rezerva komsostav na kurskah "Vistrel" i pri voennoi Akademii im M.V. Frunze, No.0461, 2 dekabria 1941 g.; in *RA T.13 (2–2)*, pp.200–1 and 128 respectively.

73 Doklad F.I. Golikova I.V. Stalinu o resul'tatakh proverki voennoi podgotovki komandirov rot i batal'onov pekhoti desitvuiushchei armii, No. GUK/OMU-2/470456, 25 maia 1944 g., in S.V. Kudriashov (gen. ed.), *Vestnik Arkhiva Prezidenta Rossiiskoi Federatsii. Voina: 1941–1945. Vipusk 2*, p.444.

74 Doklad F.I. Golikova I.V. Stalinu 'O generalitete Krasnoi Armii', No. 461422, 18 maia 1944 g., in ibid., p.427.

75 Prikaz ob ustanovlenii srokov obucheniia kursantov v artilleriiskikh uchilishchakh in na kursakh Glavnogo upravlenniia nachal'nika artillerii Krasnoi armii, No. 0713, 11 sentiabria 1942 g.; Prikaz ob ustanovlenii srokov obucheniia kursantov v voenno-inzhenirnikh uchilishchakh, No. 0733, 16 sentiabria 1942 g.; in *RA T.13 (2–2)*, pp.305–6 and 306–7 respectively.

76 ...on the composition of the Mozhaisk defence line, 13 October 1941, in Alexander Hill, *The Great Patriotic War*, p.70.

77 As former chief of staff for 62nd Army noted in his memoirs, a number of cadet regiments fought as part of the army during fighting for the Don bend during the summer of 1942, including from the Krasnodar, Groznii, Vinnitsa

and Ordzhonikidze schools, with only one such regiment still intact by mid-August. See N.I. Krilov, *Stalingradskii rubezh. Izdanie vtoroe* (Moscow: Voennoe izdatel'stvo, 1984), p.23.

78 Michael K. Jones, *Stalingrad: How the Red Army Triumphed* (Barnsley: Pen and Sword Books Ltd, 2007), p.40.

79 G.K. Zhukov, *Vospominaniia i razmishleniia. ...Tom 2*, p.285.

80 Evan Mawdsley, *Thunder in the East*, p.142.

81 A.M. Vasilevskii, *Delo vsei zhizni. Kn.1*, p.206.

82 G.K. Zhukov, *Vospominaniia i razmishleniia. ...Tom 2*, p.285.

83 Ibid., pp.285–6. I. Kh. Bagramian, *Tak shli mi k pobede* (Kiev: Politizdat Ukraini, 1988), pp.40–5.

84 See Evan Mawdsley, *Thunder in the East*, pp.132–3.

85 V.A. Pavlov, 'Na pomoshch' Leningradu', in B.I. Gavrilov (ed.), *Cherez "Dolinu smerti". Podvig i tragediia voinov Volkhovskogo fronta. Ianvar'-iiun' 1942 g. Tom 2. Vospominaniia, dokumenti i materiali* (Moscow: Institut rossiiskoi istorii RAN, 2004), pp.53–63. For an overtly sympathetic consideration of Vlasov and his German-sponsored Russian Liberation Movement that sought to raise troops against the Stalinist regime, see Catherine Andreyev, *Vlasov and the Russian Liberation Movement: Soviet reality and émigré theories* (Cambridge: Cambridge University Press, 1990). Despite Vlasov's 'movement' and the so called 'Russian Liberation Army' associated with it that only really became a meaningful force at the very end of the war, Great Russian participation in German-sponsored military units was overall far from enthusiastic. Such participation seems more often than not to have been primarily reason to get out of the even later in the war harsh conditions in German PoW camps. Many such units defected at the first suitable opportunity – many formed only once Germany's fortunes on the Eastern Front were declining. Perhaps unsurprisingly, collaboration amongst groups only incorporated in to the Soviet Union in 1939–1940 or amongst groups culturally most distinct from the Great Russian core was more enthusiastic, at least when Germany seemed to be faring military well or even subsequently in the case of SS units such as 14th SS Volunteer Division 'Galician'. For an introduction to the military collaboration of Soviet citizens with Germany, see Alexander Dallin's classic work, *German Rule in Russia 1941–1945: A Study of Occupation Policies* (London: Macmillan, 1981), first published in 1957. German military historian Joachim Hoffmann has produced a number of detailed works on Soviet peoples in German military units, such as *Die Ostlegionen 1941–1943...*(Freiburg: Verlag Rombach, 1986).

86 V.M. Domnichenko, 'Vospominaniia', in B.I. Gavrilov (ed.), *Cherez "Dolinu smerti"*, pp.36–7.

87 A good summary of these operations is provided in Evan Mawdsley, *Thunder in the East*, pp.136–41.

88 Ibid., p.141.

89 On the nature and timing of Operation 'Kremlin', see Earl F. Ziemke, 'Operation Kreml: Deception, Strategy and the Fortunes of War', in *Perameters*, Volume IX, Number 1 (1979), pp.77–8.

90 I. Kh. Bagramian, *Tak shli mi k pobede*, pp.43–5, 51 and From Report No 00137/op of the Southwestern Direction High Command to the Stavka VGK...concerning the situation in mid March 1942 of Southwestern Direction fronts and proposals on prospective military operations...during the spring-summer period of 1942, 22 March 1942, in David Glantz (ed.), *Kharkov 1942: Anatomy of a Military Disaster through Soviet Eyes* (Hersham, Surrey: Ian Allen Publishing, 2010), pp.358–9.

91 G.K. Zhukov, *Vospominaniia i razmishleniia. ...Tom 2*, pp.285–6.

92 I. Kh. Bagramian, *Tak shli mi k pobede*, pp.40–41 and From Report No 00137/op of the Southwestern Direction High Command to the Stavka VGK...concerning the situation in mid March 1942 of Southwestern Direction fronts and proposals on prospective military operations...during the spring-summer period of 1942, 22 March 1942, in David Glantz (ed.), *Kharkov 1942*, pp.358–9.

93 I. Kh. Bagramian, *Tak shli mi k pobede*, pp.52, 58.

94 In the case of Dieppe, neither having the clear character of a raid or constituting the opening of a second front!

95 From Operational Directive No 00275 of the Southwestern Direction High Command to Southwestern Front forces..., 28 April 1942, in David Glantz (ed.), *Kharkov 1942*, p.371.

96 Iurii Vladimirov, *Voina soldata-zenitchika*, pp.240, 248, 259, 264.

97 David Glantz (ed.), *Kharkov 1942*, pp.316, 318–19; Robert M. Citino, *Death of the Wehrmacht: The German Campaigns of 1942* (Lawrence, Kansas: University Press of Kansas, 2007), p.101.

98 Iurii Vladimirov, *Voina soldata-zenitchika*, p.312.

99 David Glantz (ed.), *Kharkov 1942*, p.388.

100 Evan Mawdsley, *Thunder in the East*, p.140.

CHAPTER 15

1 Führer Headquarters, 5 April 1942. Directive No. 41, in Hugh Trevor-Roper (ed.), *Hitler's War Directives, 1939–1945*, p.178.

2 Ibid., p.180.

3 Robert M. Citino, *Death of the Wehrmacht: The German Campaigns of 1942*, pp.114, 160, 165–7, 172–80.

4 Zapis' peregovorov po priamomu provodu Verkhovnogo glavnokomanduiushchego i nachal'nika General'nogo shtaba s komandovaniem Brianskogo fronta, 1 iiulia 1942, in *RA T.16 (5–2)*, pp.276–9.

5 M.E. Katukov, *Na ostrie glavnogo udara*, p.154.

6 Zapis' peregovorov po priamomu provodu Verkhovnogo glavnokomanduiushchego s komandovaniem Brianskogo fronta, 30 iiunia 1942, in *RA T16.(5–2)*, p.271.

7 Zapis' peregovorov po priamomu provodu Verkhovnogo glavnokomanduiushchego i nachal'nika General'nogo shtaba s komandovaniem Brianskogo fronta, 1 iiulia 1942, in *RA T.16 (5–2)*, p.279.

8 M.E. Katukov, *Na ostrie glavnogo udara*, p.163.

9 Zapis' peregovorov po priamomu provodu Verkhovnogo glavnokomanduiushchego i nachal'nika General'nogo shtaba s komandovaniem Brianskogo fronta, 1 iiulia 1942, in *RA T.16 (5–2)*, p.279.
10 Direktiva Stavki VGK No.170475 komanduiushchemu voiskami Brianskogo
fronta ob organizatsii kontrudara, 3 iiulia 1942 g. 00 ch. 30 min., in *RA T.16
(5–2)*, p.284.
11 I.M. Anan'ev, *Tankovie armii v nastuplenii*, pp.50, 55–6.
12 David Glantz, *Colossus Reborn*, pp.254–5; Prikaz o sostave i organizatsii tan-
kovokh chastei v tankovikh korpusakh i tankovikh armiiakh, No. 00106,
29 maia 1942 g, in *RA T.13 (2–2)*, p.245; Ibid., p.51.
13 Direktiva Stavki VGK No. 994021 komanduiushchemu 5-i tankovoi armiei o
formirovanii armii, 25 maia 1942 g., in *RA T.16 (5–2)*, p.217; I.M. Anan'ev,
Tankovie armii v nastuplenii, p.56; Prikaz o sostave i organizatsii tankovikh
chastei v tankovikh korpusakh i tankovikh armiiakh, No. 00106, 29 maia 1942
g, in *RA T.13 (2–2)*, p.245.
14 Direktiva Stavki VGK No. 944023 komanduiushchim 3-i i 5-i tankovimi
armiiami o formirovanii upravlenii armii, 26 maia 1942 g., in *RA T.16
(5–2)*, p.219.
15 Direktiva Stavki VGK No.170451 komanduiushchemu voiskami Brianskogo
fronta o peregruppirovke 5-i tankovoi armii, 4-go i 16-go tankovikh korpusov,
15 iiunia 1942 g. 18 ch 15 min, in *RA T.16 (5–2)*, p.249.
16 P.A. Rotmistrov, *Vremia i tanki* (Moscow: Voennoe izdatel'stvo Ministerstva
oboroni SSSR, 1972), p.130; David Glantz, *Colossus Reborn*, p.271.
17 Direktiva Stavki VGK No. 944023 komanduiushchim 3-i i 5-i tankovimi
armiiami o formirovanii upravlenii armii, 26 maia 1942 g., in *RA T.16
(5–2)*, p.219; Katukov, *Na ostrie glavnogo udara*, p.193.
18 State Defence Committee. Decree GOKO No. 2791ss of 28 January 1943....
On the formation of ten tank armies, in Alexander Hill, *The Great Patriotic
War*, p.112.
19 Robert M. Citino, *Death of the Wehrmacht: The German Campaigns of 1942*,
p.166.
20 M.I. Kazakov, *Nad kartoi bilikh srazhenii* (Moscow: Voennoe izdatel'stvo
Ministerstvo oboroni SSSR, 1965), p.122.
21 K.K. Rokossovskii, *Soldatskii dolg*, p.131.
22 Direktiva Stavki VGK No.170488 komanduiushchemu 5-i tankovoi armiei i
komanduiushchemu voiskami Brianskogo fronta o neudovletvoritel'nikh
deistviiakh 5-i tankovoi armii, 9 iiunia 1942 g. 04 ch 15 min, in *RA T.16
(5–2)*, p.295.
23 K.K. Rokossovskii, *Soldatskii dolg*, pp.131–3.
24 Rotmistrov, *Vremia i tanki*, pp.130–2.
25 Katukov, *Na ostrie glavnogo udara*, p.166.
26 M.I. Kazakov, *Nad kartoi bilikh srazhenii*, p.123.
27 Katukov, *Na ostrie glavnogo udara*, pp.166–7; Rokossovskii, *Soldatskii dolg*,
p.133.
28 Direktiva Stavki VGK No.170489 komanduiushchemu voiskami Voronezhskogo fronta i predstaviteliu Stavki o nanesenii udara v mezhdurech'i Dona i
Voronezha, 9 iiulia 1942 g. 21 ch 00 min, in *RA T.16 (5–2)*, p.296.

29 David Glantz, 'Forgotten battles of the German-Soviet war (1941–1945), part 7: the summer campaign (12 May-18 November 1942): Voronezh, July 1942', in *JSMS*, Volume 14, Number 3 (2001), p.199.

30 Franz Halder, *War Journal of Franz Halder. Volume VII*, pp.341, 344–5, 347–50.

31 G.F. Krivosheev, *Soviet Casualties and Combat Losses*, p.123.

32 Ibid., p.124.

33 Führer Headquarters, 23 July 1942. Directive Number 45 for the continuation of Operation 'Braunschweig', in Alexander Hill, *The Great Patriotic War*, p.99.

34 Ibid., pp.100–2.

35 E.E. Mal'tsev, *V godi ispitanii*, p.121.

36 P.A. Mikhin, *'Artilleristi, Stalin dal prikaz!'. Mi umirali, chtobi pobedit'* (Moscow: Iauza, Eksmo, 2006), p.43.

37 Polozhenie o shtrafnikh batal'onakh deistvuiushchei armii, and Polozhenie o shtrafnikh rotakh…, 26 sentiabria 1942 g., in P.N. Knishevskii, *Skritaia Pravda voini: 1941 god*, pp.360–5 and *RA T. 13 (2–2)*, pp.312–15.

38 Alex Statiev, 'Penal Units in the Red Army', in *Europe-Asia Studies*, Volume 62, Number 5 (2010), p.735.

39 Mikhail Shelkov, *Zapiski komandira strelkovogo batal'ona. Ot Rzheva do Vostochnoi Prussii. 1942–1945* (Moscow: ZAO Izdatel'stvo Tsentrpoligraf, 2010), pp.45–6.

40 Dokladnaia zapiska OO NKVD DF v UOO NKVD SSSR 'O rabote osoborganov po bor'be s trusami i panikerami v chastiakh Donskogo fronta za period s 1 oktiabria 1942 goda po 1 fevrala 1943 goda', 17 fevrala 1943 g., in V.K. Vinogradov et al (eds.), *Stalingradskaia epopeia: Vpervie publikuemie dokumenti rassekrechennie FSB RF: …* (Moscow: "Zvonnitsa-MG", 2000), p.380.

41 Polozhenie o shtrafnikh batal'onakh deistvuiushchei armii, and Polozhenie o shtrafnikh rotakh…, 26 sentiabria 1942 g., in P.N. Knishevskii, *Skritaia Pravda voini: 1941 god*, pp.362,364 and *RA T.13 (2–2)*, pp.313, 315.

42 Mikhail Suknev, *Zapiski komandira shtrafbata*, pp.158–9.

43 To the People's Commissar…Beria, [October] 1941, in Alexander Hill, *The Great Patriotic War*, pp.68–9.

44 See Decree of the State Committee of Defence No. 187ss on the re-establishment of the organs of the 3rd Board of the NKO SSSR as special sections of the NKVD SSSR, 17 July 1941, in Alexander Hill, *The Great Patriotic War*, p.55, and Prikaz NKVD SSSR No. 00941 o sformirovanii chastei voisk NKVD pri osobikh otdelakh, 19 iiulia 1941 g, in V.P. Iampol'skii (gen.ed.) et al, *Organi gosudarstvennoi bezopasnosti…Tom vtoroi. Kniga 1. Nachalo. 22 iiunia-31 avgusta 1941 goda*, p.366. At divisional level NKVD troops were to be provided to the Special Sections in company strength, at front level in battalion strength.

45 See Alexander Statiev, 'Blocking Units in the Red Army', in *The Journal of Military History*, Volume 76, Number 2 (April 2012), p.487.

46 Note of the OO NKVD STF to UOO NKVD USSR on the activities of blocking detachments of the Stalingrad and Don Fronts [no earlier than 15 October], in Alexander Hill, *The Great Patriotic War*, p.103.

47 Spravka OO NKVD STF v UOO NKVD SSSR o deiatel'nosti zagraditel'-
nikh otriadov Stalingradskogo i Donskogo frontov [ne ranee 15 oktiabria]
1942 g., in V.K. Vinogradov et al (eds.), *Stalingradskaia epopeia*, p.223.
48 Ibid., pp.222–4.
49 Dokladnaia zapiska OO NKVD DF v UOO NKVD SSSR o nastupatel'nikh
operatsiiakh 66-i armii, 30 oktiabria 1942 g., in V.K. Vinogradov et al (eds.),
Stalingradskaia epopeia, p.245.
50 Alexander Statiev, 'Blocking Units in the Red Army', p.494.
51 See Order of the People's Commissar for Defence Number 0349, 29 October
1944..., in Alexander Hill, *The Great Patriotic War*, pp.247–8.
52 Alex Statiev, 'Penal Units in the Red Army', p.733.
53 Prikaz o napravlenii v shtrafnie chasti voennosluzhashchikh, osuzhdennikh
voennim tribunalami s primeneniem otsrochki ispolneniia prigovora do
okonchaniia voini, No, 323, 16 oktiabria 1942 g., in *RA T.13 (2-2)*, pp.332–3.
54 Alex Statiev, 'Penal Units in the Red Army', pp.729–30, 733.
55 For norms of September 1941 – very much an ideal - see Prikaz o vvedenii
novikh norm prodovol'stvennogo snabzheniia Krasnoi armii, No.312, 22 sentiabria 1941 g., in *RA T.13 (2-2)*, pp.95–102.
56 Prikaz o naznachenii odnogo iz chlenov voennogo soveta fronta i armii otvetst-
vennim za snabzhenie chastei, No.0437, 20 noiabria 1941 g., in ibid., p.124.
57 Dokladnaia zapiska OO NKVD STF v UOO NKVD SSSR 'O nedochetakh v
sushchestviushchei sisteme prodovol'stvennogo snabzheniia voisk deistvuiushchei armii', 27 oktiabria 1942 g., in V.K. Vinogradov et al (eds.),
Stalingradskaia epopeia, p.237.
58 Iurii Vladimirov, *Voina soldata-zenitchika*, pp.178–80, 190.
59 See Roger Munting, 'Soviet Food Supply and Allied Aid in the War,
1941–1945', in *Soviet Studies*, Volume XXXVI, Number 4 (October 1984),
p.588. For more recent detail on this issue, in Russian see Mikhail Suprun,
'Prodovol'stvennie postavki v SSSR po Lend-lizu v godi Vtoroi mirovoi
voini', in *Otechestvennaia istoriia*, Number 3 (1996), pp.46–54.
60 Anastas Mikoian, *Tak bilo*, p.430.

CHAPTER 16

1 Ivan Tiulenev, *Cherez tri voini*, pp.327–9.
2 Sokolov, Grigorii Grigor'evich, in V.Iu. Rusanov (ed.), *Velikaia Otechestvennaia. Komandarmi. Voenno-biograficheskii slovar'* (Moscow/Zhukovskii: Kuchkovo pole, 2005), p.217.
3 Zapis' peregovorov po priamomu provodu Verkhovnogo glavnokomanduiushchemu i zamestitelia nachal'nika General'nogo shtaba s komandovaniem Volkhovskogo fronta, 10 ianvaria 1942 g., in *RA T.16 (5-2)*, pp.36–7.
4 K.A. Meretskov, *Na sluzhbe narodu*, pp.264–5.
5 See on the establishment of full unitary command and the abolition of the
institute of commissars in the Red Army. Decree of the Presidium of the
Supreme Soviet..., 9 October 1942, in Alexander Hill, *The Great Patriotic
War*, p.114 and S. Zakharov, 'Povishenie urovnia voennikh znanii politrabotnikov v godi minuvshei voini', in *Vizh*, Number 12 (1966), pp.3–10.

6 See Postanovlenie Gosudarstvennogo Komiteta Oboroni o zamestiteliakh Narkoma oboroni, Np. GKO-3399 ot 20 maia 1943 g., Moskva, Kreml', in Iurii Gor'kov, *Gosudarstvennii Komitet Oboroni postanovliaet (1941–1945)*. *Tsifri, dokumenti* (Moscow: OLMA-PRESS, 2002), p.527.

7 A.V. Gorbatov, *Godi i voini* (Moscow: Voennoe izdatel'stvo, 1989), p.209 and A.A. Pechenkin, 'Narkom oboroni SSSR I.V. Stalin i ego zamestiteli', in *Vizh*, Number 8 (2005), p.24.

8 Iu.V. Rubtsov, 'Lev Zakharovich Mekhlis', in *Voprosii istorii*, Number 10 (1998), pp.79–83; On the Pavlov case, see I.A. Basiuk, 'General armii D.G. Pavlov i tragediia iiunia 1941 g.', in *Voprosii istorii*, Number 5 (2010), pp.41–51.

9 Iu.V. Rubtsov, 'Lev Zakharovich Mekhlis', p.83.

10 Ibid., pp.83–8.

11 Direktiva Stavki VGK No.170375 Glavnokomanduiushchemu voiskami Severo-kavkazskogo napravleniia ob organizatsii oboroni na Turetskom valu, 11 maia 1942 g. 23 ch 50 min, in *RA T.16 (5–2)*, p.201.

12 Direktiva Stavki VGK No.170285 komanduiushchemu voiskami Krimskogo fronta ob oboroni Kerchi, 15 maia 1942 g. 01 ch 10 min, in ibid., p.205.

13 Direktiva Stavki VGK No.170375 Glavnokomanduiushchemu voiskami Severo-kavkazskogo napravleniia ob organizatsii oboroni na Turetskom valu, 11 maia 1942 g. 23 ch 50 min, in ibid., p.201.

14 Direktiva Stavki VGK No.155452 voennim sovetam frontov i armii o prichinakh porazheniia Krimskogo fronta v Kerchenskoi operatsii, 4 iiunia 1942 g., in ibid., pp.236–8.

15 Iu.V.Rubtsov, 'Lev Zakharovich Mekhlis', p.90.

16 See A.A. Chernobaev (ed.), *Na prieme u Stalina. Tetradi (zhurnali) zapisei lits, priniatikh I.V. Stalinim (1924–1953 gg.). Spravochnik* (Moscow: Novii khronograf, 2010), p.376 onwards.

17 Iu.A. Siakov, 'Pervaia Siniavinskaia nastupatel'naia operatsiia (sentiabr' 1941 g.)', in *Voprosi istorii*, Number 3 (2007), p.123.

18 Zapis' peregovorov po priamomu provodu Verkhovnogo glavnokomanduiushchego i nachal'nika General'nogo shtaba s komanduiushchim 54-i armiei, 16 sentiabria 1941 g. Okoncheni v 23 ch 30 min; Zapis' peregovorov po priamomu provodu Verkhovnogo glavnokomanduiushchego s komanduiushchim 54-i armiei, 20 sentiabria 1941 g. Okoncheni v 23 ch 00 min; Direktiva Stavki VGK No. 002285 komanduiushchemu voiskami Leningradskogo fronta o smene komanduiushchego 54-i armiei, 24 sentiabria 1941 g. 02 ch 45 min; im *RA T.16 (5–1)*, pp.187, 194 and 200 respectively.

19 V.Iu. Rusanov (ed.), *Velikaia Otechestvennaia. Komandarmi. Voennii biograficheskii slovar'*, pp.120–1.

20 Soobshchenie Stavki VGK No.004684 komanduiushchemu voiskami Krima o viezde v Kerch' predstavitelia Stavki, 8 noiabria 1941 g., in *RA T.16 (5–1)*, p.279; Prikaz o Kulike G.I., No.0041, 2 marta 1942 g., in *RA T.13 (2–2)*, pp.161–2.

21 V.Iu. Rusanov (ed.), *Velikaia Otechestvennaia. Komandarmi. Voennii biograficheskii slovar'*, pp.120–1.

22 Oleg V. Khlevniuk, *Stalin: New Biography of a Dictator*, p.222.

23 Viktor Anfilov, 'Timoshenko', in Harold Shukman (ed.), *Stalin's Generals*, pp.249–52.

24 Konstantin Simonov, *Glazami cheloveka moego pokoleniia*, pp.386–7.

25 Roger R. Reese, *Red Commanders*, p.161.

26 Aleksandr Vasilevskii and Matvei Zakharov, 'Nachal'nika Genshtaba (fragmenti iz predsloviia k Vospominaniiam B.M. Shaposhnikova)', in E.V. Rusakova, *Polkovodtsi. Sbornik* (Moscow: Izdatel'stvo "Roman-gazeta", 1995), pp.362–3.

27 Oleg Rzheshevsky, 'Shaposhnikov', in Harold Shukman (ed.), *Stalin's Generals*, p.229.

28 Postanovlenie GKO 'O preobrazovanii Stavki Glavnogo komandovaniia i sozdanii Glavnikh komandovanii Severo-Zapadnogo, Zapadnogo, i Iugo-zapadnogo napravlenii', sekretno No.83ss ot 10/VII 41 g., in Iurii Gor'kov, *Gosudarstvennii Komitet Oboroni postanovliaet (1941–1945)*, p.501.

29 A.M. Vasilevskii, *Delo vsei zhizni. Kn.1*, p.178.

30 Iurii Gor'kov, *Gosudarstvennii Komitet Oboroni postanovliaet (1941–1945)*, pp.103–4.

31 Reshenie Politburo TsK VKP(b) (Protokol No.36 Punkt 356) o rabote Voroshilova K.E., 1 aprelia 1942 g., in *RA T.20 (9)*, p.112.

32 Postanovleniia Gosudarstvennogo komiteta oboroni No.2246ss ob izmenenii v rukovodstve partizanskim dvizheniem, 6 sentiabria 1942 g., in ibid., p.135.

33 Direktiva Stavki VGK No.220014 komanduiushchemu Otdel'noi primorskoi armiei, predstaviteliu Stavki o perenesenii napravleniia glavnogo udara v operatsii po osvobozhdeniiu Kerchi, 27 ianvaria 1944 g., in *RA T.16 (5–4)*, p.37.

34 Boris Sokolov, *Budennii. Krasnii miurat* (Moscow: Molodaia gvardiia, 2007), p.291.

35 Postanovlenie Soveta narodnikh komissarov Soiuza SSR, 27 avgusta 1942g. Moskva, Kreml'. O pervom zamestitele Norodnogo komissara oboroni, in *RA T.13(2–2)*, p.287 and ibid., p.292.

36 David Glantz, *Colossus Reborn*, p.482–3.

37 Zapiska F.I. Golikova I.V. Stalinu o generalakh i ofitserakh Krasnoi armii, No. GUK4/607121, 20 maia 1945 g., in S.V. Kudriashov (gen.ed.), *Vestnik Arkhiva Prezidenta Rossiiskoi Federatsii. Voina: 1941–1945. Vipusk 2*, p.555; Cherniakhovskii, Ivan Danilovich, in V.Iu. Rusanov (ed.), *Komandarmi*, pp.257–8. Cherniakovskii was killed in action in February 1945.

38 Roger R. Reese, *Red Commanders*, pp.154–6.

39 Geoffrey Roberts. *Stalin's General: The Life of Georgy Zhukov* (New York: Random House Inc., 2012), pp.311–13 and 317. Here I have drawn from material from my 2013 review of this book in the journal *Slavic Review*. See *Slavic Review*, Volume 72, Number 2 (2013), pp.422–3.

40 Zh. Lopez [J. Lopez] and L. Otkhmezuri, Zhukov. *Portret na fone epokhi*, pp.369, 678–86.

41 Prikaz Stavki Verkhovnogo Glavnokomandovaniia ob utverzhdenii v dolzhnosti nachal'nika General'nogo shtabaKrasnoi armii general-polkovnika Vasilevskogo A.M., No.199, 26 iiunia 1942 g., in *RA T.13 (2–2)*, p.262.

42 A.M. Vasilevskii, *Delo vsei zhizni. Kn.1*, pp.137, 145–6.

43 G.K. Zhukov, *Vospominaniia i razmishleniia...Tom 2*, p.112.

44 Evan Mawdsley, 'Stalin: Victors are not Judged', in *JSMS*, Volume 19, Number 4 (2006), p.715.

45 G.K. Zhukov, *Vospominaniia i razmishleniia...Tom 2*, p.113.

46 Ibid.

47 Rasporiazhenie Verkhovnogo glavnokomanduiushchego No. 170605 predstaviteliu Stavki ob ispol'zovanii 4-go i 16-go tankovikh korpusov, 9 sentiabria 1942 g. 22 ch 30 min, in *RA T.16 (5–2)*, p.389.

48 Rasporiazhenie Verkhovnogo glavnokomanduiushchego No. 170608 predstaviteliu Stavki i chlenu GKO o vosstanovlenii tankovikh korpusov i smene ikh komandirov, 11 sentiabria 1942 g, 03 ch 30 min, in *RA T.16 (5–2)*, p.390.

49 See Direktiva Stavki VGK No.170603 komanduiushchemu voiskami Stalingradskogo fronta ob otstranenii ot zanimaemoi dolzhnosti komanduiushchego 62-i armiei, 8 sentiabria 1942 g., in *RA T.16 (5–2)*, p.389 and V.Iu. Rusanov (ed.), *Velikaia Otechestvennaia. Komandarmi. Voennii biograficheskii slovar'*, p.130.

50 Nachal'niku shtaba Zakavkazskogo fronta ob organizatsii podgotovki ofitserov shtabov, 6 dekabria 1942 g., in *RA T.23 (12–2)*, p.402.

51 See Prikaz o rezul'tatakh poverki uchebnikh i zapasnikh strelkovikh brigad i polkov, No.0782, 3 oktiabria 1942 g., in *RA T.13 (2–2)*, pp.318–20.

52 Mikhail Suknev, *Zapiski komandira shtrafbata*, p.30.

53 On the establishment of full unitary command and the abolition of the institute of commissars in the Red Army. Decree of the Presidium of the Supreme Soviet..., 9 October 1942, in Alexander Hill, *The Great Patriotic War*, p.114.

54 Dokladnaia zapiska OO NKVD DF v UOO NKVD SSSR 'O reagirovaniiakh lichnogo sostava Donskogo fronta na Ukaz Prezidiuma Verkhovnogo Soveta ob uprazdnenii institute komissarov i na prikaz NKO No.307', in V.K. Vinogradov et al (eds.), *Stalingradskaia epopeia*, pp.230–1.

55 Mukhail Suknev, *Zapiski komandira shtrafbata*, pp.43–8.

56 Dokladnaia zapiska OO NKVD DF v UOO NKVD SSSR 'O reagirovaniiakh lichnogo sostava Donskogo fronta na Ukaz Prezidiuma Verkhovnogo Soveta ob uprazdnenii institute komissarov i na prikaz NKO No.307', in V.K. Vinogradov et al (eds.), *Stalingradskaia epopeia*, p.231.

57 N. Bobkov, 'K istorii voinskikh zvanii v sovetskikh vooruzhennikh silakh', in *Vizh*, Number 9 (1970), pp.89–90.

58 I.M. Golushko, *Stab tila Krasnoi Armii v godi voini*, pp.162–3.

59 Mikhail Shelkov, *Zapiski komandira strelkovogo batal'ona*, pp.75–6.

60 Mikhail Suknev, *Zapiski komandira shtrafbata*, p.134.

61 Dokladnaia zapiska OO NKVD DF v UOO NKVD SSSR o reagirovanii voennosluzhashchikh na vvedenie novikh znakov razlichiia, 19 ianvaria 1943 g., in V.K. Vinogradov et al (eds.), *Stalingradskaia epopeia*, pp.366, 368. On this matter, see also Catherine Merridale, *Ivan's War*, p.164.

62 Alexander Werth, *Russia at War 1941–1945* (London: Pan Books Ltd, 1965), p.382.

63 S.M.Shtemenko, *General'nii shtab v godi voini: Ot Stalingrada do Berlina* (Moscow: AST/Tranzitkniga. 2005), pp.184–5.

64 N.D. Saltikov, *Dokladivaiu v General'nii shtab* (Moscow: Voenizdat, 1983), p.7.
65 S.M.Shtemenko, *General'nii shtab v godi voini: Ot Stalingrada do Berlina*, pp.186–7 and Prikaz Narodnogo komissara oboroni o nedochetakh v rabote ofitserov General'nogo shtaba i perakh po ee ulucheniiu, No.0391, 22 iiunia 1943 g., in *RA T.13(2–3)*, pp.184–5.
66 Direktiva Stavki VGK No.170601 komanduiushchemu voiskami Voronezhskogo fronta o vremmenoi otmene operatsii po osvobozhdeniiu Voronezha i otpravke divizii v raion Stalingrada, 7 sentiabria 1942 g. 18 ch. 10 min., in *RA T.16 (5–2)*, p.388.

CHAPTER 17

1 P.P. Lebedenko, *V izluchine Dona* (Moscow: Voennoe izdatel'stvo Ministerstva oboroni SSSR, 1965), pp.122–6, 138, 142–7.
2 Ibid., p.148.
3 Ibid., p.149.
4 See David Glantz with Jonathan M. House, *To the Gates of Stalingrad: Soviet-German Combat Operations, April-August 1942. The Stalingrad Trilogy, Volume 1* (Lawrence, KA: The University Press of Kansas, 2009), pp.481–3.
5 Alexander Hill, *The Great Patriotic War*, p.106.
6 Ibid., pp.103–4 and David Glantz with Jonathan M. House, *Endgame at Stalingrad: The Stalingrad Trilogy, Volume 3. Book One: November 1942* (Lawrence, KA: The University Press of Kansas, 2014), p.29.
7 To military soviets of fronts and armies on the defence of population centres, 24 November 1941, in Alexander Hill, *The Great Patriotic War*, p.78.
8 Extracts from the Directive of the Supreme High Command... of 14 October 1942 on measures for the defence of Stalingrad, in ibid., p.104.
9 David Glantz with Jonathan N. House, *Armageddon in Stalingrad, September-November 1942: The Stalingrad Trilogy, Volume 2* (Lawrence, KA: The University Press of Kansas, 2009), p.391. See also V.I. Chuikov, *Srazhenie veka* (Moscow: Izdatel'stvo "Sovetskaia Rossiia", 1975), p.231.
10 V. Chuikov, 'Upravlenie i sviaz' v boiakh pod Stalingradom', in *Vizh*, Number 2 (1978), p.76.
11 V.I. Chuikov, *Srazhenie veka*, p.238.
12 David Glantz with Jonathan N. House, *Armageddon in Stalingrad, September-November 1942: The Stalingrad Trilogy, Volume 2*, p.391.
13 N.I. Krilov, *Stalingradskii rubezh*, pp.123, 266.
14 I.I. Liudnikov, *Doroga dlinoiu v zhizn'* (Moscow: Voennoe izdatel'stvo Ministerstva oboroni SSSR, 1969), pp.24–5, 44; David Glantz with Jonathan N. House, *Armageddon in Stalingrad, September-November 1942: The Stalingrad Trilogy, Volume 2*, pp.400, 407, 420, 422, 650–2, 675, 680–1.
15 David Glantz with Jonathan N. House, *Armageddon in Stalingrad, September-November 1942: The Stalingrad Trilogy, Volume 2*, pp.391 and 782n17.
16 N.I. Krilov, *Stalingradskii rubezh*, p.271.
17 Ibid., pp.271–2; David Glantz with Jonathan N. House, *Armageddon in Stalingrad, September-November 1942: The Stalingrad Trilogy, Volume 2*, pp.508, 510–12.

18 I Khorikov, 'Snaiping', in *Pravda*, 25 April 1936, p.2.

19 M. Moskvin, 'Luchshchie strelki', in *Pravda*, 6 June 1939, p.4.

20 V.N. Stepakov, "Legendi i mifi sovetsko-finlandskoi voini", in *Voprosi istorii*, Number 3 (1993), pp.171–2.

21 Narodnii Komissariat Oboroni, *Boevoi ustav pekhoti Krasnoi Armii. Chast' II (batal'on, polk)* (Moscow:Voennoe Izdatel'stvo Narodnogo Komissariata Oboroni, 1942), p.22.

22 See F.F. Viktorov (gen.ed.), *Istoriia Ordena Lenina Leningradskogo voennogo okruga*, p.276 and I.V. Skikin and I.Ia. Fomichenko, 'Istoricheskaia pobeda (k 30-letiiu proriva blokadi Leningrada)', in *Voprosi istorii*, Number 1 (1973), pp.111–12.

23 N. Mal'tsev, 'Snaiperskoe dvizhenie v Stalingradskoi bitve', in *Vizh*, Number 2 (1970), p.90.

24 V.I. Chuikov, *Srazhenie veka*, pp.174–5.

25 Narodnii Komissariat Oboroni Soiuza SSR, *Boevoi ustav pekhoti RKKA (BUP-38). Chast' pervaia (boets, otdelenie, vzvod)* (Moscow: Gosudarstvennoe Voennoe Izdatel'stvo Narkomata Oboroni Soiuza SSR, 1939), p.30; Narodnii Komissariat Oboroni, *Boevoi ustav pekhoti Krasnoi Armii. Chast' I (boets, otdelenie, vzvod, rota)* (Moscow: Voennoe Izdatel'stvo Narodnogo Komissariata Oboroni, 1942), p.31.

26 Gottlob Herbert Bidermann (Derek S. Zumbro trans. and ed.), *In Deadly Combat: A German Soldier's Memoir of the Eastern Front* (Lawrence, Kansas: University Press of Kansas, 2000), p.180.

27 N. Mal'tsev, 'Snaiperskoe dvizhenie v Stalingradskoi bitve', p.93.

28 Nachal'niku Glavnogo upravleniia formirovaniia i ukomplektovaniia voisk o napravlenii v 52-iu armiiu snaiperov, 12 iiulia 1943 g., in *RA T.23 (12 -3)*, p.205.

29 Testimony of Chechetov Mikhail Fomich. http://iremember.ru/snayperi/che chetov-mikhail-fomich/stranitsa-3.html to http://iremember.ru/snayperi/che chetov-mikhail-fomich/stranitsa-5.html. [Accessed 15 August 2014].

30 Narodnii Komissariat Oboroni Soiuza SSR, *Vremennii Polevoi Ustav RKKA 1936 (PU 36)*, pp.182–4.

31 Instruktsiia po organizatsii i vedeniiu boevikh deistvii za ovladenie nasilennimi punktami, 28 dekabria 1942 g., in *SBD17*, pp.14–15.

32 Vipiski iz intruktsii komanduiushchego 47-i armiei ot 28 dekabria 1942 g. po organizatsii i vvedeniiu boevikh deistvii za ovladenie naselennimi punktami, in ibid., pp.81–2.

33 Narodnii Komissariat Oboroni, *Boevoi ustav pekhoti Krasnoi Armii. Chast' II (batal'on, polk)*, pp.70–1.

34 Chuikov, *Srazhenie veka*, p.303.

35 Ibid., p.325.

36 Ibid., pp.326, 330.

37 See for example, ibid., p.226.

38 David Glantz with Jonathan N. House, *Armageddon in Stalingrad, September-November 1942: The Stalingrad Trilogy, Volume 2*, pp.462, 775, 778.

39 N. Popov, 'Razvitie samokhodnoi artillerii', in *Vizh*, Number 1 (1977), pp.27–9.

40 N.I.Krilov, *Stalingradskii rubezh*, p.274.

41 Leonid Fialkovskii, *Stalingradskii apokalipsis. Tankovaia brigade v adu* (Moscow: Iauza/Eksmo, 2011), pp.203–7.

42 Transcript of interview with Major Pyotr Andreyevich Zayonchkovsky, May 28, 1943, in Jochen Hellbeck (trans. Christopher Tauchen and Dominic Bonfiglio), *Stalingrad: The City that Defeated the Third Reich*, pp.382–3.

43 Direktiva Stavki VGK No. 170668 komanduiushchemu voiskami Donskogo fronta o nanisenii udara v napravlenii Orlovki, 15 oktiabria 1942 g. 05 ch 23 min, in *RA T.16 (5–2)*, pp.434–5.

44 Doklad komanduiushchego voiskami Donskogo fronta No.0053/op zamestiteliu Verkhovnogo glavnokomanduiushchego plana operatsii po razgromu orlovskoi gruppirovki protivnika, 15 oktiabria 1942 g. 19 ch 45 min, in *RA T.16 (5–2)*, pp.552–3.

45 Direktiva Stavki VGK No.170670 komanduiushchemu voiskami Donskogo fronta ob izmenenii v plane operatsii po naneseniiu udara na Orlovku, 16 oktiabria 1942 g. 03 ch 00 min, in ibid., p.436.

46 Rokossovskii, *Soldatskii dolg*, pp.149–50. See also A.S. Zhadov, *Chetire goda voini* (Moscow: Voenizdat, 1978), pp.54–7.

47 David Glantz with Jonathan N. House, *Armageddon in Stalingrad, September-November 1942: The Stalingrad Trilogy, Volume 2*, pp.712–13.

48 See Oleg Shein, *Neizvestnii front Velikoi Otechestvennoi. Krovavaia bania v kalmitskikh stepiakh* (Moscow: "Iauza"/"Eksmo", 2009).

49 Ivan Tiulenev, *Cherez tri voini*, p.326.

50 N. Voronkov and N. Zakuvaev, 'Topogeodezicheskoe obespechenie voisk', in *Vizh*, Number 12 (1982), p.29.

51 Ivan Tiulenev, *Cherez tri voini*, pp.324, 326.

52 Direktiva Stavki VGK No. 170579 komanduiushchemu voiskami Zakavkazskogo fronta ob usilenii oboroni Glavnogo kavkazskogo khrebta, 20 avgusta 1942 g. 23 ch. 50 min, in *RA T.16 (5–2)*, pp.369–70. See also Direktiva Stavki VGK No. 170580 Voennomu sovetu Zakavkazskogo fronta ob usilenii oboroni perevalov, 23 avgusta 1942 g. 13 ch 37 min, in *RA T.16 (5–2)*, pp.371–2.

53 A.A. Grechko, *Bitva za Kavkaz* (Moscow: Voennoe izdatel'stvo, 1967), pp.103–4.

54 See for example Ernst Rebentisch, *The Combat History of the 23rd Panzer Division in World War II* (Mechanicsburg, PA: Stackpole Books, 2009), pp.165–6.

55 I.V. Tiulenev, *Cherez tri voini. Izd. 2-e ispr. i dopoln.* (Moscow: Voenizdat, 1972), p.176; V.V. Dichko,'"Dvadtsatii" bronepoezd v iarostnikh boiakh', in *Poklonnaia gora. Gazeta Tsentral'nogo muzeia Velikoi Otechestvennoi voini*, Number 6 (14) (December 2012), p.7. www.poklonnayagora.ru/ord_img/doc/1360228573_82.pdf [Accessed 7 February 2015]; M.V. Kolomiets, *Bronepoezda v boiu 1941–1945. "Stal'nie kreposti" Krasnoi Armii* (Moscow: Strategiia KM/Iauza/Eksmo, 2010), pp.291, 293.

56 See M.V. Kolomiets, *Bronepoezda v boiu 1941–1945* for pre-war and wartime construction and deployment of Soviet armoured trains.

57 David Glantz with Jonathan M. House, *Endgame at Stalingrad: The Stalingrad Trilogy, Volume 3. Book One: November 1942*, p.27.

58 A.M. Vasilevskii, 'Mezhdu Donom i Volgoi', in Z.S. Sheinis (ed.), *Stalingrad: Uroki istorii. Vospominaniia uchastnikov bitvi. Vtoroe izdanie* (Moscow: Izdatel'stvo 'Progress', 1980), p.37; G.K. Zhukov, *Vospominaniia i razmishleniia. …Tom 2*, pp.311–12.

59 Tovarishchu Stalinu [from Eremenko and Khrushchev], No. 2889, 9.10.42 g. 11.17, in V.A. Zhilin (ed.), *Stalingradskaia bitva. Khronika, fakti, liudi: V 2-x kn. Kn.1* (Moscow: OLMA-PRESS, 2002), pp.707–9.

60 Alexander Hill, *The Great Patriotic War*, p.106.

61 V.A. Zhilin (ed.), *Stalingradskaia bitva. Khronika, fakti, liudi: V 2-x kn. Kn.2*, p.13.

62 Ibid., pp.11–13.

63 Richard L. DiNardo, *Germany and the Axis Powers*, pp.140–1, 150.

64 State Defence Committee. Decree GOKO No. 2791ss of 28 January 1943. … On the formation of ten tank armies, in Alexander Hill, *The Great Patriotic War*, p.112.

65 I.M. Anan'ev, *Tankovie armii v nastuplenii*, p.52.

66 Prikaz o sformirovanii mekhanizirovannikh korpusov, No. 00220, 22 oktiabria 1942 g., in *RA T.13 (2–2)*, pp.346–7.

67 Direktiva Stavki VGK No.994277 nachal'niku Glavnogo avtobrenetankovogo upravleniia, komanduiushchemu voiskami Stalingradskogo fronta o napravlenii v sostav fronta mekhanizirovannikh brigad, 1 noiabria 1942 g., in *RA T.16 (.5–2)*, p.447.

68 David Glantz with Jonathan N. House, *Armageddon in Stalingrad, September-November 1942: The Stalingrad Trilogy, Volume 2*, p.693.

69 Document 82, in Alexander Hill, *The Great Patriotic War*, pp.110–11.

70 Petr Bograd, *Ot zapoliar'ia do Vengrii. Zapiski dvadtsatichetirekhletnogo podpolkovnika. 1941–1945* (Moscow: ZAO Tsentpoligraf, 2009), pp.70–1.

71 M.I. Suknev, *Zapiski komandira shtrafbata*, pp.31 and 37.

72 Prikaz Stavki Verkhovnogo Glavnokomandovaniia No.46175 o perevooruzhenii strelkovikh podrazdelenii avtomatami, 23 maia 1943 g., in *RA T.16 (5–3)*, p.153.

73 V. Iakubov and D. Dmitriev, 'Taktika ognemetnikh chastei v Velikoi Otechestvennoi voini', in *Vizh*, Number 1 (1976), p.79.

74 David Glantz with Jonathan M. House, *Endgame at Stalingrad: The Stalingrad Trilogy, Volume 3. Book One: November 1942* (Lawrence, KA: The University Press of Kansas, 2014).

75 David Glantz with Jonathan N. House, *Armageddon in Stalingrad, September-November 1942: The Stalingrad Trilogy, Volume 2*, p.656.

76 S.G. Drobiazko, *Put' soldata. S boiami ot Kubani do Dnepra. 1942–1944* (Moscow: ZAO Tsentrpoligraf, 2008), p.41.

77 See Zapis' peregovorov po priamomu provodu Verkhovnogo glavnokomanduiushchego i…nachal'nika General'nogo shtaba s komandovaniem Iugozapadnogo fronta, 20 iiunia 1942 g., in *RA T.16 (5–2)*, pp.257–8.

78 Testimony of Colonel General Raus, in Steven H. Newton (trans. and ed.), *Kursk: The German View. Eyewitness Reports of Operation Citadel by the German Commanders* (Cambridge, MA: Da Capo Press, 2002), p.261.

79 Otdel po ispolzovaniiu opita voini General'nogo shtaba Krasnoi Armii, *Sbornik takticheskikh primerov po opitu Velikoi Otechestvennoi voini. No.2. mai-iiun'*

1943 g. (Moscow: Voennoe izdatel'stvo Narodnogo Komissariata Oboroni, 1943), pp.3–5.

80 Ivan Tiulenev, *Cherez tri voini*...(Moscow : ZAO Tsentrpoligraf, 2007) p.293.

81 David Glantz with Jonathan M. House, *Endgame at Stalingrad: The Stalingrad Trilogy, Volume 3. Book One: November 1942*, pp.250–1, 256–7, 347–8.

82 See Joel S. A. Hayward, *Stopped at Stalingrad*, pp.233–44.

83 David Glantz with Jonathan M. House, *Endgame at Stalingrad: The Stalingrad Trilogy, Volume 3. Book One: November 1942*, pp.467–70.

84 Führer Headquarters, 23 July 1942. Directive No. 45. Continuation of 'Operation Braunschweig', in Hugh Trevor-Roper (ed.), *Hitler's War Directives, 1939–1945*, p.196.

85 Joel S.A. Hayward, *Stopped at Stalingrad*, p.245.

86 Zapiska P.F. Zhigareva I.V. Stalinu o perestroike upravleniia VVS, No. 331838ss, 21 marta 1942 g., in S.V. Kudriashov (gen.ed.), *Vestnik Arkhiva Prezidenta Rossiiskoi Federatsii. Voina: 1941–1945. Vipusk 2*, p.194.

87 Gorelov Sergei Dmitrievich, in A. Drabkin (ed.), *Ia dralsia na istrebitele*, pp.335–42.

88 Von Hardesty and Ilya Grinberg, *Red Phoenix Rising: The Soviet Air Force in World War II* (Lawrence, Kansas: University Press of Kansas, 2012), p.171.

89 Gorelov, in A. Drabkin (ed.), *Ia dralsia na istrebitele*, pp.354–5. See also Viacheslav Kondrat'ev, 'Sravnitel'nii analiz...sovetskikh i germanskikh istrebitelei...', in A. Drabkin (ed.), *Ia dralsia na istrebitele*, p.432; M. Mukhin, *Sovetskaia aviapromishlennost' v godi Velikoi Otechestvennoi voini*, p.342. On the development of the La-5 and La-7, see Yefim Gordon and Dmitri Khazanov, *Soviet Combat Aircraft of the Second World War. Volume One: Single-Engined Fighters*, pp.41–58.

90 On the problem of large regiments, see Directive of the Headquarters of the Supreme Command to commanders of the forces of fronts, armies and military districts, 15 July 1941, in Alexander Hill, *The Great Patriotic War*, p.58; E. Simakov, 'Sovershenstvovanie organizatsionnoi strukturi Voenno-Vozdushnikh Sil', in *Vizh*, Number 9 (1978), p.30.

91 E. Simakov, 'Sovershenstvovanie organizatsionnoi strukturi Voenno-Vozdushnikh Sil', pp.28–30.

92 Ibid., pp.30–31; Yefim Gordon and Dmitri Khazanov, *Soviet Combat Aircraft of the Second World War. Volume 2: Twim-Engined Fighters, Attack Aircraft and Bombers*, p.136.

93 M. Kozhevnikov, 'Sozdanie i ispol'zovanie aviatsionnikh rezervov Stavki VGK', in *Vizh*, Number 10 (1976), p.33.

94 M. Kozhevnikov, 'Vozdushnaia blokada', in *Vizh*, Number 11 (1974), p.20.

95 Joel S.A. Hayward, *Stopped at Stalingrad*, p.255.

96 Generalleutnant a.D. Walter Schwabedissen, *The Russian Air Force in the eyes of German Commanders* (USAF Historical Division, Research Studies Institute, Air University, June 1960), pp.191, 204–5; Joel S.A. Hayward, *Stopped at Stalingrad*, p.284.

97 I. Timokhovich, 'Vzaimodeistvie aviatsii s sukhoputnimi voiskami vo frontovoi nastupatel'noi operatsii', in *Vizh*, Number 7 (1977), p.21.

98 L. Mikriukov, 'Osnovnie napravleniia razvitiia taktiki shturmovoi aviatsii', in *Vizh*, Number 1 (1979), p.36.

99 Doklad predstavitel'ia Stavki Verkhovnomu Glavnokomanduiushchemu plana razgroma okruzhennoi v Stalingrade gruppirovki protivnika, 27 dekabria 1942 g., in *RA T.16 (5–2)*, pp.568–9.

100 Leonid Fialkovskii, *Stalingradskii apokalipsis*, pp.353, 400, 403. See also Izvlechenie iz operativnoi svodki No.27(700) General'nogo shtaba Krasnoi Armii na 8.00 27.01.43 g., 57-ia armiia, and Izvlechenie iz operativnoi svodki No.29(702) General'nogo shtaba Krasnoi Armii na 8.00 29.01.43 g., 57-ia armiia in V.A. Zhilin (ed.), *Stalingradskaia bitva. Khronika, fakti, liudi: V 2-x kn. Kn.2*, pp.499 and 507 respectively.

101 Combat report of the Headquarters of the Supreme High Command representative of the Don Front on the liquidation of enemy forces in the Stalingrad region, 2 February 1943, in Alexander Hill, *The Great Patriotic War*, p.108.

102 G.F. Krivosheev et al, *Soviet Casualties and Combat Losses*, pp.124–7.

CHAPTER 18

1 Svetlana Gerasimova (trans. and ed. Stuart Britton), *The Rzhev Slaughterhouse: The Red Army's Forgotten 15-month Campaign Against Army Group Center, 1942–1943* (Solihull, West Midlands: Helion and Company, 2013). I have cited an earlier Russian version of this work.

2 Svetlana Gerasimova, *Rzhevskaia boinia. Poteriannaia pobeda Zhukova* (Moscow: Iauza/Eksmo, 2009), pp.221–5.

3 Alexander Hill, *The Great Patriotic War*, p.106.

4 Direktiva Stavki VGK No. 170700 komanduiushchim voiskami Zapadnogo i Kalininskogo frontov o zadachakh po razgromu Rzhevsko-Sichevsko-Olenino-Beliiskoi gruppirovki protivnika, 8 dekabria 1942 g, in *RA T.16 (5–2)*, p.462.

5 A.L. Getman, *Tanki idut na Berlin*, pp.76–7.

6 Ibid., p.61.

7 Thomas L. Jentz (ed.), *Panzertruppen...1943–1945*, p.24.

8 A.L. Getman, *Tanki idut na Berlin*, p.72 and David M. Glantz, *Zhukov's Greatest Defeat*, pp.91–9.

9 David M. Glantz, *Zhukov's Greatest Defeat*, pp.223–5.

10 Ibid., pp.252–6; A.L. Getman, *Tanki idut na Berlin*, p.74.

11 David M. Glantz, *Zhukov's Greatest Defeat*, pp.306–8; A.L. Getman, *Tanki idut na Berlin*, pp.74–5.

12 David M. Glantz, *Zhukov's Greatest Defeat*, p.285.

13 Zapis' peregovorov po priamomu provodu Verkhovnogo Glavnokomanduiushchego s predstavitelem Stavki i komanduiushchim voiskami Iugo-Zapadnogo fronta, 27 noiabria 1942 g., In *RA T.16 (5–2)*, p.454.

14 Direktiva Stavki VGK No.170697 komanduiushchim voiskami Iugo-Zapadnogo i Voronezhskogo frontov, predstaviteliu Stavki ob utverzhdenii plana operatsii "Saturn", 3 dekabria 1942 g., in ibid., p.459.

15 Rasporiazhenie Verkhovnogo Glavnokomanduiushchego No. 170708 predstaviteliu Stavki on izmenenii poriadka razgroma okruzhennoi pod Stalingradom gruppirovki protivnika, 14 dekabria 1942 g., in ibid., p.467.

16 Direktiva Stavki VGK komanduiushchim voiskami Iugo-Zapadnogo i Voro-nezhskogo frontov, predstaviteliu Stavki ob izmenenii plana operatsii "Saturn", 13 dekabria 1942 g., in ibid., pp.466–7; G.K. Zhukov, *Vospomina-niia i razmishleniia. ...Tom 2*, p.364.

17 A.S. Zheltov, 'Operatsiia "Malii Saturn"', in A.S. Davidov et al (eds.), *Operatsiia "Malii Saturn"* (Rostov-na-Donu: Rostizdat, 1974), p.123.

18 Abteilung Ia. H-Qu., den 10 Dezember 1942. Tagesmeldung der Angriffs-gruppe Hollidt. NARA T-311 Roll 268 frame 001196.

19 A.S. Zheltov, 'Operatsiia "Malii Saturn"', in A.S. Davidov et al (eds.), *Operatsiia "Malii Saturn"*, pp.123–4; D.I. Stankevskii, 'Severo-vostochnee Rostova', in A.S. Davidov et al (eds.), *Operatsiia "Malii Saturn"*, pp.129–30; Iu. Plotnikov and V. Safronov, 'Razgrom 8-i ital'ianskoi armii v operatsii "Malii Saturn"' (dekabria 1942 g.), in *Vizh*, Number 12 (1982), p.39. In fact 46 out of 170 airworthy aircraft were reported as lost at Tatsins-kaia airfield – 22 Ju-52s and 24 Ju-86s involved in the Stalingrad airlift, along with considerable quantities of supplies intended for 6th Army. See Joel S.A. Hayward, *Stopped at Stalingrad*, p.272.

20 Zapis' peregovorov po priamomu provodu Verkhovnogo Glavnokoman-duiushchego i ego zamestitelia s komanduiushchim voiskami Iugo-Zapadnogo fronta, 28 dekabria 1942 g., in *RA T.16 (5–2)*, pp.470–2. The additional tank corps were to be 3rd and 10th. See *RA T.16 (5–2)*, p.474.

21 See David Glantz with Jonathan M. House, *Endgame at Stalingrad: The Stalingrad Trilogy, Volume 3. Book Two: December 1942 – February 1943* (Lawrence, KA: The University Press of Kansas, 2014), pp.239–40, and more broadly pp.232–43 for his description and analysis of this and associated events.

22 Komanduiushchemu voiskami Brianskogo fronta o peredislokatsii 5-go Mekhanizirovannogo korpusa, 25 noiabria 1942 g., in *RA T.23 (12–2)*, pp.399–400.

23 M. Shaposhnikov, 'Boevie deistviia 5-go Mekhanizirovannogo korpusa zapadnee Surovkino v dekabre 1942 goda', in *Vizh*, Number 10 (1982), pp.33–7.

24 Prikaz Stavki VGK No.00495, 28 dekabria 1942 g., in *RA T.16 (5–2)*, p.473.

25 For a German perspective, see for example Erich von Manstein, *Lost Victories*, pp.388–90.

26 Richard L. DiNardo, *Germany and the Axis Powers*, pp.154–5.

27 N. Maliugin, 'Razvitie i sovershenstvovanie tila strelkovoi divizii v godi voini', in *Vizh*, Number 11 (1978), pp.88, 92.

28 I. Golushko, 'Rabota tila v vazhneishikh operatsiiakh vtorogo perioda voini', in *Vizh*, Number 11 (1974), pp.38–9, and N. Maliugin, 'Razvitie i sover-shenstvovanie tila strelkovoi divizii v godi voini', p.93.

29 A.M. Vasilevskii, *Delo vsei zhizni. Kn.1*, p.243.

30 I. Golushko, 'Rabota tila v vazhneishikh operatsiiakh vtorogo perioda voini', pp.35, 37–8.

31 S. Lipatov and V. Kolomiets, 'Frontovaia industriia remonta tankov', in *Vizh*, Number 2 (1979), p.31.

32 I.E. Krupchenko (gen.ed.), *Sovetskie tankovie voiska 1941–1945 gg.*, pp.10–11.

33 S. Lipatov and V. Kolomiets, 'Frontovaia industriia remonta tankov', p.32; Otchet pomoshchnika nachal'nika REU GABTU o sostoianii i rabote remontnikh baz NKO SSSR, 9 dekabria 1941 g., and Prikaz NKO SSSR o formirovanii podvizhnikh remontnikh baz, No.0126, 20 fevralia 1942 g, in *Glavnoe avtobronetankovoe upravlenie. Liudi, sobitiia, fakti v dokumentakh – 1940–1942 gg.*, pp.129–34 and pp.198–9 respectively.

34 S. Lipatov and V. Kolomiets, 'Frontovaia industriia remonta tankov', p.32.

35 Gary A. Dickson, 'Tank Repair and the Red Army in World War II', in *JSMS*, Volume 25, Number 3 (September 2012), pp.390–1.

36 S. Lipatov and V. Kolomiets, 'Frontovaia industriia remonta tankov', pp.33–5.

37 David Glantz, 'Prelude to Kursk: Soviet strategic operations, February-March 1943', in *JSMS*, Volume 8, Number 1 (1995), p.7.

38 Doklad komanduiushchego voiskami Iugo-Zapadnogo fronta No. 01583 Verkhovnomu glavnokomanduiushchemu plana operatsii po razgromu Donbasskoi gruppirovki protivnika, 9 fevralia 1943 g. 23 ch 10 min, in *RA T.16 (5–3)*, p.277.

39 A.M. Vasilevskii, *Delo vsei zhizni. Kn.2*, pp.6–7.

40 Direktiva Stavki VGK No.30059 komanduiushchim voiskami Voronezhskogo i Iugo-Zapadnogo frontov, predstaviteliu Stavki o perepodchinenii 3-i Tankovoi armii, 28 fevralia 1943 g., in *RA T.16 (5–3)*, p.83.

41 Erich von Manstein, *Lost Victories*, pp.435–6.

42 Doklad komanduiushchego voiskami Voronezhskogo fronta No.03/op Verkhovnomu Glavnokomanduiushchemu plana perekhoda k vremmenoi oborone pod Khar'kovom, 1 marta 1943 g, in *RA T.16 (5–3)*, p.233; Direktiva Stavki VGK No.30061 komanduiushchemu voiskami Voronezhskogo fronta ob utverzhdenii resheniia na perekhod k oborone, 2 marta 1943 g., in *RA T.16 (5–3)*, p.86.

43 David Glantz, 'Prelude to Kursk: Soviet strategic operations, February-March 1943', pp.13–15, 29.

44 Manstein, *Lost Victories*, p.436.

45 S.M. Davtian, *Piataia vozdushnaia. Voenno-istoricheskii ocherk boevogo puti 5-i vozdushnoi armii v godi Velikoi Otechestvennoi voini* (Moscow: Voenizdat, 1990), pp.44–5.

46 A.A. Grechko, *Bitva za Kavkaz*, p.330; M.N. Kozhevnikov, *Komandovanie i shtab VVS Sovetskoi Armii v Velikoi Otechestvennoi voine 1941–1945*, p.123.

47 Georgii Pshenianik, *Krakh plana "Edel'veis". Sovetskaia aviatsiia v bitve za Kavkaz. 1942–1943* (Moscow: ZAO Izdatel'stvo Tsentrpoligraf, 2013), p.273–4, 301.

48 S.M. Davtian, *Piataia vozdushnaia: Voenno-istoricheskii ocherk boevogo puti 5-i vozdushnoi armii*, p.43; M.N. Kozhevnikov, *Komandovanie i shtab VVS Sovetskoi Armii v Velikoi Otechestvennoi voine 1941–1945*, p.122.

49 Georgii Pshenianik, *Krakh plana "Edel'veis"*, pp.279–80, 317.

50 Prikaz o poriadke napravleniia iz gospitalei voennosluzhashchikh gvardeiskikh chaste i kursantskikh brigad posle ikh vizdorovleniia, No. 354, 13 dekabria 1941 g., in *RA T.13 (2–2)*, pp.128–9.

51 B.A. Gubin and V.A. Kiselev, *Vos'maia vozdushnaia. Voenno-istoricheskii ocherk boevogo puti 8-i vozdushnoi armii v godi Velikoi Otechestvennoi voini* (Moscow: Voennoe izdatel'stvo, 1986), pp.102–3.

52 Aleksandr Pokrishkin, *Poznat' sebia v boiu. "Stalinskie sokoli" protiv asov Liuftvaffe. 1941–1945 gg.* (Moscow: ZAO Tsentrpoligraf, 2008), pp.297–8.

53 Von Hardesty and Ilya Grinberg, *Red Phoenix Rising*, p.201.

54 M.N. Kozhevnikov, *Komandovanie i shtab VVS Sovetskoi Armii v Velikoi Otechestvennoi voine 1941–1945*, p.124.

55 Von Hardesty and Ilya Grinberg, *Red Phoenix Rising*, p.205.

56 Generalleutnant a.D. Walter Schwabedissen, *The Russian Air Force in the Eyes of German Commanders*, pp.195, 207–8; S.M. Davtian, S.M. Davtian, *Piataia vozdushnaia: Voenno-istoricheskii ocherk boevogo puti 5-i vozdushnoi armii*, p.52.

57 Generalleutnant a.D. Walter Schwabedissen, *The Russian Air Force in the Eyes of German Commanders*, pp.228–9.

CHAPTER 19

1 Burkhart Mueller-Hillebrand, *Das Heer 1933–1945. Entwicklung des organisatorischen Aufbaues. Band III. Der Zweifrontenkrieg. Das Heer vom Beginn des Feldzuges gegen die Sowjetunion bis zum Kriegsende* (Frankfurt am Main: Verlag E.S. Mittler and Sohn, 1969), pp.124–5; David M. Glantz, *Stumbling Colossus*, pp.155, 275–6.

2 See for example Nachal'nikam shtabov frontov, voennikh okrugov i otdel'-nikh armii ob organizatsionnom ukreplenii strelkovikh rot, 17 iiunia 1943 g., signed Vasilevskii, in *RA T.23(12–3)*, pp.173–4.

3 Prikaz Stavki verkhovnogo glavnokomandovaniia No.46175 o perevooruzhenii strelkovikh podrazdelenii avtomatami, 23 maia 1943 g., in *RA T.16 (5–3)*, p.153.

4 G.K. Zhukov, *Vospominaniia i razmishleniia. . . .Tom 3*, p.8.

5 Doklad chlena Voennogo soveta Voronezhskogo fronta zamestiteliu predsedatelia SNK A. I. Mikoianu i nachal'niku tila Krasnoi Armii o polozhenii s avtobenzinom, 5 marta 1943 g., in *RA T.15 (4–3)*, p.110.

6 G.F. Krivosheev et al, *Soviet Casualties and Combat Losses*, pp.130–1.

7 Zapiska Voennogo soveta Voronezhskogo fronta I.V. Stalinu o doykomplektovanii voisk fronta, No.00679/a, 30 marta 1943 g., in S.V. Kudriashov (gen. ed.), *Vestnik Arkhiva Prezidenta Rossiiskoi Federatsii. Voina: 1941–1945. Vipusk 2*, pp.291–2.

8 Spravka Glavnogo upravleniia formirovaniia i ukomplektovaniia voisk Krasnoi Armii o podache marshevogo popolneniia Voronezhskomu frontu s 1 ianvaria po 1 maia 1943 g., 7 maia 1943 g, in *RA T.15 (4–3)*, pp.316–17.

9 Spravka shtaba Voronezhskogo fronta o kolichestve postupivshego popolneniia dlia chastei fronta s dekabria 1942 g. po aprel' 1943 g., [undated], in ibid., p.315.

10 116/837 tanks, broken down as 9/45 KV, 33/398 T-34, 24/290 T-70, 7/10 Matilda, 20/46 Valentine, 10/16 Lee and 10/35 Stuart tanks. Zapiska Voennogo soveta Voronezhskogo fronta I.V. Stalinu o doykomplektovanii voisk fronta, No.00679/a, 30 marta 1943 g., in S.V. Kudriashov (gen.ed.), *Vestnik Arkhiva Prezidenta Rossiiskoi Federatsii. Voina: 1941–1945. Vipusk 2*, pp.292, 295.

11 A.M. Vasilevskii, *Delo vsei zhizni. Kn.2*, p.16.

12 Doklad predstavlitelia Stavki VGK Verkohvnomu Glavnokomanduiush-chemu o vozmozhnikh deistviiakh protivnika i sovetskikh voisk vesnoi i letom 1943 goda, 8 aprelia 1943 g., in *RA T.15 (4–4)*, pp.17–18 and G.K. Zhukov, *Vospominaniia i razmishleniia. ...Tom 3*, pp.13–15; A.M. Vasilevskii, *Delo vsei zhizni. Kn.2*, p.16.

13 Direktiva General'nogo shtaba komanduiushchim voiskami frontov o pre-dstavlenii imi soobrazhenii po otsenke obstanovki, 10 aprelia 1943 g., in *RA T.15 (4–4)*, p.18; G.K. Zhukov, *Vospominaniia i razmishleniia. ...Tom 3* pp.17–21; A.M. Vasilevskii, *Delo vsei zhizni. Kn.2* , p.16–17.

14 A.M. Vasilevskii, *Delo vsei zhizni. Kn.2* , pp.17–18; G.K. Zhukov, *Vospominaniia i razmishleniia. ...Tom 3*, pp.23–4.

15 A.M. Vasilevskii, *Delo vsei zhizni. Kn.2*, pp.20–1.

16 See Third speech of I.V. Stalin to graduating officers, the Kremlin, Moscow, 5 May 1941, in Alexander Hill, *The Great Patriotic War*, p.29.

17 Direktiva Stavki VGK No.46101 komanduiushchemu voiskami Rezervnogo fronta o pereimenovanii upravleniia fronta v upravlenie Stepnogo voennogo okruga, 13 aprelia 1943 g., in *RA T.16 (5–3)*, p.116 and Direktiva Stavki VGK No.30107 komanduiushchemu voiskami Stepnogo voennogo okruga o podgotovke oboroni i zadachakh boevoi podgotovki, 23 aprelia 1943 g., in *RA T.16 (5–3)*, pp.127–8.

18 Komanduiushchemu voiskami Tsentral'nogo fronta o merakh po srivu per-edvizhenii i sosredotocheniia protivnika u Orla, 5 maia 1943 g., in *RA T.23 (12–3)*, p.134.

19 Direktiva Stavki VGK No.30123 komanduiushchim voiskami Brianskogo, Tsentral'nogo, Voronezhskogo i Iugo-Zapadnogo frontov o date vozmozh-nogo nastupleniia protivnika, 8 maia 1943 g 23 ch 35 min, and Direktiva Stavki VGK No.30124 komanduiushchemu voiskami Stepnogo voennogo okruga o date vozmozhnogo nastupleniia protivnika, 8 maia 1943 g. 24 ch 00 min, in *RA T.16(5–3)*, p.148; Direktiva Stavki VGK No.30129 koman-duiushchim voiskami ... o vremmenoi prekrashchenii deistvii aviatsii po aerodromam i kommunikatsiiam protivnika, 13 maia 1943 g., in RA *T.16 (5–3)*, p.151; Direktiva Stavki VGK No.30131 komanduiushchim voiskami ... o srokakh vozmozhnogo nastupleniia protivnika, 20 maia 1943 g. 03 ch 30 min, in *RA T.16 (5–3)*, p.153.

20 G.K. Zhukov, *Vospominaniia i razmishleniia. ...Tom 3*, p.32.

21 A.M. Vasilevskii, *Delo vsei zhizni. Kn.2*, pp.24–5. See also G.K. Zhukov, *Vospominaniia i razmishleniia. ...Tom 3*, pp.31–2.

22 A.M. Vasilevskii, *Delo vsei zhizni. Kn.2*, p.25.

23 See V.V. Kondrashov, *Znat' vse o protivnike. Voennie razvedki SSSR i fashists-koi Germanii v godi Velikoi Otechestvennoi voini*, p.168.

24 Prikaz o reorganizatsii upravleniia voiskovoi razvedki General'nogo shtaba Krasnoi Armii, No.0071, 19 aprelia 1943 g, and Prilozhenie k prikazu NKO SSSR ot 19 aprelia 1943 g. No.0071, in *RA T.13 (2–3)*, pp.124–7.

25 Prikaz o sostoianii organov voiskovoi razvedki i o meropriatiiakh po uluche-niiu ee boevoi deiatel'nosti, No.0072, 19 aprelia 1943 g, in *RA T.13 (2–3)*, pp.127–9.

26 Prikaz ob uluchshenii razvedivatel'noi raboti partizanskikh otriadov, No.0073, 19 aprelia 1943 g., in *RA T.13 (2–3)*, p.129.

27 Nachal'nikam shtabov frontov, otdel'nikh armii o nedostatkakh v vedenii razvedki i merakh po ee sovershenstvovaniiu, 25 dekiabria 1943 g., in *RA T.23 (12–3)*, pp.456–7.

28 A.M. Vasilevskii, *Delo vsei zhizni. Kn.2*, p.25.

29 I.V. Parot'kin (ed.), *Kurskaia bitva* (Moscow: Izdatel'stvo "Nauka", 1970), pp.476, 479, 485, 487.

30 Soliankin et al, *Otechestvennie bronirovannie mashini. XX vek....1941–1945 gg.*1941–1945 , p.342; Prikaz ob ispitanii 152-mm samokhodnoi pushki, 10 ianvaria 1943 g., in *RA T.13 (2–3)*, pp.22–3; Postanovlenie No.GOKO 2889ss ot 14 fevralia 1943 g. Moskva, Kreml'. O sformirovanii tiazhelikh samokhodnikh artilleriiskikh polkov RGK. www.soldat.ru/doc/gko/scans/2889-01-1.jpg. [Accessed 9 August 2014].

31 Ibid., www.soldat.ru/doc/gko/scans/2889-03-1.jpg. [Accessed 9 August 2014].

32 Elektron Priklonskii, *Dnevnik samokhodchika. Boevoi put' mekhanika-voditelia ISU-152. 1942–1945* (Moscow: ZAO Tsentropoligraf, 2008), p.73.

33 I.V. Parot'kin (ed.), *Kurskaia bitva*, pp.476–7, 479.

34 Ibid., p.488 and later.

35 Postanovlenie No. GOKO-3164ss. 12 aprelia 1943 g. Moskva, Kreml'. O sformirovanii chetirekh artilleriiskikh korpusov proriva i vos'mi otdel'nikh tiazhelikh pushechnikh artilleriiskikh brigad. www.soldat.ru/doc/gko/scans/3164-01-1.jpg and www.soldat.ru/doc/gko/scans/3164-02-1.jpg [Accessed 9 August 2014]

36 Postanovlenie No. GOKO-3247ss ot "23" aprelia 1943 g. Moskva, Kreml'. O sformirovanii dopolnitel'no odnogo artilleriiskogo korpusa proriva i vneseniia izmenenii v organizatsiiu artilleriiskoi divizii proriva. www.soldat.ru/doc/gko/scans/3247-01-1.jpg . [Accessed 9 August 2014]

37 Postanovlenie No. GOKO-3248ss ot "23" aprelia 1943 g. Moskva, Kreml'. O sformirovanii desiati otdelnikh istrebilel'no-protivotankovikh artilleriiskikh brigad rezerva Glavnokomandovaniia. www.soldat.ru/doc/gko/scans/3248-01-1.jpg, www.soldat.ru/doc/gko/scans/3248-02-1.jpg and www.soldat.ru/doc/gko/scans/3248-03-1.jpg. [Accessed 9 August 2014].

38 Testimony of Mat'ianov Viktor Nikolaevich. http://iremember.ru/artilleristi/matyanov-viktor-nikolaevich.html. [Accessed 9 August 2014].

39 4,648 Dodge ¾ ton and 37,122 Studebaker 6x4 or 6x6 2½ ton shipped by 30 June 1943 according to Soviet figures. Otchet ob otgruzke tovarov iz SSha v SSSR s 1.10.41 do -1.07.45 gg.. ...SPZK, Washington, 29.08.45. RGAE f.413.o.9.d.438.ll.16–17.

40 Niklas Zetterling and Anders Frankson, *Kursk 1943: a statistical analysis* (Abingdon, Oxon: Frank Cass, 2000), pp.18, 46, 58, 65–6.

41 This section has been prepared on the basis of a lengthy description of the period from the beginning of training in a tank school to reaching jumping off positions for his first engagement with the enemy, in Elektron Priklonskii, *Dnevnik samokhodchika*, pp.26–81.

42 Shlemotov, Aleksandr Sergeevich, in Artem Drabkin (ed.), *Ia dralsia na T-34*, pp.304–8.

43 Prikaz Stavki VGK No.46194 o formirovanii 4-i tankovoi armii, 26 iiunia 1943 g., in *RA T.16(5–3)*, p.171.

44 A.Kh. Babadzhanian, 'Bronetankovie i mekhanizirovannie voiska v Kurskoi bitve', in I.V. Parot'kin, *Kurskaia bitva*, p.194.

45 Valerii Zamulin, 'The Battle of Kursk: New Findings', in *JSMS*, Volume 25, Number 3 (2012), p.413.

46 F.W. von Mellenthin, *Panzer Battles*, p.266.

47 Nachal'nikam shtabov frontov i otdel'nikh armii ob uluchshenii maskirovki voisk, 20 iiunia 1943 g., in *RA T.23 (12–3)*, pp.176–7.

48 Komanduiushchim voiskami frontov, voennikh okrugov i otdel'nimi armiiami ob uluchshenii maskirovki voennikh ob"ektov, 30 iiunia 1943 g., in *RA T.23 (12–3)*, p.191.

49 Komanduiushchemu voiskami Stepnogo voennogo okruga o merakh po dezinformatsii protivnika otnositel'no peredvizhenii voisk okruga, 30 maia 1943 g., in *RA T.23(12–3)*, p.151.

50 P. Mel'nikov, 'Operativnaia maskirovka', in *Vizh*, Number 4 (1982), p.21.

51 K.S. Moskalenko, 'Voronezhskii front v Kurskoi bitve', in I.V. Parot'kin (ed.), *Kurskaia bitva*, pp.103–5.

52 Z. Shutov, 'Strelkovii batal'on v oborone na Kurskoi duge', in *Vizh*, Number 4 (1978), p.52.

53 A Bublikov, 'Nas razdelial tol'ko ruchei', in V.Ia. Zhilin (ed.), *"Eto bilo na ognennoi duge" (Vospominaniia gubkintsev-uchasnikov Kurskoi bitvi)* (Gubkin: Gubkinskii gorodskoi Sovet veteranov, 1993), p.11.

54 O.E. Ashcheulov, *Artilleriia Krasnoi armii 1941–1943 gg. Istoriia organizatsii i boevogo primeneniia* (Moscow: "MPPA BIMPA", 2009), pp.184–5, 213.

55 David M. Glantz and Harold S. Orenstein (trans. and ed.), *The Battle of Kursk: The Soviet General Staff Study* (London and Portland, OR: Frank Cass Publishers, 1999), p.44.

56 N.S. Fomin, 'Artilleriia v Kurskoi bitve', in I.V. Parot'kin (ed.), *Kurskaia bitva*, pp.218–19.

57 Ibid., p.219 and G.T. Khoroshilov, 'Nekotorie voprosi boevogo primeneniia artillerii v Kurskoi bitve', in ibid., p.231.

58 N.S. Fomin, 'Artilleriia v Kurskoi bitve', in ibid., p.220.

59 Direktiva Stavki VGK No.30144 komanduiushchim voiskami Zapadnogo, Brianskogo, Tsentral'nogo, Iugo-Zapadnogo i Iuzhnogo frontov o srokakh vozmozhnogo nastupleniia protivnika, 2 iiulia 1943 g. 02 ch. 10 min, in *RA T.16(5–3)*, p.175.

60 David M. Glantz and Harold S. Orenstein (trans. and ed.), *The Battle of Kursk: The Soviet General Staff Study*, p.26.

61 Steven H. Newton (trans. and ed.), *Kursk: The German View*, p.49. See also Erhard Raus (Steven H. Newton trans. and ed.), *Panzer Operations: The Eastern Front Memoir of General Raus, 1941–1945* (Cambridge, MA: Da Capo Press, 2003), p.200.

62 F.W. von Mellenthin, *Panzer Battles*, p.267.

63 Ibid., p.277.

64 A Bublikov, 'Nas razdelial tol'ko puchei', in V.Ia. Zhilin (ed.), *"Eto bilo na ognennoi duge"*, p.12.

65 Z. Shutov, 'Strelkovii batal'on v oborone na Kurskoi duge', p.57.

66 A.I. Radzievskii (gen.ed.), *Taktika v boevikh primerakh. Polk* (Moscow: Voenizdat, 1974), pp.124, 241.

67 Pis'mo I.I. Ladigin G.K. Zhukovu o prichinakh neudach v Krasnoi armii, 3 maia 1944 g., in in S.V. Kudriashov (gen.ed.), *Vestnik Arkhiva Prezidenta Rossiiskoi Federatsii. Voina: 1941–1945. Vipusk 2*, pp.422–3.

68 A.Kh. Babadzhanian, 'Bronetankovie i mekhanizirovannie voiska v Kurskoi bitve', in I.V. Parot'kin, *Kurskaia bitva*, p.195.

69 Valerii Zamulin, 'The Battle of Kursk: New Findings', pp.410–11.

70 Direktiva Stavki VGK No.46196 komanduiushchemu voiskami Stepnogo voennogo okruga o pereimenovanii okruga vo front, 9 iiulia 1943 g. 23 ch 00 min, in *RA T.16 (5–3)*, p.176.

71 A.S. Zhadov, '5-ia gvardeiskaia armiia v Kurskoi bitve', in in I.V. Parot'kin (ed.), *Kurskaia bitva*, pp.302–3.

72 I.M. Anan'ev, *Tankovie armii v nastuplenii*, p.67.

73 P. Rotmistrov, 'V srazhenii pod Prokhorovkoi i Korsun'-Shevchenkovskim', in *Vizh*, Number 2 (1978), p.79 and P.A. Rotmistrov, 'O roli broenetankovikh voisk v Kurskoi bitve', in I.V. Parot'kin (ed.), *Kurskaia bitva*, p.187.

74 P. Rotmistrov, 'V srazhenii pod Prokhorovkoi i Korsun'-Shevchenkovskim', p.80; David M. Glantz and Harold S. Orenstein (trans. and ed.), *The Battle of Kursk: The Soviet General Staff Study*, p.224.

75 On some of the origins of these exaggerations, see Valeriy N. Zamulin, 'Prokhorovka: The Origins and Evolution of a Myth', in *JSMS*, Volume 25, Number 4 (2012), pp.582–95.

76 E.F. Ivanovskii, *Ataku nachinali tankisti* (Moscow: Voennoe izdatel'stvo, 1984), pp.123–31.

77 Niklas Zetterling and Anders Frankson, *Kursk: A Statistical Analysis*, pp.103–5.

78 Ibid., p.108.

79 P.A. Rotmistrov, 'O roli broenetankovikh voisk v Kurskoi bitve', in I.V. Parot'kin (ed.), *Kurskaia bitva*, p.188.

80 David M. Glantz and Harold S. Orenstein (trans. and ed.), *The Battle of Kursk: The Soviet General Staff Study*, p.224.

81 Niklas Zetterling and Anders Frankson, *Kursk: A Statistical Analysis*, p.66.

82 P.A. Rotmistrov, 'O roli broenetankovikh voisk v Kurskoi bitve', p.188.

83 E.F. Ivanovskii, *Ataku nachinali tankisti*, p.131.

84 P.A. Rotmistrov, 'O roli broenetankovikh voisk v Kurskoi bitve', in I.V. Parot'kin (ed.), *Kurskaia bitva*, p.187 and V. Zamulin, *Zasekrechennaia Kurskaia bitva. Sekretnie dokumenti svidetel'stvuiut*, pp.770–1.

85 Donesenie N.S. Khrushchev I.V. Stalinu o tankovom srazhenii v raione Prokhorovka Kurskoi oblasti, 14 iiulia 1943 g., in S.V. Kudriashov (gen. ed.), *Vestnik Arkhiva Prezidenta Rossiiskoi Federatsii. Voina: 1941–1945. Vipusk 2*, p.324.

86 Niklas Zetterling and Anders Frankson, *Kursk: A Statistical Analysis*, p.103.

87 Doklad predstavitelia Stavki VGK Verkhovnomu Glavnokomanduiushchemu o boevikh deistviiakh v raione Prokhorovki, 14 iiulia 1943 g., in *RA T.15 (4–4)*, p.53 and Niklas Zetterling and Anders Frankson, *Kursk: A Statistical Analysis*, pp.102–3.

88 Doklad predstavitelia Stavki VGK Verkhovnomu Glavnokomanduiushchemu o boevikh deistviiakh v raione Prokhorovki, 14 iiulia 1943 g., in *RA T.15 (4–4)*, p.53. A brief extract of this document is available in English in Alexander Hill, *The Great Patriotic War*, p.130.

89 Iz operativnoi svodki shtaba 5-i gv. TA No.03, in V. Goncharov (ed.), *Bitva pod Kurskom: Ot oboroni k nastupleniiu* (Moscow: AST/Khranitel', 2006), p.619; V. Zamulin, *Zasekrechennaia Kurskaia bitva*, p.768.

90 Niklas Zetterling and Anders Frankson, *Kursk: A Statistical Analysis*, p.108.

91 Boevoe donesenie shtaba Voronezhskogo fronta No.01398 nachal'niku General'nogo shtaba o poteriakh, 24 iiulia 1943 g., in V. Goncharov (ed.), *Bitva pod Kurskom: Ot oboroni k nastupleniiu*, p.653.

92 G.F. Krivosheev et al, *Soviet Casualties and Combat Losses*, p.132.

93 David M. Glantz and Harold S. Orenstein (trans. and ed.), *The Battle of Kursk: The Soviet General Staff Study*, p.228.

94 Niklas Zetterling and Anders Frankson, *Kursk: A Statistical Analysis*, pp.108–9.

95 Karl-Heinz Friesner et al, *Das Deutsche Reich und der Zweite Weltkrieg. Band 8. Die Ostfront 1943/44*, pp.121, 150.

CHAPTER 20

1 Doklad predstavitelia Stavki VGK Verkhovnomu Glavnokomanduiushchemu o nachale operatsii "Kutuzov", 12 iiulia 1943 g., in *RA T.15 (4–4)*, pp.50–1.

2 Boevoe rasporiazhenie komanduiushchego voiskami Voronezhskogo fronta komanduiushchim 5-i i 6-i gvardeiskimi armiiami na utochnenie zadach v nastuplenii, 24 iiulia 1943 g., in V. Goncharov (ed.), *Bitva pod Kurskom*, pp.652–3; Boevoe rasporiazhenie komanduiushchego voiskami Voronezhskogo fronta komanduiushchemu 5-i gvardeiskoi armiei na provedenie silovoi razvedki, 29 iiulia 1943 g, in V. Goncharov (ed.), *Bitva pod Kurskom*, p.654; and Rasporiazhenie predstavitelia Stavki VGK komanduiushchim voiskami Voronezhskogo i Stepnogo frontov ob ispol'zovanii artilleriiskikh divizii proriva, 15 avgusta 1943 g., in *RA T.15 (4–4)*, p.83.

3 Direktiva Stavki VGK No. 30160 predstaviteliam Stavki o zadachakh i koordinatsii deistvii frontov v khode Belgorodsko-Khar'kovskoi i Donbasskoi nastupatel'nikh operatsii, 6 avgusta 1943 g., in *RA T.16 (5–3)*, p.187. See also Report of Stavka Representative No.12255 of 8 August, pp.302–5, on the Donbass Offensive Operation plan, and Stavka directive No.10165 of 12 August, pp.189–90, on the co-ordination of these operations.

4 Prikaz komanduiushchego voiskami Voronezhskogo fronta No.010/op komanduiushchim 5-i i 6-i gvardeiskimi 5 gvardeiskoi i 1-i tankovimi armiiami na ustranenie nedostatkov dopushchennikh v pervie dni nastupleniia, 5 avgusta 1943 g., in V. Goncharov (ed.), *Bitva pod Kurskom*, pp.658–9; Komanduiushchemu voiskami Voronezhskogo fronta ob udarnikh gruppirovkakh 5-i gvardeiskoi i 1-i tankovoi armii, 7 avgusta 1943 g., in *RA T.23 (12–3)*, p.243.

5 Doklad starshego ofitsera General'nogo shtaba pri Zapadnom fronte nachal'niku operativnogo upravleniia General'nogo shtaba o rezul'tatakh provedeniia nastupatel'nikh operatsii voiskami fronta za period s 12 po 31 iiulia 1943 g., in *RA T.15(4–4)*, pp.366–8, 370–1.

6 M.E. Katukov, *Na ostrie glavnogo udara*, pp.248–51.

7 Direktiva General'nogo shtaba No.13551 komanduiushchemu voiskami Tsentral'nogo fronta o nedostatkakh v ispol'zovanii 3-i gvardeiskoi tankovoi armii v nastuplenii, 13 avgusta 1943, in *RA T.15(4–4)*, p.82.

8 Mansur Abdulin, *Ot Stalingrada do Dnepra. Pekhotinets. God na fronte* (Moscow: Iauza/Eksmo, 2010), p.188.

9 Thomas L. Jentz (ed.), *Panzertruppen...*, *1943–1945*, p.43.

10 Panzer-Artillerie-Regiment 103. II. Abteilung. Kommandeur. Abt. Gef.St., den 20.8.1943. Taktische und artl. Erfahrungen in den Angriffs- und Abwehrkämpfen südl. Orel vom 5.7.43–18.8.43. NARA T-78 Roll 619 frame 000795.

11 Thomas L. Jentz (ed.), *Panzertruppen...*, *1943–1945*, p.43.

12 G.F. Krivosheev et al, *Soviet Casualties and Combat Losses*, p.252.

13 P.V. Mel'nikov (ed.), *Razvitie taktiki sukhoputnikh voisk v Velikoi Otechestvennoi voine*, p.298.

14 Thomas L. Jentz (ed.), *Panzertruppen...*, *1943–1945*, pp.52–3, 282, 284, 286 and David Doyle, *Standard Catalog of German Military Vehicles* (Lola, WI: Krause Publications, 2005), pp.109–11, 219, 222.

15 Upravlenie bronetankovikh i mekhanizirovannikh voisk 1 Belorusskogo Fronta. "15" 01 1945 g. 4/0239. Kratkii doklad po analizu boevikh povrezhdenii tankov i SU 1-go Belorusskogo Fronta po operatsiiam. 1. Orlovsko-Kurskaia operatsiia. TsAMO f.233.o.2309.d.165.ll.216–17.

16 See pp.167–8, 211, 216 and entries for 5 June 1942, 24 December and 27 December 1943 in V.A. Malishev, "'Proidet desiatok let, i eti vstrechi ne vosstanovish' uzhe v pamiati'", in *Vestnik Arkhiva...*, Number 5 (1997), pp.118–9, 123–4.

17 Thomas L. Jentz (ed.), *Panzertruppen...*, *1943–1945*, p.44.

18 N. Kireev and N. Dovbenko, 'Iz opita boevogo primeneniia peredovikh otriadov tankovikh (mekhanizirovannikh) korpusov', in *Vizh*, Number 9 (1982), p.21.

19 Sturmgeschütz Ers. U Ausb.Abt.200. Kommandeur. Bericht über die Ostfrontreise des Kommandeurs der Sturmgeschütz Ers.u.Ausb.Abt. 200 vom 30.8.1943 bis 22.9.1943. NARA T-78 Roll 619 frames 00752 and 00754.

20 See Soliankin et al, *Otechestvennie bronirovannie mashini. XX vek....1941–1945 gg.*, p.166.

21 Testimony of Koshechkin Boris Kuz'mich. http://iremember.ru/tankisti/koshechkin-boris-kuzmich/stranitsa-2.html [Accessed 14 August 2014].

22 Ibid.

23 A.I. Radzievskii, *Tankovii udar (tankovaia armiia v nastupatel'noi operatsii fronta po opitu Velikoi Otechestvennoi voini)* (Moscow: Voenizdat, 1977), p.34.

24 Of 43,148 radio sets of less than 1 KW power, only 728 were recorded as lost by the end of the war. See Otchet o rabote Imushestvennogo Upravleniia po importu i eksportu vooruzhenii i oborudovanii s 22.06.41 g. po 01.01. 1946 g. No earlier than 1 January 1946. RGAE f.413.o.9.d.555.l.58, and on when they were shipped according to the Soviet side Otchet ob otgruzke tovarov iz SSha v SSSR s 1.10.41 do -1.07.45 gg.. ...SPZK, Washington, 29.08.45. RGAE f.413.o.9.d.438.l.15.

25 The supply of No.18 sets with the British convoy PQ-12 is noted in Chapter 14. On the No.19 sets produced in Canada with labels in cyrillic, see Louis Meulstee, *Wireless for the Warrior. Radio Communications Equipment in the British Army. Compendium 1. Spark to Larkspur (Wireless Sets 1910–1948)*, pp.213–16. Various US-manufactured sets such as the SCR -284 were also supplied. See Otchet o rabote Imushestvennogo Upravleniia po importu i eksportu vooruzhenii i oborudovanii s 22.06.41 g. po 01.01. 1946 g. No earlier than 1 January 1946. RGAE f.413.o.9.d.555.ll.54–5.

26 Komanduiushchemu voiskami Voronezhskogo fronta o sovershenstvovanii vzaimodeistviia rodov voisk, 10 iiulia 1943, in *RA T.23 (12–3)*, p.205.

27 See for example Elektron Priklonskii, *Dnevnik samokhodchika*, pp.95–6 and Mansur Abdulin, *Ot Stalingrada do Dnepra*, pp.180–1.

28 Walter Bußman, 'Kursk-Orel-Dnjepr. Erlebnisse und Erfahrungen im Stab des XXXXVI. Panzerkorps während des "Unternehmens Zitadelle"', in *Vierteljahrshefte für Zeitgeschichte*, 41. Jahrg., 4.H (October 1993), p.514.

29 See Karl-Heinz Friesner et al, *Das Deutsche Reich und der Zweite Weltkrieg. Band 8. Die Ostfront 1943/44*, pp.269–74.

30 Walter Bußman, 'Kursk-Orel-Dnjepr. Erlebnisse und Erfahrungen im Stab des XXXXVI. Panzerkorps während des "Unternehmens Zitadelle"', p.517.

31 K.S. Moskalenko, *Na iugo-zapadnom napravlenii. 1943–1945. Vospominaniia komandarma* (Moscow: izdatel'stvo "Nauka", 1972), p.128.

32 Direktiva Stavki VGK No. 30187 voennim sovetam frontov i armii o predstavlenii k nagradam komandirov za forsirovanie vodnikh pregrad, 9 sentiabria 1943 g., in *RA T.16(5–3)*, p.201.

33 Komanduiushchim 60-i, 13-i armiiami, voiskami Voronezhkogo fronta o predstavlenii spiskov lichnogo sostava, otlichivshegosia pri forsirovanii Dnepra, 12 oktiabria 1943 g., in *RA T.23(12–3)*, p.368.

34 K.S. Moskalenko, *Na iugo-zapadnom napravlenii. 1943–1945*, p.128.

35 Ibid., pp.130–2.

36 Testimony of Georgii Nikolaevich Krivov, in Artem Drabkin (ed.), *Ia dralsia na T-34*, pp.199–202.

37 K.S. Moskalenko, *Na iugo-zapadnom napravlenii. 1943–1945*, p.135.

38 Zapiska A.G. Kapitokhina I.V. Stalinu o Dneprovkoi vozdushno-desantnoi operatsii, 6 oktiabria 1943 g., in S.V. Kudriashov (gen.ed.), *Vestnik Arkhiva Prezidenta Rossiiskoi Federatsii. Voina: 1941–1945. Vipusk 2*, pp.362–4.

39 Testimony of Georgii Nikolaevich Krivov, in Artem Drabkin (ed.), *Ia dralsia na T-34*, pp.200–2.

40 Ivan Novokhatskii, *Vospominaniia komandira batarei*, pp.70–3.

41 K.S. Moskalenko, *Na iugo-zapadnom napravlenii. 1943–1945*, p.133.

42 A. Ovsienko, 'Tili podkrepliaiut front', in I.G. Anisimov et al (eds.), *Nasha strel'kovaia. Veterani 252-i divizii vspominaiut. Izdanie vtoroe, pererabotannoe i dopolnennoe* (Perm': Permskoe knizhnoe izdatel'stvo, 1987), p.136.

43 As previously noted, on this matter see Alexander Hill, *The Great Patriotic War*, pp.186–7, 190.

44 Direktiva Stavki VGK No.30232 predstaviteliu Stavki, komanduiushchemu voiskami 1-go Ukrainskogo fronta na utochnenie plana operatsii po ovladeniiu Kievom, 24 oktiabria 1943 g 23 ch 00 min, in *RA T.16 (5–3)*, p.227.

45 Ibid., p.228.
46 I.I. Iakubovskii, *Zemlia v ogne* (Moscow: Voenizdat, 1975), pp.198–202, 206, 213.
47 Ibid., p.214.
48 See Komanduiushchemu voiskami 1-go Urainskogo fronta o priniatii mer k ulucheniiu upravleniia voiskami fronta i rabota sviazi, 9 noiabria 1943 g., in *RA T.23(12–3)*, pp.415–16.
49 K.S. Moskalenko, *Na iugo-zapadnom napravlenii. 1943–1945*, pp.179–83.
50 F.W. von Mellenthin, *Panzer Battles*, pp.302–3.
51 Erich von Manstein, *Lost Victories*, p.489.
52 I.I. Iakubovskii, *Zemlia v ogne*, p.247.
53 David Glantz, *Colossus Reborn*, p.280.
54 See Erich von Manstein, *Lost Victories*, pp.484–6.
55 G.F. Krivosheev et al, *Soviet Casualties and Combat Losses*, pp.138–9.
56 A. Kuznetsov, *Bol'shoi desant. Kerchensko-El'tigenskaia operatsiia* (Moscow: Veche, 2011), pp.380–6, 392–3.
57 V.P. Istomin, *Smolenskaia nastupatel'naia operatsiia (1943 g.)* (Moscow: Voenizdat, 1975), p.4.
58 A.P. Beloborodov, *Vsegda v boiu* (Moscow: Voennoe izdatel'stvo Ministerstvo oboroni SSSR, 1978), p.237.
59 V.P. Istomin, *Smolenskaia nastupatel'naia operatsiia*, pp.42–3, 55.
60 Ibid., pp.36–7, 48.
61 Ibid., p.61.
62 I.P. Galitskii, *Dorogu otkrivali saperi* (Moscow: Voenizdat, 1983), p.137.
63 Ibid., pp.139–47.
64 A.P. Beloborodov, *Vsegda v boiu*, pp.237–41, 243.
65 Doklad predstavitelia Stavki i komanuiushchego voiskami Zapadnogo fronta No. 11909 Verkhovnomu Glavnokomanduiushchemu plana razvitiia Smolenskoi operatsii, 21 avgusta 1943, in *RA T.16 (5–3)*, pp.308–9.
66 V.P. Istomin, *Smolenskaia nastupatel'naia operatsiia*, p.26.
67 A.P. Beloborodov, *Vsegda v boiu*, pp.241–3.
68 Komanduiushchemu voiskami Kalininskogo fronta ob ustranenii nedostatkov v maskirovke voisk, 10 avgusta 1943 g. In *RA T.23 (12–3)*, p.250.
69 N.M. Khlebnikov, *Pod grokhot soten batarei*, p.234.
70 V.P. Istomin, *Smolenskaia nastupatel'naia operatsiia*, pp.30–1.
71 A.P. Beloborodov, *Vsegda v boiu*, p.244.
72 Prikaz Stavki VGK No.03605 o smene komanduiushchego 4-i gvardeiskoi armiei, 22 sentiabria 1943 g., in *RA T.16 (5–3)*, p.206; Direktiva Stavki VGK No.30205 komanduiushchim voiskami frontov i armiiami o merakh po inzhenernoi razvedke i razminirovaniiu dorog, 30 sentiabria 1943 g., pp.211–12.
73 A.P. Beloborodov, *Vsegda v boiu*, pp.244–5.
74 N.M. Khlebnikov, *Pod grokhot soten batarei*, p.236.
75 A.P. Beloborodov, *Vsegda v boiu*, p.247–8.
76 Direktivi Stavka VGK No. 30191 (and 30192, 30193) komanduiushchemu voiskami Brianskogo fronta...plana nastupleniia na Minsk (...Kalininskogo fronta...po ovladeniiu Vitebskom and ...Zapadnogo fronta...na razgrom

Smolenskoi gruppirovki protivnika), 20 sentiabria 1943 g, in *RA T.16 (5–3)*, pp.204–6.

77 Direktivi Stavka VGK No. 30208 (and 30210) komanduiushchemu voiskami Tsentral'nogo fronta na...ovladenie Minskom (...Zapadnogo fronta...ovladeniia g. Vil'nius), 1 oktiabria 1943 g., in *RA T.16 (5–3)*, pp.213–15.
78 G.F. Krivosheev et al, *Soviet Casualties and Combat Losses*, pp.134–5.
79 Ibid., p.129.
80 See Otto Carius, *Tigers in the Mud: The Combat Career of German Panzer Commander Otto Carius* (Mechanicsburg, PA: Stackpole Books, 2003), pp.26–7.
81 William Lubbeck, *At Leningrad's Gates: The Story of a Soldier with Army Group North* (Newbury and Havertown, PA: Casemate Publishers, 2006), pp.138–9.
82 Mikhail Suknev, *Zapiski komandira shtrafbata*, pp.119, 123–4, 126, 132.
83 Gottlob Herbert Bidermann, *In Deadly Combat: A German Soldier's Memoir of the Eastern Front*, pp.177–81.
84 K.A. Meretskov, *Na sluzhbe narodu*, pp.344–6.
85 Ibid., p.344; Direktiva Stavki VGK No.30175 komanduiushchim voiskami Volkhovskogo i Leningradskogo frontov na perekhod k oborone, 22 avgusta 1943 g, in N.L. Volkovskii (ed.), *Blokada Leningrada v dokumentakh rassekrechennikh arkhivov*(Moscow/Saint Petersburg: OOO "Izdatel'stvo AST"/ OOO Izdatel'stvo "Poligon", 2004), p.149.
86 See for example documents in N.L. Volkovskii (ed.), *Blokada Leningrada v dokumentakh rassekrechennikh arkhivov*, pp.361–8, pp.582–4.
87 K.A. Meretskov, *Na sluzhbe narodu*, p.346.
88 G.F. Krivosheev et al, *Soviet Casualties and Combat Losses*, pp.175, 179.
89 Werner Haupt, *Army Group North*, pp.382–3.
90 G.F. Krivosheev et al, *Soviet Casualties and Combat Losses*, pp.141–2.
91 See V.K. Kopitko and E.L. Korshunov, 'General-leitenant F.N. Starikov: "Ogromnii opit, kotorii mi imeem na protiazhenii trekh let Otechestvennoi voini ... ne izuchaetsia"', in *Vizh*, Number 2 (2014), p.29.
92 Werner Haupt, *Army Group North*, p.382. On the failings of the Soviet offensive, see V.K. Kopitko and E.L. Korshunov, 'General-leitenant F.N. Starikov: "Ogromnii opit, kotorii mi imeem na protiazhenii trekh let Otechestvennoi voini ... ne izuchaetsia"', pp.22–30.
93 Gottlob Herbert Bidermann, *In Deadly Combat: A German Soldier's Memoir of the Eastern Front*, p.178 and K.A. Meretskov, *Na sluzhbe narodu*, p.345.
94 Vladimir Kotel'nikov, *"Bostoni" v Sovetskom soiuze* (Moscow: BTV-MN, 2002), pp.15, 26, 34 and 38 and Yefim Gordon and Dmitri Khazanov, *Soviet Combat Aircraft of the Second World War. Volume Two: Twin-Engined Fighters, Attack Aircraft and Bombers*, p.169.
95 See for example Elektron Priklonskii, *Dnevnik samokhodchika*, pp.91, 116–17.
96 Ibid., pp.95–6.
97 F.W. von Mellenthin, *Panzer Battles*, pp.259–60, 267.
98 S.I. Rudenko, 'Zavoevanie gospodstva v vozdukhe i osobennosti boevikh deistvii aviatsii v Kurskoi bitve', in I.V. Parot'kin (ed.), *Kurskaia bitva*, p.206.

99 Vitalii Gorbach, *Aviatsiia v Kurskoi bitve* (Moscow: Iauza/Eksmo, 2008), p.62.
100 Ibid., pp.475, 486.
101 Ibid., pp.448–9.
102 Iz doklada starshego ofitsera General'nogo shtaba pri Voronezhskom fronte nachal'niku General'nogo shtaba ob oboronitel'noi operatsii voisk fronta s 4 po 23 iiulia 1943 g., 23 avgusta 1943 g., in *RA T.15 (4–4)*, pp.379–80 and 385–6.
103 I.V. Timokhovich, *Operativnoe iskusstvo Sovetskikh VVS v Velikoi Otechesvennoi voine*, pp.280–3.
104 Hans Seidemann, 'Luftflotte Four', in Steven H. Newton (trans. and ed.), *Kursk: The German View*, pp.186–8.
105 Vitalii Gorbach, *Aviatsiia v Kurskoi bitve*, pp.482, 485, 488, 497.
106 Erhard Raus, 'Armeeabteilung Kempf', in Steven H. Newton (trans. and ed.), *Kursk: The German View*, pp.48, 51–2.
107 Erhard Raus, 'VI Corps in the Battles for Belgorod and Kharkov', in Steven H. Newton (trans. and ed.), *Kursk: The German View*, pp.259, 281.
108 Vitalii Gorbach, *Aviatsiia v Kurskoi bitve*, p.432.
109 F.W. von Mellenthin, *Panzer Battles*, p.341.
110 Spravka sostavlena po trofeinim dokumentam otdel'nogo razvedivatel'nogo batal'ona nemetskoi 167-i pekhotnoi divizii, 19.08.1943 g., in Valerii Zamulin, *Prokhorovka – neizvestnoe srazhenie velikoi voini* (Moscow; AST/Transitkniga, 2006), pp.707–9.
111 Colonel General Erhard Raus, 'IX Corps in the Battles for Belgorod and Kharkov', in Steven H. Newton (trans. and ed.), *Kursk: The German View*, pp.259–81.
112 Ibid., p.289.
113 Walter Bußman, 'Kursk-Orel-Dnjepr. Erlebnisse und Erfahrungen im Stab des XXXXVI. Panzerkorps während des "Unternehmens Zitadelle"', p.514.

CHAPTER 21

1 A translation of this speech is available in Alexander Hill, *The Great Patriotic War*, pp.220–1.
2 G.F. Krivosheev et al, *Soviet Casualties and Combat Losses*, p.140.
3 F.W. von Mellenthin, *Panzer Battles*, pp.303 and 319.
4 *Boevoi ustav bronetankovikh i mekhanizirovannikh voisk Krasnoi Armii. Chast' 1 (tank, tankovii vzvod, tankovaia rota)* (Moscow: Voennoe izdatel'stvo Narodnogo Komissariata Oboroni, 1944), pp.5–6.
5 See Otchet o rabote Imushestvennogo Upravleniia po importu i eksportu vooruzhenii i oborudovanii s 22.06.41 g. po 01.01. 1946 g. No earlier than 1 January 1946. RGAE f.413.o.9.d.555.ll. 32, 58. See also Alexander Hill, 'The Bear's New Wheels (and Tracks): US-Armored and Other Vehicles and Soviet Military Effectiveness during the Great Patriotic War in Words and Photographs', in *JSMS*, Volume 25, Number 2 (2012), p.211.
6 *Boevoi ustav bronetankovikh i mekhanizirovannikh voisk Krasnoi Armii. Chast' 1 (tank, tankovii vzvod, tankovaia rota)*, p.8.

7 Upravlenie bronetankovikh i mekhanizirovannikh voisk 1 Belorusskogo
   Fronta. "15" 01 1945 g. 4/0239. Kratkii doklad po analizu boevikh povrezh-
   denii tankov i SU 1-go Belorusskogo Fronta po operatsiiam. 1. Orlovsko-
   Kurskaia operatsiia. TsAMO f.233.o.2309.d.165.l.219.

8 Ibid., ll.219–20.

9 Dmitrii Degtev and Dmitrii Zubov, *"Chernaia smert'"*. *Pravda i mifi o boevom
   priminenii shturmovika Il-2. 1941–1945* (Moscow: ZAO Izdatel'stvo Tsentrpoligraf, 2013), pp.213–14; M. Iu. Mukhin, *Sovetskaia aviapromishlennost' v
   godi Velikoi Otechestvennoi voini*, p.342.

10 See David M. Glantz and Harold S. Orenstein (trans. and ed.), *The Battle for
   the Ukraine: The Red Army's Korsun'-Shevchenkovskii Offensive, 1944* (London
   and New York: Routledge, 2003), pp.1–4 and Niklas Zetterling and Anders
   Frankson, *The Korsun Pocket: The Encirclement and Breakout of a German Army
   in the East, 1944* (Drexel Hill, PA and Newbury, Berkshire: Casemate, 2008),
   pp.25–9.

11 Niklas Zetterling and Anders Frankson, *The Korsun Pocket*, p.53.

12 Direktiva Stavki VGK No. 220006 komanduiushchim voiskami 1-go i 2-go
   Ukraiinskikh frontov, predstaviteliu Stavki na razgrom Zvenigorodsko-
   Mironovskoi gruppirovki protivnika, 12 ianvaria 1944 g., in *RA T.16 (5–4)*,
   p.31. See also David M. Glantz and Harold S. Orenstein (trans. and ed.), *The
   Battle for the Ukraine: The Red Army's Korsun'-Shevchenkovskii Offensive, 1944*,
   pp.87–8.

13 I.S. Konev, *Zapiski komanduiushchego frontom. 1943–1945* (Moscow:
   "Nauka", 1985), p.89 and David M. Glantz and Harold S. Orenstein (trans.
   and ed.), *The Battle for the Ukraine: The Red Army's Korsun'-Shevchenkovskii
   Offensive, 1944*, p.8.

14 David M. Glantz and Harold S. Orenstein (trans. and ed.), *The Battle for the
   Ukraine: The Red Army's Korsun'-Shevchenkovskii Offensive, 1944*, p.152.

15 P. Rotmistrov, 'V srazhenii pod Prokhorovkoi i Korsun'-Shevchenkovskim',
   in *Vizh*, Number 2 (1978), pp.81–2. See also Niklas Zetterling and Anders
   Frankson, *The Korsun Pocket*, pp.73–82.

16 P. Rotmistrov, 'V srazhenii pod Prokhorovkoi i Korsun'-Shevchenkovskim',
   p.82 and Niklas Zetterling and Anders Frankson, *The Korsun Pocket*, p.111.

17 See Earl F. Ziemke, 'Military Effectiveness in the Second World War', in
   Allan R. Millett and Williamson Murray (eds.), *Military Effectiveness. Volume
   3*, p.304.

18 Niklas Zetterling and Anders Frankson, *The Korsun Pocket*, pp.22, 24, 29, 42,
   100–2 and David M. Glantz and Harold S. Orenstein (trans. and ed.), *The
   Battle for the Ukraine: The Red Army's Korsun'-Shevchenkovskii Offensive, 1944*,
   pp.100–1.

19 Niklas Zetterling and Anders Frankson, *The Korsun Pocket*, pp.148–53.

20 Directive of the Headquarters of the Supreme High Commander Number
   220021 to the Stavka representative on the destruction of the Korun'
   grouping of enemy forces, 12 February 1944, 16:45, in Alexander Hill, *The
   Great Patriotic War*, p.225 and David M. Glantz and Harold S. Orenstein
   (trans. and ed.), *The Battle for the Ukraine: The Red Army's Korsun'-Shevchen-
   kovskii Offensive, 1944*, pp.90–1.

21 G. Mikhailovskii and I. Virodov, 'Vishie organi rukovodstva voinoi', in *Vizh*, Number 4 (1978), p.24.

22 Direktiva Stavki VGK predstaviteliu Stavki o neobkhodimosti ezhednevnikh dokladov ob obstanovke, 17 avgusta 1943 g., in *RA T.16 (5–3)*, p.193.

23 Evan Mawdsley, *Thunder in the East*, pp.208–9.

24 After battle report of the Commander of forces of the 2nd Ukrainian Front of 17 February 1944 to the Supreme High Commander…, in Alexander Hill, *The Great Patriotic War*, p.226; David M. Glantz and Harold S. Orenstein (trans. and ed.), *The Battle for the Ukraine: The Red Army's Korsun'-Shevchenkovskii Offensive, 1944*, pp.91–2; Niklas Zetterling and Anders Frankson, *The Korsun Pocket*, p.277.

25 Niklas Zetterling and Anders Frankson, *The Korsun Pocket*, pp.277, 292.

26 Ibid., p.294; David M. Glantz and Harold S. Orenstein (trans. and ed.), *The Battle for the Ukraine: The Red Army's Korsun'-Shevchenkovskii Offensive, 1944*, p.153.

27 Earl F. Ziemke, 'Military Effectiveness in the Second World War', in Allan R. Millett and Williamson Murray (eds.), *Military Effectiveness. Volume 3*, p.304.

28 Karl-Heinz Friesner et al, *Das Deutsche Reich und der Zweite Weltkrieg. Band 8. Die Ostfront 1943/44*, p.556.

29 G.F. Krivosheev et al, *Soviet Casualties and Combat Losses*, pp.144–5.

30 These documents, dated 31 May, are reproduced in *RA T.16 (5–4)*, pp.93–5.

31 A.M. Vasilevskii, 'Vospominaniia o Belorusskoi operatsii', in A.M. Samsonov (ed.), *Osvobozhdenie Belorussii 1944* (Moscow: Izdatel'stvo "Nauka", 1970), pp.48–9, 57, 60–5.

32 G.K. Zhukov, 'Razgrom fashistskikh voisk v Belorussii', in A.M. Samsonov (ed.), *Osvobozhdenie Belorussii 1944*, p.32.

33 See Führer Headquarters, 8 March 1944. Führer Order No. 11 in Hugh Trevor-Roper (ed.), *Hitler's War Directives, 1939–1945*, pp.234–6 and Karl-Heinz Friesner et al, *Das Deutsche Reich und der Zweite Weltkrieg. Band 8. Die Ostfront 1943/44*, pp.519–20.

34 Karl-Heinz Friesner et al, *Das Deutsche Reich und der Zweite Weltkrieg. Band 8. Die Ostfront 1943/44*, pp.529–34.

35 David M. Glantz and Harold S. Orenstein (trans. and ed.), *Belorussia 1944: The Soviet General Staff Study* (London/New York: Frank Cass, 2001), p.65 and ibid., p.529.

36 Spravka o boevom i chislennom sostave partizanskikh soedinenii, deistvuiushchikh pered 1-m Pribaltiiskim frontom po sostoianiiu na 1 maia 1944 g., 26 maia 1944 g., in *RA T.20 (9)*, pp.534–5.

37 Alexander Brakel, 'The Relationship between Soviet Partisans and the Civilian Population in Belorussia under German occupation, 1941–4', in Ben Shepherd and Juliette Pattinson (eds.), *War in a Twilight World: Partisan and Anti-Partisan Warfare in Eastern Europe, 1939–1945* (Basingstoke, Hampshire/New York: Palgrave Macmillan, 2010), p.94.

38 Cited in Ben Shepherd, *War in the Wild East*, pp.223–4.

39 See Alexander Statiev, *The Soviet Counterinsurgency in the Western Borderlands* (Cambridge/New York: Cambridge University Press, 2010), pp.213–14.

40 David M. Glantz and Harold S. Orenstein (trans. and ed.), *Belorussia 1944: The Soviet General Staff Study*, pp.48, 63.
41 Ibid., p.63 and G.F. Krivosheev et al, *Soviet Casualties and Combat Losses*, p.145.
42 David M. Glantz and Harold S. Orenstein (trans. and ed.), *Belorussia 1944: The Soviet General Staff Study*, pp.63–4.
43 See Chapter 18.
44 Karl-Heinz Friesner et al, *Das Deutsche Reich und der Zweite Weltkrieg. Band 8. Die Ostfront 1943/44*, pp.507–13 and David M. Glantz and Harold S. Orenstein (trans. and ed.), *Belorussia 1944: The Soviet General Staff Study*, pp.44–5.
45 Karl-Heinz Friesner et al, *Das Deutsche Reich und der Zweite Weltkrieg. Band 8. Die Ostfront 1943/44*, p.510.
46 K.N. Galitskii, 'Gvardeitsi 11-i v boiakh za Belorussiiu', in A.M. Samsonov (ed.), *Osvobozhdenie Belorussii 1944*, pp.447–8.
47 Thomas L. Jentz (ed.), *Panzertruppen...1943–1945*, p.205.
48 Hans Schäufler (ed.), *Knight's Cross Panzers: The German 35th Panzer Regiment in WWII*, pp.308–10.
49 M.M. Minasian, *Pobeda v Belorussii. Piatii stalinskii udar* (Moscow: Voenizdat MVS SSSR, 1952), p.43. http://militera.lib.ru/h/minasyan_mm/06.html [Accessed 17 September 2014].
50 David M. Glantz and Harold S. Orenstein (trans. and ed.), *Belorussia 1944: The Soviet General Staff Study*, pp.78, 82–5.
51 V.T. Obukhov, '3-i gvardeiskii mekhanizirovannii korpus v boiakh za osvobozhdenie Belorussii', in in A.M. Samsonov (ed.), *Osvobozhdenie Belorussii 1944*, p.568.
52 Ibid., pp.586–7.
53 Ibid., p.579.
54 K.N. Galitskii, 'Gvardeitsi 11-i v boiakh za Belorussiiu', in A.M. Samsonov (ed.), *Osvobozhdenie Belorussii 1944*, pp.445, 449–56.
55 I.V. Timokhovich, *Bitva za Belorussiiu. 1941–1944* (Minsk: "Belarus", 1994), p.230.
56 Prikaz Stavki VGK No. 220146 o nedostatkakh v organizatsii vvoda v boi 11-go tankovogo korpusa, 16 iiulia 1944 g., in *RA T.16 (5–4)*, p.112.
57 Direktiva Stavki VGK No. 220136 komanduiushchim voiskami 1-go Pribaltiiskogo, 3,2,1-go Belorusskikh frontov ob uluchenii upravleniia voiskami pri presledovanii protivnika, 6 iiulia 1944 g., in *RA T.16(5–4)*, p.107.
58 David M. Glantz and Harold S. Orenstein (trans. and ed.), *Belorussia 1944: The Soviet General Staff Study*, p.49.
59 E.I. Filippov, *Frontovie budni komandira batarei. Vospominaniia o Velikoi Otechestvennoi voine* (Saint-Petersburg: Nestor-Istoriia, 2009), pp.84–6.
60 Ibid., pp.79–80.
61 Testimony of Pankin Aleksandr Fedorovich. http://iremember.ru/samokhodchiki/pankin-aleksandr-fedorovich/stranitsa-4.html [Accessed 22 September 2014].
62 Testimony of Zarubin Apollon Grigor'evich. http://iremember.ru/artilleristi/zarubin-apollon-grigorevich/stranitsa-2.html and http://iremember.ru/artilleristi/zarubin-apollon-grigorevich/stranitsa-3.html [Accessed 22 September 2014].

63 I.V. Timokhovich, *Bitva za Belorussiiu. 1941–1944*, p.231.
64 N.A. Antipenko, *Na glavnom napravlenii. Vosopominaniia zamestitelia koman-duiushchego frontom* (Moscow: Izdatel'stvo Nauka, 1967), p.153, 167–8.
65 I.V. Timokhovich, *Bitva za Belorussiiu. 1941–1944*, p.231.
66 A.D. Tsirlin et al, *Inzhinernie voiska v boiakh za sovetskuiu Rodinu* (Moscow: Voennoe izdatel'stvo Ministerstvo oboroni SSSR, 1970), pp.227–8.
67 N.A. Antipenko, *Na glavnom napravlenii*, pp.182, 195–6.
68 See Alexander Hill, *The Great Patriotic War*, pp.235–6.
69 See for example M.A. Polushkin, *Na sandomirskom napravlenii. L'vovsko-Sandomirskaia operatsiia (iiul'-avgust 1944 g.)* (Moscow: Voennoe izdatel'stvo, 1969), p.154.
70 G.F. Krivosheev et al, *Soviet Casualties and Combat Losses*, pp.145–6.
71 Ibid., p.146 and Karl-Heinz Friesner et al, *Das Deutsche Reich und der Zweite Weltkrieg. Band 8. Die Ostfront 1943/44*, pp.692–4.
72 Alexander Hill, *The Great Patriotic War*, p.238; David M. Glantz and Harold S. Orenstein, *The Battle for L'vov, July 1944: The Soviet General Staff Study*, pp.94–7; G.F. Krivosheev et al, *Soviet Casualties and Combat Losses*, p.146.
73 Voennim sovetam Karel'skogo, Leningradskogo, 3, 2, 1-go Belorruskikh, 1-go i 4-go Ukrainskikh frontov o ekonomnom raskhodovanii boepripasov, 31 avgusta 1944 g., in *RA T.23 (12–4)*, pp.389–90.
74 'Iassko-Kishinevskaia operatsiia v tsifrakh', in *Vizh*, Number 8 (1964), p.88. For details of this operation see David M. Glantz, *Red Storm over the Balkans: The Failed Soviet Invasion of Romania, Spring 1944* (Lawrence, KA: University Press of Kansas, 2007).
75 Alexander Hill, *The Great Patriotic War*, pp.239–40.

CHAPTER 22

1 Testimony of Vladimir Adamovich Storozhuk. http://iremember.ru/razved chiki/storozhuk-vladimir-adamovich/stranitsa-3.html and … stranitsa-6.html [Accessed 6 November 2014].
2 Mikhail Suknev, *Zapiski komandira shtrafbata*, p.147.
3 Mikhail Shelkov, *Zapiski komandira strelkovogo batal'ona*, pp.147, 177.
4 Prikaz Stavki Verkhovnogo glavnokomandovaniia o poriadke priziva voennoo-biazannikh v osvobozhdaemikh ot nemetskoi okkupatsii raionakh, No. 0430, 15 oktiabria 1943 g., in *RA T.13(2–3)*, p.216.
5 Gosudarstvennii komitet oboroni. Postanovlenie No. GOKO-5460ss ot "23" marta 1944 g. Moskva, Kreml'. O formirovanii chetirekh zapasnikh strelkovokh brigad dlia obucheniia sovetskikh grazhdan, mobilizuemikh v osvobozhdaemikh ot nemetskoi okkupatsii raionakh Zapadnoi Ukraini i Zapadnoi Belorussii. www.soldat.ru/doc/gko/scans/5460-1.jpg [Accessed 20 October 2014].
6 N.A. Antipenko, 'Til v Berlinskoi operatsii', in A.M. Samsonov (ed.), *9 maia 1945 goda*, p.723.
7 N. Maliugin, 'Razvitie i sovershenstvovanie tila strelkovoi divizii v godi voini', p.92.

8 Gosudarstvennii komitet oboroni. Postanovlenie GOKO No. 6785ss ot 25 oktiabria 1944 g. Moskva, Kreml'. O mobilizatsii voennoobiazannikh zapasa v osvobozhdennikh raionakh zapadnikh oblastei Ukrainskoi i Belorusskoi SSR i na territorii Moldavskoi SSR do 45 letnego vozrasta. www.soldat.ru/doc/gko/scans/6785-1.jpg [Accessed 20 October 2014].

9 Prikaz o ser'eznikh nedostatakh v 50-i Litovskoi zapasnoi strel'kovoi divizii i nakazanii vinovnikh, No. 0049, 23 dekabria 1944 g., in *RA T.13(2–3)*, p.341.

10 David M. Glantz, *Colossus Reborn*, pp.592, 595.

11 Tezisi doklada komandarma 4 Gv.TA Gv. General-polkovnika Leliushenko o boevikh deistviiakh 4 Gv.TA 1 Ukrainskogo fronta v Visla-Oderskoi operatsii s Sandomirskogo platsdarma s 12 ianvaria po 22 fevralia 1945 g. na sbore General'skogo sostava Tsentral'noi gruppi voisk sentiabr' 1945 g. TsAMO f.236.o.2673.d.2393.l.51.

12 Gosudarstvennii komitet oboroni. Postanovlenie No. GOKO-5907s ot "16" maia 1944 g. Moskva, Kreml'. O prizive v armiiu 25,000 zhenshchin dobrovol't-sev. www.soldat.ru/doc/gko/scans/5907-01-1.jpg [Accessed 20 October 2014].

13 Mikhail Shelkov, *Zapiski komandira strelkovogo batal'ona*, p.209.

14 Testimony of Boris Karpovich Zhurenko. http://iremember.ru/samokhodchiki/zhurenko-boris-karpovich/stranitsa-5.html. [Accessed 29 September 2014].

15 S.M. Shtemenko, *The Soviet General Staff at War. 1941–1945* (Moscow: Progress Publishers, 1970), p.310.

16 F.M. Zinchenko, *Geroi shturma reikhstaga* (Moscow: Voenizdat, 1983), pp.66–7.

17 A. Zhadov, 'Proriv gluboko esheliirovannoi oboroni protivnika', in *Vizh*, Number 1 (1978), pp.17–18.

18 Ibid., p.15.

19 V.M. Zhagala, *Raschishchaia put' pekhote...* (Moscow: Voennoe izdatel'stvo, 1985), pp.194–5.

20 I.S. Konev, *Sorok piatii. Izdanie vtoroe, ispravlennoe i dopolnennoe* (Moscow: Voennoe izdatel'stvo Ministerstva oboroni SSSR, 1970), pp.80–1.

21 Ibid., pp.77, 80–1. The 4th Tank Army became 4th Guards Tank Army on 17 March 1945.

22 G.F. Krivosheev et al, *Soviet Casualties and Combat Losses*, p.253.

23 I.S. Konev, *Sorok piatii*, pp.78–80.

24 D.D. Leliushenko, *Moskva-Stalingrad-Berlin-Praga. Zapiski komandarma* (Moscow: Izdatel'stvo 'Nauka', 1971), p.302.

25 Tezisi doklada komandarma 4 Gv.TA Gv. General-polkovnika Leliushenko o boevikh deistviiakh 4 Gv.TA 1 Ukrainskogo fronta v Visla-Oderskoi operatsii s Sandomirskogo platsdarma s 12 ianvaria po 22 fevralia 1945 g. na sbore General'skogo sostava Tsentral'noi gruppi voisk sentiabr' 1945 g. TsAMO f.236.o.2673.d.2393.ll.41,54.

26 Ibid., ll.44,46.

27 Dmitrii Shein, *Tanki vedet Ribalko. Boevoi put' 3-i Gvardeiskoi tankovoi armii* (Moscow: "Iauza"/Eksmo, 2007), pp.286, 289.

28 D.A. Dragunskii, *Godi v brone. Izdanie tret'e, dopolnennoe* (Moscow: Voennoe izdatel'stvo Ministerstva oboroni SSSR, 1983), pp.258–9.

29 Dmitrii Shein, *Tanki vedet Ribalko. Boevoi put' 3-i Gvardeiskoi tankovoi armii*, p.286.

30 I.S. Konev, *Sorok piatii*, pp.80–1.

31 Dmitrii Shein, *Tanki vedet Ribalko. Boevoi put' 3-i Gvardeiskoi tankovoi armii*, pp.287–8.

32 Tezisi doklada komandarma 4 Gv.TA Gv. General-polkovnika Leliushenko... TsAMO f.236.o.2673.d.2393.ll.3–9, 48. These can be compared to resources provided at the outset of Uranus in Chapter 17.

33 Deistviia 3 Gvardeiskoi tankovoi armii v operatsiiakh Pervogo ukrainskogo fronta 1945 g. (Plan-konspekt doklada Komanduiushchego 3 gv. TA Marshala broentankovikh voisk Ribalko). TsAMO f.236.o.2673.d.2393.l.99.

34 Tezisi doklada komandarma 4 Gv.TA Gv. General-polkovnika Leliushenko... TsAMO f.236.o.2673.d.2393.ll.18–20, 26, 31.

35 With 86 under repair. Ibid., ll.31, 34, 45.

36 I.S. Konev, *Sorok piatii*, p.78.

37 E. Smirnov, 'Deistviia 47 gv.tbr v peredom otriade tankovogo korpusa', in *Vizh*, Number 1 (1978), pp.58–9.

38 A.I. Radzievskii, 'Tanki idut na Berlin', in A.M. Samsonov, *9 maia 1945 goda*, p.690.

39 Erik Wallin (ed. Thorolf Hillblad), *Twilight of the Gods: A Swedish Volunteer in the 11th SS Panzergrenadier Division 'Nordland' on the Eastern Front* (Mechanicsburg, PA: Stackpole Books, 2009), pp.73–4.

40 Testimony of Vladimir Adamovich Storozhuk. http://iremember.ru/razvedchiki/storozhuk-vladimir-adamovich/stranitsa-5.html [Accessed 6 November 2014].

41 A.I. Radzievskii, 'Tanki idut na Berlin', in A.M. Samsonov, *9 maia 1945 goda*, p.690.

42 Otchet ob organizatsii i boevikh deistviiakh razvedki 7 Gv. TK v Berlinskoi operatsii. Maia 1945. TsAMO f.236.o.2673.d.2360.ll.60, 80–1.

43 Ibid., l.81.

44 G.F. Krivosheev et al, *Soviet Casualties and Combat Losses*, pp.151–2.

45 It is worth reitterating that Soviet-sponsored Rumanian, Yugoslav and indeed Czechoslovak units drawing often on former PoWs fought alongside Red Army units with Soviet equipment and organisation as well as regular Rumanian units and home-grown Czechoslovak and Yugoslav resistance forces. See Chapter 13.

46 See Kamen Nevenkin, *Take Budapest!: The Struggle for Hungary, Autumn 1944* (Stroud, Gloucestershire: Spellmount, 2012), pp.42–3; M.V. Zakharov (gen. ed.), *Osvobozhdenie iugo-vostochnoi i tsentral'noi Evropi voiskami 2-go i 3-go Ukrainskikh frontov. 1944–1945* (Moscow: Izdatel'stvo "Nauka", 1970), p.199; Evan Mawdsley, *Thunder in the East*, pp.353–4.

47 See Kamen Nevenkin, *Take Budapest!*, pp.27–9.

48 S.M. Shtemenko, *General'nii shtab v godi voini. Ot Stalingrada do Berlina*, p.357 and ibid., pp.21–4.

49 I.Ia. Virodov et al, *V srazheniiakh za pobedu*, p.436.

50 See S.M. Shtemenko, *General'nii shtab v godi voini. Ot Stalingrada do Berlina*, pp.358–60.

51 Gans Frisner [Hans Frießner], *Proigrannie srazheniia* (Moscow: Voennoe izdatel'stvo Ministerstva oboroni SSSR, 1966), pp.141–2, 152, and Karl-Heinz

Friesner et al, *Das Deutsche Reich und der Zweite Weltkrieg. Band 8. Die Ostfront 1943/4*, pp.872–3.

52 Direktiva Stavki VGK No.220243 komanduiushchemu voiskami 2-go Ukrainskogo fronta o likvidatsii Debretsenskoi gruppirovki protivnika i podgotovke nastupleniia na Budapesht, 18 oktiabria 1944 g. 02 ch 00 min, in *RA T.16(5–4)*, p.160, and Kamen Nevenkin, *Take Budapest!*, pp.43–4.

53 4th Rumanian Infantry Division. See Mark Axworthy et al, *Third Axis, Fourth Ally*, pp.201–2.

54 Kamen Nevenkin, *Take Budapest!*, p.45 and p.260n22; Gans Frisner [Hans Frießner], *Proigrannie srazheniia*, p.156.

55 Direktiva Stavki VGK No. 220251 komanduiushchemu voiskami 2-go Ukrainskogo fronta o podgotovke udara na Budapesht, 28 oktiabria 1944 g. 22 ch 00 min, in *RA T.16(5–4)*, p.163.

56 Kamen Nevenkin, *Take Budapest!*, pp.47–54.

57 Ibid., pp.55, 70–3.

58 A very detailed description of this attack is provided in Kamen Nevenkin, *Take Budapest!*, chapters 8 and 9.

59 Ibid., pp.202–3, 213, 220–3.

60 I.A. Pliev, *Dorogami voini* (Moscow: Veche, 2015), p.179.

61 Direktiva Stavki VGK No.220256 komanduiushchemu voiskami 2-go Ukrainskogo fronta ob organizatsii nastupleniia na Budapesht, 4 noiabria 1944 g. 20 ch 00 min, in *RA T. 16 (5–4)*, p.165 and Kamen Nevenkin, *Take Budapest!*, pp.173–4.

62 Karl-Heinz Friesner et al, *Das Deutsche Reich und der Zweite Weltkrieg. Band 8. Die Ostfront 1943/4*, p.879.

63 Fold out table, in Burkhart Mueller-Hillerbrand, *Das Heer 1933–1945...Band III. Der Zweifrontenkrieg...*, between pp.274 and 275.

64 'Iassko-Kishinevskaia operatsiia v tsifrakh', in *Vizh*, Number 8 (1964), p.88 and Karl-Heinz Friesner et al, *Das Deutsche Reich und der Zweite Weltkrieg. Band 8. Die Ostfront 1943/4*, p.736n21.

65 Karl-Heinz Friesner et al, *Das Deutsche Reich und der Zweite Weltkrieg. Band 8. Die Ostfront 1943/4*, p.889.

66 'Vislo-Oderskaia operatsiia v tsifrakh', in *Vizh*, Number 1 (1965), p.71 and Horst Boog et al, *Das Deutsche Reich und der Zweite Weltkrieg. Band 10. Erster Halbband. Der Zusammenbruch des Deutschen Reiches, 1945. Die militärische Niederwerfung der Wehrmacht* (München: Deutsche Verlags-Anstalt, 2008), p.509.

67 Krisztián Ungváry, *The Siege of Budapest: 100 Days in World War II* (New Haven, CT and London: Yale University Press, 2005), pp.417–21.

68 See Norbert Számvéber's *Days of Battle: Armoured operations north of the River Danube, Hungary 1944–1945* (Solihull, West Midlands: Helion and Company Limited, 2013).

69 G.F. Krivosheev et al, *Soviet Casualties and Combat Losses*, pp.151–2.

70 Soliankin et al, *Otechestvennie bronirovannie mashini. XX vek....1941–1945 gg.1941–1945*, p.14.

71 Komanduiushchemu voiskami 3-go Ukrainskogo fronta o pribitii v sostav fronta samokhodnoi artilleriiskoi brigadi, and ...2-go Ukrainskogo

fronta...dvukh..., both of 12 fevralia 1945 g., and Komanduiushchemu 2-go i 3-go Ukrainskikh frontov o perepodchinenii ...dvukh samokhodnikh artilleriiskikh brigad, 8 marta 1945 g., in *RA T.23 (12–4)*, pp.631 and 652.

72 N.N. Velikolepov, *Ogon' radi pobedi* (Moscow: Voennoe izdatel'stvo Ministerstvo oboroni SSSR, 1977), p.157.

73 A.I. Shebunin, *Skol'ko nami proideno...*(Moscow: Voennoe izdatel'stvo Ministerstvo oboroni SSSR, 1971), pp.149–53.

74 Ibid., p.155.

75 Ibid., pp.157–60.

76 See Vladimir Poliakov, *Vozdushnie razvedchiki – glaza fronta. Khronika odnogo polka. 1941–1945* (Moscow: ZAO Izdatel'stvo Tsentrpoligraf, 2014), pp.115, 128, 149, 161, and V. Miagkov, 'Vvedenie takticheskoi vozdushnoi razvedki istrebitel'nim aviapolkom', in *Vizh*, Number 8 (1976), pp.46–50.

77 Boevoe rasporiazhenie komanduiushchego voiskami 1-go Belorusskogo fronta komanduiushchim 3-i i 5-i udarnimi, 8-i gvardeiskoi, 69-i, 33-i, 47-i i 16-i vozdushnoi armiiami na provedenie razvedki boem, No. 00535 ot 11 aprelia 1945 g. 02:25, in *RA T.15(4–5)*, p.67.

78 M.A. Voloshin, *Razvedchiki vsegda vperedi* (Moscow: Voenizdat, 1977), pp.224–6.

CHAPTER 23

1 Protokol doprosa komanduiushchego oboronoi Berlina nemetskogo generala G. Veidlinga, sdavshegosia v plen 2 maia 1945 g., in V. Goncharov (ed.), *Bitva za Berlin: Zavershaiushchee svrazhenie Velikoi Otechestvennoi voini* (Moscow and Vladimir: AST and VKT, 2008), p.751.

2 G.K. Zhukov, *Vospominaniia i razmishleniia. ...Tom 3*, p.228.

3 A.V. Gorbatov, *Godi i voini*, p.334.

4 N.A. Antipenko, 'Til v Berlinskoi operatsii', in A.M. Samsonov (ed.), *9 maia 1945 goda*, pp.724–5, 732.

5 Siegfried Knappe, *Soldat: Reflections of a German Soldier, 1936–1949*, p.9.

6 Politicheskoe donesenie nachal'nika politicheskogo otdela 69-i armii nachal'niku politicheskogo upravleniia 1-go Belorusskogo fronta o nekotorikh itogakh i nedostatkakh pervogo dnia boia na oderskom platsdarme, No. 0471, 18 aprelia 1945 g., in *RA T.15 (4–5)*, pp.91–2.

7 Prikaz komanduiushchego voiskami 1-go Belorusskogo fronta vsem komanduiushchim armiiami i komandiram otdel'nikh korpusov o neobkhodimosti ustraneniia nedostatkov i aktivizatsii nastupatel'nikh deistvii na Berlin, 17 aprelia 1945, 20:30, in RA *T.15 (4–5)*, p.85.

8 M.E. Katukov, *Na ostrie glavnogo udara*, p.400.

9 A detailed description and analysis of the advance of 1st Ukrainian Front to the fighting in the Zossen region is provided in Ivan Konev's memoirs for 1945, I.S. Konev, *Sorok piatii*, pp.102–27.

10 Ibid., pp.117–20.

11 Ukazanie Verkhovnogo Glavnokomanduiushchego komanduiushchemu voiskami 1-go Belorusskogo fronta o vazhnosti skoreishego vziatiia Berlina

sovetskimi voiskami, No. 11069, 17 aprelia 1945 g., 17:50, in *RA T.15 (4–5)*, pp.84–5.

12 Prikaz komanduiushchego voiskami 1-go Belorusskogo fronta vsem komanduiushchim armiiami i komandiram otdel'nikh korpusov o neobkhodimosti ustraneniia nedostatkov i aktivizatsii nastupatel'nikh deistvii na Berlin, 17 aprelia 1945, 20:30, in RA *T.15 (4–5)*, p.85.

13 Stalin's speech on the German invasion of the Soviet Union (radio address, Moscow, July 3, 1941), in Alexander Hill, *The Great Patriotic War*, p.50.

14 Doklad komanduiushchego voiskami 3-go Belorusskogo fronta No.215/k Verkhovnomu Glavnokomanduiushchemu plana razgroma Kenigsbergskoi gruppirovki protivnika, 16 marta 1945 g., in *RA T.16 (5–4)*, pp.333–4.

15 On the attack see Horst Boog et al, *Das Deutsche Reich und der Zweite Weltkrieg. Band 10. Erster Halbband. Der Zusammenbruch des Deutschen Reiches, 1945*, pp.554–5 and map, p.602 and Earl F. Ziemke, *Stalingrad to Berlin: The German Defeat in the East* (Washington, D.C: Center of Military History, United States Army, 1987), p.447.

16 David M. Glantz, 'Stalin's Strategic Intentions, 1941–1945: Soviet Military Operations as Indicators of Stalin's Postwar Territorial Ambitions', in *JSMS*, Volume 27, Number 4 (2014), pp.704–5; G.K. Zhukov, *Vospominaniia i razmishleniia. ...Tom 3*, pp.202–7; Earl F. Ziemke, *Stalingrad to Berlin*, p.448.

17 V.I. Chuikov, *Konets tret'ego reikha* (Moscow: Izdatel'stvo "Sovetskaia Rossiia", 1973), p.168. An attempt by Zhukov to silence Chuikov in an April 1964 letter to Nikita Khrushchev is reproduced at www.alexanderyakovlev.org/fond/issues-doc/1004776 [Accessed 23 February 2015].

18 Earl F. Ziemke, *Stalingrad to Berlin*, p.446.

19 David M. Glantz, 'Stalin's Strategic Intentions, 1941–1945: Soviet Military Operations as Indicators of Stalin's Postwar Territorial Ambitions', p.703.

20 G.K. Zhukov, *Vospominaniia i razmishleniia. ...Tom 3*, pp.206–7.

21 Testimony of Budnitskii Aleksandr Naumovich. http://iremember.ru/saperi/budnitskiy-aleksandr-naumovich/stranitsa-3.html [Accessed 6 October 2014].

22 Operativnii otdel shtaba 1-go Belorusskogo fronta. Kratkaia svodka No.22 obobshchennogo boevogo opita voisk fronta za aprel' 1945 g. 5 iiunia 1945 g. Prilozhenie No.2. Sostav shturmovikh grupp v ulichnikh boiakh v g. Berlin. TsAMO f.233.o.2356.d.775.l.33.

23 Opit vedeniia ognia RS priamoi navodki v ulichnikh boiakh v g. Berlin. Ibid., ll.57–63.

24 Otchet o boevikh deistviiakh 6 Gvardeiskogo Tankovogo Kievskogo Krasnoznammenogo...korpusa v Berlinskoi i Prazhskoi operatsiiakh za period s 16.4.45 po 9.5.1945 goda. 24.5.1945. TsAMO f.236.o.2673. d.2360.ll.20–1.

25 Komanduiushchim artillerii Krasnoi Armii, voiskami 2-go Belorusskogo fronta o vkliuchenii v sostav fronta 74-i zenitnoi artilleriiskoi divizii i 317-go otdel'nogo artilleriiskogo diviziona osoboi moshchnosti, 29 noiabria 1944 g., in *RA T.23 (12–4)*, p.549.

26 Prikaz komanduiushchego voiskami 1-go Belorusskogo fronta vsem komanduiushchim armiiami i komandiram otdel'nikh korpusov o neobkhodimosti

ustraneniia nedostatkov i aktivizatsii nastupatel'nikh deistvii na Berlin, 17 aprelia 1945, 20:30, in *RA T.15 (5–4)*, p.85.

27 Gershman Matvei L'vovich. Interview by Grigorii Koifman, in A.V. Drabkin (ed.), *"I vse-taki mi pobedili!" Ia pomniu* (Moscow: Iauza/Eksmo, 2010), p.305.

28 Zhurnal boevikh deistvii pervogo Belorusskogo fronta za aprel' i pervuiu dekadu maia 1945 goda. TsAMO f.233.o.2356.d.739.l.243.

29 Testimony of Levin Natan Markovich. http://iremember.ru/saperi/levin-natan-markovich/stranitsa-5.html [Accessed 6 October 2014]

30 I.S. Konev, *Sorok piatii*, pp.101–2.

31 Testimony of Bukin Anton Dmitrievich. http://iremember.ru/tankisti/bukin-anton-dmitrievich/stranitsa-2.html [Accessed 6 October 2014].

32 Kratkaia svodka No.22. Obobshchenno boevogo opita voisk 1 Belorusskogo fronta za aprel' 1945 goda. 5 iiunia 1945 g. Prilozhenie No.2. Sostav shturmovikh grupp v ulichnikh boiakh v g. Berlin.TsAMO f.233.o.2356.d.775. ll.33–4.

33 Otchet o boevikh deistviiakh 6 Gvardeiskogo Tankovogo Kievskogo Krasnoznammenogo...korpusa v Berlinskoi i Prazhskoi operatsiiakh za period s 16.4.45 po 9.5.1945 goda. 24.5.1945. TsAMO f.236.o.2673.d.2360. ll.20–1.

34 Kratkaia svodka No.22. Obobshchenno boevogo opita voisk 1 Belorusskogo fronta za aprel' 1945 goda. 5 iiunia 1945 g. Prilozhenie No.9. Boi za most Briumebriuke (iz opita ulichnikh boev v g. Berlin). TsAMO f.233.o.2356. d.775.l.49.

35 Ibid., ll.45–8 and 50.

36 I.P. Roslii, *Poslednii prival – v Berline* (Moscow: Voennoe izdatel'stvo, 1983), pp.276–83; V.S. Antonov, *Put' k Berlinu* (Moscow: Izdatel'stvo "Nauka", 1975), pp.307–19 and Zhurnal boevikh deistvii pervogo Belorusskogo fronta za aprel' i pervuiu dekadu maia 1945 goda. TsAMO f.233.o.2356.d.739. ll.242, 250, 258, 268 and 276 [22, 23 and 24 April].

37 See Mark Edele, 'Soviet liberations and occupations, 1939–1949', in Richard J.B. Bosworth and Joseph A. Maiolo (eds.), *The Cambridge History of the Second World War. Volume II. Politics and Ideology* (Cambridge: Cambridge University Press, 2015), pp.489–94.

38 On looting, see the Conclusion. On rape, revenge and wider discipline, in addition to Mark Edele's piece above, see Catherine Merridale, *Ivan's War*, pp.317–28 and 349–51. See also Anthony Beevor, *The Fall of Berlin 1945* (London: Penguin Books, 2003), pp.326–7 and 408–15 and Karel C. Berkhoff, *Motherland in Danger*, p.193.

39 Otchet o boevikh deistviiakh 6 Gvardeiskogo Tankovogo Kievskogo Krasnoznammenogo...korpusa v Berlinskoi i Prazhskoi operatsiiakh za period s 16.4.45 po 9.5.1945 goda. 24.5.1945. TsAMO f.236.o.2673.d.2360.l.22.

40 Tezisi doklada komandarma 4 Gv.TA Gv. General-polkovnika Leliushenko o boevikh deistviiakh 4 Gv.TA 1 Ukrainskogo fronta v Visla-Oderskoi operatsii s Sandomirskogo platsdarma s 12 ianvaria po 22 fevralia 1945 g. na sbore General'skogo sostava Tsentral'noi gruppi voisk sentiabr' 1945 g. TsAMO f.236.o.2673.d.2393.l.55.

41 F.M. Zinchenko, *Geroi shturma reikhstaga*, pp.75–7.

42 P.I. Batov, *Operatsiia 'Oder'. Boevie deistviia 65-i armii v Berlinskoi operatsii aprel'-mai 1945 goda* (Moscow: Voennoe izdatel'stvo Ministerstva oboroni SSSR, 1965), p.89.

43 V.I. Chuikov, *Konets tret'ego reikha*, pp.212–13.

44 V.M. Shatilov, *Znamia nad reikhstagom* (Moscow: Voennoe izdatel'stvo Ministerstva oboroni SSSR, 1966), p.245.

45 Ibid., p.287.

46 Direktiva Stavki VGK No.11036 komanduiushchim voiskami frontov ob uluchshenii organizatsii boevikh deistvii, 6 marta 1945 g., in *RA T.16 (5–4)*, p.207.

47 See Mervyn Matthews, *Privilege in the Soviet Union: A Study of Elite Life-Styles under Communism* (London: George Allen and Unwin, 1978), pp.101–2, 123–4.

48 Tezisi doklada komandarma 4 Gv.TA Gv. General-polkovnika Leliushenko o boevikh deistviiakh 4 Gv.TA 1 Ukrainskogo fronta v Visla-Oderskoi operatsii s Sandomirskogo platsdarma s 12 ianvaria po 22 fevralia 1945 g. na sbore General'skogo sostava Tsentral'noi gruppi voisk sentiabr' 1945 g. TsAMO f.236.o.2673.d.2393.l.31.

49 G.G. Semenov, *Nastupaet udarnaia* (Moscow: Voennoe izdatel'stvo, 1986), p.268.

50 Protokol doprosa komanduiushchego oboronoi Berlina nemetskogo generala G. Veidlinga, sdavshegosia v plen 2 maia 1945 g., in V. Goncharov (ed.), *Bitva za Berlin: Zavershaiushchee srazhenie Velikoi Otechestvennoi voini*, p.752.

51 A.V. Gorbatov, *Godi i voini*, p.335.

52 G.S. Nadisev, *Na sluzhbe shtabnoi. Izdanie vtoroe, ispravlennoe i dopolnennoe* (Moscow: Voennoe izdatel'stvo Ministerstva oboroni SSSR, 1976), pp.191, 193–4.

53 Siegfried Knappe, *Soldat: Reflections of a German Soldier, 1936–1949*, p.9.

54 Plan-doklad dlia generalov i visshego ofitserskogo sostava Tsentral'noi Gruppi voisk. Tema: "Vozdushnaia Armiia v nastupatel'noi operatsii". Sentiabria 1945 goda. TsAMO f.236.o.2673.d.2393.l.137 and "Berlinskaia operatsiia v tsifrakh", in *Vizh*, Number 4 (1965), p.81.

55 Plan-doklad dlia generalov i visshego ofitserskogo sostava Tsentral'noi Gruppi voisk. Tema: "Vozdushnaia Armiia v nastupatel'noi operatsii". Sentiabria 1945 goda. TsAMO f.236.o.2673.d.2393.ll.132 and 140–1, 143.

56 Ibid., ll.145–6.

57 Obzor boevikh deistvii voisk 2 vozdushnoi armii v Berlinskoi nastupatel'noi operatsii...(chast' 2). TsAMO f.236.o.2673.d.2742.ll.143–60.

58 See Gordon and Khazanov, *Soviet Combat Aircraft of the Second World War. Volume One: Single-Engined Fighters*, pp.53–8 and 160–5.

59 Plan-doklad dlia generalov i visshego ofitserskogo sostava Tsentral'noi Gruppi voisk. Tema: "Vozdushnaia Armiia v nastupatel'noi operatsii". Sentiabria 1945 goda. TsAMO f.236.o.2673.d.2393.l.152.

60 G.F. Krivosheev et al, *Soviet Casualties and Combat Losses*, pp.152–9.

CONCLUSION

1 See A.N. Mertsalov and L.A. Mertsalova, *Stalinizm i voina. Iz neprochitannikh stranits istorii (1930–1990-e)* (Moscow: Izdatel'stvo "Rodnik", 1994), pp.346–52.

2 See Chapter 12.

3 F.W. von Mellenthin, *Panzer Battles*, pp.319–20.

4 Mark Harrison, *Accounting for War: Soviet employment, accounting and the defence burden, 1940–1945* (Cambridge: Cambridge University Press, 1996), p.152.

5 CSDIC (UK) SR report, SRGG 1271 [TNA, WO 208/4170]. Lecture on conditions on the Russian front given by Generalleutnant Heim, captured 23 September 1944 at Boulogne, to fellow officers on 23 May 1945, in Sönke Neitzel (ed.), *Tapping Hitler's Generals: Transcripts of Secret Conversations, 1942–45* (Bansley, South Yorkshire and St Paul, MN: Frontline Books and MBI Publishing Co., 2007), pp.160, 164.

6 G.F. Krivosheev et al, *Soviet Casualties and Combat Losses*, pp.244, 247, 253.

7 Generalleutnant a.D. Walter Schwabedissen, *The Russian Air Force in the Eyes of German Commanders*, p.271.

8 P.V. Mel'nikov (gen.ed.), *Razvitie taktiki sukhoputnikh voisk v Velikoi Otechestvennoi voine*, pp.296–7.

9 Generalleutnant a.D. Walter Schwabedissen, *The Russian Air Force in the Eyes of German Commanders*, p.271.

10 See A.P. Beloborodov (gen.ed.), *Voennie kadri sovetskogo gosudarstva v Velikoi Otechestvennoi voine 1941–1945 gg.*, chapter 5.

11 Oleg Khlevniuk, 'Stalin na voine. Istochniki i ikh interpretatsiia', in *Cahiers du Monde russe*, Volume 52, Number 2–3 (April-September 2011), p.214. See also Oleg V. Khlevniuk, *Stalin: New Biography of a Dictator*, p.227.

12 G.A. Kumanev, *Problemi voennoi istorii otechestva (1938–1945 gg.)* (Moscow: OOO Izdatel'stvo "Sobranie", 2007), pp.546–8.

13 British Air Marshal Slessor, cited in John Ellis, *Brute Force: Allied Strategy and Tactics in the Second World War* (New York: Viking Penguin, 1990), p.532.

14 David French, *Raising Churchill's Army: The British Army and the War Against Germany 1919–1945* (Oxford: Oxford University Press, 2000), pp.283, 285.

15 See for example John Ellis, *Brute Force*, p.539.

16 David French, *Raising Churchill's Army*, p.285.

17 Transcript of interview with Major Pyotr Andreyevich Zayonchkovsky, May 28, 1943, in Jochen Hellbeck (trans. Christopher Tauchen and Dominic Bonfiglio), *Stalingrad: The City that Defeated the Third Reich*, p.394.

18 On this cultural phenomenon, see *Russkii avos'* in Anna Bezhbitskaia, *Semanticheskie universalii i bazisnie kontsepti* (Moscow: Iaziki slavianskikh kul'tur, 2011), pp.375–7. In English, Anna Wierzbicka, *Semantics, Culture, and Cognition: Universal Human Concepts in Culture-Specific Configurations* (New York/ Oxford: Oxford University Press, 1992), pp.433–6.

19 Oleg Khlevniuk, 'Stalin na voine. Istochniki i ikh interpretatsiia', pp.216–17.

20 Transcript of interview with Comrade Lieutenant General Vasily Chuikov, Stalingrad, January 5, 1943, in Jochen Hellbeck (trans. Christopher Tauchen and Dominic Bonfiglio), *Stalingrad: The City that Defeated the Third Reich*, p.282. See also p.280.

21 On these issues, in addition to work cited earlier on this matter see the excellent work of for example Mark Edele, 'Towards a Sociocultural History of the Soviet Second World War', in *Kritika: Explorations in Russian and Eurasian History*, Volume 15, Number 4 (Fall 2014), pp.829–35 and 'What Are We Fighting for? Loyalty in the Soviet War Effort, 1941–1945', in *International Labor and Working-Class History*, Number 84 (Fall 2013), pp.248–68; Roger R. Reese, *Why Stalin's Soldier's Fought*, pp.306–12; Oleg Budnitskii and Jason Morton, 'The Great Patriotic War and Soviet Society: Defeatism, 1941–42', in *Kritika: Explorations in Russian and Eurasian History*, Volume 15, Number 4 (Fall 2014), pp.767–97.

22 By the top of the chain of command, looted items being shipped back by the trainload and clearly making a mockery of the nominal upper limit of 16 kg per month. See Catherine Merridale, *Ivan's War*, pp.323–6. See also Anthony Beevor, *The Fall of Berlin*, pp.407–8. The relative riches enjoyed by many Germans must at times have provoked anger amongst Soviet forces, and the suffering inflicted on the Soviet Union provided ample justification for a looting that was however not only limited to German and 'enemy' territory even if it was less likely to be tolerated elsewhere. See Mark Edele, 'Soviet Liberations and Occupations, 1939–1949', in Richard J.B. Bosworth and Joseph A. Maiolo (eds.), *The Cambridge History of the Second World War. Volume II. Politics and Ideology*, pp.489–94.

23 As I have argued regarding the partisan war on German-occupied territory, the likelihood of Soviet victory was undoubtedly an important factor in whether many peasants were willing to commit to the Soviet regime and participate in the partisan movement – or face the consequences. With the return of the Red Army increasingly likely, the partisan movement was far more successful in recruitment. See Alexander Hill, *The War Behind the Eastern Front*, pp.164–77.

24 For example, on the enemy armed forces see General'nii shtab Krasnoi Armii, Kratkii *spravochnik po vooruzhennikh silam Germanii* (Moscow: Veon-noe izdatel'stvo Narodnogo Komissariata Oboroni Soiuza SSR, 1941) (pod-pisano k pechati 29.8.41) and Geroi sovetskogo soiuza general-maior A.I. Liziukov, *Chto nado znat' voini Krasnoi Armii boevikh priemakh nemtsev iz boevogo opita frontovika* (Moscow: Voenizdat NKO SSSR, 1942) (podpisano k pechati 1.1.42).

25 Prikaz voiskam Brianskogo fronta No.08, "5" sentiabria 1941 g. Soderzha-nie: Ob uporiadochenii ucheta i opisaniia boevogo opita. TsAMO f.202.o.5. d.9.l.1.

26 V.K. Kopitko and E.L. Korshunov, 'General-leitenant F.N. Starikov: "Ogromnii opit, kotorii mi imeem na protiazhenii trekh let Otechestvennoi voini ... ne izuchaetsia"', p.29.

27 G.F. Krivosheev et al, *Soviet Casualties and Combat Losses*, pp.160–1.

Appendix 1   The Destruction of the Upper Echelons of the RKKA in 1937–1941

Category	Number serving in 1936	Shot	Died in captivity	Suicide	Returned from captivity alive	% of those serving in 1936 killed
Marshals of the Soviet Union	5	2	1	-	-	60
Komandarm (1st and 2nd rank)	15	19	-	-	1	133
Flagman of the Fleet (1st and 2nd rank)	4	5	-	-	-	125
Komkor	62	58	4	2	5	112.6
Flagman (1st rank)	6	5	-	-	1	100
Komdiv	201	122	9	-	22	76
Kombrig	474	201	15	1	30	52.1
Total	767	412	29	3	59	65.6

Source: O.F. Suvenirov, *Tragediia RKKA 1937–1938* (Moscow: Terra, 1998), p.315.

Appendix 2 Soviet Armoured Strength and Serviceability in the Western Military Districts of the Soviet Union as of 1 June 1941

Military district	Total[1]	Total including					
		Category 1 serviceability[2] [KV-series/ T-34]	Category 2 serviceability [KV-series/ T-34]	Total (%) Category 1 and 2 serviceability	Category 3 serviceability [KV-series/ T-34]	Category 4 serviceability [KV-series/ T-34]	Total (%) Category 3 and 4 serviceability
Leningrad VO	1,857	7 [3/4]	1,536 [3/4]	1,543 (83.1)	210	104	314 (16.9)
Pribaltic OVO	1,549	378 [53/50]	896 [23/0]	1,274 (82.2)	203 [2/0]	72	275 (17.8)
Western OVO	2,900	470 [88/228]	1,722 [9/0]	2,192 (75.6)	385	323	708 (24.4)
Kiev OVO	5,465	1,124 [245/ 462]	3,664 [32/ 33]	4,788 (87.6)	298 [1/1]	379	677 (12.4)
Odessa VO	1,011	178 [10/50]	565	743 (73.5)	151	117	268 (26.5)
Total	12,782	2,157 [399/ 794]	8,383 [67/ 37]	10,540 (82.5)	1,247 [3/1]	995	2,242 (17.5)

Sources: N.P. Zolotov and S.I. Isaev, 'Boegotovi bili... Istoriko-statisticheskoe issledovanie kolichestvenno-kachestvennogo sostoianiia tankovogo parka Krasnoi Armii nakanune Velikoi Otechestvennoi voini', in *Vizh*, Number 11 (1993), pp.76–7 and N.P. Zolotov et al, *Boevoi i chislennii sostav vooruzhennikh sil SSSR v period Velikoi Otechestvennoi voini (1941–1945 gg.). Statisticheskii sbornik No.1 (22 iiunia 1941 g.)* (Moscow: Institut voennoi istorii MO RF, 1994), pp.136, 140, 144, 148, 152, 156.

[1] From 31 May to 21 June an additional 41 KV-series, 138 T-34 and 27 T-40 tanks – a total of 206 tanks – were delivered by factories to the field forces of the Western and Kiev Special Military Districts – some crews clearly had little time to familiarize themselves with their new equipment before 'Barbarossa'.

[2] Serviceability categories: Category 1 – new; Category 2 – used, may require day-to-day maintenance with field units; Category 3 – requiring mid-level maintenance at the military district level; Category 4 – requiring major (capital) repair at central facilities or in factories.

Glossary

boekomplekt	*boevoi komplekt*	A full load/reload of munitions
	divizion	A Soviet military unit, distinct from a division, by the Great Patriotic War typically of artillery or related and of equivalent size to a battalion.
	fel'dsher	A member of medical staff perhaps best described in contemporary Western terms as having a role incorporating many of the functions of paramedic and nurse practitioner.
GABTU	*Glavnoe Avtobronetankovoe Upravlenie*	Main Auto-Armour Board of the Red Army
GAU	*Glavnoe Artilleriiskoe Upravlenie*	Main Artillery Board of the Red Army
GAZ	*Gosudarstvennii avtomobil'nii zavod*	State Automobile Factory
Genshtab		see GSh KA
GKO/GOKO	*Gosudarstvennii Komitet Oboroni*	State Defence Committee – effectively the Soviet war cabinet, chaired by Stalin.
GlavPU KA	*Glavnoe Politicheskoe Upravlenie Krasnoi Armii*	Main Political Directorate of the Red Army. Responsible for ideological work within the Red Army, which to a large extent meant discipline, including the appointment and supervision of political officers below front level and appointing political members to military soviets.

692

GRU	*Glavnoe Razvedivatel'noe Upravlenie*	Main Reconnaissance Board [of the Red Army]
GSh KA	*General'nii shtab Krasnoi armii*	General Staff of the Red Army
GU	*Glavnoe upravlenie*	Main Board or Central Administration of ...
HPSSS		Harvard Project on the Soviet Social System
JSMS		Journal of Slavic Military Studies
KOP	*Korpus Obrony Pogranicza*	Polish border forces
KMG	*konno-mekhanizirovannaia gruppa*	Cavalry-Mechanised Group
***Komsomol* – see also VLKSM**	*Kommunisticheskii soiuz molodozhi*	Communist Youth League
	maskirovka	Concealment and deception of Soviet intentions through such means as camouflage, dummy units and radio traffic between units not actually in situ in the areas from which transmission were being made.
MP-41	*Mobilizatsionnii Plan-41*	Mobilisation Plan-1941
NK/ *Narkom*	*Narodnii komissar* or *Narodnii komissariat*	People's Commissar or People's Commissariat – equivalent of a minister or ministry
NKO	*Narodnii Komissariat Oboroni*	People's Commissariat for Defence – the Soviet Ministry of Defence
NKGB	*Narodnii Komissariat Gosudarstvennoi Bezopasnosti*	People's Commissariat for State Security – a new ministry that acquired responsibilities, including foreign intelligence and counter-espionage on Soviet

		territory, from the NKVD for a brief period in early 1941 and then again from 1943–1946.
NKVD	*Narodnii Komissariat Vnutrennikh Del*	People's Commissariat for Internal Affairs
	oblast'	Soviet administrative region
OKH	*Oberkommando des Heeres*	German High Command of the Army, increasingly as the war progressed only concerned with the Eastern Front.
OMSBON	*Otdel'naia motostrelkovaia brigada osobogo naznacheniia*	Independent Special Service Motor Rifle Brigade (of the NKVD)
OO NKVD	*Osobii otdel* NKVD	Special Section of the NKVD – responsible for counter-intelligence in military units from 1941–1943. Replaced by SMERSH
OSOAVIAKHIM		A compound of OSO and AVIAKHIM or the Society for Co-operation in Defence and Society for Aviation-Chemical Construction respectively – provider of pre-conscription military training.
OVO	*Osobii voennii okrug*	Special military district – a military district located in sensitive border regions.
PVO	*protivovozdushnaia oborona*	Air defence - Soviet air defence forces – including anti-aircraft guns and fighter aircraft.
PU-36	*Polevoi Ustav RKKA 1936*	1936 Red Army Field Regulations
PTRD	*Protivotankovoe ruzh'e Degtiareva*	Anti-tank rifle

PzKpfw	*Panzerkampfwagen*	Tank
	raion	Soviet administrative district
RA	*Russkii arkhiv.*	See Bibliography
	Velikaia	
	Otechestvennaia	
	rasputitsa	Russian term for the period in autumn and spring when dirt roads became difficult going due to rain and the spring thaw respectively.
RGAE	*Rossiiskii*	Russian State Archive for the
	Gosudarstvennii	Economy
	Arkhiv Ekonomiki	
RGASPI	*Rossiiskii*	Russian State Archive for
	Gosudarstvennii	Socio-Political History
	Arkhiv Sotsial'no-	
	Politicheskoi Istorii	
RGA VMF	*Rossiiskii*	Russian State Archive for the
	gosudarstvennii arkhiv	Navy
	Voenno-Morskogo Flota	
RKKA	*Rabochaia i*	Workers' and Peasants' Red
	Krest'ianskaia	Army
	Krasnaia Armiia	
RVS SSSR	*Revvoensovet SSSR*	Revolutionary Military Soviet – supreme administrative body for the army during the 1920s and early 1930s.
RS	*Reaktivnie snariadi*	Soviet rocket artillery, typically known as *Katiusha*.
RSFSR	*Rossiiskaia*	Russian Socialist Federated
	Sotsialisticheskaia	Soviet Republic –
	Federativnaia	incorporated within the
	Sovetskaia Respublika	USSR.
RVGK	*Rezerv Verkhovnogo*	Reserve of the Supreme
	Glavnokomandovaniia	High Command
SAU/SU	*samokhodnaia*	Self-propelled, typically
	(artilleriiskaia)	tracked, artillery or anti-tank
	ustanovka	gun.
SBD	*Sbornik boevikh*	See Bibliography
	dokumentov	

SMERSH	*Smert' spionam*	Lit. 'death to spies' – Soviet military counterintelligence from 1943.
SNK / *Sovnarkom*	*Sovet narodnikh komissarov*	Council of People's Commissars – effectively the highest tier for the Soviet governmental, as opposed to Party, structure.
Stavka **GK**	*Stavka Glavnogo Komandovaniia*	Headquarters of the High Command (established 23 June 1941)
Stavka **VK**	*Stavka Verkhovnogo Komandovaniia*	Headquarters of the Supreme Command (established 10 July 1941)
Stavka **VGK**	*Stavka Verkhovnogo Glavnogo Komandovaniia*	Headquarters of the Supreme High Command (established 8 August 1941)
STZ	*Stalingradskii traktornii zavod*	Stalingrad Tractor Factory
	Supreme Soviet	The equivalent of the Soviet parliament, to which the *Sovnarkom* was theoretically answerable.
SVE	*Sovetskaia Voennaia Entsiklopediia*	See Bibliography
TNA		The National Archives (UK)
TsAMO	*Tsentral'nii arkhiv Ministerstva oboroni*	Central Archive of the Ministry of Defence (of the Russian Federation)
TsK	*Tsentral'nii Komitet*	Central Committee (of the Communist Party) – Party equivalent of the Supreme Soviet.
TsMVS	*Tsentral'nii Muzei Vooruzhennikh Sil*	Central Museum of the Armed Forces (photograph source)
TsShPD	*Tsentral'nii Shtab Partizanskogo Dvizheniia*	Central Headquarter of the Partisan Movement

TsVMM	*Tsentral'nii Voenno-Morskoi Muzei*	Central Naval Museum (photograph source)
Vizh	*Voenno-istoricheskii zhurnal*	See Bibliography
VKP(b)	*Vsesoiuznaia Kommunisticheskaia Partiia (bolshevikov)*	All-Union Communist Party (Bolsheviks)
VLKSM	*Vsesoiuznii Leninskii kommunisticheskii soiuz molodezhi*	All-Union Leninist Communist Union of Young People – see also *Komsomol*
VMF	*Voenno-morskoi flot*	The Soviet navy
VO	*voennii okrug*	Military district – military-administrative region, converted to a *front* if playing a frontline role in wartime.
VVS	*Voenno-vozdushnie sili*	Soviet air forces

Bibliography

ARCHIVAL SOURCES:

Central Archive of the Ministry of Defence (of the Russian Federation) (TsAMO), f.38.o.11351.d.5; f.38.o.11355.d. 236; f.81.o.12104.d.9; f.202. o.5.d.9; f.208.o.2511.d.206; f.213.o.2002.d.31; f.217.o.1217.d.127; f.217. o.1221.d.93; f.219.o.679.d.26; f.233.o.2309.d.165 and o.2356.d.739 and 775; f.236.o.2673.d.2360, 2393, 2736 and 2742; f.249.o.1544.d.33; f.251. o.646.d.13; f.450.o.11158.d.89; f.500.o.12451.d.271 and 279.

National Archives and Records Administration (NARA), T-78 Roll 619; T-311, Rolls 51 and 268; T-315, Rolls 205, 206, 1817.

Harvard Project on the Soviet Social System (HPSSS). Schedule A, Vol.5, Case 56 ; A, Vol. 13, Case 175; A, Vol. 18, Case 341; A, Vol. 21, Case 431; A, Vol. 22, Cases 433 and 445; Schedule B, Vol. 1, Case 77; B, Vol. 6, Case 193; B, Vol. 7, Case 135; B, Vol. 9, Cases 375 and 497.

Russian State Archive of the Economy (RGAE) f.413.o.9.d.438, 555.

Russian State Archive of the Navy (RGA VMF) f.r-1483.o.1.d.200; f.r-1483.o.3. d.49

Russian State Archive for Socio-Political History (RGASPI), f.644.o.1.d.3, 21, 24, 26; f.625.o.1.d.38

The National Archives (UK) (TNA), WO 208/4170

PUBLISHED DOCUMENTS (INCLUDING SERVICE DIARIES):

'K istorii territorial'nogo-militsionnogo stroitel'stva v Krasnoi Armii', in *Vizh*, Number 11 (1960), pp.87–97.

KPSS o Vooruzhennikh Silakh Sovetskogo Soiuza. Dokumenti 1917–1981 (Moscow: Voennoe Izdatel'stvo Ministerstva Oboroni SSSR, 1981).

Organizatsiia sviazi v Rostovskoi nastupatel'noi operatsii (s 24 noiabria po 12 dekabria 1941 g.) (Shtab 56 deistvuiushchei armii – otdel sviazi, 1942).

O vvedenii personal'nikh voennikh zvanii nachal'stvuiushchego sostava RKKA.... Postanovlenie TsIK i SNK SSSR ot 22 sentiabria 1935 g. (Moscow: Otdel izdatel'stva NKO SSSR, 1935).

'Plenum TsK VKP(b), 23 fevralia–5 marta 1937 g. Stenograficheskii otchet. Vipusk II', in *Voenno-istoricheskii arkhiv*, Number 1 (1997), pp.150–72.

Artsibashev, V.A. et al (eds.), *Reforma v Krasnoi Armii. Dokumenti i materiali. 1923–1928 gg. V 2 kn. Kn. 2* (Moscow/Saint Petersburg: Letnii sad, 2006).

Balashov, E. (ed.), *Prinimai nas Suomi krasavitsa!"Osvoboditel'nii" pokhod v Finlandiiu 1939–1940 gg. (Sbornik dokumentov i fotomaterialov). Chast' I* (St Petersburg: OOO "Galeia Print", 1999).

Basik, I.I. et al (eds.), *Voennii sovet pri narodnom kommissare oboroni SSSR. Oktiabr' 1936. : Dokumenti i materiali* (Moscow: Rossiiskaia politicheskaia entsiklopediia (ROSSPEN), 2009).

Boevoi ustav bronetankovikh i mekhanizirovannikh voisk Krasnoi Armii. Chast' 1 (tank, tankovii vzvod, tankovaia rota) (Moscow: Voennoe izdatel'stvo Narodnogo Komissariata Oboroni, 1944).

Biriukov, N., *Tanki frontu! Zapiski sovetskogo generala* (Smolensk: Rusich, 2005).

Bobilev, P.N. (gen.ed.) et al, *Glavnii voennii sovet RKKA. 13 marta 1938–20 iiunia 1941 gg.: Dokumenti i materiali* (Moscow: ROSSPEN, 2004).

Voennii sovet pri narodnom kommissare oboroni SSSR. Noiabr' 1937 g.: Dokumenti i materiali (Moscow: "Rossiiskaia politicheskaia entsiklopediia" (ROSSPEN), 2006).

Voennii sovet pri narodnom kommissare oboroni SSSR. 1938, 1940 gg.: Dokumenti i materiali (Moscow: "Rossiiskaia politicheskaia entsiklopediia" (ROSSPEN), 2006).

Chernobaev, A.A. (ed.), *Na prieme u Stalina. Tetradi (zhurnali) zapisei lits, priniatikh I.V. Stalinim (1924–1953 gg.). Spravochnik* (Moscow: Novii khronograf, 2010).

Cienciala, A.M. et al (eds.), *Katyn: A Crime without Punishment* (Annals of Communism) (New Haven and London: Yale University Press, 2007).

Condell, B. and Zabecki, D.T. (trans. and ed.), *On the German Art of War: Truppenführung* (Mechanicsburg, PA: Stackpole Books, 2009).

Efimenko, A.R. et al (eds.), *Vooruzhennii konflikt v raione reki Khalkhin-Gol. Maisentiabr' 1939 g. Dokumenti i materiali* (Moscow: Novalis, 2014).

Förster, J. and Mawdsley, E., 'Hitler and Stalin in Perspective: Secret Speeches on the Eve of Barbarossa', in *War in History*, Volume 11, Number 1 (2004), pp.61–103.

Gatagova, L.S. et al (eds.), *TsK VKP(b) i natsional'nii vopros. Kniga 2. 1933–1945* (Moscow: ROSSPEN, 2009).

Gavrilov, B.I. (ed.), *Cherez "Dolinu smerti". Podvig i tragediia voinov Volkhovskogo fronta. Ianvar'-iiun' 1942 g. Tom 2. Vospominaniia, dokumenti i materiali* (Moscow: Institut rossiiskoi istorii RAN, 2004).

Gavrilov, V.A. (ed.), *Voennaia razvedka informiruet. Dokumenti Razvedupravleniia Krasnoi Armii. Ianvar' 1939-iiun' 1941 g.* (Moscow: Mezhdunarodnii fond "Demokratiia", 2008).

Getty, J.A. and Naumov, O.V. (eds.), *The Road to Terror: Stalin and the Self-Destruction of the Bolsheviks, 1932–1939* (New Haven and London: Yale University Press, 1999).

Glantz, D., 'Prelude to Kursk: Soviet Strategic Operations, February-March 1943', in *JSMS*, Volume 8, Number 1 (1995), pp.1–35.

'Forgotten Battles of the German-Soviet War (1941–45), Part 4: The Winter Campaign (5 December 1941–April 1942): The Demiansk Counteroffensive', in *JSMS*, Volume 13, Number 3 (2000), pp.145–64.

'Forgotten Battles of the German-Soviet War (1941–1945), Part 7: The Summer Campaign (12 May–18 November 1942): Voronezh, July 1942', in *JSMS*, Volume 14, Number 3 (2001), pp.150–220.

Glantz, D.M., (ed.), *Kharkov 1942: Anatomy of a Military Disaster through Soviet Eyes* (Hersham, Surrey: Ian Allen Publishing, 2010).

Glantz, D.M. and Orenstein, H.S. (trans. and ed.), *The Battle of Kursk: The Soviet General Staff Study* (London and Portland, OR: Frank Cass Publishers, 1999).

Belorussia 1944: The Soviet General Staff Study (London/New York: Frank Cass, 2001).

The Battle for the Ukraine: The Red Army's Korsun'-Shevchenkovskii Offensive, 1944 (London and New York: Routledge, 2003).

Glavnoe upravlenie sviazi, *Spravochnik po voiskovim i tankovim radiostantsiiam. Chast' 1 and 2 iz 3* (Moscow: Voennoe izdatel'stvo Narodnogo Komissariata Oboroni, 1943).

Gnedovets, P.P. et al (eds.), *Sbornik boevikh dokumentov Velikoi Otechestvennoi voini. Vipusk 17, 35, 38* (Moscow: Voennoe izdatel'stvo Voennogo ministerstva soiuza SSR, 1952–1959).

Goncharov, V. (ed.), *Bitva pod Kurskom: Ot oboroni k nastupleniiu* (Moscow: AST/Khranitel', 2006).

Grazhdanskaia voina v Ispanii: Deistviia na Tsentral'nom fronte (oktiabr' 1936-aprel' 1937 goda) (Saint Petersburg: Izdatel'stvo Sankt-Peterburgskogo universiteta, 2006).

Bitva za Berlin: Zavershaiushchee svrazhenie Velikoi Otechestvennoi voini (Moscow and Vladimir: AST and VKT, 2008).

Gor'kov, I., *Gosudarstvennii Komitet Oboroni postanovliaet (1941–1945). Tsifri, dokumenti* (Moscow: OLMA-PRESS, 2002).

Hill, A., 'The Allocation of Allied "Lend-Lease" Aid to the Soviet Union arriving with Convoy PQ-12, March 1942 – A State Defence Committee Decree', in *JSMS*, Volume 19, Number 4 (2006), pp.727–38.

The Great Patriotic War of the Soviet Union, 1941–1945: A Documentary Reader (London and New York: Routledge, 2009).

Iampol'skii, V.P. (gen.ed.), Organi gosudarsrvennoi bezopasnosti SSSR v Velikoi Otechestvennoi voine. Sbornik dokumentov. Tom vtoroi. Kniga 1 *and* 2. Nachalo. 22 iiunia-31 avgusta 1941 goda *and* 1 sentiabria – 31 dekabria 1941 goda (Moscow: Izdatel'stvo "Rus'", 2000).

Ivanchishin, P.A. and Chugunov, A.I. (eds.), *Pogranichnie voiska SSSR, 1929–1938. Sbornik dokumentov i materialov* (Moscow: "Nauka", 1972).

Khaustov, V.N. et al (eds.), *Lubianka. Stalin i NKVD-NKGB-GUKR 'Smersh'. 1939–1946. Dokumenti...* (Moscow: Mezhdunarodnii fond "Demokratiia"/ izdatel'stvo "Materik", 2006).

Kiselev, V.N. (ed.), '...variantov planov strategicheskogo razvertivaniia...', in *Vizh*, Number 2 (1992), pp.18–19.

Knishevskii, P.N. (gen.ed.), *Skritaia pravda voini: 1941 god. Neizvestnie dokumenti* (Moscow: "Russkaia kniga", 1992).

Koval'chuk, V.M. (gen.ed.), *V tilu vraga. Bor'ba partisan i podpol'shchikov na okkupirovannoi territorii Leningradskoi oblasti. 1944 g.: Sbornik dokumentov* (Leningrad: Lenizdat, 1985).

Kolomiets, M., 'Boi u reki Khalkhin-Gol mai-sentiabr' 1939 goda', in *Frontovaia illiustratsiia*, Number 2 (2002).

Kopitko, V.K. and Korshunov, E.L., 'General-leitenant F.N. Starikov: "Ogromnii opit, kotorii mi imeem na protiazhenii trekh let Otechestvennoi voini ... ne izuchaetsia"', in *Vizh*, Number 2 (2014), pp.22–30.

Kudriashov, S. (ed.), *Krasnaia Armiia v 1920-e godi* (Moscow: Vestnik Arkhiva Prezidenta Rossiiskoi Federatsii, 2007).

Kudriashov, S.V. (gen.ed.), *Vestnik Arkhiva Prezidenta Rossiiskoi Federatsii. Partizanskoe dvizhenie v godi Velikoi Otechestvennoi voini* (Moscow: Izdatel'stvo "Istoricheskaia literature", 2015).

Vestnik Arkhiva Prezidenta Rossiiskoi Federatsii. Voina: 1941–1945. Vipusk 2 (Moscow: Izdatel'stvo "Istoricheskaia literatura", 2015).

Kul'kov, E.N. and Rzheshevskii, O.A. (gen.eds.), *Zimnaia voina 1939–1940. Kniga vtoraia. I.V. Stalin i finskaia kampaniia (Stenogramma sovershchaniia pri TSK VKP(b))* (Moscow: "Nauka", 1999).

Murin, Iu. G. (ed.), 'Uroki voini s Finlandiei. Neopublikovannii doklad narkoma oboroni SSSR K.E. Voroshilova na plenume TsK VKP(b), 28 marta 1940 g.', in *Novaia i noveishaia istoriia*, Number 4 (1993), pp.100–122.

Narodnii Komissariat Oboroni, *Boevoi ustav pekhoti Krasnoi Armii. Chast' I (boets, otdelenie, vzvod, rota) and Chast' II (batal'on, polk)* (Moscow: Voennoe Izdatel'stvo Narodnogo Komissariata Oboroni, 1942).

Narodnii Komissariat Oboroni Soiuza SSR, *Boevoi ustav pekhoti RKKA (BUP-38). Chast' pervaia (boets, otdelenie, vzvod)* (Moscow: Gosudarstvennoe Voennoe Izdatel'stvo Narkomata Oboroni Soiuza SSR, 1939).

Proekt Polevoi Ustav RKKA (PU 39) (Moscow: Gosudarstvennoe voennoe izdatel'stvo Narkomata Oboroni Soiuza SSR, 1939).

Vremennii Polevoi Ustav RKKA 1936 (PU 36) (Moscow: Gosudarstvennoe voennoe izdatel'stvo Narkomata Oboroni SSSR, 1937).

Naumov, V.P. (gen.ed.), *1941 god: V 2 kn. Kn.1* and *2* (Moscow: Mezhdunarodnii fond "Demokratiia", 1998).

Neitzel, S. (ed.), *Tapping Hitler's Generals: Transcripts of Secret Conversations, 1942–45* (Bansley, South Yorkshire and St Paul, MN: Frontline Books and MBI Publishing Co., 2007).

Otdel po ispolzovaniiu opita voini General'nogo shtaba Krasnoi Armii, *Sbornik takticheskikh primerov po opitu Velikoi Otechestvennoi voini. No.2. mai–iiun' 1943 g.* (Moscow: Voennoe izdatel'stvo Narodnogo Komissariata Oboroni, 1943).

Pravda, 25 April 1936; 11 September 1936; 15 March 1939; 6 June 1939; 8 May 1940.

Radionov, A.M. et al (eds.), *Glavnoe avtobronetankovoe upravlenie. Liudi, sobitiia, fakti v dokumentakh – 1940–1942 gg.* (Moscow: GABTU, 2005).

Safir, V.M., 'Oborona Moskvi. Narofominskii proriv 1–5 dekabria 1941 goda (chto bilo i chego ne bilo v deistvitel'nosti)', in *Voenno-istoricheskii arkhiv*, vipusk 1 (1997), pp.77–125.

Samsonov, A.M., *Znat' i pomnit': Dialog istorika s chitatelem* (Moscow: Politizdat, 1988).

Tarkhova, N.S. (gen.ed.) et al, *Voennii sovet pri narodnom komissare oboroni SSSR. 1–4 iiunia 1937 g.: Dokumenti i materiali* (Moscow: ROSSPEN, 2008).

Trevor-Roper, H. (ed.), *Hitler's War Directives, 1939–1945* (London: Pan Books Ltd, 1966).

Veremeev, Iu., *Krasnaia Armiia v nachale Vtoroi mirovoi: Kak gotovilis' k voine soldati i marshali* (Moscow: Eksmo/Algoritm-izdat, 2010).

Povsednevnaia zhizn' vermakhta i RKKA nakanune voini (Moscow: Eksmo/Algoritm, 2011).

Vinogradov, V.K. et al (eds.), *Stalingradskaia epopeia: Vpervie publikuemie dokumenti rassekrechennie FSB RF: . . .* (Moscow: "Zvonnitsa-MG", 2000).

Voennaia elektrotekhnicheskaia akademiia sviazi im. SM. Budennogo. Kafedra voennoi radiotekhniki, *Kratkii spravochnik po voennim radiostantsiiam (dlia nachal'nika sviazi polka)* (Leningrad: Izdanie VETAS, 1941).

Volkovskii, N.L. (ed.), *Blokada Leningrada v dokumentakh rassekrechennikh arkhivov* (Moscow/Saint Petersburg: OOO "Izdatel'stvo AST"/OOO "Izdatel'stvo "Poligon", 2004).

Zamulin, V. (ed.), *Zasekrechennaia Kurskaia bitva. Neizvestnie dokumenti svidetel'stvuiut* (Moscow: Iauza/Eksmo, 2007).

Zhilin, V.A. (gen.ed.), *Bitva pod Moskvoi. Khronika, fakti, liudi: V 2-x kn. Kn.1 and 2* (Moscow: OLMA-PRESS, 2001 and 2002).

Stalingradskaia bitva. Khronika, fakti, liudi: V 2-x kn. Kn.1 and Kn.2 (Moscow: OLMA-PRESS, 2002).

Zhuravlev, V.P. et al (eds.), 'Pervie dni voini v dokumentakh', in *Vizh*, Number 5 (1989), pp.42–56.

Zolotarev, V.A. (gen.ed.) et al, *Russkii arkhiv: Velikaia Otechestvennaia.* T.12 (1), T.13 (2–1, 2–2 and 2–3), T.15 (4–1, 4–3, 4–4 and 4–5), T.16 (5–1, 5–2, 5–3 and 5–4), T.17–6 (1–2), T.20 (9), T.21 (10), T.23 (12–1, 12–2, 12–3 and 12–4), T.25 (14) (Moscow: "TERRA", 1994–1998).

PERSONAL DIARIES, INTERVIEWS, MEMOIRS AND OTHER EYEWITNESS TESTIMONY

Abdulin, M., *Ot Stalingrada do Dnepra. Pekhotinets. God na fronte* (Moscow: Iauza/Eksmo, 2010).

Anisimov, I.G.. et al (eds.), *Nasha strel'kovaia. Veterani 252-i divizii vspominaiut. Izdanie vtoroe, pererabotannoe i dopolnennoe* (Perm': Permskoe knizhnoe izdatel'stvo, 1987).

Antipenko, N.A., *Na glavnom napravlenii. Zapiski zamestitelia komanduiushchego frontom* (Moscow: Izdatel'stvo "Nauka", 1967).

Antonov, V.S., *Put' k Berlinu* (Moscow: Izdatel'stvo "Nauka", 1975).

Artem'ev, I.N., 'Radiosviaz' v sovetskom partizanskom dvizhenii v godi Velikoi Otechestvennoi voini', in *Voprosii istorii*, Number 5 (1969), pp.108–17.

Bagramian, I.Kh., *Tak nachalas' voina* (Moscow: Voenizdat, 1971).

Tak shli mi k pobede (Kiev: Politizdat Ukraini, 1988).

Batov, P.I., *Operatsiia "Oder". Boevie deistviia 65-i armii v Berlinskoi operatsii aprel'-mai 1945 goda* (Moscow: Voennoe izdatel'stvo Ministerstva oboroni SSSR, 1965).

Beloborodov, A.P., *Vsegda v boiu* (Moscow: Voennoe izdatel'stvo Ministerstvo oboroni SSSR, 1978).

Belov, P.A., *Za name Moskva* (Moscow: Voennoe izdatel'stvo Ministerstva Oboroni SSSR, 1963).

Bidermann, G.H., (Derek S. Zumbro trans. and ed.), *In Deadly Combat: A German Soldier's Memoir of the Eastern Front* (Lawrence, Kansas: University Press of Kansas, 2000).

Bograd, P., *Ot zapoliar'ia do Vengrii. Zapiski dvadtsatichetirekhletnogo podpolkovnika. 1941–1945* (Moscow: ZAO Tsentpoligraf, 2009).

Cherepanov, A.I., *Pole ratnoe moe* (Moscow: Voenizdat, 1984).

Chistiakov, I.M., *Sluzhim otchizne* (Moscow: Voennoe izdatel'stvo Ministerstva oboroni SSSR, 1975).

Chudodeev, Iu.V., (ed.), *V nebe Kitaia. 1937–1940. Vospominaniia sovetskikh letchikov-dobrovol`tsev. Izd. 2-e* (Moscow: Glavnaia redaktsiia vostochnoi literaturi izdatel'stva "Nauka", 1988).

Chuikov, V.I., *Konets tret'ego reikha* (Moscow: Izdatel'stvo "Sovetskaia Rossiia", 1973).

'O konflikte na KVZhD', in *Vizh*, Number 7 (1976), pp.49–57.

'Upravlenie i sviaz' v boiakh pod Stalingradom', in *Vizh*, Number 2 (1978), pp.72–8.

Drabkin, A.V. and Irincheev, B. (eds.), *"A zore zdes' gromkie". Zhenskoe litso voini* (Moscow: Eksmo/Iauza, 2012).

Drabkin, A.V. (ed.), *Ia dralsia na istrebitele. Priniavshie pervii udar. 1941–1942* (Moscow: Iauza, Eksmo, 2007).

Ia dralsia na T-34. Obe knigi odnim tomom! (Moscow: Iauza/Eksmo, 2010).

"I vse-taki mi pobedili!" Ia pomniu (Moscow: Iauza/Eksmo, 2010).

Drabkin, A. and Mikhin, P. (eds.), *Mi dralis' s "Tigrami"* (Moscow: Iauza/Eksmo, 2010).

Dragunskii, D.A., *Godi v brone. Izdanie tret'e, dopolnennoe* (Moscow: Voennoe izdatel'stvo Ministerstva oboroni SSSR, 1983).

Drobiazko, S.G., *Put' soldata. S boiami ot Kubani do Dnepra. 1942–1944* (Moscow: ZAO Tsentrpoligraf, 2008).

Dunaevskaia, I., *Ot Leningrad do Kenigsberga. Dnevnik voennoi perevodchitsi (1942–1945)* (Moscow: ROSSPEN, 2010).

Egorov, A.V., *S veroi v pobedu (zapiski komandira tankovogo polka)* (Moscow: Voenizdat, 1974).

Fediuninskii, I.I., *Podniatie po trevoge* (Moscow: Voennoe izdatel'stvo Ministerstvo oboroni SSSR, 1961).

Na Vostoke (Moscow: Voenizdat, 1985).

Frisner, G. [Hans Frießner], *Proigrannie srazheniia* (Moscow: Voennoe izdatel'stvo Ministerstva oboroni SSSR, 1966).

Fialkovskii, L., *Stalingradskii apokalipsis. Tankovaia brigade v adu* (Moscow: Iauza/Eksmo, 2011).

Filippov, E.I., *Frontovie budni komandira batarei. Vospominaniia o Velikoi Otechestvennoi voine* (Saint-Petersburg: Nestor-Istoriia, 2009).

Filippov, P., 'Kavaleristi v boiakh pod Tikhvinom', in *Vizh*, Number 1 (1976), pp.34–9.

Galitskii, I.P., *Dorogu otkrivali saperi* (Moscow: Voenizdat, 1983).

Getman, A.L., *Tanki idut na Berlin (1941–1945)* (Moscow: Izdatel'stvo "Nauka", 1973).

'112-ia tankovaia diviziia v bitve pod Moskvoi', in *Vizh*, Number 11 (1981), pp.49–52.

Glazunov, A., *Voina: v plenu, v partizanakh, v deistvuiushchei armii* (Moscow: Izdatel'stvo "Kanon+"/ROOI "Reabilitatsiia", 2012).

Golikov, F.I., *V Moskovskoi bitve. Zapiski komandarma* (Moscow: "Nauka", 1967).

Golovanov, A.E., *Dal'niaia bombardirovochnaia... Vospominaniia Glavnogo marshala aviatsii. 1941–1945* (Moscow: ZAO Tsentrpoligraf, 2008).

Gorbatov, A.V., *Godi i voini* (Moscow: Voennoe izdatel'stvo, 1989).

Grechko, A.A., *Bitva za Kavkaz* (Moscow: Voennoe izdatel'stvo, 1967).

Grigorenko, P.G., *Memoirs* (New York/London: WW. Norton and Company, 1982).

Guderian, H., *Panzer Leader* (London: Arrow Books Limited, 1990).

Gurney, J., *Crusade in Spain* (London: Faber and Faber Ltd, 1974).

Gurvits, L.A., *Vospominaniia frontovogo radista. Ot KV-radiostantsii - do morskikh krilatskikh raket* (Saint-Petersburg: "Kul't-inform-press", 2008).

Hager, E. (David Garden and Kenneth Andrew, eds.), *The War Diaries of a Panzer Soldier: Erich Hager with the 17th Panzer Division on the Russian Front 1941–1945* (Atglen, PA: Schiffer Military History, 2010).

Halder, F., *War Journal of Franz Halder. Volume VI [21 February 1941 – 31 July 1941] and Volume VII [1 August 1941 – 24 September 1942]* (Historical Division, SSUSA, 1950).

Hellbeck, J. (trans. Christopher Tauchen and Dominic Bonfiglio), *Stalingrad: The City that Defeated the Third Reich* (New York: Public Affairs, 2015).

Iakovlev, N.D., *Ob artillerii i nemnogo o sebe* (Moscow: Voennoe izdatel'stvo Ministerstva Oboroni SSSR, 1981).

Iakubovskii, I.I., *Zemlia v ogne* (Moscow: Voenizdat, 1975).

Iutilainen, I. [Ilmari Juutilainen], *Ia bil "stalinskikh sokolov". Luchshii finskii as Vtoroi Mirovoi* (Moscow: Iauza press, 2013).

Ivanovskii, E.F., *Ataku nachinali tankisti* (Moscow: Voennoe izdatel'stvo, 1984).

Katukov, M.E., *Na ostrie glavnogo udara. Izdanie tret'e* (Moscow: "Visshaia shkola", 1985).

Kazakov, M.I., *Nad kartoi bilikh srazhenii* (Moscow: Voennoe izdatel'stvo Ministerstvo oboroni SSSR, 1965).

Kazar'ian, A.V., *Prisiaga na vsiu zhizn'* (Moscow: Voennoe izdatel'stvo, 1988).

Khlebnikov, N.M., *Pod grokhot soten batarei* (Moscow: Voenizdat, 1974).

Khrenov, A.F., *Mosti k pobede* (Moscow: Voennoe izdatel'stvo Ministerstvo oboroni SSSR, 1982).

Kobilianskii, I.G., *Priamoi navodkoi po vragu* (Moscow: Iauza/Eksmo, 2005).

Konev, I.S., *Sorok piatii. Izdanie vtoroe, ispravlennoe i dopolnennoe* (Moscow: Voennoe izdatel'stvo Ministerstva oboroni SSSR, 1970).

Zapiski komanduiushchego frontom. 1943–1945 (Moscow: "Nauka", 1985).

Koshelev, A.I. (ed.), *Sovetsko-iaponskie voini 1937–1945: sbornik* (Moscow: Iauza; Eksmo, 2009).

Knappe, S. with Brusaw, T., *Soldat: Reflections of a German Soldier, 1936–1949* (New York: Dell Publishing, 1992).

Krilov, N.I., *Stalingradskii rubezh. Izdanie vtoroe* (Moscow: Voennoe izdatel'stvo, 1984).

Kumanev, G.A., 'Otvet P.K. Ponomarenko na voprosi G.A. Kumaneva. 2 noiabria 1978 g.', *Otechestvennaia istoriia*, Number 6 (1998), pp.133–49.

Kurochkin, P.M., *Pozivnie fronta* (Moscow: Voennoe izdatel'stvo Ministerstvo oboroni SSSR, 1969).

Kuznetsov, N.G., 'Voenno-Morskoi Flot nakanune Velikoi Otechestvennoi voini', in *Vizh*, Number 9 (1965), pp.59–76.

Nakanune (Moscow: Voennoe izdatel'stvo Ministerstva oboroni SSSR, 1966).

Na dalekom meridian. Vospominaniia uchastnika natsional'n-revolutsionnoi voini v Ispanii. 3-e izd., ispr. (Moscow: "Nauka", 1988).

Lebedenko, P.P., *V izluchine Dona* (Moscow: Voennoe izdatel'stvo Ministerstva oboroni SSSR, 1965).

Leliushenko, D.D., *Zaria pobedi* (Moscow: Voennoe izdatel'stvo Ministerstva oboroni SSSR, 1966).

Moskva-Stalingrad-Berlin-Praga. Zapiski komandarma (Moscow: Izdatel'stvo "Nauka", 1971).

Liashchenko, N.G., *Vremia vibralo nas* (Moscow: Voennoe izdatel'stvo, 1990).

Liudnikov, I.I., *Doroga dlinoiu v zhizn'* (Moscow: Voennoe izdatel'stvo Ministerstva oboroni SSSR, 1969).

Lubbeck, W., *At Leningrad's Gates: The Story of a Soldier with Army Group North* (Newbury and Havertown, PA: Casemate Publishers, 2006).

Lukinov, M.I., 'Notes on the Polish Campaign (1939) and the War with Finland (1939–1940)', in *JSMS*, Volume 14, Number 3 (September 2001), pp.120–49.

Maistrovskii, M.Ia. (ed.), *Na pravom flange Moskovskoi bitvi* (Tver': Moskovskii rabochii, 1991).

Malishev, V.A., '"Proidet desiatok let, i eti vstrechi ne vosstanovish' uzhe v pamiati"', in *Vestnik Arkhiva Prezidenta Rossiiskoi Federatsii*, Number 5 (1997), pp.103–47.

Mal'tsev, E.E., *V godi ispitanii* (Moscow: Voennoe izdatel'stvo Ministerstva oboroni SSSR, 1979).

Mannerheim, M., *The Memoirs of Marshal Mannerheim* (New York: E.P. Dutton and Company, inc., 1954).

Field Marshal von Manstein, E., *Lost Victories* (Minneapolis, MA: Zenith Press, 2004).

Lieutenant-General Martel, S.G., *The Russian Outlook* (London: Michael Joseph Ltd, 1947).

Maslov, A.G., 'I Returned From Prison! 1', in *JSMS*, Volume 18, Number 2 (June 2005), pp.305–45.

von Mellenthin, F.W., *Panzer Battles* (London: Futura Publications Ltd, 1973).

Meretskov, K.A., *Na sluzhbe narodu. Stranitsi vospominanii* (Moscow: Izdatel'stvo politicheskoi literaturi, 1968).

Mikhin, P.A., *"Artilleristi, Stalin dal prikaz!". Mi umirali, chtobi pobedit'* (Moscow: Iauza, Eksmo, 2006).

Mikoian, A., *Tak bilo. Razmishleniia o minuvshem* (Moscow: Tsentrpoligraf, 2014).

Moskalenko, K.S., *Na iugo-zapadnom napravlenii. 1943–1945. Vospominaniia komandarma* (Moscow: izdatel'stvo "Nauka", 1972).

General-major Morzik, a.D., *German Air Force Airlift Operations* (Research Studies Institute, Air University, USAF Historical Division, June 1961).

Moshliak, I.N., *Vspomnim mi pekhotu* (Moscow: Voennoe izdatel'stvo Ministerstvo oboroni SSSR, 1978).

Nadisev, G.S., *Na sluzhbe shtabnoi. Izdanie vtoroe, ispravlennoe i dopolnennoe* (Moscow: Voennoe izdatel'stvo Ministerstva oboroni SSSR, 1976).

Newton, S.H. (trans. and ed.), *Kursk: The German View. Eyewitness Reports of Operation Citadel by the German Commanders* (Cambridge, MA: Da Capo Press, 2002).

Nikulin, Iu.V., *Sem' dolgikh let* (Moscow: AST, 2014).

Nikulin, N.N., *Vospominaniia o voine* (Moscow: AST, 2014).

Novikov, M.V., 'U ozera Khasan', in *Vizh*, Number 8 (1968), pp.205–8.

Novokhatskii, I., *Vospominaniia komandira batarei. Divizionnaia artilleriia v godi Velikoi Otechestvennoi voini. 1941–1945* (Moscow: ZAO Tsentropoligraf, 2007).

Parot'kin, I.V., (ed.), *Kurskaia bitva* (Moscow: Izdatel'stvo "Nauka", 1970).

Pliev, I.A., *Dorogami voini* (Moscow: Veche, 2015).

Pokrishkin, A., *Poznat' sebia v boiu. "Stalinskie sokoli" protiv asov Liuftvaffe. 1941–1945 gg.* (Moscow: ZAO Tsentrpoligraf, 2008).

Popov, N.S. (gen.ed.), *Konstruktor boevikh mashin* (Leningrad: Lenizdat, 1988).

Ponomarenko, P.K., 'Bor'ba Sovetskogo naroda v tilu vraga', in *Vizh*, Number 4 (1965), pp.26–36.

Priklonskii, E., *Dnevnik samokhodchika. Boevoi put' mekhanika-voditelia ISU-152. 1942–1945* (Moscow: ZAO Tsentropoligraf, 2008).

Raus, E. (Steven H. Newton trans. and ed.), *Panzer Operations: The Eastern Front Memoir of General Raus, 1941–1945* (Cambridge, MA: Da Capo Press, 2003).

Resis, A. (ed.), *Molotov Remembers: Inside Kremlin Politics. Conversations with Felix Chuev* (Chicago: Ivan R. Dee, 1993).

Richardson, W. and Freidlin, S. (eds.), *The Fatal Decisions: Six Decisive Battles of WWII from the Viewpoint of the Vanquished* (Mechanicsburg, PA: Stackpole Books, 2013).

Rokossovskii, K.K., *Soldatskii dolg* (Moscow: Voenizdat, 1972).

'Soldatskii dolg', in *Vizh*, Number 4 (1989), pp.52–7.

Roslii, I.P., *Poslednii prival – v Berline* (Moscow: Voennoe izdatel'stvo, 1983).

Roth, H. (Christine Alexander and Mason Kunze (eds.)), *Eastern Inferno: The Journals of a German Panzerjäger on the Eastern Front, 1941–43* (Havertown, PA and Newbury: Casemate Publishers, 2010).

Rotmistrov, P.A. *Vremia i tanki* (Moscow: Voennoe izdatel'stvo Ministerstva oboroni SSSR, 1972).

'V srazhenii pod Prokhorovkoi i Korsun'-Shevchenkovskim', in *Vizh*, Number 2 (1978), pp.78–84.

Russiianov, I.N., *V boiakh rozhdennaia...* (Moscow: Voenizdat, 1982).

Saltikov, N.D., *Dokladivaiu v General'nii shtab* (Moscow: Voenizdat, 1983).

Samsonov, A.M. (ed.), *Proval gitlerovskogo nastupleniia na Moskvu. 25 let razgroma nemetsko-fashistskikh voisk pod Moskvoi. 1941–1966* (Moscow: "Nauka", 1966).

9 maia 1945 goda (Moscow: Izdatel'stvo "Nauka", 1970).

Osvobozhdenie Belorussii 1944 (Moscow: Izdatel'stvo "Nauka", 1970).

Sandalov, L.M., *Perezhitoe* (Moscow: Voennoe izdatel'stvo Ministerstva oboroni SSSR, 1966).

Na Moskovskom napravlenii (Moscow: Veche, 2010).

Schäufler, H. (ed.), *Knight's Cross Panzers: The German 35th Panzer Regiment in WWII* (Mechanicsburg, PA: Stackpole Books, 2010).

Generalleutnant Schwabedissen, a.D., *The Russian Air Force in the eyes of German Commanders* (USAF Historical Division, Research Studies Institute, Air University, June 1960).

Semenov, G.G., *Nastupaet udarnaia* (Moscow: Voennoe izdatel'stvo, 1986).

Shaposhnikov, M., 'Boevie deistviia 5-go Mekhanizirovannogo korpusa zapadnee Surovkino v dekabre 1942 goda', in *Vizh*, Number 10 (1982), pp.32–38.

Shatilov, V.M., *Znamia nad reikhstagom* (Moscow: Voennoe izdatel'stvo Ministerstva oboroni SSSR, 1966).

Shebunin, A.I., *Skol'ko nami proideno...* (Moscow: Voennoe izdatel'stvo Ministerstvo oboroni SSSR, 1971).

Shoror, V.Ia.(ed.), *Khalkhin-Gol: Kniga druzhbi i pamiati* (Moscow: Voenizdat, 1990).

Sheinis, Z.S.(ed.), *Stalingrad: Uroki istorii. Vospominaniia uchastnikov bitvi. Vtoroe izdanie* (Moscow: Izdatel'stvo 'Progress', 1980).

Shelkov, M., *Zapiski komandira strelkovogo batal'ona. Ot Rzheva do Vostochnoi Prussii. 1942–1945* (Moscow: ZAO Izdatel'stvo Tsentrpoligraf, 2010).

Shtemenko, S.M., *The Soviet General Staff at War. 1941–1945* (Moscow: Progress Publishers, 1970).

General'nii shtab v godi voini. Ot Stalingrad do Berlina (Moscow: AST/Tranzit-kniga, 2005).

Simonov, K., *Glazami cheloveka moego pokoleniia* (Moscow: Izdatel'stvo Agenstva pechati Novosti, 1988).

Skvirskii, L.S., 'Vospominaniia. V predvoennie godi', in *Voprosii istorii*, Number 9 (1989), pp.55–68.

Slobodin, K.M. and Listrovoi, V.D. (eds.), *T-34: put' k Pobede: Vospominaniia tankostroitelei i tankistov. 2-e izd., dop.* (Kiev: Politizdat Ukraini, 1989).

Sobolev, A., *Razvedka boem. Zapiski voiskovogo razvedchika* (Moscow: Moskovski rabochii, 1975).

Srazhenie veka (Moscow: Izdatel'stvo "Sovetskaia Rossiia", 1975).

Suknev, M., *Zapiski komandira shtrafbata. Vospominaniia kombata. 1941–1945* (Moscow: ZAO Tsentrpoligraf, 2006).

Sverdlov, F.D., 'What's New about A Well-Known Raid: A Selection from A Suppressed Memoir', in *JSMS* Volume 8, Number 4 (1995), pp.861–71.

Tarasenko, A., 'Tankisti-remontniki v boiakh pod Moskvoi', in *Vizh*, Number 1 (1982), pp.53–58.

Tiulenev, I., *Cherez tri voini. Vospominaniia komanduiushchego Iuzhnim i Zakavkazkim frontam. 1941–1945* (Moscow: ZAO Tsentpoligraf, 2007).

Tributz, V.F., *Baltiitsi srazhaiutsia* (Moscow: Veche, 2015).

Vakhromeev, V., *Vizhit' i vernut'sia. Odisseia sovetskogo voennoplennogo. 1941–1945* (Moscow: ZAO Izdatel'stvo Tsentrpoligraf, 2011).

Vannikov, B.L., 'Zapiski narkoma', in *Znamia*, Number 1 (1988), pp.130–60.

Vasilevskii, A.M., *Delo vsei zhizni. Kn.1 and 2. 6-e izd.* (Moscow: Politizdat, 1989).

Vasilevskii, A. and Zakharov, M., 'Nachal'nika Genshtaba (fragmenti iz predsloviia k "Vospominaniiam B.M. Shaposhnikova)', in Rusakova, E.V. (ed.), *Polkovodtsi. Sbornik* (Moscow: Izdatel'stvo "Roman-gazeta", 1995), pp.352–64.

Velikolepov, N.N., *Ogon' radi pobedi* (Moscow: Voennoe izdatel'stvo Ministerstvo oboroni SSSR, 1977).

Vetrov, A.A, 'V boiakh na Ebro', in *Vizh*, Number 4 (1969), pp.72–82.

'Neprevzoidennaia "Tridtsat'chetverka"', in *Voprosi istorii*, Number 5 (1982), pp.89–100.

Tak i bilo (Moscow: Voennoe izdatel'stvo Ministerstvo oboroni SSSR, 1982).

Vladimirov, Iu. V., *Voina soldata-zenitchika: ot studencheskoi skam'i do Khar'kovskogo kotla. 1941–1942* (Moscow: ZAO Tsentrpoligraf, 2010).

Voloshin, M.A., *Razvedchiki vsegda vperedi* (Moscow: Voenizdat, 1977).

Voronov, N.N., *Na sluzhbe voennoi* (Moscow: Voennoe izdatel'stvo Ministerstva oboroni SSSR, 1963).

Wallin, E. (T. Hillblad ed.), *Twilight of the Gods: A Swedish Volunteer in the 11th SS Panzergrenadier Division "Nordland" on the Eastern Front* (Mechanicsburg, PA: Stackpole Books, 2009).

Werth, A., *Russia at War 1941–1945* (London: Pan Books Ltd, 1965).

Zakharov, *General'nii shtab v predvoennie godi* (Moscow: Voennoe izdatel'stvo, 1989).

Zhadov, A.S., *Chetire goda voini* (Moscow: Voenizdat, 1978).

Zhagala, V.M., *Raschishchaia put' pekhote...* (Moscow: Voennoe izdatel'stvo, 1985).

Zherebov, D.K. (ed.), *Tikhvin, god 1941-i* (Leningrad: Lenizdat, 1974).

Zhilin, V.Ia. (ed.), *"Eto bilo na ognennoi duge"* (*Vospominaniia gubkintsev-uchasnikov Kurskoi bitvi*) (Gubkin: Gubkinskii gorodskoi Sovet veteranov, 1993).

Zhukov, G.K., *Vospominaniia i razmishleniia. V 3-x tomakh. T.1 – 12-e izdanie. Tom 1 to 3* (Moscow: AO 'Izdatel'stvo "Novosti"', 1995).

Zinchenko, F.M., *Geroi shturma reikhstaga* (Moscow: Voenizdat, 1983).

SELECTED SECONDARY SOURCES

'Moskovskaia bitva v tsifrakh (period oboroni)', in *Vizh*, Number 3 (1967), pp.69–79.

'Moskovskaia bitva v tsifrakh (period kontrnastupleniia)', in *Vizh*, Number 1 (1967), pp.89–101.

Abrosov, S.B., 'Sovetskaia aviatsiia v grazhdanskoi voine v Ispanii', in *Vizh*, Number 8 (2012), pp.36–40.

Anan'ev, I.M., *Tankovie armii v nastuplenii: Po opitu Velikoi Otechestvennoi voini 1941–1945 gg.* (Moscow: Voenizdat, 1988).

Armstrong, J.A. (ed.), *Soviet Partisans in World War II* (Madison, Wisconsin: The University of Wisconsin Press, 1964).

Åselius, G., *The Rise and Fall of the Soviet Navy in the Baltic, 1921–1941* (London/ New York: Frank Cass, 2005).

Ashcheulov, O.E., *Artilleriia Krasnoi armii 1941–1943 gg. Istoriia organizatsii i boevogo primeneniia* (Moscow: "MPPA BIMPA", 2009).

Bellamy, C., *Absolute War: Soviet Russia in the Second World War* (London: Pan Books, 2009).

Beloborodov, A.P. (gen.ed.), *Voennie kadri sovetskogo gosudarstva v Velikoi Otechestvennoi voine 1941–1945 gg. (spravochno-statistichekie materiali)* (Moscow: Voennoe izdatel'stvo Ministerstva oboroni SSSR, 1963).

Berkhoff, K.C., *Motherland in Danger: Soviet Propaganda in World War II* (Cambridge, Massachusetts/London, England: Harvard University Press, 2012).

Bistrova, I.V., *Sovetskii voenno-promishlennii kompleks: problem stanovleniia i razvitiia (1930–1980-e godi)* (Moscow: Ros. Akad. Nauka, In-t ros. istorii, 2006).

Bobrov, M.A., 'Strategicheskoe razvertivanie VVS Krasnoi armii na zapade strani pered Velikoi Otechestvennoi voinoi', in *Vizh*, No.5 (2006), pp.3–7.

Boog, H. et al, *Germany and the Second World War. Volume IV. The Attack on the Soviet Union* (Oxford: Clarendon Press, 1998).
   Das Deutsche Reich und der Zweite Weltkrieg. Band 10. Erster Halbband. Der Zusammenbruch des Deutschen Reiches, 1945. Die militärische Niederwerfung der Wehrmacht (München: Deutsche Verlags-Anstalt, 2008).

Bosworth, R.J.B. and Maiolo, J.A. (eds.), *The Cambridge History of the Second World War. Volume II. Politics and Ideology* (Cambridge: Cambridge University Press, 2015)

Budnitskii, O., 'Muzhchini i zhenshchini v Krasnoi armii (1941–1945)', in *Cahiers du Monde russe*, Volume 52, Number 2–3 (April–September 2011), pp.405–22.

Budnitskii, O. and Morton, J. 'The Great Patriotic War and Soviet Society: Defeatism, 1941–42', in *Kritika: Explorations in Russian and Eurasian History*, Volume 15, Number 4 (Fall 2014), pp.767–97.

Carrell, P., *Hitler Moves East, 1941–1943* (New York: Bantam Books, 1966).

Citino, R.M., *Death of the Wehrmacht: The German Campaigns of 1942* (Lawrence, Kansas: University Press of Kansas, 2007).

Coox, A.D., *Nomonhan: Japan against Russia, 1939* (Stanford, California: Stanford University Press, 1985).

Davtian, S.M., *Piataia vozdushnaia. Voenno-istoricheskii ocherk boevogo puti 5-i vozdushnoi armii v godi Velikoi Otechestvennoi voini* (Moscow: Voenizdat, 1990).

DiNardo, R.L., *Germany and the Axis Powers: From Coalition to Collapse* (Lawrence, Kansas: University Press of Kansas, 2005).

Drig, E., *Mekhanizirovannie korpusa RKKA v boiu: Istoriia avtobronetankovikh voisk Krasnoi Armii v 1940–1941 godakh* (Moscow: AST/Tranzitkniga, 2005).

van Dyke, C., *The Soviet Invasion of Finland, 1939–1940* (London/Portland, OR: Frank Cass, 1997).

Edele, M., 'What Are We Fighting for? Loyalty in the Soviet War Effort, 1941–1945', in *International Labor and Working-Class History*, Number 84 (Fall 2013), pp.248–68.
   'Towards a Sociocultural History of the Soviet Second World War', in *Kritika: Explorations in Russian and Eurasian History*, Volume 15, Number 4 (Fall 2014), pp.829–35.

Erickson, J., *The Soviet High Command: A Military-Political History, 1918–1941* (London: Macmillan and Company Ltd, 1962).

The Road to Stalingrad: Stalin's War with Germany: Volume One (London: Weidenfeld and Nicholson, 1993).

Ermolov, A.Iu., *Gosudarstvennoe upravlenie voennoi primishlennost'iu v 1940-e godi: Tankovaia promishlennost'* (Saint-Petersburg: Aleteiia, 2013).

Ferris, J. and Mawdsley, E. (eds.), *The Cambridge History of the Second World War. Volume I. Fighting the War* (Cambridge: Cambridge University Press, 2015).

Friesner, K. et al, *Das Deutsche Reich und der Zweite Weltkrieg. Band 8. Die Ostfront 1943/44. Der Krieg im Osten und an den Nebenfronten* (Munich: Deutsche Verlags-Anstalt, 2007).

Gladkikh, P.F. and Loktev, A.E., *Ocherki istorii otechestvennoi voennoi meditsini. Sluzhba zdorov'ia v Velikoi Otechestvennoi voine 1941–1945 gg.* (St Petersburg: "Dmitrii Bulganin", 2005)

Glantz, D.M, *Soviet Military Intelligence in War* (Abingdon, Oxon/New York: Frank Cass, 1990).

Colossus Stumbling: The Red Army on the Eve of World War (Lawrence, Kansas: University Press of Kansas, 1998).

Zhukov's Greatest Defeat: The Red Army's Epic Disaster in Operation Mars, 1942 (Lawrence, Kansas: University Press of Kansas, 1999).

Reborn Colossus: The Red Army at War, 1941–1943 (Lawrence, KA: University Press of Kansas, 2005).

'Stalin's Strategic Intentions, 1941–1945: Soviet Military Operations as Indicators of Stalin's Postwar Territorial Ambitions', in *JSMS*, Volume 27, Number 4 (2014), pp.676–720.

Glantz, D.M., with House, J.M., *Armageddon in Stalingrad, September-November 1942: The Stalingrad Trilogy, Volume 2* (Lawrence, KA: The University Press of Kansas, 2009).

To the Gates of Stalingrad: Soviet-German Combat Operations, April-August 1942. The Stalingrad Trilogy, Volume 1 (Lawrence, KA: The University Press of Kansas, 2009).

Endgame at Stalingrad: The Stalingrad Trilogy, Volume 3. Book One: November 1942 (Lawrence, KA: The University Press of Kansas, 2014).

Endgame at Stalingrad: The Stalingrad Trilogy, Volume 3. Book Two: December 1942 – February 1943 (Lawrence, KA: The University Press of Kansas, 2014).

Golushko, I.M., *Shtab tila krasnoi armii v godi voini 1941–1945* (Moscow: Izdatel'stvo "Ekonomika i informatika", 1998).

Gorbach, V., *Aviatsiia v Kurskoi bitve* (Moscow: Iauza/Eksmo, 2008).

Gorbunov, E.A., *Vostochnii rubezh. OKDVA protiv iaponskoi armii* (Moscow: Veche, 2010).

Gordon, Y. and Khazanov, D., *Soviet Combat Aircraft of the Second World War. Volume One: Single-Engined Fighters* (Earl Shilton, Leics: Midland Publishing Limited, 1998) and *Volume Two: Twin-Engined Fighters, Attack Aircraft and Bombers* (Earl Shilton, Leics: Midland Publishing Limited, 1999).

Gradosel'skii, V.V., 'National'nie voinskie formirovaniia v Velikoi Otechestvennoi voine', in *Vizh*, Number 1 (2002), pp.18–24.

Gross, J.T., *Revolution from Abroad: The Soviet Conquest of Poland's Western Ukraine and Western Belorussia. Expanded Edition* (Princeton and Oxford: Princeton University Press, 2002).

Hardesty, V. and Grinberg, I., *Red Phoenix Rising: The Soviet Air Force in World War II* (Lawrence, Kansas: University Press of Kansas, 2012).

Harrison, M., *Accounting for War: Soviet Employment, Accounting and the Defence Burden, 1940–1945* (Cambridge: Cambridge University Press, 1996).

Harrison, R.W., *Architect of Soviet Victory in World War II: The Life and Theories of G.S. Isserson* (Jefferson, NC: McFarland and Company Inc., 2010).

Hayward, J.S.A., *Stopped at Stalingrad: The Luftwaffe and Hitler's Defeat in the east, 1942–1943* (Lawrence, Kansas: University Press of Kansas, 1998).

Heer, H. and Naumann, K. (eds.), *War of Extermination: The German Military in World War II, 1941–1944* (New York/Oxford: Berghann Books, 2004).

Hill, A., *The War Behind the Eastern Front: The Soviet Partisan Movement in North-West Russia, 1941–1944* (Abingdon, Oxon: Frank Cass, 2005).

'British Lend-Lease Aid and the Soviet War Effort, June 1941-June 1942', in *The Journal of Military History*, Volume 71, Number 3 (July 2007), pp.773–808.

'Russian and Soviet Naval Power in the Arctic from the XVI Century to the Beginning of the Great Patriotic War', in *JSMS*, Volume 20, Number 3 (July–September 2007), pp. 359–92.

'British Lend-Lease Tanks and the Battle of Moscow, November–December 1941 – Revisited', in *JSMS*, Volume 22, Number 4 (October–December 2009), pp.574–87.

'Offense, Defence, or the Worst of Both Worlds? Soviet strategy in May-June 1941', in *The Journal of Military and Strategic Studies*, Volume 13, Number 1 (Fall 2010), pp.61–74.

'The Bear's New Wheels (and Tracks): US-Armored and Other Vehicles and Soviet Military Effectiveness during the Great Patriotic War in Words and Photographs', in *JSMS*, Volume 25, Number 2 (2012), pp.204–19.

Howell, E.M., *The Soviet Partisan Movement 1941–1944. DA Pam 20–244* (Washington DC: Department of the Army, 1956).

Istomin, V.P., *Smolenskaia nastupatel'naia operatsiia (1943 g.)* (Moscow: Voenizdat, 1975).

Jentz, T.L. (ed.), *Panzertruppen: The Complete Guide to the Creation and Combat Employment of Germany's Tank Force, 1933–1942* and *1943–1945* (Atglen, PA: Schiffer Military History, 1996).

Khlevniuk, O.V, 'Stalin na voine. Istochniki i ikh interpretatsiia', in *Cahiers du Monde russe*, Volume 52, Number 2–3 (April–September 2011), pp. 205–19.

Stalin: New Biography of a Dictator (New Haven and London: Yale University Press, 2015).

Kirsanov, N.A., 'Natsional'nie formirovaniia Krasnoi Armii v Velikoi Otechestvennoi voine 1941–1945 godov', in *Otechestvennaia istoriia*, Number 4 (1995), pp. 116–26.

'Mobilizatsiia zhenshchin v Krasnuiu armiiu v godi fashistskogo nashestviia', in *Vizh*, Number 5 (2007), pp. 15–17.

Kochanski, H., *The Eagle Unbowed: Poland and the Poles in the Second World War* (London/New York: Allen Lane, 2012).

Kondrashov, V.V., *Znat' vse o protivnike. Voennie razvedki SSSR i fashistskoi Germanii v godi Velikoi Otechestvennoi voini (istoricheskaia khronika)* (Moscow: Izdatel'skii dom "Krasnaia Zvezda", 2010).

Kondrat'ev, V.I., *Bitva nad step'iu. Aviatsiia v sovetsko-iaponskom vooruzhennom konflikte na reke Khalkhin – Gol* (Moscow: Fond sodeistviia aviatsii "Russkie vitiazi", 2008).

Kovalev, I.V., *Transport v Velikoi Otechestvennoi voine (1941–1945 gg.)* (Moscow: "Nauka", 1981).

Kozhevnikov, M.N., *Komandovanie i shtab VVS Sovetskoi Armii v Velikoi Otechestvennoi voine 1941–1945 gg.* (Moscow: Izdatel'stvo "Nauka", 1977).

Kozlov, M.M. (ed.), *Akademiia General'nogo shtaba. Istoriia . . .akademii General'nogo staba Vooruzhennikh Sil SSSR imeni K.E. Voroshilova. Izdanie vtoroe. . .* (Moscow: Voennoe izdatel'stvo, 1987).

Krivosheev, G.F., 'O poteriiakh sredi zhenshchin-voennosluzhashchikh i vol'nonaemnogo sostava', in *Vizh*, Number 1 (2005), p.5.

Krivosheev, G.F. (ed.), *Soviet Casualties and Combat Losses in the Twentieth Century* (London: Greenhill Books, 1997).

Krylova, A., *Soviet Women in Combat: A History of Violence on the Eastern Front* (New York: Cambridge University Press, 2010).

Kumanev, G.A., *Problemi voennoi istorii otechestva (1938–1945 gg.)* (Moscow: OOO "Izdatel'stvo "Sobranie", 2007).

Lopez, Zh. [J. Lopez] and Otkhmezuri, L., *Zhukov. Portret na fone epokhi* (Moscow: ZAO Izdatel'stvo Tsentrpoligraf, 2015).

Lopukhovsky, L. (trans. and ed. Stuart Britton), *The Viaz'ma Catastrophe, 1941: The Red Army's Disastrous Stand Against Operation Typhoon* (Solihull: Helion and Company, 2013).

Losik, O.A. (gen.ed.), *Istoriia tankovikh voisk Sovetskoi armii. V trekh tomakh. Tom pervii. Zarozhdenie i razvitie tankovikh voisk Sovetskoi armii do Velikoi Otechestvennoi voini (1917–1941 gg.)* (Moscow: Izdanie Akademii bronetankovikh voisk imeni Marshala Sovetskogo soiuza Malinovskogo, 1975).

Maier, K.A. et al, *Germany and the Second World War, Volume 2: Germany's Initial Conquests in Europe* (Oxford: Oxford University Press, 1991).

Maliugin, N., 'Razvitie i sovershenstvovanie tila strelkovoi divizii v godi voini', in *Vizh*, Number 11 (1978), pp.87–94.

Marwick, R.D. *and* Cardona, E.C., *Soviet Women on the Frontline in the Second World War* (Basingstoke, Hampshire: Palgrave Macmillan, 2012).

Mawdsley, E., 'Crossing the Rubicon: Soviet Plans for Offensive War in 1940–1941', in *The International History Review*, Volume 25, Number 4 (December 2003), pp.818–65.

'Stalin: Victors are not Judged', in *JSMS*, Volume 19, Number 4 (2006), pp.705–25.

Thunder in the East: The Nazi-Soviet War 1941–1945 (Oxford: Hodder Arnold, 2005).

Mel'nikov, P.V. (gen.ed.), *Razvitie taktiki sukhoputnikh voisk v Velikoi Otechestvennoi voine* (Moscow: Izdanie akademii [imeni M.V. Frunze], 1981).

Mel'tiukhov, M., *Pribaltiiskii platsdarm (1939–1940 gg.). Vozvrashchenie Sovetskogo Soiuza na berega Baltiiskogo moria* (Moscow: Izdatel'stvo Algoritm, 2014).

Sovetsko-pol'skie voini. 2-e izd. Ispr. i dop. (Moscow: "Iauza", "Eksmo", 2004).

Merridale, P.V., *Ivan's War: Life and Death in the Red Army, 1939–1945* (New York: Picador, 2006).

Mertsalov, A.N. and Mertsalova, L.A., *Stalinizm i voina. Iz neprochitannikh stranits istorii (1930–1990-e)* (Moscow: Izdatel'stvo "Rodnik", 1994).

Mil'bakh, V.S., *Osobaia Krasnoznamennaia Dal'nevostochnaia armiia (Krasnoznamennii Dalnevostochnii front). Politicheskie repressii komandno-nachal'stvuiushchego sostava, 1937–1938 gg.* (Saint-Petersburg: Izdatel'stvo Sankt-Peterburgskogo universiteta, 2007).

Millet, A.R. and Murray, W. (eds.), *Military Effectiveness. Volume 2: The Interwar Period. New Edition* (Cambridge: Cambridge University Press, 2010).

Military Effectiveness. Volume 3: The Second World War. New Edition (Cambridge: Cambridge University Press, 2010).

Mukhin, M.Iu., *Aviapromishlennost' SSSR v 1921–1941 godakh* (Moscow: "Nauka", 2006).

Sovetskaia aviapromishlennost' v godi Velikoi Otechestvennoi voini (Moscow: Veche, 2011).

Mueller-Hillebrand, B., *Das Heer 1933–1945. Entwicklung des organisatorischen Aufbaues. Band III. Der Zweifrontenkrieg. Das Heer vom Beginn des Feldzuges gegen die Sowjetunion bis zum Kriegsende* (Frankfurt am Main: Verlag E.S. Mittler and Sohn, 1969).

Nevenkin, K., *Take Budapest!: The Struggle for Hungary, Autumn 1944* (Stroud, Gloucestershire: Spellmount, 2012).

Nikonova, O.Iu., *Vostanie patriotov: Osoaviakhim in voennaia podgotovka naseleniia v ural'skoi provintsii (1927–1941 gg.)* (Moscow: Novii khronograf, 2010).

Novikov, V.N. (gen.ed.), *Oruzhie pobedi* (Moscow: "Mashinostroenie", 1987).

Radey, J. and Sharp, C., *The Defense of Moscow 1941: The Northern Flank* (Mechanicsburg, PA: Stackpole Books, 2012).

Radzievskii, A. I. (gen.ed.), *Taktika v boevikh primerakh. Polk* (Moscow: Voennoe izdatel'stvo Ministerstva oboroni SSSR, 1974).

Tankovii udar (tankovaia armiia v nastupatel'noi operatsii fronta po opitu Velikoi Otechestvennoi voini) (Moscow: Voenizdat, 1977).

Reese, R.R., *Stalin's Reluctant Soldiers: A Social History of the Red Army, 1925–1941* (Lawrence, Kansas: University Press of Kansas, 1996).

Red Commanders: A Social History of the Soviet Army Officer Corps, 1918–1991 (Lawrence, KS: University Press of Kansas, 2005).

Why Stalin's Soldier's Fought: The Red Army's Military Effectiveness in World War II (Lawrence, KA: University Press of Kansas, 2011).

Roberts, G., *Stalin's General: The Life of Georgy Zhukov* (New York: Random House Inc., 2012),

Rubtsov, Iu.V., *Iz-za spini vozhdia. Politicheskaia i voennaia deiatel'nost' L.Z. Mekhlis. Izd. 2-e, ispravl.* (Moscow: OOO "Kompaniia Ritm Esteit", 2003).

Rukkas, A., 'The Red Army's Troop Mobilization in the Kiev Special Military District during September 1939', in *JSMS*, Volume 16, Number 1 (March 2003), pp.105–36.

Rusanov, V.Iu. (ed.), *Velikaia Otechestvennaia. Komandarmi. Voenno-biograficheskii slovar'* (Moscow/Zhukovskii: Kuchkovo pole, 2005).

Rutherford, J., *Combat and Genocide on the Eastern Front: The German Infantry's War, 1941–1944* (Cambridge: Cambridge University Press, 2014).

Sakharov, A.N. and Khristoforov, A.N. (gen.eds.), *K 70-letiiu nachala Vtoroi mirovoi voini. Issledovaniia, dokumenti, kommentarii* (Moscow: Institut rossiiskoi istorii RAN, 2009).

Shepherd, B., *War in the Wild East: The German Army and Soviet Partisans* (Cambridge, MA/London: Harvard University Press, 2004).

Shein, D., *Tanki vedet ribalko. Boevoi put' 3-i Gvardeiskoi tankovoi armii* (Moscow: "Iauza"/Eksmo, 2007).

Shukman, H. (ed.), *Stalin's Generals* (London: Wiedenfeld and Nicholson, 1993).

Shunkov, V.N., *Artilleriia Krasnoi Armii i Vermakhta Vtoroi mirovoi voini* (Moscow: AST/Minsk: Kharvest, 2005).

Shutov, Z., 'Strelkovii batal'on v oborone na Kurskoi duge', in *Vizh*, Number 4 (1978), pp.52–7.

Simonov, N., *Voenno-promishlennii kompleks SSSR v 1920–1950-e godi* (Moscow: ROSSPEN, 1996).

Soliankin, A.G. et al, *Otechestvennie bronirovannie mashini. XX vek.: Nauchnoe izdanie: V 4 t. Tom 1. Otechestvennie bronirovannie mashini. 1905–1941 gg.* (Moscow: OOO Izdatel'skii tsentr "Eksprint", 2002) and *Otechestvennie bronirovannie mashini. Tom 2. 1941–1945* (Moscow: Izdatel'skii tsentr "Eksprint", 2005).

Sokolov, B., *Budennii. Krasnii miurat* (Moscow: Molodaia gvardiia, 2007).

Rokossovskii (Moscow: Molodaia gvardiia, 2010).

Soshnikov, A.Ia. et al, *Sovetskaia kavaleriia: Voenno-istoricheskii ocherk* (Moscow: Voenizdat, 1984).

Srazhenie veka (Moscow: Izdatel'stvo "Sovetskaia Rossiia", 1975).

Stahel, D., *Operation Barbarossa and Germany's Defeat in the East* (Cambridge: Cambridge University Press, 2009).

Kiev 1941: Hitler's battle for supremacy in the East (Cambridge: Cambridge University Press, 2012).

Operation Typhoon: Hitler's march on Moscow, October 1941 (Cambridge: Cambridge University Press, 2013).

Statiev, A., 'Penal Units in the Red Army', in *Europe-Asia Studies*, Volume 62, Number 5 (2010), pp.721–47.

'Blocking Units in the Red Army', in *The Journal of Military History*, Volume 76, Number 2 (April 2012), pp.475–95.

Stepanov, A.S., *Razvitie sovetskoi aviatsii v predvoennii period (1938 god – pervaia polovina 1941 goda)* (Moscow: Russkii fond sodeistviia obrazovaniiu i nauke, 2009).

Sterrett, J., *Soviet Air Force Theory, 1918–1945* (Abingdon, Oxon/New York: Routledge, 2007).

Stone, D.R., *Hammer and Rifle: The Militarization of the Soviet Union, 1926–1933* (Lawrence, Kansas: University Press of Kansas, 2000).

Suvenirov, O.F., *Tragediia RKKA 1937–1938* (Moscow: Terra, 1998).

Suvorov, V. (pseud.), 'Who was Plannig to Attack Whom in June 1941, Hitler or Stalin?', in *Journal of the Royal United Services Institute for Defence Studies*, Volume 130, Number 2 (1985), pp.50–5.

Thomas, H., *The Spanish Civil War. Third Edition. Revised and Enlarged* (London: Penguin Books, 1986).

Timokhovich, I.V., *Operativnoe iskusstvo Sovetskikh VVS v Velikoi Otechestvennoi voine* (Moscow: Voenizdat, 1976).

Bitva za Belorussiiu. 1941–1944 (Minsk: 'Belarus', 1994).

Virodov, I.Ia. et al, *V srazheniiakh za pobedu* (Moscow: Izdatel'stvo "Nauka", 1974).

Vorsin, V.F., 'Motor Vehicle Transport Deliveries Through "Lend-Lease"', in *JSMS*, Volume 10, Number 2 (June 1997), pp.153–75.

Wegner, B. (ed.), *From Peace to War: Germany, Soviet Russia and the World, 1939–1941* (Oxford: Berghann Books, 1997).

Zakharov, M.V. (gen.ed.), *Osvobozhdenie iugo-vostochnoi i tsentral'noi Evropi voiskami 2-go i 3-go Ukrainskikh frontov. 1944–1945* (Moscow: Izdatel'stvo "Nauka", 1970).

Zaloga, S.J., 'Soviet Tank Operations in the Spanish Civil War', in *JSMS*, Volume 12, Number 3 (September 1999), pp.134–62.

Zetterling, N. and Frankson, A., *Kursk 1943: A Statistical Analysis* (Abingdon, Oxon: Frank Cass, 2000).

The Korsun Pocket: The Encirclement and Breakout of a German Army in the East, 1944 (Drexel Hill, PA and Newbury, Berkshire: Casemate, 2008).

Ziemke, E.F., *Stalingrad to Berlin: The German Defeat in the East* (Washington, D.C: Center of Military History, United States Army, 1987).

Zolotov, N.P. et al, *Boevoi i chislennii sostav vooruzhennikh sil SSSR v period Velikoi Otechestvennoi voini (1941–1945 gg.). Statisticheskii sbornik No.1 (22 iiunia 1941 g.)* (Moscow: Institut voennoi istorii MO RF, 1994).

Zolotov, N.P. and Isaev, S.I., 'Boegotovi bili... Istoriko-statisticheskoe issledovanie kolichestvenno-kachestvennogo sostoianiia tankovogo parka Krasnoi Armii nakanune Velikoi Otechestvennoi voini', in *Vizh*, Number 11 (1993), pp. 75–7.

WEBSITES:

http://army.armor.kiev.ua/titul/
www.germandocsinrussia.org/ru/nodes/1-rossiysko-germanskiy-proekt-po-otsi frovke-trofeynyh-kollektsiy
http://iremember.ru
http://militera.lib.ru
www.podvig-naroda.ru
www.soldat.ru/doc/gko/scans

Index

Abdulin, M.: 458
aircraft (in Soviet service):
  Airacobra (P-39); 291, 426
  Boston (A-20); 480, 482
  DB-3; 91, 161, 321, 345, 480
  DC-3 (Dakota); 323
  DI-6; 138
  Fokker D-XI; 34
  Hurricane; 291–2, 336
  I-301; 187
  I-5; 38, 404
  I-7; 38
  I-15; 111–12, 114–17
  I-16; 38–9, 111–19, 138, 162, 186, 404,
    427, 622–3n74
  Il-2; 182, 186, 192, 337, 404–5, 463,
    480–2, 494–5
  K-7; 40
  La-5; 405, 426
  La-7; 405, 558, 566
  LaGG-3; 186–7, 192, 404, 427
  Lisunov-2; 323
  Pe-2; 192, 439, 480–2, 534
  Pe-3; 534
  R-5 and derivatives; 111–12, 115, 138,
    161, 182, 303
  R-10; 91, 138
  SB; 91, 112, 114–15, 117, 119, 138,
    161–2
  Spitfire; 426
  superior to late-war German; 494
  TB-3; 88, 117, 138, 406
  TB-7; 406
  Tomahawk (P-40); 291–2
  Tu-2; 426
  U-2; 38, 138, 303, 326–7, 404, 439, 482
  Yak-1 (I-26); 186–7, 192, 292, 335,
    426–7, 622–3n74
  Yak-7; 426, 482
  Yak-9; 482
aircraft (non-Soviet):
  Bf 109; 39, 112–13, 119, 187, 566

Bristol Bulldog; 38, 162
Curtiss P-6E; 38
Dornier X; 41
Fiat CR-32; 39, 111
Fokker XXI; 162
Fw 190; 494, 566
Heinkel 111; 481
Heinkel HD-37; 38
Heinkel He-51; 39, 111
Hs 129; 494
I-95 (Mitsubishi Ki-10); 114
I-96 (Mitsubishi A5M); 114
I-97 (Nakajima Ki-27); 114, 119
Ju 87 ('Stuka'); 245, 342, 466, 481, 494
air forces (Soviet), see VVS
airpower (German): 111, 207–8, 213, 245,
    259–60, 263, 303, 315, 322, 343,
    345, 349, 383, 403–7, 420, 427–8,
    466, 480–4, 494, 510, 558, 566
airpower (Soviet): 5, 32, 49, 91, 111–18,
    138, 160–2, 176, 186–7, 191–2,
    208–9, 211, 292, 303, 320, 322,
    326–7, 333, 335–6, 345, 400, 403–7,
    416, 420–1, 426–8, 436, 439, 465–6,
    478, 480–4, 494, 509, 534–5, 544,
    557–8, 563, 565–8
  reconnaissance; 34, 49, 131, 148, 303,
    400, 482–3, 534–5, 567
  strategic bombing; 5, 161, 406
Akhumov, [Captain]: 377
Aleksin: 312
Allies (Soviet):
  aid to the Soviet Union; 4, 360, 180, 220,
    261, 313, 360, 403, 418, 426, 442,
    463, 467, 486, 493, 505, 508–9, 521,
    564–5
  convoys to the Soviet Union; 260, 336,
    403, 673n25
  Second Front; 360, 403, 490, 500–1,
    651n94
Anan'ev, I.: 272
Anders, Władysław: 334